MILLER'S

antiques

MILLER'S antiques

ELIZABETH NORFOLK *GENERAL EDITOR*

VOLUME XXV

MILLER'S ANTIQUES PRICE GUIDE

Created and designed by
Miller's
The Cellars, High Street
Tenterden, Kent, TN30 6BN
Tel: 01580 766411
Fax: 01580 766100

General Editor: Elizabeth Norfolk
Managing Editor: Valerie Lewis
Production Co-ordinator: Kari Reeves
Editorial Co-ordinator: Deborah Wanstall
Editorial Assistants: Rosemary Cooke, Joanna Hill, Maureen Horner
Production Assistants: Caroline Bugeja, Gillian Charles, Helen Clarkson, Ethne Tragett
Advertising Executive: Jill Jackson
Advertising Assistants: Emma Gillingham, Carol Woodcock
Advertising Co-ordinator & Administrator: Melinda Williams
Designer: Philip Hannath
Advertisement Designer: Simon Cook
Indexer: Hilary Bird
Production: Sarah Rogers
Jacket Design: Victoria Bevan
Additional Photographers: Ian Booth, Gareth Gooch, David Mereweather,
Dennis O'Reilly, Robin Saker, Steve Tanner

First published in Great Britain in 2003, reprinted 2004
by Miller's, a division of Mitchell Beazley,
imprints of Octopus Publishing Group Ltd,
2–4 Heron Quays, London E14 4JP

Reprinted in 2005 by Bounty Books,
a division of Octopus Publishing Group Ltd,
2-4 Heron Quays, London E14 4JP

A CIP catalogue record for this book is
available from the British Library

ISBN 0 7537 1176 1
ISBN13 9780753711767

Colour origination: 1.13, Whitstable, Kent
Lab 35, Milton Keynes, Bucks
Printed and bound: Rotolito Lombarda SPA, Italy

Front cover illustrations:
A George III silver cruet, by John Delmester, London (TSC).
A Moss Agate beaker, c1960.
A brass cigarette case, c1730–50.

Half title illustration:
A silver cigarette case, Continental, 1898 (C).

Contents illustration:
A Meissen cup and saucer, with a view of Venice, c1850.

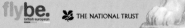

F. G. BRUSCHWEILER (Antiques) LTD.

41–67 LOWER LAMBRICKS, RAYLEIGH
ESSEX SS6 8DA

(Only 35 minutes from London, 1 hour from Gatwick and Heathrow airports)

35,000 square feet of antiques
over 10,000 items in stock at all times
always over 20 bars in stock

large oak counter bar above 12' long

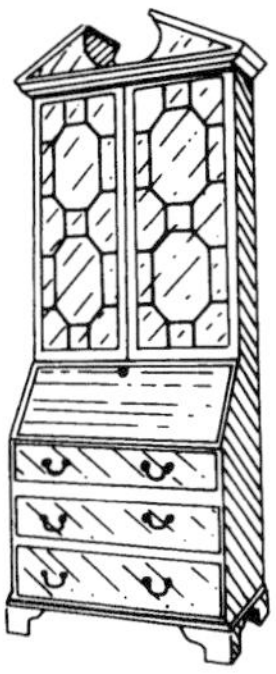

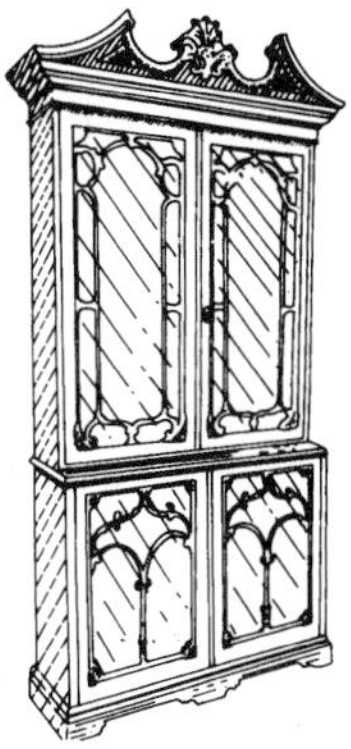

oak corner bar above 6' x 6' x 7'6" high

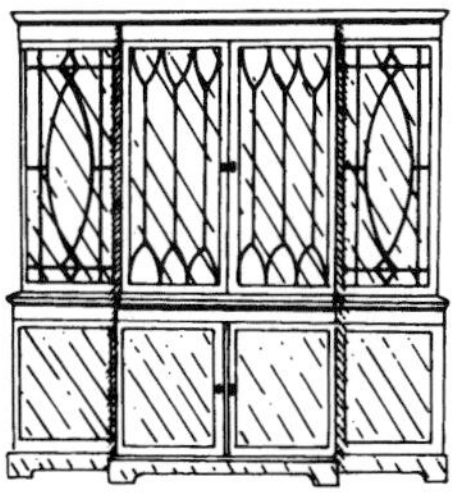

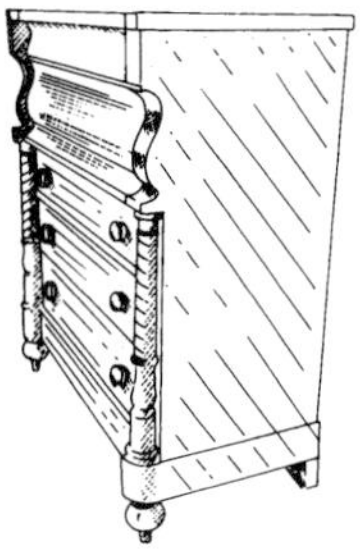

We have a varied stock of quality antiques to suit all markets, USA, Japan, Australia, Italy, Spain, Portugal, Belgium, etc.

Send for our brochure

ESTABLISHED SINCE 1963

Tel (01268) 773 761
(01268) 773 932
Fax (01268) 773 318

MEMBER OF LAPADA

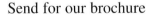

Website: www.fgbantiques.com
Email: info@fgbantiques.com

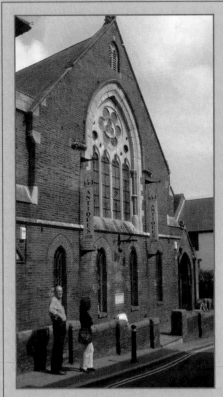

Dates	**British Monarch**	**British Period**	**French Period**
1558–1603	Elizabeth I	Elizabethan	Renaissance
1603–1625	James I	Jacobean	
1625–1649	Charles I	Carolean	Louis XIII (1610–1643)
1649–1660	Commonwealth	Cromwellian	Louis XIV (1643–1715)
1660–1685	Charles II	Restoration	
1685–1689	James II	Restoration	
1689–1694	William & Mary	William & Mary	
1694–1702	William III	William III	
1702–1714	Anne	Queen Anne	
1714–1727	George I	Early Georgian	Régence (1715–1723)
1727–1760	George II	Early Georgian	Louis XV (1723–1774)
1760–1811	George III	Late Georgian	Louis XVI (1774–1793) Directoire (1793–1799) Empire (1799–1815)
1812–1820	George III	Regency	Restauration Charles X (1815–1830)
1820–1830	George IV	Regency	
1830–1837	William IV	William IV	Louis Philippe (1830–1848) 2nd Empire Napoleon III (1848–1870) 3rd Republic (1871–1940)
1837–1901	Victoria	Victorian	
1901–1910	Edward VII	Edwardian	

<table>
<tr><th>German Period</th><th>U.S. Period</th><th>Style</th><th>Woods</th></tr>
<tr><td rowspan="2">Renaissance</td><td rowspan="3">Early Colonial</td><td>Gothic</td><td rowspan="12">Oak Period (to c1670)

Walnut period (c1670–1735)

Early mahogany period (c1735–1770)

Late mahogany period (c1770–1810)</td></tr>
<tr><td rowspan="3">Baroque (c1620–1700)</td></tr>
<tr><td rowspan="3">Renaissance/ Baroque (c1650–1700)</td></tr>
<tr><td>William & Mary</td></tr>
<tr><td>Dutch Colonial</td><td rowspan="3">Rococo (c1695–1760)</td></tr>
<tr><td>Baroque (c1700–1730)</td><td>Queen Anne</td></tr>
<tr><td>Rococo (c1730–1760)</td><td>Chippendale (from 1750)</td></tr>
<tr><td>Neo–classicism (c1760–1800)

Empire (c1800–1815)</td><td>Early Federal (1790–1810)

American Directoire (1798–1804)

American Empire (1804–1815)</td><td>Neo–classical (c1755–1805)

Empire (c1799–1815)</td></tr>
<tr><td>Biedermeier (c1815–1848)</td><td rowspan="2">Late Federal (1810–1830)</td><td>Regency (c1812–1830)</td></tr>
<tr><td rowspan="3">Revivale (c1830–1880)

Jugendstil (c1880–1920)</td><td rowspan="2">Eclectic (c1830–1880)

Arts & Crafts (c1880–1900)</td></tr>
<tr><td>Victorian</td></tr>
<tr><td>Art Nouveau (c1900–1920)</td><td>Art Nouveau (c1900–1920)</td></tr>
</table>

contents

20 Acknowledgments
21 How to use this book
22 Baca Awards
25 Introduction

26 Furniture
156 Oak & Country Furniture
191 Pine Furniture
219 Bamboo & Wicker Furniture
220 Kitchenware
224 Pottery
267 Porcelain
308 Chinese Ceramics
327 Japanese Ceramics
332 Glass
353 Silver
374 Silver Plate
376 Wine Antiques
378 Clocks
431 Watches
437 Barometers
445 Decorative Arts
499 Twentieth-Century Design
509 Lamps & Lighting
514 Rugs & Carpets
524 Textiles
538 Fans
540 Jewellery
551 Enamel
552 Fabergé
553 Gold
554 Asian Works of Art
574 Islamic Works of Art
578 Architectural Antiques
592 Sculpture
597 Metalware
604 Leather
605 Papier Mâché
606 Treen
610 Tunbridge Ware
612 Boxes
619 Music
628 Icons
633 Portrait Miniatures
638 Silhouettes
639 Artists' Materials
640 Antiquities
646 Pre-Columbian Art
647 Tribal Art
652 Books & Book Illustrations
658 Maps & Atlases
663 Dolls
671 Dolls' Houses
672 Teddy Bears
674 Soft Toys
675 Toys
687 Ephemera
693 Rock & Pop
698 Scientific Instruments
707 Marine
713 Cameras
716 Optical Devices & Viewers
717 Photographs
721 Arms & Armour
734 Militaria
745 Sport

760 Glossary
764 Directory of Specialists
771 Directory of Auctioneers
794 Key to Illustrations
801 Index to Advertisers
804 Index

Acknowledgments

The publishers would like to acknowledge the great assistance given by our consultants. We would also like to extend our thanks to all auction houses and their press offices, as well as dealers and collectors, who have assisted us in the production of this book.

FURNITURE:	Edward Reily Collins, Hallidays, The Old College, High Street, Dorchester-on-Thames, Oxfordshire OX10 7HL
CAMPAIGN FURNITURE:	Sean Clarke, Christopher Clarke Antiques, The Fosse Way, Stow-on-the-Wold, Gloucestershire GL54 1JS
	Information on care and restoration of furniture supplied by Billy Cook, High Trees House, Savernake Forest, Nr Marlborough, Wiltshire SN8 4NE
OAK & COUNTRY FURNITURE:	Paul Hopwell, 30 High Street, West Haddon, Northamptonshire NN6 7AP
POTTERY:	John Axford, Woolley & Wallis, 51–61 Castle Street, Salisbury, Wiltshire SP1 3SU
LUSTREWARE:	Ian Sharp, 23 Front Street, Tynemouth, Tyne & Wear NE30 4DX
PORCELAIN:	John Sandon, Bonhams, 101 New Bond Street, London W1Y 0AS
ASIAN CERAMICS:	Peter Wain, Anglesey
GLASS:	Andy McConnell decanterman@freezone.co.uk
SILVER & SILVER PLATE:	Nicholas Shaw, Virginia Cottage, Lombard Street, Petworth, West Sussex GU28 0AG
CLOCKS:	Michael Turner, Sotheby's Olympia, Hammersmith Road, London W14 8UX
BAROMETERS:	Kym Walker, Weather House Antiques, Foster Clough, Hebden Bridge, West Yorkshire HX7 5QZ
DECORATIVE ARTS:	Eric Knowles, Bonhams, 101 New Bond Street, London W1Y 0AS
TWENTIETH-CENTURY DESIGN:	Jeremy Morrison, Sotheby's Olympia, Hammersmith Road, London W14 8UX
RUGS & CARPETS:	Richard Purdon, 158 The Hill, Burford, Oxfordshire OX18 4QY
ASIAN WORKS OF ART:	Peter Wain, Anglesey
BOXES:	Alan & Kathy Stacey, PO Box 2771, Yeovil, Somerset BA22 7DZ
ANTIQUITIES:	Peter A. Clayton FSA, Seaby Antiquities, 14 Old Bond Street, London W1X 4JL
TRIBAL ART:	Fiona McKinnon, Elms Lester, 1–3–5 Flitcroft Street, Soho, London WC2H 8DH
TOYS:	Glenn Butler, Wallis & Wallis, West Street Auction Galleries, Lewes, East Sussex BN7 2NJ
ROCK & POP:	Paul Wane & Jason Cornthwaite, Tracks, PO Box 117, Chorley, Lancashire PR6 0UU
SCIENTIFIC INSTRUMENTS & MARINE:	Jon Baddeley, Bonhams, 65–69 Lots Road, Chelsea, London SW10 0RN
MILITARIA:	John Wright, Q & C Militaria, 22 Suffolk Road, Cheltenham, Gloucestershire GL50 2AQ

How to use this book

In order to find a particular item, consult the contents list on page 19 to find the main heading – for example, Silver. Having located your area of interest, you will find that larger sections have been sub-divided. If you are looking for a particular factory, designer or craftsman, consult the index which starts on page 804.

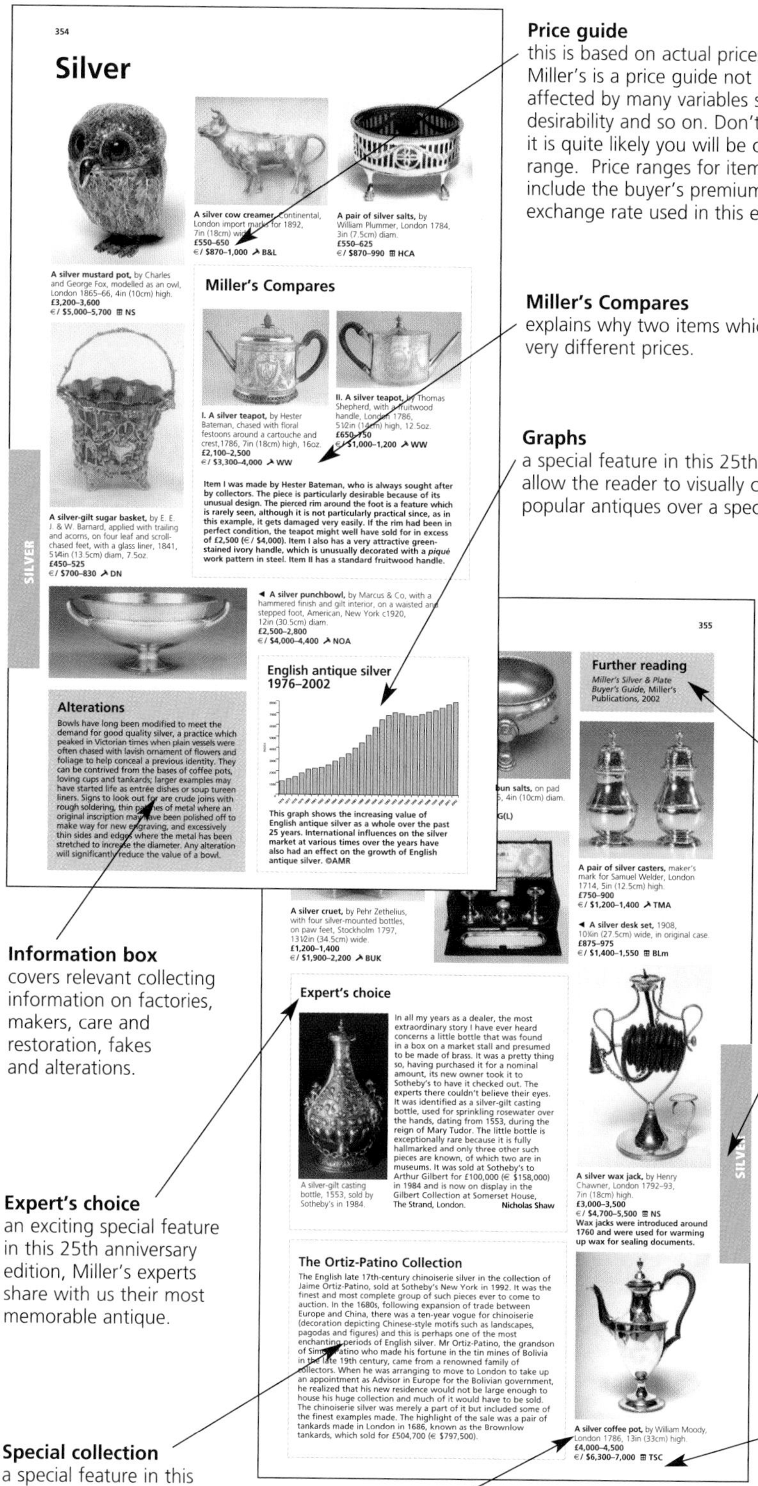

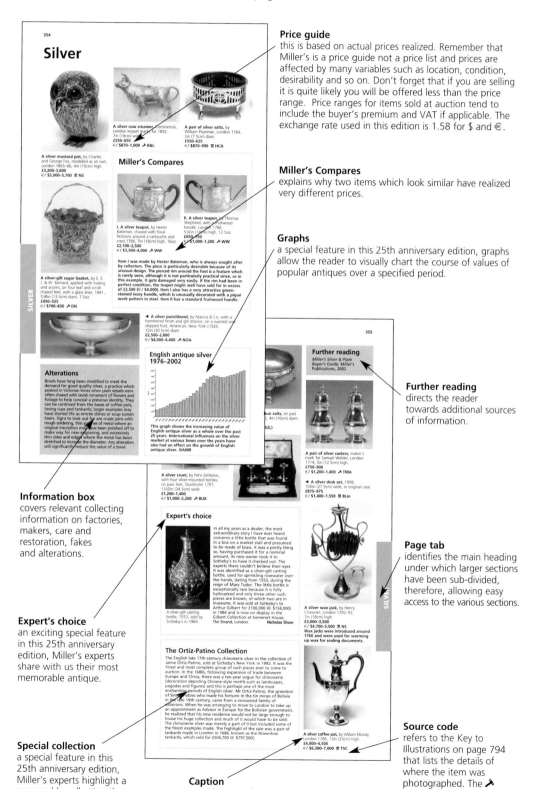

Price guide
this is based on actual prices realized. Remember that Miller's is a price guide not a price list and prices are affected by many variables such as location, condition, desirability and so on. Don't forget that if you are selling it is quite likely you will be offered less than the price range. Price ranges for items sold at auction tend to include the buyer's premium and VAT if applicable. The exchange rate used in this edition is 1.58 for $ and €.

Miller's Compares
explains why two items which look similar have realized very different prices.

Graphs
a special feature in this 25th anniversary edition, graphs allow the reader to visually chart the course of values of popular antiques over a specified period.

Further reading
directs the reader towards additional sources of information.

Information box
covers relevant collecting information on factories, makers, care and restoration, fakes and alterations.

Page tab
identifies the main heading under which larger sections have been sub-divided, therefore, allowing easy access to the various sections.

Expert's choice
an exciting special feature in this 25th anniversary edition, Miller's experts share with us their most memorable antique.

Source code
refers to the Key to Illustrations on page 794 that lists the details of where the item was photographed. The 🔨 icon indicates the item was sold at auction. The ⊞ icon indicates the item originated from a dealer.

Special collection
a special feature in this 25th anniversary edition, Miller's experts highlight a memorable collection that was offered for sale or auction during the past 25 years.

Caption
provides a brief description of the item including the maker's name, medium, year it was made and in some cases condition.

The BACA *Winners...*

CATEGORY 1
General Antiques Dealer

UK: NORTH OF M62
Haughey Antiques
Kirkby Stephen, Cumbria

M62 SOUTH, TO M4 / M25
The Country Seat
Huntercombe, Manor Barn,
Henley-on-Thames

LONDON (INSIDE M25)
Gordon Watson
50 Fulham Road, London

SOUTH AND SOUTH-WEST OF ENGLAND
Lennox Cato Antiques
1 The Square, Edenbridge

CATEGORY 2
Specialist Antiques Dealers

FURNITURE
Adams Antiques
Churches Mansion, Hospital Street,
Nantwich

COLLECTABLES
sponsored by ebay.co.uk
The Girl Can't Help It
Alfies Antique Market, Marylebone,
London

SILVER & PLATE
Sanda Lipton
Elliot House, 28A Devonshire Street,
London

PRINTS
Elizabeth Harvey-Lee
1 West Cottages, Middle Aston Road,
North Aston, Oxfordshire

WATERCOLOUR
Chris Beetles Ltd
10 Ryder Street, St James, London

CERAMICS
Simon Spero
109 Kensington Church Street,
London

GLASS
Mallet & Son (Antiques Ltd)
129 Mount Street, London

JEWELLERY
Joseph H. Bonnar
72 Thistle Street, Edinburgh

CATEGORY 3
Auction Houses

UK: NORTH OF M62
Bonhams Auctioneers
17a East Parade, Leeds

M62 SOUTH, TO M4 / M25
Bonhams Auctioneers
Knowle, Solihull

INSIDE M25
Sotheby's Auctions
34–35 New Bond Street, London

SOUTH AND SOUTH-WEST OF ENGLAND
Woolley & Wallis
51–61 Castle Street, Salisbury

CATEGORY 4
Associated Awards

AON AWARD FOR AUCTIONEER OF THE YEAR
sponsored by AON
David Lay
Penzance Auction Rooms, Alverton, Penzance

BEST ANTIQUES CENTRE
The Swan at Tetsworth
High Street, Tetsworth, Oxfordshire

ANTIQUES ON THE INTERNET
www.welshantiques.com

BBC HOMES AND ANTIQUES MAGAZINE AWARD FOR BEST ANTIQUES SHOPPING STREET
sponsored by BBC HOMES & ANTIQUES MAGAZINE
High Street, Burford, Oxfordshire

ANTIQUES TRADE GAZETTE AWARD FOR IN-HOUSE EXHIBITION
sponsored by Antiques Trade GAZETTE THE ANTIQUES TRADE WEEKLY
Christopher Clarke Antiques
"Campaign Furniture"

Introduction

It is interesting to reflect on the many conversations I have had with dealers and collectors about lucky finds. Tales of barns that revealed Chinese export porcelain packed in cider barrels or the Gillows sideboard pulled out of the bonfire in the fading light of a past and distant 5 November.

There was, according to those involved in what purported to be the antique trade of post-war Britain, no shortage of 'kit'. The biggest problem, for most people, was once bought, who on earth to sell it to. Such a dilemma would be considered unthinkable today, although at the time of writing plenty of dealers involved in brown furniture might well be able to identify with their predecessors operating in a Britain that apparently had never had it so good.

It is a sobering exercise to look back on the many changes witnessed by those of us who have spent 25 years and more engrossed in this fascinating business. This has been a period dominated by such diverse personalities as Elton John whose sale back in 1988 is reviewed on page 474, or the Hunt brothers, who were determined to gain control of the silver bullion market, which saw the price of silver soar to £34 (€/ $54) per ounce only then to plummet to £7 (€/ $11).

Today many children find it simply impossible to imagine how anyone managed to live a life without a personal computer and display visible horror at the prospect of life without the precious mobile phone or Playstation II. Twenty five years ago the antiques scene was not too dissimilar to that of today. What has encroached into the business during the interim years has been the 'collectable'. Its emergence has been part and parcel of the ever growing parameter of a business intent on filling the void left by the more standard areas of antiques, many of which have become noticeably depleted in volume. This expansion has resulted in a wide variety of new markets in which can be included Rock and Pop memorabilia, post-war design, contemporary ceramics and many more.

Another significant area of expansion has been the veritable growth of reference books, specialist magazines and periodicals resulting in many a bookcase overflowing. The thirst for knowledge has also been quenched by the media in response to the public's escalating interest in all things antique.

The ball started rolling way back in the days of black and white television with the arrival of the first 'antique superstar', a certain Mr Arthur Negus. It was Arthur who set about demystifying the antique business on his not to be missed Sunday afternoon programme *Going for a Song* – revised in the mid-1990s to feature yours truly and much lamented after almost 400 programmes second time around. At the time of writing we find ourselves with wall-to-wall television antiques programmes, the majority of which place a decided emphasis towards 'value' and suggest a business where you can 'get rich quick'. Oh, if only it were quite so simple.

The quantum leap in technology has without question altered the structure of trading patterns. The arrival of the worldwide web and the internet auction site was greeted with trumpets sounding in much the same way as the thousands of dotcoms, but now many of these have been and gone in what can only be described as a techno rationalization. Today the world of ebay continues to prosper alongside the traditional form of auction and the influence of the web cannot be understated. The effects of this global awareness are considered in the introductions provided by both Edward Reily Collins (Furniture) and John Sandon (Porcelain). Whereas Edward's comments focus on the practical demise of the bureau and its failure to accommodate present day computer hardware, John is quick to forewarn readers of the many pitfalls presented by buying porcelain off the web.

Despite all the remarkable advances in technology the antiques business is not immune to global wars, terrorism and life-threatening disease on either side of the Atlantic. However, in spite of the turmoil in world finance and the political upheavals in the Middle East this business has displayed a remarkable resilience.

As a result I am left to reflect on what the next 25 years might hold in store. The only thing I truly hope for is the same amount of fun that I have been lucky enough to experience in the previous quarter of a century.

Eric Knowles

Christies aggregate 1976–2002

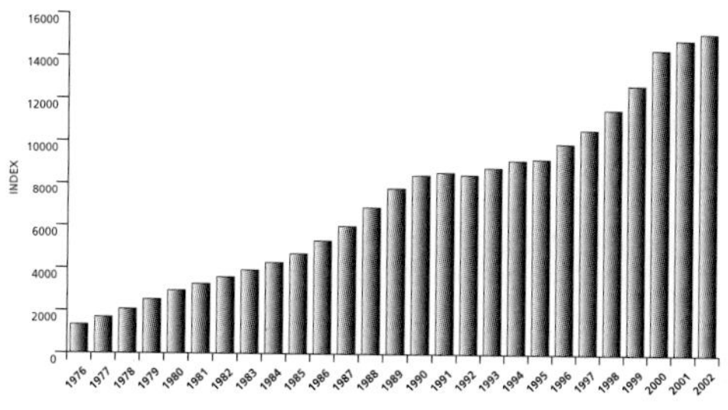

This graph shows the increasing value of antiques as a whole over the past 25 years. Individual collecting areas such as furniture or glass may not follow this graph exactly. ©AMR

Furniture

The 1980 edition of *Miller's Antiques Price Guide* states that increased public awareness of antiques has led to the demand for more and more information about the subject. That demand has turned into a flood as evidenced by the proliferation of television programmes, magazines and radio interviews, all dealing with antiques. One only has to compare the editorial of the 1979 *Miller's Antiques Price Guide* with this year's to notice not only the increased variety of stock but also the amount of technical information included.

Looking back over the last 25 years, the price of good mahogany furniture has fluctuated widely, due to political and economic factors as well as fashion trends. As a collector, one has to be careful to spot these trends – in 1999, for instance, a Queen Anne walnut bureau was priced at £2,700–3,300 (€/ $4,300–5,200), but in this year's Guide an almost identical piece (page 39) was priced at only £2,000–2,500 (€/ $3,200–3,500). The culprit for this decline in value is the computer, because there simply is not enough room to fit all the paraphernalia associated with the machine on a bureau. However, don't sell your bureau just yet. With computers, like mobile phones, becoming smaller each year, the hardware will probably become so compact that they will soon fit back in the bureau again and prices will rise once more.

Although the current political and economic uncertainty may have affected the middle market for English furniture, the market for untouched furniture with provenance, good colour and patination and excellent condition, has gone from strength to strength over the last few years. As for middle range Georgian furniture we have seen similar situations in the market in 1991 and 1992, and experience shows that once the economy improves, prices increase.

If we compare period Georgian pieces with the late 19th- and early 20th-century copies that were produced in huge quantities to fill the large houses of manufacturing and trading barons, or indeed with the soulless utility furniture of today, it is plain to see that beautiful workmanship can be purchased for little more than its mass-produced imitations.

Edward Reily Collins

Beds & Cradles

A rococo painted and parcel-gilt bed, Swedish, mid-18thC, 67in (170cm) wide.
£6,000–7,500
€/ $9,500–11,800 ⚒ S(NY)

Chippendale

- An item described as Chippendale was actually made by Thomas Chippendale.
- An item described as being Chippendale period was made during the Chippendale period but not by Thomas Chippendale.
- An item described as Chippendale-style is a later copy.

A George III mahogany tester bed, with arched canopy, drapery and twin reeded posts, 74¾in (190cm) long.
£1,200–1,400
€/ $1,900–2,200 ⚒ S(O)

A Chippendale period stained maple and pine tester bed, posts possibly reduced in height, American, probably Massachusetts, c1780, 63½in (161.5cm) long.
£2,000–2,400
€/ $3,200–3,800 ⚒ S(NY)

► An Empire mahogany *lit en bateau*, with folding box spring base and spring interior mattress, French, early 19thC, 93¼in (237cm) wide.
£1,700–2,000
€/ $2,700–3,200 ⚒ S(O)

A mahogany four-poster bed, with tapering front posts and acanthus leaf decoration, c1835, 66in (167.5cm) wide.
£8,000–9,000
€/ $12,600–14,200 ⊞ SeH

A walnut tester bed, with drapery hangings, Continental, 19thC, 42¼in (107.5cm) wide.
£1,700–2,000
€/ $2,700–3,200 S(O)

A mahogany and cane cradle, the caned canopy top above a caned body, on turned end supports, with turned stretchers, on outswept feet, 19thC, 43¼in (110cm) wide.
£120–150
€/ $190–240 B(W)

A mahogany and cane cradle, the arched cover with acorn finials, the stand with ring-turned uprights, with conforming stretchers, 19thC, 18in (45.5cm) long.
£500–600
€/ $800–950
GAK

► A Victorian burr-walnut-veneered half-tester double bed, with moulded cornice and twin lobed hanging pendants, fitted with side rails and curtain hoops, the back hung with curtains, the domed footboard with panelled, foliate and column mouldings, on casters, 63in (160cm) wide.
£1,800–2,000
€/ $2,800–3,200 FHF
The relatively low value is due to practical reasons. Most modern houses do not have high enough ceilings for such an item. However, to make one today using such well-matched walnut veneer would cost at least three times this price.

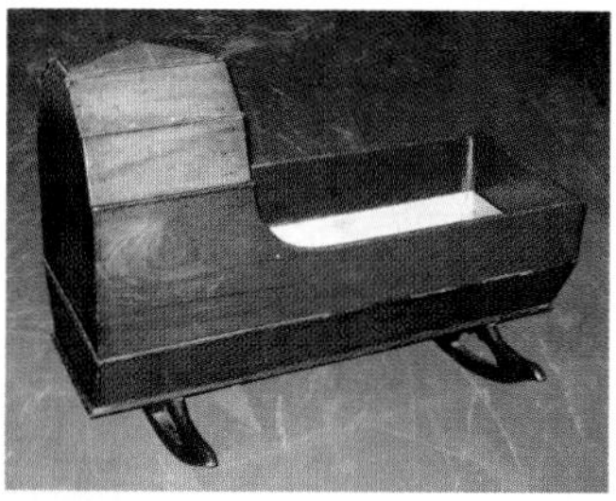

► A Victorian mahogany cradle, c1860, 36in (91.5cm) long.
£150–200
€/ $250–300
BWL

◄ A Victorian carved rosewood bed, the headboard with five inset panels surmounted by a crest of carved fruit, with melon urn finials, 82in (208.5cm) wide.
£2,800–3,200
€/ $4,400–5,000
JDJ

► A brass bed, 19thC, 56in (142cm) wide.
£150–180
€/ $250–290
DuM
This is missing the side rails to hold the base, hence the low price.

A Victorian mahogany half-tester bed, with serpentine-front cornice and curved footboard, 60in (152.5cm) wide.
£2,500–3,000
€/ $4,000–4,700 ⊞ SWA

A mahogany half-tester bed, c1870, 60in (152.5cm) wide.
£1,250–1,400
€/ $1,900–2,200 ⊞ NAW

A beech and walnut carved and ivory-inlaid bed, attributed to Gabriel Viardot, Paris, the headboard carved with a dragon, French, c1880, 66½in (169cm) wide.
£6,500–7,750
€/ $10,200–12,200 S(O)
Gabriel Viardot took over the family firm in rue Rambuteau from his father, Charles, in 1861. He specialized in exotic furniture and was influenced by Chinese and Vietnamese styles. Viardot was a jury member and medal winner at the 1867, 1878 and 1889 International Exhibitions in Paris.

A cedarwood four-poster bed, the posts with spiral-turned decoration and panelling surmounted by a fluted band canopy, with a carved scrolling headboard, Australian, New South Wales, c1845, 54¾in (139cm) wide.
£3,500–4,200
€/ $5,500–6,600 LJ

An Empire-style mahogany upholstered bed, French, c1875, 54in (137cm) wide.
£1,600–2,000
€/ $2,500–3,000 ⊞ SeH

A brass bed, c1890, 54in (137cm) wide.
£2,400–2,800
€/ $3,800–4,400 ⊞ SeH

► A Louis XVI-style walnut bed, with decorative carved headboard, French, c1895, 60in (152.5cm) wide.
£1,200–1,500
€/ $1,900–2,400 ⊞ SeH

An Empire painted bed, recovered, French, c1860, 60in (152.5cm) wide.
£2,250–2,500
€/ $3,200–3,800 ⊞ DAC

A rococo-style mahogany half-tester bed, with flame mahogany veneer, c1875, 72in (183cm) wide.
£8,000–9,000
€/ $12,600–14,200 ⊞ SeH

A Renaissance-style mahogany bed, with ormolu mounts, quarter-veneered panels and original wooden side rails, c1890, 66in (167.5cm) wide.
£1,800–2,000
€/ $2,800–4,700 ⊞ SWA

A mahogany bed, with parquetry work and ormolu decoration, French, c1895, 60in (152.5cm) wide.
£1,500–1,800
€/ $2,300–2,800 ⊞ SeH

A Gothic-style carved walnut bed, c1895, 60in (152.5cm) wide.
£5,000–6,000
€/ $8,000–9,500 ⊞ SeH

A pair of Louis XVI-style carved beechwood beds, the headboards upholstered in damask, the posts modelled as arrow quivers, c1900, 42½in (108cm) wide.
£1,200–1,500
€/ $1,900–2,400 ⚒ NOA

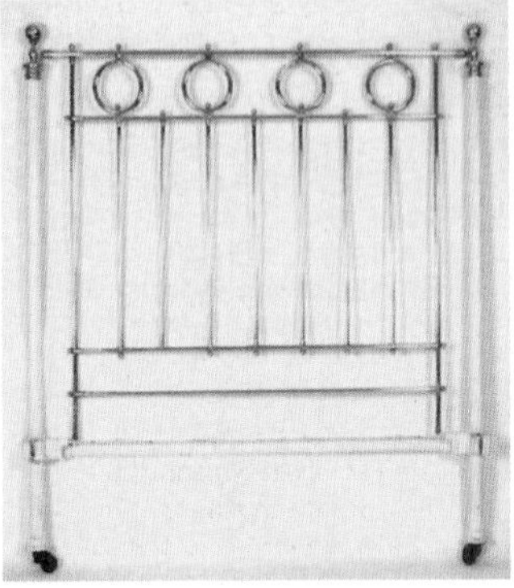

An Edwardian brass and painted bed, the head with brass hoops and rails, surmounted by ball finials, 54¼in (140.5cm) wide.
£280–350
€/ $440–550 ⚒ B(W)

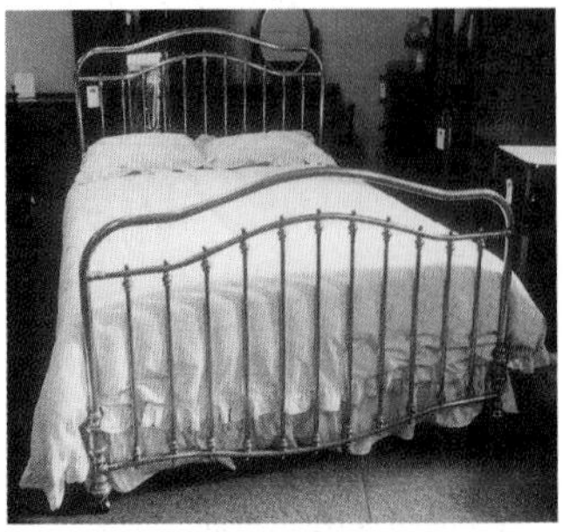

A brass bed, c1910, 60in (152.5cm) wide.
£1,600–1,800
€/ $2,500–2,800 ⊞ SWA

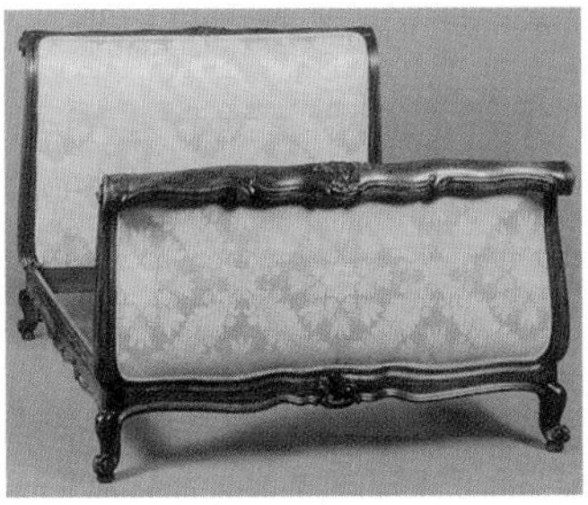

A Louis XV-style carved and stained beech bed, French, 19thC, 61in (155cm) wide.
£1,600–2,000
€/ $2,500–3,200 ⚒ S(O)

A painted wooden bed, with upholstered headboard, French, c1900, 42in (106.5cm) wide.
£1,200–1,500
€/ $1,900–2,400 ⊞ SeH

An Edwardian mahogany bed, with inlaid stringing, 54in (137cm) wide.
£700–900
€/ $1,100–1,400 ⊞ SeH

A Belle Epoque Louis XV boudoir-style bed, with lacquered finish, French, c1910, 60in (152.5cm) wide.
£5,000–5,500
€/ $8,000–8,700 ⊞ SeH

A bedstead, the ends painted with landscape scenes by moonlight, Italian, c1900, 36in (91.5cm) wide.
£1,600–2,000
€/ $2,500–3,200 ⊞ SeH

A Louis XV-style walnut bed, with original wooden side rails, with quartered veneered panels, c1900, 60in (152.5cm) wide.
£1,300–1,500
€/ $2,000–2,400 ⊞ SWA

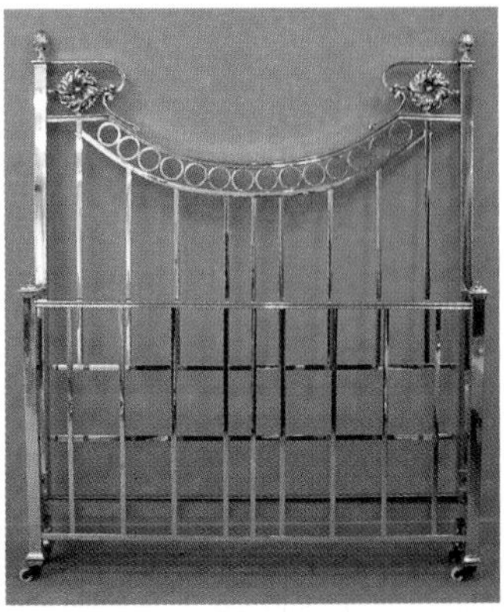

An Edwardian brass bed, 54in (137cm) wide.
£1,400–1,700
€/ $2,200–2,700 ⊞ SeH

A burr-walnut-veneered bed, Italian, c1910, 72in (183cm) wide.
£5,000–6,000
€/ $8,000–9,500 ⊞ SeH

Benches

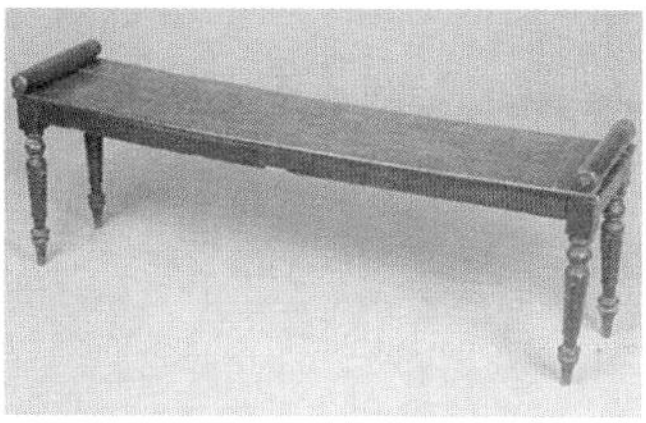

A Regency mahogany hall bench, seat split, 54in (137cm) wide.
£1,500–1,800
€/ $2,400–2,800 B(Ba)

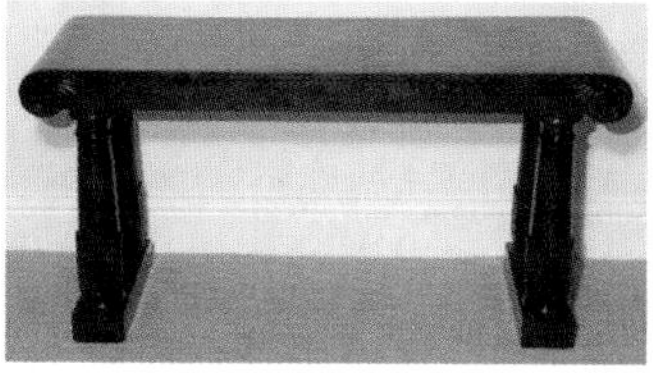

A mahogany hall seat, stamped 'James Winter, London', c1825, 36in (91.5cm) wide.
£6,000–7,000
€/ $9,500–11,000 CAT

A William IV mahogany bench, 107in (272cm) wide.
£650–800
€/ $1,000–1,300 S(O)

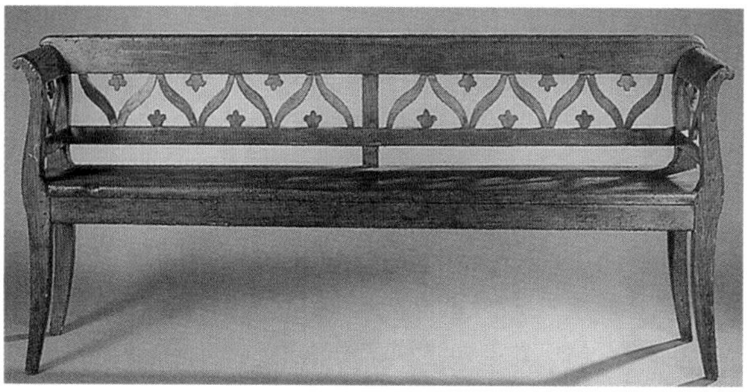

A Biedermeier softwood hall bench, the open backrest pierced with S-scrolls and stylized fleur-de-lys, the outscrolled open armrests with conforming decoration, on sabre legs, South German, mid-19thC, 74¾in (190cm) wide.
£4,000–5,000
€/ $6,300–7,900 S(Am)

A mahogany hall bench, with bobbin-turned decoration, c1835, 55in (139.5cm) wide.
£3,750–4,500
€/ $6,000–7,000 S(O)

Bonheurs du Jour

A George III satinwood and kingwood cross-banded bonheur du jour, 32¼in (82cm) wide.
£2,200–2,750
€/ $3,500–4,400 S(O)

A maple and mahogany bonheur du jour, c1790, 24in (61cm) wide.
£3,000–3,500
€/ $4,700–5,500 S(O)

A black-japanned bonheur du jour, distressed, c1800, 20½in (52cm) wide.
£1,000–1,200
€/ $1,600–1,900 S(O)

A burr-maple and rosewood-banded bonheur du jour, with step-up centre and pierced gilt-brass gallery above an arched and mirrored compartment flanked by two cupboards with Sèvres portrait panels, French, early 19thC, 39in (99cm) wide.
£2,000–2,500
€/ $3,200–4,000 MEA

◄ **A Victorian rosewood bonheur du jour,** with thuya-wood inlay and Sèvres plaques, on plain square supports and moulded plinth above turned feet, 24½in (62cm) wide.
£1,700–2,200
€/ $2,700–3,400
TEN

◄ **A black-lacquered papier mâché bonheur du jour,** in the style of Jennens & Bettridge, c1840, 24½in (62cm) wide.
£3,750–4,500
€/ $6,000–7,000 S(O)

Jennens & Bettridge were well-known papier mâché manufacturers who, in 1816, took over the Birmingham factory of H. Clay. In 1831 they invented a technique of painting onto papier mâché and later patented a type of inlay using coloured glass, mother-of-pearl, tortoiseshell and ivory. The company was active until c1864.

A figured walnut bonheur du jour, the arched mirrored door enclosing a shelved cupboard, flanked by two side cupboards, crossbanded throughout and with ormolu mounts, mid-19thC, 41in (104cm) wide.
£1,500–1,800
€/ $2,400–2,500 TMA

A kingwood bonheur du jour, with Sèvres-style porcelain mounts, gallery possibly altered, French, c1890, 30¾in (78cm) wide.
£2,500–3,000
€/ $4,000–4,700 S(O)

An ebonized and parcel-gilt amboyna-veneered bonheur du jour, decorated with painted porcelain panels, the upper section with a central compartment flanked by two side cupboards, the base fitted with one long writing drawer flanked by two short drawers, late 19thC, 48½in (123cm) wide.
£2,400–3,000
€/ $3,800–4,700 TMA
This piece represents excellent value for money, particularly if the purchaser can regard this as an investment for 10 years or so.

A mahogany bonheur du jour, Baltic, 1850–75, 45¾in (116cm) wide.
£650–800
€/ $1,000–1,300 B(Ba)

A parquetry bonheur du jour, with ormolu mounts, on turned and fluted legs, French, 19thC, 31in (78.5cm) wide.
£2,500–3,200
€/ $4,000–5,000 G(B)

A Louis XV-style mahogany, ebonized and marquetry bonheur du jour, with sliding writing surface, French, c1900, 29½in (75cm) wide.
£2,800–3,200
€/ $4,400–5,000 S(O)

A kingwood, amboyna, satinwood and marquetry bonheur du jour, with ormolu mounts, c1880, 30in (76cm) wide.
£6,750–7,500
€/ $10,700–12,000 ⊞ Che

A walnut bonheur du jour, French, 19thC, 38½in (98cm) wide.
£450–550
€/ $700–870 B(Ba)

◄ A kingwood-veneered bonheur du jour, with gilt-metal mounts and Sèvres-style porcelain plaques, the serpentine front with a blue velvet inset slide above a drawer, on cabriole legs, French, late 19thC, 30in (76cm) wide.
£3,000–3,750
€/ $4,700–6,000 WW

A mahogany and inlaid bonheur du jour, the rear of the cupboard doors fitted with letter racks, the fold-over top with gilt-tooled green leather inset, c1910, 32¾in (83cm) wide.
£2,000–2,400
€/ $3,200–3,800 S(O)

A Louis XV-style kingwood and tulipwood bonheur du jour, with central mirrored door and drawer, flanked by shelves, the protruding lower part with leather inset top, above a bow-shaped frieze drawer flanked by dummy drawers, on cabriole legs with gilt-bronze foliate-cast mounts, c1880, 46½in (118cm) wide.
£2,000–2,400
€/ $3,200–3,800 S(Am)

A carved walnut bonheur du jour, late 19thC, 38in (96.5cm) wide.
£2,000–2,250
€/ $3,200–3,500 ⊞ RPh

An ebonized and amboyna bonheur du jour, with ormolu mounts, the central mirror flanked by cupboards, surmounted by a pierced-brass gallery, the base with elaborate frieze and two open shelves, with classical ceramic plaques at intervals, French, late 19thC, 55in (139.5cm) wide.
£2,800–3,500
€/ $4,400–5,500 JM

Items in the Furniture section have been arranged in date order within each sub-section.

Bookcases

A George III mahogany bookcase, with astragal-glazed doors, 46in (117cm) wide.
£5,700–6,300
€/ $9,000–10,000 ⊞ APO

A mahogany bookcase, the cushion-moulded cornice above two doors, the upper two-thirds glazed and with applied Gothic tracery, the lower-third panelled, on bun feet, 1825–50, 55½in (141cm) wide.
£4,500–5,700
€/ $7,000–9,000 ⚒ NOA

A Regency rosewood and simulated rosewood bookcase, inlaid with satinwood bands, the moulded cornice above bead- and reel-carved frieze, the two arched astragal-glazed doors enclosing three shelves, the lower section with one long drawer and two panelled doors enclosing a shelf, on turned tapering feet, 37in (94cm) wide.
£2,000–2,500
€/ $3,200–4,000 ⚒ B

A mahogany bookcase, the frieze with two drawers, probably American, New York, c1835, 43¾in (111cm) wide.
£3,500–4,200
€/ $5,500–6,600 ⚒ S(O)

◄ **A mahogany bookcase,** the upper section with two glazed doors, the top carved with scrolls and foliage, the base with two drawers and two cupboard doors, on a plinth base, c1860, 41½in (105.5cm) wide.
£550–700
€/ $870–1,100 ⚒ E

A mahogany bookcase, the upper section with two glazed doors, c1825, 42in (106.5cm) wide.
£7,000–7,800
€/ $11,000–12,300 ⊞ SAW

► **A mahogany bookcase,** the moulded cornice above open shelves and two panelled cupboards, c1840, 61in (155cm) wide.
£2,200–2,700
€/ $3,500–4,200 ⚒ S(O)

A mahogany bookcase, with astragal-glazed doors over six drawers, c1850, 60in (152.5cm) wide.
£4,250–4,750
€/ $6,700–7,500 ⊞ MTay

Generally speaking, smaller bookcases are more valuable than larger examples as they fit more easily into modern rooms. However, it is important to check that they haven't been reduced. Look at the divisions for the shelves. The distance from the top shelf to the roof of the bookcase should be the same as that from the bottom shelf to the floor of the bookcase. Glazed bookcases were often converted from bedroom wardrobes. Check that the glazing bars have the same amount of wear and patination as the styles on the door.

Georgians had a great sense of proportion. Step back from a piece and take a good look: if it looks out of proportion, it's wrong!

A Victorian Reformed Gothic oak breakfront bookcase, the foliate-carved and spindle gallery pediment over three bays of open shelves flanked by rosette-carved fluted uprights, on a plinth base, 123¾in (314.5cm) wide.
£2,200–2,750
€/ $3,500–4,400 ⚒ Bri
Reformed Gothic was a late 19th century revivalist movement based on Arts and Crafts construction ideals but with Gothic detailing.

A carved oak bookcase, with two glazed doors, possibly Welsh, c1860, 44in (112cm) wide.
£375–425
€/ $600–670 ⊞ MTay

A mahogany bookcase, stamped 'J. Stewart, Maidenhead', 1875, 48in (122cm) wide.
£1,000–1,250
€/ $1,600–1,900 L

A mahogany bookcase, the upper section with a stepped cornice above two reeded glazed doors enclosing three shelves, the lower section with two reeded drawers, above two reeded cupboard doors enclosing a shelf, on a plinth base, late 19thC, 34in (86.5cm) wide.
£750–880
€/ $1,200–1,400 PFK

A mahogany bookcase, with two glazed doors, c1860, 49in (124.5cm) wide.
£5,250–5,850
€/ $8,300–9,200 ⊞ RAN

A Renaissance revival walnut and burr-walnut bookcase, the moulded cornice over two arched glazed doors, each with original glass, on a projecting base fitted with two panelled doors enclosing four shelves, American, 1875–1900, 50in (127cm) wide.
£2,500–3,000
€/ $4,000–4,700 NOA

A Victorian oak breakfront library bookcase, with moulded dentil cornice, the three glazed doors enclosing adjustable shelves, the base with central frieze drawer above six short drawers, flanked by two cupboards, on a box base, 80in (203cm) wide.
£2,000–2,500
€/ $3,200–4,000 LVS

A mid-Victorian Gothic revival-style mahogany and ebonized bookcase, the dentil-moulded cornice above an astragal-glazed door with Gothic arches enclosing shelves, flanked by moulded uprights, on a plinth base, 22in (56cm) wide.
£1,300–1,600
€/ $2,000–2,500 B

A mahogany bookcase, American, c1900, 45in (114.5cm) wide.
£400–500
€/ $630–800 DuM

A Victorian mahogany-veneered bookcase, the fixed ogee cornice above arched glazed doors with horizontal bars enclosing adjustable shelves, the base with two panelled doors enclosing adjustable shelves, the sides with scroll volutes, on a plinth base, 40¾in (103.5cm) wide.
£1,400–1,750
€/ $2,200–2,700 WW

A carved oak bookcase, retailed by Hamptons, London, c1885, 52¼in (132.5cm) wide.
£3,400–3,750
€/ $5,400–6,000 ⊞ MTay

► **An Edwardian oak bookcase,** the glazed upper section over a base with two drawers and two cupboard doors, 49in (124.5cm) wide.
£1,100–1,200
€/ $1,700–1,900 ⊞ WiB

Bureau Bookcases

A George II mahogany bureau bookcase, the glazed doors enclosing shelves, folio compartments and drawers, 41¾in (106cm) wide.
£3,500–4,250
€/ $5,500–6,700 ⚒ TEN

A Sheraton period mahogany cylinder bureau bookcase, c1790, 39in (99cm) wide.
£13,000–14,500
€/ $21,000–23,000 ⊞ Che

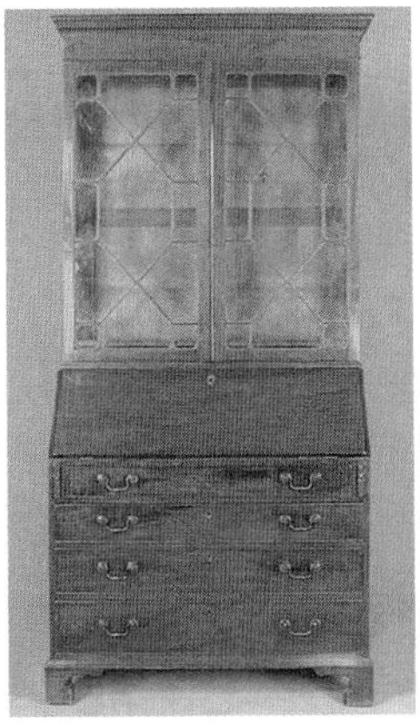

A George III mahogany bureau bookcase, the associated top with two astragal-glazed doors, 43¼in (110cm) wide.
£1,000–1,250
€/ $1,600–1,900 ⚒ B(Ba)

A bureau bookcase, associated, restored, c1800, 48½in (123cm) wide.
£4,250–4,750
€/ $6,700–7,500 ⊞ MTay

► An Edwardian Sheraton-style mahogany bureau bookcase, 26in (66cm) wide.
£800–1,000
€/ $1,300–1,600 ⚒ JM

A George III mahogany bureau bookcase, the associated upper section with replaced swan-neck pediment with cast-brass oval medallion terminals, the two glazed doors with wooden tracery, enclosing two shelves, the lower section with a fall-front enclosing drawers and pigeonholes, above three long drawers with Chippendale-style pierced-brass backplate bale handles, on bracket feet, some pigeonholes missing, 42in (106.5cm) wide.
£500–625
€/ $800–1,000 ⚒ PFK

A George III mahogany bureau bookcase, the associated upper section with two glazed doors enclosing adjustable shelves, the lower section with fall-front enclosing a fitted interior of a central cupboard and six drawers, 46in (117cm) wide.
£3,300–4,000
€/ $5,200–6,300 ⚒ S(O)

A rococo revival rosewood mechanical cylinder bureau bookcase, the upper section with a bonnet top over two conforming glazed doors, the interior with four period maple shelves, the base with mechanical cylinder top which extends the writing surface as the top opens, revealing a fitted interior with pigeonholes, on a base with a projecting drawer over two recessed cupboard doors, American, 1875–1900, 47in (119.5cm) wide.
£4,500–5,000
€/ $7,000–8,000 ⚒ NOA

◄ A Queen Anne-style walnut bureau bookcase, 31½in (80cm) wide.
£700–850
€/ $1,100–1,300 ⚒ S(O)

English 18th-century furniture 1976–2002

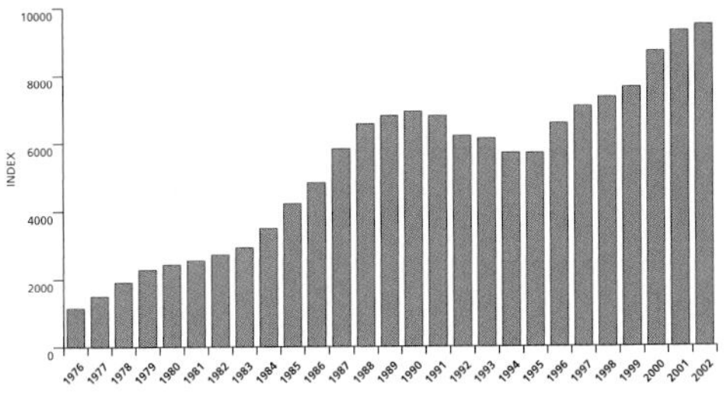

This graph shows the increasing value of English furniture as a whole over the past 25 years. Individual collecting areas such as chairs or tables and from different periods may not follow this graph exactly. ©AMR

FURNITURE

Low Bookcases

A Regency mahogany dwarf bookcase, with two drawers, 34¾in (88.5cm) wide.
£600–750
€/ $950–1,200 ⚒ S(O)

A mahogany open bookcase, the galleried top above a waterfall section to a rectangular lower part, with moulded edges, on turned legs with brass casters, one end of galleried top missing, stamped 'B.B. & Co Patent', early 19thC, 27in (68.5cm) wide.
£1,200–1,500
€/ $1,900–2,400 ⚒ WW

◀ A pair of ebonized and parcel-gilt open bookcases, each with a shaped top and four fixed shelves flanked by turned pillars, on turned tapering legs, repainted, 19thC, 21¾in (55.5cm) wide.
£1,100–1,400
€/ $1,700–2,200 ⚒ DN

A Regency mahogany double-sided bookcase, with a pierced-brass gallery, on brass casters, 30½in (77.5cm) wide.
£2,300–2,750
€/ $3,600–4,300 ⚒ NOA

A Victorian walnut floor-standing open bookcase, on a moulded plinth base, 34in (86.5cm) wide.
£2,300–2,800
€/ $3,600–4,400 ⚒ CGC

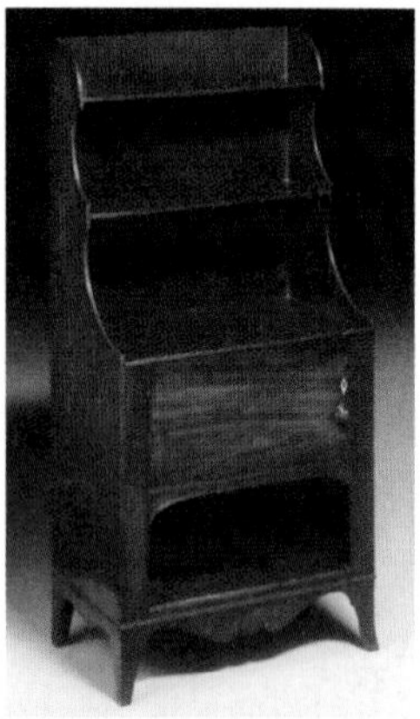

A late Regency mahogany bookcase cupboard, the upper section with shaped sides and two open shelves, the lower section with a cupboard above an open compartment, on splayed bracket feet, 22¾in (58cm) wide.
£1,500–2,000
€/ $2,400–3,200 ⚒ B

A Victorian mahogany dwarf open bookcase, 45¼in (115cm) wide.
£420–525
€/ $650–800 ⚒ B(Ch)

Revolving Bookcases

An oak revolving bookcase, one spindle missing, one damaged, mid-19thC, 22½in (57cm) wide.
£520–650
€/ $800–1,000 ⚒ B(Ch)

▶ An Edwardian mahogany revolving bookcase, 23¾in (60.5cm) wide.
£520–650
€/ $800–1,000 ⚒ L

◀ An Edwardian walnut revolving bookcase, 21in (53.5cm) wide.
£420–525
€/ $650–830 ⚒ B(Ba)

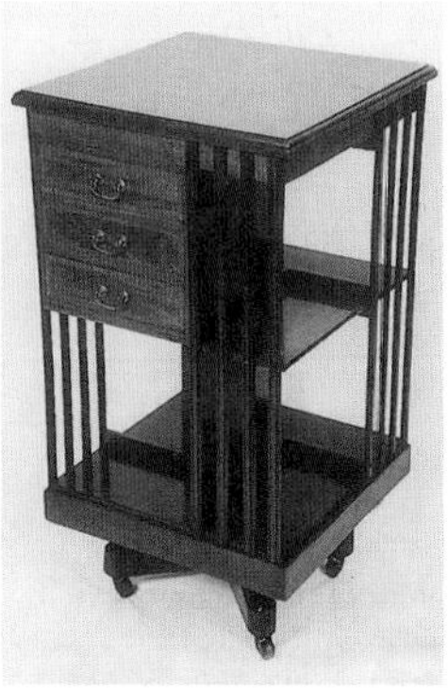

A mahogany inlaid revolving bookcase, fitted with three drawers, c1910, 19in (48.5cm) wide.
£1,400–1,500
€/ $2,200–2,400 ⊞ MTay

An Edwardian mahogany revolving bookcase, the moulded square top over pierced fretwork sides, the stand with a bowed apron, on cabriole legs and pad feet, with a shaped serpentine undertier, 18in (45.5cm) square.
£460–575
€/ $720–900 ⚒ EH

The revolving bookcase was first produced c1800, but achieved its greatest popularity in Edwardian times.

Secretaire Bookcases

A George III mahogany secretaire bookcase, the moulded cornice above a dentil frieze and two glazed doors enclosing shelves, the lower section with a shaped apron, on bracket feet, 44in (112cm) wide.
£2,000–2,500
€/ $3,200–4,000 CGC

A Regency mahogany secretaire bookcase, with a pair of bar-tracery glazed doors, the fall-front enclosing pigeonholes, drawers and a central cupboard, the base with panelled doors enclosing three sliding shelves, on splayed bracket feet, 50in (127cm) wide.
£3,200–4,000
€/ $5,000–6,300 DA

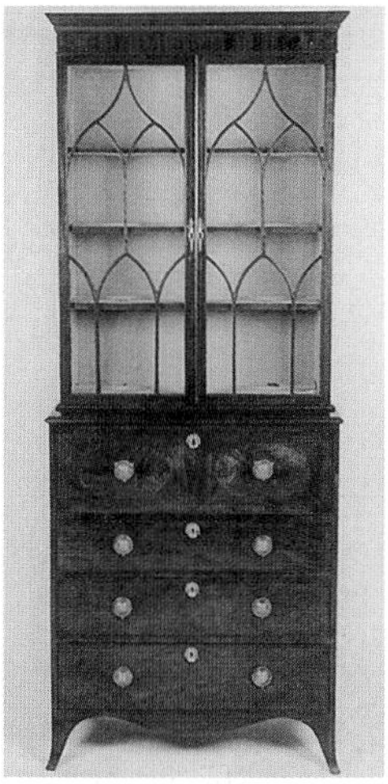

A George III mahogany secretaire bookcase, in the style of Hepplewhite, with plain frieze and moulded cornice above Gothic arched glazed doors enclosing interior shelves, the base with inlaid fall-front frieze drawer and writing surface, secretaire drawers and pigeonholes above three long graduated drawers with neo-classical brass handles, on splayed bracket feet, 34in (86.5cm) wide.
£3,800–4,750
€/ $6,000–7,500 HYD

A Regency mahogany secretaire bookcase, with ebony stringing, on swept feet, 44in (112cm) wide.
£2,600–3,250
€/ $4,100–5,000 G(L)

◄ **A Victorian walnut-veneered secretaire bookcase,** with adjustable shelves enclosed by two glazed doors over a fitted secretaire drawer, above an adjustable shelf enclosed by two panel doors, 50in (127cm) wide.
£1,300–1,600
€/ $2,000–2,500 WW

Miller's Compares

I. A late George III mahogany secretaire bookcase, the secretaire drawer fitted with pigeon-holes and satinwood-faced drawers, 42in (106.5cm) wide.
£1,400–1,800
€/ $2,200–2,800 L

II. A late George III mahogany secretaire bookcase, the upper part enclosed by a pair of glazed doors, the lower part with a fitted drawer above long drawers, 44¼in (112.5cm) wide.
£800–1,000
€/ $1,300–1,600 L

The superior quality of Item I is demonstrated by the satinwood-faced drawers inside the secretaire drawer. The wood is of a better colour and the veneering, particularly of the upper part, is more interesting than that of Item II. The design of the astragal bars and also the presence of feet on Item I give it a more elegant appearance.

A Regency mahogany secretaire bookcase, with ebony stringing, the swan-neck pediment above two astragal-glazed doors, the fitted drawer above three further graduated drawers, on turned feet, 42¼in (107.5cm) wide.
£1,850–2,250
€/ $2,800–3,700 Bea

A mahogany secretaire bookcase, with ebony moulding and a fitted secretaire drawer, on a plinth base, c1840, 54in (137cm) wide.
£5,500–6,250
€/ $8,700–9,800 ⊞ RPh
The addition of the ebony moulding makes this a more desirable item.

Items in the Furniture section have been arranged in date order within each sub-section.

Boxes-on-Stands

A marquetry and laburnum oyster box, on a later stand, the hinged top enclosing a mirrored interior, c1700, 21¼in (54cm) high.
£1,700–2,000
€/ $2,700–3,200 S(O)

An Edwardian inlaid mahogany drinks cabinet, with rising interior and galleried undertier, on square tapered legs, with brass casters, 28¾in (73cm) wide.
£950–1,200
€/ $1,500–1,900 B&L

A mahogany sewing box-on-stand, early 20thC, 33in (84cm) high.
£720–800
€/ $1,150–1,300 RPh

Buckets

A late George III brass-bound mahogany peat bucket, 13in (33cm) high.
£350–450
€/ $500–700 Bea(E)

A pair of brass-bound teak coopered buckets, c1820, 11½in (29cm) diam.
£820–900
€/ $1,300–1,400 S(O)

A brass-bound mahogany coopered bucket, c1830, 13¾in (35cm) high.
£140–155
€/ $220–245 F&F

Buffets

A Louis XVI provincial mahogany and brass-mounted *console desserte*, the white marble inset top with pierced brass gallery above a frieze drawer, on turned fluted legs with undertier, the feet with turned brass sabots, 31½in (80cm) wide.
£1,200–1,500
€/ $1,900–2,400 B
This piece originally belonged to the Rev. Lord Augustus Fitzclarence, Vicar of Mapledurham, the illegitimate son of William IV.

A William IV mahogany two-tier buffet, by James Winter & Sons, with two drawers in the apron, on reeded legs with brass casters, maker's stamp to one drawer, 43in (109cm) wide.
£1,100–1,400
€/ $1,700–2,200 B
James Winter is listed at 101 Wardour Street, Soho, London as a furniture broker, appraiser and undertaker (1823–40). The business continued to trade until 1870 and it is unlikely that any of the furniture so marked was made by James Winter.

A Victorian mahogany two-tier buffet, with figured back, turned finial decoration and moulded edge, over a flat top with figured frieze, on baluster-turned supports with undertier below, on casters, 59¾in (152cm) wide.
£650–800
€/ $1,000–1,300 BIG

LOCATE THE SOURCE
The source of each illustration in Miller's can be found by checking the code letters below each caption with the Key to Illustrations, pages 794–800.

Bureaux

A Queen Anne walnut bureau, the fall-front enclosing a stepped interior of four drawers and pigeonholes flanking a central cupboard with pillar drawers and a well below, above two short and two long drawers, on later bracket feet, restored, the top later veneered, 27¼in (69cm) wide.
£2,000–2,500
€/ $3,200–4,000 🔨 B
The fact that the top of this item was veneered at a later date is reflected in the low price.

A Chippendale-style mahogany bureau, the fall-front enclosing a writing surface and a fitted interior, the centre with an arched panelled drawer with secret compartments each side, the four oak-lined graduated and cockbeaded drawers with brass bail handles and escutcheon plates, on ogee bracket feet, c1770, 39in (99cm) wide.
£4,000–4,500
€/ $6,300–7,300 ⊞ JC
This piece attracted a higher price because of its good original condition. Untouched items with good patination will always be more sought after.

A George III inlaid and crossbanded mahogany writing bureau, the fall-front enclosing a fitted interior, over four graduated drawers, on bracket feet, 43¼in (110cm) wide.
£600–750
€/ $950–1,200 🔨 WilP

► **A George III mahogany bureau,** the fall-front enclosing a stepped, fitted interior, 33in (84cm) wide.
£820–1,000
€/ $1,300–2,400 🔨 L

A George III mahogany bureau, the sloping fall-front enclosing pigeonholes above two moulded frieze drawers and a shaped apron, on shell-carved cabriole legs with pad feet, base 19thC, 26¾in (68cm) wide.
£600–750
€/ $950–1,200 🔨 B(L)

A plum pudding mahogany bureau, with a secret drawer, late 18thC, 40in (101.5cm) wide.
£2,500–2,800
€/ $4,000–4,400 ⊞ RPh

A serpentine walnut bureau, the fall-front enclosing eight drawers and pigeonholes, German, c1770, 45in (114.5cm) wide.
£2,200–2,750
€/ $3,500–4,400 🔨 S(O)

A mahogany tambour-top bureau, the tambour enclosing a slide with ratcheted adjustable reading slope, four small drawers and pigeonholes, c1800, 34in (86.5cm) wide.
£2,800–3,400
€/ $4,400–5,400 🔨 S(O)

A mahogany cylinder bureau, early 19thC, 48½in (123cm) wide.
£10,000–12,500
€/ $16,000–20,000 ⊞ W&C

A Georgian mahogany bureau, with satinwood crossbanding, 42in (106.5cm) wide.
£2,500–2,850
€/ $4,000–4,500 ⊞ MHA

A walnut serpentine bureau, Italian, 1800–50, 43¼in (110cm) wide.
£600–725
€/ $950–1,150 ⚒ B(Ba)

A marquetry cylinder bureau, inlaid with hunting scenes depicting hounds and rabbits, the interior fitted with small drawers, the kneehole with a drawer flanked by two further small drawers, on turned fluted tapering supports, Continental, early 19thC, 48in (122cm) wide.
£2,500–3,200
€/ $4,000–5,000 ⚒ BWL

A Victorian mahogany cylinder bureau, the upper section with glazed doors, the cylinder enclosing drawers and pigeonholes and a leather-lined slide, 51½in (131cm) wide.
£1,100–1,400
€/ $1,700–2,200 ⚒ L

► An Edwardian mahogany satinwood-banded *bureau de dame*, with floral marquetry inlay, 30¼in (77cm) wide.
£900–1,100
€/ $1,400–1,700 ⚒ B(Ch)

A Victorian rosewood and inlaid cylinder bureau, with a pierced three-quarter gallery above an inlaid fall-front enclosing a leather-lined writing slide and fitted interior, a further frieze drawer below, on square tapered legs with casters, 31¼in (79cm) wide.
£1,800–2,200
€/ $2,800–3,500 ⚒ TEN

A kingwood and parquetry *bureau de dame*, French, c1880, 34in (86.5cm) wide.
£2,000–2,350
€/ $3,200–3,700 ⊞ Che

A Victorian mahogany cylinder bureau, probably by Gillows, the single-tier bookshelf top with three-quarter brass gallery on, the cylinder enclosing satinwood-fronted drawers and curtained pigeonholes, with a pull-forward green morocco leather writing surface, each with four graduated drawers, on a plinth base, losses and damage to gallery, 51½in (131cm) wide.
£3,000–3,750
€/ $4,700–6,000 ⚒ HAM

► An Edwardian mahogany bureau, 26in (66cm) wide.
£750–825
€/ $1,200–1,300 ⊞ MHA

An Edwardian rosewood cylinder bureau, the cylinder enclosing a bird's-eye maple-faced interior and a pull-out leather-lined slide, inlaid with foliate scrolls, 30in (76cm) wide.
£900–1,150
€/ $1,400–1,800 ⚒ L

A walnut and marquetry cylinder bureau, with floral-inlaid fall-front over two long drawers, on square tapering legs, Dutch, 19thC, 34in (86.5cm) wide.
£1,000–1,250
€/ $1,600–1,900 ⚒ G(B)

An Edwardian mahogany bureau, the tambour front enclosing a fitted interior with drawers, pigeonholes, and a pull-out leather-inset writing surface on a ratchet action, above two short drawers, on ring-turned legs, altered, 36¼in (92cm) wide.
£500–625
€/ $800–1,000 ⚒ RbF

Cabinets

A walnut and cherrywood-banded cabinet, the ogee-moulded cornice above two doors inlaid with stylized flowerheads, decorative lines and bands, flanked on each side with strapwork panels, the sides and back with decorative lines and banding, on block feet, Austrian, mid–18thC, 74¾in (190cm) wide.
£550–700
€/ $1,300–1,700 B

Further reading

Miller's Late Georgian to Edwardian Furniture Buyer's Guide, Miller's Publications, 2003

A marquetry cabinet, Dutch, early 19thC, 46in (117cm) wide.
£1,000–1,200
€/ $1,600–1,900 S(O)

► **An Edwardian mahogany and satinwood-banded coal cabinet,** 15¾in (40cm) wide.
£100–125
€/ $160–200 B(Ch)

A black-japanned chinoiserie cabinet, attributed to S. Hille & Co, the top decorated with birds in flight above two doors decorated with figures in chinoiserie landscapes, with a pierced and engraved lock plate and strap hinges, above two further doors, on cabriole legs, early 20thC, 40¼in (102cm) wide.
£550–700
€/ $870–1,100 B

The firm of Hille was founded by Salamon Hille in 1906. Their Old Street, London, workshop aimed at high-quality production with an emphasis on materials and craftsmanship. They produced furniture in a number of revivalist tastes and supplied top retailers such as Hamptons, Maples and Waring and Gillow. Chinese Chippendale-style lacquer suites were introduced around 1914, with the more exclusive pieces being produced in satinwood with lacquer panels and gold leaf decoration.

Bedside Cabinets

A George III mahogany tray-top commode, the shaped sides with handles, the rising front above a commode drawer, 21¼in (54cm) wide.
£700–850
€/ $1,100–1,300 TRM

◄ **A George III mahogany night commode,** the rising top above four false drawers opening as a cupboard, 27¾in (70.5cm) wide.
£300–375
€/ $500–600 L

► **A mahogany tray-top bedside cabinet,** with boxwood inlay and stringing, c1790, 31in (78.5cm) wide.
£1,000–1,100
€/ $1,600–1,700 BMi

A mahogany tray-top cabinet, with two doors above two drawers, c1790, 22in (56cm) wide.
£2,400–2,650
€/ $3,800–4,200 RGa

A George III mahogany and boxwood-strung bedside cabinet, the raised shaped back with a shelf, over a tambour door with a brass handle, on square tapering legs, 16in (40.5cm) wide.
£2,300–2,800
€/ $3,600–4,400 DN

A George III mahogany tray-top bedside cabinet, the galleried top with cut-out handles, above a door with a brass handle, on square tapering legs with a platform stretcher, 13in (33cm) wide.
£1,000–1,100
€/ $1,600–1,700 ⊞ JC

A late George III mahogany bedside commode, with boxwood inlay and stringing, the tambour door over a commode drawer inlaid with a swag, on square section legs, 19¼in (49cm) wide.
£520–650
€/ $800–1,000 ⚒ B(Ch)

A mahogany bedside cabinet, Dutch, early 19thC, 18½in (47cm) wide.
£250–320
€/ $400–500 ⚒ L

A mahogany bedside cabinet, c1870, 16in (40.5cm) wide.
£525–575
€/ $830–900 ⊞ MTay

A walnut bedside cabinet, the grey marble top over a banded drawer and fall-front compartment, on moulded cabriole legs, with undertier, French, late 19thC, 15in (38cm) wide.
£120–150
€/ $190–240 ⚒ EH

◄ A matched pair of Edwardian mahogany bedside cabinets, 16in (40.5cm) wide.
£175–200
€/ $275–300 ⊞ PaA

Restoration & repair

When the time comes to repair or restore a piece of furniture try to select a member of the British Antique Furniture Restorers' Association (BAFRA) who will be happy to provide a written quotation before work begins. It is a good idea to ask to see examples of previous restoration work or seek recommendations from a client.

Some work can be done at home, such as applying candle wax to the runners and sides of drawers to prolong their life. Other tasks will need to be done in a workshop. Every 30 or 40 years chairs need to be knocked apart and the old glue removed, before regluing and reassembly. This work should be undertaken promptly if a chair becomes loose; otherwise the chair may collapse and a standard restoration task will become a costly repair.

A walnut bedside cabinet, with marble top, on cabriole legs, French, c1885, 16in (40.5cm) wide.
£135–150
€/ $200–240 ⊞ PaA

A pair of kingwood side cabinets, with gilt-brass galleries and mounts, c1900, 39in (99cm) high.
£1,250–1,380
€/ $2,000–2,200 ⊞ RAN

► A pair of painted bedside cabinets, with a single shallow drawer over a double dummy drawer cupboard door, Italian, c1920, 25in (63.5cm) wide.
£1,500–1,700
€/ $2,400–2,700 ⊞ SSW

A light oak bedside cabinet, with rosewood crossbanding, with a tambour cupboard door modelled as book spines, on tapering legs, c1900, 18in (45.5cm) wide.
£500–625
€/ $800–1,000 ⚒ GAK

An Edwardian mahogany bedside cabinet, with satinwood banding, on casters, door stamped 'Edwards and Roberts', 16in (40.5cm) wide.
£350–400
€/ $550–630 ⊞ RPh

Bureau Cabinets

A baroque inlaid figured-walnut bureau cabinet, with serpentine front, the central door with a shaped panel enclosing a fitted interior flanked by two banks of five drawers, over a hinged fall-front and three serpentine-front drawers with gilt-metal rococo handles, on compressed bun feet, restored, German, early 18thC, 47¼in (120cm) wide.
£3,400–4,250
€/ $5,400–6,700 ⚒ Bri

For further information on antique furniture see the full range of Miller's books at **www.millers.uk.com**

A tiger maple bureau cabinet, the two panelled doors above a fall-front opening to reveal six cubbyholes and five drawers, with three graduated drawers below, brass handles and hinges replaced, American, 18thC, 36¼in (92cm) wide.
£12,000–14,000
€/ $19,000–22,000 ⚒ JDJ

► **A parquetry bureau cabinet,** the upper section with a serpentine cornice enclosed by two doors, with mirror cartouche outlines, the base with a sloping front above a long drawer, the central recess with a kneehole drawer, on cabriole legs with moulded scroll outlines, Italian, 18thC, 36in (91.5cm) wide.
£2,000–2,500
€/ $3,200–4,000 ⚒ L

► **A walnut bureau bookcase,** with mirrored door, c1720, 41in (104cm) wide.
£17,500–20,000
€/ $28,000–32,000 ⊞ Che

A mahogany bureau cabinet, north German, c1760, 43¾in (111cm) wide.
£1,100–1,400
€/ $1,700–2,200 ⚒ S(O)

Cabinets-on-Chests

A William and Mary walnut cabinet-on-chest, fitted with a cushion frieze drawer and further drawers surrounding a central cupboard, enclosed by two doors, all with feather stringing, the base with two short and two long drawers, 47in (119.5cm) wide.
£5,500–6,500
€/ $8,700–10,300 ⚒ L

A William and Mary walnut and featherbanded cabinet-on-chest, the ogee-moulded cornice above a cushion drawer and two burr-walnut quarter-veneered drawers enclosing a central cupboard door revealing three short drawers, the base above two long graduated drawers, on shaped bracket feet, extra height added to the feet, 43¼in (110cm) wide.
£2,300–2,800
€/ $3,600–4,400 ⚒ B

A Queen Anne burr-walnut-veneered cabinet-on-chest, with feather-banding throughout, the cushion frieze drawer above two short and two long drawers, on later oak ball feet, 42¼in (107.5cm) wide.
£3,700–4,700
€/ $5,800–7,400 ⚒ Bea

An Edwardian mahogany cabinet-on-chest, with satinwood and parquetry banding, moulded and dentil cornice, two brass-trimmed astragal-glazed doors enclosing shelving, the base with two short over two long drawers, on bracket feet, 43in (109cm) wide.
£650–800
€/ $1,000–1,200 ⚒ AH

Items in the Furniture section have been arranged in date order within each sub-section.

Corner Cabinets

A japanned corner cabinet, the door with an arched fielded reserve decorated with gilt chinoiserie, on a 19thC stand decorated en-suite, mid-18thC, 76¼in (193.5cm) high.
£650–800
€/ $1,000–1,200 B(S)

A mahogany corner cupboard, with arched doors, c1760, 27in (68.5cm) wide.
£1,500–1,650
€/ $2,400–2,600 F&F

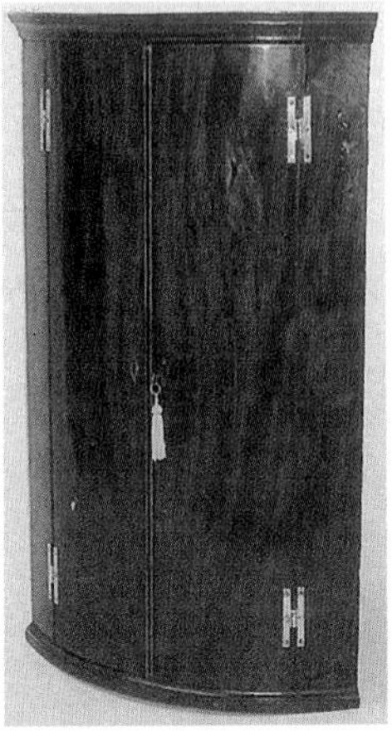

A George II walnut hanging corner cabinet, 26¾in (68cm) wide.
£600–750
€/ $950–1,200 B(Ch)

A mahogany bowfronted corner cabinet, with block moulding and brass H-hinges, c1760, 28in (71cm) wide.
£2,700–3,000
€/ $4,300–4,700 ChC

A mahogany glazed corner cupboard, with flame veneers and boxwood stringing, c1800, 52in (132cm) wide.
£4,750–5,250
€/ $7,500–8,300 MTay

◄ **A George III mahogany bowfronted hanging corner cabinet,** the doors with brass H-hinges, 43in (109cm) high.
£1,100–1,400
€/ $1,700–2,200 BWL

A lacquered bowfronted hanging corner cabinet, with chinoiserie decoration, mid-18thC, 17¾in (45cm) wide.
£800–1,000
€/ $1,300–1,600 S(O)

A George III mahogany hanging corner cabinet, slight damage, 52in (132cm) high.
£600–750
€/ $950–1,200 RbF

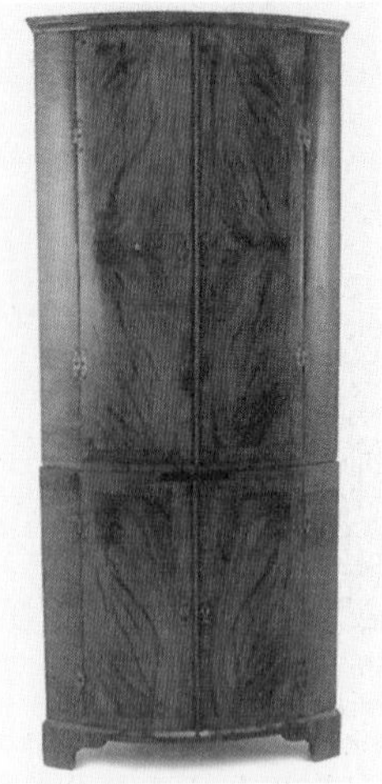

A late George II walnut bowfronted corner cabinet, inlaid with feather stringing, 36in (91.5cm) wide.
£1,700–2,200
€/ $2,700–3,500 L

A George III mahogany bowfronted corner cabinet, enclosed by two doors inlaid with oval paterae, later inlay, 26in (66cm) wide.
£300–375
€/ $475–600 L

A Victorian figured walnut corner cupboard, enclosed by a glazed door, 26in (66cm) wide.
£300–375
€/ $475–600 HOLL

◄ **A Napoleon III mahogany and kingwood bowfronted corner cabinet,** the single door with a matchbook-veneer panel, on a panelled plinth base, French, 14½in (37cm) wide.
£850–1,000
€/ $1,300–1,600 NOA

A rosewood corner collector's cabinet, with glazed upper section, and music trays to base, on square tapering supports, stamped 'Sneider & Hanau', Frankfurt, 19thC, 42in (106.5cm) wide.
£380–475
€/ $600–750 HOLL

An Edwardian inlaid mahogany corner cabinet, with satinwood banding and boxwood stringing, 27½in (70cm) wide.
£850–1,100
€/ $1,300–1,600 B(Ba)

An Edwardian mahogany glazed-front corner cabinet, the central bowfronted door enclosing fitted shelving, the tapering square supports joined by a solid undertier, on splayed feet, 24½in (62cm) wide.
£360–450
€/ $580–700 GAK

A lacquered corner cupboard, c1920, 72in (183cm) high.
£1,350–1,500
€/ $2,200–2,400 Che

Display Cabinets

A Chippendale period display cabinet, the astragal-glazed doors with two panelled cupboards below, on a plinth base, c1760, 48in (122cm) wide.
£13,500–15,000
€/ $21,000–24,000 CAT

A George III mahogany display cabinet, 56in (142cm) wide.
£1,800–2,200
€/ $2,800–3,500 S(O)

A boullework and gilt-metal-mounted dwarf cabinet, mid-19thC, 33¾in (85.5cm) wide.
£320–400
€/ $500–630 B(Ba)

◄ **A George III mahogany display cupboard,** c1790, 45in (114.5cm) wide.
£3,200–3,500
€/ $5,000–5,500 Che

An ebonized mahogany two-door cabinet, with brass embellishments and velvet-lined interior, c1860, 37in (94cm) wide.
£550–625
€/ $870–1,000 PaA

A figured walnut credenza, with tulipwood angled crossbanding, the matchbook-veneered top with a moulded edge and wide tulipwood crossbanding with a skirting board overhang, with rounded ends and concave centre above a glazed central door enclosing a central shelf, the interior lined with raw silk, flanked by two pilasters with gilt-metal mounts to the top and base, either end with bowfronted open display shelves, on a breakfront and bow-ended plinth, c1860, 53¾in (136.5cm) wide.
£2,500–2,850
€/ $4,000–4,500 JC

A Victorian walnut floor-standing display cabinet, with marquetry-inlaid frieze and two glazed doors enclosing shelves, flanked by ormolu-mounted inlaid uprights, standing on a plinth base with a shaped apron, label for 'Windsor & Neate, Complete House Furnishers, Newbury', 42½in (108cm) wide.
£1,100–1,400
€/ $1,800–2,200 CGC

A Victorian walnut and floral marquetry credenza, with gilt-metal mounts and four glazed doors enclosing shelves, on a plinth base with bracket feet, 60in (152.5cm) wide.
£2,500–3,200
€/ $4,000–5,000 ⚒ AH

A Victorian inlaid figured walnut breakfront side cabinet, with gilt-metal mounts, the central glazed door flanked by two curved glazed doors enclosing a red velvet-lined interior, on a plinth base and raised feet, 60in (152.5cm) wide.
£2,600–3,250
€/ $4,100–5,000 ⚒ PF

A Victorian painted vitrine, on a stand, 44in (112cm) wide.
£4,200–4,700
€/ $6,600–7,400 ⊞ SAW

A line-inlaid satinwood display cabinet, with glazed door and sides, c1890, 73in (185.5cm) high.
£3,200–3,500
€/ $5,000–5,500 ⊞ JSt

A mahogany vitrine, with crossbanded panel and ormolu mounts, French, c1900, 28in (71cm) wide.
£2,000–2,200
€/ $3,200–3,500 ⊞ DAC

A walnut and bowed glass curio cabinet, American, c1900, 40in (101.5cm) wide.
£500–625
€/ $800–1,000 ⚒ Dum

An Edwardian mahogany and inlaid serpentine-fronted display cabinet, by Thomas Justice & Co, Dundee, the projecting and banded cornice and plain frieze above two bowed cupboard doors, flanked by two shaped glazed cupboard doors and glazed sides, 48in (122cm) wide.
£2,000–2,500
€/ $3,200–4,000 ⚒ B(Ed)

► **An Edwardian mahogany breakfront display cabinet,** the moulded cornice with applied vase and swag decoration, above a centre glazed door, flanked on either side by a glazed panel, each with wooden astragals and enclosing a pair of shelves, the base having a frieze with central oval paterae and bellflower swag decoration above an open shelf, on six square tapered legs with fretwork spandrels and terminating in spade feet, 55in (139.5cm) wide.
£450–565
€/ $700–870 ⚒ Mit

Decorative features in detail

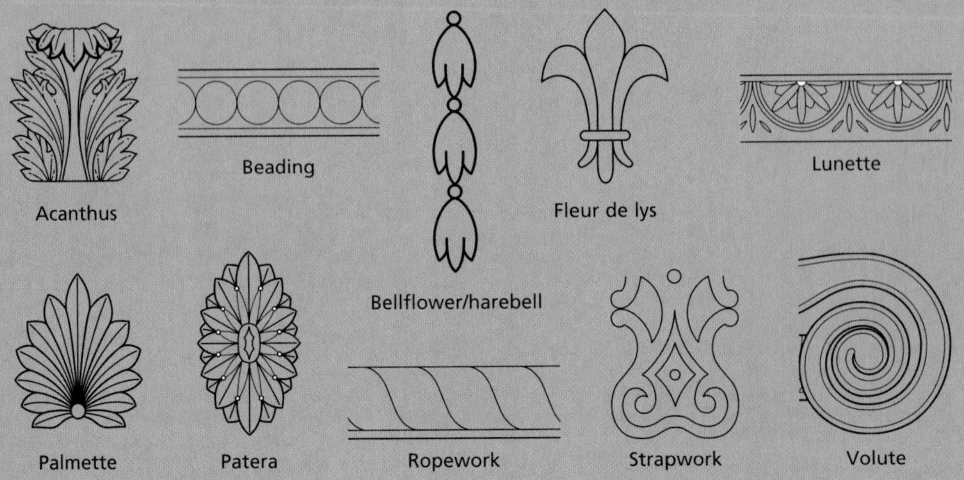

An Edwardian marquetry-inlaid mahogany display cabinet, with an astragal-glazed door, on square tapered legs and spade feet, 27in (68.5cm) wide.
£320–400
€/ $500–630 EH

An Edwardian mahogany display cabinet, with glazed rounded sides, the lower part inlaid with burrwood panels, 44¾in (113.5cm) wide.
£2,400–3,000
€/ $3,800–4,700 L

An Edwardian mahogany boxwood and ebony line-inlaid display cabinet, with dentil-moulded cornice above two astragal-glazed doors enclosing a shelved interior, over two cupboard doors decorated with cartouches, with undertier, on square tapered spade feet, 51in (129.5cm) high.
£1,000–1,250
€/ $1,600–1,900 G(B)

An Edwardian mahogany display cabinet, with stringing, the moulded edged top with raised ledge back, astragal-glazed doors and glazed sides enclosing shelving, on square tapering legs with undershelf and spade feet, 24in (61cm) wide.
£520–650
€/ $800–1,000 AH

A mahogany two-door display cabinet, 1920s, 62¼in (158cm) wide.
£400–500
€/ $630–800 SWO

◄ **A pair of Louis Martin-style glass-fronted demi-lune display cabinets,** painted, with gilt decoration, French, c1940, 67in (170cm) high.
£2,500–2,800
€/ $4,000–4,400 RAN

► **An Edwardian mahogany inlaid cabinet,** the glazed upper section with a pair of inlaid bowed doors below, 40in (101.5cm) wide.
£1,650–1,850
€/ $2,600–3,000 MHA

An Edwardian inlaid display cabinet, on splayed legs, 43in (109cm) wide.
£450–570
€/ $700–900 SWO

► **An Edwardian Sheraton-style mahogany display cabinet,** with boxwood line and floral marquetry inlay, moulded cornice and two glazed doors over a two-door serpentine base, on square tapering legs, 33in (84cm) wide.
£850–1,100
€/ $1,300–1,700 JM

Music Cabinets

◄ **A mid-Victorian mahogany music cabinet,** 30in (76cm) wide.
£650–800
€/ $1,000–1,200 B(Ba)

A late Victorian inlaid walnut music cabinet, one foot loose, 23¼in (59cm) wide.
£500–625
€/ $800–900 B(Ch)

◄ **An Edwardian inlaid mahogany music cabinet,** 19in (48.5cm) wide.
£120–150
€/ $190–350 B(Ch)

An Edwardian inlaid mahogany music cabinet, with a glazed door over two drawers, 19in (48.5cm) wide.
£440–485
€/ $700–770 CHAC

A pair of Edwardian mahogany music cabinets, with stringing, moulded edged top with three-quarter gallery, inlaid fluted frieze, five drawers with brass drop handles, panelled sides, on collared square tapering legs joined by shaped stretchers, label for Arthur Wilson, Pick & Co, Sheffield, 21½in (54.5cm) wide.
£500–625
€/ $800–1,000 AH

Pedestal Cabinets

A pair of satinbirch and marquetry pedestal cabinets, with ebony stringing and tulipwood banding, the inlaid tops with scrolling engraved foliage and stiff leaves to the edge, the frieze drawers above panel doors enclosing three mahogany drawers, on tapered square feet, alterations, 19thC, 20½in (52cm) wide.
£4,000–5,000
€/ $6,300–7,900 S

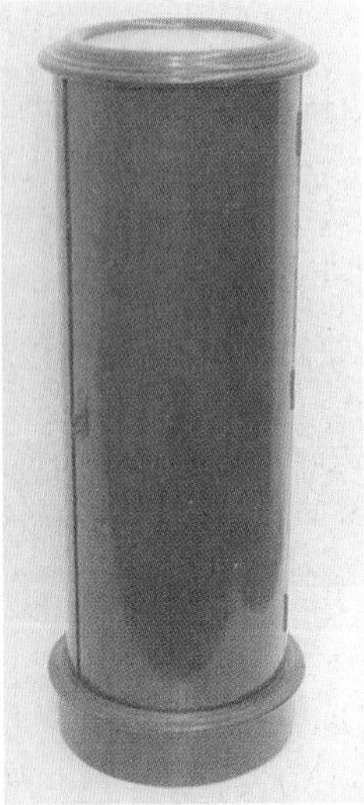

◄ **A Victorian mahogany pedestal cabinet,** with an inset marble top, two interior shelves, on a plinth base, marble cracked, 15in (38cm) diam.
£580–725
€/ $925–1,150 FHF

► **A bird's-eye maple pedestal cabinet,** late 19thC, 14½in (37cm) wide.
£500–625
€/ $800–1,000 B(Ba)

A pair of Biedermeier-style birchwood cabinets, Swedish, c1910, 15¼in (38.5cm) wide.
£2,600–3,000
€/ $4,100–4,800 CAV

A flame mahogany pedestal cabinet, c1900, 32in (81.5cm) wide.
£1,700–2,000
€/ $2,700–3,200 GBr

Pairs

It is not uncommon to find that pairs of pedestal cabinets are not exactly the same size. This is because they were often made at different times, the second one being ordered by the client when he could afford it, after the first one had been delivered. It was usually made from memory or perhaps copied from works day books that had not been accurately kept.

Secretaire Cabinets

A William and Mary walnut secretaire cabinet, the upper section with a cushion frieze drawer, the burrwood fall-front enclosing drawers and pigeonholes around a central cupboard, all with feather stringing, the associated base with three long drawers and a half sunburst to the recess and the bottom drawer, 42¾in (108.5cm) wide.
£4,200–5,000
€/ $6,600–8,000 ⚒ L

A satinwood and kingwood secretaire, with marble top, ormolu mounts and parquetry sides, French, c1880, 30in (76cm) wide.
£2,500–2,800
€/ $4,000–4,400 ⊞ DAC

A George III mahogany secretaire cabinet, the swan-neck pediment above two fielded panelled doors enclosing four sliding trays, the base with a secretaire drawer above three graduated long drawers with brass swan-neck handles, on bracket feet, 51½in (131cm) wide.
£2,000–2,500
€/ $3,200–4,000 ⚒ GTH

► A mahogany secretaire cabinet, 19thC, 33in (84cm) wide.
£1,500–1,700
€/ $2,300–2,700 ⊞ WAW

An Edwardian satinwood secretaire, with stringing and rosewood crossbanding, the fall-front with dummy drawers enclosing a fitted interior, over one long drawer and two doors, on splayed bracket feet, 28¼in (72cm) wide.
£2,000–2,500
€/ $3,100–3,900 ⚒ SWO

◄ A maple secretaire cabinet, with brass handles, American, 1930, 31in (78.5cm) wide.
£230–280
€/ $360–440 ⚒ DUM

A marquetry *secrétaire à abattant,* c1800, 24in (61cm) wide.
£4,200–4,600
€/ $6,600–7,300 ⊞ SAW

A Biedermeier satinbirch *secrétaire à abattant,* possibly north German, 19thC, 29in (73.5cm) wide.
£700–850
€/ $1,100–1,300 ⚒ B(Ba)

A mahogany secretaire side cabinet, the flap enclosing four small drawers and pigeonholes, c1835, 37in (94cm) wide.
£900–1,100
€/ $1,400–1,700 ⚒ S(O)

Side Cabinets

A George III mahogany D-shaped side cabinet, with crossbanded top, fitted with two frieze drawers, flanked by false drawers, 42in (106.5cm) wide.
£4,000–4,700
€/ $6,300–7,400 ⚒ L

A mahogany side cabinet, with two doors enclosing a cellaret drawer, early 19thC, 49in (124.5cm) wide.
£580–725
€/ $920–1,100 ⚒ L

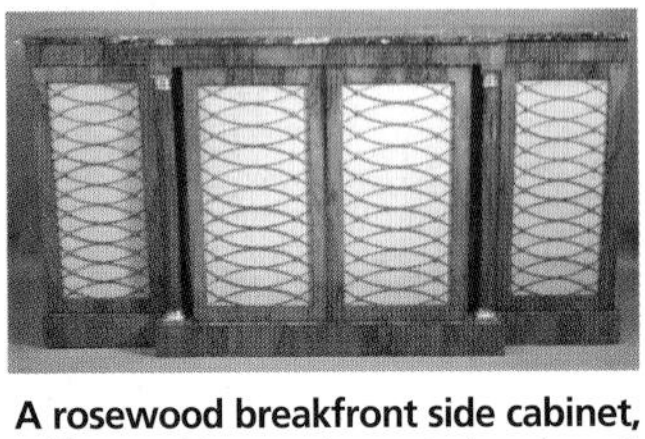

A rosewood breakfront side cabinet, with a marble top, the central cupboard enclosed by two doors flanked by capped pillars and two further cupboards, all with gilt-metal grilled curtain doors, on a plain base, early 19thC, 71½in (181.5cm) wide.
£1,400–1,750
€/ $2,200–2,700 ⚒ TMA

A rosewood breakfront side cabinet, with glazed tapestry doors, c1835, 56in (142cm) wide.
£3,000–3,400
€/ $4,700–5,300 ⊞ MTay

A mahogany and marquetry side cabinet, inlaid with stringing, Dutch, c1790, 43in (109cm) wide.
£3,300–4,000
€/ $5,200–6,300 ⚒ S(O)

A Regency mahogany chiffonier, the round cornered top over two frieze drawers and two panelled cupboards below enclosing shelves, on turned feet, 55½in (141cm) wide.
£2,000–2,400
€/ $3,100–3,800 ⚒ TEN

A mahogany chiffonier, the shelved superstructure with three small drawers, over two drawers and two cupboard doors, c1825, 47in (119.5cm) wide.
£4,200–4,600
€/ $6,600–7,200 ⊞ APO

► **A mahogany chiffonier,** with a carved back, two cushion-moulded frieze drawers, above two cupboard doors, on squat bun feet, 19thC, 40½in (103cm) wide.
£680–850
€/ $1,100–1,300 ⚒ SWO

A mahogany side cabinet, the block-rail inlaid with satinwood, Continental, c1800, 36in (91.5cm) wide.
£5,000–5,750
€/ $8,000–9,000 ⊞ NAW

A Regency satinwood and calamander-banded cabinet base, in the style of George Oakley, the top above two doors with re-entrant panels and scrolling ebony lines, the side pilasters applied with ebonized mounts, above shaped bracket feet painted with anthemia, evidence of a superstructure, 50¾in (129cm) wide.
£800–1,000
€/ $1,300–1,600 ⚒ B

The firm of George Oakley (1773–1840) produced high-quality Grecian-style furniture, often using fashionable materials such as rosewood, mahogany and calamander, with inlays of satinwood, ebony and boullework.

A walnut side cabinet, with a marble top, top in two pieces, French, early 19thC, 67¼in (171cm) wide.
£600–750
€/ $950–1,200 ⚒ B(Ch)

A walnut credenza, the moulded top above two small frieze drawers, with two panelled cupboards below, Italian, 19thC, 37½in (95.5cm) wide.
£500–625
€/ $800–1,000 TEN

A giltwood and gesso pier cabinet, with marble top, the central door with a pastel of a muse, flanked by open shelves, French, 19thC, 44in (112cm) wide.
£900–1,100
€/ $1,400–1,700 G(L)

A teak and marquetry side cabinet, the panel door enclosing trays, French, c1870, 30in (76cm) wide.
£700–800
€/ $1,100–1,300 S(O)

A Victorian mahogany chiffonier, 55in (139.5cm) wide.
£1,200–1,350
€/ $1,900–2,200 ⊞ RPh

A Victorian ebonized credenza, with gilt-metal-mounts, brass inlay and cherub-mounted stiles, 62½in (159cm) wide.
£1,000–1,250
€/ $1,600–1,200 B(Ba)

A Victorian burr-walnut credenza, the two central solid panelled doors with satinwood inlay, flanked by two quarter-round glazed doors fronted by two pairs of ebonized fluted columns with gilt-metal mounts, 72in (183cm) wide.
£3,200–4,000
€/ $5,100–6,300 BWL

A Victorian rosewood-veneered demi-lune side cabinet, the moulded edge marble top above a moulded frieze above a central pierced fret panel, flanked by two moulded outline panel doors enclosing a shelf, on a plinth, 52¼in (132.5cm) wide.
£500–625
€/ $800–1,000 WW

An ebonized side cabinet, in the style of Lamb of Manchester, with inlay detail, gilt work and Wedgwood plaque, c1880, 66in (167.5cm) wide.
£3,000–3,250
€/ $4,700–5,200 RAN

A Sheraton revival mahogany side cabinet, painted overall with flowers, musical trophies and a farm scene, the top with a reeded edge above two panelled doors enclosing shelves, on a plinth base, late 19thC, 37½in (95.5cm) wide.
£1,700–2,200
€/ $2,700–3,500 DN

A George III-style mahogany demi-lune side cabinet, c1900, 41¼in (107.5cm) wide.
£520–650
€/ $800–1,000 B(Ba)

A Victorian gilt-metal-mounted burr-walnut double side cabinet, the top with a gilt metal gallery above four glazed doors, the outer doors enclosing velvet-lined shelves, the projecting base of similar form, the two central doors with mirror plates, on a plinth, associated, 72in (183cm) wide.
£3,000–3,750
€/ $4,700–6,000 PF

A pair of satinwood-veneered demi-lune commodes, with inlaid marquetry, the crossbanded top inlaid with an urn and ribbon-tied fruiting vines, above a shelf enclosed by a mahogany-banded door inlaid with an urn, flanked by oval paterae, with protruding inlaid flat pilasters on square tapering feet, minor damage, late 19thC, 49in (124.5cm) wide.
£42,000–52,000
€/ $66,000–82,000 WW
Estimated at £4,000–6,000 (€/ $6,300–9,500), these commodes, which had been owned by two different members of the same family and brought together for the sale, finally sold for £42,000 (€/ $66,300), underlining the current strength of the market for such decorative items. Although there was minor damage, the quality of the marquetry was superb, and the satinwood veneer was a further desirable factor. They are quite narrow in depth and would therefore fit comfortably in most rooms – practicality is always an important point.

A mahogany demi-lune commode cabinet, with original decorative paintwork and fitted interior with slides, c1910, 50in (127cm) wide.
£2,400–2,650
€/ $3,800–4,200 RAN

A Victorian walnut and inlaid breakfront credenza, with ormolu mounts, the solid centre door flanked by glazed doors, 72in (183cm) wide.
£1,500–1,800
€/ $2,400–2,800 HOLL

An ebonized amboyna credenza, with ebony banding, ormolu moulding and mounts, with similar porcelain plaques, twin glazed side cupboards and central open shelf with double cupboard under, on turned feet, late 19thC, 72in (183cm) wide.
£2,800–3,500
€/ $4,400–5,400 JM

A Viardot-style side cabinet, c1890, 55in (139.5cm) high.
£650–725
€/ $1,000–1,100 SAW

A mahogany bow-end side cabinet, in Regency style, c1920, 35in (89cm) wide.
£1,150–1,300
€/ $1,800–2,000 Che

Cabinets-on-Stands

A walnut cabinet-on-stand, the cushion frieze with a drawer, the two cupboard doors below revealing a central cupboard enclosing a drawer and ten further drawers, the later stand with two drawers, late 17thC and later, 41¾in (106cm) wide.
£2,500–3,000
€/ $4,000–4,700 S(O)

A stained beech, mother-of-pearl and gilt-bronze side cabinet-on-stand, attributed to Gabriel Viardot, Paris, with cast mouldings, French, c1885, 30in (76cm) wide.
£1,800–2,200
€/ $2,800–3,500 S(O)

A kingwood *vernis Martin* cabinet-on-stand, with gilt-metal mounts, French, 1890, 37in (94cm) wide.
£3,200–4,000
€/ $5,000–6,300 WW

▶ **An Edwardian satin-wood and rosewood collector's cabinet-on-stand,** with two panelled doors enclosing six drawers, on swept feet, 20in (51cm) wide.
£1,500–2,000
€/ $2,400–3,200 G(L)

A Louis XVI-style mahogany cabinet-on-stand, Swedish, 1900–10, 12½in (32cm) wide.
£1,750–2,000
€/ $2,800–3,200 ⊞ CAV

Expert's choice

A *pietra dura* cabinet, Florence, c1726, sold at Christie's on 5th July 1990.

There have been many exciting items that have come up for sale during the last 25 years, but, to me, the most memorable must be the Badminton Cabinet. I cannot think of any other piece of furniture that is so exuberant, impressive and beautifully decorative.

The cabinet is made of *pietra dura* and ebony and is mounted with ormolu. It was made in Florence c1726 for the third Duke of Beaufort. This architectural piece is of huge proportions – measuring 152in (386cm) high and 91in (23cm) wide. It is surmounted with a clock, a coat-of-arms with its Ducal coronet and, to either side, ormolu swags encrusted with semi-precious stones and the four corners mounted with ormolu figures depicting the Four Seasons. Below this is a collection of drawers centred by a cupboard door, which opens to reveal a further three purple heart and ebony drawers. The fronts of the drawers and cupboards, together with the side of the cabinet, are inlaid with the most amazing vibrantly colourful semi-precious stones with birds, some in flight around bouquets of flowers and some perched among flowers, all amazingly lifelike. To add to this already dramatic effect, the panels are edged with ormolu and bordered with amethyst quartz. The whole piece is supported on eight lapis-lazuli and red-jasper-mounted legs.

To me, the Badminton Cabinet is a piece that, once seen, can never be forgotten. It sold for £8,580,000 (€/ $13,556,400). **Edward Reily Collins**

Table Cabinets

A mahogany-veneered writing cabinet, early 19thC, 22½in (57cm) wide.
£260–325
€/ $410–510 WW

An Edwardian bird's-eye maple and brass-bound cigar cabinet, 19¾in (50cm) wide.
£250–320
€/ $400–500 B

A Victorian oak table collector's cabinet, the doors enclosing two banks of nine drawers, 30¼in (77cm) wide.
£220–275
€/ $350–435 SWO

Canterburies

A six-section mahogany music canterbury, with two side drawers, c1790, 26in (66cm) wide.
£3,800–4,250
€/ $6,000–6,700 ⊞ CAT

A Regency mahogany canterbury, 19in (48.5cm) wide.
£2,200–2,400
€/ $3,200–3,800 ⊞ APO

A Victorian figured walnut canterbury, on carved turned feet and casters, 21½in (54.5cm) wide.
£1,300–1,600
€/ $2,000–2,500 ⚒ TEN

A Victorian burr-walnut-veneered canterbury, the scroll legs with brass casters, 22in (56cm) wide.
£680–850
€/ $1,100–1,300 ⚒ WW

A George III mahogany canterbury, 16½in (42cm) wide.
£520–650
€/ $825–1,000 ⚒ L

A Regency mahogany canterbury, restored, 19¾in (50cm) wide.
£750–950
€/ $1,200–1,500 ⚒ B(Ba)

A Victorian rosewood canterbury, 18in (45.5cm) high.
£1,250–1,400
€/ $2,000–2,200 ⊞ BrL

A mahogany canterbury, c1810, 20in (51cm) wide.
£2,000–2,200
€/ $3,200–3,500 ⊞ Che

A rosewood canterbury, with a single drawer, on brass casters, 19thC, 20in (51cm) wide.
£1,100–1,200
€/ $1,700–1,900 ⊞ WAW

A walnut canterbury, c1880, 19in (48.5cm) wide.
£325–360
€/ $520–600 ⊞ PaA

◄ **A Victorian walnut music canterbury,** the three divisions supported by turned pillars, above a single long drawer, on turned legs with ceramic casters, 21in (53.5cm) wide.
£400–500
€/ $630–800 ⚒ G(B)

Open Armchairs

A mahogany cockpen armchair, in the Chinese Chippendale style, the drop-in seat inset with a later solid panel, above a blind fret-carved seat rail, minor losses and faults, c1760.
£3,000–3,500
€/ $4,700–5,500 BR

During the 17th and 18th century, Europe had a fascination with the orient and Chippendale incorporated many Chinese features into his furniture using fretwork, lacquerwork, pagodas etc.

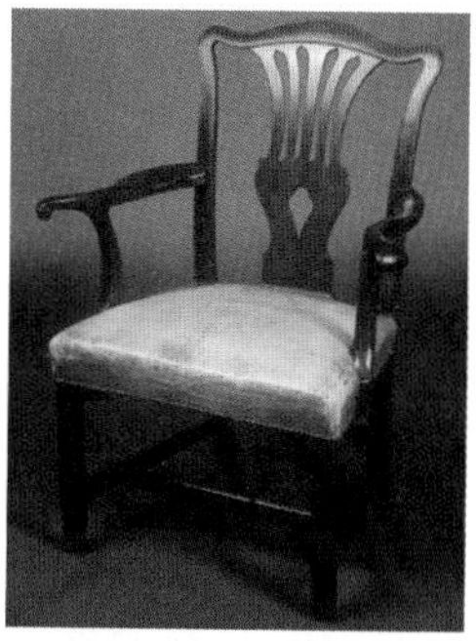

A George III mahogany open-scroll armchair, in the Chippendale style, with leather stuff-over seat, the back legs stamped with a Gothic C below a crown.
£550–700
€/ $870–1,100 B(WM)

► **A painted and parcel-gilt elbow chair,** with padded back and bowfronted stuff-over seat, late 18thC.
£1,200–1,500
€/ $1,900–2,400 TEN

A rococo giltwood *fauteuil en cabriolet*, the shield-shaped backrest within a moulded frame surrounded by a floral garland, with padded out-curved scrolled arms on leaf-carved supports, with a bow-shaped seat, the seat rail and cabriole legs with carved decoration, probably Spanish, c1760.
£2,300–2,700
€/ $3,600–4,300 S(Am)

A George III carved mahogany armchair, Irish.
£800–1,000
€/ $1,300–1,600 S(O)

◄ **A pair of carved walnut *fauteuils*,** with padded backs, scroll arms and stuff-over seat, one chair with insect damage, French, late 18thC.
£900–1,100
€/ $1,400–1,700 JDJ

A George III mahogany armchair.
£400–500
€/ $630–800 L

A mahogany-framed Gainsborough chair, on square legs and casters, late 18thC.
£800–1,000
€/ $1,300–1,600 HOLL

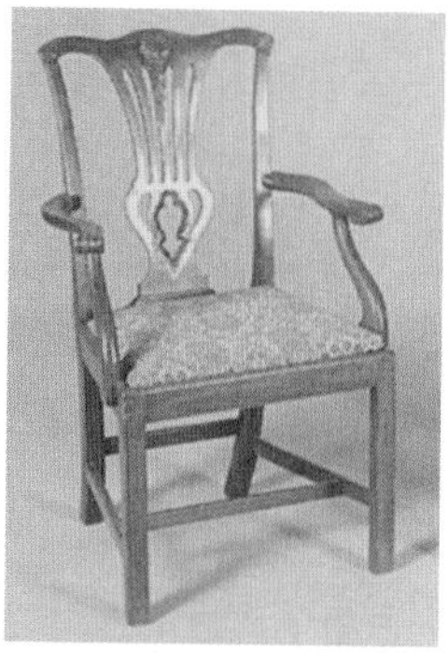

A pair of George III mahogany provincial armchairs, some restoration and later arms.
£140–175
€/ $300–280 B(Ba)

A George III mahogany and leather armchair.
£1,600–1,800
€/ $2,500–2,800 APO

A pair of mahogany armchairs, the curved panelled bar back above open-pierced reeded splats with carved central paterae, the reeded arms on ring-turned vertical supports, with drop-in upholstered seats, on square tapered legs, c1810.
£2,400–2,650
€/ $3,800–4,200 ⊞ JC

A mahogany armchair, the arms with dolphin-shaped supports, c1820.
£350–420
€/ $550–670 ⚒ S(O)

A late Regency carved pollarded oak armchair, the panelled bar top-rail with moulded scroll terminals and rectangular splats, with stuff-over seat, on sabre legs and casters.
£1,700–2,200
€/ $2,700–3,500 ⚒ B(Nor)

A Georgian mahogany elbow chair, with pierced splat back, shaped top rail, scroll arms and an upholstered drop-in seat, on square chamfered supports.
£370–470
€/ $580–750 ⚒ BWL

A pair of neo-classical birch tub chairs, the curved back and sides with inlaid stringing and a central inlaid patera, the padded seat raised on splayed legs, 1800–25.
£2,500–3,250
€/ $4,000–5,500 ⚒ NOA

A pair of George IV mahogany elbow chairs, the figured swept bar backs with acanthus carving and downswept reeded arms and supports, with stuff-over seats, supported on palmette-carved and turned legs.
£900–1,100
€/ $1,400–1,700 ⚒ HAM

◄ **A simulated rosewood upholstered armchair,** with a reclining back and sliding footrest, c1835.
£350–420
€/ $550–650 ⚒ S(O)

A Regency salon armchair, with hand-painted floral decoration and upholstered seat, on turned legs.
£120–150
€/ $190–240 ⚒ WilP

A pair of Restauration armchairs, with padded backs, scrolling arms and bowed padded seats, on sabre legs, together with a similar side chair, French, 1815–30.
£1,500–2,000
€/ $2,400–3,200 ⚒ B

A rope-back carver chair, c1830.
£580–650
€/ $900–1,000 ⊞ RPh

A Regency mahogany open armchair, with leather drop-in seat.
£260–325
€/ $400–500 ⚒ B(Ba)

A mahogany open armchair, the back with five spindle splats, with flat arms and cushion seat and turned legs with brass caps and casters, 1825–50.
£1,300–1,500
€/ $2,000–2,400 ⚒ NOA

A mahogany Patent Reclining Chair, by Robert Daws, c1835.
£2,700–3,000
€/ $4,300–4,700 ⊞ ChC
Robert Daws traded from 17 Margaret Street, near Oxford Circus in London, from 1820–39, when he moved to new premises in Edgware Road. He patented his 'Improved Recumbent Easy Chair' in 1827.

◄ **A William IV mahogany elbow chair.**
£650–725
€/ $1,000–1,150 ⊞ RPh

A mahogany *fauteuil*, the padded back above scrolling arms, the bowed padded seat on lapetted sabre legs, French, 1830–48.
£800–975
€/ $1,300–1,500 B

A mid-Victorian cast-iron and brass decorated rocking chair, attributed to R. W. Winfield & Co, the ringed padded back between uprights surmounted by leaf-cast terminals, the downswept padded arms and over-scrolled seat on shaped rolling rockers.
£1,800–2,250
€/ $2,800–3,500 B

A version of this model was shown by Winfield at the Great Exhibition in 1851 and again at the London International Exhibition in 1862. The design seemed to go against the over ornamentation that was dominant at the time. It is thought that it may have been designed by Peter Cooper (New York, 1793–1883), who founded the Canton Iron Works in Baltimore and built the Tom Thumb, one of the earliest American locomotives, and who was to become one of the leaders of the American iron industry. The firm of Winfield was founded at Cambridge Street in Birmingham in 1829 and specialized in the production of decorative brass objects, particularly bedsteads.

► **A pair of mahogany open armchairs,** Danish, c1870.
£1,200–1,350
€/ $1,900–2,200 RPh

A Victorian walnut open armchair, with moulded balloon-shaped padded back and serpentine-shaped seat, on cabriole front legs and down-scroll rear legs.
£1,450–1,800
€/ $2,300–3,000 MEA

A Victorian mahogany reclining easy chair, on brass casters.
£220–245
€/ $350–380 PaA

A pair of walnut Burgomaster chairs, with walnut-veneered backrest, out-curved scrolled arms on incurved supports and padded seat, on scrolled legs, alterations, Italian, 19thC.
£3,400–3,750
€/ $5,400–6,000 S(Am)

A Victorian mahogany X-framed chair, with leather upholstery.
£800–900
€/ $1,300–1,400 SAW

An ebonized armchair, with curved padded backrest, padded arms and S-scrolled reeded supports carved with leaves and topped with a reeded finial, on leaf-carved turned toupie feet with casters, probably American, 19thC.
£2,300–2,750
€/ $3,600–4,300 S(Am)

A Renaissance revival walnut open armchair, the uprights formed as caryatids, American, 1850–75.
£575–700
€/ $900–1,100 NOA

A pierced laminated-rosewood open armchair, in the Tuthill King pattern, attributed to John Henry Belter, the high back with a crest, the serpentine front with carved rose decoration, on French-style cabriole legs on brass caster feet, 19thC.
£15,000–17,000
€/ $24,000–27,000 JDJ

German-born John Henry Belter (1804–63) emigrated to the United States in 1833 and developed a range of sumptuously carved furniture of heavy proportions, which was intended to grace the houses of the country's *nouveau riche*. These designs are said to have given rise to the term 'a belter of a piece'. Items were seldom marked and rarely exported and therefore examples are hardly ever found outside the United States.

A walnut X-framed Savanorola armchair, the back with a grotesque and shell-carved top rail, with hide-covered padded central panel, with a padded seat, the foliate moulded legs terminating in paw feet, Italian, 19thC.
£200–250
€/ $300–400 PF

◄ **A pair of walnut armchairs,** the padded backs flanked with acanthus-carved uprights, downswept arms with animal carved terminals and stuff-over seat with acanthus-carved apron, Continental, 19thC.
£450–550
€/ $700–870 CGC

A mahogany Gainsborough chair, with brocade upholstery, c1880.
£1,650–1,850
€/ $2,600–3,000 ⊞ RAN

A pair of ebonized elbow chairs, by L. Hitchcock, each with a stencilled crest and back rail, the downswept arms with turned supports, the rush seat on turned legs and stretchers, stencilled 'L. Hitchcock, Hitchcocksville, Conn. Warrented', American, late 19thC.
£500–650
€/ $800–1,000 ⚒ DN

A pair of Chippendale-style mahogany chairs, c1900.
£2,800–3,200
€/ $4,400–5,000 ⊞ Che

► An Edwardian painted satinwood elbow chair, the caned shield back with a centre portrait splat, on shaped legs, Waring's label.
£600–725
€/ $950–1,150 ⚒ SPF

A mahogany armchair, Continental, c1880.
£800–900
€/ $1,300–1,400 ⊞ RPh

A walnut, ebony and bone-inlaid armchair, in the Moorish style, inlaid with flowerheads and patterns created from bone *tesserae,* the back with an ebonized swan-neck pediment above a portrait of a gentleman in 17thC costume, surmounted by an ivory-inlaid grotesque mask, flanked by further inlaid panels on an ebony ground, the downswept arms above a solid seat with a shaped apron on trestle supports, Italian, late 19thC.
£620–775
€/ $1,000–1,200 ⚒ B

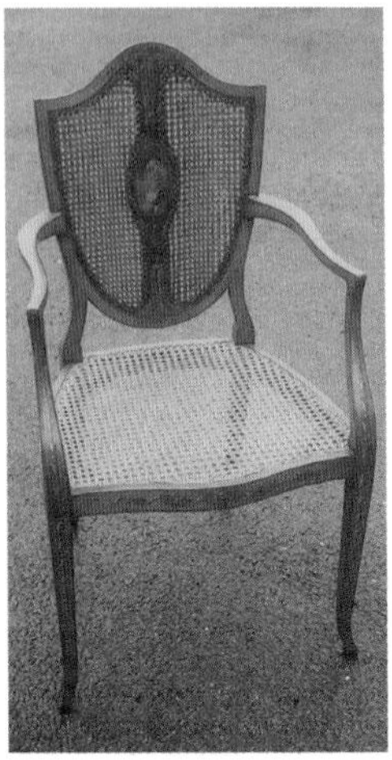

A pair of Louis XV-style walnut armchairs, recovered, c1890.
£1,600–1,800
€/ $2,500–2,800 ⊞ DAC

A maple rocking chair, with scrolling arms and a modified curule base joined to rockers, Anglo-American, late 19thC.
£1,500–2,000
€/ $3,500–3,200 ⚒ NOA

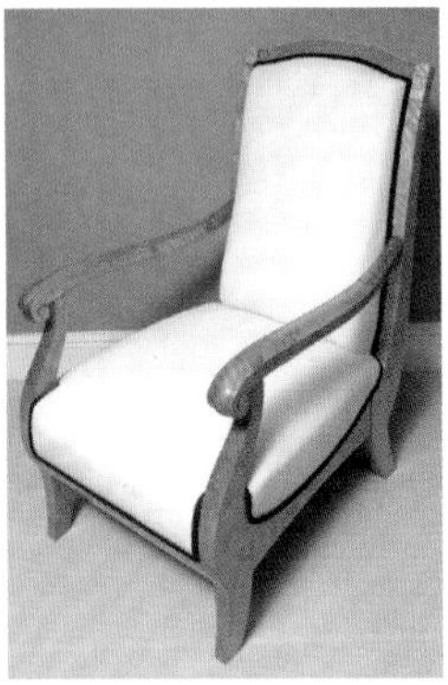

A pair of Biedermeier-style birchwood armchairs, Swedish, 1900–10.
£5,000–5,600
€/ $8,000–8,800 ⊞ CAV

A pair of rosewood open armchairs, inlaid with musical instruments and satinwood stringing, with upholstered seats and backs, on square tapering legs, spade feet and casters, late 19thC.
£650–820
€/ $1,000–1,300 ⚒ RTo

A carved walnut armchair, American, c1900.
£550–700
€/ $870–1,100 ⚒ DuM

An inlaid mahogany elbow chair, c1905.
£340–375
€/ $550–600 ⊞ RPh

◄ A pair of Louis XV-style walnut *fauteuils,* c1930.
£1,000–1,100
€/ $1,500–1,600 ⊞ MLL

Upholstered Armchairs

A walnut wing armchair, with padded back, sides and outscrolled arms, repairs to front legs, replacement back legs, early 18thC.
£1,500–1,800
€/ $2,400–2,800 ⚒ B

A George III mahogany chair, with stuff-over back, arms and seat.
£150–200
€/ $240–300 ⚒ L

An early Victorian rose-wood-framed button-back chair, on turned legs with casters.
£450–575
€/ $700–900 ⚒ JAd

A walnut armchair, the shaped padded back, arms and seat above a walnut-veneered frieze and cabriole legs, 18thC.
£500–600
€/ $800–1,000 ⚒ WW

A mid-Georgian mahogany wing armchair, with deep button back, wings and scroll-over arms, cabriole front legs with compressed ball feet.
£850–1,100
€/ $1,300–1,700 ⚒ PFK

A George III-style mahogany barrel-back wing armchair, 19thC.
£450–565
€/ $700–900 ⚒ B(Ba)

◄ A Victorian mahogany spoon-back armchair, with buttoned back and padded arms and seat, on cabriole front legs.
£140–170
€/ $220–270 ⚒ EH

A Chippendale-style cherrywood lolling chair, with serpentine top crest rail, American, Connecticut, 18thC.
£1,500–2,000
€/ $2,400–3,200 ⚒ JDJ

A stained-wood upholstered armchair, French, mid-18thC.
£400–500
€/ $630–800 ⚒ BERN

A pair of stained wood upholstered armchairs, French, mid-18thC.
£800–975
€/ $1,300–1,500 ⚒ BERN

A late Regency simulated rosewood armchair.
£400–500
€/ $630–800 ⚒ S(O)
Beech was often used instead of solid rosewood because it was stronger and found locally, therefore keeping down costs. The wood was then painted to simulate rosewood.

A Victorian walnut-framed tub chair, the buttoned back above down-swept scrolling arms and stuff-over seat, on cabriole legs with brass casters.
£400–500
€/ $630–800 **CGC**

A Victorian mahogany-framed armchair, on scroll-carved French-style legs and casters.
£800–900
€/ $1,300–1,400 **BWL**

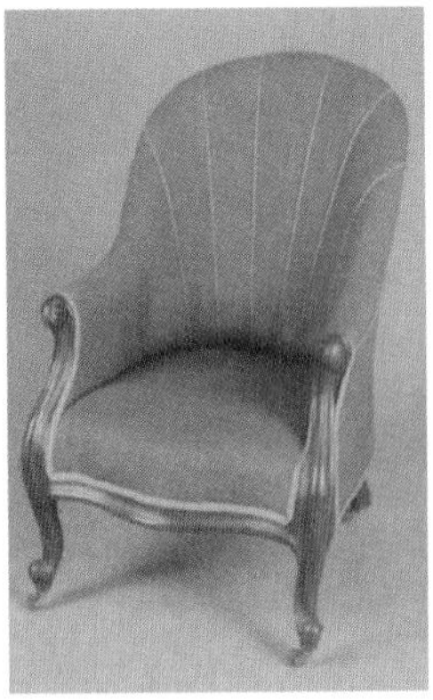

A mid-Victorian mahogany tub chair.
£180–225
€/ $285–350 **B(Ba)**

A pair of button-back armchairs, on ebonized turned legs, French, c1860.
£1,000–1,200
€/ $1,600–1,900 **S(O)**

A pair of giltwood tub-shaped *fauteuils*, c1870.
£2,100–2,350
€/ $3,300–3,700 **RAN**

A Queen Anne-style walnut-framed wing armchair, the upholstered back with out-scrolled arms, on ball-turned front legs, cut down, reupholstered, 19thC.
£420–525
€/ $950–830 **B(W)**

A pair of Louis XV-style walnut *fauteuils*, reupholstered, French, c1880.
£1,700–2,000
€/ $2,700–3,200 **DAC**

A mahogany and leather armchair, the concave padded back and sloping arms above a bowed seat, on cabriole legs with claw-and-ball feet, 1875–1900.
£1,200–1,400
€/ $1,900–2,200 **NOA**

A late Victorian easy chair, on ring-turned tapering front legs with brass caps and casters.
£230–300
€/ $360–470 **PFK**

A button-upholstered armchair, on ebonized turned legs and ceramic casters, late 19thC.
£650–750
€/ $1,000–1,200 **S(O)**

A Gothic-style carved oak armchair, late 19thC.
£700–900
€/ $1,100–1,400 **B(Ba)**

A late Victorian mahogany-framed wing armchair, the acanthus-carved cabriole legs with ball-and-claw feet.
£270–340
€/ $425–800 **B(Ch)**

A giltwood wing armchair, with upholstered back, sides and seat, the frame carved with scrolls, on cabriole legs, late 19th–early 20thC.
£700–875
€/ $1,100–1,400 **DN**

A pair of walnut and leather upholstered armchairs, French, late 19thC.
£700–875
€/ $1,100–1,400 **B(Ch)**

A pair of Howard-style upholstered armchairs, early 20thC.
£1,800–2,250
€/ $2,800–3,500 **B(Ch)**

Bergères

A Restauration mahogany bergère, with padded back and arms above a cushioned seat, on sabre legs, French, 1800–25.
£1,000–1,200
€/ $1,600–1,900 NOA

A mahogany bergère, with a reeded frame and caned back, arms and seat, on square tapering legs, with brass casters, early 19thC.
£800–1,000
€/ $1,300–1,600 DN

A Regency ebonized bergère, with original decoration.
£1,250–1,400
€/ $1,900–2,200 CAT

A Regency mahogany bergère, with reeded frame.
£650–800
€/ $1,000–1,300 L

► **An Empire-style giltwood bergère,** the cove back with reeded back-rail and scroll ends, the sides and seat upholstered, the arms with carved dolphin-head supports, on squared sabre legs, French, 19thC.
£300–375
€/ $475–600 B&L

◄ **A William IV rosewood and caned bergère.**
£700–875
€/ $1,100–1,400 B(Ba)

A Sheraton revival satinwood and decorated bergère, c1890.
£2,000–2,300
€/ $3,200–3,600 Che

Children's Chairs

A child's George III mahogany chair, the arched back above a pierced vase splat, drop-in seat and moulded chamfered square legs, on a later square-legged stand, c1780.
£950–1,200
€/ $1,500–1,900 S(O)

A child's Georgian mahogany open armchair, with serpentine top-rail, pierced vase splat, rush drop-in seat, on square legs, restored.
£380–475
€/ $600–750 Bea

A child's mahogany high chair, with horizontal splat and drop-in seat, the turned tapering front supports and sabre back legs joined by stretchers, 19thC.
£160–200
€/ $250–300 FHF

A child's mahogany high chair and table, 19thC, table 12½in (32cm) high.
£625–700
€/ $1,000–1,100 SDA

Safety

The children's furniture illustrated in this guide no longer complies with EC safety regulations and must not be used for its original purpose.

► **A child's Victorian oak and caned bergère,** on turned supports with cross-stretcher.
£85–100
€/ $135–160 WilP

Corner Chairs

A Chippendale-style carved and figured walnut corner chair, repairs to one leg, American, Philadelphia, 1760–80.
£2,000–2,400
€/ $3,200–3,800 S(NY)

A George III mahogany high-back corner chair, the scrolled top-rail above pierced splats, gun barrel columns and a drop-in seat, on square legs joined by stretchers, restored.
£1,200–1,500
€/ $1,900–2,400 B(L)

A mahogany corner armchair, altered and restored, 18thC.
£1,200–1,500
€/ $1,900–2,400 B(Ba)

A marquetry corner armchair, Dutch, c1850.
£770–950
€/ $1,200–1,500 S(O)

A pair of oak corner chairs, c1880.
£800–875
€/ $1,300–1,400 GBr

A Victorian carved oak corner chair, with a coronet and a painted leather seat.
£130–160
€/ $200–250 SWO

A pair of Edwardian rosewood corner chairs, the top-rails and splat backs inlaid with satinwood, above stuff-over seats, on square tapering legs, with spade feet.
£450–565
€/ $700–900 RTo

An Edwardian light mahogany corner chair, the splat back inlaid with boxwood stringing and a panel, over three open fret and carved supports, on cabriole legs joined by a cross-stretcher.
£220–270
€/ $350–425 DA

Dining Chairs

A George I walnut dining chair, with splat back and drop-in seat, on cabriole legs carved with shell knees, on pad feet joined by an H-stretcher.
£280–350
€/ $440–550 RTo

A walnut dining chair, with scroll top-rail, pierced waisted splat and drop-in seat, on cabriole legs with shell-carved hips and claw-and-ball feet, 18thC.
£340–425
€/ $550–670 G(L)

Further reading

Miller's Antiques Encyclopedia, Miller's Publications, 1998

A set of six George III mahogany dining chairs, after a design by Thomas Sheraton, each with a curved and overlapping cresting rail, over a diamond trellis splat with leaf-capped reeded frame, flanked by reeded tapering uprights, above a stuff-over seat, on reeded knop-turned tapering front legs, repaired.
£1,700–2,200
€/ $2,700–3,500 B(WM)

► **A set of eight Hepplewhite-period mahogany dining chairs,** c1790.
£10,000–11,000
€/ $11,800–17,500
CAT

A set of six mahogany brander-back dining chairs, including two armchairs, the goblet-shaped backs enclosing five moulded splats above drop-in seats, on square tapering legs, c1800.
£1,400–1,750
€/ $2,200–2,800 ⚒ B(Ed)

The 'brander back' was a pattern frequently used in common chairs from the eastern counties of Scotland during the last quarter of the 18th century. These were probably made for an improved farmhouse and have been given an extra fashionable lift by the curvature of their stiles – a reference to the shield-back shape seen in Hepplewhite's *Cabinet and Upholsterer's Guide* 1788.

Valuing sets of chairs

Sets of dining chairs are worth proportionally more the larger the set. For good quality 19th-century copies of Georgian chairs, for example:
2: approx 3 x price of a single
4: approx 6 x price of a single
6: approx 10 x price of a single
8: approx 16 x price of a single
10: approx 25 x price of a single
The reason that the unit price between a pair and four is the same is that the latter are difficult to sell unless looking for chairs for a card table. Pairs and sets of six or more are more desirable.

A set of four George III mahogany dining chairs.
£400–500
€/ $630–800 ⚒ L

A set of six mahogany dining chairs, Dutch, early 19thC.
£750–950
€/ $1,200–1,500 ⚒ L

A set of six mahogany chairs, with gilt-metal mounts, Scandinavian, early 19thC.
£1,500–2,000
€/ $2,400–3,200 ⚒ S(O)

A pair of Regency mahogany dining chairs, the bar backs with brass inlay, cane seats, damaged.
£300–375
€/ $475–600 ⚒ SWO

◄ A set of eight Regency mahogany dining chairs, with two armchairs, the bar backs above pierced shell and circle motifs, on turned tapering legs.
£1,100–1,400
€/ $1,700–2,200 ⚒ BWL

A set of four rosewood dining chairs, with caned seats and squab cushions, c1810.
£1,750–2,000
€/ $2,800–3,200 ⊞ RPh

A set of six mahogany dining chairs, the backs with moulded top-rails and single horizontal bars joined by reeded X-shaped splats, with drop-in seats, on square tapered legs joined by stretchers, early 19thC.
£650–800
€/ $1,000–1,300 ⚒ PF

► A set of six late George III mahogany dining chairs, with boxwood stringing throughout, the backs with stick splats, above upholstered seats and tapering turned legs.
£900–1,150
€/ $1,400–1,800 ⚒ Bea

A set of eight Regency mahogany dining chairs, including two armchairs, with gadrooned top-rails, palmette-carved crossbars, upholstered seats, on tapering turned legs, restored.
£2,400–3,000
€/ $3,800–4,700 ⚒ Bea

A set of six late George III mahogany bar-back dining chairs, including two carvers.
£800–1,000
€/ $1,300–1,600 ⚒ B(Ba)

A pair of Regency Gothic-style dining chairs.
£750–850
€/ $1,200–1,300 ⊞ SAW

A set of four William IV mahogany dining chairs.
£900–1,000
€/ $1,400–1,600 ⊞ DY

A set of four William IV mahogany dining chairs.
£1,440–1,550
€/ $2,300–2,400 ⊞ RPh

A set of five George IV mahogany dining chairs.
£450–575
€/ $700–900 ⚒ L

A set of seven William IV mahogany bar-back dining chairs.
£6,200–6,850
€/ $9,800–11,000 ⊞ RAN

A set of six mahogany dining chairs, c1840.
£2,250–2,500
€/ $3,500–4,000 ⊞ DY

◄ **A set of six early Victorian walnut dining chairs,** restored.
£600–750
€/ $950–1,200 ⚒ B(Ba)

A set of eight rosewood dining chairs, with carved backs and back-rails, on turned and carved legs, c1825.
£7,000–8,000
€/ $11,000–12,500 ⊞ BERA

A pair of William IV mahogany dining chairs, upholstered in leather.
£150–200
€/ $250–300 ⚒ B(Ba)

A set of six William IV mahogany dining chairs, with upholstered drop-in seats, on tapered front legs.
£650–820
€/ $1,000–1,300 ⚒ WL

A set of eight rosewood dining chairs, with button-upholstered seats, c1850.
£2,500–2,800
€/ $4,000–4,400 ⊞ NoC

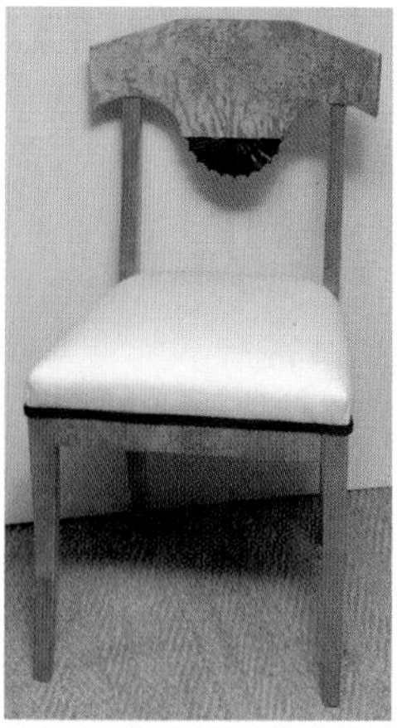

A pair of Biedermeier birchwood and masur birch dining chairs, Swedish, 1820–30.
£2,000–2,300
€/ $3,200–3,600 ⊞ CAV

A set of four William IV rosewood dining chairs, the top- and centre-rails profusely carved with acanthus leaf scrolls and flowerheads, above cane seats, on reeded tapering legs.
£650–820
€/ $1,000–1,300 ⚒ RTo

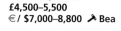

A set of 12 George III-style mahogany dining chairs, the arched backs with foliate-carved stick splats and gilt-brass mounts, above leather-upholstered seats, on tapering square legs, damaged, one chair distressed, 19thC.
£4,500–5,500
€/ $7,000–8,800 ⚒ Bea

A pair of Victorian inlaid walnut dining chairs.
£430–475
€/ $680–750 ⊞ RPh

A set of six Victorian mahogany dining chairs, on turned reeded supports.
£620–775
€/ $1,000–1,200 ⚒ MAR

A set of six Victorian mahogany dining chairs.
£400–500
€/ $630–800 ⚒ L

A set of four Victorian walnut balloon-back dining chairs.
£500–650
€/ $800–1,000 ⚒ L

A set of six Victorian walnut dining chairs, with scroll-moulded waisted balloon backs, the sprung serpentine seats on cabochon-moulded turned legs.
£550–700
€/ $870–1,100 ⚒ PF

A set of eight late Victorian mahogany dining chairs, by Lamb of Manchester, with leather-upholstered back and seats, on cabriole legs with pad feet and ceramic casters, stamped 'Lamb, Manchester'.
£1,000–1,200
€/ $1,600–1,900 ⚒ DN

◄ **A set of six Edwardian walnut dining chairs,** with floral-carved top-rail and spindle back, above a stuff-over seat, on ring-turned legs.
£240–300
€/ $380–475 ⚒ AMB

► **A set of eight Victorian mahogany dining chairs,** with padded leather backs and seats, on turned and fluted tapering legs.
£1,800–2,200
€/ $2,800–3,500
⚒ G(L)

A set of four Victorian carved rosewood balloon-back dining chairs, on French cabriole legs.
£1,000–1,250
€/ $1,600–2,000 ⚒ WilP

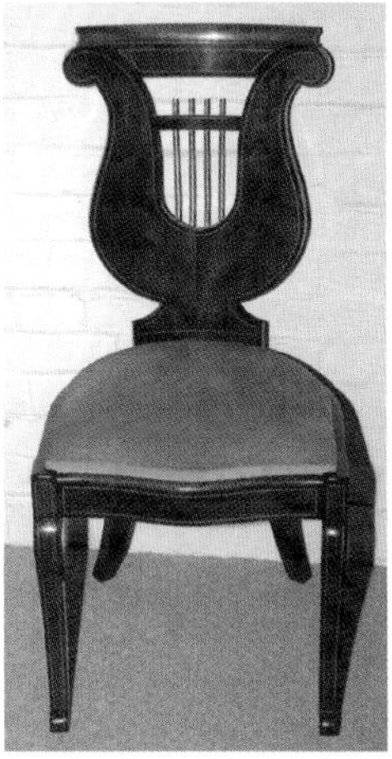

A set of seven mahogany lyre-back dining chairs, Continental, c1880.
£5,300–6,000
€/ $8,400–9,500 ⊞ SAW

Hall Chairs

A pair of George III mahogany hall chairs.
£2,200–2,400
€/ $3,500–3,800 ⊞ APO

A pair of Regency mahogany hall chairs, with shaped backs, on ring-turned leg supports.
£900–1,100
€/ $1,400–1,700 AMB

► **A pair of William IV mahogany hall chairs,** the scroll-bordered waisted backs centred with stylized carved scallop shell motifs.
£630–800
€/ $1,000–1,300
Bri

◄ **A pair of late Victorian walnut hall chairs.**
£100–140
€/ $160–220
B(Ba)

A set of six early Victorian mahogany hall chairs, each with a shield-shaped back with a central painted crest, the solid serpentine seat on turned tapering legs.
£1,700–2,200
€/ $2,700–3,500 DN

A carved walnut hall chair, the back ornately decorated with a mask and scrolling and pierced foliage, the shaped solid seat with a dished centre, on trestle legs.
£220–275
€/ $350–430 WW

Library Chairs

An oak library chair, with a cane seat, c1830.
£600–725
€/ $1,000–1,150 S(O)

An oak metamorphic library chair, possibly by Gillows, c1835.
£4,700–6,000
€/ $7,500–9,500 S(O)
The top portion of this chair folds forward, converting to steps.

A William IV rosewood and simulated rosewood library chair, the shaped back, scroll arms and seat upholstered in brown leather, the arms carved with diagonal reeding and florets, on turned tapered reeded legs with brass casters.
£1,700–2,200
€/ $2,700–3,500 B&L

An early Victorian leather library chair, with button-upholstered back.
£3,000–3,400
€/ $4,700–5,400 ⊞ SAW

◄ **A pair of mahogany-framed upholstered library chairs,** the arms with painted and carved swan supports, on square tapering front legs and rear swept legs, Continental, mid-19thC.
£1,100–1,400
€/ $1,700–2,200 TMA

► **A mahogany library chair,** with upholstered back and seat, the arms carved with lion's heads, the front legs with claw-and-ball feet, 19thC.
£1,150–1,400
€/ $1,800–2,200 SWO

Nursing Chairs

An early Victorian rosewood nursing chair, on cabriole front legs.
£200–240
€/ $300–380 CHTR

A Victorian mahogany balloon-back nursing chair.
£180–225
€/ $300–350 B(Ba)

A Victorian walnut nursing chair.
£130–160
€/ $200–250 B(Ba)

A walnut nursing chair, on original casters, c1860.
£680–760
€/ $1,100–1,200 SAW

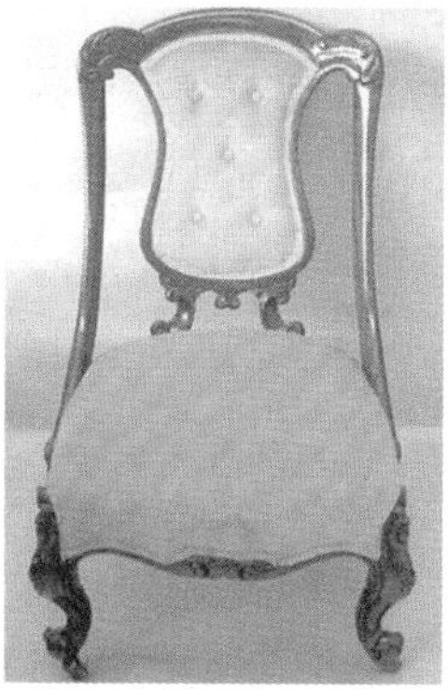

A Victorian rosewood nursing chair, with button-upholstered lyre-shaped back on scroll supports, with serpentine-front upholstered seat, on cabriole legs with scroll feet and china casters.
£150–200
€/ $250–300 WW

LOCATE THE SOURCE

The source of each illustration in Miller's can be found by checking the code letters below each caption with the Key to Illustrations, pages 794–800.

A Victorian nursing chair, with button-upholstered back.
£170–185
€/ $270–300 WiB

A walnut-framed nursing chair, late 19thC.
£180–225
€/ $290–350 SWO

Salon Chairs

A matched set of six Victorian walnut salon chairs, with pierced wavy-ladder backs and stuff-over seats, on moulded rails and slender moulded cabriole legs with tripod feet, four chairs labelled by Marsh, Jones, Cribb & Co, and two by J. H. Cooper & Sons, Ilkley, Yorkshire.
£850–1,100
€/ $1,300–1,600 TEN

Marsh & Jones was founded in 1865 when John Marsh and Edward Jones acquired the Leeds upholstery and cabinet making business of John Kendell & Co.

Sets/pairs

Unless otherwise stated, any description which refers to 'a set' or 'a pair' includes a guide price for the entire set or the pair, even though the illustration may show only a single item.

A pair of Victorian walnut-framed button-backed salon chairs, reupholstered.
£2,600–3,000
€/ $4,000–4,700 JSt

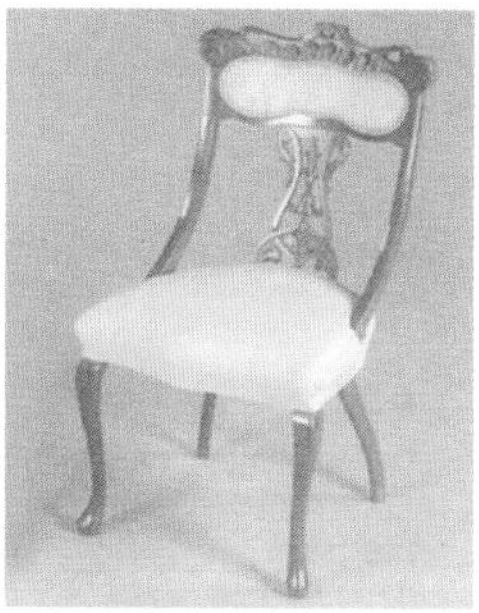

A set of four Edwardian mahogany salon chairs, with marquetry inlay, carved backs and satinwood ground marquetry panels, the seat rails with boxwood stringing, on cabriole legs, one leg repaired.
£340–425
€/ $700–670 HoG

◄ **A set of four Louis Philippe-style mahogany salon chairs,** French, early 20thC.
£130–160
€/ $200–250 B(Ch)

Side Chairs

A walnut high-back chair, with corresponding scrolling top-rail and stretcher, and caned back and seat, 17thC.
£200–250
€/ $300–400 G(L)

A pair of walnut side chairs, the shaped backs with solid curved central splats, above slip-in upholstered seats, within stepped and rounded frames, on cabriole front legs with corner ears and pad feet, joined by rounded stretchers, the rear legs with additional stretcher, c1720.
£1,650–1,850
€/ $2,600–3,000 ⊞ JC

A set of four marquetry and walnut side chairs, the shaped backs with vase-shaped splats inlaid with bird and flower marquetry with cupid in the cresting rail, in various stained hardwoods and ivory, above shaped drop-in seats, on cabriole legs with shoe-shaped feet, Dutch, 18thC.
£3,800–4,750
€/ $6,000–7,500 HAM

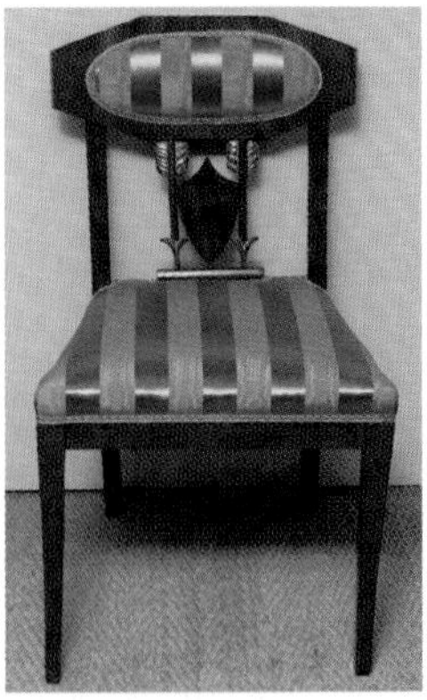

A pair of Empire mahogany chairs, Swedish, 1810–20.
£2,600–3,000
€/ $4,000–4,800 ⊞ CAV

A pair of rosewood-framed side chairs, Continental, c1870.
£700–800
€/ $1,100–1,300 ⊞ RPh

A set of four mahogany Queen Anne-style side chairs, late 19thC.
£720–800
€/ $1,100–1,300 ⊞ PaA

► A set of three rosewood and marquetry side chairs, c1910.
£350–400
€/ $550–630 ⊞ Che

◄ An ebonized and marquetry side chair, by Herter Brothers, with original velvet-upholstered seat, rail stamped '4718', 1877–79.
£3,000–3,750
€/ $4,700–6,000 B
By the late 1850s, Gustav and Christian Herter were established as prominent New York furniture-makers. Their furniture covered a variety of styles and they worked on many high-profile commissions.

Miscellaneous Chairs

A rosewood tub chair, 19thC.
£350–400
€/ $550–630 ⊞ SAW

◄ A Victorian rococo revival carved walnut sewing chair, with brocade upholstery, on cabriole legs with casters.
£120–150
€/ $200–250 BR

► A walnut prie-dieu, 1860.
£325–360
€/ $500–570 ⊞ PaA

Chaise Longues

A rosewood chaise longue, with hide upholstery and brass inlay, c1810, 81in (205.5cm) long.
£5,000–5,650
€/ $7,900–8,900 ⊞ APO

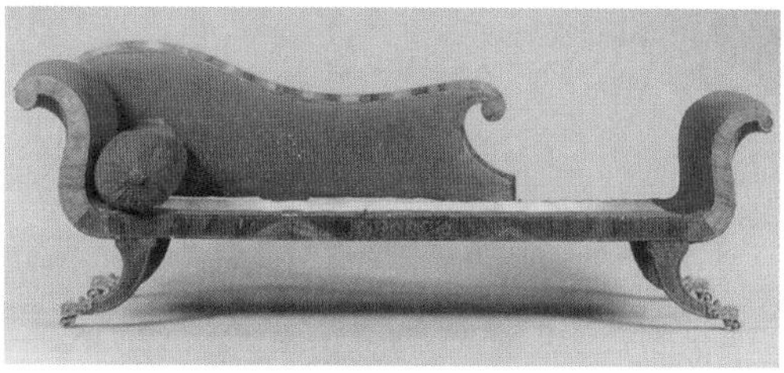

A rosewood chaise longue, seat cushion missing, c1825, 89in (226cm) long.
£3,500–4,200
€/ $5,500–6,650 ⚒ S(O)

A neo-classical painted and parcel-gilt chaise longue, Swedish, 19thC, 57in (145cm) long.
£5,000–6,250
€/ $8,000–10,000 ⚒ S(NY)

An early Victorian mahogany chaise longue, the back and stuff-over arms with concentric disc terminals, the hinged seat with bedding box below, on inverted tulip-form legs with brass caps and casters, 70in (178cm) long.
£400–500
€/ $630–800 ⚒ PFK

A Victorian rosewood chaise longue, with sprung seat on cabriole legs with casters, 78in (198cm) long.
£600–750
€/ $950–1,185 ⚒ PF

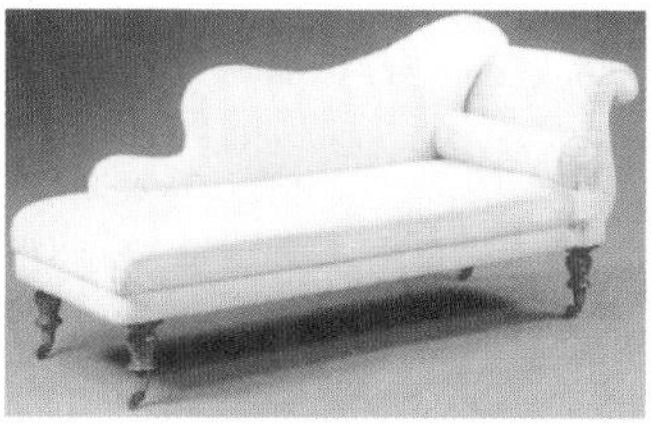

A chaise longue, on walnut baluster legs with brass caps and casters, c1860, 72in (183cm) long.
£1,800–2,200
€/ $2,850–3,475 ⚒ S(O)

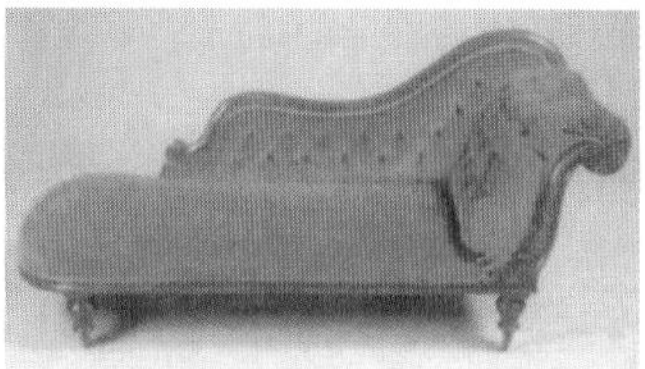

A late Victorian mahogany chaise longue, 73¼in (186cm) long.
£300–375
€/ $475–600 ⚒ B(Ba)

► An ebonized wooden-framed chaise longue, with pierced foliate and carved decoration, and velour upholstery, early 20thC, 70in (178cm) long.
£140–175
€/ $220–275 ⚒ FHF

Chests & Coffers

A carved walnut *cassone*, with arched panels and paw feet, Italian, c1620, 53in (134.5cm) wide.
£5,200–5,800
€/ $8,200–9,200 ⊞ DJH

A mahogany blanket chest, with hinged cover and four apron drawers, c1770, 67¾in (172cm) wide.
£1,100–1,300
€/ $1,750–2,000 ⚒ S(O)

A George III mahogany mule chest, on ogee bracket feet, base to bracket feet missing, 50½in (128.5cm) wide.
£700–875
€/ $1,100–1,380 ⚒ DN

The mule chest has a lifting lid with drawers below and was mainly used in the 17th century and went on to develop into the chest of drawers.

Chests of Drawers & Commodes

A walnut chest, with marquetry inlay of sycamore, boxwood, bog oak and holly, with two short over three long drawers, on replacement bun feet, c1690, 35in (89cm) wide.
£12,000–13,500
€/ $19,000–21,000 ⊞ HA

A George II inlaid mahogany chest of drawers, the crossbanded and parquetry line-inlaid top above a brushing slide and four graduated drawers with later turned wood handles, on bracket feet, 26½in (67.5cm) wide.
£1,100–1,400
€/ $1,750–2,200 ⚒ Bri

A figured walnut veneered and crossbanded chest, with two short over three long drawers, on bun feet, c1710, 36in (91.5cm) wide.
£7,000–7,800
€/ $11,000–12,300 ⊞ RGa

A Queen Anne inlaid walnut chest of drawers, with original cast-brass fittings, extensive damage, American, Pennsylvania, c1750, 40in (101.5cm) wide.
£11,000–13,000
€/ $17,500–20,500 ⚒ S(NY)

American furniture termed, for example, 'Queen Anne' does not necessarily date from the actual period of Queen Anne. This is because the latest fashions took about 20 years to cross the Atlantic but the style is nevertheless of that period.

A walnut commode, with shaped front, the crossbanded and quartered top with double herringbone inlay, matching four long drawers with ornate brass handles, plain sides and high bracket feet, Continental, early 18thC, 34in (86.5cm) wide.
£6,250–7,500
€/ $9,900–12,000 ⚒ JNic

A George II walnut chest of drawers, the top with ovolo-moulded edge, over a slide and three long drawers, on bracket feet, 31½in (80cm) wide.
£4,000–4,800
€/ $6,300–7,600 ⚒ TEN

A George III mahogany bowfronted chest of drawers, with rosewood crossbanding and stringing, brass ring handles and later ogee-bracket feet, 39¼in (99.5cm) wide.
£500–600
€/ $800–950 ⚒ AH

The Parry Collection

The Parry Collection of predominantly oak and walnut furniture that was sold by Christie's on 24 April 1997 was notable for its wonderful near original condition, colour and deep rich patination. The Parrys had an exceedingly critical eye, and obviously only wanted the best. Their house must have been magnificently furnished as I do not think I have seen so many oak dressers and *cwrpwrdds* (cupboards) or magnificently patinated walnut chests of drawers in one sale. I had set my heart on two pieces in particular, both of which had unusual features and glorious colour and patination. The first, a late 18th-century north Wales oak architectural dresser was notable for its spindle gallery as well as its attractive scroll fret-carved frieze. It sold for three times my original estimate! The second, a George I burr-walnut bachelor's chest with a most unusual superstructure incorporating small drawers and a hinged writing surface, with a collection of three rows of small drawers and two further long drawers below, all with delicate herringbone inlay, sold for a staggering £265,000 (€/ $420,000). **Edward Reily Collins**

A walnut commode, with a marble top, Italian, c1770, 28in (71cm) wide.
£2,600–3,000
€/ $4,100–4,750 ⊞ Che

A mahogany parquetry commode, stamped with the crowned coat-of-arms of Amsterdam and J. G. of St Joseph Guild, Dutch, c1771, 23¾in (60.5cm) wide.
£3,200–3,800
€/ $5,000–6,000 S(Am)

In most major Dutch cities French-style marquetry furniture was produced from the 1760s onwards, both to meet public demand and to counteract the large amount of French furniture being imported. Following a complaint from the Amsterdam Guild of St Joseph, import regulations were tightened, and the remaining foreign stock was allowed to be sold only if it was stamped with the mark of the Guild of St Joseph. In the case of this commode, its French style probably led the officials to apply the stamp in the belief that it was of foreign origin.

A George III mahogany Lancashire chest, the fascia with five dummy drawers over four drawers with brass drop handles, flanked by cluster columns, on ogee bracket feet, 68in (172.5cm) wide.
£1,500–2,000
€/ $2,370–3,170 AH

A George III mahogany serpentine chest of drawers, the three long graduated drawers with a shaped apron, on splayed bracket feet, 43½in (110.5cm) wide.
£1,750–2,200
€/ $2,750–3,475 BWL

A George III mahogany dressing chest, with a caddy top, brushing slide and four graduated long drawers, on shaped bracket feet, restored, 33in (84cm) wide.
£1,100–1,400
€/ $1,750–2,200 Bea

◄ **A walnut bachelor's chest of drawers,** probably Dutch, 18thC, 32in (81.5cm) wide.
£6,000–6,800
€/ $9,500–10,700
⊞ APO

► **A mahogany chest of drawers,** with two short and three long graduated drawers, on shaped bracket feet, c1780, 41¼in (105cm) wide.
£2,300–2,650
€/ $3,650–4,250
⊞ JC

◄ **A mahogany chest of drawers,** on bracket feet, c1780, 40in (101.5cm) wide.
£800–875
€/ $1,260–1,380
⊞ PaA

A George III mahogany chest of drawers, the four long graduated drawers with foliate-cast swing handles, 34in (86.5cm) wide.
£1,750–2,200
€/ $2,750–3,500 TMA

A mahogany bowfronted chest of drawers, the crossbanded top above five drawers, c1800, 37in (94cm) wide.
£4,000–4,500
€/ $6,325–7,225 RGa

A mahogany bowfronted chest of drawers, with two short and two long graduated drawers with original knob handles, above a shaped apron, on splay bracket feet, early 19thC, 35½in (90cm) wide.
£620–775
€/ $975–1,225 DMC

A mahogany chest, the reeded top above a brushing slide and three long drawers, on bracket feet, 19thC, 36¾in (93.5cm) wide.
£800–1,000
€/ $1,260–1,580 SWO

A mahogany bowfronted chest of drawers, c1800, 42in (106.5cm) wide.
£1,600–1,850
€/ $2,500–3,000 DUK

A Federal mahogany-inlaid figured birchwood bowfronted chest of drawers, sections of drawer facing later reveneered, American, New Hampshire, c1800, 42in (106.5cm) wide.
£3,200–3,800
€/ $5,000–6,000 S(NY)

A Federal mahogany bowfronted chest of drawers, American, c1810, 44in (112cm) wide.
£9,000–10,000
€/ $14,200–15,800 Che

A mahogany chest of drawers, with two short and three long drawers, on ogee bracket feet, early 19thC, 53in (134.5cm) wide.
£900–1,000
€/ $1,425–1,575 MHA

► **A mahogany commode,** with three drawers, Dutch, early 19thC, 31in (78.5cm) wide.
£3,200–3,500
€/ $5,000–5,500 DOA

A George III mahogany chest of drawers, on bracket feet, 31in (78.5cm) wide.
£2,800–3,250
€/ $4,400–5,300 JSt

A mahogany Lancashire chest of drawers, the lifting top above five dummy drawers with four drawers beneath, on shaped bracket feet, c1800, 67in (170cm) wide.
£4,250–4,750
€/ $6,750–7,500 HA

A mahogany and crossbanded serpentine chest of drawers, the two short and three long graduated drawers with lozenge ivory escutcheons and brass knop handles, above a shaped apron and short splayed feet, c1820, 41in (104cm) wide.
£9,500–12,000
€/ $15,000–19,000 WL

The colour and grain of the mahogany of this piece are exceptional, the top being formed of concentric bands of decreasing size, and the serpentine front has attractive crossbanding and cockbeading. This is a quality piece of furniture by a fine craftsman and is in completely original condition. A further plus factor is that it has been very well cared for over the years.

A mahogany chest of drawers, with original handles, restored, c1820, 41in (104cm) wide.
£1,200–1,350
€/ $2,000–2,150 ⊞ MTay

A George IV mahogany chest, the frieze with a Tunbridge ware band, above two short and four long graduated drawers with ivory escutcheons and turned wooden handles, on bracket feet, 41¼in (105cm) wide.
£480–600
€/ $750–1,000 DD

A pair of walnut and marquetry commodes, with marble tops, French, c1830, 53in (134.5cm) wide.
£17,500–20,000
€/ $27,500–31,500 ⊞ Che

A mahogany and line-inlaid commode, south German, 19thC, 33½in (85cm) wide.
£500–625
€/ $790–985 B(Ba)

A mahogany bowfronted chest of drawers, c1820, 42in (106.5cm) wide.
£430–480
€/ $675–750 ⊞ PaA

A Sheraton-style figured maple chest of drawers, the two over three graduated drawers with floral-moulded pressed glass pulls, flanked by turned pilasters, American, 1825–50, 43½in (110.5cm) wide.
£2,300–2,750
€/ $3,600–4,300 NOA

A mahogany chest of drawers, the marble top above two short and three long panelled drawers with gilt-metal handles, with canted sides, on a plinth base with bun feet, French, 19thC, 39½in (100.5cm) wide.
£1,200–1,500
€/ $1,900–2,375 DN

An Empire walnut commode, with a marble top, French, c1820, 50in (127cm) wide.
£2,000–2,300
€/ $3,150–3,600 ⊞ SIE

A mahogany chest of drawers, with inlaid floral marquetry decoration, with six long drawers, on bracket feet, Dutch, 19thC, 37in (94cm) wide.
£3,400–4,250
€/ $5,375–6,650 CHTR

An early Victorian mahogany-veneered barrel-front chest, with four long graduated drawers, top cracked, 43in (109cm) wide.
£500–625
€/ $790–985 WW

When looking at period walnut chests of drawers, look at the inside carcass wood: if it is of pine the piece is country made, if oak it is town made, i.e. for wealthy patrons and therefore will be better made and more valuable. On late 18th-century chests the fashion was for bun feet, which the Georgians often replaced with bracket feet to 'modernize' the piece. To help tell if the chest is earlier than Georgian, take out the bottom drawer and you should be able to see the remains of the spigot (a round peg) from the bun foot.

- Up to c1660 drawers had bearers fixed to their sides which ran in grooves.
- Drawers of this period never reached the back boards – a space was left for ventilation.
- Up to c1770 boards in the bottom of drawers ran back to front. Subsequently they ran side to side. Victorian drawers tended to have just one bottom board.
- Beware of chests with three small drawers in the top: they are most certinaly the tops of chests-on-chests.

A Victorian mahogany chest of drawers, with two short over three long drawers, 42in (106.5cm) wide.
£800–900
€/ $1,260–1,420 ⊞ MHA

A flame mahogany commode, with a marble top, above four oak-lined drawers, Continental, c1850, 50in (127cm) wide.
£800–900
€/ $1,260–1,420 ⊞ PaA

A Louis XV-style burr-walnut and walnut commode, with four graduated drawers, damaged, Dutch, 19thC, 35½in (90cm) wide.
£1,400–1,700
€/ $2,200–2,700 ⚒ S(Am)

A mahogany serpentine chest of drawers, with four long graduated drawers, on shaped bracket feet, early 20thC, 30in (76cm) wide.
£480–600
€/ $775–950 ⚒ PF

A Victorian mahogany chest of drawers, 40½in (103cm) wide.
£620–685
€/ $980–1,000 ⊞ WiB

A neo-classical mahogany and brass commode, with two square and two long drawers, Russian, 1850–1900, 24¾in (60.5cm) wide.
£2,200–2,500
€/ $3,475–4,000 ⚒ S(Am)

A kingwood commode, with a marble top, French, c1880, 47in (119.5cm) wide.
£3,300–3,650
€/ $5,200–5,700 ⊞ RAN

Daily care

Never lift a chest by the top as it may come away from the base, always open a drawer and lift it by the carcase. Be aware of tables with drawers which, if the table is tipped, may fall out. Prevent scratches to polished surfaces by placing felt pads under clocks, caddies etc., and by wrapping furniture in a clean blanket when transporting it. Never lock a bureau fall; if someone broke into it the damage could be greater than the value of the contents. Furniture should remain unlocked during transit as a small jolt can result in a jammed lock. Small piles of sawdust are a sign of live woodworm and a reputable company will fume the furniture for 48 hours without damaging timber or upholstery.

A late Victorian satinwood chest of drawers, with two short and three long drawers, on turned feet, 42in (106.5cm) wide.
£420–525
€/ $650–830 ⚒ DA

An Edwardian mahogany serpentine chest of drawers, with a brushing slide, 32in (81.5cm) wide.
£1,400–1,600
€/ $2,200–2,500 ⊞ HiA

◄ A mahogany and boxwood-strung serpentine chest of drawers, by Maple & Co, the two short and three long graduated drawers with rosewood parquetry and brass handles, on a plinth base, early 20thC, 48in (122cm) wide.
£450–565
€/ $700–1,050 ⚒ DN

Chest-on-Chests

A figured maple chest-on-chest, with original cast-brass hardware, American, New England, c1760, 38½in (98cm) wide.
£8,000–9,500
€/ $12,650–15,000
S(NY)

A walnut chest-on-chest, with herringbone banding, the drawers with later brass handles, on bracket feet, 18thC, 41in (104cm) wide.
£2,700–3,400
€/ $4,250–5,375 SWO

A Regency mahogany bowfronted chest-on-chest, the arch roundel cornice over seven long graduated drawers with original scallop plate ring handles, on swept bracket feet, 52in (132cm) wide.
£3,800–4,750
€/ $6,000–7,500 G(L)

Miller's Compares

I. A George III mahogany chest-on-chest, the upper section with a moulded cornice above two short and three long graduated drawers, the lower section with three further long graduated drawers, on bracket feet, 38½in (98cm) wide.
£6,000–7,500
€/ $9,500–12,000
CGC

II. A George III mahogany chest-on-chest, the upper section with a moulded cornice and dentil frieze above two short and three long graduated crossbanded drawers flanked by fluted canted corners, the lower section with a brushing slide above three long graduated drawers, on bracket feet, 44in (112cm) wide.
£2,200–2,750
€/ $3,500–4,300 CGC

Item I is smaller than Item II, both in height and width, and this is always a desirable factor as houses today are generally smaller than in the past and large furniture is difficult to accommodate. Item I is also of better colour, while Item II is a little 'flat' – it may have been repolished at some stage. In addition there is an attractive patina on Item I, particularly around the handle plates and escutcheons, which would indicate that the piece hasn't been touched or restored recently. Both pieces were consigned from private sources, but Item I had been bought from a reputable local dealer in the 1950s or '60s and had not been on the market since then: another plus point. Although both items had been consigned with the same estimate, Item I is from a deceased estate and the executors did not want the piece back, so it 'took off' not only because of its superior appearance, but also perhaps in part due to sale-room psychology: the 'come and get me' estimate had the desired effect of attracting much interest, and people are usually prepared to bid a little bit further once they have decided they really want something.

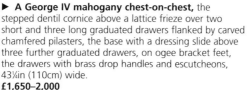

► **A George IV mahogany chest-on-chest,** the stepped dentil cornice above a lattice frieze over two short and three long graduated drawers flanked by carved chamfered pilasters, the base with a dressing slide above three further graduated drawers, on ogee bracket feet, the drawers with brass drop handles and escutcheons, 43¼in (110cm) wide.
£1,650–2,000
€/ $2,600–3,200 LJ

A George III mahogany chest-on-chest, crossbanded with stringing and parquetry banding, the moulded cornice above two short over three long drawers with gilt and embossed oval drop handles, with canted corners, the base with three further drawers, a shaped apron and splayed feet, 44¾in (113.5cm) wide.
£950–1,200
€/ $1,500–2,000 AH

A mahogany chest-on-chest, the two short and six long graduated drawers with original brass handles, on bracket feet, c1780, 74in (188cm) high.
£6,750–7,500
€/ $10,700–11,800 ⊞ JSt

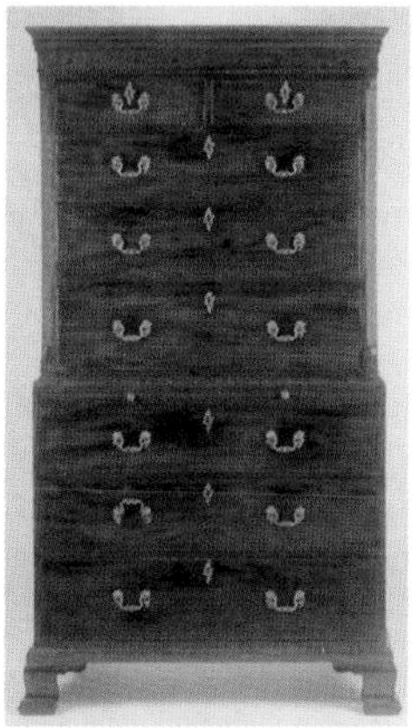

Secretaire Chests

A late George III mahogany secretaire chest, with a central secretaire drawer flanked by two pairs of drawers, above cupboards enclosing fitted small drawers with ring handles, on bracket feet, 42in (106.5cm) wide.
£500–625
€/ $800–1,000 HOLL

A mahogany secretaire chest, with rosewood-veneered drawer fronts, the secretaire drawer with a fitted interior, above three graduated long drawers, on splay bracket feet, early 19thC, 46in (117cm) wide.
£500–625
€/ $800–1,000 CHTR

A burr-walnut secretaire chest, with three long drawers and raised pilasters, 19thC, 41¼in (105cm) wide.
£340–425
€/ $550–675 SWO

A Biedermeier satinbirch inverted breakfront secretaire commode, possibly Scandinavian, 19thC, 43¼in (110cm) wide.
£500–625
€/ $800–1,000 B(Ba)

A Regency mahogany secretaire chest, c1815, 43in (109cm) wide.
£1,700–2,000
€/ $2,700–3,100 ⊞ Che

A Classical mahogany secretaire chest, the top with turreted ends above a conforming case with two shallow drawers over a secretaire drawer revealing an inset writing surface and a variety of drawers and cubbyholes, flanking a central cupboard, over three long graduated drawers, all flanked by engaged fluted pilasters, on turned bulbous feet, American, 1800–25, 49½in (125.5cm) wide.
£1,500–2,000
€/ $2,400–3,100 NOA

Chests-on-Stands

A William and Mary walnut chest-on-stand, with a cushion frieze drawer above two short and three long drawers with feather crossbanding, the stand with three short drawers to the shaped apron, on cup-and-cover-turned legs, 42in (106.5cm) wide.
£2,750–3,200
€/ $4,300–5,000 L

A William and Mary laburnum oyster-veneered and line-inlaid chest-on-stand, the moulded pediment above two short and three long graduated drawers, the stand with three further drawers above a shaped apron, on turned baluster legs and bun feet, 43¾in (111cm) wide.
£4,000–5,000
€/ $6,300–7,900 RTo

A William and Mary walnut and crossbanded chest-on-stand, the upper section with a moulded cornice above three short and three long graduated drawers, the stand with three further short drawers to the arched apron, on six turned and tapered legs joined by a curved undertier, on bun feet, with original engraved escutcheons and drop handles, stand with later components, 36in (91.5cm) wide.
£4,000–5,000
€/ $6,300–7,900 FHF

A William and Mary walnut chest-on-stand, with later legs, 40½in (103cm) wide.
£1,700–2,200
€/ $2,700–3,500 ⚒ B(Ba)

A George I walnut chest-on-stand, the burr-walnut facings with feather crossbanding, stand later, 38½in (98cm) wide.
£2,000–2,500
€/ $3,200–4,000 ⚒ L

A George II walnut chest-on-stand, stand later, 41¾in (106cm) wide.
£900–1,100
€/ $1,400–1,750 ⚒ B(Ba)

► **A William and Mary-style walnut and floral marquetry chest-on-stand,** the projecting top above two short and two long drawers, on an associated stand with spiral-turned legs, late 19thC, 38½in (98cm) wide.
£2,200–2,750
€/ $3,500–4,300 ⚒ BR

A Queen Anne walnut chest-on-stand, 39in (99cm) wide.
£2,700–3,500
€/ $4,250–5,500 ⚒ L

A George I walnut chest-on-stand, the drawers with feather stringing, stand later, 37in (94cm) wide.
£1,250–1,500
€/ $2,000–2,400 ⚒ L

A walnut chest-on-stand, c1750, 40in (101.5cm) wide.
£4,500–5,000
€/ $7,000–8,000 ⊞ RPh

A Queen Anne walnut and featherbanded chest-on-stand, the later veneered top above a moulded cornice and three short and three long drawers with double ovolo mouldings, the later stand on spiral-turned oak legs, on bun feet, stretcher restored, 40¾in (103.5cm) wide.
£900–1,100
€/ $1,450–1,750 ⚒ BR

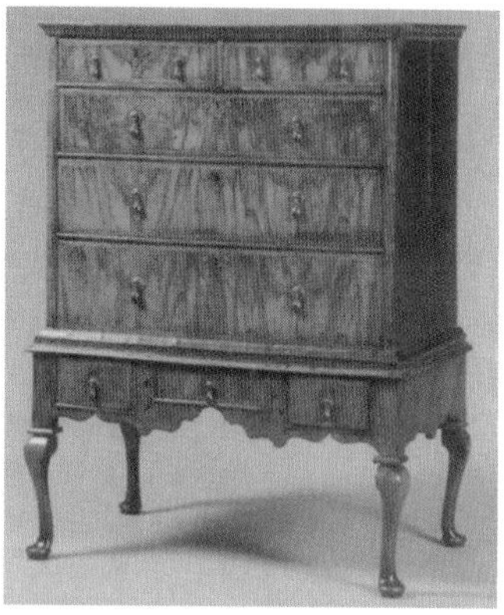

A George II walnut chest-on-stand, altered, 38¼in (97cm) wide.
£2,800–3,400
€/ $4,400–5,400 ⚒ S(O)

A carved and figured maple chest-on-stand, with original cast-brass hardware, legs later, American, Massachusetts, c1750, 38in (96.5cm) wide.
£8,000–9,500
€/ $12,650–15,000 ⚒ S(NY)

Wellington Chests

◄ **A satinbirch Wellington chest,** the upper panelled door enclosing a void interior, above four drawers, c1840, 23¾in (60.5cm) wide.
£1,100–1,400
€/ $1,750–2,200 ⚒ **S(O)**

A figured walnut secretaire Wellington chest, c1850, 22in (56cm) wide.
£4,000–4,500
€/ $6,300–7,000 ⊞ **Che**

A late Victorian Wellington chest, the later mahogany top above six graduated drawers with burr-walnut-veneered fronts and wooden knob handles, locking side pilasters, on a plinth base, 22½in (57cm) wide.
£1,450–1,800
€/ $2,300–2,850 ⚒ **WW**

A mahogany Wellington chest, on a plinth base, late 19thC, 22in (56cm) wide.
£650–820
€/ $1,000–1,300 ⚒ **PF**

Wellington chests typically have seven drawers – one for each day of the week.

► **A burr-walnut Wellington-style chest,** with six drawers, on a plinth base, c1900, 41in (104cm) wide.
£530–600
€/ $850–950 ⊞ **PaA**

A Victorian mahogany Wellington chest, with seven drawers, handles replaced, 41in (104cm) wide.
£765–850
€/ $1,200–1,350 ⊞ **HiA**

Clothes & Linen Presses

A Chippendale figured maple linen press, the cupboard doors enclosing three shelves, one foot facing and one door panel of a later date, American, New Jersey, c1770, 52in (132cm) wide.
£9,000–11,000
€/ $14,200–17,400 ⚒ **S(NY)**

A George III figured mahogany linen press, the interior with later shelves, 50½in (128.5cm) wide.
£1,300–1,600
€/ $2,000–2,500 ⚒ **L**

► **A Chippendale period mahogany linen press,** c1790, 51in (129.5cm) wide.
£4,800–5,300
€/ $7,500–8,250 ⊞ **APO**

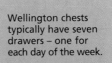

A mahogany dwarf linen press, c1780, 47in (119.5cm) wide.
£2,600–3,000
€/ $4,000–4,750 ⊞ **Che**

A George III mahogany linen press, altered, 51½in (131cm) wide.
£900–1,100
€/ $1,400–1,750 B(Ba)

A mahogany linen press, the scrolled cornice over two panelled doors enclosing slides, drawers and twist-turned columns, c1835, 56¼in (143cm) wide.
£1,800–2,200
€/ $2,800–3,500 SWO

A mahogany-veneered linen press, 18thC, 58in (147.5cm) wide.
£2,400–2,700
€/ $3,750–4,250 WAW

◄ **A George IV mahogany linen press,** the stepped moulded cresting and plain reeded frieze above a pair of single reed-moulded panelled curl-veneered doors enclosing four brushing slides, above two short and two long graduated cockbeaded drawers with turned wooden handles, on turned wooden feet, 50in (127cm) wide.
£1,000–1,250
€/ $1,500–2,000 DD

A mahogany linen press, the flared cornice above two panelled doors enclosing a brass hanging rail and slides, with later inlaid stringing and marquetry urns, the base with two long and two short drawers, on later bracket feet, 19thC, 52¼in (132.5cm) wide.
£900–1,100
€/ $1,400–1,700 WW

◄ **A mahogany linen press,** the two doors enclosing hanging space, above two short and three long drawers, restored, c1840, 51in (129.5cm) wide.
£2,350–2,600
€/ $3,700–4,000 MTay

► **A Victorian satinbirch linen press,** with mirrored doors, 43in (109cm) wide.
£1,350–1,500
€/ $2,200–2,400 MHA

A linen press, with flame mahogany panels, two doors over four drawers, c1820, 50in (127cm) wide.
£3,800–4,250
€/ $6,000–6,750 RPh

A mahogany linen press, the canted cornice above two panelled doors, enclosing sliding trays and hanging space, with two long drawers below, on a plinth base, 19thC, 52in (132cm) wide.
£650–820
€/ $1,000–1,300 DMC

A black-japanned linen press, the interior with four sliding trays and three drawers, restored, c1820, 51¼in (130cm) wide.
£3,200–3,800
€/ $5,000–6,000 S(O)

◄ **A Biedermeier-style satinwood linen press,** with rosewood, ebony and sycamore stringing, the two panelled doors over three long drawers, on square feet, north European, 19thC, 62¼in (158cm) wide.
£1,500–1,750
€/ $2,350–2,750 AMB

A mahogany linen press, the upper section with sliding trays, possibly Irish, c1835, 52¼in (133.5cm) wide.
£530–650
€/ $850–1,000 S(O)

An Edwardian fruitwood linen press, with maker's label 'Maple & Co', 49¼in (125cm) wide.
£320–400
€/ $500–630 B(Ch)

Columns & Pedestals

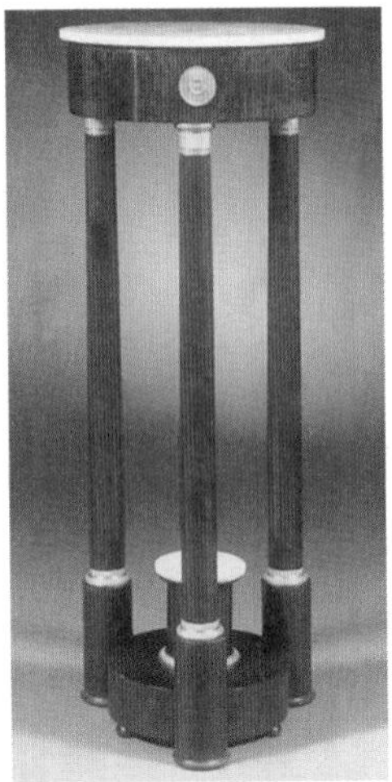

An Empire mahogany pedestal, the marble top above an ormolu-applied frieze, joined to a lower shelf by column supports, with ormolu capitals and bases, the lower shelf centred by a marble-topped pillar, on turret feet, French, early 19thC, 14¼in (36cm) diam.
£1,650–2,000
€/ $2,600–3,200 NOA

◄ **An ebonized and gilt-bronze pedestal,** c1880, 22¾in (58cm) wide.
£1,200–1,500
€/ $1,900–2,400 S(O)

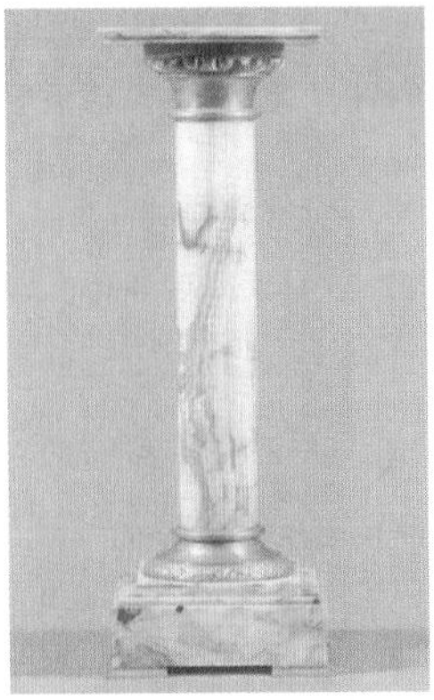

An onyx and gilt-bronze column, late 19thC, 41in (104cm) high.
£600–700
€/ $950–1,100 S(O)

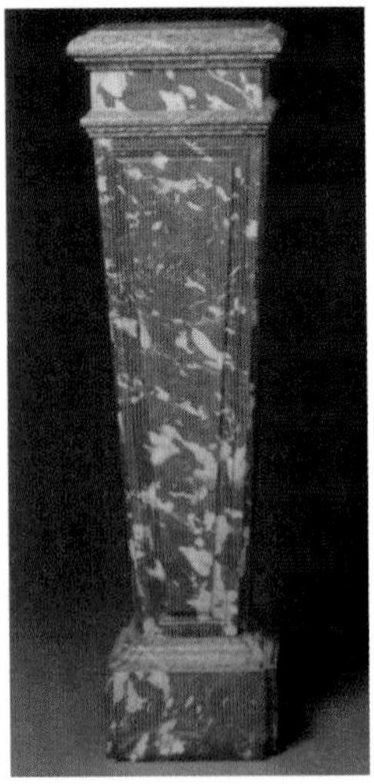

A pair of *brèche violette* and *verde* marble pedestals, the moulded tops on panelled tapering pilaster supports and moulded cut-corner plinth bases, 1875–1925, 47¾in (121.5cm) high.
£1,400–1,700
€/ $2,200–2,700 B

◄ **An Edwardian Adam-style mahogany pedestal,** the *guilloche* frieze divided by carved rams' heads holding leaf swags, on a fluted base, 43in (109cm) high.
£1,400–1,700
€/ $2,200–2,700 EH

Davenports

◄ **A Regency rosewood davenport,** on bun feet with casters, 22in (56cm) wide.
£3,200–4,000
€/ $5,000–6,300 TEN

A walnut davenport, with a hinged storage compartment above a hinged writing surface, on runner feet with casters, 1850–75, 21in (53.5cm) wide.
£530–650
€/ $850–1,000 NOA

A rosewood davenport, mid-19thC, 22in (56cm) wide.
£1,600–1,800
€/ $2,500–2,850 HiA

A Victorian walnut davenport, the sloped hinged serpentine front enclosing a series of small drawers, the back with a raised stationery compartment, the lower stage with four drawers to one side and four opposing dummy drawers, the front with foliate-carved scrolled supports, on bun feet with casters, 44in (112cm) wide.
£480–600
€/ $750–950 FHF

A Victorian mahogany davenport, the later pierced arcaded top above a leather-inset slope, lifting to reveal an interior fitted with bird's-eye maple-veneered drawers and pigeonholes, the brass lock stamped 'G. Williams, 60 Sun St' above an outline panel front with scroll support, the right side with a hinged pen drawer above four graduated drawers fitted with wooden knob handles, with opposing dummy drawers, the concave plinth on flattened bun feet with casters, writing slope cracked, 27in (68.5cm) wide.
£600–720
€/ $950–1,100 WW

◄ **A walnut davenport,** the leather-lined writing slope above a side drawer opposing a blind-fret panel on part-fluted and twist-turned support, lock stamped 'Bramah 24 Piccadilly', c1860, 22in (56cm) wide.
£2,200–2,500
€/ $3,500–4,000 S(O)

It is believed that in the late 18th century the firm of Gillows was commissioned to make a special desk to be used at sea in the cabin of a 'Captain Davenport'. In Gillows' Costs Book there is a sloping lid desk with a gallery, with working drawers to one side and opposing dummy drawers, captioned 'Captain Davenport Desk'.

A Victorian walnut davenport, with metamorphic stationery rack, the piano lid with a fitted sliding writing surface, four drawers to one side with opposing dummy drawers, 21¾in (55.5cm) wide.
£3,500–4,000
€/ $5,500–6,300 BIG

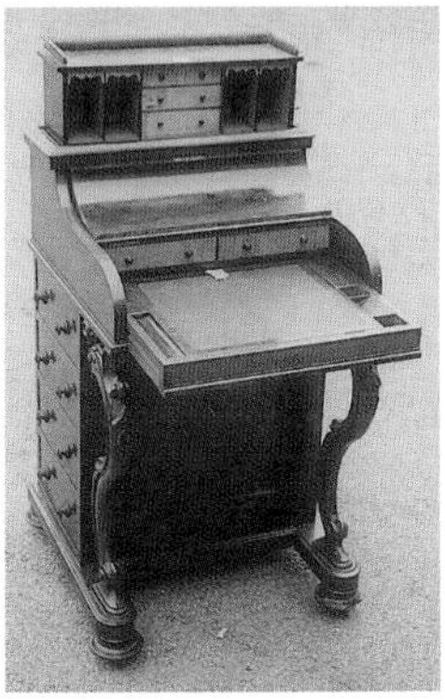

◄ **A mid-Victorian rosewood 'jack in the box' davenport,** the rising top with three satinwood drawers and four pigeonholes, the interior with two drawers and pull-out ratchet, with four real and four dummy drawers, on carved cabriole legs with bun feet, 21in (53cm) wide.
£2,200–2,750
€/ $3,500–4,300 SPF

► **An inlaid rosewood davenport,** c1890, 20in (51cm) wide.
£875–975
€/ $1,380–1,540 GBr

A late Victorian rosewood and marquetry-inlaid metamorphic davenport, the tilt-action top with leather writing surface and three-quarter gallery with hinged lid, enclosing pigeonholes and a writing fitment, above a single frieze drawer and panelled fall-front enclosing two shelves, on square legs with china casters, 23¼in (59cm) wide.
£900–1,150
€/ $1,400–1,800 BR

A banded mahogany davenport, handles replaced, c1905, 22in (56cm) wide.
£530–585
€/ $850–925 PaA

Daybeds

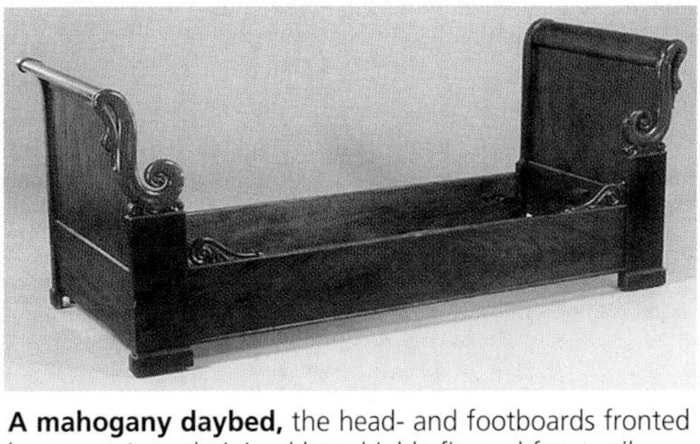

A mahogany daybed, the head- and footboards fronted by a swan's neck, joined by a highly figured front-rail, on moulded feet, French, 1825–50, 79in (200.5cm) long.
£1,200–1,500
€/ $1,900–2,400 NOA

► **A walnut daybed,** French, c1860, 74½in (189cm) long.
£2,000–2,200
€/ $3,200–3,500 SIE

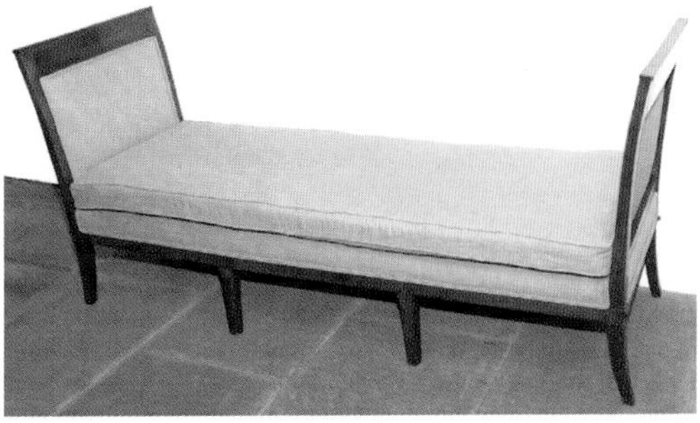

A walnut daybed, the shaped frame on scroll-carved cabriole legs, reupholstered, 19thC, 60in (152.5cm) long.
£1,700–2,000
€/ $2,700–3,200 JSt

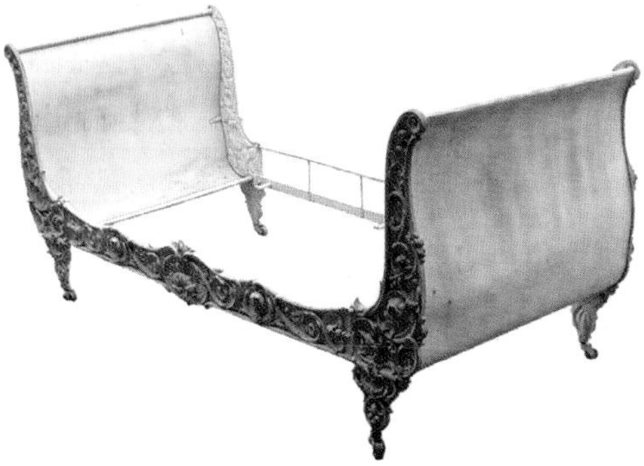

A cast-iron daybed, c1880, 72in (183cm) long.
£1,100–1,200
€/ $1,750–2,000 SeH

► **A late Victorian mahogany-framed daybed,** with floral upholstery, 74¾in (190cm) long.
£360–450
€/ $575–700
B(Ba)

Desks

An early Georgian walnut kneehole desk, with feather and crossbanding, eight drawers and a recessed door, on bracket feet, 32in (81.5cm) wide.
£1,700–2,200
€/ $2,680–3,500 SPF

A mahogany pedestal desk, the top with a reeded rim, above a central drawer, the kneehole with a recessed tambour, the pedestals each with four short drawers, one set of four being dummies forming doors, panelled to one side, on bracket feet, late 18thC, 49¼in (125cm) wide.
£1,700–2,200
€/ $2,700–3,500 HOK

A Carlton House-style mahogany writing desk, the lower section with three-quarter brass gallery, eight drawers and pigeonholes, the top with leather writing surface and ratchet-adjustable slope, above a frieze drawer flanked by four further drawers, on square tapering legs with later spade feet and casters, 19thC, 54¾in (139cm) wide.
£3,250–3,750
€/ $5,100–5,900 B

A mahogany kneehole desk, c1740, 30in (76cm) wide.
£5,200–5,800
€/ $8,200–9,200 Che

A rosewood writing desk, c1830, 45in (114.5cm) wide.
£1,750–2,000
€/ $2,700–3,200 RPh

A Gothic revival walnut kneehole writing desk, with moulded tracery decoration, the gallery with a small shaped structure to each end, above an inverted breakfront moulded edge top, inset with a leather writing surface, above a frieze drawer and kneehole, flanked by six further frieze drawers, the sides and back with tracery decoration, on spirally fluted and carved legs joined by shaped X-stretchers, on bun feet, French, mid-19thC, 51¼in (130cm) wide.
£1,600–2,000
€/ $2,500–3,200 B

◄ **An early Victorian mahogany desk,** the top with back-rail and rounded front corners, above two frieze drawers and two short drawers, all with wooden knob handles, flanking a central kneehole, on tapering reeded legs with brass caps and ceramic casters, 47¼in (120cm) wide.
£300–375
€/ $475–600 PFK

A George II walnut kneehole desk, the herringbone-inlaid and crossbanded moulded top above a featherbanded long frieze drawer, shaped apron and recessed cupboard drawer, flanked by six similar short drawers, on bracket feet, restorations and alterations, 30¾in (78cm) wide.
£1,650–2,000
€/ $2,600–3,150 CGC

A late Federal figured mahogany desk, the hinged lid opening to a well with pigeonholes, the upper right drawer inscribed 'J Button January 11th 1839 New York, Dow Beekman 1886 Middleburg N.Y.', American, c1839, 54½in (138.5cm) wide.
£2,500–3,200
€/ $4,000–5,000 S(NY)

A mahogany partner's desk, the reeded top with leather writing surface, over nine drawers opposed by nine further drawers, on bracket feet, 19thC, 49in (124.5cm) wide.
£2,600–3,250
€/ $4,000–5,000 G(L)

A Georgian-style mahogany pedestal desk, c1860, 41in (104cm) wide.
£1,700–2,000
€/ $2,700–3,200 RPh

A black-lacquered lady's desk, with polychromed chinoiserie decoration, the upper section with four drawers, the lower section with a pull-out writing surface above one long frieze drawer, on turned and panelled tapering legs with ball feet, French, 1850–75, 31¼in (79.5cm) wide.
£1,100–1,400
€/ $1,750–2,200 NOA

A mid-Victorian mahogany pedestal desk, with solid top over a centre drawer with four drawers either side, 58in (147.5cm) wide.
£1,600–1,800
€/ $2,500–2,850 RPh

A Victorian walnut writing desk, by Maple & Co, the upper section with a rear gallery and seven drawers, the lower section with sloping writing surface, with six drawers, on turned supports, with shelves under, 54¼in (138cm) wide.
£650–820
€/ $1,000–1,300 WilP

A rosewood lady's writing desk, inlaid with various woods, French, c1870, 38in (96.5cm) wide.
£3,200–3,500
€/ $5,000–5,500 MHA

Cross Reference
Bureaux (pages 39–40)
Writing Tables (pages 141–142)

A French-style olivewood and gilt-metal-mounted kneehole writing desk, by Wright & Mansfield, with two leather-inset slides and veneering to the rear, drawer stamped 'Wright & Mansfield, 104 Bond St', c1880, 36¼in (92cm) wide.
£5,750–6,750
€/ $9,000–10,600 S(O)

Wright & Mansfield were one of the pre-eminent makers of furniture from about 1860–86, trading from premises in New Bond Street and exhibiting at the International Exhibition in 1862. The desk pictured here demonstrates the fashion for French furniture at this time and its association with quality. Wright & Mansfield were among a number of British cabinet makers competing for this market.

► **A Victorian mahogany escritoire,** the raised back with a gallery and moulded cornice above a triple panelled fall-front enclosing pigeonholes, drawers and a leather inset, the base with a concealed frieze drawer above two panelled doors enclosing six drawers flanking a kneehole, 49½in (125.5cm) wide.
£450–565
€/ $700–900 DN

◄ **A Sheraton revival satinwood inlaid desk,** c1885, 54in (137cm) wide.
£2,600–3,000
€/ $4,000–4,750
Che

► **A Sheraton revival mahogany kidney-shaped desk,** on brass casters, late 19thC, 54in (137cm) wide.
£3,500–4,000
€/ $5,500–6,300
SAW

A late Victorian rosewood and satinwood marquetry writing desk, by Collinson & Lock, the marquetry possibly designed by Stephen Webb, in the Renaissance style, the stepped superstructure with pierced three-quarter gallery, with two drawers either side, above a moulded top with tooled leather writing surface and concave front with frieze drawers to each side and fluted uprights, with marquetry-panelled sides and back, on turned tapering leaf-carved and reeded legs with casters, centre drawer stamped 'Collinson & Lock, London', and numbered 109, one caster detached, 48in (122cm) wide.
£2,000–2,250
€/ $3,100–3,500 ⚒ B

A Sheraton-style mahogany Carlton House desk, c1900, 54in (137cm) wide.
£6,000–6,600
€/ $9,500–10,500 ⊞ Che

A mahogany semi-bowfronted kneehole writing desk, the leather-fitted top with a raised section to the rear comprising a bank of two drawers either side of a recess with pillared brass gallery, the front with a central bowfronted drawer above a kneehole, with four graduated drawers to either side, all with solid mahogany linings and ebony cockbeading, brass ring handles, locks and inset brass escutcheons, the top and sides inlaid and edged with lines and banding of ebony stringing, on eight square tapered legs with brass casters, c1910, 44¾in (113.5cm) wide.
£3,500–3,850
€/ $5,500–6,100 ⊞ JC

A George III-style mahogany desk, stencilled 'Jewell, High Holborn', c1890, 48in (122cm) wide.
£1,200–1,500
€/ $1,900–2,400 ⚒ B(Ba)

A rosewood and marquetry lady's desk, c1890, 39in (99cm) wide.
£3,300–3,700
€/ $5,100–5,750 ⊞ Che

Rosewood

A South American and West Indian wood imported into Europe from the mid-18th century onwards, rosewood has a purplish-red colour with black or dark brown streaks. It was used for veneers, banding and inlays to contrast with mahogany and satinwood.

An Edwardian inlaid mahogany writing desk, by Maple & Co, 42in (106.5cm) wide.
£3,400–3,750
€/ $5,400–5,900 ⊞ BrL

A painted satinwood Carlton House desk, 1920–30s, 52in (132cm) wide.
£17,500–20,000
€/ $28,000–32,000 ⊞ MHA

A walnut partner's desk, with leather top, c1890, 60in (152.5cm) wide.
£2,600–3,000
€/ $4,000–4,750 ⊞ SAW

A mahogany writing desk, the hinged top enclosing a fitted interior, c1900, 19in (48.5cm) wide.
£1,200–1,500
€/ $1,900–2,400 ⚒ S(O)

An Edwardian mahogany lady's desk, crossbanded with stringing, the raised mirror back with broken pediment and shelf flanked by stationery compartments with gilt-metal galleries over hinged sloping lids and drawers, leather writing surface, above two frieze drawers with brass drop handles, on square tapering legs with casters, 36in (91.5cm) wide.
£900–1,100
€/ $1,400–1,700 ⚒ AH

An oak pedestal desk, with Rexine insert top, on claw-and-ball feet, 1930s, 48½in (123cm) wide.
£260–320
€/ $400–500 ⚒ B(Ba)

Dumb Waiters

An early George III mahogany dumb waiter, with three graduated tiers, on a baluster column and tripod downswept legs, terminating in brass casters, 43in (109cm) high.
£1,100–1,400
€/ $1,700–2,200 HYD

A George III mahogany dumb waiter, with three graduated tiers, 47in (119.5cm) high.
£3,250–3,600
€/ $5,100–5,700 APO

A George III mahogany dumb waiter, with three dished tiers on gun barrel pillars, and a tripod cabriole base with casters, repairs, 40¼in (102cm) high.
£1,300–1,600
€/ $2,000–2,500 TEN

An early Victorian mahogany three-tier dumb waiter, the three graduated tiers with wavy edges, 53½in (136cm) high.
£1,500–1,800
€/ $2,400–2,850 B(Ba)

A mahogany dumb waiter, with three galleried shelves on inverted reeded columns with knopped lobed finials, on casters, c1840, 44in (112cm) high.
£1,500–1,800
€/ $2,400–2,850 HOK

An Empire-style mahogany and marble two-tier dumb waiter, c1890, 36in (91.5cm) high.
£1,000–1,150
€/ $1,600–1,800 Che

Dumb waiters were often used in pairs in large houses from the mid-18th century. When the ladies retired after dinner, the dumb waiters were placed either end of the table by the footmen and laden with drink so the gentlemen could help themselves without too much exertion and, because the staff had retired, the conversation could be more open. Hence dumb waiter!

A Georgian-style mahogany three-tier dumb waiter, early 20thC, 45in (114.5cm) high.
£1,250–1,400
€/ $2,000–2,200 RPh

Etagères

A walnut étagère, the glass-inset moulded top on splayed uprights above two conforming tiers, on fluted circular-section tapering legs, 19thC, 39¼in (100cm) wide.
£360–450
€/ $575–700 CGC

A mahogany two-tier étagère, with parcel-gilt decorated friezes, on turned supports with casters, 19thC, 16½in (42cm) wide.
£500–600
€/ $800–950 WW

A mahogany two-tier étagère, the galleried top with globe finials on square supports, 19thC, 16in (40.5cm) wide.
£260–320
€/ $410–500 WW

An ebonized three-tier étagère, with neo-classical inlay in sycamore and satinwood, c1890, 17in (43cm) wide.
£1,000–1,150
€/ $1,600–1,800 CGA

FURNITURE

Frames

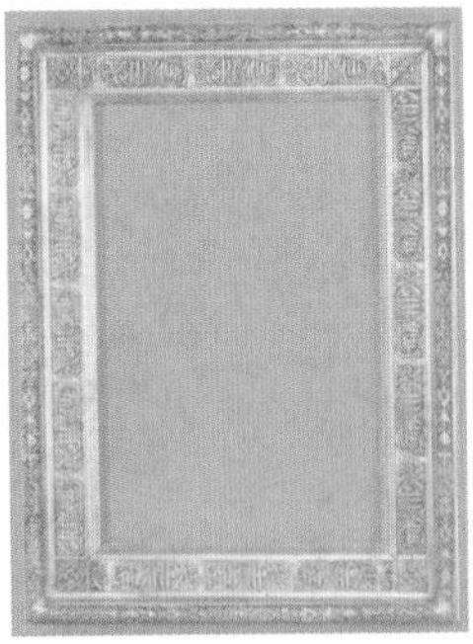

A gilded composition frame, with plain wedge sight, moresque decoration to the frieze and D-section top edge, 19thC, 29¼ x 19½in (74.5 x 49.5cm).
£340–425
€/ $550–670 B(Kn)

A gilded composition frame, 19thC, 44 x 28¼in (112 x 72cm).
£320–400
€/ $500–650 B(Ch)

A gilt gesso frame, in a glazed ebonized wood surround, c1870, 30 x 23in (76 x 58.5cm).
£400–500
€/ $630–800 S(O)

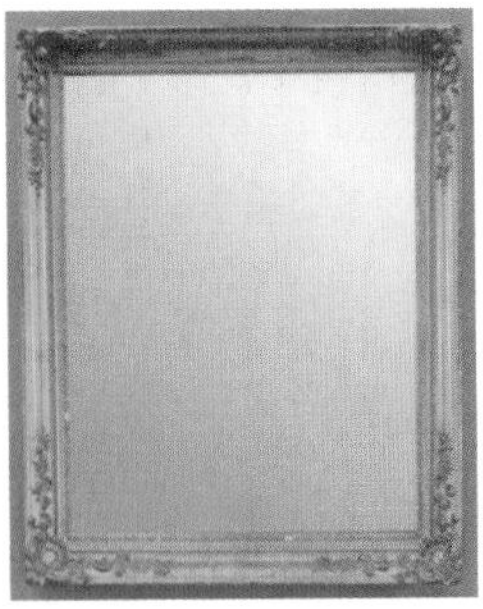

A giltwood frame, cornered by a cartouche- and floral-moulded design, 1875–1900, 43 x 35in (109 x 89cm).
£380–475
€/ $600–750 NOA

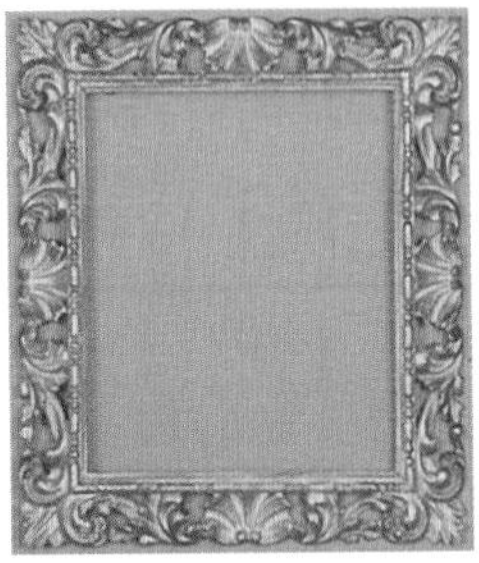

A carved, pierced and gilded frame, Italian, 19thC, 14¼ x 12½in (36 x 32cm).
£360–450
€/ $550–700 B(Ch)

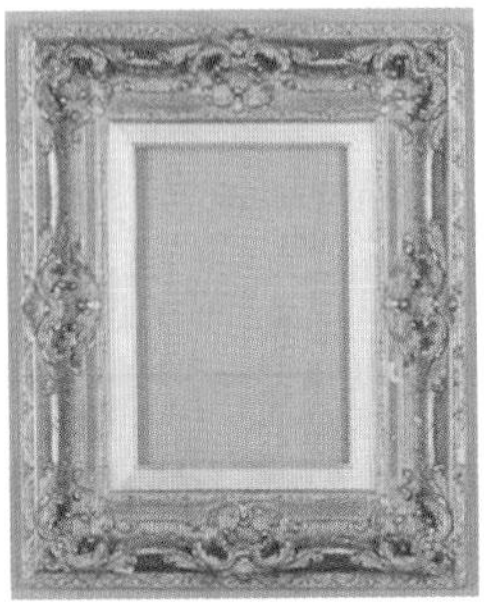

A pierced, swept and gilded composition frame, Continental, 19thC, 12½ x 9in (32 x 23cm).
£220–275
€/ $350–425 B(Ch)

A gilt composition frame, the moulded cartouche corner crestings with an intertwined foliate scroll with flowerheads and buds, late 19thC, aperture 27½ x 23½in (70 x 59.5cm).
£300–375
€/ $475–600 RTo

A gilt composition frame, with shaped gilt-wood and composition mount, the frame with foliate rococo scroll corner crestings with a foliate spandrel towards centre crestings on two sides, late 19thC, aperture 29 x 24½in (73.5 x 62.5cm).
£300–375
€/ $475–600 RTo

Hall Stands

A Victorian mahogany hall stand, the serpentine lower part with a marble top and fitted central drawer flanked by a stick stand, on carved scrolling front supports and a shaped base, requires restoration, 55in (139.5cm) wide.
£160–200
€/ $250–315 FHF

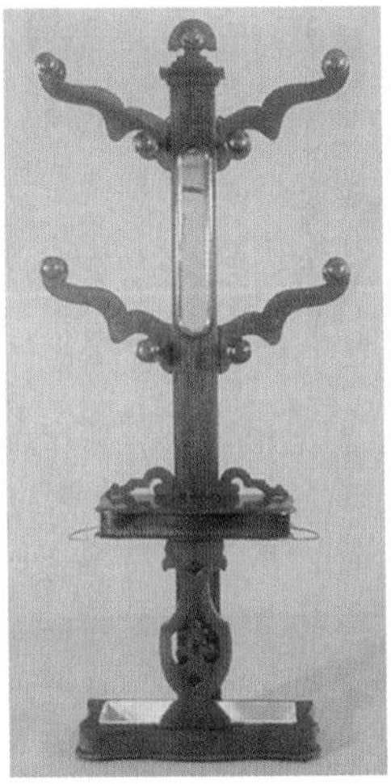

A Victorian mahogany hall stand, the central support with inset mirror and lidded box with brass rings, on a shaped base with painted zinc liner, 34in (86.5cm) wide.
£300–375
€/ $475–600 WW

A Gothic revival carved oak hall stand, with a hinged compartment above a cupboard door, c1880, 53½in (136cm) wide.
£1,100–1,300
€/ $1,750–2,000 S(O)

A Gothic revival mahogany hall stand, the upper section with an arched top above three pierced carvings, a central arched top mirror below, with carved side columns and pierced carved brackets to the projecting upper rail, the base with a marble top and a central drawer, with pierced brackets to the canted carved arched panel supports, 19thC, 50in (127cm) wide.
£500–600
€/ $800–950 TRL

Jardinières

A mahogany jardinière, with a brass liner and a swing handle, c1820, 21in (53.5cm) high.
£1,000–1,150
€/ $1,600–1,800 RPh

A Louis XVI-style yew wood, ebonized and boxwood marquetry jardinière table and cover, with gilt-metal mounts and a green tin liner, 19thC, 24in (61cm) wide.
£520–650
€/ $800–1,000 B(Ch)

A carved wood pedestal jardinière, modelled as a flowering rustic trug, on carved column and root-form tripod feet, German, Black Forest, 19thC, 38in (96.5cm) high.
£400–500
€/ $630–800 HOLL

A giltwood jardinière, the caned panels hung with floral swags, the lower part with a lattice and flowerhead frieze centred by shells, on floral-carved cabriole legs joined by an arched X-stretcher, on scroll feet, French, late 19thC, 36¾in (93.5cm) high.
£1,700–2,200
€/ $2,700–3,500 B(O)

A satinwood-veneered *bombé* jardinière, with polychrome decoration, on cabriole legs, veneer missing, Continental, late 19thC, 15in (38cm) wide.
£300–375
€/ $475–600 WW

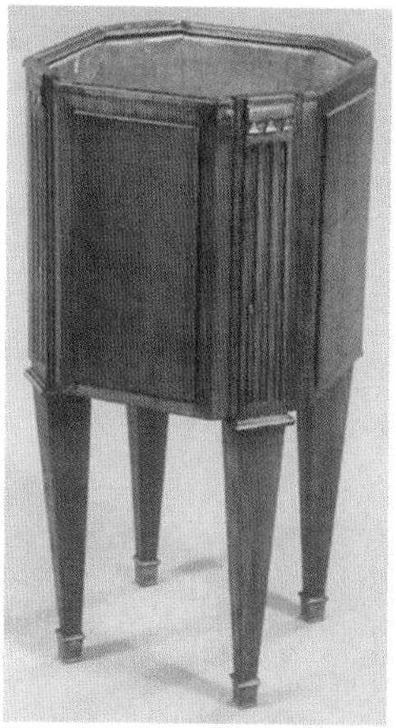

◀ **A Louis XVI-style fruitwood jardinière,** the sides panelled and flanked by fluted pilasters, on tapering square legs, with metal liner, c1900, 25½in (65cm) high.
£400–500
€/ $630–800 NOA

▶ **An Edwardian inlaid mahogany jardinière,** 36in (91.5cm) high.
£625–700
€/ $980–1,100 RPh

Lowboys

Miller's Compares

I. A burr-elm-veneered lowboy, the moulded fruitwood top with crossbanding, over a long frieze drawer and two small frieze drawers with line-inlaid stringing, with a shaped apron, on walnut cabriole legs, mid-18thC, 30in (76cm) wide.
£12,500–15,000
€/ $20,000–24,000 B(O)

II. A mahogany lowboy, restored, mid-18thC, 32¼in (82cm) wide.
£680–850
€/ $1,000–1,350 B(Ba)

Item I is in wonderful, untouched condition, and a little cleaning and waxing will result in a glorious colour. Item II appears to have lost all traces of original colour and finish, and is 'flat' in appearance.

A mid-Georgian walnut lowboy, 30in (76cm) wide.
£900–1,100
€/ $1,400–1,750 L

A Queen Anne-style walnut lowboy, with three drawers, late 19thC, 24in (61cm) wide.
£900–1,000
€/ $1,400–1,600 HiA

Miniature Furniture

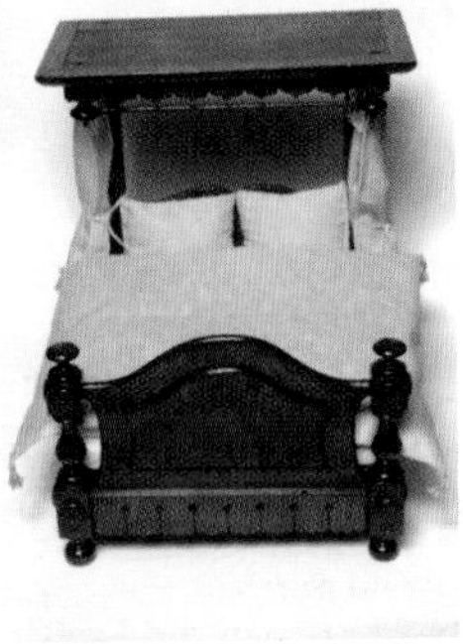

A late Victorian mahogany miniature half-tester bed, possibly an apprentice piece, with later bedding, 17½in (44.5cm) high.
£1,300–1,450
€/ $2,000–2,250 ⊞ SDA

An oak and mahogany-veneered miniature waterfall bookcase, with reeded edges and two shelves, the base with a drawer with gilt-brass handle, on ball feet, 19thC, 11in (28cm) high.
£150–200
€/ $235–315 WW

A Victorian mahogany miniature chest, modelled as an organ case with gilt pipes and enclosing three drawers, on bun feet, 7in (18cm) high.
£200–250
€/ $315–400 CGC

A late Victorian rosewood miniature side cabinet, with raised mirrored back and one long drawer above a bevelled mirror-glazed single door enclosing a shelved cupboard, 12½in (32cm) wide.
£480–600
€/ $750–950 TMA

► **A walnut miniature chest of drawers,** on bun feet, c1710, 14in (35.5cm) wide.
£3,800–4,200
€/ $6,000–6,600 ⊞ CAT
This is a very attractive piece of early date.

A Victorian mahogany miniature chest of drawers, the three long drawers with wooden knob handles, over a shaped apron, on integral bracket feet, 12½in (32cm) wide.
£260–325
€/ $400–500 PFK

A Victorian mahogany miniature chest of drawers, with two short over two long drawers decorated with Tunbridge ware butterfly panels, all with brass knobs, on bun feet, 13in (33cm) wide.
£200–250
€/ $315–400 HoG

A mahogany miniature apprentice chest of drawers, with four long graduated drawers, on bracket feet, 19thC, 14½in (37cm) wide.
£280–350
€/ $440–550 B(W)

A Victorian mahogany miniature chest of drawers, the three graduated drawers with glass knobs, on turned feet, 10in (25.5cm) wide.
£300–380
€/ $475–600 BWL

A mahogany miniature linen press, c1830, 11in (28cm) wide.
£3,000–3,300
€/ $4,750–5,250 ⊞ BBo

◄ **A Victorian figured and burr-walnut miniature Wellington chest,** the moulded-edge top above six drawers with fitted knob handles, with a side locking pilaster, on a plinth base, one knob missing, 15in (38cm) wide.
£600–750
€/ $950–1,180 WW

Cheval Mirrors

A George III mahogany cheval mirror,
25¼in (64cm) wide.
£360–450
€/ $575–700 L

A George IV mahogany cheval mirror,
31in (78.5cm) wide.
£1,350–1,500
€/ $2,150–2,375 WAW

A George IV mahogany cheval mirror, with a bevelled plate, on bobbin-turned supports decorated with ebonized stringing, on splay legs with brass paw feet and casters, 21in (53.5cm) wide.
£500–600
€/ $800–950 AG

A Victorian mahogany cheval mirror,
mirror not attached, 37½in (95.5cm) wide.
£300–375
€/ $475–600 L

A Victorian mahogany cheval mirror,
35in (89cm) wide.
£600–750
€/ $950–1,185 B(Ba)

◄ **An Edwardian mahogany cheval mirror,** with inlaid stringing, the plate on tapering supports with acorn finials, the scroll legs with brass sabots and casters, 28in (71cm) wide.
£300–375
€/ $475–600 WW

A beechwood *faux* bamboo cheval mirror, French, c1870, 34in (86.5cm) wide.
£670–850
€/ $1,000–1,350 S(O)

Dressing Table Mirrors

A walnut dressing table mirror, the arched plate with a shaped surmount, the shaped platform base with three drawers, on turned feet, early 18thC, 17in (43cm) wide.
£1,000–1,200
€/ $1,500–2,000 BWL

A George I walnut dressing table mirror, the base with a concave-fronted drawer, 16½in (42cm) wide.
£575–675
€/ $900–1,000 S(O)

A George I walnut dressing table mirror, with swing frame, the plate with a moulded border flanked by uprights surmounted by turned brass finials, above three frieze drawers, on shaped feet, one finial missing, uprights possibly later, 13¾in (35cm) wide.
£850–1,100
€/ $1,350–1,750 B

A mahogany dressing table mirror, c1750, 16in (40.5cm) wide.
£700–775
€/ $1,100–1,225 ⊞ RPh

A Georgian Hepplewhite-style mahogany dressing table mirror, 25in (63.5cm) wide.
£700–800
€/ $1,100–1,250 ⊞ RPh

A late George III mahogany dressing table mirror, 23¼in (59cm) wide.
£140–175
€/ $220–275 ⚒ L

A mahogany bowfronted dressing table mirror, early 19thC, 18in (45.5cm) wide.
£350–400
€/ $550–630 ⊞ RPh

A Regency maple and rosewood crossbanded dressing table mirror, 24in (61cm) wide.
£180–225
€/ $285–350 ⚒ B(Ba)

A Regency mahogany dressing table mirror, the bowfronted base with three drawers, on later bracket feet, minor restorations, 18½in (47cm) wide.
£360–450
€/ $550–700 ⚒ B(W)

A mahogany dressing table mirror, c1830, 19½in (49.5cm) wide.
£150–170
€/ $235–270 ⊞ PaA

A mahogany dressing table mirror, with two drawers, c1835, 21¾in (55.5cm) wide.
£250–300
€/ $400–475 ⚒ S(O)

Mirrors or looking glasses

Early looking glasses were made of highly polished gold, silver or bronze and set into decorative frames. Poorer people often used polished pewter, which was much less expensive. In the Middle Ages steel and crystal were used and Venetian glass began to appear. In 1663 the Duke of Buckingham established a glass house at Vauxhall, and in 1664 the importation of foreign glass was forbidden by law, which resulted in the emergence of a large home production of ever increasing sizes of plate glass.

◄ **A mid-Victorian mahogany dressing table mirror,** attributed to Gillows, with reeded scroll supports, the platform base with bun feet, 17¾in (45cm) wide.
£150–200
€/ $235–315 ⚒ B(L)
This was a standard Gillows dressing table mirror design. It was produced with or without a drawer underneath from c1829 onwards. Some also had 'tray bottoms'.

A mahogany dressing table mirror, the backplate between turned uprights, the base fitted with two short drawers, 19thC, 18½in (47cm) wide.
£150–200
€/ $235–315 ⚒ AMB

A gilded dressing table mirror, French, c1880, 23in (58.5cm) high.
£1,000–1,200
€/ $1,500–2,000 ⊞ HA

Wall Mirrors

A Queen Anne walnut-veneered cushion-framed wall mirror, with a moulded frame, alterations and restorations, 24¾ x 22½in (63 x 57cm).
£550–700
€/ $870–1,100 B(W)

A George II giltwood wall mirror, with a bevelled plate, 26¾in (68cm) wide.
£800–1,000
€/ $1,250–1,500 L

A George III figured mahogany and gilt-decorated fret-cut wall mirror, with a *ho-o* bird surmount and swan-neck cresting, the bevelled plate within a gilt slip, 24in (61cm) wide.
£800–1,000
€/ $1,250–1,700 B(Pr)

► **A George III gilt-gesso wall mirror,** 18½in (47cm) wide.
£800–1,000
€/ $1,250–1,580 DN

A giltwood wall mirror, with a floral- and husk-carved border, surmounted by an arched top and shaped cresting with conforming decoration, on a punched ground, with later brass candle brackets, restored, early 18thC, 19¼in (49cm) wide.
£1,400–1,750
€/ $2,200–2,750 B(WM)

► **A parcel-gilt walnut wall mirror,** with a convex frame, the arched solid cresting moulded with a central shell flanked by dolphins, the base fret cut, mid-18thC, 23in (58.5cm) wide.
£600–750
€/ $950–1,200 PF

A George II giltwood wall mirror, carved with rope-twist and egg-and-dart borders and pendant foliage, 37in (94cm) wide.
£400–500
€/ $630–800 SWO

A George I gilt-framed wall mirror, with later bevelled plate, 18in (45.5cm) wide.
£800–1,000
€/ $1,250–1,500 S(O)

A silvered wall mirror, the later plate within a carved and moulded frame, the border plates divided by florettes, the sides hung with Greek key leaf carvings, the apron with fluted tapering leaf-carved feet, some damage, Italian, Piedmont, 18thC, 25½in (65cm) wide.
£360–450
€/ $550–700 B

► **A George III wall mirror,** the painted and parcel-gilt frame carved with bellflowers and beading, 37¼in (95.5cm) wide.
£2,000–2,500
€/ $3,200–4,000 WW

A George II mahogany wall mirror, with a giltwood border and shaped scroll frame, 26in (66cm) wide.
£800–1,000
€/ $1,250–1,500 JAd

A carved giltwood wall mirror, with floral and foliate decoration and floral urn surmount, the inner frame with egg-and-dart carved decoration, 18thC, 36in (91.5cm) high.
£1,000–1,250
€/ $1,500–2,000 BWL

A George III walnut and parcel-gilt wall mirror, 37½in (95.5cm) high.
£340–425
€/ $550–675 SWO

A Federal giltwood and *verre églomisé* pier mirror, minor damage, American, New York, c1800, 46½in (118cm) high.
£11,000–14,000
€/ $17,500–22,000
S(NY)
This is a very attractive mirror and such pieces invariably sell well in the USA.

A gilt-framed wall mirror, with a five-branch candleholder beneath, c1810, 39in (99cm) wide.
£2,000–2,250
€/ $3,200–3,500 MTay

A Regency giltwood pier mirror, the figural frieze over a bevelled plate, flanked by Egyptian-headed pilaster strips terminating in feet, 29¼in (74.5cm) wide.
£420–525
€/ $675–825 SWO

◀ **A giltwood mirror,** the plate surrounded by raised intertwining palmetto- and floral-decorated frame, American, 1825–50, 34in (86.5cm) wide.
£900–1,100
€/ $1,400–1,750 NOA

Gilt furniture

There are two types of gilding: water gilding, which has a yellow tone, and oil gilding with its distinctive deeper orange tone. Most English 18th- and 19th-century furniture was water gilded. Layers of gesso were applied to the carved wood base, then recut to define the decoration. A liquid clay base, or bole, was applied, and the gold leaf laid upon it before being burnished to achieve the final tone.

Oil gilding was less common and involved the application of an oil size to which the gold leaf was then stuck. Great care must be taken with gilt furniture. Never apply water as the gold will wash off; instead, seek the advice of a specialist gilder. Likewise, avoid hanging mirrors in bathrooms or other rooms with high humidity. To prevent damage to elaborately-carved furniture, dust lightly using a feather duster.

A pier mirror, the bevelled plate with a reeded ebonized slip, the ball-decorated cornice above a key frieze, with ribbon-tied cluster pilasters later painted, early 19thC, 26in (66cm) wide.
£300–375
€/ $475–600 WW

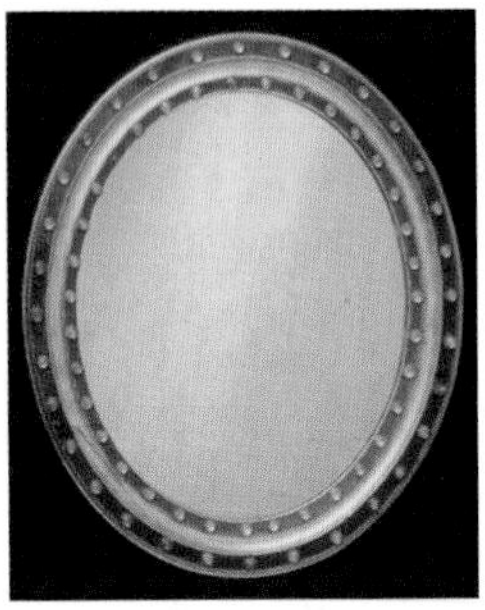

A Regency ebonized and parcel-gilt mirror, with cut-glass beads, the later plate within moulded borders, Irish, 21¼in (54cm) wide.
£700–875
€/ $1,100–1,400 B

A William IV gilt and composition convex mirror, 30¼in (77cm) diam.
£1,000–1,250
€/ $1,500–1,900 B(Ba)

A pair of giltwood wall mirrors, with cartouche-shaped frames and pierced crest and foliate scrolls, 19thC, 13¼in (33.5cm) wide.
£600–775
€/ $950–1,200 DN

A Regency giltwood convex girandole, gilding refreshed, 23¾in (60.5cm) wide.
£750–950
€/ $1,200–1,500 B(Ba)

A giltwood and gesso wall mirror, the moulded frame with a later plate, the eagle surmount with a chain and ball hanging from its beak, the base with a scroll leaf and fan design, the reverse with paper label 'William Wade, Picture Frame Maker, Carver, Gilder & Printseller, No. 86 Leadenhall Street, London', early 19thC, 19in (48.5cm) wide.
£600–725
€/ $950–1,150 WW
William Wade traded at Leadenhall Street from 1784 until after 1840.

A carved giltwood wall mirror, the plate within a scrolling foliage frame with a shell surmount, 19thC, 24½in (62cm) wide.
£550–700
€/ $870–1,100 WW

A giltwood and gesso wall mirror, the inverted breakfront half-round and foliate pilaster frame enclosing a plate with an ebonized reeded slip, 19thC, 30in (76cm) wide.
£500–650
€/ $800–1,000 WW

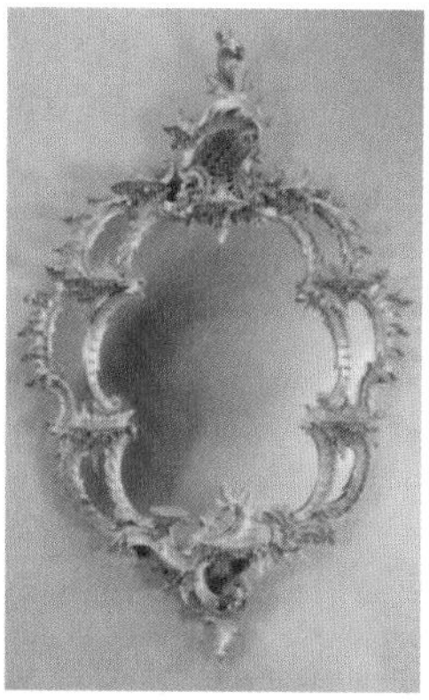

A rococo-style giltwood wall mirror, the frame with foliate scrolls and nine small shelves, 19thC, 32in (81.5cm) wide.
£1,100–1,300
€/ $1,750–2,000 DN

An ebonized and gilded wall mirror, Scandinavian, 19thC, 30in (76cm) wide.
£1,500–1,700
€/ $2,400–2,700 S(O)

A Louis XVI-style over-mantel mirror, French, 19thC, 42in (106.5cm) wide.
£450–575
€/ $700–900 L

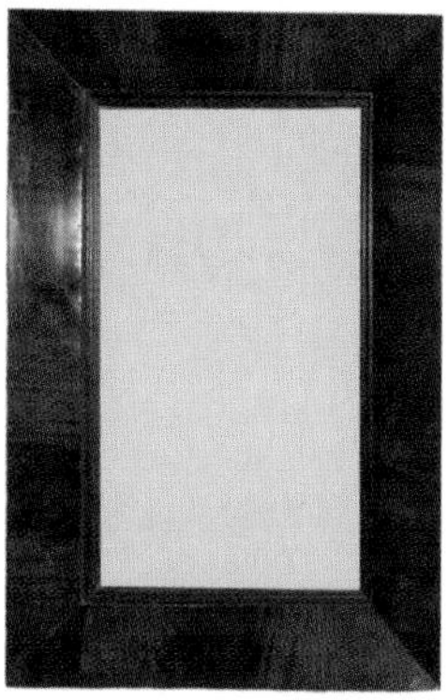

◄ A mahogany wall mirror, c1840, 22in (60cm) wide.
£235–260
€/ $370–400 MHA

► A Victorian giltwood wall mirror, the bevelled plate within a ribboned frame, 36¾in (93.5cm) wide.
£340–425
€/ $500–675 SWO

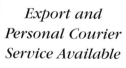

An ebonized and silvered wood wall mirror, the bevelled plate within a moulded frame supporting two gilt-metal branches, Irish, c1860, 16½in (42cm) wide.
£400–500
€/ $650–800 S(O)

◄ **A Victorian overmantel mirror,** with a scrolled pediment and swagged frieze, the plate flanked by architectural columns, 41in (104cm) wide.
£240–300
€/ $380–480 SWO

A giltwood wall mirror, the broken scroll pediment between a campana urn finial with fruiting vine and inner ribbon-tied husk border above a swagged floral spray, c1880, 30¼in (77cm) wide.
£600–750
€/ $1,000–1,200 WL

A rosewood overmantel mirror, with ivory inlay, c1880, 46in (117cm) wide.
£700–800
€/ $1,100–1,250 GBr

A mahogany, ebonized and painted mirror, the arched pediment enclosing a scantily clad winged angel, within a foliate border above the mirror plate, Baltic, 1850–1900, 25½in (65cm) wide.
£600–750
€/ $950–1,200 S(Am)

A Victorian gilt gesso wall mirror, the frame moulded with rococo scrolls, leaves and flowering stems, 61in (155cm) high.
£700–875
€/ $1,100–1,375 B(S)

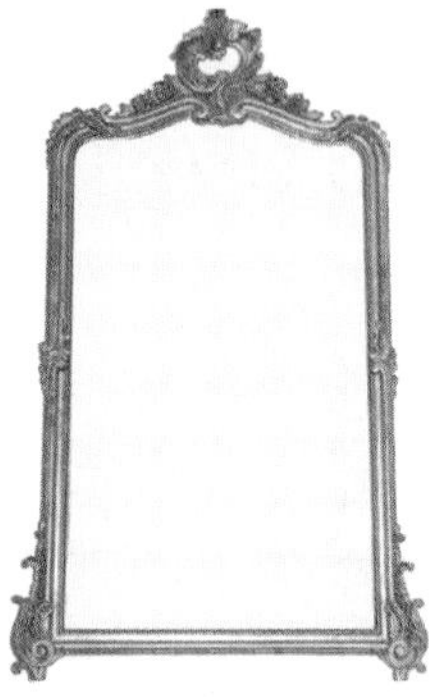

A giltwood overmantel mirror, French, c1890, 34in (86.5cm) wide.
£1,450–1,600
€/ $2,300–2,500 DAC

A gilt gesso over-mantel mirror, with ribboned top, glass with defects, late 19thC, 60¼in (153cm) wide.
£500–625
€/ $800–1,000 SWO

A glass and micro-mosaic wall mirror, the bevelled plate within a border of etched glass marginals and a further border of micro-mosaic flora on a gold *tesserae* ground, within a further border of etched glass marginals, Venetian, late 19thC, 30¾in (78cm) wide.
£2,300–2,800
€/ $3,600–4,400 B

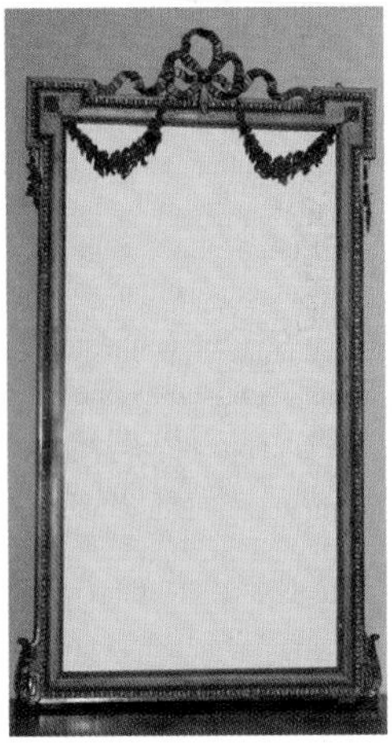

A giltwood overmantel mirror, French, c1880, 38in (96.5cm) wide.
£1,600–1,800
€/ $2,500–2,850 DAC

A Directoire-style painted wood *trumeau*, partly constructed of antique elements, the upper oval panel painted *en grisaille* with the figure of an 18thC soldier, French, c1900, 38in (96.5cm) wide.
£750–950
€/ $1,200–1,500 NOA

A George III-style giltwood and gesso overmantel mirror, with a swan-neck pediment, c1900, 54in (137cm) wide.
£700–875
€/ $1,100–1,400 S(O)

◄ **A pair of mahogany and gilt wall mirrors,** c1920, 19in (48.5cm) wide.
£475–525
€/ $750–825 GBr

Ottomans

An early Victorian ottoman, the hinged woolwork top above silk-upholstered sides, on a rosewood base with bun feet, 30in (76cm) wide.
£700–850
€/ $1,100–1,350 DN

A mahogany ottoman, upholstered in needlework, mid-19thC, 16in (40.5cm) square.
£160–180
€/ $250–285 HiA

A mahogany ottoman, with a deep-button, leather-padded lidded top revealing a storage space over a padded concave base, on squat bun feet, 1850–75, 21in (53.5cm) wide.
£1,200–1,500
€/ $1,900–2,400 NOA

Screens

A painted six-fold screen, one side with an Italian landscape, the reverse with random floral motifs, Italian, 18thC, each fold 28in (71cm) wide.
£6,000–7,500
€/ $9,500–11,750 B

This is remarkable value when compared to what one might have to pay for a framed oil painting of a similar size and date. Such pieces are often used nowadays as a less expensive alternative to oil paintings.

An embossed leather four-fold screen, painted with foliate scrolls and flowers to one side, some splits and repairs, 19thC, 72½in (184cm) wide.
£950–1,200
€/ $1,500–1,900 DN

A late Victorian mahogany and bevelled glass three-fold screen, each fold 24in (61cm) wide.
£220–275
€/ $350–440 BR

Fire Screens

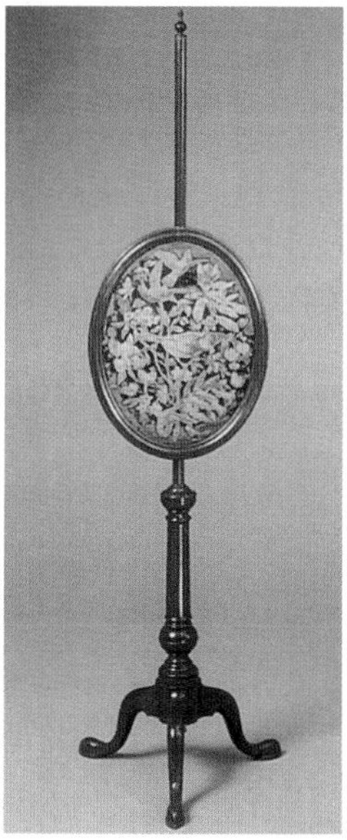

◄ **A Chippendale-style mahogany pole screen,** panel distressed, repairs to two legs, American, Philadelphia, c1765, 56in (142cm) high.
£1,100–1,300
€/ $1,700–2,000 S(NY)

► **A late George III mahogany pole screen,** the silkwork panel depicting a bird, the baluster-turned stem with an urn finial, the three cabriole legs with turned toes, restored, screen 11½in (29cm) wide.
£150–180
€/ $235–285 WW

A Regency mahogany and triple-glass fire screen, decorated with roundels and with brass top corners and handle, with two fitted sliding panels and a pull-out panel, on moulded splay legs with brass terminals and casters, 42in (106.5cm) high.
£550–700
€/ $870–1,100 MCA

A rosewood fire screen, with barley-twist columns, on moulded cabriole legs with brass casters, early 19thC, 29in (73.5cm) wide.
£765–850
€/ $1,200–1,350 ⊞ JSt

A pair of rosewood pole screens, with original needlework panels, c1835, 55in (139.5cm) high.
£3,300–3,700
€/ $5,200–5,800 ⊞ REI

A mahogany fire screen, with foliate carved crest over a tapestry panel depicting a mother and child, the frame on cabriole legs, 19thC, 27in (68.5cm) high.
£200–250
€/ $300–400 🔨 G(L)

► An Edwardian carved walnut fire screen, the framed needlework panel above outsplayed feet, 29½in (75cm) high.
£250–320
€/ $400–500 🔨 SWO

A pair of rosewood pole screens, c1825, 57in (145cm) high.
£3,000–3,250
€/ $4,750–5,200 ⊞ CAT

An early Victorian mahogany pole screen, the fabric panel in a frame of C-scrolls and cartouches, the pole with a carved baluster collar, on three out-scrolled legs, finial missing, 54in (137cm) high.
£230–280
€/ $360–440 🔨 Mit

A rosewood fire screen, with a needlework panel depicting two girls, c1830, 28in (71cm) wide.
£450–500
€/ $700–800 ⊞ NoC

An early Victorian rosewood pole screen, with a raised woolwork banner, screen 17½in (44.5cm) diam.
£450–550
€/ $700–850 🔨 L

An Edwardian mahogany-framed fire screen, with a needlework panel in the style of Morris & Co, 41in (104cm) high.
£160–180
€/ $250–280 ⊞ HiA

► A walnut fire screen, with claw feet, early 20thC, 43¼in (110cm) high.
£80–100
€/ $125–160 🔨 B(W)

A William IV mahogany pole screen, the banner with fleur-de-lys corners, the floral study worked with chenille and woolwork, on a vase and plain turned column with a spire finial, 62in (157.5cm) high.
£250–320
€/ $400–500 🔨 DD

A Victorian pole screen, the floral needlework panel with a moulded frame, the turned pole on an octagonal baluster stem, the base with scroll feet, 18in (45.5cm) wide.
£120–150
€/ $200–240 🔨 WW

Settees & Sofas

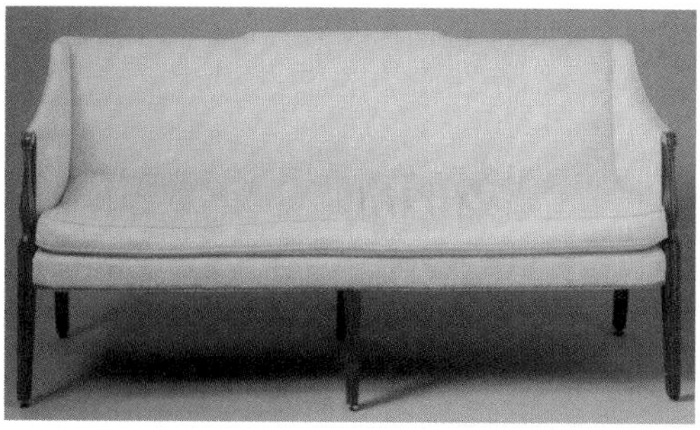

A Federal mahogany sofa, central rear leg replaced, American, Philadelphia, c1800, 73½in (186.5cm) wide.
£2,400–2,750
€/ $3,800–4,300 S(NY)

A pair of mahogany-framed sofas, with acanthus-carved rails, and swept carved feet, c1815, 57in (145cm) wide.
£32,000–35,000
€/ $50,000–55,000 HA
It is very unusual to find sofas of such compact size. Both are in excellent condition and the carving is of the highest quality, which makes them very desirable pieces.

◄ **A Regency mahogany-framed sofa,** the scrolling reeded arms terminating in spiral twist columns, with narrow front frieze and similar spiral-twist front supports, 57in (145cm) wide.
£500–600
€/ $800–950 TRL

A Regency mahogany bergère settee, possibly by Gillows, the back with paterae above a cane panel and conforming openwork band, with a cane seat below, 46in (117cm) wide.
£2,000–2,500
€/ $3,200–4,000 MEA

► **An Empire-style mahogany carved sofa,** the back-rail with painted stringing and trailing leaf decoration with applied ormolu paterae, the sides carved as recumbent winged harpies with gilt wings and simulated bronze bodies, the seat-rail on square tapering legs, c1820, 73¼in (186cm) wide.
£1,800–2,250
€/ $2,850–3,500 B&L

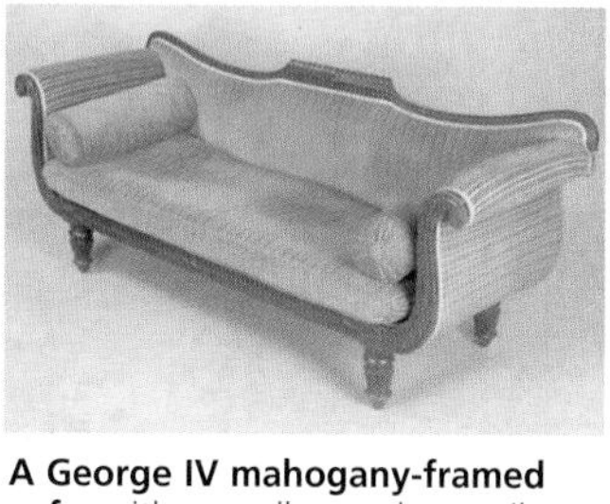

A George IV mahogany-framed sofa, with a scroll-carved top-rail and arms, on melon fluted legs, 85¾in (218cm) wide.
£950–1,200
€/ $1,500–1,900 B(Ch)

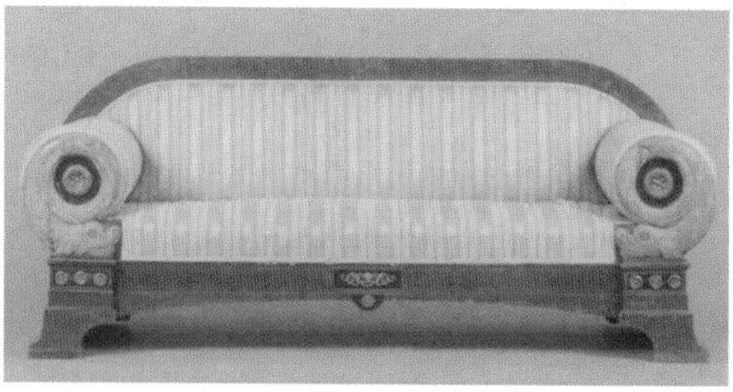

◄ **A mahogany and upholstered sofa,** part ebonized and with gilt-metal mounts, Swedish, c1830, 85½in (217cm) wide.
£1,800–2,200
€/ $2,850–3,500 S(O)

A mahogany and leather sofa, c1835, 84in (213.5cm) wide.
£5,200–5,700
€/ $8,200–9,000 GBr

A Chippendale-style mahogany double chair-back sofa, with a foliate-embroidered seat, the back joined by splayed arms terminating in scrolls, with curved uprights above an apron, 19thC, 66in (167.5cm) wide.
£1,200–1,500
€/ $1,900–2,400 GAK

A giltwood-framed canapé, French, mid-19thC, 88in (223.5cm) wide.
£6,000–6,800
€/ $9,500–10,750 ⊞ RAN

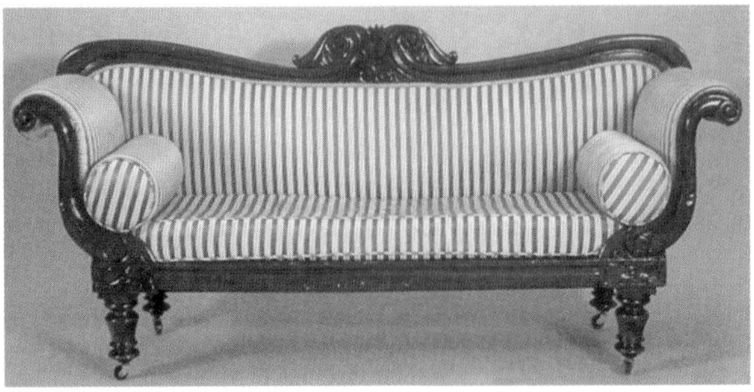

An early Victorian mahogany-framed settee, the shaped back with centred carved scrolls, on turned legs, 79in (200.5cm) wide.
£380–475
€/ $600–750 ⚒ WW

A leather and oak conversation seat, in the style of A. W. N. Pugin, with three seats, the leaf-carved legs with flower-carved feet, c1860, 86½in (219.5cm) wide.
£2,000–2,400
€/ $3,200–3,800 ⚒ S(O)

Augustus Welby Northmore Pugin (1812–52) was commissioned, at the age of only 15, to design a set of chairs for Windsor Castle. He established his own cabinet-making firm in Hart Street, Covent Garden, (1829–31) and produced furniture in the Gothic, Elizabethan and Jacobean styles. He was also responsible for the design of all the internal decorative furniture and furnishings for the New Palace of Westminster. The leaf and flower carving on this item has similarities to carving seen in his later work.

A rosewood double-ended button-back sofa, on carved cabriole legs with casters, c1860, 70in (178cm) wide.
£3,000–3,250
€/ $4,750–5,150 ⊞ JSt

The term settee, possibly a corruption of the word settle, was used from the early 17th century to describe a modified chair for two people to sit upright. From the 1760s, the term sofa (from the Ottoman *sopha*) was introduced as the settee became longer, with padded arms and back, and was deep enough to recline in comfort. Nowadays the two terms have become interchangable.

A walnut bench, the oblong padded back above a stuffed seat, the padded arms with baluster supports on turned tapering legs with beaded collars, c1860, 67in (170cm) wide.
£700–850
€/ $1,100–1,350 ⚒ S(O)

A carved mahogany-framed settee, on turned and fluted legs, French, c1870, 52in (132cm) wide.
£2,500–2,850
€/ $4,000–4,500 ⊞ RAN

A Victorian ebonized love seat, 41¾in (106cm) wide.
£350–450
€/ $550–700 ⚒ B(Ba)

A carved giltwood-framed canapé, French, c1870, 65in (165cm) wide.
£2,400–2,650
€/ $3,800–4,200 ⊞ RAN

A George III-style mahogany triple chair-back settee, c1880, 54¾in (139cm) wide.
£800–1,000
€/ $1,250–1,600 ⚒ S(O)

A Louis XV-style sofa, c1885, 55in (139.5cm) wide.
£3,200–3,500
€/ $5,000–5,500 ⊞ Che

A Victorian mahogany-framed button-back double-ended settee, on turned legs, reupholstered, 81½in (207cm) wide.
£420–525
€/ $670–830 HoG

A Victorian walnut-framed parlour sofa, the padded back with pierced scrolling foliate surround, the padded arms on carved and scrolled supports, with serpentine stuff-over seat, on cabriole legs and casters, 73in (185.5cm) wide.
£1,100–1,400
€/ $1,750–2,200 AH

A pair of rococo-style giltwood canapés, the frames centred by a floral and foliate cartouche, Italian, 19thC, 62in (157.5cm) wide.
£7,000–7,800
€/ $11,000–12,500 RAN

A Victorian walnut serpentine settee, with a shaped back, on turned front legs, 52in (132cm) wide.
£600–750
€/ $950–1,200 SWO

A Chippendale-style mahogany couch, c1880, 46in (117cm) wide.
£1,650–1,850
€/ $2,600–2,900 GBr

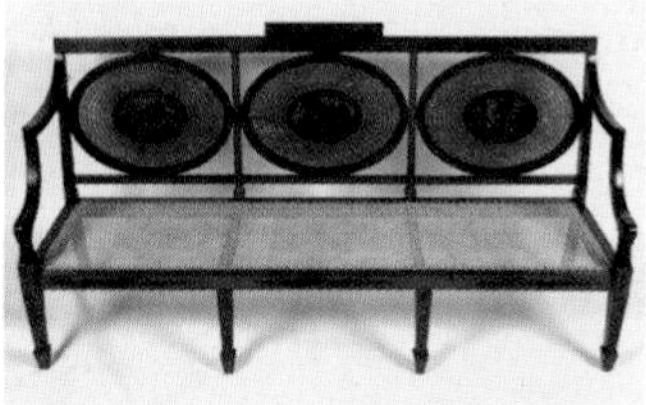

◄ **A Victorian painted satinwood sofa,** by Gillows, 68in (172.5cm) wide.
£6,000–6,750
€/ $9,500–10,650 SAW

A late Victorian mahogany Chesterfield sofa, button-upholstered in leather, the out-scrolled sides and serpentine seat close-nailed, on turned legs with later casters, 78¾in (200cm) wide.
£2,200–2,750
€/ $3,500–4,300 B

► **An Edwardian rosewood-framed settee,** 59in (150cm) wide.
£350–450
€/ $550–700 B(Ba)

A Louis XV-style walnut-framed settee, French, c1900, 48in (122cm) wide.
£1,000–1,150
€/ $1,600–1,800 MLL

An Edwardian mahogany shaped-back sofa, 47in (119.5cm) wide.
£400–450
€/ $650–700 HiA

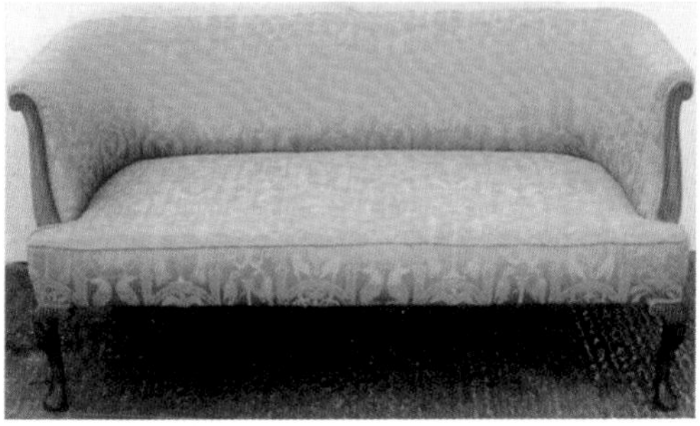

A Georgian-style mahogany-framed sofa, the upholstered back terminating in carved scrolls, on cabriole legs with foliate-carved knees, 1920s, 62in (157.5cm) wide.
£300–375
€/ $475–600 TRL

Shelves

A mahogany graduated hanging shelf, early 19thC, 24in (61cm) wide.
£330–400
€/ $525–650 S(O)

A mahogany four-tier graduated open bookshelf, with X-frame bracing bars, on turned feet, 19thC, 37in (94cm) wide.
£300–375
€/ $475–600 DMC

A mahogany hanging shelf, c1820, 18in (45.5cm) wide.
£300–335
€/ $475–525 F&F

A mahogany three-tier graduated hanging shelf, the shaped sides with turned paterae, on turned feet, 19thC, 33in (84cm) wide.
£340–425
€/ $550–675 DMC

A rosewood open wall shelf, the three serpentine shelves on moulded spiral-twist and baluster supports, some replacements, 19thC, 32in (81.5cm) wide.
£320–375
€/ $500–600 WW

A Victorian mahogany open shelf, the shaped scroll top above three graduated shelves and scroll supports, 24¼in (61.5cm) wide.
£320–375
€/ $500–600 WW

A mahogany five-tier wall shelf, with stamped patent mark, c1885, 18in (45.5cm) wide.
£400–450
€/ $650–700 RPh

A mahogany three-tier bowfronted wall shelf, with fretwork sides, late 19thC, 15in (38cm) wide.
£475–575
€/ $750–900 G(L)

Sideboards

A George III mahogany bowfronted sideboard, with a central drawer, the single side drawers with inlaid doors below, 90in (228.5cm) wide.
£4,500–5,000
€/ $7,000–8,000 WAW

A George III mahogany serpentine sideboard, with a single frieze drawer above a shaped apron, on boxwood-strung tapering legs with spade feet, 40½in (103cm) high.
£450–565
€/ $700–900 RTo

A George III mahogany sideboard, with line, shell and floral lozenge inlay, the upper section with sliding doors, the three central drawers flanked by two further drawers, 84in (213.5cm) wide.
£1,000–1,250
€/ $1,600–2,000 WilP

◄ **A George III mahogany sideboard,** with reeded top, above one shallow and two deep drawers, with lion mask and ring handles, some old repairs, 45in (114.5cm) wide.
£1,000–1,250
€/ $1,600–2,000 BWL

A George III inlaid mahogany breakfront sideboard, the central frieze drawer above a cupboard with panelled doors, all decorated with satinwood crossbanding and stringing, 61in (155cm) wide.
£1,500–1,800
€/ $2,400–2,800 JAd

A Sheraton mahogany bowfronted sideboard, with Edwardian inlay, c1780, 54in (137cm) wide.
£8,500–9,500
€/ $13,500–15,000 ⊞ REI
The brass galleries on sideboards were for curtains, used to protect the expensive (often silk) wall coverings from being splashed when food was being served.

◄ A mahogany serpentine sideboard, crossbanded in purple heart and boxwood, c1780, 44in (112cm) wide.
£11,500–13,000
€/ $18,000–20,000 ⊞ CAT

A mahogany serpentine pedestal sideboard, with tambour doors, c1790, 66in (167.5cm) wide.
£2,600–3,000
€/ $4,000–4,750 ⊞ Che

A Federal walnut serpentine sideboard, with tulipwood and mahogany inlay, American, North Carolina, c1800, 65¾in (167cm) wide.
£12,500–16,000
€/ $20,000–25,000 ⚒ S(NY)
The sideboard was a new form introduced during the Federal period as the object for serving food in American dining rooms. It was an expensive and unusual form designed with drawers and cupboards intended for the storage of silver plate, dishes, glasses, tablecloths, bottles and other articles necessary for dining. George Hepplewhite praised the form in *The Cabinet Maker and Upholsterer's Guide* (London, 1788), noting the 'great utility of this piece of furniture has procured it a very general reception; and the conveniences it affords render a dining room incomplete without a sideboard'.

A Federal inlaid walnut sideboard, majority of inlaid collars missing, American, North Carolina, c1795, 56½in (143.5cm) wide.
£12,000–14,000
€/ $19,000–22,000 ⚒ S(NY)

A mahogany bowfronted sideboard, with satinwood inlay and banding, c1790, 58in (147.5cm) wide.
£9,000–10,000
€/ $14,000–16,000 ⊞ DJH

► A late George III mahogany and satinwood-banded bowfronted sideboard, with later fitted interior, 59½in (151cm) wide.
£2,000–2,400
€/ $3,150–3,800
⚒ B(Ba)

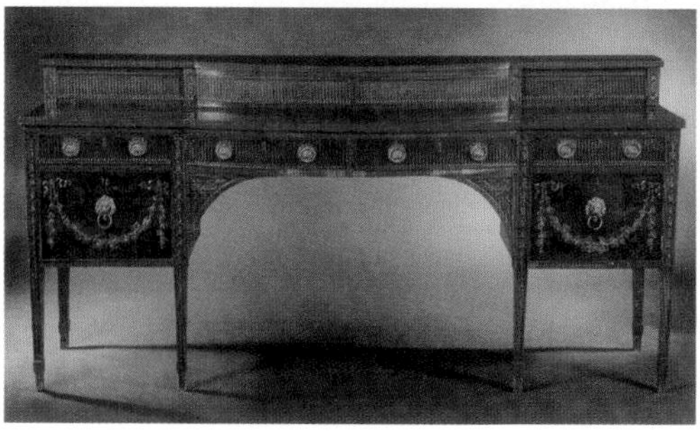

A mahogany sideboard, the crossbanded and carved raised back with sliding fluted cupboards and centre sections, above a shaped top, over four frieze drawers, a cellaret drawer to one side and a cupboard to the other, both with lion mask handles and carved with ribbon-and-vine swags, early 19thC, 96in (244cm) wide.
£1,500–1,800
€/ $2,400–2,850 ⚒ B(Ed)
This sideboard has the characteristic Scottish feature of a rear stage with sliders or sliding panels that reveal storage space for glasses. Because of its size, it can be identified as a Glasgow example. Glasgow cabinet makers began their sideboards at 84in (213.5cm) long, instead of 72in (183cm), as in Edinburgh.

A Sheraton period mahogany sideboard, with boxwood stringing, the raised back enclosed by twin sliding tambour shutter doors, with three frieze drawers flanked by deep cellaret drawers, with end pot cupboard, early 19thC, 88in (223.5cm) wide.
£2,000–2,400
€/ $3,200–3,800 ⚒ DMC

A Regency mahogany sideboard, the D-shaped top with outset tower corners, over a frieze drawer and arched apron, flanked by bowed deep drawers, one fitted as a cellaret, 60¼in (153cm) wide.
£3,200–3,750
€/ $5,000–6,000 ⚒ TEN

A Regency mahogany breakfront sideboard, the top with a three-quarter gallery over a central frieze drawer, flanked by bowed fitted cellaret drawers with cupboards below, on ball feet, stamped 'Gillows, Lancaster', 66in (167.5cm) wide.
£2,800–3,500
€/ $4,500–5,500 ⚒ TEN

A mahogany and ebonized inlaid breakfront sideboard, the crossbanded top above a central frieze drawer and a recess arcaded deep drawer, flanked by part-bowed drawers, a cupboard door and a cellaret drawer, panelled pilasters, later brass rosette ring handles, top split, early 19thC, 77½in (197cm) wide.
£1,700–2,200
€/ $2,700–3,500 ⚒ WW

A Regency mahogany sideboard, the raised triangular back over a crossbanded top, the central sunk panelled frieze drawer flanked by inversely tapered pedestals, with panelled doors between fluted pilasters, enclosing shelves to one side and fitted cellaret drawers to the other, on ebonized ball feet, 72½in (184cm) wide.
£2,200–2,750
€/ $3,500–4,300 ⚒ TEN

A Regency mahogany pedestal sideboard, with black line decoration, 76½in (194.5cm) wide.
£2,200–2,500
€/ $3,500–4,000 ⚒ B(Ba)

A Regency mahogany bowfronted sideboard, 42in (106.5cm) wide.
£400–500
€/ $650–800 ⚒ B(Ba)

A Regency mahogany sideboard, the crossbanded top above a bowed centre drawer with frieze drawer below, flanked by a cellaret drawer and a cupboard, 60¼in (153cm) wide.
£700–875
€/ $1,100–1,400 ⚒ GTH

A late Regency mahogany bow-fronted sideboard, surmounted by a tubular brass curtain rail, with a long drawer above an arched apron flanked by a cupboard and a deep cellaret drawer, with a small cupboard to one side, 78in (198cm) wide.
£2,200–2,500
€/ $3,500–4,000 ⚒ B(S)

A carved mahogany rosewood sideboard, with brass mounts, the doors opening to shelves, the side fitted with retractable slides, repairs to both right feet, American, c1815, 72in (183cm) wide.
£3,000–3,500
€/ $4,800–5,500 ⚒ S(NY)

A mahogany sideboard, the frieze with three drawers, each pedestal with a hinged compartment in the top, above a drawer and cupboard, one with a cellaret drawer, c1820, 95in (241.5cm) wide.
£1,300–1,500
€/ $2,000–2,400 ⚒ S(O)

A George IV mahogany breakfront pedestal sideboard, with spiral twist and lappet-carved stiles, 68½in (174cm) wide.
£600–750
€/ $950–1,200 B(Ch)

A George IV mahogany bowfronted sideboard, with one short drawer, one deep drawer, and two cupboards with brass lion mask ring handles, 50in (127cm) wide.
£800–1,000
€/ $1,300–1,600 AG

► A mahogany four-door sideboard, c1865, 60in (152.5cm) wide.
£2,000–2,250
€/ $3,150–3,500 ⊞ Che

A George IV mahogany pedestal sideboard, on a plinth base, 78¼in (199cm) wide.
£1,300–1,600
€/ $2,000–2,500 DN

Many 18th-century sideboards have a small cupboard in one of the sides towards the back. Known as the 'pot cupboard', this is exactly what it contained. After dinner, when the ladies had retired, a butler would produce the pot (often silver) and the gentlemen would relieve themselves as it was passed around the table!

A George IV Gothic-style mahogany twin pedestal sideboard, with an architectural panelled back, above a bowfronted frieze drawer, with Gothic arched panel cupboards to the pedestals, flanked by turned columns, on inverted breakfront bases, 61in (155cm) wide.
£950–1,200
€/ $1,500–2,000 HYD

A mahogany bowfronted sideboard, the shaped top above two short drawers, flanked by two cupboard doors modelled as dummy drawers, 19thC, 54¼in (138cm) wide.
£800–1,000
€/ $1,250–1,600 CGC

A Victorian carved figured mahogany mirrored-back sideboard, the shaped-top glass with foliate trail-carved crest and side uprights, over an inverted breakfront base with a central frieze drawer and twin panel-fronted cupboards, flanked by oval-panel-inset doors with fitted interiors of slides and cellaret drawer, on a plinth base, damaged, 78in (198cm) wide.
£750–950
€/ $1,200–1,500 Bri

A late Victorian walnut mirrored-back sideboard, with original handles and mirrors, 72in (183cm) wide.
£1,600–1,800
€/ $2,500–2,850 ⊞ SWA

A Victorian mahogany sideboard, with a leaf-and-scroll-carved back, fitted with three frieze drawers, one pedestal with a cellaret section and a centre cupboard with panelled doors, on a plinth base, 71in (180.5cm) wide.
£900–1,100
€/ $1,400–1,750 HOLL

► **An inlaid walnut sideboard,** German, 19thC, 93¾in (238cm) wide.
£900–1,100
€/ $1,400–1,750 B(Ch)

A rosewood and satinwood crossbanded sideboard, with boxwood stringing, the top with a raised three-quarter gallery and moulded edge, above five drawers with brass handles around a kneehole, late 19thC, 46in (117cm) wide.
£800–1,000
€/ $1,300–1,600 DN

A Victorian mahogany inverted breakfront pedestal sideboard, superstructure missing, 71in (180.5cm) wide.
£280–350
€/ $450–550 B(Ba)

A pollarded oak and figured walnut mirrored-back sideboard, with copper mounts and carved panels, c1900, 78in (198cm) wide.
£2,700–3,000
€/ $4,300–4,700 S(O)

A Victorian mahogany pedestal sideboard,with an inverted break-front top, and three frieze drawers above cupboard doors, with trays, 82in (208.5cm) wide.
£425–525
€/ $675–825 SWO

◄ **An Edwardian Sheraton-style inlaid mahogany sideboard,** 53in (134.5cm) wide.
£1,800–2,000
€/ $2,850–3,200 ⊞ RPh

An Edwardian inlaid mahogany bowfronted sideboard, 49in (124.5cm) wide.
£850–950
€/ $1,350–1,500 ⊞ MHA

An Edwardian Sheraton-style mahogany inverted breakfront sideboard, with satinwood and boxwood banding and stringing, the central frieze drawer above an arched frieze and open shelf, flanked by two curved front drawers, 54in (137cm) wide.
£500–650
€/ $800–1,000 TRL

An Edwardian crossbanded mahogany serpentine sideboard, 45¾in (116cm) wide.
£375–475
€/ $600–750 SWO

Items in the Furniture section have been arranged in date order.

Cake Stands

A mahogany three-tier cake stand, c1890, 38in (96.5cm) high.
£380–425
€/ $600–670 ⊞ GBr

An Edwardian mahogany cake stand, with three dished plates and central carrying handle, on three splayed legs, 31½in (80cm) high.
£110–140
€/ $175–220 ⚒ FHF

► An Edwardian mahogany three-tier cake stand, 38in (96.5cm) high.
£600–675
€/ $950–1,100 ⊞ RPh

► A mahogany cake stand, the serpentine top with moulded edge, the fall-sides each revealing a base-lined dished tray, on four splayed feet, early 20thC, 29½in (75cm) high.
£100–125
€/ $160–200 ⚒ BIG

An Edwardian inlaid mahogany three-tier cake stand, 38in (96.5cm) high.
£170–220
€/ $270–350 ⚒ JAd

Hat & Stick Stands

A carved walnut coat stand, with umbrella support, the base with inset drip pan, on spool feet, German, 19thC, 85¾in (218cm) high.
£5,500–7,000
€/ $8,700–11,000
⚒ B(EA)

These Black Forest-type carved bear and tree coat stands are currently very popular, particularly with decorators in US ski resorts.

A cast-iron stick stand, attributed to Sheffield, Edwin & Theophilus Smith, in the form of a boy standing among reeds and grappling with a serpent, with removable leaf-cast drip tray, with registration design lozenge, c1866, 33in (84cm) high.
£1,500–2,000
€/ $2,400–3,200 ⚒ S

► A brass-bound coopered mahogany stick stand, with brass mask handles, late 19thC, 26in (66cm) high.
£1,300–1,500
€/ $2,000–2,400 ⚒ S(O)

A cast-iron stick stand, with pierced foliate-cast back, diamond registration mark, c1880, 33in (84cm) high.
£565–680
€/ $900–1,100 ⚒ S(O)

A Victorian painted-wood stick stand, with turned supports and lead-lined base, on turned feet, 61½in (156cm) wide.
£300–375
€/ $475–600 ⚒ WW

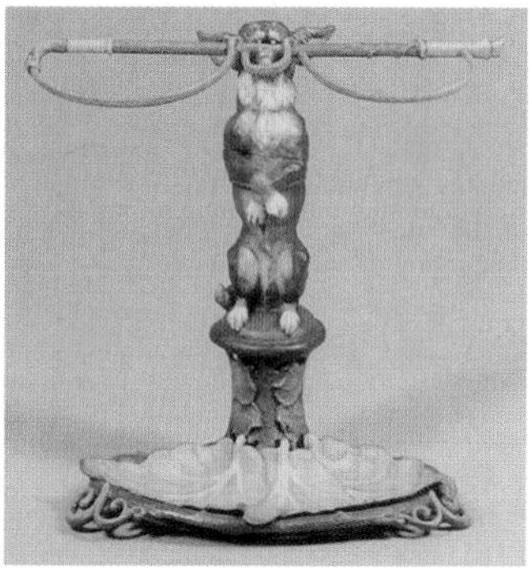

A cast-iron stick stand, after a design by Coalbrookdale, in the form of a begging dog supported on a pierced leaf-cast pedestal and holding a riding crop in its jaw, the removable tray cast as three leaves, on a moulded base with pierced scroll-cast supports, redecorated, late 19thC, 24in (61cm) high.
£4,300–4,750
€/ $6,800–7,500 ⚒ S

Folio Stands

A mahogany folio stand, c1830, 27in (68.5cm) wide.
£2,600–3,000
€/ $4,000–4,700 GBr

A carved mahogany folio stand, c1870, 34in (86.5cm) wide.
£6,000–6,850
€/ $9,600–10,800 RAN

A mahogany folio rack, the slatted two-division top on square tapering legs, early 19thC, 28in (71cm) wide.
£2,700–3,000
€/ $4,300–4,700 S(O)

A rosewood folio stand, mid-19thC, 26½in (67.5cm) wide.
£375–475
€/ $600–750 S(O)

► **A walnut folio stand,** the moulded top on baluster supports and an undertier, c1900, 37in (9cm) wide.
£775–900
€/ $1,100–1,400 S(O)

A late Regency mahogany folio stand, 25¼in (64cm) wide.
£1,300–1,600
€/ $2,000–2,500 B(Ba)

A walnut folio stand, French, 19thC, 41in (104cm) wide.
£300–375
€/ $475–600 WW

Kettle & Urn Stands

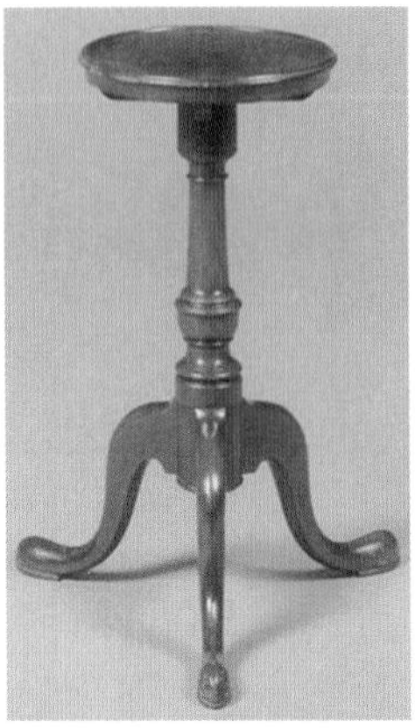

A George III mahogany kettle stand, with an associated dished top, one leg later, 18¼in (46cm) high.
£1,400–1,600
€/ $2,200–2,500 S(O)

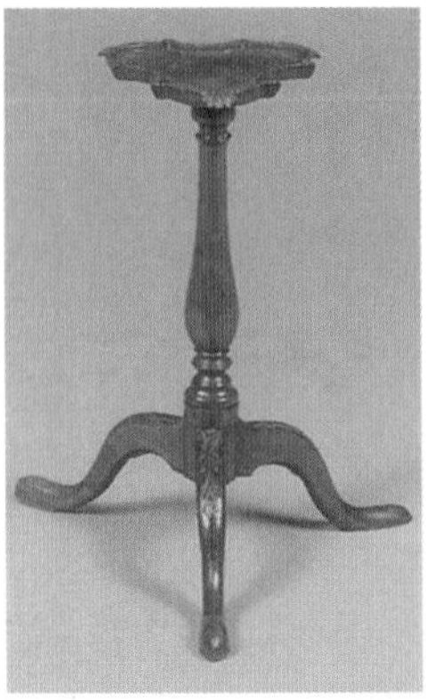

A George III mahogany urn stand, with associated triform top, on later-carved cabriole legs, 23¾in (60.5cm) high.
£550–650
€/ $870–1,000 S(O)

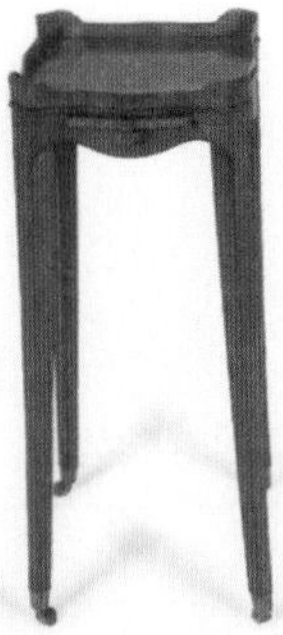

A pair of satinwood and tulipwood urn tables, with brass caps and casters, c1770, 25in (63.5cm) high.
£16,000–18,000
€/ $25,000–28,000 REI
Being made of satinwood and in excellent condition, these tables are particularly desirable.

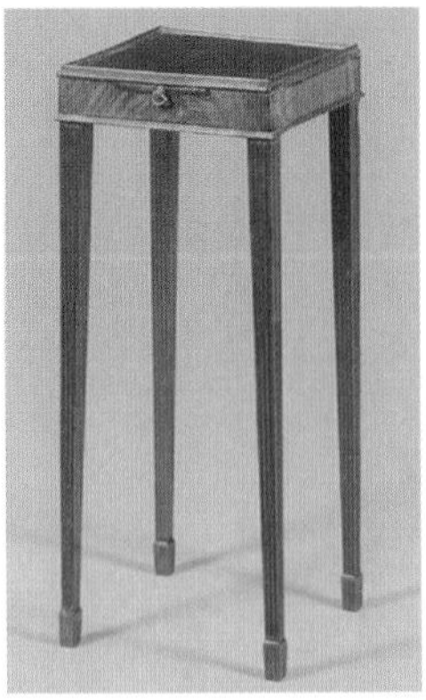

A George III mahogany kettle stand, with a moulded tulipwood and crossbanded top above a moulded frieze fitted with a slide, on tapered stop-fluted legs and spade feet, top repositioned, 26¾in (68cm) high.
£3,200–3,500
€/ $5,000–5,500 S

Music Stands

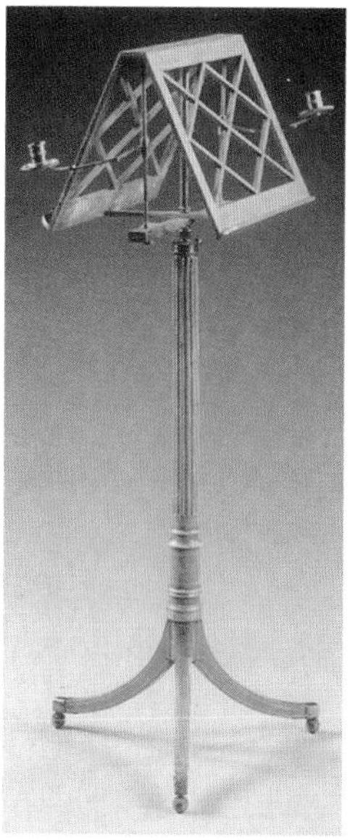

◄ **A satinbirch duet stand,** by Erard's, London, the trellis rest with candle arms, on a fluted turned and tapering adjustable column and sabre-legged tripod, early 19thC, 48in (122cm) high.
£7,000–8,000
€/ $11,000–12,500 S(O)

The distinguished Parisian firm Erard's were in practice between 1777–1960. The business was founded by Sébastien Erard, who had been apprentice to a Parisian harpsichord maker for two years before establishing his own workshop in the rue de Bourbon. In 1786 the company expanded by opening a branch in London, and in 1789 his brother Jean-Baptiste joined as partner.

A pair of mahogany music stands, with adjustable height and inclination, on ring-turned pillars and tripod bases with hipped sabre legs, early 19thC, 29½in (75cm) minimum height.
£1,800–2,250
€/ $2,800–3,500 TEN

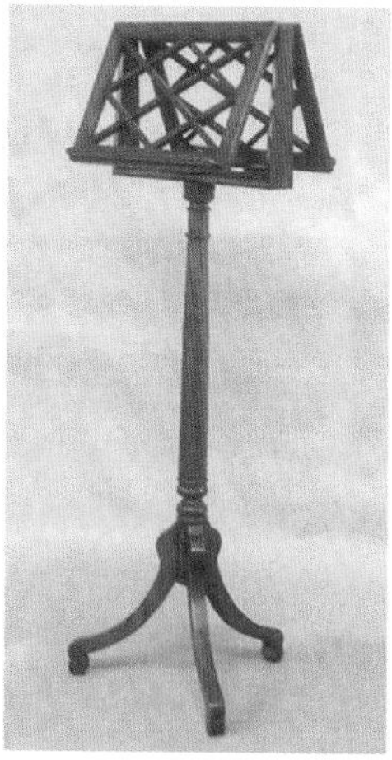

A mahogany tripod duet stand, the top with a pair of folding lattice-work music rests, on a turned tapered column on hipped sabre legs with scroll feet, early 19thC, 54in (137cm) high.
£400–500
€/ $630–800 PF

Plant Stands

◄ **A carved and painted limewood jardinière,** in the form of a cloth-draped surface on a carved cupid support with a carved tripod case, 19thC, 31in (78.5cm) high.
£500–600
€/ $800–950
HOLL

An arched top split-cane plant stand, after a design by George Smith, on turned legs with brass casters, c1820, 50in (127cm) wide.
£1,800–2,200
€/ $2,800–3,500 ⊞ GKe

A walnut two-tier plant stand, the marquetry-inlaid top with gilt mounts, French, late 19thC, 30in (76cm) high.
£900–1,100
€/ $1,400–1,700 SWO

Shaving Stands

A mahogany shaving stand, minor damage, c1840, 67in (170cm) high.
£550–600
€/ $800–950 ⊞ PaA

◄ **A shaving stand,** by James Shoolbred, with maker's enamel plaque, c1870, 58¾in (149cm) high.
£530–635
€/ $850–900 S(O)

James Shoolbred & Co were operating from an address in Tottenham Court Road, London, during the late 19th century and were described by the *Art Journal* as 'Eminent among the most extensive cabinet makers and upholsterers in England.'

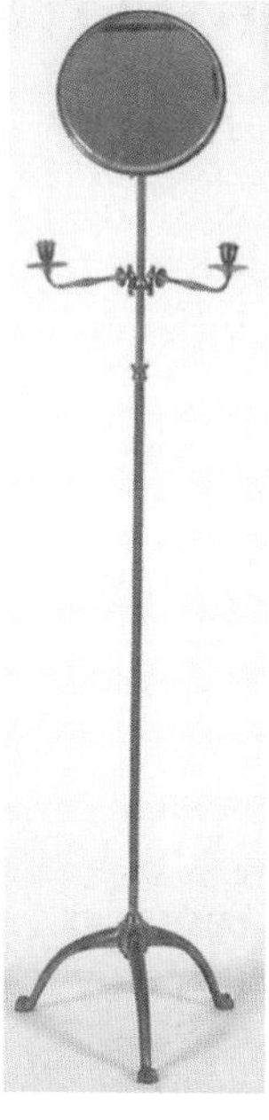

► **An adjustable brass shaving stand,** late 19thC, 61½in (156cm) high.
£150–200
€/ $240–300 DMC

Miscellaneous Stands

A George III mahogany bottle stand, 13in (33cm) square.
£600–750
€/ $950–1,200 B(Ba)

◀ **An early Victorian oak lamp stand,** the top inlaid with burr-oak, rosewood and bird's-eye maple, on a tapering column and triform base, 56in (142cm) high.
£650–800
€/ $1,000–1,300 SWO

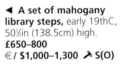

◀ **A late Victorian mahogany luggage stand,** the slatted top on ring-turned tapering legs, one slat stamped 'W.B.Ld', 25½in (65cm) wide.
£320–400
€/ $500–630
WW

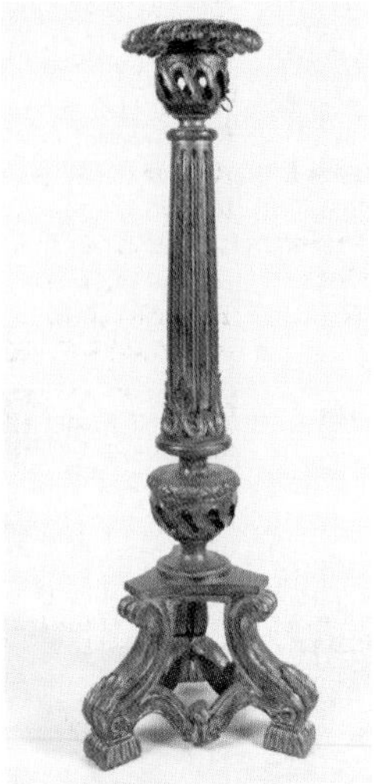

A carved limewood stand, Venetian, c1870, 36in (91.5cm) high.
£700–800
€/ $1,100–1,300 GBr

◀ **A pair of giltwood candle stands,** on a rococo base, c1910, 48in (122cm) high.
£1,250–1,385
€/ $2,000–2,200 RAN

Steps

◀ **A set of mahogany library steps,** early 19thC, 50½in (138.5cm) high.
£650–800
€/ $1,000–1,300 S(O)

A set of mahogany bed steps, the treads with leather insets, with two storage compartments, c1850, 26in (66cm) high.
£1,200–1,350
€/ $1,900–2,200 GBr
The middle step concealed a chamber pot.

A set of library steps, the ring-turned support on four spiral steps, on pad feet, early 19thC, 46in (117cm) high.
£900–1,100
€/ $1,400–1,700 B(L)

A set of mahogany bed steps, the three fabric-lined treads above ebony-strung panels, on ring-turned tapering legs, early 19thC, 26in (66cm) high.
£950–1,200
€/ $1,500–1,900 S(O)

A late Victorian set of stained-wood library steps, with galleried top-rail, the top stage with storage compartment, on turned supports, 22½in (57cm) high.
£200–250
€/ $300–400 FHF

A Regency mahogany bed-step commode, minor alterations, 26½in (67.5cm) high.
£600–700
€/ $950–1,100 B(Ba)

A set of mahogany metamorphic library steps, the treads inset with tooled leather, on ring-turned legs, 19thC, 27¾in (70.5cm) high extended.
£1,100–1,400
€/ $1,700–2,200 B(WM)
The top two steps fold down to make a leather-topped table.

Stools

A William and Mary walnut stool, the padded seat with later damask top panel, on square-section panelled tapering legs, upper capitals to legs and feet replaced, seat rails with paper label from Leamington Spa Art Gallery Treasures of Warwickshire Exhibition, July 1948, 21¼in (54cm) wide.
£1,500–2,000
€/ $2,400–3,200 ⚒ B

A George III mahogany stool, with drop-in seat, 20in (51cm) wide.
£280–350
€/ $440–550 ⚒ SWO

A giltwood footstool, in the style of Thomas Hope, the milled seat-rail on fluted square section end supports, on turned and tapered feet with roundel mouldings, with later button-upholstered seat, restorations and replacements, 19thC, 30¼in (77cm) wide.
£2,500–3,200
€/ $4,000–5,000 ⚒ S

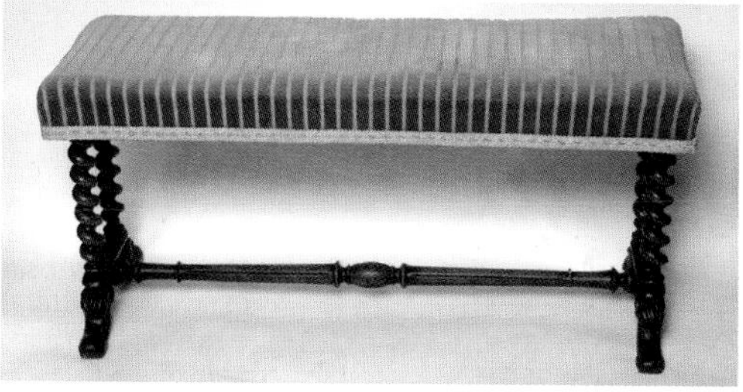

◄ **A mahogany stool,** with spiral-twist column legs, 1860, 38in (96.5cm) wide.
£280–320
€/ $440–500
⊞ PaA

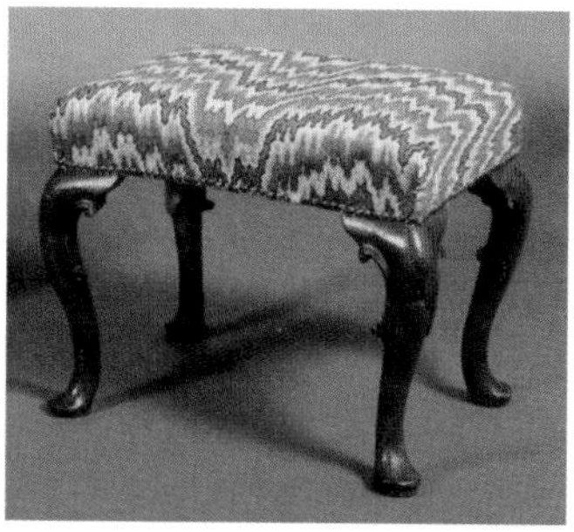

A pair of George II walnut stools, with stuff-over seats, on C-scroll-carved cabriole legs with pad feet, minor restoration, 20¾in (52.5cm) wide.
£3,200–4,000
€/ $5,000–6,300 ⚒ B(WM)

A mahogany stool, in the style of Duncan Phyfe, the scrolling tapered seat on U-shaped supports, on inward-curved scrolling feet, American, early 19thC, 20½in (52cm) wide.
£5,000–6,000
€/ $8,000–9,500 ⚒ B

Duncan Phyfe (1768–1854) is the best-known New York cabinet maker of the early and mid-19th century. He made use of the forms and ornament of classical Greece and Rome and gave his name to the generic term for American furniture in the neo-classical style. Phyfe-type furniture was made into the mid-19th century, with a revival in the late 19th/early 20th century.

◄ **A carved mahogany X-frame stool,** on casters, c1845, 21½in (54.5cm) wide.
£380–425
€/ $600–670 ⊞ MTay

A George III mahogany stool, on turned legs with pad feet, 13¾in (35cm) diam.
£220–275
€/ $350–435 ⚒ AMB

A pair of Regency upholstered footstools, 15in (38cm) wide.
£1,700–2,000
€/ $2,700–3,200 ⊞ APO

A pair of carved oak footstools, 19thC, 34in (86.5cm) wide.
£7,500–8,500
€/ $12,000–13,500 ⊞ CAT

A Victorian walnut stool, the upholstered drop-in top on scrolled X-shaped supports, 21in (53.5cm) wide.
£160–220
€/ $250–350 ⚒ TRM

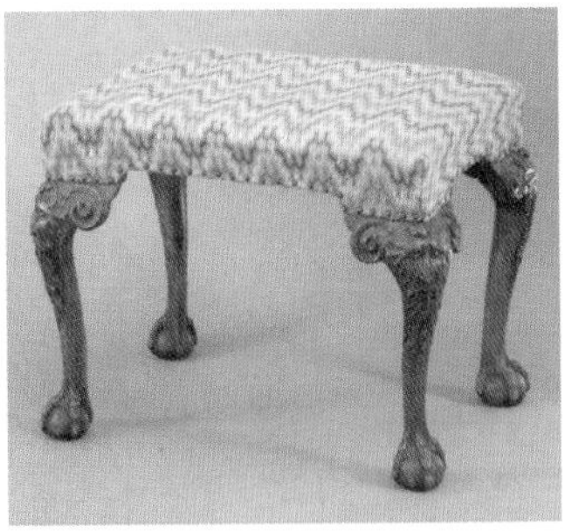

A Victorian carved mahogany stool, with upholstered seat and cabriole legs with satyr masks, on claw-and-ball feet, 24in (61cm) wide.
£260–325
€/ $400–500 G(L)

A Victorian rosewood stool, with drop-in seat on curved X-supports, 21½in (54.5cm) wide.
£300–375
€/ $475–600 B&L

A carved walnut stool, covered with floral tapestry, on cabriole legs, c1875, 28in (71cm) wide.
£1,150–1,300
€/ $1,800–2,000 ⊞ MTay

A pair of Victorian giltwood footstools, 13½in (34.5cm) wide.
£600–720
€/ $950–1,100 L

A pair of faded mahogany footstools, covered with floral tapestry, c1880, 15in (38cm) wide.
£200–225
€/ $300–350 ⊞ GBr

► A pair of mahogany and Tunbridge ware-inlaid footstools, with beadwork coverings, c1880, 11in (28cm) diam.
£600–675
€/ $950–1,100 ⊞ JSt

A walnut stool, with caned back, c1910, 25in (63.5cm) high.
£300–325
€/ $475–500 ⊞ RPh

Music Stools

◄ A rosewood and brass-inlaid piano chair, c1815.
£2,000–2,250
€/ $3,200–3,600 ⊞ Che

A Victorian mahogany and inlaid music stool, the string-inlaid frieze over out-splayed front legs, 36in (91.5cm) high.
£140–175
€/ $220–275 DA

◄ An Edwardian inlaid mahogany adjustable piano stool, 19¾in (50cm) high.
£280–350
€/ $440–550 SWO

A mahogany revolving piano stool, c1825, 20in (51cm) high.
£330–370
€/ $520–580 ⊞ GBr

◄ A walnut adjustable duet stool, on ring-turned supports and splayed feet, c1905, 34in (86.5cm) wide.
£350–450
€/ $550–700
GAK

A Victorian walnut piano stool, by Gillows, 24in (61cm) wide.
£2,000–2,200
€/ $3,200–3,500 ⊞ SAW

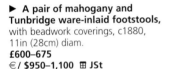

Bedroom Suites

A mahogany bedroom suite, comprising triple wardrobe, marble-topped dressing table, pot cupboard, side chair and washstand, late 19thC.
£500–625
€/ $800–1,000 B(Ba)

A walnut four-piece bedroom suite, consisting of marble-topped chest of drawers, commode with marble top and splash-back, bed and mirror, bed shortened in height, some veneer loss, American, late 19thC, headboard 60in (152.5cm) high.
£900–1,100
€/ $1,400–1,700 JDJ

An Edwardian inlaid mahogany three-piece bedroom suite, comprising wardrobe, dressing table and bedside cupboard, wardrobe 72in (183cm) wide.
£1,000–1,250
€/ $1,600–1,900 SWO

Salon Suites

A painted beechwood five-piece salon suite, with cushions and cane seats, paint worn, settee with unmatched cushion, c1800, settee 50½in (128.5cm) wide.
£2,200–2,750
€/ $3,500–3,800 S(O)

A walnut and inlaid salon suite, comprising a sofa, two side chairs, a tub chair and a nursing chair, late 19thC.
£550–700
€/ $870–1,100 B(Ba)

► **A mahogany salon suite,** comprising a sofa, two elbow chairs and four dining chairs, with pierced splat backs, serpentine aprons and cabriole front legs, late 19thC.
£800–1,000
€/ $1,300–1,600 GAK

A chinoiserie green-painted and gilt three-piece bergère suite, comprising a settee and a pair of armchairs, c1920, settee 67in (170cm) wide.
£1,500–2,000
€/ $2,400–3,200 S(O)

An Edwardian mahogany-framed three-piece salon suite, comprising two tub armchairs and a sofa, on turned and reeded legs.
£750–950
€/ $1,200–1,500 B&L

An Edwardian mahogany salon suite, comprising a settee, four side chairs and two armchairs.
£600–750
€/ $950–1,200 B(Ba)

Architects' Tables

An early George III mahogany architect's table, the top sloping on a ratchet, the frieze with a pull-out drawer, the sides with pull-out candle slides, 34½in (87.5cm) wide.
£1,600–2,000
€/ $2,500–3,100 ⚒ L

A mahogany architect's table, with ratchet top and a single drawer on turned legs, c1790, 39in (99cm) wide.
£3,800–4,300
€/ $6,000–6,700 ⊞ SAW

▶ A mahogany architect's table, the ratchet and adjustable top above two frieze drawers and two side slides, on turned legs with turned feet and casters, restored, 36¼in (92cm) wide.
£1,500–1,800
€/ $2,400–2,800 ⚒ B(W)

▶ A mahogany architect's table, the adjustable top above a supported drawer, with writing slide and compartments, 18thC, 35in (89cm) wide.
£1,000–1,200
€/ $1,600–1,900 ⚒ LAY

An early George III mahogany architect's table, with adjustable hinged top and drop flaps above a frieze drawer with brass swan-neck handle, on chamfered legs with brass toes and casters, 30in (76cm) wide.
£3,500–4,250
€/ $5,500–6,700 ⚒ HYD

A Directoire mahogany architect's table, the hinged leather-inset writing surface above a frieze drawer enclosing a sliding writing surface and various compartments, with sliding padded side leaves, on tapered legs with casters, stamped 'Chapuis', 38½in (98.5cm) wide.
£14,000–16,000
€/ $22,000–25,000 ⚒ S(Am)
Jean-Joseph Chapuis (1765–1864) from Brussels is best known for his quality mahogany furniture. In 1798 he started workshops in rue de Borgval and after his marriage moved to 264 rue de Loxum. He appeared in the *Almanachs du Commerce* until 1824 and was active until about 1830.

Bedside Tables

A pair of Louis XV-style kingwood bedside tables, with marble tops and ormolu mounts, French, c1880, 28in (71cm) wide.
£1,250–1,400
€/ $1,900–2,200 ⊞ DAC

A mahogany drop-leaf bedside table, with undertier, late 19thC, 27¼in (69cm) wide.
£220–260
€/ $350–400 ⚒ B(Ch)

A pair of satinwood bedside tables, with marble tops and ormolu mounts, French, c1900, 31in (78.5cm) high.
£1,000–1,150
€/ $1,600–1,800 ⊞ BrL

A pair of Louis XV-style kingwood and marquetry bedside tables, c1920, 25in (63.5cm) high.
£1,150–1,300
€/ $1,800–2,000 ⊞ Che

Card Tables

A George II mahogany card table, with baize-lined fold-over top, the frieze enclosing a drawer, on turned tapering legs and pad feet, 30in (76cm) wide.
£1,300–1,500
€/ $2,000–2,350 WW

A George III mahogany card table, on brass casters, 37in (94cm) wide.
£3,000–3,400
€/ $4,800–5,400 APO

A George III mahogany card table, the shaped top on cabriole legs, 35in (89cm) wide.
£900–1,000
€/ $1,400–1,600 WAW

A late Georgian mahogany card table, 36in (91.5cm) wide.
£750–850
€/ $1,180–1,350 HiA

A Sheraton mahogany card table, attributed to Samuel Field McIntire, on tapering reeded legs, American, c1800, 37½in (95.5cm) wide.
£1,300–1,500
€/ $2,000–2,350 JDJ

A George III mahogany card table, the fold-over top enclosing recessed counter wells and candle sconces, on cabriole legs with paw feet, Irish, 89in (226cm) wide.
£4,000–4,800
€/ $6,400–7,600 JAd

A George III demi-lune satinwood card table, the tulipwood-banded fold-over top inlaid with a large shell motif, on tapered legs, 38¼in (97cm) wide.
£2,000–2,400
€/ $3,200–3,800 G(B)

A Sheraton card table, inlaid with rosewood, c1805, 36in (91.5cm) wide.
£6,200–7,000
€/ $9,800–11,000 F

A brass-bound mahogany demi-lune card table, with a later suede-lined interior above a panelled frieze, on fluted, tapering legs with gilt-brass sabots, two legs replaced, Russian, early 19thC, 43¼in (110cm) wide.
£1,100–1,400
€/ $1,750–2,200 B

A Regency zebrawood card table, the top on a scissor-action frame, the curved supports on sabre legs with brass caps and casters, 36in (91.5cm) wide.
£2,400–3,000
€/ $3,800–4,800 TEN

A Regency rosewood card table, with baize-lined fold-over top, on tapering column support with lion-paw feet, 36in (91.5cm) wide.
£400–500
€/ $650–800 ⚒ AMB

A William IV rosewood card table, the fold-over top on a leaf-carved and turned column, on a quatrefoil base with lion-paw feet, 36in (91.5cm) wide.
£600–775
€/ $950–1,200 ⚒ TMA

A Victorian walnut card table, the quatrefoil base above turned columns on scrolled legs with brass and porcelain casters, 54in (137cm) wide.
£1,100–1,400
€/ $1,700–2,200 ⚒ JM

A Victorian walnut card table, 36in (91.5cm) wide.
£1,100–1,250
€/ $1,750–1,900 ⊞ NAW

A Sheraton-style mahogany card table, inlaid with boxwood, c1820, 36in (91.5cm) wide.
£1,250–1,400
€/ $1,900–2,200 ⊞ DUK

A William IV rosewood card table, the baize-lined fold-over top above a tablet frieze, on a tapering column with scroll and paw feet and recessed casters, one caster missing, 35¾in (91cm) wide.
£800–1,000
€/ $1,250–1,600 ⚒ DN

A rosewood-veneered card table, the carved, reeded column above a platform base with claw feet, 19thC, 38in (96cm) wide.
£500–600
€/ $800–950 ⚒ HoG

A Victorian walnut card table, with a baize-lined fold-over serpentine top, on cabriole legs with scroll feet and ceramic casters, 38in (96cm) wide.
£750–850
€/ $1,200–1,350 ⚒ CGC

A late Regency mahogany card table, on turned, tapering legs, 31¾in (80.5cm) wide.
£1,650–1,850
€/ $2,500–3,000 ⊞ JC

A mahogany crossbanded card table, with baize-lined demi-lune top, inlaid panelled frieze, on square tapering legs and spade feet, 19thC, 37¼in (94.5cm) wide.
£750–950
€/ $1,200–1,500 ⚒ AH

A Victorian rosewood card table, the fold-over top on carved, quadripartite legs, 19thC, 36¼in (92cm) wide.
£700–875
€/ $1,100–1,400 ⚒ SWO

A Victorian walnut card table, on a central column with carved feet, 36in (91.5cm) wide.
£600–700
€/ $950–1,100 ⊞ WAW

A figured-walnut card table, on swept supports and cabriole legs with scrolled splay feet and casters, c1870, 36in (91.5cm) wide.
£2,700–3,000
€/ $4,250–4,800 ⊞ JSt

A Louis XV-style ebonized boulle card table, the fold-over top inlaid with turtle shell and brass, on cabriole legs and sabots, French, late 19thC, 35¾in (91cm) wide.
£1,000–1,250
€/ $1,600–1,900 Gam

A red boulle and ormolu card table, with baize-lined fold-over top, with beaded borders and cherub-head mounts, on square tapering legs, 19thC, 36in (91.5cm) wide.
£700–900
€/ $1,100–1,400 JM

An Edwardian inlaid mahogany demi-lune card table, 30in (76cm) wide.
£1,000–1,100
€/ $1,600–1,800 ⊞ RPh

An Edwardian mahogany envelope card table, with stringing and parquetry banding, the frieze drawer with brass handles, on square tapering legs, 21½in (54.5cm) wide.
£250–320
€/ $400–500 AH

A pair of George III-style mahogany demi-lune card tables, c1910, 33in (84cm) wide.
£5,250–5,850
€/ $8,250–9,250 ⊞ RAN

Centre Tables

A rosewood centre table, with three short frieze drawers, on ring-turned baluster legs with brass mounts, Portuguese, 17thC, 53in (134.5cm) wide.
£2,000–2,500
€/ $3,200–4,000 L

A mahogany centre table, the dished marble top above a plain frieze, on shaped legs above a fluted acorn standard on splayed brass-inlaid legs with caps and casters, Baltic, c1825, 28in (71cm) wide.
£900–1,100
€/ $1,500–1,800 NOA

A rosewood centre table, with maker's label 'Thomas Mills, Bradford', c1840, 23¾in (60.5cm) wide.
£700–850
€/ $1,100–1,350 S(O)

A kingwood and tulipwood marquetry centre table, with gilt-metal mounts, the frieze with a drawer, above foliate sabots, French, c1860, 45in (114.5cm) wide.
£3,200–3,500
€/ $5,000–5,500 JSt

A Louis XVI-style mahogany marquetry centre table, inlaid with later floral marquetry, on square tapering legs, Dutch, c1800, 35¼in (89.5cm) wide.
£2,500–3,000
€/ $4,000–4,800 S(Am)

A flame mahogany centre table, the tilt-top on a central column, c1835, 47in (119.5cm) diam.
£2,400–2,700
€/ $3,800–4,300 GBr

A rococo revival mahogany centre table, with a fruit and floral carved frieze, on cabriole legs, American, 1850–75, 39in (99cm) wide.
£650–820
€/ $1,000–1,300 NOA

A burr-walnut centre table, with boxwood inlay, c1860, 53in (134.5cm) wide.
£2,000–2,250
€/ $3,200–3,500 GBr

A rosewood and ormolu centre table, attributed to Gillows of Lancaster, the top composed of mixed specimen marbles, c1810, 32in (81.5cm) wide.
£5,000–5,500
€/ $8,000–8,700 HA
This table was made for the Ponsonby family of Ponsonby Hall, near Kirkby Lonsdale, Cumbria.

A rosewood centre table, 19thC, 30in (76cm) wide.
£450–500
€/ $710–790 SWO

A marquetry serpentine centre table, with ormolu mounts, veneered in various coloured woods, the frieze enclosing one side drawer, mid-19thC, 51½in (131cm) wide.
£3,200–3,750
€/ $5,000–5,800 TMA

A pollarded oak centre table, 19thC, 54in (137cm) diam.
£9,000–10,000
€/ $14,000–16,000 SAW

Colour & patination

- These are two of the most important factors when valuing furniture
- Patination is produced by decades of waxing combined with dirt, grease and dust, all hardened by regular dusting.
- When valuing furniture, check for darker colour where the piece would be handled, i.e. chair arms, front of drawers under handles etc.
- Colour, if original, should vary from one side to the other as the side nearest the window will fade more because of the sun. If a piece has been repolished the colour will be even all over.
- On carved furniture dirt will have accumulated in the carving, producing darker patches. If repolished, there will be no contrast.

A Victorian walnut centre table, the top inlaid with satinwood and ebony, on splayed legs, with wavy block feet, 41¾in (106cm) wide.
£550–700
€/ $870–1,100 CGC

A walnut and ebonized centre table, by Lamb of Manchester, 19thC, 38in (96.5cm) wide.
£1,250–1,400
€/ $1,900–2,200 ⊞ WAW

A Victorian oak centre table, on cabriole legs, 40in (101.5cm) wide.
£700–780
€/ $1,100–1,225 ⊞ MHA

► A pollarded oak centre table, c1880, 45in (114.5cm) wide.
£1,100–1,200
€/ $1,750–1,900 ⊞ SAW

An Edwardian satinwood crossbanded and inlaid centre table, the top radially veneered above shaped stretchers, on tapering legs and paw feet, 49¼in (125cm) wide.
£3,350–4,200
€/ $5,200–6,650 B(EA)
This is an example of quality Edwardian cabinet making.

Console & Pier Tables

A Louis XV carved oak console table, with a marble top, Liège, Belgium, 18thC, 23in (58.5cm) wide.
£1,800–2,250
€/ $2,800–3,500 BERN

A Biedermeier walnut console table, the figured top above a frieze enclosing one central drawer, joined by a mirrored back and front square columns on a lower plinth shelf, northern European, 1800–25, 39½in (100.5cm) wide.
£2,600–3,200
€/ $4,100–5,000 NOA

A Federal painted poplar pier table, extensively damaged, American, c1810, 35¾in (91cm) wide.
£2,800–3,200
€/ $4,400–5,000 S(NY)
The very poor condition of the top has badly affected the price.

A Regency carved giltwood console table, after a design by Holland & Son, with a mottled yellow ochre top on a plinth base, 54¼in (138cm) wide.
£4,500–5,500
€/ $7,000–8,500 Gam

A late Regency rosewood console table, with a later *verde antico* top, 29½in (75cm) wide.
£1,100–1,400
€/ $1,700–2,200 B(Ba)

A William IV mahogany console table, with a beaded top, on scrolled supports and paw feet, on a platform base, Irish, 48in (122cm) wide.
£1,600–2,000
€/ $2,500–3,000 JAd

Miller's Compares

I. A painted satinwood pier table, the crossbanded top painted with foliage, on ribbed, tapering legs, Irish, late 18thC, 39¼in (99.5cm) wide.
£13,000–16,000
€/ $20,000–25,000 HOK

II. A satinwood side table, the fan-inlaid top on square tapering legs, Irish, 19thC, 50in (127cm) wide.
£1,250–1,600
€/ $1,900–2,500 HOK

There may be only 20-odd years' difference in the date of these two tables, but Item I is smaller in size than item II and therefore of better proportion. The quality of the decoration is also far superior in Item I, but the most important factor is that it has provenance: it had once been owned by the Overend family of Airfield House, Dublin, who were keen collectors of good-quality 18th-century furniture.

A Louis XV-style gilt console table, with an onyx top, French, c1880, 54in (137cm) wide.
£1,700–2,000
€/ $2,700–3,200 DAC

A Victorian oak console table, with a plain top and frieze, on scroll supports and feet, 54in (137cm) wide.
£850–1,100
€/ $1,350–1,750 JAd

Dining Tables

Items in the Furniture section have been arranged in date order.

A George II mahogany drop-leaf dining table, on turned tapering legs with pad feet, 47in (119.5cm) wide.
£1,000–1,200
€/ $1,600–1,900 JDJ

A mahogany single drop-leaf dining table, the crossbanded frieze with one long drawer with brass handles, on tapering legs, early 19thC, 44½in (113cm) wide.
£800–1,000
€/ $1,300–1,600 DD

An early George III mahogany drop-leaf dining table, 48in (122cm) wide, extended.
£200–250
€/ $315–400 L

A mahogany drop-leaf dining table, on turned legs with pointed pad feet, mid-18thC, 52in (132cm) extended.
£650–800
€/ $1,000–1,260 BR

A George III cuban mahogany drop-leaf dining table, repolished, slight restoration, 65½in (166.5cm) wide.
£1,000–1,250
€/ $1,600–1,900 B(Ch)

◄ **A George III mahogany D-end dining table,** each half on four tapering legs, 47¼in (120cm) wide.
£850–1,100
€/ $1,350–1,750 SWO

A mahogany tilt-top dining table, on a turned baluster column with splay legs, 19thC, 55in (139.5cm) wide.
£1,300–1,600
€/ $2,000–2,500 JM

A mid-Victorian mahogany wind-out extending dining table, with an additional central leaf, the extending action labelled 'Samuel Hawkins Patentee Bishopsgate, London', on carved, turned tapering legs, further leaf missing, 96in (244cm) extended.
£1,700–2,200
€/ $2,700–3,500 PFK

A Victorian walnut extending dining table, with five extra leaves, 156in (396cm) extended.
£2,300–2,800
€/ $3,600–4,400 B(Ba)

A Victorian mahogany concertina-action extending dining table, with two extra leaves, on turned and fluted tapering legs, 96in (244cm) extended.
£1,600–2,000
€/ $2,500–3,200 PFK

A goncalo alves-veneered dining table, the central pedestal on four legs with brass casters, 1820–30, 54in (137cm) wide.
£5,000–6,000
€/ $8,000–9,500 MHA

A Victorian mahogany extending dining table, with three extra leaves, 125½in (319cm) extended.
£4,500–5,500
€/ $7,000–8,750 SWO

A Victorian walnut extending dining table, with three extra leaves, on tapering legs, 115¾in (194cm) extended.
£1,500–2,000
€/ $2,400–3,200 DN

A Victorian mahogany extending dining table, with three extra leaves, 103½in (263cm) extended.
£2,000–2,500
€/ $3,200–4,000 Bea(E)

A mahogany extending banqueting table, by Crace & Co, London, with five extra leaves, with four turned and lobed legs, mid-19thC, 167½in (426cm) extended.
£8,000–10,000
€/ $12,500–16,000 HOK

The family firm of Crace & Co was founded in the mid-18th century and rose to prominence in the 19th century. Their commissions included decorating the Royal Pavilion in Brighton for the Prince Regent, and various properties for William Waldorf Astor.

◄ An early Victorian mahogany drop-leaf dining table, 61½in (156cm) wide.
£450–565
€/ $700–900 B(Ba)

A Victorian mahogany extending dining table, with two extra leaves, on cabriole legs with paw feet, 98½in (250cm) extended.
£2,500–3,200
€/ $4,000–5,000 JAd

A Victorian mahogany dining table, with three legs on a central column, 48in (122cm) diam.
£1,250–1,400
€/ $2,000–2,200 MHA

A Victorian oak wind-out extending dining table, with two extra leaves and handle, on turned carved legs, 93¼in (237cm) extended.
£700–900
€/ $1,100–1,400 B(Ch)

A Victorian oak wind-out extending dining table, with one extra leaf, on turned legs, 124in (315cm) extended.
£1,100–1,200
€/ $1,700–1,900 ⊞ PaA

Daily care

Climate can greatly affect furniture and a few simple steps can be taken to prevent damage. Avoid leaving furniture in direct strong sunlight and allow some draught into a room; a small humidifier may be beneficial if the atmosphere is particularly dry. Warped table leaves should be put in a damp atmosphere where they may straighten themselves, and card tables which develop a 'smile' will benefit from being opened overnight. If this does not work, the help of a qualified restorer will be required.

A chestnut extending dining table, with two extra leaves, French, late 19thC, 94½in (240cm) extended.
£800–1,000
€/ $1,300–1,600 ⚒ B(Ch)

A mahogany extending dining table, with one extra leaf, on carved and fluted legs, two leaves missing, early 20thC, 47¾in (121.5cm) wide.
£900–1,100
€/ $1,400–1,700 ⚒ SWO

A Regency-style mahogany dining table, early 20thC, 108¼in (275cm) wide.
£1,200–1,500
€/ $1,900–2,400 ⚒ B(Ba)

A mahogany extending dining table, with two extra leaves, on claw-and-ball feet, c1920, 94in (239cm) extended.
£3,400–3,750
€/ $5,400–6,000 ⊞ MTay

Display Tables

A mahogany and gilt-metal-mounted vitrine table, French, 1848–70, 22in (56cm) wide.
£550–700
€/ $870–1,100 ⚒ B(Ch)

A Louis XV-style kingwood and ormolu *bijouterie* table, French, c1880, 26in (66cm) wide.
£2,350–2,600
€/ $3,600–4,000 ⊞ Che

An 18thC-style giltwood and gesso *bijouterie* table, late 19thC, Italian, 36¼in (92cm) wide.
£950–1,200
€/ $1,500–1,900 ⚒ S(O)

A stained hardwood and mahogany display table, with a glazed top, on carved cabriole legs, with undertier, c1900, 27in (68.5cm) wide.
£1,100–1,250
€/ $1,750–1,900 ⊞ MTay

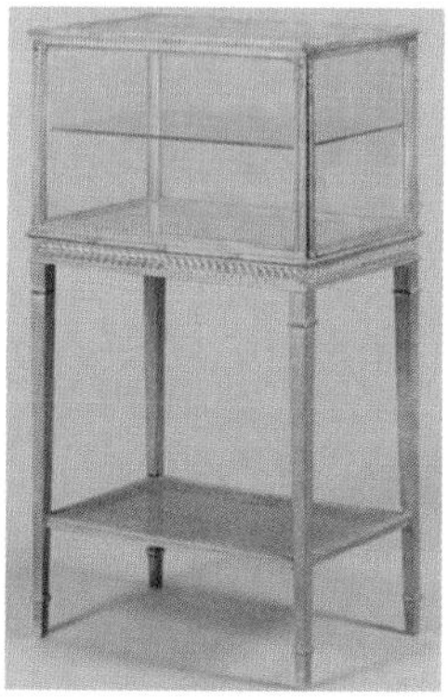

◄ **A late 18thC-style giltwood and gesso display table,** early 20thC, 24½in (62cm) wide.
£1,500–1,800
€/ $2,350–2,850 ⚒ S(O)

► **An Edwardian mahogany display table,** with a glazed top and sides, 16in (40.5cm) wide.
£315–350
€/ $500–550 ⊞ HiA

An Edwardian walnut vitrine table, restored, 24½in (62cm) wide.
£250–325
€/ $400–500 ⚒ B(Ba)

Dressing Tables

An early George III mahogany dressing table, the hinged and divided top with figural panels and chequered line inlay, the interior with a mirror, beaker apertures and lidded compartments, the fret-carved frieze with later lopers, legs possibly later, 26in (66cm) wide.
£1,400–1,700
€/ $2,200–2,700 ⚒ B

A mahogany bowfronted dressing table, with inlaid stringing, a frieze drawer above a kneehole and two short drawers, with later brass-plate lion mask ring handles, on tapering legs with socket feet, 19thC, 35¾in (91cm) wide.
£450–550
€/ $700–870 ⚒ WW

A Transitional rococo revival *faux* rosewood dressing table, the mirror flanked by a pair of cupboards, the base with a marble top over three drawers with pie crust moulding, on bracket feet, American, mid-19thC, 42in (106.5cm) wide.
£900–1,100
€/ $1,400–1,700 ⚒ NOA

A George III gentleman's mahogany dressing table, serpentine-shaped, with central lifting mirror above drawers and doors, on square tapering legs, 35¾in (91cm) wide.
£700–850
€/ $1,100–1,300 ⚒ SWO

A George III mahogany gentleman's travelling dressing table, with a slide and a central drawer flanked by five small drawers, on tapered legs, 19in (48.5cm) wide.
£400–450
€/ $630–710 ⚒ HOLL

► **A Victorian bird's-eye maple dressing table,** 59in (150cm) wide.
£400–450
€/ $630–710 ⚒ B(Ba)

A Victorian figured walnut dressing table, by Heal & Son, the mirror above four jewellery drawers and three frieze drawers, on pedestal supports with three drawers, on plinth bases, 52in (132cm) wide.
£600–700
€/ $950–1,100 ⚒ HOLL

An Empire mahogany dressing table, the mirror plate tilting between columns with engine-turned capitals, the top inset with a marble top above a long drawer, on turned legs, French, 37¾in (96cm) wide.
£750–900
€/ $1,200–1,400 ⚒ B

A satinwood kneehole dressing table, with central lifting mirror, c1825, 34in (86.5cm) wide.
£400–440
€/ $630–700 ⊞ PaA

A Chippendale revival mahogany dressing table, c1885, 38in (96.5cm) wide.
£1,450–1,600
€/ $2,300–2,500 ⊞ Che

◄ **A Sheraton revival satinwood, tulipwood-crossbanded and ebony-strung dressing table,** the quarter-veneered top above three drawers with brass handles, flanking a kneehole, on tapering legs with brass caps and casters, late 19thC, 36¼in (92cm) wide.
£750–900
€/ $1,200–1,400 DN

An Edwardian mahogany dressing table, the three mirrors above a central drawer flanked by two pairs of drawers, on turned legs with brass casters, 53in (134.5cm) wide.
£880–1,000
€/ $1,400–1,600 MHA

A George II-style walnut dressing table, with featherbanding, the five drawers flanking a kneehole, on shell-carved cabriole legs, early 20thC, 48in (122cm) wide.
£1,000–1,100
€/ $1,600–1,700 S(O)

◄ **An Edwardian inlaid mahogany dressing table,** the mirror suspended between scroll uprights, over a central well with fitted trinket drawers and an arrangement of five crossbanded drawers, on tapering legs, 48in (122cm) wide.
£400–475
€/ $630–750 AMB

Drop-Leaf Tables

An early George III mahogany single-leaf side table, 29in (73.5cm) wide.
£320–375
€/ $500–590 L

Cross Reference
See Dining Tables (pages 121–123)

A mahogany drop-leaf table, inlaid with floral marquetry, the legs with inlaid fluted decoration, 19thC, 43¼in (110cm) wide.
£850–1,000
€/ $1,300–1,600 AMB

A mahogany drop-leaf table, with a drawer, on turned tapering legs and pad feet, 18thC, 33in (84cm) wide.
£500–575
€/ $790–900 BWL

A mahogany double drop-leaf wake table, with boxwood stringing, on tapering legs, 19thC, Irish, 73¾in (187.5cm) wide.
£1,100–1,300
€/ $1,700–2,000 JAd

A George III mahogany drop-leaf table, 48in (122cm) wide.
£800–950
€/ $1,300–1,500 B(Ch)

A Renaissance revival inlaid and ebonized drop-leaf table, decorated with a central classical urn, Greek key and foliate scroll roundel within a berried-laurel diamond reserve, American, c1875, 60in (152.5cm) wide.
£10,000–12,000
€/ $16,000–19,000 S(NY)
The Renaissance revival became the leading fashion in America by 1860. Rather than strictly reproducing forms popular during the Renaissance, the style consisted of creative adaptations of Renaissance architectural ornament.

Drum Tables

A late Regency rosewood drum table, damaged, 41in (104cm) diam.
£5,800–6,500
€/ $9,200–10,300 ⊞ WAW

A Regency-style drum table, with a tooled-leather inset top, late 19thC, 33in (84cm) diam.
£850–1,000
€/ $1,300–1,600 ⚒ B(Ch)

A Regency elm and burr-elm drum table, the crossbanded top above an arrangement of two real and two dummy drawers with turned knobs and inlaid shield-shaped escutcheons, on a baluster-turned column and downswept legs with brass caps and casters, 24in (61cm) diam.
£7,000–8,000
€/ $11,000–12,600 ⚒ HYD

► A mahogany drum table, the revolving top fitted with two frieze drawers with brass knobs, the baluster-turned stem on three scroll legs, 19thC, 20½in (52cm) diam.
£350–420
€/ $550–670 ⚒ WW

A Victorian mahogany drum table, the top with leatherette inset above a frieze fitted with four real and four dummy drawers, on four fluted legs with downswept scroll feet with casters, 48in (122cm) diam.
£900–1,100
€/ $1,400–1,700 ⚒ Mit

Games Tables

A Federal inlaid birchwood and maple games table, American, c1810, 35in (89cm) wide.
£4,500–5,000
€/ $7,000–8,000 ⚒ S(NY)

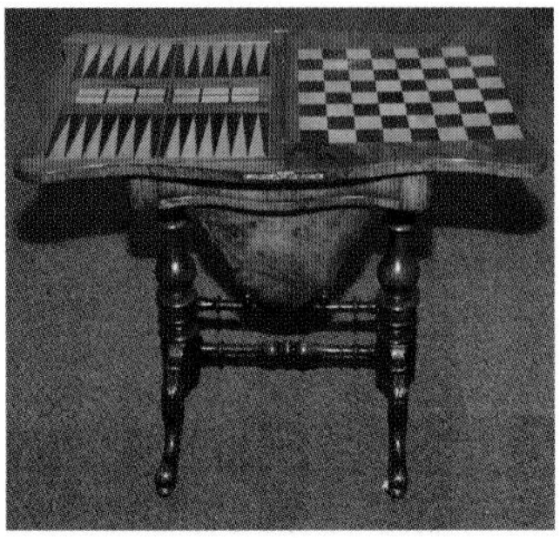

► A walnut games table, with reversible bagatelle top, c1870, 29in (73.5cm) diam.
£2,500–2,750
€/ $4,000–4,400 ⊞ MTay

A Victorian walnut games table, on a turned stretcher base, 31in (78.5cm) wide.
£200–230
€/ $300–350 ⊞ PaA

◄ A Victorian walnut serpentine fold-over and swivel-top games/sewing table, on turned legs, 27in (68.5cm) high.
£1,750–2,000
€/ $2,700–3,200 ⊞ BrL

An Edwardian inlaid mahogany and leather games table, 28in (71cm) wide.
£765–850
€/ $1,200–1,350 ⊞ RPh

Library Tables

A late Regency rosewood library table, the three-quarter pierced gilt-metal gallery above a leather-inset top and gadrooned frieze, with two drawers, the turned and reeded legs with casters, 44in (112cm) wide.
£2,200–2,500
€/ $3,500–4,000 TF

A Victorian rosewood library table, the top with two shaped frieze drawers, on turned tapering and lotus-moulded column legs and moulded scroll feet with brass casters, 48in (122cm) wide.
£1,300–1,500
€/ $2,000–2,400 DD

A yew wood oyster-veneered library table, the moulded top with a central medallion and crossbanded edge, above an inlaid frieze with two drawers, on turned tapering legs and pad feet, Dutch, late 19thC, 49¾in (126.5cm) wide.
£1,300–1,500
€/ $2,000–2,400 BR

A William IV mahogany library table, probably by Williams & Gibton, the moulded top above two real and two dummy drawers, on two tapering cylindrical columns and bun feet, stamped 'No. 11771', Irish, 59in (150cm) wide.
£1,500–1,750
€/ $2,400–2,750 MEA

A Victorian rosewood library table, with gilt-tooled leather inset to the crossbanded top, with two frieze drawers, on lotus-carved tapering baluster legs with brass casters, 56¾in (144cm) wide.
£2,000–2,200
€/ $3,200–3,500 Bea(E)

► **A Victorian mahogany library table,** 48in (122cm) wide.
£800–900
€/ $1,300–1,400 PaA

A rosewood library table, with thumb-moulded edge and two frieze drawers, on baluster-turned legs, Spanish, 19thC, 57½in (146cm) wide.
£2,800–3,200
€/ $4,400–5,000 JAd

A William IV mahogany library table, with gilt-tooled leather inset top over two short drawers with brass knobs, on baluster legs and splayed and scrolled feet, 42in (106.5cm) wide.
£1,000–1,200
€/ $1,600–1,900 MCA

A Victorian walnut library table, the moulded top with inlaid satinwood crossbanding, above two drawers, on turned tapering baluster columns, stamped 'Holland & Sons', 47¾in (121.5cm) wide.
£2,400–2,750
€/ $3,800–4,350 Gam

A late Victorian oak library table, with a leatherette inset top, 68¼in (173.5cm) wide.
£320–375
€/ $500–590 B(Ba)

A Gothic revival oak library table, the moulded top above three real and three dummy drawers, with blind tracery carving to all sides, the ring-turned legs on bun feet, c1900, 78in (198cm) wide.
£7,000–8,500
€/ $11,000–13,500 S

Waxing

To maintain and improve patination, furniture should be waxed once a month with a wax-based (never silicone-based) polish. Over-waxing can result in a smeared finish. Apply a thin layer of wax, leave for a short time and burnish with a soft clean cloth, remembering to follow the direction of the grain. Damage can be avoided by ensuring that belt buckles, rings and buttons are not allowed to come into contact with the furniture while cleaning. Always use place mats to protect polished surfaces from hot or cold dishes. The cold water in a vase can produced a white 'chill' mark which will need the attention of an expert. When cleaning brasses use a wadding cleaner to avoid liquid spillages to the patinated surfaces. A beautiful finish can be achieved by polishing the highlights of brass handles and leaving a natural build up of wax around the backplates and knobs.

Nests of Tables

► **A mahogany nest of three tables,** on foliate-carved cabriole legs with pad feet, c1900, 22in (56cm) wide.
£350–425
€/ $550–670 NOA

A walnut nest of tables, the tops with raised beading, on sabre legs, c1910, 17½in (45cm) wide.
£700–775
€/ $1,100–1,200 ⊞ MTay

An oak nest of tables, with bobbin-turned legs, c1930, 17in (43cm) wide.
£170–185
€/ $270–300 ⊞ CHAC

Miller's Compares

I. A set of Regency rosewood and mahogany quartetto tables, with ebonized and boxwood stringing, on turned legs, early 19thC, the largest table 18¼in (46.5cm) wide.
£4,500–5,500
€/ $7,000–8,700 S

II. A set of Regency figured mahogany and satinwood-crossbanded quartetto tables, on ring-turned legs, 18¼in (46.5cm) wide.
£2,400–2,750
€/ $3,800–4,350 S(O)

Item I has all the quality points that are sought after by collectors. The set, with its well-figured veneer, ring-turned legs, bowed rear stretchers and swept trestle feet, has a more elegant appearance than Item II.

Occasional Tables

A partridgewood-veneered and boxwood-strung occasional table, with two drawers, on tapering legs, c1790, 27in (68.5cm) wide.
£2,650–3,000
€/ $4,200–4,700 ⊞ HA

A Regency mahogany and plumwood occasional table, with baluster column and hipped sabre legs, on turned feet, base repaired, 24in (61cm) wide.
£1,000–1,100
€/ $1,600–1,700 Bon

A Regency rosewood occasional table, with fluted tapering column and concave platform base, 21in (53.5cm) wide.
£550–700
€/ $870–1,100 BWL

A yew wood occasional table, with parquetry top and incised carving to the pedestal base, Irish, c1820, 23¼in (59cm) wide.
£2,000–2,200
€/ $3,200–3,500 S(O)

► **A William IV occasional table,** the top veneered with a fan and alternate concentric borders of yew and rosewood, on a tapering cluster column with platform base, the bun feet with recessed brass casters, 25in (63.5cm) diam.
£4,500–5,000
€/ $7,100–7,900 BWL

A burr-maple and purple heart-inlaid occasional table, with two drawers, on brass casters, French, c1835, 30in (76cm) wide.
£5,200–5,700
€/ $8,200–9,000 ⊞ CAT

A Louis XV-style kingwood and marquetry occasional table, c1880, 26in (66cm) wide.
£1,400–1,600
€/ $2,200–2,500 ⊞ Che

Parquetry or marquetry?

Parquetry: inlays of variously coloured small pieces of wood veneer in geometric patterns on the carcass.
Marquetry: a decorative coloured veneer of wood and other decorative materials inlaid into furniture to form arabesque or floral patterns, and sometimes pastoral or figurative designs.

A Charles Baker's patent folding occasional table, the top with a piecrust edge, on tapering legs, c1898, 30in (76cm) diam.
£100–120
€/ $160–190 GAK

A tulipwood-veneered parquetry occasional table, with ormolu mounts, French, 19thC, 20in (51cm) wide.
£3,250–3,600
€/ $5,000–5,700 REI

A painted satinwood occasional table, c1890, 33in (84cm) wide.
£3,000–3,300
€/ $4,700–5,200 SAW

A Gothic revival rosewood occasional table, the top with an ogee-moulded frieze, on scroll supports with scroll feet, American, 1825–50, 33in (84cm) wide.
£600–700
€/ $950–1,100 NOA

► A parquetry occasional table, minor losses to veneer, Italian, 19thC, 30¼in (77cm) diam.
£1,200–1,400
€/ $1,900–2,200 B(Ba)

Olivewood

Olivewood is a hard, close-grained wood from southern Europe and has a green-to-yellow colour with interesting black-grey marking. It was used in the mid-17th century for marquetry inlay, because its colour provided contrasting decoration to walnut, which is a darkish brown with black veining. Olivewood was also frequently seen as cross-graining on chests of drawers from the mid-17th century onwards.

A Victorian olivewood occasional/display table, the rotating three-tier superstructure on spiral-turned supports, the octagonal top with moulded edge and plain frieze, on a tapering octagonal column and scroll feet, 24½in (62cm) diam.
£1,500–1,800
€/ $2,400–2,800 TEN

A pair of Louis XVI-style mahogany occasional tables, with pierced brass galleries enclosing variegated marble tops, each with two drawers and two candle slides to the frieze, on tapering legs with brass caps, French, c1900, 18in (45.5cm) diam.
£1,000–1,200
€/ $1,600–1,900 NOA

◄ A Victorian rosewood occasional table, on a tapering octagonal column and tripod base, 21¾in (55.5cm) diam.
£260–325
€/ $400–500 CHTR

► A rosewood *guéridon* table, with brass mounts, French, c1900, 30in (76cm) high.
£450–500
€/ $700–800 DAC

Pembroke Tables

A Sheraton mahogany Pembroke table, with satinwood crossbanding, c1780, 28in (71cm) wide.
£4,700–5,200
€/ $7,400–8,200 ⊞ REI

A George III manchineel Pembroke table, with one real and one dummy drawer, on chamfered legs with casters, 25¼in (64cm) wide.
£450–540
€/ $700–850 ⚒ TEN

A mahogany Pembroke table, decorated with inlaid marquetry in exotic woods, late 18thC, 45in (114.5cm) wide.
£3,500–4,000
€/ $5,500–6,300 ⊞ BMi

A Sheraton sabicu-veneered Pembroke table, with padouk crossbanding, c1790, 40in (101.5cm) wide.
£2,000–2,400
€/ $3,200–3,800 ⊞ CAT

A George III Sheraton-style satinwood Pembroke table, the top inlaid with tulipwood banding edged with boxwood and ebony stringing, with one real and one dummy frieze drawer, on tapering legs with casters, 28in (71cm) wide.
£3,700–4,500
€/ $5,800–7,100 ⚒ HYD

A mahogany Pembroke table, with a single drawer and tapering legs, early 19thC, 31in (78.5cm) wide.
£280–320
€/ $440–500 ⊞ PaA

◄ **A mahogany Pembroke table,** with reeded top, on ring-turned legs with casters, early 19thC, 39in (99cm) wide.
£320–400
€/ $500–630 ⚒ BWL

► **A mid-Victorian mahogany Pembroke table,** 36in (91.5cm) wide.
£300–325
€/ $475–500 ⊞ WiB

A George III mahogany and crossbanded Pembroke table, with serpentine leaves, restored, c1790, 35½in (90cm) wide.
£2,400–2,800
€/ $3,800–4,400 ⚒ S(O)

A George III satinwood Pembroke table, the crossbanded top over a single drawer, on tapering legs with socket feet, alterations, 32¼in (82cm) wide.
£750–875
€/ $1,200–1,400 ⚒ B(W)

A mahogany Pembroke table, with one real and one dummy frieze drawer with ebonized stringing and fitted with later brass knob handles, on ring-turned legs with brass casters, 19thC, 21in (53.5cm) wide.
£350–450
€/ $550–700 ⚒ WW

Reading Tables

An early George III mahogany reading table, with ratchetted lift-up top, 29½in (75cm) wide.
£550–625
€/ $870–990 L

A late Georgian mahogany adjustable reading table, on a turned column with scroll feet, 18¼in (46.5cm) wide.
£550–700
€/ $870–1,100 WiLP

A Regency mahogany reading table, with hinged adjustable top, the trestle feet with beaded moulding, 20in (51cm) wide.
£550–625
€/ $870–990 Bea(E)

A Regency rosewood reading table, the ratchetted top over a frieze drawer, on carved scroll supports, with undertier, 21¼in (54cm) wide.
£400–475
€/ $630–750 B(EA)

◄ A Victorian walnut adjustable reading table, 36in (91.5cm) wide.
£3,700–4,000
€/ $5,800–6,300 SAW

► A Victorian rosewood and rosewood-veneered adjustable reading table, 33in (84cm) wide.
£450–525
€/ $710–830 SWO

Serving Tables

A late George III neo-classical-style mahogany breakfront serving table, crossbanded and inlaid with boxwood and purplewood lines, the shaped top above a painted and parcel-gilt base, decoration later, 76¾in (195cm) wide.
£3,500–4,250
€/ $5,500–6,700 B

A mahogany serving table, with a single drawer, on carved legs, c1830, 53in (134.5cm) wide.
£1,700–2,000
€/ $2,700–3,200 RPh

A mahogany breakfront serving table, the central drawer flanked by shallow bowed drawers, the turned baluster legs headed by reeded panels, Irish, early 19thC, 78¾in (200cm) wide.
£850–1,100
€/ $1,350–1,750 HOK

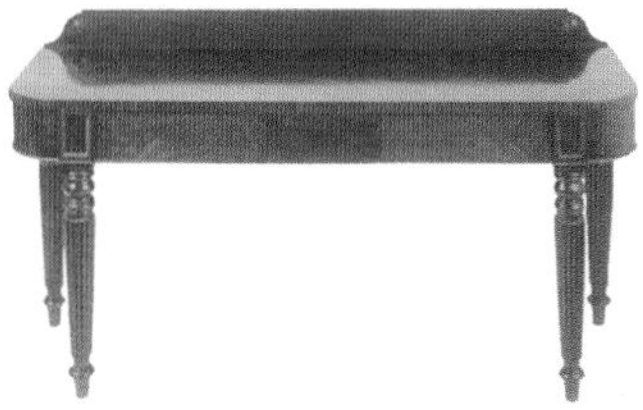

A George IV mahogany serving table, the rounded top above two frieze drawers, on turned and reeded tapering legs headed by bead-moulded tablets, later raised back, 72¼in (183.5cm) wide.
£1,300–1,600
€/ $2,000–2,500 Bea(E)

An early Victorian mahogany serving table, the mirror-back surmounted by a foliate cartouche and scroll supports, above a base with a central frieze drawer, flanked by foliate terminals on acanthus-scrolled legs with scroll feet, 65¾in (167cm) wide.
£1,300–1,600
€/ $2,000–2,500 JAd

A Regency-style mahogany serving table, with three frieze drawers, early 20thC, 60¼in (153cm) wide.
£1,400–1,600
€/ $2,200–2,500 S(O)

Side Tables

A William and Mary walnut side table, with inlaid banded top, above a frieze drawer, on spiral-turned legs, 30in (76cm) wide.
£2,800–3,500
€/ $4,500–5,500 BWL

A late Georgian mahogany bowfronted side table, 35¾in (91cm) wide.
£1,000–1,125
€/ $1,500–1,750 WiB

A mahogany side table, with a frieze drawers and shaped apron, on square chamfered legs, apron restored, early 19thC, 30¾in (78cm) wide.
£400–500
€/ $630–800 DN

An early Victorian mahogany side table, the moulded-edge top above two frieze drawers with brass swan-neck bale handles, on turned tapering legs with brass caps and casters, 48in (122cm) wide.
£180–225
€/ $280–350 PFK

A George III John Cobb-style side table, the serpentine top centred by a harewood marquetry panel, a geometric panel with geometric trelliswork surrounding a floral marquetry medallion, and flanked by burr-yew wood-veneered panels, the conforming frieze with a central drawer flanked by burr-maple panels, with rosewood crossbandings throughout, later drawer, some later veneers and marquetry, 45in (114.5cm) wide.
£3,500–4,200
€/ $5,500–6,650 S(O)
The marquetry decoration to this table incorporates several elements which relate to the work of the great 18th century cabinet maker John Cobb, of St Martin's Lane, London. He was the son-in-law of the celebrated cabinet maker Giles Grendey and was in business until 1777.

A mahogany side table, with associated ormolu mounts, alterations, early 19thC, 32¼in (82cm) wide.
£420–520
€/ $670–820 B(Ba)

A late George III mahogany serpentine side table, with a frieze drawer, on square tapering legs, 34in (86.5cm) wide.
£320–400
€/ $500–600 G(L)

A Regency figured rosewood side table, the drop-leaf top on a tulip-carved column and quatrefoil base, 29½in (75cm) wide.
£1,000–1,250
€/ $1,500–2,000 B(Ch)

A William IV mahogany side table, with panelled gallery back, two short drawers with turned knop handles, on ring-turned tapering legs, Irish, 44in (112cm) wide.
£1,850–2,300
€/ $2,850–3,650 WL
Mack, Williams and Gibton was the leading firm of cabinet makers in the city of Dublin in the early 19th century. In 1806, they were appointed upholsterers and cabinet makers to the king. This table dates to between 1829–44, when, on the death of John Mack in 1829, the firm traded as Williams & Gibton. In 1844, William Gibton died and the firm traded as Williams & Sons, ceasing business in 1952.

◄ **A rosewood stretcher table,** c1840, 22in (56cm) wide.
£1,000–1,150
€/ $1,500–1,750 SAW

A Queen Anne-style walnut side table, the banded top above a frieze with a long drawer, on cabriole legs headed by carving, with claw-and-ball feet, mid-19thC, 30¾in (78cm) wide.
£1,800–2,200
€/ $2,850–3,500 NOA

A Victorian walnut and line-inlaid side table, with two drawers, on reeded turned end supports, with scroll-carved legs and casters, 42in (106.5cm) wide.
£600–770
€/ $1,000–1,200 E

A rosewood side table, with three marquetry drawers, c1880, 40in (101.5cm) wide.
£1,000–1,150
€/ $1,500–1,800 RPh

A mahogany side table, with a single drawer, on turned tapering legs with brass casters, stamped 'Cope's Patent', 19thC, 29in (73.5cm) wide.
£1,200–1,500
€/ $2,000–2,400 BWL

An inlaid mahogany side table, with two drawers, c1880, 52in (132cm) wide.
£6,200–6,850
€/ $9,750–10,750 RAN

A pair of ebony and inlaid side tables, the tops with panels depicting figures, masks and sea horses enclosed by foliage, the panels interspersed by ivory and mother-of-pearl geometric designs, with frieze drawers, the cylindrical section legs joined by pierced X-stretchers with finials, on peg feet, Italian, Milanese, 19thC, 28¾in (73cm) wide.
£3,500–4,200
€/ $5,500–6,600 B(Ch)

Silver Tables

A George II and later Giles Grendey-style red japanned silver table, with gilded chinoiserie decoration and carved scroll brackets, on cabriole legs and pad feet, 32½in (82.5cm) wide.
£6,500–7,500
€/ $10,300–11,800 HOLL

A George III mahogany silver table, alterations, 27½in (70cm) wide.
£3,200–3,500
€/ $5,000–5,500 S(O)

A George III mahogany silver table, with pierced gallery, 29½in (75cm) wide.
£1,200–1,500
€/ $2,000–2,400 S(O)

Tables with galleried edges were designed by Chippendale in 1754 and used for displaying objects and for serving tea in the 18th century. These are often now known as silver tables. In the 19th century French-style tables with metal galleries were popular.

◄ **A Georgian mahogany silver table,** the top with a shallow moulded gallery, the shaped apron centred on two sides by a carved scallop shell, on scroll-moulded cabriole legs with faceted pad feet, Irish, 32in (81.5cm) wide.
£7,000–8,200
€/ $11,000–13,000 S

A Chippendale-style mahogany silver table, restored, late 19thC, 39¾in (101cm) wide.
£600–700
€/ $950–1,100 B(Ch)

Sofa Tables

A mahogany drop-leaf sofa table, with crossbanding, on outswept legs, c1790, 43in (109cm) wide.
£6,250–7,000
€/ $9,800–11,000 ⊞ GKe

A Regency rosewood sofa table, 37in (94cm) wide.
£2,000–2,400
€/ $3,200–3,800 L

A Regency Thomas Hope-style rosewood sofa table, with brass stringing and gilt-metal mounts, with one real and one dummy drawer with egg-and-dart-style gilt-metal moulding, on four carved giltwood lion-paw feet with original casters, 67in (170cm) extended.
£3,700–4,500
€/ $5,750–7,100 TF

A Regency satin-banded mahogany sofa table, with two frieze drawers, on reeded downswept legs with brass caps and casters, 36in (91.5cm) wide.
£1,200–1,500
€/ $2,000–2,400 G(L)

English Regency period

- At present Regency furniture is quite sought after as its classical style, influenced by Egyptian, Etruscan, Greek and Roman periods, complements some minimalist styles.
- Many ideas were copied from French Consulate and Empire designs.
- Some of the more exuberant pieces were inlaid with brass patterns and after c1805, ebony inlay.
- Woods most frequently used include mahogany, rosewood, simulated rosewood in the form of painted beechwood, and coromandel.
- Some of the finest Regency styles are found in pieces by Thomas Hope.

A Regency mahogany sofa table, with a rosewood-crossbanded top, above two frieze drawers, on a cheval frame with a turned stretcher, the reeded scroll feet with brass toe caps and casters, 38in (96.5cm) wide.
£1,200–1,500
€/ $2,000–2,400 BWL

A Regency George Bullock-style rosewood-veneered sofa table, the top with a crossbanded edge, the similarly inlaid frieze with two drawers, on a square baluster stem, the four hipped splayed legs with foliate-cast brass caps and casters, 22½in (57cm) wide.
£2,700–3,400
€/ $4,250–5,400 Bea

A neo-classical walnut sofa table, the highly figured top above a single frieze drawer, on a stand with swan-neck and acanthus carving, the concave base on splayed legs with paw feet, north European, early 19thC, 35½in (90cm) wide.
£1,200–1,500
€/ $2,000–2,400 NOA

A Victorian rosewood sofa table, with two drawers, the ring- and baluster-turned stem with gadrooned collar, on a concave platform base with scrolled feet and casters, 57in (145cm) extended.
£850–1,100
€/ $1,350–1,750 AH

A mahogany and floral marquetry sofa table, the outswept top above a frieze drawer, on scrolling legs joined by a baluster-turned stretcher, Dutch, 19thC, 47¼in (120cm) wide.
£1,800–2,250
€/ $2,850–3,500 B

A mahogany banded sofa table, with lyre end supports, early 20thC, 54in (137cm) wide.
£700–800
€/ $1,100–1,250 HiA

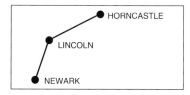

Sutherland Tables

A Victorian walnut Sutherland table, the figured drop-leaf top with a moulded border, on multi-carved cabriole legs, 29½in (75cm) wide.
£550–625
€/ $870–1,000 ⚒ RbF

A Victorian burr-walnut Sutherland table, 34½in (87.5cm) wide.
£500–600
€/ $800–950 ⚒ L

A mid-Victorian mahogany Sutherland table, 35¾in (91cm) wide.
£280–350
€/ $450–550 ⚒ B(Ba)

An Edwardian mahogany double Sutherland table, each top with moulded edge, on ring-turned supports, upper table 22in (56cm) wide.
£350–450
€/ $550–700 ⚒ FHF

A Victorian inlaid walnut Sutherland table, 34¾in (88.5cm) wide.
£550–625
€/ $870–1,000 ⚒ SWO

An Edwardian inlaid mahogany Sutherland table, 24in (61cm) wide.
£200–250
€/ $300–400 ⚒ SWO

Sutherland tables were introduced in the 19th century and named after the Duchess of Sutherland.

Tea Tables

A George II mahogany tea table, the fold-over top above a later frieze drawer, restored, Irish, 33½in (85cm) wide.
£1,000–1,250
€/ $1,500–2,000 ⚒ B(Ch)

A mahogany tea table, c1760, 34¼in (87cm) wide.
£650–800
€/ $1,000–1,250 ⚒ S(O)

A mahogany metamorphic combined tea and writing table, the double fold-over top with adjustable rising sloping writing inset and three small drawers, c1790, 35¾in (91cm) wide.
£1,500–1,800
€/ $2,400–2,850 ⚒ S(O)

◄ A Hepplewhite period mahogany serpentine tea table, the fold-over top above a banded frieze with a single drawer, on moulded channelled square tapering legs, c1790, 36in (91.5cm) wide.
£1,100–1,400
€/ $1,750–2,200 ⚒ MCA

► A George III mahogany tea table, 33¾in (85.5cm) wide.
£350–450
€/ $550–700 ⚒ L

A mahogany tea table, on sabre legs, c1820, 36¼in (92cm) wide.
£800–900
€/ $1,250–1,400 ⚒ S(O)

A Regency inlaid maple tea table, 36in (91.5cm) wide.
£3,000–3,400
€/ $4,750–5,400 ⊞ APO

A rosewood folding tea table, on a carved and turned central column, c1820, 43in (109cm) wide.
£3,300–3,700
€/ $5,200–6,000 ⊞ SAW

A George IV mahogany tea table, the hinged top above a plain frieze, on turned and reeded tapering legs, 36in (91.5cm) wide.
£650–800
€/ $1,000–1,270 ⚒ AG

A mahogany tea table, the veneered fold-over top above a veneered frieze with ebony stringing, on moulded square tapering legs, early 19thC, 36in (91.5cm) wide.
£280–350
€/ $450–550 ⚒ WW

A William IV mahogany and rosewood tea table, with crossbanding and brass inlay, 35¾in (91cm) wide.
£450–550
€/ $700–875 ⚒ B(Ba)

Tripod Tables

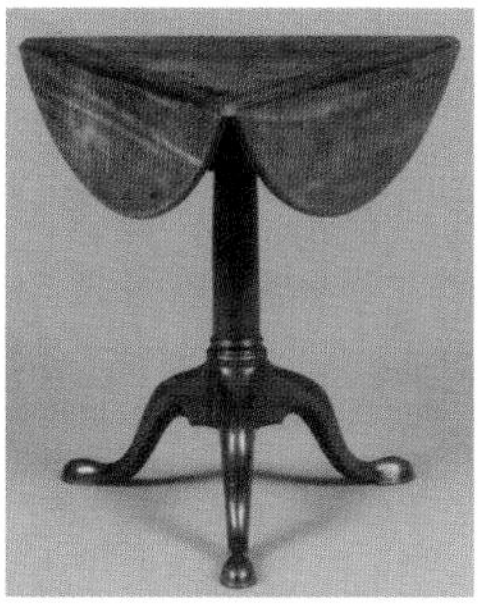

A George II mahogany tripod table, the drop-leaf top with three hinged flaps rising in conjunction with a swivel action, on cabriole legs with pad feet, 33in (84cm) diam.
£3,800–4,200
€/ $6,000–6,700 ⚒ S

A George II mahogany tripod table, the tilting top with a floral-carved border, on a baluster-turned twist column and tripod downswept legs carved with acanthus leaves, on claw-and-ball feet, 22in (56cm) diam.
£3,000–3,750
€/ $4,750–6,000 ⚒ HYD

◄ A George III carved mahogany tripod table, the shaped snap top with a pierced baluster gallery, on a fluted tapering column, the decorated tripod splayed supports with paw feet, 29¼in (74.5cm) wide.
£2,500–3,000
€/ $4,000–4,750 ⚒ B(EA)

A Chippendale period mahogany birdcage tripod table, c1750, 30in (76cm) diam.
£1,900–2,100
€/ $3,000–3,300 ⊞ SAW

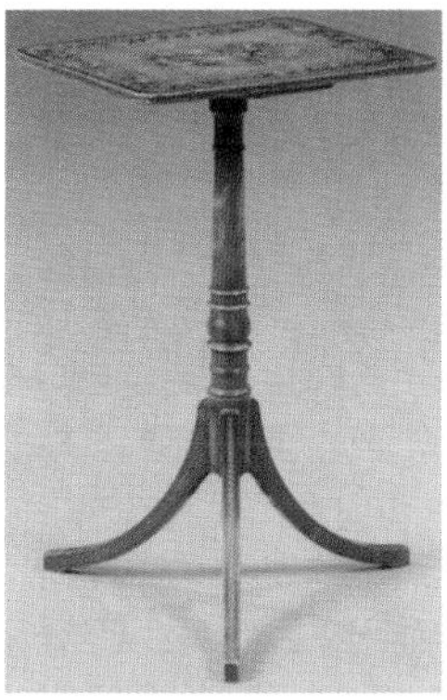

An early George III mahogany tripod table, the later dished top on a birdcage support, 26½in (67.5cm) diam.
£650–775
€/ $1,000–1,200 ⚒ L
This description means that the table had a plain circular top that was lobed and dished at a later date. The Victorians were keen on 'enhancing' furniture, and this piece would be worth more today if it had not been altered.

◄ A satinwood and painted tripod table, decorated with neo-classical motifs, the rounded top on a baluster stem, the tripod with sabre legs, some later painting, c1795, 17in (43cm) wide.
£1,800–2,200
€/ $2,850–3,500 ⚒ S(O)

A George III mahogany tripod table, with tilt-top, the central barrel- and vase-turned column with cabriole legs, 31in (78.5cm) diam.
£450–550
€/ $700–870 ⚒ PF

A George III mahogany tripod table, the tilt-top on a bird-cage support, the three carved legs with shaped pad feet, 26½in (67.5cm) diam.
£2,000–2,500
€/ $3,200–4,000 ⚒ TMA

A George III mahogany tripod table, on a turned central column, 31in (78.5cm) diam.
£2,250–2,500
€/ $3,500–4,000 ⊞ APO

A child's tripod table, the walnut tilt-top on a beech stem with oak legs, c1790, 11in (28cm) diam.
£1,250–1,400
€/ $2,000–2,200 ⊞ HA
This is of the correct proportions to go with a child's chair and therefore was not made for adult use.

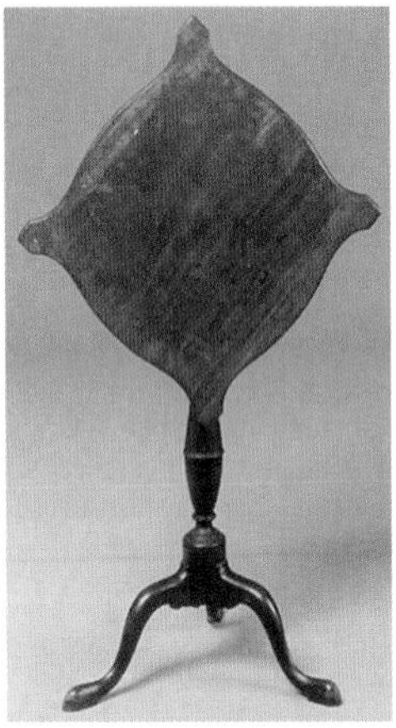

A Federal turned and figured mahogany tripod table, with traces of possibly original finish, cleats later, American, Massachusetts, c1800, 26¾in (68cm) wide.
£2,500–2,750
€/ $4,000–4,400 ⚒ S(NY)

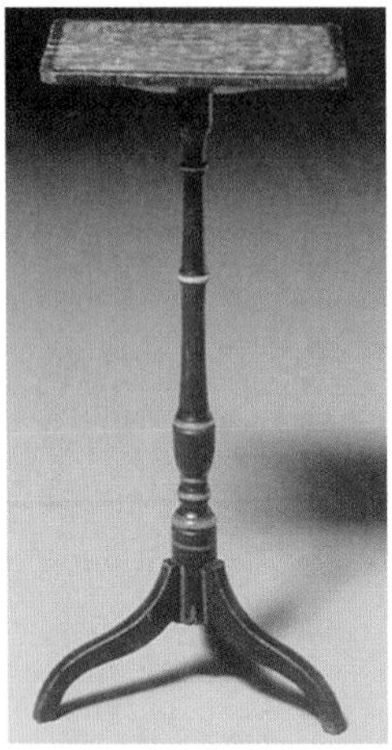

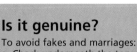

A Regency ebonized and decorated tripod table, the top paper-mounted with classical objects and antiquities, on a turned urn-shaped column with arched legs, 11¾in (30cm) wide.
£260–325
€/ $400–500 ⚒ B

An early Victorian rosewood-veneered tripod table, the tilt-top inlaid with marquetry flowers within sun rays, enclosed by a border of flowers and leaf motifs, the tapering faceted stem on three floral marquetry-inlaid cabriole legs with roundels to the toes, 25in (63.5cm) wide.
£700–820
€/ $1,100–1,300 ⚒ WW

An early Victorian rosewood tripod table, the veneered top on a turned stem and cabriole legs, 29in (73.5cm) high.
£830–925
€/ $1,300–1,450 ⊞ RPh

◄ A rosewood and banded tripod table, the tilt-top on a turned column and quadruped base, with brass terminals and casters, 19thC, 39in (99cm) diam.
£700–900
€/ $1,100–1,400 ⚒ E

A walnut tripod table, the veneered top above a carved stem, c1870, 20in (51cm) diam.
£340–375
€/ $550–600 ⊞ MTay

A marquetry tripod table, on a turned column and three flat legs, 19thC, 25½in (65cm) wide.
£320–400
€/ $500–630 ⚒ SWO

Is it genuine?

To avoid fakes and marriages:

- Check underneath the top: there should be a dark shadow of approximately 1½–2in (4–5cm) in a band around the edge, caused by dirt from the fingers when the table is lifted.
- Check that the lopers (the strengthening supports found under the table top) haven't been cut back. If they have, there will be a shadow left behind that will 'run off' to the edge which indicates that the top has been reduced.
- Check that the block on the column has left a shadow where it meets the underside of the table. If there is a difference, it means that the stem and table top are not original to each other.
- Georgian tavern tables with good bold swept legs were often later carved by Victorians to enhance value. This resulted in very thin-looking legs out of balance with the column.

► A George II-style mahogany tripod table, on tapering legs with pad feet, c1900, 28in (71cm) diam.
£1,300–1,450
€/ $2,000–2,275 ⊞ RAN

Two-Tier Tables

A mahogany two-tier table, with a drawer, originally a whatnot, c1830, 20in (51cm) wide.
£650–725
€/ $1,000–1,150 ⊞ RPh

◄ A near pair of Victorian walnut two-tier occasional tables, one with a square top, the other with rounded corners, on splayed legs, the undertiers with pierced galleries, stamped '1020', 22¾in (58cm) wide.
£900–1,100
€/ $1,400–1,700 ⚒ TRM

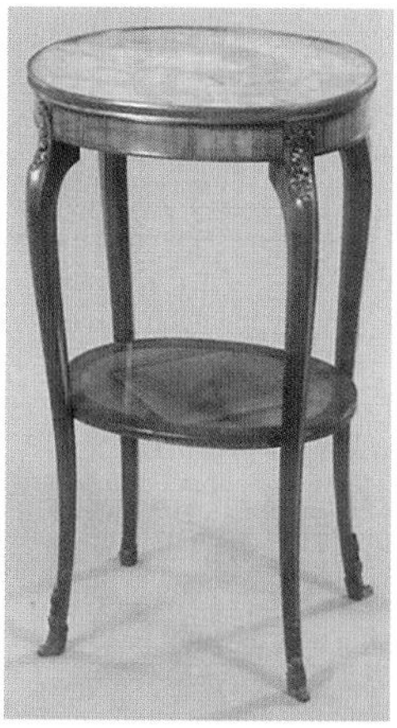

A mahogany and kingwood two-tier table, the inset marble top above a quarter-veneered stretcher shelf, on cabriole legs with sabots, French, 1850–75, 17in (43cm) diam.
£600–750
€/ $1,000–1,200 ⚒ NOA

A mahogany and inlaid two-tier table, with a tray, c1890, 35in (89cm) wide.
£2,700–3,000
€/ $4,250–4,750 ⊞ SAW

An inlaid walnut and kingwood two-tier table, French, late 19thC, 33in (84cm) wide.
£300–375
€/ $475–600 ⚒ SWO

A mahogany two-tier occasional table, c1890, 20in (51cm) wide.
£260–300
€/ $400–475 ⊞ GBr

► An Edwardian inlaid rosewood two-tier table, on square tapering legs, 24in (61cm) wide.
£140–175
€/ $225–275 ⚒ AMB

Work Tables

◄ A George III satinwood work table, by Gillows, Lancaster, with a frame for a workbasket, on square tapering legs, stamped 'Gillows, Lancaster', 19¼in (49cm) wide.
£4,500–5,500
€/ $7,000–8,700 ⚒ B(NW)

Designs for several similar tables normally described as 'work-bag tables' were drawn in Gillow's Estimate Sketch Books between 1793 and 1803. They were fitted with a frame under the drawer from which silk work bags were suspended. The escutcheon and knobs are in ivory and appear to be original. These knobs would have cost Gillows 4d each in 1798 and the lock 1s 2d. The total cost to Gillows in materials and labour for making a similar pieces (in satinwood with a mahogany top) was £2 7s 1/2d: the journeyman received one guinea. This piece too would originally have had a fitted work bag.

A Regency rosewood work table, the crossbanded ratcheted top over a side drawer and a silk-covered pull-out box, on swept legs with brass paw casters, 14¼in (36cm) wide.
£1,800–2,250
€/ $2,850–3,550 ⚒ SWO

◄ A Regency mahogany Pembroke work table, with dummy cupboard drawers, on square tapering legs with brass casters, 29in (73.5cm) wide.
£1,450–1,600
€/ $2,300–2,500 ⊞ APO

◄ A Regency mahogany Pembroke work table, with a frieze drawer over a deep drawer with double dummy drawer front, 16in (40.5cm) wide.
£3,500–3,850
€/ $5,500–6,000 ⊞ BERA

A Regency mahogany and inlaid workbox, the hinged lid with box stringing, enclosing an open interior above a material compartment, on a concave support with a platform base and four splayed tapering and inlaid legs with brass caps and casters, 16in (40.5cm) wide.
£1,100–1,400
€/ $1,750–2,200 ⚒ TRM

A mahogany Pembroke work table, with two small drawers and two opposing dummy drawers, a sliding work well, on turned and fluted legs with brass cup casters, early 19thC, 15¾in (40cm) wide.
£900–1,100
€/ $1,400–1,700 ⚒ DMC

An early Victorian mahogany work table, the baize-lined fold-over top above a frieze and an embroidered bag section, on column support with circular base and feet, 20in (51cm) wide.
£550–675
€/ $870–1,000 ⚒ AMB

A George IV mahogany bowfronted work table, with ebony stringing, the hinged top above three dummy drawers above a fitted drawer, all with turned rosewood knob handles with mother-of-pearl inlay, on ring-turned legs, 17in (43cm) wide.
£1,200–1,500
€/ $2,000–2,400 ⚒ G(L)

A bird's-eye maple work table, on a pedestal base, American, 19thC, 18in (45.5cm) wide.
£450–550
€/ $710–870 ⚒ DuM

A walnut drum work table, with gilt-bronze mounts, the galleried swivel top above a compartment with pendant piastre mounts and two apron drawers, on cabriole legs, Dutch, c1840, 12¼in (31cm) wide.
£3,000–3,500
€/ $4,750–5,500 ⚒ S(O)

A mahogany work table, on ring-turned tapering legs with brass casters, c1820, 29in (73.5cm) high.
£1,000–1,100
€/ $1,600–1,750 ⊞ JSt

An early Victorian rosewood work table, with a fitted silk interior, 20in (51cm) wide.
£1,650–1,850
€/ $2,600–3,000 ⊞ RPh

► An early Victorian mahogany work table, the moulded top over two drawers and a silk box, on turned tapering legs with brass caps and casters, 23in (58.5cm) wide.
£450–550
€/ $700–900 ⚒ BR

A mid-Victorian burr-walnut and marquetry work table, the moulded-edge top enclosing the original papered and satin-lined interior, on a carved socle, with carved cabriole legs and scroll feet, 18½in (47cm) wide.
£600–750
€/ $1,000–1,200 ⚒ B
This design is known as a 'trumpet table'.

A rosewood work table, the top inlaid with a chess board, above a frieze drawer, c1830, 18in (45.5cm) wide.
£1,500–1,650
€/ $2,400–2,600 ⊞ GBr

A mahogany work table, on fret-cut trestle ends joined by turned balusters, c1840, 21in (53.5cm) wide.
£2,200–2,450
€/ $3,500–3,900 ⊞ RAN

A Victorian walnut work table, the serpentine top above four drop finials, a conforming frieze drawer and separate satin-covered work slide, on pierced and scroll-carved supports, and four leaf-capped outswept legs with casters, 23¼in (59cm) wide.
£1,400–1,600
€/ $2,200–2,500 ⚒ LJ

A walnut work and vanity table, with drawers, and a fitted interior with a mirror, c1890, 21in (53.5cm) wide.
£250–275
€/ $400–430 ⊞ PaA

► **An ebonized and parcel-gilt papier mâché work table,** the serpentine hinged top with a fitted interior, on a baluster column, shaped platform and four scrolled feet, gilding rubbed, 19thC, 19in (48.5cm) wide.
£450–550
€/ $700–870 ⚒ JM

A Victorian mahogany work table, 30in (76cm) wide.
£1,200–1,325
€/ $1,900–2,100 ⊞ SAW

► **A Victorian mahogany work table,** on a triform base, 29in (73.5cm) diam.
£800–900
€/ $1,250–1,400 ⊞ RPh
The basket is for holding balls of wool.

An Edwardian mahogany work table, the divided hinged top enclosing a silk-lined interior with a lift-out fitted drawer, the whole outlined with a satinwood band and boxwood stringing, on square tapering supports with spade feet, 15¾in (40cm) wide.
£500–600
€/ $800–950 ⚒ DD

A walnut sewing table, early 20thC, 36in (91.5cm) wide.
£800–900
€/ $1,250–1,450 ⊞ RPh

Papier mâché

Papier mâché, possibly first known in the Orient, but recorded in France in the mid-17th century, had reached England by 1672. Henry Clay (d.1812) patented a process of using heat to bond together sheets of prepared material (pulped paper, chalk and glue) which formed panels that could be japanned and had heat-resistant properties. These sheets were made into items of furniture, boxes, dishes and trays.

Writing Tables

A George II mahogany writing table, with a rising stationery compartment and ratchet adjustable writing slope, 30in (76cm) wide.
£3,500–4,500
€/ $5,500–7,000 ⚒ HYD

A George III acacia wood writing table, 30in (76cm) wide.
£3,500–4,000
€/ $5,500–6,300 ⊞ APO

A George III satinwood writing table, with an adjustable dual reading slope, 34in (86.5cm) wide.
£11,250–12,500
€/ $17,500–19,750 ⊞ CAT
The adjustable slope and the wood of which it is made makes this piece particularly desirable.

◄ **A George III mahogany harlequin writing table,** with an adjustable writing slope, 25¾in (65.5cm) wide.
£3,000–3,500
€/ $4,750–5,500 ⚒ S(O)

► **A George III mahogany writing table,** with a divided drawer and secret drawer behind, 35¾in (91cm) wide.
£1,400–1,700
€/ $2,200–2,700 ⚒ B

A Regency amboyna writing table, with two drawers, 39in (99cm) wide.
£4,200–4,600
€/ $6,650–7,300 ⊞ APO

A partners' mahogany writing table, c1840, 48in (122cm) wide.
£750–850
€/ $1,200–1,350 ⊞ GBr

A Victorian walnut writing table, labelled 'Richardson of Hull', c1871, 45in (114.5cm) wide.
£4,700–5,200
€/ $7,400–8,200 ⊞ SAW

A Victorian maple writing table, the leather-inset top above two frieze drawers, on moulded sleigh feet with brass casters, 50¾in (129cm) wide.
£700–850
€/ $1,100–1,350 ⚒ CGC

An oak writing table, by Gillows, c1900, 36in (91.5cm) wide.
£500–565
€/ $780–880 ⊞ WiB

A Biedermeier cherrywood writing table, the top inset with gilt-tooled leather, above a frieze with three drawers, northern European, early 19thC, 39½in (100.5cm) wide.
£1,000–1,250
€/ $1,600–1,900 ⚒ NOA

An early Victorian mahogany writing table, the galleried top above five drawers, the kneehole with carved leaf brackets, fitted with later brass handles, 41¼in (105cm) wide.
£475–575
€/ $750–900 ⚒ WW

A mahogany kidney-shaped writing table, French, c1880, 43in (109cm) wide.
£3,800–4,200
€/ $6,000–6,600 ⊞ Che

A kingwood, rosewood and tulipwood writing table, the top inset with red gilt-tooled leather, on cabriole legs, French, 19thC, 66in (167.5cm) wide.
£5,500–6,500
€/ $8,700–10,300 ⚒ HAM

A rosewood and marquetry writing table, gallery probably later, German, c1830, 41¼in (105cm) wide.
£2,800–3,200
€/ $4,400–5,000 ⚒ S(O)

A walnut and marquetry writing table, the leather-lined top above a frieze drawer, labelled 'Edwards & Roberts', c1850, 52in (132cm) wide.
£5,300–6,250
€/ $8,300–10,000 ⚒ S(O)

Edwards & Roberts were among the foremost English cabinet makers of the second half of the 19th century. Founded in London in 1845, the firm rapidly expanded and by 1854 was trading as 'Edwards & Roberts, Antique and Modern Cabinet Makers and Importers of Ancient Furniture'. The firm produced furniture of modern design, as well as copies of 18th- and early 19th-century English and French pieces. They also retailed a great deal of second-hand furniture, so the presence of a label does not necessarily mean that the item was actually made by the firm.

An satinwood inlaid writing table, with rosewood and mahogany bandings, lock stamped 'Deutsches 202324 Reichs-Patent' and signed, Dutch or German, early 20thC, 43¼in (110cm) wide.
£1,200–1,400
€/ $2,000–2,200 ⚒ S(O)

◄ A parquetry writing table, signed 'Linke', French, c1920, 37in (94cm) wide.
£14,000–16,000
€/ $22,000–25,000 ⊞ HA

François Linke (1855–1946) was one of the most popular French cabinet makers of his time. He specialized in copying Louis XV & XVI styles.

Teapoys

A George III mahogany teapoy, the hinged cover enclosing a fitted interior, 15in (38cm) wide.
£2,000–2,200
€/ $3,200–3,500 RPh

A mahogany teapoy, inlaid with ebony, c1820, 29in (73.5cm) wide.
£1,500–1,700
€/ $2,400–2,700 BMi

A George IV mahogany teapoy, the hinged lid enclosing a fitted interior, on cast-brass paw feet with casters, 45in (114.5cm) wide.
£1,000–1,200
€/ $1,600–1,900 JAd

A George IV rosewood teapoy, the hinged lid enclosing two lidded lift-out caddies and a vacant recess, 14¾in (37.5cm) wide.
£450–525
€/ $710–830 L

A William IV rosewood teapoy, the hinged top enclosing lidded compartments and apertures, 19¾in (50cm) wide.
£470–570
€/ $740–900 B(Ch)

◄ A William IV rosewood teapoy, the rising top enclosing two cylindrical caddies and two cut-glass bowls, the scrolled feet with recessed casters, 19¼in (49cm) wide.
£1,000–1,250
€/ $1,600–1,900 DN

► A Victorian burr-walnut and walnut-veneered teapoy, the hinged top enclosing two lidded compartments, 47¼in (120cm) high.
£675–820
€/ $1,100–1,300 SWO

Torchères

A carved mahogany torchère, with later gilt-brass gallery, on cabriole legs with claw-and-ball feet, c1760, 41¾in (106cm) high.
£7,000–8,500
€/ $11,000–13,500 S

A pair of giltwood torchères, the velvet-lined tops on open scrolled supports, labelled 'Edwards & Roberts', c1860, 34in (86.5cm) high.
£2,400–2,700
€/ $3,800–4,300 S(O)

A yew-veneered torchère, the top with a lift-out cover, on paw feet, 19thC, 43in (109cm) high.
£2,200–2,600
€/ $3,500–4,000 WW

A pair of George I-style green painted torchères, c1900, 37in (94cm) high.
£1,350–1,500
€/ $2,000–2,400 APO

Towel Rails

A mahogany double-gate towel rail, on a stretchered platform and scroll feet, early 19thC, 33¾in (85.5cm) wide.
£280–350
€/ $450–550 WW

A walnut towel rail, with turned reeded supports, late 19thC, 25¾in (65.5cm) wide.
£100–120
€/ $160–190 SWO

A mahogany and boxwood-strung towel rail, the twin-facetted rails within a lyre-shaped support and panel sides, on splayed feet, late 19thC, 38½in (98cm) wide.
£200–240
€/ $320–380 BIG

Trays

A Regency period lacquer tray, on a later stand, c1810, 30in (76cm) wide.
£2,400–2,700
€/ $3,800–4,300 ⊞ REI

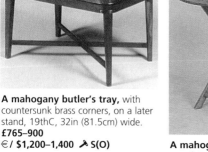

A mahogany butler's tray, with countersunk brass corners, on a later stand, 19thC, 32in (81.5cm) wide.
£765–900
€/ $1,200–1,400 S(O)

A mahogany butler's tray, on a later stand, 19thC, 30in (76cm) wide.
£180–225
€/ $280–350 B(Ba)

A mahogany butler's tray, on a later folding stand, 19thC, 34¾in (88.5cm) wide.
£450–550
€/ $700–850 B(Ba)

◄ **A Sheraton revival decorated satinwood tray table,** c1900, 23in (58.5cm) diam.
£585–650
€/ $900–1,000 ⊞ Che

► **An Edwardian satinwood tray table,** 27in (68.5cm) wide.
£400–450
€/ $630–700 ⊞ RPh

A mahogany butler's tray, on a stand, 19thC, 22in (56cm) wide.
£400–450
€/ $630–700 S(O)

An ebonized tray, on a simulated walnut stand, late 19thC, 24¾in (63cm) wide.
£280–320
€/ $440–500 B(Ch)

Wall Brackets

A carved limewood and walnut wall bracket, modelled as a tapering cascade of flowers, hops, barley ears, pea-pods and a snail, surmounted by a shaped plateau with a leaf-carved edge above, 18thC, the plateau later, 15in (38cm) wide.
£1,300–1,600
€/ $2,000–2,500 TEN

A giltwood wall bracket, carved and pierced with C-scrolls and shells, 1750–1800, 13½in (34.5cm) high.
£800–950
€/ $1,250–1,500 S(O)

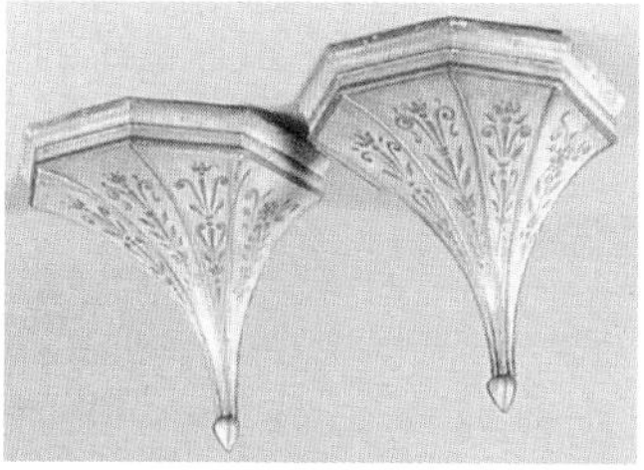

◄ A pair of George III painted wall brackets, with later decoration, 17¼in (44cm) wide.
£1,300–1,500
€/ $2,000–2,400 S(O)

A pair of giltwood and gesso wall brackets, c1830, 10¾in (27.5cm) wide.
£2,200–2,700
€/ $3,500–4,300 S(O)

A pair of gilt gesso and carved wood wall brackets, the D-shaped plateau tops with flower- and foliate-carved supports, 1850–75, 13½in (34.5cm) high.
£2,000–2,500
€/ $3,200–4,000 B

A Chinese Chippendale-style mahogany wall bracket, with a shaped frieze and pierced fret triform support, fret gallery damaged, late 19thC, 13in (33cm) wide.
£150–200
€/ $230–300 WW

A pair of carved mahogany wall brackets, in the shape of a *ho-o* bird on foliage, 1875–1925, 15¼in (38.5cm) high.
£340–425
€/ $550–670 SWO

Wardrobes

A mahogany wardrobe, c1795, 97in (246.5cm) high.
£2,600–3,000
€/ $4,000–4,750 ⊞ Che

A George IV mahogany wardrobe, the moulded cornice above a plain frieze and two drawers enclosing hanging space, modelled as two dummy cupboard doors and six short dummy drawers, above a single long drawer, on bracket feet, 61½in (156cm) wide.
£900–1,000
€/ $1,400–1,600 ⚒ CGC

A late George III mahogany wardrobe, the scroll cresting with gilt-metal mounts, the frieze with chequered stringing, above two panelled doors, on splayed bracket feet, 50in (127cm) high.
£2,000–2,300
€/ $3,200–3,600 ⚒ G(L)

An early Victorian mahogany wardrobe, the moulded cornice above six drawers, on a plinth base, 86¼in (219cm) wide.
£3,000–3,750
€/ $4,750–6,000 ⚒ B(L)
The quality of the timber and construction, together with the recessed panelled frieze and rounded turned knobs, suggest the work of Gillows of Lancaster.

◄ **A mahogany wardrobe,** with three doors above two drawers, c1835, 82in (208.5cm) wide.
£1,650–1,800
€/ $2,500–2,800 ⚒ S(O)

Auction or dealer?

When buying at auction, prices can be lower than those of a dealer, but a buyer's premium and VAT will be added to the hammer price. Equally, when selling at auction, commission, tax and photography charges will be deducted from the hammer price. Dealers will often restore pieces before putting them back on the market.

► **A mid-Victorian walnut wardrobe,** with two doors, 54in (137cm) wide.
£850–950
€/ $1,350–1,500 ⊞ HiA

A Regency mahogany 'fiddleback' wardrobe, the two panelled doors with ebony beading, on flowerhead-carved scroll feet, 51½in (131cm) wide.
£900–1,100
€/ $1,400–1,750 ⚒ Bea

An early Victorian mahogany-veneered inverted breakfront wardrobe, the central architectural pediment above six long drawers with turned wood handles, on a plinth base, 80½in (204.5cm) wide.
£550–625
€/ $870–990 ⚒ WW

A figured mahogany and stencil-decorated wardrobe, the doors opening to a divided interior with a drawer, shelves and a hanging rail, minor patches and repairs to doors at hinges, American, New York, c1820, 54in (137cm) wide.
£16,000–20,000
€/ $25,000–32,000 ⚒ S(NY)
The relatively small size of this wardrobe, the arcaded frieze, column supports and carved winged lion paw feet make this a perfect decorator's piece

An early Victorian mahogany inverted breakfront wardrobe, the centre with two arched panelled doors enclosing slides, flanked by panelled doors enclosing a hanging space, on a plinth base, 100¼in (254.5cm) wide.
£1,600–2,000
€/ $2,500–3,200 ⚒ AH

◄ **A mahogany fitted wardrobe,** with three doors, c1860, 83in (211cm) wide.
£2,200–2,450
€/ $3,500–3,900 ⊞ MHA

A late Victorian mahogany wardrobe, 55½in (141cm) wide.
£450–550
€/ $700–870 ⚒ B(Ba)

A Victorian lady's Biedermeier-style mahogany wardrobe/ linen cabinet, the top of convex stepped design on D-formed side quarters, the two figured mahogany doors with applied convex moulding, on squat circular feet, 45in (114.5cm) wide.
£420–520
€/ $660–820 GAK

A Victorian mahogany wardrobe, the moulded cornice with ovolu banding, the two arched leaf-carved doors enclosing hanging space and drawers, on a plinth base, 59in (150cm) wide.
£800–950
€/ $1,300–1,500 AH

◄ **A Victorian oak wardrobe/ compactum,** 82in (208.5cm) wide.
£900–1,000
€/ $1,400–1,600 WiB

► **A Victorian mahogany wardrobe,** on turned feet, 51¼in (130cm) wide.
£550–625
€/ $870–990
JAd

A Victorian burr-walnut breakfront wardrobe, with a mirrored central door and two side doors, 76in (193cm) wide.
£2,000–2,300
€/ $3,200–3,650 RPh

A late Victorian satinbirch compactum, 107in (272cm) wide.
£280–320
€/ $440–500 B(Ch)

A gentleman's walnut compactum, with two cupboard doors enclosing fitted pull-out hangers, with five graduated drawers below a cupboard door, the two lower section drawers on a plinth base, c1900, 66¼in (168.5cm) wide.
£420–520
€/ $670–820 SWO

An inlaid mahogany wardrobe, c1900, 73in (185.5cm) wide.
£3,800–4,250
€/ $6,000–6,650 MTay

A walnut and mahogany triple wardrobe, with hanging space, the single door enclosing three sliding trays above three small drawers, on a plinth base, c1900, 76½in (194cm) wide.
£420–500
€/ $670–800 SWO

► **An Edwardian banded mahogany triple wardrobe,** with mirrored doors, and two hanging compartments, 72in (183cm) wide.
£765–850
€/ $1,200–1,350 PaA

An Edwardian inlaid mahogany wardrobe, with mirrors, drawers and cupboards, 82in (208.5cm) wide.
£1,300–1,450
€/ $2,000–2,300 DUK

Washstands

A George III mahogany washstand, the galleried lift-off top revealing apertures, above two cupboard doors, two frieze drawers and a deep drawer with dummy fronts, the square legs with an X-undertier, 17in (43cm) wide.
£450–550
€/ $700–870 WW

A mahogany washstand, the top enclosing a mirror and spaces for wash bowls, above a tambour compartment and drawer to the side, c1780, 20½in (52cm) wide.
£700–850
€/ $1,100–1,400 S(O)

A Regency Gillows-style mahogany washstand, the three-quarter gallery back with a shelf and applied rosette terminals to the side panels, over a marble top and single frieze drawer, on four turned reeded supports, with concave-fronted undertier and brass casters, 30¼in (77cm) wide.
£800–1,000
€/ $1,300–1,600 Bri

A George III mahogany enclosed washstand, with a tambour door, 22in (56cm) wide.
£1,100–1,200
€/ $1,750–1,900 WAW

A George III mahogany washstand, the crossbanded divided top opening to reveal a now vacant interior, fitted with a false drawer above a cupboard and two long drawers, 18in (45.5cm) wide.
£340–425
€/ $550–675 L

A walnut washstand, French, c1880, 32½in (82.5cm) wide.
£240–265
€/ $380–415 PaA

A George III mahogany enclosed washstand/ writing cabinet, the hinged top with fittings, above a slide with a baize-lined slope, and five drawers simulating nine drawers, with brass lion-mask handles, on square tapering legs with brass terminals and casters, 28in (71cm) wide.
£650–800
€/ $1,000–1,300 DN

A George III mahogany washstand, with a hinged splash-back, the tambour shutter door enclosing a pot cupboard, with one small drawer and two dummy drawers, 25in (63.5cm) wide.
£1,500–1,650
€/ $2,350–2,550 RGa

A Victorian washstand, with a marble top, 42in (106.5cm) wide.
£450–500
€/ $700–800 RPh

◄ **A mahogany washstand,** with a marble top, early 20thC, 41¾in (106cm) wide.
£150–180
€/ $240–280 B(Ba)

A George III mahogany enclosed washstand, the top rising to reveal a fitted interior with adjustable mirror and compartments with hinged covers, a slide and two small drawers under, with pierced foliate-carved corner brackets, and a shaped undertier, on straight legs, 24in (61cm) wide.
£400–475
€/ $630–750 E

A George III mahogany bowfronted corner wash-stand, the galleried back above three apertures, the central tier with a central drawer, on square outsplayed legs joined by an undertier, 22in (56cm) wide.
£300–375
€/ $475–600 DMC

A late Victorian/Edwardian mahogany washstand, the lift-up top with a dummy drawer enclosing a wash bowl and space for a toothbrush holder, over a single panel door, on a plinth base, 23½in (59.5cm) wide.
£100–120
€/ $160–190 BIG

Whatnots

A mahogany four-tier whatnot, with a drawer, c1780, 20in (51cm) wide.
£1,200–1,400
€/ $1,900–2,200 S(O)

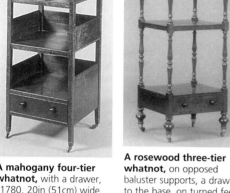

A rosewood three-tier whatnot, on opposed baluster supports, a drawer to the base, on turned feet and casters, early 19thC, 16½in (42cm) wide.
£1,500–1,800
€/ $2,400–2,850 TEN

A rosewood three-tier whatnot, with centre drawer, c1825, 40in (101.5cm) high.
£4,200–4,600
€/ $6,600–7,300 ⊞ F

A William IV rosewood four-tier whatnot, with a drawer to the base, 55in (139.5cm) high.
£2,400–2,650
€/ $3,800–4,200 ⊞ MTay

A mahogany four-tier whatnot, with a fretwork galleried top, a drawer at the base, on turned legs, c1835, 55in (139.5cm) high.
£2,600–2,850
€/ $4,100–4,500 ⊞ BERA

A rosewood three-tier whatnot, on barley-twist uprights, c1850, 15in (38cm) wide.
£2,000–2,250
€/ $3,200–3,600 ⊞ RGa

A rosewood five-tier whatnot, with barley-twist uprights, mid-19thC, 34in (86.5cm) wide.
£600–680
€/ $950–1,100 ⊞ HiA

A walnut four-tier whatnot, with serpentine outline and barley-twist uprights, c1850, 49in (124.5cm) high.
£1,100–1,250
€/ $1,750–1,900 ⊞ MTay

A walnut three-tier whatnot, with ormolu mounts, c1860, 36in (91.5cm) high.
£2,200–2,400
€/ $3,500–3,800 ⊞ SAW

► **A Victorian ebonized four-tier whatnot,** with burr-walnut banding, 26in (66cm) wide.
£260–300
€/ $400–475 ⊞ PaA

A rosewood four-tier whatnot, 19thC, 19in (48.5cm) wide.
£1,000–1,150
€/ $1,600–1,800 ⊞ SAW

A rosewood whatnot/display cabinet, inlaid with brass stringing, with marble shelves, each tier on ring-turned supports, on short turned legs, French, c1880, 24in (61cm) wide.
£2,000–2,250
€/ $3,200–3,500 ⊞ JC

Window Seats

A mahogany window seat, c1770, 38¼in (97cm) wide.
£1,650–1,800
€/ $2,500–2,800 ⚒ S(O)

An oak window seat, on turned legs, c1870, 43in (109cm) wide.
£2,200–2,450
€/ $3,500–3,800 ⊞ CAT

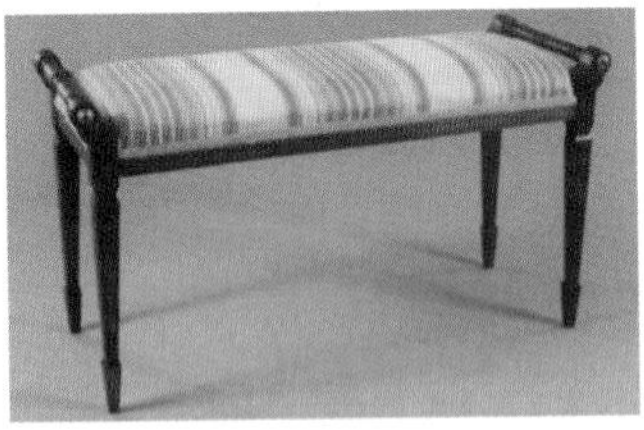

A turned and carved mahogany Sheraton-style window seat, the roll ends with turned giltwood bosses, c1900, 38in (96.5cm) wide.
£500–600
€/ $800–950 ⚒ NOA

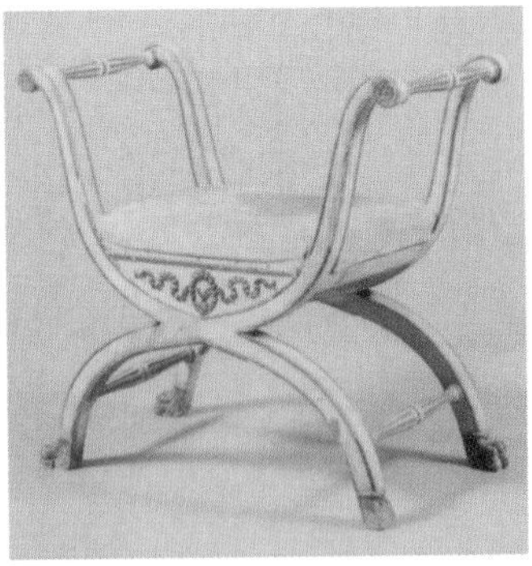

A painted window seat, Italian, early 19thC, 28¾in (73cm) wide.
£900–1,100
€/ $1,400–1,700 ⚒ S(O)

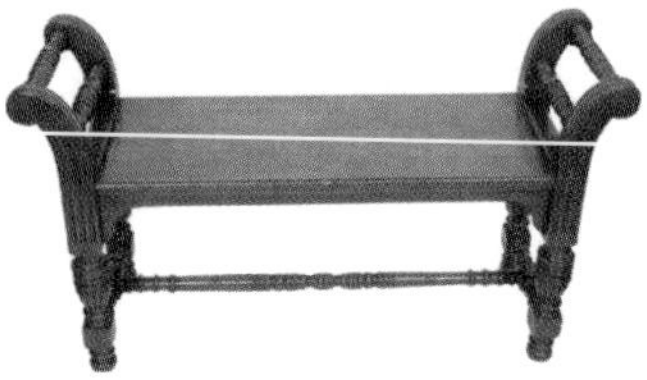

A carved and turned oak window seat, late 19thC, 44in (112cm) wide.
£2,000–2,300
€/ $3,200–3,600 ⊞ APO

A Regency Charles Tatham-style mahogany window seat, on rounded tapering legs, 59¾in (152cm) wide.
£3,800–4,750
€/ $6,000–7,500 ⚒ B
Charles Heathcote Tatham first published his design upon which this stool is based in his *Etchings of Ancient Ornamental Architecture* drawn from the originals in Rome and other parts of Italy during the years 1794–96. This book was tremendously popular, going into three editions by 1810, and was probably used by Thomas Hope in his *Household Furniture* of 1807.

A beechwood window seat, with carved frieze and turned legs, 1920s, 55in (140cm) wide.
£600–720
€/ $950–1,100 ⚒ SWO

◄ **An Edwardian mahogany and satinwood window seat,** on square-section legs with spade feet, 41in (104cm) wide.
£550–700
€/ $870–1,100 ⚒ B(Ch)

Wine Coolers

A Chippendale period mahogany wine cooler, with later stand, c1765, 22in (56cm) diam.
£6,000–7,000
€/ $9,500–11,000 ⊞ REI

A late George III mahogany wine cooler, the hinged top opening to reveal a later tin liner, with brass-bound sides and carrying handles, the stand with cabriole legs and pad feet, restorations, some parts missing, 27¼in (69cm) diam.
£1,600–2,000
€/ $2,500–3,200 ⚒ B(Ch)

A George III inlaid mahogany cellaret, the legs with pierced spandrels, 21¼in (54cm) diam.
£1,200–1,500
€/ $1,900–2,400 ⚒ S(O)

Items in the Furniture section have been arranged in date order within each sub-section.

Ice houses

Since Roman times, beautiful wine coolers and the ice they contained were both symbols of status and wealth as a large staff was needed to make ice. In winter, vast quantities of blocks of ice were cut from the rivers or lakes on a country estate and then packed in straw in caves which would enable it to last until the summer. If there were no caves, an ice house was built with no windows, a very small door and a roof that overhung the walls to keep the sun off. This was lined with straw and then packed with ice in the winter. Many country houses still have ice houses which make very good tool sheds!

A George III mahogany cellaret, the concave-moulded and ebony-strung hinged lid enclosing an interior with nine compartments, the sides with carrying handles, on bracket feet with casters, 16¼in (41.5cm) wide.
£500–625
€/ $800–1,000 B&L

A George III mahogany cellaret, outlined with satinwood and ebonized bandings, with two brass handles and an ivory escutcheon, on square tapering legs, 15in (38cm) wide.
£650–825
€/ $1,000–1,300 DD

A George IV mahogany cellaret, the canted lid carved with fruit, enclosing a lead-lined interior, with lion-mask handles to either side of the base, on a moulded plinth and turned lotus-carved feet with casters, some damage, 30in (76cm) wide.
£1,400–1,700
€/ $2,200–2,700 TEN

A mahogany cellaret, c1800, 20in (51cm) wide.
£1,450–1,600
€/ $2,200–2,500 Che

A mahogany and boxwood-strung bowfronted cellaret, the lid enclosing a baize-lined interior, interior divisions missing, early 19thC, 20in (51cm) wide.
£1,000–1,250
€/ $1,600–2,000 DN

A George IV mahogany sarcophagus-shaped cellaret, 36in (91.5cm) wide.
£2,600–3,000
€/ $4,100–4,700 WAW

◄ **A brass-bound mahogany wine cooler,** on turned tapering feet, c1835, 35¾in (91cm) wide.
£6,000–6,500
€/ $9,500–10,500 S(O)

A late George III mahogany bowfronted cellaret, inlaid with boxwood stringing, 21½in (54.5cm) wide.
£200–250
€/ $300–400 L

A mahogany butler's bowfronted cellaret, the hinged top enclosing lead-lined compartments, c1820, 38¼in (97cm) wide.
£2,500–3,000
€/ $4,000–4,750 S(O)

A Victorian walnut wine cooler, with hinged top and brass finial and handle, 21in (53.5cm) high.
£750–900
€/ $1,200–1,400 BWL

Campaign Furniture

An old copy of the The Army and Navy Stores' catalogue will show numerous items available at the end of the 19th century to ease the life of the soldier or traveller. Officers of the armed forces, who created the demand for this furniture were also conscious of the fashion of the day and this was reflected in the work of the cabinet makers they commissioned. Although most 18th-century campaign pieces are unattributable, designs for portable furniture are known by such recognized names as Chippendale or Sheraton. The end of the 18th century saw the rise of specialist makers of camp equipage with the names of Thomas Butler and Morgan & Sanders perhaps being the most recognized. The number of such specialists increased in the 19th century fuelled by military needs, the popularity of the Grand Tour and the increase of Europeans moving to the colonies. This demand for campaign furniture encouraged many makers to be inventive in their designs thus creating many unusual and interesting pieces.

Many of the original reasons for the popularity of campaign furniture hold true today. It is practical, versatile, and by definition very easy to move about. The fold-out bed is not a modern invention and its early 19th-century forebear is just as useful for that extra guest, although far more elegant. As you would expect, Georgian campaign furniture on the whole has a greater demand than Victorian for the same reasons that apply to antique furniture. However there are factors that break this basic rule of thumb: the ingenuity of design seen in the late 19th century is one, while a good maker's name on a piece is another. Although most furniture by Ross & Co of Dublin (see the chiffonier, cabinet, ballon-back chairs and mirror on the following pages) is typically Victorian, their name enjoys a very good reputation. They were the army's preferred suppliers in their day and have a good following among collectors. Provenance is also important and if an item's history can be traced it will have a bearing on its value.

The strength of campaign furniture in today's market can be put down to a number of reasons, some of which have already been mentioned. The recent publication of the first book on the subject, *British Campaign Furniture* by Nicholas Brawer, has increased awareness in this field and so created more collectors. However, perhaps the main reason for the renewed popularity of campaign furniture is one that is true right across the antiques world – if something is different to the norm it will be more sought after.

Sean Clarke

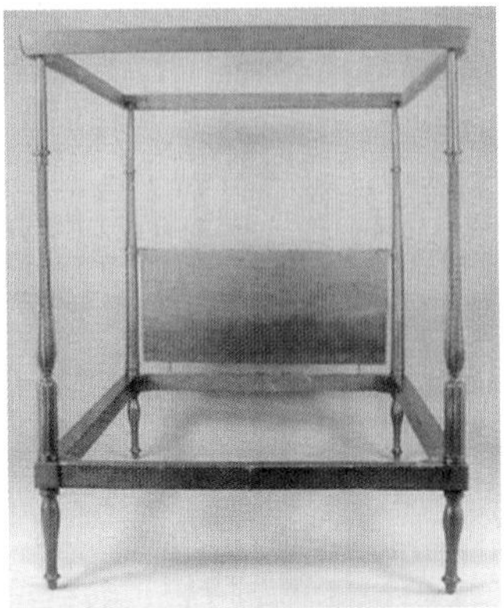

A Regency mahogany and brass four-poster campaign bed, with brass plate engraved 'Butlers Patent, Catherine St', 58¾in (149cm) wide.
£2,500–3,200
€/ $4,000–5,000 B(Ba)

Items in the Campaign Furniture section have been arranged alphabetical order.

A mahogany and stained-pine campaign bookcase, the two sections joined by a piano hinge, the panelled doors enclosing three adjustable pine shelves, two short drawers with ivory knobs to one side of base, mid-19thC, 19¼in (49cm) wide.
£750–850
€/ $1,100–1,400 ⊞ ChC

A mahogany portable campaign bookshelf, painted to resemble rosewood, early 19thC, 24in (61cm) wide.
£500–550
€/ $800–870 ⊞ ChC

The simple but effective design of this type of campaign shelf ensured that they were made during most of the 19th century and into the 20th century. The three shelves are supported and divided by brass standards that have a steel rod running through them; this is held in place by decorative brass nuts to the top and bottom. The shelves could either be set on a surface, such as a campaign chest, or hung.

A mahogany campaign box, fittings missing, c1780, 6in (15cm) wide.
£25–30
€/ $40–48 ⊞ MB

◄ **A mahogany campaign dispatch box,** the underside of the lid with a removable mahogany tablet containing a paper notepad, enclosing three divided sections for pens, mid-19thC, 9½in (24cm) wide.
£180–200
€/ $280–320 ⊞ ChC

A mahogany and brass-bound campaign box, the hinged top centred by an inset brass plaque engraved 'A. D. B. Martinez' below a Maltese Cross surmounted by a coronet, on a later moulded stand, 19thC, 44½in (113cm) wide.
£4,000–5,000
€/ $6,300–8,000 S

A walnut campaign cabinet, by Ross & Co, the front and removable side mouldings of solid and veneered walnut, the sides, back and top painted black, 1850–75, 42in (106.5cm) wide.
£1,000–1,100
€/ $1,500–1,750 ⊞ ChC
The inside edge of the moulding has remnants of canvas glued to it and this, along with pinholes to the edges of each side of the cabinet, suggests that a length of material was fitted to the two mouldings to cover up the unsightly top and sides when set up. The cabinet has a Ross brass label and a paper label to the inside giving packing instructions. It can be seen from this label that it originally had a bookshelf superstructure, designed to be removed for transport. The label also gives instructions for packing four chairs and a couch into the carcass. The interior has two shelves. The bun feet unscrew for packing, and the iron fittings to the front edge of the top and bottom suggest that a protective cover would be fixed over the doors for travel.

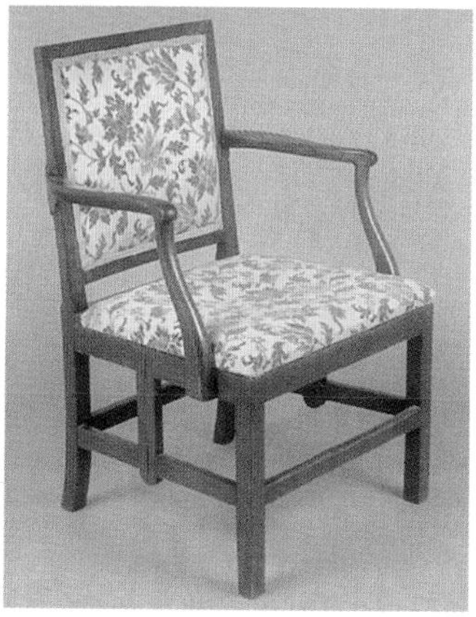

A camphorwood campaign writing box, with tambour top drawer, on a chamfered stand, 19thC, 18¾in (47.5cm) wide.
£320–400
€/ $500–600 SWO

A mahogany campaign chair, 1825–50.
£1,600–1,750
€/ $2,500–2,750 ⊞ ChC
This officer's armchair breaks down very quickly for packing. Unscrewing the arm bolts allows them to be removed and the hinged back to drop down against the back legs. The legs fold with a concertina action once the drop-in seat has been removed. The iron fittings to each leg were made to bear carrying struts to give the chair a further use.

A Victorian mahogany campaign chest, with a hinged lid and base drawer, damaged, 22¾in (58cm) wide.
£85–110
€/ $135–175 SWO

◄ A late George III mahogany campaign chair, with removable arms and inward-folding sides.
£500–625
€/ $800–1,000 L

A mahogany campaign bureau, the fall-front enclosing a fitted interior with pigeonholes and four drawers, on a stand with square tapering legs, c1870, 27½in (70cm) wide.
£1,600–1,800
€/ $2,500–2,850 ⊞ ChC
For ease of transport the bureau section lifts off its stand. It is marked with a 'Colonel Kemp' stamp to the back of both sections, and although little is known of the Colonel it does highlight that the desk was made for military purposes.

A set of four Ross & Co walnut balloon-back campaign chairs, 1850–75.
£1,600–1,750
€/ $2,500–2,750 ⊞ ChC
This set of chairs was probably made to fit inside a chiffonier or other similar piece of cased furniture. The front legs unscrew from the seat and the back legs, which screw through the seat into the chairback, have an additional small thumb bolt to further secure them. Each piece is stamped with a number which corresponds to its position on the chair, thus ensuring that parts from one chair don't get mixed up with those from another. Two of the chairs have the brass Ross & Co label to the underside of the seat, and it is typical of the firm that not all chairs in a set would be labelled.

A teak campaign chest of drawers, with two short over three long drawers, early 19thC, 35½in (90cm) wide.
£1,800–2,000
€/ $2,850–3,200 ⊞ ChC
The use of teak suggests that this chest of drawers was either made or destined for use in the colonies, the oily nature of the wood being more resilient to the eastern climate. The upper section has a brass fitting to each side which houses a bolt that slides down to fix the two sections together. This system of locking the two parts of the chest together is relatively unusual, as is the fact that the base is fitted with steel threads to receive the removable feet.

A teak campaign chest, 19thC, 36in (91.5cm) wide.
£1,800–2,000
€/ $2,850–3,200 ⊞ APO

Items in the Campaign Furniture section have been arranged in alphabetical order.

A teak campaign chest, 19thC, 39in (99cm) wide.
£2,200–2,400
€/ $3,500–3,800 ⊞ SAW

A pine cupboard case for a campaign chest, with mahogany and satinwood door panels with brass knobs, early 19thC, 41½in (105.5cm) wide.
£1,800–2,000
€/ $2,850–3,200 ⊞ ChC
Double cupboards such as this one, although very useable in their own right, are often associated with being made to contain a two-part chest. The Army and Navy catalogue describes them as 'Cases for Chest of Drawers'.

A mahogany campaign chest, c1870, 39in (99cm) wide.
£2,200–2,450
€/ $3,500–3,800 ⊞ GBr

A black-painted pine campaign chest, by Hill & Millard, the upper section with iron handles and mounts, the panelled doors painted 'Captain Gerard, 23rd Regiment W. Fusiliers', late 19thC, 41½in (105.5cm) wide.
£600–750
€/ $1,000–1,200 🔨 HAM
Army General order 13(7) from 1879 specified that all packing cases of campaign furniture must have the owner's name and regiment marked on it. Army General order 131(D) from 1871 specified a maximum size for campaign chests of drawers of 42 x 24 x 24in (106.5 x 61 x 61cm), although there were always exceptions to the rules, especially among the wealthy officers.

A Victorian teak and brass-bound campaign chest, the fitted central secretaire drawer flanked by two short drawers, over three long drawers, on turned feet, 39in (99cm) wide.
£2,300–2,800
€/ $3,600–4,400 🔨 G(B)

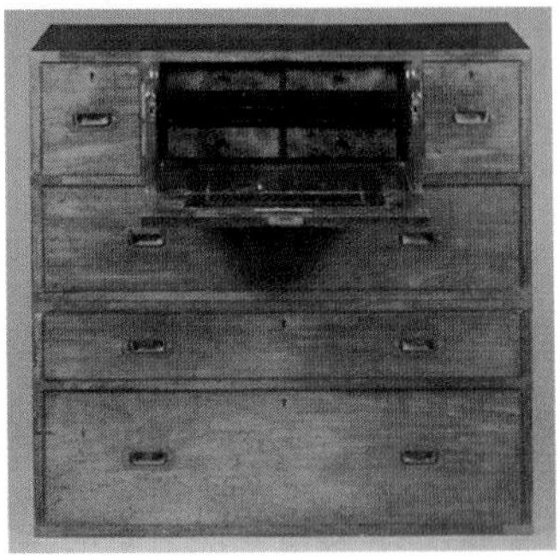

A teak campaign secretaire chest, in two sections, the central secretaire compartment enclosing secret drawers, on detachable feet, label for Hill & Millard, London, c1878, 39in (99cm) wide.
£2,500–3,000
€/ $4,000–4,750 🔨 S(O)
Hill & Millard were upmarket military outfitters and trunk makers formed by John Hill and Richard Millard. In the London commercial directories from 1855 to 1865, the firm is recorded as 'military outfitters and trunk makers, 7 Duncannon St., Strand'.

A walnut campaign chiffonier, by Ross & Co, 1850–75, 44½in (113cm) wide.
£1,600–1,750
€/ $2,500–2,750 ⊞ ChC

A brass, steel and bronze luggage stand, by Tonks of Birmingham, with X-frame supports, late 19thC, 21½in (54.5cm) wide.
£75–85
€/ $120–135 ⊞ ChC
When open, this folding rack forms a low table on which to rest a piece of luggage to raise it up to a more practical height. It also has the added advantage of keeping luggage off the ground in a country where it might be susceptible to vermin.

A mahogany campaign dining table, with two extra leaves, 1750–1800, 117in (297cm) extended.
£7,000–7,500
€/ $11,000–11,850 ⊞ ChC

A mahogany campaign Pembroke table/washstand, mid-19thC, 36¾in (93.5cm) wide.
£1,250–1,400
€/ $2,000–2,200 ⊞ ChC
The central, hinged section of the top is released by pressing a button concealed under one of the drop leaves. A mirror with adjustable angle is on the underside of the top, and the table well is fitted for a bowl, jug and soap dish, as well as having a drawer to one side. The turned table legs unscrew for carriage. These tables are sometimes referred to as 'ship tables'.

A mahogany collapsible campaign mirror, by Ross & Co, the base with a hinged three-position easel arm, maker's label, reverse of mirror plate inscribed 'March 1876', 11½in (29cm) wide.
£270–300
€/ $425–475 ⊞ ChC

A tortora wood campaign occasional table, on turned legs, New Zealand, c1860, 26in (66cm) wide.
£1,100–1,250
€/ $1,750–2,000 ⊞ ChC
Tortora wood, native to New Zealand, is a very striking timber with distinctive figuring and a colour similar to satinwood. The table was designed to fold away when not in use. A sprung ash bar underneath the top keeps the legs in place, and releasing the spring enables the legs to fold underneath the top.

A teak and brass-bound campaign trunk, c1800, 31in (78.5cm) wide.
£700–785
€/ $1,100–1,300 ⊞ GBr

► A leather and iron-bound campaign trunk, 1875–1925, 30in (76cm) wide.
£320–350
€/ $500–550 ⊞ ChC
The iron loops on the back of this trunk indicate that it was made to be strapped to a mule for transport.

A mahogany campaign card/tea table, 1790–1810, 33in (84cm) square.
£600–650
€/ $950–1,000 ⊞ ChC
The top of this table is hinged so that it can be opened out, like a standard tea table, to double its size. In order that both sides of the top are supported it is swiveled on its box to a right angle. In doing this the storage space for the turned beech legs is revealed.

A satinwood campaign writing table, c1910, 24in (61cm) wide.
£1,250–1,400
€/ $1,900–2,200 ⊞ RPh

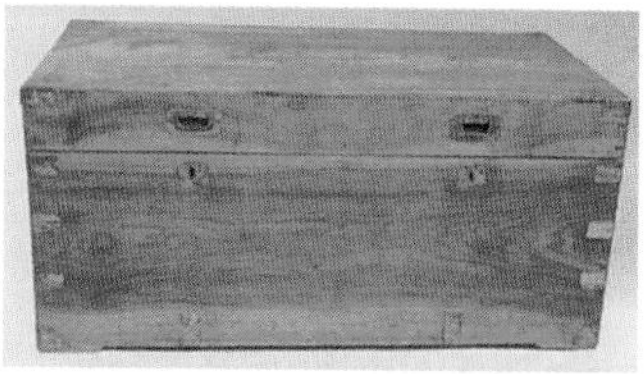

A camphorwood campaign trunk, with brass corner brackets and carrying handles, 19thC, 41in (104cm) wide.
£300–375
€/ $475–600 HoG
Camphorwood was used in making this trunk because of its pungent smell which would discourage moths and other pests.

Oak & Country Furniture

During the last two and a half decades, we have seen the availability of good, unrestored oak furniture decline year by year. For example, 25 years ago we bought 30 good dressers a year, now it's two or three; similarly, then we bought ten good court cupboards, now it's one or two. Naturally, as the scarcity of these items increases, so does the value, a situation that attracts the forger. Almost every collection I value these days includes fake items and I am being offered more all the time. To avoid such pieces buy only from experienced specialist dealers with good reputations. If you want to see the best you must build up a relationship and keep in regular contact with them.

Recent downward trends in the stock market have created an atmosphere of unpredictability for investors. However, I think that they could do very well by investing in oak furniture which, providing they focus on the three most important criteria: condition, colour and patination, will stand them in good stead for the next 25 years. Early oak in good condition, with attractive colour and patination, is now rare and extremely desirable. Its track record speaks for itself. The *Antiques Trade Gazette* recently reported that the housing market had outstripped furniture as an investment for the first time in 35 years; if the market begins to cool, as is now predicted, this leaves oak and country furniture looking good once again as a secure long-term investment.

Do not dismiss a piece you like because it has been restored. Bear in mind that nowadays the quality of restoration, with the use of recycled timber and the availability of original handles, hinges, etc, has enabled us to return many pieces of oak furniture back to the market place after being skillfully and sympathetically restored.

Always buy a piece because you like it, and you will enjoy it every day of your life. This way you will definitely get your money's worth. Treat the investment as the perk at the end of the day.

Paul Hopwell

Beds, Cradles & Daybeds

An oak cradle, 17thC, 36in (91.5cm) long.
£400–475
€/ $630–750 L

An oak cradle, 19thC and earlier, 46in (117cm) long.
£800–900
€/ $1,250–1,450 SeH

An oak bedstead, with a panelled tester on moulded and scroll-carved rails, the baluster front supports ending in a geometric-moulded triple-panel footboard, with shaped oak side panels, restored, German, early 18thC, footboard 61in (155cm) wide.
£4,750–5,750
€/ $7,500–9,150 S(O)

An oak cradle, the bonnet-shaped top over a scalloped frieze, on a rocking platform, 1725–50, 24½in (62cm) long.
£225–280
€/ $350–450 NOA

A carved oak daybed, with slatted base, c1880, 42in (106.5cm) wide.
£450–500
€/ $700–800 PaA

◄ **An oak daybed,** carved with figures and mythical beasts, late 19thC, 48in (122cm) wide.
£1,800–2,000
€/ $2,850–3,200 SeH

An oak country bed, French, c1900, 54in (137cm) wide.
£800–900
€/ $1,250–1,400 ⊞ SeH

◄ **A carved chestnut bed,** with original carved side rails, Breton, c1900, 54in (137cm) wide.
£1,150–1,300
€/ $1,750–2,000 ⊞ SWA

► **A carved oak bedstead,** with upholstered panels, Continental, c1900, 60in (152.5cm) wide.
£5,500–6,000
€/ $8,750–9,500 ⊞ SeH

A country bedstead, French, c1900, 60in (152.5cm) wide.
£800–900
€/ $1,250–1,400 ⊞ SeH

Benches

17th-century oak benches, even if paired, seem to make only half the price of the equivalent joint stool because benches are not a convenient size for today's modern homes. They are difficult to sell, so any restoration will lower the price even further. A new top, for example, can reduce the value by 75 per cent, even for a pair. Continental benches are not as popular with the British market.

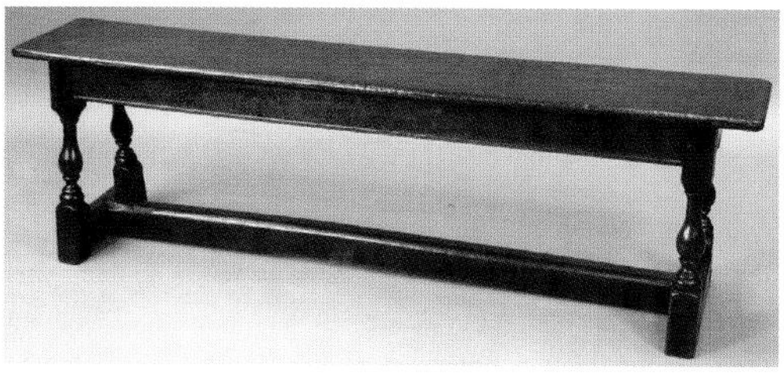

An oak bench, with a later top, 17thC, 66¼in (168.5cm) wide.
£650–775
€/ $1,000–1,200 SWO

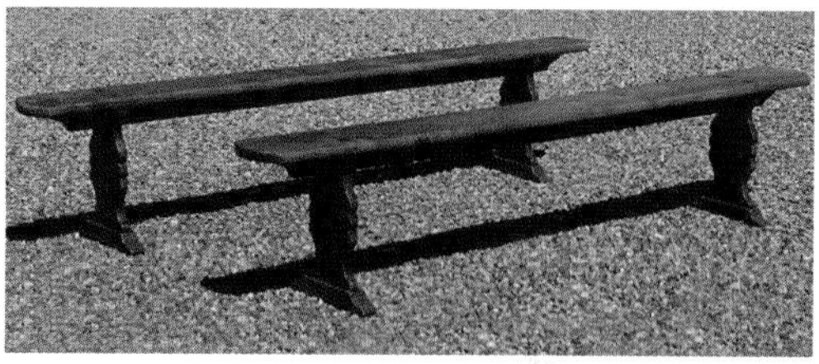

► **A pair of fruitwood benches,** French, c1840, 94in (239cm) wide.
£1,250–1,400
€/ $2,000–2,200 ⊞ DeG

Bookcases

A Regency oak bookcase, the moulded cornice over two Gothic arch astragal-glazed doors enclosing three adjustable shelves, the base with two panelled doors enclosing a single shelf, 50½in (128.5cm) wide.
£800–1,000
€/ $1,250–1,500 Bri

A Victorian Jacobean revival-style oak bookcase, the upper section with two arched shelf compartments flanked by fluted columns, the base with drawers and a cupboard, with all-over carving of human masks, scrolls and foliage, 59in (150cm) wide.
£900–1,100
€/ $1,400–1,700 JAd

A provincial Louis XV-style fruitwood bookcase, the two doors fitted with wire grilles, enclosing three shelves, French, 1850–75, 35½in (90cm) wide.
£830–1,000
€/ $1,300–1,600 NOA

An Edwardian oak bookcase, the moulded cornice above two astragal-glazed doors, the projecting base with two panelled doors, 39in (99cm) wide.
£550–650
€/ $870–1,000 DMC

Boxes

An oak writing box, with a single drawer, Low Countries, c1660, 16in (40.5cm) wide.
£700–775
€/ $1,100–1,200 ⊞ SEA

A carved oak Bible box, with fitted interior and secret drawer, c1680, 23in (58.5cm) wide.
£1,400–1,550
€/ $2,200–2,400 ⊞ TRI

An oak Bible box, with geometrical carving and outline, late 17thC, 21½in (54.5cm) wide.
£270–300
€/ $425–475 ⊞ CHAC

An oak Bible box, the front carved with a bearded mask and scrolling flowers and foliage, 17thC, 30¾in (78cm) wide.
£240–300
€/ $375–475 ⚒ L

An oak box, with iron banding, c1860, 70in (178cm) wide.
£180–200
€/ $285–315 ⊞ AL

◀ An oak candle box, with cross-banding, c1780, 21in (53.5cm) high.
£240–265
€/ $375–415 ⊞ PaA

Buffets

A provincial oak buffet, the top with canted corners and a moulded edge, above a central drawer over three cupboard doors with diamond-carved panels, on scrolling feet, Italian, 1775–1800, 62½in (159cm) wide.
£2,700–3,200
€/ $4,250–5,000 ⚒ NOA

A carved oak sideboard, with a central drawer over two doors, French, mid-18thC, 41¾in (106cm) wide.
£2,400–3,000
€/ $3,800–4,800 ⚒ BERN

A Victorian carved oak three-tier buffet, 45in (114.5cm) wide.
£380–425
€/ $600–670 ⊞ PaA

◀ A walnut *buffet à deux corps,* French, c1840, 59in (150cm) wide.
£3,200–3,500
€/ $5,000–5,500 ⊞ MHA

A walnut *buffet à deux corps,* with four doors, French, Burgundy, early 19thC, 56in (142cm) wide.
£2,700–3,000
€/ $4,250–5,000 ⊞ MLL

A painted buffet, on knurl feet, French, 19thC, 50½in (128.5cm) wide.
£600–720
€/ $1,000–1,150 ⚒ B(Ba)

Bureaux

A Queen Anne oak bureau, the fall-front enclosing a fitted interior with a well, above a frieze, with two short and two long drawers, on later bracket feet, maker's label 'John Gatehouse, Cabinet Maker, Nr. Holbourn Bridge, London', 30in (76cm) wide.
£1,700–2,200
€/ $2,700–3,500 CHTR
John Gatehouse's trade label states that he sold '... all Sorts of Cabinet Work, viz Chests of Drawers, Book-cases, Cabinets, Scrutores; All Sorts of Glasses, Pier-Glasses, Chimney Glasses and Sconces; Also all Sorts of Joiners-Work; as Oval-Tables, Cane-Chairs etc.' He is listed in a 1695 directory of inhabitants of the parish of St Andrew, Holbourn.

An ash bureau, mid-18thC, 34in (86.5cm) wide.
£675–750
€/ $1,000–1,200 HiA

An oak, holly and bog oak bureau, with chequerbanded decoration, the fall-front enclosing a fitted interior with pigeonholes, drawers, a slide-concealed well, pilaster drawers and secret compartments, with original brass mounts, probably Cheshire, 1760–80, 36in (91.5cm) wide.
£6,000–7,200
€/ $9,500–11,400 RYA

◄ **A George III provincial oak bureau,** restored, 39in (99cm) wide.
£550–625
€/ $870–990 B(Ba)

A George II oak bureau, the fall-front enclosing a stepped interior and a well, 32in (81.5cm) wide.
£650–750
€/ $1,000–1,200 L

Items in the Oak & Country section have been arranged in date order within each sub-section.

A George III oak bureau, the fall-front enclosing a fitted interior, over two short and three long drawers with later brass handles and escutcheons, on bracket feet, 37½in (95.5cm) wide.
£1,100–1,300
€/ $1,750–2,000 DN

Bureau Cabinets

A George III oak bureau cabinet, 33½in (85cm) wide.
£1,400–1,700
€/ $2,200–2,700 L

Look carefully when you are buying a bureau cabinet. The top section could have been reduced and even if it is all original, check that it is well-proportioned. It will be a poor investment if extensive restoration has to be carried out.

► **A late George III oak bureau cabinet,** with later brass handles and escutcheons, feet possibly later, 34½in (87.5cm) wide.
£600–720
€/ $1,000–1,150 DN

An oak bureau cabinet, c1780, 42in (106.5cm) wide.
£5,800–6,500
€/ $9,000–10,250 Che

A George II oak three drawer dresser base on baluster turned legs.
English c1730

A bold George I oak single drawer side table with barrel turned legs and moulded 'H' stretcher.
English c1725

A Charles II oak moulded chest of drawers.
English c1680

Chairs

An oak *caqueteuse* jointed armchair, with a wide seat and elbowed arms, Salisbury, 1580–1630.
£11,000–12,000
€/ $17,500–19,000 ⊞ KEY
A *caqueteuse* is a type of chair with a tall back and widely splayed arms capable of accommodating the full dresses of ladies in the late 16thC.

An oak wainscot armchair, the panelled back with a moulded inset top-rail surmounted by a central fan-shaped fluted crest, the open-scrolled arms on turned supports, the moulded seat above a moulded seat-rail, on turned legs, early 17thC.
£900–1,100
€/ $1,400–1,700 PF

An oak wainscot open armchair, the ebony-inlaid top-rail above a carved panel back, with a later seat, 17thC.
£700–820
€/ $1,100–1,300 AMB

A carved oak chair, South Yorkshire, c1650.
£2,250–2,500
€/ $3,500–4,000 ⊞ SEA

Wainscot chairs

Wainscot chairs have to be in good condition to reach their best price. Check the seat: if replaced the value will be reduced by half. Height is very important – low chairs reduce in value by approximately a third while those around 44in (112cm) high provide the best value. As a general rule 17th-century chairs are worth 30 per cent more than 18th-century examples.

An ash, elm and pine armchair, the cresting initialled 'IM', feet retipped, c1660.
£525–625
€/ $850–1,000 S(O)

An oak chair table, with a hinged plank table top, scroll-carved open arms, baluster ring-turned arm supports and front stretcher rail, with block-carved stretcher rails and legs, one arm damaged, 17thC.
£680–820
€/ $1,000–1,300 TMA

An elm dog-kennel dug-out armchair, with a pine seat and a painted surface, Cornwall, 1700–60.
£12,000–15,000
€/ $19,000–24,000 ⊞ RYA
This chair was hewn from a single tree trunk and fitted with a plank seat. The owner has been unable to trace another example which incorporates a dog kennel.

An oak country chair, with later restorations and a pine seat, 1675–1725.
£380–425
€/ $600–675 ⊞ CHAC

A black-painted maple armchair, with a rush seat, reduced in height, backrests repaired, American, New England, 1710–40.
£1,350–1,500
€/ $2,100–2,400 S(NY)

◀ An elm commode, with metal repairs, c1730.
£750–850
€/ $1,180–1,300 ⊞ TRI

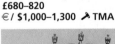

A yew wood armchair, with chequered frieze, on bobbin-turned legs, the cresting initialled and dated 'GB 1711'.
£4,200–5,000
€/ $6,600–7,900 S(O)

A painted pine and oak primitive boarded Windsor chair, c1740.
£4,000–5,000
€/ $6,350–7,900 ⊞ RYA

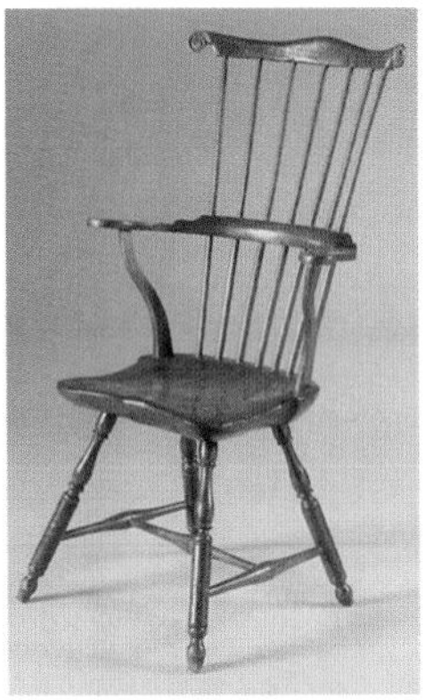

A fan-back Windsor armchair, both arm terminals repaired, American, Pennsylvania, late 18thC.
£2,500–2,750
€/ $4,000–4,300 ⚒ S(NY)

An oak lambing chair, the panelled winged back with arched top, the scrolled arms on baluster-turned supports, with a box seat and turned feet, 1775–1825.
£1,000–1,250
€/ $1,600–2,000 ⚒ AH

An oak country chair, with panelled back, with later alterations and restorations, mid-18thC.
£700–765
€/ $1,100–1,900 ⊞ CHAC

An elm elbow chair, c1790.
£580–650
€/ $900–1,000 ⊞ WELL

An ash rocking chair, with a shaped top-rail, the high back with turned wing supports and turned twin spindle rails, with a rush seat, on turned front legs, North Country, early 19thC.
£200–240
€/ $315–380 ⚒ TRM

Lambing chairs

Now is a good time to buy, as many lambing chairs are coming onto the market, perhaps due to the depressed state of farming. Tall chairs approximately 44in (112cm) high with large arms and big wings are the ones to look for. Chairs made in the 18th century make double their 19th-century equivalents.

A pair of Hepplewhite-style chairs, with rush seats, c1780.
£850–950
€/ $1,300–1,500 ⊞ SEA

A painted chair, French, Provence, 18thC.
£400–450
€/ $630–700 ⊞ SWN

An ash carver chair, with a ladder back, c1820.
£300–340
€/ $475–550 ⊞ SWN

A yew, elm and fruitwood Windsor chair, with a pierced splat and saddle seat, on cabriole front legs, 18thC.
£1,600–1,900
€/ $2,500–3,000 ⚒ G(L)

A pair of painted Gustavian-style chairs, Swedish, late 18thC.
£1,500–1,650
€/ $2,400–2,600 ⊞ CAV

◄ **An ash and elm tub chair,** East Anglian, early 19thC.
£300–360
€/ $475–575 ⚒ S(O)

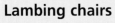

An elm and fruitwood Windsor elbow chair, the pierced vertical rails with central bosses, on a turned underframe, mid-19thC.
£260–320
€/ $400–500 ⚒ BR

An oak *sugán* chair, Irish, Co Clare, c1860.
£70–80
€/ $110–125 ⊞ Byl

A set of six Victorian Gothic-style oak chairs, with cane seats, repaired, c1880.
£325–360
€/ $515–575 ⊞ PaA

A set of six Old Hickory-style chairs, with spindle backs and oak slat seats, American, early 20thC.
£2,800–3,200
€/ $4,400–5,000 ⊞ NART

A mahogany and elm Darvel chair, by Hugh Sheilds, the turned stick back with a curved top-rail and hoop elm arms, the solid seat on turned legs, Scottish, 19thC.
£300–375
€/ $475–600 ⚒ B(Ed)

Hugh Sheilds was an inn keeper and wright in Newmilns, to the west of Darvel, Ayrshire. He trained with Darvel chair maker John McMath and developed his chair design, introducing elaborate stretchers for the early 19th century pattern. Darvel chairs by Hugh Sheilds usually have ten spindles (as opposed to 11 on earlier chairs) and are characteristically varnished with shellac, which gives them a distinguishing ginger colour. Like the early Darvel chairs, this example has spindles that were made using a rounding plane, not turned on a lathe. The peg housings were made using an auger, rather than a spoon bit, which accounts for the very thick seat slabs. Such a generous seat ensured that the leg sockets could be a good size without the risk of the lead screw piercing the surface of the seat. The use of mahogany for the seat is unusual; American birch seems to have been the standard timber employed for these chairs during the 19th century.

A set of six chestnut Breton chairs, each with a different carved scene on the back, c1900.
£1,200–1,300
€/ $1,900–2,000 ⊞ SWA

A set of four elm and ash primitive stick-back chairs, 19thC.
£1,100–1,200
€/ $1,750–1,900 ⊞ HiA

A set of four ash and elm dining chairs, Irish, c1875.
£270–300
€/ $425–475 ⊞ Byl

An oak, ash and sycamore stick-back chair, 1860–80.
£900–1,000
€/ $1,400–1,600 ⊞ SDA

An oak wood-turner's chair, 19thC.
£320–350
€/ $500–550 ⊞ APO

Children's Chairs

A child's ash primitive stick-back Windsor armchair, c1790.
£1,150–1,275
€/ $1,800–1,900 ⊞ F&F

A child's ash chair, with a later rush seat, c1825.
£450–500
€/ $700–800 ⚒ S(O)

A child's armchair, with remains of original paint, Welsh, 19thC.
£400–440
€/ $630–675 ⊞ MFB

A child's birchwood armchair, with a rush seat, French, c1850.
£270–300
€/ $425–475 ⊞ F&F

A child's mahogany rocking commode chair, with hinged seat, 19thC.
£720–820
€/ $1,100–1,300 ⚒ AH

A child's ash and elm training rocking chair, 1860–80.
£350–400
€/ $550–630 ⊞ SDA

A child's oak chair, North Country, c1880.
£100–120
€/ $160–190 ⊞ WiB

A child's ash and beech chair, c1900.
£120–135
€/ $190–215 ⊞ SDA

Chests & Coffers

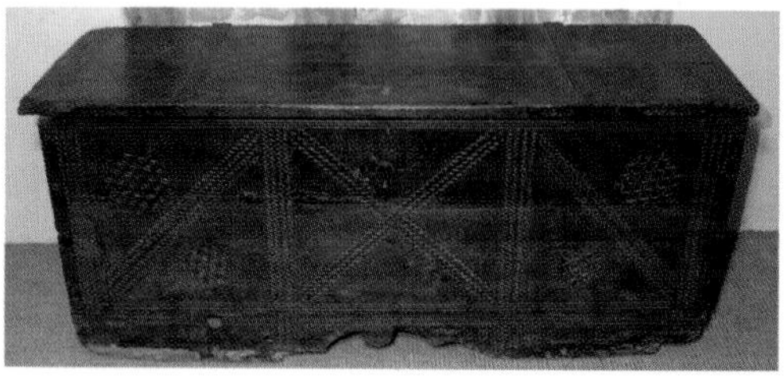

A walnut chip-carved coffer, with original paintwork, 1450–1500, 63in (160cm) wide.
£4,000–4,500
€/ $6,300–7,200 ⊞ NMA

An oak chest, the hinged panelled lid enclosing a plain interior, the front with four linenfold panels and decorated lock plate, on block feet, key missing, French, 16th–17thC, 63in (160cm) wide.
£1,200–1,400
€/ $1,900–2,200 ⚒ S(Am)

A panelled oak mule chest, with a carved frieze and two drawers with brass handles, c1615, 43¼in (110cm) wide.
£750–875
€/ $1,200–1,400 ⚒ GTH

A storage box, with primitive decoration, early 17thC, 33in (84cm) wide.
£135–150
€/ $215–235 ⊞ CHAC

A dower/mule chest, West Country, c1640, 48in (122cm) wide.
£2,500–3,000
€/ $4,000–4,750 ⊞ REF

An oak chest, the triple-panelled hinged cover containing a candle box, the front carved with *guilloche* and arched ornament between panelled foliage, on square legs with block feet, cover initialled 'WL' and dated 1676, 48½in (123cm) wide.
£1,500–1,800
€/ $2,350–2,850 ⚒ WL

A carved oak coffer, the front with three architectural arched panels, with a carved frame and stiles, 17thC, 54¼in (138cm) wide.
£2,000–2,500
€/ $3,200–4,000 ⚒ SWO

An oak coffer, the hinged top with three panels above a front with a flute-moulded top-rail and two panels, iron lock, late 17thC, 48in (122cm) wide.
£900–1,100
€/ $1,400–1,700 ⚒ PF

An oak mule chest, the wire-hinged cover over a carved front with three panels over two drawers, early 18thC, 50½in (128.5cm) wide.
£1,200–1,400
€/ $1,900–2,200 ⚒ TMA

An oak coffer, the two-piece top with a moulded edge and original iron strap hinges, on a two-piece plain front and panelled sides, one end stile replaced, 17thC, 48½in (123cm) wide.
£350–425
€/ $550–670 ⚒ PFK

An oak coffer, the domed plank lid with iron strap hinges, the panelled fascia with a lock plate, with panelled sides and moulded stiles, Continental, 17thC, 48in (122cm) wide.
£320–375
€/ $500–590 ⚒ AH

An oak-planked coffer, late 17thC, 34in (86.5cm) wide.
£720–800
€/ $1,150–1,250 ⊞ HiA

A carved cedarwood chest, carved 'ANO HOS 1710 KEG', lid now locked, Alpine, 1710, 20½in (52cm) wide.
£850–1,000
€/ $1,350–1,580 ⚒ S(O)

An oak coffer, with a plank top, 17thC, 52in (132cm) wide.
£450–525
€/ $710–830 ⚒ L

An elm chest, 17thC, 64½in (164cm) wide.
£500–550
€/ $800–870 ⚒ S(O)

An oak coffer, with carved decoration, late 17thC, 56in (142cm) wide.
£1,500–1,650
€/ $2,300–2,600 ⊞ KEY

An oak coffer, with plank sides, late 17thC, 39½in (100.5cm) wide.
£220–250
€/ $350–400 ⚒ HOLL

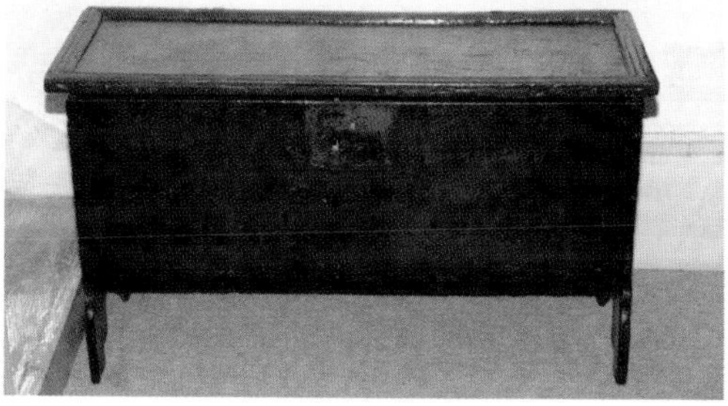

◄ **An oak coffer,** c1720, 41in (104cm) wide.
£850–950
€/ $1,350–1,500
⊞ TDS

An oak coffer-on-stand, with four drawers, c1740, 36¾in (93.5cm) wide.
£800–1,000
€/ $1,250–1,600 ⚒ S(O)

A Georgian fruitwood coffer, with domed lid, original handles and lock, 33in (84cm) wide.
£1,150–1,300
€/ $1,800–2,000 ⊞ APO

A carved and panelled oak coffer, 18thC, 45in (114.5cm) wide.
£500–550
€/ $800–870 ⊞ HiA

An oak coffer, the three-quarter hinged top above a plain front with a brass keyplate, on a shaped plinth, Welsh, late 18thC, 26in (66cm) wide.
£375–450
€/ $590–710 ⚒ PF

An elm dowry chest, Irish, c1865, 48in (122cm) wide.
£550–600
€/ $870–950 ⊞ Byl

A George III oak and mahogany-banded mule chest, the lift-up top above four fielded panels, with two drawers below with brass escutcheons and swing handles, on shaped bracket feet, 54¼in (138cm) wide.
£350–425
€/ $550–670 ⚒ M

An elm coffer, 18thC and later, 39½in (100.5cm) wide.
£160–200
€/ $250–300 ⚒ B(Ba)

A painted walnut chest, the front with three fielded panels, c1830, 46in (117cm) wide.
£800–900
€/ $1,250–1,450 ⊞ DMe

An oak and iron-bound chest, c1870, 38in (96.5cm) wide.
£350–400
€/ $550–630 ⊞ GBr

An oak coffer, 18thC, 44in (112cm) wide.
£700–800
€/ $1,100–1,250 ⊞ MHA

An oak coffer, the front with three carved panels, on bracket feet, repaired, late 18thC, 48in (122cm) wide.
£280–320
€/ $440–500 ⊞ PaA

A leather and brass-studded marriage chest, probably Flemish or Dutch, c1830, 40in (101.5cm) wide.
£1,200–1,400
€/ $1,900–2,200 ⊞ REF

A painted elm mule chest, with dummy drawers above a single long drawer, Irish, Co Kilkenny, c1870, 44in (112cm) wide.
£1,100–1,200
€/ $1,750–1,900 ⊞ DMe

◄ **A late Victorian carved oak coffer,** the front with three panels, 42in (106.5cm) wide.
£200–225
€/ $300–350
⊞ PaA

An elm six-plank coffer, 19thC, 46½in (118cm) wide.
£230–275
€/ $360–430 ⚒ SWO

(*above*) Oak refectory table, fine colour, c1640

We are the vendors of early English country furniture from the 16th to early 19th century specializing in refectory dining tables. Also sets of chairs, coffers, Windsor chairs, dressers, chests of drawers, court cupboards, lowboys always in stock.

(*left*) Oak and walnut chest of drawers, c1680

(*right*) West Country box seat, c1650

(*left*) Rare confessional box, c1450

(*below*) West Country dresser, oak and cherry, c1790

(*below*) Box seat settle, dated 1756

The Refectory

38 WEST STREET · DORKING · SURREY RH4 1BU

Tel/Fax: 01 306 742111

www.therefectory.co.uk

Chests of Drawers

An oak chest of drawers, with four moulded drawers, on bracket feet, early 17thC and later, 37in (94cm) wide.
£400–500
€/ $630–790 GAK

An oak chest of drawers, on later bracket feet, late 17thC, 37¾in (96cm) wide.
£850–1,000
€/ $1,350–1,600 S(O)

An oak geometrically moulded chest of drawers, with two short and three long graduated drawers, with split-baluster pilaster spindles, with later top and panelled ends, late 17thC, 41¼in (105cm) wide.
£950–1,100
€/ $1,500–1,700 B(NW)

LOCATE THE SOURCE

The source of each illustration in Miller's can be found by checking the code letters below each caption with the Key to Illustrations, pages 794–800.

An oak chest of drawers, with four long drawers, raised on later elm bun feet, 17thC, 37½in (95.5cm) wide.
£1,300–1,500
€/ $2,000–2,400 AMB

A panelled oak chest of drawers, the upper section with two short and two deep inlaid drawers flanking a conforming door, the lower section with two geometrically panelled long drawers, on later bun feet, alterations, late 17thC, 44in (112cm) wide.
£1,000–1,100
€/ $1,600–1,700 Bea

A carved and painted chest of three drawers, probably walnut, Italian, Piedmonte, c1740, 43in (109cm) wide.
£20,000–22,000
€/ $32,500–35,000 RYA
This piece retains its original paint and metalwork and is of extremely good proportions.

► **A George III oak chest of drawers,** on ogee bracket feet, originally surmounted by a screw-press, 33in (84cm) wide.
£550–650
€/ $870–1,000 L

An oak chest of drawers, with panelled sides, the four drawers with panelled fronts, on later bracket feet, 17thC, 41in (104cm) wide.
£650–750
€/ $1,000–1,200 E

An oak chest of drawers, the moulded top above four geometrically moulded drawers, with panelled ends, on stile feet, drawer linings replaced, late 17thC, 29½in (75cm) wide.
£950–1,100
€/ $1,500–1,700 HAM

A panelled oak and pine chest of drawers, restored, American, Massachusetts, c1700, 37½in (95.5cm) wide.
£2,200–2,500
€/ $3,500–4,000 S(NY)

A George III oak and mahogany crossbanded chest of drawers, with two short and three long drawers flanked by reeded pilasters, on bracket feet, formerly the top part of a chest-on-chest, 43¾in (111cm) wide.
£470–570
€/ $750–900 DN

An oak chest of drawers, with two short and three long geometrically moulded drawers, with panelled sides, on block feet, 18thC, 36¼in (92cm) wide.
£475–575
€/ $750–900 B(W)

An oak bowfronted corner chest of drawers, the moulded top above two short and two long drawers, Dutch, 18thC, 29¼in (74.5cm) wide.
£5,000–6,000
€/ $7,900–9,500 S(O)

◄ **A Chippendale-style figured cherrywood chest of drawers,** with original cast-brass handles, restorations to base, American, probably Connecticut, c1780, 38¼in (97cm) wide.
£1,250–1,500
€/ $1,900–2,400 S(NY)

A provincial oak chest of drawers, in two sections, restored, 18thC, 43¾in (111cm) wide.
£280–340
€/ $440–540 B(Ch)

A pair of inlaid oak commodes, Continental, c1800, 53in (134.5cm) wide.
£7,500–8,500
€/ $11,750–13,500 APO

OAK & COUNTRY FURNITURE

A late George III provincial oak chest of drawers, with mahogany crossbanding, restorations and alterations, 43in (109cm) wide.
£320–375
€/ $500–590 B(Ba)

◄ An oak chest of drawers, on ogee bracket feet, c1800, 47in (119.5cm) wide.
£550–600
€/ $850–950 ⊞ PaA

► A Victorian pollarded oak chest, the rounded top above a panelled frieze drawer, over two short and three long drawers, on bun feet, 44in (112cm) wide.
£550–625
€/ $870–990 BR

An elm dowry chest-on-stand, the upper section with six dummy drawers, the lower section with two short drawers over one long drawer, with brass plaque inscribed 'Margaret Coonan', Irish, Co. Kilkenny, c1840, 49in (124.5cm) wide.
£800–900
€/ $1,250–1,400 ⊞ HON

Chests-on-Chests

A mid-Georgian oak chest-on-chest, on bracket feet, with later wooden knob handles, lower section possibly shortened, 40¼in (102cm) wide.
£650–750
€/ $1,000–1,200 PFK

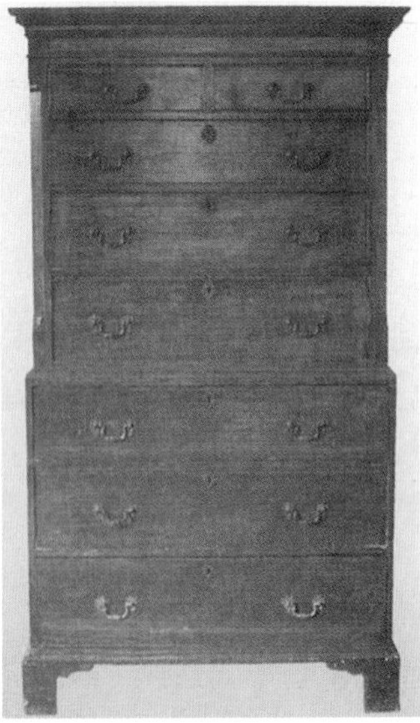

◄ A George III oak chest-on-chest, the upper section with a moulded Greek key cornice, above two short and three long graduated cock-beaded drawers, flanked by canted corners, the base with three long graduated cock-beaded drawers, all with brass drop handles with foliate backplates, on bracket feet, 42in (106.5cm) wide.
£1,100–1,400
€/ $1,750–2,200
Mit

A George III provincial oak and mahogany chest-on-chest, restored, 45in (114.5cm) wide.
£2,000–2,250
€/ $3,150–3,500 B(Ba)

Items in the Oak & Country section have been arranged in date order within each sub-section.

Chests-on-Stands

An oak chest-on-stand, with two short and two long drawers, on a later stand, 17thC, 37½in (95.5cm) wide.
£700–820
€/ $1,100–1,300 B(W)

► A William and Mary oak chest-on-stand, alterations and restorations, 37¾in (96cm) wide.
£780–875
€/ $1,200–1,400
B(Ba)

An oak chest-on-stand, the two short and three long drawers with brass drop handles, the stand with turned legs, late 17thC, 38in (96.5cm) wide.
£2,000–2,250
€/ $3,150–3,500 JNic

A George I oak chest-on-stand, with two short and five long drawers, on later pad feet, 41¼in (105cm) wide.
£1,800–2,150
€/ $2,850–3,400 SWO

An oak and walnut-cross-banded chest-on-stand, c1740, 40¼in (102cm) wide.
£2,200–2,500
€/ $3,500–4,000 S(O)

A George III oak chest-on-stand, with two short and four long drawers, the later stand with a shaped apron, on cabriole legs, 37½in (95.5cm) wide.
£900–1,100
€/ $1,400–1,750 L

A provincial oak chest-on-stand, on later feet, restorations, alterations, 18thC, 39½in (100.5cm) wide.
£600–700
€/ $950–1,100 B(Ba)

► **A Georgian oak chest-on-stand,** the top with a plain cornice and fluted chamfered corners, above two short and three long drawers, the base with three frieze drawers, on cabriole legs, 37¾in (96cm) wide.
£1,300–1,500
€/ $2,000–2,400 B&L

► **A Carolean-style oak chest-on-stand,** with geometric mitred drawer fronts, the upper section with two deep drawers, above a projecting base with a single drawer, on stile feet, c1900, 32in (81.5cm) wide.
£350–400
€/ $550–630 BR

OAK & COUNTRY FURNITURE

Clothes & Linen Presses

A George III oak linen press, the moulded cornice with plain mahogany frieze, above two arch-panelled press doors, over two short and two long drawers, with a serpentine apron and bracket feet, 54in (137cm) wide.
£900–1,100
€/ $1,400–1,700 B(W)

A George III oak linen chest-on-stand, with brass carrying handles, 44½in (113cm) wide.
£850–1,000
€/ $1,350–1,600 B(Ba)

A George III oak linen press, 49in (124.5cm) wide.
£1,800–2,000
€/ $2,800–3,200 APO

A George III oak linen press, with later interior shelf, 54½in (138.5cm) wide.
£1,200–1,400
€/ $1,900–2,200 L

► **An early Victorian oak linen press,** the applied reeded-edge top above slides and a cupboard enclosed by three doors with outline panels and reeded stiles, the base with two drawers, on turned feet, 68½in (174cm) wide.
£650–750
€/ $1,000–1,200 WW

A Gothic revival oak linen press, late 19thC, 47in (119.5cm) wide.
£2,000–2,300
€/ $3,200–3,650 WAW

Cupboards

A Charles II oak cupboard, adapted from a larger piece, 35½in (90cm) wide.
£1,100–1,250
€/ $1,700–2,000 ⚒ S(O)

An oak food cupboard, with wainscot-panelled door, c1690, 36in (91.5cm) wide.
£5,000–6,000
€/ $8,000–9,500 ⊞ PHA

An oak mural livery cupboard, with yew spindles, mid-17thC, 41in (104cm) wide.
£4,700–5,200
€/ $7,500–8,200 ⊞ KEY

An oak livery cupboard, the moulded-edge plank top above a lunette-carved frieze, and panelled fascia with a central door, on turned and block supports, 17thC, 38½in (98cm) wide.
£1,300–1,500
€/ $2,000–2,400 ⚒ AH

An oak cupboard, with pierced sides, 17thC, 51¾in (131.5cm) wide.
£1,500–1,800
€/ $2,400–2,850 ⚒ L

◀ **An oak cupboard,** the top above a plain frieze and panelled door, enclosing shelves, flanked by ribbed pilasters, on sledge feet, restorations, Dutch, 17thC and later, 31in (78.5cm) wide.
£450–550
€/ $700–870 ⚒ S(Am)

An oak press cupboard, the carved frieze with turned pendants, above two carved cupboard doors flanking a panel, with flowerhead-centred *guilloche*-carved stiles, and foliate-carved end stiles, the lower section with a moulded top above a foliate and pokerwork frieze, with two panelled doors, the moulded end stiles extending as legs, boarded top replaced, later shelf, 17thC and later, 61in (155cm) wide.
£1,600–2,000
€/ $2,500–3,200 ⚒ PFK

An oak cabinet-on-stand, with the date 1703 carved on the doors, c1703, 42½in (108cm) wide.
£2,200–2,375
€/ $3,500–3,700 ⊞ CHAC

A carved oak cupboard, Flemish, 17thC, 58in (147.5cm) wide.
£7,000–8,000
€/ $11,000–12,500 ⊞ APO

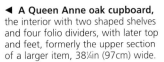

◀ **A Queen Anne oak cupboard,** the interior with two shaped shelves and four folio dividers, with later top and feet, formerly the upper section of a larger item, 38¼in (97cm) wide.
£600–720
€/ $950–1,150 ⚒ S(O)

An elm wall-hanging corner cupboard, c1720, 33in (84cm) wide.
£1,500–1,800
€/ $2,400–2,800 ⊞ RYA

LOCATE THE SOURCE
The source of each illustration in Miller's can be found by checking the code letters below each caption with the Key to Illustrations, pages 794–800.

► **An oak cupboard,** the moulded cornice above two raised and fielded panel doors, the slightly projecting base with three raised and fielded panels, on stile supports, early 18thC, 51¼in (130cm) wide.
£600–700
€/ $950–1,100 ⚒ DD

An oak corner cupboard, the panelled door enclosing shelves, early 18thC, 30in (76cm) wide.
£280–320
€/ $440–500 ⚒ DN

► **A carved elm armoire,** French, c1750, 86in (218.5cm) high.
£4,500–5,000
€/ $7,000–8,000
⊞ TDS

A yew wood and cherrywood armoire, French, c1760, 91in (231cm) high.
£3,500–4,000
€/ $5,500–6,300 ⊞ TDS

An oak press cupboard, the top section with Gothic-shaped fielded panels, over a base with three drawers, Welsh, Meirionnydd, c1760, 42in (106.5cm) wide.
£5,000–6,000
€/ $8,000–9,500 ⊞ CoA

An oak wall cupboard, with a single three-panel door, Welsh, 1760–80, 27in (68.5cm) wide.
£1,750–2,000
€/ $2,700–3,200 ⊞ KEY

An oak hanging corner cabinet, with a moulded shaped door, 1770, 26in (66cm) wide.
£315–350
€/ $480–550 ⊞ PaA

A mid-Georgian oak hanging cupboard, with a drawer to the base, 24in (61cm) wide.
£500–600
€/ $800–950 ⚒ L

◄ **An oak and pine bread and cheese cupboard,** with three internal shelves and two drawers, the upper double doors with spindle ventilation, Welsh, Anglesey, c1780, 73½in (186.5cm) high.
£5,300–6,000
€/ $8,300–9,500 ⊞ MFB

A painted chestnut armoire, c1780, 49½in (125.5cm) wide.
£1,300–1,450
€/ $2,000–2,300 ⊞ SIE

An oak livery cupboard, c1790, 51in (129.5cm) wide.
£2,250–2,500
€/ $3,500–4,000 ⊞ NoC

An oak housekeeper's cupboard, c1790, 56in (142cm) wide.
£2,800–3,250
€/ $4,400–5,000 ⊞ WELL

A George III oak and mahogany crossbanded corner cupboard, the doors with moulded panels, with inlaid ivory lock escutcheons and reeded sides, 41in (104cm) high.
£400–500
€/ $650–790 ⚒ HOLL

A cherrywood armoire, with brass hinges and lock, French, 18thC, 52in (132cm) wide.
£1,500–1,700
€/ $2,400–2,700 ⊞ DUK

A provincial chestnut cabinet, the moulded cornice enclosed by a fielded panel door with a drawer below, on turned legs, with gallery base and slat foot, French, 18thC, 24½in (62cm) wide.
£250–300
€/ $400–475 ⚒ TRM

◄ **An oak and mahogany corner cupboard,** c1790, 31in (78.5cm) wide.
£1,000–1,125
€/ $1,600–1,800 ⊞ MHA

A George III oak cupboard, the upper section with crossbanded doors, 54in (137cm) wide.
£800–950
€/ $1,250–1,500 ⚒ L

◄ **An oak press cupboard,** the two doors over three short and two long drawers, late 18thC, 51in (129.5cm) wide.
£1,000–1,100
€/ $1,600–1,750 ⊞ WAW

◄ **A George III oak corner cupboard,** the bowfront enclosed by solid doors with mahogany crossbanding, with a shaped apron, 26¼in (66.5cm) wide.
£300–350
€/ $475–550 ⚒ L

A fruitwood armoire, the door panels carved with birds, French, c1800, 51in (129.5cm) wide.
£5,500–6,200
€/ $8,500–9,800 ⊞ HA

A George IV oak and mahogany-crossbanded cabinet-on-chest, the stepped cornice and inlaid frieze above two panelled cupboard doors enclosing three shelves, the lower section with two short and three long graduated cockbeaded drawers with ivory lozenge escutcheons, on a shaped apron and short splayed feet, probably Welsh, 48in (122cm) wide.
£1,200–1,400
€/ $1,900–2,200 ⚒ WL

A fruitwood cupboard, with solid panel doors, French, 19thC, 44in (112cm) wide.
£300–350
€/ $475–550 ⚒ B(Ba)

A neo-classical oak cabinet, the arched pediment carved with an urn and foliage above a plain frieze and two panelled doors flanked by columns, the lower section with three long drawers flanked by fluted pilasters, on square fluted tapering feet, Dutch, c1800, 67in (170cm) wide.
£1,500–1,800
€/ $2,400–2,800 ⚒ S(Am)

A chestnut armoire, French, c1830, 57in (145cm) wide.
£1,450–1,600
€/ $2,250–2,500 ⊞ GD

A Gothic-style oak side cabinet, with brass strapwork mounts and *guilloche* and roundel embossed panels, c1875, 40in (101.5cm) wide.
£1,800–2,000
€/ $2,800–3,200 ⊞ NAW

An oak cupboard, with blind and fielded panels, the base with a fall-front and two secret drawers, Welsh, c1800, 40in (101.5cm) wide.
£7,000–8,000
€/ $11,000–12,500 ⊞ PHA

A Louis XV provincial fruitwood armoire, the moulded cornice above two doors, with shaped panels, a scalloped apron below, on scrolled toes, French, 1800–25, 74½in (189cm) wide.
£2,300–2,750
€/ $3,600–4,300 ⚒ NOA

A carved oak hall cupboard, the top with a carved boar's head, German, 19thC, 99in (251.5cm) high.
£1,100–1,200
€/ $1,750–1,900 ⊞ HiA

▶ A carved chestnut food cupboard, Breton, c1900, 39in (99cm) wide.
£1,100–1,200
€/ $1,750–1,900 ⊞ SWA

An oak and pine panelled food cupboard, with a moulded cornice, the two doors with pierced central panels, with two drawers and two doors below, on bracket feet, early 19thC, 42½in (108cm) wide.
£1,600–2,000
€/ $2,500–3,200 ⚒ Bea(E)

An oak double corner cupboard, the moulded cornice above a glazed door enclosing shelves, the lower section with two arched panelled doors, with canted angles, on a shaped plinth, Welsh, mid-19thC, 37in (94cm) wide.
£900–1,100
€/ $1,400–1,700 ⚒ PF

Spice Cupboards

An oak spice cupboard, 17thC, 15in (38cm) wide.
£1,350–1,500
€/ $2,100–2,400 ⊞ SEA

An inlaid oak spice cupboard, the five short drawers with ring handles, c1700, 14½in (36.5cm) wide.
£320–375
€/ $500–590 TEN

An oak wall-hanging spice cupboard, the fielded panel door enclosing a fitted interior, the drawers with paper spice labels and later handles, c1780, 22in (56cm) wide.
£1,000–1,200
€/ $1,600–1,900 S(O)

Spices and herbs were used extensively from the Middle Ages to either add flavour to unexciting food or disguise tainted meat and game.

Desks

An oak writing desk, the fall-front enclosing an interior with a lidded well and open compartments, on turned fluted legs, c1720, 28¼in (72cm) wide.
£1,500–1,800
€/ $2,400–2,800 S(O)

Further reading

Miller's Pine & Country Furniture Buyer's Guide, Miller's Publications, 1995

A Victorian carved oak kneehole desk, on bobbin-turned legs, 31in (78.5cm) wide.
£350–400
€/ $550–650 ⊞ PaA

A Victorian oak writing desk, by John Taylor & Son, Edinburgh, the leather-inset top fitted with a leather-inset slide, with one central drawer and four short drawers, on reeded legs with casters, one drawer stamped, Scottish, 48in (122cm) wide.
£1,000–1,250
€/ $1,600–2,000 B(W)

► **A Victorian carved oak pedestal desk,** with three frieze drawers and six pedestal drawers, 48in (122cm) wide.
£300–350
€/ $475–550 SWO

Dough Bins

An elm dough bin, with a hinged plank lid, on baluster-turned and block legs and turned feet, 18thC, 36½in (92.5cm) wide.
£475–575
€/ $750–910 AH

An elm dough bin, on turned legs, 18thC, 24in (61cm) wide.
£550–600
€/ $870–950 ⊞ SWN

A provincial fruitwood dough table, the removable planked top revealing a dough bin, on square legs, now altered to coffee table height, French, mid-19thC, 48in (122cm) wide.
£700–800
€/ $1,100–1,300 NOA

Dressers

A George II oak dresser, Welsh, 55½in (141cm) wide.
£4,250–5,000
€/ $6,700–7,900 S(O)

An early George III oak dresser, with a boarded rack and three frieze drawers, on low ogee bracket feet, Welsh, 73½in (186.5cm) wide.
£9,500–11,500
€/ $15,000–18,000 B(SW)

An oak pot board dresser, Welsh, Cardiganshire, c1760, 74in (188cm) wide.
£7,000–7,800
€/ $11,000–12,500 ⊞ CoA

◄ **An oak dresser,** with original brass handles, Welsh, 1760–80, 63in (160cm) wide.
£8,750–9,750
€/ $14,000–15,500 ⊞ NMA

► **A George III oak dresser,** with mahogany banding and brass drop handles, 62in (157.5cm) wide.
£2,300–2,800
€/ $3,650–4,500 AH

An oak pot board dresser, Welsh, Carmarthenshire, c1780, 72in (183cm) wide.
£8,500–9,500
€/ $13,500–15,000 ⊞ CoA

An oak dresser, with stained-pine back boards and baseboard, Welsh, c1780, 63¾in (162cm) wide.
£2,200–2,500
€/ $3,500–4,000 S(O)

An oak dresser, with a boarded rack, on square legs with a pot board base, 18thC, 53in (134.5cm) wide.
£4,000–4,750
€/ $6,300–7,500 BWL

A George III oak dresser, with associated superstructure, 64½in (164cm) wide.
£2,000–2,500
€/ $3,200–4,000 B(Ba)

An oak dresser, the boarded rack with three shelves, above a base with three frieze drawers and three ogee arched panelled cupboards, on stile legs, rack associated, Welsh, 18thC, 58¾in (149cm) wide.
£2,000–2,500
€/ $3,200–4,000 ⚒ B(SW)

A cherrywood dresser, the open delft rack with an ogee-moulded cornice and three shelves, with shaped sides, above a base with three short drawers flanked by two flush-panelled cupboards revealing a shelf, on a plinth base, late 18thC, 76in (193cm) wide.
£4,750–5,750
€/ $7,500–9,100 ⚒ HAM

An oak dresser, the canopied structure with three shelves, the base with three cockbeaded frieze drawers, above three graduated cockbeaded central dummy drawers, flanked by two doors with turned wooden knob handles and inlaid bone keyplates, on bracket feet, Welsh, mid-19thC, 62in (157.5cm) wide.
£3,000–3,600
€/ $4,750–5,750 ⚒ PF

An oak dresser, the boarded rack with a moulded cornice and plain frieze above two shelves, the lower section with three moulded drawers above two twin-fielded panelled cupboard doors, centred by a fielded panel, on extended stile supports, Denbighshire, 18thC, 60½in (153.5cm) wide.
£2,500–3,000
€/ $4,000–4,750 ⚒ B(NW)

A fruitwood dresser, the boarded rack with a moulded cornice above four shelves, the base with three frieze drawers above two cupboards, each enclosed by a panelled door, spaced by a central panel, on shaped bracket feet, early 19thC, 75¼in (191cm) wide.
£4,000–4,800
€/ $6,300–7,500 ⚒ B(NW)

A pear, apple and walnut dresser, French, Burgundy, 19thC, 56in (142cm) wide.
£1,500–1,700
€/ $2,400–2,700 ⊞ MLL

An oak dresser, the delft rack with two shelves, with moulded cornice and shaped side supports, the base with ebonized cockbeading and escutcheons, the three drawers with brass drop handles, on square tapering legs, rack associated, 18thC, 59in (150cm) wide.
£1,400–1,700
€/ $2,200–2,700 ⚒ JM

An oak dresser, the upper section with central open shelves, flanked by a glazed cupboard and a drawer on each side, the base with three drawers and two panelled doors, flanking a central 'kennel', on turned feet with turned column sides, 19thC, 62in (157.5cm) wide.
£700–840
€/ $1,100–1,300 ⚒ E

An oak dresser, with original brass fittings, late 19thC, 60in (152.5cm) wide.
£1,250–1,400
€/ $2,000–2,200 ⊞ SWA

Low Dressers

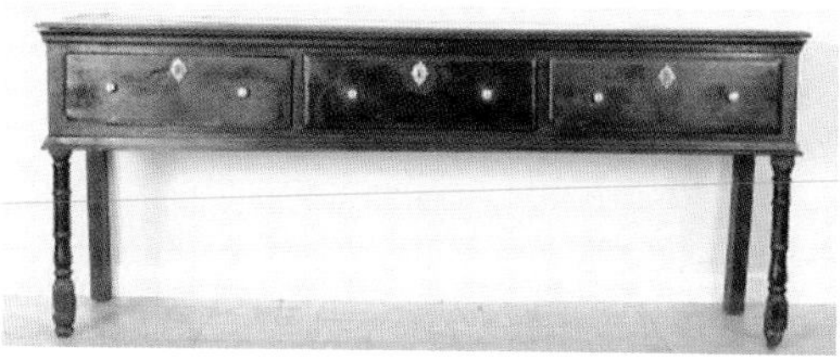

An oak dresser base, with three frieze drawers, c1700, 75in (190.5cm) wide.
£1,700–2,000
€/ $2,700–3,150 BWL

A Queen Anne and later oak low dresser, with three frieze drawers, 77¼in (196cm) wide.
£1,300–1,600
€/ $2,000–2,500 CGC

► **An oak low dresser,** the frieze with three moulded drawers, above a cupboard flanked by two drawers, with iron drop handles, early 18thC and later, 68in (172.5cm) wide.
£2,400–3,000
€/ $3,800–4,800 AH

An oak low dresser, the two drawers with replacement brass handles, early 18thC, 54in (137cm) wide.
£2,200–2,500
€/ $3,500–4,000 JNiC

◄ **An oak low dresser,** the three central drawers flanked by two side cupboards, early 18thC, 71½in (181.5cm) wide.
£1,000–1,200
€/ $1,600–1,900
TMA

An oak low dresser, with original handles, Lancashire, c1760, 70in (178cm) wide.
£11,250–12,250
€/ $17,500–19,500 ⊞ NMA
This completely original piece has cushion-moulded drawers and is a superb colour.

► **A mid-Georgian elm dresser base,** the three frieze drawers with swan-neck handles, above a shaped apron, 67¾in (172cm) wide.
£1,600–1,900
€/ $2,500–3,000
Bri

◄ **A George III oak dresser base,** with 17thC components, doors reversed, restored, 75¼in (191cm) wide.
£1,400–1,700
€/ $2,200–2,700
S(O)

An oak dresser base, the two drawers with original brass handles, c1780, 59in (150cm) wide.
£8,000–9,000
€/ $12,500–14,000 ⊞ REI

Expert's choice

A farmer turned up at our workshop in the 1970s with two of the smallest Charles II geometrically-moulded oak dresser bases with turned baluster legs that I have ever seen. One was turned upside down and screwed to the other. The legs of the top one and all of the drawers had been removed. The drawer cavities were covered with chicken mesh as the piece was being used as bantam nest boxes – the drawers were being used to set potatoes.

We bought the pair for £225 (€/ $350), fitted the legs back, removed the chicken wire and droppings and fully restored them. The drawers still had their original brass furniture, and the wood had excellent colour and patina. We sold them for approximately £1,000 (€/ $1,600) each. Today those dressers would make a minimum of £18,000 (€/ $28,000).

Paul Hopwell

A George III oak low dresser, with three long and two short drawers over two central drawers flanked by panelled cupboard doors, with brass drop handles, 70in (178cm) wide.
£1,800–2,200
€/ $2,800–3,500 AH

An oak dresser base, altered and restored, 18thC, 58¾in (149cm) wide.
£550–625
€/ $870–1,000 B(Ba)

An oak low dresser, with three drawers over two cupboard doors and two further drawers, reduced in height, feet lacking, 18thC, 75½in (192cm) wide.
£3,000–3,500
€/ $4,750–5,500 TEN

An oak and mahogany-banded low dresser, with three frieze drawers above a cupboard flanked by two pairs of drawers, with brass swan-neck handles, 1775–1825, 77½in (197cm) wide.
£4,200–5,000
€/ $6,600–8,000 WW

An oak dresser base, with original handles and metalwork, French, c1800, 82in (208.5cm) wide.
£3,400–3,800
€/ $5,400–6,000 PICA

◄ **A late George III oak dresser base,** with three drawers over a central open section with pot board, flanked by two pairs of panelled doors, later alteration and additions, 36¼in (92cm) wide.
£2,200–2,800
€/ $3,500–4,400 BIG

Many dresser bases, potboards and cupboards started life with racks which are now missing. As a general rule only buy pieces whose proportions still seem right without a rack and which have a bold top with good moulding. Many original dresser cornices were removed and then replaced at a later date. If this is the case check that the colour and patina are a good match. Such marriages reduce the value by half.

◄ **An oak side cabinet,** the two doors and ends with Gothic tracery carving, late 19thC, 35½in (90cm) wide.
£150–180
€/ $240–280
SWO

Lowboys

A Georgian oak lowboy, the three cockbeaded drawers with swan-neck handles, on pad feet, 30in (76cm) wide.
£550–700
€/ $870–1,100 HoG

A Georgian oak lowboy, the centre drawer replaced, 29in (73.5cm) wide.
£780–875
€/ $1,200–1,400 RPh

An oak lowboy, the banded top above three drawers with brass handles, a shaped frieze below, the cabriole legs on spade feet, later carving to back legs, 18thC, 32in (81.5cm) wide.
£420–525
€/ $675–825 WW

Settles & Seats

A Charles II oak monk's bench, the two-plank rising top above scroll arms and a solid rising seat, on turned legs with block feet, 36¾in (93.5cm) wide.
£1,000–1,250
€/ $1,600–1,900 CGC

An oak settle, with a leather-studded seat, on turned bulbous and square block legs with hoof feet, mid-18thC, 76in (193cm) wide.
£600–750
€/ $1,000–1,200 WL

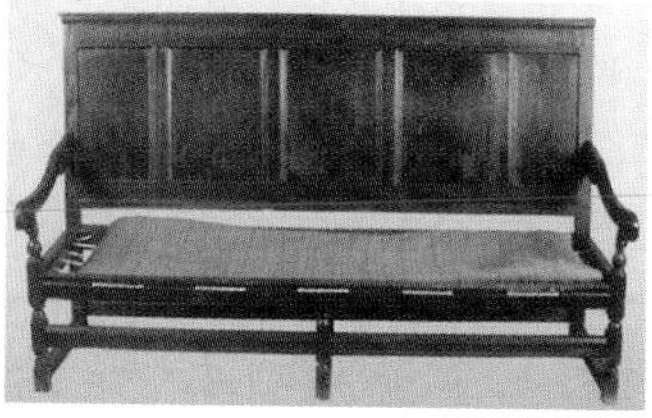

An oak settle, the back with five panels above downcurved arms, on partially-turned legs, early 18thC, 72½in (184cm) wide.
£500–650
€/ $800–1,000 Mit

An elm settle, with a box seat, Welsh borders, mid-18thC, 42in (106.5cm) wide.
£3,500–3,800
€/ $5,500–6,000 ⊞ KEY

An oak settle, the panelled back above shaped arms and a squab seat, on cabriole legs with pad feet, mid-18thC, 71¾in (182.5cm) wide.
£700–850
€/ $1,100–1,350 DN

A panelled oak settle, the box seat with a removable central lid, lid formerly hinged, restored, c1780, 68in (172.5cm) wide.
£2,400–2,800
€/ $3,800–4,400 S(O)

An elm high-back settle, the box seat with a single door, 18thC, 42in (106.5cm) wide.
£3,200–3,600
€/ $5,000–5,700 ⊞ NMA

An oak and fruitwood box settle, the back with eight panels above a hinged seat, with scroll-ended downswept arms, the front triple panelled, on baluster and ring-turned front legs and later ball feet, 18thC, 53½in (136cm) wide.
£2,300–2,800
€/ $3,700–4,400 B(NW)

A painted metamorphic settle/table, the base with a half lid, with mortice and tenon joints, 18thC, 29½in (75cm) wide.
£1,500–1,800
€/ $2,400–2,800 JDJ

A turned ash and poplar Windsor settee, with rod back, initials and dates to underside of seat, some parts possibly of a later date, American, Pennsylvania, c1800, 76in (193cm) wide.
£2,400–2,800
€/ $4,000–4,400 S(NY)

A carved and panelled oak settle, the base is an early 18thC coffer, 19thC, 46in (117cm) wide.
£700–800
€/ $1,100–1,250 ⊞ HiA

An oak box settle, carved with kings, queens and knights, the arms carved with lions' heads, c1880, 66in (167.5cm) wide.
£1,600–1,800
€/ $2,500–2,800 ⊞ REF

◀ **A painted beech settee,** with a rush seat, French, c1880, 48in (122cm) wide.
£800–900
€/ $1,250–1,450 ⊞ MLL

▶ **An oak metamorphic settle,** the gouge-carved panelled back above a slatted seat unfolding to create a single bed with a slatted base, late 19thC, 42½in (108cm) wide.
£350–420
€/ $550–670 B(Ch)

Stools

An oak box stool, with a hinged top, c1640, 15in (38cm) wide.
£4,300–4,800
€/ $6,800–7,600 ⊞ TRI

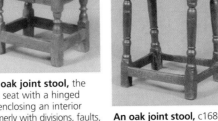

An oak joint stool, the box seat with a hinged lid enclosing an interior formerly with divisions, faults, c1660, 16in (40.5cm) wide.
£2,000–2,200
€/ $3,150–3,500 S(O)

An oak joint stool, c1680, 18¼in (46.5cm) wide.
£1,100–1,300
€/ $1,750–2,000 S(O)

A pair of oak joint stools, 17thC, 17¼in (44cm) wide.
£800–1,000
€/ $1,250–1,600 L

For further information on antique furniture see the full range of Miller's books at **www.millers.uk.com**

An oak joint stool, the thick top above turned legs, 1650–1700.
£2,250–2,500
€/ $3,500–4,000 ⊞ KEY

An elm joint stool, c1780, 18in (45.5cm) high.
£180–200
€/ $280–315 ⊞ F&F

An oak stool, the stuff-over needlework seat with brass nails, on square tapering chamfered legs, early 19thC, 18in (45.5cm) wide.
£200–250
€/ $300–400 ⚒ WW

A pair of primitive elm stools, 19thC, larger 32in (81.5cm) wide.
£1,150–1,300
€/ $1,800–2,000 ⊞ SAW

An oak joint stool, with an upholstered top, late 17thC, 16in (40.5cm) square.
£1,000–1,100
€/ $1,600–1,750 ⊞ SuA

An elm milking stool, with ash legs, 18thC, 11in (28cm) diam.
£110–125
€/ $175–200 ⊞ CHAC

A mahogany stool, c1820, 25in (63.5cm) high.
£200–220
€/ $300–350 ⊞ F&F

An ash stool, c1780, 30in (76cm) wide.
£580–650
€/ $900–1,000 ⊞ SEA

A sycamore and elm milking stool, early 19thC, 19in (48.5cm) wide.
£150–180
€/ $230–280 ⚒ S(O)

An elm stool, c1860, 16in (40.5cm) wide.
£350–400
€/ $550–650 ⊞ SSW

A beech stool, c1880, 11in (28cm) high.
£280–320
€/ $440–500 ⊞ HRQ

◄ **An ash country stool,** c1900, 9in (23cm) high.
£130–145
€/ $200–230 ⊞ SDA

Tables

An oak gateleg table, c1660, 42in (106.5cm) wide.
£2,700–3,000
€/ $4,250–4,750 ⊞ SEA

A walnut side table, on turned supports and stretchers, c1670, 28in (71cm) wide.
£2,800–3,250
€/ $4,500–5,000 ⊞ WELL

An oak side table, with a single drawer, on turned legs, 17thC, 28in (71cm) wide.
£3,500–4,000
€/ $5,500–6,300 ⊞ APO

An oak occasional table, restored, 17thC, 20in (51cm) wide.
£800–1,000
€/ $1,250–1,500 ⚒ B(Ch)

Miller's Compares

I. A Charles II oak gateleg table, with a plain frieze, on bobbin-turned legs with inverted cup feet, 38½in (98cm) wide.
£950–1,200
€/ $1,500–1,900 ⚒ CGC

II. A Charles II oak drop-leaf table, with opposing frieze drawers, on bobbin-turned legs with ball feet, 38½in (98cm) wide.
£320–400
€/ $500–630 ⚒ CGC

The top of Item I belongs to the base (in other words it is not a marriage), which is always an important factor to look for, whereas the ends of the leaves of Item II have been restored and the drawers are replacements. The bobbin turning on the legs of Item I are also bolder than that of Item II, and this appeals to some buyers. Because of the repairs that have been carried out on Item II, the colour is not uniform, whereas that of Item I is richer and much more even. Item I has come from a good, private source and has been looked after over the years, which almost invariably helps to lift the price.

An oak refectory table, with a plank top on square chamfered legs, length reduced, 17thC, 71¾in (182.5cm) long.
£1,200–1,500
€/ $1,900–2,400 ⚒ SWO

An oak centre table, with silhouette legs, c1680, 27in (68.5cm) wide.
£5,500–6,500
€/ $8,700–10,250 ⊞ RYA

An oak gateleg table, c1680, 36in (91.5cm) wide.
£2,000–2,200
€/ $3,200–3,500 ⊞ DJH

◀ **An elm and oak side table,** with a carved frieze, on baluster-turned legs joined by moulded stretchers, 17thC, 45in (114.5cm) wide.
£600–725
€/ $1,000–1,150 ⚒ CGC

A child's oak cricket table, with turned legs, c1690, 22in (56cm) diam.
£3,500–3,850
€/ $5,500–6,000 ⊞ SuA

An oak side table, with a long frieze drawer, on a bobbin- and block-turned frame, late 17thC, 26in (66cm) wide.
£550–650
€/ $870–1,000 TMA

An oak refectory table, with a panel top above a carved frieze, on cup and cover legs, 1675–1725, 63in (160cm) long.
£2,000–2,500
€/ $3,200–4,000 JNic

► **A Queen Anne oak silver table,** 26in (66cm) long.
£1,300–1,450
€/ $2,000–2,300 SuA

An oak gateleg table, with alterations, late 17thC, 50¾in (129cm) wide.
£350–420
€/ $550–670 B(Ba)

An oak gateleg table, with baluster-turned legs, c1690, 39in (99cm) extended.
£4,500–5,500
€/ $7,100–8,700 RYA

◄ **An oak gateleg table,** on bobbin-turned legs with square feet, formerly with drawer, late 17thC, 66in (167.5cm) wide.
£750–875
€/ $1,200–1,400 PF

An oak gateleg table, c1710, 60in (152.5cm) wide.
£2,800–3,250
€/ $4,400–5,000 SEA

An oak side table, the moulded-edge top above a frieze drawer, on turned tapered legs, early 18thC, 27in (68.5cm) wide.
£650–750
€/ $1,000–1,200 DMC

An oak cricket table, early 18thC, 27in (68.5cm) diam.
£800–950
€/ $1,250–1,500 L

An oak gateleg table, with a single drawer and a wavy apron, on baluster-turned legs with turned feet, early 18thC, 60in (152.5cm) wide.
£400–480
€/ $630–760 PF

An oak side table, with a single drawer, c1725, 35½in (90cm) wide.
£3,500–4,200
€/ $5,500–6,600 PHA

An oak tripod table, with original revolving birdcage, on spider legs, bearers replaced, 1740–60, 28½in (72.5cm) diam.
£2,250–2,800
€/ $3,500–4,500 RYA

An oak and fruitwood country side table, the frieze drawer above a shaped apron, on turned tapering legs with pad feet, spliced leg and other repairs, mid-18thC, 27¼in (69cm) wide.
£380–450
€/ $600–710 DN

An oak side table, the drawer with brass escutcheons and swing handles, on turned tapering legs and pad feet, c1750, 30¼in (77cm) wide.
£650–820
€/ $1,000–1,300 WL

An oak refectory table, with three drawers, French, c1750, 79in (200.5cm) wide.
£2,250–2,500
€/ $3,500–4,000 DAC

A Georgian provincial elm and fruitwood cricket table, on three tapering splayed legs, 22½in (57cm) diam.
£650–750
€/ $1,000–1,200 Bea(E)

An elm tavern table, on an X-frame, c1770, 52in (132cm) wide.
£2,000–2,500
€/ $3,150–4,000 RYA

◄ **A Georgian oak, elm and fruitwood country wine table,** 16in (40.5cm) diam.
£875–975
€/ $1,400–1,550 CGA

An oak tilt-top table, 1760–80, 30in (76cm) diam.
£950–1,100
€/ $1,500–1,750 KEY

An oak side table, c1770, 29¾in (75.5cm) wide.
£900–1,000
€/ $1,400–1,600 ⚒ S(O)

A chestnut farmhouse table, French, c1780, 80in (203cm) long.
£6,000–6,500
€/ $9,500–10,000 ⊞ REI

An elm and pine tilt-top table, with a painted top, c1790, 23in (58.5cm) wide.
£1,000–1,150
€/ $1,580–1,750 ⊞ SuA

An oak side table, with a drawer, 18thC, 27in (68.5cm) wide.
£1,700–2,000
€/ $2,700–3,200 ⊞ WAW

A George III oak side table, 30¾in (78cm) wide.
£420–525
€/ $670–830 ⚒ L

An oak table, Spanish, c1780, 24in (61cm) wide.
£420–465
€/ $675–725 ⊞ SSW

An oak-top farmhouse table, 18thC, 74½in (189cm) wide.
£1,350–1,500
€/ $2,200–2,400 ⊞ SWN

A walnut side table, French, Alsace, c1780, 39in (99cm) wide.
£850–950
€/ $1,350–1,500 ⊞ TDS

A provincial cherrywood dressing table, opening to reveal a mirror and compartments, with a writing surface and two drawers, French, 18thC, 31¼in (79.5cm) wide.
£800–950
€/ $1,250–1,500 ⚒ S(P)

An oak cricket table, with a plank top, over a shaped apron, on three tapering legs, 18thC, 26in (66cm) diam.
£1,000–1,200
€/ $1,600–1,900 ⚒ BWL

◄ **An oak cricket table,** with a plank top and undertier, 18thC, 33in (84cm) diam.
£650–750
€/ $1,000–1,200 ⚒ HOLL

A beech and chestnut trestle table, French, 18thC, 63in (160cm) long.
£2,250–2,500
€/ $3,500–4,000 ⊞ AMS

◄ **An oak cricket table,** c1800, 22in (56cm) diam.
£850–950
€/ $1,350–1,500 ⊞ REF

A painted wood folding peasant table, with original paint, c1800, 40¼in (102cm) wide.
£800–950
€/ $1,250–1,500 BUK(F)

An oak farmhouse table, with a partially stripped three-plank top, a frieze drawer to each end, on square tapering legs, early 19thC, 69in (175.5cm) long.
£400–475
€/ $630–750 PFK

An ash and pine cricket table, c1820, 22in (56cm) high.
£430–475
€/ $675–750 ⊞ SEA

A cherrywood farmhouse table, c1830, 75in (190.5cm) long.
£2,700–3,000
€/ $4,300–4,750 ⊞ DeG

A Louis Philippe-style provincial cherrywood side table, with a marble top, above a frieze with one drawer, on turned bulbous legs with ball feet, French, 1850–75, 31½in (80cm) wide.
£280–320
€/ $440–500 NOA

A Victorian carved oak refectory-style table, the plank top above a strapwork-carved front frieze, on turned and carved legs, 84¾in (215.5cm) long.
£2,200–2,700
€/ $3,500–4,250 B(NW)

◄ **A Victorian oak dining table,** 120in (305cm) extended.
£4,700–5,200
€/ $7,500–8,200
⊞ REF

An oak farmhouse table, 19thC, 66in (167.5cm) long.
£750–850
€/ $1,200–1,350 ⊞ WAW

◄ **A fruitwood farmhouse table,** French, 19thC, 75½in (192cm) wide.
£600–700
€/ $950–1,100 SWO

A 17thC-style oak refectory table, with three drawers, Flemish, c1900, 70½in (179cm) wide.
£1,100–1,300
€/ $1,750–2,000 S(O)

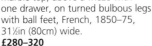

An end table, the two tiers decorated with twigs, American, Adirondacks, 1875–1925, 31½in (80cm) wide.
£2,000–2,400
€/ $3,200–3,800 ⊞ NART

Pine Furniture

Beds

A pine bed, German, c1890, 36in (91.5cm) wide.
£280–320
€/ $440–500 ⊞ HRQ

A pine bed, central European, c1900, 39in (99cm) wide.
£450–500
€/ $700–800 ⊞ COF

A pine bed, Continental, c1900, 39in (99cm) wide.
£315–350
€/ $500–550 ⊞ COF

Bookcases

A pine bookcase, with four shelves, mid-19thC, 68in (173cm) wide.
£530–630
€/ $840–1,000 ⚒ S(O)

A Victorian pine open bookcase, on a plinth base, 72in (183cm) wide.
£315–350
€/ $500–550 ⊞ PaA

A Victorian glazed pine bookcase, 36in (91.5cm) wide.
£330–365
€/ $520–575 ⊞ P&T

◄ **A pine bookcase,** Irish, c1870, 47in (119.5cm) wide.
£450–500
€/ $700–790 ⊞ Byl

► **A late Victorian pine bookcase,** the upper section with two glazed doors, 41in (104cm) wide.
£720–800
€/ $1,150–1,250 ⊞ P&T

A pine bookcase, the upper section with four glazed doors, over four panelled doors, c1890, 102in (259cm) wide.
£1,800–2,000
€/ $2,800–3,200 ⊞ TPC

◄ **A pine bookcase,** with two glazed doors above two panelled doors, c1880, 42in (106.5cm) wide.
£380–430
€/ $600–680 ⊞ DFA

A stepped pine bookcase, c1900, 46in (117cm) wide.
£70–80
€/ $110–135 ⊞ DFA

Boxes

A Shaker stained pine lap desk, the top drawer with a divided interior, American, early 19thC, 20¼in (51.5cm) wide.
£4,000–4,800
€/ $6,300–7,500 ⚒ S(NY)

This desk represents a rare form made by a Shaker craftsman, a group formed in 1776 by Mother Ann Lee, a proponent of an existence focused on simplicity, purity and integrity of workmanship. This piece follows the classic elements of Shaker design philosophy taught by Mother Ann, who advised that things be made 'plain and simple...unembellished by any superfluities which add nothing to its goodness or durability'.

A carved and open fret-cut pine wall-hanging candle box, with a single drawer, Scottish, c1860, 8¾in (22cm) wide.
£320–400
€/ $510–630 ⊞ RYA

A cabinet maker's painted pine tool box, the interior with parquetry decoration and fitted with drawers and lidded compartments, the top later-decorated with a winged figure and hieroglyphics, 19thC, 36¾in (93.5cm) wide.
£250–300
€/ $400–475 ⚒ SWO

A pine blanket box, with iron handles, c1880, 37in (94cm) wide.
£115–130
€/ $180–200 ⊞ DFA

A pine box, with inlaid decoration, c1860, 13in (33cm) wide.
£75–85
€/ $120–135 ⊞ AL

A pine box, with a domed lid, c1880, 29in (73.5cm) wide.
£400–450
€/ $630–700 ⊞ COF

A pine blanket box, c1880, 30in (76cm) wide.
£100–120
€/ $160–190 ⊞ DFA

A pine box, c1880, 23in (58.5cm) wide.
£100–115
€/ $160–180 ⊞ AL

A pine document box, Irish, c1880, 29in (73.5cm) wide.
£110–120
€/ $175–190 ⊞ Byl

A pine box, with steel brackets, c1890, 25in (63.5cm) wide.
£90–100
€/ $140–160 ⊞ AL

A pine box, with a domed lid, c1900, 30in (76cm) wide.
£80–90
€/ $125–140 ⊞ HRQ

A pine blanket box, with wooden handles, c1900, 26in (66cm) wide.
£100–120
€/ $160–190 ⊞ HRQ

► **A pine box,** with rope handles, c1920, 13in (33cm) wide.
£80–90
€/ $125–135 ⊞ DFA

Chairs

◄ **A turned maple, pine and hickory Windsor armchair,** underside of seat branded 'CMD', American, New England, c1780.
£3,000–3,500
€/ $4,750–5,500 ⚒ S(NY)

A pine chair, with original paint, c1900.
£40–45
€/ $65–70 ⊞ DFA

A carved and turned pine chair, c1880.
£55–60
€/ $85–95 ⊞ DFA

► **A set of four pine kitchen chairs,** Continental, c1910.
£200–220
€/ $300–350 ⊞ PaA

A pine country chair, Hungarian, c1880.
£45–50
€/ $70–80 ⊞ Byl

A pine country chair, Irish, c1870.
£130–145
€/ $200–230 ⊞ Byl

A child's pine chair, c1920.
£70–80
€/ $110–125 ⊞ AL

Chests & Coffers

A pine chip-carved dowry chest, with original iron fittings, Norwegian, c1700, 21in (53.5cm) wide.
£2,400–2,700
€/ $3,800–4,250 ⊞ RYA

A polychrome-painted pine chest, the panelled front now with two hinged doors, German, 1700–50, 55¼in (140.5cm) wide.
£1,350–1,600
€/ $2000–2,600 ⚒ S(O)

A pine coffer, c1800, 80in (203cm) wide.
£240–265
€/ $380–420 ⊞ AL

A pine marriage chest, with original decoration, c1850, 45in (114.5cm) wide.
£265–300
€/ $420–475 ⊞ PaA

A pine dwarf trunk, with a domed lid, c1820, 10¾in (27.5cm) wide.
£115–130
€/ $180–200 ⊞ CHAC

An early Victorian pine mule chest, with a single drawer, 35in (89cm) wide.
£300–345
€/ $475–550 ⊞ P&T

A pine blanket chest, the interior with a candle tray, with iron handles, late 19thC, 54in (137cm) wide.
£200–240
€/ $315–380 ⚒ DA

► **A stained pine coffer,** the interior with lidded candle box, late 19thC, 48in (122cm) wide.
£160–200
€/ $250–315 ⚒ SWO

Chests of Drawers

A painted elm and pine nest of apothecary drawers, c1800, 39½in (100.5cm) wide.
£2,700–3,000
€/ $4,250–4,750 ⊞ RYA

A pine and maple chest of drawers, the hinged top opening to reveal a well with two dummy and three real drawers, American, Massachusetts, 1700–30, 45in (114.5cm) wide.
£2,750–3,250
€/ $4,300–5,000 ⚒ S(O)

A Georgian pine chest of drawers, with two short over two long drawers, 36in (91.5cm) wide.
£500–550
€/ $800–870 ⊞ P&T

► **A pine chest of drawers,** with two short over three long drawers, c1810, 40in (101.5cm) wide.
£600–670
€/ $950–1,000 ⊞ AL

A pine chest of drawers, on bracket feet, c1820, 40in (101.5cm) wide.
£720–800
€/ $1,150–1,250 ⊞ COF

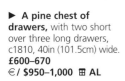

A pine chest of drawers, American, 19thC, 40in (101.5cm) wide.
£165–200
€/ $260–315 DuM

A Victorian pine chest of drawers, with splashback and two short over two long drawers, with original knobs, 40in (101.5cm) wide.
£360–400
€/ $575–650 P&T

A Victorian pine chest of drawers, with two short over two long drawers, 34in (86.5cm) wide.
£270–300
€/ $425–475 CHAC

A Victorian painted pine chest of drawers, 41¼in (105cm) wide.
£130–160
€/ $200–250 B(Ba)

A Victorian pine chest of drawers, with china knobs, 35in (89cm) wide.
£200–230
€/ $315–360 PaA

A pine chest of drawers, with splashback, c1860, 36in (91.5cm) wide.
£325–360
€/ $515–570 HRQ

A grained pine apprentice chest of drawers, mid-19thC, 11in (28cm) wide.
£160–180
€/ $250–290 SWN

A pine chest of drawers, with original paint, Swedish, Stockholm, c1870, 46in (117cm) wide.
£2,500–3,000
€/ $4,000–4,750 JF

Items in the Pine Furniture section have been arranged in date order.

A painted pine chest of drawers, with splashback, c1870, 37in (94cm) wide.
£850–1,000
€/ $1,350–1,600 S(O)

A Louis-Philippe-style chest of drawers, Continental, c1870, 41in (104cm) wide.
£350–400
€/ $550–630 HRQ

A pine chest of drawers, with turned pillars and original paint, c1870, 62in (157.5cm) wide.
£600–660
€/ $950–1,000 ⊞ DMe

A pine chest of drawers, with turned decoration, c1880, 42in (106.5cm) wide.
£240–265
€/ $380–420 ⊞ DFA

A pine chest of drawers, with turned decoration, Romanian, c1880, 50in (127cm) wide.
£270–300
€/ $425–475 ⊞ Byl

A pine chest of six drawers, on bun feet, c1880, 39in (99cm) wide.
£450–500
€/ $700–800 ⊞ TPC

A pine chest of drawers, with turned pillars and bun feet, c1870, 46in (117cm) wide.
£330–370
€/ $520–580 ⊞ DMe

A stripped pine chest of drawers, with two short over three long drawers, late 19thC, 42½in (108cm) wide.
£200–240
€/ $315–380 B(W)

A pine chest of drawers, with two short over two long drawers, Irish, c1880, 38in (96.5cm) wide.
£240–265
€/ $380–420 ⊞ Byl

A pine chest of drawers, c1890, 34in (86.5cm) wide.
£430–475
€/ $680–750 ⊞ COF

◄ **A pine chest of drawers,** with shaped top and decoration to drawer fronts, Continental, c1890, 45in (114.5cm) wide.
£260–300
€/ $400–475 ⊞ PaA

A pine chest of drawers, with turned decoration, eastern European, c1875, 46in (117cm) wide.
£270–300
€/ $425–475 ⊞ Byl

A pine chest of drawers, with original handles, c1880, 30in (76cm) wide.
£320–350
€/ $500–550 ⊞ HRQ

A pine chest of drawers, with two short over three long drawers, with original handles, c1880, 38in (96.5cm) wide.
£350–400
€/ $550–630 ⊞ HRQ

A pitch pine four-drawer commode, with a marble top, early 20thC, 39in (99cm) wide.
£450–500
€/ $700–800 ⊞ MHA

Cupboards

A painted pine corner cupboard, the glazed upper section with two shelves, the base with a fall-front enclosing an open interior above panel doors enclosing a shelf, Norwegian, 18thC, 68½in (174cm) high.
£1,300–1,500
€/ $2,000–2,400 B(Ed)

A fret-carved pine corner cupboard, the upper section with three shelves, the lower section with a panelled door, refinished, 1775–1800, 39in (99cm) wide.
£900–1,000
€/ $1,400–1,600 NOA

A pine hanging corner cupboard, with original paint, 18thC, 44in (112cm) high.
£580–650
€/ $900–1,000 ⊞ SWN

A George III bowfronted painted pine corner cupboard, the upper section with a moulded cornice over a pair of glazed doors, the base with a pair of panelled doors, 54in (137cm) wide.
£2,400–2,800
€/ $3,800–4,400 HYD

A provincial pine cupboard, the arched cornice above a pair of glazed panel doors, over a further pair of doors, with later feet, French, late 18thC, 53½in (136cm) wide.
£850–1,000
€/ $1,350–1,600 B(Ch)

◄ **A pine butler's cupboard,** c1800, 48in (122cm) wide.
£650–750
€/ $1,000–1,200 ⊞ TPC

A stained pine cupboard, the panelled doors opening to reveal two shelves, losses, American, New York, 1750–1800, 53½in (136cm) wide.
£5,000–6,000
€/ $8,000–9,500 S(NY)

A George III pine four-door corner cupboard, c1780, 42in (106.5cm) wide.
£1,125–1,250
€/ $1,800–1,900 ⊞ HRQ

A pine corner cupboard, with original paint, late 18thC, 39in (99cm) wide.
£2,000–2,300
€/ $3,150–3,600 ⊞ PICA

A provincial pine glazed cupboard, the lower cupboard doors opening to reveal a pair of drawers, French, 1750–75, 55½in (141cm) wide.
£1,200–1,400
€/ $1,900–2,200 S(O)

A pine cupboard, the doors with fielded pudding panels, Irish, c1790, 57in (145cm) wide.
£4,300–4,600
€/ $6,800–7,300 ⊞ DMe

LOCATE THE SOURCE
The source of each illustration in Miller's can be found by checking the code letters below each caption with the Key to Illustrations, pages 794–800.

A Biedermeier pine cupboard, German, c1800, 56in (142cm) wide.
£550–600
€/ $870–950 ⊞ HRQ

A painted pine cupboard, the glazed upper section over two reeded-panel doors, c1810, 97in (246.5cm) high
£4,000–5,000
€/ $6,300–8,000 ⊞ JF

A painted pine armoire, with panelled doors, Irish, c1830, 64in (162.5cm) wide.
£7,000–8,000
€/ $11,000–12,500
⊞ DMe

A pine larder cupboard, with four panelled doors, c1840, 61in (155cm) wide.
£750–820
€/ $1,200–1,300 ⊞ DFA

A pine linen press, the upper section with a moulded cornice over a pair of panel doors and spirally-reeded quarter columns, the base fitted with six drawers, early 19thC, 69¼in (176cm) wide.
£1,200–1,400
€/ $1,900–2,200 🔨 B(Pr)

A pine marriage cupboard, with painted folk art decoration, central European, dated 1835, 42in (106.5cm) wide.
£3,200–3,800
€/ $5,000–6,000 ⊞ RYA

A pine housekeeper's cupboard, the lower section with six drawers, south Derbyshire, c1840, 65in (165cm) wide.
£1,500–1,650
€/ $2,400–2,500 ⊞ HRQ

◀ **A pine cupboard,** with panelled sides and doors, with original paint, Irish, Co Roscommon, 1840–50, 54in (137cm) wide.
£900–1,000
€/ $1,400–1,600 ⊞ HON

▶ **A pine cupboard,** the moulded cornice above a reeded frieze, over four panelled cupboard doors and two drawers, on bracket feet, 1800–25, 62in (157.5cm) wide.
£1,000–1,200
€/ $1,600–1,900 🔨 NOA

A stained pine corner cupboard, 19thC, 74¾in (190cm) high.
£480–540
€/ $760–850 🔨 SWO

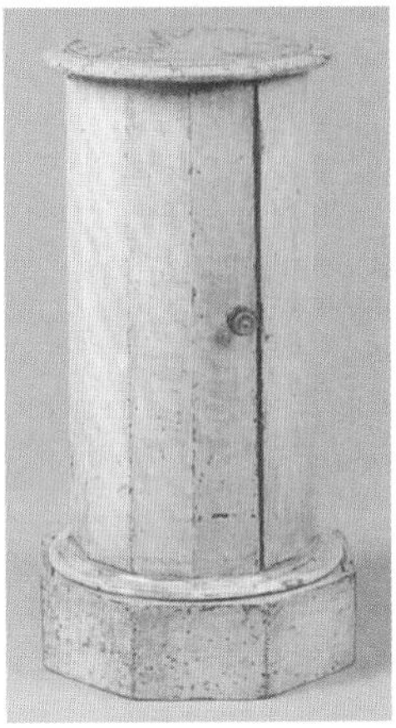

A painted pine pot cupboard, with a simulated marble top, c1840, 14½in (37cm) diam.
£1,000–1,200
€/ $1,600–1,900 🔨 S(O)

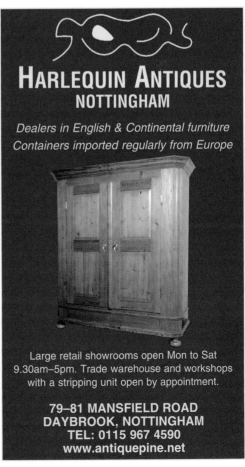

PINE FURNITURE

A painted pine cupboard, by Mangan Bros, with two panelled doors, Irish, Co Kildare, c1840, 63in (160cm) wide.
£2,200–2,600
€/ $3,500–4,100 ⊞ DMe

A pine wall cupboard, c1850, 19in (48.5cm) wide.
£100–120
€/ $160–190 ⊞ HRQ

A pine cupboard, with two doors, eastern European, c1870, 36in (91.5cm) wide.
£85–95
€/ $135–150 ⊞ HRQ

A pine cupboard, c1845, 25in (63.5cm) wide.
£270–300
€/ $425–475 ⊞ P&T

A pine cupboard, the four doors with carved sunburst decoration, with original scumble finish, c1860, 60in (152.5cm) wide.
£900–1,000
€/ $1,400–1,600 ⊞ HON

◄ **A pine cupboard,** the glazed upper section over two doors, Irish, c1865, 40in (101.5cm) wide.
£520–625
€/ $820–990 ⊞ Byl

A pine step-back cupboard, with four doors, Irish, c1870, 48in (122cm) wide.
£550–600
€/ $870–950 ⊞ Byl

► **A pine larder cupboard,** with four doors, c1870, 42in (106.5cm) wide.
£375–425
€/ $590–670 ⊞ DFA

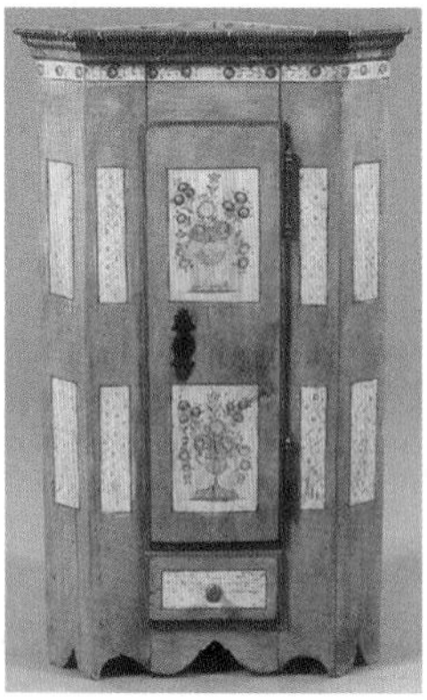

A painted pine corner cupboard, the single door over a short drawer, Dutch, mid-19thC and later, 27in (68.5cm) wide.
£550–600
€/ $870–950 ⚒ NOA

A glazed pine display cupboard, Irish, c1860, 50in (127cm) wide.
£475–525
€/ $750–830 ⊞ DMe

A pine panelled cupboard, the two-door upper section over one short and two long drawers and two further doors, Irish, Co Tipperary, c1850, 59in (150cm) wide.
£950–1,100
€/ $1,500–1,750 ⊞ HON

A painted pine cupboard, the upper section with two glazed doors, over three central drawers and two doors, c1860, 45in (114.5cm) wide.
£500–560
€/ $790–880 ⊞ DFA

◄ **A pine cupboard,** c1870, 41in (104cm) wide.
£300–330
€/ $475–520 ⊞ Byl

A pine cupboard, European, c1875, 36in (91.5cm) wide.
£270–300
€/ $420–4750 ⊞ Byl

A pine corner cupboard, French, c1880, 33in (84cm) wide.
£650–735
€/ $1,000–1,150 ⊞ AL

A pine corner cupboard, with a glazed top, Irish, c1880, 45in (114.5cm) wide.
£450–500
€/ $710–790 ⊞ Byl

A pine cupboard, with two panelled doors, Irish, c1880, 46in (117cm) wide.
£300–330
€/ $475–520 ⊞ Byl

A pitch pine panelled cupboard, with four doors, Irish, Co Galway, c1880, 96in (244cm) high.
£900–980
€/ $1,400–1,600 ⊞ HON

◄ A pine bedside cupboard, c1880, 30in (76cm) high.
£115–130
€/ $180–200 ⊞ HRQ

► A pine cupboard, the two doors enclosing a shelved interior, over two drawers, c1880, 47in (119.5cm) wide.
£300–330
€/ $475–520 ⊞ DFA

A pine corner cupboard, c1885, 22in (56cm) wide.
£550–600
€/ $870–950 ⊞ COF

A pine cupboard, the four doors with Gothic panels, with two drawers, Irish, c1890, 40in (101.5cm) wide.
£650–720
€/ $1,000–1,100 ⊞ Byl

A pine cupboard, with a single drawer over a panelled door, on turned bun feet, c1890, 25in (63.5cm) wide.
£150–165
€/ $240–260 ⊞ DFA

A painted pine cupboard, with glazed upper section, American, 19thC, 38in (96.5cm) wide.
£80–100
€/ $130–160 ⚒ DuM

► A pine wall cupboard, European, c1910, 24in (61cm) wide.
£225–250
€/ $350–400 ⊞ COF

A pine cupboard, with shelf over, c1890, 14½in (37cm) wide.
£55–60
€/ $85–95 ⊞ AL

A pine cupboard, with four doors, c1890, 51in (129.5cm) wide.
£550–625
€/ $870–1,000 ⊞ DFA

A pine wardrobe, with an arched top, central European, c1900, 39in (99cm) wide.
£625–700
€/ $1,000–1,100 ⊞ COF

A pine bread cupboard, eastern European, c1890, 63in (160cm) wide.
£280–320
€/ $440–520 ⊞ PaA

A pine corner cupboard, c1890, 18in (45.5cm) wide.
£450–500
€/ $700–800 ⊞ COF

A pine cupboard, German, c1890, 43in (109cm) wide.
£550–600
€/ $870–950 ⊞ HRQ

A pine cupboard, with a glazed upper section, c1890, 34in (86.5cm) wide.
£420–470
€/ $660–740 ⊞ AL

◄ A pair of pine side cupboards, eastern European, c1900, 32in (81.5cm) wide.
£245–270
€/ $380–430 ⊞ PaA

A pine bedside cupboard, German, c1910, 17in (43cm) wide.
£115–130
€/ $180–200 ⊞ HRQ

◄ A pair of pine bedside cupboards, central European, c1920, 28in (71cm) high.
£400–450
€/ $630–700 ⊞ COF

PINE FURNITURE

Desks & Bureaux

A pine bureau, with fully fitted interior, c1800, 38in (96.5cm) wide.
£1,500–1,800
€/ $2,400–2,850 ⊞ TPC

A pine bureau, Irish, Co Kilkenny, 1850–60, 41in (104cm) wide.
£750–820
€/ $1,200–1,300 ⊞ HON

A pine bureau, c1870, 56in (142cm) wide.
£2,000–2,200
€/ $3,200–3,500 ⊞ COF

► A pine writing desk, German, c1900, 47in (119.5cm) wide.
£500–550
€/ $800–870 ⊞ HRQ

A pine partner's desk, c1900, 49in (124.5cm) wide.
£1,350–1,500
€/ $2,150–2,350 ⊞ COF

◄ A pine pedestal desk, the moulded drawers flanked by reeded columns, original paintwork, c1900, 48in (122cm) wide.
£1,100–1,200
€/ $1,700–1,900
⊞ TPC

A pine pedestal desk, Continental, c1920, 51in (129.5cm) wide.
£630–700
€/ $1,000–1,100 ⊞ HRQ

Dressers

A George III stained pine dresser, Welsh, c1800, 66in (167.5cm) wide.
£1,400–1,600
€/ $2,200–2,500 S(O)

A pine chicken coop dresser, cornice replaced, Irish, early 19thC, 49½in (125.5cm) wide.
£950–1,100
€/ $1,500–1,700 S(O)

◄ **A painted pine dresser,** with carved sunburst decoration and reeded sides, original paint, Irish, c1840, 57in (145cm) wide.
£600–660
€/ $950–1,000 HON

A painted pine dresser, original paint, losses refreshed, c1840, 67in (170cm) wide.
£7,200–8,000
€/ $11,500–12,500 RYA

◄ **A painted pine *buffet à deux corps*,** French, early 19thC, 50in (127cm) wide.
£1,300–1,500
€/ $2,000–2,400 PICA

► **A pine dresser,** with two plate shelves above six frieze drawers and three doors, c1850, 82in (208.5cm) wide.
£2,500–3,000
€/ $4,000–4,800 TPC

A painted pine dresser, original paint, Irish, c1850, 61in (155cm) wide.
£1,100–1,200
€/ $1,700–1,900 DMe

◄ **A painted pine dresser,** the top with fret-carved decoration and reeded corners, Irish, Co Galway, c1860, 49in (124.5cm) wide.
£750–820
€/ $1,200–1,300 HON

A pine dresser, Irish, c1860, 49in (124.5cm) wide.
£550–620
€/ $870–1,000 Byl

A pine dresser, Irish, c1860, 43in (109cm) wide.
£450–500
€/ $700–800 DMe

A Victorian pine dresser, with pot board base, 54in (137cm) wide.
£700–800
€/ $1,100–1,300 ⊞ WiB

A pitch pine dresser, with carved shamrock decoration above two glazed doors flanking shelves, Irish, Co Clare, c1870, 56in (142cm) wide.
£900–1,000
€/ $1,400–1,600 ⊞ HON

A pine dresser, c1870, 57in (145cm) wide.
£850–920
€/ $1,350–1,450 ⊞ DMe

A pine dresser, Irish, c1875, 52in (132cm) wide.
£500–560
€/ $800–880 ⊞ Byl

A Victorian pine dresser, restored, Irish, 81in (205.5cm) wide.
£950–1,100
€/ $1,500–1,700 ⚒ S(O)

A pine dresser, c1870, 51in (129.5cm) wide.
£300–330
€/ $475–525 ⊞ DFA

A pine dresser, with two glazed doors, Irish, c1875, 51in (129.5cm) wide.
£500–560
€/ $800–880 ⊞ Byl

A pine dresser, with two glazed doors, eastern European, c1875, 42in (106.5cm) wide.
£450–500
€/ $710–790 ⊞ Byl

A pine dresser, the upper section with three doors, Welsh, c1870, 59in (150cm) wide.
£1,800–2,000
€/ $2,800–3,200 ⊞ COF

A pine dresser, Irish, Co Donegal, c1870, 58in (147.5cm) wide.
£500–560
€/ $800–880 ⊞ Byl

A painted pine dresser, c1870, 51in (129.5cm) wide.
£450–500
€/ $700–800 ⊞ DFA

A pine dresser, Irish, c1870, 54in (137cm) wide.
£300–330
€/ $475–525 ⊞ Byl

A pine dresser, with glazed doors, European, c1880, 54in (137cm) wide.
£450–500
€/ $710–790 ⊞ Byl

A pine dresser, c1880, 40in (101.5cm) wide.
£650–750
€/ $1,000–1,200 ⊞ TPC

A pine dresser, with glazed top, eastern European, c1890, 42in (106.5cm) wide.
£450–500
€/ $710–790 ⊞ PaA

A pine dresser, c1880, 41in (106.5cm) wide.
£200–225
€/ $315–350 ⊞ DFA

A pine dresser, with glazed top, c1890, 47in (119.5cm) wide.
£720–800
€/ $1,200–1,300 ⊞ HRQ

A pine dresser, with glazed top, German, c1900, 36in (91.5cm) wide.
£630–700
€/ $990–1,100 ⊞ HRQ

A pine dresser, the upper section with a glazed door over a drawer flanked by two panelled doors, the base with four drawers flanked by two panelled doors, c1880, 53in (134.5cm) wide.
£1,800–2,000
€/ $2,900–3,200 ⊞ COF

A pine dresser, with glazed top, Irish, c1890, 51in (129.5cm) wide.
£900–1,000
€/ $1,400–1,600 ⊞ P&T

A pine apothecary dresser, some drawers replaced, eastern European, c1900, 62in (157.5cm) wide.
£1,500–1,700
€/ $2,400–2,799 ⊞ PaA

Dresser Bases & Side Cabinets

A painted pine side cabinet, Swedish, c1800, 42in (106.5cm) wide.
£3,500–4,000
€/ $5,500–6,500 ⊞ CAV

A George III pine dresser base, with two doors and three drawers, 74in (188cm) wide.
£800–950
€/ $1,300–1,500 ⚒ PFK

A Victorian pine dresser base, handles replaced, 61½in (156cm) wide.
£320–400
€/ $500–630 ⚒ B(Ba)

A Victorian pine chiffonier, 35in (89cm) wide.
£480–550
€/ $780–870 ⊞ P&T

A pine dresser base, c1870, 44in (112cm) wide.
£165–185
€/ $260–290 ⊞ DFA

► **A pine chiffonier,** with carved splashback, Irish, Co Galway, c1870, 50in (127cm) wide.
£325–360
€/ $515–560 ⊞ HON

◀ **A pine dresser base,** on turned feet, c1870, 56in (142cm) wide.
£400–450
€/ $630–700 ⊞ DFA

A pine side cabinet, Romanian, c1875, 47in (119.5cm) wide.
£200–230
€/ $300–360 ⊞ Byl

A pine chiffonier, Irish, c1875, 48in (122cm) wide.
£250–280
€/ $400–440 ⊞ Byl

◀ **A Victorian pine chiffonier,** handles replaced, Lincolnshire, c1880, 58in (147.5cm) wide.
£1,100–1,250
€/ $1,700–1,900 ⊞ COF

A pine side cabinet, with carved decoration, Continental, c1900, 43in (109cm) wide.
£475–525
€/ $750–830 ⊞ P&T

A pine dresser base, c1900, 43in (109cm) wide.
£280–320
€/ $440–500 ⊞ HRQ

◀ **A pine chiffonier,** with carved decoration, Irish, c1880, 45in (114.5cm) wide.
£230–260
€/ $360–400 ⊞ Byl

Dressing Chests & Tables

A painted pine dressing chest, with mirror, c1890, 36in (91.5cm) wide.
£270–300
€/ $425–480 ⊞ HRQ

A pine dressing table, with mirror, c1890, 42in (107cm) wide.
£400–440
€/ $630–690 ⊞ AL

A pine dressing table, c1895, 36in (91.5cm) wide.
£550–600
€/ $870–950 ⊞ COF

▶ **A Victorian pine dressing table,** with simulated bamboo edging and legs, 43¾in (111cm) wide.
£300–340
€/ $475–540 ⚒ B(W)

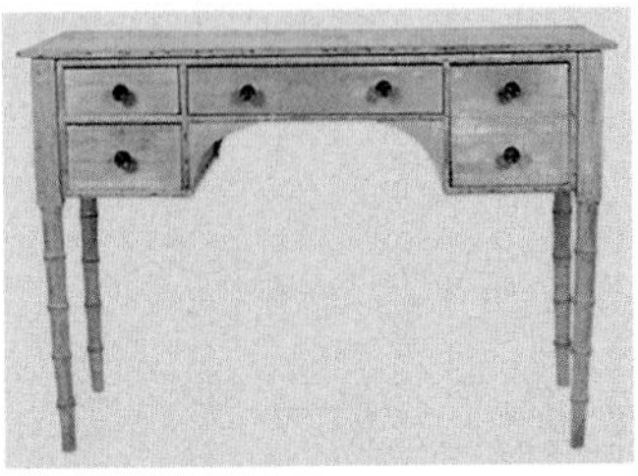

PINE FURNITURE

Ladders & Steps

◄ **A Victorian pine step ladder,** with patented mechanism, 69in (175.5cm) high.
£200–225
€/ $310–350 ⊞ GBr

A pine library ladder, late 19thC, 94½in (240cm) high.
£280–320
€/ $440–500 ⚒ DN

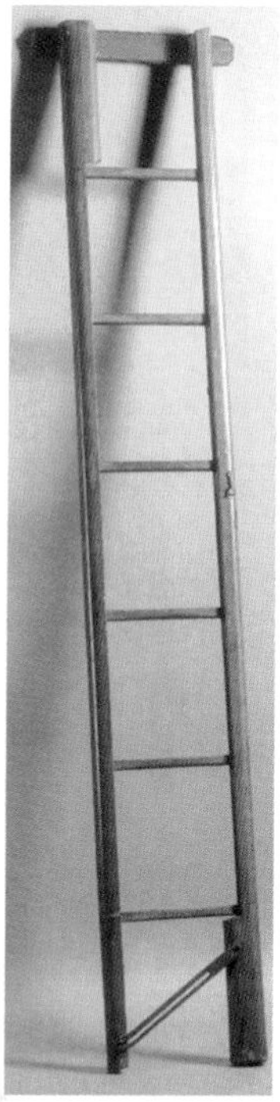

► **A stained pine folding library ladder,** labelled 'J. H. Heathman, Endell St, London', late 19thC, 84in (213.5cm) high.
£800–900
€/ $1,250–1,400 ⚒ S(O)

Linen Presses

◄ **A pine linen press,** c1830, 83in (211cm) high.
£1,800–2,000
€/ $2,900–3,200 ⊞ P&T

A Victorian pine linen press, the interior with slides, 42in (106.5cm) wide.
£1,000–1,200
€/ $1,600–1,900 ⊞ TPC

An early Victorian pine linen press, 85in (216cm) high.
£800–900
€/ $1,260–1,500 ⊞ P&T

◄ **A pine linen press,** c1860, 82in (208.5cm) high.
£550–650
€/ $870–1,000 ⊞ DFA

► **A Victorian pine linen press,** the interior with slides, c1875, 86in (218.5cm) high.
£1,300–1,500
€/ $2,000–2,300 ⊞ PaA

PINE FURNITURE

Settles & Settees

A painted pine settle, Welsh, c1780, 56in (142cm) wide.
£3,500–4,000
€/ $5,500–6,400 ⊞ SEA

A pair of pine settles, with winged sides, one with applied horseshoe, probably Devon, 19thC, 57½in (146cm) wide.
£6,500–8,000
€/ $10,300–13,000 ⚒ HOK
These settles were formerly the property of the painter Jack B. Yeats (1870–1957), and as they were kept in his studios, they were frequently used as backgrounds in his illustrations.

► A Victorian pine settle, 109in (277cm) wide.
£1,000–1,100
€/ $1,600–1,700 ⚒ S(O)

A pine settle, c1800, 75in (190.5cm) wide.
£500–560
€/ $800–880 ⊞ DFA

A pine settle, with hinged box seat, Continental, 19thC, 46in (117cm) wide.
£220–240
€/ $350–380 ⊞ HRQ

A pine settle, c1860, 48in (122cm) wide.
£270–300
€/ $425–475 ⊞ DFA

A provincial grained pine settle, 19thC, 75in (190.5cm) wide.
£1,000–1,200
€/ $1,600–1,900 ⚒ Bea(E)

A pine settle, with carved decoration and a hinged box seat, damaged, 19thC, 63in (160cm) wide.
£500–600
€/ $790–950 ⚒ SWO

A painted pine settle, c1870, 69in (175.5cm) wide.
£1,350–1,500
€/ $2,100–2,400 ⊞ SWN

A pine settle, Romanian, c1880, 69in (175.5cm) wide.
£300–330
€/ $475–525 ⊞ Byl

A pine settle, with one long drawer, original paint, c1890, 70in (178cm) wide.
£400–500
€/ $630–800 ⊞ TPC

Tables

A pine cricket table, Welsh, c1800, 29in (73.5cm) diam.
£720–800
€/ $1,150–1,300 ⊞ COF

A pine cricket table, early 19thC, 33in (84cm) diam.
£475–575
€/ $750–910 ⚒ HYD

A pine table, with a single drawer, European, early 19thC, 30in (76cm) wide.
£325–360
€/ $510–570 ⊞ HRQ

◄ An early Victorian pine table, with three drawers, 52in (132cm) wide.
£350–400
€/ $550–630
⊞ P&T

A painted pine drop-leaf table, Swedish, c1820, 44½in (113cm) extended.
£2,300–2,800
€/ $3,600–4,400 ⊞ RYA

An early Victorian pine table, with two drawers, Irish, 60in (152.5cm) wide.
£425–475
€/ $670–750 ⊞ P&T

◄ A Victorian pine table, in the Gothic revival style, 75¼in (191cm) wide.
£380–450
€/ $600–710
⚒ B(Ch)

► A Victorian pine side table, by Howard & Sons, the galleried top above two frieze drawers, on turned simulated bamboo legs, 48in (122cm) wide.
£750–875
€/ $1,200–1,400
⚒ DN

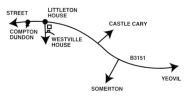

PINE FURNITURE

◄ **A pine table,** with a single drawer, on cabriole legs, German, c1840, 43in (109cm) wide.
£215–240
€/ $340–380 ⊞ HRQ

A Victorian painted pine side table, 51½in (131cm) wide.
£400–450
€/ $630–700 ⊞ WiB

A painted pine and fruitwood games table, c1840, 18in (45.5cm) diam.
£2,300–2,800
€/ $3,600–4,400 ⚒ RYA

A pine cricket table, c1850, 28in (71cm) diam.
£300–350
€/ $480–550 ⊞ TPC

A Victorian pine dining table, on turned legs, c1850, 91in (231cm) wide.
£1,500–1,700
€/ $2,400–2,700 ⊞ P&T

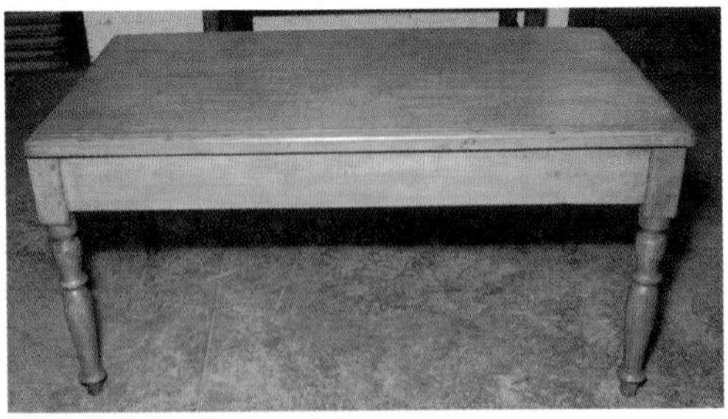

A pine table, on turned legs, Irish, c1865, 64in (162.5cm) wide.
£315–350
€/ $500–550 ⊞ Byl

A pine table, on turned legs, Irish, c1870, 83in (211cm) wide.
£300–330
€/ $475–525 ⊞ DMe

A pine table, with a painted base, c1870, 75in (190.5cm) wide.
£350–400
€/ $550–630 ⊞ DFA

◄ **A pine table,** the column base with original paint, c1870, 46in (117cm) diam.
£260–300
€/ $400–475
⊞ DFA

A pine drop-leaf table, Irish, c1870, 44in (112cm) wide.
£225–250
€/ $350–400 ⊞ Byl

◀ **A pine table,** c1880, 35in (89cm) wide.
£90–100
€/ $140–160 ⊞ DFA

▶ **A pine table,** with a central drawer, c1880, 50in (127cm) wide.
£210–230
€/ $330–350 ⊞ Byl

A pine drop-leaf table, with one drawer, c1880, 42in (106.5cm) wide.
£280–320
€/ $440–500 ⊞ AL

A pine side table, with shelf underneath, c1880, 32in (81.5cm) wide.
£215–235
€/ $340–370 ⊞ AL

For further information on antique furniture see the full range of Miller's books at **www.millers.uk.com**

◀ **A pine table,** with a central drawer, c1880, 61in (155cm) wide.
£160–180
€/ $250–280
⊞ DFA

A pine drop-leaf table, c1880, 44in (112cm) wide.
£200–225
€/ $315–350 ⊞ HRQ

A pine table, with a painted base, c1880, 48in (122cm) wide.
£145–160
€/ $230–250 ⊞ DFA

A pine table, on turned legs, Irish, c1880, 66in (167.5cm) wide.
£350–400
€/ $550–630 ⊞ Byl

A pine wine table, with fold-over top, French, c1880, 31in (78.5cm) diam.
£480–530
€/ $750–830 ⊞ AL

A pine table, on six walnut legs, Welsh, c1880, 138in (350.5cm) wide.
£1,800–2,000
€/ $2,800–3,200 ⊞ COF

A pitch pine drop-leaf table, Irish, c1880, 48in (122cm) diam.
£225–250
€/ $350–400 ⊞ Byl

A pine drop-leaf table, on turned legs, Irish, c1880, 48in (122cm) wide.
£200–230
€/ $315–350 ⊞ Byl

A pine table, with beech top, on turned legs, c1890, 42in (106.5cm) wide.
£315–350
€/ $500–550 ⊞ HRQ

A pine table, with one drawer, c1890, 41in (104cm) wide.
£280–320
€/ $440–500 ⊞ HRQ

A pine table, Irish, c1890, 56in (142.5cm) wide.
£350–400
€/ $550–640 ⊞ HRQ

A pine table, c1890, 52in (132cm) wide.
£265–330
€/ $420–520 ⊞ TPC

A pine side table, top replaced, c1890, 25in (63.5cm) wide.
£180–200
€/ $285–315 ⊞ AL

Further reading

Miller's Pine & Country Furniture Buyer's Guide, Miller's Publications, 1995

A Victorian pine table, c1895, 72in (183cm) wide.
£535–600
€/ $845–950 ⊞ COF

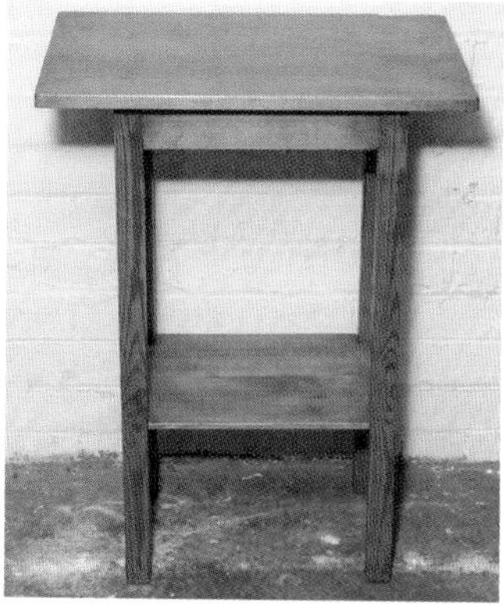

A pine side table, German, c1920, 24in (61cm) wide.
£100–120
€/ $160–190 ⊞ HRQ

◄ **A Victorian pine library table,** on turned legs, 63in (160cm) wide.
£715–800
€/ $1,125–1,300
⊞ PaA

A painted pine side table, with a yew top, c1930, 36in (91.5cm) wide.
£80–90
€/ $125–145 ⊞ DFA

Wardrobes

A Biedermeier-style pine wardrobe, with original lock, on turned feet, German, c1840, 60in (152.5cm) wide.
£675–750
€/ $1,100–1,200 ⊞ HRQ

A pine wardrobe, with three doors, c1870, 79in (200.5cm) wide.
£450–500
€/ $700–800 ⊞ DFA

A pine wardrobe, Irish, c1875, 52in (132cm) wide.
£270–300
€/ $425–475 ⊞ Byl

A pine wardrobe, with panelled doors, Irish, c1875, 50in (127cm) wide.
£1,300–1,500
€/ $2,000–2,400 ⊞ COF

A pine wardrobe, the interior with internal drawers and a secret compartment, German, c1880, 57in (145cm) wide.
£630–700
€/ $990–1,100 ⊞ HRQ

A pine wardrobe, the two doors above a single drawer, German, c1880, 45in (114.5cm) wide.
£550–620
€/ $870–980 ⊞ HRQ

A pine wardrobe, the two doors above a single drawer, c1880, 52in (132cm) wide.
£300–330
€/ $475–525 ⊞ DFA

A pine wardrobe, c1890, 37in (94cm) wide.
£225–250
€/ $350–400 ⊞ DFA

A Victorian gesso-decorated pine wardrobe, 40in (101.5cm) wide.
£500–600
€/ $790–950 ⊞ TPC

◄ **A pine wardrobe,** c1900, 44in (112cm) wide.
£400–450
€/ $630–450 ⊞ HRQ

A pine wardrobe, the two doors above a single drawer, c1900, 46in (117cm) wide.
£320–350
€/ $510–550 ⊞ PaA

A pine wardrobe, c1900, 36in (91.5cm) wide.
£380–435
€/ $600–690 ⊞ AL

◄ **A pine wardrobe,** the three doors above two drawers, German, c1900, 68in (172.5cm) wide.
£800–900
€/ $1,250–1,500 ⊞ HRQ

► **A pine wardrobe,** with decorative carving, German, c1910, 64in (162.5cm) wide.
£800–900
€/ $1,250–1,500 ⊞ HRQ

Washstands

A pine washstand, c1820, 27in (68.5cm) wide.
£300–335
€/ $475–530 ⊞ AL

A pine washstand, c1880, 35in (84cm) wide.
£235–260
€/ $365–410 ⊞ HRQ

A pine washstand, c1880, 19in (48.5cm) wide.
£65–70
€/ $100–110 ⊞ Byl

A pine washstand, c1900, 24in (61cm) wide.
£90–100
€/ $140–160 ⊞ DFA

Miscellaneous

A pair of pine bedside cabinets, eastern European, c1880, 45in (114.5cm) high.
£200–230
€/ $315–360 ⊞ Byl

A pine butcher's block, with two drawers, c1880, 48in (122cm) wide.
£450–500
€/ $700–800 ⊞ DFA

A pine food safe, c1900, 20in (51cm) wide.
£100–115
€/ $160–180 ⊞ AL

▶ **A painted pine grain bin,** c1880, 61in (155cm) wide.
£80–90
€/ $125–140 ⊞ DFA

A pine grain bin, c1890, 30in (76cm) wide.
£175–200
€/ $275–315 ⊞ AL

◀ **A pine plate rack,** Irish, Co Tipperary, c1850, 49in (124.5cm) wide.
£500–560
€/ $800–880 ⊞ HON

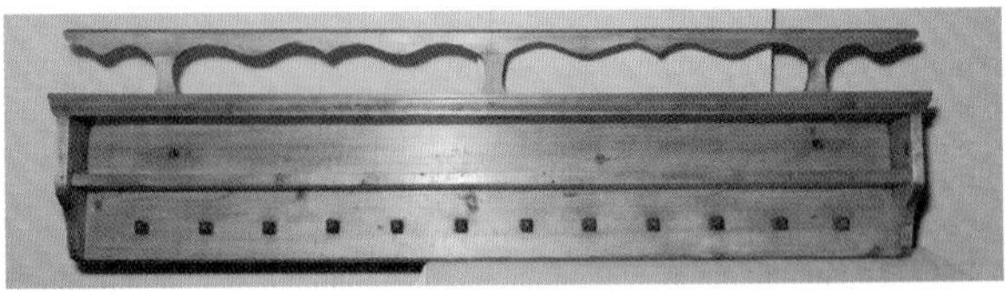

A pine pot rack, Romanian, c1890, 70in (178cm) wide.
£250–280
€/ $395–445 ⊞ HRQ

▶ **A pine shoe bench,** with two doors, Continental, c1920, 42in (106.5cm) wide.
£150–175
€/ $250–275 ⊞ COF

A pine shop counter, c1890, 42in (106.5cm) wide.
£450–500
€/ $700–800 ⊞ COF

A pine towel rail, c1890, 32in (81.5cm) wide.
£60–65
€/ $90–100 ⊞ AL

◀ **A pine wall rack,** 19thC, 39in (99cm) wide.
£145–160
€/ $230–250 ⊞ HRQ

Bamboo & Wicker Furniture

A Victorian bamboo open bookcase, the shelves and back covered in seagrass, 39in (99cm) wide.
£320–375
€/ $500–590 WW

A pair of bamboo chairs, c1890.
£240–265
€/ $380–420 ⊞ AL

A chinoiserie bamboo and lacquer writing desk, with leather top, 19thC, 35in (90cm) wide.
£900–1,000
€/ $1,400–1,600 ⊞ CoHA

◄ A bamboo jardinière, the sides formed by four Wedgwood tiles entitled 'Oberon', 'Peasblossom', 'Herodia' and 'Cobweb', metal-lined, late 19thC, 26in (66cm) high.
£475–565
€/ $750–890 TRM

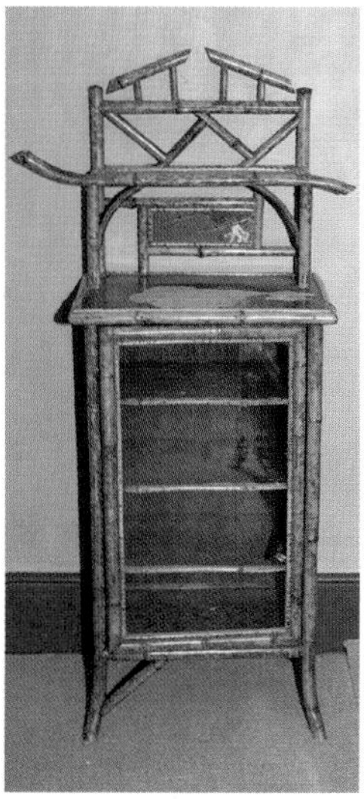

◄ A chinoiserie bamboo music cabinet, with a glazed door, late 19thC, 30in (76cm) wide.
£900–1,000
€/ $1,400–1,600 ⊞ CoHA

A bamboo and lacquer table, restored, late 19thC, 21in (53.5cm) diam.
£145–160
€/ $230–250 ⊞ CoHA

A bamboo table, with Art Nouveau tiles, c1890, 20in (51cm) square.
£175–200
€/ $275–315 ⊞ GBr

A bamboo wardrobe, with central mirror, c1890, 37in (94cm) wide.
£600–670
€/ $950–1,100 ⊞ AL

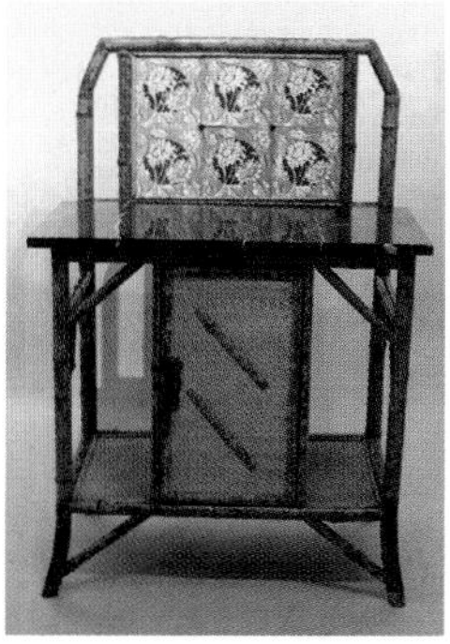

A Victorian bamboo washstand, with a marbled top and tiled splashback, 19thC, 30in (76cm) wide.
£230–275
€/ $360–430 BWL

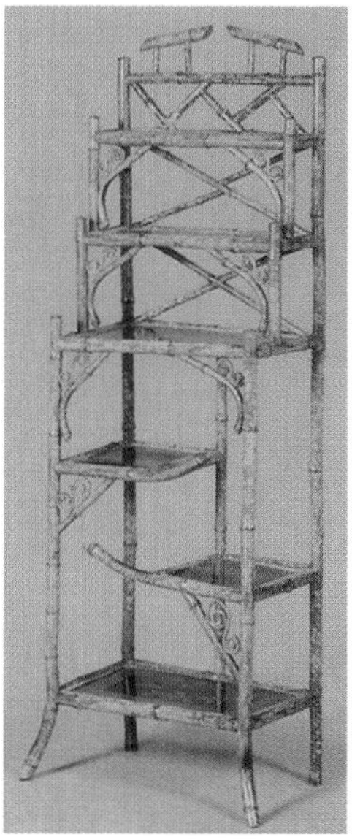

A Victorian bamboo and lacquer whatnot, the legs with applied gilt-metal caps, 24½in (62cm) wide.
£950–1,150
€/ $1,500–2,400 S(O)

A wicker and maple three-tier whatnot, by Haywood-Wakefield, American, c1900, 17½in (44.5cm) wide.
£1,300–1,500
€/ $2,000–2,400 ⊞ NART

Kitchenware

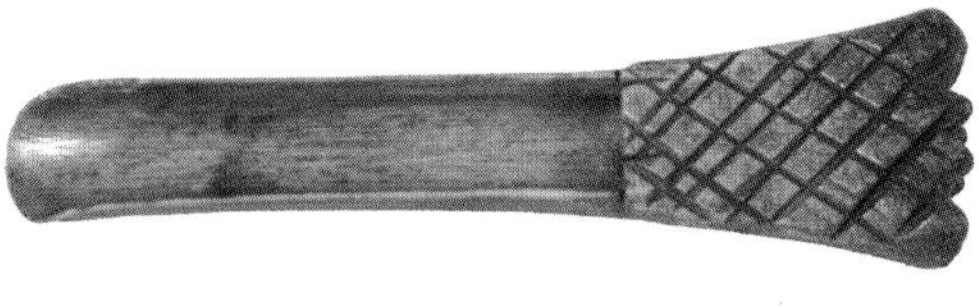

A bone apple corer, Welsh, 18thC, 4½in (11.5cm) wide.
£135–150
€/ $215–240 ⊞ SEA

A pair of star-shaped baking tins, c1915, 9¼in (23.5cm) diam.
£40–45 each
€/ $60–70 ⊞ MSB

► A sycamore butter churn, Welsh, c1840, 24in (61cm) high.
£440–490
€/ $700–780 ⊞ MFB

A sycamore butter print, c1870, 3½in (9cm) diam.
£60–65
€/ $90–100 ⊞ AL

◄ An oak and iron-bound pump-action butter churn, 19thC, 38in (96.5cm) high.
£115–125
€/ $180–195 ⊞ CHAC

A sycamore butter print, Welsh, c1880, 8in (20.5cm) wide.
£200–220
€/ $315–350 ⊞ MFB

A sycamore butter wheel, c1860, 6½in (16.5cm) long.
£70–80
€/ $110–125 ⊞ SDA

► A wooden cider keg, West Country, c1850, 8in (20.5cm) high.
£340–380
€/ $540–600 ⊞ SEA

A Victorian coffee grinder, by Peugeot Frères, French, c1880, 14in (35.5cm) high.
£170–200
€/ $270–315 ⊞ PaA

A china cream pail, c1920, 9½in (24cm) high.
£550–600
€/ $870–950 ⊞ SMI

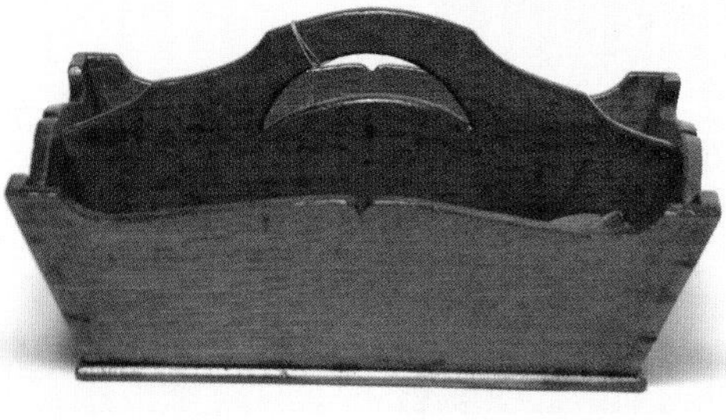

An oak cutlery box, Welsh, c1780, 13in (33cm) wide.
£400–450
€/ $630–710 ⊞ SEA

A set of toleware wall kitchen drawers, c1920, 14in (35.5cm) wide.
£130–150
€/ $200–240 ⊞ B&R

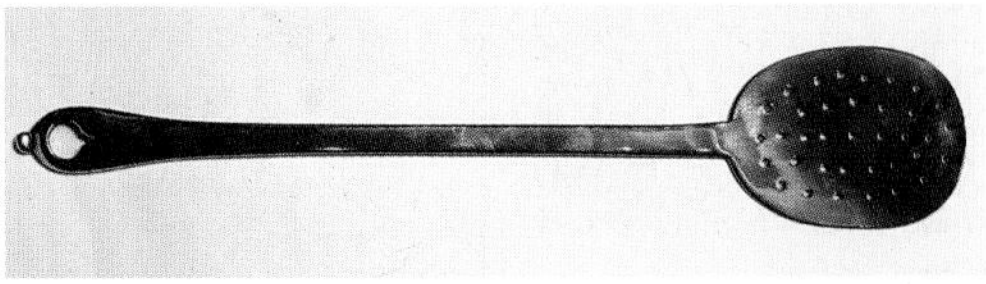

A brass fish slice, early 18thC, 18in (45.5cm) long.
£340–375
€/ $540–600 ⊞ SEA

A wooden flour barrel, 1890–1920, 12in (30.5cm) diam.
£70–75
€/ $110–120 ⊞ CHAC

A goffering iron, late 19thC, 3in (7.5cm) high.
£80–90
€/ $125–140 ⊞ WeA
Goffering irons are used to iron cuffs and sleeves.

A brass griddle, Scottish, 19thC, 4in (10cm) diam.
£135–150
€/ $215–240 ⊞ SEA

A late Victorian silver-plated ham-bone holder, of plain baluster form with a pierced, key-type screw, 5½in (14cm) long.
£80–100
€/ $125–160 ⚒ WW

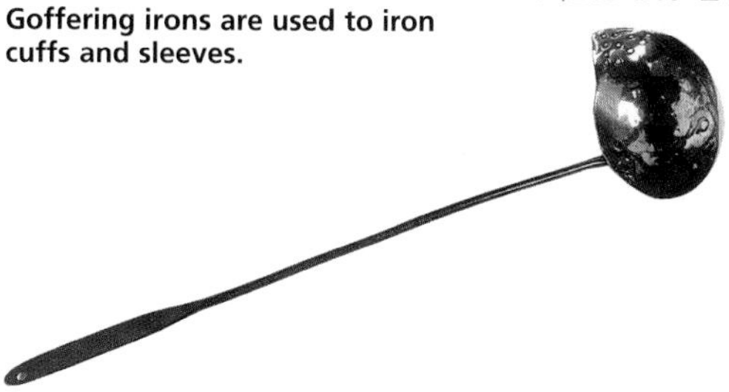

A brass straining ladle, with iron handle, c1780, 24in (61cm) long.
£200–225
€/ $315–350 ⊞ MFB

A pine maid's box, c1890, 11½in (29cm) high.
£90–100
€/ $140–160 ⊞ AL

A cast-iron mangle, by C. E. Sheldon, Irish, c1860, 60in (152.5cm) high.
£160–180
€/ $250–280 ⊞ HON

An Eddystone milk boiler, c1910, 7½in (19cm) high.
£75–85
€/ $120–135 ⊞ WeA

◄ **A brass and tin milk can,** c1900, 18in (45.5cm) high.
£180–200
€/ $285–315 ⊞ SMI

► **A brass and tin milk can,** c1910, 7in (18cm) high.
£80–90
€/ $125–145 ⊞ WeA

A Royal Doulton ceramic milk pail, c1890, 10in (25.5cm) high.
£180–200
€/ $285–315 ⊞ SMI

A brass milk skimmer, with steel handle, early 19thC, 21½in (54.5cm) long.
£200–220
€/ $315–350 ⊞ WeA

A Wilson creamware jelly mould, each face painted with fruit and flowers, impressed 'Wilson', 1790–1800, 9¾in (25cm) diam.
£3,500–4,000
€/ $5,500–6,300 ⚒ WW
This is a rare item.

A pewter one and a half pint ice cream mould, c1870, 6in (15cm) high.
£200–220
€/ $315–350 ⊞ MFB

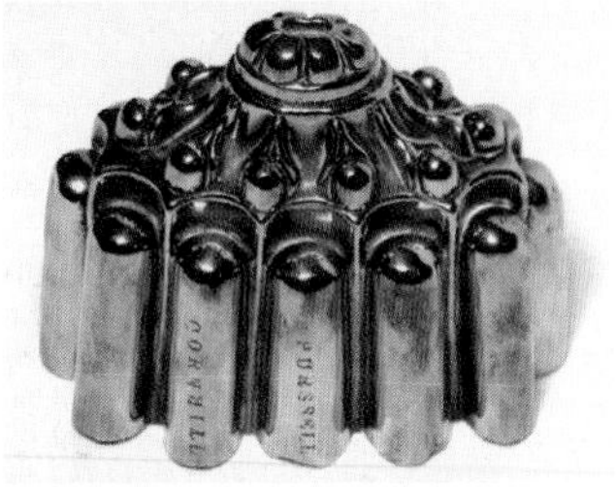

A Purssell Cornhill copper jelly mould, 19thC, 7in (18cm) diam.
£350–400
€/ $550–630 ⊞ SEA

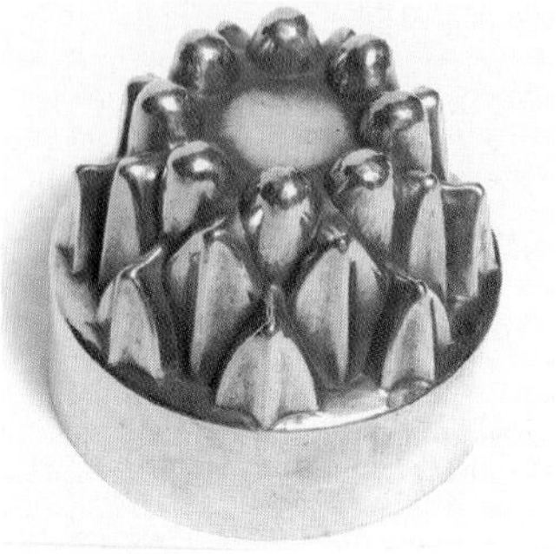

A Victorian copper jelly mould, 4in (10cm) diam.
£160–175
€/ $250–275 ⊞ WiB

A copper and tin jelly mould, c1880, 7in (18cm) wide.
£160–200
€/ $250–315 ⊞ WeA

A metal chocolate mould, in the shape of a fish, 1900–20, 13in (33cm) wide.
£70–75
€/ $110–120 ⊞ CHAC

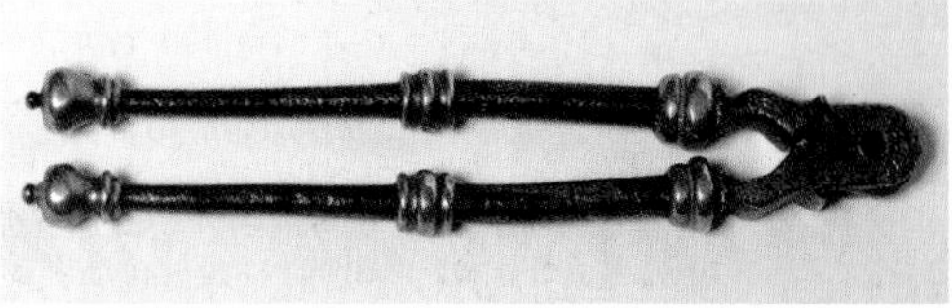

A wrought-iron and brass nut cracker, c1770, 5in (12.5cm) long.
£340–375
€/ $540–600 ⊞ SEA

An elm oatmeal crusher, Scottish, c1880, 14in (35.5cm) long.
£80–90
€/ $125–140 ⊞ MFB

A tinplate oven, with an open back and superstructure to hold a clockwork spit jack, early 19thC, 48in (122cm) high.
£250–300
€/ $400–475 ⚒ S(O)

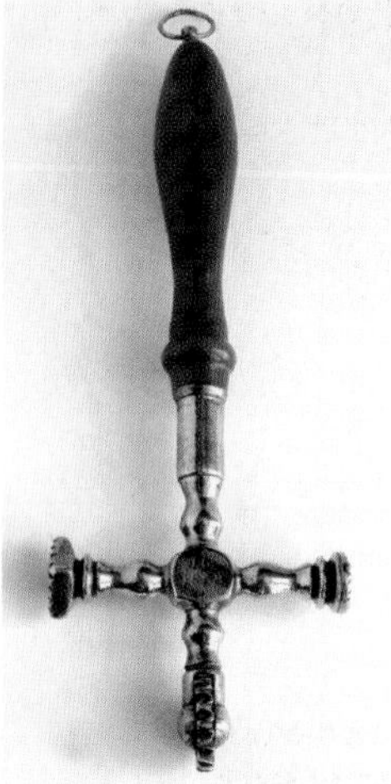

A brass pastry cutter, with a wooden handle, c1860, 11in (28cm) long.
£160–180
€/ $250–285 ⊞ WeA

► An elm pestle and mortar, 19thC, 36¼in (92cm) high.
£525–625
€/ $830–990 ⚒ SWO

An oak potato press, Romanian, c1880, 22in (56cm) wide.
£55–60
€/ $85–95 ⊞ Byl

A pair of cast-iron and brass butcher's scales, French, c1880, 26in (66cm) wide.
£180–200
€/ $285–315 ⊞ SMI

A painted tin biscuit tin, c1900, 6½in (16.5cm) wide.
£100–120
€/ $160–190 ⊞ SWN

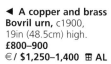

A Denby storage jar, c1910, 14in (35.5cm) high
£100–120
€/ $160–190 ⊞ SMI

◄ A copper and brass Bovril urn, c1900, 19in (48.5cm) high.
£800–900
€/ $1,250–1,400 ⊞ AL

A three-tier boxwood spice tower, c1810, 6in (15cm) high.
£260–300
€/ $410–475 ⊞ F&F

A T. G. Green Streamline storage jar, c1930, 4in (10cm) high.
£65–75
€/ $100–120 ⊞ CAL

Pottery

The last year has certainly seen difficulties in the market place as a whole with many investments in share portfolios and pensions proving disastrous. Auction houses have had their fair share of turmoil, some showing huge losses. With wars in Afghanistan and now in Iraq, there is plenty of uncertainty and reasonable cause for concern about the year ahead. However, despite all this doom and gloom, the housing market remains high and the collectors' market for pottery, particularly at the top end, looks as strong as ever. Collectors and dealers are still fighting hard over rarities such as the English delft cat jug dated 1677, which recently fetched £45,000 (€/ $71,000) at auction having been discovered lurking behind a Royal Crown Derby saucer worth about £25 (€/ $40). The market for majolica remains good with rare game pie dishes still fetching their expected four- and five-figure sums. The majolica highlight this year was the £105,000 (€/ $166,000) achieved for the Minton Museum Collection life-size peacocks by Paul Comolera dating from 1873.

Various other collections have appeared on the market including the sale of Staffordshire figures and animals from the Margaret Cadman Collection held at Christie's and some very fine Wood family models that were offered at Sotheby's. I have handled two collections of printed political satire pottery in the last six months and both proved sell-outs, with London specialist dealers complaining bitterly at the seemingly extortionate prices collectors and museums are willing to pay.

This in part might be accounted for by the amazing advances in communication over the last five years. With hundreds of auctioneers and thousands of dealers all posting their sale catalogues and stock online, anyone interested has easy access to anything new in the market place. It also shows that despite a difficult market with plenty of uncertainty, terrorist threats and wars, there is still a lot of enthusiasm for old pots, particularly the best pieces, from collectors across the country and around the world.

John Axford

Animals

A Staffordshire creamware model of a water buffalo, possibly Whieldon, c1755, 6in (15cm) wide.
£5,800–6,500
€/ $9,200–10,200 ⊞ JHo
Fragments of a very similar model with a rider were found on the site of Thomas Whieldon's pottery at Fenton Vivian.

A Staffordshire salt-glazed stoneware bear baiting jug and cover, the applied clay chippings simulating fur, the snout pierced with two chain links, c1760, 10in (25.5cm) high.
£3,500–4,200
€/ $5,500–6,600 WW
This piece was exhibited at the Northern Ceramic Society Exhibition in 1974: a useful provenance as there are many fakes of these jugs.

◀ **A Ralph Wood model of a goat,** lying on a rocky base, decorated in translucent glazes, with hollow unglazed underside, 1775–85, 6½in (16.5cm) high.
£2,500–3,000
€/ $4,000–4,800 G(L)

A pair of De Porceleyne Claeuw Dutch Delft peewit butter dishes and covers, with polychrome decoration, claw mark and numerals in blue inside covers, restored, c1765, 5½in (14cm) long.
£5,500–6,500
€/ $8,700–10,500 S(NY)

A tin-glazed group of a spaniel and three puppies, shaded in manganese, her tail and shaggy fur around the head and neck in bright yellow and black, the puppies with brown markings, possibly German, c1770, 9½in (24cm) wide.
£620–775
€/ $975–1,225 B

A Ralph Wood model of a ram, c1790, 7in (18cm) wide.
£2,000–2,300
€/ $3,200–3,600 HOW

A pearlware group of a cow and milkmaid, decorated in Pratt colours, the base with sponged decoration, Staffordshire or Yorkshire, minor restoration to tail, c1800, 6in (15cm) high.
£1,100–1,200
€/ $1,750–1,900 HOW

A Staffordshire pearlware model of a lioness, on a shaped foliate scroll-moulded base, bocage missing, minor restoration and overpainting, 1810–15, 5½in (14cm) high.
£950–1,200
€/ $1,500–1,900 S(NY)

A pair of Staffordshire pigeons, early 19thC, 3in (7.5cm) wide.
£800–880
€/ $1,250–1,400 JHo

A Staffordshire pearlware dog whistle, lower part restored, snout chipped, c1790, 2¼in (5.5cm) high.
£900–1,100
€/ $1,400–1,700 S(O)

A Staffordshire pearlware model of a cockerel, on a rock base, decorated with polychrome enamels, c1800, 9¾in (25cm) high.
£1,600–2,000
€/ $2,500–3,200 G(L)

A Staffordshire model of a pug, early 19thC, 3¾in (9.5cm) high.
£500–550
€/ $800–870 JHo

A pottery model of a pig, Scottish, c1830, 6in (15cm) high.
£1,600–1,800
€/ $2,500–2,800 HOW

A Prattware model of a horse, possibly Staffordshire, late 18thC, 3½in (9cm) wide.
£1,100–1,200
€/ $1,700–1,900 JHo

A Staffordshire model of a pointer, early 19thC, 6½in (16.5cm) wide.
£1,500–1,700
€/ $2,400–2,700 JHo

A Staffordshire model of a retriever, with light brown markings, on a green and brown rockwork base, c1820, 6½in (16.5cm) wide.
£450–550
€/ $700–870 F&C

An Obadiah Sherratt-style Staffordshire bull baiting group, entitled 'Bull.Beating' and 'Now Captin Lad', modelled as a chained bull tossing a terrier over one shoulder, and being bitten on its nose by another, a man with his arms raised by the bull's hind quarters, on a flat-footed table base, minor restoration and hairline crack, c1830, 13½in (34.5cm) long.
£3,500–4,200
€/ $5,500–6,600 B(Kn)

A Staffordshire buff-glazed model of a lion, on a fixed stand, 19thC, 13½in (34.5cm) wide.
£650–750
€/ $1,000–1,150 LVS

A pair of Dutch Delft blue and white models of cows, minor glaze chips, painted A/I:H mark, 19thC, 9in (23cm) wide.
£1,500–1,800
€/ $2,400–2,850 S(O)

A pair of Staffordshire models of poodles, c1850, 8in (20.5cm) high.
£320–350
€/ $500–550 NAW
These are of good quality, with separate front legs and applied sieved-clay coats. Poodles are harder to find than spaniels and therefore command a higher price, particularly when they are a good matching pair, such as these.

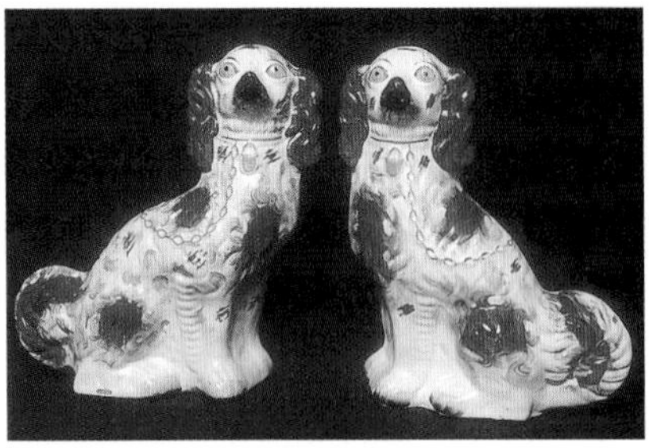

A pair of Staffordshire models of spaniels, c1850, 13in (33cm) high.
£450–500
€/ $700–800 TUN

A Staffordshire group of three dogs, c1850, 7½in (19cm) high.
£1,700–1,900
€/ $2,700–3,000 HOW

A glazed terracotta model of a spaniel, by James Bailey, restoration damage to ear, Canadian, Ontario, 1850s, 6¾in (17cm) high.
£1,100–1,200
€/ $1,700–1,900 RIT

A pair of Staffordshire models of circus ponies, c1855, 6in (15cm) high.
£800–875
€/ $1,300–1,400 HOW

A Staffordshire model of a hen on a nest with chicks, c1855, 7in (18cm) high.
£725–800
€/ $1,150–1,300 HOW

A Staffordshire model of an Afghan hound, with a figure of a girl by its side, c1860, 13in (33cm) high.
£850–950
€/ $1,350–1,500 ML

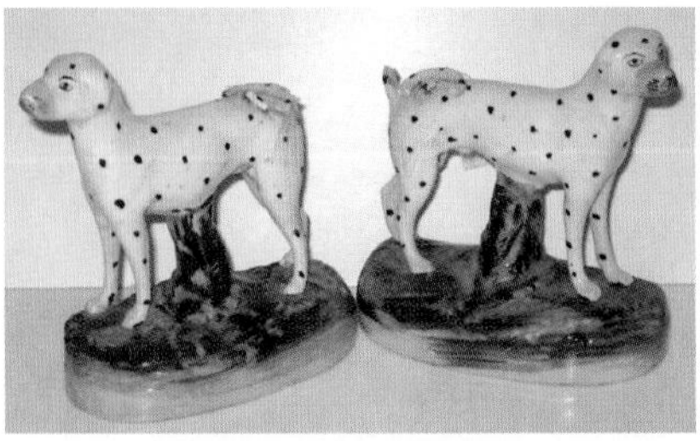

◄ **A pair of Staffordshire models of Dalmations,** on painted bases, tails damaged, c1860, 6½in (16.5cm) wide.
£220–260
€/ $350–400 BWL

► **A pair of Staffordshire spill vases,** modelled as sporting dogs standing before trees, c1860, 10in (25.5cm) high.
£1,200–1,400
€/ $1,900–2,200 HOW

A pair of Staffordshire models of Jackfield-style cats, c1860, 8in (20.5cm) high.
£775–850
€/ $1,200–1,350 HOW

A pair of Staffordshire models of spaniels, each holding a basket of flowers in its mouth, 1860–80, 7½in (19cm) high.
£475–565
€/ $750–900 TMA

A pair of Victorian Staffordshire models of spaniels, with painted features, gilt collars and chains, 8¾in (22cm) high.
£220–250
€/ $350–400 PF

A pair of Staffordshire models of spaniels, 1860–80, 7½in (19cm) high.
£240–265
€/ $380–420 CHAC

Miller's Compares

I. A pair of Staffordshire models of spaniels, c1870, 9½in (24cm) high.
£350–400
€/ $550–630 CHAC

II. A pair of Staffordshire models of spaniels, c1875, 9½in (24cm) high.
£220–250
€/ $350–400 CHAC

Item I depicts a pair of Staffordshire dogs which are commonly known as 'Disraeli spaniels' because the kiss curls on the tops of their heads are reminiscent of the hairstyle of the Victorian prime minister Benjamin Disraeli. They are only found in black and white, and are much scarcer and therefore more desirable than those without the curls, as in Item II.

A Brown-Westhead and Moore majolica group of a camel and an Arab, shape No. 1285, both seated before an open stone forming a flower holder, on a mound base, one ear of camel repaired, small chip to noseband, impressed mark, c1870, 16in (40.5cm) wide.
£2,700–3,200
€/ $4,300–5,000 S(O)

A Staffordshire pottery model of a King Charles spaniel, seated on a cushion, haircrack to base, 19thC, 5in (12.5cm) high.
£300–350
€/ $475–550 B(W)

A pottery majolica stick stand, modelled as a heron with a fish, some damage, stamped '7765/12', Continental, 19thC, 31in (78.5cm) high.
£470–565
€/ $740–900 SWO

A pair of Jackfield-style models of spaniels, c1870, 9in (23cm) high.
£380–420
€/ $600–670 DAN

► **A pair of Staffordshire spill vases,** modelled as spaniels, c1875, 12in (30.5cm) high.
£450–550
€/ $710–870 TUN

A Staffordshire model of a spaniel, with a painted face, incised initials 'WM' and 'NT' to underside, 19thC, 10¾in (27.5cm) high.
£140–160
€/ $220–250 SWO

A pair of Staffordshire pottery models of pugs, each wearing a collar with a gilt locket, one back leg reglued, late 19thC, 11in (28cm) high.
£525–625
€/ $830–985 B(W)

A Staffordshire porcellaneous spill vase, modelled as a goat standing before a tree trunk, c1880, 4in (10cm) high.
£170–185
€/ $270–300 SER

A Staffordshire model of an elephant, c1880, 8in (20.5cm) high.
£1,200–1,300
€/ $1,900–2,000 HOW

A Wedgwood majolica crocus pot and stand, modelled as a hedgehog, unmarked, late 19thC, 10½in (26.5cm) wide.
£680–820
€/ $1,100–1,300 S(O)

A Staffordshire model of a lamb, c1880, 3in (7.5cm) high.
£170–185
€/ $270–290 SER

A pair of Victorian Staffordshire models of reclining deer, 3in (7.5cm) high.
£85–100
€/ $135–160 CoCo

► **A majolica gurgler jug,** 19thC, 9¾in (25cm) high.
£105–115
€/ $165–180 CHAC
This jug makes a gurgling sound when water is poured and therefore is often known as a gurgler.

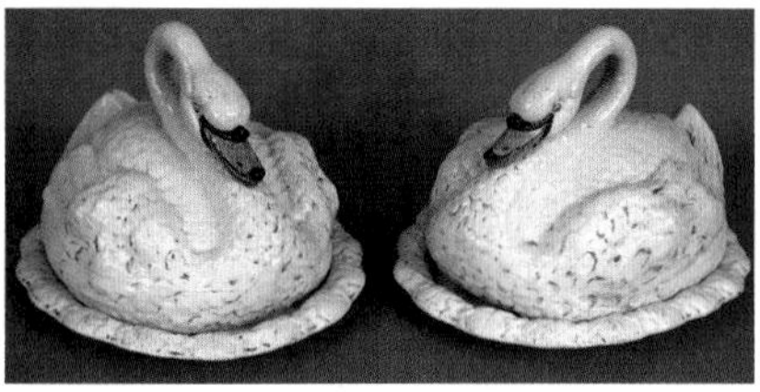

A pair of Staffordshire pottery dishes and covers, modelled as swans, 19thC, 8in (20.5cm) high.
£550–650
€/ $870–1,000 SWO

A pair of Staffordshire pottery models of zebras, damaged, 1875–1925, 7¾in (19.5cm) high.
£500–600
€/ $800–950 RTo

A pair of Staffordshire spill vases, modelled as lambs beneath rustic tree trunks, minor damage, 19thC, 5in (12.5cm) high.
£380–450
€/ $600–700 BWL

A Victorian Staffordshire group of a cow and calf, on a gilt-lined grassy base, horns restored, 7in (18cm) high.
£170–200
€/ $270–315 PFK

A Sarreguemines majolica tobacco box, modelled as a monkey playing a piano, piano cover and monkey's left hand missing, impressed marks, French, late 19thC, 9½in (24cm) wide.
£450–525
€/ $700–830 DN

Baskets

A Staffordshire pearlware blue and white basket-on-stand, printed with Grazing Rabbits pattern, within a floral border, c1820, 11½in (29cm) wide.
£850–1,000
€/ $1,300–1,600 WL

A Wedgwood Imperial Queen's Ware reticulated basket, with rope-twist borders, the sides hung with floral garlands, on a flared foot moulded with a Vitruvian scroll, marked 'Wedgwood', c1875, 7½in (19cm) wide.
£180–225
€/ $285–350 WW

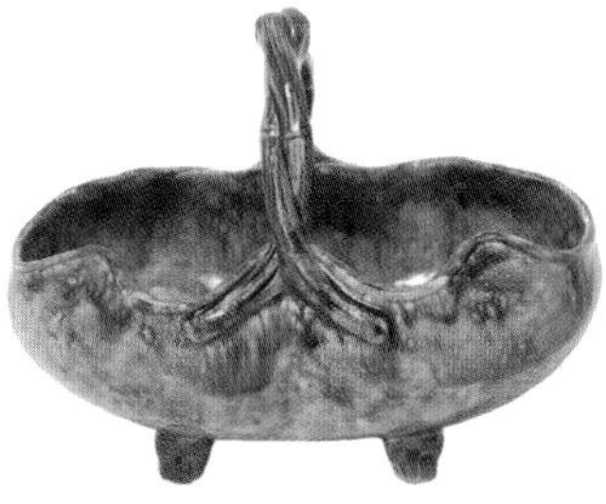

A majolica basket, c1880, 9½in (24cm) wide.
£60–70
€/ $95–110 CHAC

◄ **A George Jones majolica strawberry basket,** moulded with blossoming strawberry plants, the base with a painted design No. 3300 111 and impressed registration lozenge, 19thC, 11¾in (30cm) wide.
£525–625
€/ $830–990 SWO

A majolica strawberry basket, the handle modelled with strawberries, the curved body decorated with flowers, flanked by recesses for jars, impressed mark for the Victoria Pottery Co, late 19thC, 13in (33cm) wide.
£220–250
€/ $350–400 BR

Bowls

A Hispano-Moresque lustre bowl, painted with a bird among stylized trees and foliage, minor chip and surface wear, Spanish, Valencia, 1700–50, 15in (38cm) diam.
£920–1,100
€/ $1,450–1,750 S(O)

An English delft blue and white bowl, decorated with a bird flying over a pagoda, early 18thc, 11in (28cm) diam.
£675–750
€/ $1,000–1,200 KEY

A delft bowl, probably Bristol, c1730, 8¾in (22cm) diam.
£900–1,000
€/ $1,400–1,600 JHo

Items in the Pottery section have been arranged in date order within each sub-section.

An Enoch Booth bowl, c1743, 7in (18cm) diam.
£4,000–4,400
€/ $6,300–7,000 JHo

Enoch Booth, with Thomas Astbury and Josiah Wedgwood, is associated with the invention and development of creamware. The design for this bowl is derived from Chinese blue and white porcelain.

A maiolica bowl, the top painted with a geometric pattern, cracked, rim chips, Spanish, 18thC, 12¼in (31cm) diam.
£100–120
€/ $160–190 DN

A Neale caneware sucrier and cover, with twin handles and neo-classical-style moulding, the cover with scrolling acanthus leaves and flowers, a central fluted boss and floral knop, the base with panels containing an urn flanked by pendant husks, fine crack to flange of cover, impressed factory mark, incised 'N31', c1790, 7½in (19cm) wide.
£800–1,000
€/ $1,250–1,600 B

A Staffordshire pottery pedestal bowl, printed and enamelled with figures beside a fireplace and chair, the reverse inscribed 'Love not sleep lest thou come to poverty', c1840, 3½in (9cm) diam.
£85–100
€/ $135–160 WL

A late Victorian George Jones majolica sugar basin and milk jug, both decorated with relief-moulded flowers, the basin on three log feet, the jug with a branch handle, crack to basin, jug 3in (7.5cm) high.
£100–120
€/ $160–190 PFK

An earthenware bowl, with everted rim and dark brown splatter glazes on a red body, hairline crack, Canadian, Quebec, 19thC, 11½in (29cm) wide.
£180–220
€/ $280–340 RIT

A pottery bowl, c1860, 10in (25.5cm) diam.
£155–170
€/ $245–270 MFB

A faïence barber's bowl, polychrome-painted with floral sprays and insects, damaged, French, 19thC, 10in (25.5cm) wide.
£100–120
€/ $160–190 EH

A Furnival Pottery punch bowl, transfer-printed and coloured with Gothic arcading, late 19thC, 19½in (49.5cm) diam.
£400–500
€/ $630–800 S

Various Furnival partnerships produced pottery in Cobridge, Staffordshire, in the second half of the 19th century. Furnivals Ltd was in production from 1890–1968.

A Minton majolica bowl, modelled as a lily bowl above three crouching frogs, on a circular base, stem restored, dated 1865, 4½in (11.5cm) high.
£950–1,150
€/ $1,500–1,800 B(W)

A Wedgwood majolica punch bowl, cracks, 19thC, 13½in (34.5cm) diam.
£220–250
€/ $350–400 MAR

A Wemyss basket, painted with irises, with rope-twist handle, impressed 'Wemyss', printed retailer's mark for Thomas Goode & Co, London, early 20thC, 16in (40.5cm) long.
£2,500–3,000
€/ $4,000–4,700 S

Buildings

A Staffordshire watch stand, modelled as a castle keep on a mound base, c1820, 8in (20.5cm) high.
£1,800–1,900
€/ $2,800–3,000 JHo

A Prattware money box, modelled as a house flanked by two figures, some restoration, impressed flowerhead mark, 1800–50, 5in (12.5cm) high.
£185–220
€/ $290–350 WW

A Staffordshire porcellaneous model of a cottage, c1840, 4in (10cm) high.
£200–225
€/ $315–350 DAN

A Staffordshire model of Euston Station, c1855, 11in (28cm) high.
£1,200–1,400
€/ $1,900–2,200 HOW

Busts

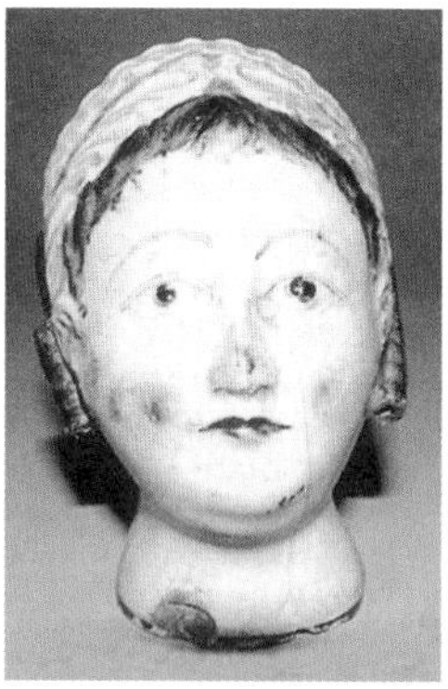

A pearlware female head, with elaborate coiffure, possibly a *bonbonnière*, screw-on cover missing, 1775–1825, 3in (7.5cm) high.
£55–65
€/ $85–100 PFK

A Staffordshire bust of Alexander I of Russia, by Wood & Caldwell, c1805, 12in (30.5cm) high.
£1,500–1,650
€/ $2,400–2,600 JHo

A Staffordshire pearlware bust of Voltaire, impressed title to reverse of pedestal, early 19thC, 6in (15cm) high.
£550–650
€/ $870–1,000 S

A Wedgwood black basalt bust of Mercury, modelled after the Antique by William Hackwood, on a waisted socle, impressed 'Wedgwood' to bust and socle, 19thC, 18½in (47cm) high.
£1,300–1,500
€/ $2,000–2,400 Bea(E)

Candlesticks

A Minton majolica candlestick, modelled as a putto supporting a sconce on his head, on a circular base, reglued through the ankles, impressed marks and date cypher for 1867, 7in (18cm) high.
£700–850
€/ $1,100–1,350 WW

► **A Minton majolica candlestick,** the bulbous gadrooned shaft on a shaped circular base, c1870, 7½in (19cm) high.
£500–600
€/ $800–950 B

Ex-Minton Sale. Masterpieces of Minton was the title of an auction held at Bonhams in July 2002. The sale comprised 380 pieces of pottery and porcelain from the Minton Museum Collection.

A pair of Wedgwood blue and white triton two-light candlesticks, each supporting two leaf- and scroll-moulded branches beneath foliage sconces, restored, impressed marks, painted '2129', c1876, 14¼in (36cm) high.
£650–750
€/ $1,000–1,200 S(O)

Cheese Domes

A stoneware cheese dome, with floral decoration, c1870, 11in (28cm) diam.
£100–120
€/ $160–190 WAC

A George Jones majolica cheese dome, the textured ground moulded with briars and leafy wildflowers, pink-glazed interior, glued repair to stand, impressed mark, black script pattern No. 5223, post-1873, 7in (18cm) high.
£1,400–1,600
€/ $2,200–2,500 S(O)

A Thomas Forester & Sons majolica cheese dome, modelled with a frieze of four panels edged in bamboo, each containing a stork wading among waterlilies and bulrushes, with a bamboo handle, rim chips, glaze wear and crazing, inscribed '28', c1883, 11¼in (28.5cm) high.
£500–625
€/ $800–1,000 B

Cow Creamers

A Prattware-style cow creamer and cover, restored, c1800, 6¼in (16cm) long.
£450–550
€/ $700–870 S(O)

A cow creamer, probably Swansea, early 19thC, 7in (18cm) long.
£375–450
€/ $600–700 DAU

A cow creamer, North Yorkshire, early 19thC, 5¼in (13.5cm) long.
£1,000–1,100
€/ $1,600–1,750 JHo

Dishes

A Liverpool or London delft sweetmeat dish, c1760, 8½in (21.5cm) diam.
£3,000–3,300
€/ $4,750–5,250 JHo

A Durlach faïence dish, painted with sprays of *indianische Blumen* and scattered sprigs, minor glaze chips to rim, German, c1760, 13½in (34.5cm) wide.
£700–800
€/ $1,100–1,250 S(O)

A Rörstrand faïence dish, Swedish, 1765, 19in (48.5cm) wide.
£450–550
€/ $700–870 BUK

Three Minton majolica oyster dishes, with moulded shell decoration, marked, 1868, 9in (23cm) diam.
£700–820
€/ $1,100–1,300 SWO

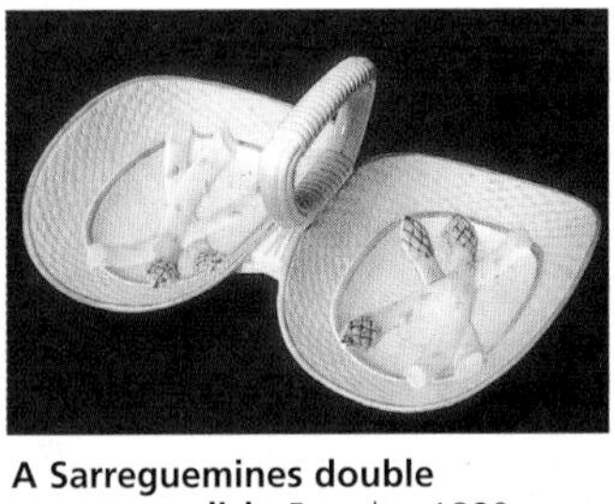

A Sarreguemines double asparagus dish, French, c1880, 15in (38cm) wide.
£270–300
€/ $425–475 MLL

A pottery dish, the exterior printed with three fish, crazing and foot chip, 19thC, 7in (18cm) diam.
£160–200
€/ $250–315 PFK
The fish are meant to represent char, which were made into a paste and stored in these vessels. The char is a fish that belongs to the *Salmonidae* family and inhabits lakes in Scotland, Ireland and Wales. It flourished years ago, but is seldom seen today.

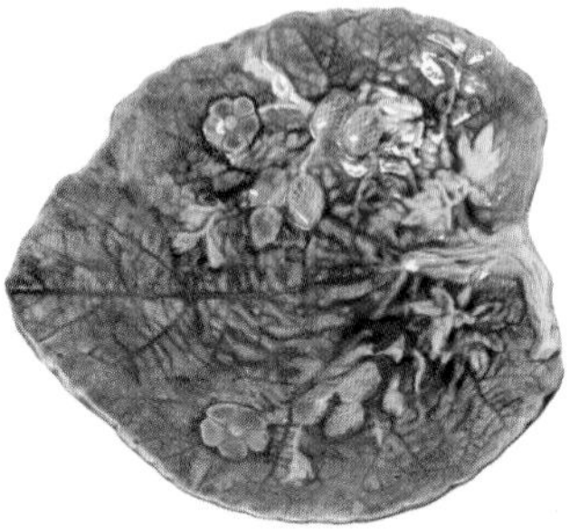

A majolica strawberry dish, 1850–1900, 10½in (26.5cm) wide.
£75–85
€/ $120–135 CHAC

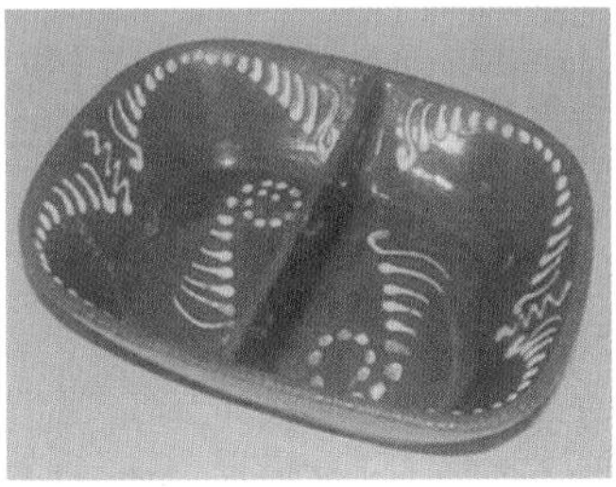

A slip-trailed pottery dish, with two compartments, a beaded rim and integral trailing, 19thC, 11¾in (30cm) wide.
£65–75
€/ $100–115 PFK

A Wemyss quaich, painted with roses, c1900, 7in (18cm) diam.
£320–350
€/ $500–550 RdeR

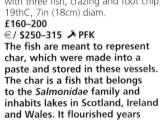

Covered Dishes

A Marieberg faïence butter dish and cover, Swedish, 1766–69, 8in (20.5cm) wide.
£1,500–1,700
€/ $2,400–2,700 BUK

A Staffordshire creamware butter dish and cover, the knop modelled as a cow, 18thC, 7in (18cm) diam.
£2,500–2,800
€/ $4,000–4,400 JHo

A Mosbach faïence butter dish and cover, on a fixed stand, painted with flower sprays and scattered leaves, the cover with a pear finial, minor glaze chips to rims, CT monogram in black, German, 1775–1825, 9½in (24cm) diam.
£500–600
€/ $800–950 S(O)

A Minton majolica game pie dish and cover, the lid with a hare, mallard and woodsnipe, the base with basketweave and oak leaves, date cypher for 1858, 14in (35.5cm) wide.
£1,000–1,200
€/ $1,600–1,900 HOLL

A Minton majolica game pie dish and cover, the cover surmounted by a gundog lying on a gun and a gamebag, relief decorated with a hare to the front and a pheasant to the reverse, on four moulded paw feet, impressed marks to base, c1870, 8in (20.5cm) wide.
£2,000–2,400
€/ $3,200–3,800 B(EA)

A sardine box, the lid with an applied dolphin finial and moulded with seaweed, decorated in cream with gilded detail on a puce ground, the base also embossed with seaweed or foliage within gilded rims, 19thC, 5½in (14cm) wide.
£100–120
€/ $160–190 GAK

Drainers & Strainers

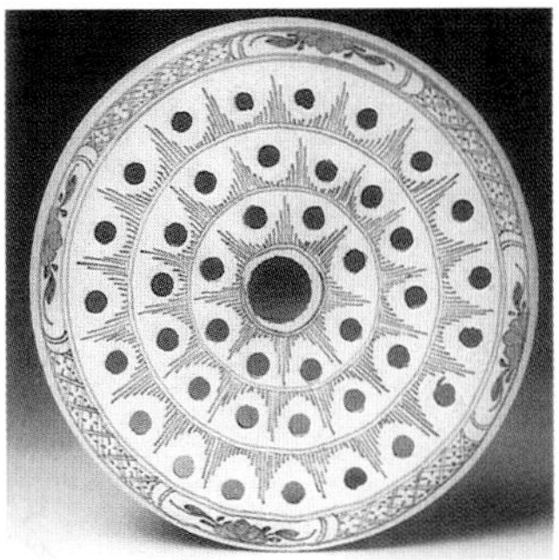

A London delft drainer, painted with radiating lines, rim chip, glaze worn, mid-18thC, 7in (18cm) diam.
£900–1,100
€/ $1,400–1,700 B

A creamware strainer, c1790, 3in (7.5cm) wide.
£200–225
€/ $315–350 DSA

A Hicks & Meigh Ironstone drainer, c1820, 13in (33cm) wide.
£280–320
€/ $440–500 CoS

Further reading

Miller's Ceramics Buyers Guide, Miller's Publications, 2000

A Spode Ironstone drainer, c1825, 15in (38cm) wide.
£360–400
€/ $550–630 CoS

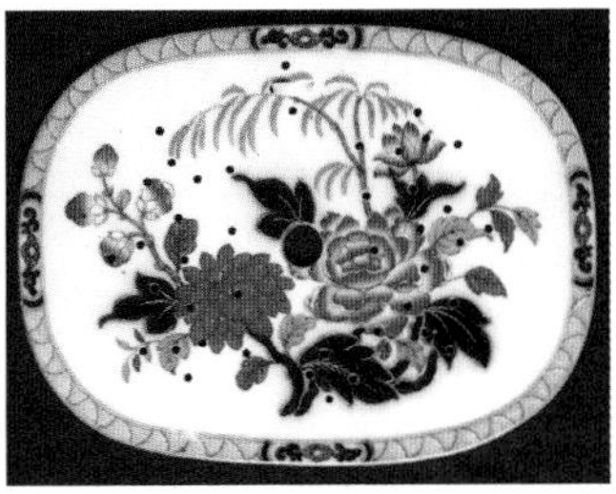

A Minton & Hollins drainer, pattern No. 5160, over-enamelled with flowers, c1843, 12in (30.5cm) wide.
£380–420
€/ $600–675 CoS

A Mason's drainer, decorated with Bandana pattern, c1850, 13in (33cm) wide.
£380–420
€/ $600–675 CoS

Figures

A faïence figure of St Louis, standing with his right arm outstretched and his left arm raised before him, his costume painted in blue, his crown, feet and the fleur-de-lys moulded on his cape picked out in ochre, base inscribed 'Saint.Louis.,1735', minor damage, French, possibly Nevers, 15¾in (40cm) high.
£350–420
€/ $550–660 B

A Staffordshire figure of Iphigenia, c1790, 8½in (21.5cm) high.
£250–280
€/ $400–440 SER

A Staffordshire pearlware group of children, entitled 'Scuffle', modelled as a boy and two girls fighting over a hat, c1810, 6¼in (16cm) high.
£375–450
€/ $600–700 S(O)

A Staffordshire figure of Faith, restored, c1780, 8in (20.5cm) high.
£170–185
€/ $270–300 SER

A Prattware figure of a fiddler, probably Staffordshire, c1790, 7½in (19cm) high.
£1,600–1,800
€/ $2,500–2,800 JHo

A pair of Staffordshire Tittensor figural groups, c1810, 6in (15cm) high.
£3,200–3,500
€/ $5,000–5,500 JHo
Charles and John Tittensor were Staffordshire figure-makers during the late 18th century and early 19th century. Some pieces have impressed marks.

A Ralph Wood pearlware figure of a shepherd, the base decorated with sheep and birds, c1785, 8½in (21.5cm) high.
£450–500
€/ $700–800 JRe

A Wood family pearlware figure of Simon, standing before a tree stump, his arms folded, on a grassy mound base, small chips, c1785, 8¾in (22cm) high.
£1,700–2,000
€/ $2,700–3,200 S(O)

The Wood family of potters

Many of the most celebrated English pottery figures of the 18th century were made by members of the Wood family working in Staffordshire. The rare and extremely expensive pew groups of c1745 are often attributed to Aaron Wood (1717–85). Ralph Wood I (1715–72) and Ralph Wood II (1748–95) are famous for their skillfully modelled Toby jugs and figures with high temperature underglaze colours. Some pieces have impressed marks or an incised rebus mark of a small clump of trees.

A Ralph Wood pearlware figural group, entitled 'The Bird Cage', decorated with overglaze enamels, impressed No. 89, c1790, 10½in (26.5cm) high.
£900–1,000
€/ $1,400–1,600 JRe

A pair of Staffordshire creamware figures of children, decorated in enamels, c1800, 8in (20.5cm) high.
£850–950
€/ $1,350–1,500 JRe

► A Staffordshire pearlware figure of Diana, decorated with overglaze enamel, c1810, 11½in (29cm) high.
£450–500
€/ $700–800 JRe

A Staffordshire pearlware spill vase rural group, of a deer, a stag, a boy and a squirrel, c1820, 8½in (21.5cm) high.
£1,500–1,700
€/ $2,400–2,700 ⊞ HOW

A Staffordshire inkwell, modelled as a boy on a dolphin, early 19thC, 5in (12.5cm) high.
£1,000–1,100
€/ $1,600–1,750 ⊞ JHo

◄ **A Staffordshire Walton figural group,** entitled 'Friendship', c1820, 7½in (19cm) high.
£850–950
€/ $1,350–1,500 ⊞ HOW

A pair of pearlware figures of The Welsh Tailor and Wife, after Derby, each modelled riding a goat with a basket on their back containing infants and kids, painted with overglaze colours, on scroll-moulded bases, damaged, early 19thC, 5½in (14cm) high.
£170–200
€/ $270–315 ⚒ PF

► **A Staffordshire figure of Dr Syntax,** early 19thC, 5in (12.5cm) high.
£900–1,000
€/ $1,400–1,600
⊞ JHo
Dr Syntax is a comic character originally depicted in a series of drawings by the cartoonist Thomas Rawlinson, c1800.

A Staffordshire pearlware figure of an old soldier, decorated with overglaze enamels, c1820, 8in (20.5cm) high.
£2,000–2,300
€/ $3,200–3,650 ⊞ JRe

POTTERY

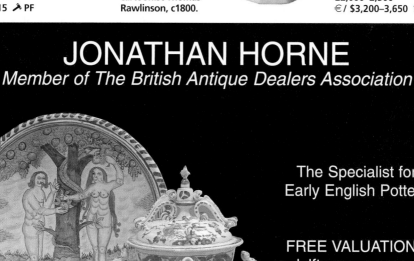

A Staffordshire pearlware pastoral group, modelled as a man and a woman sitting beneath a gnarled tree stump with two lambs and an owl, damaged, 1800–50, 8in (20.5cm) high.
£200–240
€/ $315–380 WW

A Staffordshire figural group of The Traveller, c1820, 4in (10cm) high.
£1,100–1,200
€/ $1,750–1,900 JHo

A Staffordshire pearlware spill vase group of a Vicar and clerk, christening a child, with three figures looking on, before a turreted castle flanked by flowering trees, the oval mound base moulded with a scroll, restored, c1825, 7in (18cm) high.
£850–975
€/ $1,350–1,550 LFA

An Obadiah Sherratt-style pearlware group of the Battle of the Breeches, modelled as a couple fighting over a pair of breeches, a baby and a cat at their feet, damaged, 1820–30, 7½in (19cm) high.
£2,300–2,700
€/ $3,600–4,200 S(O)

A Staffordshire pearlware group, entitled 'Petter Rising The Lame Man Acts Ch 2', c1825, 10½in (26.5cm) high.
£1,500–1,700
€/ $2,400–2,700 HOW

A Staffordshire figure of a female gardener, c1825, 7in (18cm) high.
£550–600
€/ $870–950 HOW

A Staffordshire figural group of a dancer and a musician, with a swan beneath a bridge, c1840, 7½in (19cm) high.
£155–170
€/ $245–270 CHAC

A pair of Staffordshire figures of royal chidren on ponies, by Thomas Parr, c1850, 9in (23cm) high.
£1,400–1,600
€/ $2,200–2,500 HOW

A Staffordshire figure of Garibaldi, with Liberté flag, c1850, 13in (33cm) high.
£340–375
€/ $550–600 ML

A pair of Staffordshire figures of Gringoire and Esmerelda, restored, c1850, 7in (18cm) high.
£155–170
€/ $245–270 CHAC

► **A Staffordshire spill vase,** modelled as Macomo and the lion, on a gilt-scroll base, c1850, 8¼in (21cm) high.
£850–1,000
€/ $1,350–1,600 SJH

A pair of Staffordshire figures of a girl and a boy with birds, c1850, 6in (15cm) high.
£270–300
€/ $430–470 ACO

A pair of Staffordshire figures of a man and a woman playing musical instruments, the bases decorated with vine leaves, c1850, 13in (33cm) high.
£630–700
€/ $1,000–1,100 TUN

A Staffordshire figural group of a prince and princess in a carriage, c1850, 8in (20.5cm) high.
£1,100–1,200
€/ $1,750–1,900 ⊞ HOW

A Staffordshire figure of a girl gardener, by a bridge over a stream, c1850, 7¼in (18.5cm) high.
£60–70
€/ $95–110 ⊞ CHAC

A Staffordshire pottery spill vase group, modelled as a fortune teller, 1850–60, 10in (25.5cm) high.
£200–235
€/ $315–375 ⊞ DAN

A Staffordshire figural group of a soldier and a sailor, c1854, 12in (30.5cm) high.
£300–325
€/ $475–515 ⊞ SER

A Staffordshire pottery figure, entitled 'The First Ride', c1855, 11½in (29cm) high.
£1,800–2,000
€/ $2,800–3,200 ⊞ HOW

A pair of Staffordshire figures, she entitled 'Sand', he entitled 'Beesums', c1855, 9in (23cm) high.
£765–850
€/ $1,200–1,350 ⊞ ML

Most working class cottages used to have flagstone floors which would get covered in grease and dirt. The method of cleaning them would be to spread sand liberally over the floor and leave it to be walked on for two or three days to soak up the grease. It would then be swept up with besom – a broom made of twigs tied round a stick. These itinerant traders would travel together from marketplace to marketplace selling their wares.

A Staffordshire figural group of Welsh shepherds, c1855, 14in (35.5cm) high.
£400–450
€/ $630–700 ⊞ TUN

A pair of Staffordshire figures of Scottish gardeners, wearing traditional dress, each with two pots of flowers, on a scroll-moulded base, c1860, 9¼in (23.5cm) high.
£65–80
€/ $100–125 ⚒ TMA

◄ A pair of Staffordshire pottery figures of a fisherman and a fisherwoman, each holding a basket of fish, 1860–80, 13in (33cm) high.
£120–140
€/ $190–220 ⚒ G(L)

A Staffordshire mustard pot figure, in the form of a portly gentleman, c1860, 6in (15cm) high.
£100–110
€/ $160–175 ⊞ DHA

A pair of Staffordshire figures of a girl and a boy reading, c1860, 6in (15cm) high.
£200–220
€/ $315–350 ⊞ SER

A Staffordshire figure, entitled 'Will Watch', 19thC, 15in (38cm) high.
£200–225
€/ $315–355 ⊞ CHAC

A Staffordshire group of Uncle Tom and Eva, from *Uncle Tom's Cabin*, c1860, 10in (25.5cm) high.
£300–325
€/ $475–515 ⊞ DHA

A Staffordshire figural group of a Scottish couple, seated on a clock, 19thC, 13½in (34.5cm) high.
£100–120
€/ $160–190 ⊞ CHAC

A pair of Staffordshire porcellaneous figural groups, of ladies mounted on stags, cracks, c1860, 7½in (19cm) high.
£380–450
€/ $600–700 ⚒ BR

A Staffordshire figural group of a shepherdess and a sheep, c1860, 7in (18cm) high.
£60–70
€/ $95–110 ⊞ ACO

A Staffordshire figural group of a girl with a goat, c1860, 6in (15cm) high.
£140–155
€/ $220–244 ⊞ SER

A pair of Stafforshire figural groups of a boy and a girl sitting on goats, c1865, 6in (15cm) high.
£300–335
€/ $475–525 ⊞ ML

A Staffordshire figural group of two musicians and a dog, 19thC, 12½in (32cm) high.
£120–135
€/ $190–215 ⊞ CHAC

► A Wedgwood black basalt figural group, entitled 'Cupid Disarmed', impressed 'Wedgwood', and title to the reverse, late 19thC, 13¾in (35cm) high.
£1,750–2,100
€/ $2,800–3,300 ⚒ B(WM)

A pair of Staffordshire figures of a girl and a boy with sheep, c1880, 7½in (19cm) high.
£350–400
€/ $550–630 ⊞ SER

A pair of majolica figures of women, one clutching wheat sheaves and holding a basket, the adjacent tree stump surmounted by wheat sheaves and a sickle, the other with upraised arms, the adjacent tree stump surmounted by a water jug, firing crack, 1850–1900, 21in (53.5cm) high.
£1,700–2,000
€/ $2,700–3,150 ⚒ RIT

◄ A Staffordshire figure of a grape picker, 19thC, 13½in (34.5cm) high.
£120–150
€/ $190–240 ⚒ L

A Staffordshire pottery spill vase figural group, of a young man holding a bird, and a young woman holding a bird's nest, standing above a bridge, on a gilt-lined base, 19thC, 13in (33cm) high.
£75–90
€/ $120–140 ⚒ DMC

A Staffordshire figure, entitled 'Infant Jesus', wearing a loin cloth, leaning on a pedestal surmounted by a book, on a gilt-lined base, 19thC, 11in (28cm) high.
£750–900
€/ $1,200–1,400 ⚒ SJH

POTTERY

Flatware

A maiolica dish, painted with a landscape and Cupid flanked by Venus and Mars embracing, and a bearded man, the reverse with a series of concentric rings and inscribed 'nonara e martto', Italian, possibly Urbino, 16thC, 9in (23cm) diam.
£3,000–3,600
€/ $4,750–5,700 ⚒ Bea

Items in the Pottery section have been arranged in date order within each sub-section.

A faïence dish, painted with a central flowering plant flanked by the date, the rim with four similar flower sprays, German, Zittau, dated 1685, 12in (30.5cm) diam.
£725–875
€/ $1,150–1,400 ⚒ S(O)

A maiolica dish, painted with the Madonna and Child, restored, hair crack, Italian, Venice, 1550–1600, 9½in (24cm) diam.
£2,000–2,400
€/ $3,200–3,800 ⚒ S(NY)

A Dutch Delft dish, painted with a pomegranate and objects, chips to edges, late 17thC, 13¾in (35cm) diam.
£300–350
€/ $475–550 ⚒ BR
This design was copied directly from Chinese *kraak* porcelain of 1600–40.

► A Dutch Delft royal portrait dish, commemorating Queen Mary, chip and crack to underside, initialled 'KM', numbered 20, 1675–1725, 13in (33cm) diam.
£1,400–1,600
€/ $2,200–2,500 ⚒ TEN

A pink lustre plate, with floral decoration, Hispano-Moresque, 16thC, 12½in (32cm) diam.
£2,000–2,200
€/ $3,150–3,200 ⚒ DA

An English delft charger, painted with oak leaves and cherries, late 17thC, 13¾in (35cm) diam.
£5,800–7,000
€/ $9,000–11,000 ⚒ S(O)

Expert's choice

A delft armorial plate, 1653, sold by Woolley & Wallis on 28th November 2001.

It's the unexpected that is usually the most exciting. Recently while on a valuation I discovered hanging above a kitchen sink a delft armorial plate inscribed with initials, and, more importantly, it was dated. Dated English delftware is among the 'holy grail' of English pottery, a small number of pieces having fetched over £100,000 (€/ $158,000) at auction.
On consulting *Dated English Delftware*, by Louis Lipski and Michael Archer (Sotheby's Publications 1984), I discovered a moulded dish with the same coat-of-arms and, like 'my' plate, dated 1653, the year Cromwell became Lord Protector of England. A footnote suggested that the arms were perhaps those of the Makers of Playing Cards Company, or the Paste Board Makers, although it seems these arms were not authorized in the 17th century. Unfortunately the plate had been broken into eight pieces and riveted back together. Had this been an equally rare piece of 18th-century Chinese porcelain, or Royal Worcester for that matter, it would have been nearly worthless, but English delft collectors are more pragmatic and realize that if they insist on perfect pieces, they would rarely buy anything at all. This was amply demonstrated when the plate was knocked down in the saleroom for £10,200 (€/ $16,000). **John Axford**

A London delft blue-dash charger, decorated with tulips and flowers growing from a mound, the reverse also tin-glazed, some restoration, c1700, 13½in (34.5cm) diam.
£2,800–3,200
€/ $4,400–5,000 S

A London or Bristol delft plate, c1725, 10in (25.5cm) diam.
£400–435
€/ $630–680 JHo

A Bristol delft plate, c1750, 12in (30.5cm) diam.
£675–750
€/ $1,100–1,200 SEA

Delft & delft

Delft is tin-glazed earthenware made in Holland since the 16th century, so-called from the town where so much of it was produced. From the 17th century tin-glazed earthenware was made in England using similar techniques and styles. In order to differentiate them, it is best to precede the term 'Delft' or 'Delftware' by Dutch or English. However, it has become customary for dealers and auction houses to use 'Delft' for the Dutch wares and 'delft' or 'delftware' for the English.

An English delft marriage plate, painted with cupids, the border with leaf scrolls and wheel medallions, reserving a panel with the initials 'E & EK', the reverse with repeating circles and groups of four dots, minor glaze chips and cracks, dated 1708, 8¾in (22cm) diam.
£4,000–4,750
€/ $6,300–7,500 B

A London delft dish, painted with a parrot seated on a ring, with rocks and flowers, rim chips, c1730, 13¾in (35cm) diam.
£525–625
€/ $830–980 S(O)

An English delft charger, painted centrally with flowers, rocks and a fence, within a border of repeated flower stems, mid-18thC, 13½in (34.5cm) diam.
£170–200
€/ $270–315 CGC

A Dutch Delft plate, painted with a Chinese man and a bird beside a vase of flowers, the rim with diaper border and five ribbon-bound leaf vignettes, early 18thC, 9in (23cm) diam.
£225–250
€/ $350–400 CGC

A Bristol delft plate, decorated with a peacock between trees, c1730, 8in (20.5cm) diam.
£2,200–2,400
€/ $3,500–3,800 JHo

A delft dish, possibly English, painted with chinoiserie flowers in a fenced garden, chips to rim, hairline glaze cracks, mid-18thC, 13½in (34.5cm) diam.
£200–225
€/ $315–350 RTo

► **A Moustiers faïence plate,** with central coat-of-arms, within a border of garlands, painted Olery mark, French, c1750, 9¾in (25cm) diam.
£280–340
€/ $440–550 Bea(E)

An English delft plate, painted with an exotic bird on a leafy branch, with rockwork and flowers, mid-18thC, 8¾in (22cm) diam.
£260–325
€/ $400–500 WW

A Bristol delft plate, painted with a bird on a rocky pinnacle, c1760, 12in (30.5cm) diam.
£1,100–1,200
€/ $1,700–1,790 ⊞ KEY

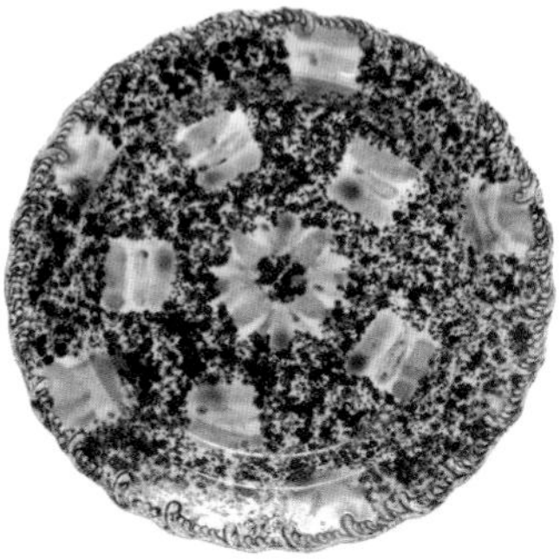

A Whieldon-style spongeware plate, c1765, 9in (23cm) diam.
£360–400
€/ $575–630 ⊞ HOW

A pair of Wedgwood creamware soup plates, from the Earl of Shaftesbury service, painted with the full arms of Anthony Ashley Cooper, 5th Earl of Shaftesbury, impressed marks, c1786, 9¾in (25cm) diam.
£525–625
€/ $830–900 B

A Dutch Delft dish, painted with a vase and jardinière of flowers, the border with five foliate panels, some glaze damage to rim, mid-18thC, 12in (30.5cm) diam.
£270–320
€/ $425–500 Bea(E)

A set of four English delft plates, painted with a Chinese pagoda set in a landscape, c1760, 9in (23cm) diam.
£585–650
€/ $925–1,000 ⊞ KEY

Thomas Whieldon

Thomas Whieldon (1719–95) was one of the principal 18th-century Staffordshire potters. He started a factory in 1740, making a wide range of wares, and partnered Josiah Wedgwood between 1754 and 1759. His name is most often associated with wares decorated with high-temperature underglaze colours, typically mottled green, grey, purple, yellow and brown, as well as the 'tortoiseshell ware' with sponged manganese decoration. Unfortunately for the ceramic historian his pieces were never marked.

An English delft plate, with floral decoration, 18thC, 9in (23cm) diam.
£400–450
€/ $630–700 ⊞ SEA

A Dutch Delft plate, painted with a pot issuing flowers, c1750, 14in (35.5cm) diam.
£360–400
€/ $575–625 ⊞ SEA

A salt-glazed plate, decorated with a Liverpool Sadler & Green printed design, c1765, 9in (23cm) diam.
£700–780
€/ $1,100–1,200 ⊞ JHo

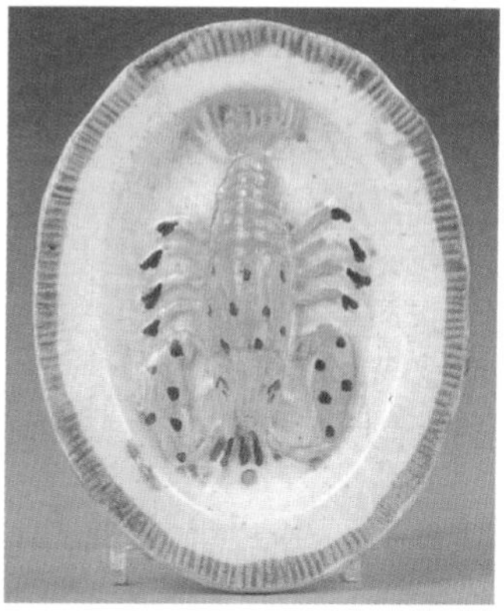

A creamware miniature platter, the centre moulded with a lobster, with a feather-moulded edge, c1780, 4¼in (11cm) wide.
£315–375
€/ $500–600 HAM

A Bristol delft charger, painted with stylized flowers and foliage, 18thC, 13in (33cm) wide.
£1,000–1,200
€/ $1,600–1,900 HYD

A Dutch Delft plate, painted with a vase of flowers, 18thC, 9in (23cm) diam.
£100–120
€/ $160–190 SWO

A Swansea Pottery arcaded plate, painted with a heron, c1815, 8in (20.5cm) diam.
£1,000–1,100
€/ $1,600–1,700 HOW

A child's plate, decorated with turkeys, within a moulded rim, c1840, 7½in (19cm) diam.
£145–160
€/ $230–250 HOW

A plate, printed with a view of the Philadelphia Exhibition 1876, decorated with a star device rim, 1876, 8¾in (22cm) diam.
£85–100
€/ $130–160 SAS

A Delft dish, painted with Oriental flowers within a flower and leaf border, rim chips, probably Dutch, 18thC, 12in (30.5cm) diam.
£120–150
€/ $190–240 TMA

A pearlware plate, commemorating Alderman Wood, the Lord Mayor of London, giving up his house to Queen Caroline on her arrival in London, 1820, 8in (20.5cm) diam.
£1,100–1,300
€/ $1,700–2,000 RdV

A nursery plate, painted with flowers and the name 'Alice', mid-19thC, 5½in (14cm) diam.
£135–150
€/ $215–240 SWN

A majolica 'corn on the cob' bread platter, some chips, 19thC, 14½in (37cm) wide.
£135–150
€/ $215–240 CHAC

A delft plate, painted with a hot air balloon above a house and garden, within a swag border, some fritting, late 18thC, 8¾in (22cm) diam.
£1,300–1,500
€/ $2,000–2,400 CHTR

An enamelled plate, commemorating the coronation of Queen Victoria, the centre painted with a portrait and inscription, the border relief-moulded with stylized flowers, c1837, 6¾in (17cm) diam.
£350–420
€/ $550–650 DD

A spongeware cream pottery dish, by Mann & Co, Hanley, 1858–60, 14in (35.5cm) diam.
£270–300
€/ $425–475 MFB

A Wemyss plate, painted with greengages, c1900, 5in (12.5cm) diam.
£270–300
€/ $425–475 RdeR

Flower Bricks

A London or Bristol delft flower brick, c1740, 6¼in (16cm) wide.
£1,000–1,100
€/ $1,600–1,700 ⊞ JHo

A pair of London delft flower bricks, each side painted with a vase of flowers, rim chips, c1750, 5¾in (14.5cm) wide.
£2,000–2,400
€/ $3,200–3,800 ⚒ S

A delft flower brick, possibly Liverpool, each side painted with a cottage, the ends painted with a bird, chips, c1760, 6in (15cm) wide.
£900–1,100
€/ $1,400–1,700 ⚒ S(O)

Garden Seats

A majolica garden seat, modelled as a blackamoor child among bulrushes, supporting a cushion, the base on three bun feet, c1870, 17½in (44.5cm) high.
£850–1,000
€/ $1,350–1,600 ⚒ S(NY)

► A George Jones majolica garden seat, modelled as a tripod of vine sticks roped together and hung with fruiting vines at the top, chips, with applied pad mark inscribed 'stoke-on-trent', with GJ monogram, foot chipped, c1870, 18in (45.5cm) high.
£750–900
€/ $1,200–1,400 ⚒ B

A Minton majolica garden seat, shape No. 1219, decorated in low relief with cranes and stylized flowering foliage, incised shape No., impressed Minton mark and date cipher for 1885, 17¾in (45cm) high.
£900–1,100
€/ $1,400–1,700 ⚒ B
Ex-Minton Sale.

Inkstands & Inkwells

A delft inkstand, probably Liverpool, each side painted with buildings, the ends with a man in a boat, c1760, 5in (12.5cm) wide.
£800–950
€/ $1,250–1,500 ⚒ S(O)

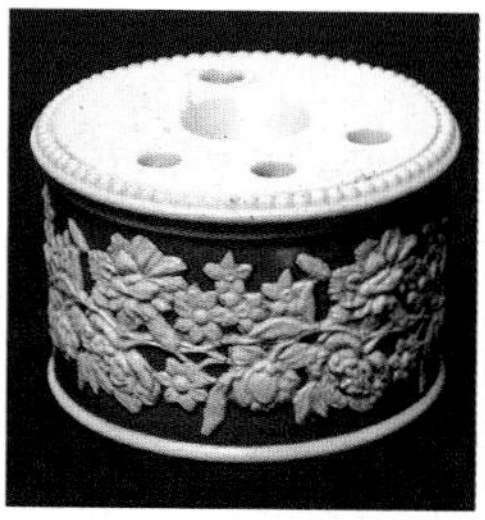

A stoneware inkwell, probably by Wilson, with raised sprigged decoration, c1800, 1¾in (4.5cm) high.
£225–250
€/ $350–400 ⊞ DIA

◄ A delft ink stand, with twin wells with covers and a drawer to each end, painted with Chinese figures and landscapes on a scrolling ground, monogrammed AR, 19thC, 7¾in (19.5cm) wide.
£135–160
€/ $215–250 ⚒ WW

Stoneware

'Stoneware' is a general heading for a wide range of ceramic wares which are fired at a high temperature (1200°–1400°C), so that the body becomes vitrified and impervious to liquids. Stonewares are always hard but, unlike porcelain, are seldom translucent and not usually white. The earliest stonewares were made in China in the 7th century AD as forerunners to porcelain, but it was not until the 15th century that they appear in Europe, initially in northern parts of Germany. Stonewares can be grey, red, brown, black or white and are often decorated with a salt glaze with the characteristic 'orange peel' surface. Fine and very hard red stonewares were made by Böttger at Meissen in the early 18th century and by the Elers Brothers in England, who were copying the red wares from Yixing in South China. Other centres in England include Nottingham, Derbyshire and London, while in Staffordshire fine white stonewares were produced, often decorated with vibrant coloured enamels to compete with the new porcelain trade.

Jardinières

A Victorian majolica jardinière, moulded in high relief with Chinese dragons chasing a flaming pearl among clouds, damaged, 15in (38cm) high.
£375–450
€/ $600–700 PF

▶ A Victorian pottery jardinière, on a matching stand, 34¼in (87cm) high.
£100–120
€/ $160–190 SWO

A pair of majolica jardinières, modelled as tree trunks, one cracked, 19thC, 8in (20.5cm) high.
£140–160
€/ $220–250 G(L)

A majolica jardinière, modelled as a woven basket with twin handles, with a stand of rustic twig design, 19thC, 23¾in (60.5cm) high.
£260–325
€/ $400–500 TRM

An earthenware flower pot, attributed to Dion family, with ruffled rim and base, decorated with a dark brown streaky glaze on a red body, cracks, Canadian, Quebec, 19thC, 8in (20.5cm) diam.
£160–200
€/ $250–315 RIT

A majolica jardinière, with moulded morning glory flowers and stems entwined around the side, late 19thC, 7in (18cm) high.
£200–225
€/ $315–350 CHAC

A late Victorian Wardle majolica jardinière and stand, both with relief-moulded foliage decoration, impressed marks, 30in (76cm) high.
£220–250
€/ $350–400 PFK

A majolica jardinière and stand, French, 1850–1900, 80in (203cm) high.
£3,800–4,300
€/ $6,000–6,800 BrL

A majolica jardinière and stand, probably by Bretby, the jardinière with lobed spirally moulded rim, the stand with balustroid stems on a spirally moulded foot, 1875–1925, 29½in (75cm) high.
£130–160
€/ $200–250 PFK

An earthenware jardinière and stand, German, c1900, 46in (117cm) high.
£630–750
€/ $990–1,200 DuM

▶ A Wemyss pottery Combe jardinière, painted with dog roses between bands, impressed 'Wemyss Ware R. H. & S.', cracks, c1900, 7in (18cm) high.
£420–500
€/ $670–800 S(O)

A Wemyss 'Rothes' flower pot, painted with four sandmartins among sponged trees, haircracks and chip, impressed Wemyss Ware, R.H. & S, early 20thC, 8in (20.5cm) high.
£500–600
€/ $790–950 S

Jars

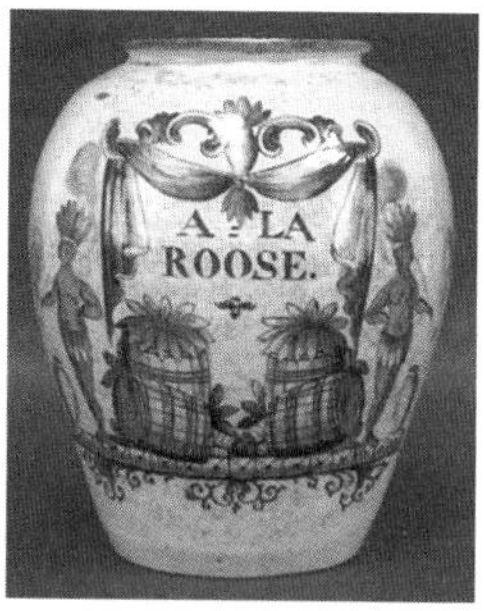

A Dutch Delft tobacco jar, painted with two Native Americans flanking barrels of tobacco beneath festooned drapery, inscribed 'A = La Roose', damage to rim, 1675–1725, 10½in (26.5cm) high.
£900–1,100
€/ $1,400–1,750 RTo

A Bristol or London delft jar, 1700–15, 7in (18cm) high.
£6,000–6,800
€/ $9,500–10,750 JHo

A Castelli maiolica apothecary jar, painted with a figure seated by a tortoise and enclosed by flowering plants, inscribed 'Flemmatico Pea1 Acqua' above larger label inscribed 'Aq. Chelid', one handle and base missing, rim repair, early 18thC, 14½in (37cm) high.
£600–700
€/ $950–1,100 S(O)

A maiolica wet drug jar, with a spout and a loop handle, with foliate decoration and the initials 'M.B.', Italian, 18thC, 9½in (24cm) high.
£200–240
€/ $315–380 TRM

Two Dutch Delft tobacco jars, by De Drie Klokken (The Three Bells) factory, each decorated with a jar labelled 'St Domingo' and 'Hanover', flanked by a Native American smoking, barrels and ships, 18thC, 10¼in (26cm) high.
£1,200–1,400
€/ $1,900–2,200 Bri

A Dutch Delft tobacco jar and brass cover, painted with a flower and scrollwork medallion, inscribed 'Romano' in a reserve, marked P:C in underglaze blue, glaze wear and abrasion, 18thC, 13¼in (33.5cm) high.
£550–650
€/ $870–1,000 S(Am)

A Minton majolica two-handled pedestal jar and cover, moulded in relief with oak leaves and acorns, date code for 1856, 11½in (29cm) high.
£720–850
€/ $1,150–1,350 DN

A Farrar Pottery earthenware tobacco jar, by James Black, with dark brown glaze and applied relief foliage and pipes, the cover with cylindrical finial, Canadian, Quebec, 1880–1908, 8½in (21.5cm) high.
£200–240
€/ $315–380 RIT

Jugs & Ewers

A stoneware jug, German, c1580, 12in (30.5cm) high.
£1,200–1,400
€/ $1,900–2,200 SEA

A Westerwald stoneware jug, German, c1670, 8in (20.5cm) high.
£600–660
€/ $950–1,000 JHo

A Staffordshire solid agateware cream jug, with a shaped rim and scroll handle, on lion-paw feet, each with a lion mask at the knee, one foot repaired, 1745–55, 4in (10cm) high.
£1,400–1,600
€/ $2,200–2,500 B

A Wedgwood jug, printed in Liverpool with a couple taking tea in the garden, c1765, 5in (12.5cm) high.
£170–185
€/ $270–300 ⊞ JHo

A Farrar's Pottery stoneware jug, buff-glazed with hand-painted cobalt floral decoration, chips to base, American, Vermont, early 19thC, 15in (38cm) high.
£160–200
€/ $250–315 ⚒ RIT

A pearlware Pan's head jug, decorated with colourful knots, small chips, marked 'Shorthose & Co', c1820, 6¼in (16cm) high.
£240–280
€/ $380–440 ⚒ WW

A Neale pearlware jug, decorated with floral sprays, c1790, 7in (18cm) high.
£450–500
€/ $700–800 ⊞ DSA

A commemorative jug, with a named portrait of 'Admiral Lord Nelson', c1805, 8in (20.5cm) high.
£1,700–1,900
€/ $2,700–3,000 ⊞ RdV

A Mason's Ironstone china foot-bath jug, the lobed bulbous body surmounted by a cylindrical neck with an inset angular spout, a reeded handle, and a further dragon-head-moulded handle beneath the spout, decorated with a Japanese pattern, minor faults, crown and drape mark, 1820–40, 12in (30.5cm) high.
£1,300–1,600
€/ $2,000–2,500 ⚒ DN

A creamware puzzle jug, with a pierced border and spout, and scroll handle, painted with sprays of flowers and inscribed and dated 1792 to the frieze and base, 18thC, 9in (23cm) high.
£900–1,100
€/ $1,400–1,700 ⚒ HYD

Ironstone

'Ironstone', or 'Ironstone china', is a trade name for a hard, durable earthenware patented by Charles Mason in 1813, and which was claimed to contain slag of iron as an ingredient. Although this claim has since been proved false, nearly 200 years later clever marketing ensured 'Mason's Patent Ironstone China' is still a household name. Early examples are highly sought after by collectors and are very expensive. Other Staffordshire makers of Ironstone include Davenport, Spode, Ridgway and the Ashworth Brothers.

A Devon slipware jug, by Fishley, with central panel of two birds, the reverse inscribed 'Beware as the potter said to the lump of clay, I'll be burnt first saucily responded the mud', below a border of leaves, 19thC, 11½in (29cm) high.
£5,750–6,750
€/ $9,000–10,700 ⚒ SJH
Devon slipware is very collectable and pieces by the Fishley family don't often come onto the market.

► A pair of pottery puzzle jugs, each with moulded decoration depicting windmills, oak trees and figures drinking, 19thC, larger 8½in (21.5cm) high.
£55–70
€/ $85–110 ⚒ TRM

A pottery Coronation jug, the body moulded with a trellis design and scrolling cartouche printed with portraits and panels of Coronation trophies, 1831, 7¼in (18.5cm) high.
£300–375
€/ $475–600 ⚒ SAS

A Robert Burns stoneware mask-head jug, by Machin & Potts, moulded with scenes of merrymaking, with Tam O'Shanter to the reverse, centred by a named portrait, moulded mark and dated 1834, 8¼in (21cm) high.
£60–75
€/ $95–120 ⚒ SAS

► A majolica jug, c1880, 6in (15cm) high.
£60–70
€/ $95–110 ⊞ CHAC

A Minton 'Henri Deux' ornamental ewer, by Charles Toft, the fixed overhead handle with a seated dog finial, the spout above a bearded male mask, with Renaissance-style arabesques and Celtic motifs, the foot and middle section applied with scrolls, signed 'C. Toft Minton & Co,' c1878, 10½in (26.5cm) high.
£1,600–2,000
€/ $2,500–3,200 ⚒ B
Ex-Minton Sale.

A majolica pitcher, by Eureka Pottery, decorated in low relief with a fan, dragonfly, prunus and waterlily motifs, American, New Jersey, 1883–87, 7¼in (18.5cm) high.
£270–330
€/ $430–530 ⚒ RIT

► A Minton majolica 'Tower' jug, the hinged cover with a jester's head finial, with Britannia metal mounts, above an entwined branch rustic handle continuing around the rim band, above a frieze of four dancing figures, finial chipped, impressed 'Mintons, 1231', year cypher for 1881, 12½in (32cm) high.
£525–625
€/ $830–1,000 ⚒ TEN

◄ A Mason's Patent Ironstone china footbath jug, with a relief serpent mask handle to the front and a tail to the rear, 19thC, 13in (33cm) high.
£820–975
€/ $1,300–1600 ⚒ SWO

A graduated set of three Mason's Ironstone Hydra-shaped jugs, floral-decorated, with serpent-form handles, printed mark, 19thC, largest 6½in (16.5cm) high.
£140–160
€/ $220–250 ⚒ DMC

► A Wemyss ewer, possibly by Edwin Sandland, painted with dragonflies above reeds, within line borders, impressed and painted Wemyss, early 20thC, 9½in (24cm) high.
£1,000–1,200
€/ $1,600–1,900 ⚒ S

Mugs & Tankards

A Nottingham salt-glazed stoneware mug, inscribed 'William Bomer 1723', incised with two bands of scrolling flowers, 4½in (11.5cm) high.
£2,300–2,800
€/ $3,600–4,400 WW

A pearlware tankard, with a leaf-capped loop handle, painted *en grisaille* with a classical maiden seated by a tree, with gilt embellishment, base inscribed 'Swansea', 1775–1825, 5¾in (14.5cm) high.
£3,500–4,250
€/ $5,500–6,700 AH
This mug was identified as being decorated by William Weston Young, who worked at Swansea for only four years from 1803–07. Only three such pieces have been on the market in the last ten years.

A Leeds creamware mug, with moulded gadrooned borders and reeded cross-over scroll handles, with applied floral terminals, 18thC, 3¾in (9.5cm) high.
£625–750
€/ $1,000–1,175 PFK

Items in the Pottery section have been arranged in date order within each sub-section.

A creamware mug, printed with two children and a dog at play, c1800, 3½in (9cm) high.
£500–550
€/ $800–880 DSA

A delft tankard, probably London, chips, mid-18thC, 5½in (14cm) high.
£3,500–3,850
€/ $5,500–6,000 JHo

A creamware Masonic mug, printed and painted with an armorial shield and emblems, and inscribed 'Richd & Thomason Rodgers, West Herrington', base crack, c1800, 5¾in (14.5cm) high.
£900–1,100
€/ $1,400–1,700 WW

► **A pearlware mug,** inscribed 'My Dear Boy', above floral sprigs, chipped and cracked, c1820, 3½in (9cm) high.
£100–120
€/ $160–190 HAM

A Thuringian pewter-mounted faïence tankard, painted with a scrollwork cartouche enclosing a standing elephant, flanked by flowering branches, the cover inscribed 'RW' and '1745' below an inlaid portrait medallion of Louis XV, some wear and repair, maker's mark, HL monogram to base, German, mid-18thC, 9½in (24cm) high.
£750–875
€/ $1,200–1,400 S(O)

The Rous Lench Collection

Many ceramics aficionados will agree with me that the heavyweight champion of English auctions over the last 25 years was the sale of Thomas George Burne's wonderful collection of pottery and porcelain. It was formed over many years to fill the fine 16th-century timbered house Rous Lench Court, in Worcestershire, that he was given as a 21st birthday present in 1928. The rarity of the pieces and the fantastic prices they realized is legendary and still act as a benchmark for prices well over a decade after they were sold. Following his death in 1985, his collection was sold in two parts by Sotheby's in 1986 and by Christie's in 1990. The collection included some 140 pieces of 16th–18th century English delft, among them a single candlestick dating from the Commonwealth period of 1653 which fetched £154,000 (€/ $243,000). From the non-Delft pottery a silver-mounted Tudor jug of c1550 fetched £275,000 (€/ $435,000). Quintessentially English 17th-century slipware was well represented and other pottery included fine Staffordshire white salt-glazed stonewares, Whieldon ware, Astbury figures and a charming Pew group of the type attributed to Aaron Wood dated to c1745.

The wonderful 18th-century English porcelain was among the best ever seen on the market, so for collectors of English pottery or porcelain, the two sale catalogues are simply a must for the reference library. Even in those days, 25 lots sold at over £40,000 (€/ $63,000) and one wonders about the sanity of such prices. A question easy to ask but harder to answer is 'Would these items make such high prices today?' Some pieces, although they appeared astonishingly expensive at the time, certainly would be very pricey in the sale rooms today and could quite conceivably make more, but for the most expensive pieces, it is more difficult to say. The market at that time was polarized between two extremely determined American collectors who, to the auction houses' delight, would neither compromise nor stop bidding.

John Axford

A Mason's Ironstone moulded mug, painted with flowers and foliage, with an animal mask handle, early 19thC, 6in (15cm) high.
£230–280
€/ $350–450 WW

A nursery mug, inscribed 'A Present for Hannah', mid-19thC, 3in (7.5cm) high.
£135–150
€/ $215–240 SWN

An Orange Order mug, printed and decorated with Masonic emblems, a lustre rim, restored chip, 1800–1850, 4¾in (12cm) high.
£200–250
€/ $300–380 WW

A majolica mug, decorated with birds and lillies, c1880, 4½in (11.5cm) high.
£175–200
€/ $275–315 CHAC

A majolica mug, decorated with a grape vine, 19thC, 4½in (11.5cm) high.
£50–60
€/ $80–95 CHAC

A Wemyss mug, painted by Karol Nekola with thistles, Wemyss mark to base, early 20thC, 5½in (14cm) high.
£375–450
€/ $590–710 DAU

POTTERY

Plaques

A Makkum plaque, painted with a quayside with sailing vessels and windmills, minor glaze wear, the reverse dated 1704, Dutch, 14½in (36.5cm) high.
£320–400
€/ $500–625 S(Am)

LOCATE THE SOURCE

The source of each illustration in Miller's can be found by checking the code letters below each caption with the Key to Illustrations, pages 794–800.

▶ **An Enoch Wood blue jasper medallion,** applied with a relief figure of Minerva, impressed 'Minerva The Goddess of Wisdom, War and Wool "Heathen Mythology" Enoch Wood Sculpsit', minor chip, c1790, 4¾in (12cm) high.
£350–425
€/ $550–670 B

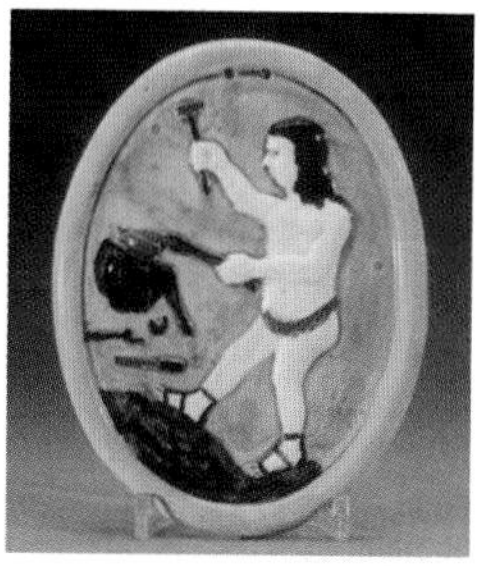

A Pratt-style plaque, moulded with Vulcan standing at a forge, pierced for hanging, rim chips, c1800, 7½in (19cm) high.
£650–750
€/ $1,000–1,200 S(O)

A faïence wall plaque, painted with a view of Mont Saint Michel, French, late 19thC, 9 x 8in (23 x 20.5cm).
£140–175
€/ $220–280 SWO

A pottery wall plaque, entitled 'No Surrender', commemorating the Battle of the Boyne in 1698, late 19thC, 9in (23cm) wide.
£60–70
€/ $95–110 STA

Pot Lids

A portrait of Wellington, with clasped hands, Ball No. 160B, with an overglazed pot decorated with fruiting vines, c1850, 4in (10cm) diam.
£200–220
€/ $315–350 SAS

'Napirima, Trinidad', Ball No. 225, c1853, 4¼in (11cm) diam.
£120–140
€/ $190–220 SAS

'Charity', Ball No. 362, with a decorative border, c1860, 2¾in (7cm) diam.
£220–250
€/ $350–400 SAS

► 'The Best Card', Ball No. 254, with a decorative border, c1860, 4in (10cm) diam.
£100–110
€/ $160–175 SAS

American Dentifrice inscribed 'C.J. Peacock D. D. S. Pennsylvania College of Dental Surgery 2 West Park Terrace Scarborough', minor wear, c1880, 3½in (9cm) diam.
£280–340
€/ $440–540 BBR

'Dressing My Lady's Hair', Ball No. 434, framed, c1880, 4in (10cm) diam.
£850–1,000
€/ $1,350–1,600 SAS

◄ Price & Co Alexandra Cherry Paste, inscribed 'The Celebrated Alexandra Cherry Paste prepared by Price & Co late Price & Gosnell Perfumers to the Royal Family for the Teeth and Gums 246 Regent Street, London', wear, crazing and chips, c1880, 3½in (9cm) diam.
£350–420
€/ $550–660 BBR

Pots

A delft posset pot, painted with chinoiserie figures in a garden, early 18thC, 6in (15cm) high.
£1,300–1,600
€/ $2,000–2,500 KEY

► A delft posset pot and cover, painted with a Chinese figure in a boat approaching a dwelling, damage to rim, mid-18thC, 9½in (24cm) wide.
£675–825
€/ $1,000–1,300 TEN

► A salt-glazed stoneware crock, by W. Hart, decorated with a spotted fish, hairline crack, American, New York, mid-19thC, 11in (28cm) high.
£3,500–4,200
€/ $5,500–6,700 S(NY)

A Wemyss pot, painted with fruit, late 19thC, 3in (7.5cm) high.
£165–185
€/ $260–290 SER

Dessert Services

A Hicks & Meigh stone china part dessert service, comprising 13 pieces, decorated in the Imari palette with willow and peony within fenced gardens, heightened in gilt, minor faults and one dish repaired, printed factory marks to bases, early 19thC.
£820–975
€/ $1,300–1,500 RTo

A Minton stone china part dessert service, comprising 39 pieces, decorated with Amherst Japan pattern, some damage and repair, blue-printed marks, red script pattern No. 824, c1840.
£675–820
€/ $1,000–1,300 S(O)

► **A majolica dessert service,** comprising 18 pieces, decorated with a waterlily and leaf pattern, two pieces chipped, 19thC.
£625–750
€/ $980–1,185 AG

A Mason's Ironstone part dessert service, comprising 15 pieces, decorated with flowers, leaves and fruit, one dish chipped, impressed factory marks, c1820.
£3,300–4,000
€/ $5,200–6,300 WW

A Copeland & Garrett fruit service, comprising 13 pieces, decorated with poppies and forget-me-nots, 19thC.
£100–120
€/ $160–190 TRM

POTTERY

Dinner Services

An Ironstone dinner service, comprising 62 pieces, decorated with flowers and heightened with gilding, minor damage, impressed marks and painted pattern No. 2/7129, mid-19thC.
£520–625
€/ $820–1,000 S(O)

A Victorian dinner service, comprising 77 pieces, transfer-decorated with vases of flowers within floral panelled borders, heightened with colour.
£1,900–2,200
€/ $3,000–3,500 B(Pr)

◄ **An Ironstone dinner service,** comprising 66 pieces, 19thC.
£2,700–3,200
€/ $4,250–5,000 JAd

A Mason's Ironstone part dinner service, comprising 75 pieces, with Oriental-style decoration, 19thC.
£925–1,100
€/ $1,400–1,700 RTo

A Staffordshire pottery part dinner service, comprising 71 pieces, decorated in the Pekin pattern, some damage, c1880.
£725–875
€/ $1,100–1,375 DN

Tea Services

A Staffordshire part tea service, pattern No. 247, comprising six pieces, decorated with stylized flowers and rockwork, c1830.
£130–160
€/ $200–250 WW

A Staffordshire drabware part tea service, comprising three pieces, applied with trailing leaves and flowers, chips and losses, incised marks, c1840.
£200–225
€/ $300–350 S(O)

► A George Jones majolica Japanese-style cabaret service, model Nos. 3450 and 3465, comprising ten pieces, damaged, marked, registration lozenges for 1875.
£9,200–11,000
€/ $14,500–17,000 B
Despite the damage to this service, George Jones is always popular and commands high prices.

Stands

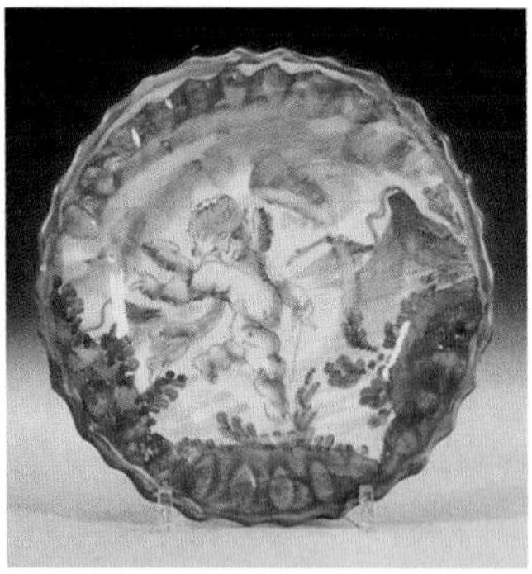

A Savona faïence stand, moulded with a stand ring in the centre and a lobed rim, painted with a putto in a landscape, small chip to rim, blue tower mark, 1700–50, 7in (18cm) diam.
£320–350
€/ $500–550 S(O)

A London delft stand, with polychrome decoration, on claw feet, c1730, 5½in (14cm) diam.
£3,400–3,800
€/ $5,400–6,000 JHo

► A Wedgwood lazy Susan, with a printed border, impressed mark, 19thC, 19in (48.5cm) diam.
£275–325
€/ $430–515 SWO

A Dublin delft tureen stand, probably by Henry Delamain, painted with Peony and Fence pattern, minor frits, blue-painted 7 to reverse, 1755–60, 22in (56cm) wide.
£2,600–3,000
€/ $4,150–4,750 S(O)

Tea Canisters

A Durlach faïence tea canister, painted with Oriental flowers in a fenced garden, the shoulder with two insects, minor glaze chips, German, c1770, 4½in (11.5cm) high.
£500–600
€/ $790–950 S(O)

A Prattware tea canister, decorated with Macaroni figures, c1790, 5½in (14cm) high.
£300–320
€/ $475–500 KEY

A Prattware tea canister, decorated with Macaroni figures, c1790, 5½in (14cm) high.
£300–320
€/ $475–500 KEY

Tea, Coffee & Punch Pots

A Staffordshire salt-glazed miniature teapot, c1740, 3in (7.5cm) high.
£880–980
€/ $1,400–1,550 ⊞ KEY

A Staffordshire lead-glazed red ware teapot, possibly Astbury, decorated with creamware, c1760, 3½in (9cm) high.
£1,200–1,400
€/ $1,900–2,200 ⊞ JRe

A creamware teapot, attributed to William Greatbatch, with double C-scroll handle, foliate spout and pierced collar, metal cap to spout, repair to collar, c1780, 5in (12.5cm) high.
£175–200
€/ $275–325 ⚒ RIT

A Leeds creamware coffee pot, the lid with a rose knop, with acanthus-moulded spout, the entwined handle with leafy terminals, c1780, 10in (25.5cm) high.
£620–680
€/ $980–1,000 ⊞ KEY

A Pratt-style pearlware punch pot, decorated with floral garlands, initials to body, spout and lid chipped, 1780–90, 9½in (24cm) high.
£180–220
€/ $280–350 ⚒ SWO

A Minton majolica teapot and cover, shape No. 1838, modelled as a seated chinaman wearing a kimono and trousers, holding a Noh mask, the spout issuing from its mouth, restoration and hairline crack, impressed Minton and date cypher, 1875, 5¾in (14.5cm) high.
£1,300–1,500
€/ $2,000–2,400 ⚒ B
Ex-Minton Sale.

Prattware

Prattware is a lightweight pottery made in Staffordshire, Scotland and the North East of England, characterized by the use of high temperature underglaze colours, typically a dirty orange, sludgey green, a rather drab blue, manganese and brown. As the colours are underglaze, they do not flake as enamel colours so often do. Named after a family of Staffordshire potters, the wares mostly date from the late 18th and early 19th centuries, and include figures, animals, relief-moulded jugs and tea canisters, Toby jugs and plaques. Later in the 19th century, the Pratt family pottery became famous for the production of colour-printed pottery pot lids.

► **A majolica teapot,** decorated with a bamboo and bird design, repair to inner rim, c1880, 6½in (16.5cm) high.
£100–120
€/ $160–190
⊞ CHAC

◄ **A jasper ware teapot,** c1890, 5in (12.5cm) high.
£70–80
€/ $110–125
⊞ CoCo

Tiles

A Dutch Delft tile, 1600–20, 4¼in (11cm) square.
£400–435
€/ $630–700 ⊞ JHo

An English delft tile, painted in Fazackerly colours, mid-18thC, 5¼in (13.5cm) square.
£270–325
€/ $425–500 ⚒ WW

A Liverpool delft tile, printed with the fox and cockerel from *Aesop's Fables*, c1770, 5in (12.5cm) square.
£350–400
€/ $550–630 ⊞ RdV

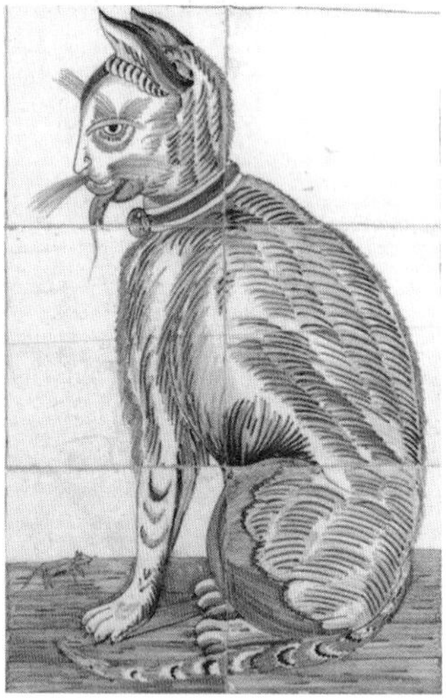

A tile picture, comprising six tiles, depicting a seated cat with two mice, restored, mounted onto board, Dutch, 1770–90, 15¼in x 10in (38.5 x 25.5cm).
£1,700–1,900
€/ $2,700–3,000 ⚒ S(Am)

A *pâte-sur-pâte* tile, by P. Ipsen, Danish, Copenhagen, c1870, 8in (20.5cm) square.
£290–320
€/ $460–480 ⊞ KMG

A Trent Tile Co tile, signed by Isaac Broome, American, c1890, 6in (15cm) square.
£240–265
€/ $380–420 ⊞ KMG

► **A tile picture,** comprising six tiles, 19thC, 11¾ x 17¼in (30 x 44cm).
£80–95
€/ $120–150 ⚒ SWO

Toby & Character Jugs

A Staffordshire Prattware character jug, modelled as Bacchus, c1790, 12in (30.5cm) high.
£1,700–1,900
€/ $2,700–3,000 ⊞ JRe

A Ralph Wood The Squire Toby jug, pipe missing, c1790, 11in (28cm) high.
£3,500–4,000
€/ $5,500–6,300 ⊞ JBL
The Toby's hand has a hole to take a pipe which, was usually the first thing to break. Later moulds did not incorporate this aperture.

It is thought that Toby jugs derive their name from a humorous song written in the mid-18th century about Toby Fillpot, a fellow who was more than a little fond of his drink. Long after he had died, his body turned into clay in the ground, and an enterprising potter made it into a jug. A mezzotint was produced to accompany this song which proved very popular in Georgian Britain.

A Wood-style Toby jug, wearing a tricorn hat, holding a frothing beer cup and an empty beer jug, damaged, late 18thC, 14¼in (36cm) high.
£1,100–1,300
€/ $1,750–2,000 ⚒ HAM

A Prattware Martha Gunn Toby jug, with a pearlware glaze, c1790, 10in (25.5cm) high.
£1,800–2,000
€/ $2,800–3,200 ⊞ JBL
Martha Gunn, 'the Queen of the Dippers', was a celebrated Brighton character who assisted ladies in bathing in the sea, from bathing machines, in the latter half of the 18th century and early 19th century. It is said that she also bathed the Prince of Wales (later George IV).

A Staffordshire pearlware Warty Face Toby jug and cover, seated holding a foaming jug and a pipe, chips to pipe, early 19thC, 9½in (24cm) high.
£270–320
€/ $430–500 S(O)

A Toby jug, possibly Enoch Wood, decorated in enamels, c1820, 10in (25.5cm) high.
£450–500
€/ $700–800 ⊞ JBL

◄ A Staffordshire pearlware George Whitfield jug, 1820–25, 8in (20.5cm) high.
£500–550
€/ $800–870 ⊞ JRe
George Whitfield (1714–70) was a famous Methodist preacher and a friend of John Wesley. This Toby is often mistakenly called The Nightwatchman.

A spongeware Portobello Toby jug, c1820, 10in (25.5cm) high.
£520–585
€/ $800–900 ⊞ JBL
This Toby's hat lifts out and can be used as a measure to drink from.

A pair of Punch and Judy character jug, c1880, 10in (25.5cm) high.
£580–650
€/ $915–1,000 ⊞ JBL

Tureens

A Staffordshire salt-glazed tureen and cover, minor restoration, c1740, 11in (28cm) wide.
£1,000–1,100
€/ $1,600–1,750 ⊞ JRe

A Rörstrand faïence tureen and cover, Swedish, c1758, 16½in (42cm) wide.
£1,700–2,000
€/ $2,700–3,200 ⚒ BUK

A Mosbach faïence soup tureen and cover, the domed cover with a fruit finial, decorated with flower sprays and scattered sprigs, restored, cracked, rim chip to cover, CT monogram in manganese, German, c1780, 12½in (32cm) wide.
£375–450
€/ $600–700 ⚒ S(O)

A Neale & Co creamware sauce tureen, the cover with a floral finial, decorated with a frilled band and flowers, chips, impressed mark, 18thC, 8¼in (21cm) wide.
£140–160
€/ $220–250 ⚒ AG

A Leeds creamware sauce tureen and cover, the cover with a pomegranate finial, with moulded handles, late 18thC, 7in (18cm) wide.
£325–375
€/ $500–600 ⚒ TRM

A Davenport pearlware tureen and cover, the finial modelled as a bunch of grapes, painted with flowers, chips and staining, impressed 'Davenport' above an anchor, incised 22 to foot and cover, 1810–25, 7¾in (19.5cm) wide.
£800–950
€/ $1,300–1,500 ⚒ S(O)

POTTERY

◀ A Mason's Ironstone soup tureen, cover and stand, heightened with enamels, printed marks, 19thC, 14in (35.5cm) wide.
£350–420
€/ $550–650 ⚒ SWO

▶ A Victorian Ironstone tureen and cover, transfer-printed in the Imari palette, 11in (28cm) wide.
£80–90
€/ $120–140 ⚒ BR

Vases & Urns

A Caltagirone maiolica bottle vase, painted with flowers and scrolling foliage, chips and repairs, Italian, 17thC, 9in (23cm) high.
£650–775
€/ $1,000–1,225 ⚒ S(O)

A Clérissy faïence tulip vase, probably by Moustier, decorated *en camaïeu* after the engravings by J. Bérain, rim chips, French, c1730, 9½in (24cm) high.
£2,000–2,200
€/ $3,200–3,500 ⚒ S(Am)

Jean Bérain (1640–1711) was influenced by the Renaissance period and worked as a designer to the Court of Louis XIV.

A Dutch Delft vase, c1740, 11in (28cm) high.
£340–375
€/ $550–600 ⊞ SEA

▶ A faïence *bouquetière*, possibly Durlach, chips and cracks, German, c1770, 6¼in (16cm) high.
£420–500
€/ $670–800 ⚒ S(O)

A London blue and white delft vase, decorated with flowers, c1760, 8in (20.5cm) high.
£1,000–1,100
€/ $1,600–1,700 ⊞ JHo

A Marieberg faïence vase, Swedish, 1777, 11½in (29cm) high.
£625–725
€/ $1,000–1,200 ⚒ BUK

A Davenport creamware urn and cover, painted with chinoiserie figures in a garden setting, the shoulder reserved with four gilt scroll-edged cartouches of river landscapes, repeated on the cover beneath a gilt border reserved with acanthus leaves around a gilt knop, mounted with a silver spigot, restored, c1810, 22½in (57cm) high.
£3,200–3,800
€/ $5,000–6,000 ⚒ S(NY)

An earthenware vase, by Simon Humberstone, with relief horizontal bands and mottled green and yellow glazes on a buff body, rim chips, Canadian, Ontario, late 19thC, 10in (25.5cm) high.
£450–500
€/ $700–800 ⚒ RIT

A Wedgwood & Bentley Queensware basalt cassolet, with a reversible cover, the urn with twin scroll handles decorated with swags, raised on a basalt base, late 18thC, 11in (28cm) high.
£920–1,100
€/ $1,400–1,700 ⚒ TRM

A cassolet has a reversible cover so that it can be used as either an urn or a candle holder.

A Wedgwood amphora-shaped vase, painted with a wide band depicting villages by a rustic stile with a church and a cottage in the background, a figure in a country lane approaching a cottage, the shoulders and base with gilt line decoration, 19thC, 7in (18cm) high.
£100–110
€/ $160–175 ⚒ TMA

A Victorian Staffordshire pottery vase, with printed enamel and gilt decoration, 11¾in (30cm) high.
£75–90
€/ $120–140 ⚒ SWO

A pair of Wedgwood and Bentley black basalt vases, with ram's head masks and loop handles, the shoulders with laurel leaf borders, covers missing, damage to one handle, impressed marks, late 18thC, 3¾in (9.5cm) high.
£380–450
€/ $600–700 ⚒ S(O)

A Davenport vase, decorated with a flying bird pattern, c1820, 16in (40.5cm) high.
£780–850
€/ $1,250–1,300 ⊞ SCO

A Wedgwood jasper ware vase, decorated with paterae and floral swags hung from fluted pilasters, impressed Wedgwood mark, 1794–1800, 5in (12.5cm) high.
£375–425
€/ $600–675 ⚒ WW

A Staffordshire pearlware spill vase, moulded with a clock face within a garter, flanked by royal supporters, on a table base, 1825–35, 10¼in (26cm) high.
£2,000–2,400
€/ $3,100–3,800 ⚒ S(NY)

Miscellaneous

A Minton earthenware beer set, by Henry Stacy Marks, comprising a tray, a jug and two mugs, inscribed 'Chaucer, ye be welcome withouten any greeve', slight damage, minor restoration, dated 1873, tray 15¼in (38.5cm) wide.
£600–720
€/ $950–1,100 ⚒ B

► A Wedgwood transfer-printed cup and saucer, c1770, saucer 5in (12.5cm) diam.
£200–220
€/ $315–350 ⊞ JHo
This was probably sent from the Wedgwood factory to Liverpool to be printed.

A Bristol pearlware thread box, with sliding cover, c1820, 7 x 3in (18 x 7.5cm) wide.
£530–585
€/ $840–920 ⊞ DAN

A pearlware condiment set, on integral stand, c1820, 6in (15cm) high.
£250–300
€/ $400–475 ⚒ SWO

A Nottingham salt-glazed stoneware loving cup, decorated with trailing leaf and flower sprays, inscribed 'Thos Lowe 1813', rim chips, 6½in (16.5cm).
£450–550
€/ $710–870 ⚒ B

A Staffordshire Prattware pipe, c1790, 9in (23cm) long.
£800–900
€/ $1,200–1,400 ⊞ JRe

► A Marieberg faïence snuff box, decorated with cameos, Swedish, 1758–66, 3½in (9cm) wide.
£600–720
€/ $950–1,145 ⚒ BUK

A Leeds creamware sauce boat, moulded in the form of a shell, 1770–80, 6in (15cm) high.
£300–340
€/ $475–540 ⊞ KEY

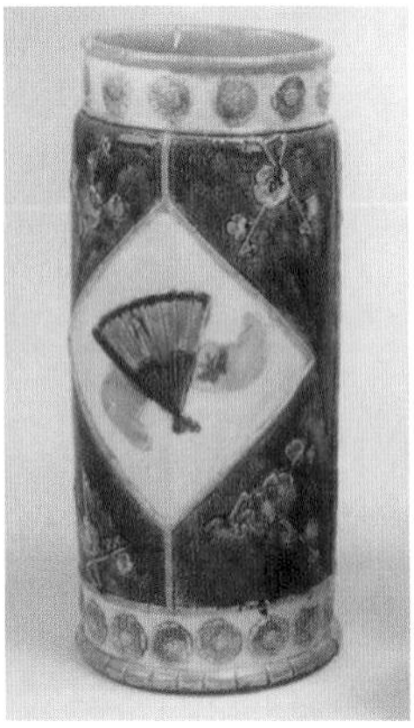

A majolica stick stand, decorated with lozenge-shaped panels of fans, within borders of flowering prunus, cracked, Continental, late 19thC, 21¾in (55.5cm) high.
£120–150
€/ $190–240 ⚒ DN

A salt-glazed stoneware cornucopia wall pocket, moulded with a cartouche of Flora carrying a cornucopia of flowers, with a rocaille border under a rim with three pierced rings, c1770, 11in (28cm) high.
£320–375
€/ $500–590 ⚒ TEN

A Wemyss wash set, comprising ewer, basin, sponge dish and strainer, soap dish with cover and drainer, painted with cherries, minor damage, impressed marks, c1900, basin 15in (38cm) diam.
£600–720
€/ $950–1,150 ⚒ S(O)

Transfer-Printed Pottery

A Davenport pearlware pierced basket and stand, transfer-printed with castle views, 1825–30, 12in (30.5cm) wide.
£385–425
€/ $600–670 ⊞ DSA

A Heath Pottery bowl and ewer, transfer-printed with Willow pattern, c1810, jug 8in (20.5cm) high.
£550–600
€/ $870–950 ⊞ SCO

A bowl, transfer-printed with Gun Dogs pattern, 1815–25, 7½in (19cm) diam.
£200–225
€/ $315–350 ⊞ GRe

► A Minton footed bowl, transfer-printed with Camel and Giraffe pattern, c1820, 11¾in (30cm) wide.
£170–200
€/ $270–315 ⚒ SWO

A Spode slop bowl and cover, transfer-printed with Musicians pattern, blue printed marks, some damage, 1820–30, 13in (33cm) high.
£1,400–1,700
€/ $2,200–2,700 ⚒ B(Kn)

A Clews cheese coaster, transfer-printed with Castle pattern and fleur-de-lys, with scroll handles, on a moulded oval foot, minor damage, early 19thC, 16in (40.5cm) wide.
£1,300–1,500
€/ $2,000–2,400 ⚒ EH
The Castle pattern was popular at Spode and was copied by many other makers. It is supposed to be based on an aquatint by Merigot entitled 'The Gate of Sebastian' (1796), with the foreground taken from another aquatint, 'Ponte Molle'.

A creamware coffee pot, transfer-printed with a pastoral landscape, 11¾in (30cm) high.
£250–320
€/ $400–500 ⚒ JAd

A Spode dessert comport, transfer-printed with The Lion in Love on the top and the Leopard and Fox on the underside, from the *Aesop's Fables* series, c1830, 6in (15cm) diam.
£500–550
€/ $790--870 ⊞ GN

An Andrew Stevenson pearlware tea bowl and saucer, transfer-printed with a rural scene, impressed mark, c1820, saucer 5in (12.5cm) diam.
£170–200
€/ $270–315 ⊞ DSA

A Copeland cup and saucer, commemorating the Arctic Expedition of 1875, transfer-printed with a polar bear within an inscribed and dated band, the reverse with three anchors fouled with inscribed ribbons, cup chipped, saucer 4in (10cm),diam.
£500–575
€/ $790–910 ⚒ SAS
The Arctic Expedition of 1875 was led by Sir George Strong Nares.

A pickle dish, transfer-printed with a chinoiserie pattern, c1820, 5in (12.5cm) wide.
£145–160
€/ $230–250 ⊞ CoCo

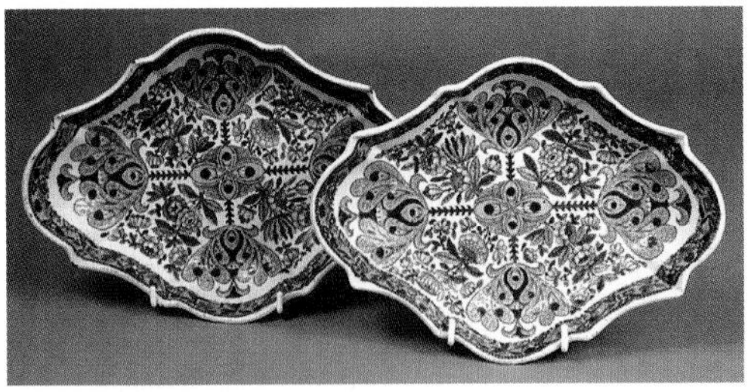

A pair of Spode dishes, transfer-printed with Flower Cross pattern, c1820, 10in (25cm) wide.
£80–100
€/ $125–160 SWO

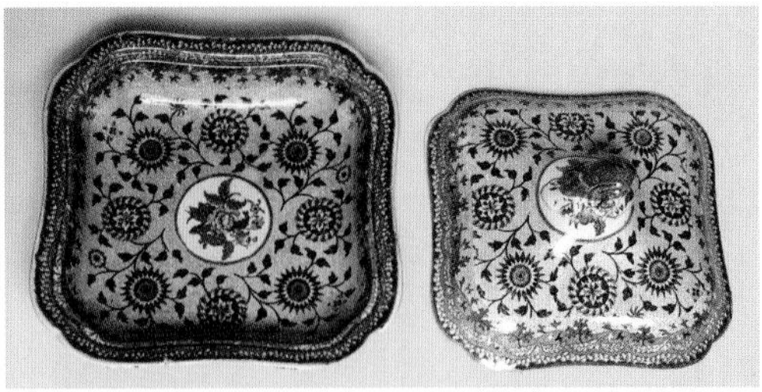

A Minton dish and cover, transfer-printed with Pin Wheel pattern, c1820, 9½in (24cm) wide.
£135–150
€/ $215–235 ⊞ SCO

A Spode egg stand, transfer-printed with Chinese Flowers pattern, c1820, 7½in (19cm) diam.
£90–100
€/ $145–160 ⊞ SCO

A Spode earthenware meat dish, transfer-printed with Shooting a Leopard pattern from the Indian Sporting series, with canted corners, impressed and printed marks, c1810, 20¾in (52.5cm) wide.
£2,400–2,800
€/ $3,800–4,400 RTo

A meat dish, transfer-printed with Pashkov House, Moscow pattern, 1815–25, 21in (53.5cm) wide.
£900–1,100
€/ $1,400–1,700 B(Kn)

A Minton pearlware meat dish, transfer-printed with Benevolent Cottagers pattern, 1815–20, 15in (38cm) wide.
£500–550
€/ $790–870 ⊞ DSA

An Andrew Stevenson plate, transfer-printed with a pattern from the Ornithological series, 1816–30, 6¼in (16cm) diam.
£60–65
€/ $95–105 ⊞ CHAC

A Ridgway pearlware meat dish, transfer-printed with a pattern from the Angus Seats series within a landscape-panelled border, c1820, 17¾in (44cm) wide.
£260–325
€/ $410–515 LFA

A Clews plate, transfer-printed with a scene of Dr Syntax taking possession of his living, c1820, 10in (25.5cm) diam.
£325–360
€/ $515–565 ⊞ CoS

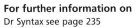

For further information on
Dr Syntax see page 235

A Mason plate, transfer-printed with Tyburn Turnpike pattern from the Beaded Frame series, c1820, 8in (20.5cm) diam.
£180–200
€/ $285–315 ⊞ GRe

A pair of plates, transfer-printed in blue and white with Ladies of Llangollen pattern within a shaped floral border, impressed mark, probably Staffordshire, c1820, 10in (25.5cm) diam.
£420–500
€/ $650–790 F&C

The 'Ladies of Llangollen', Eleanor Butler and Sarah Ponsonby, the first sapphic couple of polite society, lived in a black and white timbered cottage, 'Plas Newydd', in North Wales.

A meat dish, transfer-printed with a view of Lancaster North East from the Antique Scenery series, 1825–35, 21½in (54.5cm) wide diam.
£800–880
€/ $1,250–1,400 ⊞ GRe

A pair of Staffordshire meat dishes, transfer-printed with a chinoiserie motif, c1825, 16in (40.5cm) wide.
£530–585
€/ $850–900 ⊞ DAN

A Copeland meat dish, transfer-printed with Horse and the Loaded Ass pattern from the *Aesop's Fables* series, 1825–50, 18in (45.5cm) wide.
£500–600
€/ $800–950 ⚒ PFK

A Ridgway stoneware meat dish, transfer-printed with Regina pattern from Asiatic Pheasants series, 1830–40, 21½in (54.5cm) wide.
£450–500
€/ $700–800 ⊞ PGO

◄ A meat dish, transfer-printed with Willow pattern, c1850, 17½in (44.5cm) wide.
£70–80
€/ $110–125 ⊞ CHAC

A Rogers pottery meat dish, transfer-printed with Boston State House pattern, impressed marks, 19thC, 18¾in (47.5cm) wide.
£1,000–1,200
€/ $1,580–1,900 ⚒ TMA
This dish was made for export to the American market.

► A meat dish, by Wagstaff & Brunt, transfer-printed with Belfast Views pattern, dated 1883, 13in (33cm) wide.
£135–150
€/ $215–235 ⊞ STA

A pair of Ridgway plates, transfer-printed with a floral motif, 1880–90, 10in (25.5cm) diam.
£70–80
€/ $110–125 ⊞ CHAC

A jug, transfer-printed with an Indian scene from the Parrot Border series, minor restoration, 1815–25, 12½in (32cm) high.
£300–350
€/ $475–550 ⚒ B(Kn)

A William Adams double-ended garden seat, transfer-printed with Seasons pattern showing July/August, c1830, 18½in (47cm) wide.
£2,000–2,200
€/ $3,200–3,500 ⊞ GN

A jug, transfer-printed with two identical Italianate scenes, impressed mark 'S', 1825–50, 9in (23cm) high.
£75–90
€/ $120–140 ⚒ PFK

A Thomas Fell pearlware jug, transfer-printed with rural scenes, c1840, 10in (25.5cm) high.
£385–425
€/ $600–670 ⊞ DSA

A Farmer's Arms jug, transfer-printed with Masonic symbols within a union border, inscribed 'E R Broom', dated 1841, 9½in (24cm) high.
£850–950
€/ $1,400–1,500 ⊞ GN

A cider tankard, transfer-printed with a floral design, 1835–45, 5in (12.5cm) diam.
£115–130
€/ $180–200 ⊞ CoCo

A mug, transfer-printed with a chinoiserie pattern and 'Hunter's Improved Soda Font London', with internal partition, 19thC, 4¼in (11cm) high.
£450–525
€/ $710–830 ⚒ BBR

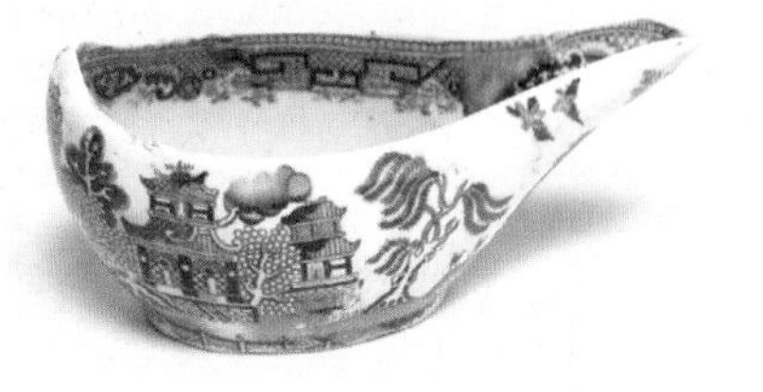

A John Meir pap feeder, transfer-printed with Willow pattern, c1830, 5in (12.5cm) wide.
£135–150
€/ $215–235 ⊞ GN

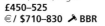

◄ A part dinner service, attributed to Minton, comprising 33 pieces, transfer-printed with Royal Persian pattern, minor rim chips, impressed marks, 1825–40.
£220–250
€/ $350–400 ⚒ DN

A Dawson's Low Ford Pottery part dinner service, comprising 79 pieces, transfer-printed with figures in a landscape, some damage, restoration, impressed marks, 1840–60.
£1,100–1,300
€/ $1,700–2,000 ⚒ S(O)

An Elkin & Newbon part dinner service, comprising 38 pieces, transfer-printed with Botanical Beauties pattern, 19thC, meat dish 15¾in (40cm) wide.
£180–220
€/ $284–350 ⚒ SWO

◄ A Herculaneum pearlware teapot, transfer-printed with a fishing scene, c1820, 5in (12.5cm) high.
£440–485
€/ $700–770 ⊞ CoS

A toast rack, probably by William Hackwood, the dividers decorated as towers, 1825–40, 8in (20.5cm) wide.
£270–475
€/ $425–750 ⊞ GRe

A Copeland & Garrett tureen, cover and stand, transfer-printed with Byron Group floral pattern, 1838–40, 7in (18cm) wide
£300–325
€/ $475–515 ⊞ DSA

A John Meir waste pail and cover, transfer-printed with Laconia pattern, rim chip, printed mark, 19thC, 13½in (34.5cm) high.
£420–525
€/ $650–800 ⚒ TMA

Lustreware

The earliest lustrewares date from 13th-century Persia and were made popular again by Wedgwood at the beginning of the 19th century. Lustreware was soon produced by many other British potteries, particularly those in north east England. Pink lustre was the most popular in the early to mid-19th century, with orange or apricot appearing around 1855.

The earliest lustrewares from north east England seem to date from around 1820. Most popular of the decorative wares produced on the Rivers Wear and Tyne were the rectangular and circular wall plaques, along with the multitude of jugs, bowls, frog mugs, chamber pots etc, decorated with transfers reflecting contemporary social events. From 1794–1890, a large number of pieces were decorated with various transfers commemorating the opening of the Sunderland Bridge. It is interesting to note transfers of the Sunderland 'New Bridge' can be safely dated post-1859, as this is when the old bridge was levelled due to structural faults and then reconstucted.

The term Sunderland Ware seems to derive from the transfer decoration of the Sunderland Bridge. This term can be confusing as there were more potteries on the River Tyne producing Sunderland Ware than there were on the River Wear. The Wear potteries of Dixon & Co, Anthony Scott, Dawson & Co and Samuel Moore, excelled in lustre-decorated wares. Tyneside factories on the Tyne such as C. T. Maling, Thomas Fell, Joseph Sewell and John Carr of North Shields made equally good quality wares. The range of subjects seemed never ending: Royalty, politics, religion, murders, births, disasters were all captured.

Lustreware production peaked in the North East around 1845, but cheap imports from the Staffordshire potteries caused standards to fall and many potteries closed. Soon only a handful were left. John Carr of North Shields produced lustreware as late as c1890 until finally closing in 1918. The last pottery in the North East to produce lustreware was C. T. Maling & Sons, Newcastle. This factory was the largest and longest in production, initially manufacturing pottery at Sunderland in 1762 and finally extinguishing the last kiln in Newcastle in 1963, ending over 200 years of pottery manufacture in the north east of England.

Ian Sharp

POTTERY

A pair of Staffordshire lustreware models of spaniels, c1875, 12½in (32cm) high.
£220–245
€/ $345–385 ⊞ CHAC

A Dixon & Co pink lustre bowl, transfer-printed with the Mariners' Arms, c1830, 7in (18cm) diam.
£250–280
€/ $395–445 ⊞ IS

A puce lustre frog chamberpot, the inner decorated with head and shoulders of a figure, inscribed 'use me well, keep me clean, I will not tell what I have seen', the outer decorated with panels of verse, early 19thC, 8½in (21.5cm) high.
£500–575
€/ $790–910 ⚒ GAK

A Sunderland pink lustre chamber pot, the inner decorated with the head and shoulders of a figure and inscribed with a verse, the outer inscribed 'To the Wife' and 'A Present'; hairline crack, c1840, 5¼in (13.5cm) high.
£480–565
€/ $760–890 ⚒ S(O)

◀ A pink lustre pearlware model of a grandfather clock, probably by Portobello, Scotland, c1830, 4½in (11.5cm) high.
£400–450
€/ $635–715 ⊞ RdV

A pink lustre jug, relief-moulded with portraits of Princess Charlotte and Prince Leopold above a stiff-leaf border, with split-scroll handle, haircracks, c1816, 6in (15cm) high.
£380–430
€/ $600–680 ⚒ S

A lustre jug, relief-moulded with a stag hunting scene, painted in brightly coloured enamels with bands of purple lustre, slight damage, c1830, 7¼in (18.5cm) high.
£220–250
€/ $350–400 ⚒ F&C

A Newcastle Pottery lustre creamware jug, decorated with the Gardener's Arms, c1830, 7in (18cm) high.
£500–550
€/ $790–870 ⊞ IS
This type of decoration was once mistakenly attributed to Addison, Faulkener & Co.

A North Shields Pottery jug, decorated with a view of the Iron Bridge at Sunderland, c1840, 5½in (14cm) high.
£400–450
€/ $635–715 ⊞ IS

A pink lustre jug, transfer-printed with the sailing ship *William the IV*, flanked by oval panels inscribed with verses, cracked, early 19thC, 8¼in (21cm) high.
£280–320
€/ $440–500 ⚒ RTo

A Sunderland lustre jug, with decorated panels inscribed 'Ancient Order of Foresters' and 'Manchester Unity', c1830, 9in (23cm) high.
£630–700
€/ $1,000–1,100 ⊞ RdV

A pink lustre Masonic jug, inscribed 'Mason's Arms', c1840, 6½in (16.5cm) high.
£800–900
€/ $1,300–1,500 ⊞ RdV

A Tyneside lustre jug, inscribed 'The Mariners' Compass', the reverse with verse, c1855, 5½in (14cm) high.
£250–280
€/ $395–445 ⊞ IS

◄ A Staffordshire lustre jug, transfer-printed and overpainted with a band seated and playing musical instruments, with printed verse 'I wish I was in Dixy Land' and 'Sally is the girl for me', 19thC, 6¼in (16cm) high.
£400–470
€/ $630–740 ⚒ TMA

A Dixon & Co lustre creamware jug, transfer-printed with a view of the Cast Iron Bridge over the River Wear, Sunderland, factory mark, c1825, 6½in (16.5cm) high.
£430–480
€/ $680–760 ⊞ IS

A Sunderland pink lustre jug, attributed to Dawson's, transfer-printed with inscriptions of various free trade societies, c1835, 6½in (16.5cm) high.
£400–450
€/ $630–715 ⊞ IS

A lustre and enamelled jug, attributed to Anthony Scott, Southwick Pottery, decorated with a cartouche entitled 'Return to his True Love', c1850, 6½in (16.5cm) high.
£400–450
€/ $635–715 ⊞ IS
This type of 'squiggle' lustre decoration is typical of Anthony Scott.

A lustre jug, attributed to Anthony Scott, Southwick Pottery, decorated with the 'Sailors Farewell' c1860, 7in (18cm) high.
£430–480
€/ $680–760 ⊞ IS

A lustre jug, decorated with Masonic symbols and cartouches of Justice, Charity and Hope, c1820, 6in (15cm) high
£675–750
€/ $1,100–1,200 ⊞ RdV

A Northumberland Pottery lustre mug, commemorating the 1826 Northumberland election, decorated with a cartouche inscribed 'Bell and Victory', 4½in (11.5cm) high.
£675–750
€/ $1,100–1,200 ⊞ IS

A Sunderland lustre mug, decorated with a ship in full sail, and 'Peace & Plenty' legend in a cartouche, c1835, 5in (12.5cm) high.
£500–550
€/ $790–870 ⊞ HOW

A Sunderland lustre mug, c1835, 5in (12.5cm) high.
£400–450
€/ $630–715 ⊞ HOW

► **A Sunderland pink lustre frog mug,** transfer-printed with a view of the Cast Iron Bridge over the River Wear, Sunderland, c1840, 4¾in (12cm) high.
£425–470
€/ $670–750 ⊞ RdV

A Sunderland pink lustre pearlware mug, depicting 'The Sailors' Farewell' and the 'Cast Iron Bridge', c1840, 5in (12.5cm) high.
£520–575
€/ $820–900 ⊞ RdV

A Sunderland orange lustre frog mug, decorated with the '*Norah Creina* Steam-Yacth', and a verse, over-painted with enamel colours, minor damage to girdle, c1850, 7in (18cm) high.
£220–260
€/ $350–400 ⚒ BR

A Sunderland lustre frog mug, commemorating the Crimean War, decorated with the flags of Great Britain and France, c1855, 5in (12.5cm) high.
£440–500
€/ $700–800 ⊞ RdV

A Sunderland lustre jug, attributed to Anthony Scott, Southwick Pottery, decorated with a view of the New Sunderland Bridge, c1860, 5in (12.5cm) high.
£250–280
€/ $400–450 ⊞ IS

A Victorian lustre frog mug, decorated with a ship, inscribed 'Health to the sick', 5¼in (13.5cm) high.
£85–100
€/ $135–160 ⚒ BIG

POTTERY

A Sunderland lustre plaque, decorated with a portrait of John Wesley, inscribed 'The best of all God is with us', c1830, 6¾ x 5¾in (17 x 14.5cm) high.
£400–450
€/ $630–715 ⊞ RdV

A Sunderland lustre plaque, inscribed 'The Token or Jack's Safe Return', c1830, 9½ x 8¼ in (24 x 21cm).
£430–475
€/ $680–750 ⊞ PSA

A Garrison Pottery pink and copper lustre plaque, decorated with a Middle Eastern scene, impressed 'Dixon, Phillips & Co', c1835, 8in (20.5cm) wide.
£340–380
€/ $540–600 ⊞ IS

A Sunderland lustre plaque, inscribed 'God Speed the Plough', c1835, 8 x 9in (20.5 x 23cm).
£430–475
€/ $680–750 ⊞ HOW

A Sunderland lustre plaque, decorated with a ship in full sail, c1840, 8 x 9½in (20.5 x 24cm).
£430–475
€/ $680–750 ⊞ HOW

A Low Lights Pottery pink lustre plaque, by John Carr, c1845, 9½ x 8in (24 x 20.5cm).
£200–225
€/ $315–350 ⊞ NAW

A Sunderland lustre plaque, transfer-printed 'Thou God Seest me', indistinct impressed mark, probably Dixon, 19thC, 8in (20.5cm) wide.
£100–120
€/ $160–190 ⚒ DAU

A Tyneside pink lustre plaque, decorated with a view of the Iron Bridge over the River Wear, Sunderland, damaged, c1850, 8½in x 7½in (21.5 x 19cm).
£100–110
€/ $160–175 ⊞ NAW

A Sunderland orange lustre script plaque, attributed to Anthony Scott, Southwick Pottery, c1865, 8½in (21.5cm) wide.
£250–275
€/ $400–430 ⊞ IS

A lustre commemorative plate, inscribed 'Charlotte in Memoriam', c1820, 8in (20.5cm) diam.
£550–620
€/ $870–980 ⊞ RdV

A Sunderland lustre named plate, inscribed 'Stephen Hill', impressed Dixon & Co, c1820, 7½in (19cm) diam.
£630–700
€/ $1,000–1,100 ⊞ RdV

A pair of lustre vases, possibly St Anthony's Pottery, Newcastle-upon-Tyne, all-over decorated in variegated pink lustre, rim chip, c1815, 5¾in (14.5cm) high.
£475–565
€/ $750–890 ⚒ B

Porcelain

Many people are frightened to collect porcelain because it feels fragile and breakable, but to a porcelain enthusiast, this very fragility makes it special. There is a real joy in owning a delicate vase that has survived unbroken through many generations. Cracks, repair or restoration make an enormous difference to the value of a piece of fine porcelain. However, over recent years, attitudes have changed and many collectors now view damage in a different light.

Bonhams' sale last year of part of the Minton Museum collection focused attention on the subject of damage, as a surprising amount of pieces offered in this sale were cracked or broken. This is because it was a reference collection of samples, retained by Minton for exhibitions and to train new decorators and many pieces had travelled the world, or been handled repeatedly in a working factory. Damaged porcelain is difficult to sell, but nevertheless, the saleroom was packed with private collectors who saw beyond the cracks and over-painting. They realized these were unique Minton pieces with a historic provenance. Broken vases sold for the same price I would expect to achieve for perfect examples without such provenance.

Collectors who cannot afford rare and historic porcelain in fine condition are often happy to buy damaged examples to have repaired. Many collectors favour 'museum-type' repairs that clean the dirt from old cracks to leave pieces looking attractive, but without extensive surface spraying. A damaged item can be transformed by careful conservation but only special pieces justify the cost of fine repair. Just remember, no matter how skilful the repair, restored porcelain will always be worth much less than perfect.

As the volume of porcelain sold on the internet increases, an alarming trend is emerging. Descriptions of damage are often woefully inadequate, cracks are frequently ignored, and a worrying amount is professionally restored. Don't take anything at face value. Before you buy, ask for a guarantee that the condition is as described. Wherever possible, though, try to buy undamaged porcelain, as this will give much more pleasure in the long term. **John Sandon**

Animals

A model of a pigeon, nesting on a basket-work base, chipped, Spanish, probably Alcora, 1775–1800, 6in (15cm) high.
£375–450
€/ $600–700 ⚒ B

A Kloster Veilsdorf group of a leopard attacking a mule, modelled by Pfränger, on a scroll-edged base, German, c1775, 8¼in (21cm) wide.
£1,100–1,300
€/ $1,700–2,000 ⚒ S(O)
This is a very rare group, but the gruesome subject may have been the reason for the modest price realized.

A Belleek spill vase, modelled as a fish, Irish, First Period, 1863–90, 7in (18cm) high.
£585–650
€/ $900–1,000 ⊞ MLa

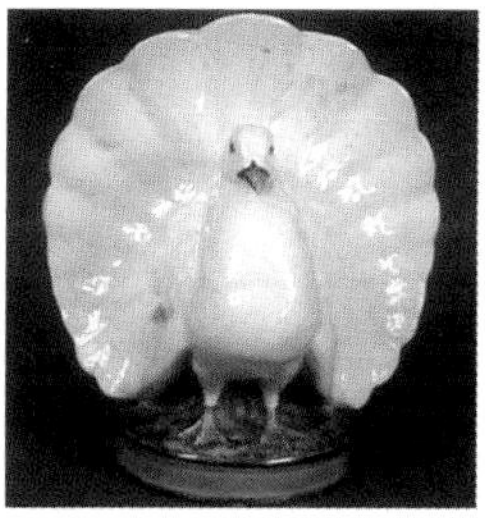

A Minton vase, modelled as a fantail dove, c1870, 6in (15cm) high.
£275–330
€/ $430–520 ⚒ SWO

A Belleek Parian group of greyhounds, Irish, First Period, 1863–90, 8in (20.5cm) high.
£5,200–6,200
€/ $8,200–9,800 ⚒ JAd

A Moore Bros table centrepiece, modelled as two swans flanking a bulrush-moulded vase on a waterlily-moulded base, damaged, impressed 'Moore' and printed T. Goode', c1875, 12¼in (31cm) wide.
£180–200
€/ $280–315 ⚒ RTo
In good condition this group would have realized considerably more.

Expert's choice

A Limehouse cat, 1746–48, sold by Bonhams in September 1991.

When I was shown this porcelain cat in 1990, it was totally unrecorded. The owner thought it was delft, but I knew it was a significant piece of early English porcelain. Just a few months earlier, archaeologists digging on a site in east London had discovered one of the first porcelain factories. The few dozen broken fragments identified the products of the Limehouse porcelain manufactory. Among the shards from Limehouse, being sorted at the Museum of London, I recognized a fragment of the foot of a cat. It matched the cat I had been asked to sell. Until these shards were found, this distinctive porcelain had been incorrectly identified as Liverpool. Research continues and archaeology has many new lessons to teach collectors of porcelain. The cat realized £5,280 (€/ $8,300) in September 1991. No others have turned up since, and today it would be worth £12,000–15,000 (€/ $19,000–24,000). **John Sandon**

► **A Chamberlain Worcester model of a cat and a kitten,** the cat painted with tabby markings, on a cushion base with gilded edge detail, minor damage, impressed 'Chamberlains', 1820–30, 2½in (6.5cm) high.
£900–1,000
€/ $1,400–1,600 B

A Saint Cloud soft paste snuff box, modelled as a recumbent dog, decorated with figures and houses, 1740–50, 1¾in (4.5cm) high.
£4,200–5,000
€/ $6,600–7,900 S(P)

► **A model of a tabby cat,** with puce printed retailer's mark for John Mortlock, Orchard St, London, mid-19thC, 11½in (29cm) high.
£1,500–1,800
€/ $2,400–2,800 S(O)

A Royal Worcester model of a swan holding a basket between its wings, mark with date code for 1901, 7¼in (18.5cm) high.
£250–280
€/ $400–440 SWO

A monkey band group, comprising 9 pieces, some damage, German, early 20thC, 7in (18cm) high.
£650–750
€/ $1,000–1,200 G(L)

Baskets

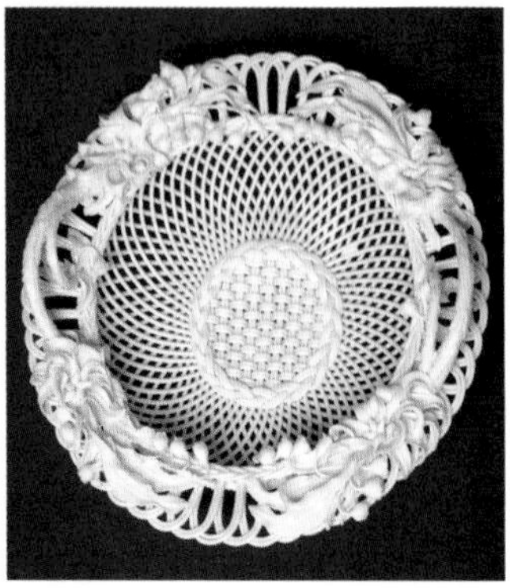

A Belleek two-strand lily of the valley basket, Irish, First Period, 1863–90, 10in (25.5cm) diam.
£1,800–2,000
€/ $2,800–3,200 MLa

A Bow basket, the centre painted with a floral spray, chipped foot and restoration, c1760, 11in (28cm) wide.
£220–250
€/ $350–400 SWO
The low price realized for this basket reflects extensive restoration.

A Coalport basket, the sides, bail handle and rim applied with flowers, the interior painted with flowers and gilt scrolls, handle repaired, 'CD' mark, c1840, 8½in (21.5cm) wide.
£170–200
€/ $270–315 WW
The low price realized for this basket reflects the damage.

A Worcester basket, the sides pierced with interlaced circles applied with florets at the intersections, the centre painted with Staghunt pattern, side of rim restored, c1756, 6¼in (16cm) diam.
£750–875
€/ $1,200–1,400 B
The price reflects the damage and restoration.

Miller's Compares

I. **A Worcester basket,** the sides pierced with interlocking circles, applied externally with florets at the intersections, the exterior washed in yellow, the centre painted with a floral spray surrounded by smaller sprigs, the sides with further small trailing sprigs, 1763–65, 7¾in (19.5cm) diam.
£2,000–2,200
€/ $3,200–3,500 B

II. **A Worcester dessert basket,** the sides pierced with overlapping circles, applied externally at the intersections with florets, the centre painted with a floral spray, with a foliate scroll border, minor wear and crack, 1758–60, 7¾in (19.5cm) diam.
£650–775
€/ $1,000–1,200 B

These two baskets are the same size and of a similar date, but Item I is more desirable because of its yellow exterior which gives it a more attractive appearance. Item II, moreover, has a minor crack to the rim – damage will nearly always reduce an item's value, unless the item is particularly rare.

A Worcester basket, the sides pierced with interlocking circles, applied externally with florets, the centre painted with a spray of flowers and a smaller sprig, c1760, 5in (12.5cm) diam.
£1,000–1,200
€/ $1,600–1,900 B

► **A Worcester basket,** the reticulated sides applied with flowerheads, the interior painted with flowers, damaged, c1765, 8in (20.5cm) diam.
£250–300
€/ $400–500 WW
The low price achieved by this basket reflects the amount of damage it has sustained.

Bowls

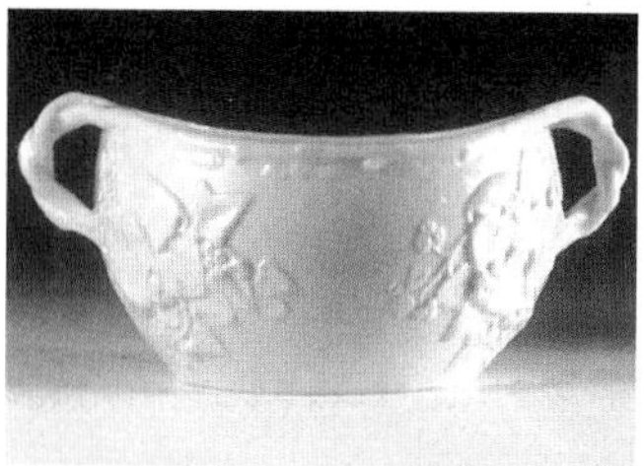

◄ **A Belleek sugar bowl,** moulded with ivy leaves and berries, Irish, First Period, 1863–90, 6in (15cm) wide.
£80–100
€/ $125–160 WW

► **A Belleek coral and cardium shell bowl,** Irish, Second Period, 1891–1926, 4½in (11.5cm) high.
£450–500
€/ $700–800 MLa

A Belleek bowl, the exterior applied with flowers below the frilled rim, on three scroll feet, minor chips and losses to flowers, black printed mark, Irish, Second Period, 1891–1926, 10in (25.5cm) diam.
£375–450
€/ $600–700 S(O)

A Belleek Celtic fruit bowl, heightened in enamel and gilding, the interior washed in yellow, Irish, 1926–39, 10in (25.5cm) diam.
£420–500
€/ $670–800 S(O)

A Belleek bowl, Irish, Third Period, 1926–46, 11in (28cm) diam.
£1,100–1,200
€/ $1,700–1,900 ⊞ MLa

► A Bow bowl, painted in the *famille rose* palette with flowers, leaves and rockwork, and a figure in a boat, workman's mark, 1752–53, 6½in (16.5cm) diam.
£600–700
€/ $950–1,100 ⚒ WW

◄ A Caughley bowl, enamel-painted, probably by Fidelle Duvivier, with two figures in an extensive wooded river landscape, and with three similar vignettes, the interior similarly decorated, beneath a leaf-scroll and ribbon band, minor rim chip, c1790, 8¼in (21cm) diam.
£2,000–2,200
€/ $3,200–3,500 ⚒ LFA

A pair of Adolph Hamann hand-painted monteiths, each with a gilded rim and two branch handles, decorated with floral sprays, inscribed decorator's mark, German, Dresden, 1875–1925, 6in (15cm) wide.
£300–350
€/ $475–550 ⚒ RIT

► An Imperial Porcelain Manufactory bowl, painted with floral sprays, slight wear, Russian, St Petersburg, 1855–81, 12¼in (31cm) diam.
£700–820
€/ $1,100–1,300
⚒ BUK

A Sèvres bowl, painted by Edmé-François Bouillat or Geneviève-Louise Bouillat, with three oval panels of buildings and small figures in river landscapes, including a fire scene, alternating with medallions, the border with trailing flowers above a gilt floral swag border, minor wear to gilt rim, interlaced 'LL', date code 00 and painter's mark 'y', French, dated 1791, 7in (18cm) diam.
£1,500–1,800
€/ $2,400–2,800 ⚒ S(O)

A Royal Worcester bowl, hand-painted by Ricketts with apples and blackberries, dated 1926, 7in (18cm) diam.
£420–500
€/ $670–800 ⚒ B(W)

A Worcester porringer, with an ozier-moulded border below the rim, the twin rustic handles with a moulded scroll at the lower terminal, the upper terminal flanked by applied flowers, leaves and stalks, the interior printed and overpainted with *Les Garçons Chinois*, the exterior painted with scattered flower sprays, minor losses to handles, c1757, 7in (18cm) wide.
£4,500–5,200
€/ $7,000–8,200 ⚒ B
The shape appears to be unrecorded. Related moulding is found on rare covered *écuelles* usually decorated in blue, but no similar handles have been recorded. The extensive decoration inside strongly suggests this shape was complete without a cover and that it may have served as a wine cup or quaich.

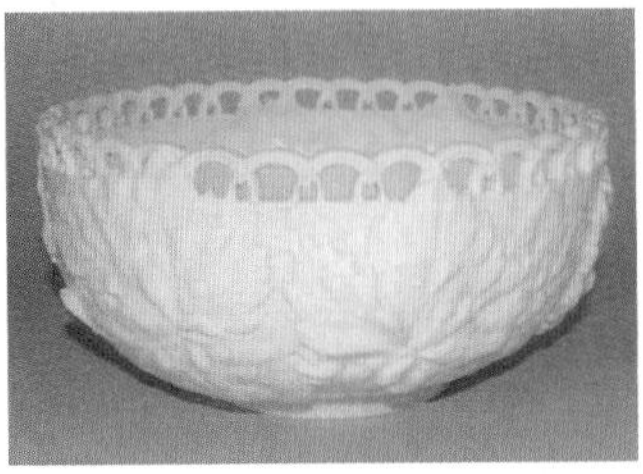

A Royal Worcester fruit bowl, moulded with fruiting foliage on a basketweave ground, with pierced arcaded rim, puce mark, date code for 1890, 9½in (24cm) diam.
£80–100
€/ $125–160 ⚒ PFK

◄ A miniature bowl-on-stand, the bowl with gilded ram's head-handles, both painted with flowers against gilt borders, chips to pedestal base, 1815–20, bowl 3½in (9cm) diam.
£230–275
€/ $360–430 ⚒ G(L)

Covered Bowls

A Caughley sucrier and cover, with rounded knop, decorated in gold with leaf garlands suspended from bands gilt with leaf scrolls, c1790, 4½in (11.5cm) high.
£375–450
€/ $600–700 LFA

A Gaudy Welsh sucrier, c1840, 6in (15cm) high.
£90–100
€/ $140–160 ⊞ WAC

A Sèvres écuelle, cover and stand, French, c1774, stand 10in (25.5cm) wide.
£1,500–1,650
€/ $2,400–2,600 ⊞ DHu

Reticulation

The art of 'reticulation' was perfected at the Royal Worcester factory. Initially Worcester craftsmen cut formal honeycomb patterns out of lightly moulded teawares. More elaborate productions copied carved ivories imported from India.

By the 1880s truly magnificent pierced vases were made in the Persian taste. The Grainger factory also made equally fine reticulated work. The holes were cut out one by one while the clay was still wet, following complicated moulded scroll-work patterns. George Owen excelled above all other craftsman, dispensing with moulded guidelines and producing unbelievable pierced patterns using hand and eye alone. His signed vases are testament to his genius and deserve the high prices they now command.

A pair of Grainger's Worcester reticulated bowls and covers, pierced with foliate and floret chamfered rectangles, date code for 1893, 4½in (11.5cm) diam.
£475–550
€/ $750–870 L

◄ A Royal Worcester reticulated bowl and cover, by George Owen, the cover with a pierced band of unique design, the finial surrounded by a band of applied 'pearls', a wide band of honeycomb below a border of scrolls and anthemia in raised gold, supported on a plinth by a row of gilded 'pearls', gold mark, shape No. 2521, incised 'G Owen', 1920–21, 5in (12.5cm) diam.
£10,000–12,000
€/ $16,000–19,000 B

Boxes

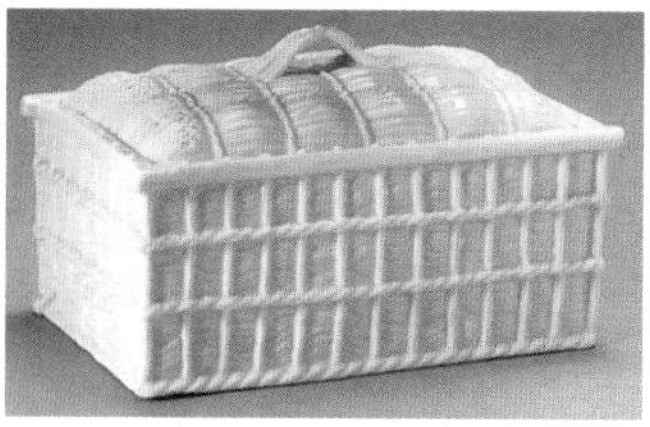

◄ A Belleek biscuit box and cover, modelled as a straw-moulded crate bound by string, cover with retouched chip, impressed and black printed marks, Irish, First Period, 1863–90, 7¾in (20.5cm) wide.
£420–500
€/ $670–790 S(O)

A Royal Worcester reticulated casket and cover, by George Owen, the cover with a pierced boss, flanked by honeycomb panels, with pierced borders edged in raised gold, the twin handles applied with beaded rings, further bands of 'pearls' applied to the base and cover, the shoulder pierced with scrollwork and flowers picked out in gold, above a wide band alternately pierced with diamonds and circles within tall upright panels, on a scroll-moulded base and ball feet, small chip to inner rim partly refilled, gold mark, shape No. 2412, incised signature, dated 1909, 6¼in (16cm) wide.
£12,500–15,000
€/ $20,000–24,000 B
The minor damage to this piece is reflected in the realized price.

A trinket box, with Sèvres-style decoration, French, late 19thC, 5in (12.5cm) wide.
£585–650
€/ $925–1,000 ⊞ MAA

A Dresden box, with gilt-metal mounts, the lid with a hand-painted courting scene, a landscape to the base, pseudo crossed swords mark, German, late 19thC, 2in (5cm) diam.
£100–120
€/ $160–190 SWO

Busts

A Copeland Parian bust of The Veiled Bride, after Raphael Monti, impressed 'R. Monti 1861 Copeland', on a socle base impressed 'Crystal Palace Art Union', 15in (38cm) high.
£3,000–3,400
€/ $4,700–5,400 ⚒ Mit

A W. H. Goss Parian bust of the Earl of Derby, 1876–91, 6½in (16.5cm) high.
£165–185
€/ $260–300 ⊞ G&CC

A Minton biscuit bust of Lord Brougham, on a glazed pedestal with gilt borders, the base titled in gilding, minor crack, 1830–40, 6in (15cm) high.
£900–1,100
€/ $1,400–1,700 ⚒ S

► A pair of busts of Princess Charlotte and Prince Leopold, by J. & R. Riley, prince restored at neck, signed and dated 1819, 15¾in (40cm) high.
£4,800–5,700
€/ $7,600–9,000 ⚒ S

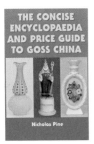

A Sèvres biscuit bust of General Desaix de Veygoux, impressed 'Sèvres' and incised 'D 81.10', the base with printed circle mark and date code 'S.82', French, c1882, 16in (40.5cm) high.
£1,000–1,200
€/ $1,600–1,900 ⚒ S(NY)

Louis Charles Antoine Desaix de Veygoux (1768–1800) was a general in the French Revolutionary Wars. He died at the Battle of Marengo in northern Italy on June 14 1800.

For further information on antique porcelain see the full range of Miller's books at **www.millers.uk.com**

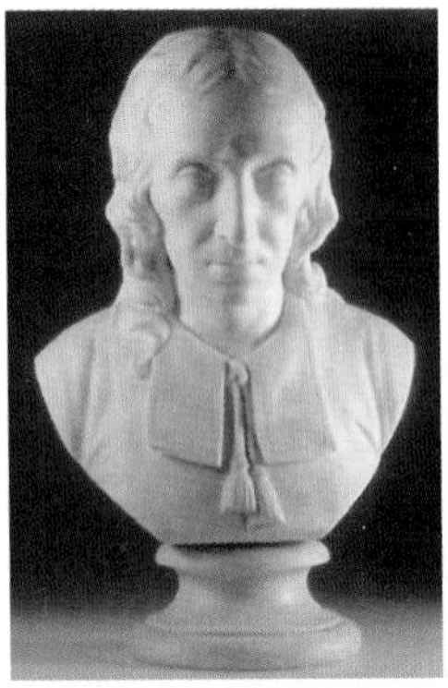

A Wedgwood Parian bust of Milton, after the model by E. W. Wyon, titled to the reverse, collar chip, c1860, 14¼in (36cm) high.
£250–280
€/ $400–440 ⚒ WW

PORCELAIN

Candlesticks & Chambersticks

► **A Coalport chamberstick,** with encrusted floral decoration, c1830, 2in (5cm) high.
£660–700
€/ $1,000–1,100 ⊞ DIA

A Barr, Flight & Barr 'Music' candlestick, painted with an upright panel of Beauchief Abbey, Derbyshire, within gilded neo-classical borders applied with bands of 'pearls', some scratches and wear, script marks, c1810, 5¼in (13.5cm) high.
£375–450
€/ $600–700 ⚒ B
The Flight factory invoices use the name 'Music' for sticks of this shape.

A Chamberlain Worcester taperstick, decorated with Japan pattern, No. 240, c1810, 2¾in (7cm) high.
£800–880
€/ $1,300–1,400 ⊞ DIA

A Worcester Barr, Flight & Barr chamberstick, the base painted with four shells, with a reattached gilt handle, impressed and painted marks, 1807–13, 3¼in (8.5cm) high.
£1,000–1,200
€/ $1,600–1,900 ⚒ G(L)

A chamberstick, the shell-moulded base with encrusted floral decoration, c1830, 2in (5cm) high.
£550–600
€/ $870–950 ⊞ DIA

Centrepieces

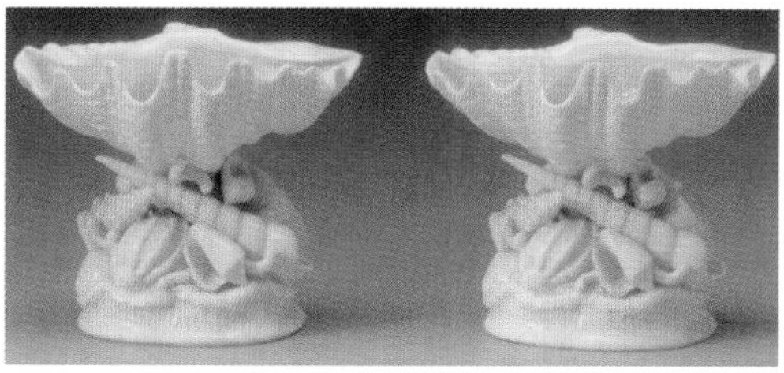

A pair of Belleek centrepieces, the open clam shells on a pile of smaller shells above a water-moulded base, small chips, black printed mark, First Period, 1863–90, 5in (12.5cm) high.
£650–750
€/ $1,000–1,200 ⚒ S(O)

LOCATE THE SOURCE
The source of each illustration in Miller's can be found by checking the code letters below each caption with the Key to Illustrations, pages 794–800.

► **A Belleek centrepiece,** black printed mark, Third Period, 1926–46, 12in (30.5cm) high.
£1,000–1,100
€/ $1,600–1,700 ⊞ MLa

A Berlin figural centrepiece, the centre of the bowl painted with an arrangement of flowers, supported by three biscuit putti around a parcel-gilt biscuit foliate column, on a tripartite base, restored chip to column, sceptre mark in underglaze blue, red printed 'KPM' and orb, German, c1840, 8½in (21.5cm) high.
£2,800–3,200
€/ $4,400–5,000 ⚒ S(NY)

A John Bevington Meissen-style centrepiece, modelled as a lady and a gentleman running around a flower-encrusted column supporting a pierced basket, minor losses, marked, c1860, 18in (45.5cm) high.
£1,000–1,100
€/ $1,600–1,800 ⚒ B(Kn)

A William Cookworthy pickle stand, the dishes modelled as three clam shells, on a tripod pedestal foot supported at the corners by three dolphins surrounded by shells, a pyramid of shells at the top forming the handle, a flower spray inside each dish, chips and restoration, 1768–73, 6¾in (17cm) high.
£1,700–2,000
€/ $2,700–3,200 ⚒ B

A pair of Royal Crown Derby comports, decorated in the Imari palette, pattern No. 2444, date code for 1901, 9in (23cm) diam.
£320–375
€/ $500–600 ⚒ SWO

◄ A Minton *pâte-sur-pâte* centrepiece, with a pieced scroll rim, the sides decorated with a medallion of a maiden and cherub, and strips decorated with neo-classical motifs, on four scroll feet, cracked, c1892, impressed and printed marks, indistinct date cypher and shape number, 16½in (42cm) wide.
£3,200–3,800
€/ $5,000–6,000 ⚒ B
Ex-Minton Sale.

A Plaue centrepiece, the pierced basket encrusted with roses, on a scroll-moulded stem applied with three putti, small chips, crossed lines in underglaze blue, German, c1900, 12in (30.5cm) high.
£380–450
€/ $600–700 ⚒ S(O)

A Spode dessert centrepiece, painted with roses, c1820, 13in (33cm) wide.
£1,600–1,800
€/ $2,500–2,900 ⊞ DAN

A Swansea centrepiece, painted with groups of flowers, firing crack to rim and some wear, Welsh, 1814–26, 13½in (34.5cm) wide.
£2,200–2,500
€/ $3,500–4,000 ⚒ S(O)

A centrepiece, the flower-encrusted bowl pierced with lattice panels and decorated with flowers, on a flower-encrusted stem, the base modelled as a figural group of a lady and gallant playing chess, watched by a female attendant, damaged, Continental, late 19thC, 22¾in (58cm) high.
£200–225
€/ $315–350 ⚒ RTo

A Carl Thieme Potschappel centrepiece, applied with flowers and figures of cherubs, the interior painted with flowers, minor damage, blue marks, German, c1900, 16½in (42cm) wide.
£300–360
€/ $475–575 ⚒ DORO

A centrepiece, the dish supported by a satyr, cracked and stained, 19thC, 9¼in (23.5cm) high.
£250–300
€/ $400–475 ⚒ SWO

Coffee & Teapots

A Belleek teapot, decorated with Thorn pattern, Irish, First Period, 1863–90, 4in (10cm) high.
£720–800
€/ $1,100–1,200 MLa

► **A Belleek 'Grass' tea kettle and cover,** with a ribbon-bound handle, rubbing, black printed mark, the interior of the cover with black printed instructions for warming the pot, First Period, 1863–90, 6in (15cm) high.
£320–375
€/ $500–600 S(O)

◄ **A Belleek teapot,** with enamelled floral decoration, Second Period, 1891–1926, 5in (12.5cm) high.
£1,000–1,100
€/ $1,600–1,800 MLa

◄ **A Caughley coffee pot and cover,** the domed cover applied with a flower finial, painted in bright enamels with four Chinese 'bubblehead' figures beside an iron red fence, including a small child holding a stick, the reverse with three similar figures, small chips to cover, c1775, 7½in (19cm) high.
£1,000–1,200
€/ $1,600–1,900 B

A Derby teapot and stand, c1810, 6in (15cm) high.
£675–750
€/ $1,000–1,200 CoS

A Ludwigsburg coffee pot and cover, painted by Gottlieb Friedrich Kirschner with a large flower spray, a smaller sprig on the reverse and further scattered flowers, the domed cover with a fruit knop, the gilt-edged spout and handle moulded with rocailles and acanthus leaves, chips, wear and some restoration, crowned interlaced 'CC' monogram in underglaze blue, painter's mark 'K' in green, impressed 4 and 3, incised A, German, c1775, 8¼in (21cm) high.
£2,500–3,000
€/ $4,000–4,800 S(O)
Gottlieb Friedrich Kirschner (1748–89) was a painter of birds and flowers and an engraver who was active at the Ludwigsburg manufactory between about 1770 and 1787.

A Worcester teapot and cover, painted with a Chinese family, the cover with a floral knop, c1770, 5¾in (14.5cm) high.
£450–525
€/ $700–830 S(O)

◄ A Christian's Liverpool palm tree teapot, the fluted lid and acanthus-moulded panelled body painted in blue with formal floral groups, chips, haircrack to finial, c1770, 7¼in (18.5cm) high.
£1,300–1,500
€/ $2,000–2,400 LAY

A New Hall coffee jug and cover, the high-domed cover with a pine-cone knob, the spout with a shaped bridge across the widest part, small chips and cracks, 1782–85, 10¼in (26cm) high.
£3,700–4,400
€/ $5,700–7,000 B

A Worcester teapot, painted with floral sprays, the spout and handle with puce scrollwork, damaged, old collectors' labels to underside, 1765–68, 5in (12.5cm) high.
£90–110
€/ $140–175 PFK

► A Worcester Flight, Barr & Barr teapot, cover and stand, c1815, 8in (20.5cm) high.
£540–600
€/ $850–950 CoS

◄ A Worcester Flight teapot, c1790, 7in (18cm) high.
£400–450
€/ $630–700 DSA

A Lowestoft miniature teapot, with domed lid, the body painted with floral sprays, cracked, spout detached but present, old collector's label '445 Lowestoft' to base, c1775, 3¼in (8.5cm) high.
£1,500–1,800
€/ $2,400–2,800 PFK
Lowestoft miniature teawares are very rare in colours other than blue and white, hence this high price for a badly damaged piece.

A Worcester teapot and cover, painted with Conjurer pattern, the cover with a flower finial, chips to spout and finial, 1768–70, 6in (15cm) high.
£550–625
€/ $870–990 B

A Worcester teapot and cover, painted with panels of Chinese figures and smaller panels of landscapes, some restoration, c1770, 7in (18cm) wide.
£550–625
€/ $870–1,000 WW

◄ A Worcester teapot, painted with a floral pattern in the Chinese style, c1770, 5in (12.5cm) high.
£480–530
€/ $750–830 DSA

Coffee & Tea Services

A Caughley part coffee and tea service, comprising 27 pieces, fluted and painted with French sprigs, some damage, c1785.
£625–725
€/ $990–1,150 B(Kn)

An assembled Caughley tea service, comprising 25 pieces, decorated with Pagoda pattern, some damage, blue S marks, c1785.
£650–750
€/ $1,000–1,200 B(Kn)

A Copeland & Garrett part coffee and tea service, comprising 13 pieces, painted with panels of garden flowers with scroll-moulded and gilt reserves, printed mark in green, c1840.
£300–350
€/ $475–550 Bea(E)

A Derby tea service, comprising 52 pieces, decorated in the Japanese style with flowers and foliage, c1825.
£1,100–1,200
€/ $1,700–1,900 E

◄ A Coalport John Rose part tea service, comprising 27 pieces, painted and gilt in the Japanese style with shrubs issuing flowers, and baluster panels with C-scroll borders, minor wear, one can with restored handle, c1810.
£1,300–1,500
€/ $2,000–2,400 DN

A Royal Crown Derby coffee service, comprising 15 pieces, decorated in the Imari palette with a floral design, printed mark and various date cyphers, c1900.
£300–340
€/ $475–550 GAK

► A Derby Crown Porcelain Co cabaret service, comprising 15 pieces, printed and painted with Japan pattern, haircrack to one saucer, printed and impressed factory marks, painted pattern No. 198, c1884, tray 14in (35.5cm) wide.
£500–575
€/ $800–900 S(O)

A Fürstenberg coffee service, comprising 22 pieces, painted with various landscape vignettes including buildings and rural figures supported by scrollwork cartouches with suspended flower garlands, minor damage, painted marks, impressed numerals, German, 1770–75, coffee pot 10½in (26.5cm) high.
£1,800–2,000
€/ $2,800–3,200 S(Am)

A Hilditch part tea service, comprising 17 pieces, decorated with chinoiserie scenes, some damage, printed factory marks, c1825.
£275–325
€/ $430–500 WW

► A Minton *pâte-sur-pâte* cabaret set, comprising nine pieces, by Thomas Mellor, each with a panel depicting putti in different attitudes, the ground with neo-classical ornament, edged with running patterns of gilt scrolls and leaves, some restoration, impressed factory marks and date codes, one saucer with monogram 'TM', 1878–80.
£7,500–9,000
€/ $12,000–14,000 B

A New Hall composite part tea and coffee service, comprising 52 pieces, printed and coloured with Window pattern, restoration and damage, painted No. 425, 1775–1825.
£1,500–1,850
€/ $2,400–2,900 ⚒ S(O)

A Paris coffee service, comprising 13 pieces, with gilt decoration of leaf garlands, gilding worn, coffee pot knop repaired, French, c1820.
£650–750
€/ $1,000–1,200 ⚒ BUK

A Sèvres-style 'jewelled' solitaire, comprising 7 pieces, each reserved with panels enclosing titled scenes from medieval history, including Joan of Arc, battle and bedside scenes, the saucer with trophies, some restoration and chips, pseudo-Sèvres mark, date letters, incised marks and blue script titles, French, late 19thC, tray 9½in (24cm) wide.
£2,500–3,000
€/ $4,000–4,800 ⚒ S(O)

◄ A Staffordshire rococo revival tea service, comprising 41 pieces, with gilt-enriched borders, pattern No. 1/1698, some damage, lozenge mark, c1845.
£80–90
€/ $125–145 ⚒ PFK

► A Swansea part tea service, comprising four pieces, decorated in the Japanese Imari style with flowers and panels, teapot stand and plate marked 'Swansea', pattern No. 194, Welsh, 1816–20.
£850–1,000
€/ $1,300–1,600 ⚒ WW

A Swansea part tea service, comprising 43 pieces, painted with flower sprigs on a spiral- and ozier-moulded ground, minor restoration and cracks, gilt script mark, Welsh, c1820.
£2,200–2,500
€/ $3,500–4,000 ⚒ S(O)

A Vienna coffee and tea service, comprising 20 pieces, decorated with flowers and gilt rims, wear and damage to one rim, c1800, coffee pot 6¼in (16cm) high.
£525–625
€/ $830–990 ⚒ DORO

Items in the Porcelain section have been arranged in factory order, with non-specific pieces appearing at the end of each sub-section.

A Chamberlain Worcester tea service, comprising 36 pieces, impressed and printed marks, c1830.
£850–1,000
€/ $1,300–1,600 ⚒ TEN

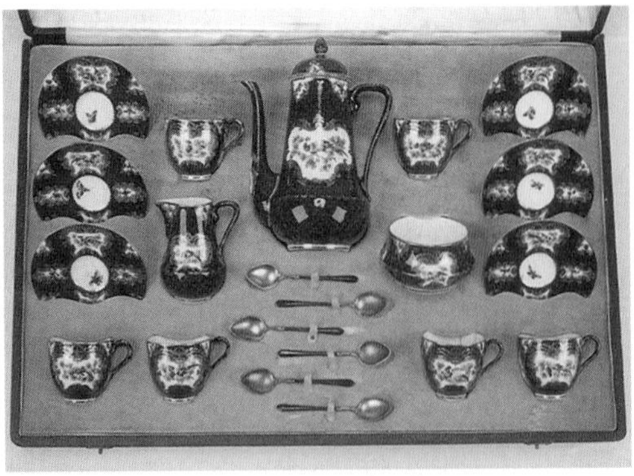

A Royal Worcester boxed coffee set, comprising 22 pieces, painted by George Johnson, with panels of exotic birds in the 18thC-style, some damage, import marks and date code for 1927, in a fitted box.
£625–725
€/ $990–1,200 ⚒ DN

Clocks

A Chelsea chinoiserie-style clock case, modelled as a lady seated on the steps of a rococo pavilion, the upper section with a harebell three-tiered roof containing a clock cavity, the rear with a rocky base applied with florets, some restoration, chips and losses, red anchor mark, 1756–58, 10¼in (26cm) high.
£5,000–5,500
€/ $7,900–8,700 ⚒ B

A Jacob Petit mantel clock, stand and finial, the dial set in a rococo-moulded surround, painted with two lovers in an interior, the reverse and sides painted with flower panels, surmounted by a floral cluster finial, restoration and losses, painted mark, French, mid-19thC, 28in (71cm) high.
£3,000–3,500
€/ $4,700–5,500 ⚒ S(O)

A mantel clock, in a Jacob Petit-style case enriched with gilding and floral panels, with looking plate strike and silk suspension with radiating *guilloche* silvered dial, steel Breguet hands, the detachable base with a scene of Oriental fisherfolk, French, mid-19thC, 16in (40.5cm) high.
£650–750
€/ $1,000–1,200 ⚒ TEN

A rococo-style mantel clock and stand, encrusted and painted with flowers, surmounted by three cherubs above an enamel dial signed 'Leroy', the two-train brass movement with anchor escapement and outside count wheel, striking on a bell, French, c1900, 15½in (39.5cm) high.
£340–400
€/ $550–630 ⚒ BR

Cups

A Berlin coffee can and saucer, probably decorated outside the factory, painted by Charlotte Bose, with a gilt-edged panel of a shepherd tending his flock, a small town in the distance, the saucer inscribed 'Souvenir de l'année 1778', chips, impressed and incised marks, script signature, German, dated 1811.
£750–875
€/ $1,200–1,400 ⚒ S(O)

▶ **A Bow coffee cup,** painted in the *famille rose* style with a floral pattern, c1755, 2½in (6.5cm) high.
£340–380
€/ $550–590 ⊞ DSA

A Chelsea tea bowl, painted in the Kakiemon style with scattered flowerheads, hair crack and chip, c1752, 2¾in (7cm) wide.
£425–500
€/ $$670–790 ⚒ WW

A Coalport breakfast cup and saucer, from the Earl Nelson service, the border with Greek key pattern between gold bands, painted with the two crests of the *San Josef* and the *Chelengk* awarded to Admiral Lord Nelson, beneath an Earl's coronet, chip to foot rim of saucer, 1806–08, saucer 6in (15cm) diam.
£1,600–1,900
€/ $2,500–3,000 ⚒ B
This rare set was commissioned by William, 1st Earl Nelson, who inherited the title following the death of his brother Horatio. A selection of pieces from this set is in the National Maritime Museum, Greenwich.

A Caughley tea bowl and saucer, painted with Target pattern, 1793–95, 2in (5cm) high.
£300–330
€/ $475–525 ⊞ DSA

A Champion Bristol coffee cup and saucer, painted with floral sprays, c1775, 2in (5cm) high.
£540–600
€/ $850–950 ⊞ DSA

Further reading

Miller's Collecting Porcelain,
Miller's Publications, 2002

◀ **A Coalport coffee can,** c1805, 2½in (6.5cm) high.
£65–75
€/ $100–120 ⊞ JAY

A Derby Crown Porcelain Co cup and saucer, c1880, 5in (12.5cm) high.
£160–175
€/ $250–275 ⊞ CoS

King Street Derby

Derby was home to two major porcelain factories, Royal Crown Derby and King Street Derby. Aside from Royal Crown Derby, another manufactory was established across the city in King Street. Between 1862 and 1866 the King Street works were managed by George Stephenson and Sampson Hancock. They were continued by Hancock alone until 1935.

The King Street factory mark copied the old Derby crowned D, but with added initials SH. Most productions were revivals of traditional Derby shapes and patterns. This lack of originality means that King Street Derby is generally cheaper than Royal Crown Derby.

A Lowestoft tea bowl and saucer, printed with Fisherman Crossing a Bridge pattern, 1775–80, 3in (7.5cm) diam.
£430–475
€/ $680–750 ⊞ DSA

A New Hall coffee can, decorated with pseudo Tobacco leaf pattern, pattern No. 856, c1810, 2¼in (5.5cm) high.
£160–175
€/ $250–275 ⊞ CoS

A Derby King Street tea cup and saucer, possibly painted by Annie Bailey with floral sprays, painted marks, 1900–25.
£170–200
€/ $270–315 ⚒ DN

A Lowestoft blue and white tea bowl and saucer, painted with a pagoda in a fenced garden, within diaper borders, c1780.
£480–565
€/ $750–870 ⚒ DN

A Nymphenburg cabinet cup and saucer, the cup painted with a flower bouquet on a medallion, with a band of gilt classical urns and swags, the handle and cup interior gilt, impressed marks, German, c1815.
£1,200–1,400
€/ $1,900–2,200 ⚒ S(O)

A Derby coffee cup, with a wishbone handle, painted with a Chinese lady seated on a rock, another lady, a child and a dog to her left, rim chip, c1758, 2½in (6.5cm) high.
£480–565
€/ $750–870 ⚒ B

A Fürstenberg chocolate cup and *trembleuse* saucer, the cup modelled with a tied ribbon forming the handle, painted with floral bouquets, one in the shape of the initial S, cover missing, saucer chipped, script mark, German, c1775, saucer 5½in (14cm) diam.
£55–65
€/ $85–100 ⚒ BR

A New Hall coffee can, c1805, 2½in (6.5cm) high.
£85–100
€/ $135–160 ⊞ JAY

A Paris cup and saucer, red stamped marks, French, early 19thC, cup 2½in (6.5cm) high.
£170–200
€/ $270–315 ⚒ DORO

A Schlaggenwald cup and saucer, marked, Bohemian, 1844, cup 2¾in (7cm) high.
£180–200
€/ $280–315 ⚒ DORO

A Sèvres cabinet cup and saucer, painted by Jacques-Nicolas Sinsson with garden flowers, with gilt *faux* gadroons and foliate borders in gold and platinum, the cup with scrolling handle with biting snake terminals, fine crack to base of handle, printed mark of Charles X, painter's initials and date markings, dated 1828, saucer 6in (15cm) diam.
£1,000–1,200
€/ $1,600–1,900 ⚒ B

A Swansea cup, painted with colourful flowers, with gilt border designs, small chip, marked 'Swansea', Welsh, 1814–20, 4in (10cm) high.
£1,200–1,400
€/ $1,900–2,200 ⚒ WW

A Vauxhall tea bowl and saucer, printed and overpainted with sprays of flowers and insects, a further spray to the inside base of the tea bowl, several chips and fine cracks, 1758–60, saucer 4½in (11.5cm) diam.
£700–820
€/ $1,100–1,300 ⚒ B

A Worcester tea bowl, decorated with Fruit pattern, c1780, 3¼in (8.5cm) diam.
£100–110
€/ $160–175 ⊞ JAY

◄ **A Vienna cup and saucer,** painted mark, Austrian, 1827, saucer 6in (15cm) diam.
£750–900
€/ $1,200–1,400 ⚒ DORO

A Worcester tea bowl and saucer, transfer-printed with Bat pattern, c1785, saucer 5in (12.5cm) diam.
£150–165
€/ $240–260 ⊞ WAC

A Worcester reeded cup and saucer, with floral and gilt decoration, 1780–85, 2½in (6.5cm) high.
£350–400
€/ $550–650 ⊞ DSA

A Chamberlain Worcester tea cup, painted with a view 'Doniquaik, Scotland', the name in script beneath, against a marbled gilt ground, painted mark, c1815, 2½in (6.5cm) high.
£240–275
€/ $380–430 ⚒ G(L)

A Royal Worcester reticulated tea cup and saucer, painted with sprays of roses alternating with pierced sections highlighted in gold, beneath pansy flowers, printed mark, c1870, saucer 4¼in (11cm) diam.
£625–725
€/ $990–1,100 ⚒ S(O)

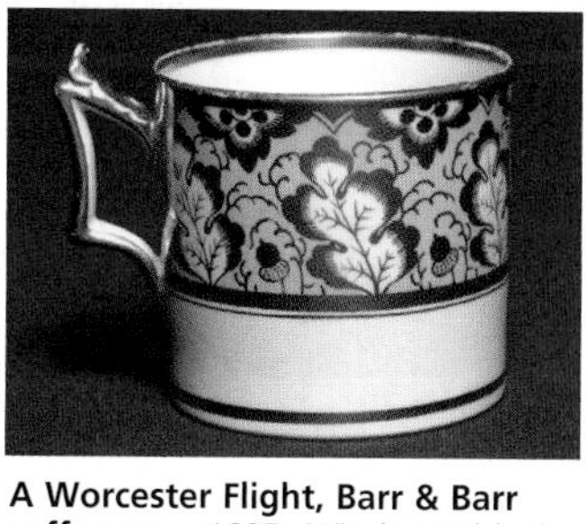

A Worcester Flight, Barr & Barr coffee can, c1825, 2½in (6.5cm) high.
£130–145
€/ $200–230 ⊞ CoS

► **A cup and saucer,** each painted with a bird and shrub, within gilded borders, some wear to gilding, c1820, saucer 5in (12.5cm) diam.
£135–150
€/ $210–240 ⚒ G(L)

Custard Cups

A Caughley custard cup and cover, printed in blue with Willow Nankin pattern and a dagger border, 1785–90, 3in (7.5cm) high.
£420–500
€/ $670–790 ⚒ B

A Marieberg set of four custard cups and covers, damage to knops, Swedish, 1769–88.
£750–900
€/ $1,200–1,400 ⚒ BUK

A Chamberlain Worcester set of eight armorial custard cups and covers, painted with panels of flowers within gilt C-scroll borders, the two-handled tray set with recesses and painted with a central bunch of flowers, small restored areas, the covers with grey printed marks, c1820.
£1,700–2,000
€/ $2,700–3,200 ⚒ DN

Dessert & Dinner Services

A Samuel Alcock part dessert service, comprising 25 pieces, painted with flowers, c1845.
£750–850
€/ $1,200–1,300 ⚒ S(O)

A Caughley part dessert service, comprising 28 pieces, gilt with a central flower within a border of interlinked ovals, some damage and wear, c1790.
£380–450
€/ $600–700 ⚒ S(O)

A Cauldon dessert service, comprising 29 pieces, painted with flowers, the borders with gilt floral decoration, c1910.
£1,000–1,200
€/ $1,600–1,900 ⚒ B(Kn)

► **A Coalport part dessert service,** comprising 22 pieces, painted with fruits within geometric and fruiting vine borders, 19thC.
£850–1,000
€/ $1,350–1,600
⚒ B(Ed)

A Derby dinner service, comprising 49 pieces, painted with cornflowers, with gilt foliate decoration, some cracks and restoration, 1820–30, dinner plate 10in (25.5cm) diam.
£800–950
€/ $1,300–1,500 ⚒ AG

◄ **A Derby part dessert service,** comprising 41 pieces, painted with a bouquet of flowers within gilt borders, some damage and wear, marked, c1810.
£2,400–2,800
€/ $3,800–4,400 ⚒ S(O)

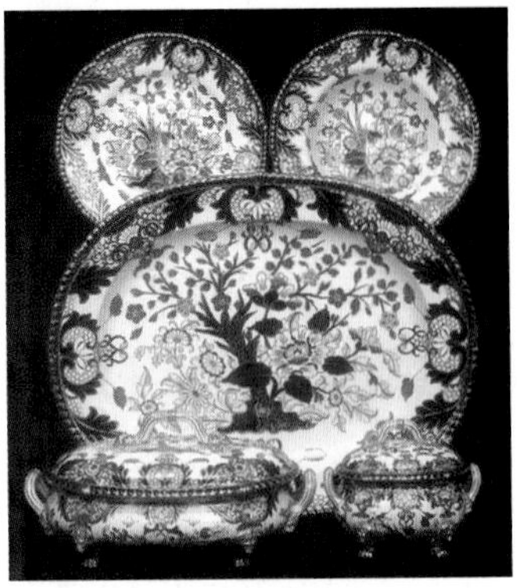

A Royal Crown Derby Imari pattern dinner service, comprising 62 pieces, painted with a floriate pattern, printed and impressed marks, c1890.
£4,200–5,000
€/ $6,600–7,900 ⚒ LJ

A Frank Haviland Limoges part dinner service, comprising 83 pieces, decorated with a floral pattern, retailer's mark, French, c1900, dinner plate 10in (25.5cm) diam.
£750–900
€/ $1,200–1,400 NOA

A Minton dessert service, comprising 17 pieces, each painted with a botanical specimen, one plate with small crack, impressed diamond registration marks, dated 1857.
£650–750
€/ $1,000–1,200 B
Ex-Minton Sale.

◄ A Minton part dessert service, comprising eight pieces, each with a hand-painted topographical scene, c1870.
£300–350
€/ $475–550
SWO

A Ridgway dessert service, comprising 21 pieces, each piece painted with a different flower species, with gilt scrolled panels and pierced borders with flower sprays, minor damage, painted pattern No. 2 over 5183, 1840–45, dessert plate 9¼in (23.5cm) diam.
£550–625
€/ $870–990 BR

► A Royal Worcester part dessert service, by Richard Sebright, comprising five pieces, painted with a group of fruits against a mossy ground, reserved on a border with raised and flat gilding, minor damage, puce marks, 1913–19, plates 8¾in (22cm) diam.
£1,500–1,800
€/ $2,400–2,800 B(NW)

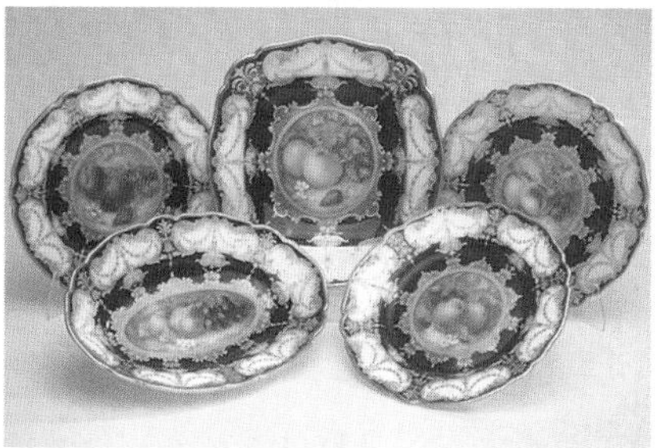

◄ A Vienna-style dessert service, comprising nine pieces, painted by Riemer, with gilt panels around a central Kauffman-style classical panel, titles in black script, blue enamel shield/ beehive marks, late 19thC, plate 9in (23cm) diam.
£1,800–2,200
€/ $2,800–3,500
TEN

A Staffordshire dessert service, comprising 37 pieces, painted with a floral spray, within a shaped border gilded with scrolls, pattern No. 5903, cracks, 1845–50.
£1,500–1,800
€/ $2,400–2,800 B(EA)

Dishes

A Berlin dish, decorated with flower sprays within 'Königsglatt' pattern borders, German, c1785, 13in (33cm) wide.
£800–900
€/ $1,300–1,400 US

A Caughley dessert dish, painted with a floral spray to the centre and a border pattern, 1780–85, 10in (25.5cm) wide.
£470–520
€/ $750–830 DSA

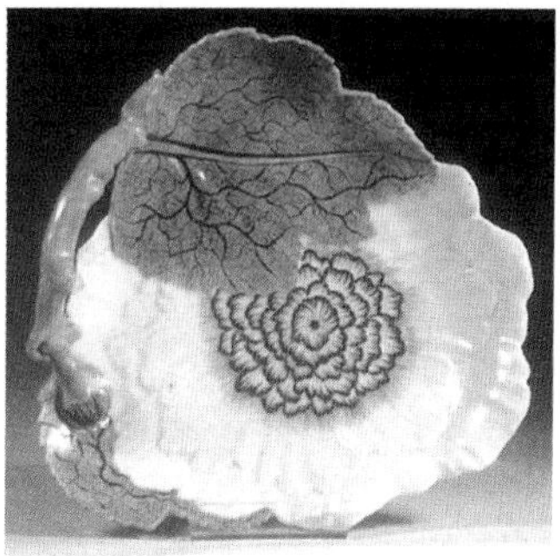

A Chelsea peony dish, moulded with a large flowerhead and leaves, the stalk handle issuing a flower bud, red anchor mark, c1755, 8¾in (22cm) diam.
£1,700–2,000
€/ $2,700–3,200 WW

A Derby dish, from the Ducie service, the fluted border decorated with *faux* pearls, reserved with a panel bearing the cypher of Francis Reynolds Moreton, 3rd Baron Ducie, and a coronet within a ribboned wreath, on a low foot, minor rubbing, painted and impressed marks, c1791, 12½in (31.5cm) wide.
£800–950
€/ $1,300–1,500 B

A Limehouse pickle dish, moulded in the form of a scallop shell, painted with a Chinese hut by a pine tree surrounded by scroll and feather motifs, a shell flanked by two leaves at the base, the underside with floral sprays, 1746–48, 4in (10cm) diam.
£2,500–3,000
€/ $4,000–4,700 B

▶ A Vauxhall dish, the well with geometric moulding, the edge panels enclosing pierced trellis motifs, bordering smaller panels with diaper designs, some cracks and chips, 1755–58, 10in (25.5cm) diam.
£3,000–3,600
€/ $4,700–5,700 B

A Derby shell-shaped dessert dish, painted with a flower, *Gladiolus Cardinalis*, within gilt-line borders, slight wear, some regilding, pattern No. 197 and title in blue, c1800, 9½in (24cm) diam.
£400–475
€/ $630–750 B

A Sèvres dessert dish, painted with rose sprigs within a border of gilt-centred flowerheads, within a network of *oeils-de-perdrix* reserved with gilt-framed panels enclosing a single rose, French, dated 1771, 8½in (21.5cm) square.
£950–1,100
€/ $1,500–1,700 S(NY)

A Derby King Street dish, painted by H. S. Hancock, with sprays of flowers within a gilt border and gilt-gadrooned rim, signed, script marks, 1900–25, 11in (28cm) wide.
£1,300–1,500
€/ $2,000–2,400 DN

A Spode pineapple serving dish, painted with roses and forget-me-nots, the central holder raised on a moulded base, painted mark, c1820, 9in (23cm) diam.
£300–350
€/ $475–550 TRM

A Worcester dessert dish, moulded with leafy vine branches lying on a basket, the centre and arcaded borders painted with flowers, a crack and some wear, double anchor mark, 1765–68, 12in (30.5cm) wide.
£2,000–2,200
€/ $3,200–3,500 B

A Worcester moulded leaf dish, painted with bouquets of flowers with gilt rococo reserves, c1775, 10in (25.5cm) wide.
£700–765
€/ $1,100–1,200 RAV

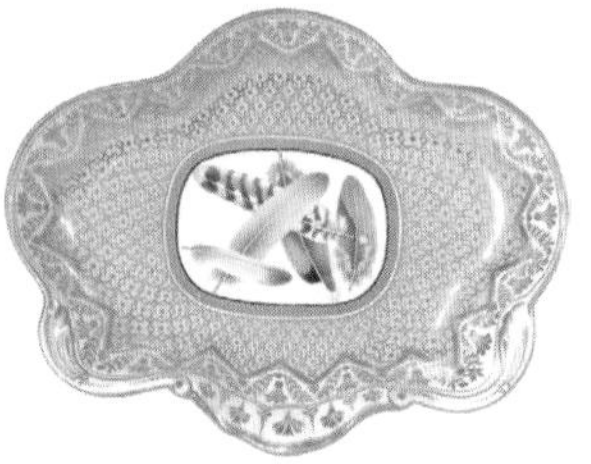

A Chamberlain Worcester dessert dish, painted with feathers within a panel, the undulating rim gilded with foliage and scrolls, footrim chipped, c1815, 9½in (24cm) wide.
£525–625
€/ $830–990 G(L)

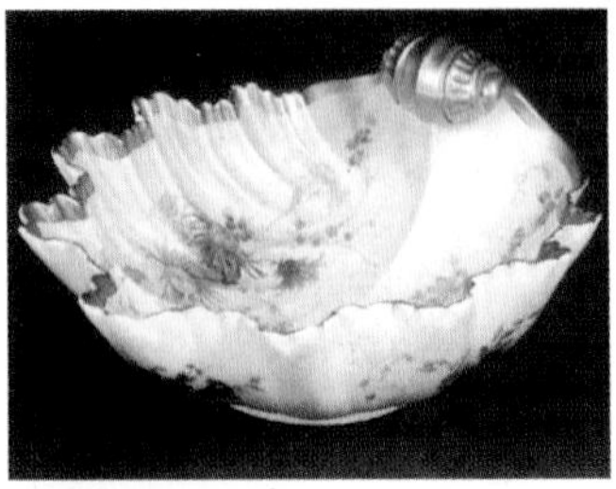

A Royal Worcester shell-shaped dish, decorated with sprays of flowers on a blush ivory ground, No. 1274, dated 1893, 9in (23cm) wide.
£220–240
€/ $350–380 HYD

Figures

A pair of Belleek figures, representing Affection and Meditation, Irish, First Period, 1863–90, 14in (35.5cm) high.
£5,500–6,000
€/ $8,700–9,500 ⊞ MLa
These pieces are large and rare.

► **A Chelsea figural scent bottle,** modelled as a bearded friar carrying a basket and a sack, on a mound painted with flower sprigs, minor chips, stopper missing, c1755, 3¾in (9.5cm) high.
£1,300–1,500
€/ $2,000–2,400 ⚒ B

A Copeland Parian figure of Night, after Raphael Monti, modelled as a woman with arms outstretched, a sleeping child at her feet, with a separate plinth base moulded in relief with a frieze of masks and putti above a Vetruvian scroll lower section, some damage, impressed and incised marks, c1862, 26in (66cm) high.
£1,400–1,600
€/ $2,200–2,500 ⚒ DN

A Berlin figure of Amphiaraus, German, 19thC, 9in (23cm) high.
£170–185
€/ $270–300 ⊞ SER

A Copeland Parian figure, after an original by Joseph Durham, entitled 'Go to Sleep', modelled as a young girl seated on a rock, wagging a finger at a dog on her lap, impressed marks for 'Copeland' and the 'Art Union of London', 1862'z,17¾in (45cm) high.
£900–1,100
€/ $1,400–1,700 ⚒ Bea(E)

► **A pair of Bow figures of a shepherd and shepherdess,** c1765, 6in (15cm) high.
£3,200–3,500
€/ $5,000–5,500
⊞ DMa

► **A Bow figure of Juno and the eagle,** representing Air, after Etienne Le Hongre, restored, red anchor mark, c1765, 10in (25.5cm) high.
£400–475
€/ $630–750 ⚒ WW

A Chelsea figural flower holder, after a Saint Cloud original, modelled as a fish seller with a basket, seated on a rockwork base, chips and crack, red anchor mark, c1755, 9in (23cm) high.
£800–950
€/ $1,300–1,500 ⚒ LFA

► **A Copeland Parian figure of Beatrice,** by E. Papworth, c1860, 22in (56cm) high.
£675–750
€/ $1,000–1,200 ⊞ JAK

English 18th-century porcelain 1976–2002

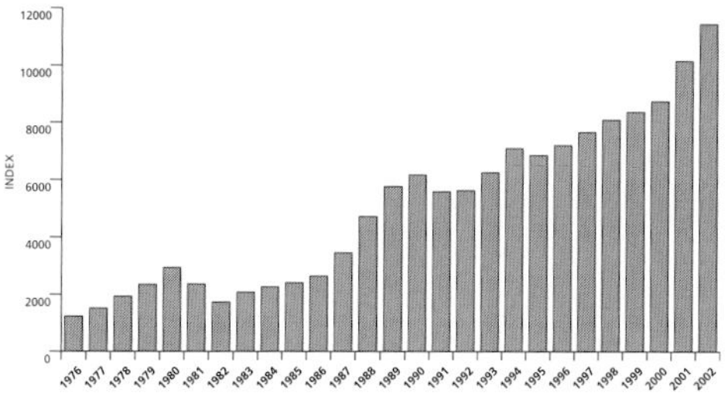

This graph shows the increasing value of English 18th-century porcelain as a whole over the past 25 years. Individual collecting areas from different periods may not follow this graph exactly. ©AMR

◄ **A pair of Derby figures of Milton and Shakespeare,** each resting on a stack of books supported on a column, on rococo bases, 18thC, larger 12¼in (31cm) high.
£550–650
€/ $870–1,000 B(Pr)

A Derby biscuit figural group, entitled 'Poetry', the base incised with crown and crossed batons, 216 and the mark of Isaac Farnsworth, 1775–80, 10¼in (26cm) high.
£900–1,100
€/ $1,400–1,700 TMA

A Derby figure of a putto, minor losses, c1800, 4½in (11.5cm) high.
£165–185
€/ $260–290 ⊞ SER

► **A Derby King Street figure of Dr Syntax,** seated, with a sketch book and pencil, a pair of ducks at his feet, chip to beak of one duck, 19thC, 5¼in (13.5cm) high.
£275–325
€/ $430–515 TMA

A pair of Derby King Street figures, c1890, 8½in (21.5cm) high.
£850–950
€/ $1,300–1,500 ⊞ DAN

A Derby King Street candle snuffer, modelled as Sarah Gamp, late 19thC, 4in (10cm) high.
£400–440
€/ $630–700 ⊞ TH
Sarah Gamp is a character in Charles Dickens's novel *Martin Chuzzlewit*.

A Frankenthal figure of a Chinese man, holding a jug in one hand and waving with the other, modelled by C. Lück, underglaze blue crowned CT mark, German, c1775, 5in (12.5cm) high.
£1,000–1,200
€/ $1,600–1,900 DORO

A biscuit model of a peasant woman, impressed and printed marks for the Gardner factory, Russian, late 19thC, 8in (20.5cm) high.
£350–400
€/ $550–630 WW

A W. H. Goss figure of an angel holding a stoup, 1862–86, 6in (15cm) high.
£400–450
€/ $630–700 ⊞ G&CC
This is a copy of the font at St John's Church, Barmouth, north Wales.

A biscuit model of Spinario, after the Antique, the boy sitting removing a thorn from his foot, impressed marks for Gustavsberg, Swedish, early 20thC, 10¾in (27cm) high.
£380–450
€/ $600–700 WW

► **A Höchst figure of a boy gardener,** standing with a rake on a grassy mound, minor damage, wheel mark in blue, German, c1770, 5¼in (13.5cm) high.
£450–525
€/ $710–830 B

◄ **A Le Nove figural group,** dressed in 18thC costume, on a rustic base, Italian, 18thC, 7in (18cm) high.
£1,100–1,300
€/ $1,700–2,000 HYD

► **A Limbach figure of a lady,** depicting Autumn, from a set of The Seasons, wearing a wide-brimmed hat, holding a basket of grapes, the base with scrollwork, some restoration, German, c1780, 5¼in (13.5cm) high.
£950–1,100
€/ $1,500–1,700 S(O)

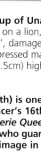

A Minton Parian figure of Margaret of Anjou, dated 1851, 17in (43cm) high.
£240–275
€/ $380–430 G(B)

◄ **A Minton Parian figural group of Una and the Lion,** the maiden seated on a lion, the base relief-moulded 'John Bell', damaged, moulded registration lozenge, impressed marks and date codes, c1860, 14¾in (37.5cm) high.
£380–450
€/ $600–700 RTo
Una (the representation of Truth) is one of the characters in Edmund Spencer's 16th-century allegorical poem *The Faerie Queene*. She was accompanied by a lion who guarded her virtue. This was a popular image in Victorian times, since in 1838 the young Queen Victoria had been portrayed as Una on the reverse of a gold £5 coin engraved by William Wyon, the Chief Engraver at the Royal Mint. It is regarded as one of the most beautiful coins ever made.

A Minton Parian figure, entitled 'Comedy', by John Bell, c1864, 16in (40.5cm) high.
£1,100–1,200
€/ $1,700–1,900 JAK

PORCELAIN

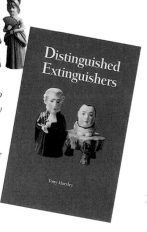

A Minton Parian figure of Lalage, after the model by John Bell, depicted sitting holding her knee and a floral wreath, titled and with impressed marks, c1864, 16¼in (41.5cm) high.
£650–775
€/ $1,000–1,200 WW

A biscuit group, probably Niderviller, modelled as four rustic figures holding flowers, around a central tree, on a rocky mound base with later gilt-metal mount, some chips and losses, French, late 18thC, 14¼in (36cm) high.
£300–350
€/ $475–550 DN

A Royal Dux figure of a cavalier, seated on a chair, pouring ale from a jug, raised and painted marks, Bohemian, late 19thC, 11½in (29cm) high.
£850–975
€/ $1,350–1,50 SJH

A Vienna figural group, representing Winter, modelled as a man holding a pipe in one hand and a glass of schnapps in the other, the girl sitting at his feet holding a bottle, minor damage, Austrian, c1755, 5¼in (13.5cm) high.
£750–900
€/ $1,200–1,400 DORO

A pair of figural scent bottles, modelled as actors, each holding a mask, with apertures in their hats, French, mid-19thC, 10¼in (26cm) high.
£250–300
€/ $400–475 SWO

A pair of Royal Worcester figures of Egyptian musicians, crack to one base, dated 1886, 13in (33cm) high.
£2,100–2,300
€/ $3,300–3,600 MER

A Royal Worcester figure of a woman, probably Cleopatra, partially draped, wearing a snake armlet, dated 1865, 9½in (24cm) high.
£650–750
€/ $1,000–1,200 GTH

► A pair of coloured biscuit figures, each holding a dove for the purpose of receiving and sending a love letter, on gilt-decorated bases, French, c1875, 16in (40.5cm) high.
£400–480
€/ $630–750 TMA

A pair of figures, of a man and a woman, wearing 18thC costume, each with a jug beside a well, Continental, 19thC, 13¾in (35cm) high.
£280–325
€/ $440–500 GTH

A biscuit porcelain figural group, of a satyr with an infant satyr and a child, entwined with flower garlands, impressed 'Clodion', French, late 19thC, 9¾in (25cm) high.
£220–260
€/ $350–400 HOLL

Matching pairs

Most figures were sold as matching pairs, such as a male and female. When a pair was ordered, two figures were selected at random from the warehouse, and so were not necessarily a perfect match. They might have been coloured by different decorators and have different painter's marks underneath. Some pairs were totally mismatched at the time. Others were bought separately, or a companion figure may be a later replacement. Collectors take this seriously. A matching pair must comprise the two correct models with corresponding colouring, made at the same time. Ideally they should have identical marks. Matching painter's marks, while not essential, are always an advantage. A married pair, assembled later and with differences in colouring, is always worth less than a true pair.

Flatware

A Belleek dessert plate, decorated with a Greek pattern, Irish, Second Period, 1891–1926, 9½in (24cm) diam.
£350–400
€/ $550–630 ⊞ MLa

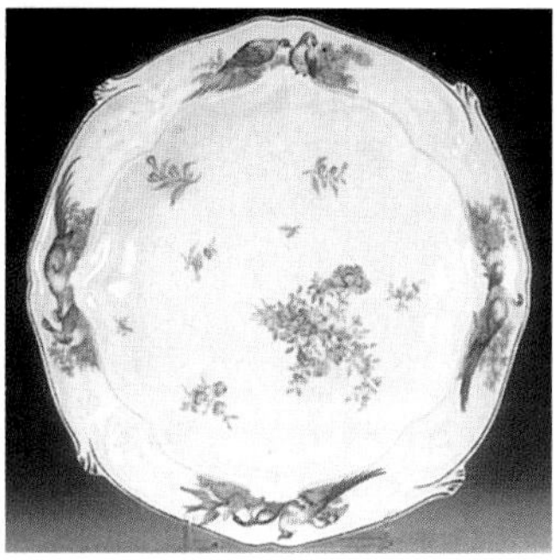

A Chelsea plate, painted with sprays and sprigs of flowers, within a scroll-moulded border painted with four pairs of birds among foliage, red anchor mark, c1755, 8½in (21.5cm) diam.
£700–850
€/ $1,100–1,300 ⚒ S(O)

A Copeland cabinet plate, by Charles Ferdinand Hürten, the pierced basketweave reticulated border reserved with four panels painted with blackberry sprays, the centre painted with tumbling rose sprays, decorated with tooled gold, printed mark, c1880, 9in (23cm) diam.
£3,500–4,200
€/ $5,500–6,500 ⚒ B

LOCATE THE SOURCE
The source of each illustration in Miller's can be found by checking the code letters below each caption with the Key to Illustrations, pages 794–800.

A Berlin cabinet plate, the centre painted with a lady borne aloft by Time, putti and the winds, within a tooled gilt border of foliate scrollwork, impressed and painted marks, German, 1817–23, 9¾in (25cm) diam.
£1,000–1,200
€/ $1,600–1,900 ⚒ S(O)

A Chelsea plate, enamel-painted in the Hans Sloane style with a turnip, two butterflies, flowers, a leaf and an insect, riveted crack, red anchor mark and No. 2, c1755, 9½in (24cm) diam.
£750–900
€/ $1,200–1,400 ⚒ LFA

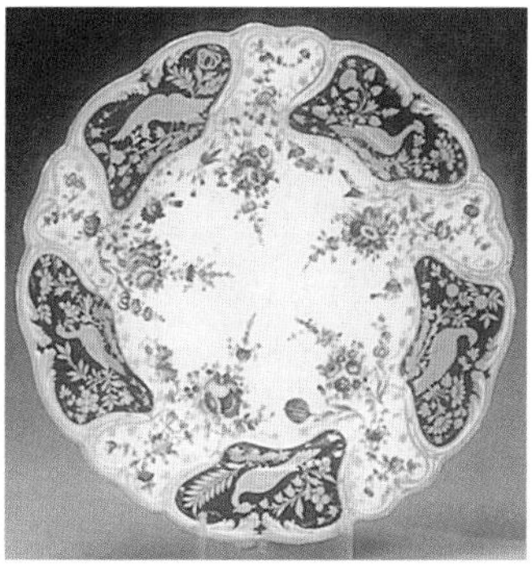

A Derby plate, in the Chelsea style, the border panels with long-tailed birds and foliage in tooled gold, separated by spiralling flower sprays, the rim moulded with scrollwork, minor wear, painted marks, c1815, 9½in (24cm) diam.
£320–375
€/ $500–600 ⚒ B

▶ **A pair of Doccia plates,** painted with flowers, Italian, c1770, 9in (23cm) diam.
£1,200–1,300
€/ $1,900–2,000 ⊞ DAN

A Bow saucer dish, painted with a butterfly and flower sprays, with scattered sprigs, 1765–70, 8¼in (21cm) diam.
£550–625
€/ $870–1,000 ⚒ B

A pair of Coalport plates, painted with bird and flower panels inside gilt frames around a central gilt foliate medallion, minor wear, c1820, 9¾in (25cm) diam.
£500–600
€/ $800–950 ⚒ S(O)

A Derby dessert plate, by 'Quaker' Pegg, painted with a flower, *Passiflora Alata*, within a plain gilt rim, painted marks, c1815, 6in (15cm) diam.
£1,300–1,500
€/ $2,000–2,400 ⚒ B

A W. H. Goss commemorative plate, decorated with possibly a royal gravedigger carrying a spade in one hand and keys in the other, inscribed with a verse and 'July 2nd of 1594 R.S. Oetatis 98', and printed mark and registration No. for 1885–86, 9in (23cm) diam.
£140–160
€/ $220–250 GAK

A plate, painted by Yelizaveta Verngardovna Rosendorf on an Imperial Porcelain Factory blank, sickle mark, Russian, dated 1920, 9½in (24cm) diam.
£320–375
€/ $500–600 HYD

A set of four Minton plates, painted in the Chinese style with exotic birds perched on tree branches, impressed marks and date ciphers, dated 1865, 9¾in (25cm) diam.
£900–1,100
€/ $1,500–1,700 B
Ex-Minton Sale.

A Minton cabinet plate, painted by Antonin Boullemier, with a Watteau-style scene of 'Le Bougeois Gentilhomme', depicting a cavalier fencing with two ladies, within gilt-decorated borders, painted and impressed marks, dated 1875, 9¾in (25cm) diam.
£375–450
€/ $600–700 B
Ex-Minton Sale.

A Minton *pâte-sur-pâte* cabinet plate, by Alboin Birks, the pierced lobed reticulated rim moulded with shells and waves, the centre decorated with a pebble-gilt ground reserved with a *pâte-sur-pâte* panel depicting a cherub with a skipping rope, signed, printed and impressed marks, c1895, 9in (23cm) diam.
£3,000–3,500
€/ $5,000–5,500 B
Alboin Birks devised the process of moulded *pâte-sur-pâte* panels on porcelain items. These were particularly popular in the USA.

A Nantgarw floral soup plate, with a moulded C-scroll and foliate border, impressed marks, Welsh, c1820, 9½in (24cm) diam.
£4,300–5,000
€/ $6,500–8,000 S(O)

A Nantgarw charger, with a central spray of flowers and fruit, within a gilt mosaic border with six floral panels, restored, impressed mark, Welsh, 1818–20, 21in (53.5cm) diam.
£1,700–2,000
€/ $2,700–3,200 B

► **A pair of Nantgarw dessert plates,** painted with flowers inside a C-scroll and foliate-moulded border, minor wear, one with impressed mark, Welsh, c1820, 8¼in (21cm) diam.
£2,200–2,500
€/ $3,500–4,000 S(O)

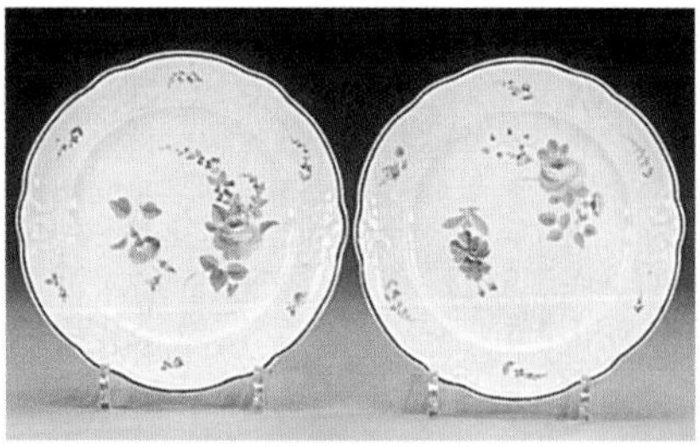

A Nantgarw dessert plate, probably painted in the Sims workshop, London, with a border of flower sprigs surrounding a central rose, impressed mark, Welsh, 1818–20, 9¼in (23.5cm) diam.
£1,000–1,200
€/ $1,600–1,900 B(SW)

A pair of Neuberg-Gieshübl plates, both painted with finches among fruit beneath a tree trunk, within a pierced acanthus border, overlaid in gold, impressed marks, German, mid-19thC, 10in (25.5cm) diam.
£320–375
€/ $500–600 RTo

A Paris cabinet plate, painted with a harbour scene, French, c1830, 9½in (24cm) diam.
£530–585
€/ $840–925 DAN

PORCELAIN

◄ **A set of six Paul Delvaux dinner plates,** in the style of Jean Pillement, the centres decorated with chased gilt chinoiserie figural vignettes, one chip and wear, French, c1900, 10in (25.5cm) diam.
£160–200
€/ $250–300 NOA

A Wedgwood plate, with a pierced border, the centre painted with cattle and signed by Henry Mitchell, brown-printed Wedgwood mark, c1880, 9in (23cm) diam.
£950–1,100
€/ $1,500–1,700 DIA

Henry Mitchell was a fine painter of animals, and is best known for his work at Minton. After leaving Minton he worked for other Staffordshire makers, including Doulton.

A Swansea soup plate, from the Lysaght service, probably painted by Henry Morris, with a basket of flowers to the centre, minor wear to gilding, Welsh, c1820, 9½in (24cm) diam.
£2,200–2,500
€/ $3,500–4,000 S(O)

Swansea

Swansea porcelain is special in many ways. The porcelain body has a unique beauty that sets it apart from contemporary English bone china. Elegant shapes are decorated in the French taste with the emphasis on feminine prettiness: delicate painted flowers sit so comfortably on the pure white porcelain. While much Swansea porcelain was enamelled in London, collectors prefer the work of artists based at the Swansea factory. Attaching the name of a painter adds much to the value. Care must be taken, though, as Staffordshire, Coalport and even Paris porcelain is frequently mistaken for Swansea.

► **A Worcester saucer dish,** painted with a bridge and buildings, surrounded by a border of scattered flowers and insects, edged with a gilt-decorated border, painted mark, c1780, 7in (18cm) diam.
£700–820
€/ $1,100–1,300 S(O)

◄ **A Worcester plate,** painted with two exotic birds by trees, within a gilt border, seal mark, c1772–75, 7½in (19cm) diam.
£400–500
€/ $630–800
CGC

► **A Worcester plate,** with a scalloped edge, decorated with Old Mosaic pattern, pseudo-Oriental mark, c1768, 8½in (21.5cm) diam.
£475–575
€/ $750–900
HYD

◄ **A Chamberlain Worcester plate,** painted with the arms and crest of Hay, Earl of Errol, the border with Rich Queens pattern, c1805, 9in (23cm) diam.
£900–1,000
€/ $1,400–1,600
DHu

A Royal Worcester plate, painted by John Stinton, the gilt rim acid-etched with neo-classical designs, minor damage, signed, puce mark, dated 1912, 10¼in (26cm) diam.
£1,000–1,200
€/ $1,600–1,900 B

A saucer, painted with a variety of shells, the border decorated with enamel, cracked, c1825, 6in (15cm) diam.
£100–120
€/ $160–190 G(L)

An anti-slavery plate, the centre painted with an African figure, the scroll-moulded border with four inscriptions, chipped, c1835, 9in (23cm) diam.
£220–260
€/ $350–400 SAS

Ice Pails & Wine Coolers

A pair of Coalport ice pails and covers, painted with sprays of flowers beneath gilt dentil-edged borders, the covers similarly decorated, on gilt paw feet on square bases, liners missing, hair-crack, c1820, 14¾in (37.5cm) diam.
£3,000–3,600
€/ $4,700–5,700 S(NY)

A pair of Derby ice pails, with liners, decorated with Imari pattern, with gilt shell-moulded handles, the covers with foliate loop handles, cover handles repaired, chips, painted marks, c1815, 12¾in (32.5cm) diam.
£800–900
€/ $1,300–1,400 S(O)

A Derby ice pail and cover, decorated with bands of flowers and leaves with gilt borders, with a scroll knop, restored, painted marks, early 19thC, 12¼in (31cm) diam.
£275–320
€/ $430–500 WW

A pair of Chamberlain Worcester wine coolers, applied with fruiting vines around the rim, the body embossed with rose, shamrock and thistle sprays around painted floral sprays, the handles formed of entwined wheat sheaves, on a marbled base, restored, chips, losses and wear, 1816–20, 9in (23cm) high.
£900–1,100
€/ $1,400–1,700 B

A Derby ice pail and cover, gilded and enamelled in the Imari palette with birds, flowers and blossoming branches, with two handles, hairline crack and discolouration, painted mark, early 19thC, 9¾in (25cm) high.
£380–450
€/ $600–700 RTo

A Nymphenburg wine cooler, painted with a flower spray and further scattered flowers, with pierced gilt-edged scrollwork handles with moulded rocaille terminals, impressed marks, German, c1765, 6¼in (16cm) high.
£750–875
€/ $1,200–1,400 S(O)

Further reading

Miller's Porcelain Antiques Checklist,
Miller's Publications, 1991

► **A pair of ice pails,** decorated in the Imari palette with flowers, with twin handles, the covers waisted with a high collar, c1815, 11in (28cm) high.
£900–1,100
€/ $1,400–1,700 Bri

Inkstands & Inkwells

A Royal Crown Derby inkwell, decorated in the Imari palette, 1919, 3in (7.5cm) high.
£430–470
€/ $670–750 ⊞ DIA

► A Staffordshire inkwell, decorated with a panel of peasants in a landscape, attributed to William Pollard, c1825, 3in (7.5cm) high.
£1,100–1,200
€/ $1,700–1,900 ⊞ DIA

A Worcester Flight, Barr & Barr inkwell, painted with a panoramic landscape and three figures, the well gilded with palmettes and seaweed, the handle with a mask terminal, two chips, cover missing, 1813–40, 5½in (14cm) wide.
£1,300–1,500
€/ $2,000–2,400 G(L)

◄ An inkwell, painted with flowers, within gilt dentil borders, cover missing, early 19thC, 1½in (4cm) high.
£40–50
€/ $60–80 TMA

A Chamberlain inkwell, the cover surmounted by a biscuit figure of a seated classical lady writing, a gilded quillholder to her right, one side of the base painted with a view of Moxhull Hall, Warwickshire within Gothic-style gilded borders, painted marks, losses and wear, c1823, 4¾in (12cm) high.
£1,000–1,200
€/ $1,600–1,900 B

Jardinières

A Coalport jardinière and stand, decorated with a silhouette portrait of George III, within the gilt inscription 'A Token from Cheltenham', with gilt ring-moulded handles, minor chips, 1805–10, 6¾in (17cm) high.
£1,000–1,100
€/ $1,600–1,700 S(O)

► A Worcester Flight & Barr jardinière, with moulded ring handles and spreading foot, painted with feathers over a gilt net ground, reserved within a panel with a sprig and foliate border, crack and wear, incised mark, c1800, 6¼in (16cm) high.
£2,200–2,600
€/ $3,500–4,000 B

A Nymphenburg jardinière, with *bombé*-shaped sides, each corner with an angel's-head finial, the side panels painted with *deutsche Blumen* and flower sprays within moulded and scrolled borders, painted marks, German, early 20thC, 12¼in (31cm) wide.
£280–320
€/ $440–520 BR

A Samson, Paris jardinière, on a raised foot, decorated in the *famille rose* style, painted mark, French, late 19thC, 19in (48cm) diam.
£450–550
€/ $700–870 SWO

A Royal Worcester jardinière, with gilded everted rim and scroll-moulded shoulder details, painted with studies of roses, on a stepped foot, signed 'W.E. Jarman', printed and painted marks, dated 1913, 10¼in (26cm) diam.
£900–1,100
€/ $1,400–1,700 DD

Jugs & Ewers

A Belleek jug, Irish, First Period, 1863–90, 6in (15cm) high.
£700–800
€/ $1,100–1,300 ⊞ MLa

A Du Paquier ewer, painted with flowers, the foot with restored firing crack, Austrian, Vienna, c1735, 6in (15cm) high.
£1,600–2,000
€/ $2,500–3,200
⚒ DORO

A Bow jug, the grooved strap handle applied with a heart at the lower terminal, decorated with three fan-shaped panels depicting Chinese river scenes, alternating with floral panels, irregular panels below the rim, replacement metal spout, base detached and restuck, c1760, 8½in (21.5cm) high.
£400–500
€/ $630–800 ⚒ B

A Lowestoft sparrow beak cream jug, polychrome-painted with Oriental figures in a garden, 1770–75, 3¼in (8.5cm) high.
£675–750
€/ $1,000–1,200 ⊞ DSA

◄ **A Sèvres jug,** with a part-fluted body, on a flared foot, printed mark, French, c1876, 4in (10cm) high.
£130–150
€/ $200–240 ⚒ WW

A Caughley mask jug, with cabbage-leaf-moulded body, decorated with Fisherman pattern, printed mark, late 18thC, 8¾in (22cm) high.
£550–650
€/ $870–1,000 ⚒ Bea

► **A New Hall 'Robin' jug,** decorated with a Chinese lady with a parasol and a boy with a kite by a fence in a garden, pattern No. 20, 1782–87, 2¾in (7cm) high.
£1,400–1,700
€/ $2,200–2,700 ⚒ B

A ewer, with a high gilt-scroll handle and tooled gilt spout, painted with a continuous frieze of various birds alternating with fruits, French or Bohemian, early 19thC, 10½in (26.5cm).
£700–850
€/ $1,100–1,300 ⚒ S(O)

A Derby jug, decorated with a pictorial vignette, handle restored, inscribed 'In Italy' to base, c1820, 4½in (11cm) high.
£140–160
€/ $220–250 ⚒ SWO

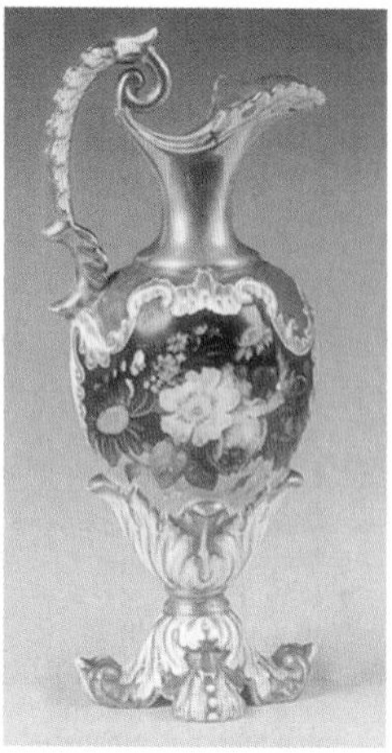

A pair of Rockingham ewer vases, painted with botanical subjects, on rococo-moulded quatrefoil bases, some damage, printed marks, c1830, 9¼in (23.5cm) high.
£3,700–4,200
€/ $5,800–6,600 ⚒ HAM

◄ **A Staffordshire mask jug,** moulded and enamelled with titled portrait busts of Brougham and Denman flanked by patriotic flowers, some restoration and cracks, c1820, 5½in (14cm) high.
£400–450
€/ $630–700 ⚒ S
Brougham and Denman were legal advisers to Queen Caroline, the estranged wife of the Prince Regent.

Rockingham

The Rockingham china works at Swinton, Yorkshire, made very individual English porcelain. Elaborate teapots and eccentric vases epitomize English taste in the 1830s. Rockingham figures and tea services bearing the factory mark of a griffin were keenly collected 100 years ago. Unfortunately, unmarked teawares from other makers were incorrectly identified as Rockingham and enormous confusion resulted. The Rockingham name is still widely misused, even though comprehensive reference books now enable collectors to recognize the real thing.

A graduated set of four Staffordshire lobed jugs, heightened with gold, c1830, largest 8in (20.5cm) high.
£350–420
€/ $550–660 TMA
These jugs are decorated with roses, thistles and shamrock, known as 'Union' sprigs representing the United Kingdom.

A Vienna jug, painted with flowers, minor restoration to edge, shield mark, c1770, 6¾in (17cm) high.
£250–300
€/ $400–475 DORO

A Worcester sparrow beak jug, transfer-printed with The Fence pattern, 1770–75, 5in (12.5cm) high.
£230–260
€/ $370–400 WAC

A Worcester cream jug, painted in the Chinese style with figures on terraces, the gilt flower and leaf-scroll ground decorated with flowers and leaves within scroll borders, c1772, 3½in (9cm) high.
£750–900
€/ $1,200–1,400 LFA

A Royal Worcester jug, painted with flowers and foliage, gilt handle, clay and date mark for 1888, 9in (23cm) high.
£300–340
€/ $475–540 AG

A Grainger's Worcester jug, the panel-moulded ground decorated with relief-moulded and painted flowers, the handle decorated with a key pattern, heightened with gold, dated 1892, 8in (20.5cm) high.
£120–140
€/ $190–220 B(W)

A Factory X ewer, the ribbed body painted with flowers, the interior with a border of leaves, flowers and festoons, pattern No. 134, c1790, 5in (12.5cm) high.
£230–270
€/ $360–430 WW

Mugs & Tankards

◄ **A Bloor Derby porter mug,** painted by Daniel Lucas, hair crack, printed circular mark, c1830, 5in (12.5cm) high.
£380–440
€/ $600–700 B

A Bow mug, painted with a floral pattern, c1760, 3½in (9cm) high.
£580–650
€/ $900–1,000 DSA

Cookworthy

William Cookworthy was a chemist who discovered in Cornwall the raw materials for making hard paste porcelain. He obtained a patent in March 1768 and his factory at Plymouth commenced full production soon afterwards. Sadly, kiln losses were heavy and much Plymouth porcelain suffered from a burnt glaze. The last firing at Plymouth was in November 1770. Thanks to new backing from a fellow Quaker, Richard Champion, Cookworthy moved his factory to Bristol, where he continued as before until his retirement in 1774. Because it is so hard to distinguish the porcelain made at Plymouth from early productions at Bristol, many collectors prefer to call it Cookworthy porcelain, rather than Plymouth.

A Bristol mug, painted with a floral spray and scattered sprigs beneath a laurel leaf border, minor wear to gilt rim, marked, c1775, 3¾in (9.5cm) high.
£1,000–1,200
€/ $1,600–1,900 S(O)

A Cookworthy tankard, with a grooved loop handle, painted with birds among leafy trees and foliage, cracks and repairs, enamels worn, tin mark, c1770, 5¼in (13.5cm) high.
£750–875
€/ $1,200–1,400 B

A Worcester mug, with grooved strap handle, painted with Prunus Fence pattern, small flake to foot rim, workman's mark, 1755–60, 2½in (6.5cm) high.
£850–1,000
€/ $1,300–1,600 ⚒ Bea

◄ **A Worcester mug,** printed with the King of Prussia and emblems of war, small rim chips, dated 1757, 3½in (9cm) high.
£650–750
€/ $1,000–1,200 ⚒ G(L)

► **A Worcester mug,** decorated in the Imari palette with exotic birds among foliage, 1753–54, 3¼in (8.5cm) high.
£27,000–32,000
€/ $43,000–50,000 ⚒ HYD
This mug is an exceptionally rare piece of early Worcester in very good condition.

A Worcester Flight & Barr mug, painted in London, probably by Thomas Baxter with two boys playing shuttlecock, within a panel, the reverse with a couple walking in the grounds of a country house, a border below the rim painted with fruit, flowers, scrollwork, a bird, a butterfly and a caterpillar, slight wear to gilding, unmarked, 1802–05, 4¼in (11cm) high.
£900–1,100
€/ $1,400–1,700 ⚒ B

Plaques

A George Jones *pâte-sur-pâte* plaque, by Frederick Schenk, decorated with two nymph-like figures beside a rock pool, impressed factory mark, gilt No. 5661, c1880, 11in (28cm) diam.
£1,100–1,300
€/ $1,700–2,000 ⚒ S(O)

A Royal Worcester plaque, painted by John Stinton with Highland cattle grazing beside a river, hills in the distance, signed, printed mark for 1930, 4in (10cm) diam, in a gilt and swept frame.
£1,100–1,300
€/ $1,700–2,000 ⚒ M

A pair of plaques, one painted with flowers, berries and a dragonfly, the other with grapes, foliage and other fruit, c1830, 9½ x 8in (24 x 20.5cm), framed.
£1,100–1,300
€/ $1,700–2,000 ⚒ B(Pr)

A plaque, hand-painted with a lady wearing a feather hat within a border of ornate foliate scrolls and grotesques, German, 19thC, 13¾in (35cm) square.
£200–225
€/ $320–350 ⚒ B(W)

A pair of plaques, painted with Jesus Christ and Mary, set in a gilt-tooled leather travelling case, Continental, late 19thC, 5½ x 3½in (14 x 9cm).
£200–240
€/ $320–380 ⚒ G(L)

A plaque, decorated with a young girl with a parrot perched on her hand, some fruit to the side, German, c1880, 4in (10cm) wide.
£375–450
€/ $600–700 ⚒ HAM

Pot-Pourri Jars & Vases

A Spode pot-pourri jar and cover, with inner cover and gilt handles, decorated with cherubs and acanthus leaves, pattern No. 2063, impressed mark, early 19thC, 9in (23cm) high.
£230–275
€/ $360–430 TRM

A pot-pourri vase and cover, the cover and foot pierced and moulded with oak leaves and acorns, set with branch handles, painted with a panel of birds, the reverse with flowers, 1840s, 17¾in (45cm) high.
£650–750
€/ $1,000–1,200 S(O)

A Tournai pot-pourri vase and cover, the pierced cover with a grapevine finial, the pierced body with gilt ram's head handles, the gadrooned lower section applied with swags of fruiting vines, on a gilt-edged rocky base with a putto reclining on an urn spilling water, and a seated dog, decoration later, minor damage and putto's head restuck, French, c1765, 8in (20.5cm) high.
£300–350
€/ $475–550 S(O)
This would have been worth much more if the decoration had been contemporary.

► A pair of pot-pourri vases and covers, each with scroll side handles and four lion-paw feet, decorated with gilt vines, one handle repaired, 1826–30, 5in (12.5cm) high.
£250–300
€/ $400–475 WW

A Royal Worcester rose pot-pourri jar and cover, by George H. Cole, the pierced cover with a gilded finial, the body with a reserved cartouche painted with garden flowers, signed 'Cole' within a C-scroll border in raised gilding, damaged, transfer-printed factory mark, date mark for 1903, 9½in (24cm) high.
£700–820
€/ $1,100–1,300 PF

A Royal Worcester pot-pourri vase and two covers, decorated with flowers, c1914, 13in (33cm) high.
£1,400–1,600
€/ $2,200–2,500 ⊞ JUP

A pair of pot-pourri vases and covers, after Derby originals, painted with swags of roses, gilding worn, Continental, early 20thC, 8¾in (22cm) high.
£550–650
€/ $870–1,000 S(O)

PORCELAIN

Sauce & Cream Boats

◄ A Bow sauce boat, on three lion-paw feet, the sides painted in *famille rose* colours with peony sprays, a further spray inside the base, the rim with a diaper pattern reserved with flowerhead panels, damaged, 1752–54, 8¾in (22cm) wide.
£300–350
€/ $475–550 B

A Bow sauce boat, decorated with Desirable Residence pattern, footrim repaired, c1765, 7½in (19cm) long.
£200–225
€/ $320–350 SWO

A pair of Caughley cream boats, printed with the Apple Prints pattern, 1780–85, 2½in (6.5cm) high.
£1,100–1,300
€/ $1,700–2,000 LFA

► A Pennington's Liverpool cream boat, painted with floral sprays, chip to spout, c1785, 5in (12.5cm) wide.
£500–550
€/ $800–870
⊞ DSA

◄ **A Lowestoft sauce boat,** hairline crack and restoration, workman's mark to underside, c1765, 7½in (19cm) long.
£180–220
€/ $280–340 ⚒ SWO

A Vienna sauce boat, painted with flowers, fruit and vegetables, edge and foot restored, shield mark, c1760, 9in (23cm) wide.
£160–200
€/ $250–315 ⚒ DORO

A Worcester cream boat, rim chips, c1752, 4¼in (11cm) wide.
£2,200–2,500
€/ $3,500–4,000 ⚒ B

► **A Worcester two-handled sauce boat,** painted with Two-Handled Sauceboat Landscape pattern, rim chip and haircrack, workman's mark, c1757, 7½in (19cm) wide.
£650–750
€/ $1,000–1,200 ⚒ S(O)

A pair of Worcester sauce boats, painted with a version of Little Fisherman pattern, one chipped, crescent mark, c1765, 5¼in (13.5cm) wide.
£650–750
€/ $1,000–1,200 ⚒ Bea

The Watney Collection

The Watney collection of English porcelain sold for £2million (€/ $3million) in 1999–2000, but its value was much more than monetary. It was a working and learning collection, and as such it made a massive contribution to the study and understanding of early blue and white.

During a lifetime spent trawling the stalls of London's Portobello Road, Bernard Watney bought nearly 2,000 pieces, the majority of which were not identified. As a doctor, Bernard used his analytical approach to sort his collection into distinct groups and then investigated likely makers. Many pieces in the collection were damaged and broken in some way, but when they were auctioned after Bernard's death, the prices achieved showed that collectors valued rarity and provenance far above condition. **John Sandon**

Scent Bottles

A Derby scent bottle, stopper regilded, 1830, 4in (10cm) high.
£320–350
€/ $500–550 ⊞ CoS

A Dresden scent bottle, modelled as a cushion with a flame finial on a domed stopper, the body painted with alternating panels of figures and flowers, with moulded tasselled corners and gilt highlights, German, 19thC, 3½in (9cm) wide.
£130–150
€/ $200–240 ⚒ AH

► **A Fürstenberg gilt-metal-mounted scent flask,** after a Chelsea model, the basket-moulded body reserved with a raised panel inscribed 'Eau de Senteur' hanging from a moulded gilt chain, the neck painted with a flower sprig, the foliate pierced metal stopper attached with a chain, marked, German, c1770, 3½in (9cm) high.
£600–720
€/ $950–1,100 ⚒ S(O)

► **A pair of Rockingham scent bottles,** encrusted with flowers and heightened with gold, the necks with raised gilt rings, the stoppers encrusted with flowers, damaged, 1830–35, 5in (12.5cm) high.
£650–750
€/ $1,000–1,200 ⚒ TMA

► **A Spode scent bottle,** minor restoration, pattern No. 4650, c1825, 5in (12.5cm) high.
£260–285
€/ $400–450
⊞ CoS

Tea Canisters

A Fürstenberg tea canister and cover, with moulded floral decoration, painted in puce with floral sprays within shaped gilt reserves, minor chips, finial missing, German, c1775, 4¾in (12cm) high.
£100–120
€/ $160–190 F&C

A pair of Worcester-style Samson tea canisters and covers, moulded with flutes and panels painted with buildings and flowers, one with a seal mark, the other with a cross mark, French, 1880, 4¾in (12cm) high.
£350–400
€/ $550–630 WW

A Worcester tea canister, transfer-printed and hand-coloured with figures and ruins, Knowles Boney Collection label, cracked, cover missing, c1765, 5¼in (13.5cm) high.
£320–375
€/ $500–600 S(O)

Trays

A Belleek tray, decorated with a dragon, Irish, First Period, 1872, 15in (38cm) diam.
£3,300–3,600
€/ $5,200–5,700 ⊞ MLa

A Vienna cabaret tray, with a gilt and pierced rim, the central panel painted with Rubens' Boys and signed 'Bauer, Wien', within a classical-style border of grotesques, small chip to one corner, impressed and shield marks, Austrian, mid-19thC, 13in (33cm) wide.
£1,500–1,800
€/ $2,400–2,800 B

A Caughley spoon tray, decorated with a patera and leaf swags, marked, c1785, 6¾in (17cm) wide.
£160–200
€/ $250–315 WW

A Minton tray, painted by Lucien Boullemier with a Bacchic putto within a Sèvres-style border of flowers and a gilt foliate rim, hairline crack, globe mark, 1900–25, 14in (35.5cm) wide.
£1,100–1,300
€/ $1,700–2,000 DN

► A Sèvres-style tray, decorated with flowers, with a relief-moulded border heightened in gold, gilt pseudo-Sèvres mark, Bohemian, c1900, 21¼in (54cm) wide.
£320–375
€/ $500–600 DORO

A Caughley/Coalport spoon tray, painted with Tower pattern, the fluted border with a butterfly and diaper border, c1798, 6in (15cm) wide.
£1,300–1,500
€/ $2,000–2,400 LFA

A Chamberlain's Worcester topographical card tray, painted with a titled view of the Houses of Parliament within a shell-encrusted border, damaged, painted factory mark and title, c1840, 11¾in (30cm) wide.
£750–900
€/ $1,200–1,400 S(O)

PORCELAIN

Tureens

◄ **A Derby dessert tureen, cover and stand,** painted with botanical specimen sprays within gilt leaf-band borders, each piece inscribed in blue with botanical names, blue baton marks, c1790, stand 9in (23cm) wide.
£1,600–2,000
€/ $2,500–3,200 DN

A Bloor Derby tureen and cover, hand-painted with flowers, edged in gold, with a scrolled gilt handle, minor restoration, c1830, 10in (25.5cm) wide.
£200–225
€/ $320–350 B(W)

A Höchst tureen and cover, the cover applied with an artichoke finial, the rim moulded with the *Altbrandenstein* pattern, the body painted with flowers, some restoration, impressed initials, German, 1760–65, 10¼in (26cm) diam.
£950–1,100
€/ $1,500–1,750 S(Am)

◄ **A Nantgarw dessert tureen with matching Swansea cover and stand,** painted in London, some restoration, gilding worn, tureen impressed 'Nantgarw C.W.', stand impressed 'Swansea', 1814–23, 7½in (19cm) wide.
£7,000–8,000
€/ $11,000–12,500 S(O)
The price for this piece reflects the present strength of the Welsh porcelain market.

► **A pair of Spode porcelain dessert tureens, covers and stands,** painted and sprigged with flower sprays, some wear to gilding, c1815, 7in (18cm) high.
£420–500
€/ $670–790 S(O)

A Vienna tureen and cover, heightened with gold, impressed mark and Vienna shield mark, Austrian, date mark for 1846, 6½in (16.5cm) high.
£160–200
€/ $250–315 DORO

PORCELAIN

Vases

A Belleek ram's head cornucopia vase, Irish, First Period, 1863–90, 4in (10cm) high.
£850–950
€/ $1,350–1,500 MLa

A pair of Belleek bronze-effect vases, with cherubs, Irish, First Period, 1863–90, 12in (30.5cm) high.
£5,000–5,500
€/ $8,000–8,700 DeA

► **A pair of Chelsea vases,** on four scrolled feet, painted on both sides with birds perched on rocks and fruiting branches, surrounded by garlands of applied flowers, buds and leaves, covers possibly missing, flowers damaged, gold anchor marks, c1765, 9½in (24cm) high.
£750–900
€/ $1,200–1,400 B

► **A garniture of Derby frill vases,** comprising a central vase and a pair of trumpet vases, minor damage, restoration, the pair of vases possibly lacking covers, patch marks, 1760–65, centre vase 11¾in (30cm) high.
£2,400–2,700
€/ $3,800–4,300 B

A Royal Crown Derby waisted vase, decorated with Imari pattern, dated 1911, 5in (12.5cm) high.
£240–275
€/ $380–430 SWO

A Staffordshire vase, possibly Mayer & Newbold, painted in enamels with flowers and leaves within gilt cartouches, regilded rim, 1820–25, 5in (12.5cm) high.
£440–485
€/ $680–780 ⊞ CoS

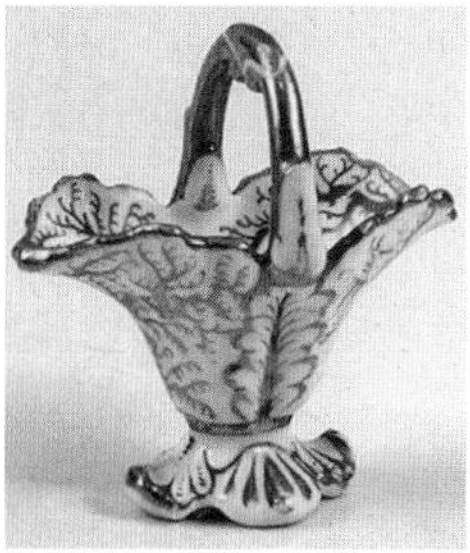

A Rockingham miniature basket, with loop handle, moulded with leaves and decorated with gold, on a lobed base, red number, c1835, 2¾in (7cm) high.
£1,000–1,200
€/ $1,600–1,900 LFA

► **A pair of Sèvres-style vases,** with 'jewelled' decoration, c1860, 10in (25.5cm) high.
£2,300–2,500
€/ $3,600–4,000 ⊞ DHu

A pair of Jagetet Pinon vases, each gilt and silvered with a wreath medallion enclosing two birds, with scattered acorns and oak leaves, gilt dragon handles, one foot repaired, gilt painted mark, French, Tours, early 20thC, 24¾in (63cm) high.
£575–650
€/ $900–1,000 S(O)

A Minton vase, painted with hanging game and hunting trophies, the borders with foliage and butterflies, with gilt leaf and ring handles, slight wear to border, c1850, 9½in (24cm) high.
£450–525
€/ $700–830 B
Ex-Minton Sale.

A Christian's Liverpool baluster vase, painted with a willow tree flanked by peony and bamboo, cracked, c1770, 3½in (9cm) high.
£550–650
€/ $870–1,000 S(O)

A Minton quadruple bottle vase, painted with rural vignettes and a scene of the Houses of Parliament beneath rose festoons, the four handles extending upwards to form a crown studded with cabochons, minor damage, c1870, 8¾in (22cm) high.
£350–400
€/ $550–630 B
Ex-Minton Sale.

A pair of Sèvres-style vases, with 'jewelled' decoration, one finial restored, c1880, 10in (25.5cm) high.
£3,200–3,500
€/ $5,000–5,500 ⊞ MAA

A Longton Hall rococo vase, painted with panels of exotic birds in landscapes and applied with flowers and foliage, on a foot painted with scattered flowers, cracks and chips, c1755, 8½in (21.5cm) high.
£900–1,100
€/ $1,400–1,700 S(O)

A pair of Paris two-handled vases, with gilt swan handles, painted with a continuous scene of a stylized garden with fountains, trellis arbours and pots of roses, the waisted feet on marble bases, French, c1820, 13¼in (33.5cm) high.
£2,500–3,000
€/ $4,000–4,700 S(NY)

A Spode trumpet vase, with everted gilt rim, painted with two bouquets of flowers against a gilded scale ground, with beaded borders, star crack, pattern No. 1166, painted mark, c1810, 6¼in (16cm) high.
£200–240
€/ $320–380 G(L)

A Willets Manufacturing Co 'Belleek' vase, painted by E. Welcher, probably outside the factory, with roses beneath a gilt rim, green printed mark 'Willets Belleek' and serpent, American, dated 1904, 20¾in (52.5cm) high.
£1,600–2,000
€/ $2,500–3,200 ⚒ S(NY)

The Willets Manufacturing Co of Trenton, New Jersey, was established in 1879 by brothers Joseph, Daniel and Edmund Willets. They made American Belleek from c1894–1909, Trenton having become a major centre for the production of American Belleek after china clay had been discovered there in the 1860s. Enthusiasm for these wares had been fired by the Irish Belleek factory's exhibition at the 1876 Philadelphia Exhibition.

A pair of Worcester Flight, Barr & Barr miniature vases, each painted with an exotic bird in a landscape, minor chips to gadrooned rims, puce mark, c1825, 2in (5cm) high.
£1,400–1,600
€/ $2,200–2,500 ⚒ G(L)

A Locke & Co Worcester vase, with dolphin shoulder handles, hand-painted with violets and a butterfly, small rim chips, c1890, 4¼in (11cm) high.
£240–275
€/ $380–430 ⚒ B(W)

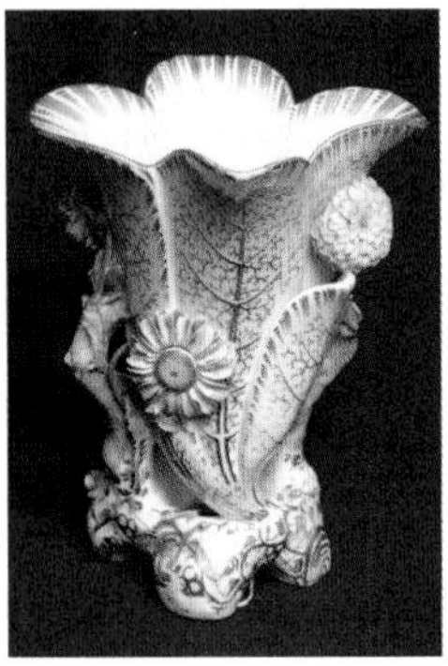

► **A flower vase,** c1840, 8in (20.5cm) high.
£400–450
€/ $630–700 ⊞ DAN

A pair of Royal Worcester vases, with gilt scroll handles, painted with flowers and foliage, date code for 1895, 5¾in (14.5cm) high.
£375–425
€/ $600–670 ⚒ L

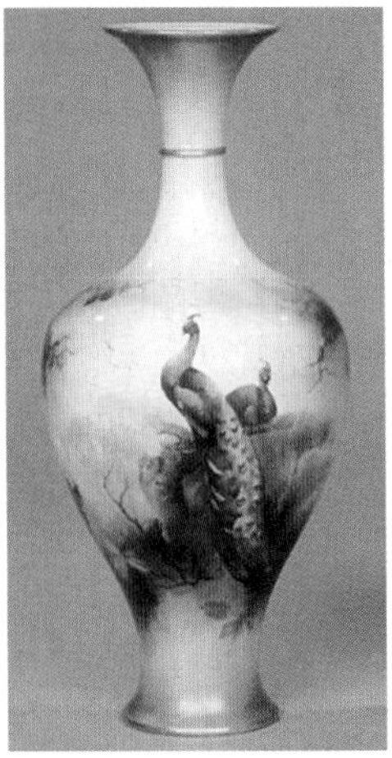

A pair of Royal Worcester Hadley Ware vases, decorated with a pair of peacocks in the branches of a pine tree against a misty twilight, etchings coloured in by Reginald H. Austin, artist's signature, green factory mark, date codes, 1903, 12in (30.5cm) high.
£1,400–1,600
€/ $2,200–2,500 ⚒ TEN

A pair of Grainger's Worcester vases, moulded as shells, c1900, 3in (7.5cm) high.
£130–145
€/ $200–230 ⊞ PSA

For further information on antique porcelain see the full range of Miller's books at
www.millers.uk.com

A rococo vase and cover, the cover with gilded scroll and floral ornament, twin handles, the body decorated with roses, convolvulus and other flowers, on a pierced rococo base with scrollwork and dragons, Bohemian, c1860, 23½in (59.5cm) high.
£320–375
€/ $500–600 ⚒ TRM

Wall Brackets

◄ **A pair of Dresden-style mirror-back wall brackets,** each with a floral painted back panel surround, with putti over a demi-lune ebonized platform, above a pierced and floral-encrusted basket support with a further putto mounted beneath, each on a velvet-covered backboard, damaged, German, late 19thC, 34¼in (87cm) high.
£1,300–1,500
€/ $2,000–2,400 ⚒ Bri

A pair of Grainger's Worcester wall brackets, painted mark, c1870, 8in (20.5cm) high.
£1,000–1,200
€/ $1,600–1,900 ⚒ G(B)

A Royal Worcester wall bracket, the shaped top supported by a winged cherub head, two impressed marks, c1870, 8in (20.5cm) high.
£250–300
€/ $400–475 ⚒ EH

Miscellaneous

A Du Paquier beaker, painted with Oriental flowers, two exotic birds in flight and insects, the interior rim with a formal border heightened with gold, spot and glaze abrasion to rim, Austrian, Vienna, c1730, 2¾in (7cm) high.
£775–900
€/ $1,200–1,400 S(Am)

A Caughley eye bath, moulded with leaf scrolls and printed with Fisherman pattern, beneath a cell diaper and pendant flowerhead border, on a scroll-moulded baluster stem and fluted foot, c1785, 2in (5cm) high.
£1,400–1,700
€/ $2,200–2,700 LFA

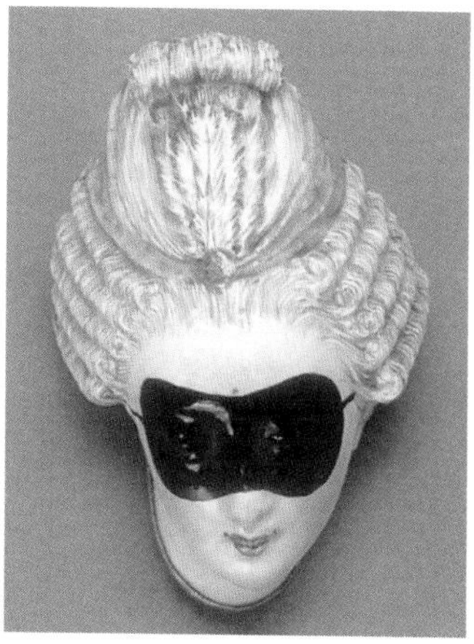

A *bonbonnière*, modelled as a female head wearing a mask beneath elaborately-coiffured hair, the reverse mounted with a gilt-metal cover engraved with scrolling foliage and flowers, German, possibly Thuringian, 1750–1800, 3in (7.5cm) wide.
£1,000–1,200
€/ $1,600–1,900 S(O)

A needle case, hand-painted with vines and a cupid at one end, German, c1760, 5in (12.5cm) long.
£1,200–1,400
€/ $1,900–2,200 US

Three tulip flowerheads, modelled with overlapping petals around a central aperture, one petal chipped, probably German, 1775–1800, 2¼in (5.5cm) high.
£500–600
€/ $800–950 S(O)

A Spode pastille burner, modelled as a cottage with a pitch roof cover, enamelled with encrusted flowers on a mound base, minor cracks, Feldspar porcelain mark, c1830, 4¾in (12cm) high.
£420–475
€/ $670–750 G(L)

A Worcester spitoon, decorated with Three Flowers pattern, c1770, 4½in (11.5cm) high.
£600–650
€/ $950–1,000 WWW

A Sèvres ice cup, from the Louis XVI service, painted by Philippine l'aîné with an allegory of Justice, scales in her right hand, a sceptre in her left, books by her side, enclosed by tooled *guilloche* gilding, the ground gilt with foliate scrolls and flower swags, minor damage, French, 1790, 2½in (6.5cm) high.
£2,200–2,500
€/ $3,500–4,000 B
While the majority of the Louis XVI service was sold by the French Revolutionary government in 1793 and was later acquired by George IV in 1811, it is known that several items, which appear in the records, became separated from the main service. This cup would appear to be one of these items.

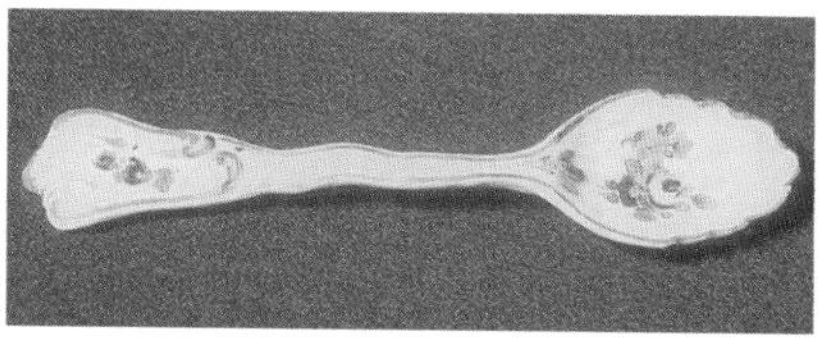

A Bristol Champions spoon, painted with flowers, c1775, 4in (10cm) long.
£630–700
€/ $1,000–1,100 JUP

► **A Worcester cornucopia wall pocket,** painted with insects and flower sprays, damaged, 1755–60, 10in (25.5cm) high.
£450–525
€/ $700–830 WW
Coloured Worcester cornucopia are very rare and the price of this reflects the damage.

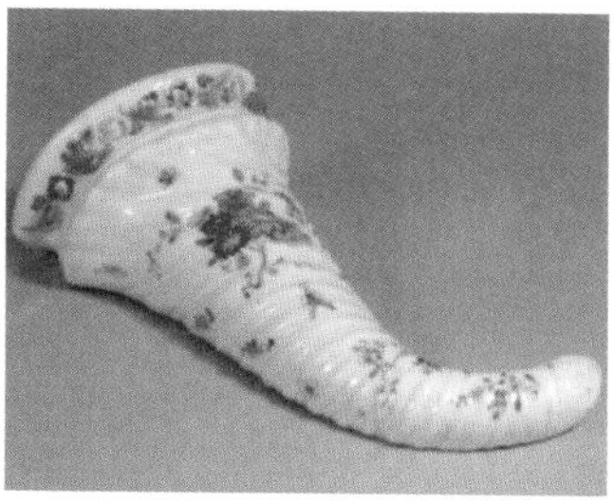

PORCELAIN

Meissen

Meissen is Europe's oldest successful porcelain factory, the earliest pieces dating from c1710. These are known today as 'Böttger porcelain' after Johann Böttger, the alchemist who discovered the secret of making 'hard paste' porcelain to rival the valuable imports from China and Japan.

Some early Meissen directly copied Oriental prototypes, although most productions were totally original. The brilliant painter J. G. Herold specialized in chinoiserie subjects. Other enamellers painted landscapes, detailed figure subjects or the finely-executed flowers known as *deutsche Blumen*. Every piece of 18th-century Meissen was decorated to the highest possible standards. Their principal figure modeller, Johann Kändler, is best known for his harlequins and figures of street vendors. By the 19th century, such pieces had become enormously popular in Britain and the United States, and they were reissued in new colouring, every piece being carefully hand-decorated.

Recently 19th-century Meissen has rocketed in value and some pieces are nearly as valuable as 18th-century examples. Mostly, though, earlier productions are worth more, and for this reason identifying the date of manufacture is crucial. Fortunately almost every piece is clearly marked with the famous crossed swords, derived from the arms of Saxony. In the 18th century each sword was painted as a neat, straight line. During the 'Academic' period (1763–74), a dot was placed between the sword hilts, and during the 'Marcolini' period (1774–1813) a star or asterisk was painted above the hilts. Somewhat scruffy marks were used until the 1840s and then, until the early 20th century, the swords were carefully painted, each gently curved, and a 'pommel' (dark spot) placed at the tip of each hilt. From 1926 to 1939 a dot was placed between the blades of the swords. Post-WWII pieces have thin, curved swords, with no dot or pommels.

The crossed swords marks are extensively faked, for Meissen is the most widely copied porcelain. Many other makers in the Dresden area have reproduced popular Meissen shapes and patterns. It is therefore essential to distinguish between actual Meissen factory productions and 'Dresden'-style porcelain, which is always inferior. **John Sandon**

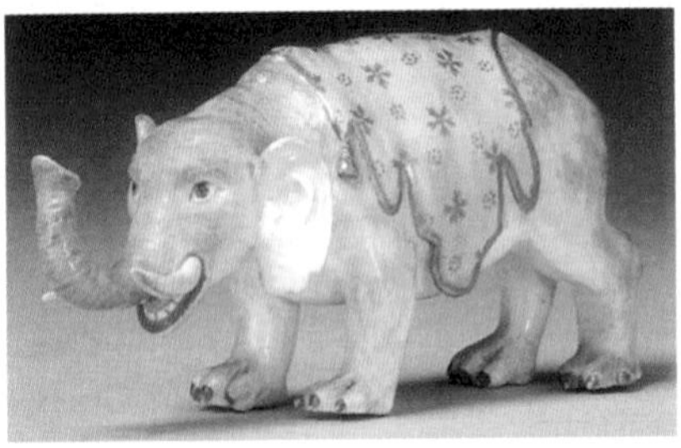

A Meissen model of an elephant, by J. J. Kändler, wearing a caparison hung with gilt tassels and gilt with florets, minor restoration, c1750, 5¾in (14.5cm) long.
£1,200–1,500
€/ $1,900–2,400 B

A Meissen model of pug dog, by J. J. Kändler, one foreleg repaired, c1750, 3in (7.5cm) long.
£1,600–2,000
€/ $2,500–3,200 S(O)

A Meissen model of a bullfinch, c1880, 3½in (9cm) high.
£300–340
€/ $475–550 BROW

A Meissen model of a Bolognese terrier, damaged, blue crossed swords mark and incised numerals, 1850–1900, 9in (23cm) high.
£600–700
€/ $950–1,100 HYD

◄ **A Meissen model of an Alsatian,** No. V188, first modelled by Eric Hösel in 1927, crossed swords mark, c1928, 7¼in (18.5cm) long.
£1,200–1,300
€/ $1,900–2,000 DAV

► **A Meissen beaker,** painted with *deutsche Blumen*, crossed swords mark, c1745, 3¼in (8.5cm) diam.
£240–275
€/ $380–430 WW

A Meissen trinket box, painted with a view of Albrechtsburg Castle at Meissen, crossed swords mark, c1900, 4in (10cm) diam.
£580–650
€/ $900–1,000 DAV

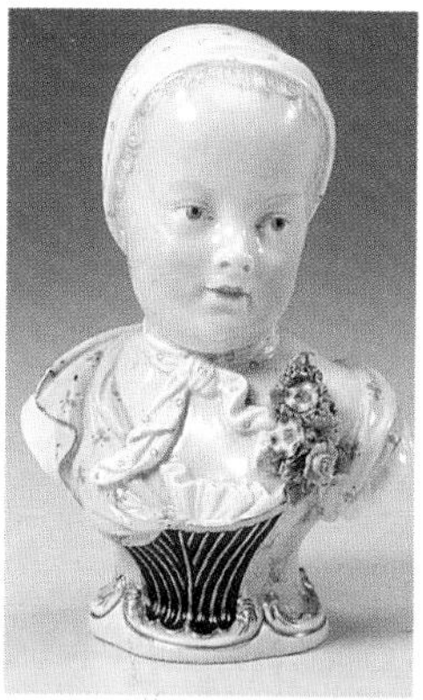

◄ **A Meissen *Kinderkopf* bust of a girl,** a nosegay on her left shoulder, incised and impressed numerals, mid-19thC, 6in (15cm) high.
£600–700
€/ $950–1,100 TMA

► **A Meissen candle snuffer,** encrusted with flowers and painted with two insects, marked, c1860, 8¼in (8.5cm) high.
£200–240
€/ $320–380 SWO

A Meissen candlestick, c1850, 3in (7.5cm) high.
£270–300
€/ $425–475 DAN

A pair of Meissen chamber sticks, modelled with miniature figures of child gardeners, c1860, 5½in (14cm) high.
£1,500–1,700
€/ $2,400–2,700 MAA

◄ **A pair of Meissen candlesticks,** heightened in gold with a panel of flowers to front and back, crossed swords marks, c1870, 5½in (14cm) high.
£700–800
€/ $1,100–1,200 DAV

A Meissen tea bowl and saucer, c1735, 3in (7.5cm) diam.
£1,400–1,500
€/ $2,200–2,400 US

◄ **A Meissen cup and saucer,** with deep base for hot water, mid-19thC, 5in (12.5cm) high.
£1,000–1,100
€/ $1,600–1,700
BROW

A Meissen egg cup, painted with scattered sprigs of *deutsche Blumen*, gilt-edged rim, crossed swords mark, 1755–60, 2¼in (5.5cm) high.
£750–875
€/ $1,200–1,400 S(O)
The double egg cup can be used to place the egg either horizontally or vertically, depending on whether the custom is to break open its end or side, the latter being the case in Germany and Austria, the former in France and Italy.

A Meissen Comedia Dell'Arte figure of Pantaloon, by J. J. Kändler, on a floral-moulded base, c1738–40, 6in (15cm) high.
£7,000–8,200
€/ $11,000–13,000 EH
This is a rare earlier version of the model. The later version is slightly smaller and Pantaloon has one arm raised.

A Meissen figure of a pipe smoker, c1747, 5in (12.5cm) high.
£3,500–4,000
€/ $5,500–6,300 ⊞ BHa

► A Meissen figure of a fishmonger, minor restoration, c1760, 6in (15cm) high.
£1,400–1,600
€/ $2,200–2,500 ⚒ DORO

A Meissen figure of a boy on a hobby horse, c1860, 6½in (16.5cm) high.
£1,300–1,500
€/ $2,000–2,400 ⊞ BROW

A Meissen figural group of child gardeners, leaves restored, crossed swords mark, c1900, 8¾in (22cm) high.
£1,100–1,300
€/ $1,700–2,000 ⚒ DORO

A Meissen figure of a Turkish gentleman, by J. F. Eberlein, c1748, 7in (18cm) high.
£3,400–3,800
€/ $5,400–6,000 ⊞ BHa

A Meissen flower seller, c1870, 5½in (14cm) high.
£1,200–1,400
€/ $1,900–2,200 ⊞ BHa

A Meissen figure of a young man, c1750, 5in (12.5cm) high.
£1,400–1,500
€/ $2,000–2,300 ⊞ MAA

A Meissen figure of a seamstress, by J. J. Kändler, holding pieces from a jacket, on a scroll-moulded base, minor chips and losses, crossed swords mark, c1760, 9in (23cm) high.
£1,600–1,800
€/ $2,500–2,800 ⚒ S(NY)

18th-century Meissen 1976–2002

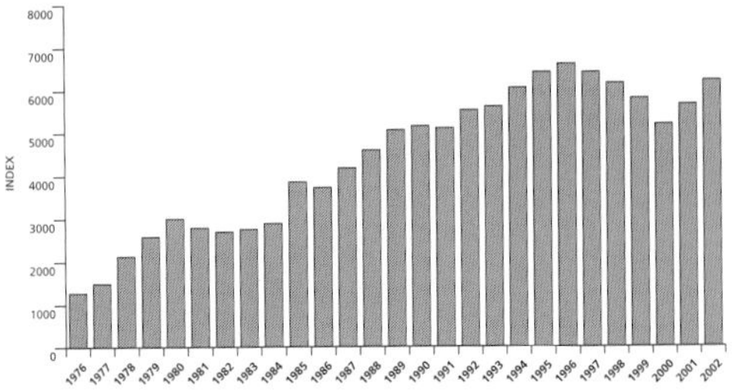

This graph shows the changing value of 18th-century Meissen porcelain as a whole over the past 25 years. Individual collecting areas and different periods, such as the 19th century, may not follow this graph exactly. ©AMR

A Meissen figure of a man reading, restored, 19thC, 5in (12.5cm) high.
£225–250
€/ $350–400 ⊞ SER

A Meissen group of cherubs, carrying flowers, c1900, 6½in (16.5cm) high.
£1,800–1,900
€/ $2,800–3,000 ⊞ MAA

◄ A pair of Meissen figures of Malabar Musicians, playing musical instruments, wearing Chinese hats and flowered clothing, on scrolled bases, damaged, crossed swords mark, 1860–80, 13in (33cm) high.
£1,200–1,400
€/ $1,900–2,200 ⚒ JNic

A Meissen plate from the Swan service, by J. J. Kändler, the shell-moulded ground with two swans swimming among bulrushes in the centre, a crane in flight overhead, the rim painted with the arms of Brühl and Kolowrat-Krakowsky, scattered sprigs and *indianische Blumen* with a gilt-dashed rim, minor wear, crossed swords and impressed potter's mark of four radiating triangles, 1738–39, 9in (23cm) diam.
£8,500–10,000
€/ $13,500–16,000 ⚒ S(O)

The Swan service was ordered in 1736 for the director of the factory, Count Heinrich von Brühl (1700–63). The service originally comprised over 2,200 pieces, most of which remained at the family seat, Schloss Pförten, until 1945, when Russian troops destroyed much of the service and the castle was burned to the ground.

A set of four Meissen soup plates, painted with *deutsche Blumen* within basket weave borders, one with foot rim crack, gilding worn, c1760, 8¾in (22cm) diam.
£500–600
€/ $800–950 ⚒ BUK

A Meissen cabinet plate, the central panel painted with a scene after Boucher, depicting Venus bathing attended by a nymph, within a lobed and pierced rim moulded with panels of forget-me-nots, crossed swords mark, impressed and incised numerals, c1870, 10¼in (26cm) diam.
£2,200–2,500
€/ $3,500–4,000 ⚒ B

A pair of Meissen plates, with enamelled floral sprays, within basket weave borders, crossed swords mark, mid-18thC, 11¾in (30cm) diam.
£350–420
€/ $550–670 ⚒ SWO

A Meissen miniature teapot and cover, with scroll handle, painted with *deutsche Blumen* and scattered sprigs, the cover with a flower bud finial, traces of crossed swords mark, c1760, 4in (10cm) high.
£625–725
€/ $1,000–1,200 ⚒ S(O)

A Meissen topographical vase, painted with a titled view of Pillnitz within a moulded rococo cartouche, further cartouches enclosing flowers, crossed swords mark, incised and impressed numerals, mid-19thC, 12in (30.5cm) high.
£1,600–2,000
€/ $2,500–3,200 ⚒ RTo

A Meissen vase, decorated with flowers and fruit, c1860, 10in (25.5cm) high.
£1,600–1,800
€/ $2,500–2,800 ⊞ MAA

► A Meissen vase, decorated with flowers and fruit and Watteau-style figures within a panel, c1880, 5½in (14cm) high.
£1,200–1,300
€/ $1,900–2,000 ⊞ MAA

A Selection of Chinese Dynasties & Marks

Early Dynasties

Neolithic	10th – early 1st millennium BC	Tang Dynasty	618–907
Shang Dynasty	16th century–c1050 BC	Five Dynasties	907–960
Zhou Dynasty	c1050–221 BC	Liao Dynasty	907–1125
Warring States	480–221 BC	Song Dynasty	960–1279
Qin Dynasty	221–206 BC	*Northern Song*	960–1127
Han Dynasty	206 BC–AD 220	*Southern Song*	1127–1279
Six Dynasties	222–589	Xixia Dynasty	1038–1227
Wei Dynasty	386–557	Jin Dynasty	1115–1234
Sui Dynasty	581–618	Yuan Dynasty	1279–1368

Ming Dynasty Marks

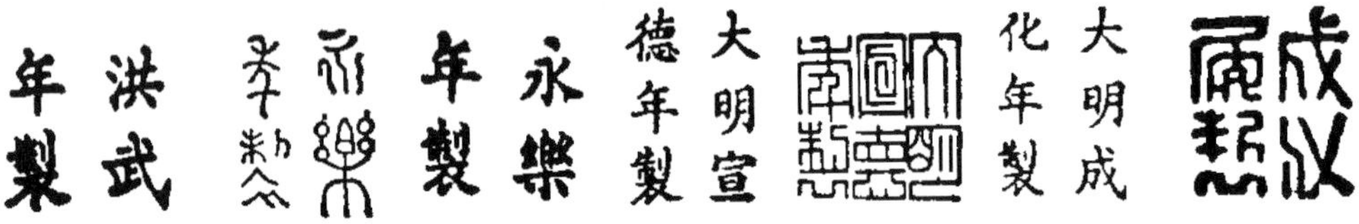

Hongwu 1368–1398 | Yongle 1403–1424 | Xuande 1426–1435 | Chenghua 1465–1487

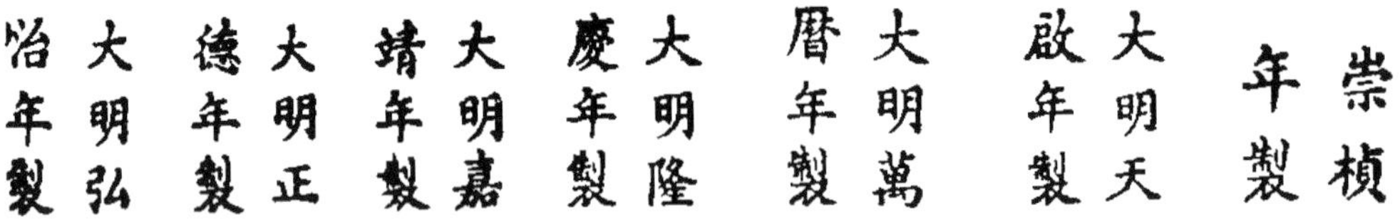

Hongzhi 1488–1505 | Zhengde 1506–1521 | Jiajing 1522–1566 | Longqing 1567–1572 | Wanli 1573–1619 | Tianqi 1621–1627 | Chongzhen 1628–1644

Qing Dynasty Marks

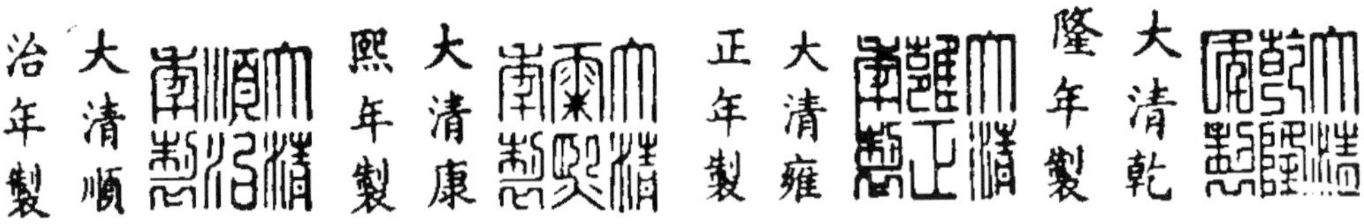

Shunzhi 1644–1661 | Kangxi 1662–1722 | Yongzheng 1723–1735 | Qianlong 1736–1795

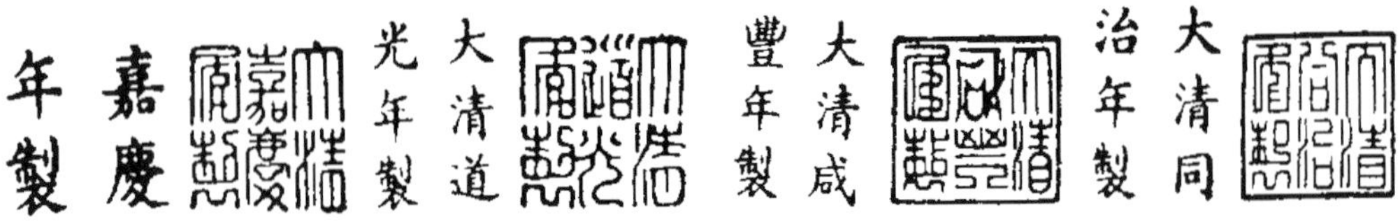

Jiaqing 1796–1820 | Daoguang 1821–1850 | Xianfeng 1851–1861 | Tongzhi 1862–1874

Guangxu 1875–1908 | Xuantong 1909–1911 | Hongxian 1916

CHINESE CERAMICS

Chinese Ceramics

The international demand for Chinese ceramics has, until now, ensured that prices were unaffected by localized recessions, but the global recession of the past two years has affected the market, especially for pristine, well-documented pieces in the £1,000–20,000 (€/ $1,700–32,000) price range. Large decorative pieces are still sought by interior designers but demand is slowing. The Chinese mainland market is only expanding for large, highly decorated, 19th-century items considered to be of 'Chinese taste'. The finest and rarest pieces are still in demand, however, especially as alternative investments, and academic collectors are always keen to acquire small, interesting examples of various types or kilns.

The last 25 years have seen many changes in collecting fashions and market values. The systematic looting of tombs in China, and improved 'faking' techniques, has led to a serious downturn in values of Tang and Han Dynasty excavated ceramics. Figures considered very rare 25 years ago are now commonplace, and thermoluminescence testing has become the norm. Imperial porcelains of the Qing Dynasty (1662–1911) have increased ten-fold in value due to Chinese demands, arising from a shortage of Ming and earlier Imperial works. Collectors recognized that high quality and rare objects of any period should be obtained while still available. Early 20th-century 'official wares' have sold for up to £30,000 (€/ $47,000) each.

Even in depressing times, the beauty and perfection of the best Chinese ceramics continue to attract connoisseurs and collectors. This is particularly evident with Chinese Export ceramics, where the market has slowed for routine goods but still realizes record prices for exceptional pieces.

The next 25 years will see a huge increase in the value of Imperial ceramics as the full purchasing power of mainland China takes effect. Lesser-quality tomb figures will continue to drop in price due to market saturation and lack of confidence in authenticity, and at least another five ship-wrecks of ceramics (already located) will surface, thus further diminishing a slow market.

Peter Wain

Animals

A pottery model of a dog, Oxford T/L tested, Han Dynasty, 206 BC–AD 220, restored, 21in (53.5cm) high.
£1,800–2,000
€/ $2,800–3,200 GLD

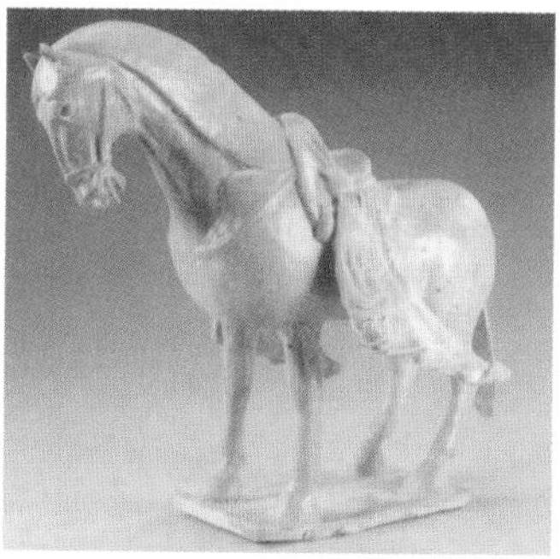

A straw-glazed pottery model of a horse, Oxford T/L tested, Sui Dynasty, 581–618, 11in (28cm) high.
£1,500–1,700
€/ $2,400–2,700 S(O)

A pottery model of a boar, Tang Dynasty, 618–907, 13¼in (34cm) high.
£700–850
€/ $1,100–1,300 S(O)

A pottery model of a horse, Oxford T/L tested, some damage and restoration, Tang Dynasty, 618–907, 9½in (24cm) high.
£240–275
€/ $380–420 WW

A *sancai*-glazed model of a camel, Tang Dynasty, 618–907, 20in (51cm) high.
£3,000–3,500
€/ $4,800–5,800 B

A glazed Yueyao model of a ram, with an aperture on the forehead, Jin Dynasty, 1115–1234, 6in (15cm) high.
£2,000–2,200
€/ $3,200–3,500 S(Am)

T/L test

Oxford T/L test refers to a test certificate awarded by Oxford Authentication Ltd to those genuine pieces of ceramics which have passed their thermoluminescence test which is accurate to plus or minus 200 years.

◄ **A pair of *famille verte* models of Dogs of *Fo*,** with vases on their backs, raised on plinths, both damaged, Kangxi period, 1662–1722, 7¾in (19.5cm) high.
£150–175
€/ $240–280 ⚒ WW

A pair of *famille rose* candle holders, in the form of recumbent lions, one looking to the left, the other to the right, restored, Canton, 19thC, 7½in (19cm) wide.
£2,500–3,000
€/ $4,000–4,800 ⚒ B

A glazed model of a dog, 18thC, 3in (7.5cm) high.
£300–350
€/ $475–550 ⚒ L

Items in the Chinese Ceramics section have been arranged in date order within each sub-section.

A pair of glazed models of cockerels, standing on rocks, one with gilt-metal base, 18thC, 6¼in (15.5cm) high.
£600–720
€/ $950–1,200 ⚒ S(O)

A pair of models of cockerels, late 19thC, 9in (23cm) high.
£850–950
€/ $1,400–1,600 ⊞ AUA

Bowls

A glazed porcelain bowl, Song Dynasty, 960–1279, 9in (23cm) diam.
£1,600–1,800
€/ $2,500–2,800 ⊞ GLD

A Provincial bowl, decorated with scrolling foliage, commendation mark, 1550–75, 4¾in (12cm) diam.
£1,500–1,800
€/ $2,400–3,000 ⚒ L

A Junyao stoneware tea bowl, with hare's fur glaze, Song Dynasty, 960–1279, 4¾in (12cm) diam.
£1,100–1,300
€/ $1,700–2,000 ⊞ PCA

A bowl, decorated in the centre with a crane, below *ruyi* heads and pendants, 16thC, 8½in (21.5cm) diam.
£700–820
€/ $1,100–1,300 ⚒ G(L)

◄ **A Swatow bowl,** decorated with flowers and birds, late Ming Dynasty, 17thC, 9¾in (25cm) diam.
£400–500
€/ $600–720 ⚒ S(O)

A Henan bowl, Jin Dynasty, 1115–1234, 4¾in (12.5cm) diam.
£2,500–3,000
€/ $4,000–4,800 ⚒ B

A bowl, c1643, 8in (20.5cm) diam.
£100–125
€/ $160–200 ⊞ McP
This piece is from the Hatcher cargo, retrieved from a shipwreck that occurred in the South China Sea c1643, and named after the diver who arranged the salvage operation. The cargo consisted of predominantly blue and white wares from Jingdezhen.

A *famille verte* fluted basin, decorated in the centre with birds, surrounded by floral sprays, Kangxi period, 1662–1772, 11in (28cm) diam.
£3,400–3,800
€/ $5,400–6,000 ⊞ G&G

An Immortal basin, the centre painted with an Immortal dressed in flowing robes, standing on a dragon, within a barbed border, Kangxi mark and period, 1662–1772, 16¼in (41cm) diam.
£5,500–6,500
€/ $8,600–10,200 ⚒ S(HK)
It is unusual to find a powder-blue dish of this type with a large blue and white figure design depicting an Immortal.

A Chinese export *famille rose* bowl, decorated with floral sprays, 1775–1825, 9in (23cm) diam.
£180–220
€/ $280–350 ⚒ PFK

A bowl, European decorated with a couple in front of a column and trees, the exterior yellow-glazed and incised with dragons, 19thC, 5in (12.5cm) diam.
£600–700
€/ $950–1,100 ⚒ G(L)

A bowl, Kangxi mark and period, 1662–1722, 8in (20.5cm) diam.
£2,000–2,300
€/ $3,200–3,600 ⊞ GLD

A blue and white bowl, from the *Vung Tau* cargo, late 17thC, 6in (15cm) diam.
£130–145
€/ $200–230 ⊞ McP
The Chinese ship the *Vung Tau* was wrecked off the coast of Vietnam c1696 and salvaged c1990.

A bowl, painted with eight Immortals, Qianlong mark and period, c1780, 10in (25.5cm) diam.
£1,300–1,500
€/ $2,000–2,400 ⊞ CHT

A porcelain bowl, both the exterior and interior decorated with figures playing games, floral internal border, with blue-gilt fret borders, Canton, 19thC, 13½in (34.5cm) diam.
£575–675
€/ $900–1,000 ⚒ DMC

A porcelain bowl, the exterior painted with four dragons among cloud scrolls, the interior with a single dragon, with everted rim, minor flake to rim, character marks, Kangxzi period, 1662–1772, 7¼in (18.5cm) diam.
£4,500–5,500
€/ $7,000–8,400 ⚒ Bea(E)
The quality, mark and pattern of this bowl all indicate it is an Imperial piece, that is, made for the Royal Court. In perfect condition it would be worth £12,000–15,000 (€/ $18,000–24,000).

A bowl, from the Nanking cargo, c1752, 6in (15cm) diam.
£160–185
€/ $250–300 ⊞ McP
The Dutch East India Company's ship *Geldermalsen* sank near Java in 1751. Included in its cargo was a particular type of Chinese blue and white porcelain known as Nanking, hence the name. Although there was little in the cargo to excite the purist collector of Asian ceramics, the story of the salvage attracted intense public interest, which was reflected in the prices achieved when the pieces were sold at auction. Items from this cargo still, nearly 20 years later, command a premium over comparable pieces of Chinese export porcelain.

A pair of *famille rose* bowls, the sides painted with four medallions enclosing the characters *wu fu wan shou*, one cracked, Guangxu mark and period, 1875–1908, 5½in (14cm) diam.
£700–850
€/ $1,100–1,400 ⚒ S(Am)
The characters *wu fu wan shou* mean five blessings for 10,000 years.

◀ **A fish bowl,** the exterior painted with a pair of peacocks and other birds among seasonal flowers between diaper bands, the interior with five goldfish and weed, Canton, early 20thC, 14¼in (36cm) diam.
£300–350
€/ $475–550 ⚒ CGC

Boxes

A Chinese export *famille rose* box and cover, painted with sprays of flowers and leaves, both rivetted, Qianlong period, 1736–95, 5½in (14cm) diam.
£250–300
€/ $400–480 LFA

A box and cover, painted with a flower medallion reserved on a scrolling butterfly ground, marks, 19thC, 12in (30.5cm) diam.
£700–850
€/ $1,100–1,300 S(O)

▶ A blue and white box and cover, inscribed, 1820–40, 5in (12.5cm) wide.
£60–70
€/ $95–110 McP

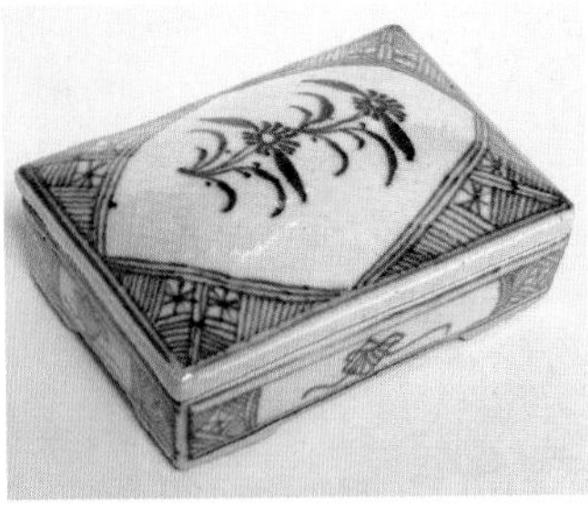

A *famille rose* box and cover, the rounded sides painted with flowering branches, the top centred with a large flower, Guangxu mark and period, 1875–1908, 12¼in (31cm) diam.
£10,000–12,000
€/ $16,000–19,000 S(HK)
This box is an Imperial piece and much sought after by Chinese ceramics collectors as it is rare to find good-quality items of this period.

▶ A *famille rose* box and cover, decorated with boys on a terrace, 19thC, 3in (7.5cm) diam.
£160–200
€/ $250–315 G(L)

Brushpots

A brushpot, painted with figures and a horse in a landscape, c1640, 7½in (19cm) high.
£4,700–5,700
€/ $7,500–9,000 B

A brushpot, painted with scholars in a bamboo grove, above a raised narrow border, c1640, 8½in (21.5cm) diam.
£1,800–2,200
€/ $2,800–3,500 S(O)

▶ A *famille verte* brushpot, painted with a long-tailed bird and prunus, rim chips, Kangxi period, 1662–1722, 5½in (14cm) high.
£600–700
€/ $950–1,100 G(L)

A brushpot, painted with a large phoenix, Shunzhi/Kangxi period, 1650–70, 8in (20.5cm) diam.
£8,000–10,000
€/ $12,500–15,800 S(NY)

A *famille rose* brushpot, painted on each side with a fruiting flower branch, on bracket feet, 18thC, 5¼in (13.5cm) high.
£600–720
€/ $950–1,100 S(O)

Cups

A stoneware offering tray, with seven fixed cups, Six Dynasties period, 222–589, 7in (18cm) diam.
£400–500
€/ $630–800 ⊞ GLD

A *wucai* month cup, painted with a white prunus tree emblematic of the 11th month, the side inscribed with a poem, Kangxi period, 1662–1722, 2¾in (6.5cm) high.
£5,200–6,200
€/ $8,200–9,800 ⚒ S(HK)
A full set of 12 month cups would command a very high price.

A wine cup, painted with two birds, one perched in a fruiting peach tree, the other in a flowering magnolia issuing from rockwork, Kangxi mark and period, 1662–1722, 1¾in (4.5cm) high.
£4,000–5,000
€/ $6,400–7,900 ⚒ B

A *famille verte* tea bowl and saucer, Kangzi period, 1662–1722, bowl 3in (7.5cm) diam.
£320–360
€/ $500–570 ⊞ McP

A footed cup, the sides painted with boys flying a kite below a splashed border, glaze chips to rim, c1640, 4¼in (11cm) high.
£2,200–2,500
€/ $3,500–4,000 ⚒ B

◄ A tea bowl and saucer, decorated with a huntsman, a mountainous landscape in the background, Kangxi period, 1662–1722, saucer 4¼in (11cm) diam.
£270–300
€/ $420–500 ⊞ GLD

Expert's choice

The outstanding Peony Pavilion Collection sold by Christie's London, in 1989 was formed in Japan by one family over six generations. It consisted of 200 lots (approximately 1,000 pieces) of late Ming Chinese export ceramics made specifically for use in the Japanese tea ceremony. The porcelain was made during the reign periods of Tianqi and Chongzhen (1621–43) and showed an extensive range of rare designs and shapes. The latter decades of the Ming Dynasty (known as the Transitional period) was a period of some obscurity in Chinese porcelain production. It was a time of national disintegration and civil war that resulted in the disruption of ceramic production in China and loss of traditional markets. Despite local troubles these wares suggest a spirit of innovation in a search for new markets. New shapes and designs were produced, in underglaze blue and white and on-glaze enamels, reflecting Japanese taste. This resulted in an unusual mix of cultures. Many designs had never been seen in Europe before. The whole collection was a revelation. These late Ming pieces were assessed as of a little-understood period and as an insight into the contemporary neo-Confucian culture in Japan.

This collection would have been formed at very little financial cost in Japan, but it could only have been so comprehensive as a result of the inherited passion and enthusiasm of five generations.

Peter Wain

A pair of *famille rose* tea bowls and saucers, painted with a winged cherub below a multi-coloured eight-panelled border, Yongzheng period, 1723–35.
£1,400–1,600
€/ $2,200–2,600 ⚒ G(L)

A tea bowl and saucer, Kangxi period, 1662–1722, saucer 4in (10cm) diam.
£400–450
€/ $640–700 ⊞ CHT

A tea bowl and saucer, Dutch-decorated, Qianlong period, 1736–95, cup 4in (10cm) diam.
£160–180
€/ $250–280 ⊞ GLD

A Chinese export tea bowl and saucer, c1740, 2½in high.
£235–260
€/ $370–400 ⊞ DAN

A Mandarin palette trio, comprising tea bowl, coffee cup and saucer, c1770, saucer 5in (12.5cm) diam.
£160–180
€/ $250–280 ⊞ DAN

A Chinese export porcelain tea bowl, painted *en grisaille* with Britannia and a reclining soldier, the reverse with Venus and Cupid seated on a cloud, the interior with a central sprig and a gilt rim, 19thC, 3in (7.5cm) diam.
£140–160
€/ $220–250 SWO

A pair of Chinese export tea bowls and saucers, decorated with initials within a cartouche, with C-scroll and flower borders, cracks, mid-18thC.
£200–225
€/ $320–350 DN

A coffee cup, decorated with Masonic symbols, Qianlong period, 1736–95.
£750–875
€/ $1,200–1,400 G(L)

◄ A tea bowl and saucer, from the *Tek Sing* cargo, c1822, saucer 4in (10cm) diam.
£115–125
€/ $180–200
⊞ DAN
The *Tek Sing* sank in the Gaspar Straits in Indonesia in 1822.

► A Libation cup, of archaic *yi* form, with coffee glaze, 19thC, 5¼in (13.5cm) diam.
£850–1,000
€/ $1,300–1,500
S(O)

Dishes

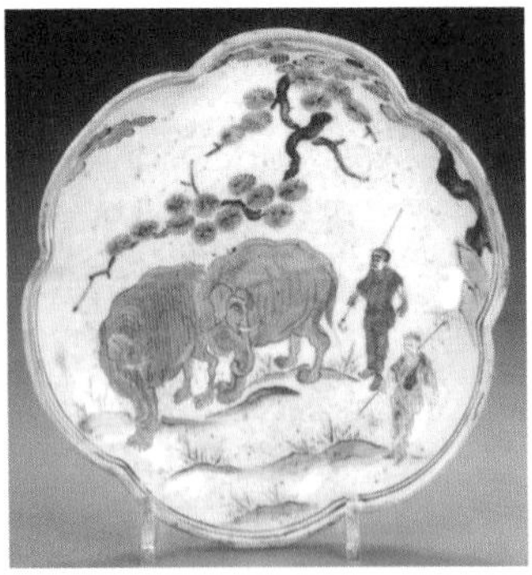

A *wucai* dish, made for the Japanese market, decorated with two elephants and their keepers near a pine tree, 1621–27, 9¾in (25cm) diam.
£2,500–3,000
€/ $4,000–4,700 S(Am)

A silver-mounted dish, Kangxi/Yongzheng period, 1710–50, mounts Dutch, 19thC, 9in (23cm) diam.
£415–460
€/ $640–720 ⊞ McP

► A teapot stand, enamel-painted in the workshop of James Giles, London, with a pair of exotic birds perched among rocks and foliage, two smaller birds flying overhead, gilt rim, minor wear, 1765–70, 5¼in (13.5cm) wide.
£1,300–1,500
€/ $2,000–2,400 B

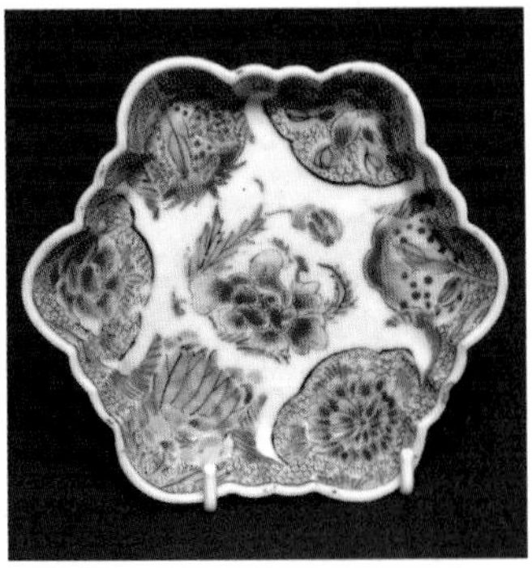

A *famille rose* teapot stand, c1760, 5in (12.5cm) wide.
£260–285
€/ $400–450 ⊞ DAN

Miller's Compares

I. **A pair of Chinese Imari shell dishes,** painted with radiating sprays of chrysanthemums within a geometric border, minor frits, Qianlong period, 1736–95, 7in (18cm) wide.
£1,100–1,300
€/ $1,700–2,000 ⊞ G&G

II. **A pair of shell dishes,** with floral decoration, Qianlong period, 1736–95, 6½in (16.5cm) wide.
£750–850
€/ $1,000–1,400 ⊞ G&G

These pairs of mid-18th century shell dishes were both made in Jingdezhen for the European market. Item I is decorated in the much rarer and therefore more desirable Chinese Imari palette and is worth much more than Item II which is a blue and white example.

A spoon tray, decorated with the 'Arms of Liberty' depicting John Wilkes and his opponent Lord Mansfield, c1770, 4¾in (12cm) wide.
£1,200–1,400
€/ $1,900–2,200 ⚒ G(L)

◀ **A *famille rose* pedestal dish,** painted with butterflies, the exterior with roses and other flowers, Canton, Qing Dynasty, 19thC, 15in (38cm) wide.
£320–360
€/ $500–570 ⚒ B(B)

A *famille rose* porcelain dish, the centre with a medallion depicting figures in a lakeside landscape, within a field of butterflies and birds among flowers, the border decorated with scrolls and swords, silvered and gilt-enriched, 19thC, 9¼in (23.5cm) square.
£160–200
€/ $250–300 ⚒ PFK

Ewers & Kendi

A Yue ware ewer and cover, Warring States period, 480–221 BC, 8in (20.5cm) high.
£4,000–4,500
€/ $6,300–7,000 ⊞ GLD
Yue are high-fired green wares.

A Yingqing glazed ewer and cover, with curved spout, the C-shaped handle applied with a loop, the cover and finial set with a smaller loop, Song Dynasty, 960–1279, 6in (15cm) high.
£1,700–2,000
€/ $2,700–3,200 ⚒ S(Am)

A blue and white *kendi*, painted in underglaze blue with panels of flowers and precious objects, Wanli period, 1573–1619, 8½in (21.5cm) high.
£450–525
€/ $700–830 ⚒ B(WM)

A *kendi*, from the Hatcher cargo, c1643, 5in (12.5cm) high.
£770–860
€/ $1,200–1,400 ⊞ McP

◀ **A *kendi*,** painted with panelled foliage, with brass-mounted spout, early 17thC, 8in (20.5cm) high.
£350–425
€/ $550–670 ⚒ G(L)

▶ **An octagonal lobed ewer,** with phoenix-head spout, decorated with peony, lotus and other flowers, cover missing, Kangxi period, 1662–1722, 8¾in (22cm) high.
£4,000–5,000
€/ $6,300–7,900 ⚒ G(L)

Figures

A set of five pottery equestrian figures, each soldier in military attire, the saddlecloths and trappings richly painted, traces of mud encrustation, Han Dynasty, 206 BC–AD 220, 11¼in (28.5cm) high.
£5,500–6,000
€/ $8,700–9,500 ⚒ S(NY)
Various pottery figures of similar models are recorded but this is remarkable as one figure bears an impressed potter's seal. The inscription reads '*Guo nan*' (Baron Guo), which suggests that these figures were made for the tomb of a member of the Han aristocracy.

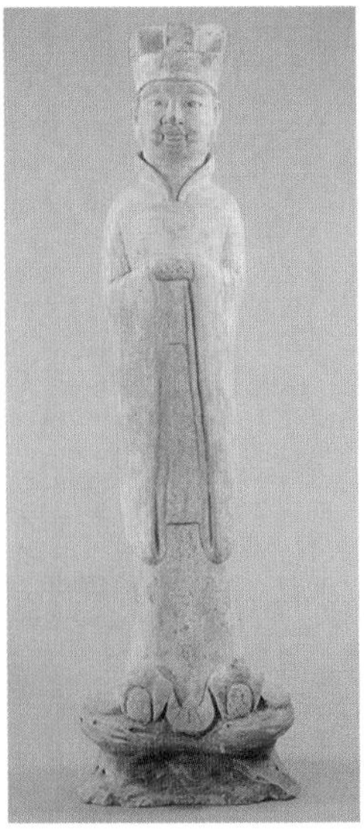

A painted pottery figure of a courtier, traces of pigment to gown, the head later, Tang Dynasty, 618–907, 41¾in (106cm) high.
£1,200–1,400
€/ $1,900–2,200 ⚒ S(O)

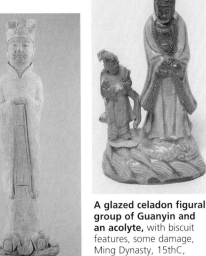

A glazed celadon figural group of Guanyin and an acolyte, with biscuit features, some damage, Ming Dynasty, 15thC, 10in (25.5cm) high.
£650–700
€/ $1,000–1,100 ⊞ GLD

◄ A porcelain figure of Guanyin, decorated in blue and white, a bird perched on her left hand, damaged, Kangxi period, 1662–1722, 8¼in (21cm) high.
£280–325
€/ $440–500 ⚒ F&C

A Chinese export *blanc de Chine* figure, Qianlong period, 1736–95, 9½in (24cm) high.
£1,400–1,600
€/ $2,200–2,500 ⊞ McP

A *famille rose* figure of an Immortal, restored, Qianlong period, 1736–95, 9¼in (23.5cm) high.
£320–350
€/ $475–550 ⊞ G&G

A celadon figure, Qianlong period, c1750, 5in (12.5cm) high.
£230–260
€/ $360–400 ⊞ McP

A *famille rose* figure of a jovial boy, kneeling, holding a pomegranate and a *ruyi* fungus, Jiaqing period, 1796–1820, 6¼in (16cm) high.
£320–350
€/ $480–550 ⚒ S(O)

◄ A *blanc de Chine* figure of Wenzhu, seated on a lion, holding the scroll of knowledge (*putsaka*) in his hand, minor chips, early 18thC, 7½in (19cm) wide.
£950–1,100
€/ $1,500–1,700 ⚒ TEN
Wenzhu is the Bodhisattva of Wisdom.

A pair of figures of the He-He Erxien, holding *ruyi* sceptres and other Buddhist objects, 18thC, 8in (20.5cm) high.
£250–300
€/ $400–475 ⚒ CGC
The He-He Erxien are the twin genii of mirth and harmony, and the patron deities of merchants, potters and lime burners.

Flatware

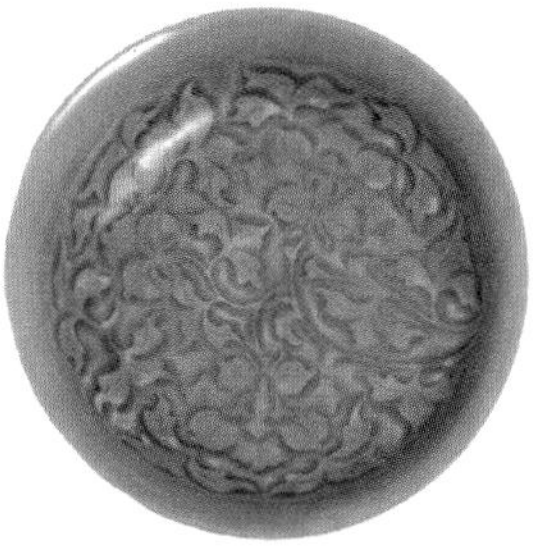

A celadon moulded dish, Northern Song Dynasty, 960–1127, 6in (15cm) diam.
£1,600–1,800
€/ $2,500–2,800 ⊞ GLD

A Junyao plate, with a flattened rim and covered with a thick glaze, 12th–13thC, 8¼in (21cm) diam.
£1,300–1,500
€/ $2,000–2,400 ⚒ S(O)

An offering dish, carved with a roundel of plum blossom encircled by the Eight Buddhist Emblems, early Ming Dynasty, 8¾in (22cm) diam.
£450–550
€/ $700–870 ⚒ S(O)
The Eight Buddhist Emblems or happy omens are the Chakra (wheel), the Conch Shell, the Umbrella, the Canopy, the Lotus, the Vase, the Pair of Fish and the Endless Knot.

A dish, damaged, 16thC, 14in (35.5cm) diam.
£600–670
€/ $950–1,000 ⊞ NAW

A dish, Jiajing period, 1522–66, 14in (35.5cm) diam.
£1,100–1,300
€/ $1,700–2,000 ⊞ GLD

Kraak porselein

In 1603 the Dutch captured the Portugese carrack *Santa Carterina*. Its cargo of fine porcelain, known as *kraak porselein*, was auctioned in Amsterdam amid great excitement. With the subsequent founding of the Dutch East India Company, there was a huge expansion in the export trade.

◄ A *kraak porselein* plate, Wanli period, c1600, 8in (20.5cm).
£600–700
€/ $950–1,100
⊞ McP

► A *kraak porselein* dish, damaged, Wanli period, c1600, 14in (35.5cm) diam.
£675–750
€/ $1,000–1,200 ⊞ McP

A *kraak porselein* dish, the centre decorated with a hanging flower basket with trailing roots, rivetted, 1610–25, 19in (48.5cm) diam.
£2,200–2,500
€/ $3,500–4,000 ⊞ AUA

A *kraak porselein* saucer, c1620, 4in (10cm) diam.
£225–250
€/ $350–400 ⊞ CHT

A 'Master of the Rocks' dish, painted with a man on land and two fishermen, on an inverted foot, Shunzhi period, 1644–61, 33½in (85cm) diam.
£2,500–3,000
€/ $4,000–4,700 S(O)
'Master of the Rocks' is a style of blue and white painting (usually showing rocks and mountains) of the Shunzi/early Kangxi period. The quality of pieces decorated in this style is always excellent.

A *famille verte* octagonal saucer, the border painted with flowering plants, Kangxi period, 1662–1722, 5in (12.5cm) diam.
£250–300
€/ $400–475 L

A pair of Chinese Imari armorial plates, 1710–20, 8½in (21.5cm) diam.
£700–800
€/ $1,100–1,300 McP

A *famille rose* plate, decorated with a boating scene, Qianlong period, 1736–95, 14¾in (37.5cm) wide.
£800–880
€/ $1,200–1,400 G&G

A *famille verte* dish, painted with figures on a café-au-lait ground, Kangxi period, 1662–1722, 11in (28cm) diam.
£280–320
€/ $440–500 McP

A *famille verte* plate, painted with flowers on a café-au-lait ground, Kangxi period, c1700, 8in (20.5cm) diam.
£100–125
€/ $160–200 DAN

A plate, with six-character Chengua mark, Kangxi period, c1720, 9in (23cm) diam.
£630–700
€/ $1,000–1,100 CHT

A pair of Chinese export *famille rose* plates, enamelled with European figures in a rural landscape within gilt floral borders, the rims decorated with fruit and flower sprays, Qianlong period, 1736–95, 9in (23cm) diam.
£1,600–2,000
€/ $2,500–3,200 B

A *famille verte* dish, painted with flowers, Kangxi period, 1662–1722, 11in (28cm) diam.
£1,300–1,500
€/ $2,000–2,400 GLD

A Chinese Imari plate, Kangxi period, c1710, 9in (23cm) diam.
£450–500
€/ $700–800 CHT

A soup plate, decorated with a coat-of-arms within a spearhead border, Qianlong period, c1740, 9in (23cm) diam.
£750–875
€/ $1,200–1,400 G(L)

A Chinese export octagonal plate, painted with two Continental armorials in a vase-shaped cartouche, within radiating lotus petals and a scale band, c1745, 8¼in (21cm) diam.
£1,300–1,500
€/ $2,000–2,400 LFA
This is a very rare item.

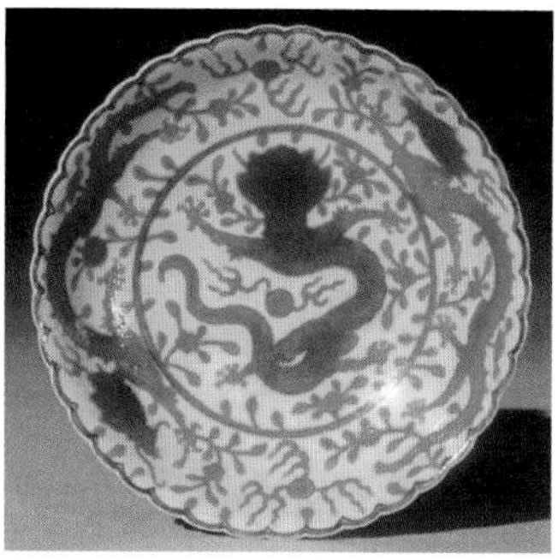

A dish, painted with a leaping dragon among scrolling foliage, encircled by two further dragons, Qianlong period, 1736–95, 5¼in (13.5cm) diam.
£3,800–4,500
€/ $6,000–7,100 S(HK)

A glazed plate, with six-character mark, Qianlong period, 1736–95, 9½in (24cm) diam.
£380–450
€/ $600–700 S(O)

A *famille rose* saucer dish, painted with long-tailed birds and peonies issuing from rockwork, Qianlong period, 1736–95, 8¾in (22cm) diam.
£170–200
€/ $270–320 G(L)

A Chinese export plate, the centre decorated with figures in a garden, c1770, 8in (20.5cm) diam.
£260–300
€/ $400–475 DAN

The Edward T. Chow & T. Y Chao Collections

The past 25 years have seen some spectacular sales of Chinese ceramics and works of art. Two of the most important were the Edward T. Chow collection, sold in three sales over 1980–81 and the T. Y. Chao collection, sold over 1986–87. Any piece from these collections will be greatly enhanced by its provenance.

Edward Chow (b1910) worked in a gallery in Shanghai and already had a small collection of Chinese ceramics by the age of 20. He met, and was influenced by, many famous western collectors, including Sir Percival David. After a brief spell in New York during WWII, Chow settled in 1949 in Hong Kong, where most of his collection was formed. He moved to Switzerland in 1966 and died in 1980. Chow kept an open mind in his collecting and, following the tenets of rarity, quality and perfection, would get just as excited by a Daoguong period (1821–50) tea bowl as he would a Xuande period (1426–35) stem cup.

T. Y. Chao was also a Hong Kong-based businessman with a good eye, keen interest and the financial means to form a major collection. His first interest was Qing Dynasty (1644–1911) Imperial porcelain, but his interests broadened to include Chinese ceramics and fine jades of all periods. His Ming Dynasty (1368–1644) Imperial Wares contained an extraordinary group of early 15th-century blue and white, which had been enhanced by purchases from the Edward T. Chow sale.

It will be many years before a private collector can build up a comparable collection, as so many items of this quality have now been acquired by museums and permanent collections. **Peter Wain**

A pair of fluted saucer dishes, painted with flowering plants issuing from rockwork, Qianlong period, 1736–95, 10in (25.5cm) diam.
£275–325
€/ $430–500 L

A Chinese export *famille rose* dinner plate, of European silver shape, minor damage, Qianlong period, c1770, 9¼in (23.5cm) diam.
£850–1,000
€/ $1,300–1,600 BUK

A meat plate, painted with a river landscape within Fitzhugh-style diaper pattern borders, minor chips, Qianlong period, 1736–95, 18½in (47cm) wide.
£170–200
€/ $270–320 BR

The Fitzhugh pattern is characterized by a border of four split pomegranates and butterflies and was made for the American market, being named after the person who first ordered it.

A *famille rose* meat dish, painted in enamels with leaves and flowers, heightened with gilt, 18thC, 13in (33cm) wide.
£1,200–1,500
€/ $1,900–2,400 TMA

◄ **A pair of dishes,** Jiaqing period, 1796–1820, 12in (30.5cm) wide.
£340–380
€/ $550–600 McP

Garden Seats

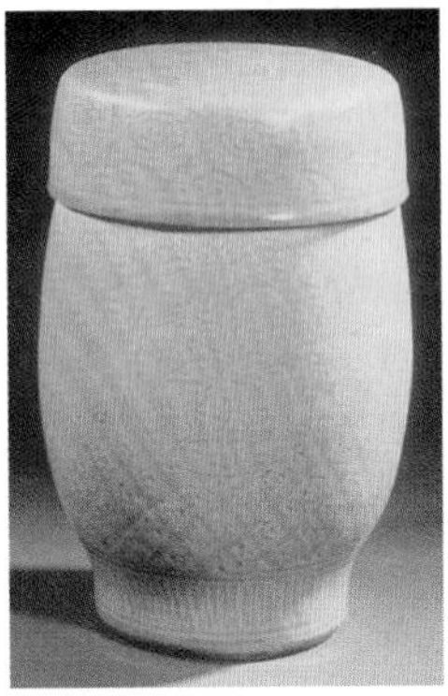

A celadon garden seat, carved with roundels of lotus reserved on a diaper ground, cracked, Ming Dynasty, 16thC, 15¾in (40cm) high.
£2,500–3,000
€/ $4,000–4,700 S(Am)

► **A reticulated *famille verte* garden seat,** painted with formal lotus scrolls and with moulded lion masks, between bands of *ruyi*-shaped collars decorated with lions, Kangxi period, 1662–1722, 19¾in (50cm) high.
£8,500–10,000
€/ $14,000–16,000 S(HK)
Surviving Kangxi garden seats are very rare – particularly decorated in 'Chinese taste' that is, not for export. This piece would appeal greatly to the Chinese mainland market.

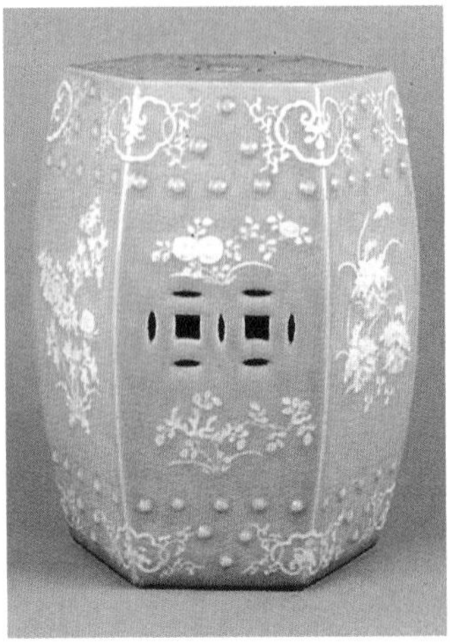

► **A Chinese export celadon hexagonal garden seat,** with raised enamel decoration, 19thC, 18½in (47cm) high.
£200–250
€/ $320–400 L

A pair of garden seats, painted with birds among flowers and rockwork within borders of reticulated medallions, scholar's objects and studs, Qing Dynasty, c1900, 18in (45.5cm) high.
£1,800–2,200
€/ $2,800–3,500 B

Jars

A glazed jar, with applied decoration, Tang Dynasty, 618–907, 4in (10cm) high.
£1,800–2,000
€/ $2,800–3,200 GLD

A glazed miniature jar, the two-tone clay with an even marbled effect, Tang Dynasty, 618–907, 3½in (9cm) high.
£250–300
€/ $400–475 S(O)

A Junyao jar, Jin Dynasty, 1115–1234, 5¼in (13.5cm) high.
£450–500
€/ $700–800 S(O)

A jar, painted with four dragons chasing flaming pearls below a *ruyi*-lappet collar, minor frits, Wanli period, 1573–1619, 5¼in (13.5cm) high.
£1,600–2,000
€/ $2,500–3,200 B

A *wucai* jar, decorated with Buddhist boys, minor damage and restoration, Chongzhen period, 1628–44, 9in (23cm) high.
£750–850
€/ $1,200–1,350 G&G

A baluster jar and cover, painted with three rows of landscape and garden scene panels beneath a foliate border, damaged, Kangxi period, 1662–1722, 22½in (57cm) high.
£1,000–1,200
€/ $1,600–1,900 Bri

A pair of *wucai* jars, c1670, 6½in (16.5cm) high.
£850–950
€/ $1,350–1,500 ⊞ CHT

► **A lidded jar,** from the *Vung Tau* cargo, c1700, 6in (15cm) high.
£400–450
€/ $630–700 ⊞ McP

A jar, the panels decorated with a musician, scholar and a lady beneath a diaper border, leaf mark, 17thC, 7in (18cm) high.
£350–400
€/ $550–630 ⚒ DN

A jar, the central fluted band decorated with four panels of scholars and a warrior, with a hardwood cover, Kangxi period, c1722, 9¼in (23.5cm) high.
£500–575
€/ $800–900 ⚒ G(L)

A jar, Qianlong/Jiaqing period, 1780–1820, 10in (20.5cm) high.
£420–460
€/ $670–725 ⊞ McP

◄ **A streaky-glazed jar,** of Han Dynasty bronze form, with applied loop handles, 19thC, 13in (33cm) high.
£350–400
€/ $550–630 ⚒ S(O)

A jar, decorated with figures, rocks and plantains, 19thC, 15½in (39.5cm) high.
£900–1,100
€/ $1,400–1,700 ⚒ DN

► **A *famille rose* jar and cover,** painted with a courtyard scene between borders of gilt raised protrusions, applied with mock mask ring handles, the cover with peach finial, Canton, 19thC, 8¼in (21cm) high.
£1,600–1,800
€/ $2,500–2,800 ⚒ S(Am)

◄ **A *wucai* jar and cover,** painted with flying horses, 19thC, 11¾in (30cm) high.
£700–800
€/ $1,100–1,300 ⚒ S(O)

Jugs

A jug and cover, of European shape, Qianlong period, c1750, 7in (18cm) high.
£550–620
€/ $850–1,000 ⊞ McP

A sparrow beak jug, 1775–1825, 4in (10cm) high.
£170–200
€/ $270–320 ⚒ SWO

A Chinese Imari jug and cover, the fluted body decorated with symmetrical foliate designs, cover and handle with original apertures for metal mounts, 18thC, 8¾in (22cm) high.
£300–350
€/ $475–550 ⚒ S(O)

Mugs & Tankards

◄ **A tankard,** painted with lotus, peony, chrysanthemum and prunus sprays, with curved strap handle, restored, Kangxi period, 1662–1722, 4in (10cm) high.
£650–750
€/ $1,000–1,200 ⚒ B

A Chinese export porcelain mug, with Mandarin-style panel, c1770, 5in (12.5cm) high.
£200–235
€/ $320–370 ⊞ DAN

A Compagnie des Indes tankard, painted in *famille rose* enamels with an urn and scattered sprigs, with entwined strap handle, Qianlong period, 1736–95, 6in (15cm) high.
£300–350
€/ $475–550 ⚒ G(B)

A gilt-decorated tankard, painted with classic lotus below a pair of lions and a brocade ball, Kangxi period, 1662–1722, 4½in (11.5cm) high.
£650–750
€/ $1,000–1,200 ⚒ S(O)

Items in the Chinese Ceramics section have been arranged in date order within each sub-section.

A *famille rose* mug, c1760, 5in (12.5cm) high.
£400–450
€/ $630–700 ⊞ DAN

A Chinese Imari porcelain tankard, painted with flowers and vases of peacock feathers, 19thC, 6in (15cm) high.
£120–140
€/ $190–220 ⚒ AH

Tea, Chocolate & Coffee Pots

An enamelled 'Cadogan' teapot, painted with a dignitary attended by two boys, the reverse with another official and two retainers, minor damage, c1640, 5½in (14cm) high.
£6,000–7,000
€/ $9,500–11,000 ⚒ TEN
This piece is rare because of its early date.

A *famille verte* teapot and cover, painted with a garden scene of birds and trees, Kangxi period, 1662–1722, 4in (10cm) high.
£600--700
€/ $950–1,100 ⚒ S(O)

Cadogan teapots

Earl Cadogan was the first Englishman to own a curiosity piece from China known as a 'wine pourer'. During the voyage from the east in the 18th century, these items were packed with tea to avoid damage, and therefore the British assumed these pots were used for brewing tea. Today, a Cadogan teapot refers to a type of lidless pot into which water is poured through a hole in the bottom and the pot is then quickly turned the right way up. An interior funnel prevents the water from leaking out through the hole.

A reticulated teapot and cover, painted with flowers, minor frits, Kangxi period, 1662–1722, 7in (18cm) wide.
£2,000–2,400
€/ $3,200–3,800 ⚒ G(L)

A Chinese Imari teapot, with white metal attachments, c1720, 6in (12.5cm) high.
£550–600
€/ $870–950 ⊞ CHT

◄ **A 'Cadogan' teapot,** Qianlong period, 1736–95, 5in (12.5cm) high.
£200–220
€/ $320–350 ⊞ McP

◄ **A Chinese Imari chocolate pot,** painted with flowers on a terrace, crack, cover restored, early 18thC, 6¾in (17cm) high.
£200–250
€/ $315–400 G(L)

► **A Chinese export chocolate pot and cover,** reserved with four panels of peonies on a daisy meander ground, c1735, 7¼in (18.5cm) high.
£1,500–1,800
€/ $2,400–2,800 S(NY)

Chocolate pots can be easily identified as the handle is at right angles to the spout.

A Compagnie des Indes *famille rose* coffee pot, decorated with figures in a landscape, chipped, Qianlong period, 1736–95, 10¼in (26cm) high.
£400–500
€/ $630–790 BERN

A teapot and cover, decorated in enamels with tobacco leaves, 18thC, 7¼in (18.5cm) diam.
£1,400–1,700
€/ $2,200–2,700 S(O)

A Yixing teapot and cover, with gilt-metal mounts, 18thC, 4½in (11.5cm) high.
£450–550
€/ $700–870 G(L)

A double teapot and covers, decorated with squirrels on grape vines, the reverse with a bird on willow trees, early 19thC, 5in (12.5cm) high.
£600–700
€/ $950–1,100 S(O)

Tureens

A pomegranate tureen, cover and stand, painted with a continuous landscape scene, with moulded stalk and twig handles, the cover moulded in high relief with three pomegranates, with lobed stand, Qianlong period, 1736–95, stand 9½in (24cm) diam.
£3,750–4,500
€/ $6,000–7,000 B

A Chinese export tureen, decorated in *famille rose* colours with European flowers, on shell feet, slight chips to glaze, wear to enamel, Qianlong period, 1736–95, 12½in (32cm) wide.
£1,400–1,600
€/ $2,200–2,500 BUK

A Meissen-style tureen and cover, decorated in *famille rose* colours with floral sprays, the cover with a crown finial and the base with Prince of Wales feather handles terminating in European masks, damaged and restored, Qianlong period, 1736–95, 15in (38cm) wide.
£4,300–4,800
€/ $6,700–7,500 ⊞ G&G

A tureen and cover, decorated in *famille rose* colours, enamelled with musicians and figures at leisure, cracked and rivetted, Qianlong period, 1736–95, 14in (35.5cm) wide.
£400–500
€/ $630–800 B(Kn)

A soup tureen and cover, decorated in *famille rose* colours with a pavilioned landscape, the pierced cover with a pineapple finial, with bracket handles, on a splayed foot, 18thC, 11½in (29cm) high.
£1,400–1,600
€/ $2,200–2,500 S(O)

A Chinese export porcelain tureen and cover, decorated with flowers, the cover with a rose knop, damaged and repaired, Qianlong period, 1736–95, 12½in (32cm) wide.
£1,000–1,200
€/ $1,600–1,900 BUK

Vases

A *cizhou* slip-painted vase, with a band of stylized foliage, a further band with lotus, between freely-drawn characters, Song/Yuan Dynasty, 13thC, 16¼in (41.5cm) high.
£1,000–1,200
€/ $1,600–1,900 ⚒ G(L)

A vase, painted on one side of the neck with an armoured figure on horse-back, a lady and a small child, a five-column poem inscribed below, rim crack, c1640, 18in (45.5cm) high.
£3,500–4,200
€/ $5,500–6,600 ⚒ B

A *yen yen* vase, Kangxi period, c1720, 9in (23cm) high.
£850–950
€/ $1,300–1,500 ⊞ CHT

A *meiping*, painted with classical lotus on undulating leafy stems, between lappets and cloud-head borders, Ming Dynasty, 16thC, 9in (23cm) high.
£650–800
€/ $1,000–1,300 ⚒ S(O)

A vase, painted with landscapes and fishermen, Transitional period, c1640, 10in (25.5cm) high.
£2,000–2,200
€/ $3,200–3,500 ⊞ GLD

A Chinese export bottle vase, with applied foliate and pierced handles, decorated with a band of birds on flowering branches and flower sprays, Kangxi period, 1662–1722, 9¾in (25cm) high.
£2,200–2,700
€/ $3,500–4,300 ⚒ DN

A stoneware vase, Ming Dynasty, 15th–16thC, 25in (63.5cm) high.
£1,600–1,800
€/ $2,500–2,800 ⊞ GLD

A *yen yen* vase, painted and lightly moulded with prunus branches reserved around the flowerheads with a blue wash, 1662–1722, 18½in (47cm) high.
£3,500–4,000
€/ $5,500–6,300 ⚒ G(L)
This vase is decorated with a very beautiful and rare design. Such a piece could sell for as much as £5,000–6,000, (€/ $7,900–9,500).

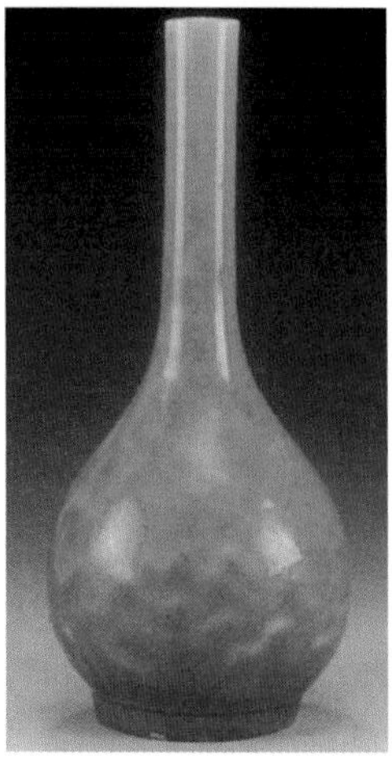

A Chinese Imari baluster vase and cover, painted with long-tailed birds on rockwork issuing peony, some cracks, finial incomplete, 17thC, 26in (66cm) high.
£1,400–1,600
€/ $2,200–2,500 ⚒ G(L)

A gilded vase, restoration to rim, Kangxi period, early 18thC, 17in (43cm) high.
£2,700–3,000
€/ $4,300–4,700 ⊞ GLD

A *famille verte* vase, Kangxi period, 1662–1722, 9½in (24cm) high.
£425–475
€/ $670–750 ⊞ McP

◄ A glazed bottle vase, with a tall neck, 18thC, 7¼in (18.5cm) high.
£500–550
€/ $800–870 ⚒ S(O)

A flambé-glazed bottle vase, with moulded bands around the waist and shoulder, surmounted by a ribbed neck with cupped mouth and lipped rim, on a spreading foot, Qianlong period, 1736–95, 14½in (37cm) high.
£3,200–3,700
€/ $5,000–6,000 ⚒ B

A baluster vase, decorated with landscape and pagoda scenes, the reverse with two boats, 18thC, 16in (40.5cm) high.
£250–300
€/ $400–475 ⚒ DMC

A pair of Transitional-style vases, each decorated with infant Buddhas running through lotus scrolls, with hardwood covers and stands, 19thC, 10½in (26.5cm) high.
£1,000–1,200
€/ $1,600–1,900 ⚒ RTo

A *ru*-style baluster vase, with canted corners, broad shoulder and waisted neck, restored chip, Qianlong period, 1736–95, 13¼in (33.5cm) high.
£2,000–2,500
€/ $3,200–4,000 ⚒ B

***Ru* is a thick, smooth, greenish-blue glaze first used in the Song Dynasty (960–1279) on Imperial wares from Henan Province.**

A flambé-glazed bottle vase, of garlic-clove form surmounted by a cylindrical neck, with flambé glaze, 18thC, 13¾in (35cm) high.
£1,700–1,900
€/ $2,700–3,000 ⚒ S(O)

A pair of porcelain bottle vases, each underglaze-painted with dragons among clouds and precious objects, 19thC, 25½in (65cm) high.
£800–1,000
€/ $1,300–1,600 ⚒ Bri

Chinese ceramics 1976–2002

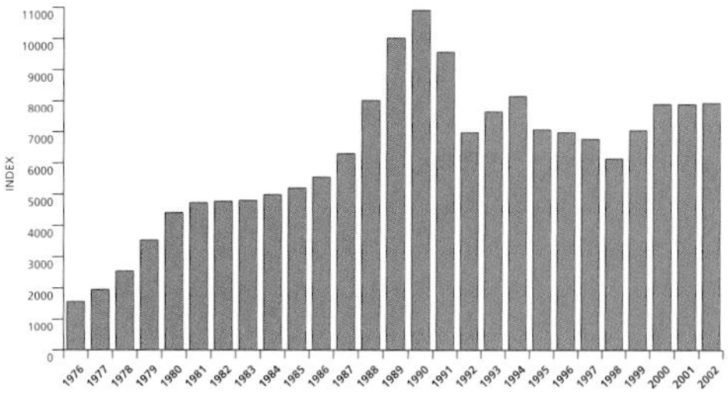

This graph shows how the value of Chinese ceramics as a whole has fluctuated over the past 25 years. Specific collecting areas such as tomb figures or Imperial porcelain of the Qing Dynasty will deviate from this graph. ©AMR

A baluster vase, with a slender neck, the incised and enamelled decoration depicting four figures with vases of flowers and butterflies, handles damaged, Canton, 18thC, 9¼in (23.5cm) high.
£80–100
€/ $125–160 ⚒ TMA

A pair of celadon-glazed vases, of fluted chrysanthemum shape with bulbous necks, applied with stylized handles, 19thC, 8in (20.5cm) high.
£1,400–1,600
€/ $2,200–2,500 ⚒ S(Am)

A square-section vase, each face decorated with watery landscapes, 1800–50, 14¼in (36cm) high.
£1,400–1,600
€/ $2,200–2,500 ⚒ WW

A flambé vase, decorated in *famille rose* colours, with flowers issuing from rockwork, 19thC, 16¼in (41.5cm) high.
£650–750
€/ $1,000–1,200 ⚒ S(O)

► **A pair of panelled vases,** decorated in enamel with Oriental figures on a bridge and in garden landscapes, 19thC, 22in (56cm) high.
£550–650
€/ $870–1,000 ⚒ JAd

A *hu*-shaped vase, decorated in *famille rose* colours, painted with figures in various pursuits, with side handles, 19thC, 10¾in (27.5cm) high.
£475–575
€/ $750–900 WW
A *hu* is a bronze vessel for ritual use.

A pair of baluster vases, with flared rims and gilt handles, painted with a travelling sage, on a ground of birds and butterflies, among floral sprays, Canton, 19thC, 8¾in (22cm) high.
£320–375
€/ $500–600 Mit

◄ **A vase,** painted in *famille rose* colours with travellers and fishermen in a lakeside setting, the neck inscribed with a poem, the base with a seal mark, early 20thC, 8in (20.5cm) high.
£2,200–2,700
€/ $3,500–4,300 S(HK)

◄ **A baluster vase and cover,** painted with scrolling floral designs, between formal borders, the cover with a dog of *Fo* finial, 19thC, 19¼in (49cm) high.
£100–125
€/ $160–200 PFK

A pair of vases, relief-decorated with lizards and dogs of *Fo*, buds and garden landscapes, Canton, 1875–1925, 22in (56cm) high.
£275–320
€/ $430–500 DD

◄ **An earthenware baluster vase,** with low-relief geometric and floral decoration in enamels, impressed character mark, early 20thC, 17¼in (44cm) high.
£130–150
€/ $200–240 AMB

Miscellaneous

A Chinese Imari fishbowl or jardinière, the interior decorated with fish, the exterior with the Three Friends of Winter, some damage, 17th–18thC, 15¼in (38.5cm) diam.
£1,000–1,200
€/ $1,600–1,900 B(Kn)
In Chinese culture, the Three Friends of Winter are prunus (wild plum), pine and bamboo, all emblems of longevity. They are also symbolic of the qualities of a gentleman – Prunus: good looks and independence; Pine: constancy of friendship in a time of adversity; Bamboo: durability, integrity and loyalty. They are also symbolic of the three religions of China: Daoism, Buddhism and Confucianism.

A Chinese export *famille rose* tea canister and cover, c1760, 5½in (14cm) high.
£300–340
€/ $475–500 DAN

► **A *blanc-de-Chine* wine pot and cover,** applied with two writhing *chilong*, one forming the handle, the other forming the spout, the cover surmounted by a pierced coiled *chilong*, chips and star crack to base, 17thC, 5¼in (13.5cm) high.
£1,800–2,200
€/ $2,800–3,500 B

A Kangxi wine kettle, with metal mounts to the handle, c1710, 9in (23cm) high.
£900–1,000
€/ $1,400–1,600 CHT

Japanese Ceramics

Japanese chronology chart

Jomon (Neolithic) period	c10,000–100 BC	Muromachi (Ashikaga) period	1333–1568
Yayoi period	c200 BC–AD 200	Momoyama period	1568–1600
Tumulus (Kofun) period	200–552	Edo (Tokugawa) period	1600–1868
Asuka period	552–710	*Genroku period*	*1688–1703*
Nara period	710–794	Meiji period	1868–1911
Heian period	794–1185	Taisho period	1912–1926
Kamakura period	1185–1333	Showa period	1926–1989

Bowls

An Arita bowl, c1700–30, 5½in (14cm) diam.
£420–460
€/ $650–720 ⊞ McP

A Kakiemon-style bowl, with everted iron-oxide rim, decorated with additional enamels and gilt with birds and flowers, marked *'kin'*, 18thC, 9½in (24cm) diam.
£775–900
€/ $1,200–1,400 S(O)

An Imari barber's bowl, decorated in underglaze blue, iron-red and gold, late 18thC, 10¾in (27.5cm) diam.
£525–625
€/ $830–1,000 B(WM)

► **A Satsuma bowl,** the interior depicting the story of The Moon and The Moor, Meiji period, c1890, 5in (12.5cm) diam.
£1,400–1,500
€/ $2,200–2,400 ⊞ AUA
The Moon and The Moor relates the story of two brothers, Yasuma, the flute player and Kidomaru, the outlaw.

A bowl, decorated in Imari palette, three-character mark on the base, Arita, c1900, 9½in (24cm) diam.
£950–1,100
€/ $1,500–1,700 BUK
This well-known group of bowls decorated with ships was produced in Arita for export, c1900–10.

Cups

◄ **An Imari tea bowl and saucer,** damaged, c1730, saucer 5in (12.5cm) diam.
£60–70
€/ $95–110 ⊞ McP

For further information on
Eggshell porcelain see page 330

► **A cased set of six eggshell porcelain coffee cans and saucers,** early 20thC, case 15in (38cm) wide.
£180–220
€/ $280–350
BR

Miller's Compares

I. A pair of Kakiemon cups, painted with flowers in iron-red and enamels, 18thC, 2½in (6.5cm) diam.
£1700–2,000
€/ $2,700–3,200 S(O)

II. A Kakiemon tea bowl, painted in enamels with flying birds and flowers emerging behind rocks, 18thC, 4in (10cm) diam.
£500–600
€/ $800–950 S(O)

Naturally, a pair is likely to be worth more than a single item, but Item I had the advantage over Item II by also being of a more pleasing shape. The decoration of Item I is also classic Kakiemon, a plus-point with collectors. Furthermore, a footnote included with Item I referred to a similar piece and therefore made it attributable to one that was already well-documented.

Dishes

A pair of Kakiemon-style dishes, 1662–1722, 6in (15cm) square.
£2,200–2,500
€/ $3,500–4,000 ⊞ McP

An Imari dish, 19thC, 6in (15cm) wide.
£100–120
€/ $160–190 ⊞ McP

► An Imari dish, late 19thC, 18½in (47cm) wide.
£180–220
€/ $280–350 CHTR

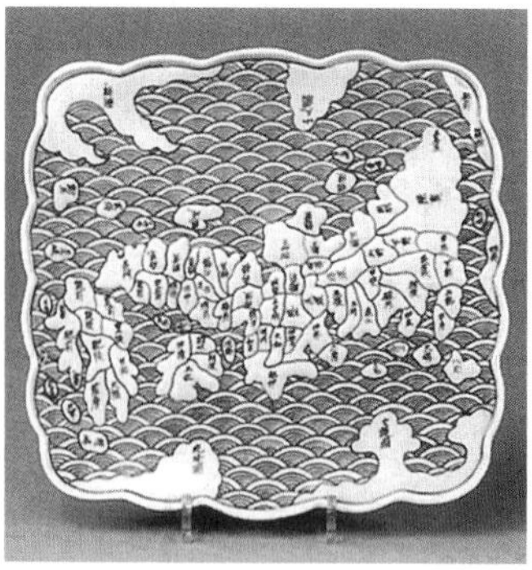

An Arita map dish, decorated in relief with a map of Japan, the sea in a stylized fish-scale pattern, dated 1830, 12½in (32cm) wide.
£900–1,000
€/ $1,400–1,600 S(O)
These dishes are decorated with a popular pattern on imported Japanese porcelain 1830–40. They were a production of Arita ware and were produced mainly by the Kama-no-tani kiln.

Figures

A pair of Imari figures of actors, wearing robes decorated with morning glory, c1700, 17¾in (45cm) high.
£4,500–5,000
€/ $7,000–7,900 S(O)
These export figures are very popular with decorators. Often damaged, this pair appears to be perfect and of a good size.

◄ An Imari figure of a *bijin*, her kimono painted with flower branches and meander diaper patterns, restoration to foot, 19thC, 18¾in (47.5cm) high.
£1,200–1,400
€/ $1,900–2,200 S(Am)

A Satsuma group of a young woman and her child, with enamel decoration, early 20thC, 5½in (14cm) high.
£475–575
€/ $750–900 RTo

Flatware

An Imari dish, the centre painted with a Mandarin duck, 17th/18thC, 8½in (21.5cm) diam.
£200–240
€/ £300–380 G(L)

An Arita Ko-Imari-style dish, early 18thC, 5in (12.5cm) diam.
£380–420
€/ $600–670 ⊞ McP

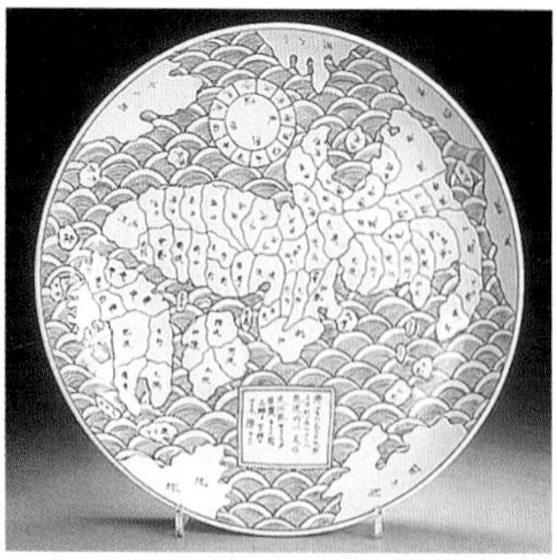

A map dish, moulded in relief with the map of Japan, each of the provinces named, with a wind dial and the signs of the Zodiac, spurious six-character mark, 1830–44, 18in (45.5cm) diam.
£2,500–3,000
€/ $4,000–4,700 S(Am)
This map dish is rare because of the addition of the Zodiac signs.

A charger, the underglaze blue central *mon* framed with an Imari panel, decorated with pheasants and prunus blossoms, 19thC, 16¼in (41.5cm) diam.
£160–200
€/ $250–300 ⚒ BR

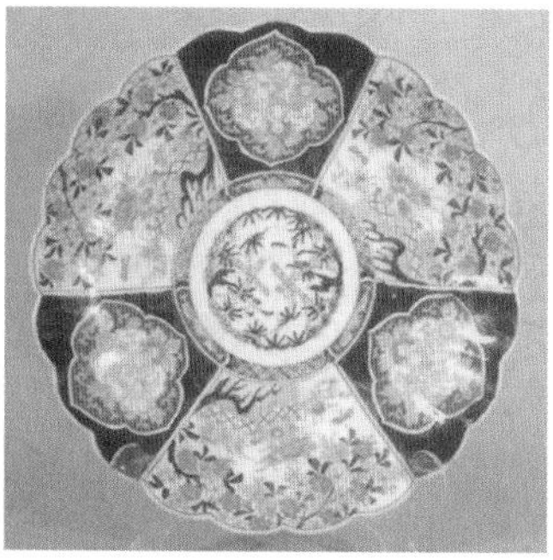

An Imari charger, late 19thC, 14¾in (37.5cm) diam.
£130–160
€/ $200–250 ⚒ PFK

◄ A pair of chargers, decorated with carp, early 20thC, 18in (45.5cm) diam.
£800–900
€/ $1,300–1,400 ⚒ S(O)
Although quite late, these chargers are very attractive and therefore desirable to decorators as well as collectors, which results in this high price.

A Fukugawa porcelain charger, decorated in underglaze blue, coloured enamels and gilding, with bamboo, irises and flowering shrubs, the reverse with sprays of flowers, signed, Meiji period, 1868–1911, 18¾in (47.5cm) diam.
£320–375
€/ $500–600 ⚒ F&C
Fukugawa was a family of potters in Arita with a distinctive style of work.

Jars

A pair of Imari jars and covers, one cover restored, c1690, 15¼in (38.5cm) high.
£950–1,200
€/ $1,500–1,800 ⚒ BERN

An Imari jar and cover, painted and gilt with chrysanthemum, the shoulders with a band of floral branches, with a bud finial, 18thC, 21in (53cm) high.
£3,500–4,000
€/ $5,300–6,300 ⚒ S(Am)

A pair of Imari jars and covers, painted and gilt with peonies and prunus, with inner lids, 19thC, 7¾in (19.5cm) high.
£220–250
€/ $350–400 ⚒ PFK

A Satsuma earthenware jar, decorated with a procession of figures including *samurai* and *geisha* among musicians and dancers, between bands of dragons and formal designs incorporating the Satsuma *mon*, signed *Hosen zo*, Meiji period, 1868–1911, 11½in (29cm) high.
£1,300–1,500
€/ $2,000–2,400 ⚒ S(O)

Koros

A koro and cover, the knop modelled as a *shishi*, signed 'Kinkozan', Meiji period, 1868–1911, 4¼in (11cm) high.
£1,000–1,200
€/ $1,600–1,900 ⚒ S(O)

A koro and metal cover, painted with chrysanthemums, signed 'Hododa', Meiji period, 1868–1911, 4¼in (11cm) high.
£1,700–2,000
€/ $2,700–3,200 ⚒ S(O)

An Imari koro and cover, the segmented cover with piercing and a Dog of *Fo* knop, handles glued, 19thC, 11¾in (30cm) high.
£140–160
€/ $220–250 ⚒ B(W)

A Satsuma earthenware koro and cover, hand-painted and gilded, on three mask-form feet, signed, c1900, 6¾in (17cm) high.
£375–450
€/ $600–700 ⚒ AMB

Tea & Coffee Services

A tea service, comprising 22 pieces, detailed in enamels and gilt with six scenes of birds in seasonal settings, signed 'Senzan', Meiji period, 1868–1911, teapot 4in (10cm) high.
£600–720
€/ $950–1,100 ⚒ S(O)

► **An eggshell porcelain tea service,** comprising 21 pieces, painted with battle scenes, early 20thC, tray 18¼in (46.5cm) square.
£300–350
€/ $475–550 ⚒ PFK

A cased Satsuma tea service, comprising 18 pieces, painted with Thousand Lohan pattern, with dragon handles and cover knops, signed 'Ariyama', Satsuma *mon* marks, early 20thC.
£320–375
€/ $500–600 ⚒ CGC

Eggshell porcelain

Japanese porcelain tea services, often eggshell thin, were produced in their many thousands during the period 1900–1920. Always highly decorative and of good quality, they were the most popular souvenir purchase of merchant seamen visiting the Far East. Almost every family in Europe with sea-faring traditions owns the remnants of such a service. A complete service should contain a teapot, milk jug, sugar pot, six tea cups and saucers, six side plates and two bread/cake plates. The service was sold in a fitted box. A complete undamaged boxed set is worth about £300 (€/ $475), whereas an individual tea cup and saucer is worth about £10 (€/ $15) or £15 (€/ $24) if a geisha girl can be seen through the base of the cup.

Vases

◄ **An Arita vase,** c1690, 16in (40.5cm) high.
£600–680
€/ $950–1,100 ⊞ McP

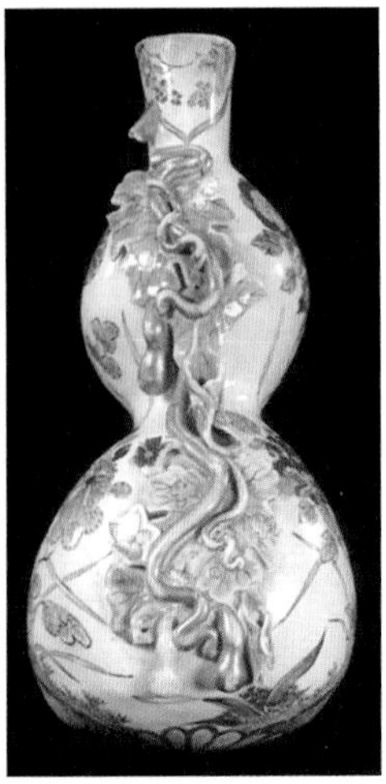

An Imari wall vase, modelled as a double gourd with applied leaves and tendrils, painted in enamels and gilt with floral designs, early 18thC, 8¼in (21cm) high.
£1,800–2,000
€/ $2,800–3,200 ⚒ S(O)

A Satsuma vase, by the Kinkozan Studio, signed 'Sozan', Meiji period, 1868–1911, 4in (10cm) high.
£3,700–4,200
€/ $6,000–6,600 ⊞ MER

An Arita bottle vase, decorated with flowerheads and bamboo leaves, early 18thC, 2½in (6.5cm) high.
£350–400
€/ $550–650 ⊞ AUA

A pair of Satsuma earthenware vases, enamelled and gilt with chrysanthemum sprays, figures within landscapes to either side, painted marks, Meiji period, 1868–1911, 4¾in (12cm) high.
£80–100
€/ $125–160 ⚒ WL

► **A Satsuma vase,** decorated with panels of landscapes, signed 'Kinkozan', Meiji period, 1868–1911, 5in (12.5cm) high.
£2,500–2,800
€/ $4,000–4,500 ⊞ MER

A pair of Satsuma vases, decorated with Samurai warriors and ladies, maker's mark and Satsuma *mon*, late 19thC, 14½in (37cm) high.
£400–500
€/ $630–800 ⚒ SWO

A Satsuma earthenware vase, with a short waisted neck, decorated with circular emblems, late 19thC, 5in (12.5cm) high.
£140–160
€/ $220–250 Bea(E)

► A Satsuma vase, decorated with quails, signed, impressed mark for Taizan, Meiji period, c1890, 13in (33cm) high.
£2,000–2,200
€/ $3,200–3,500 AUA

A Kutani vase, decorated with panels of figures and flowers, with a spreading neck and *shishi* handles, late 19thC, 10¼in (26cm) high.
£140–160
€/ $220–250 WW

An Imari porcelain vase, with a flared rim, decorated with exotic birds and foliage, late 19thC, 25½in (65cm) high.
£700–850
€/ $1,100–1,300 DMC

◄ A pair of Satsuma earthenware vases, decorated with scholars, early 20thC, 10in (25.5cm) high.
£130–150
€/ $200–240 SWO

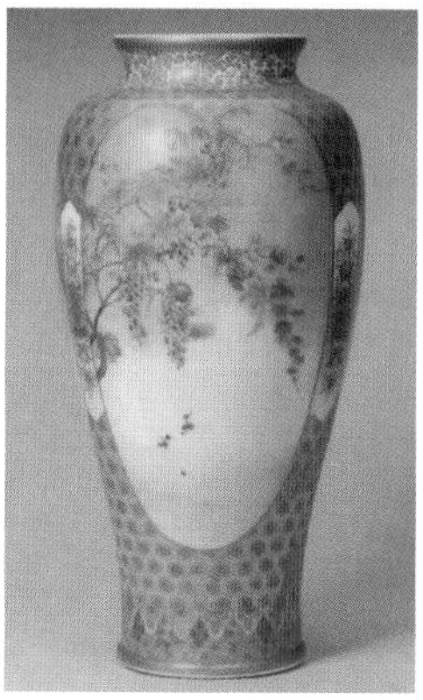

◄ A Satsuma vase, decorated with three panels depicting blossoming branches, on a ground of hexagonal geometric motifs, signed 'Kinkozan', c1912, 23¼in (59cm) high.
£4,000–4,800
€/ $6,300–7,500 B

Miscellaneous

A Satsuma earthenware belt buckle, c1900, 1¾in (4.5cm) diam.
£80–100
€/ $120–160 DuM

A Satsuma model of a cottage, with hens on the roof, c1900, 7in (18cm) wide.
£1,500–1,700
€/ $2,400–2,700 GLD

A pair of European-decorated Arita wine flasks, the sides printed with four chinoiserie scenes, damaged, late 17thC, 8½in (21.5cm) high.
£550–625
€/ $870–1,000 TEN

A Satsuma jardinière, decorated with butterflies among flowers, painted signature, 1875–1925, 9¾in (25cm) high.
£320–375
€/ $500–600 SWO

An Arita oil or vinegar jug, from a condiment set, made for the Dutch market, 1710–20, 4in (10cm) high.
£470–520
€/ $750–830 McP

An Arita teapot and cover, painted with a European wooded landscape with buildings and passing travellers, damage, c1700, 4¼in (11cm) high.
£3,000–3,500
€/ $4,700–5,500 B
This is a rare piece and attractively decorated.

Glass

Exhibitions, books and the dispersal of notable collections can have marked effects on the appreciation and demand for particular categories of decorative antiques, and glass has proved no exception over the past 25 years. The publication of new literature generates an understanding, appreciation and interest among collectors that boosts demand and inflates prices. The popularity of 18th-century English drinking-glasses rose sharply after the sales of the Smith Collection in 1967–68, waned during the 1980s, rallied after the appearance in 1987 of L. M. Bickerton's *Eighteenth Century Drinking Glasses* and is currently at a new peak. Interest in British glass made between the wars, initially stimulated by an exhibition in 1987 at the Broadfield House Glass Museum, near Stourbridge, continues to grow.

The irony particular to glass is that most collectors remain narrowly focused. For example, 18th-century drinking glasses, lighting pieces, scent bottles and Victorian rock crystal and cameo are extremely sought after, and Irish pieces command prices disproportionate to English equivalents of superior quality. However, a vast majority of old glass remains relatively cheap and available. The most obvious laggard is cut-glass, the British and Irish speciality, which remains widely neglected. Others include 18th-century jellies, syllabubs, sweetmeats and salts, most 19th-century glassware including drinking glasses, and almost all decanters. It is hard to predict whether interest in these will rise although, as wine consumption increases, decanters might be considered a hot tip for the future.

The greatest complicating factor when attempting to predict future values is the general health of the economy. For example, the financial problems that have afflicted Germany for the past decade have undermined demand for all central European antiques, including Bohemian glass.

In the coming decades 20th-century British cut glass might be expected to rise ahead of the market. Most examples bear a maker's mark, and the stark and stylized contemporary designs are well suited to modern homes. It is already fetching prices that would have been laughed at just a decade ago. **Andy McConnell**

Ale, Spirit & Wine Glasses

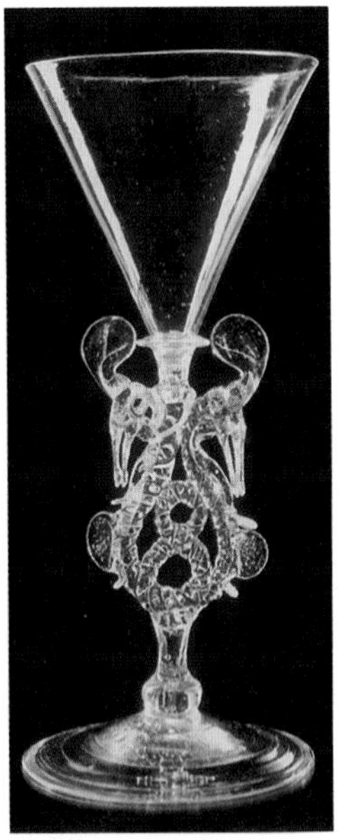

A *façon de Venise* winged goblet, the conical bowl over an openwork stem, the interlaced section inset with coloured spiralling threads applied with pinched ornament, the coiled tubing terminating in pincered serpent-style heads, above a baluster section and a conical foot, probably Lowlands, c1680, 7¼in (18.5cm) high.
£2,000–2,200
€/ $3,200–3,500 ⚒ S

► A *latticinio* wine glass, the bowl set on a multi-knopped stem with mereses above and below, the bowl and foot composed of *vetro a retorti* with repeated gauze cable, lace and spiral-thread ribs, the stem with *vetro a fili*, Venetian, 17thC, 5½in (14cm) high.
£1,700–2,000
€/ $2,700–3,200 ⚒ B

A baluster wine glass, the bell bowl with a solid teared base, on a plain teared stem with an annular shoulder knop and a basal knop, on a folded foot, c1725, 6¼in (16cm) high.
£1,200–1,300
€/ $1,900–2,000 ⊞ GS

A *façon de Venise* wine glass, the conical bowl over a hollow baluster stem, with a folded foot, traces of glass disease, Swedish, Kungsholm, 1675–1700, 6¾in (17cm) high.
£500–575
€/ $800–900 ⚒ BUK
Glass disease is also called 'crizzling'. It is caused by poorly prepared ingredients and results in an irreparable maze of silvery cracks in the glass.

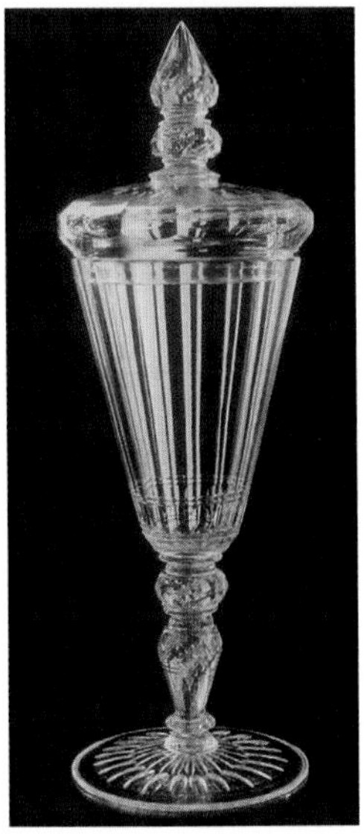

◄ A goblet and cover, the facet-cut bowl over a faceted knopped stem and inverted baluster section, all enclosing spiralling threads, on a conical foot with a rosette-cut base, the domed cover with a knopped finial inset with spiralling threads, Bohemian, 1720–30, 11½in (29cm) high.
£2,300–2,700
€/ $3,600–4,300 ⚒ S

The Parkington Collection

It was not long ago that interest in antique glassware was limited to up until the end of the Regency period. The sale in 1997 and 1998 at Christie's of Michael Parkington's vast glass collection helped shatter this date boundary. Parkington started by collecting 18th-century drinking glasses but gradually shifted his interest to Victorian and Edwardian cut, engraved, coloured and pressed glass. He also collected 20th-century pieces by Whitefriars, Keith Murray, Gray-Stan and Monart. The results of the sale provided benchmark prices for the public and trade, and spurred further interest in the subject.

Tales of Parkington's acquisitive fever remain legendary, with almost as many pieces jokingly said to have been housed under his floorboards as displayed on his shelves. Yet glass collecting inspired a passion within him that provided a sanctuary from his life as an international lawyer whose clients included the incarcerated Nelson Mandela. **Andy McConnell**

A wine glass, the trumpet bowl with a swelling shoulder teared knop, on a plain drawn stem, with a folded conical foot, c1730, 6¼in (16cm) high.
£235–260
€/ $370–400 ⊞ Som

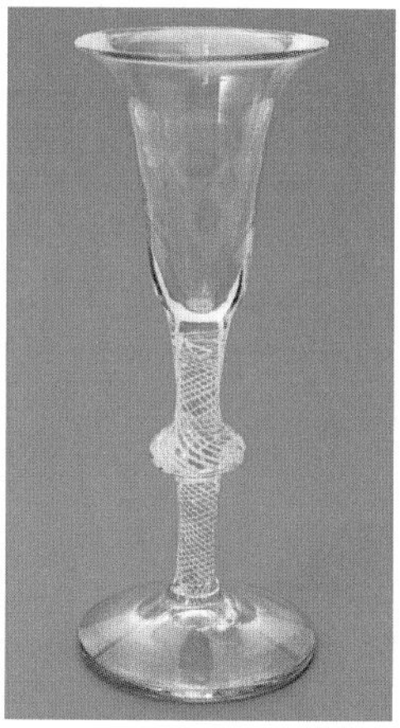

A wine glass, the bell bowl with a knopped spiral air-twist stem, on a conical foot, c1750, 6½in (16.5cm) high.
£400–440
€/ $630–700 ⊞ PSA

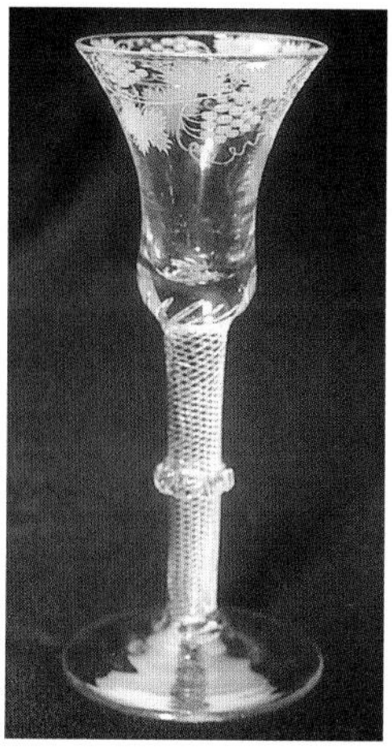

A wine glass, the bell bowl engraved with a band of fruiting vine, on a multi-spiral air-twist stem with a vermicular collar, on a conical foot, c1750, 6½in (16.5cm) high.
£550–600
€/ $870–950 ⊞ Som

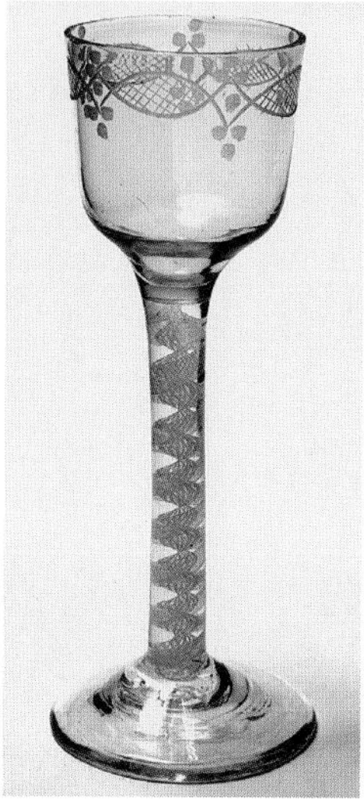

A wine glass, with an engraved bowl above an opaque twist stem, c1750, 6in (15cm) high.
£200–225
€/ $320–350 ⊞ CHAC

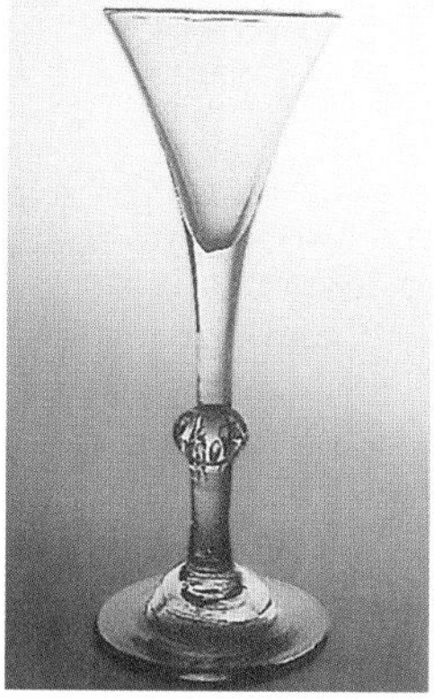

A Kit-Kat wine glass, with a drawn trumpet bowl, the stem with a beaded knop, on a domed foot, c1730, 7¼in (18.5cm) high.
£750–875
€/ $1,200–1,400 ⚒ LFA

These glasses are so-named because they are of a type seen in Sir Geoffrey Kneller's early 18th-century paintings of London's Kit-Kat Club.

A wine glass, with a drawn trumpet, on a plain stem, with a folded foot, c1730, 7in (18cm) high.
£160–180
€/ $250–290 ⊞ JHa

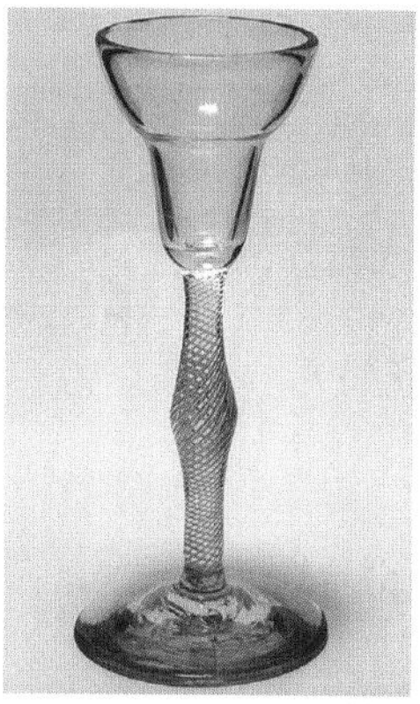

► **A cordial glass,** with a pan-top funnel bowl, over a multiple-series air-twist stem with a swollen central knop, c1750, 5½in (14cm) high.
£500–600
€/ $790–950 ⊞ BrW

A light baluster wine glass, the bell bowl on a swelling knop, over an inverted baluster and basal-knop stem, on a conical foot, c1750, 7¼in (18.5cm) high.
£950–1,100
€/ $1,500–1,700 ⊞ GS

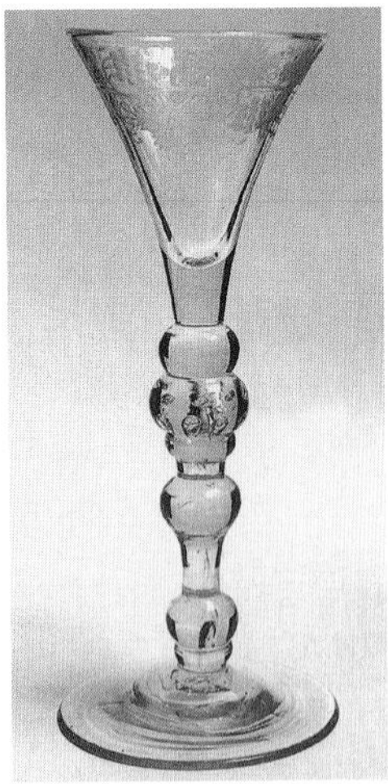

A light baluster wine glass, the trumpet bowl engraved with a band of fruiting vine, on a multi-knopped stem, on a conical foot, c1750, 7in (18cm) high.
£1,300–1,400
€/ $2,100–2,500 ⊞ GS

A wine glass, the funnel bowl with basal fluting, on a double-knopped multi-spiral air-twist stem, c1750, 5½in (14cm) high.
£420–465
€/ $670–730 ⊞ WMa

► A Dutch-engraved light baluster goblet, the round funnel bowl engraved with arms of four lions rampant, beneath a coronet and flanked by lion supporters, on a bobbin-knopped stem, the central knop filled with bead inclusions, on a conical foot, small chip, c1750, 7½in (19cm) high.
£2,000–2,200
€/ $3,200–3,500 ⚒ DN

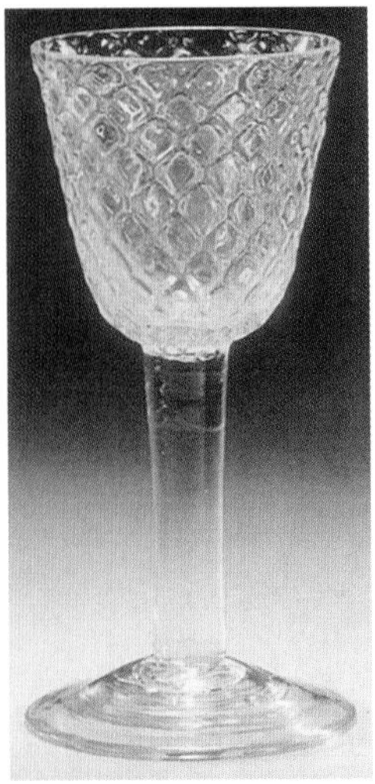

A wine glass, the honeycomb-moulded funnel bowl on a plain stem, on a conical foot, c1755, 6½in (16.5cm) high.
£600–700
€/ $950–1,100 ⚒ S(O)

◄ An ale flute, the panel-moulded bowl on a double-series air-twist stem, c1760, 8in (20.5cm) high.
£1,000–1,200
€/ $1,600–1,900 ⊞ WMa

A wine glass, the round funnel bowl engraved with a rose, two buds and a moth, on a multi-spiral air-twist double-knopped stem, c1750, 6¼in (16cm) high.
£850–950
€/ $1,300–1,500 ⊞ BrW

An ale flute, the deep round funnel bowl on a double-series opaque-twist stem, on a conical foot, c1760, 8in (20.5cm) high.
£350–400
€/ $550–630 ⊞ Som

A wine glass, the drawn trumpet bowl with a multi-spiral air-twist composite stem and a beaded short inverted baluster, on a domed foot, c1750, 7in (18cm) high.
£775–900
€/ $1,200–1,400 ⚒ S(O)

A wine glass, the rounded funnel bowl over an inverted baluster knop and cylindrical stem, on a domed spreading folded foot, c1755, 5¾in (14.5cm) high.
£260–300
€/ $400–475 ⊞ PSA

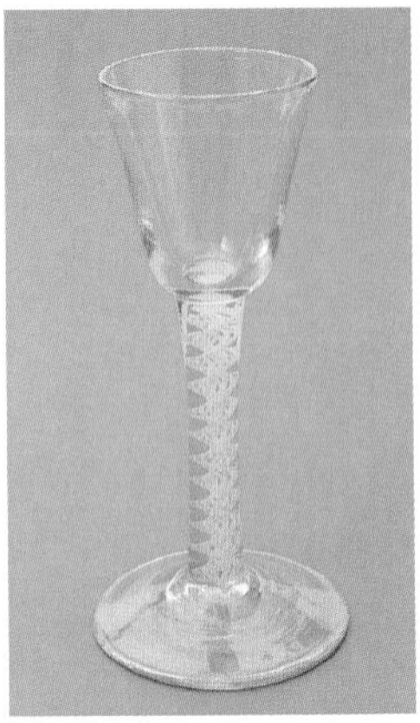

A glass, the funnel bowl with a double-series opaque air-twist stem, on a conical foot, c1760, 5½in (14cm) high.
£300–330
€/ $475–515 ⊞ PSA

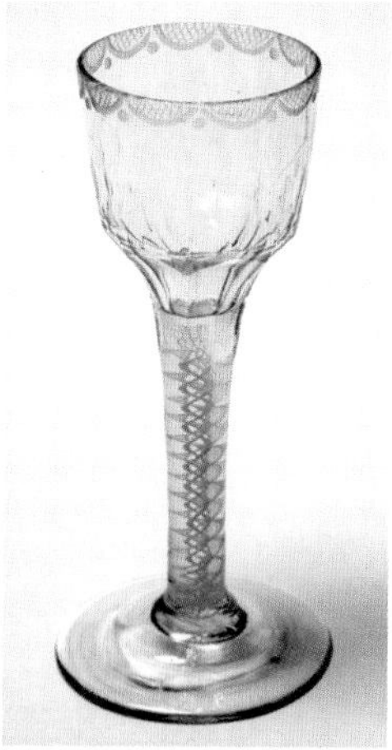

A wine glass, the bowl with a swag-engraved lip, on an opaque double-twist stem, c1760, 5¾in (14.5cm) high.
£400–450
€/ $630–710 ⊞ CHAC

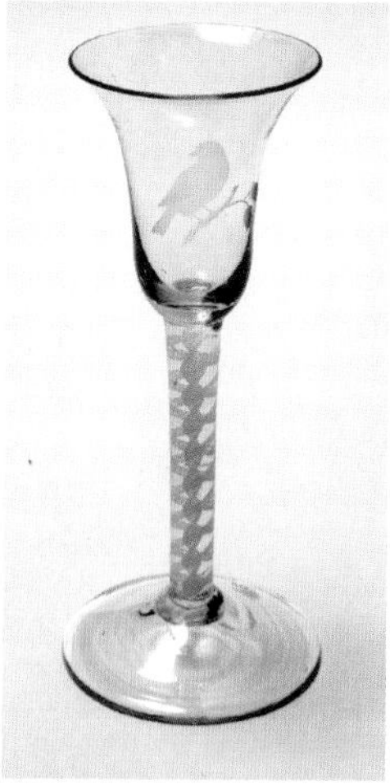

A wine glass, the bowl engraved with a bird, on an air-twist stem, c1760, 5¾in (14.5cm) high.
£360–400
€/ $550–630 ⊞ CHAC

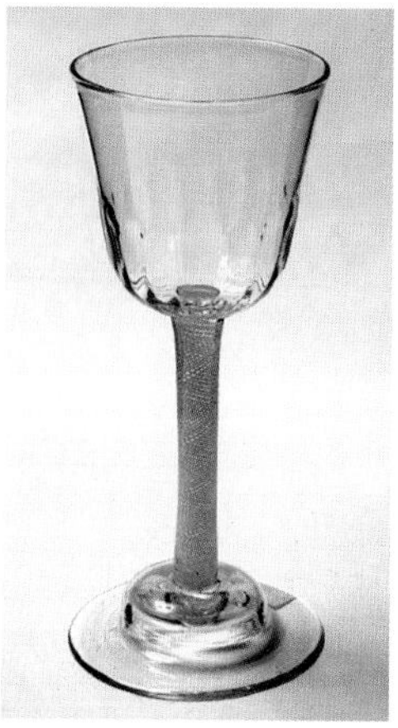

A wine glass, the moulded bowl on a single-series opaque-twist stem, and domed foot, c1765, 6in (15cm) high.
£630–700
€/ $1,000–1,100 ⊞ Del

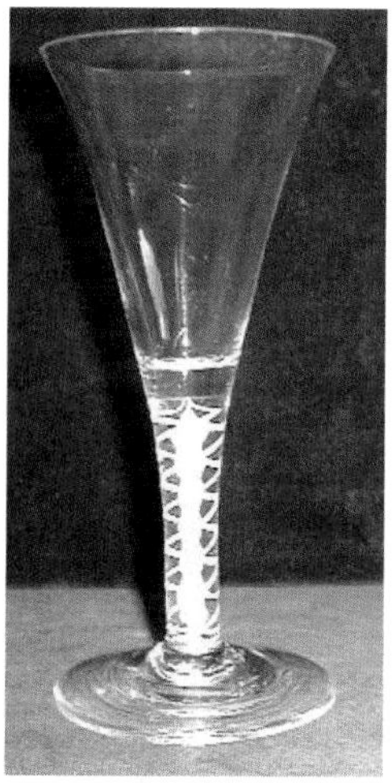

A wine glass, the drawn trumpet bowl on an opaque-twist stem, c1760, 7½in (17.5cm) high.
£280–320
€/ $440–500 ⊞ BrW

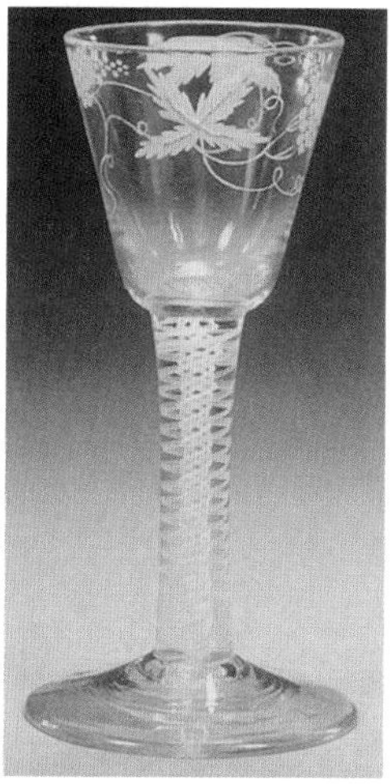

A Beilby enamelled wine glass, the funnel bowl painted with fruiting vine, on a double-series opaque-twist stem, on a conical foot, c1765, 6in (15cm) high.
£1,800–2,000
€/ $2,800–3,200 ⚒ S(O)

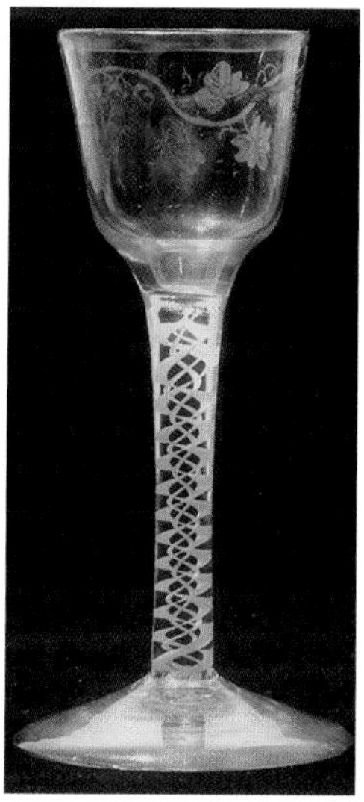

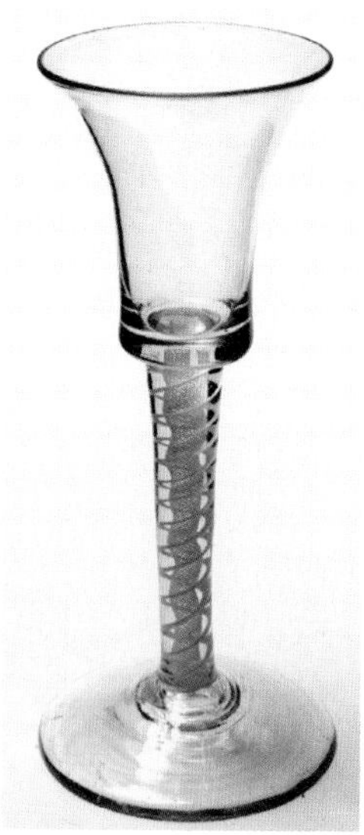

A wine glass, with an opaque double-twist stem, c1760, 6¾in (17cm) high.
£315–350
€/ $480–550 ⊞ CHAC

► **A wine glass,** the bucket bowl on a double-series opaque-twist and gauze stem, with a conical foot, c1765, 5½in (14cm) high.
£265–300
€/ $420–475 ⊞ PSA

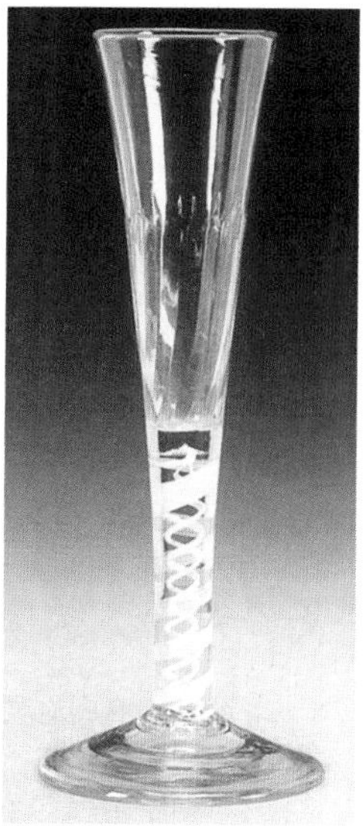

A ratafia flute, the conical bowl with rib-moulding on a double-series opaque-twist stem, with a conical foot, c1765, 7¼in (18.5cm) high.
£1,200–1,400
€/ $1,900–2,200 ⚒ S(O)

◄ **A wine glass,** the ogee bowl gilt-decorated in the Giles Workshop, with trailing fruiting vines, with a gilt rim, on an opaque-twist stem with two spiral threads enclosed by two corkscrew twists, on a conical foot, 1765–68, 6in (15cm) high.
£900–1,100
€/ $1,400–1,700 ⚒ B

A wine goblet, on a multi-spiral opaque-twist stem with a shoulder and base knop, c1760, 7in (18cm) high.
£800–875
€/ $1,300–1,400 ⊞ WMa

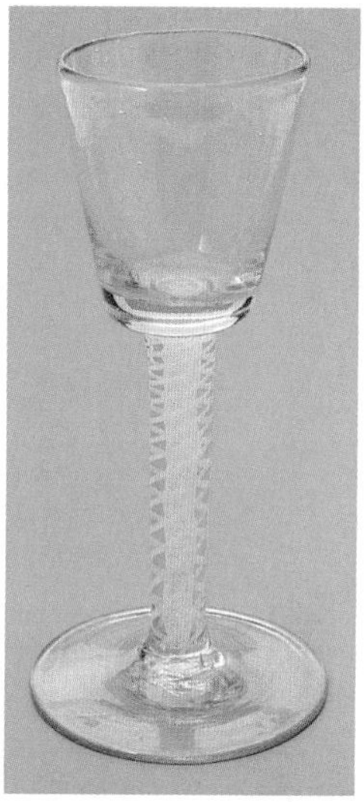

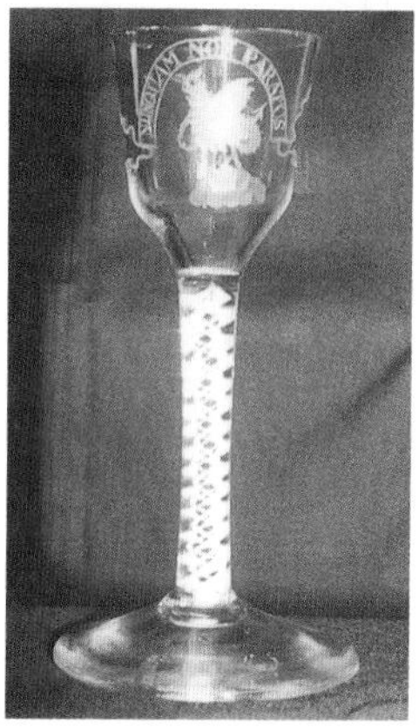

A wine glass, the ogee bowl engraved 'Nunquam Non Paratus' (Never Unprepared), above a cockatrice, on a double-series opaque stem, on a conical foot, c1765, 6in (15cm) high.
£800–900
€/ $1,300–1,400 ⊞ RAP

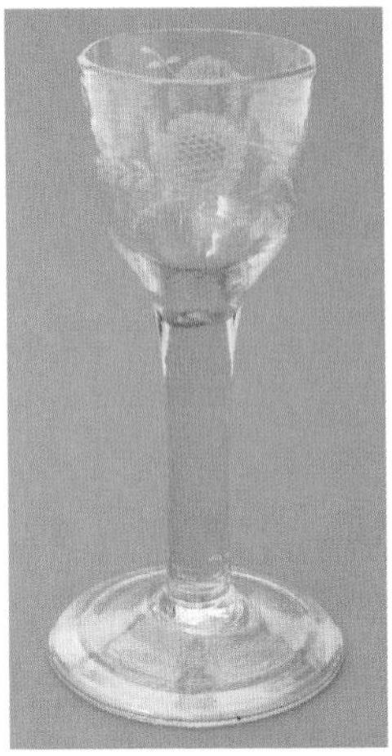

A wine glass, the ogee bowl with engraved rococo motifs, on a folded foot, 18thC, 5½in (14cm) high.
£165–185
€/ $260–290 ⊞ PSA

A wine glass, the bowl engraved with a thistle, on a faceted stem, c1770, 6in (15cm) high.
£320–350
€/ $510–550 ⊞ JHa

A wine glass, the bowl engraved with a flower and a bee, the shoulder knobbed, on a facet stem with a row of shield cuts, c1770, 5in (12.5cm) high.
£340–380
€/ $550–600 ⊞ JHa

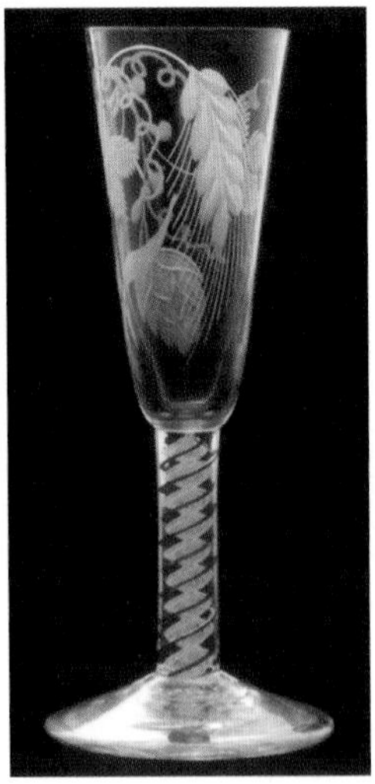

A colour-twist ale flute, the tapering bowl engraved with hops and barley, the stem with spiral threads enclosing a central lace twist, on a conical foot, c1770, 7½in (19cm) high.
£3,000–3,500
€/ $4,700–5,500 ⚒ B
The blue spiral increases the price by at least half as much again compared to a standard white air-twist glass.

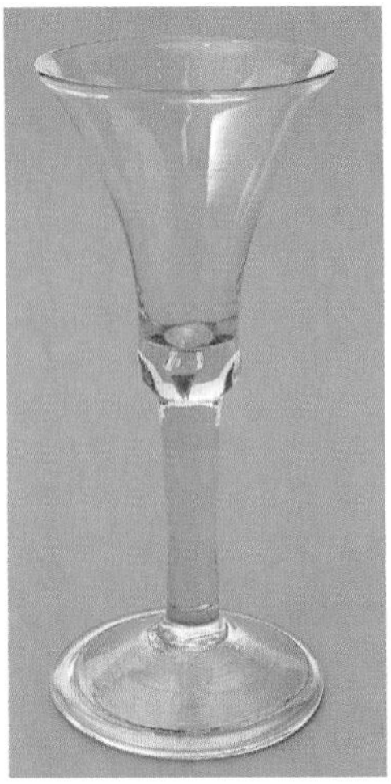

A wine glass, the bell bowl on a domed folded foot, c1770, 6¾in (17cm) high.
£250–280
€/ $400–440 ⊞ PSA

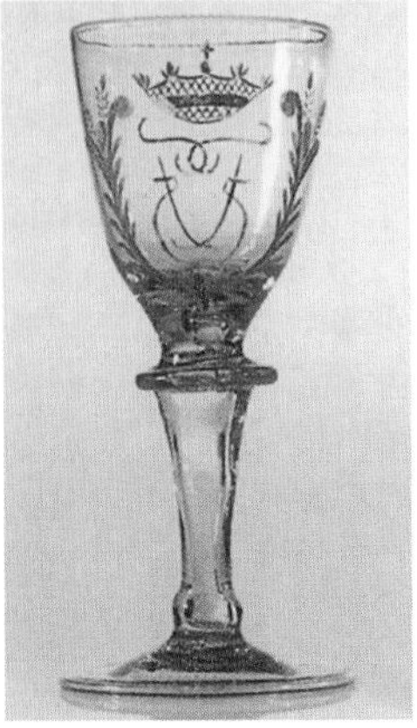

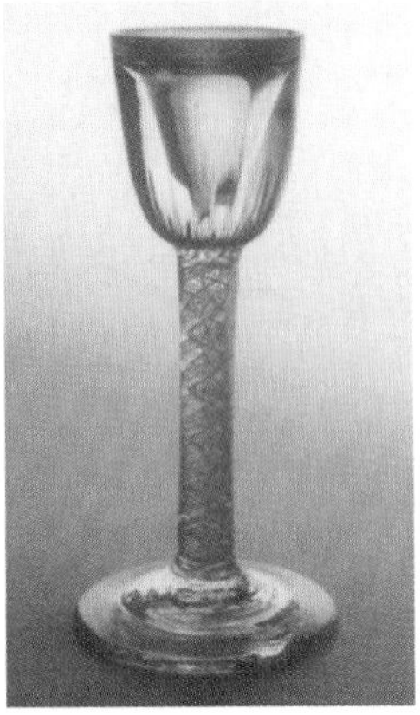

A wine glass, the deceptive rounded bowl with basal flutes, on a multi-spiral opaque-twist stem, the ply bands outside a corkscrew, c1770, 5¾in (14.5cm) high.
£2,000–2,400
€/ $3,200–3,800 ⚒ LFA
The deceptive bowl is more unusual than regular ones.

A wine glass, the diamond facet-cut bowl with an Adam-style swag and medallion, with bucrania and patera engraving, c1770, 5in (12.5cm) high.
£880–975
€/ $1,400–1,500 ⊞ WMa

Neo-classical design in glass

The architect Robert Adam's return from his Grand Tour in 1758 was the prime catalyst in the decorative revolution that overthrew rococo in favour of the neo-classical style that has since remained the preferred expression of British taste. Neo-classical motifs were applied, usually in symmetrical cutting, but sometimes engraved, onto British glassware from 1765–95. James Giles applied in gold motifs such as wheel-like paterae and ox-skull *bucraniae*, taken from Roman funerary carvings, to decanter and cruet bottles. Similarly engraved pieces have also been linked to his workshop, and that of Fleet Street merchant/decorator William Parker.

A wine glass, the lipped cup bowl with faceting to the base, on a faceted stem, c1770, 5½in (14cm) high.
£220–250
€/ $350–400 ⊞ PSA

◄ **A Nöstetangen wine glass,** the bowl with the engraved and gilt royal monogram of Frederik V, Norwegian, c1770, 6¼in (16cm) high.
£450–550
€/ $710–870 ⚒ BUK

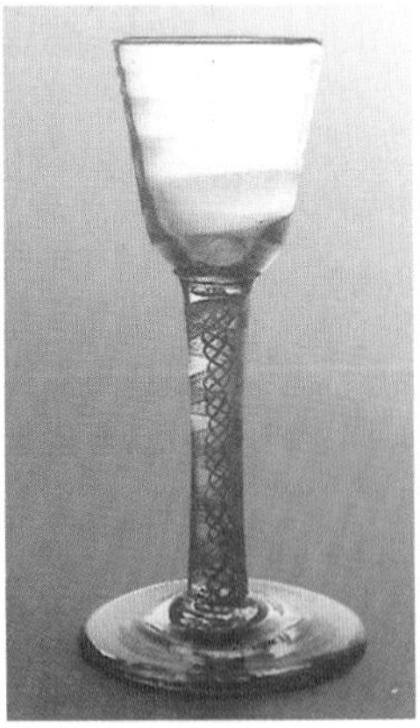

A 'Lynn' wine glass, the funnel bowl with five ribs, on a multi-spiral opaque-twist stem, with a ply band enclosing two spiral cables, c1770, 5½in (14cm) high.
£750–875
€/ $1,200–1,400 ⚒ LFA
'Lynn' glasses, with their distinctive grooved horizontal rings around the bowl, are so-called because it used to be thought that they were made in Kings Lynn, Norfolk.

An ale glass, the drawn trumpet bowl engraved with hops and barley, on a plain foot, 18thC, 6½in (16.5cm) high.
£60–70
€/ $95–110 ⊞ JHa

A glass goblet, engraved with an armorial and scrolling foliage between bands of printies, on a hollow-knopped stem and an engraved foot, Continental, 18thC, 9¾in (25cm) high.
£280–320
€/ $440–500 ⚒ WW

A pair of Yarmouth gilt rummers, attributed to William Absolon, each bowl inscribed 'From rocks & sands & dangers free Pray God protect the ship & we', within grasses and formal star and flowers, the reverse with an anchor, below a gilt line band, above a collar and spreading foot, gilding rubbed, c1800, 5in (12.5cm) high.
£2,000–2,200
€/ $3,200–3,500 ⚒ S(O)

A Regency rummer, the bucket bowl etched with thistles and flowers, over a slice-cut and hobnail band, on a star-cut foot, 7½in (19cm) high.
£200–240
€/ $315–380 ⚒ EH

A rummer, the bucket bowl engraved with looped laurel leaves and ribbon bows, on a bladed-knop stem and conical foot, Irish, c1825, 5in (12.5cm) high.
£45–50
€/ $70–80 ⊞ Som

A firing glass, the ogee bowl on a thick tapering stem and terraced foot, mid-18thC, 3½in (9cm) high.
£100–120
€/ $160–190 ⚒ PFK

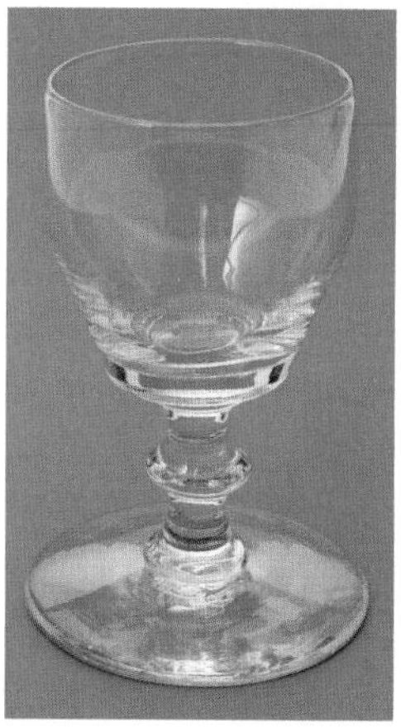

A set of six dram glasses, the ovoid bowls on single-knop stems and conical feet, c1840, 4½in (11.5cm) high.
£135–150
€/ $215–240 ⊞ PSA

► **A goblet,** possibly Harrach Glasshouse or Schachtenbach, the thistle-shaped bowl and conical foot gilt with scroll and Gothic arched panels, applied with pincered trails, the clear hexagonal stem with opaque twist spirals between gilt collars, Bohemian, c1850, 11¾in (30cm) high.
£800–900
€/ $1,300–1,400 ⚒ S(O)

A pan-topped rummer, with a petal-moulded bowl, c1800, 4½in (11.5cm) high.
£55–60
€/ $85–95 ⊞ JHa

◄ **A rummer,** the petal-moulded bowl above a short stem, on a conical foot, c1800, 4½in (11.5cm) high.
£65–75
€/ $100–120 ⊞ Som

A rummer, engraved with a ship in full sail, dated 1819, 5in (12.5cm) high.
£315–350
€/ $480–550 ⊞ Del

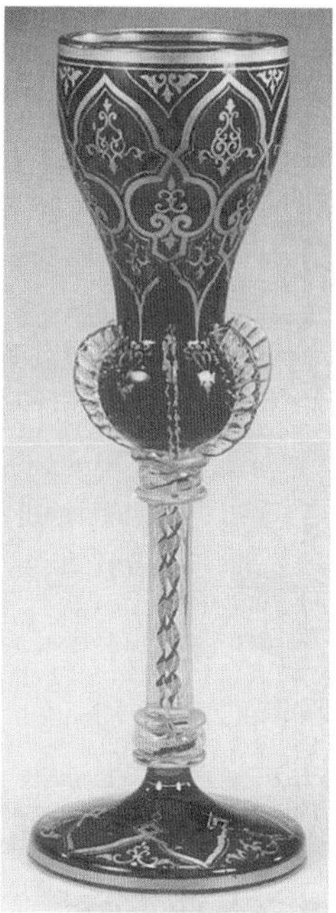

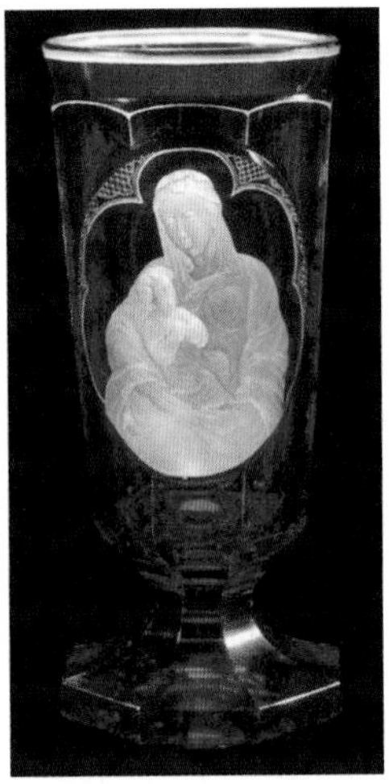

A ruby-stained goblet, possibly by Anton Heinrich Pfeiffer, the bowl cut with eight facets, cut with a raised oval medallion and intaglio-engraved with the Virgin and Child, the reverse cut with a lens framed by fruiting vine branches, Bohemian, 1850–1900, 6¾in (17cm) high.
£800–1,000
€/ $1,300–1,600 S

A goblet, the bowl decorated with leaves, birds and red deer, on a clear glass foot, foot damaged, Bohemian, c1860, 5in (12.5cm) high.
£350–420
€/ $550–670 DORO

A lidded goblet, engraved with a coat-of-arms in a cartouche, Bohemian, c1860, 8¾in (22cm) high.
£275–325
€/ $430–520 DORO

A goblet, engraved with snowdrops and ferns, c1880, 6in (15cm) high.
£100–110
€/ $160–175 JHa

◀ **A set of 18 roemers,** possibly Theresienthal, each with a cup-shaped bowl on a clear baluster stem with trailing and three applied raspberry prunts, Bohemian, c1880, 6¼in (16cm) high.
£575–675
€/ $900–1,100 S(O)

Expert's choice

The Hinnenburg Goblet, c1715, sold by Sotheby's in 2000.

The Hinnenburg Goblet was made in Dresden, c1715, for Augustus the Strong, Elector of Saxony, and was listed as an 'Emperor Goblet' in a royal inventory of 1739. It was discovered by Simon Cottle of Sotheby's in the cellars of a German castle. Formed in three sections, lid, body and screwing stem/foot, it is decorated with deep swag cutting and polished engraving, and has a teared-ball knop above a hollow baluster stem. However, its greatest attribute is a series of 12 silver-gilt medallion busts of Roman Emperors inserted into its bowl. A group of Meissen red stoneware medallions with similar modelling known to be by Johann Böttger confirm a link between the ceramics and glassware produced at the Saxon court. The goblet fetched £133,500 (€/ $211,000) at Sotheby's in 2000. **Andy McConnell**

A glass goblet, decorated with a coat-of-arms, with historismus-style enamelling, the rim with a pearl border, Bohemian, c1880, 8in (20.5cm) high.
£240–300
€/ $380–475 DORO

▶ **A glass goblet and cover,** engraved on one side with a Danish inscription, the reverse with a building in Bredgade, Copenhagen, c1880, 14in (35.5cm) high.
£1,100–1,200
€/ $1,700–1,900 G&G

A Murano Glass Co goblet and cover, by Dr Antonio Salviati, the funnel bowl with a partly-gilt rim, on an openwork stem with aventurine inclusions, above a conical foot with a folded rim, the domed cover with a similar openwork finial, c1880, 28¾in (73cm) high.
£3,500–4,000
€/ $5,500–6,300 S

Beakers & Tumblers

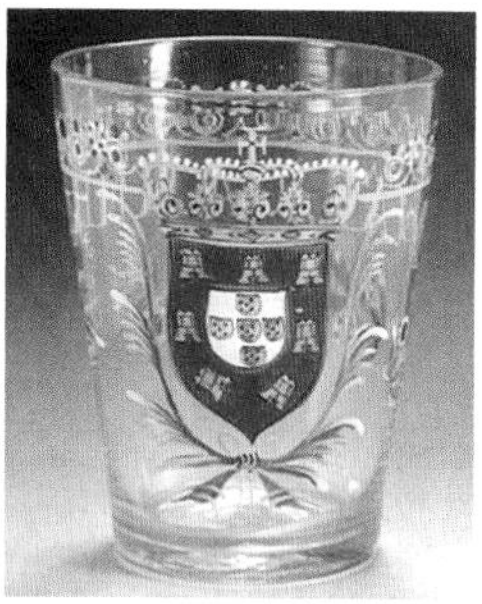

An enamelled armorial beaker, painted with a shield and coronet, the reverse inscribed 'Vivat Joannes.V.' above stylized flowers, below a scroll border, German, Saxony, 18thC, 6¼in (16cm) high.
£775–900
€/ $1,200–1,400 S(O)

An alabaster glass footed beaker, decorated in the rococo style with rocailles, flowers and leaves, Bohemian, c1830, 5in (13cm) high.
£650–750
€/ $1,000–1,200 DORO

A coloured sulphide tumbler, by Baccarat or Val St Lambert, decorated with a central roundel containing a sulphide depicting a dove and a wreath of flowers, flanked by lobes cut with fine diamonds, the footrim facet-cut, chip under footrim, Belgian, c1850, 3½in (8.5cm) high.
£200–240
€/ $300–380 B

A Henrikstorp beaker, with engraved decoration of trailing foliage and a monogram, minor foot chips, Swedish, 1700–50, 3¼in (8.5cm) high.
£850–1,000
€/ $1,300–1,600 BUK

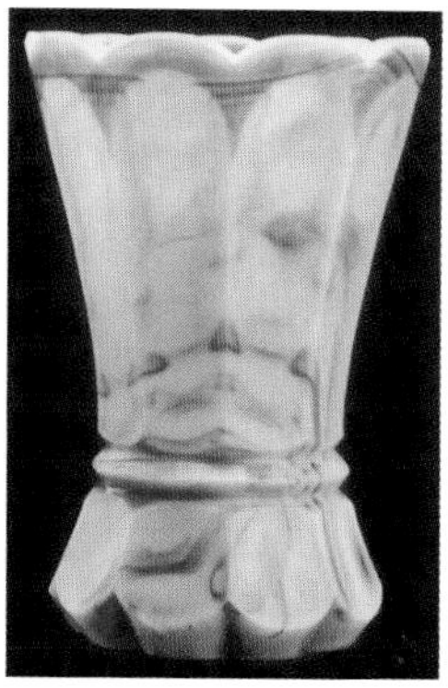

An Agatin or Lithyalin marbled beaker, the faceted bowl waisted towards the bottom and cut with a waistband, Bohemian, c1830, 5¼in (13.5cm) high.
£1,000–1,200
€/ $1,600–1,900 S

A beaker, enamel-decorated with a band of silver flowers, Bohemian, c1860, 5in (13cm) high.
£280–340
€/ $440–550 DORO

► **A beaker,** painted with humorous representations of the months of the year, rim slightly damaged, German, c1900, 5½in (14cm) high.
£240–280
€/ $380–440 DORO

A Kosta beaker, engraved with wedding motifs of birds, a heart and stylized flowers, Swedish, 1750–1800, 8¼in (21cm) high.
£320–375
€/ $500–600 BUK

► **A footed beaker,** with enamel overlay and gilt decoration, gilt slightly rubbed, Bohemian, c1840, 5in (12.5cm) high.
£350–420
€/ $550–670 DORO

A transparent-enamelled spa beaker, the waisted cylindrical bowl painted with a scene within an amber-stained frame inscribed in gilding 'Brandenburgerthor. Berlin. 1825', the reverse cut with a lens, below an amber-stained band, gilt rim and star-cut base, gilding rubbed, Bohemian, 19thC, 4½in (11.5cm) high.
£775–900
€/ $1,200–1,400 S(O)

A beaker, with a gilt rim and gilt decoration of a huntsman in a wooded landscape with a castle, Bohemian, c1760, 3¾in (9.5cm) high.
£320–375
€/ $500–600 DORO

An enamelled beaker, possibly by Lobmeyr or Meyr's Neffe, the tapering bowl enamelled in *Schwartzlot* in transparent enamels, the four panels of classical maidens alternating with floral garlands entwined around torches, the border with amber flashing and a gold foliate band, Bohemian, c1900, 4½in (11.5cm) high.
£500–570
€/ $790–900 B

Schwartzlot **means 'black lead' decoration. This is a Historismus piece: a reproduction of a style of decoration pioneered c1700 in Silesia/Bohemia by Ignaz Preissler (born 1670).**

GLASS

Bottles, Carafes & Decanters

A mallet-shaped wine bottle, applied with a string rim, with a deep pontil-scarred base, with all-over iridescent patination, 1720–30, 6½in (16.5cm) high.
£240–275
€/ $380–440 BBR

A square-section case decanter, with an engraved cartouche for 'Rum' and floral motifs, c1780, 9in (23cm) high.
£165–185
€/ $260–290 CHAC

A pair of club-shaped decanters, with lozenge stoppers, c1800, 9½in (24cm) high.
£450–500
€/ $700–800 CHAC

A wine bottle, applied with a seal inscribed 'B. Greive, 1727', 6½in (16.5cm) high.
£3,000–3,500
€/ $4,700–5,500 L
This is an unrecorded bottle. Collectors of bottles are prepared to pay substantial sums for rare items, particularly pieces of early date, such as this example. A seal, especially a dated one, can increase the price by about ten times.

A pair of club-shaped cruet bottles, 1790–1820, 5in (12.5cm) high.
£400–450
€/ $630–700 Del

A pair of glass bottles, cold-painted with titled portraits of 'Peter Floirs, Vice-Admiraal van Friesland' and 'Adriaan Bankert, Admiraal van Zeeland', over scenes of naval engagements, Dutch, early 19thC, 14¼in (36cm) high.
£1,500–1,800
€/ $2,400–2,800 TEN

A Nailsea-type globular-shaped bottle, with white flecks, with applied collar, pontil scar to the base, 1770–80, 6in (15cm) high.
£375–450
€/ $600–700 BBR

A decanter, engraved with panels of Masonic emblems and figures, above a chequered band with drapery below, the neck with three triple-annular rings, stopper missing, one ring chipped, c1800, 8½in (21.5cm) high.
£600–700
€/ $1,000–1,100 S(O)

A set of three barrel-shaped spirit decanters, with original stoppers, c1830, 8½in (21.5cm) high.
£350–400
€/ $550–650 PSA

A decanter, with cut fluting and a neo-classical engraved band, c1780, 12in (30.5cm) high.
£315–350
€/ $500–550 JHa

A pair of Bristol blue club-shaped decanters, for rum and brandy, the club-shaped bodies decorated in gilt, gilding worn, 1790–1820, 8¾in (22cm) high.
£350–400
€/ $550–630 PSA

An engraved shaft-and-globe bottle, inscribed 'Walter Galbraith' and dated 1837 within a scroll, depicting agricultural implements including a plough, scythe, rake, fork and shovel, above a thistle and a rose, Scottish, 10¼in (26cm) high.
£375–450
€/ $600–700 B(Ed)

An opaline glass carafe and stand, with hand-painted floral enamelling, 1840–60, 8in (20.5cm) high.
£100–125
€/ $160–200 ⚒ SWO

◄ A pair of shaft-and-globe decanters, cut with flutes and printies, with scale-cut necks and cut stoppers, c1860, 8¾in (22cm) high.
£170–200
€/ $270–300 ⊞ Som

A claret decanter, on a star-cut base, stopper missing, small chips, 19thC, 11¾in (30cm) high.
£220–260
€/ $350–400 ⚒ TMA

A decanter, by Fritz Heckert, decorated in gilt with enamel highlights, pommel damaged, Bohemian, c1880, 9¾in (25cm) high.
£400–500
€/ $630–800 ⚒ DORO
This type of decoration is known as 'Jodphur style'.

◄ A silver-mounted decanter, the stopper modelled as a beaker, silver hallmarked Chester 1906, 10¾in (27.5cm) high.
£150–175
€/ $230–280 ⚒ FEN

A Lobmeyr decanter, engraved in the Baroque style with half figures below canopied thrones within foliate scrollwork with animals and birds, the domed stopper with a ball finial, the faceted neck with a scroll band, on a flared faceted foot, engraved mark, c1880, 10½in (26.5cm) high.
£1,800–2,000
€/ $2,800–3,200 ⚒ S(O)

GLASS

Bowls

◄ **A cut-glass fruit bowl,** with wave rim, on a star-cut base, rim chipped, Irish, c1790, 9¾in (25cm) high.
£350–400
€/ $550–630 G(L)

A finger bowl, 1820, 3¾in (9.5cm) high.
£60–65
€/ $95–100 PSA

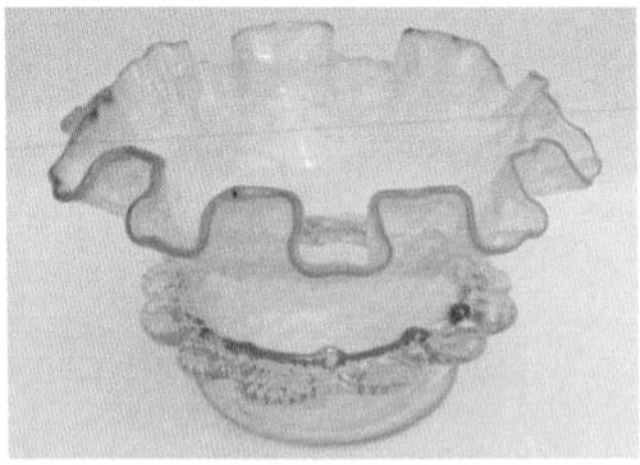

A Stourbridge-style opalescent glass preserve bowl, c1900, 3in (8.5cm) high.
£85–100
€/ $130–160 GRI

A bowl, cut with strawberry diamonds, on a star-cut base, 1810–20, 8in (20.5cm) diam.
£100–120
€/ $160–190 TMA

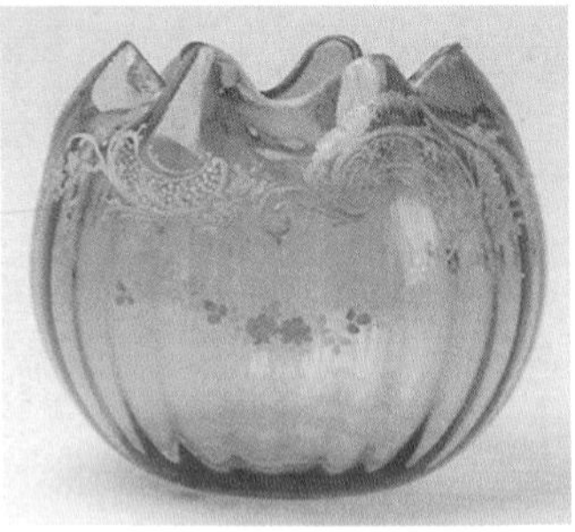

A rib-moulded glass rose bowl, with rococo-revival gilding, late 19thC, 9¼in (23.5cm) diam.
£130–160
€/ $200–250 JDJ

A lidded bowl, with blue-flashed and gilded neo-classical decoration, Russian, 1750–1800, 9in (23cm) diam.
£3,800–4,500
€/ $6,000–7,000 BUK

A tea caddy bowl, with a fan-cut rim, the arched and diamond-cut body on a star-cut foot, c1830, 4in (10cm) diam.
£145–160
€/ $230–250 Som

Boxes

A cut-glass casket, with ormolu mounts, the hinged cover cut with strawberry diamonds, the body cut with pillars and serrated vertical bands, on a star-cut base, chipped, French, c1830, 4¾in (12cm) high.
£450–500
€/ $700–800 S(O)

A blue-flashed casket, with gilt decoration and engraved with scenes of Karlsbad, Bohemian, 1840–50, 6in (15cm) wide.
£650–775
€/ $1,000–1,200 BUK

► **A Moser-style cranberry glass casket,** with ormolu mounts, cold-painted with floral and foliate scrollwork, Bohemian, 1860–80, 4¾in (12cm) square.
£400–475
€/ $630–750 GTH

A ruby-flashed sugar box and cover, with enamel decoration, Bohemian, c1860, 5¼in (13.5cm) wide.
£150–180
€/ $240–280 DORO

Centrepieces

A cut-glass *épergne*, the scroll arms hung with baskets and surmounted by a chevron- and diamond-cut bowl with Van Dyck-style rim, on a diamond-cut dome scalloped base, baskets matched, Continental, late 18thC, 22in (56cm) high.
£3,500–4,200
€/ $5,500–6,500 ⚒ B

A ruby-flashed table centrepiece, decorated with rococo scrolls in enamel and gold, rim slightly damaged, Bohemian, c1860, 5¾in (14.5cm) high.
£180–220
€/ $280–350 ⚒ DORO

A uranium glass table centrepiece, with gilded and enamel decoration, Bohemian, c1840, 6½in (16.5cm) high.
£400–500
€/ $630–800 ⚒ DORO

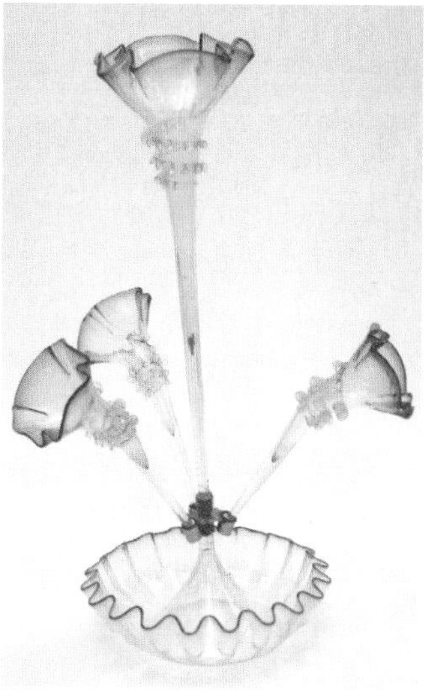

An *épergne*, with frill rims, with four trumpet vases, on a stand, 19thC, 21in (53.5cm) high.
£160–200
€/ $250–300 ⚒ G(L)

A Clichy paperweight tazza, the rims applied with a spiralling ribbon, the bowl inset with a central rose within five interlaced cane garlands alternating with a single cane, above a knopped baluster stem and domed foot, French, c1850, 4in (10cm) high.
£3,000–3,500
€/ $4,700–5,700 ⚒ S(O)

A Lobmeyr Persian-style tazza, the bowl inscribed with Kufic lettering within gilt scrollwork, the interior with a central medallion enclosing a stylized flower, on an annulated collar and trumpet foot, painted grid mark, c1880, 3½in (9cm) high.
£2,500–3,000
€/ $4,000–4,700 ⚒ S(O)
This is Lobmeyr's equivalent of Heckert's 'Jodhpur style' (see Bottles, Carafes & Decanters page 341).

A table centrepiece, with a crimped rim, c1880, 4¼in (11cm) high.
£120–135
€/ $190–215 ⊞ PSA

◄ **A late Victorian four-vase *épergne*,** with clear glass trailed banding, frilled opaque and overlaid rims, on a shaped dished opaque base, 14in (35.5cm) high.
£130–160
€/ $200–250 ⚒ TMA

A four-vase *épergne*, on a wavy-edge bowl, c1890, 18½in (47cm) high.
£750–850
€/ $1,200–1,300 ⊞ CB

An *épergne*, with a cut-glass vase, on a gilt-metal base modelled with two birds among fruit and foliage, stamped 'Defreville', 19thC, 15½in (39.5cm) high.
£375–450
€/ $600–700 ⚒ HYD

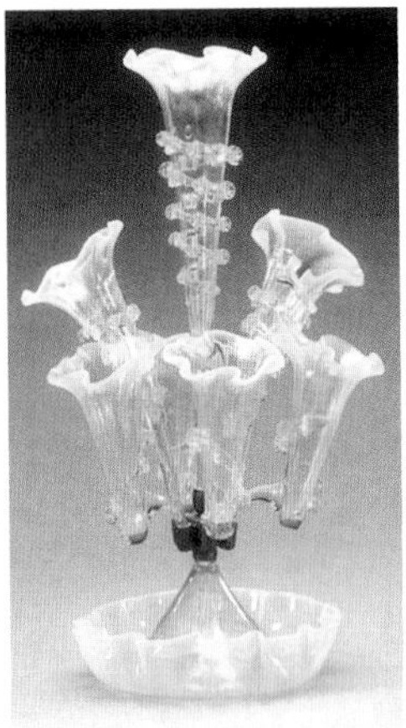

A six-vase *épergne*, the vases applied with pinched trailing ornament, below fluted rims, Bohemian, late 19thC, 17¼in (44cm) high.
£900–1,000
€/ $1,400–1,700 ⚒ S(O)

◀ An opaque glass centrepiece, the spirally crimped dish on a plated stand pierced with vine decoration, on a beaded foot, 19thC, 11in (28cm) diam.
£65–80
€/ $100–125
⚒ PFK

Eight crimp-edged vases, in a silver-plated frame, c1900, 18in (45.5cm) wide.
£400–500
€/ $630–800 ⊞ CB

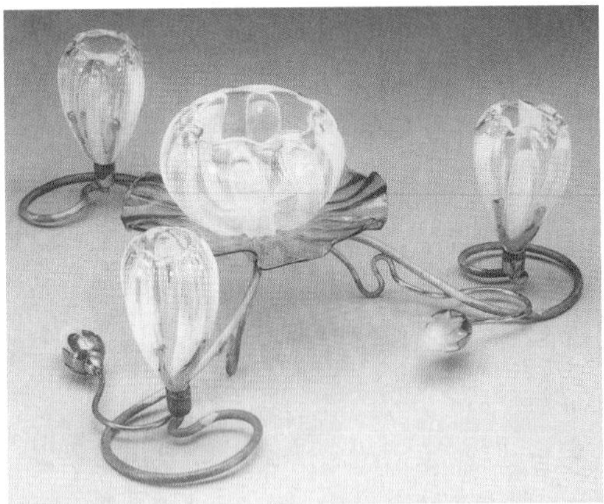

A John Walsh Walsh ormolu-mounted *épergne*, with five opalescent glass bowls on a stand and a spiralling frame, early 20thC, 14¼in (36cm) wide.
£850–1,000
€/ $1,300–1,600 ⚒ S(O)

John Walsh Walsh

The fame of Victorian Britain's leading glassworks – Richardson, Thomas Webb and Stevens & Williams – has obscured the existence of scores of others that operated principally in the Midlands, the North and North-East. They include the bizarrely named John Walsh Walsh, which produced a wide range of cut, engraved, etched, cameo, art and reproduction 'antique' glassware in Birmingham from 1850–1951. The company grew gradually to a peak during the 1930s, when it employed around 400 staff.
It remains best known for its ranges designed by William 'Clyne' Farquharson.

Flasks

A *façon de Venise* mottled glass barillet, the narrow aperture moulded with a folded rim and flanked by two scroll handles, French, c1700, 4¾in (12cm) wide.
£1,000–1,100
€/ $1,600–1,700 ⚒ S(O)

Items in the Glass section have been arranged in date order within each sub-section.

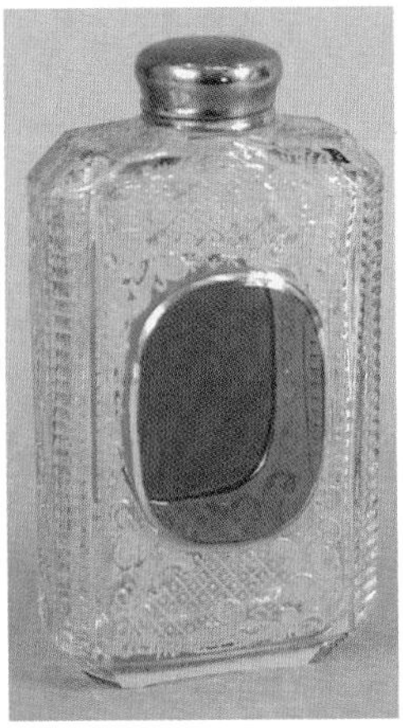

An amber-flashed and cut-glass flask, with metal screw-stopper, Bohemian, c1860, 5¼in (13.5cm) high.
£120–140
€/ $190–220 ⚒ SWO

A Stourbridge Oriental-style gilt and silvered moonflask, by Thomas Webb & Sons, attributed to Jules Barbe, one side depicting two carp, one chasing an eel, the reverse with a frog among lily pads flanked by flowering grasses within stylized scroll borders, c1890, 9½in (24cm) high.
£7,200–8,000
€/ $11,500–12,600 ⚒ S
This rare piece is an example of outstanding craftsmanship.

Jugs & Ewers

A *milchglas* **jug and cover,** decorated in gold and enamels in the rococo style, the cover with a pear knop, Bohemian, c1760, 9¾in (25cm) high.
£250–300
€/ $400–475 ⚒ DORO

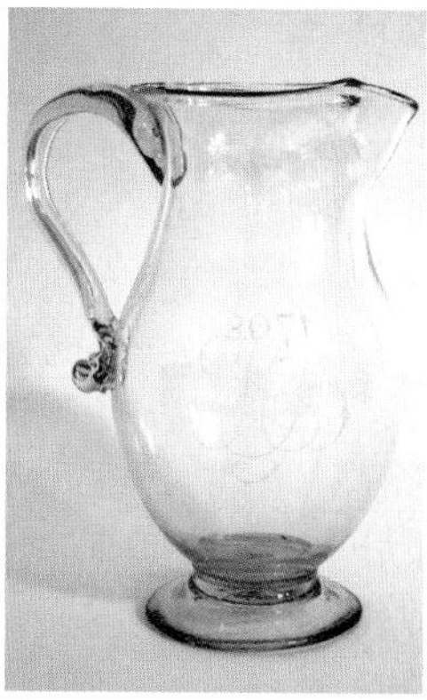

A glass water jug, with applied scroll handle, engraved with a monogram, the reverse dated 1798, 8¾in (22cm) high.
£600–700
€/ $1,000–1,100 ⚒ G(L)

A glass water jug, with scroll handle, decorated with Adam-style neo-classical cut motifs, on a facet-cut foot, Irish, c1810, 9¾in (25cm) high.
£400–450
€/ $630–700 ⚒ LFA
This type of decoration is typical of Irish works.

An enamelled and gilt glass ewer, by Harrachor Glasshouse, painted with floral bouquets, with a scroll handle, gilding rubbed, chipped, Bohemian, c1845, 10¼in (26cm) high.
£1,500–1,800
€/ $2,400–2,800 ⚒ S

Anglo-Bohemian Victorian engraving

Demand for engraved glassware between 1850 and 1890 created a skills shortage that drew scores of Bohemian engravers to Britain. Working principally in Edinburgh, Stourbridge and London, they developed new decorative styles that saw their traditional subject matter, such as stags in woodland, supplanted by a range of classical and naturalistic decorative themes and the development of 'rock crystal' glassware. The leading exponents included William Fritsche and Frederick Kny, who spent a combined 80 years working in Stourbridge, mostly for Thomas Webb & Sons. Kny's son Ludwig was the chief designer at Stuart Crystal between the world wars.

A ruby-flashed glass claret jug, by James Charles Edington, the fluted and Gothic-arch cut glass with silver vine stock handle and girdle, shaped collar and cover with vine tendril ring finial, London 1847, 11½in (29cm) high.
£3,000–3,400
€/ $4,700–5,400 ⚒ Bri

► **A glass ewer,** etched with trailing vines and baskets of flowers beneath a waisted neck with engraved arched panels, on a pedestal base, c1870, 12½in (32cm) high.
£575–675
€/ $900–1,000 ⚒ HAM

A cranberry glass water jug, with a clear scroll handle, 19thC, 8in (20.5cm) high.
£160–200
€/ $250–300 ⚒ SWO

A Lobmeyr rococo revival opalescent glass ewer and goblet, engraved and gilt with a scrolling foliate rocaille ground and 'jewelled' with opaque dots, chipped and cracked, monogram mark, c1880, ewer 9¾in (25cm) high.
£400–475
€/ $630–750 ⚒ DN

Champagne decanters

Champagne decanters have existed for over three centuries, generally containing a stoppered bubble or tube of glass into which crushed ice is inserted to chill their contents. In 1755, examples were priced at six shillings each, making them cheaper than their contents, which cost eight shillings a bottle. While their function may appear illogical, their use for dispensing vintage Champagnes remains recommended by connoisseurs. This is because decanting allows the taste of the Champagne to develop, reduces the number of bubbles and slightly raises its temperature to above the point at which it numbs tastebuds.

A cranberry ice glass champagne decanter and stopper, with clear handle, 19thC, 15in (38cm) high.
£140–160
€/ $220–250 ⚒ GTH

Lustres

A pair of glass lustres, with Albert drops, c1840, 8in (20.5cm) high.
£1,100–1,200
€/ $1,700–1,900 ⊞ Del

The term 'lustre' can be confusing as it has been applied to a number of different items over the past 300 years. They have included a chandelier (18th century), a cut-glass table centrepiece supporting a single candlestick (19th century), or a single drop suspended from a chandelier, centrepiece or candlestick (current usage).

A pair of clear glass lustres, with cut drops, 1840–50, 7¾in (19.5cm) high.
£350–400
€/ $550–630 ⚒ SWO

► **A pair of enamelled glass lustres,** decorated with enamelled portrait medallions of children and floral sprays with gilded foliage, beneath a scrolling, scalloped rim, hung with cut-glass prisms, on domed feet with further medallions, Bohemian, late 19thC, 11in (28cm) high.
£800–950
€/ $1,200–1,500 ⚒ RIT

Mugs & Tankards

A glass mug, with a swirled body, pontil scar to base, 1775–1825, 3in (7cm) high.
£80–90
€/ $125–145 ⚒ BBR

◄ **A ruby-stained glass tankard and cover,** with pewter mounts, engraved with a stag and deer in a woodland scene, the cover engraved 'FAK' in Gothic lettering, with a rounded star-cut base, late 19thC, 7in (18cm) high.
£850–1,000
€/ $1,300–1,600 ⚒ S

A ruby-flashed and enamelled glass tankard and cover, with pewter mounts, decorated in colours and gilt with flowers, thumbpiece missing, Bohemian, c1830, 5¼in (13.5cm) high.
£220–250
€/ $350–400 ⚒ DORO

Panels & Pictures

A reverse glass painting, depicting the Biblical story of Noah and his three sons, Ham, Sem and Japheth, inscribed, south German, 18thC, in a later ebonized and gilt frame, 16¼ x 20in (41 x 51cm).
£700–800
€/ $1,100–1,200 ⚒ S(Am)

A leaded and stained glass Historismus panel, depicting a coat-of-arms above an inscribed banner, German, 19thC, 17in (43cm) high.
£400–500
€/ $630–800 ⚒ RTo

A Victorian stained and leaded glass window, depicting a hunter against a background of trees, birds in flight and snow-covered ground, some cracks and bulging, 34 x 27½in (86.5 x 70cm), mounted in a light box.
£800–950
€/ $1,200–1,500 ⚒ JDJ

Paperweights

A Baccarat concentric millefiori paperweight, French, c1848, 2½in (6.5cm) diam.
£350–400
€/ $550–630 ⊞ DLP

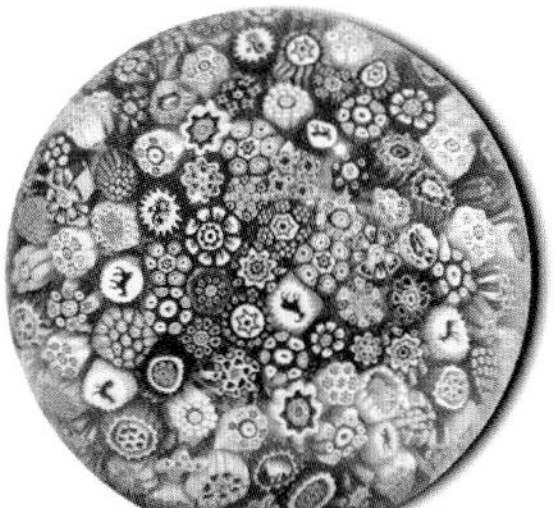

A Baccarat close-pack millefiori paperweight, with 15 silhouettes, initialled 'B', French, 1848, 3½in (9cm) diam.
£8,000–9,000
€/ $12,700–14,200 ⊞ SWB

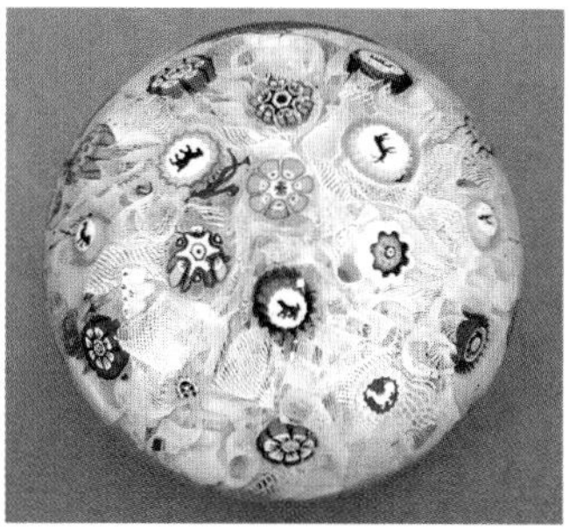

A Baccarat scattered millefiori paperweight, with a variety of canes, one inscribed 'B1848', on a tossed muslin ground, French, dated 1848, 3¼in (8.5cm) diam.
£1,000–1,200
€/ $1,600–1,900 G(L)

A specimen flower paperweight, probably Baccarat, decorated with a pansy with central star motif, on a star-cut foot, bruised and scuffed, French, 19thC, 3in (7.5cm) diam.
£475–550
€/ $750–870 BR

A Boston & Sandwich Glass Co poinsettia paperweight, American, c1860, 3in (7.5cm) diam.
£700–800
€/ $1,100–1,300 ⊞ DLP

A Clichy miniature paperweight, with a central rose, on a carpet ground of fine canes, French, mid-19thC, 1¾in (4.5cm) diam.
£4,000–4,800
€/ $6,300–7,500 B

GLASS

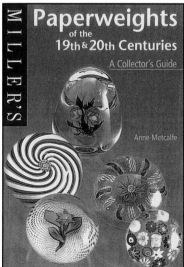

A Clichy rose paperweight, with a central rose, French, 1845–60, 2in (5cm) diam.
£2,200–2,400
€/ $3,300–3,800 ⊞ SWB

A Pantin rose paperweight, French, c1878, 3in (7.5cm) diam.
£9,000–10,000
€/ $14,000–16,000 ⊞ DLP

Pantin paperweights are arguably the finest glass paperweights ever made. They have a 3-dimensional quality and realism that is spectacular. Fewer than 20 rose weights are known to exist from this maker, one of about 200 weights documented from Pantin.

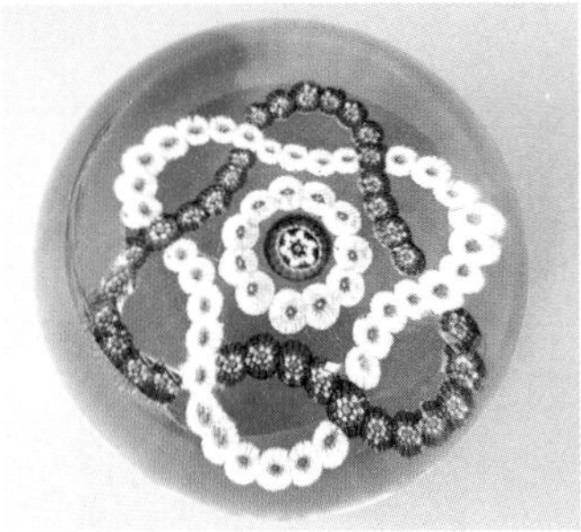

A Clichy paperweight, the central cluster within a garland design, bruise to base, French, 19thC, 3in (7.5cm) diam.
£240–275
€/ $380–430 ⚒ G(B)

A St Louis miniature crown paperweight, the twisted *latticinio* threads alternating with lengths of twisted ribbon around a central cane, minor damage, French, mid-19thC, 2in (5cm) diam.
£220–250
€/ $350–400 ⚒ B

A pair of scrambled paperweights, possibly Franchini, set with a variety of colourful canes, *latticinio* tubing and aventurine, pontil scar, Venetian, mid-19thC, 2½in (6.5cm) diam.
£550–650
€/ $870–1,000 ⚒ S(O)

Further reading

Miller's Paperweights of the 19th & 20th Centuries: A Collector's Guide,
Miller's Publications, 2000

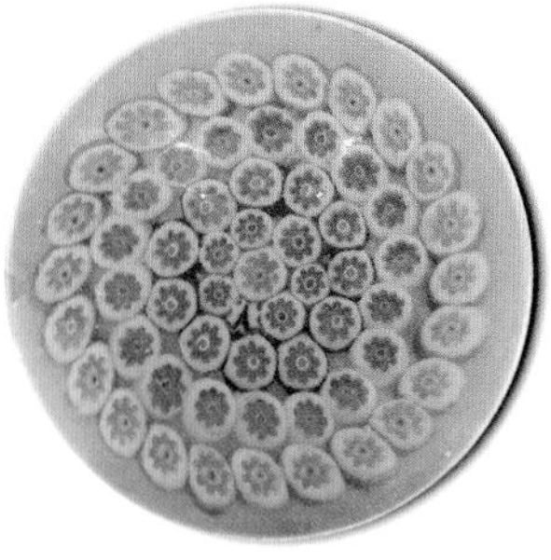

A Salvador Ysart Y-cane paperweight, 1930s, 3in (7.5cm) diam.
£330–365
€/ $520–580 ⊞ SWB

Scent Bottles

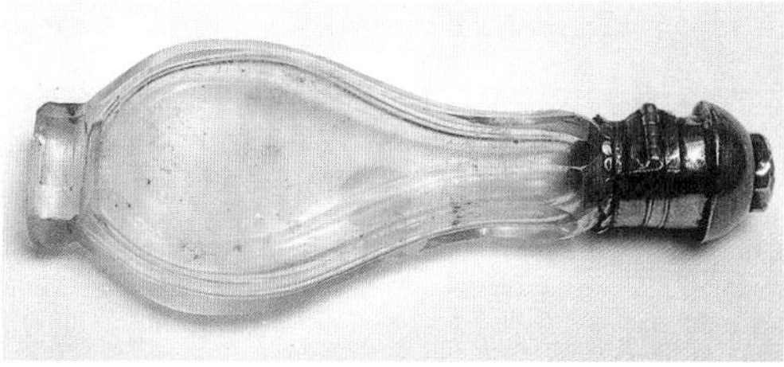

A glass scent bottle, the hinged silver top inset with Stuart crystal, c1690, 3½in (9cm) high.
£530–600
€/ $850–950 ⊞ LBr

James Giles

James Giles (1718–80) has long been recognized as one of England's finest 18th-century porcelain decorators. However, it is now known that glassware amounted to around 15 per cent of his workshop output. He applied a wide range of rococo and neo-classical motifs in gold to items of table glass, including decanters and drinking glasses, and in gold and polychrome vitreous enamels to a series of small coloured and cut-glass scent or 'smelling bottles', as they were known. The latter, dated 1760–65, were often inscribed with mottoes such as 'Fidelité' and 'Toujours' and were presented between clandestine lovers.

A glass scent bottle, probably James Giles, London, the front gilt with a flaming heart and tree and 'Pour vous seul', the reverse gilt with a floral spray, with a swirl-chased gold cap, c1760, 3in (7.5cm) high, in original fishskin case.
£1,400–1,600
€/ $2,200–2,500 S(O)

A cut-glass scent flask and stopper, the shoulder cut with oval facets below the three-ringed neck, on a solid foot cut with strawberry diamonds, with similarly-cut stopper, c1830, 10in (25.5cm) high.
£475–575
€/ $750–900 S(O)

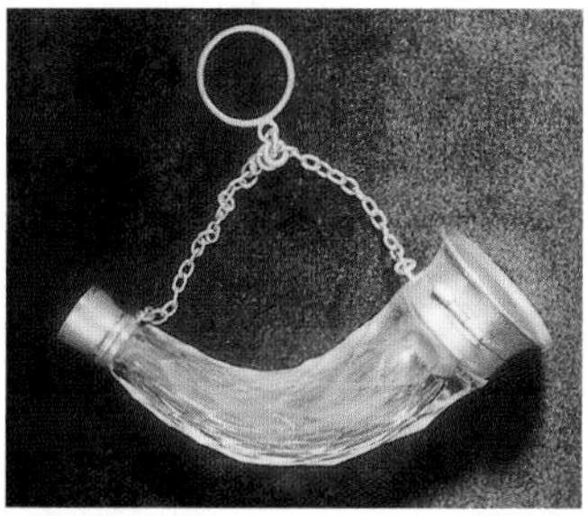

► A diamond-cut-glass scent bottle, modelled as a horn, with engine-turned silver mount, chain and finger ring, c1850, 4in (10cm) long.
£270–300
€/ $430–470
⊞ Som

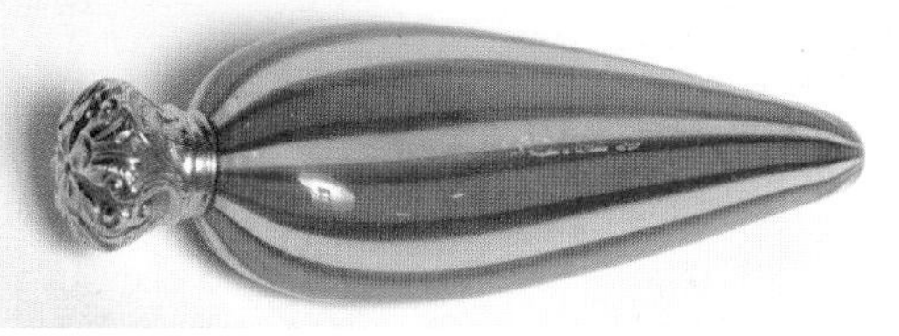

A Stourbridge glass scent bottle, with a silver top, c1870, 5in (12.5cm) high.
£500–550
€/ $800–870 ⊞ CoS

◄ A Sampson Mordan scent flask and vinaigrette, with silver-gilt mounts, London 1873, 4in (10cm) long.
£550–600
€/ $870–1,000
HAM

► A glass scent bottle, overlaid with a plaque painted with a female portrait bust against gilded foliage, Bohemian, 19thC, 4¾in (12cm) high.
£160–200
€/ $250–300 G(L)

Sampson Mordan

Founded in 1815, Sampson Mordan & Co became one of the leading makers of late Victorian novelties, often in designs that married wood, ceramics, silver and glass. Typically, they produced a scent bottle modelled as a Champagne bottle (1869), a chased silver egg containing sewing tools (1876), a miniature barrel-shaped spirit flask (1882), an inkwell disguised as a tortoise (1881), an owl pincushion (1895) and a ceramic walnut scent bottle with silver mounts (1885). The company mark also appeared on silver-mounted claret jugs shaped as an eagle (1881) and a kangaroo (1882).

A Stourbridge cameo glass scent bottle, carved with passion flowers and leaves, with a hinged silver mount, late 19thC, 5½in (14cm) high.
£900–1,100
€/ $1,400–1,700 B

A glass scent bottle, encased in brass foliate work, Continental, 19thC, 4in (10cm) high.
£200–250
€/ $300–400 SWO

Sets & Services

A glass hock decanter, with a set of six matching glasses, c1840, 14in (35.5cm) high.
£550–600
€/ $870–950 ⊞ Del
This colour is usually attributed to Richardson's of Stourbridge and is typical of early Victorian glass.

► **A gilt part drinking set,** comprising seven pieces, decorated with scattered floral sprays, chips and minor rubbing to gilding, Continental, c1850, goblet 5¾in (14.5cm) high.
£525–625
€/ $830–1,000 ⚒ S(O)

◄ **A cut-glass service,** comprising 66 pieces, 1930s.
£200–240
€/ $300–380
⚒ TRM

Sweetmeat & Jelly Dishes

◄ **A pan-topped jelly glass,** with moulded panels and a scroll handle, on a domed foot, c1750, 4½in (11.5cm) high.
£250–300
€/ $400–475 ⚒ LFA
Glasses like this, filled with colourful syllabubs, jellies and mousses were often arranged on dining tables, on a series of glass salvers, ranging from large to small, as described in Mrs Glasse's cookery book of the 1740s.

A sweetmeat glass, with a flute- and petal-cut rim, on a domed radially-moulded foot, c1760, 6in (15cm) high.
£400–450
€/ $630–700 ⊞ Som

A sweetmeat glass, the honeycomb-moulded double-ogee bowl on an octagonal pedestal and domed foot, foot trimmed, c1760, 6½in (16.5cm) high.
£300–350
€/ $475–550 ⚒ DN

Vases & Urns

◄ **A pair of covered glass urns,** the covers with facet-cut finials and fluted rims, the bodies with a band of fluting above a band of leaves, on square feet, Irish, c1795, 11¾in (30cm) high.
£2,000–2,200
€/ $3,200–3,500 ⚒ HOK

► **An Empire-style flashed glass urn,** with Regency-style cutting, on an ormolu base, slight damage to rim, 1800–15, 16in (40.5cm) high.
£2,800–3,200
€/ $4,400–5,000 ⚒ BUK

A pair of cut-glass covered urns, the high domed covers with lapidary-cut finials, the bodies panel-cut with diamond-cut bands, Anglo-Irish, c1800, 14½in (37cm) high.
£850–1,000
€/ $1,300–1,600 ⚒ NOA

An overlay glass vase, with an opaline panel enamelled with polychrome massed flowers, the body decorated with gilt flowers, Bohemian, mid-19thC, 12½in (32cm) high.
£280–320
€/ $440–500 PFK

An opaline glass baluster vase, possibly by Baccarat, decorated in gold and polychrome enamels, French, c1850, 14in (35.5cm) high.
£170–200
€/ $270–300 BUK

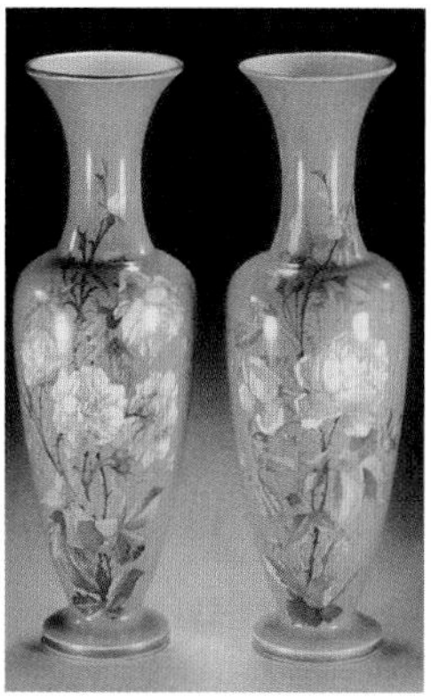

A pair of Baccarat opaline glass vases, painted with roses and foliage within gilt borders, enamels and gilding rubbed, c1855, 19¾in (50cm) high.
£1,800–2,000
€/ $2,800–3,200 S(O)

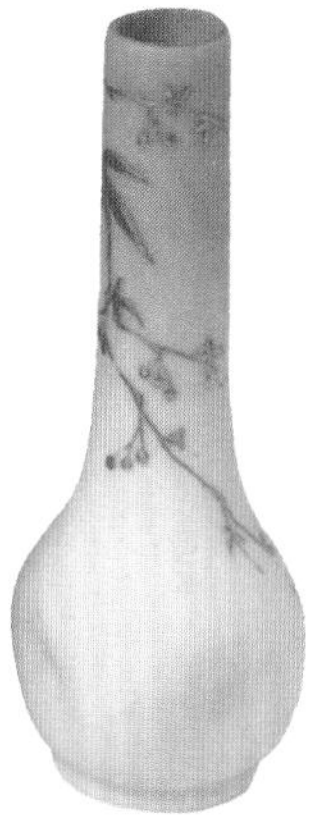

A pair of Thomas Webb & Sons 'Queen's Burmese Ware' glass stick vases, gilt with leaf and berry sprays in the workshop of Jules Barbe, with dimpled bases, 1885–90, 6in (15cm) high.
£240–275
€/ $380–430 B

Burmese glass, characterized by a body colour that graduates from yellow to pale pink, was originally produced in the United States in 1886 by the Mount Washington Glass Company. In Britain that same year, this style of glass was patented by Thomas Webb & Sons under the name 'Queen's Burmese', so-called because it was favoured by Queen Victoria. This distinctive colour was created by using a combination of gold and uranium oxides, together with sodium nitrate: the glass changed colour when reheated quickly, as seen at the top of this vase. Burmese wares were mainly ornamental pieces such as vases.

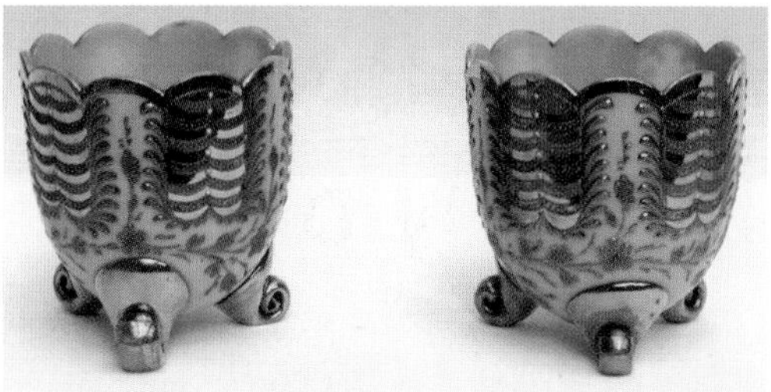

► **A pair of glass posy vases,** with gilt decoration, Continental, 1880–90, 3in (7.5cm) high.
£100–120
€/ $160–190 GRI

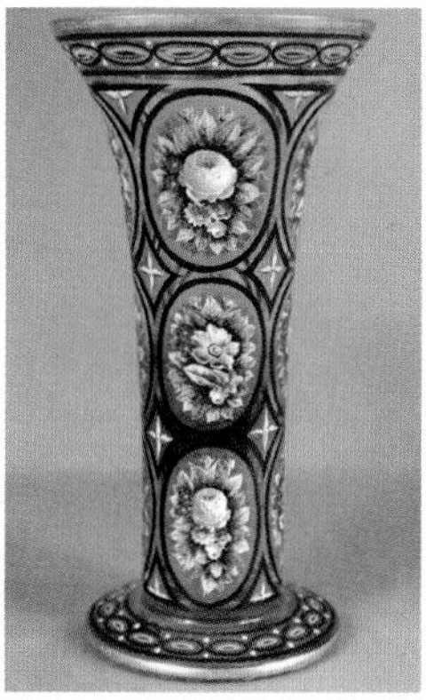

A glass vase, hand-painted in enamels with panels of flowers, 19thC, 13in (33cm) high.
£200–225
€/ $300–350 SWO

A pair of Japonaise opaque overlay glass vases, decorated in relief with prunus blossom and flying fish beneath scroll and beaded rims, on stepped bases, the four corner feet modelled as elephants' masks, 19thC, 15in (38cm) high.
£150–180
€/ $240–280 TMA

A pair of opaque glass vases, hand-painted with parrots and gilded leaf sprays, one chipped, Continental, 19thC, 15¾in (40cm) high.
£1,200–1,500
€/ $1,900–2,400 JAd

The decoration of these vases is of superior quality and they therefore achieved a high price at auction.

► **A ruby-flashed glass trumpet vase,** engraved with a continuous scene of deer in a forest landscape, on a domed and fluted foot with a floral band, minor damage, Bohemian, late 19thC, 18in (45.5cm) high.
£1,000–1,200
€/ $1,600–1,900 DN

The decoration of this vase is of a very high standard.

A glass vase, decorated with alternate panels of enamelled flowers and diamond cutting within gilt bands, c1900, 15½in (39.5cm) high.
£400–450
€/ $630–700 DORO

Miscellaneous

◀ **A glass carafe,** enamelled with flowers and the bear emblematic of the city of Berne, applied string-ring to neck, Swiss, c1730, 6¾in (17cm) high.
£1,100–1,300
€/ $1,700–2,000 ⊞ G&G

An oval glass dish, cut with strawberry diamonds and intersecting prisms, beneath a notched rim, c1820, 11½in (29cm) wide.
£320–350
€/ $500–550 ⊞ Som

A flatware set, with Bohemian millefiori glass handles, c1850.
£700–800
€/ $1,100–1,300 ⊞ DLP

A frigger of a seaside town, modelled with a locomotive travelling along a bridge between two tunnels, the bay beneath with two sailing ships, the cliffs with houses and a lighthouse, on a wooden stand, beneath a glass dome, late 19thC, 19¾in (50cm) high.
£650–750
€/ $1,000–1,200 ⚒ DN
A frigger is a decorative or novelty glass object apparently made by glassworkers in their own time, using surplus glass that remained in the furnace pots.

A *façon de Venise* glass inkwell, applied with two cylindrical sconces or pen-holders with trailed and pincered ornament, scroll handle, applied flowers with ruby beads, on a wide foot with upturned rim, probably Venetian, c1800, 4in (10cm) high.
£400–450
€/ $630–700 ⚒ S(O)

A cranberry glass patch pot, with opaque decoration, inscribed 'Firenze', c1885, 2½in (6.5cm) diam.
£180–200
€/ $280–300 ⊞ GRI

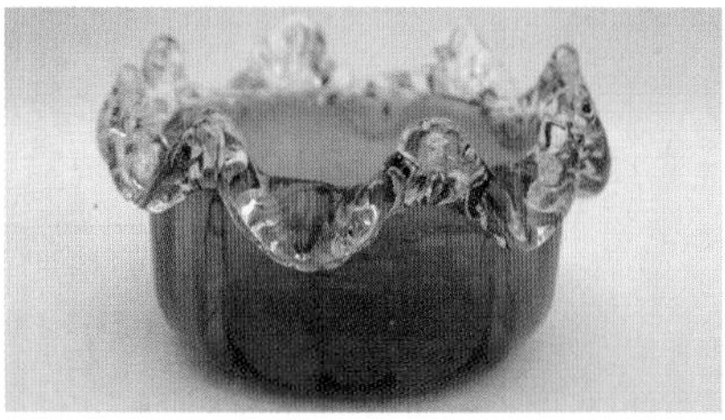

A ribbed cranberry glass salt, with colourless coronet frill, c1900, 2½in (6.5cm) diam.
£80–90
€/ $125–145 ⊞ GRI

◀ **A set of 24 glass rinsers,** each with a facet-cut band, minor damage, 19thC, 3½in (9cm) diam.
£650–750
€/ $1,000–1,200 ⚒ S(O)
These were used for rinsing wine glasses during meals, to save having to change them between different wines.

▶ **A toddy lifter,** the flute-cut neck with two cut rings, c1810, 5¼in (13.5cm) high.
£120–150
€/ $190–240 ⊞ Som
Toddy lifters are relics of an age when punch was a staple beverage across the English-speaking world. Made in Britain and Ireland during the 18th and 19th centuries, they were used for transferring punch 'toddies' from bowl to glass without requiring a messy ladle. Generally formed as vertically stretched miniature decanters, they had holes bored in both ends. The bulbous end was immersed into a bowl of punch until full and a thumb closed the upper hole, creating a vacuum to suspend the contents. The thumb was then removed to release the measure into a waiting glass.

An amethyst glass vinaigrette, with a silver top, cut with Regency-style strawberry diamonds, 1860, 1in (2.5cm) high.
£425–475
€/ $670–750 ⊞ CoS

Silver

Around the time the first edition of *Miller's Antiques Price Guide* was published, strange things were happening in the silver world. In 1980, a small group, headed by the millionaire Hunt brothers of Texas, decided to purchase all available bullion silver to gain control of the market and act as a hedge against inflation. Prices went through the roof and peaked at £34 (€/ $54) per ounce. As a result beautiful old pieces of silver were being sold for their bullion rather than their antique value and melted down. Silver had never cost so much, and anyone who purchased at that time is unlikely to ever get their money back as within a few months the trading rules on the New York Metals Market were changed and the Federal Reserve intervened. The Hunts' game was over and immediately prices plummeted to about £7 (€/ $11) per ounce. The speculators disappeared, and so had a great deal of antique silver.

Prices were just beginning to recover when, from 1983–92, a few private individuals competed against each other to buy large, top grade silver items, thus lifting the prices for such pieces to new heights. As the best pieces became virtually impossible to afford, an enthusiastic market for middle-range English silver developed. Much was being purchased by European dealers, until the value of the pound became so strong in the early 1990s that such pieces were no longer in demand abroad. However, a market for more affordable items, 'collectables' such as card cases, snuff boxes, vinaigrettes and provincial silver began to emerge.

The picture today is that the value of English domestic silver from 1600–1840, in good condition, has appreciated above inflation, although prices for coffee pots and some later Georgian tankards have remained fairly static since, in spite of the Hunt brothers, there are still plenty of them about. Wine-related objects and collectable pieces are keenly sought after but standard items such as tea sets from c1900–50 are not selling well due to the absence of the export market.

Top range antique silver is becoming ever more rare and beyond the means of many collectors. At present the average age of the collector of antique silver is rising. It is important to attract younger blood into the field and with the large range of more affordable items available there is plenty to choose from, even for those on a limited budget. **Nicholas Shaw**

Animals

A silver mustard pot, by Charles and George Fox, modelled as an owl, London 1865–66, 4in (10cm) high.
£3,200–3,600
€/ $5,000–5,700 ⊞ NS

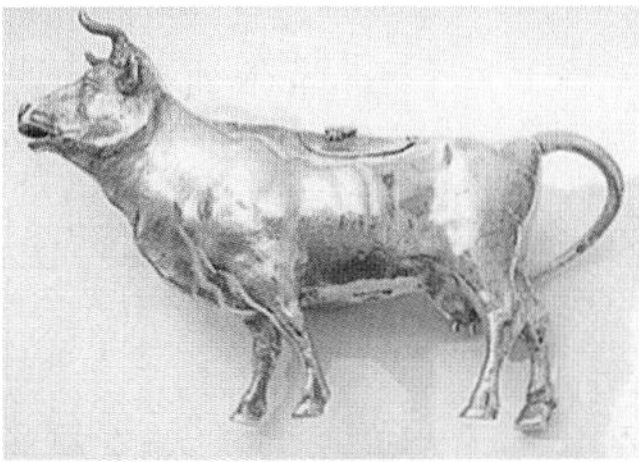

A silver cow creamer, Continental, London import marks for 1892, 7in (18cm) wide.
£550–650
€/ $870–1,000 ⚒ B&L

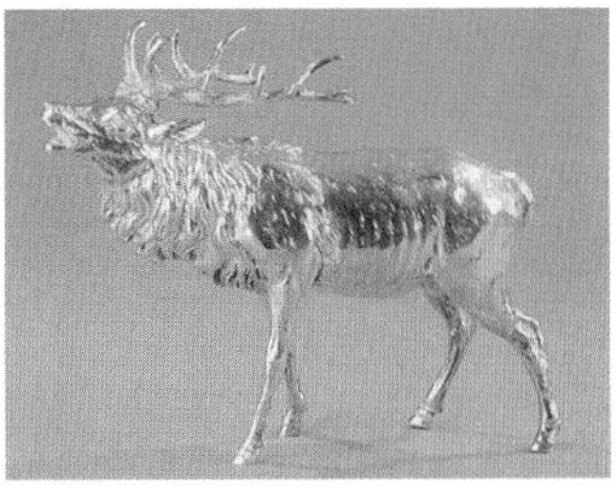

A silver model of a stag, Continental, c1890, 9¾in (25cm) wide, 25oz.
£1,300–1,500
€/ $2,000–2,400 ⚒ TEN

A silver jardinière, by Durgin Division of Gorham, modelled as a swan, with a removable gilt-metal flower grid, marked on base, American, c1900, 13in (33cm) wide, 54oz.
£5,000–6,000
€/ $7,900–9,500 ⚒ S(NY)

A silver fish *étui*, Continental, 19thC, 5in (12.5cm) long.
£1,300–1,500
€/ $2,000–2,400 ⊞ SHa

A pair of silver pin cushions, modelled as hedgehogs, Birmingham 1904, 1¼in (3cm) wide.
£380–450
€/ $600–700 ⚒ G(L)

A silver parasol handle, by W.B., modelled as a parrot's head, mounted on a parasol with a bamboo shaft, London 1910, 35in (89cm) long.
£160–200
€/ $250–320 ⚒ SWO

Baskets

A silver bread basket, by William Plummer, engraved with the armorials of the King family within a rococo floral cartouche, below a crest and above a motto, the sides pierced with panels of scrolls, roundels, crosses and other motifs between curved beaded straps, handle missing, London 1768, 13in (33cm) wide, 17oz.
£700–800
€/ $1,100–1,300 S(O)

A silver basket, by Jonas Nylander, decorated with a coat-of-arms, Swedish, Skara 1824, 12in (30.5cm) wide.
£1,100–1,300
€/ $1,700–2,000 BUK

A silver cake basket, pierced and embossed with flowers, scrolls and shells, Chester 1896, 12¼in (31cm) wide, 10.5oz.
£160–200
€/ $250–320 DN

A silver-gilt sugar basket, by Tudor & Leader, the pierced gallery sides below embossed paterae and husk swags with bead-edge borders, on a pedestal foot, with a glass liner, Sheffield 1776, 4¾in (12cm) high, 2.5oz.
£800–950
€/ $1,300–1,500 B(L)

► **A silver-gilt sugar basket,** by E. E. J. & W. Barnard, applied with trailing oak leaves and acorns, on four leaf and scroll-chased feet, with a glass liner, London 1841, 5¼in (13.5cm) diam, 7.5oz.
£450–525
€/ $700–830 DN

A silver basket, by Peter and Ann Bateman, with floral swag decoration and engraved initials, on a shaped base, London 1792, 6¼in (16cm) wide, 8oz.
£500–600
€/ $800–950 RIT

◄ **A silver fruit basket,** by Henry Matthews, the shaped rim cast with flowers and C-scrolls above pierced and embossed sides, on a raised foot cast with flowers and scrolls, Birmingham 1903, 13¾in (35cm) wide.
£750–875
€/ $1,200–1,400 RTo

Beakers

A silver beaker, by Jean-Nicholas Saget, with a moulded girdle between applied fruiting vine decoration, engraved with an armorial, the date 1789 and inscribed below the rim and to the foot, French, Paris c1787, 4¾in (12cm) high, 5oz.
£320–380
€/ $500–600 CGC

A silver christening mug, by John Anton Bunning, the tapering body with applied rim and friezes of engraved decoration centred by a scroll cartouche with initials, traces of gilding, maker's mark, South African, Capetown, c1790, 2½in (6.5cm) high, 2oz.
£160–200
€/ $250–320 WW

A silver beaker, by Paul Storr, engraved with a contemporary coat-of-arms, London 1802–03, 3¾in (9.5cm) high, 4oz.
£2,500–2,800
€/ $4,000–4,400 NS

► **A silver beaker,** by M. Koshov, Russian, Moscow 1875, 2¾in (7cm) high.
£160–175
€/ $250–280 GRe

A pair of horn and silver beakers, with threaded rims, mid-19thC, 4in (10cm) high.
£180–220
€/ $280–350 TMA

SILVER

Bowls

A silver christening bowl, engraved with initials 'MN', maker's mark PD, Channel Islands, c1700, 5½in (14cm) wide, 3oz.
£1,800–2,200
€/ $2,800–3,500 ⚒ B&L

A silver quaich, by J. Hay, Scottish, Edinburgh 1875–76, 5in (12.5cm) wide.
£1,500–1,700
€/ $2,400–2,700 ⊞ NS

A silver rose bowl, with flower-moulded loop handles, on pad feet, with a glass liner, Continental, 19thC, 17in (43cm) wide, 38oz.
£800–950
€/ $1,300–1,500
⚒ AH

A silver bowl and cover, probably by William Darker, with a plain waisted band, London 1728, 4in (10cm) diam.
£1,800–2,200
€/ $2,800–3,500 ⚒ HOLL

A silver bowl, by Charles Stuart Harris, London 1886, 3¾in (9.5cm) high.
£270–300
€/ $425–470 ⊞ GRe

A silver bowl, possibly by Charles Townsend of Dublin, with shaped rim and chased wrythen fluting, engraved with two crests, on three shell-capped short scroll legs and hoof feet, maker's mark, Irish, c1760, 5in (12.5cm) diam.
£375–425
€/ $590–670 ⚒ G(L)

A silver punch bowl, by Alexander Clark, with gadrooned rim, the bowl half fluted and reeded with wrythen decoration, on a flared foot, Sheffield 1899, 11in (28cm) diam.
£750–900
€/ $1,200–1,400 ⚒ RTo

► A silver rose bowl, with repoussé, floral and scrolled decoration, London 1902, 8¼in (21cm) diam, on an ebonized stand.
£150–175
€/ $240–280
⚒ WilP

◄ A silver rose bowl, by F.B. & Sons, with embossed C-scroll vacant cartouches, Sheffield 1902, 8½in (21.5cm) diam.
£240–275
€/ $380–440
⚒ DMC

A silver punchbowl, by Marcus & Co, with a hammered finish and gilt interior, on a waisted and stepped foot, American, New York c1920, 12in (30.5cm) diam.
£2,500–2,800
€/ $4,000–4,400 ⚒ NOA

SILVER

Boxes

A silver counter box, by B. B. & Crescent, London c1685, 1¾in (4.5cm) high.
£800–900
€/ $1,300–1,400 ⊞ BEX

A silver tea caddy, by Daniel Smith and Robert Sharp, with a foliate knop, the body with an engraved armorial, London 1764, 3¼in (8.5cm) wide.
£2,000–2,400
€/ $3,200–3,800 ⚒ SWO

A silver box, with repoussé decoration of cherubs' heads, 1902, 1¾in (4.5cm) square.
£200–235
€/ $320–370 ⊞ BLm

Items in the Silver section have been arranged in date order within each sub-section.

Caddy Spoons

◄ A silver caddy spoon, by William Eley, London 1815, 4½in (11.5cm) long.
£110–120
€/ $175–190
⊞ GRe

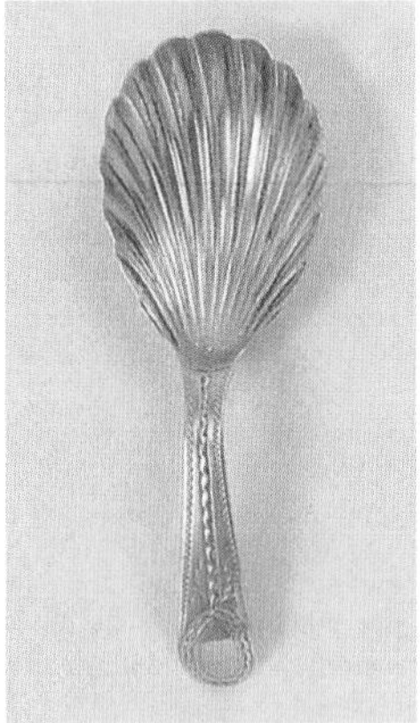

A silver caddy spoon, probably by William Marshall, with a fluted bowl and a bright-cut stem with a vacant cartouche, Scottish, Edinburgh c1800, 3¾in (9.5cm) long, 0.75oz.
£100–120
€/ $160–190 ⚒ WW

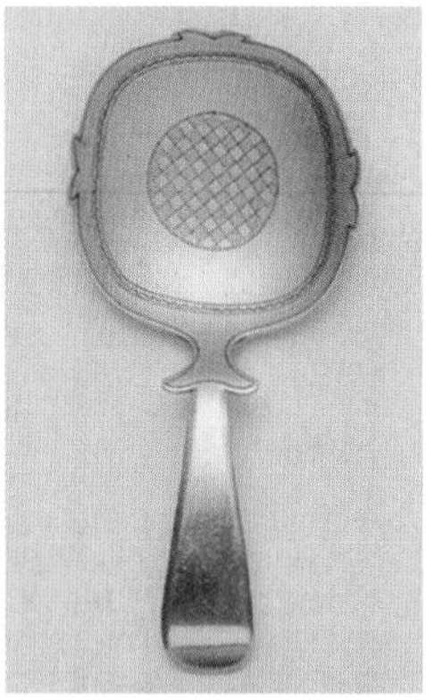

A silver caddy spoon, by Thomas Hames, the rounded square bowl with a bright-engraved band around a central roundel of diaper-work, the plain handle with a fish-tail projection at the base, 1814, 4in (10cm) long.
£320–375
€/ $500–600 ⚒ B

A silver caddy spoon, by Henry Lias, London 1856, 4in (10cm) long.
£70–80
€/ $110–130
⊞ GRe

► A silver caddy spoon, by James Collins, with foliate engraving, Birmingham 1850, 3¼in (8.5cm) long.
£70–85
€/ $110–135
⚒ WW

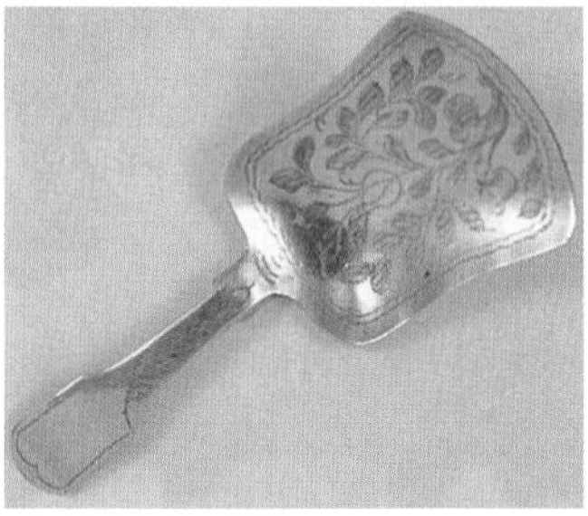

Candlesticks & Chambersticks

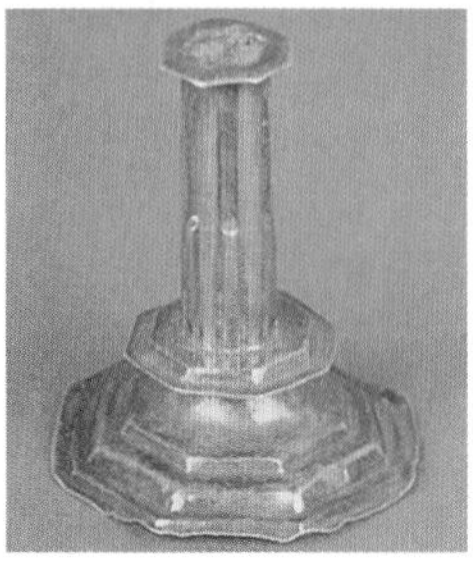

A silver miniature candlestick, possibly by William Matthew, the stop-fluted stem on a stepped base, London 1703, 2in (5cm) high.
£500–565
€/ $800–900 ⚒ RTo

A pair of silver candlesticks, by William Comyns, with repoussé-decorated stems, 1899, 6½in (16.5cm) high.
£900–1,000
€/ $1,400–1,600 ⊞ CoHA

► A silver dwarf candlestick, Sheffield 1822, 4¼in (11cm) high.
£160–200
€/ $250–320 ⚒ SWO

◄ A silver chamberstick, by James Dixon & Sons, Sheffield 1897, 5¼in (13.5cm) wide.
£900–1,000
€/ $1,400–1,600
⊞ BLm

SILVER

Card Cases

A silver card case, by Nathaniel Mills, depicting St Paul's Cathedral, Birmingham 1843–44, 4in (10cm) high.
£1,300–1,500
€/ $2,000–2,400 NS

A silver card case, by Nathaniel Mills, engraved with flowers and acanthus scrolls, on an engine-turned ground, initialled 'E.R.', Birmingham 1845, 4in (10cm) high.
£200–220
€/ $320–350 B(WM)

A silver card case, embossed with a cathedral within a floral and scroll frame, the reverse with a panel filled with a quiver, arrows and a torch, framed by foliate scrolls, late 19thC, 3½in (9cm) high, cased.
£200–225
€/ $320–350 RTo

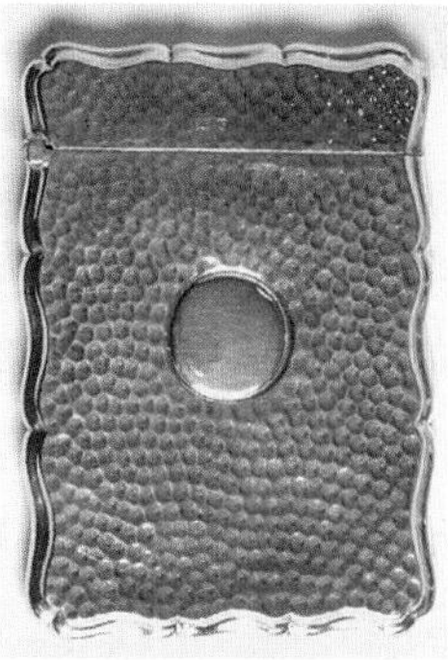

A silver card case, by A. & J. Zimmermann, Birmingham 1902, 3¾in (9.5cm) high.
£130–145
€/ $200–230 GRe

Insurance values

Always insure your valuable antiques for the cost of replacing them with similar items, regardless of the original price paid. Both dealers and auctioneers can provide a valuation service for a fee.

► **A silver card case,** by William Comyns, decorated with repoussé cherubs, London 1904, 4in (10cm) high.
£350–400
€/ $550–630 BLm

Casters

A pair of silver casters, maker's mark for Samuel Welder, London 1714, 5in (12.5cm) high.
£750–900
€/ $1,200–1,400 TMA

Expert's choice

A silver-gilt casting bottle, 1553, sold by Sotheby's in 1984.

In all my years as a dealer, the most extraordinary story I have ever heard concerns a little bottle that was found in a box on a market stall and presumed to be made of brass. It was a pretty thing so, having purchased it for a nominal amount, its new owner took it to Sotheby's to have it checked out. The experts there couldn't believe their eyes. It was identified as a silver-gilt casting bottle, used for sprinkling rosewater over the hands, dating from 1553, during the reign of Mary Tudor. The little bottle is exceptionally rare because it is fully hallmarked and only three other such pieces are known, of which two are in museums. It was sold at Sotheby's to Arthur Gilbert for £100,000 (€/ $158,000) in 1984 and is now on display in the Gilbert Collection at Somerset House, The Strand, London. **Nicholas Shaw**

A set of three silver casters, maker ES, Exeter 1727, largest 6¼in (16cm) high.
£5,000–6,000
€/ $8,000–9,500 G(L)

◄ **A silver sugar caster,** by Haseler & Haseler, with a blue glass liner, London 1898, 7½in (19cm) high, 4oz.
£230–275
€/ $360–430 WW

► **A silver sugar caster,** by Charles and George Asprey, London 1904, 9in (23cm) high.
£200–235
€/ $320–370 PGO

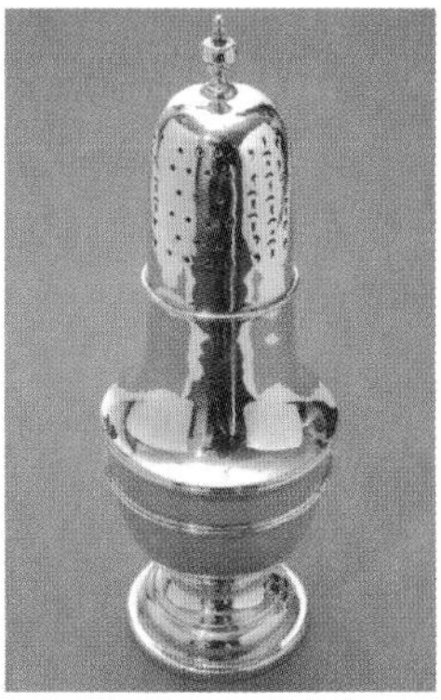

Centrepieces

A silver centrepiece, by John and Joseph Angell, with pierced foliate decoration, on foliate scrolling feet, London 1843, 10in (25.5cm) high.
£450–525
€/ $700–830 SWO

Items in the Silver section have been arranged in date order within each sub-section.

A neo-Renaissance-style silver *épergne*, by HW, the central reeded stem and three arched arms supporting etched glass sweetmeat bowls on later silver sconces, on a circular base with three cast hairy-paw feet, London 1877, 17¼in (44cm) high, 57oz.
£2,200–2,500
€/ $3,500–4,000 WL

A Victorian silver centrepiece, with gilt interior and repoussé decoration, 19in (48.5cm) wide.
£1,700–2,000
€/ $2,700–3,200 JDJ

A silver centrepiece, by Gorham Manufacturing Co, with wavy embossed and pierced rim, numbered, American, Providence, Rhode Island 1901, 18¼in (46.5cm) wide, 45oz.
£1,400–1,600
€/ $2,200–2,500 S(NY)

A silver *épergne*, the baskets with glass liners, Sheffield 1909, 11½in (29cm) high.
£3,200–3,500
€/ $5,000–5,500 BLm

A silver *épergne*, the lobed central dish flanked by two similar smaller dishes, supported by scrolled branches, on a spreading base with scroll feet, Birmingham 1910, 9in (23cm) high, 56oz.
£650–750
€/ $1,000–1,200 G(B)

A silver centrepiece, with a glass liner, London 1911, 8½in (21.5cm) high.
£2,300–2,500
€/ $3,600–4,000 BLm

Chocolate, Coffee & Teapots

A silver coffee pot, by Gabriel Sleath, with later chased decoration and a crest, London 1732, 9¾in (25cm) high, 26oz.
£1,000–1,200
€/ $1,600–1,900 S(O)

◄ **A silver teapot,** by James Ker, Scottish, Edinburgh 1737–38, 5in (12.5cm) high.
£5,000–5,500
€/ $8,000–8,700 NS

► **A silver coffee jug,** by John Craig, Irish, Dublin 1772, 12in (30.5cm) high.
£4,700–5,200
€/ $7,400–8,200 WELD

A silver chocolate pot, by Pehr Zethelius, the sliding knop modeled as a flower, with ebonized handle, Swedish, Stockholm 1782, 6¾in (17cm) high.
£3,500–4,000
€/ $5,500–6,400 BUK

Miller's Compares

I. A silver teapot, by Hester Bateman, chased with floral festoons around a cartouche and crest, with green-stained ivory handle, London 1786, 7in (18cm) high, 16oz.
£2,100–2,500
€/ $3,300–4,000 WW

II. A silver teapot, by Thomas Shepherd, with a fruitwood handle, London 1786, 5½in (14cm) high, 12.5oz.
£650–750
€/ $1,000–1,200 WW

Item I was made by Hester Bateman, who is always sought after by collectors. The piece is particularly desirable because of its unusual design. The pierced rim around the foot is a feature which is rarely seen, although it is not particularly practical since, as in this example, it gets damaged very easily. If the rim had been in perfect condition, the teapot might well have sold for in excess of £2,500 (€/ $4,000). Item I also has a very attractive green-stained ivory handle, which is unusually decorated with a *piqué* work pattern in steel. Item II has a standard fruitwood handle.

A silver coffee pot, by William Moody, London 1786, 13in (33cm) high.
£4,000–4,500
€/ $6,300–7,000 TSC

A silver teapot, by Jabez Halsey, with a monogram in a cartouche, swags and a cluster of strawberries, with a pineapple finial, maker's mark, American, New York c1790, 6½in (16.5cm) high, 18oz.
£3,300–3,800
€/ $5,200–6,000 S(NY)

An early Victorian silver-gilt coffee pot, by Charles Reily and George Storer, the body engraved with a ducal coronet above a cypher, the spout with a hinged cover, the handle hinged to fold, on a heater base, 6¾in (17cm) high, 16.75oz.
£850–1,000
€/ $1,300–1,600 CGC

A silver coffee pot, by Giulio II Zanetti, the body decorated with bands of leaves and palmettes, the spout terminating in a bird's head, with an ebonized wood handle, Italian, Bologna c1840, 12in (30.5cm) high.
£1,400–1,600
€/ $2,200–2,500 DORO

A silver teapot, by Martin Hall & Co, embossed with rococo-style decoration, with an eagle finial, on four scroll feet, Sheffield 1909, 7½in (19cm) high, 25.5oz.
£280–325
€/ $440–510 BR

SILVER

Cigar & Cigarette Cases

A silver cigar case with a hinged lid, by Nathaniel Mills, one side engraved with the Crystal Palace within a floral and scroll frame, the reverse engraved with a foliate scroll cartouche on an engine-turned band ground, Birmingham 1850, 5in (12.5cm) high.
£550–625
€/ $870–1,000 RTo

A silver cigarette case, with a silver-gilt interior, initialled 'MM', Russian, 19thC, 3½in (9cm) wide.
£100–120
€/ $160–190 SWO

► **A silver and gold-mounted officer's cheroot case,** Russian, Moscow 1908–17, 6in (15cm) wide.
£2,500–2,800
€/ $4,000–4,400 SHa

A silver cigar case, Birmingham 1903, 5in (12.5cm) wide.
£80–100
€/ $125–160 G(L)

Clocks & Watches

A Victorian silver heart-shaped desk timepiece, with foliate scroll engraving, 4in (10cm) high.
£120–140
€/ $190–220 G(L)

◄ **A silver-cased carriage clock,** by William Comyns, with an enamel dial and French platform movement, on four bun feet, London 1901, 3¾in (9.5cm) high.
£650–750
€/ $1,000–1,200 DMC

A silver watch, by Mappin & Webb, on a hobnail-cut glass inkwell, Birmingham c1905, 4in (10cm) wide.
£1,100–1,300
€/ $1,700–2,000 HCA

English antique silver 1976–2002

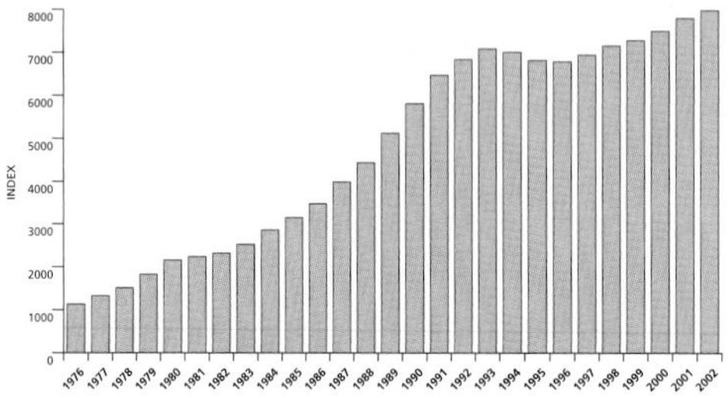

This graph shows the increasing value of English antique silver as a whole over the past 25 years. International influences on the silver market at various times over the years have also had an effect on the growth of English antique silver. ©AMR

A silver carriage clock, with eight-day French movement, and platform lever escapement, inscribed 'Goldsmith & Silversmiths Co, Regent Street', London 1905, 3in (7.5cm) high.
£670–750
€/ $1,100–1,200 PSA

► **A silver miniature longcase clock,** with an easel back, Birmingham 1912, 6¼in (16cm) high.
£140–160
€/ $220–250 SWO

Coffee & Tea Services

A silver three-piece tea service, by William Fountain, the milk jug and sugar bowl with gilt interiors and wrythen handles cast in the shape of entwined horns of plenty, all on pedestal bases with gadrooned borders, London 1805–08, 57oz.
£800–1,000
€/ $1,300–1,600 WW

A silver three-piece tea service, with half-fluted bodies, the hinged teapot lid with an embossed finial, the loop handle moulded with acanthus leaf, on bun feet, London 1822 and 1823, 36oz.
£700–850
€/ $1,100–1,300 AH

► **A silver five-piece tea and coffee service,** by William Forbes for Ball, Tomkins & Black, the sides flat-chased with rococo cartouches and engraved with a monogram, American, New York c1845, coffee pot 10in (25.5cm) high, 100oz.
£2,000–2,400
€/ $3,200–3,800 S(NY)

A silver four-piece tea and coffee service, by Charles Reily and George Storer, with flower-spray finials, chased with leaves and flowers, engraved with an ermine crest, with leafy S-scroll handles, on scroll panel feet, London 1840, coffee pot 10in (25.5cm) high, 87oz.
£1,300–1,500
€/ $2,000–2,400 Bri

A silver neo-classical four-piece tea and coffee service, by Edward Barnard & Sons, the teapot and coffee pot with pineapple finials, each piece decorated in relief with human masks, floral swags and leaves, chased with ribbons, swags, bellflowers and medallions, London 1868, 83oz.
£2,800–3,200
€/ $4,400–5,000 PFK

SILVER

A silver five-piece tea and coffee service, by Charles Stuart Harris, London 1886–87, 100oz.
£4,300–4,800
€/ $6,800–7,600 ⊞ JC
Charles Stuart Harris entered his mark in 1852 as a 'Spoon Maker'. Later in 1896 he was described as a silver worker. He carried on in business until 1904, when the firm became known as C. S. Harris & Sons Ltd.

A silver three-piece tea service, by Elkington, Birmingham 1891, teapot 4in (10cm) high.
£1,200–1,300
€/ $1,900–2,000 ⊞ BLm

A silver three-piece tea service, by Barnard Bros, London 1898, 3in (7.5cm) high.
£550–600
€/ $870–950 ⊞ GRe

A silver and porcelain coffee set, by Elkington & Co, with Copelands China coffee cans and saucers, on bun feet, one coffee can and saucer missing, Birmingham 1899, stand 14¼in (36cm) wide.
£350–420
€/ $550–670 ⚒ RTo

A silver part tea and coffee service, by Sebastian Garrard, the engine-turned baluster bodies with ivory handles, the covers with a crest in the form of a ram's head, 1910, 124oz.
£900–1,100
€/ $1,400–1,700 ⚒ L

Condiment Pots

A pair of silver bun salts, on pad feet, London 1735, 4in (10cm) diam.
£100–120
€/ $160–190 ⚒ G(L)

► **A silver novelty salt,** modelled as an open sack, 1874, 2½in (6.5cm) high.
£200–225
€/ $315–350 ⚒ G(L)

A silver hexagonal mustard pot, with associated mustard spoon, 1859, 3½in (9cm) high.
£200–250
€/ $315–400 ⚒ SWO

► **A silver mustard pot,** London 1911, 3½in (9cm) high.
£260–300
€/ $400–475 ⊞ GRe

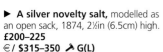

A pair of silver salts, by William Plummer, London 1784, 3in (7.5cm) diam.
£550–625
€/ $870–990 ⊞ HCA

A pair of silver parcel-gilt salts, by Henry Chawner, of pedestal design with twin-reeded loop handles and conforming banding, London 1796, 3in (7.5cm) high.
£300–350
€/ $470–550 ⚒ GTH

A pair of cut-glass mustard pots, with silver mounts, Birmingham 1903, 3in (7.5cm) high.
£120–135
€/ $190–215 ⊞ BrL

A pair of silver salts, by Gorham & Co, each with three drop ring handles and Greek key border, on three cast winged sphinx feet, incised '410', American, 1913, 3½in (9cm) diam.
£200–225
€/ $315–350 ⚒ WW

Cruets

A silver cruet, by Thomas Daniell, the central beaded loop handle incorporating a pierced spacer for the eight cut-glass silver-mounted bottles, on claw-and-ball feet, London 1784, 9¾in (25cm) high.
£900–1,100
€/ $1,400–1,700 CGC

A silver cruet, by Pehr Zethelius, with four silver-mounted bottles, on paw feet, Stockholm 1797, 13½in (34.5cm) wide.
£1,200–1,400
€/ $1,900–2,200 BUK

A silver cruet, by Rebecca Emes and Edward Barnard, on anthemion-cast feet, three bottles missing, London 1827, 7½in (19cm) wide.
£250–300
€/ $400–475 BR

► **A silver condiment set,** comprising three pieces, by Barnards, London 1899, largest 4in (10cm) high.
£240–265
€/ $380–420
GRe

Cups & Goblets

A silver tumbler cup, the base marked 'AW, probably by Clement Reed, York 1694, 3in (7.5cm) high, 2oz.
£4,200–5,000
€/ $6,600–8,000 TEN

A Britannia standard silver tea cup, by VN, with a scrolled handle and a moulded base, engraved with a crest, London 1697, 2½in (6.5cm) high.
£4,200–5,000
€/ $6,600–8,000 TRM

A silver wine goblet, by Henry Chawner, the bell bowl engraved with a coat-of-arms, on a reel-shaped base, London 1789–90, 6½in (16.5cm) high, 9.75oz.
£1,800–2,000
€/ $2,800–3,200 NS

Cutlery

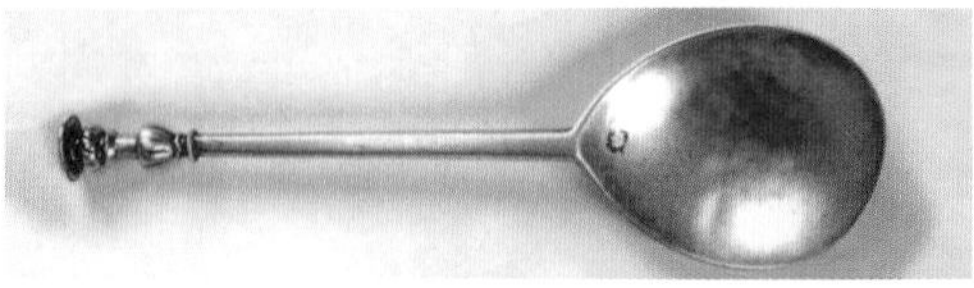

A silver spoon, with a fig-shaped bowl, the silver-gilt baluster terminal pricked with initials 'E P', London 1572.
£1,700–2,000
€/ $2,700–3,200 DN

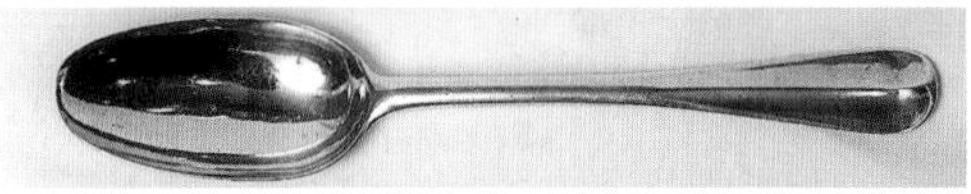

A silver tablespoon, by Jeremiah Morgan, Irish, Clonmel c1750, 8in (20.5cm) long.
£2,500–2,800
€/ $4,000–4,400 WELD
Items from Clonmel are very rare.

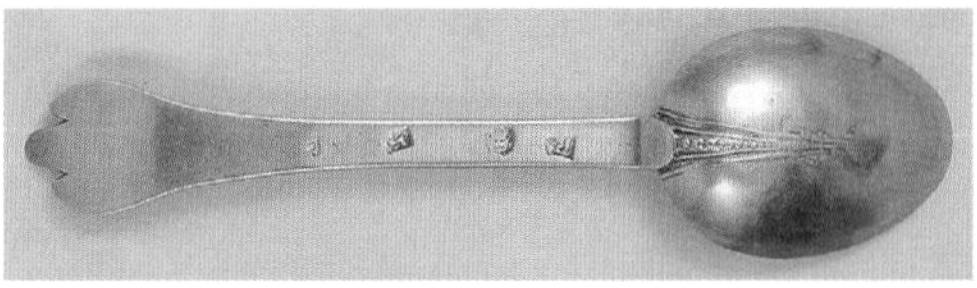

A silver trefid spoon, by William Matthew, with a bead and reeded rat-tail, reverse of stem marked, London c1690, 8in (20.5cm) long, 2.25oz.
£275–325
€/ $430–515 WW

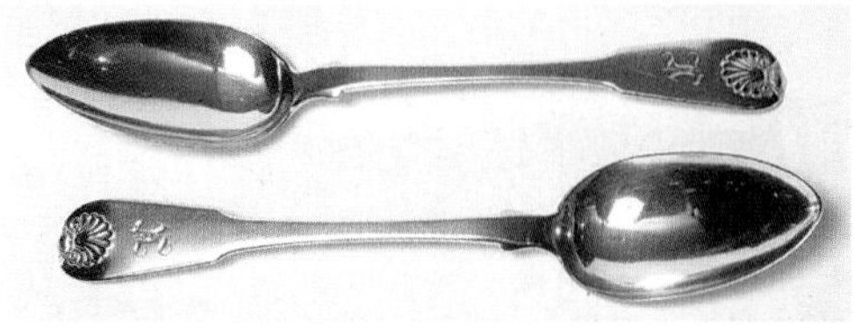

A pair of silver table spoons, by W & PC, Edinburgh 1826, 9in (23cm) long.
£80–90
€/ $125–140 WAC

Dishes

A pair of silver-gilt dishes, with scroll borders and trellis-pierced panels engraved with armorials, on scroll feet, 19thC, 10in (25.5cm) diam.
£625–725
€/ $1,000–1,100 G(L)

A silver bonbon dish, by Mappin & Webb, relief decorated with shells and flowerheads, with scroll-edged lattice-pierced panels, hallmarked Sheffield 1906, 10½in (26.5cm) diam, 10oz.
£120–150
€/ $190–240 PFK

A silver dish, embossed with the mask of a mastiff dog surrounded by a whip, Sheffield 1909, 4¾in (12cm) diam, 21oz.
£120–150
€/ $190–240 HOLL

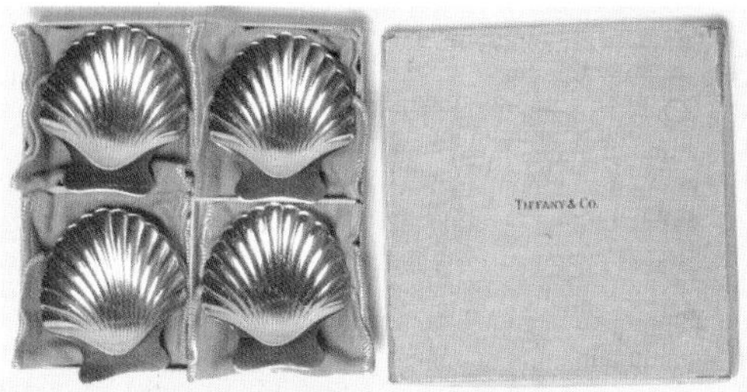

◄ **A set of four silver dishes,** by Tiffany & Co, c1910, boxed, 5½in (14cm) wide.
£675–750
€/ $1,100–1,200
SHa

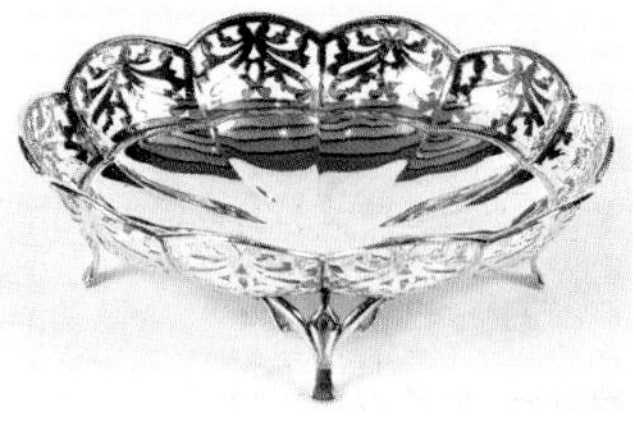

A silver bonbon dish, by H. Vale & Co, with pierced decoration, Chester 1911, 8in (20.5cm) wide.
£270–300
€/ $430–475 CoHA

Covered Dishes

A pair of silver entrée dishes, with gadrooned rims and detachable foliate-scrolled loop handles, with chased crests, maker's mark 'J.A.', London 1777–78, 11½in (29cm) wide, 100oz.
£2,200–2,500
€/ $3,500–4,000 AH

► **A silver-gilt covered dish and stand,** with a fruit finial, French, 19thC, 7in (18cm) wide, 16oz.
£200–250
€/ $315–400 TRM

► **A pair of silver entrée dishes and covers,** by The Goldsmiths & Silversmiths Co, crested, London 1903, 9½in (24cm) wide, 73oz.
£800–1,000
€/ $1,300–1,600 CGC

A silver revolving breakfast dish, with a rotating lid and two removeable trays, Sheffield 1908, 13in (33cm) wide.
£550–650
€/ $870–1,000 B(W)

Dish Rings & Crosses

A silver dish cross, by Hester Bateman, with a pear-shaped lamp, London 1782, 12½in (32cm) extended, 13oz.
£1,600–1,900
€/ $2,500–3,000 S(NY)

A silver dish ring, with a glass liner, Sheffield 1907, 4in (10cm) high.
£1,300–1,400
€/ $2,000–2,200 BLm

A silver dish ring, decorated with hounds within chased and engraved foliage, Irish, Dublin 1909, 4in (10cm) high, 15oz.
£1,800–2,200
€/ $2,800–3,500 JAd

Dressing Table Sets

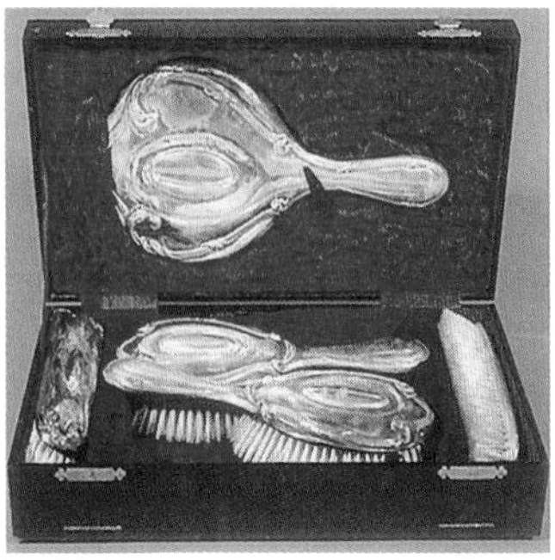

A six-piece silver-backed dressing table set, Chester 1909, cased.
£80–100
€/ $130–160 WilP

A silver dressing table set, Sheffield 1918, in fitted inlaid wood case, 15in (38cm) wide.
£380–425
€/ $600–670 GRe

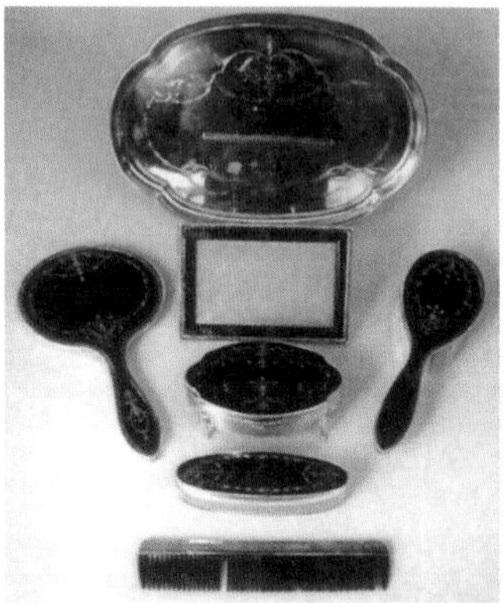

A silver and tortoiseshell seven-piece dressing table set, Birmingham 1920.
£650–750
€/ $1,000–1,200 BR

Ewers & Jugs

A small coin silver creamer, by Thomas Barton Simpkins, the bulbous body with a scroll handle on three trifid feet, decorated with a crest and three inscriptions, American, 1724–1804, 3¾in (9.5cm) high.
£4,500–5,300
€/ $7,000–8,300 JDJ

A silver cream jug, by John Bridge, London 1826, 5in (12.5cm) wide.
£270–300
€/ $430–475 CoHA

A silver wine ewer, by Andrew Fogelberg, London 1780, 11in (28cm) high.
£1,800–2,000
€/ $2,800–3,200 TSC

A silver water jug, by J. Mackay, with a mask spout, bracket handle and foliate finial, engraved with a coat-of-arms, Edinburgh 1840, 10½in (26.5cm) high, 33oz.
£1,400–1,600
€/ $2,200–2,500 B(Ed)

A silver jug, engraved with two opposing shell and scroll cartouches, with a mask spout, scrolling figurative handle and a finial modelled as a cherub riding a swan, 19thC, 30in (76cm) high.
£320–375
€/ $500–600 TMA

A silver hot water jug, with an ebony handle, 1900, 11in (28cm) high.
£270–300
€/ $430–475 EXC

◄ **A silver pitcher,** by the International Silver Co, engraved with swags and navette-shaped cartouches, with a waisted top and a C-scroll handle, American, Connecticut, c1930, 9½in (24cm) high.
£350–400
€/ $550–630 NOA

A silver cream jug, by Rebecca Emes and Edward Barnard, London 1820, 4½in (11.5cm) high.
£260–285
€/ $400–450 PGO

A Victorian Cellini pattern Renaissance-style ewer, by John Samuel Hunt, with a chased crest, gilded interior, and original cork stopper, 11½in (29cm) high, 38oz.
£1,200–1,400
€/ $1,900–2,200 AH

The Cellini pattern ewer was a standard design of claret jug made throughout the second half of the 19th century. It was so named because it was similar to a piece made by the 16th-century Italian goldsmith Benvenuto Cellini.

Figures

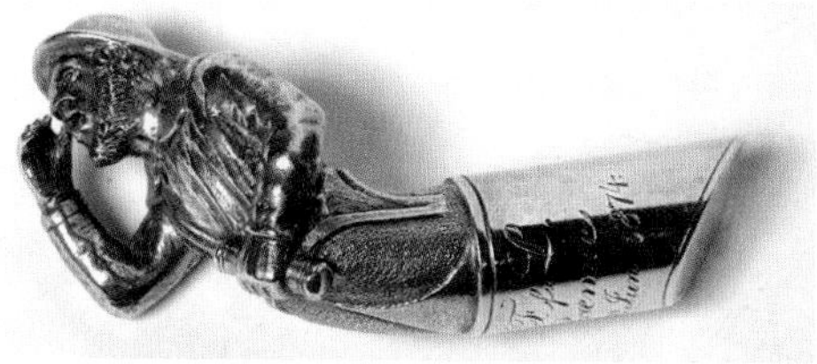

A silver whistle, in the form of a sailor, Continental, probably Danish, c1874, 3in (7.5cm) long.
£765–850
€/ $1,200–1,300 ⊞ NS

◀ A silver-gilt wager cup, in the form of a young lady holding a swinging cup above her head, probably by Joseph Angell, London 1828, 6¾in (17cm) high, 7oz.
£4,000–4,800
€/ $6,300–7,600 ⚒ HOLL
This piece had been stored in a bank vault for approximately 100 years and is still in mint condition.

A silver figure of a knight, with an ivory face, the armour elaborately chased, on a quatrefoil-shaped plinth, import marks for 1905, Austrian, c1900, 15¾in (40cm) high, 43oz.
£1,700–2,000
€/ $2,700–3,200 ⚒ TEN

Flasks

◀ A silver flask, maker's mark JW, early 18thC, 5in (13cm) high, 5oz.
£900–1,100
€/ $1,400–1,700 ⚒ S(O)

▶ A silver-mounted hip flask, by James Dixon & Sons, engraved with a crest and a motto, with a crocodile skin sleeve, Sheffield 1895, 6¾in (17cm) high.
£85–100
€/ $135–160 ⚒ BR

A silver hip flask, Birmingham 1920, 7in (18cm) high.
£260–285
€/ $400–450 ⊞ GRe

Frames

A late Victorian silver-mounted easel dressing table mirror, embossed with C-scrolls and flowers around an engraved cartouche, bevelled glass, 14½in (37cm) high.
£280–320
€/ $440–500 ⚒ EH

▶ A silver frame, Birmingham 1902, 8in (20.5cm) high.
£220–245
€/ $350–380 ⊞ WAC

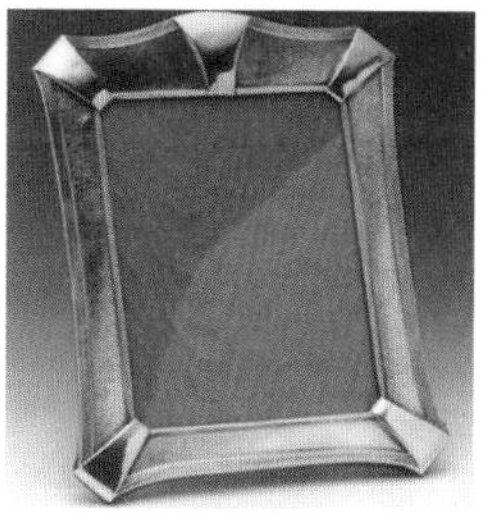

A silver frame, by Sothers, Orchard & Co, with lightly hammered surface, Birmingham 1907–08, 11¼in (28.5cm) high.
£675–750
€/ $1,100–1,200 ⊞ NS

A silver frame, Birmingham 1903, 7in (18cm) high.
£160–175
€/ $250–275 ⊞ BrL

▶ A silver-gilt frame, with engine-turned decoration and Greek key border, London 1913, 4¾in (12cm) high.
£120–150
€/ $190–240 ⚒ TMA

Inkstands & Inkwells

A silver inkstand, by Messrs Angell, the raised pierced borders decorated with scrolls, shells and foliage, with two silver-mounted cut-glass inkpots and a chamberstick and snuffer, retailer's stamp, London 1840, 13½in (34.5cm) wide, 42.5oz.
£1,500–1,800
€/ $2,400–2,800 E

► **A silver and copper inkstand,** by Black, Starr & Frost, the cartouche-shaped stand with applied bearskin above a pen tray, with applied border of whiplash scrolls, the cut-glass inkwell applied with a bull's head, American, New York c1905, 13½in (34.5cm) wide.
£3,000–3,500
€/ $4,700–5,500 S(NY)

◄ **A silver inkstand,** by William Hutton & Son, Sheffield 1908, 9in (23cm) wide.
£350–385
€/ $550–600
GRe

Kettles

◄ **A silver 'toy' tea kettle,** probably by David Clayton, London c1715, 3¾in (9.5cm) high.
£650–775
€/ $1,000–1,200 HYD

► **A silver tea kettle and stand,** by Pezé Pilleau, engraved with armorials and a crest within rococco cartouches below a chased shoulder of flowers and scrolls, the stand with floral aprons and shell feet, London 1751, 11½in (29cm) high, 52oz.
£1,300–1,500
€/ $2,000–2,400 S(O)

A silver kettle and stand, by J. T. Heath & J. H. Middleton, with fluted decoration, London 1891, 10¼in (26cm) high, 36oz.
£400–470
€/ $630–740 WW

Lamps

A silver storm chamber lamp, with a gadrooned base, ring handle and bayonet fitting glass shade, initialled, maker's mark HE?, London 1817, 4¾in (12cm) diam, 6.5oz.
£525–625
€/ $830–1,000 WW

A silver-gilt hanging lamp, in the form of an angel's head, maker's mark 'C.H.', Workmaster Alexander N. Mitin, Russian, St Petersburg 1851, 21¾in (55.5cm) long, 15oz.
£1,100–1,300
€/ $1,700–2,000 DORO

► **A silver carriage lamp,** by Frederick Perry, with hinged cover and door and sprung candle holder, 1882, 6in (15cm) high, 15oz.
£800–1,000
€/ $1,300–1,600 G(L)

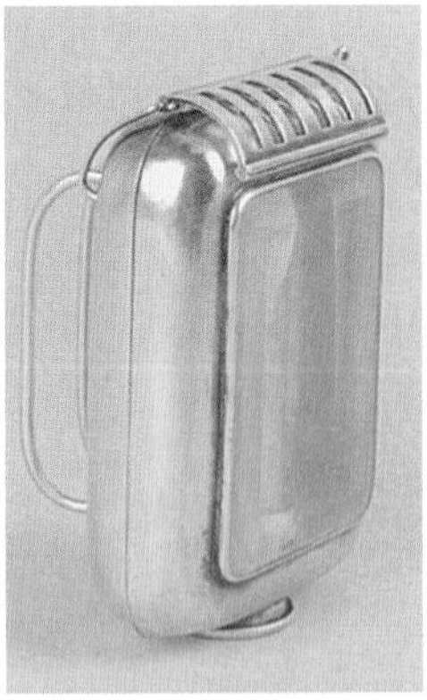

A silver hand lantern, by Drew & Sons, with hinged, glazed cover, the back with finger grips and engraved crest and initials, 1894, 4¼in (11cm) high.
£950–1,100
€/ $1,500–1,700 L

Items in the Silver section have been arranged in date order.

Menu Holders

A parcel-gilt menu holder, by Sampson Mordan & Co, modelled as a stack of four grenades, London c1881, 2¼in (5.5cm) high.
£160–200
€/ $250–315 WW

► **A pair of silver menu holders,** by Mappin & Webb, in the shape of galleons, London 1899–1900, 2in (5cm) high, 1.75oz.
£340–375
€/ $550–600 NS

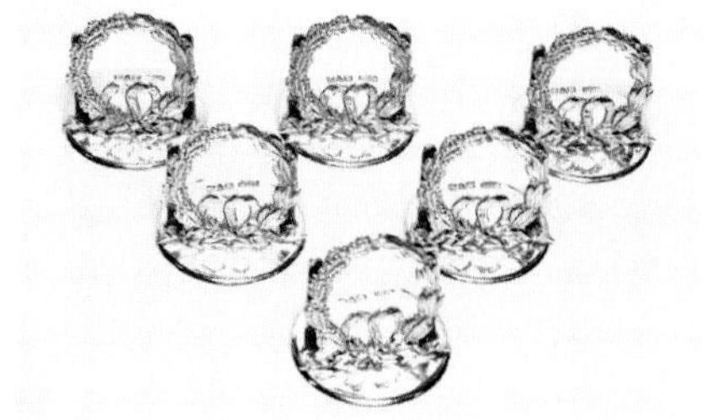

◄ **A set of six silver menu holders,** Chester 1913, 1½in (4cm) high.
£400–450
€/ $630–700 EXC

Mirrors

A silver toilet mirror, embossed and chased with flowers and scrolls, maker's initials for A. & J. Zimmerman, Birmingham 1886, 14in (35.5cm) high.
£280–325
€/ $440–515 G(L)

A silver-mounted dressing table mirror, by William Comyns, with an easel back, decorated in relief with C-scrolls, floral sprays and husks, London 1899, 12in (30.5cm) high.
£350–425
€/ $550–670 WW

A silver mirror, Chester 1900, 17in (43cm) high.
£675–750
€/ $1,100–1,200 GRe

An Edwardian silver presentation toilet mirror, embossed with scrolls and flowerheads, with velvet backing, 20in (51cm) high.
£320–400
€/ $500–630 AH

Mugs & Tankards

◄ **A lady's silver tankard,** by William Andrews, 1697–98, 5in (12.5cm) high.
£4,500–5,500
€/ $7,100–8,700
NS

A silver miniature christening mug, London 1855, 3in (7.5cm) high, with original case.
£250–275
€/ $400–440 CoHA

A silver tankard, by John Cuthbert, with a hollow scroll handle, Irish, Dublin 1704–06, 4in (10cm) high, 7oz.
£1,100–1,300
€/ $1,700–2,000 HOK

► **A silver christening mug,** London 1863, 4in (10cm) high.
£315–350
€/ $500–550 BrL

A silver tankard, by P. Muller, Russian, St Petersburg 1830, 6in (15cm) high.
£1,600–1,800
€/ $2,500–2,800 SHa

Napkin Rings

◄ **A pair of silver napkin rings,** by E. J. & W. Barnard, chased with floral scrolls, London 1874, in an Elkington & Co box.
£180–220
€/ $285–350 FEN

A pair of silver napkin rings, London 1891, in box 5½in (14cm) wide.
£220–245
€/ $350–380 ⊞ BLm

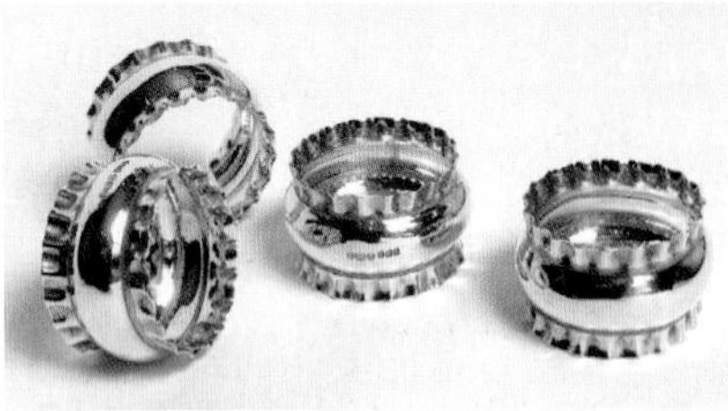

A set of four silver napkin rings, Sheffield 1899, 1¾in (4.5cm) diam.
£180–200
€/ $285–315 ⊞ GRe

◄ **A set of four silver napkin rings,** by H. W. Ltd, with C-scroll edges and foliate-chased decoration, Birmingham 1907, in original case.
£150–175
€/ $240–275 PFK

Rattles

◄ **A baby's silver rattle,** by Joseph Willmore, with eight bells, coral teether and whistle, Birmingham 1807, 5in (12.5cm) long.
£575–675
€/ $900–1,100
G(B)

A baby's silver rattle, by Joseph Willmore, with chased decoration, four bells, coral teether and whistle, Birmingham c1825, 5in (12.5cm) long.
£275–325
€/ $440–500 WW

A Victorian baby's silver rattle, with six bells, ivory ring and whistle, 5in (12.5cm) long.
£330–400
€/ $520–630 JDJ

Salvers & Trays

A silver salver, by Samuel Reily, Irish, Cork c1795, 6in (15cm) wide.
£2,100–2,300
€/ $3,300–3,600 ⊞ WELD

For more Salvers & Trays
see Papier Mâché page 605

A silver salver, by Walter and John Barnard, London 1892, 10in (25.5cm) diam, 16oz.
£350–400
€/ $550–630 ⊞ GRe

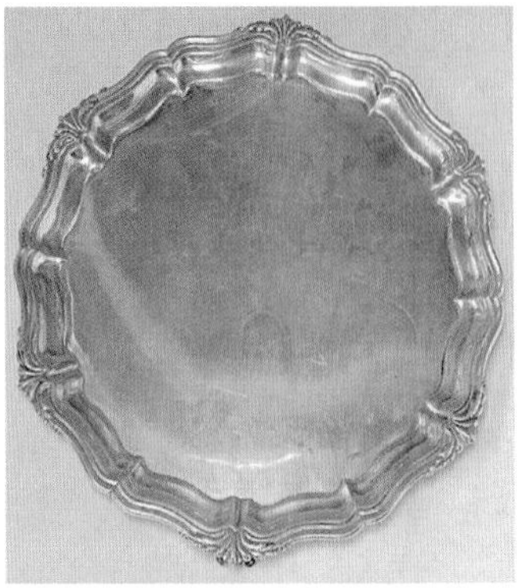

A silver salver, with piecrust border and scroll feet, Sheffield 1909, 15in (38cm) diam.
£320–375
€/ $500–600 G(L)

Sauce Boats

A pair of silver sauce boats, by Robert Innes, with an armorial, London 1748, 8in (20.5cm) wide.
£4,500–5,000
€/ $7,000–8,000 ⊞ PAY

A pair of silver sauce boats, by Tiffany & Co, Director's mark for Edward Moore, American, c1870, 7in (18cm) wide.
£2,500–2,800
€/ $4,000–4,400 ⊞ SHa

► A pair of silver sauce boats, by Charles Stuart Harris, with gadrooned rims and leaf-capped double scroll handles, London 1897, 7¾in (19.5cm) wide, 30oz.
£950–1,100
€/ $1,500–1,700 ⚒ WW

A pair of silver sauce boats, by Stewart Dawson, London 1911, 4in (10cm) high.
£600–670
€/ $950–1,100 ⊞ GRe

Scent Bottles

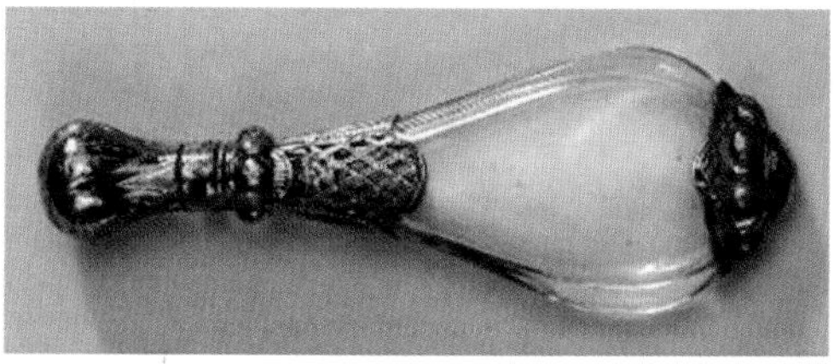

A silver-mounted glass scent bottle, with hinged domed cover and stopper, Continental, 19thC, 4¼in (11cm) high.
£150–175
€/ $240–275 ⚒ TMA

► A silver scent bottle, engraved in the Kate Greenaway style with a child by a church, with hinged cover, London 1882, 2½in (6.5cm) high.
£220–280
€/ $350–440 ⚒ G(L)

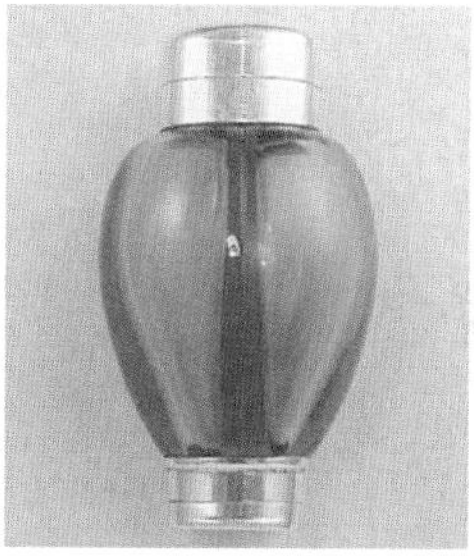

A Victorian silver-mounted glass scent bottle/ vinaigrette, by Sampson Mordan & Co, with two hinged covers opening to reveal glass stoppers at one end, the other end a vinaigrette, incised maker's mark and registration lozenge, 3¾in (9.5cm) high.
£650–750
€/ $1,000–1,200 ⚒ WW

SILVER

Serving Implements

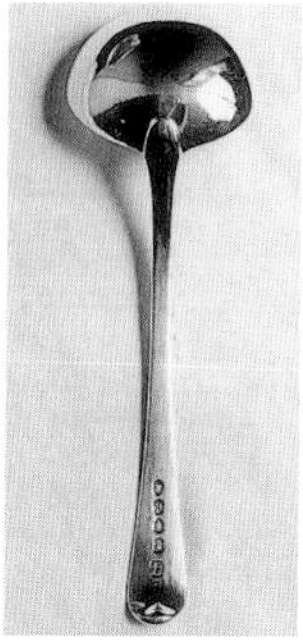

A silver sauce ladle, by W. Eley and W. Fearn, London 1805, 7in (18cm) long.
£150–165
€/ $240–260
⊞ BEX

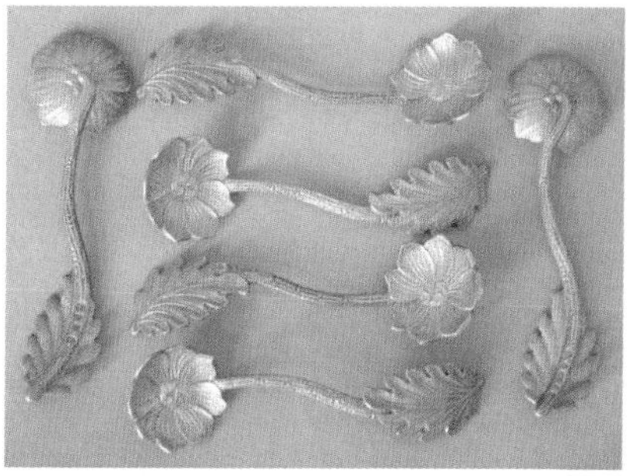

◄ A set of six silver salt spoons, by Joseph Willmore, in the shape of buttercups, with leaf handles, Birmingham 1827.
£375–425
€/ $600–670
⚒ G(L)

A silver soup ladle, London 1865, 13in (33cm) long.
£250–285
€/ $400–450 ⊞ PGO

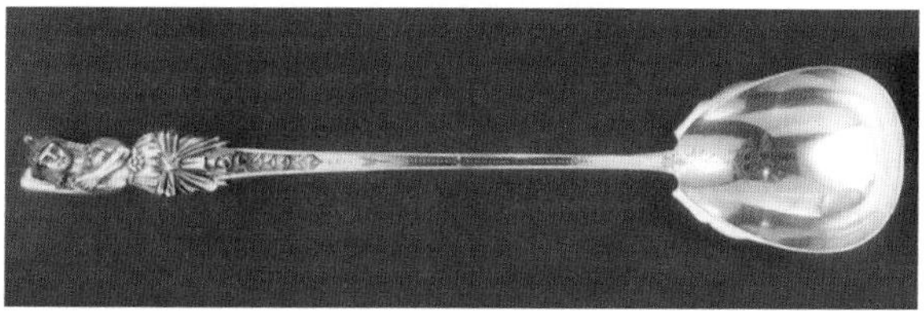

◄ A silver punch ladle, the finial formed as a female Egyptian term, the bowl engraved with a monogram, American, c1870, 15in (38cm) long, 9oz.
£1,400–1,600
€/ $2,200–2,500 ⚒ S(NY)

Snuff Boxes

A silver snuff box, by Richard Lockwood, with bright-engraved diaper border, the cover with a crest, 1805, 2½in (6.5cm) wide.
£550–650
€/ $870–1,000 B(Wm)

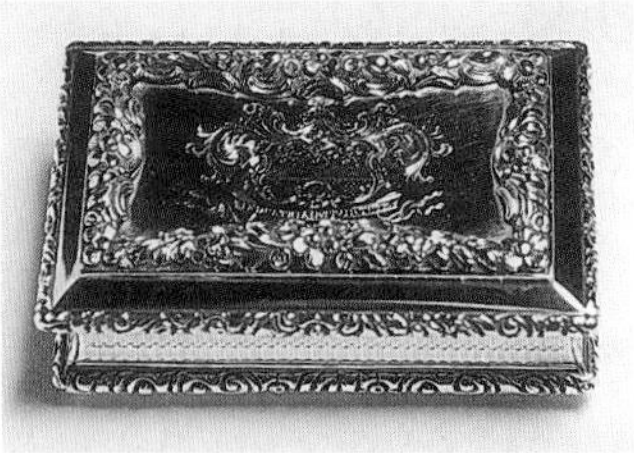

A silver table snuff box, by Nathaniel Mills, Birmingham 1834, 3½in (9cm) wide.
£2,400–2,700
€/ $3,800–4,300 ⊞ BEX

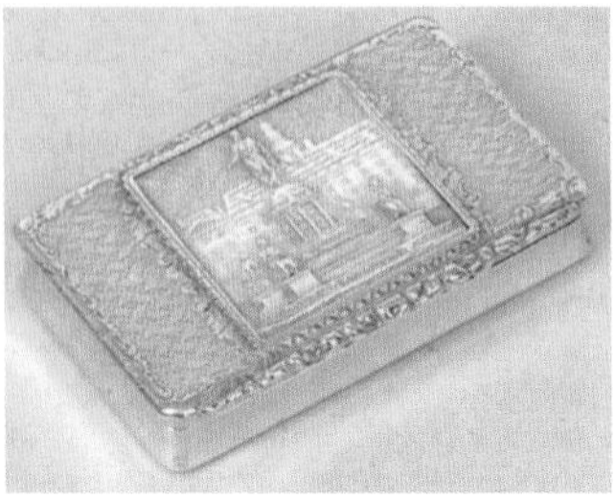

► **A silver snuff box,** with gilt interior, the top engraved with a view of the Kaiser Franz memorial, Vienna, silversmith Josef Witek, Austrian, Vienna 1846, 3¼in (8.5cm) wide, 3.5oz.
£400–475
€/ $630–750 DORO

A silver snuff box, by Joseph and John Angell, London 1846–47, 4in (10cm) wide, in a fitted case.
£6,800–7,500
€/ $10,700–11,800 ⊞ NS
This piece is in immaculate condition and is therefore very desirable.

A silver trompe l'oeil snuff box, engraved with warrants and trade label to simulate those on a Havana cigar box, maker's mark, Russian, Moscow 1896–1905, 3in (7.5cm) wide, 2.25oz.
£280–325
€/ $440–515 WW

Snuffer Trays

A silver-gilt snuffer tray, by Johann Martin Satzger, engraved with a cypher below a coronet within flat-chased rococo decoration, German, Augsburg 1753–55, 7½in (19cm) wide, 8.75oz.
£1,200–1,400
€/ $1,900–2,200 S(O)

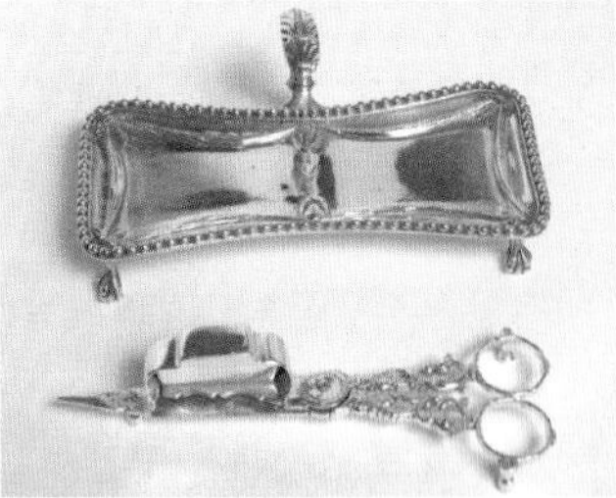

► **A pair of silver snuffers and tray,** tray by John Carter, snuffers by John Baker, London 1771, tray 6½in (16.5cm) wide.
£1,100–1,300
€/ $1,700–2,000 ⊞ GRe

◄ **A silver snuffer tray,** by John Emes, with a reeded rim, engraved frieze and vacant wreath cartouche, London 1801, 10in (25.5cm) wide, 4.5oz.
£320–400
€/ $500–630 WW

Table Bells

A silver twist bell, Birmingham 1895, 3in (7.5cm) high.
£630–700
€/ $1,000–1,100 ⊞ BLm

► **A silver-mounted table bell,** by William Comyns, with push button top and pierced sides of scrolling shamrock, London 1903, 4¼in (11cm) diam.
£475–550
€/ $750–870 B(L)

► **A silver table bell,** the handle cast as a boy with a goblet and bottle in his hands, the bell with a cast frieze of dancers and a musician in a rural setting, import marks for London 1902, Continental, early 20thC, 5½in (14cm) high, 4.25oz.
£150–175
€/ $140–275 GTH

Tea Caddies

A silver tea caddy, by Peter, Anne and William Bateman, with wooden finial, with key, London 1805, 6¾in (17cm) wide, 16.5oz.
£1,000–1,200
€/ $1,600–1,900 ⚒ CGC

A silver tea caddy, embossed with leaf and scroll decoration, the hinged cover with leaf and ball finial, maker's marks for John Harrison & Co, Sheffield 1852, 4¼in (11cm) high.
£320–375
€/ $500–600 ⚒ FEN

A silver tea caddy, London 1860, 6½in (16.5cm) high.
£1,100–1,300
€/ $1,700–2,000 ⊞ BLm

A silver tea caddy, of lobed form, on lion-paw feet, Chester 1895, 5in (12.5cm) high.
£300–350
€/ $475–550 ⚒ G(L)

LOCATE THE SOURCE
The source of each illustration in Miller's can be found by checking the code letters below each caption with the Key to Illustrations, pages 794–800.

► **A silver tea caddy,** by West & Son, London 1908, 4in (10cm) high.
£270–300
€/ $425–475 ⊞ GRe

Toast Racks

A silver toast rack, by Thomas Halford, London 1810, 6in (15cm) wide.
£430–475
€/ $680–750 ⊞ GRe

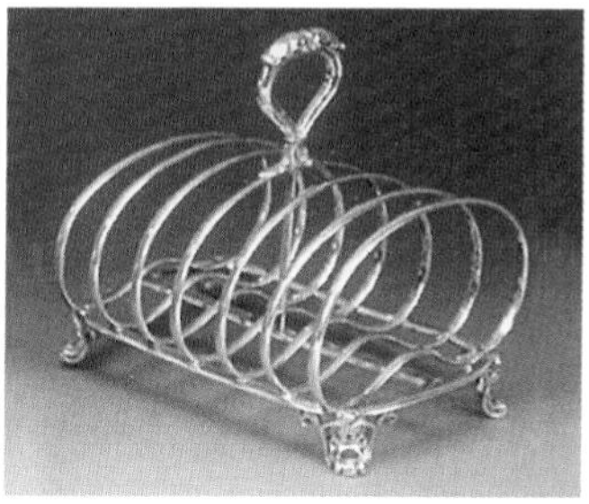

A silver toast rack, by Paul Storr (Storr & Mortimer), London 1832, 5¼in (13.5cm) high, 11.75oz.
£1,000–1,200
€/ $1,600–1,900 ⚒ CGC

A silver toast rack, c1890, 4in (10cm) wide.
£100–115
€/ $160–180 ⊞ EXC

Vesta Cases

A silver vesta case, 1894, 2in (5cm) wide.
£50–60
€/ $80–95 ⊞ EXC

A silver table vesta/stamp case, by Samuel Jacobs, London 1894–95, 3in (7.5cm) high.
£1,500–1,700
€/ $2,400–2,700 ⊞ NS

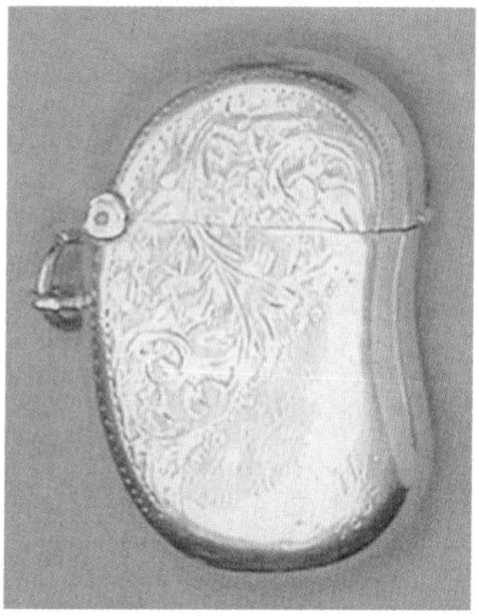

A silver vesta case, by W. H. Haseler, partially scroll-engraved, with inscription, Birmingham 1912, 2in (5cm) wide.
£80–100
€/ $125–160 ⚒ WW

Vinaigrettes

A silver vinaigrette, by Joseph Taylor, in the shape of a purse, engraved with flowers and scrolls and pricked borders to simulate stitching, initialled, Birmingham 1810–15, 1in (2.5cm) wide.
£220–260
€/ $350–400 WW

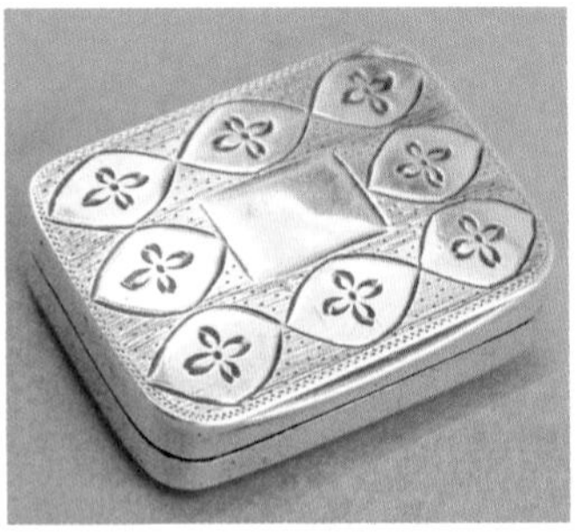

A silver vinaigrette, with wire-work grille, Birmingham 1813, 1in (2.5cm) wide.
£180–220
€/ $280–350 G(L)

A silver and parcel-gilt vinaigrette, with raised foliate borders, pierced grille and suspension ring, maker's mark, Birmingham 1835, 1½in (4cm) wide, 0.75oz.
£140–170
€/ $220–275 DMC

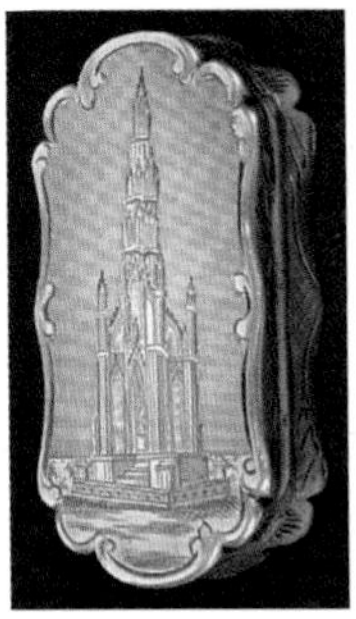

◄ **A silver vinaigrette,** by Nathaniel Mills, depicting the Albert Memorial, Birmingham 1853, 2in (5cm) wide.
£600–675
€/ $950–1,100
CoHA

A silver vinaigrette, by George Knight, with chased floral and scrolling decoration, the hinged grille chased and pierced, Birmingham 1870, 1¾in (4.5cm) wide.
£200–225
€/ $315–350 BR

A silver novelty vinaigrette, in the shape of a shoe, 1891, 2¾in (7cm) wide.
£100–125
€/ $160–200 G(L)

◄ **A silver-mounted horn vinaigrette,** the cover with chased decoration and set with a cairngorm, with gilt interior, Edinburgh 1898, 4in (10cm) wide.
£475–550
€/ $750–870 EH

Further reading

Miller's Silver & Plate Buyer's Guide, Miller's Publications, 2002

Wax Jacks

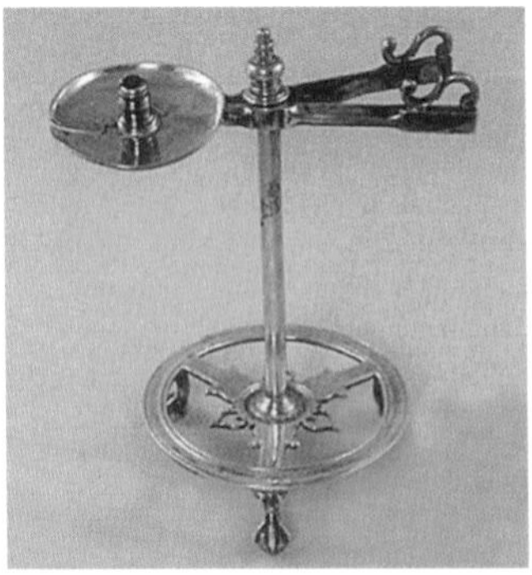

A silver wax jack, by Gawen Nash, the spring-loaded taper holder with plain drip pan and a pierced scroll surmount on each arm, the central pole with acorn knop finial and three bird's claw-and-ball feet, London c1745, 5½in (14cm) high, 6oz.
£1,800–2,200
€/ $2,800–3,500 WW

A silver wax jack, by Joseph Lock, London 1777–78, 6in (15cm) high.
£3,000–3,500
€/ $4,700–5,500 NS

A silver wax jack, by Henry Chawner, London 1792–93, 7in (18cm) high.
£3,000–3,500
€/ $4,700–5,500 NS
Wax jacks were introduced around 1760 and were used for warming up wax for sealing documents.

Miscellaneous

A silver desk set, Birmingham 1908, 10¾in (27.5cm) wide, in original case.
£875–975
€/ $1,400–1,550 ⊞ BLm

A silver table lighter, by Hawksworth, Eyre & Co, Sheffield 1907, 4in (10cm) high.
£260–285
€/ $400–450 ⊞ GRe

Items in the Silver Miscellaneous section have been arranged in alphabetical order.

► **A pair of silver tea glass holders,** by Gustav Klingert, Russian, Moscow 1896, 3½in (9cm) high.
£340–375
€/ $550–600 ⊞ SHa

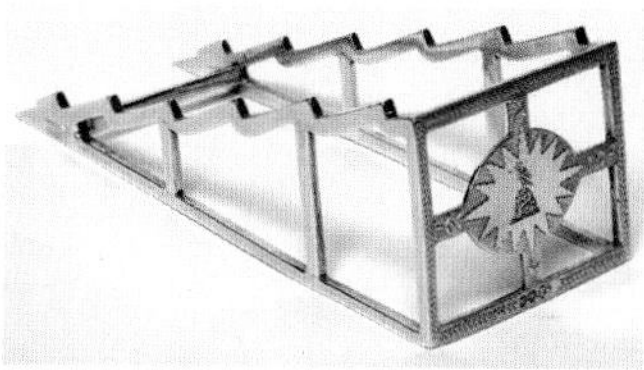

A silver dish wedge, by Peter and William Bateman, London 1808–09, 6in (15cm) wide.
£1,000–1,100
€/ $1,600–1,700 ⊞ NS

A silver plate, by Paul de Lamerie, the twisted rope rim interspersed with shells and foliage, the border with the arms of the Corporation of London, London 1737, 10in (25.5cm) diam, 20oz.
£2,800–3,400
€/ $4,400–5,400 ⚒ HAM
Paul de Lamerie is among the foremost English silversmiths and his pieces are highly desirable.

A silver hot water jug, by William Eaton, with semi-fluted body and cover with shell and gadrooned borders, the spout with acanthus decoration, London 1821, 8½in (21.5cm) high, 29oz.
£250–300
€/ $400–475 ⚒ G(B)

A coin silver platter, by Newell Harding & Co, the centre engraved with a rococco cartouche with presentation inscription, on cast and applied acanthus feet, American, Boston, c1856, 13¼in (33.5cm) wide, 43oz.
£1,200–1,500
€/ $1,900–2,400 ⚒ NOA

A silver sugar urn, by Frank Knöll, chased with a band of floral decoration, the cover with a flower knop, old repairs, Austrian, Vienna 1814, 6¾in (17cm) high.
£1,500–1,800
€/ $2,400–2,800 ⚒ DORO

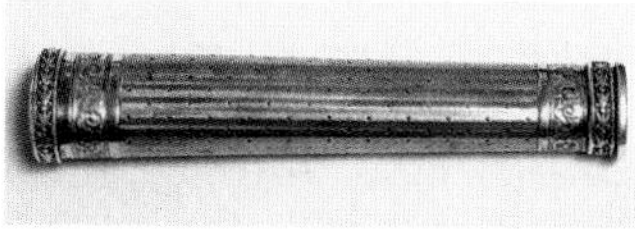

A silver wax holder, French, 18thC, 5in (12.5cm) long.
£150–165
€/ $240–260 ⊞ EXC

The Ortiz-Patino Collection

The English late 17th-century chinoiserie silver in the collection of Jaime Ortiz-Patino, sold at Sotheby's New York in 1992. It was the finest and most complete group of such pieces ever to come to auction. In the 1680s, following expansion of trade between Europe and China, there was a ten-year vogue for chinoiserie (decoration depicting Chinese-style motifs such as landscapes, pagodas and figures) and this is perhaps one of the most enchanting periods of English silver. Mr Ortiz-Patino, the grandson of Simon Patino who made his fortune in the tin mines of Bolivia in the late 19th century, came from a renowned family of collectors. When he was arranging to move to London to take up an appointment as Advisor in Europe for the Bolivian government, he realized that his new residence would not be large enough to house his huge collection and much of it would have to be sold. The chinoiserie silver was merely a part of it but included some of the finest examples made. The highlight of the sale was a pair of tankards made in London in 1686, known as the Brownlow tankards, which sold for £504,700 (€/ $797,500). **Nicholas Shaw**

Silver Plate

A George III old Sheffield plate pierced cake basket, with bright-cut decoration and beaded rim, engraved with a coat-of-arms, with swing handle, on a pierced foot, 14½in (37cm) wide.
£150–175
€/ $240–275 G(L)

An old Sheffield plate swing-handle cake basket, with a fluted band below a gadrooned edge, engraved with a crest, c1820, 10½in (26.5cm) wide.
£200–240
€/ $315–380 B(L)

A Victorian electroplated biscuit box, with engraved foliate decoration, the cover with urn-shaped finial, the pierced dish base on claw-and-ball feet, 8in (20.5cm) wide.
£150–175
€/ $240–275 BR

◄ An Edwardian silver-plated cake stand, the pierced top with swing handle, on fluted legs, 10in (20.5cm) diam.
£40–50
€/ $65–80 GAK

► A pair of old Sheffield plate pillar candlesticks, with fluted columns and Corinthian capitals, the beaded bases with ram's-head masks and swags, c1800, 12½in (32cm) high.
£450–540
€/ $700–850 BWL

Items in the Silver Plate section have been arranged in alphabetical order.

A silver-plated candelabra, in the manner of Matthew Boulton, cast with rams' heads, the bases with a coursing dog crest, 19thC, 27¼in (69cm) high.
£275–325
€/ $430–515
HOLL

A Victorian silver-plated centrepiece, by Elkington & Co, the beaded plate frame over a foliate-decorated tripod supported by three figures, on three claw feet, glass missing, 22½in (57cm) high.
£750–850
€/ $1,200–1,300 CGC

A Victorian silver-plated and glass centrepiece, 15in (38cm) high.
£1,100–1,200
€/ $1,700–1,900 BrL

An old Sheffield plate coffee biggin, with winged fluting and armorials, on a gadrooned foot, c1820, 8in (20.5cm) high.
£420–460
€/ $665–725 G&G

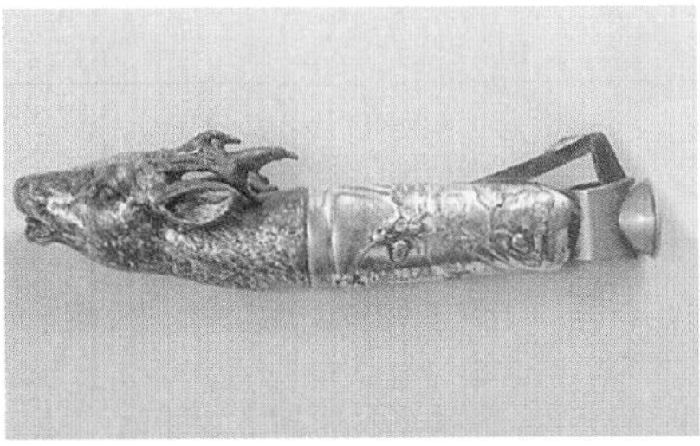

A silver-plated cigar cutter, with a stag's head terminal, 1875–1900, 5½in (14cm) long.
£275–325
€/ $430–515 WW

A Victorian EPNS tazza, the mother-of-pearl bowl supported by a putto standing on a rock- and seashell-cast domed base, on three dolphin and shell feet, 14½in (37cm) high.
£400–500
€/ $630–800 GTH

A Victorian electroplated serving dish, of neo-classical form, with a gadrooned edge, on stylized paw feet, 13¾in (35cm) wide.
£100–125
€/ $160–200 PFK

◄ **A silver-plated bacon dish,** late 19thC, 12in (30.5cm) wide.
£225–250
€/ $350–400 ⊞ GRe

► **An old Sheffield plate dish cross,** c1790, 11in (28cm) wide.
£385–430
€/ $600–680 ⊞ GRe

An old Sheffield plate dog collar, with applied moulded edges, inscribed, late 18thC, 5in (12.5cm) wide.
£650–750
€/ $1,000–1,200 ⚒ B

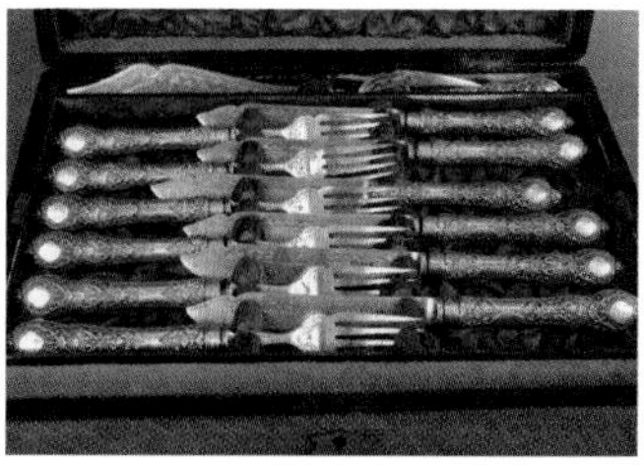

A Victorian silver-plated cutlery set, comprising 12 fish knives and forks and a pair of servers, in original case.
£160–200
€/ $250–315 ⚒ SWO

A Victorian Sheffield plate kettle and stand, engraved with flowers, scallop shells and scrolls beneath a cast scroll rim, with hinged cover, the stand with scrollwork feet, 15¾in (40cm) high.
£220–250
€/ $350–400 ⚒ RTo

An old Sheffield plate samovar, with lion-mask and ring handles, decorated with an heraldic shield, early 19thC, 18½in (47cm) high.
£380–450
€/ $600–700 ⚒ SWO

A silver-plated six-piece tea and coffee service, by Meriden Britannia Co, decorated with repoussé roses below a milled band of birds and flowers, American, Connecticut, c1900–17, pots 6in (15cm) high.
£200–225
€/ $315–350 ⚒ NOA

A Victorian silver-plated tea caddy, with engraved cartouches and borders, the cover with strawberry finial, with lion-mask and drop-ring handles and central internal divider, c1865, 6½in (16.5cm) wide.
£140–160
€/ $220–250 ⚒ WW

A silver-plated spoon warmer, by Benet Fink & Son, in the shape of Aladdin's lamp, c1880, 9in (23cm) wide.
£200–220
€/ $315–350 ⊞ BrL

A George III old Sheffield-plate teapot, with beaded borders, engraved coat-of-arms and ebony handle, 11¾in (30cm) wide.
£100–120
€/ $160–190 ⚒ G(L)

A Victorian silver-plated tray, with foliate border, engraved to centre, 30in (76cm) wide.
£240–275
€/ $380–430 ⚒ L

► **A pair of Adam-style silver-plated hot water urns,** decorated with Prince of Wales feathers, with reeded scroll handles, c1910, 23in (58.5cm) high.
£1,800–2,000
€/ $2,800–3,200 ⚒ NOA

Wine Antiques

A painted-iron bar bottle opener, c1905, 9½in (24cm) long.
£120–140
€/ $190–220 ⊞ JOL

A silver brandy saucepan, by William Fleming, London 1720–21, 3in (7.5cm) high.
£1,500–1,700
€/ $2,400–2,700 ⊞ NS

A brandy saucepan and cover, by Samuel Wheatley, crested, with turned wooden handles and knop finial, London 1829, bowl 4¼in (11cm) diam, 9oz.
£550–650
€/ $870–1,000 ⚒ WW

A silver wine coaster, by C. Clarke, with original wooden base, Irish, Dublin, c1775, 5in (12.5cm) diam.
£5,000–5,600
€/ $8,000–9,000 ⊞ WELD

► A pair of silver wine coasters, by Matthew Boulton, with pierced sides and turned wooden bases, Birmingham 1813, 5½in (14cm) diam.
£1,200–1,400
€/ $1,900–2,200 ⚒ BWL

A horn-handled corkscrew, 19thC, 4in (10cm) long.
£70–75
€/ $110–120 ⊞ SEA

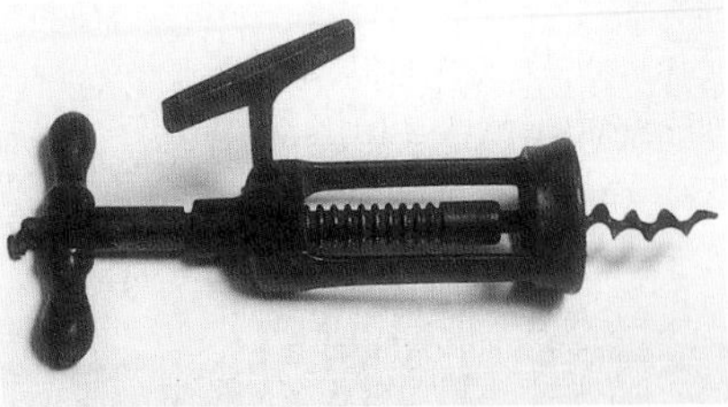

A metal double pillar corkscrew, 19thC, 7in (18cm) long.
£110–120
€/ $175–190 ⊞ JOL

A double-action corkscrew, with brush and turned base handle, the brass barrel applied with a royal coat-of-arms, 19thC, 7in (18cm) long.
£250–300
€/ $400–475 ⚒ AH

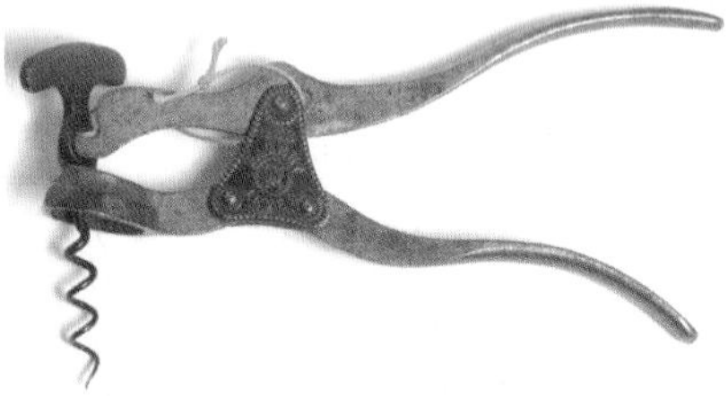

A Victorian Lunds two-part lever corkscrew, 8in (20.5cm) long.
£85–95
€/ $135–150 ⊞ WiB

◄ A folding pocket corkscrew, containing eight tools, c1820, 2¾in (7cm) wide.
£80–100
€/ $140–160 ⊞ CS

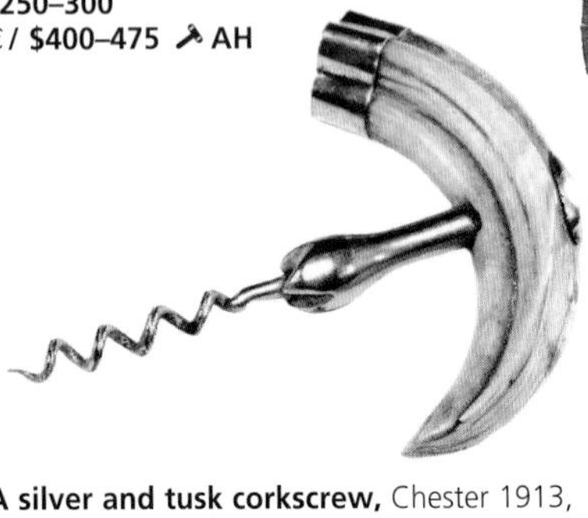

A silver and tusk corkscrew, Chester 1913, 5½in (14cm) long.
£50–60
€/ $80–100 ⚒ TMA

Items in the Wine Antiques section have been arranged in alphabetical order.

► A coromandel decanter box, the hinged lid releasing the gilt-brass mounted strap-work front doors, containing three spirit decanters, five glasses and a gilt-brass tray, c1870, 12½in (32cm) wide.
£650–725
€/ $1,000–1,100 ⚒ CGC

A silver-mounted brandy decanter, with a ribbed, moulded body inscribed 'Brandy', Birmingham 1893, 6¾in (17cm) high.
£200–225
€/ $315–355 ⚒ L

A Victorian oak tantalus, with silver-plated mounts and three decanters, 12½in (32cm) wide.
£240–275
€/ $380–430 ⚒ SWO

A William IV cast-iron wine cooler, with ring handles and foliate motifs, 36in (91.5cm) wide.
£600–700
€/ $950–1,100 ⚒ G(L)

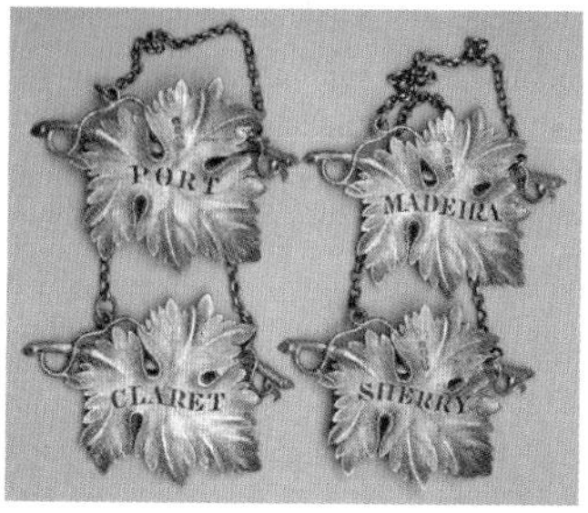

A set of four silver-gilt wine labels, by Thomas Eley, in the shape of vine leaves, 1828, 2½in (6.5cm) wide.
£220–260
€/ $350–400 ⚒ G(L)

A silver wine funnel and stand, funnel by J. Gibson, stand by Terry & Williams, Irish, Cork 1795, 5in (12.5cm) long.
£3,300–3,600
€/ $5,200–5,700 ⊞ WELD

A silver tantalus, by Frederick Elkington, with three decanters, Birmingham 1881, 14in (35.5cm) high.
£5,500–6,000
€/ $8,700–9,500 ⊞ BLm

A silver wine cooler, chased with yachts, one with enamelled gold flag, a paddle steamer, man o'war and other vessels, with cast seahorse handles, on scallop feet, possibly Martin & Hall, 1874, 10in (25.5cm) diam, 108oz.
£4,500–5,400
€/ $7,100–8,500 ⚒ TEN

A pair of silver wine labels, by D. & C. Edwards, Scottish, Glasgow 1905, 1½in (4cm) wide.
£130–145
€/ $200–230 ⊞ GRe

An Edwardian stained bird's-eye maple and ebonized musical liqueur stand, the mechanism activated by opening the six doors, 9½in (24cm) high.
£500–575
€/ $790–910 ⚒ SWO

A silver wine cooler, by R. & S. Hennell, engraved on either side with a crest, the everted gadrooned rim applied at intervals with shells, with drop-ring handles and wooden base, London 1808, 10½in (26.5cm) wide.
£5,000–5,500
€/ $8,000–8,700 ⚒ S(O)

A set of three cast-silver wine labels, by G. C., with mask, fruiting vine and shell surrounds, 18thC, 2in (5cm) wide.
£250–300
€/ $400–475 ⚒ BWL

Clocks

Any clock made before the era of mass production will have a unique tick and strike which can bring a room to life. The huge variety of timepieces produced since the 17th century means that there is always a style to suit every home, even the most minimalist contemporary setting.

English clocks by the most famous makers from the 'Golden Age' of clockmaking (1665–1725) will be expensive but it is still quite possible to find later antique clocks for three-figure sums. The longcase is perhaps the most popular domestic clock and modest 30-hour examples can be found for £1,000 (€/ $1,600) or less. There are still bargains to be found in Victorian and Edwardian chiming clocks. Housed in a variety of cases, they were all made to a very high standard with three-train fusee movements. Those with less space may prefer carriage clocks with their large choice of mechanisms from the simple timepiece to full *grande-sonnerie* striking. Cases are usually of brass with glazed panels on all sides; these are sometimes replaced with porcelain or enamel. Where a larger and more decorative clock can be accommodated it may be worth considering a French boulle bracket clock. Made in large numbers during the 18th and 19th centuries, they usually have high quality movements and the cases are works of art in themselves. Even 18th-century examples are still very reasonably priced. Beware cases that are in poor condition, as restoration of boulle can be very expensive.

The formation of the Antiquarian Horological Society in the 1950s helped lift clock collecting onto a more respectable footing, shedding the image of the eccentric. Regular, specialized clock auctions began in the 1970s, clocks previously having been included in furniture sales.

The market for antique clocks has remained surprisingly stable for many years, and new collectors are continuing to emerge, so I foresee no slowing down of demand in the next 25 years. The difficulty will be to find enough attractive or technically interesting pieces to satisfy this demand. Inevitably, prices will continue to rise, but clocks are still extremely good value when compared with other areas of the antique market.

Michael Turner

British Bracket, Mantel & Table Clocks

An ebonized table clock, by James Snelling, London, with three subsidiary dials, 18thC, 17½in (44.5cm) high.
£3,200–3,800
€/ $5,000–6,000 E

A mahogany table clock, the brass dial with separate silvered brass chapter ring, false pendulum, date aperture and strike/silent feature to the arch, the eight-day double fusee movement with verge escapement striking and repeating the hours on a bell, on brass ogee feet, c1765, 17½in (44.5cm) high.
£11,000–13,000
€/ $17,500–21,000 PAO

A mahogany chiming table clock, by John Watson, London, the brass dial with twin subsidiary dials for date and strike/silent, the eight-day triple-train fusee movement with verge escapement, chiming and repeating the quarters on eight bells and the hour on a single bell, the backplate engraved with scrolls and foliage and maker's name, the bell-top case surmounted by brass finials, the sides with gilt-brass caryatids, frets and handles, on ogee-bracket feet, c1770, 22½in (57cm) high.
£20,000–22,500
€/ $31,500–35,500 PAO

A George III musical table clock, by James McCabe, London, the dial with silvered chapter ring with Roman numerals within foliate spandrels, three subsidiary dials, chime/silent, fast/slow and selection for seven tunes, the eight-day triple-train fusee movement with anchor escapement, striking the hours on a bell and chiming on 12 bells with pull repeat, the domed pediment surmounted by a gilt-metal ball finial and with panels of silk-backed gilt-metal sound frets, the canted corners with fluted pilasters, on four gilt-metal ogee-bracket feet, 25½in (65cm) high.
£10,000–12,000
€/ $16,000–19,000 DN

◀ **A mahogany table clock,** by Robert Cox, Christchurch, with concentric calendar, c1785, 20in (51cm) high.
£10,000–11,500
€/ $16,000–18,000 JeF

Spring-driven clocks

The coiled spring was first introduced about 1480. However, it gave poor results due to the variation in the strength of the drive it provided when fully wound up and when nearly run down. To overcome this, the fusee was invented (probably in France) which solved the problem of the uneven drive. The fusee was used throughout Germany, France and England on early portable and table clocks. As the quality of springs improved the fusee fell from use in France and Germany towards the end of the 17th century. It continued to be used in England up to the 20th century. The reluctance of English clockmakers to adapt to modern trends led to the downfall of the industry. When a fusee is fitted to a clock it is an indication of high quality.

A mahogany table clock, by William Hambly, Falmouth, the silvered dial with strike/silent and calendar ring and signed 'Willm.Hambly Falmouth', the twin fusee movement with verge escapement, striking on a bell, the backplate engraved with foliate scrolls, the moulded case with brass scale side frets and carrying handle, c1790, 18¾in (47.5cm) high.
£4,000–5,000
€/ $6,300–8,000 B(NW)

► **An ebony table clock,** by George Philip Strigels, the brass dial with strike/silent dial in the arch, the eight-day twin-train fusee movement with verge escapement and bob pendulum, striking on a bell, the front and back doors with cut-brass frets on turquoise silk, on brass bracket feet, 18thC, 17¼in (44cm) high.
£4,200–5,000
€/ $6,600–7,900 CGC

A mahogany table clock, by James Parlett Saddleton, Kings Lynn, the silvered brass dial engraved with Roman hours and Arabic minutes, with strike/silent dial to the arch, the eight-day five-pillar double fusee movement with anchor escapement, striking the hours on a bell, the backplate engraved with an urn, foliage and flowers, the broken arch top with three brass-bordered pads and brass handle, on brass ogee-bracket feet, c1795, 17in (43cm) high.
£9,500–10,500
€/ $15,000–16,500 PAO
Clocks with triple-pad tops are particularly desirable.

CLOCKS

The prices realized at auction may reflect the fact that the clocks have sometimes undergone alterations to their movements, or are in unrestored condition.

A chinoiserie-decorated bracket clock, by Richard Laurence, Bath, with original wall bracket, the silvered dial with strike/silent dial over a Roman and Arabic chapter ring and engraved centre, the twin gut fusee movement with five knopped pillars, striking on a bell, decorated with raised gilt Chinese figures and buildings, 18thC, 29in (73.5cm) high.
£9,000–11,000
€/ $14,200–17,400 B
Richard Laurence was working from Bath and Warminster between 1729 and 1773.

A mahogany and brass-inlaid table clock, by Francis Perigal, London, the painted dial with Arabic and Roman numerals and subsidiary dials to the arch, the double fusee movement with anchor escapement, striking on a bell, with engraved backplate, the case with triple-pad top and brass scale side frets, on bracket feet, c1800, 15in (38cm) high.
£3,700–4,200
€/ $5,800–6,600 HYD

A mahogany table clock, the painted convex dial with brass bezel, the brass backplate engraved 'Septimus Miles, London', with triple-train fusee movement, the case with fluted tapering pediment with pineapple finials, flanked by gilt-brass carrying handles, on ogee brass feet, c1800, 8¾in (22cm) high.
£2,400–2,800
€/ $4,000–4,400 HOK
Septimus Miles (d1847) was at 32 Ludgate St, London, between 1795 and 1829.

A partridge wood table clock, by Handley & Moore, London, the dial with Roman chapters and strike/silent feature, the eight-day double fusee movement with anchor escapement, striking and repeating the hours on a bell, the backplate with engraved border and maker's name, the engraved pendulum with calibrated rating, the case inlaid with satinwood lines, the sides with scale frets, on four brass ogee feet, c1810, 17in (43cm) high.
£6,500–7,300
€/ $10,300–11,500 ⊞ PAO

► A rosewood and brass-inlaid mantel clock, with silvered dial, the eight-day twin-chain fusee movement striking on a bell, early 19thC, 11in (28cm) high.
£4,800–5,800
€/ $7,600–9,200 SWO

► A mahogany table clock, the arched brass dial signed James Burton, Lincoln's Inn, with subsidiary calendar dial and strike/silent dial to the arch, the twin fusee movement with anchor escapement, striking on a bell, the unsigned backplate engraved with foliage and a basket of fruit, with brass carrying handle, on brass bracket feet, early 19thC, 19¼in (49cm) high.
£1,700–2,000
€/ $2,700–3,200 Bea(E)

Bracket/table clocks

Most 17th- and 18th-century English table clocks have carrying handles. A clock would have been an expensive purchase and so most households would have had only one, which would have been used downstairs during the day and carried up to the bedroom at night. These clocks often had quarter repeating work which could be set into action at will during the dark hours thereby audibly indicating the time to the nearest quarter hour. Handles continued to be fitted to the cases of later clocks but these were usually intended only to be decorative.

A mahogany and brass-inlaid mantel timepiece, by Stedman, Godalming, with convex painted dial and fusee movement, on brass ball feet, early 19thC, 15in (38cm) high.
£1,200–1,400
€/ $1,900–2,200 G(L)

An inlaid mahogany table clock, by Thomas Sherwood, Leeds, the repainted dial signed for the maker, the triple-chain fusee movement with tall shouldered plates with engraved shaded edge and pendulum bob, and anchor escapement, chiming on eight bells and striking the hours on another bell, the case with a caddy top, on a stepped base with ball feet, early 19thC, 26¾in (68cm) high.
£1,500–1,800
€/ $2,400–2,700 B
Thomas Sherwood was working from Leeds between 1801 and 1834.

LOCATE THE SOURCE
The source of each illustration in Miller's can be found by checking the code letters below each caption with the Key to Illustrations, pages 794–800.

◀ **A rosewood and brass-inlaid bracket clock,** the painted dial signed 'Burlington & Co, Lynn', the twin fusee movement striking on a gong, the caddy top surmounted by a gilt-metal pineapple finial, loop carrying handles to the sides, with rosewood bracket, early 19thC, 20in (51cm) high.
£1,000–1,200
€/ $1,600–1,900 ⚒ Bea(E)

A mahogany and brass-inlaid mantel clock, the cream dial with Roman numerals and signed 'James McCabe, Royal Exchange, London', with eight-day twin fusee movement, striking on a bell, early 19thC, 18½in (47cm) high.
£2,000–2,400
€/ $3,200–3,800 ⚒ TF

A Regency mahogany mantel clock, by Whitehurst & Son, Derby, with silvered dial and twin fusee movement, backplate and dial engraved with maker's name, finial missing, 17¼in (44cm) high.
£2,700–3,200
€/ $4,300–5,000 ⚒ SWO

A Regency bronze and ormolu mantel time-piece, by Parkinson & Frodsham, with drum case and Roman dial, the plinth with a floral swag, on hatched pad feet, dial and back of movement signed, 8¼in (21cm) high.
£1,600–1,900
€/ $2,500–3,000 ⚒ G(L)

A Regency ormolu timepiece, by Viner & Co, London, with an engine-turned dial and single fusee movement, the rococo case with scroll sides, on four feet, hands missing, 8¼in (21cm) high.
£950–1,100
€/ $1,500–1,700 ⚒ B(W)

▶ **A Regency mahogany and brass-inlaid table timepiece,** with painted dial signed 'W. Tanner, Lewes', the inlaid case with acanthus ring handles, surmounted by a fir cone finial, the sides with scale frets, on brass ball feet, 17in (43cm) high.
£1,600–2,000
€/ $2,500–3,200 ⚒ BR

Striking/chiming/musical clocks

Over the centuries various forms of striking and chiming have been used to announce the time audibly but the terms are often confused.

- Striking: The simplest form of striking is called passing strike. This is when the timepiece does not have a separate striking train but will trip a hammer to strike a single blow on a bell or a gong at the hour. The most usual form of sounding the time is to strike the full number of the hour and sometimes, in addition, the half-hour with a single blow. A more complicated form of striking is often used in Holland and is known as Dutch striking. The hour is sounded on a large bell and at the half hour the next hour is sounded in full on a small bell. Some early English makers used Dutch striking. Another complicated form of striking called Roman striking was used exclusively by the Knibb family of clockmakers.
- Quarter striking: Two different bells or gongs are usually employed to sound ting-tang striking at the quarters. This is sometimes known as *petite sonnerie*. The more complicated form known as *grande sonnerie* is when the hour is sounded at every quarter in addition to the quarter hour.
- Chiming: The clock plays a tuneful phrase on a number of bells or gongs at each quarter. One phrase is played at quarter past the hour, increasing to four phrases at the hour. The most usual form is the Westminster chime used on Big Ben.
- Musical: Some clocks will have a musical train, perhaps in addition to a chiming or striking train. The clock will often play quite a long tune on several bells, usually once every three hours.

A Regency mahogany table clock, the convex painted dial with Roman numerals, the eight-day twin-train fusee movement with anchor escapement, striking on a bell, the brass-inlaid case surmounted by a gilt-metal acorn finial, feet missing, damaged, 24in (61cm) high.
£1,200–1,400
€/ $1,900–2,200 ⚒ DN

A George IV mahogany and brass-inlaid table clock, the enamel dial with Roman numerals and inscribed 'Chas. Watts, Oxford', with eight-day fusee movement, striking on a bell, the backplate with engraved border, fruiting cornucopia plate ring handles to the sides, above pierced scale frets, on ball feet, 16in (40.5cm) high.
£1,500–1,800
€/ $2,400–2,800 ⚒ WW

A mahogany mantel clock, by Arnold, London, the engraved silvered dial with strike/silent and rise and fall in the arch, the triple-train fusee movement with deadbeat escapement, wood rod pendulum and maintaining power, chiming on eight bells, the case with barley-twist columns and carved scrolls, c1840, 24¾in (63cm) high.
£2,800–3,200
€/ $4,400–5,000 ⚒ TEN

A mahogany mantel timepiece, by Andrew Millar, Edinburgh, with Roman numerals and eight-day movement, the case with ebonized moulding, on pad feet, c1840, 13¾in (35cm) high.
£320–380
€/ $500–600 ⚒ TRM

► **A rosewood mantel clock,** the lancet dial with Roman numerals and inscribed 'S. Hart - Devizes', the eight-day twin-train fusee movement with anchor escapement, striking on a bell, the pediment with radiating gadroons surmounted by a gilt-metal pineapple finial, 19thC, 12½in (32cm) high.
£2,000–2,200
€/ $3,200–3,500 ⚒ DN

A table clock, made of West Indian specimen wood, with painted dial and English twin-train fusee movement, c1840, 21in (53.5cm) high.
£2,600–3,000
€/ $4,000–4,700 ⊞ APO

A mahogany table clock, by E. T. Biggs, Maidenhead and Slough, the painted dial with maker's name, the double fusee movement striking on a bell, the case with carved floral decoration and metal frets to the sides and back door, feet missing, mid-19thC, 17½in (44.5cm) high.
£475–575
€/ $750–900 ⚒ TMA

A rosewood mantel timepiece, by Robert Scott, London, with engraved Roman dial within an angled bezel, the single gut fusee movement with anchor escapement, the case with gadrooned top and later finial, on a stepped base and bun feet, mid-19thC, 11¾in (30cm) high.
£2,000–2,200
€/ $3,200–3,400 ⚒ B

A patinated- and gilt-bronze mantel clock, by E. H. Adams, Exeter, in the Gothic style, the silvered Roman dial with blued steel moon hands, the twin gut fusee movement with anchor escapement, striking on a bell, the case surmounted by three crocket finials over an embattlement above architectural tracery, pilasters and niches, on scrolled feet, mid-19thC, 15¾in (40cm) high.
£650–750
€/ $1,000–1,200 B(Kn)

Items in the Clock section have been arranged in date order.

A bronze-mounted oak bracket clock, by Wales & McCulloch, London, the silvered Roman dial with twin subsidiary dials for regulation and chime on eight bells/Westminster chimes selection, within a scroll-engraved mask, the triple-chain fusee movement with anchor escapement, chiming the quarters on eight bells and the hours on a gong, the case with four foliate and ball finials and lattice-decorated side panels, on lion-paw feet, on original carved bracket, gong block stamped 'JD', c1870, 36in (91.5cm) high.
£2,200–2,500
€/ $3,500–4,000 B

Bracket/table clocks

The term 'bracket clock' only came into general use in the 19th century. Most of the clocks that are called bracket clocks were never designed to be placed on a bracket. The British Museum is of the opinion that English 'bracket clocks' should really be known as spring clocks (as opposed to weight-driven clocks) or table clocks unless they were specifically designed to be placed on a bracket. Most 17th- and 18th-century table clocks have beautifully engraved backplates which were evidently meant to be seen. Clocks intended for display on a bracket usually have backplates that are plain except for the signature of the maker.

A walnut gallery timepiece, by Sir John Bennett, London, with signed painted dial and cast-brass bezel, the fusee and chain movement with anchor escapement, c1880, 28in (71cm) high.
£900–1,000
€/ $1,400–1,600 S(O)

A Victorian rosewood world mantel timepiece, with painted 24-hour revolving dial, the outer dial with world cities, with single fusee movement, the silvered-brass inner bezel inscribed 'A M Bezant, Hereford', 20¾in (52.5cm) high.
£950–1,100
€/ $1,500–1,700 WW

A walnut mantel clock, with Marti movement, striking on a gong, with brass mounts and cresting, on cast claw feet, late 19thC, 13½in (34.5cm) high.
£350–425
€/ $550–670 G(L)

A rosewood gallery timepiece, the painted dial with Roman numerals and inscribed 'C. Stening, Hove', with eight-day fusee movement, the case on carved foliate scroll mouldings and a pedestal base, c1885, 13in (33cm) high, with associated wall bracket.
£300–340
€/ $475–550 RTo

◀ **A mahogany mantel clock,** with painted Roman dial signed 'Parsons, London', the twin fusee movement striking on a bell, the brass-inlaid and boxwood-strung case with brass carrying handle and brass frets, on brass bracket feet, 19thC, 14¼in (36cm) high.
£1,300–1,500
€/ $2,000–2,400 Bea

An ebonized bracket clock, by Poole of London, the gilt-brass dial with Roman numerals and three subsidiary dials, the triple-train movement chiming on eight bells and striking on a gong, with carrying handles, on hairy paw feet, with matching gilt-brass-decorated bracket, c1890, 24in (61cm) high.
£2,000–2,200
€/ $3,200–3,500 HYD

For further information on antique clocks see the full range of Miller's books at **www.millers.uk.com**

A walnut-veneered table clock, retailed by Camerer, Kuss & Co, London, with eight-day quarter-striking Lenzkirch movement, pierced frets to each side, c1900, 14¼in (36cm) high.
£750–875
€/ $1,200–1,400 SWO

A late Victorian mahogany table clock, by Lund & Blockley, London, in late 17thC style, the brass matted dial with silvered chapter ring, the triple fusee movement with anchor escapement, chiming the quarters on eight bells and striking the hours on a gong, on foliate-cast and chased scrolled feet, 20in (51cm) high.
£2,000–2,300
€/ $3,200–3,600 BR

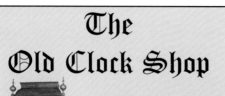

A late Victorian gilt-brass-mounted ebonized table clock, the silvered and brass dial with chime/silent and two chimes in the arch, the triple-train fusee movement with anchor escapement, chiming on eight bells and striking on a gong, on scrolling feet, 24½in (62cm) high.
£2,400–2,800
€/ $3,800–4,400 TEN

◀ **An oak bracket clock,** the silvered dial with brass Arabic numerals enclosing a matted centre, below silvered subsidiary strike/silent, slow/fast and chime on eight bells/Westminster chimes dials, with triple fusee movement chiming the quarters on eight bells, the spandrels and arch cast with shells and foliate decoration, with original oak bracket, early 20thC, 23¼in (59cm) high.
£1,600–1,900
€/ $2,500–3,000 PFK

Continental Bracket, Mantel & Table Clocks

An ormolu mantel clock, the striking movement in a case surmounted by a flower-filled vase, 1775–1800, 14in (35.5cm) high.
£2,800–3,200
€/ $4,400–5,000 S(NY)

An ormolu and biscuit porcelain *pendule à cercles tournants*, with revolving enamel rings and a striking movement, the temple enclosing a biscuit figure of a boy, French, 1775–1800, 15¼in (38.5cm) high.
£5,300–6,300
€/ $8,300–10,000 S(NY)

An ormolu-mounted marble mantel clock, the enamel dial with Roman hours, Arabic quarters and pierced hands, the circular movement with pinned pillars and silk suspension with outside countwheel, striking on a bell, surmounted by an eagle and four urn finials, on a shaped base with turned feet, French, late 18thC, 23¼in (59cm) high.
£2,200–2,500
€/ $3,500–4,000 B

An ormolu Empire timepiece, the enamel dial with Roman numerals and blued steel moon hands, signed 'Alibert à Paris', the replaced gilt verge watch movement signed 'Romilly, Paris', with pierced and engraved cock over baluster pillars, mounted on two griffins on a base, the plinth with cast feet, hair crack to dial, French, early 19thC, 9¾in (25cm) high.
£275–325
€/ $430–520 B(Kn)

An ormolu mantel clock, the Roman dial with pierced gilt-brass hands within an octagonal bezel, the circular movement with bevelled lower edge, silk suspension and outside countwheel striking on a bell, French, early 19thC, 17in (43cm) high.
£850–1,000
€/ $1,300–1,600 B(Kn)

An ormolu mantel clock, modelled as Apollo and two of his nine muses, one holding a jester's doll, the other a tambourine, the eight-day bell striking movement with silk suspension, French, c1805, 17¾in (45cm) high.
£6,500–7,300
€/ $10,300–11,500 GDO

Trade versus auctions

The apparently higher prices indicated for clocks sold by dealers than by auction can be misleading. Clocks bought at auction will not be in guaranteed working order, may need expensive restoration and may be missing keys, winders etc. Many clock dealers will be able to offer pieces from stock in guaranteed condition, and will usually provide documentation to support authenticity of the piece. In many cases a dealer will be prepared to set the clock up in your home and advise you on how to regulate it to time and to reset the strike, should it go out of sequence, as part of an after-sale service.

An ormolu clock, modelled as Pandora, the eight-day bell striking movement with silk suspension, French, c1818, 17¾in (45cm) high.
£3,800–4,300
€/ $6,000–6,800 ⊞ GDO

A bronze and gilt-bronze mantel clock, flanked by personifications of the Arts and Sciences portrayed by two bronze cherubs as sculptor and designer, repeated in the frieze below, the dial with an engine-turned centre and Roman chapters, the movement by Pons of Paris, French, c1820, 17in (43cm) high.
£8,300–9,200
€/ $13,000–14,500 ⊞ JIL

A patinated-bronze and *verde antico* marble mantel clock, modelled as Aurora lifting the veil of night, signed 'Ravrio bronzier à Paris' and 'Mesnil Hr.', the eight-day bell-striking movement with silk suspension, French, c1820, 29½in (75cm) high.
£16,000–18,000
€/ $25,000–28,500 ⊞ GDO
Ravrio and Mesnil worked together to produce very fine quality clocks. This example is large and in exceptionally good original condition.

Ormolu (mercury gilding)

The earliest form of gilding usually found on clock cases is mercury gilding. This is where the bronze or brass casting is cleaned and chased and then applied with an amalgam of gold and mercury. Great skill is required to apply the correct amount of this amalgam so that the detail of the casting is not lost. The piece is then fired (this type of gilding is sometimes known as fire gilding), which causes the mercury to evaporate but leaves the gold adhering to the bronze or brass. This is then worked with fine abrasives to produce a lustrous finish. The result is called ormolu or gilt-bronze, even though the base metal is often brass. The term ormolu has come to be used more often when referring to the gilt clocks produced during the Empire period in France and the Regency period in England when the quality of the work had reached its zenith.

An ormolu and marble mantel clock, the engine-turned dial with Roman numerals, moon hands and bezel cast with flowerheads, the twin train movement with outside countwheel striking on a bell, the plinth with a relief plaque of cupids, on winged paw feet, French, c1825, 22in (56cm) high.
£3,000–3,400
€/ $4,700–5,400 ⚒ GTH

A patinated-bronze and marble mantel clock, French, c1830, 22½in (57cm) high.
£1,800–2,000
€/ $2,800–3,200 ⚒ S(O)

A lacquered-brass perpetual calendar mantel clock, the enamel dial with recessed centre revealing the Brocot escapement, on a calendar dial with outer four-yearly chapter enclosing subsidiaries for day, month, date and phases of the moon, the movement with twin mercury jar pendulum striking on a bell, the four-glass case with moulded brass top and stepped base, French, mid-19thC, 15in (38cm) high.
£3,500–4,000
€/ $5,500–6,300 ⚒ B

A silver and gilt boudoir timepiece, with Swiss cylinder movement, surmounted by an enamelled figure of a violinist, flanked by two similar figures on enamelled columns, the glass cupola shade with figures and enamelled scenes, Austrian, 1825–50, 8¼in (21cm) high.
£1,700–2,000
€/ $2,700–3,200 ⚒ TEN
This is a rare and unusual piece.

A burrwood portico mantel clock, with gilt-bronze mounts, the silvered dial with black chapters, four gilt-bronze half-bun feet, French, 1825–50, 22¼in (56.5cm) high.
£750–900
€/ $1,200–1,400 ⚒ NOA

A Louis XV-style rococo ormolu mantel clock, the dial with enamel numerals, Raingo Frères movement, with countwheel striking on a bell, cast with C-scrolls and foliage, hands missing, French, 19thC, 18in (45.5cm) high.
£750–875
€/ $1,200–1,400 ⚒ G(L)

A patinated-metal clock, surmounted by a bronzed-spelter figure of a warrior, the enamel dial with Roman numerals, half-hourly striking mechanism, French, c1850, 26¾in (68cm) high.
£600–700
€/ $950–1,100 LCM

► An ormolu and jewelled porcelain mantel clock, the dial decorated with a courting couple, with eight-day bell-striking movement, French, c1880, 19¾in (50cm) high.
£6,000–6,800
€/ $9,500–10,700 ⊞ GDO

An ormolu mantel clock, by Raingo Frères, Paris, surmounted by figures and with hand-painted porcelain panels, French, 19thC, 11¾in (30cm) high.
£375–450
€/ $600–700 WilP

A mantel clock, the black marble base surmounted by a bronze statue of Columbus, French, c1870, 21in (53.5cm) high.
£1,700–2,000
€/ $2,700–3,200 ⊞ SET

An ormolu and Sèvres porcelain clock, with eight-day Japy Frères bell-striking movement, decorated with 18thC-style portrait miniatures to the top and sides, French, c1870, 19¾in (50cm) high.
£7,500–8,700
€/ $11,800–13,800 ⊞ GDO

◄ A tortoiseshell boulle mantel clock, the dial with individual enamel numerals, the eight-day movement striking the hours and half-hours on a bell, with glass side panels and matching plinth, c1880, 22in (56cm) high.
£1,600–1,800
€/ $2,500–2,800 ⊞ K&D

An ormolu and *bleu céleste* porcelain mantel clock, with eight-day bell-striking movement, French, c1880, 17¾in (45cm) high.
£3,400–3,800
€/ $5,400–6,000 ⊞ GDO

◄ A tortoiseshell boulle mantel clock, with bronze mounts, the cast dial with individual enamel numeral cartouches, the eight-day movement striking the hours and half-hours on a gong, French, c1890, 14in (35.5cm) high.
£1,100–1,300
€/ $1,700–2,000 ⊞ K&D

► A Gothic-style gold-fired mantel clock, the enamel dial covered by bevelled glass crystal, the eight-day time and bell-striking movement by Marti, French, late 19thC, 14in (35.5cm) high.
£750–820
€/ $1,200–1,300 ⊞ SET

A gilt-brass clock, the dial with Roman numerals, sunburst emblem and brass hands, the twin-train movement with rack striking on a bell, the case surmounted by an eagle over a caddy with applied rosette, the base engraved, French, late 19thC, 15¾in (40cm) high.
£300–350
€/ $475–550 ⚒ B(Kn)

A bronzed spelter and marble mantel clock, surmounted by two female figures flanking a lyre, the enamel dial overlaid with gilt filigree mask, with Louis Boname bell-striking movement, applied with a plaque inscribed 'Harmonie par Math. Moreau', on female term feet, French, c1895, 30in (76cm) high.
£650–780
€/ $1,000–1,200 ⚒ S(O)
Moreau sculpted numerous figures which were then reproduced in spelter for clock mounts, lamps etc.

Spelter

Spelter is a soft brittle metal, much like zinc, which was used by the French from c1850 to make large numbers of inexpensive copies of bronze figures and clock cases. It casts well and accepts a gilt or a bronze patina which resembles the more expensive patinated-bronze or ormolu. Before gilding, the spelter was usually copper plated as the gold adhered better to the copper than to the spelter. When protected from the atmosphere under a glass dome these spelter clocks can look very good, but when exposed they tend to tarnish more quickly than true ormolu clocks. The value of a gilt-spelter clock, even in good condition, is about one third that of a similar ormolu clock.

► A Moorish-style gilt-brass mantel clock, the engraved silver dial with Turkish numerals, the eight-day movement with cylinder escapement, striking on a gong, the case modelled as a Moorish pavilion with crescent finial, embellished overall with cast *champlevé* decoration of equestrian figures, birds, and other creatures, French, c1895, 11½in (29cm) high.
£1,400–1,600
€/ $2,200–2,500 ⚒ S(O)

A boulle bracket clock, with gilt-metal mounts, the beaten brass dial with enamel numerals, the glazed door decorated with the three Fates, surmounted by Minerva, French, 19thC, 60in (152.5cm) high with bracket.
£2,200–2,500
€/ $3,500–4,000 ⚒ CoH

A *champlevé* enamel and gilt-metal mantel clock, with brass chapter ring and circular movement striking on a bell, the domed-top case surmounted by a temple lion, with floral decorated panels and applied floral mounts, French, 19thC, 15¾in (40cm) high.
£1,000–1,200
€/ $1,600–1,900 ⚒ Bea

◄ A gilt-metal and tortoiseshell-mounted mantel clock, retailed by E. White, Paris and London, the enamel dial with Roman numerals and elaborate hands, the scroll case surmounted by floral relief, on a scroll base, French, 19thC, 14½in (37cm) high.
£650–750
€/ $1,000–1,200 ⚒ B(Kn)

A mantel clock, the dial with Roman numerals, on porcelain supports with ormolu mounts and flanked by ormolu cherubs, surmounted by a porcelain urn, the drum case with a *bleu céleste* floral ground, on turned feet, French, 19thC, 18in (45.5cm) high.
£750–850
€/ $1,200–1,400 ⚒ TRM

► A gilt-brass mantel clock, the dial with Roman numerals and visible Brocot escapement, striking on a bell, with mercury pendulum, enclosed by four bevelled glass plates, French, 19thC, 15in (38cm) high.
£1,300–1,500
€/ $2,100–2,400 ⚒ DD

A gilt-metal mantel clock, with enamel dial and eight-day movement striking on a bell, decorated with ribbons, on an alabaster base, French, 19thc, 12½in (32cm) high, with an ebonized stand.
£350–425
€/ $550–670 ⚒ HOLL

A gilt-bronze and marble mantel clock, the enamel dial signed 'Biesta à Paris', with Japy Frères movement striking on a bell, the case inlaid with 18thC-style watercolours, French, c1890, 14¼in (36cm) high.
£1,000–1,200
€/ $1,600–1,900 ⚒ S(O)

► A gilt-metal and porcelain mantel clock, by Henry Marc, Paris, the case with putti, swags and painted porcelain panels, on a shaped base with a glass dome, damaged, French, 19thC, 15¾in (40cm) high.
£250–300
€/ $400–475
⚒ B(W)

A boulle mantel clock, with a drum movement striking on a gong, the case with gilt-metal mounts, French, late 19thC, 11¾in (30cm) high.
£300–350
€/ $475–550 SWO

A lacquered wood timepiece, by Dunhill, Paris, the enamel dial marked with maker's name, the barrelled spring movement with a lever platform escapement, the chinoiserie decoration depicting birds, figures and foliage, French, early 20thC, 5in (12.5cm) high.
£160–200
€/ $250–320 TMA

An oak and brass-mounted mantel clock, with silvered dial and eight-day striking movement, the caddy top with foliate handle and pierced corner brackets, on a moulded base with bracket feet, French, 19thC, 19½in (49.5cm) high.
£650–775
€/ $1,000–1,200 AH

An Edwardian mahogany lancet mantel timepiece, the enamel dial supporting a full plate platform escapement movement, inlaid with a fan patera and boxwood stringing, French, early 20thC, 9¼in (23.5cm) high.
£200–240
€/ $320–380 DMC

A gilt-metal and porcelain mantel clock, the dial with Roman numerals, the circular movement striking on a bell, surmounted by an urn, with porcelain columns and panels within a foliate-decorated case, stamped '32735', 19thC, 14½in (37cm) high.
£1,000–1,200
€/ $1,600–1,900 Bea(E)

An oak mantel clock, by Winterhalder & Hofmeier, with eight-day quarter-striking movement, German, c1910, 15in (38cm) high.
£1,200–1,400
€/ $1,900–2,200 PTh

An Empire-style burr-wood mantel timepiece, the enamelled dial with Arabic numerals and painted floral swags, the single train Paris movement in a drum, French, late 19thC, 9¼in (23.5cm) high.
£650–750
€/ $1,000–1,200 PF

A mahogany mantel clock, by Gustav Becker, Freiberg, No. 2,506, with Westminster chime, case refinished, German, c1925, 12¾in (32.5cm) high.
£675–750
€/ $1,000–1,200 SET

The Joseph Meraux Collection

In the autumn of 1992 my colleagues in the New York watch department were invited to inspect a collection of clocks in New Orleans. They were so overwhelmed by what they found that they telephoned me immediately and asked me to fly over. No details were given but they promised I would not be disappointed.

I shall never forget my first day at the house. After initial introductions I started to look around. There were clocks everywhere! Every piece of furniture, most of the wall space and all of the floor, apart from a narrow passage, was covered with clocks. Even the staircase had two or three clocks on every step. This was the collection of the late Joseph Meraux, who came from an affluent and influential Louisiana family. The young Joseph Meraux first attended the New Orleans auction houses with his mother, stimulating in him what was to become a lifelong interest in collecting, particularly clocks. At the end of my time there my colleagues and I had examined and listed 3,250 clocks! The range of clocks was enormous – English, French, German and of course American – and included many rare and unusual examples. The collection was rich in 19th-century automaton or mystery clocks. Our task was further complicated because the clocks had all been removed from their figures and stored separately – I spent many hours sorting through the various pieces and bringing them together again. Every room I entered brought fresh revelations, every cupboard was filled and no flat surface was left free of a clock. It was only near the end of the appraisal that I was told that there was a coach house nearby also filled with clocks and another building elsewhere in the town containing some particularly large examples. Even my huge enthusiasm for the subject began to wane!

For me one of the chief delights was to discover the enormous French 19th-century silvered-bronze figural mystery clock by Farcot, standing nearly ten feet (three metres) high, in one of the outbuildings; at first we could find only the figure but gradually tracked down the movement and the pendulum. This wonderful clock proved to be one of many highlights when the collection was sold for £1,700,000 (€/ $2,700,000) at Sotheby's New York on 28 June 1993.

I am sure there must be many other enthusiasts forming collections of clocks but I very much doubt whether I shall ever again have the privilege of working with such an extraordinary collection as that put together by Mr Meraux.

Michael Turner

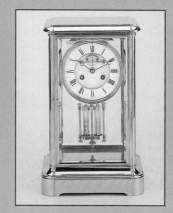

Carriage Clocks

An engraved gilt strut timepiece, by Thomas Cole, retailed by London & Ryder, c1853, 5½in (14cm) high.
£5,000–5,500
€/ $8,000–8,700 ⊞ JeF

An engraved brass carriage clock, by Brunelot, with eight-day striking movement, French, c1870, 6½in (16.5cm) high, with original carrying case.
£1,400–1,600
€/ $2,200–2,500 ⊞ BELL

Anglaise style

The *anglaise* style of carriage clock was designed by the French for the 'plain English taste'. The case components including the handle were all 'squared', giving quite a severe look. The *anglaise riche*-styled case was basically the same shape as the *anglaise* but had extra decoration, usually in the form of Corinthian columns, dentil mouldings and sometimes cloisonné enamelling or, more rarely, Limoges enamel panels.

An *anglaise riche* carriage clock, with royal blue chapter ring and alarm ring, the eight-day movement striking the hours and half hours on a gong, with silvered lever escapement and bimetallic balance, the case with Corinthian columns and key handle, French, c1880, 4in (10cm) high.
£1,700–1,900
€/ $2,700–3,000 ⊞ PSA

A gilt-brass combined timepiece, barometer and calendar, the lantern case surmounted by a compass and loop handle, thermometer missing, signed 'Mohican', French, dated 1885, 9¾in (25cm) high.
£500–600
€/ $800–950 ⚒ B(W)

A carriage clock, with enamel dial and a gilded mask, the eight-day movement striking the hours and half-hours on a gong, French, c1885, 5½in (14cm) high.
£750–850
€/ $1,200–1,400 ⊞ K&D

A brass carriage clock, 19thC, 9in (23cm) high.
£220–250
€/ $350–400 ⚒ SWO

A gilt-brass *mignonette* carriage clock, with an eight-day movement, French, c1890, 3¾in (9.5cm) high, with original leather travelling case.
£700–775
€/ $1,100–1,200 ⊞ PSA

◄ **A brass carriage time-piece,** probably by Drocourt, retailed by Benson, French, c1890, 2½in (6.5cm) high.
£950–1,100
€/ $1,500–1,700 ⊞ BELL

A gilt-brass miniature carriage timepiece, by A. Ecalle, Paris, the ivorine dial with Arabic numerals, the silvered lever escapement with a compensated bimetallic balance, the corniche case with winged term columns, French, 19thC, 3¼in (8.5cm) high.
£750–900
€/ $1,200–1,400 ⚒ B(Kn)

A gilt-brass corniche-cased carriage clock, the two-train movement with platform escapement, with push repeat striking on a gong, French, late 19thC, 6¾in (17cm) high.
£330–400
€/ $520–630 ⚒ BR

A carriage timepiece, the enamelled chapter ring with Arabic numerals, the case decorated with gilt-brass flowers between fluted pilasters supporting bevelled glass, French, late 19thC, 5¼in (13.5cm) high.
£240–275
€/ $380–440 ⚒ CGC

A brass carriage clock, the silvered dial with Arabic numerals and paste 'jewelled' decoration, the repeat movement with lever escapement, glass broken, French, 1875–1925, 5¼in (13.5cm) high.
£400–475
€/ $630–750 ⚒ AMB

Portable clocks

Portable or carriage clocks originated in Switzerland and France towards the end of the 18th century. They are usually known as *pendules d'officier* and often have complicated striking works and an alarm. The first maker to produce carriage clocks in glazed rectangular cases was Abraham Louis Breguet in the early years of the 19th century. The style evolved quickly and was taken up by other makers such as Paul Garnier and Leroy. For the next 100 years carriage clocks continued to be made by many French makers, usually in gilt-brass rectangular cases but sometimes embellished with porcelain or enamel panels. The movements vary from plain timepiece to full *grande sonnerie* with alarm.

A tortoiseshell and silver carriage timepiece, c1904, 3in (7.5cm) high.
£1,100–1,200
€/ $1,700–1,900 ⊞ BELL

An ormolu-mounted *pendule d'officier*, the dial painted with ribbon-tied floral swags and Arabic numerals, the eight-day French brass movement striking on a gong, with beaded bezel, dial damaged, early 20thC, 8¾in (22cm) high.
£850–1,000
€/ $1,300–1,600 ⚒ DD

A silver and enamel miniature timepiece, import marks for London 1910, 2¼in (5.5cm) high, with original case.
£1,100–1,300
€/ $1,700–2,000 ⊞ SHa

A gilt-brass and marble carriage timepiece, the enamel dial signed 'Walker Ltd', the movement with lever platform escapement, French, c1910, 5¼in (13.5cm) high.
£575–675
€/ $900–1,000 ⚒ S(O)

Cartel Clocks

A provincial gilt-bronze cartel clock, the dial flanked by columns surmounted by rams' heads joined by a garland and surmounted by an urn, French, c1785, 32¼in (82cm) high.
£1,700–2,000
€/ $2,700–3,200 S(P)

A carved giltwood cartel clock, with painted dial signed 'Beurling, Stockholm', decoration restored, Swedish, c1800, 35½in (90cm) high.
£2,500–2,800
€/ $4,000–4,400 BUK
Per Henrik Beurling is recorded as working between 1783 and 1806.

A Louis XV-style cartel clock, with convex dial, the eight-day movement striking the hours and half-hours on a bell, the rococo case with fretted panels, French, c1885, 19in (48.5cm) high.
£900–1,000
€/ $1,400–1,600 K&D

A Louis XVI-style gilt-metal cartel clock, signed 'Berthoud, Paris', the dial with Roman and Arabic numerals, the case surmounted by an urn and decorated with laurel swags and scrolls, French, 19thC, 26in (66cm) high.
£650–775
€/ $1,000–1,200 B(W)
French 19th-century clocks that were made in the 18th-century style were often confusingly signed with an 18th-century maker's name – as in this instance.

The word cartel may come from the Italian *cartella*, or wall bracket. It refers to decorative, spring-driven wall clocks produced mainly in France during the second half of the 18th century. The cases are invariably made of intricately cast ormolu, and they generally have elaborate decorative features such as figures, female masks, scrolling foliage, swags and classical urns. Being of cast metal, the case is very strong, allowing makers to cast crisp, detailed decoration.

◄ **An Empire-style giltwood cartel clock,** with painted dial, signed 'C. A. Lindström, Stockholm', Swedish, c1910, 35½in (90cm) high.
£2,700–3,000
€/ $4,300–4,700 CAV
C. A. Lindström was born in 1846 and was a clockmaker from 1889.

Electric Clocks

An electric mantel timepiece, by Matthäus Hipp, Neuchâtel, seconds hand missing, surface rust to steel work, Swiss, c1870, 26½in (67.5cm) high.
£4,500–5,000
€/ $7,000–8,000 S(O)

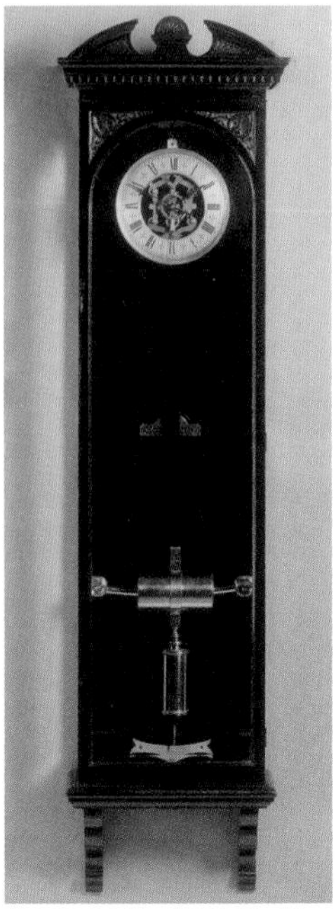

◄ **An ebonized Bentley's patent electric wall regulator,** by Cash & Skilbeck, the engraved annular silvered dial with gilt moulded bezel and centre seconds, the movement visible through the centre, the escape wheel impulsed and unlocked by two gravity arms controlled by the separately suspended wood rod pendulum with cylindrical bob and brass-cased coil oscillating over a fixed steel magnet, switching device signed 'Cash & Skilbeck, Makers, Leeds', in a dust-proofed bevel-glazed case, the interior with silvered beat plaque, with transformer power supply, c1900, 65¾in (167cm) high.
£10,000–12,000
€/ $16,000–19,000 S(O)

An electric timepiece, by Eureka Clock Co, London, the enamelled dial with Arabic numerals, with compensated balance, No. 8226, Patent No. 14614, the mahogany case with bevelled glass panels, 1906, 13½in (34.5cm) high.
£1,800–2,200
€/ $2,800–3,500 B(Kn)

Garnitures

An ormolu and marble Greco-Egyptian revival five-piece mantel clock garniture, the concave gilt dial decorated with *faux* hieroglyphics and inscribed 'G. Servant A Paris, Medaille d'Or 1867', the eight-day movement striking on a bell, the case surmounted by a Ptolemic ormolu bust with headdress signed 'Emile-Hebert', with applied mummiform caryatids to the side pieces, on lion-paw feet, with two conforming busts on fluted Ionic pedestals applied with leafy garlands and two tazzas on conforming bases, French, c1870, clock 24in (61cm) high
£4,000–4,800
€/ $6,300–7,600 ⚒ Bri

A clock garniture, with convex enamel dial and eight-day movement striking the hours and half-hours on a bell, the case set with bronze cherubs and ormolu mounts, on a marble base, French, c1875, 12in (30.5cm) high.
£1,800–2,000
€/ $2,800–3,200 ⊞ K&D

► A marble and bronze clock garniture, with parcel-gilt decoration, bronze sculpture missing from clock, French, c1880, clock 17¼in (44cm) wide.
£700–800
€/ $1,100–1,300 ⚒ S(O)

An ormolu-mounted alabaster clock garniture, by Marti, the eight-day spring-driven movement striking on a bell, top of clock urn removable, minor damage, French, c1880, 15in (38cm) high.
£1,400–1,600
€/ $2,200–2,500 ⊞ SET

◄ A gilt-spelter and porcelain clock garniture, the porcelain dial with Roman numerals, the eight-day movement striking on a gong, the case surmounted by two cherubs flanking a porcelain urn, supported by Corinthian columns flanked by a putto to either side, on reeded, scroll and paw feet, with a pair of matching urns, French, late 19thC, clock approx 20¾in (52.5cm) high.
£650–775
€/ $1,000–1,200 ⚒ RTo

For further information on antique clocks see the full range of Miller's books at **www.millers.uk.com**

Lantern Clocks

◄ A brass lantern clock, the dial with Roman numeral chapter ring and brass hand, the twin-train short duration balance wheel movement with countwheel striking on a bell, old restorations, probably West Country, c1650, 14½in (37cm) high.
£4,000–4,800
€/ $6,300–7,600 ⚒ Bri

► A brass lantern clock, the conventional movement with verge escapement, the external locking plate striking on the top-mounted bell, with a modern wall bracket, restored, c1720, 15in (38cm) high.
£2,300–2,600
€/ $3,600–4,000 ⚒ S(O)

A lantern clock, with Winterhalder & Hofmeier eight-day ting-tang movement striking the quarters on two bells, German, c1900, 14in (35.5cm) high.
£780–870
€/ $1,200–1,350 ⊞ K&D

Longcase Clocks

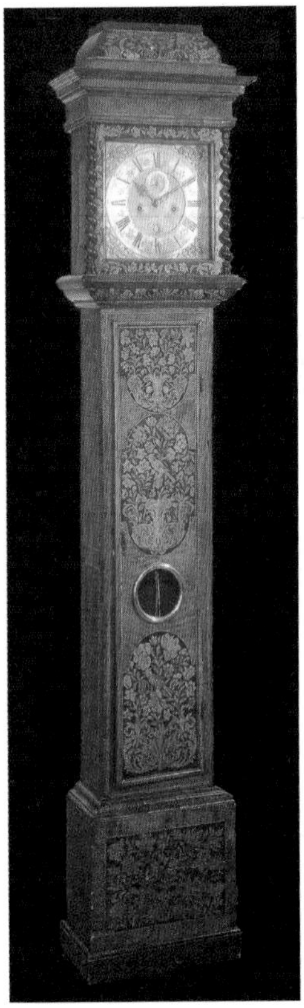

A William and Mary walnut longcase clock, by William Grimes, the brass dial with a silvered chapter ring, subsidiary seconds dial and date aperture, the eight-day movement striking on a bell, the hood with foliage marquetry and ebonized spiral-twist pilasters, the trunk door with bird and foliage marquetry and inset with a lenticle, on a conforming base, base reduced, 87in (221cm) high.
£25,000–30,000
€/ $39,000–47,000 WW

This clock sold well in excess of the auctioneer's expectations. This is probably because it is in unusually good original condition for a 300 year old clock. It has lost the back hood pillars and the original bun feet have been replaced with an apron, but the marquetry is of exceptionally fine quality. The clock looks as if it has not been touched for years, thereby adding to its desirability.

► **A chinoiserie-decorated longcase clock,** by Richard Martin, Northampton, with an eight-day movement, c1700, 98in (249cm) high.
£12,000–13,500
€/ $19,000–21,000 ALS

A walnut marquetry longcase clock, the dial with calendar aperture and seconds dial, the month-going movement with six ring-turned pillars, reversed five-wheel trains and outside countwheel, the hood formerly rising, c1690, 77¾in (197.5cm) high.
£13,500–15,000
€/ $21,000–24,000 S(O)

► **A walnut longcase clock,** by Thomas Lumpkin, London, the brass dial with a silvered Roman chapter ring, subsidiary seconds and a date aperture, with an eight-day movement, late 17thC, 87in (221cm) high.
£4,200–5,000
€/ $6,500–7,900 G(L)

A William III walnut marquetry longcase clock, by John Clows, London, the brass dial with subsidiary seconds, date aperture and ringed winding holes, with a long-plated eight-day, five ring, turned-pillar bell-striking movement, with an outside countwheel and anchor escapement, the case with a lenticle, the hood formerly rising, probably associated, 83in (211cm) high.
£5,000–6,000
€/ $7,900–9,500 B(NW)

John Clows was admitted to the Clockmakers Company in 1672, probably the date he completed his apprenticeship. He was a Warden of the company in 1713.

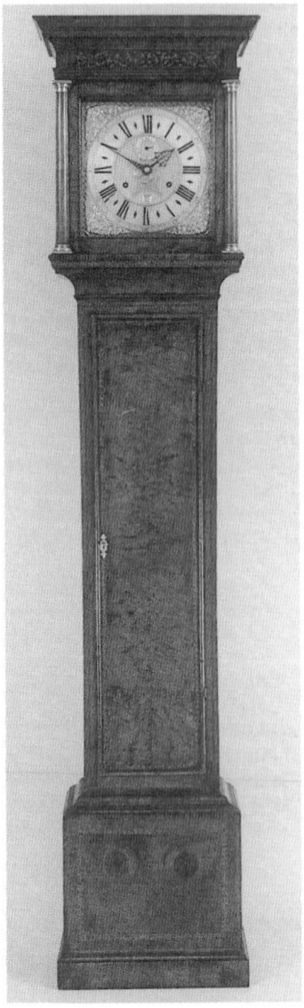

A walnut-veneered oak longcase clock, by Robert Sadler, London, the brass dial with a separate silvered-brass chapter, seconds and date rings, the month-duration five-pillar movement with a latched centre pillar, the inside rack striking the hours on a bell, the trunk door with figured veneers and marquetry border, repeated to the base with a single plinth, c1710, 86in (218.5cm) high.
£25,000–28,500
€/ $39,000–45,000 PAO

This clock is in good, clean and restored condition with the added appeal of a month-running movement. It has beautiful hands and a rich, warm colour to the case. This clock was offered in fully working condition.

An oak longcase clock, by William Snow I, Otley, the silvered dial with a Roman chapter ring, inscribed 'William Snow 584', a crescent-form date aperture and single hand, with 30-hour movement, hood finials missing, early 18thC, 81in (205.5cm) high.
£1,800–2,200
€/ $2,800–3,500 ⚒ PFK
Thirty-hour clocks can be difficult to sell, but this clock was made by a well-documented maker who numbered most of the clocks he made. This always appeals to collectors, as it demonstrates the uniqueness of each clock and assists with dating.

A mahogany crossbanded oak longcase clock, by Jacob Massy, London, the brass dial with a Roman and Arabic chapter ring with half quarter marks, subsidiary seconds and a decorated date aperture, the associated early 18thC movement with five knopped and finned pillars, high barrels and anchor escapement, rack striking on a bell, in a 19thC case, formerly with strike/not-strike lever, 84¼in (214cm) high.
£1,300–1,500
€/ $2,000–2,400 ⚒ B
This clock has a perfectly good movement and case, but they did not start life together and this is reflected in the low selling price.

Marriages

In the antiques world, a marriage is when components that did not start life together have been brought together to form a whole. This applies more frequently to longcase clocks than to any other form of antique. This is because longcase clock dials tend to be made to fairly standard sizes and so can be comfortably housed in a different case from the one for which they were intended. Check for the following clues: the style of the case and dial should complement each other, the dial should fit the aperture in the hood accurately, and the movement seatboard should sit comfortably on the case styles without too much evidence of recent alteration to the packing. Where the components are from the same period it may be regarded as a compatible marriage and may not reduce the value of the piece too much. If the movement has been changed so that there is a marriage of movement, case and dial, the value will be very much reduced.

► **An oak longcase clock,** by Robert Cutbush, Maidstone, the brass dial with Roman numerals, subsidiary seconds dial and date aperture, in a 19thC case, 1700–50 85in (216cm) high.
£750–875
€/ $1,200–1,400 ⚒ RTo

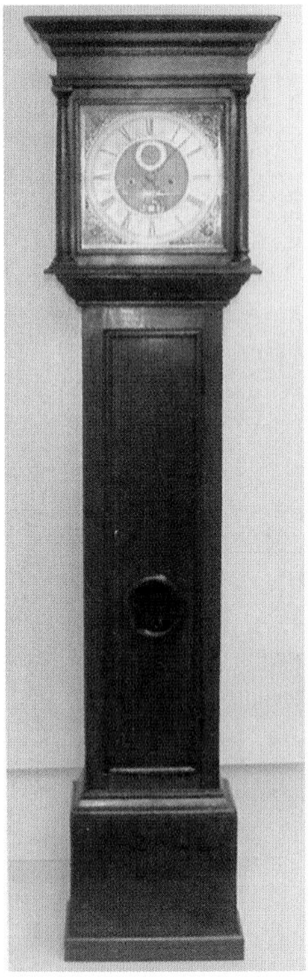

An oak longcase clock, by Thomas Deykin of Worcester, the brass and silvered dial inscribed 'Tho. Deykin Worcester No. 176', with an hourly-striking eight-day movement with five pillars, the door with a glass lenticle, replacement lock and repairs to the base, early 18thC, 80½in (204.5cm) high.
£4,200–5,000
€/ $6,600–7,900 FHF

A provincial stained-oak alarm lantern longcase clock, the relief-moulded brass dial with cartouche Roman numerals, iron hour hand and iron alarm hand, the brass and iron posted movement with verge escapement, with a knife-edge suspended pendulum, alarm and rack striking on a bell, French, c1730, 96½in (245cm) high.
£2,200–2,500
€/ $3,500–4,000 S(Am)

◄ **An oak longcase clock,** by William Avenell, Alresford, the dial with ringed winding and date apertures, with an eight-day movement, mid-18thC, 87¾in (223cm) high.
£6,800–7,500
€/ $10,700–12,000 ALS

Longcase clocks 1976–2002

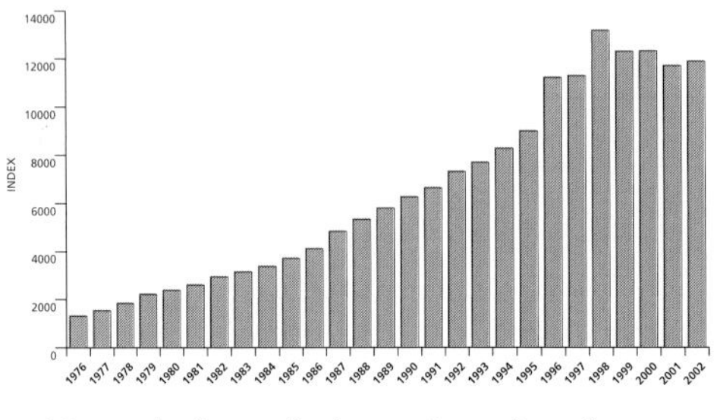

This graph shows the increasing value of antique Longcase clocks as a whole over the past 25 years. ©AMR

An oak longcase clock, by Phillip Avenell, Farnham, the dial with ringed winding and date apertures, with an eight-day movement, a lenticle to the trunk door, early 18thC, 83in (211cm) high.
£6,700–7,500
€/ $10,500–12,000 ALS

A *faux* tortoiseshell-lacquer longcase clock, by Aylmer Stopes, London, the brass dial with a separate silvered-brass chapter ring with seconds and date, the arch with a strike/silent facility, with an eight-day, five-pillar movement striking the hours on a bell, the case with gold chinoiseries to the trunk door and base, c1740, 87in (221cm) high.
£8,500–9,600
€/ $13,500–15,200 PAO

► **An oak longcase clock,** by T. Thorpe, Colchester, the brass and silvered dial with calendar aperture, with 30-hour movement, mid-18thC, 86in (218.5cm) high.
£1,400–1,600
€/ $2,200–2,500 G(B)

A longcase clock, by Thomas Budgen (Bugden), Croydon, the brass dial with a silvered chapter ring, Roman numerals and Arabic five-minute intervals, the five-pillar movement with anchor escapement rack striking on a bell, c1740, 86in (218.5cm) high.
£1,800–2,200
€/ $2,800–3,500 GTH

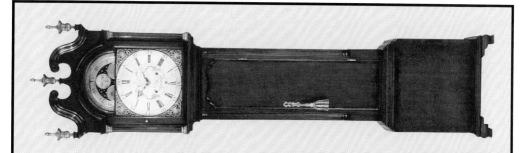

A lacquered longcase clock, by E. Whittingham, London, the brass dial with a strike/silent subsidiary, recessed seconds and date aperture, signed on an applied plaque, the five-pillar movement with anchor escapement striking on a bell, hood reduced, minor damage, mid-18thC, 82in (208.5cm) high.
£1,700–2,000
€/ $2,700–3,200 ⚒ B(Kn)
The high cost of restoring japanned or lacquered decoration has kept the price down on this London clock.

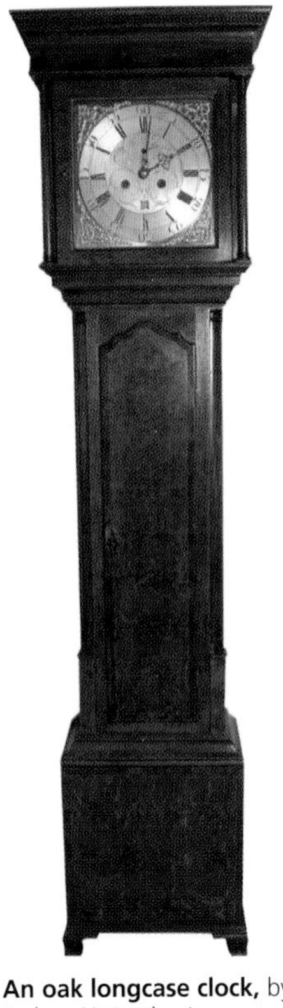

An oak longcase clock, by Joshua Harrocks, Lancaster, with an eight-day movement, the case with mahogany crossbanding, c1760, 84in (213.5cm) high.
£8,000–9,500
€/ $12,700–15,000 ⊞ JeF

A rococo lacquered longcase clock, by Petter Ernst, Stockholm, with gilt-bronze mounts and carved decoration of acanthus leaves, rocailles and shells, with later painted decoration of flowers, trailing foliage and birds, Swedish, c1760, 90½in (230cm) high.
£8,200–10,000
€/ $13,000–15,800 ⚒ BUK
This is a fine clock by one of Sweden's most respected makers. This is good value for money.

A mahogany longcase clock, by Benjamin Martin, Manchester, the dial with a rolling moon, subsidiary seconds and date aperture, the eight-day bell-striking movement with an inside countwheel, c1770, 89in (226cm) high.
£4,200–5,000
€/ $6,600–7,900 ⚒ B(NW)
Manchester clocks are popular and have distinctive cases.

An oak longcase clock, by James Smythe, Saxmundham, with an eight-day movement, c1765, 86½in (219.5cm) high.
£6,800–7,500
€/ $10,700–11,800 ⊞ ALS

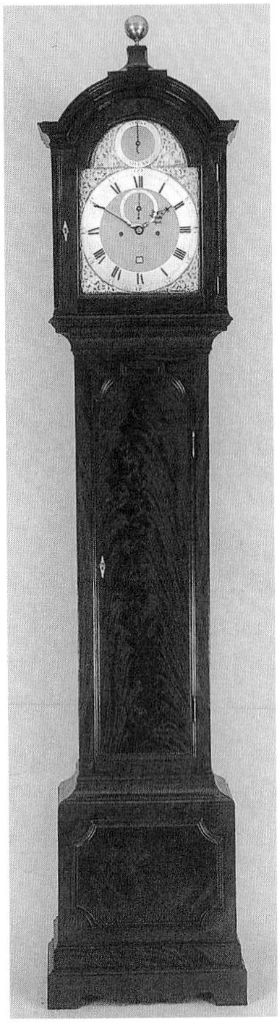

A mahogany longcase clock, by Robert Hynam, London, the brass dial with seconds ring and a strike/silent facility to the arch, the eight-day movement with five pillars and deadbeat escapement, striking the hours on a bell, c1770, 95in (241.5cm) high.
£19,500–21,500
€/ $30,000–34,000 ⊞ PAO
This is a rare clock, by the clockmaker to the Russian court at St Petersburg. This is one of the most desirable case styles, with well-figured veneers and restrained decoration to the hood.

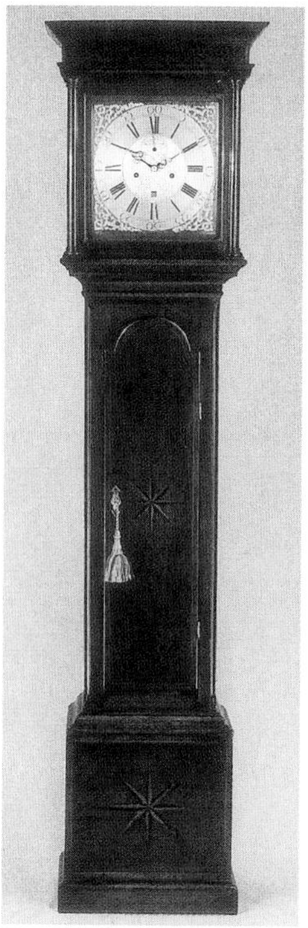

A longcase clock, by Charles Raymond, Lideway, with an eight-day movement, and inlaid decoration of a star to trunk and base, c1770, 82in (208.5cm) high.
£7,700–8,500
€/ $12,000–13,500 ⊞ ALS

An oak longcase clock, by James Webster, Shropshire, with an engraved brass dial and single hand movement, c1770, 76in (193cm) high.
£5,800–6,500
€/ $9,000–10,300 ⊞ RYA
This clock is in good original condition and the appeal of a single hand added to its value despite its 30-hour movement. James Webster is recorded as working in Shrewsbury, Shropshire, c1770.

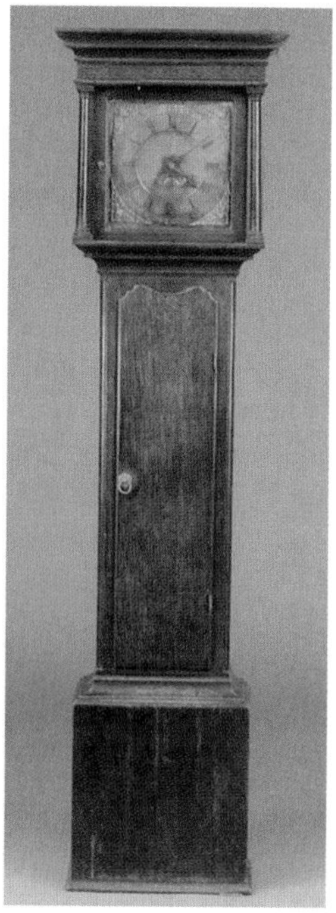

An oak longcase clock, by Wilson, Askrigg, the brass dial with date aperture, the hood with plain columns, blind fret frieze and moulded flat top, the case with a shaped headed door and quarter columns, c1770, 81in (205.5cm) high.
£2,000–2,400
€/ $3,200–3,800 ⚒ TEN

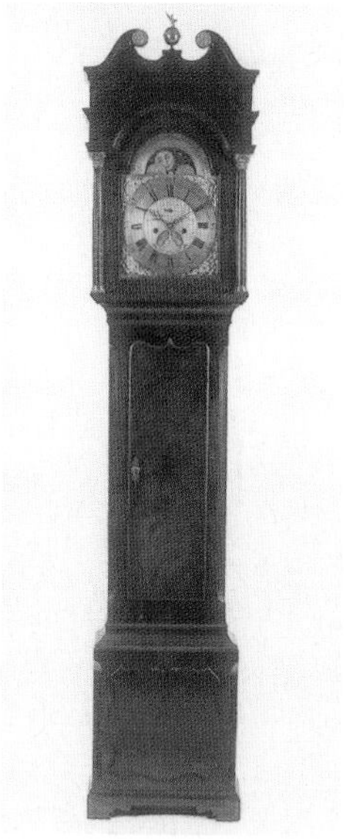

A mahogany longcase clock, by E. Bilbie, Chew Stoke, the brass dial with a silvered Roman numeral chapter ring, subsidiary seconds dial and a calendar sector, the arch with rolling moon and tidal cycle, engraved 'High Water at Bristol Key' to the border, with a four-pillar rack and bell-striking movement, c1775, 92½in (235cm) high.
£5,000–6,000
€/ $7,900–9,500 ⚒ Bri

A mahogany longcase clock, by William Mason, London, the brass dial with a separate silvered-brass chapter ring and seconds and date apertures, the arch with a rocking ship automaton, the eight-day duration five-pillar movement striking the hours on a bell, with removable pagoda top, c1775, 100in (254cm) high.
£16,500–18,500
€/ $26,000–30,000 ⊞ PAO
The rocking ship automaton in the arch is a rare feature on a London clock. It is in excellent restored condition and therefore commands a high price.

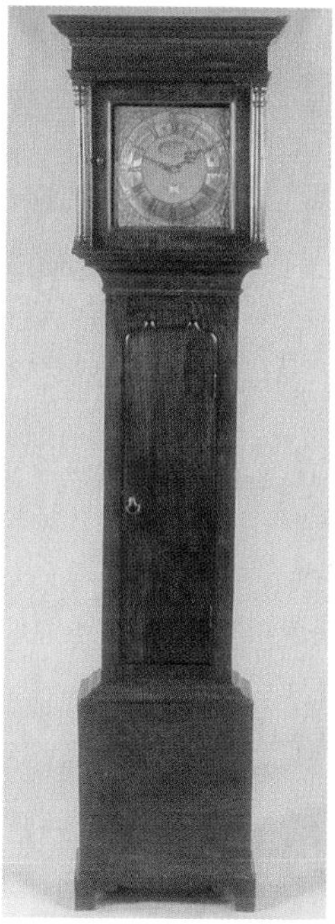

A mid-Georgian oak longcase clock, by John Porthouse I, Penrith, the dial with silvered chapter ring with Roman hours and Arabic minutes, a subsidiary calendar aperture, with an hour-striking 30-hour movement, 83½in (212cm) high.
£2,000–2,200
€/ $3,200–3,500 ⚒ PFK

The longcase clock evolved in the mid-17th century after the invention of the pendulum. Interference with the weights caused the clock to run unreliably, so they had to be protected. A short while later the long pendulum was introduced, which needed even more careful protection than the weights. From the very beginning clockmakers seized the opportunity to enhance the appeal of the clock by housing it in an attractive case. This set the trend for the next 300 years, and the design and decoration of clock cases evolved to reflect the current fashion.

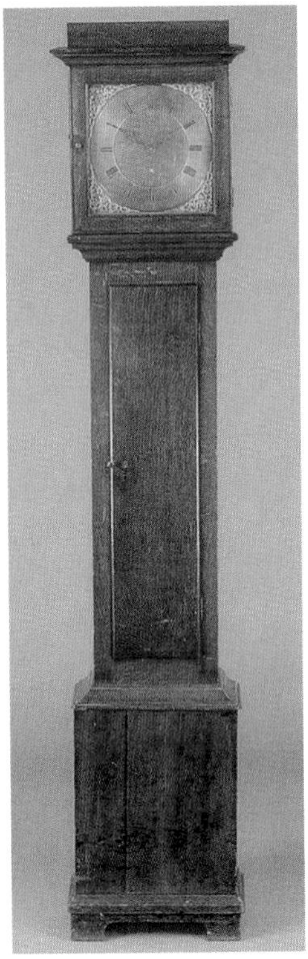

An oak longcase clock, by E. Sagar, Skipton, the brass dial with an engraved centre and date subsidiary, c1780, 80in (203cm) high.
£1,400–1,600
€/ $2,200–2,500 ⚒ TEN

An oak longcase clock, by Thomas Brown, Chester, the engraved dial with centresweep seconds and moonphases, the eight-day movement with deadbeat escapement, c1780, 90in (228.5cm) high.
£9,300–10,300
€/ $14,700–16,200 ⊞ ALS

An oak longcase clock, by Benjamin Lockwood, Swaffham, the eight-day, five-pillar movement with strike/silent and pull hour repeat, c1780, 90in (228.5cm) high.
£6,700–7,500
€/ $10,500–11,800 ⊞ ALS

A mahogany longcase clock, by Robert Fletcher, Chester, the arch with a moon feature, with an eight-day movement, c1790, 90in (228.5cm) high.
£12,500–14,000
€/ $20,000–22,000 ⊞ JeF

A mahogany longcase clock, by James Howden, Edinburgh, with an eight-day movement, the case with boxwood stringing, c1780, 87½in (222.5cm) high.
£9,300–10,300
€/ $14,700–16,000 ⊞ ALS

A mahogany longcase clock, by William Priest, Bristol, the eight-day movement with moonphases and High Water at Bristol Key, c1780, 95in (241.5cm) high.
£13,500–15,000
€/ $21,000–24,000 ⊞ ALS

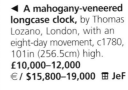

◄ **A mahogany-veneered longcase clock,** by Thomas Lozano, London, with an eight-day movement, c1780, 101in (256.5cm) high.
£10,000–12,000
€/ $15,800–19,000 ⊞ JeF

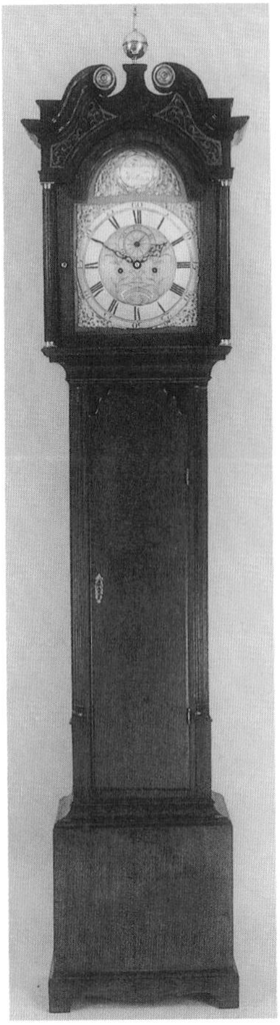

► **An oak longcase clock,** by John Turnbull, Hawick, the brass dial with silvered-brass chapter ring, seconds and date, a silvered-brass cartouche to the arch with the maker's name, the eight-day movement striking on a bell, Scottish, c1780, 90in (228.5cm) high.
£8,000–8,800
€/ $12,700–14,000 ⊞ PAO

LAPADA MEMBER

P. A. Oxley

Quality British Antique Clocks & Barometers

Established 1971

The leading UK dealer in quality restored antique longcase clocks

Very large selection always available

Prices from £3,500 to £30,000

P. A. Oxley Antique Clocks & Barometers, The Old Rectory, Cherhill, Calne, Wiltshire SN11 8UX, U.K. Tel: 01249 816227 Fax: 01249 821285
E-mail: info@paoxley.com www.british-antiqueclocks.com

Full stock with prices shown on our website

Member of the Association of Art and Antique Dealers

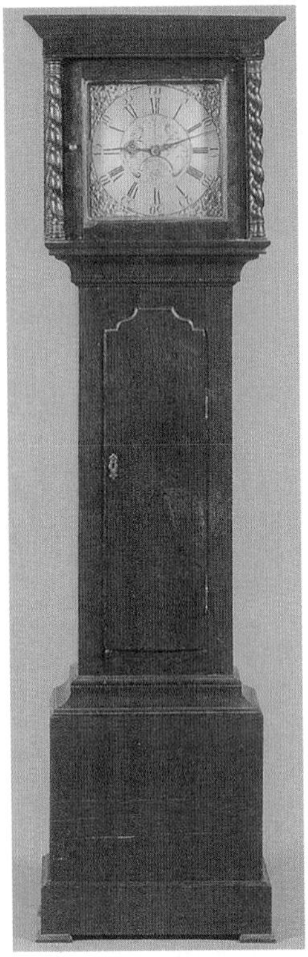

An oak longcase clock, by Winstanley, Holywell, the dial with a calendar sector and inscribed 'Time is Valuable', the plated 30-hour movement with external locking plate striking on a bell, hood pillars and base replaced, c1780, 79in (200.5cm) high.
£800–900
€/ $1,300–1,400 ⚒ S(O)
Alterations to the case kept the price to a modest level.

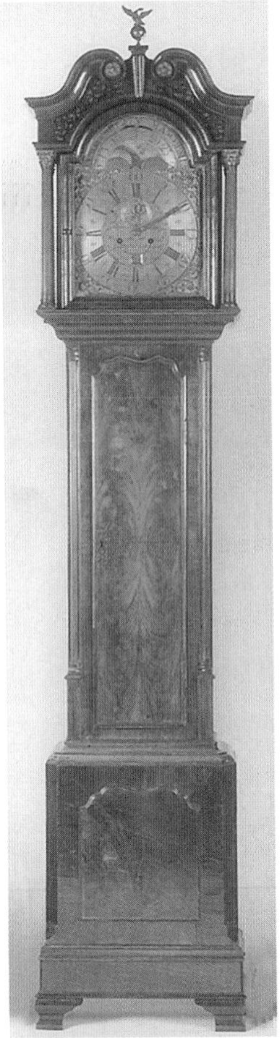

A flame-figured mahogany longcase clock, by James Wrigley, Manchester, the dial with rolling moon, subsidiary seconds, date aperture and arcaded minute ring, the rack and bell-striking eight-day movement with anchor escapement, c1780, 99½in (252.5cm) high.
£3,800–4,500
€/ $6,000–7,000 ⚒ B(NW)
James Wrigley is a hitherto unrecorded maker, though it seems probable that he is descended from the Manchester clockmakers, James Wrigley and Isaac Wrigley, who died in 1697 and 1742 respectively.

A stained wood longcase clock, the brass dial with a pewter chapter ring, Roman numerals, subsidiary seconds, pierced steel hands and a name shield signed,' Joa Chr Bartels Goslar' the posted movement with anchor escapement, rack quarter-striking on three bells, the case with a lenticle, on a *bombé* plinth with canted corners, on bracket feet, German, c1780, 93¾in (238cm) high.
£1,200–1,400
€/ $1,900–2,200 ⚒ S(Am)

A George III mahogany longcase clock, by Joseph Avard, Bristol, the brass dial with a moonphase, High Tide at Bristol Key, subsidiary seconds and a date aperture, with an eight-day movement, associated case, 85in (216cm) high.
£4,000–4,800
€/ $6,300–7,600 ⚒ G(L)
The movement and case both appear to be from the Bristol area. The shaped trunk door, fancy edge to the glazed door and crisply cut mouldings and pillars are all typical of this area.

A George III banded mahogany and walnut longcase clock, by Blaylock, Longtown, the brass dial with a silver chapter ring, Roman and Arabic numerals and subsidiary seconds and calendar dials, with an eight-day movement, 85in (216cm) high.
£3,500–4,200
€/ $5,500–6,600 ⚒ G(B)

◄ **A George III oak and crossbanded mahogany longcase clock,** by Jn. Bell, Garstang, with a seconds hand, calendar aperture and eight-day movement, 79in (200.5cm) high.
£1,500–1,800
€/ $2,400–2,800 ⚒ Mit

► **A George III oak and mahogany crossbanded longcase clock,** by W. Belman, Broughton, the painted dial with Roman numerals and a calendar aperture, with a 30-hour movement, 79in (200.5cm) high.
£525–625
€/ $830–1,000 ⚒ Mit

◄ **A George III mahogany longcase clock,** by James Brown, Portsmouth, the silvered arch dial with moonphase above a subsidiary seconds dial and a calendar aperture, the eight-day movement striking on a bell, 91½in (232.5cm) high.
£4,000–4,800
€/ $6,300–7,600 WW

► **A George III boxwood-lined mahogany longcase clock,** by Alex Duncan, Elgin, the silvered dial with subsidiary seconds dial and date aperture, the eight-day movement striking on a bell, Scottish, 84¾in (215.5cm) high.
£2,800–3,200
€/ $4,400–5,000 B(Ed)

Scottish clocks from the late 18th century usually have attractive slim cases which fit comfort-ably into modern homes, thereby increasing their appeal and value.

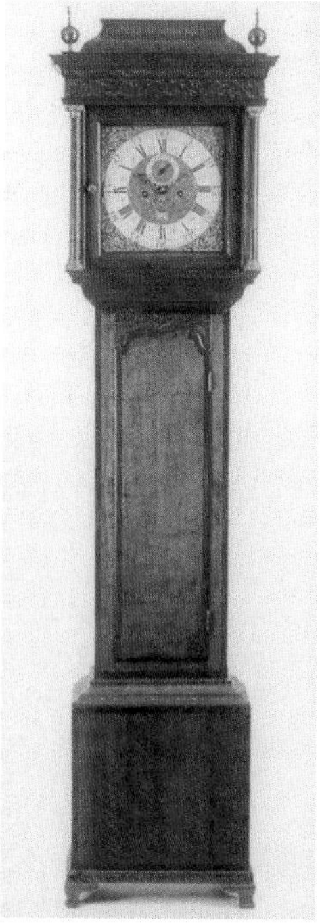

A George III oak and crossbanded longcase clock, the brass dial with a silver chapter ring, the twin-train movement with anchor escapement striking a bell, signed 'Nath. Brown, Manchester', 83¾in (212.5cm) high.
£2,200–2,600
€/ $3,500–4,100 Bea(E)

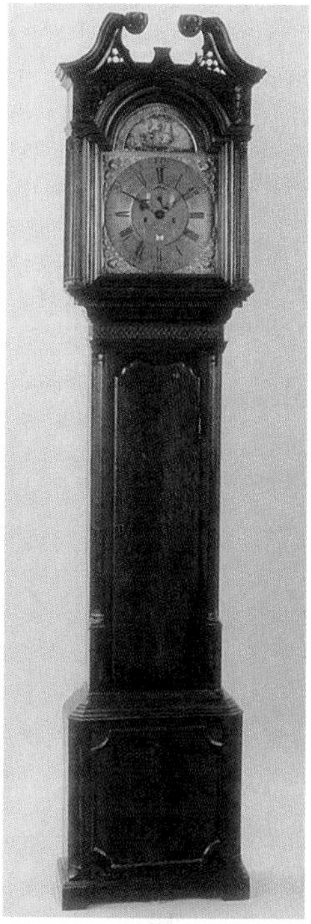

A George III mahogany longcase clock, by Thomas Fayrer, Lancaster, the brass dial with subsidiary seconds dial and date aperture, with an eight-day striking movement, pediment reduced, 92½in (235cm) high.
£4,800–5,700
€/ $7,600–9,000 B(S)

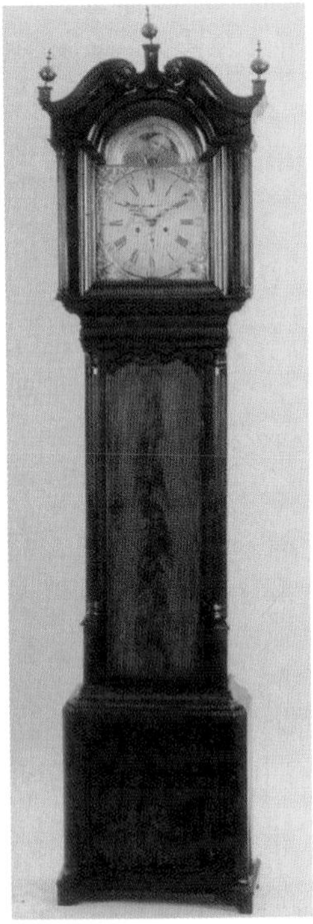

A George III mahogany longcase clock, by George Harden, Altrincham, the silvered dial with subsidiary seconds and date hands engraved with birds with painted moonphase, 89¾in (228cm) high.
£4,000–4,800
€/ $6,300–7,600 ⚒ B(S)

◀ **A George III mahogany longcase clock,** by Foot, South Brent, the painted dial with a rocking ship to the arch, Roman numerals to the chapter ring, subsidiary dial and date aperture, with a two-train eight-day movement striking on a bell, 89in (226cm) high.
£3,300–4,000
€/ $5,200–6,300 ⚒ HYD
The automaton feature in this clock helped it to make a higher than expected price.

A George III mahogany longcase clock, by B. Mitchell, Cockermouth, the painted dial with a date aperture, painted spandrels and cottage scene, with a 30-hour movement, the hood with a swan-neck pediment with punched brass terminals, 86in (218.5cm) high.
£2,500–3,000
€/ $4,000–4,700 ⚒ Mit

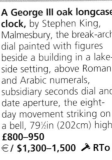

A George III oak longcase clock, by Stephen King, Malmesbury, the break-arch dial painted with figures beside a building in a lake-side setting, above Roman and Arabic numerals, subsidiary seconds dial and date aperture, the eight-day movement striking on a bell, 79½in (202cm) high.
£800–950
€/ $1,300–1,500 ⚒ RTo

► **A George III mahogany and chequer-strung longcase clock,** by W. P., Whitby, the dial painted with a girl seated by the wayside, with black Roman numerals, a subsidiary seconds dial and arched calendar sector, the twin-train movement striking on a bell, 89in (226cm) high.
£3,000–3,600
€/ $4,700–5,700 ⚒ B(Nor)

A George III mahogany-banded oak longcase clock, the dial with a date aperture, subsidiary seconds and painted Arabic numerals, with an eight-day movement, with swan neck pediment, 84in (213.5cm) high.
£800–950
€/ $1,300–1,500 EH
This is a very reasonable price for an eight-day clock, but circular dials are not as popular as square or arched ones.

An oak longcase clock, the brass dial with silvered chapter ring, date and seconds dial and signed 'William Mercer, Maidstone', the eight-day five-pillar movement striking the hours on a bell, c1785, 82in (208.5cm) high.
£3,400–3,800
€/ $5,400–6,000 K&D

A mahogany longcase clock, by John Edgecumbe, Bristol, the brass break-arch dial with a silvered Roman numeral chapter ring, subsidiary seconds dial and arch calendar aperture dial painted with a rocking ship before a castle with a flotilla beyond, inscribed 'The Nassau of Bristol' to the silvered arch border, with a four-pillar rack and bell-striking movement, hood damaged, c1785, 88½in (225cm) high.
£5,500–6,500
€/ $8,700–10,300 Bri

A figured mahogany longcase clock, by James Tregent, London, the brass dial with Roman numerals, subsidiary strike/silent dial, seconds dial and date aperture, with an eight-day bell-striking movement, early 19thC, 87¾in (223cm) high.
£4,500–5,300
€/ $7,000–8,400 RTo

A George III provincial oak and walnut boxwood-strung and walnut-banded longcase clock, the engraved brass dial with a painted moonphase, the hood with a swan-neck pediment, 92½in (235cm) high.
£2,500–3,000
€/ $4,000–4,700 JAd

An oak longcase clock, by Thos. Olive, Cranbrook, with a silvered dial and 30-hour movement, the crested hood with a fretwork frieze, giltwood ball and spire finials, c1785, 81in (205.5cm) high.
£3,300–3,600
€/ $5,200–5,700 PGO

A mid-Georgian oak longcase clock, by Christopher Caygill, Askrigg, the brass dial and chapter ring with Roman hours, Arabic minutes and a date aperture, with a 30-hour movement, 80½in (204.5cm) high.
£2,000–2,400
€/ $3,200–3,800 ⅄ PFK

An oak longcase clock, by Watkin Owen, Llanrwst, the dial with subsidiary seconds and downswept date, the eight-day rack- and bell-striking movement fixed with a false plate cast 'Wilson', Welsh, c1790, 81in (205.5cm) high.
£1,700–2,000
€/ $2,700–3,200 ⅄ B(NW)

A mahogany longcase clock, by Samuel Thorndike, Ipswich, the engraved silvered dial with strike/silent, date and seconds dial, the eight-day five-pillar movement striking the hours on a bell, c1790, 92in (233.5cm) high.
£5,200–5,700
€/ $8,200–9,000 ⊞ K&D

A yew wood longcase clock, by Swift, Coltishall, with a silvered dial and eight-day striking movement, c1790, 77in (195.5cm) high.
£5,000–5,500
€/ $8,000–8,600 ⊞ PGO

A japanned wood longcase clock, by Henry Brunwin, London, the brass dial with a date aperture and strike/silent dial, 18thC, 48¾in (124cm) high.
£2,000–2,200
€/ $3,200–3,500 ⅄ S(O)
This clock sold for a low price because the case is reduced and in need of restoration.

An oak longcase clock, by James Kenway, Bridport, the brass dial and chapter ring with an engraved centre and date aperture, 18thC, 78¾in (200cm) high.
£1,000–1,200
€/ $1,600–1,900 ⅄ WW

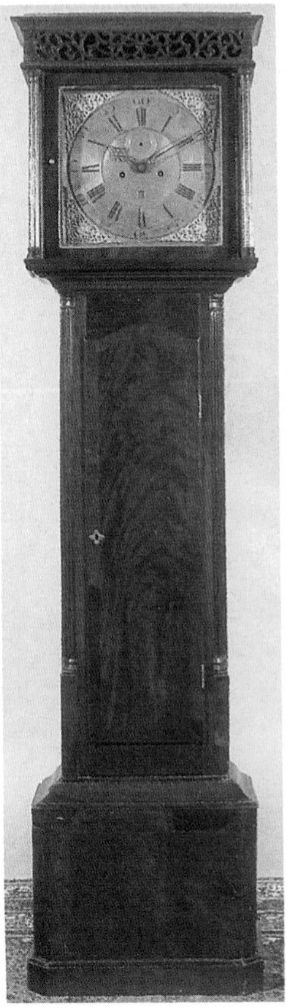

► **A mahogany longcase clock,** the brass dial with seconds dial and calendar, signed 'Chris Clarke, Dublin', top removed and replaced with blind fret cornice, Irish, 18thC, 82¾in (210cm) high.
£1,000–1,200
€/ $1,600–1,900 ⅄ HOK
This clock has an altered case, hence the low price it achieved at auction.

An oak longcase clock, by John Christian, Aylsham, the brass dial with Roman and Arabic numerals, with an eight-day four-pillar bell-striking movement, the hood with a scrolling cornice, 18thC, 82¼in (209cm) high.
£1,200–1,400
€/ $1,900–2,200 ⅄ CGC

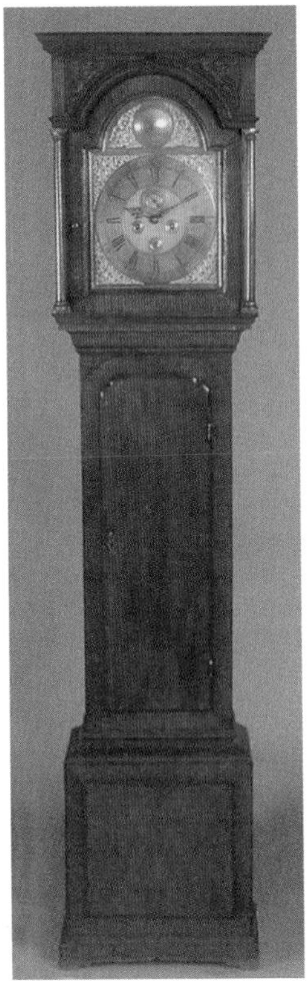

An oak and mahogany eight-day longcase clock, by Thomas Ogden, Halifax, the silvered brass dial with subsidiary dials for seconds and date and pierced steel hands, the engraved arch flanked by dolphin spandrels, 18thC, 89in (226cm) high.
£4,500–5,200
€/ $7,100–8,200 ⚒ M

A mahogany longcase clock, by Jas Monkhouse, Carlisle, with painted dial, a moonphase in the arch, date and seconds dials, the hood with swan-neck pediments above fluted Corinthian columns, the trunk with fluted pilasters and crossbanded inlay, late 18thC, 96in (244cm) high.
£2,200–2,500
€/ $3,500–4,000 ⚒ TMA

◀ A mahogany longcase clock, by Eardley Norton, London, No. 1165, the arched brass dial with a strike/silent subsidiary, a Roman and Arabic chapter ring, recessed subsidiary seconds and a date aperture, the movement with plates held by six knopped pillars, chiming the quarters on eight bells and the hours on a ninth, with deadbeat escapement and steel crutch, late 18thC, 100¼in (257cm) high.
£12,000–14,000
€/ $19,000–22,000 ⚒ B
Eardley Norton was working from 49 St John Street, Clerkenwell, London, in the mid 18th century and was free of the Clockmakers' Company from 1770–94. He was a maker of great repute of watches and complex clocks and in 1771 patented a striking mechanism. This clock has been in the vendor's family since c1870.

A *faux* tortoiseshell longcase clock, by Nicholls of Canterbury, with an eight-day movement, c1795, 81¾in (207.5cm) high.
£6,700–7,500
€/ $10,500–11,800 ⊞ ALS

An oak longcase clock, by W. Flint, Ashford, the arched plain dial with seconds and date dials, the eight-day movement striking on a bell, the hood with brass-capped and reeded-angle pillars and typical 'Kent' cresting, with three brass finials, c1800, 85in (216cm) high.
£3,800–4,350
€/ $6,000–7,000 ⊞ PAO

► An oak longcase clock, by George Suggate, Halesworth, the arched dial with Arabic chapters, seconds and date, the corners with painted shells, a painted ruin to the arch, with an eight-day bell-striking movement, c1800, 84in (213.5cm) high.
£3,500–4,000
€/ $5,500–6,300 ⊞ PAO

A mahogany longcase clock, by Henry Gamble, Bramley, the silvered dial with moonphases in the arch, the centre with a date sector, the movement with an anchor escapement striking on a bell, late 18thC, 91¾in (233cm) high.
£2,500–2,800
€/ $4,000–4,400 ⚒ B(Kn)
This is a good clock and could have realized as much as £4,000 (€/ $6,300).

A mahogany longcase clock, by Whitehurst, Derby, with a silvered dial and a rack and bell-striking movement, the inlaid boxwood-strung case with a break-arch hood, apron replaced, case later, c1800, 79in (200.5cm) high.
£2,500–3,000
€/ $4,000–4,700 S(O)

A mahogany longcase clock, by Samuel Kellett, Bredbury, the broken-arch dial with a rolling moon and calendar, a central painting of Faith, Hope and Charity, the eight-day rack and bell-striking movement with anchor escapement, in a flame-figured strung and crossbanded case, calendar hand missing, c1810, 86in (218.5cm) high.
£1,500–1,800
€/ $2,400–2,800 B(NW)

The Kelletts were something of a clockmaking dynasty during the 18th and 19th centuries in Bredbury and Woodley in Cheshire. This clock could have been made by one of two Samuel Kelletts working at the time.

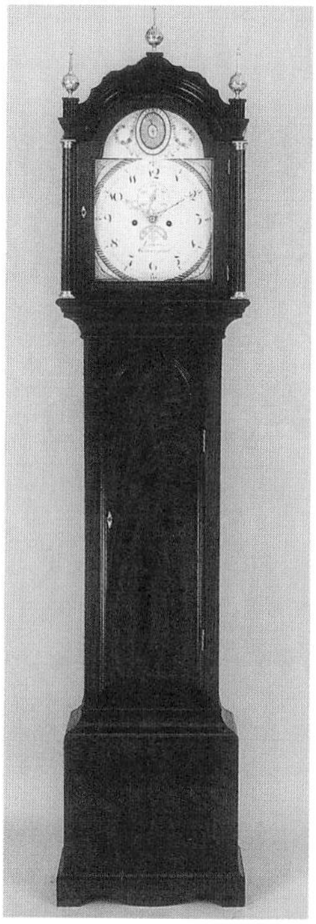

A mahogany longcase clock, by Lewis, Gravesend, the dial showing seconds and date, with Arabic chapters and matching brass hands, the eight-day movement striking on a bell, c1810, 87in (221cm) high.
£7,500–8,250
€/ $11,800–13,000 PAO

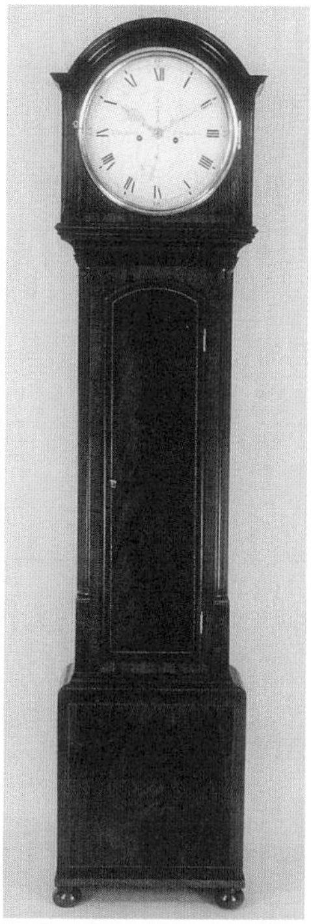

A mahogany longcase clock, by A. Oliphant, Pittenweem, the round dial showing seconds and date, with matching brass hands, and eight-day bell striking movement, Scottish, c1810, 78½in (199.5cm) high.
£6,400–7,200
€/ $10,100–11,400 PAO

A pine longcase clock, with moonphase, and carved hood, Irish, c1810, 88in (223.5cm) high.
£2,000–2,200
€/ $3,200–3,500 ⊞ HON

A late George III mahogany and line-inlaid longcase clock, by Bartley & Eggert, Bristol, the painted dial with Roman numerals, Arabic quarter-hour divisions, seconds and date subsidiary dials, the arch with an automaton of Adam and Eve in the Garden of Eden, the eight-day twin-train movement with anchor escapement and rack strike on a bell, 85¾in (218cm) high.
£3,200–3,800
€/ $5,000–6,000 ⚒ DN
The Adam and Eve automaton feature in the arch is rare.

A mahogany longcase clock, by John Black, Aberdeen, the painted dial with subsidiary seconds and calendar dials, with an eight-day striking movement, Scottish, early 19thC, 88¼in (224cm) high.
£3,800–4,500
€/ $6,000–7,000 ⚒ SWO

A mahogany longcase clock, by Thomas Blundell, Dublin, the dial with a silvered Roman chapter ring, the matted centre with ringed winding holes, calendar aperture and subsidiary seconds dial, the eight-day four-pillar movement with anchor escapement, rack striking on a bell, case and movement associated, Irish, early 19thC, 91¾in (233cm) high.
£2,500–2,800
€/ $4,000–4,400 ⚒ B(Kn)

◄ **An oak and cross-banded longcase clock,** by T. Hadfield, Chapel, the broken-arch dial with moonphase, the eight-day rack and bell-striking movement with anchor escapement, the movement associated, early 19thC, 89¾in (228cm) high.
£1,300–1,500
€/ $2,000–2,400 ⚒ B(NW)

► **An oak and mahogany longcase clock,** by Cordingley, Leeds, the dial with a stately home painted to the arch, with floral spandrels, Arabic chapters and two subsidiary dials, the eight-day movement striking on a bell, dial and movement possibly associated, early 19thC, 89¼in (226.5cm) high.
£950–1,100
€/ $1,500–1,700 ⚒ B(L)

An oak longcase clock, by Harvey, Abergavenny, the dial with Roman numerals and a calendar aperture, with a 30-hour movement, the hood with a dentil cornice, blind fret frieze and pillars, Welsh, early 19thC, 75in (190.5cm) high.
£1,000–1,200
€/ $1,600–1,900 ⚒ PF

A mahogany crossbanded longcase clock, by G. Healer, Wantage, the painted dial with Roman numerals and foliate spandrels, with a 30-hour movement striking on a bell, the hood with turned columns, early 19thC, 78¾in (200cm) high.
£450–525
€/ $700–800 DN
This is a very reasonable price for this clock.

An oak longcase clock, by James Potts, Berwick, the arched dial with a painted scene of a Chinese woman and a parasol, with a subsidiary seconds dial, date aperture and Arabic numerals, with an eight-day movement, early 19thC, 80¼in (204cm) high.
£650–750
€/ $1,000–1,200 TRM

An oak longcase clock, the arched painted enamel dial with Roman numerals, subsidiary seconds and calendar dials, the eight-day movement by J. Low, Arbroath, the hood with a swan-neck pediment, Scottish, early 19thC, 79in (200.5cm) high.
£1,000–1,200
€/ $1,600–1,900 LVS

An inlaid mahogany longcase clock, the arched dial painted with a moonphase, with Roman numerals and seconds dial, with eight-day movement, early 19thC, 88¼in (224cm) high.
£2,200–2,600
€/ $3,500–4,100 CHTR

A mahogany longcase clock, by Moseley, Neath, with enamel dial, Roman numerals, date aperture and seconds dial, the eight-day movement striking on a bell, Welsh, early 19thC, 89in (226cm) high.
£1,800–2,200
€/ $2,800–3,500 B(SW)

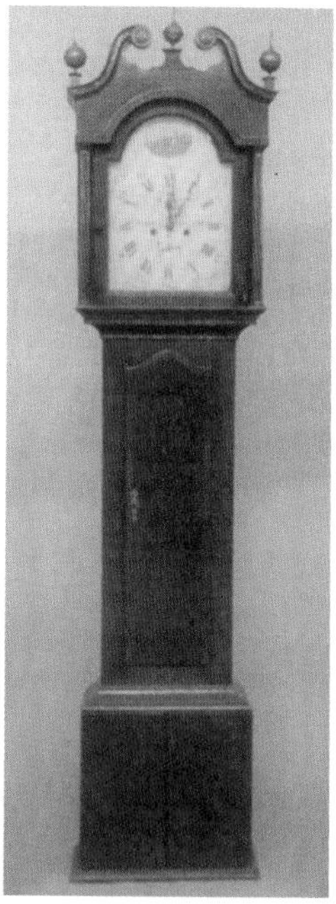

An oak longcase clock, by Jno Peacock, Lincoln, the arched painted dial with seconds and calendar dials, with eight-day, twin-train movement, the walnut banded hood with a swan-neck pediment surmounted by three brass globe finials, early 19thC, 78in (198cm) high.
£1,700–2,000
€/ $2,700–3,200 PF

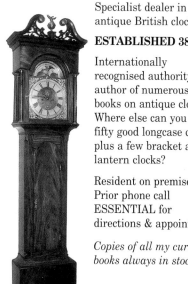

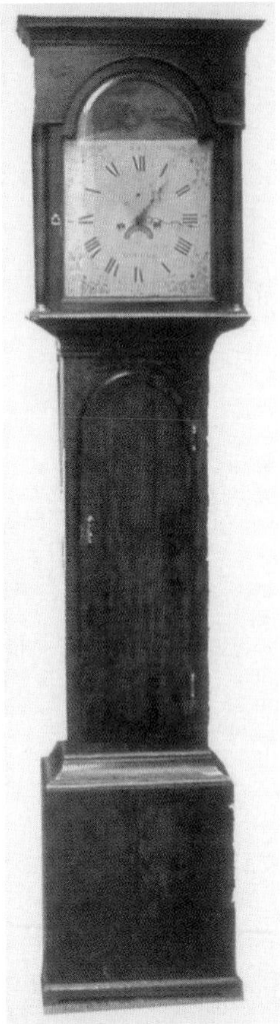

An oak longcase clock, the arched dial painted with a coaching scene and signed 'Hexham', with seconds dial and arched date aperture, the eight-day four-pillar movement with a deadbeat escapement striking on a bell, early 19thC, 83in (211cm) high.
£800–1,000
€/ $1,300–1,600 ⚒ HOLL

A late George III oak and mahogany inlaid longcase clock, by William Randall, Newbury, the painted dial with Arabic numerals, subsidiary seconds and date dials, the arch with a moon-phase, the eight-day twin-train movement with rack striking on a bell, stamped 'Walker & Hughes', 83¾in (213cm) high.
£1,400–1,600
€/ $2,200–2,500 ⚒ DN

Most longcase clocks will have either an eight-day or a 30-hour movement. The latter was no problem when someone was always at home to wind the clock every day. After the invention of the railway and the car, travel became easier and more frequent, and so owners preferred to have a clock that would not run down and stop if they went away for the weekend. As both trains are driven by the same weight, the trick is to put a clothes peg on the strike fly to prevent the strike sounding, and the timekeeping side will then run for about four days on one winding. Eight-day clocks are more sought after and so tend to command higher prices. The same increase in value applies to the rarer month-going and longer-duration clocks.

An oak longcase clock, by R. Summerhayes, Ilminster, the dial with seconds and date dials, and Arabic chapters, the eight-day movement striking on a bell, c1815, 86in (218.5cm) high.
£3,500–4,000
€/ $5,500–6,300 ⊞ PAO

A late Georgian oak and mahogany longcase clock, by Martin Roper, Penrith, the painted dial with Roman numerals and a crescent-form date aperture, with a 30-hour, hour striking movement, c1815, 80in (203cm) high.
£900–1,100
€/ $1,400–1,700 ⚒ PFK

An oak and crossbanded-mahogany longcase clock, by R. Summerhayes, Ilminster, with an eight-day movement, c1820, 78in (198cm) high.
£3,800–4,300
€/ $6,000–6,800 ⊞ ALS

◄ **A pine longcase timepiece,** by Samuel Beal, Sheffield, with original painted and grained decoration, c1820, 62in (157.5cm) high.
£4,000–4,500
€/ $6,300–7,000 ⊞ MHA

◄ **A Biedermeier birchwood longcase clock,** by Ola Larsson, Solberga, Swedish, c1820, 88in (223.5cm) high.
£5,500–6,000
€/ $8,700–9,500 ⊞ CAV
Ola Larsson (1762–1853) lived in Solberga, in the province of Skåne. He made a great variety of clocks, including longcase.

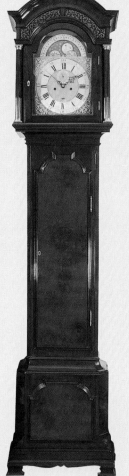

A George IV mahogany longcase clock, by William Roberts, Bath, the painted dial with date aperture and subsidiary seconds dial, the eight-day twin-train movement with anchor escapement and rack striking on a bell, 89in (226cm) high.
£1,800–2,200
€/ $2,800–3,500 ⚒ DN

An oak and mahogany longcase clock, by Richard Griffith, Denbigh, the painted dial with date aperture subsidiary seconds ring, with an eight-day movement, with a false plate cast 'Finnemore & Son', Welsh, c1830, 88in (223.5cm) high.
£1,700–2,000
€/ $2,700–3,200 ⚒ B(NW)

A mahogany longcase clock, by Dubberly, Monmouth, the enamelled dial with two subsidiary dials, flanked by spiral columns, the case on bracket supports, Welsh, c1830, 86in (218.5cm) high.
£1,700–2,000
€/ $2,700–3,200 ⚒ BWL

A mahogany longcase clock, by W. Birtwell, Burnley, the arched brass dial with a moonphase, with an eight-day movement, the hood with a swan-neck cornice and baluster columns, the trunk with a Gothic arched door between cluster column corners with inlaid stringing, 19thC, 96in (244cm) high.
£2,000–2,400
€/ $3,200–3,800 ⚒ SWO

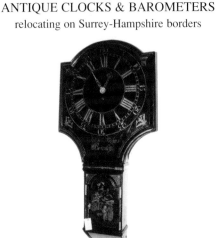

An oak longcase clock, by Marshall, Greenside, the painted dial with floral corners, the arch painted with a peacock, the 30-hour plated movement with outside countwheel striking on a bell, the hood with a flat top dentil-moulded cornice, c1830, 81in (205.5cm) high.
£750–900
€/ $1,200–1,400 ⚒ S(O)

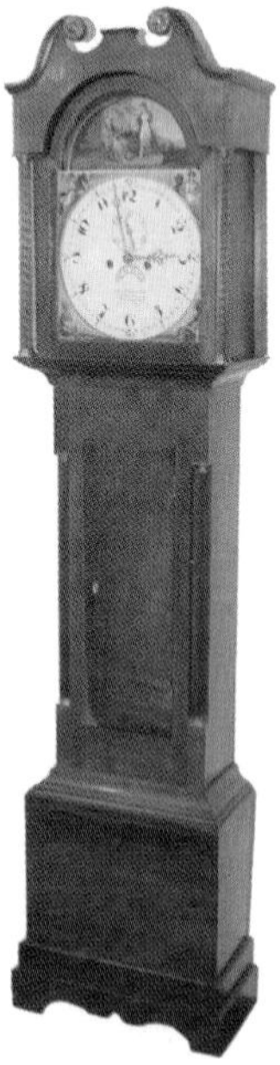

An oak longcase clock, by George Stephenson, Warminster, the painted dial with date and seconds, the eight-day movement striking the hours on a bell, c1830, 82in (208.5cm) high.
£2,400–2,700
€/ $3,800–4,300 ⊞ K&D

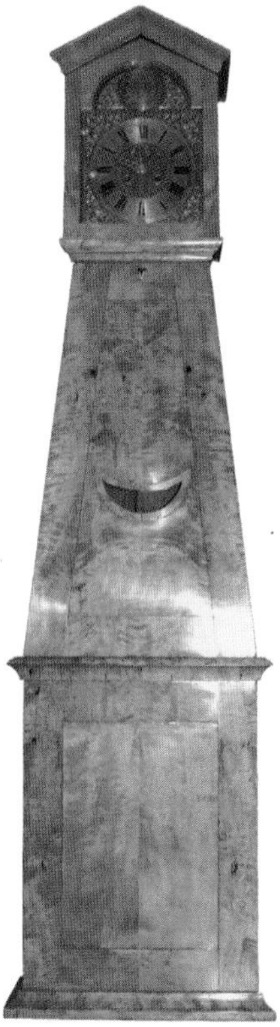

A Biedermeier birchwood longcase clock, inscribed 'sic volvitur aetas', (so time elapses), Swedish, c1830, 86in (218.5cm) high.
£5,000–5,600
€ / $7,900–8,900 ⊞ CAV

A mahogany longcase clock, by Richard Roughsedge, Twickenham, the brass dial with a silvered chapter ring and subsidiary seconds dial, the hood with a finial-mounted arched moulded cornice above a glazed door, case c1835, movement c1775, 88¼in (224cm) high.
£1,700–2,000
€ / $2,700–3,200 ⚒ CGC

► A mahogany longcase clock, by Lawrence, Bristol, the brass dial with a lunar aperture with High Water at Bristol Key, the chapter ring with Roman numerals, cast corner spandrels, engraved centre panel, date aperture and second hand, with an eight-day striking movement, the case with boxwood and ebony string inlays, case c1840, movement and dial c1770, 89in (226cm) high.
£2,200–2,600
€ / $3,500–4,100 ⚒ HoG

An early Victorian oak and mahogany-veneered longcase clock, by Pearce, Stratford, the dial painted with a pheasant, country houses and cottages, the 30-hour movement striking on a bell, 83in (211cm) high.
£500–600
€ / $800–950 ⚒ WW

An oak and mahogany longcase clock, by George Wilson, Appleby, the painted dial with Roman numerals, subsidiary seconds dial and date aperture, the arch painted with two sheep by a stream, with an eight-day hour-striking movement, c1845, 86in (218.5cm) high.
£800–1,000
€/ $1,300–1,600 PFK

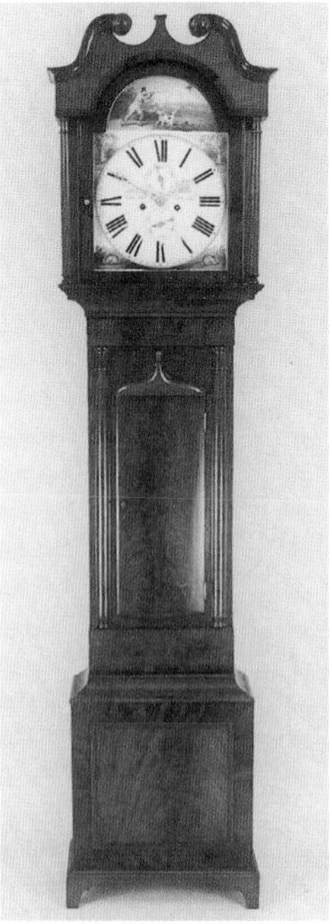

A mahogany longcase clock, by James Simm, Elgin, the dial painted with a country sporting scene in the arch, the corners with game, with seconds and date dials, the eight-day movement striking the hours on a bell, Scottish, c1850, 73in (185.5cm) high.
£5,500–6,200
€/ $8,600–9,800 PAO

A mahogany longcase clock, by Dilger & Barclay, Glasgow, the painted dial with seconds and calendar dials, with a rack and gong-striking movement, Scottish, c1850, 82in (208.5cm) high.
£2,700–3,000
€/ $4,300–4,700 S(O)
The bowfronted door is typical of mid-19th century Scottish clocks.

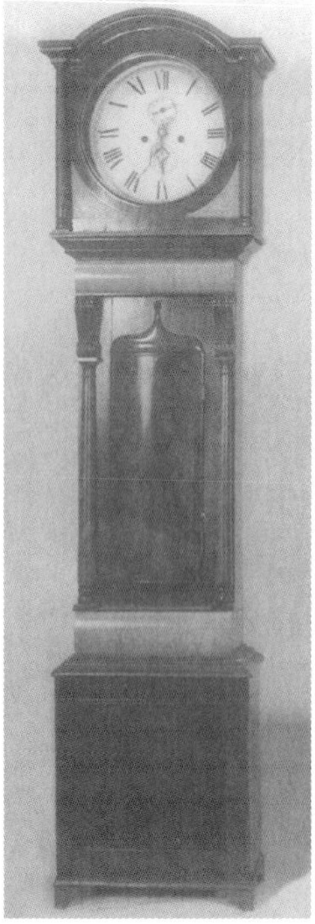

A mahogany longcase clock, the painted enamel dial with Roman and Arabic numerals, subsidiary seconds and calendar dials and an eight-day movement, with a moulded arch hood, Scottish, 19thC, 79in (200.5cm) high.
£1,100–1,300
€/ $1,700–2,000 LVS

An oak and walnut longcase clock, by W. Pibus, Caister, the arch painted with ships, the spandrels with shells, the dial with Roman numerals, second dial, and calendar aperture, mid-19thC, 84in (213.5cm) high.
£1,200–1,500
€/ $1,900–2,400 PF

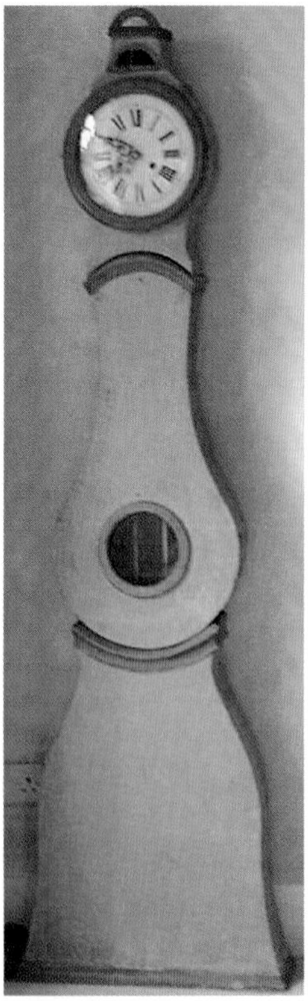

A painted pine longcase clock, Swedish, c1850, 78in (198cm) high.
£4,000–4,500
€/ $6,300–7,000 DeG

Derek Roberts

25 Shipbourne Road, Tonbridge, Kent TN10 3DN

Tel: 01732 358986 • Fax: 01732 771842 • Email: drclocks@clara.net

www.qualityantiqueclocks.com

Joseph Buckingham in Ye Minories. An exceptionally fine and small 'bird and flower' marquetry longcase with green stained bone inlay and 10 inch dial. Height 6ft 2in.

We carry an extensive range of fine clocks of all types. Details on request.

Most of our stock may be seen on our website but should you have any particular requirements do please let us know.

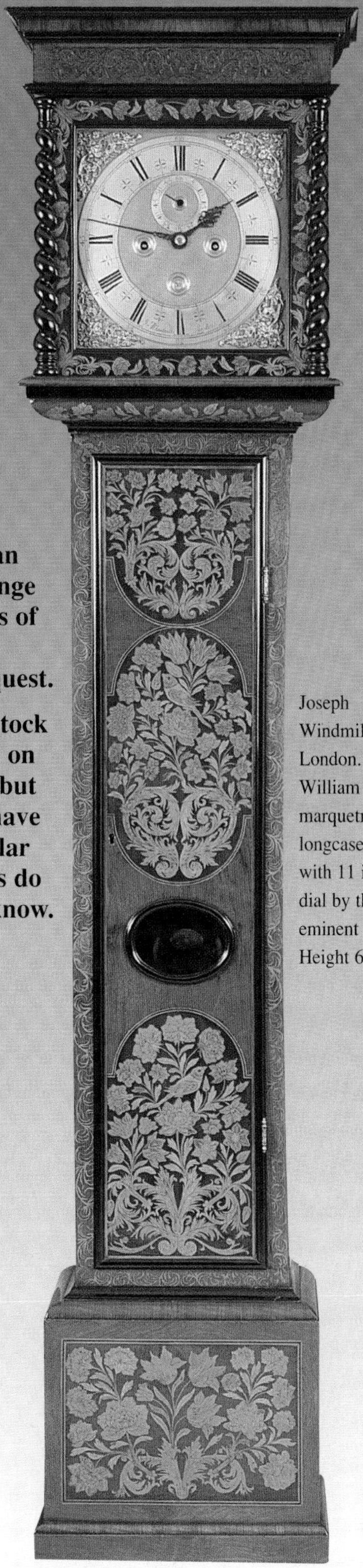

Joseph Windmills, London. A good William and Mary marquetry longcase clock with 11 inch dial by this eminent maker. Height 6ft 6in.

A mahogany longcase clock, by R. Currer, Falkirk, the dial painted with studies of Thompson, Allan Ramsay, Sir Walter Scott, Cunningham and the Lass of Gowrie, with subsidiary seconds and date dials, with an eight-day movement, the trunk with a bowfronted door, turned pilasters and ogee columns, Scottish, mid-19thC, 85¾in (218cm) high.
£2,800–3,200
€/ $4,400–5,000 B(Ed)

A mahogany longcase clock, by Josh. Stromier, Glasgow, the dial with Roman numerals, subsidiary seconds and calendar dials, with an eight-day bell-striking movement, Scottish, 19thC, 78¼in (199cm) high.
£1,400–1,600
€/ $2,200–2,500 AMB

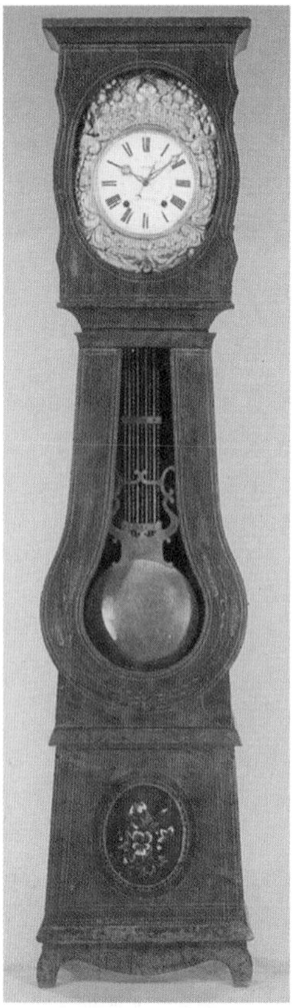

An oak and mahogany longcase clock, by Birley, Birmingham, the painted arched dial with seconds dial, date aperture and Roman numerals, with an eight-day four-pillar bell-striking movement, the hood with a swan-neck pediment and half-columns, 19thC, 87in (221cm) high.
£1,000–1,200
€/ $1,600–1,900 CGC

◄ **A grained wood *comtoise* clock,** by Duval, Beaumont-le-Roger, with an embossed gilt-brass framed enamel dial, the case graining including *faux*-marquetry and stringing, French, c1850, 88½in (225cm) high.
£1,000–1,200
€/ $1,600–1,900 NOA

A mahogany longcase clock, by Pirrie, Perth, the gilt-painted dial with seconds and subsidiary dials, the eight-day movement striking on a bell, the hood with a broken pediment with a ball finial above a brass-rimmed glazed door with anthemion-carved corners and side columns, Scottish, 19thC, 90½in (230cm) high.
£2,000–2,500
€/ $3,200–4,000 B(Ed)
The unusual appearance of this clock would be attractive to many people, and therefore it could sell for up to £3,000 (€/ $4,700).

► **A mahogany longcase clock,** by David Read, Ipswich, with painted dial, and eight-day bell striking movement, under an arched hood flanked by reeded columns, 19thC, 84¾in (215.5cm) high.
£1,600–2,000
€/ $2,500–3,200 AMB

A painted pine *comtoise* clock, French, c1860, 96in (244cm) high.
£700–800
€/ $1,100–1,300 PaA

A walnut-inlaid longcase clock, by Percy Webster, the brass dial with a silvered chapter ring, the four-pillar movement with anchor escapement rack striking on a bell, 1875–1925, 72½in (184cm) high.
£4,200–5,000
€/ $6,600–7,900 B

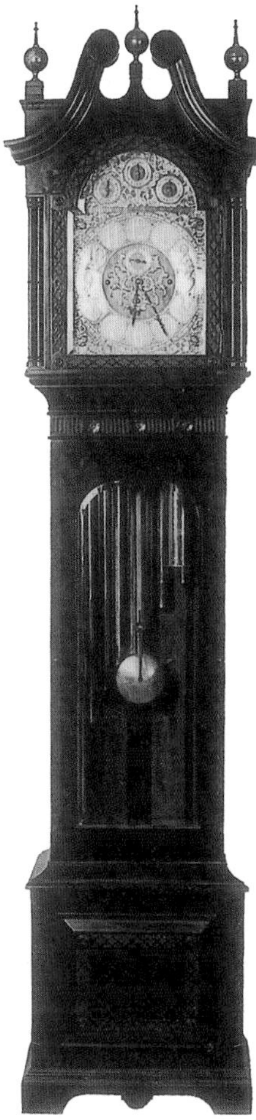

◀ **A mahogany longcase clock,** the break-arch dial applied with a silvered Arabic numeral chapter ring, subsidiary dials for seconds, Westminster/Whittington chimes, strike/silent and chime/silent, the quarter-chiming triple-train movement with anchor escapement on eight tubular bells, striking the hour on a further bell, c1900, 102in (259cm) high.
£4,000–5,000
€/ $6,300–7,900 Bri

▶ **A Gothic-revival mahogany longcase clock,** retailed by Maple & Co, London, the shaped silvered dial with subsidiaries for chime/silent and Whittington chimes/Westminster chimes, over a Roman chapter and subsidiary seconds within engraved scrolls, the quarter-chiming movement with maintaining power and deadbeat escapement, the glazed trunk door revealing the mercury pendulum and beat scale, tubular chimes missing, late 19thC, 96½in (245cm) high.
£3,200–3,800
€/ $5,000–6,000 B
The lack of tubular bells has kept the price of this clock down.

The prices realized at auction may reflect the fact that the clocks have sometimes undergone alterations to their movements, or are in unrestored condition.

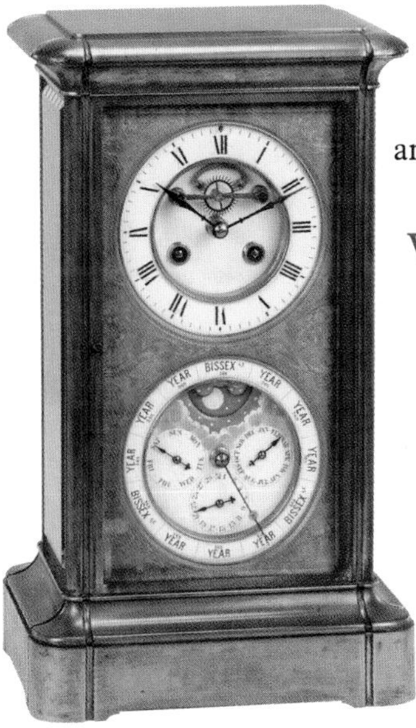

An Edwardian mahogany chiming longcase clock, the brass dial with a silvered chapter ring with Roman numerals, subsidiary seconds dial, the arch with chime/ silent dial, the eight-day triple-train movement with deadbeat anchor escapement, striking and chiming the hours on coiled gongs, 85¾in (218cm) high.
£3,200–3,800
€/ $5,000–6,000 DN

A George III-style longcase clock, the brass dial inscribed 'Tempus Fugit', the silvered boss and chapter ring with a leaf-engraved centre, with a triple-train chiming movement, the hood flanked by fluted pillars below a blind fret frieze and swan-neck pediment, early 20thC, 47¼in (120cm) high.
£5,000–6,000
€/ $7,900–9,500 B(WM)

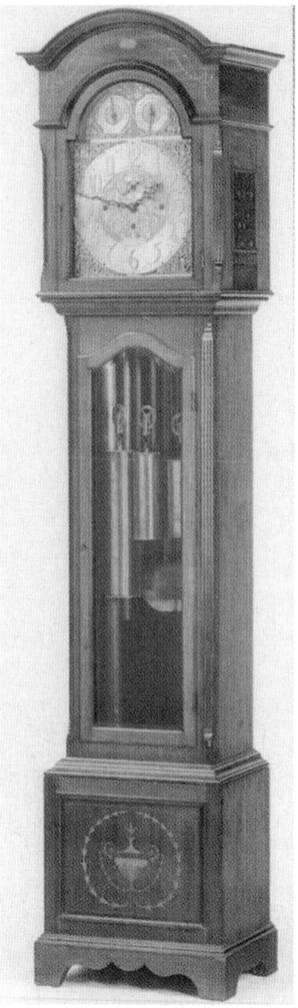

A late Edwardian mahogany longcase clock, retailed by Mappin & Webb, London, the dial with silvered chapter ring with gilt Arabic numerals, seconds dial, chimes selector and dials to the arch, the eight-day movement chiming on eight tubular bells, the hood inlaid with floral scrolls and a central fan motif, 93in (236cm) high.
£3,500–4,200
€/ $5,500–6,600 AG

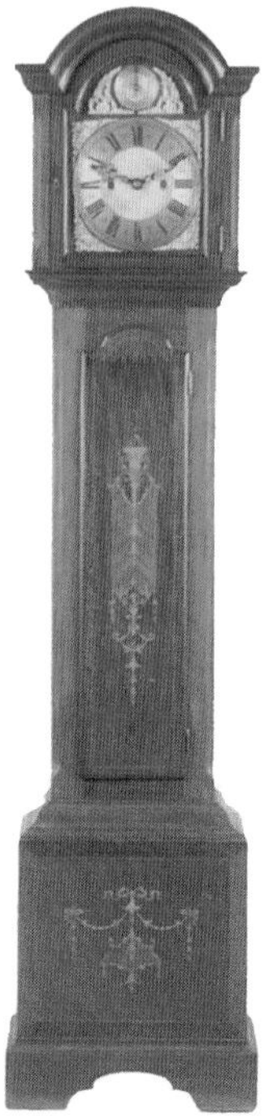

► **A mahogany longcase clock,** retailed by Yoell, Retford, the brass arched dial with foliate spandrels, the silver chapter ring with Roman numerals and subsidiary seconds dial, the arch with a chime/silent dial, the eight-day triple-train movement with anchor escapement, striking the hour and chiming the quarters on five tubular bells, early 20thC, 92½in (235cm) high.
£2,500–3,000
€/ $4,000–4,700 DN

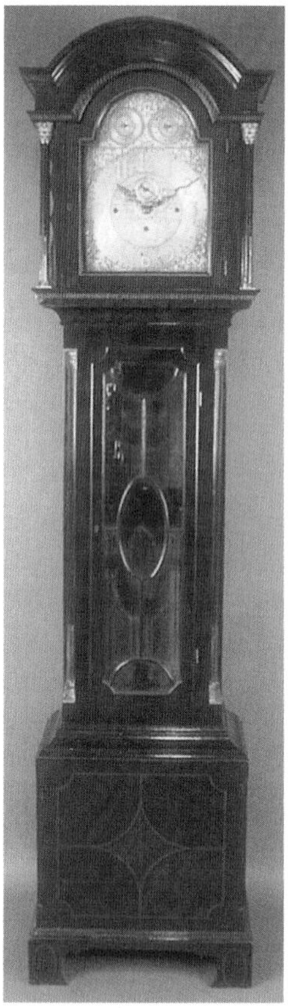

A mahogany longcase clock, the brass dial with chime/silent and Whittington/ Westminster subsidiary dials above a silvered chapter ring with gilt Arabic numerals and subsidiary seconds dial, the eight-day chiming movement striking on tubular bells, early 20thC, 88¼in (224cm) high.
£2,800–3,200
€/ $4,400–5,000 RTo

◄ **An inlaid mahogany longcase clock,** the brass dial with a silvered chapter ring with Roman hours and Arabic minutes, silvered strike/ silent ring and chapter ring, the movement striking on a gong, early 20thC, 72½in (184cm) high.
£1,300–1,500
€/ $2,000–2,400 PFK

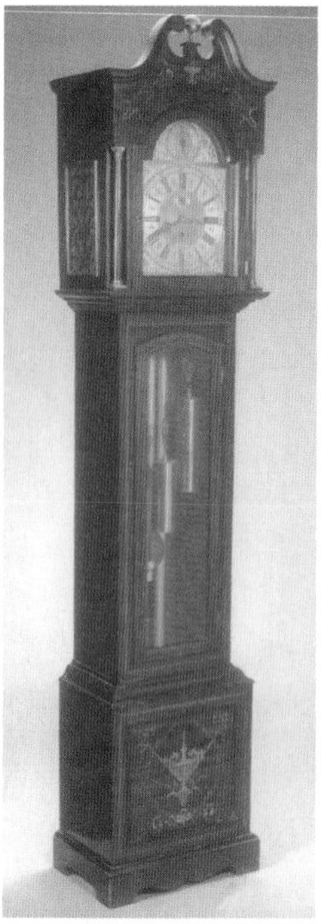

An oak Jacobean-revival-style longcase clock, the dial with a silvered chapter ring and baroque-style spandrels, the German triple-train movement by Winterhalter & Hofmeier, chiming and striking on gongs, early 20thC, 77in (195.5cm) high.
£1,700–2,000
€/ $2,700–3,200 PFK

Novelty Clocks

A bronze cathedral clock, with spring-drive eight-day time and bell-strike movement, with gilt dial, spires and figures and silk thread suspension, the sides with blue glass panels behind the arches, French, c1820, 19in (48.5cm) high.
£4,000–4,500
€/ $6,300–7,000 ⊞ SET

A patinated-brass novelty timepiece, modelled as a fountain with rotating glass 'water stream', the gilt dial with Roman numerals, the movement with silk suspension, pinned pillars and light bob, set in a brickwork arch with a lion's head spout issuing the rotating glass rod into a cut-glass bowl, on an ebonized stand, glass dome cracked, French, mid-19thC, 15¾in (40cm) high.
£625–725
€/ $1,000–1,200 ⚒ B

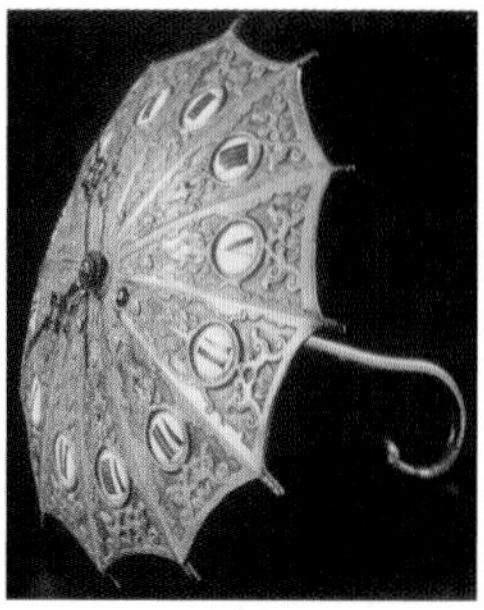

A parasol timepiece, set with 12 enamel numeral plaques, the eight-day movement signed 'W Paris' below a crown, decorated with stylized leaves and flowers, with later tin cover and later lever escapement, French, c1900, 10½in (26.5cm) diam.
£575–675
€/ $900–1,100 ⚒ S(O)

A carved oak longcase clock, modelled as a square tower, the pressed brass dial with Arabic numerals and ornate hands, the weight-driven movement striking on two coiled gongs, with carved roof tiles, brickwork, balconies and windows, over a porch and four sets of steps, German, Black Forest, c1900, 107in (272cm) high.
£2,200–2,500
€/ $3,500–4,000 ⚒ B

► **An Edwardian picture timepiece,** with watch-style movement, depicting Big Ben and the Houses of Parliament, mounted and framed, 16 x 12½in (40.5 x 32cm).
£160–200
€/ $250–320 ⚒ SWO

Expert's choice

A musical and automaton clock, late 18thC, sold by Sotheby's in October 1993.

During my time at Sotheby's I have handled some extraordinary clocks but perhaps the most astonishing was a magnificent English ormolu musical and automaton clock that had lain abandoned for nearly half a century.

The clock belonged to an elderly farmer in Wales whose mother had paid £290 (€/ $460) for it in 1946. It had never worked the whole time they owned it and now he wanted to sell it.

The first time I saw the clock it took my breath away. It was obviously English despite its richly gilded casing and fell into the category of what is sometimes known as 'sing-songs'. These are extraordinary musical and automaton clocks that were made by a number of talented London makers in the late 18th century. They were made for export to the Orient and were usually purchased by western merchants to present to the Emperors who they hoped could be persuaded by such gifts to smooth the path of commerce.

This particular clock had a richly gilded body set with brightly coloured pastes and was surmounted by a painted and silvered peacock standing in front of a chinoiserie pagoda inset on the base with glass rods simulating waterfalls.

The clock was carefully removed from the farmhouse and delivered to our London warehouse where, after some repair and oiling, it was excitedly restarted.

The peacock began its performance after more than half a century of lying silent. The organ bellows were in a poor condition and so the pipes produced no more than a wheezing sound but the bells played loudly and tunefully while the bird moved around in a most realistic way turning its head back and forth, moving its long flexible neck and displaying its beautiful tail, while the pagoda behind began to rise in the air until it was double its original height. As the music drew to a close the pagoda sank back to its previous level and the peacock concluded its performance with a small bow.

Research revealed that the clock had a documented provenance from 1835 when it was purchased in New Bond Street, London, by a wealthy landowner. The history of the clock before 1835 is not known but, although unsigned, it is likely that it was made in the workshops of the famous clockmaking entrepreneur James Cox. Ironically, the dealer who purchased it for £353,000 (€/ $558,000) in October 1993 had his premises on the same street where it had been sold in 1835. **Michael Turner**

Skeleton Clocks

A marble and brass skeleton mantel timepiece, the enamel dial with Roman numerals and Breguet hands, the movement with anchor escapement and silk suspended pendulum, on a marble base beneath a glass dome with later ebonized base, French, 1800–25, 9½in (24cm) high.
£400–500
€/ $630–800 ⚒ S(Am)

A bronzed skeleton timepiece, with silvered chapter ring and Roman numerals, the pendulum movement with passing strike, the stepped lobed marble base with bun feet, c1875, 16½in (42cm) high.
£600–700
€/ $950–1,100 ⊞ WL

Items in the Clock section have been arranged in date order within each sub-section.

A Victorian brass skeleton timepiece, with a fretted silvered Roman chapter ring, the eight-day single fusee mechanism with passing strike, four wheel crossings and anchor escapement, on a moulded mahogany plinth beneath a glass dome, 19¼in (49cm) high.
£750–875
€/ $1,200–1,400 ⚒ BIG

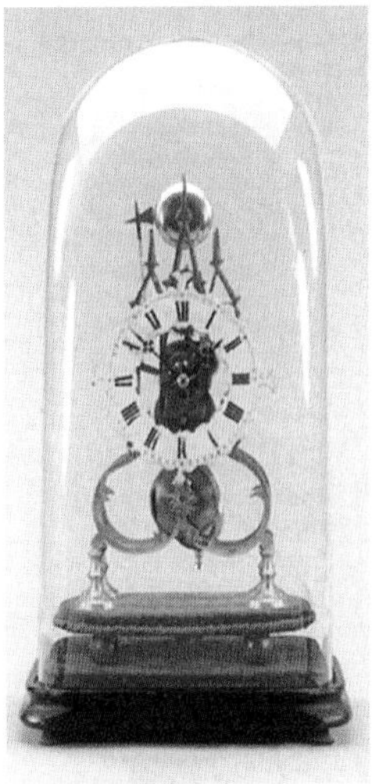

A brass skeleton timepiece, with painted chapter ring and fusee movement with anchor escapement and passing strike on a bell, the pierced Gothic frame on a velvet-covered stand and similar base, beneath a cracked glass dome, c1875, 16½in (42cm) high.
£450–500
€/ $700–800 ⚒ S(O)

Wall Clocks

For further information on antique clocks see the full range of Miller's books at **www.millers.uk.com**

A tavern clock, by Gillett & Healey, Manchester, with gilt chinoiserie decoration, late 18thC, 60in (152.5cm) high.
£14,000–16,000
€/ $22,000–25,000 ⊞ ALS

An elmwood ship's automaton alarm *staartklok*, restored, automaton later, Dutch, Frisland, c1800, 50¾in (129.5cm) high.
£850–1,000
€/ $1,400–1,600 ⚒ S(Am)

◄ A rosewood wall timepiece, with painted dial and eight-day fusee movement, inlaid with mother-of-pearl, c1830, 24in (61cm) high.
£1,100–1,300
€/ $1,700–2,000 ⊞ SET

A mahogany wall clock, by D. Meyer, Abingdon, the convex dial with Roman chapters, the eight-day fusee movement with shaped plates and anchor escapement, c1835, dial 12in (30.5cm) diam.
£1,700–2,000
€/ $2,700–3,200 ⊞ PAO

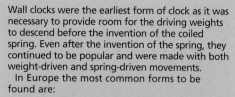

Wall clocks were the earliest form of clock as it was necessary to provide room for the driving weights to descend before the invention of the coiled spring. Even after the invention of the spring, they continued to be popular and were made with both weight-driven and spring-driven movements.
In Europe the most common forms to be found are:

- Britain: tavern clocks (weight-driven) and dial clocks (spring and fusee-driven). Both types originated in the 18th century and the dial clock continued to be made well into the 20th century.
- France: cartel clocks were made from the mid-18th century. All French wall clocks were usually spring-driven.
- Germany: cuckoo clocks and 'postman's alarm' clocks. Both were usually weight-driven although some spring and fusee cuckoo clocks exist.
- Holland: *stoelkloks* and *staartkloks*. Both types were always weight-driven.

◀ **An ebonized and gilded wall clock,** Maltese, 19thC, 23¾in (60.5cm) high.
£4,000–4,500
€/ $6,300–7,000 ⚒ B(Pr)
Maltese items are keenly sought after by the home market.

▶ **A mahogany drop-dial wall timepiece,** by Dearling, Croydon, with eight-day fusee movement, c1860, 20in (51cm) high.
£1,000–1,100
€/ $1,600–1,700 ⊞ K&D

A Biedermeier ash wall timepiece, the milk-glass dial signed 'Ignaz Lutz in Wien', the Roman numerals within shields and enclosed within a gilded pie-crust bezel, the eight-day movement with a wood rod pendulum, Austrian, c1845, 38¼in (97cm) high.
£5,200–5,800
€/ $8,200–9,200 ⊞ C&A

A musical cuckoo clock, the dial with pierced horn hands, the triple-train movement playing four airs, with eagle cresting, the front with two opening doors, one with a piper, the other a cuckoo, the front flanked by entwined oak leaves above a carved deer and hunting dog on a rockwork base, piper later, German, Black Forest, late 19thC, 43in (109cm) high.
£1,800–2,200
€/ $2,800–3,200 HAM

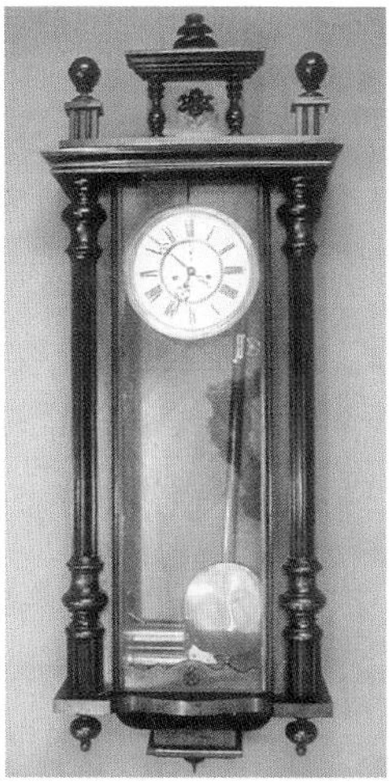

A Vienna-style walnut wall clock, by Gustav Becker, with enamel dial and eight-day twin-train weight-driven striking movement, the case with fluted columns, German, late 19thC, 45¾in (116cm) high.
£350–425
€/ $550–670 AMB

A Vienna-style walnut and ebonized wall clock, the enamelled dial with Roman numerals and subsidiary second hand, eight-day weight-driven striking movement, German, c1895, 40in (101.5cm) high.
£400–450
€/ $630–700 Mit

A mahogany wall clock, with weight-driven movement, the case with three-finial pediment top, the trunk with column sides, German, early 20thC, 52in (132cm) long.
£320–375
€/ $500–600 FHF

American Clocks

A carved and figured walnut longcase clock, with moon dial and repainted calendar wheel, the moon dial stamped (Os)bornes (Man)ufactory Birmingham, inside of backboard inscribed 'A. Miller Wyoming, PA', base moulding later, Pennsylvania, c1780, 92in (233.5cm) high.
£11,500–13,500
€/ $18,200–21,300 S(NY)

Many American longcase clocks have movements and dials that were made in England. Their rarity and value lie in the custom-made American cases.

A *faux bois* mirror wall clock, the painted wood dial with Roman numerals, gilt spandrels and matching diamond hands, the twin-train weight-driven movement with wooden wheels and anchor escapement, the countwheel striking on a bell, inside label 'Patent Clocks, manufactured & sold by David Dutton, Mont Vernon, N.H.', 1825–50, 35½in (90cm) high.
£600–720
€/ $950–1,100 S(Am)

► A carved walnut drop-dial wall clock, the paper dial with Roman numerals, mid-19thC, 31½in (80cm) high.
£400–500
€/ $630–800 SWO

A mahogany double decker shelf clock, by Birge, Peck & Co, Bristol, decorated with panels of Andrew Jackson and a beehive, replaced dial and tablets, case split, weights missing, Connecticut, 1830–56, 32¾in (83.5cm) high.
£250–300
€/ $400–475 JDJ

A mahogany Gothic-style clock, by Birge & Fuller, Bristol, with painted dial, eight-day wagon-spring movement, the case with four candlesticks, losses to dial, replaced minute hand, bottom glass replaced, Connecticut, c1845, 26in (66cm) high.
£2,500–3,000
€/ $4,000–4,700 ROSc

A rosewood shelf clock, by Atkins Clock Co, Bristol, with repainted dial and eight-day time/strike/alarm movement, restored, Connecticut, c1865, 16¾in (42.5cm) high.
£280–325
€/ $440–520 ROSc

A rosewood wall clock, by E. N. Welch, Forrestville, time and strike movement, case refinished, original label, Connecticut, c1865, 25in (63.5cm) high.
£750–825
€/ $1,200–1,300 ⊞ SET

► A mahogany trunk dial wall clock, the painted dial signed for 'T Hyde, Sleaford', with open-spring bell striking movement signed 'E. N. Welch, Forestville, Connecticut, USA', the case with carved ears and inset with a lenticle, rim and glass missing, c1890, 21¼in (54cm) high.
£550–600
€/ $870–950 ⚒ S(O)

A spelter shelf clock, by Seth Thomas Sons & Co, with 14-day spring-driven movement striking on a bell, some repainting, 1865–79, 17in (43cm) high.
£750–820
€/ $1,200–1,300 ⊞ SET

A rosewood shelf clock, Oriental, by E. Ingraham & Co, Bristol, with eight-day time and strike movement, case refinished, some veneer loss, Connecticut, c1878, 18in (45.5cm) high.
£600–720
€/ $950–1,200 ⚒ ROSc

A painted wood regulator, c1890, 36in (91.5cm) high.
£80–100
€/ $125–160 ⚒ DuM

An oak school regulator, by Seth Thomas Clock Co, with eight-day spring-driven time and strike movement, original label, c1890, 24in (61cm) high.
£500–565
€/ $800–900 ⊞ SET

A stained pine wall clock, with painted dial, and eight-day movement striking on a bell, late 19thC, 21½in (54.5cm) high.
£200–225
€/ $320–350 ⚒ DA

CLOCKS

A miniature tin mantel clock, the enamelled chapter ring dial with gilt centre, winding mechanism operated by the rear panel, stamped 'Pat.April 23rd 1878', late 19thC, 2¼in (5.5cm) diam, in original tin case.
£160–200
€/ $250–320 ⚒ FHF

A Greek revival-style enamel-painted wood mantel clock, by Gilbert, chiming on rods, some repainting, dated 1913, 12in (30.5cm) high.
£280–320
€/ $440–500 ⊞ SET

◄ An oak wall clock, Jupiter, by Seth Thomas Clock Co, with moon dial and eight-day weight-driven-movement striking on a bell, restored, c1910, 59in (150cm) high.
£5,000–6,000
€/ $7,900–9,500 ⚒ ROSc

An oak regulator wall timepiece, Observatory, by William L. Gilbert Clock Co, with eight-day movement, minor damage, c1910, 37in (94cm) high.
£300–350
€/ $475–550 ⚒ ROSc

A mahogany miniature banjo timepiece, by Waltham Clock Co, with eight-day lever movement, and Waltham's 'car clock' stem wind movement, some replacements and repairs, c1930, 21in (53.5cm) high.
£270–320
€/ $430–500 ⚒ ROSc

British Regulators

An early Victorian mahogany regulator, the painted dial with an outer ring with Arabic five-minute divisions and centre sweep hand, subsidiary seconds and hour dials, inscribed and dated 'W W Kent 1837', the single-train movement with deadbeat escapement, 73¼in (186cm) high.
£3,000–3,400
€/ $4,700–5,400 DN

A mahogany longcase regulator, by William Barr, Edinburgh, the painted dial with subsidiary hour and seconds dials, the movement with deadbeat escapement and maintaining power, a glass reverse-painted pendulum bob, c1859, 76in (193cm) high.
£5,800–6,500
€/ $9,200–10,200 K&D

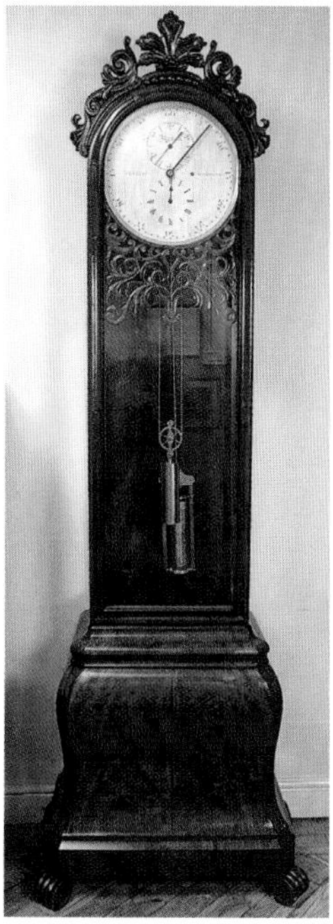

A mahogany regulator, by Jenkins, Merthyr, with mercury pendulum, restored, c1860, 83in (211cm) high.
£7,500–8,500
€/ $11,900–13,400 KHW

A mahogany-veneered regulator, the silvered dial with subsidiary seconds and hour dials, inscribed 'John Garden, Aberdeen', the single-train movement with deadbeat escapement, Scottish, 19thC, 82¼in (209cm) high.
£3,200–3,800
€/ $5,000–6,000 WW

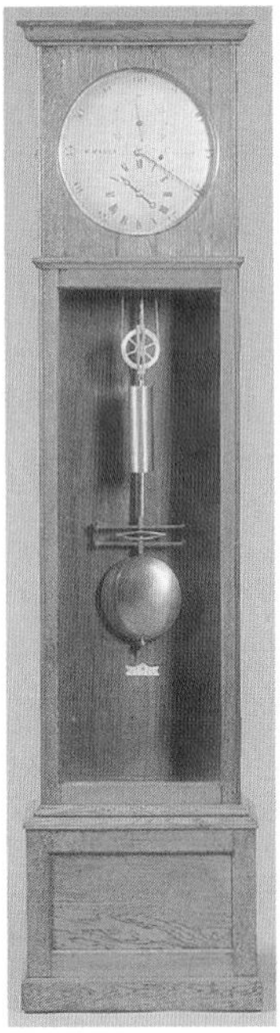

◄ **An oak longcase regulator,** by William Maule, Coldstream, with engraved and signed silvered dial, weight-driven movement and deadbeat escapement, maintaining power, five-spoke wheels and minute hand counterweight, separately suspended steel rod pendulum, c1860, 75½in (192cm) high.
£3,300–4,000
€/ $5,200–6,300 ⚒ S(O)

A mahogany table regulator, by Pewsey, London, with signed silvered dial, maintaining power and double-wheeled deadbeat escapement to twin jar mercury pendulum, the case with a glazed front door with dependent pierced cresting, 1850–1900, 22½in (57cm) high.
£4,000–4,800
€/ $6,300–7,600 ⚒ B

Regulators

A true regulator is a timepiece without strike or chime which will run so accurately (usually within a second or two a week) that other clocks can be regulated by it. A regulator will be weight driven and have some sort of compensated pendulum and a deadbeat escapement. The movement (mechanism) will be as simple as possible, and because of this the dials are distinctive, with an outer minutes ring enclosing separate seconds and hours dials. This is to eliminate additional wheel work behind the dial that would be needed if both hour and minute hands were concentric as on ordinary clocks. Many clocks such as German and Austrian 'Vienna' wall clocks and French four-glass clocks are incorrectly called regulators, even though they are capable of keeping excellent time and sometimes have a form of compensated pendulum.

Continental Regulators

A walnut *grande sonnerie Laterndluhr,* by 'Rauschmann in Ofen', the enamel dial with two subsidiary dials for the calendar work, with eight-day movement striking the quarters on two bells, the case with pen and ink decoration and ebonized backboard, lift-out side doors to the hood, Austrian, c1810, 61in (155cm) high.
£55,000–60,000
€/ $87,000–95,000 ⊞ C&A

A walnut *Dachluhr,* attributed to Marrenzeller, the enamel dial no longer signed, with a gilded engine-turned bezel, the movement with high-count pinions and maintaining power, the compensated gridiron pendulum with a brass bob, the fan-top six-light case with boxwood stringing, Austrian, c1845, 66in (167.5cm) high.
£32,000–36,000
€/ $50,000–56,000 ⊞ C&A

A rosewood and brass-inlaid mantel regulator, the two-piece enamel dial with Roman numerals, the centre signed 'Planté Sr De Lagrave A Paris', gilt Breguet hands, the movement with visible Brocot escapement stamped 'Noël A Robins A Paris 5528', the countwheels striking on a bell, heavy gridiron pendulum, French, mid-19thC, 22¾in (58cm) high.
£2,200–2,500
€/ $3,500–4,000 ⚒ S(Am)

A gold-plated brass crystal regulator, the enamel dial with second hand, signed 'Theo B. Starr', with eight-day spring-driven time and strike movement, mercury pendulum, minor repairs, case lacquered, French, c1870, 18½in (47cm) high.
£2,500–2,800
€/ $4,000–4,500 ⊞ SET
It is quite rare to have a centre seconds hand.

► **A four-glass regulator,** with Roman calibrated dial, the Japy Frères eight-day movement rack striking on a bell, with mercurial pendulum, the geometric case with flat top and moulded edge and bevelled glass sides, French, 1875–1925, 12½in (32cm) high.
£450–525
€/ $700–830 ⚒ BIG

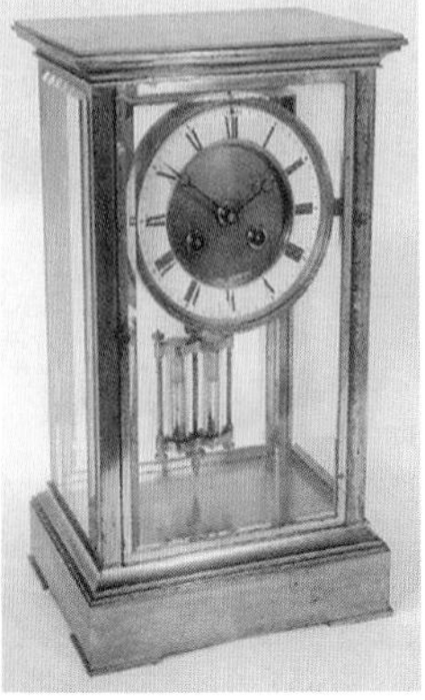

Watches

Pocket Watches

A silver mock triple-case pendulum verge watch, the full plate movement with Egyptian pillars, with later single steel hand, pendant and bow, maker's mark 'WE', signed 'Quare, London', late 17thC, 2¼in (5.5cm) diam.
£3,500–4,000
€/ $5,500–6,300 PT

A gilt-metal pair-cased verge watch, with six-hour dial, subsidiary seconds and calendar work, with full plate movement, in a polished case, seconds hand missing, 1675–1725, 2¼in (5.5cm) diam.
£2,200–2,500
€/ $3,500–4,000 B

A silver pair-cased watch, by William van der Hegge, Amsterdam, No. 73, the dial with date aperture, with pierced and engraved balance bridge, casemaker's mark 'CLP', Dutch, c1750, 2¼in (5.5cm) diam.
£600–720
€/ $950–1,100 S(Am)

A gilt-metal verge watch, the full plate movement signed 'Gibb, Rotterdam', in a consular case covered with shagreen, 1750–1800, 2in (5cm) diam.
£825–1,000
€/ $1,300–1,600 S(Am)

A gold-cased pocket watch, by Vauchez, Paris, No 7411, with enamel dial and diamond-set hands, the case with a border of brilliants, the reverse with an enamel portrait of a girl, 18thC, 1½in (4cm) diam.
£600–700
€/ $950–1,100 L

A silver and tortoiseshell triple-case verge pocket watch, the movement signed 'C. Fly, London, No. 4211', the white enamel dial with gilt hands, hallmarked London 1761, 2¼in (5.5cm) diam.
£1,400–1,600
€/ $2,200–2,500 GH

A repoussé silver air-cased pendant alarm timepiece, by Phillip Jacob Bickelman, the dial with secondary chapter ring and alarm dial, movement signed, inner case marked 'JB', outer case with remnants of stained shagreen, Austrian, mid-18thC, dial 5in (12.5cm) diam.
£3,000–3,400
€/ $4,700–5,400 HOLL

A skeletonized gold verge watch, with stone-set silver hands and full plate fusee movement, enamel dial restored, signed 'Thuilly à Genève', Swiss, c1780, 1½in (4cm) wide.
£1,800–2,000
€/ $2,800–3,200 PT

A gilt and underpainted horn pair-cased verge watch, by Arther Dodge, Goudhurst, No. 1773, signed, with later hands, c1780, 2in (5cm) diam.
£640–750
€/ $1,000–1,200 S(O)

A gold and enamel consular-cased verge watch, by L'Epaute, Paris, with gilt full plate quarter-repeating movement, signed, the frame set with paste decoration, French, c1790, 1¾in (4.5cm) diam.
£1,200–1,400
€/ $1,900–2,200 S(G)

A gold consular-cased verge watch, by L'Epine Horologers du Roy, minute hand later, with presentation case and winding key, French, c1790, 1½in (4cm) diam.
£800–900
€/ $1,300–1,400 S(O)

A gilt and enamel verge watch, the silver regulator dial with gilt indicator, Arabic numerals and gold hands, the case with restored polychrome enamel pastoral scene, signed 'Breguet, Paris', French, c1800, 2¼in (5.5cm) diam.
£2,700–3,000
€/ $4,300–4,700 PT

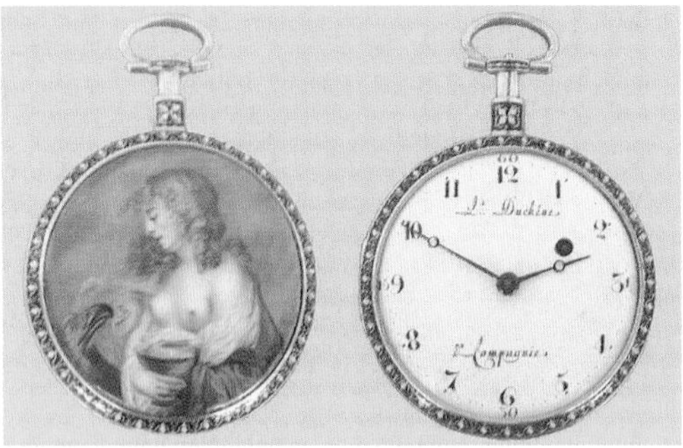

A gold pocket watch, the enamel dial signed 'Ls. Duchêne Compagnie', the painted reverse depicting Ganymede with an eagle, Swiss, late 18thC.
£3,000–3,800
€/ $4,700–6,000 G(B)

An 18ct gold pocket watch, the fusee movement by Charles Harden, London, No. 6164, with chased and engine-turned decoration, 1823, 1¾in (4.5cm) diam.
£500–550
€/ $800–870 L

A diamond fob watch, by Le Roy & Fils, with an opalescent enamel dial surrounded by a border of brilliant-cut diamonds, the reverse engraved with a monogram and date, suspended on a silver and gold brooch set with diamonds, the chain set with rose-cut diamond accents, French, c1880.
£1,700–2,000
€/ $2,700–3,200 HAM

An 18ct gold lever pocket watch, with full plate gilt keywind fusee movement and Harrison's maintaining power, the engine-turned case with chased and engraved bezels, maker's mark 'WW', London 1825, 1¾in (4.5cm) diam, in a blue morocco-covered travelling case.
£1,000–1,200
€/ $1,600–1,900 PT

An 18ct pink-gold hunting-cased keyless cylinder watch, by Patek Philippe, No. 67074, the dial with Roman numerals, the back engraved with a coat-of-arms surmounted by a coronet, with a photocopied letter from Patek Philippe, dial with hair cracks, case now with wristwatch lugs, Swiss, 1881, 1¼in (3cm) diam.
£900–1,100
€/ $1,400–1,700 S(O)

► **An 18ct gold open-faced watch,** by Breguet, No. 513, with a gilt lever movement, bi-metallic compensation balance, spiral balance with overcoil, wolf's tooth winding, and gold cuvette, French, 1889, 1¾in (4.5cm) diam, with certificate and leather box.
£1,500–1,800
€/ $2,400–2,800 S(NY)

An 18ct gold lever watch, by Smith & Gamble, Dublin, No. 2005, with three-colour gold dial, in an engine-turned case, with associated guard chain and fob, Irish, early 19thC.
£700–820
€/ $1,100–1,300 B(Kn)

A gilt-metal cylinder stopwatch, by Thomas Earnshaw, London, No. 2671, in a consular case, the inner marked with initials 'TC', the outer case containing five watch papers dated from 1844–67 and a further example with a printed image of George III and a Thomas Earnshaw watch paper, early 19thC, 2in (5cm) diam.
£850–1,000
€/ $1,300–1,600 B

An 18ct Massey gold five-lever pocket watch, the gold dial with three-colour gold border and applied gold Roman numerals, with Harrison's maintaining power, hallmarked Chester 1822, 2¼in (5.5cm) diam.
£1,100–1,200
€/ $1,700–1,900 PT

An 18ct gold open-faced pocket watch, by Charles Frodsham, London, No. 03964, the enamel dial with subsidiary seconds, the three-quarter plate gilt movement with lever escapement, London 1873, 2¼in (5.5cm) diam.
£1,900–2,300
€/ $3,000–3,600 S(NY)

◄ **An 18ct gold Victorian pocket watch,** the dial and case with engraved floral decoration, 1½in (4cm) diam.
£170–200
€/ $270–315 L

A 14ct gold keyless pocket watch, by Waltham, the case with engraved flowers and filigree patterns to the front edge, the reverse engraved with a stag, American, 1893.
£350–385
€/ $550–600 Bns

An 18ct gold half-hunter-cased keyless lever watch, by George Orm & Son, No. 17708, the enamel dial with subsidiary seconds, the case reverse with an engraved entwined monogram, London 1898, 2in (5cm) diam.
£565–675
€/ $900–1,000 S(O)

A gunmetal watch, the gilt dial with rotating rings for minutes and hours, surmounted by a radiated cross, with a gilt lever movement, c1900, 2in (5cm) diam.
£850–1,000
€/ $1,300–1,600 S(Am)

A gold-mounted fob watch, the engine-turned gilt dial with pearl-set Roman chapters, the case set with half pearls, the surmount formed as a pearl-set shell, c1900.
£3,200–3,800
€/ $5,100–6,000 B(Ed)

An 18ct gold half-hunter watch, by M. F. Dent, No. 33028, with a secondary dial and crown wind, an engraved crest to the reverse of the case, Sheffield 1904, with original box.
£700–850
€/ $1,100–1,300 HOLL

► An 18ct gold open-face pocket watch, by Longines, No. 910503, the enamel dial with subsidiary seconds dial, the keyless 15-jewel movement with monometallic balance and flat balance spring, the engine-turned case with an engraved shield, Swiss, c1910.
£200–240
€/ $315–380 DN

◄ A diamond-set platinum pendant fob watch, c1910, 1in (2.5cm) diam.
£7,000–8,000
€/ $11,100–12,700 ⊞ NBL

A silver pocket watch, the enamel dial with triple calendar and moonphase, in an engine-turned case, London 1917.
£400–450
€/ $630–710 DD

◄ A silver and enamel crucifix watch, with an enamel dial, and keywind gilt going barrel bar movement, Swiss, c1930, 3¼in (8.5cm) long.
£450–500
€/ $700–800 ⊞ PT

Wristwatches

An Arbu moonphase calendar chronograph self-winding wristwatch, with an automatic movement, in a stainless steel case with push-button adjusters, Swiss, 1950s, 1¼in (3cm) diam.
£525–585
€/ $830–920 ⊞ Bns

A Breitling Datora chronograph wristwatch, Swiss, c1953.
£900–1,000
€/ $1,400–1,600 ⊞ HARP

A Le Coultre Master Mariner automatic wristwatch, with lapis-effect dial symbolizing the stars and the solar system and raised hour markers symbolizing planets, Swiss, c1955, with original box.
£1,400–1,500
€/ $2,200–2,400 ⊞ HARP

A Baume & Mercier 18ct pink-gold triple date chronometer wristwatch, with registers and moonphase, subsidiary dials and seconds, minutes and hour recording, Swiss, c1950, 1½in (4cm) diam.
£6,300–7,000
€/ $10,000–11,000 ⊞ AGR

A Cartier stainless steel wristwatch, with Girard Perregeux movement, French, 1945.
£630–700
€/ $1,000–1,100 ⊞ HARP

A Longines silver wristwatch, Swiss, 1920s.
£580–650
€/ $900–1,000 ⊞ TEM

A J. W. Benson 9ct gold wristwatch, with enamel dial and hands, hallmarked, 1933.
£450–500
€/ $700–790 ⊞ HARP

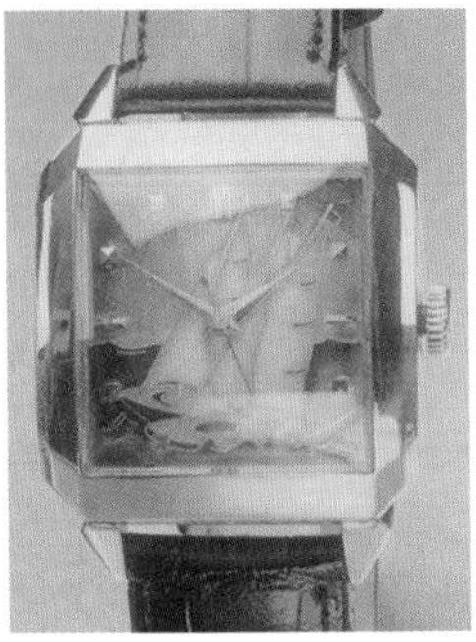

An Eska Watch Co 18ct gold automatic centre seconds wristwatch, the cloisonné dial depicting two sailing ships, with applied faceted square and baton numerals, the cushion-form case with a faceted bezel, dial cracked, Swiss, c1955, 1¼in (3cm) wide.
£3,000–3,300
€/ $4,700–5,200 ⚒ S(G)

A Longines 9ct gold wristwatch, with an enamel dial, Swiss, 1920s.
£550–625
€/ $870–1,000 ⊞ TEM

A Breitling 18ct gold triple-date chronograph wristwatch, Swiss, 1940s.
£3,200–3,600
€/ $5,000–5,700 ⊞ TEM

An International Watch Co 18ct gold wristwatch, Swiss, 1950s.
£1,100–1,300
€/ $1,700–2,000 ⊞ TEM

A Longines silver wristwatch, Swiss, 1930s.
£420–465
€/ $670–730 ⊞ TEM

◄ **A Longines stainless steel wristwatch,** the silvered dial with subsidiary seconds, with a nickel lever movement, Swiss, c1935, 1½in (3.5cm) long.
£350–400
€/ $550–630
⚒ S(Am)

► **A Movado steel wristwatch,** with day, date and month apertures, Swiss, 1950s.
£800–900
€/ $1,300–1,400 ⊞ TEM

An Omega wristwatch, Swiss, 1930s.
£800–900
€/ $1,300–1,400 ⊞ TEM

An Omega steel three-dial chronograph wristwatch, Swiss, 1950s.
£1,800–2,000
€/ $2,800–3,200 ⊞ TEM

A Rolex 9ct gold wristwatch, No. 759142, the dial with luminous numerals and subsidiary seconds, with a nickel-finished movement, Swiss, c1918, 1¼in (3.5cm) diam.
£1,000–1,200
€/ $1,600–1,800 ⚒ B

An Omega 9ct gold wristwatch, Swiss, 1930s.
£870–970
€/ $1,300–1,500 ⊞ TEM

A Patek Philippe 18ct gold wristwatch, No. 638548, movement No. 901606, the silvered dial with subsidiary seconds, the polished case with downturned lugs, Swiss, 1940s, 1in (2.5cm) square.
£1,700–2,000
€/ $2,700–3,200 ⚒ B

A silver Rolex wristwatch, with an enamel dial, Swiss, 1920s.
£750–825
€/ $1,200–1,300 ⊞ TEM

◄ A Rolex half-hunter wristwatch, Swiss, 1920s.
£1,500–1,700
€/ $2,400–2,700 ⊞ TEM

An Omega 18ct gold wristwatch, the silvered dial with subsidiary seconds, the case with a curved back, Swiss, c1935, 1½in (4cm) long.
£650–770
€/ $1,000–1,200 ⚒ S(G)

An Omega stainless steel military wristwatch, the black dial with subsidiary seconds, luminous hands and marked with the King's arrow, Swiss, c1945, 1½in (3.5cm) diam.
£350–390
€/ $550–630 ⊞ Bns

The King's arrow indicates that this watch has been issued to the British Army.

◄ A Pierce stainless steel chronograph wristwatch, the silvered dial with subsidiary seconds and dials for running seconds and minutes, c1940.
£190–230
€/ $300–360 ⚒ DN

A Rolex 9ct white-gold and diamond wristwatch, with a prima manual wind movement, the case set with 28 brilliant-cut diamonds, on a stainless steel band, c1930.
£300–360
€/ $470–570 ⚒ LJ

A Tiffany 14ct gold curved tank wristwatch, 1930s.
£1,300–1,500
€/ $2,100–2,400 ⊞ TEM

A silver hunter wristwatch, the dial with subsidiary seconds, early 20thC.
£140–160
€/ $220–250 ⚒ G(L)

A Rolex Prince stainless steel wristwatch, the brushed-steel dial with subsidiary seconds, Swiss, 1930s.
£2,400–2,800
€/ $3,800–4,400 ⚒ AH

◄ A Rolex Oyster Perpetual chronometer steel wristwatch, Swiss, c1953, 1¼in (3cm) diam.
£470–560
€/ $740–880 ⚒ BR

A Vacheron & Constantin gold, enamel and diamond-set bracelet watch, No. 360685, the bezel set with diamonds, with similarly decorated central lugs, Swiss, c1915, 1in (2.5cm) diam.
£1,400–1,600
€/ $2,200–2,500 ⚒ S(O)

A cocktail watch, the diamond-set bezel with French-cut soapphire accents, c1925.
£200–225
€/ $320–350 ⚒ HAM

A Rolex 9ct gold wristwatch, the dial with subsidiary seconds, Swiss, c1935.
£420–500
€/ $660–790 ⚒ WW

A Tiffany 18ct gold wristwatch, 1920s.
£500–565
€/ $800–900 ⊞ TEM

A Zenith stainless steel top-wind wristwatch, with subsidiary seconds, Swiss, c1948.
£450–500
€/ $700–800 ⊞ HARP

A platinum square-cut diamond watch, c1925, ¾in (2cm) wide.
£1,800–2,000
€/ $2,800–3,200 ⊞ WIM

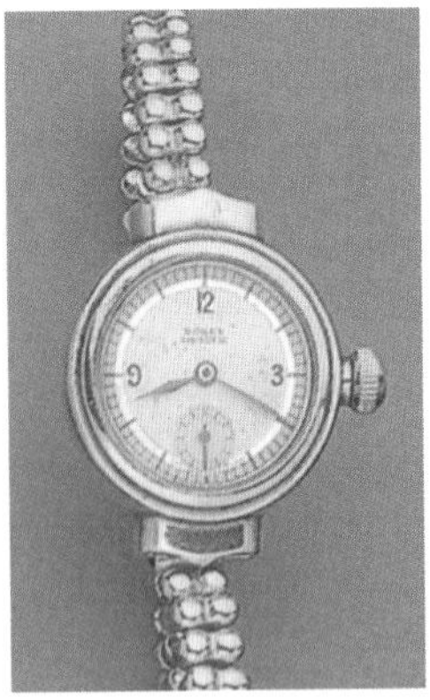

A Rolex Oyster 9ct gold wristwatch, the dial with outer seconds track and subsidiary seconds, with a 15-jewel movement, 1935, 1¼in (3cm) diam.
£420–500
€/ $660–790 ⚒ B(Kn)

A diamond wristwatch, with a blue stone cabochon winding button on a white metal mesh bracelet, c1920.
£650–820
€/ $1,000–1,300 ⚒ WW

An Art Deco platinum diamond-set cocktail watch, the case with full diamond-set bezel, shoulder and lugs, each with a larger baguettte-cut diamond and seven circular faceted diamonds, on a 9ct twin row Brazilian link bracelet, 1930s, ½in (1.5cm) diam, with box.
£1,100–1,300
€/ $1,700–2,000 ⊞ Bns

Barometers

Stick Barometers

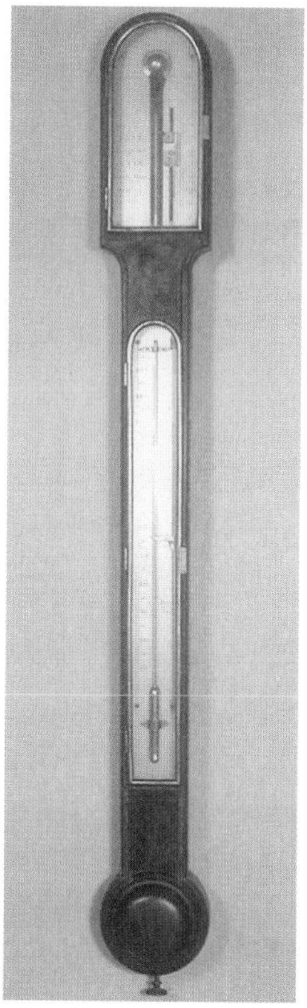

A George III mahogany stick barometer, with arched silver dial inscribed 'G. Adams, Fleet Street', above a thermometer with vernier scale and hinged brass door, 37in (94cm) high.
£6,000–6,800
€/ $9,500–10,700 WW

It is less common to find stick barometers with brass doors. Always expect to pay more for examples that have this feature.

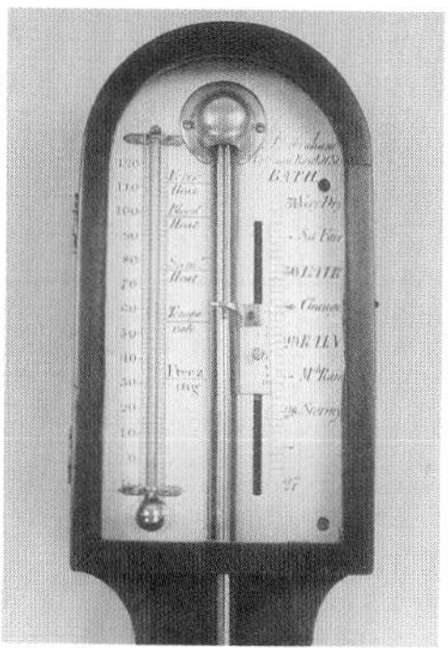

A mahogany stick barometer, by Jacob Abraham, Bath, the silvered plate with mercury thermometer, c1820, 36in (91.5cm) high.
£3,800–4,300
€/ $6,000–6,800 ⊞ PAO

A mahogany stick barometer, by Burton, London, with silvered-brass plate and oval cistern cover, c1790, 36in (91.5cm) high.
£2,300–2,600
€/ $3,600–4,100 ⊞ AW

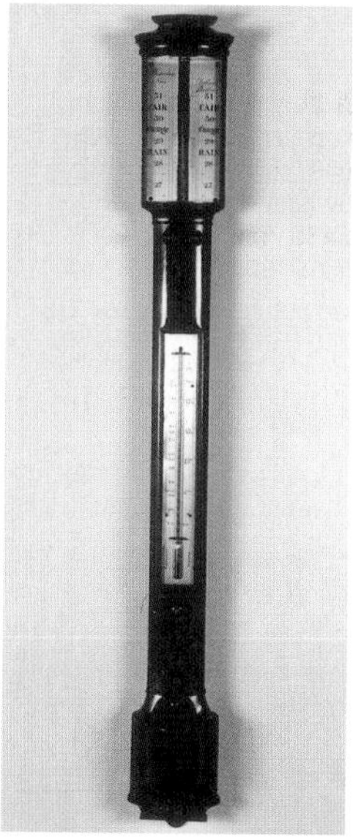

A mahogany bowfronted stick barometer, by Dollond, London, with caddy top and ebonized cistern cover, c1830, 38in (96.5cm) high.
£6,000–7,500
€/ $9,500–11,500 ⊞ RAY

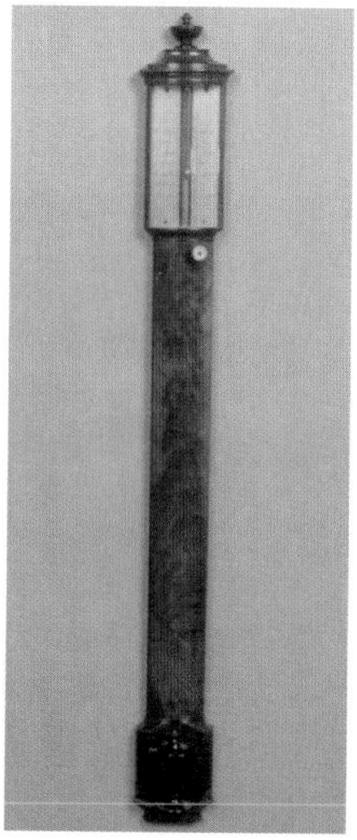

A mahogany bowfronted stick barometer, by Ramsden, London, the silvered scale with Ramsden's improved double pointer, c1800, 38in (96.5cm) high.
£10,000–12,000
€/ $15,800–19,000 TEN

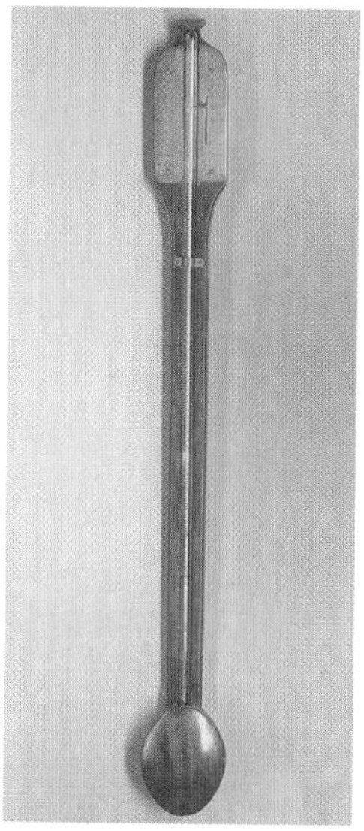

A mahogany stick barometer, by Alex Trotter, Jedburgh, the decorated plates with hand-set pointer, with oval cistern cover, Scottish, c1800, 35¾in (91cm) high.
£1,300–1,500
€/ $2,000–2,400 S(O)

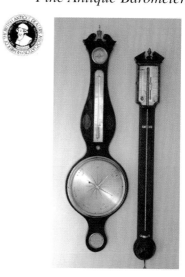

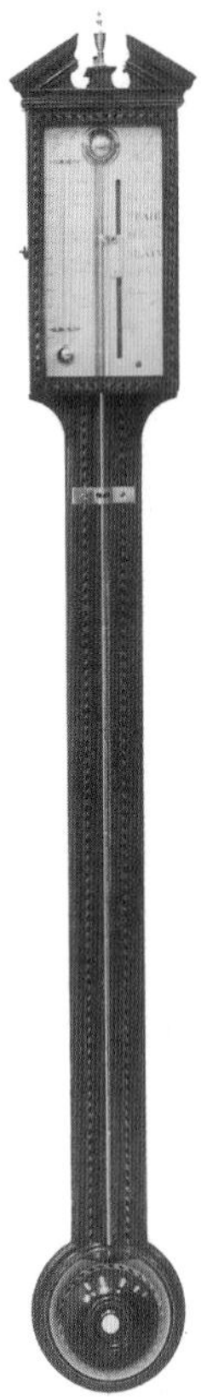

◄ **An oak stick barometer,** by H. Pascoe, Penzance, with ivory registers, 19thC, 35¾in (91cm) high.
£800–950
€/ $1,300–1,500 ⚒ AH

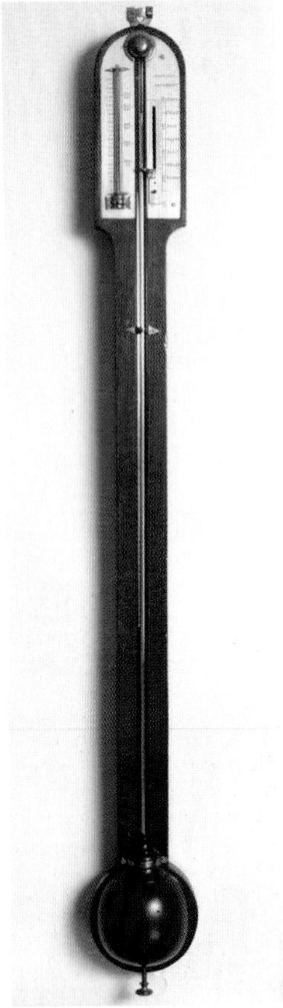

A mahogany stick barometer, by John Hay, Aberdeen, Scottish, c1850, 37in (94cm) high.
£1,800–2,000
€/ $2,800–3,200 ⊞ TRI

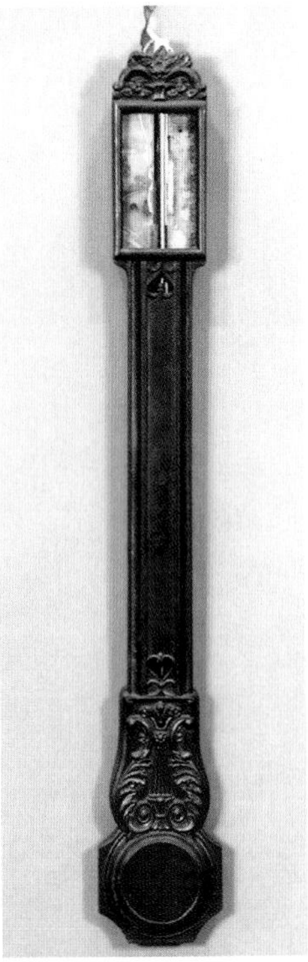

A cast-iron-fronted stick barometer, with paper register inscribed 'J.W. Smith Stowe, VT', American, Vermont, 19thC, 37in (94cm) high.
£525–625
€/ $830–980 ⚒ SWO

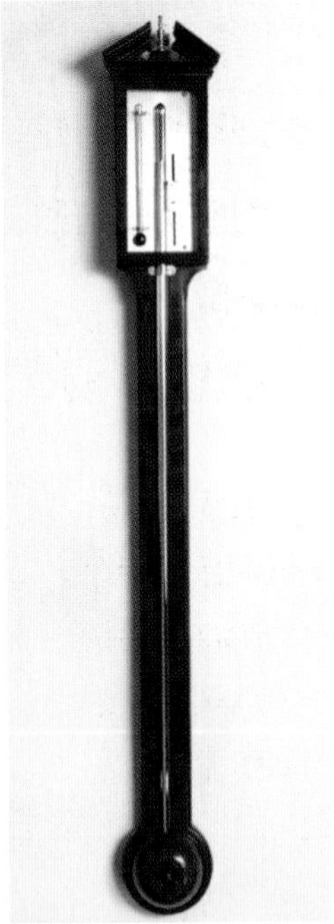

◄ **A mahogany stick barometer,** by Cox, London, c1850, 37in (94cm) high.
£2,000–2,200
€/ $3,200–3,500 ⊞ TRI

► **A mahogany stick barometer,** by Louis Pedrone, Liverpool, with signed silvered-brass register plates, c1850, 37in (94cm) high.
£5,500–6,000
€/ $8,700–9,500 ⊞ AW

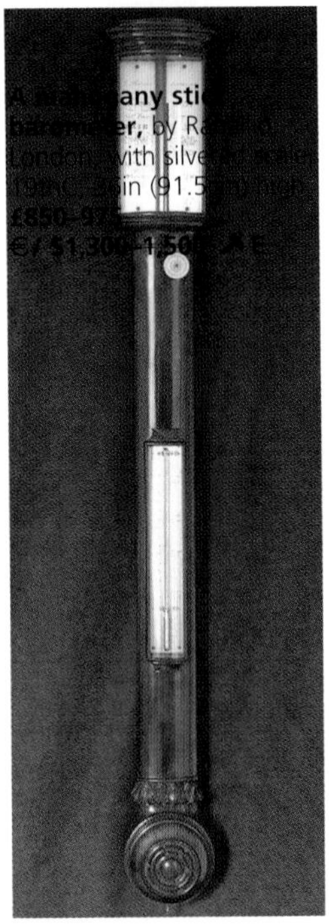

A [illegible]any stic[illegible] [illegible]er, by Ra[illegible] London, with silve[illegible] 19thC, [illegible]in (91.5[illegible]
£850–97[illegible]
€/ $1,30[illegible]–1,50[illegible] ⚒ [illegible]

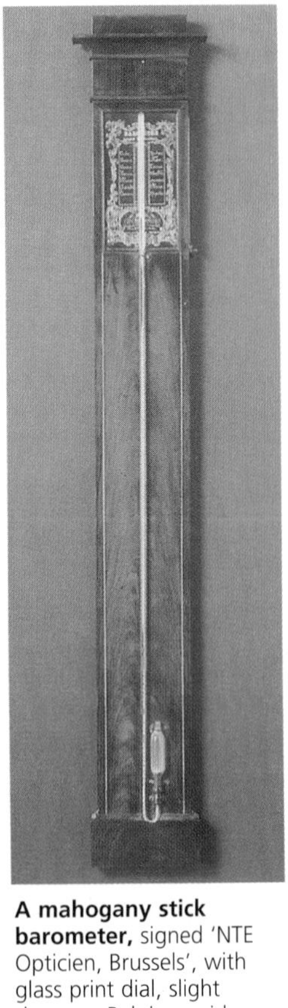

A mahogany stick barometer, signed 'NTE Opticien, Brussels', with glass print dial, slight damage, Belgian, mid-19thC, 42½in (108cm) high.
£1,500–1,700
€/ $2,400–2,700 ⚒ S(Am)

Always expect to pay more for a stick barometer than a wheel barometer of the same period. This is because fewer stick barometers were made and also demand for them today is higher. It is easy to understand when you realize that nowadays houses are smaller and it is easier to find space for an item that takes up only a few inches of space. Most stick barometers are only 4–6in (10–15cm) wide.

The popularity of the wheel barometer grew in the early 19th century because it was easier to read. The dial feature of a wheel barometer magnifies the inch scale, so smaller changes became more noticeable. The stick barometer measures the length of the mercury column in inches and so minor changes are less noticeable. An average wheel barometer has an 8in (20.5cm) dial size, fitted with a cabinet which is 10in (25.5cm) in diameter.

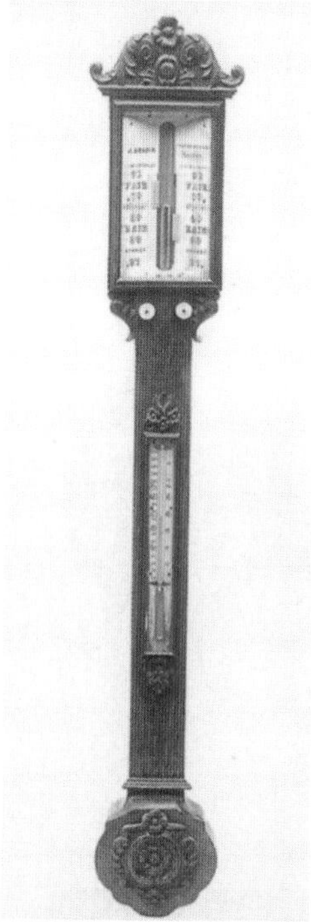

A Victorian oak stick barometer, by J. Amadio, London, with ivory scales, 42¼in (107cm) high.
£600–720
€/ $950–1,100 Bea

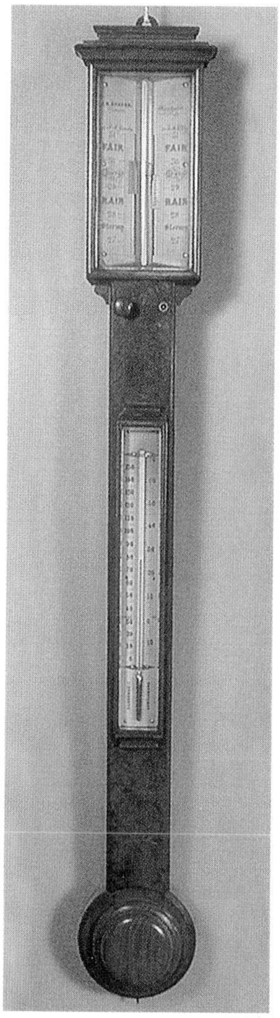

A Victorian burr-walnut stick barometer, by J. B. Dancer, Manchester, with ivory plates, vernier scale and thermometer, 38in (98cm) high.
£1,300–1,500
€/ $2,000–2,400 WW

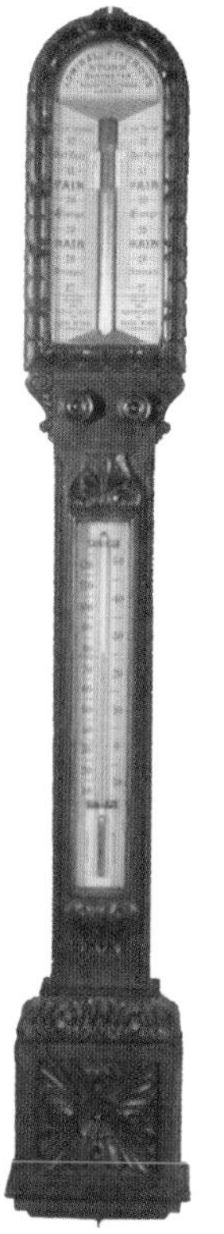

A Victorian oak Admiral Fitzroy storm barometer, by Negretti & Zambra, London, with signed ceramic plates, 41½in (105.5cm) high.
£1,800–2,200
€/ $2,800–3,500 WW

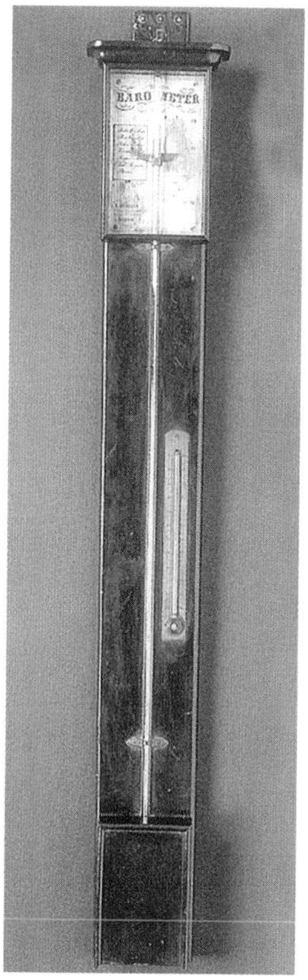

An ebonized wood stick barometer, by R. Beckmann, with signed silvered plates, losses, German, 1850–1900, 36½in (93cm) high.
£450–550
€/ $720–870 S(Am)

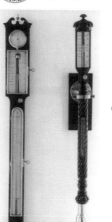

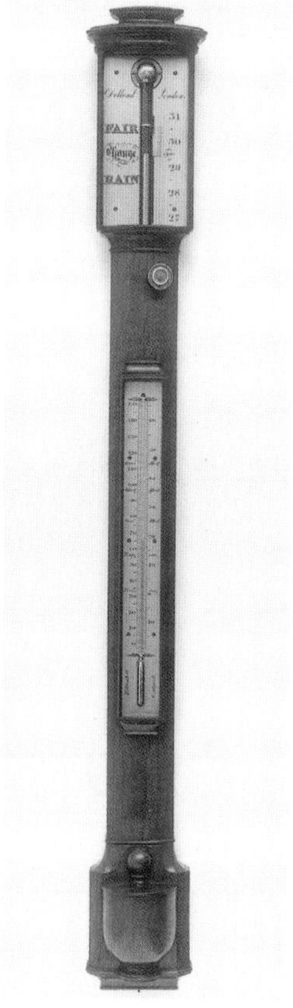

A mahogany bowfronted stick barometer, by Dollond, London, with silvered-brass plate and inset thermometer, c1870, 38½in (98cm) high.
£3,500–4,000
€/ $5,500–6,300 AW

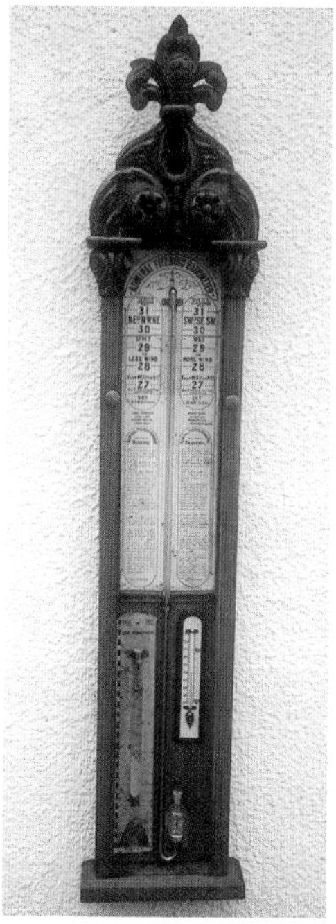

An oak Admiral Fitzroy barometer, c1880, 46in (117cm) high.
£1,600–1,800
€/ $2,500–2,800 RAY

Polytechnic barometers

Barometers of this style are interesting as they combine the advantages of the banjo barometer dial (which gives an expanded reading), with the scale and visibility of the stick barometer. The dial, instead of having the enlarged inch scale, has weather observations printed on the outer rim. These are broken into winter and summer readings, and are a modification of Fitzroy's observations. The majority of Polytechnic barometers have printed silvered-card dials, a few were made with white pottery dials and fewer still are of engraved silvered brass, the latter being the most expensive.

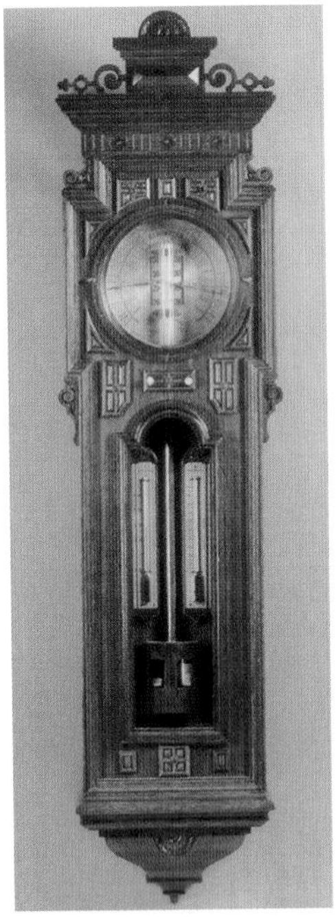

An oak Admiral Fitzroy Polytechnic barometer, by Joseph Davis, London, with signed silvered scale, two adjustable pointers for 'yesterday' and 'today' and Centigrade and Fahrenheit thermometers, c1885, 67in (170cm) high.
£2,200–2,500
€/ $3,500–4,000 ⚒ S(O)

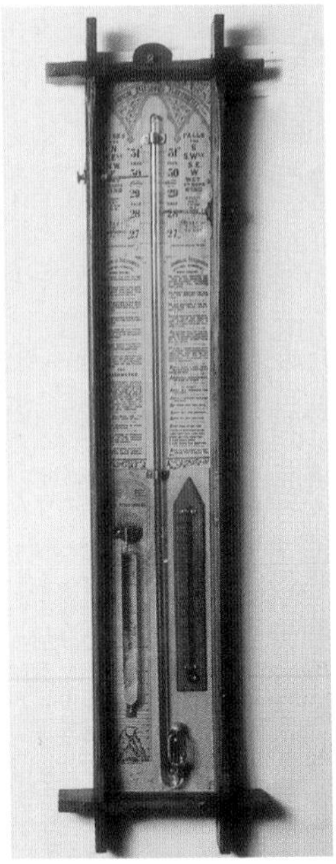

◄ An oak Admiral Fitzroy storm barometer, c1890, 40in (101.2cm) high.
£800–900
€/ $1,300–1,400 ⊞ AB

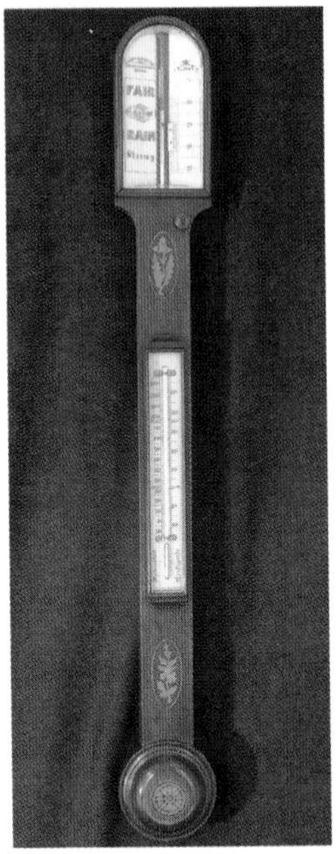

► A mahogany stick barometer, by Curry & Paxton, London, early 20thC, 36in (91.5cm) high.
£1,700–2,000
€/ $2,700–3,200 ⊞ AW

Wheel Barometers

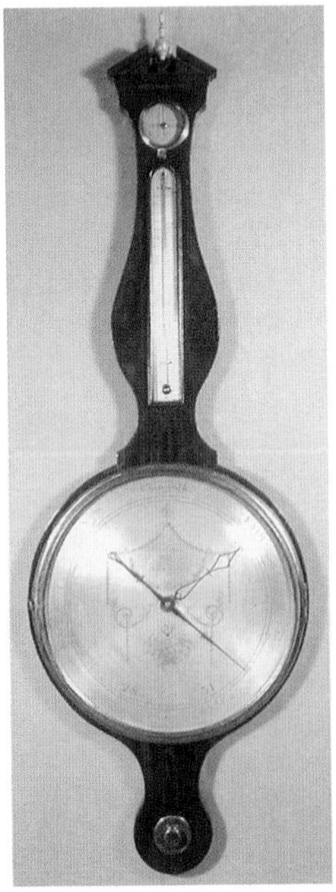

A George III mahogany wheel barometer, by J. Wilson, London, with silvered dial and register above, chevron stringing, 46¾in (119cm) high.
£5,500–6,200
€/ $8,700–9,800 ⚒ WW

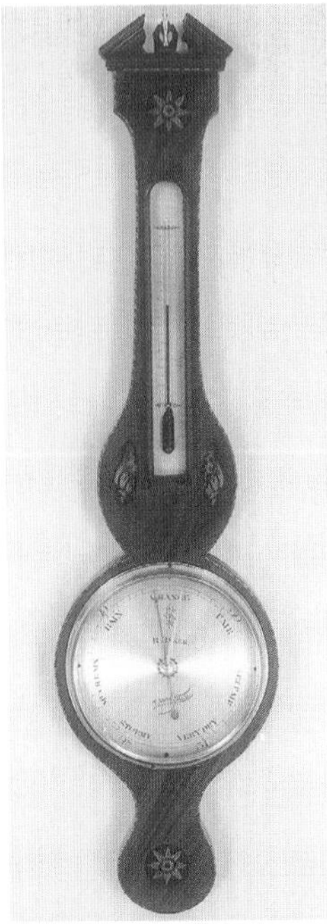

An inlaid mahogany wheel barometer, by R. Baker, Tamworth, with silvered-brass scale, c1800, 39in (99cm) high.
£1,600–1,800
€/ $2,500–2,800 ⊞ PAO

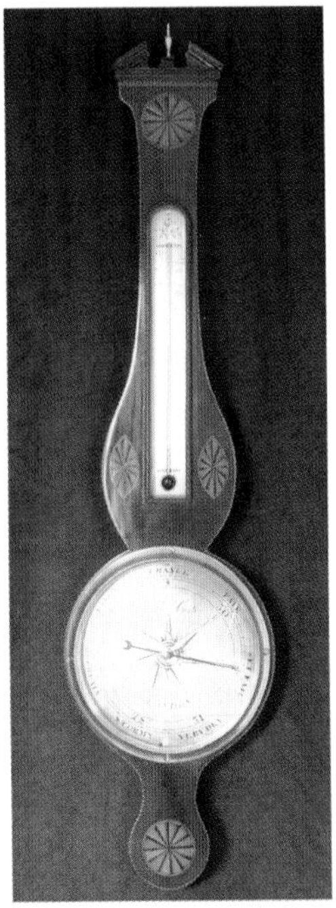

An inlaid mahogany wheel barometer, by John Corti, London, with chequer stringing, c1800, 37in (94cm) high.
£2,400–2,800
€/ $3,800–4,400 ⊞ AW

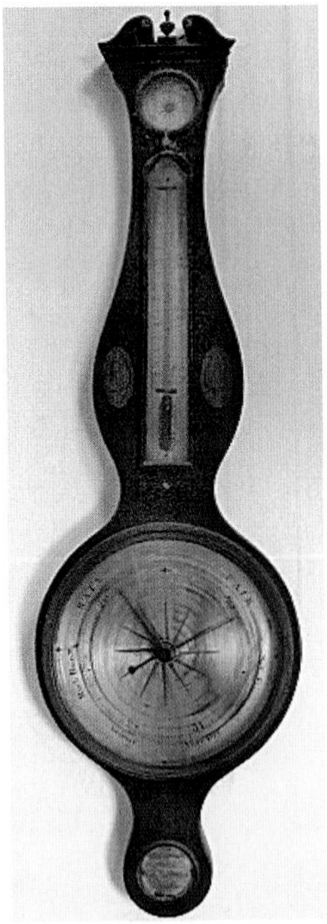

A mahogany and shell-inlaid wheel barometer, by Gough, London, with silvered register scale, alcohol thermometer and hygrometer, needs restoration, early 19thC, 38in (96.5cm) high.
£1,300–1,500
€/ $2,100–2,400 ⚒ TMA

A *verre églomisé* wheel barometer, the gilt, blue and white dial within gilt, green and red egg-and-dart border, French, c1800, 36¾in (93cm) high.
£2,000–2,200
€/ $3,200–3,500 S(Am)

A mahogany wheel barometer, by C. Camozzi, Buckingham, with dry/damp dial, thermometer and verge clock movement by Davidson, London, c1820, 46in (117cm) high.
£850–1,000
€/ $1,300–1,600 L&E

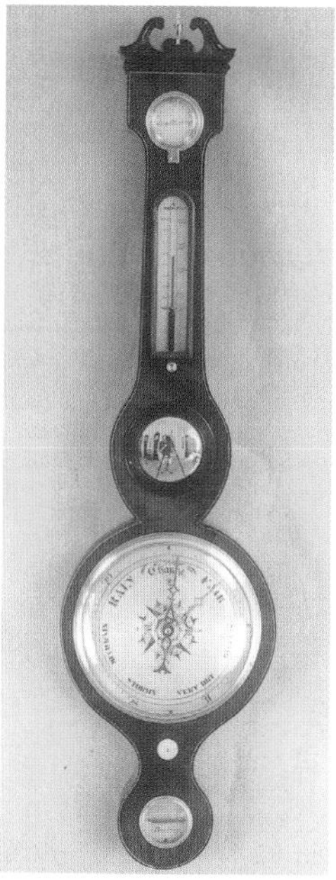

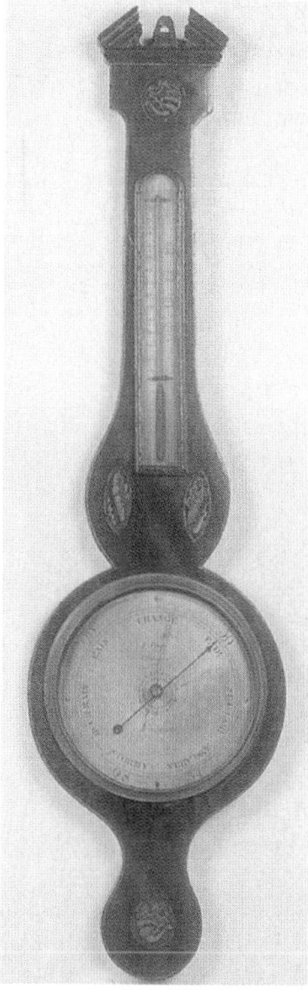

A mahogany and shell-inlaid wheel barometer, by Uago, Glasgow, with silvered dial, and alcohol thermometer, Scottish, early 19thC, 38¼in (97cm) high.
£420–500
€/ $660–790 B(L)

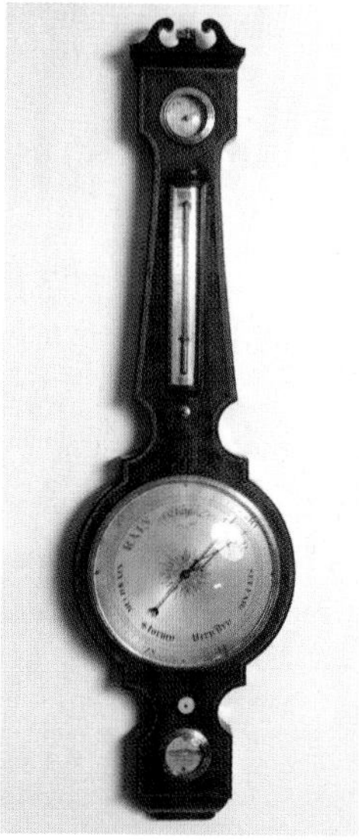

A mahogany and tulipwood crossbanded wheel barometer, by G. & C. Dixey, c1830, 43in (109cm) high.
£2,000–2,400
€/ $3,500–3,800 TRI

◄ **A mahogany wheel barometer,** by G. Kalabergo, Banbury, with silvered-brass scale, thermometer, hygrometer and spirit level, c1830, dial 8in (20.5cm) diam.
£850–950
€/ $1,300–1,500 PAO

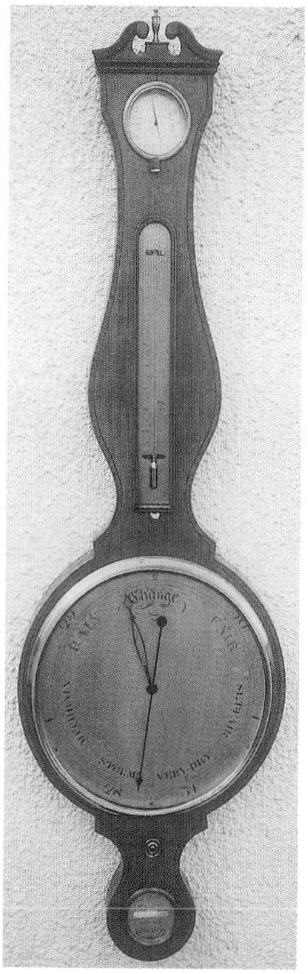

A crossbanded satinwood wheel barometer, by Lione Somalvico & Co, London, c1810, dial 12in (30.5cm) diam.
£3,500–4,000
€/ $5,500–6,300 RAY

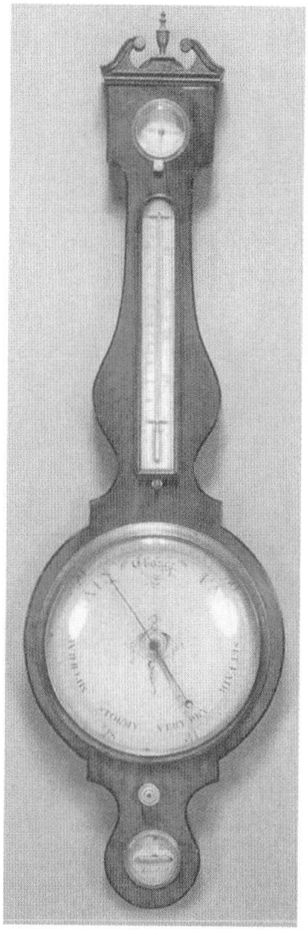

A Regency satinwood and line-inlaid wheel barometer, by J. Predary, Manchester, with silvered dial and hygrometer, thermometer and spirit level, 40¾in (103.5cm) high.
£1,800–2,200
€/ $2,800–3,500 DN

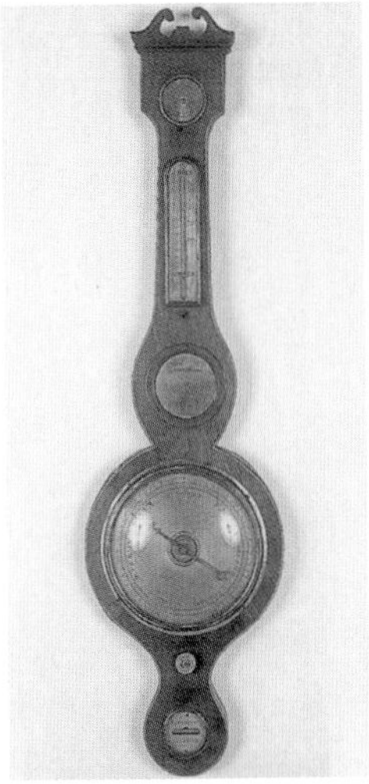

A mahogany wheel barometer, with silvered dial, alcohol thermometer, hygrometer and spirit level inscribed 'Songuini Llandilo', Welsh, 19thC, 37¾in (96cm) high.
£275–325
€/ $430–515 B(SW)

A Louis XV-style giltwood and gesso barometer, the paper dial signed 'Molteno et Baroni, Paris', French, 19thC, 43¼in (110cm) high.
£2,000–2,200
€/ $3,200–3,500 S(O)

◄ **A mahogany wheel barometer,** by L. Martinelli & Son, London, with silvered-brass dial, thermometer, hygrometer and spirit level, c1840m dial 14in (35.5cm) diam.
£2,500–2,800
€/ $4,000–4,400 ⊞ PAO

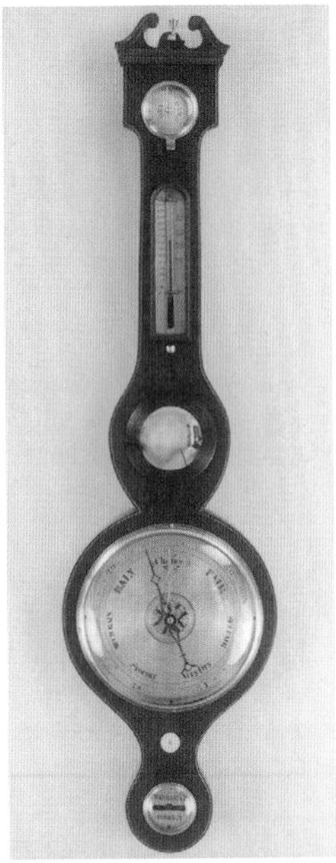

A mahogany wheel barometer, with silvered-brass scale, the thermometer mounted in a removable box, with hygrometer, spirit level and mirror, c1840, 38in (96.5cm) high.
£750–850
€/ $1,200–1,400 ⊞ PAO

► **A mahogany wheel barometer,** by Dring & Fage, London, with silvered dial, thermometer, spirit level and replaced hygrometer, mid-19thC, 42¼in (107.5cm) high.
£650–750
€/ $1,000–1,200 B(Kn)

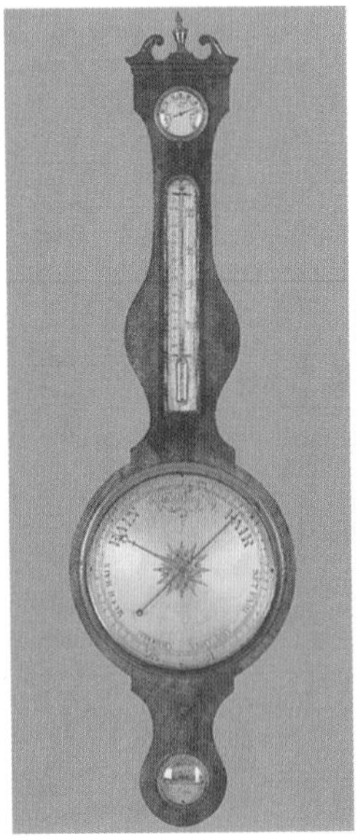

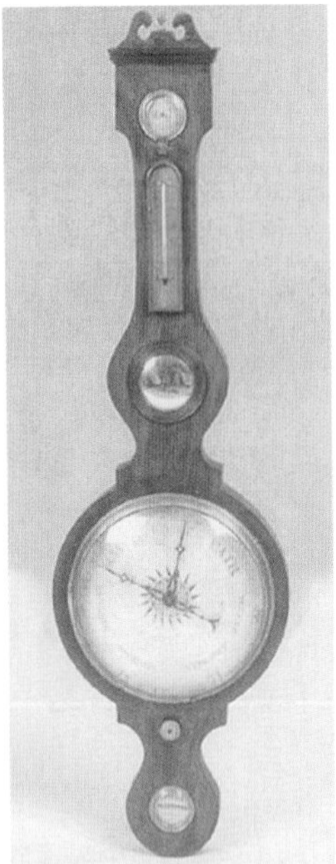

An early Victorian mahogany wheel barometer, by A. Luvate, Preston, with silvered dial, hygrometer, alcohol thermometer, spirit level and mirror, replaced swan-neck pediment, 42½in (108cm) high.
£280–320
€/ $440–500 PFK

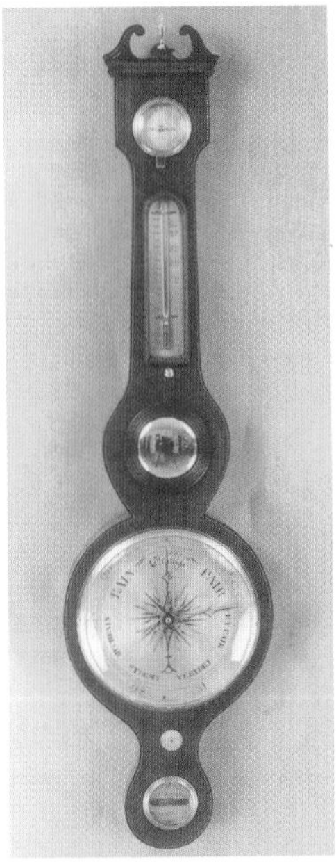

A mahogany wheel barometer, by Richard Howse, Marlborough, with silvered-brass scale, the thermometer mounted in a removable box, with hygrometer, spirit level and mirror, c1845, dial 8in (20.5cm) diam.
£875–975
€/ $1,400–1,500 ⊞ PAO

► **A Victorian wheel barometer,** by Samuel Solomon, Devizes, with silvered dial, thermometer, hygrometer, spirit level and mirror, 38¾in (98.5cm) high.
£380–450
€/ $620–700 WW

A mahogany boxwood-strung wheel barometer, with silvered dial, thermometer, hygrometer, mirror and spirit level, signed 'G. Riva & Co, Glasgow', Scottish, mid-19thC, 43½in (110cm).
£400–500
€/ $630–800 Bea

A black- and gilt-japanned and mother-of-pearl wheel barometer, by Wheeler, London, with silvered dial and thermometer, the case with chinoiserie-style decoration, thermometer damaged, c1850, 42in (106.5cm) high.
£500–600
€/ $800–950 S(O)

► **A Victorian mother-of-pearl and brass inlaid rosewood wheel thermometer,** with silvered dial, 40¼in (102cm) high.
£900–1,100
€/ $1,400–1,600 AH
This barometer has a very fine quality case and a lot of time has been spent on the cabinet-work. However, in today's market this style does not fit easily into modern homes because of the perceived fussiness of the casework. The inlay is of finely-cut mother-of-pearl interlaced with a tracery of brass. It required great expertise to complete such work. When fashions change, however, barometers of this quality will command high prices.

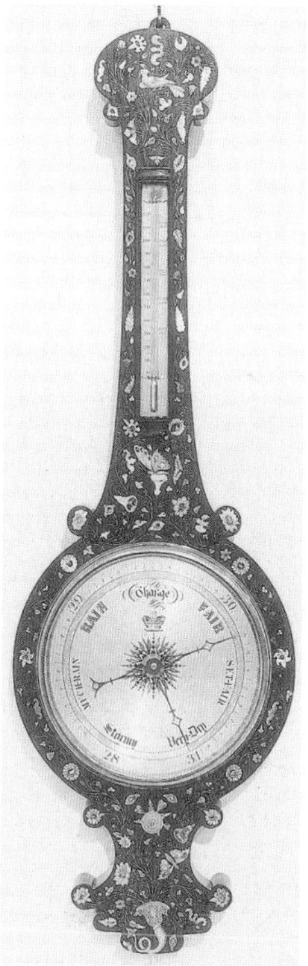

An oak and stained beech barometer, the painted glass dial signed 'Malizard', French, late 19thC, 35½in (90cm) high.
£420–500
€/ $660–800 S(O)

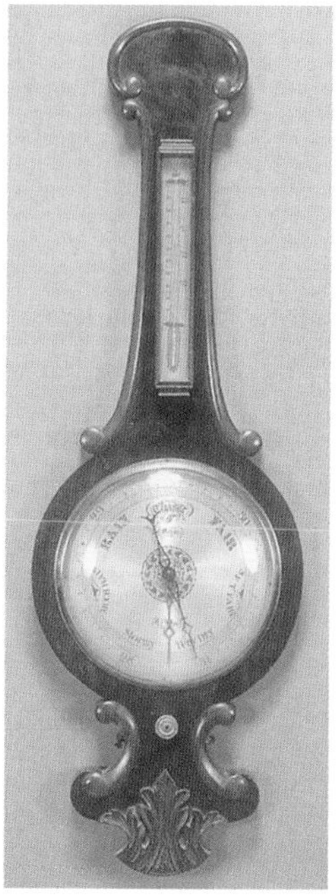

► **A mahogany wheel barometer,** by Row, Alton, with silvered dial and thermometer, late 19thC, 38½in (98cm) high.
£380–450
€/ $620–700 DN

The prices realized at auction may reflect the fact that the barometers have sometimes undergone alterations to their mechanisms, or are in unrestored condition.

Aneroid Barometers

A brass-cased aneroid barometer and thermometer, by Negretti & Zambra, London, with silvered dial and applied curved thermometer, c1860, 4¾in (12.5cm) diam, in velvet-lined glazed oak case.
£800–900
€/ $1,300–1,400 S(O)

◄ **A gilt-brass aneroid barometer and thermometer,** the dial signed F. L. West, London, on a spelter stand in the shape of a girl on a foliate base, 1860–80, 7in (18cm) high.
£160–175
€/ $250–275
B(Kn)

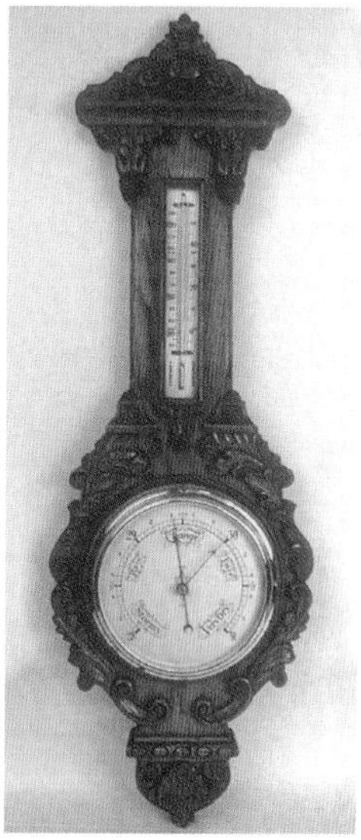

A late Victorian aneroid barometer, in an oak case, carved with sea scrolls and scallop shells, 38in (96.5cm) high.
£275–325
€/ $430–515 EH

► **An ormolu-cased aneroid barometer,** with white enamel dial signed 'Torricelli', French, 19thC, dial 13in (33cm) high.
£575–600
€/ $900–1,100 EH

An oak-cased aneroid barometer, by Negretti & Zambra, c1910, 20in (51cm) high.
£800–900
€/ $1,300–1,400 RTW

Items in the Barometers section have been arranged in date order within each sub-section.

Barographs

A mahogany-cased aneroid barograph, with single chart drawer, early 20thC, 14½in (37cm) wide.
£700–820
€/ $1,100–1,300 ⚒ GAK

A mahogany-cased barograph, by Oscar Erickson, Helsinki, with Russian marks on open barometer dial, Finnish, c1910, 14in (35.5cm) wide.
£1,300–1,400
€/ $2,000–2,200 ⊞ RTW

An oak-cased barograph, retailed by J. Lizars, Glasgow, the recording drum signed 'Gluck Co Ltd', with bevelled glass cover and a single chart drawer, early 20thC, 9in (23cm) high.
£650–775
€/ $1,000–1,200 ⚒ S(O)

A mahogany-cased barograph, retailed by Alner Coe & Co, Chicago, with bevelled glass cover and chart drawer, c1910, 14in (35.5cm) wide.
£1,600–1,800
€/ $2,500–2,800 ⊞ RTW

An oak-cased barograph, with bevelled glass cover and chart drawer, c1910, 14in (35.5cm) wide.
£900–1,000
€/ $1,400–1,600 ⊞ RTW

An oak-cased barograph, by Callaghan & Co, London, with bevelled glass cover and chart drawer, c1920, 15in (38cm) wide.
£1,000–1,100
€/ $1,600–1,700 ⊞ RTW

Further reading

Miller's Collecting Science & Technology,
Miller's Publications, 2001

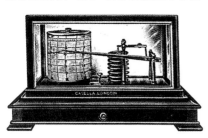

► **A mahogany-cased barograph,** by Short & Mason, c1920, 14in (35.5cm) wide.
£630–700
€/ $1,000–1,100 ⊞ RTW

◄ **A mahogany-cased weighted barograph,** by Jules Richard, French, c1925, 15in (38cm) wide.
£2,700–3,000
€/ $4,300–4,800 ⊞ RTW
This is known as a micro-barograph. The large clock drum enables an expanded reading between 28–31in (71cm–78.5cm) range, therefore small changes become more noticeable.

An oak-cased 'Regency' barograph, by Negretti & Zambra, London, with bevelled glass cover and chart drawer, c1925, 16in (40.5cm) wide.
£600–700
€/ $950–1,100 ⚒ PF

Decorative Arts

It's not when policeman start to appear younger but when your bookcase becomes too small to cope with all your *Miller's Antiques Price Guides* that you know you are getting older in our business. A quarter of a century is a significant milestone for any enterprise and having worked for at least as many years in a premier London auction house I have witnessed many ups and downs in the Decorative Arts world. Interest first focused on this period in the mid- to late 1970s, the age of flairs, punk and John Travolta gyrating to the strains of *Saturday Night Fever*. This was an age devoid of mobile phones and personal computers, populated by people limited to watching three TV channels and holding fondue parties. Although predicted then by many of the antiques old guard as merely a passing fad, where those who should know better were bound to get their fingers burnt, the following for all things Nouveau and Deco continues to grow.

So who and what have been the big movers? Starting Stateside, Tiffany lamps continue to hold the premier position with Newcomb College Pottery attracting huge interest and serious money in more recent years. Glass by Gallé, Daum and Lalique has maintained an international following although the heady prices paid in the late 1980s took a steep dive during the early '90s. In Britain the rarity of works by Charles Rennie Mackintosh, in tandem with a growing international appreciation, has ensured a constant demand and prices in excess of £1 million (€/ $1.6 million) for his more important furniture. British art pottery, particularly the work of William de Morgan and the Martin Brothers, now attracts international buyers with deep pockets. Factory-decorated pieces by Clarice Cliff have also been pursued by a growing army of fanatics prepared to pay £12,000 (€/ $19,000) and more for a rare Age of Jazz figure, whereas Susie Cooper, although discovered several years ago by the Japanese, has yet to find a real following in the United States.

As for the future, two names to watch out for might be glassmaker John Ditchfield and silversmith Stuart Devlin. **Eric Knowles**

Aesthetic Movement Ceramics

A Burmantofts Anglo-Persian-style vase, attributed to Louis Kramer, artist's monogram 'KL' and impressed marks, 1880s, 14¾in (37.5cm) high.
£6,500–7,500
€/ $10,300–11,700 ⚒ TEN

A Wileman & Co cabaret set, comprising eight pieces, c1889.
£100–120
€/ $160–190 ⚒ BR

A Minton porcelain vase, possibly designed by Christopher Dresser, in the style of Chinese cloisonné, on three gilt legs, impressed and puce printed marks, c1873, 7½in (19cm) diam.
£800–950
€/ $1,200–1,500 ⚒ S(O)

A Victorian aesthetic-style planter, the brass frame inset with four Minton ceramic tiles depicting figures emblematic of the seasons, signed 'Moyr Smith', 9½in (24cm) square.
£520–620
€/ $830–980 ⚒ PFK

A Pinder & Bourne vase, the gold-blocked sides reserved with chrysanthemum *mon*, monogrammed 'F**A**R**', impressed mark, 1879, 14½in (37cm) wide.
£700–820
€/ $1,100–1,300 ⚒ TEN

A Victorian majolica Japanese-style jug, c1880, 7½in (19cm) high.
£350–385
€/ $550–600 ⊞ CHAC

Aesthetic Movement Furniture

A pitch pine three-piece bedroom suite, comprising a triple wardrobe, dressing table and pot cupboard, with ebony stringing and geometric designs, c1880, wardrobe 89¼in (226.5cm) high.
£470–570
€/ $750–900 PFK

An ebonized satinwood and parcel-gilt credenza, in the style of Jackson & Graham, the later top above a sgraffito-decorated frieze, the glazed door flanked by six bevelled panels enclosing a velvet-lined interior, flanked by cupboards centred by Pre-Raphaelite-style oil paintings of women wearing classical dress, on a later plinth base with shaped bracket feet, reconstructed from a larger side cabinet, c1880, 81¼in (206.5cm) wide.
£2,500–3,000
€/ $4,000–4,700 B

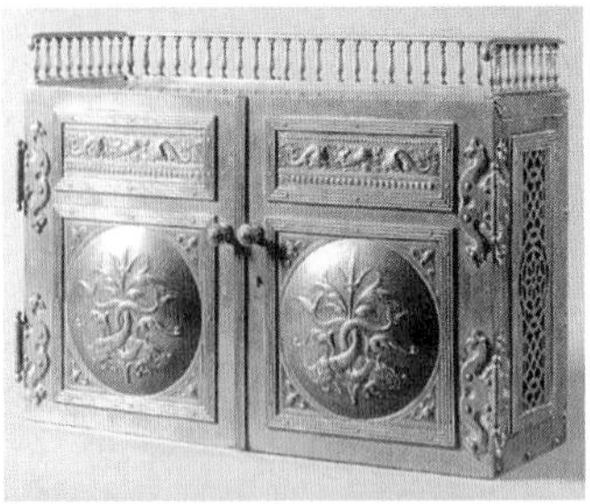

A brass cabinet, with applied embossed panels and pierced side panels, c1880, 21in (53.5cm) wide.
£400–500
€/ $630–790 S(O)

► **A pair of inlaid walnut side chairs,** attributed to Herter Brothers, American, c1870.
£2,800–3,200
€/ $4,400–5,000
S(NY)

A corner cabinet, by Gillows, 19thC, 56in (142cm) high.
£1,600–1,800
€/ $2,500–2,800 APO

An oak rocking chair, with lion-head and floral leather decoration, c1880.
£720–800
€/ $1,100–1,300 TDG

A late Victorian seat, the padded fan back on turned ebonized supports with a central burr-walnut-veneered panel, centred by a jasper ware-style plaque, on turned and veneered legs with casters, 41½in (105.5cm) wide.
£170–200
€/ $270–320 WW

A pair of Japanese-style lacquered bedside cupboards, by Howard & Son, 1880–90, 18in (45.5cm) wide.
£4,000–4,400
€/ $6,300–7,000 GKe

Items in the Aesthetic Movement sections have been arranged in alphabetical order.

An ebonized, gilt and polychrome-decorated hanging cupboard, the top with a shelf and sloping carved sides, above two panel doors with stylized flowers and bees, applied ornamental strapwork hinges, enclosing a shelf, c1875, 19¼in (49cm) wide.
£525–625
€/ $830–990 B

A mahogany and inlaid sideboard, possibly by Heal's, with engraved escutcheons, c1885, 55½in (141cm) high.
£2,000–2,200
€/ $3,200–3,500 B
This piece reflects the influence of the Aesthetic style in its decoration and has details inspired by the leading designers of the time. The superstructure with this type of pierced fret is a feature evident on other Heal's designs from the 1880s.

A Victorian inlaid oak sideboard, the frieze with ebonized 'studs', the drawers with original brass handles, previously with a mirror back or similar, 72in (183cm) wide.
£400–500
€/ $630–800 PFK

► **A walnut writing table,** the leather-lined top above two drawers, c1880, 45in (114.5cm) wide.
£1,500–1,800
€/ $2,400–2,800 S(O)

An ebonized table, the moulded-edge top inlaid with calamander, on casters, late 19thC, 28½in (72.5cm) high.
£7,500–8,800
€/ $12,000–14,000 DN
This piece carries the stamp of Lamb of Manchester, who were successful during the second half of the 19th century. It was found in the dairy of a local farmhouse, and despite being in need of restoration, it still fetched an impressive price.

An occasional table, in the style of E. W. Godwin, the underside with hand-written label 'Stansfield', late 19thC, 20in (51cm) wide.
£2,200–2,500
€/ $3,500–4,000 S(O)
The fact that this table sold for such a high price indicates that it was indeed considered to have been designed by E. W. Godwin.

A gilt centre table, with shelf and spindle-and-ball design, American, late 19thC, 31in (78.5cm) high.
£5,000–5,500
€/ $8,000–8,700 NART

For further information on tables see pages 114–142

Aesthetic Movement Metalware

A Gorham Manufacturing Co silver and mixed metal Japanese-style bowl, the spot-hammered surface applied with maple leaves in copper and brass, marked and numbered, American, Providence, 1879, 11in (28cm) diam.
£4,500–5,300
€/ $7,000–8,500 S(NY)
This bowl is an example of Gorham interpreting a Tiffany Japanese-style design by Edward C. Moore.

Further reading

Miller's Art Nouveau & Art Deco Buyer's Guide, Miller's Publications, 2001

A silver sugar bowl, cream jug and sugar tongs, by Henry Lias and James Wakely, London 1883–84, jug 2in (5cm) high, 6oz.
£1,100–1,200
€/ $1,700–1,800 NS

A brass kettle, with repoussé decoration, c1890, 9in (23cm) high.
£200–220
€/ $300–350 RUSK

◄ **A Barbour Silver Co silver hot water urn,** decorated with engraved arabesque panels, with gadrooned bone handles, on a pierced galleried foot and a detachable tripod base with gadrooned bone feet joined by a stretcher, the burner by Gorham Corporation and dated 1883, American, Hartford, c1885, 13in (33cm) high.
£750–900
€/ $1,200–1,400 NOA

Arts & Crafts Ceramics

An American Encaustic Tiling Co tile, depicting a fable, c1920, 6in (15cm) square.
£115–125
€/ $180–200 ⊞ KMG

A Burmantofts jardinière and stand, 1890–1910, 45in (114.5cm) high.
£1,000–1,100
€/ $1,600–1,700 ⊞ ASA

A Rookwood floor vase, decorated by Charles Stewart Todd with a grape-vine and fruit, beneath a matt glaze, impressed marks, American, c1915, 17¾in (45cm) high.
£2,000–2,200
€/ $3,200–3,500 ⚒ JAA

An Ashworth vase, c1900, 9½in (24cm) high.
£110–125
€/ $175–200 ⊞ DSG

A Burmantofts jardinière, c1900, 13in (33cm) high.
£520–580
€/ $820–900 ⊞ AFD

A Denby tube-lined tobacco jar, decorated with Festoon pattern, rim damaged, presser missing, c1925, 4in (10cm) high.
£130–145
€/ $200–230 ⊞ KES

A Van Briggle plate, decorated with a multi-toned matt glaze, incised marks, American, 1907–12, 6in (15cm) diam.
£320–400
€/ $500–630 ⚒ TREA

An Ault vase, moulded with six anthemia, on a lotus base, c1905, 7in (18cm) diam.
£350–385
€/ $550–600 ⊞ HUN

A William De Morgan pottery vase, decorated with a running crackle glaze, restored, Sands End mark, c1888, 9in (23cm) high.
£400–450
€/ $630–700 ⊞ RUSK

A Foley *intarsio* vase, c1890, 11in (28cm) high.
£900–1,000
€/ $1,400–1,600 ⊞ RH

Foley (1892–1925) became the trade name for Wileman & Co, which was known as Shelley from 1925. The name derived from their premises, The Foley, at Longton, Staffordshire. Their Art Nouveau wares included a range of earthenware, designed and decorated by Frederick Rhead, using a dramatic form of underglaze decoration known as *intarsio*.

A jardinière, by William Baron, with moulded loop additions, incised marks, c1900, 11½in (29cm) diam.
£230–275
€/ $360–430 ⚒ RbF

A William De Morgan lustre vase, possibly by Halsey Ricardo, impressed Sands End mark, painted initials 'HR', slightly misfired, 1888–97, 10in (25.5cm) high.
£2,200–2,600
€/ $3,500–4,000 ⚒ RTo

A Vodrey pottery vase, with beaded decoration, c1885, 5¾in (14.5cm) high.
£320–375
€/ $500–600 ⚒ JAd

Frederick Vodrey (1845–97) was born in Tunstall, Staffordshire, where his father worked in the pottery industry. His mother moved c1860 to Dublin, where she opened a retail china and glass business, which Frederick took over in 1865. By 1882 the business had expanded to include an art pottery factory, a relatively new departure in Ireland. Frederick acted as designer, while his brother Thomas was mould-maker. Like many other ceramicists of his time, Frederick became interested in recreating the forms and glazes of 17th-century Chinese pottery. His work is considered unique within the history of Irish ceramic design and won awards at all the exhibitions in Ireland in the 1880s.

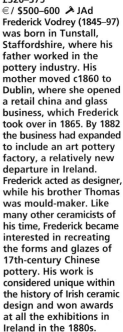

Arts & Crafts Clocks

An ebonized wood and painted tile mantel clock, possibly by Lewis F. Day, the tile face enclosed by four corner tiles painted with flora and the captions 'Childhood', 'Manhood', 'Age' and 'Death', c1880, 16½in (42cm) high.
£1,700–2,000
€/ $2,700–3,200 B

A brass and copper clock garniture, c1890, clock 13in (33cm) high.
£1,400–1,600
€/ $2,200–2,500 ASP

An oak mantel clock, with a pewter face and Swiss eight-day movement, retailed by Liberty & Co, platform replaced, c1900, 12in (30.5cm) high.
£1,800–2,000
€/ $2,800–3,200 AFD

► **A copper mantel clock,** in the style of George Walton, hammered in relief with harebells, early 20thC, 15¼in (38.5cm) wide.
£750–900
€/ $1,200–1,400 GH

Arts & Crafts Furniture

A copper-mounted oak bedroom suite, by Shapland & Petter, comprising a triple wardrobe and dressing table, c1905, dressing table 48in (122cm) wide.
£950–1,100
€/ $1,500–1,700 B

An oak bookcase, with stamped copper hinges, c1885, 46in (117cm) wide.
£2,000–2,300
€/ $3,200–3,600 WilP

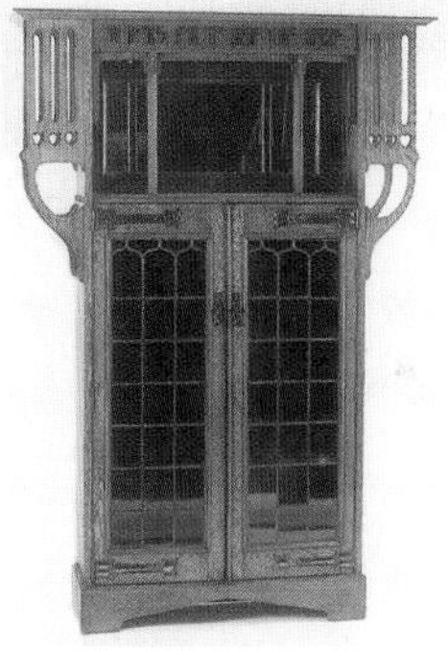

An oak bookcase, the frieze applied with a legend, the two leaded glazed doors with patinated metal furniture below, c1900, 76½in (194.5cm) high.
£1,200–1,500
€/ $1,900–2,400 Bri

An oak open bookcase, c1890, 48in (122cm) high.
£300–325
€/ $475–515 GBr

A mahogany secretaire cabinet, c1890, 59in (150cm) high.
£630–700
€/ $1,000–1,100 GBr

◄ **An oak cabinet,** the doors enclosing three sliding trays and hanging space, late 19thC, 22¾in (58cm) wide.
£600–700
€/ $950–1,100 S(O)

An inlaid mahogany display cabinet, by Shapland & Petter, c1900, 50in (127cm) wide.
£4,500–5,000
€/ $7,000–8,000 ASP

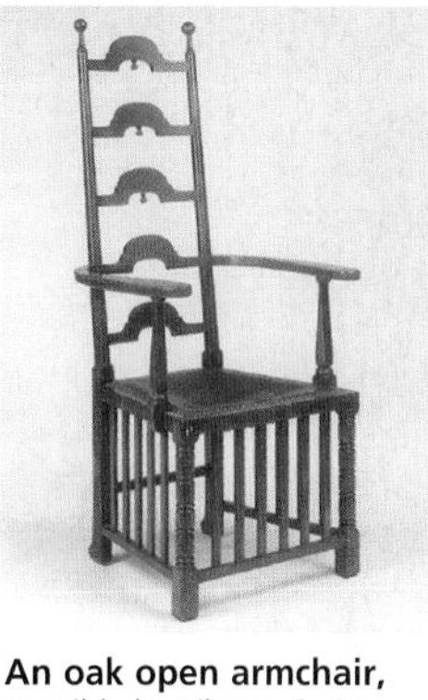

An oak open armchair, possibly by Liberty & Co, the ladderback with shaped splats between tapering uprights surmounted by ball finials, the leather-studded seat on ring-turned legs joined by stretchers supporting square-section uprights, c1900.
£500–600
€/ $800–950 B

A beechwood and walnut coffer, by Jolliffe, with gesso decoration, with the motto 'Safe Bind, Safe Find', the interior with paper label giving details of student and school, 1899, 45¼in (115cm) wide.
£4,000–4,500
€/ $6,300–5,500 ⚒ S(O)
It is probable that Jolliffe was a student at the Kensington School of Art and that this is an exam piece.

A Cotswold School oak hall stand, c1870, 41in (104cm) wide.
£1,400–1,600
€/ $2,200–2,500 ⊞ APO

A silver-plated mirror, c1900, 24in (61cm) wide.
£500–550
€/ $800–870 ⊞ TDG

An oak Sutherland table, c1890, 28in (71cm) wide.
£300–345
€/ $475–550 ⊞ GBr

A hall cupboard, attributed to Shapland & Petter, c1890, 32in (81.5cm) wide.
£1,200–1,400
€/ $1,900–2,200 ⊞ GBr

A Keswick School of Industrial Art copper mirror, c1900, 17in (43cm) wide.
£1,200–1,300
€/ $1,900–2,000 ⊞ SHa

An oak occasional table, the copper top with an engraved design, above a shaped frieze, on splayed tapering legs, c1900, 57in (145cm) wide.
£100–125
€/ $160–200 ⚒ BWL

◄ **An oak dining table,** by Gustav Stickley, No. 934-E, with two extra leaves, branded 'Als/ik/kan' with remnants of paper label, American, c1902, 76in (193cm) extended.
£6,000–7,200
€/ $9,500–11,500 ⚒ S(NY)

An embossed copper fire surround, with cast-iron grate, the copper panels decorated with stars and moons on a brick-effect ground, the moulded grate hood with a stylized forest view, flora and sunburst motifs, c1895, 54¼in (138cm) wide.
£2,400–2,800
€/ $3,800–4,400 ⚒ B

A brass wall mirror, set with Ruskin pottery roundels, c1915, 20in (51cm) wide.
£400–450
€/ $630–700 ⊞ WAC

A Liberty & Co oak sideboard, the top section with a glazed door, c1900, 70in (178cm) wide.
£1,100–1,300
€/ $1,700–2,000 ⚒ SWO

A Glasgow School oak side table, c1905, 26in (66cm) wide.
£225–275
€/ $360–430 ⊞ PVD

MITOFSKY ANTIQUES

Art Nouveau • Art Deco • Arts and Crafts

A very fine René Prou sycamore secrètaire. Made in Paris c1930 with fully fitted interior. 146cm high x 75cm wide x 40cm deep.

An outstanding carom table (billiard). Made by E. T. Curtres, Paris, 1889. Mahogany with brass inlay. Signed in brass by the artist, addressed in brass, scoreboard on four sides and signed E. Gueret. 82cm high x 300cm long x 173cm wide.

8 Rathfarnham Road, Terenure, Dublin 6, Ireland
Tel: (0353•)-4920033 Fax: (0353•)-4920188
Website: www.mitofskyartdeco.com
Email: info@mitofskyartdeco.com

Arts & Crafts Jewellery

A silver buckle, London 1904, 3in (7.5cm) wide.
£500–550
€/ $800–870 ⊞ SHa

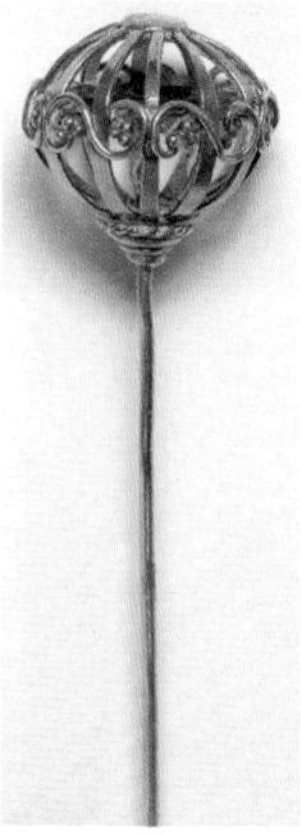

► **A Guild of Handicraft silver hat pin,** by Bertha Lilian Goff, c1890, 8in (20.5cm) long.
£170–185
€/ $270–300 ⊞ ANO

A necklace, with moonstones and a cornelian pendant, c1890, pendant 2in (5cm) long.
£475–525
€/ $750–830 ⊞ ANO

A necklace, after a design by Archibald Knox, the chain with arrow-shaped pendants, interspersed with blister pearls and turquoise, c1910, 15¾in (40cm) long.
£800–950
€/ $1,200–1,500 ⚒ B

A silver pendant, probably to a design by George Gaskin, the openwork panel set with blister pearls and chrysoprase, with a drop and similar smaller panels, c1905.
£750–875
€/ $1,200–1,400 ⚒ TEN

A silver and enamel pendant, by Charles Horner, 1908, 2in (5cm) long.
£225–250
€/ $350–400 ⊞ RGA

A silver and enamel pendant, by Charles Horner, 1909, 2½in (6.5cm) long.
£225–250
€/ $350–400 ⊞ RGA

► **A white-metal and enamel pendant,** by Murrle Bennet, stamped, on a chain, c1910, pendant 2½in (6.5cm) long.
£700–820
€/ $1,100–1,300 ⚒ B

Arts & Crafts Lighting

A pair of W. A. S. Benson brass wall lights, with spiral tendrils projecting from double-leaf supports and turned wall plates, with Powell bell-shaped vaseline glass shades, unmarked, c1900, 15in (38cm) long.
£4,800–5,300
€/ $7,600–8,400 ⊞ HUN

For further information on
W. A. S. Benson see page 456

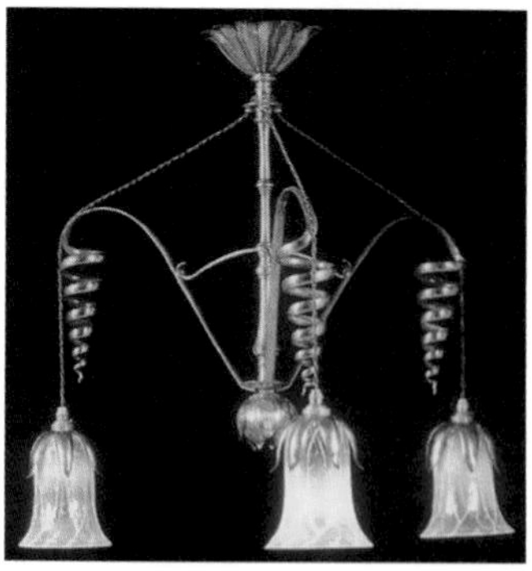

A copper and brass three-light chandelier, attributed to W. A. S. Benson, with three opalescent glass shades patterned with foliage, 26in (66cm) high.
£3,500–4,000
€/ $5,500–6,300 ⚒ S(O)

◄ **A W. A. S. Benson brass and copper two-part chandelier,** with curved tendrils and eight opaline glass shades, c1900, 49¼in (125cm) long.
£650–750
€/ $1,000–1,200 ⚒ B

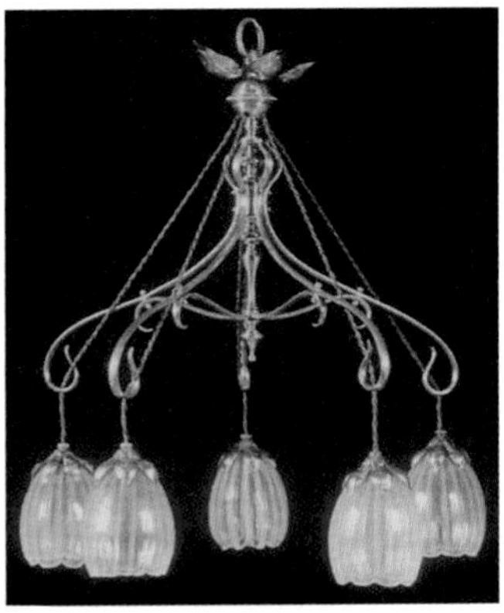

A brass five-light chandelier, in the style of W. A. S. Benson, with shaped opalescent glass shades, early 20thC, 25½in (65cm) high.
£4,500–5,000
€/ $7,000–8,000 ⚒ S(O)

A cast-brass wall lantern, with original etched tube, signed 'Osler', c1900, 15in (38cm) long.
£520–580
€/ $830–900 ⊞ JeH

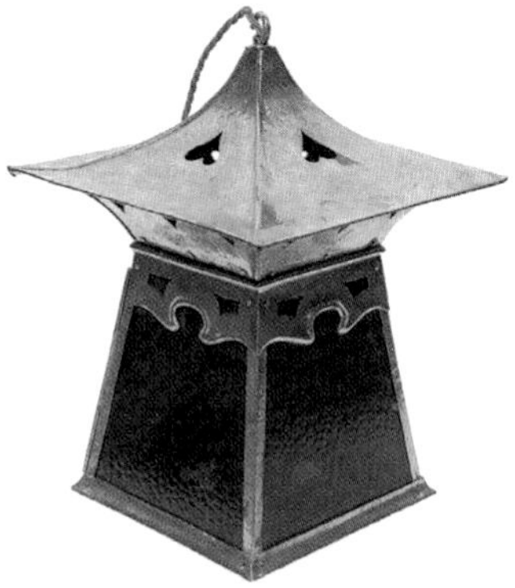

A copper hanging lantern, with original amethyst glass, c1900, 20in (51cm) high.
£1,100–1,200
€/ $1,700–1,900 ⊞ ASP

Always check that electric lighting conforms to the current safety regulations before using.

A pair of brass candelabra, c1890, 26in (66cm) high.
£700–800
€/ $1,100–1,200 ⊞ ASP

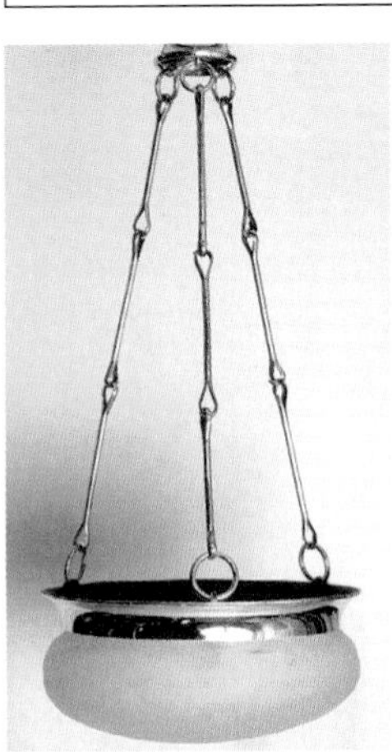

An Edwardian etched glass ceiling bowl, by Farraday & Son, with brass fittings and interlocking brass chain, marked 'F&S', 9in (23cm) diam.
£130–145
€/ $200–230 ⊞ JeH

A Glasgow School brass lantern, with coloured glass panes, 1890–1900, 11in (28cm) high.
£450–500
€/ $700–800 ⊞ JeH

An Arts & Crafts hall lantern, hand-painted with birds, 13in (33cm) high.
£720–800
€/ $1,100–1,300 ⊞ OLA

▶ **A copper hallway light,** c1900, 16in (40.5cm) high.
£580–650
€/ $900–1,000 ⊞ OLA

A hammered iron newel post lamp, 1900–10, 34in (86.5cm) high.
£350–400
€/ $550–630 ⊞ EAL

▶ **A patinated wrought-iron, copper and mica floor lamp,** by Sam Stoltz, the standard modelled as a vine-wrapped tree trunk with a cluster of wrought-iron roots, with a copper band cut with dolphins and tropical fish, the shade with a cut-copper swamp scene of herons, a deer and a cougar in a palm tree, American, c1930, 76in (193cm) high.
£3,800–4,200
€/ $6,000–6,600 ⚒ NOA

Sam Stoltz was a talented and imaginative artist, architect, contractor and landscape designer. He and his wife relocated from Chicago to Orlando, Florida in 1925 to take advantage of the sunny weather and the real estate boom. Stoltz's first designs were homes in the suburbs of Chicago – bungalows reflecting the influence of Frank Lloyd Wright's prairie style. His fascination with birds and fauna led him to embellish his houses with depictions of herons, flamingos, pelicans, cardinals, doves, fish, deer and even monkeys, painted on plaster and glass, sculpted in plaster relief and stucco, as well as in wrought iron. He remained active until 1946 and died in 1952, aged 76.

Arts & Crafts Metalware

A Keswick School of Industrial Art silver twin-handled cauldron bowl, design attributed to Harold Stabler, with embossed floral decoration, with presentation inscription, Birmingham 1899, 15½in (39.5cm) wide, 30oz.
£1,700–2,000
€/ $2,700–3,200 B(NW)

A Newlyn embossed copper rose bowl, on a detachable base with three splayed feet, stamped, early 20thC, 8½in (21.5cm) diam.
£470–570
€/ $750–900 S(O)

A pair of brass candlesticks, c1870, 8in (20.5cm) high.
£340–375
€/ $550–600
SHa

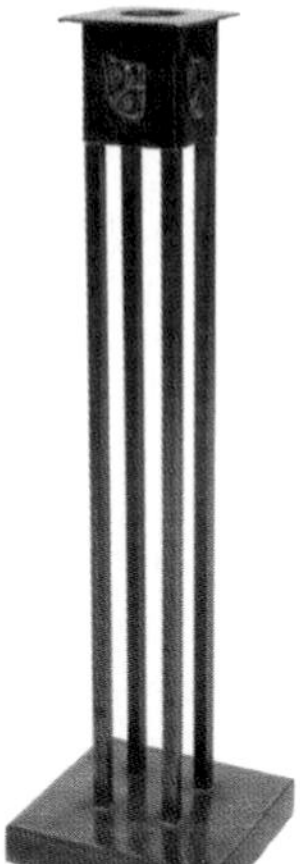

A Keswick School of Industrial Art copper charger, early 20thC, 19½in (49.5cm) diam.
£350–420
€/ $550–670 BR

A Newlyn copper bowl, c1900, 13in (33cm) diam.
£1,300–1,500
€/ $2,100–2,500 SHa

An embossed copper box, the lid embossed 'Lilly' the underside marked 'V.M. 1908', 7¼in (18.5cm) wide.
£330–400
€/ $530–630 S(O)

A pair of Newlyn-style copper chambersticks, decorated with fish, c1900, 8in (20.5cm) diam.
£350–425
€/ $550–670 G(L)

◄ **A pair of copper candlesticks,** in the style of Margaret Gilmour, Scottish, c1900, 11in (28cm) high.
£250–280
€/ $400–440 AFD

A copper charger, No. 2399, by John Pearson, the centre with a galleon, the border with leaping dolphin-like fish, signed and dated 1898, 20in (51cm) diam.
£2,300–2,600
€/ $3,600–4,100 G(L)

► **A pair of copper and brass chenets,** early 20thC, 17¾in (45cm) high.
£330–400
€/ $530–630 S(O)

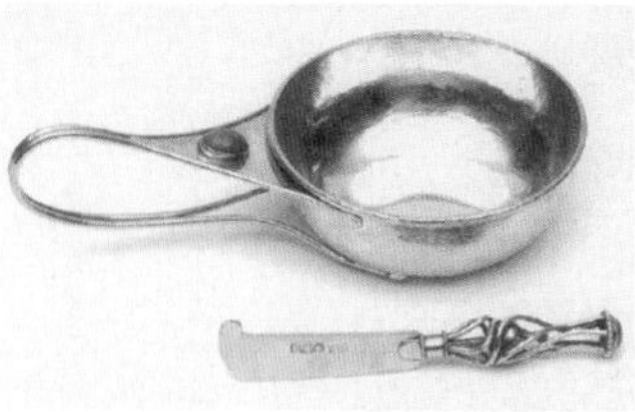

A Guild of Handicraft silver bowl, from a design by Charles Robert Ashbee, the beaten bowl with wirework hoop handle set with a cabochon, London 1901, 8in (20.5cm) wide, with a matching butter spoon.
£3,200–4,000
€/ $5,000–6,300 Bea

A pair of copper and iron candlesticks, 1880–1900, 6½in (16.5cm) high.
£100–120
€/ $160–190 AFD

A Birmingham Guild of Handicraft copper casket, c1910, 10in (25.5cm) wide.
£450–500
€/ $700–800 DAD

A Newlyn copper charger, c1890, 14½in (37cm) diam.
£765–850
€/ $1,200–1,400 SHa

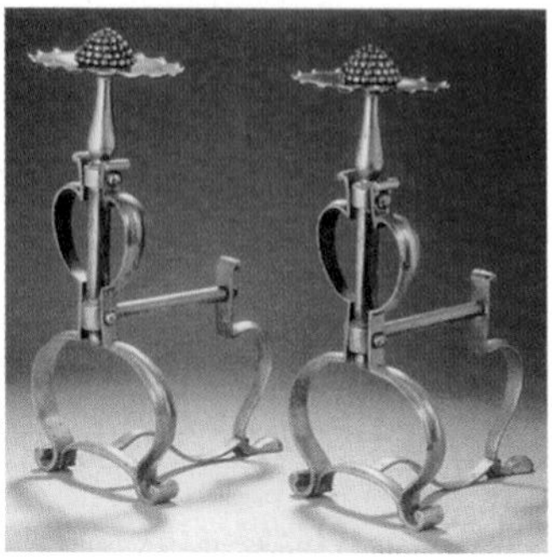

A copper coal box/log bin, c1900, 17in (43cm) wide.
£270–300
€/ $430–475 ⊞ ASP

A brass coal bucket, 1900–10, 17in (43cm) high.
£115–130
€/ $180–200 ⊞ EAL

An A. E. Jones silver three-piece coffee set, comprising a coffee pot, a cream jug and a sugar bowl, the coffee pot decorated with two bands of flowerheads to the girdle and collar, the hinged domed cover with a wooden finial and scroll handle, Birmingham 1918, coffee pot 8in (20.5cm) high.
£300–360
€/ $475–575 ⚒ CGC

A Hukin & Heath cruet stand, by Christopher Dresser, modelled as five conjoined wells centred by a handle, marked, 1879, 5½in (14cm) high.
£900–1,000
€/ $1,400–1,600 ⚒ S(O)

A Duchess of Sutherland's Cripples Guild of Handicraft silver dish and cover, with hammered design, based on a French *écuelle*, c1910, 7in (18cm) wide.
£700–800
€/ $1,100–1,300 ⊞ DAD

A brass footman, c1902, 21in (53.5cm) wide.
£325–360
€/ $500–560 ⊞ ASP

► **An Arts & Crafts W. A. S. Benson brass kettle-on-stand,** with burner and paw feet, on original tray, 11in (28cm) high.
£450–500
€/ $700–800 ⊞ HUN

Duchess of Sutherland's Cripples Guild of Handicrafts

The Guild was set up by Millicent, Duchess of Sutherland (1867–1955) in Trentham, Stoke-on-Trent, to assist crippled children who had suffered from pneumoconiosis, or lead poisoning, in the local north Staffordshire pottery industry.

The Guild produced art metal from 1902. The ouput was primarily copper and silvered-copper. Other crafts included silver, enamels and pottery in silver mounts. The majority of silver wares tend to be influenced by late 17th- and early 18th-century designs. All appear to have been submitted to the Birmingham assay office and bear the maker's mark of MS for Millicent Sutherland. The silver plate and copper wares were stamped with the letters DSCG beneath a coronet. The artist/designer Francis Arthur Edwardes was responsible for teaching metalwork, and the products were retailed until 1922, both locally and through a shop at 13–14 New Bond Street, London.

An A. E. Jones silver-gilt porringer and cover, Birmingham 1906, 6in (15cm) high.
£1,600–1,750
€/ $2,500–2,700 ⊞ SHa

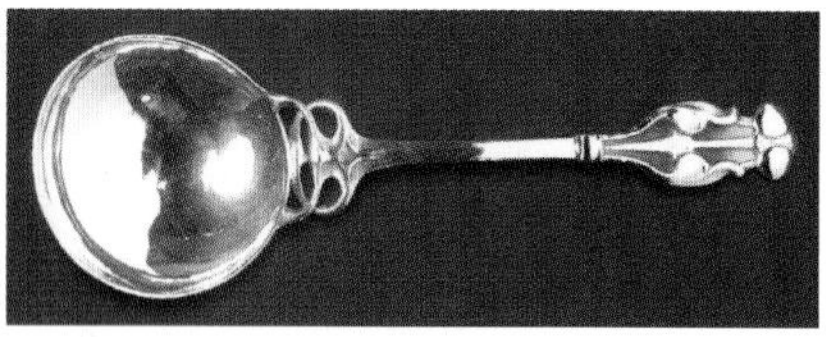

A silver and enamel spoon, by Connell, London 1906, 7in (18cm) long.
£500–550
€/ $800–900 ⊞ SHa

◀ A Duchess of Sutherland's Cripples Guild of Handicrafts silver-plated samovar, with two ivory bar handles, c1910, 20in (51cm) high.
£350–400
€/ $550–630 ⊞ DAD

A silver spoon, by H. G. Murphy, London 1935, 8in (20.5cm) long.
£500–550
€/ $800–900 ⊞ SHa

A silver four-piece tea service, comprising a teapot, stand, open sugar bowl and milk jug, the teapot with a domed hinged lid, ebonized finial and loop side handle, with beaten decoration, on three feet, the three-handled sugar bowl with trefoil leaf loop terminals, maker's mark for Charles Edwards, London 1917, 30oz.
£600–700
€/ $950–1,100 ⚒ B(W)

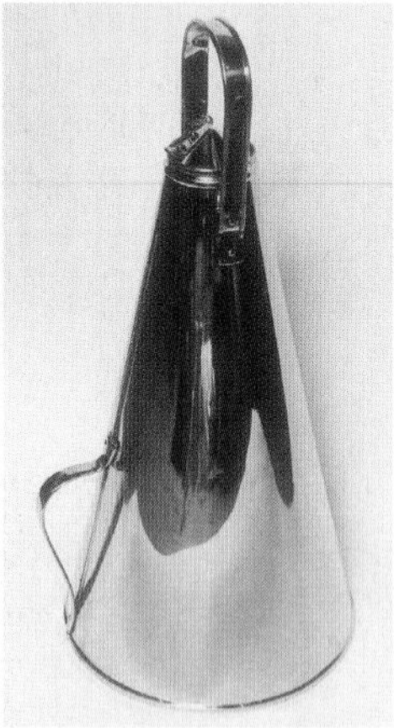

An Arts & Crafts W. A. S. Benson copper two-gallon thermos, with folding loop handle, 22in (56cm) high.
£570–635
€/ $900–1,000 ⊞ HUN

William Arthur Smith Benson (1854–1924)

W. A. S. Benson is recognized today as being perhaps the most important English designer and architect producing commercial metalware and lighting. Benson helped to establish the Art Workers' Guild in 1883 and the Arts and Crafts Exhibition Society in 1888. Production at his Hammersmith workshop commenced in 1880 with emphasis on copper and brass, although silver wares were also produced. In 1896, following the death of William Morris, Benson became a director of Morris & Co. Unlike Morris, Benson embraced the use of machines, and his metalwork designs were produced by various mechanical processes. His silver ware was shown at the Paris Exhibition of 1900 and retailed through the Maison de l'Art Nouveau of Samuel Bing. The Hammersmith workshops eventually closed in 1920.

A Newlyn copper tray, c1900, 28in (71cm) wide.
£450–500
€/ $700–800 ⊞ WAC

◀ A hammered copper tray, with birds among trailing foliage, 1900–10, 22in (56cm) wide.
£135–150
€/ $220–240 ⊞ EAL

A brass trivet, c1900, 13in (33cm) long.
£250–280
€/ $400–450 ⊞ AFD

A Hukin & Heath silver-plated tureen, No. M-057 A, by Christopher Dresser, with hardwood handles, on tripod legs, PODR mark, 1880, 12in (30.5cm) wide.
£2,200–2,500
€/ $3,500–4,000 ⚒ S(O)

A brass and copper wall sconce, c1915, 15in (38cm) high.
£150–165
€/ $240–260 ⊞ WAC

Doulton

A Royal Doulton beaker, commemorating the Diamond Jubilee of Queen Victoria, 1897, 4in (10cm) high.
£200–225
€/ $320–360 H&G

◄ **A Royal Doulton model of a bird of prey on a rock,** No. 145, with circle mark lion and crown, 1917–36, 8¾in (22cm) high.
£550–650
€/ $870–1,000 BBR

A Royal Doulton De Luxe coffee set, with printed and painted marks, 1940s, coffee pot 8¼in (21cm) high.
£150–175
€/ $240–280 SWO

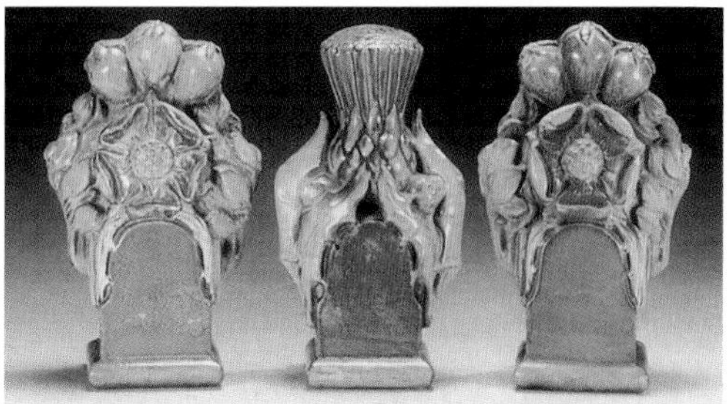

Three Doulton Lambeth salt-glazed stoneware finials, by Gilbert Bayes, some damage and repair, 1920–30, 13in (33cm) high.
£950–1,100
€/ $1,500–1,700 S(O)

A Royal Doulton ewer, c1905, 6in (15cm) high.
£175–200
€/ $275–315 PGO

◄ **A Doulton Lambeth jardinière,** by Frank Butler, c1878, 6½in (16.5cm) high.
£2,000–2,400
€/ $3,200–3,800 JE

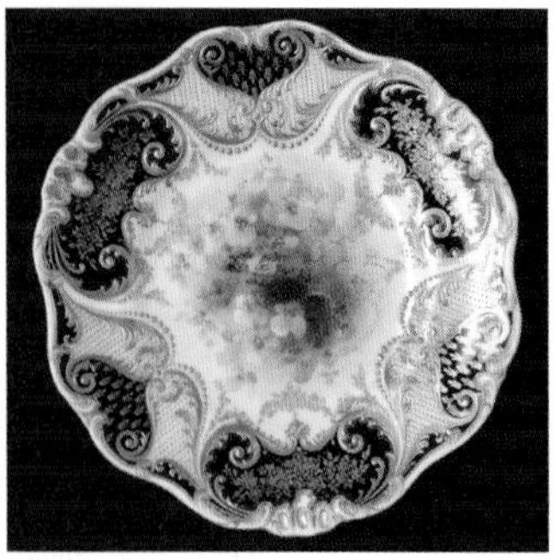

A Royal Doulton plate, by David Dewsberry, decorated with a floral bouquet and raised gilding, 1906, 9½in (24cm) high.
£780–850
€/ $1,200–1,300 ⊞ DIA

◄ A pair of Doulton Lambeth pots, with silver-plated rims, on a silver-plated stand stamped H.B., with a sifter spoon and ladle, 19thC, pots 3¼in (8.5cm) diam.
£250–300
€/ $400–470 ⚒ SWO

A Doulton Lambeth tyg, by Mark V. Marshall, with floral decoration, c1900, 6in (15cm) high.
£420–500
€/ $660–800 ⚒ G(L)

► A Doulton Kelmscott toilet set, c1900, largest 12in (30.5cm) high.
£800–900
€/ $1,300–1,400 ⊞ ASP

A pair of Royal Doulton vases, the necks with tube-lined cartouches, c1910, 8in (20.5cm) high.
£200–225
€/ $320–350 ⊞ LBr

A pair of Doulton vases, by George Tinworth, all-over-decorated with a scrolling foliate motif, incised artist's monogram and impressed factory marks, c1900, 7½in (19cm) high.
£800–1,000
€/ $1,300–1,600 ⚒ G(L)

A royal Doulton Lambeth stoneware vase, by Hannah Barlow and Florence Roberts, with an incised scene of sheep grazing, 1905, 15in (38cm) high.
£2,100–2,400
€/ $3,300–3,800 ⊞ GAA

A Royal Doulton vase, by Eliza Simmance, with stylized Art Nouveau designs, rim restored, c1910, 15in (38cm) high.
£220–250
€/ $350–400 ⚒ SWO

A Royal Doulton Titanian Ware vase, by F. Henri, c1920, 6in (15cm) high.
£900–1,000
€/ $1,400–1,600 ⊞ JE

Titanian Ware, produced from 1915–30, used titanium oxide in the glaze to give a blue colouration, ranging in tone from pale grey to dark royal blue. It was used to provide a background for fine porcelain pieces decorated by artists such as Harry Allen and F. Henri.

A Royal Doulton vase, by Eliza Simmance, c1910, 11in (28cm) high.
£600–700
€/ $950–1,100 ⊞ JE

► A Royal Doulton Art Nouveau vase, 1920s, 5½in (14cm) high.
£120–135
€/ $190–215 ⊞ PGO

A Royal Doulton flambé vase, with a printed factory mark and painted HN monogram, c1930, 7in (18cm) high.
£470–565
€/ $720–900 ⚒ S(O)

Martin Brothers

A Martin Brothers stoneware bowl, with six applied flowerhead roundels beneath a metal mount and handles, incised marks, 1895, 11in (28cm) diam.
£770–900
€/ $1,200–1,400 S(O)

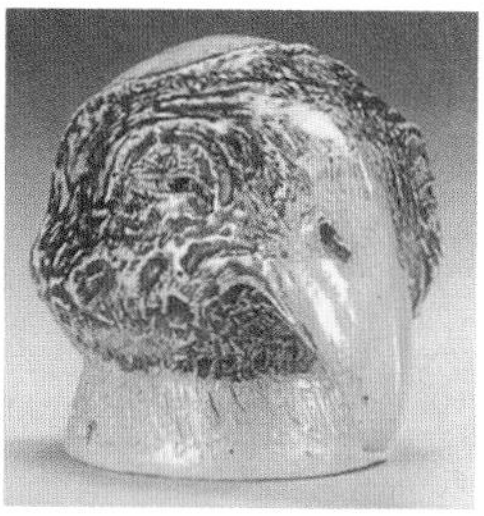

A Martin Brothers stoneware bird jar cover, small chip to beak, incised marks, 1882, 3¾in (9.5cm) high.
£900–1,000
€/ $1,400–1,600 S(O)

A Martin Brothers stoneware jardinière, modelled with a Celtic-style interlinked band pierced and modelled with overlapping fins, incised and impressed marks, rim crack and chip, 1873, 8¼in (21cm) high.
£500–600
€/ $800–950 LFA

◄ A Martin Brothers stoneware jug, with incised decoration, neck damaged and repaired, incised marks, 1885, 8½in (21.5cm) high.
£700–850
€/ $1,100–1,300
S(O)

► A Martin Brothers pottery jug, maker's signature to base, 1887, 9in (23cm) high.
£1,400–1,600
€/ $2,200–2,500 L

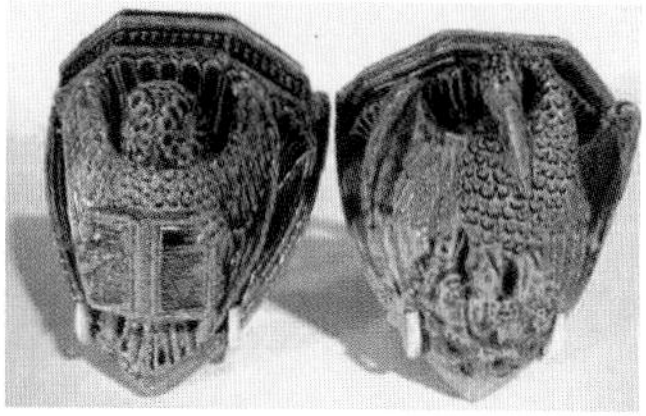

A pair of Martin Brothers stoneware wall brackets, one modelled with an owl and a book, the other with a pelican, impressed marks, one chipped, c1877, 5½in (14cm) high.
£1,100–1,300
€/ $1,700–2,000 L&E

Moorcroft

A Moorcroft bowl, decorated with Pomegranate pattern, 1913–25, 4½in (11.5cm) high.
£265–300
€/ $420–475 ⊞ PGO

A Moorcroft Macintyre jug, c1904, 7in (18cm) high.
£450–500
€/ $700–800 ⊞ MPC

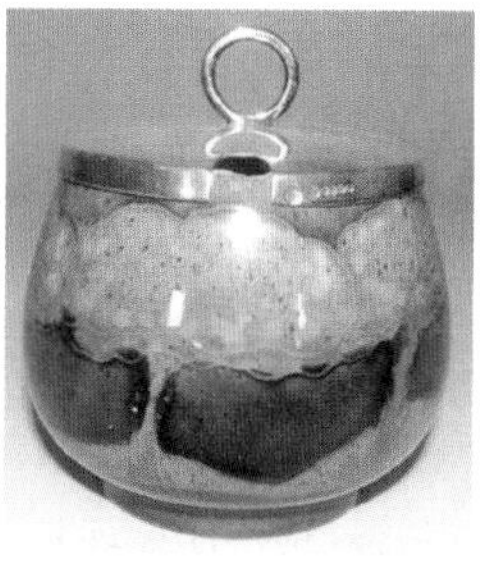

A Moorcroft jam pot, decorated with Moonlit Blue landscape pattern, with a plated cover, rim chip, impressed marks, c1925, 8½in (21.5cm) diam.
£380–450
€/ $600–700 PFK

A pair of Moorcroft Macintyre vases, the necks with panelled gilt scale, the bodies decorated with Art Nouveau poppies, printed marks, c1900, 6¼in (16cm) high.
£1,600–2,000
€/ $2,500–3,200 TEN

A Moorcroft Macintyre vase, c1904, 9in (23cm) high.
£850–950
€/ $1,300–1,500 MPC

A Moorcroft Macintyre Florian ware vase, decorated with Rose Garland pattern, printed marks and signature, c1907, 7¾in (20cm) high.
£1,500–1,800
€/ $2,400–2,800 SWO

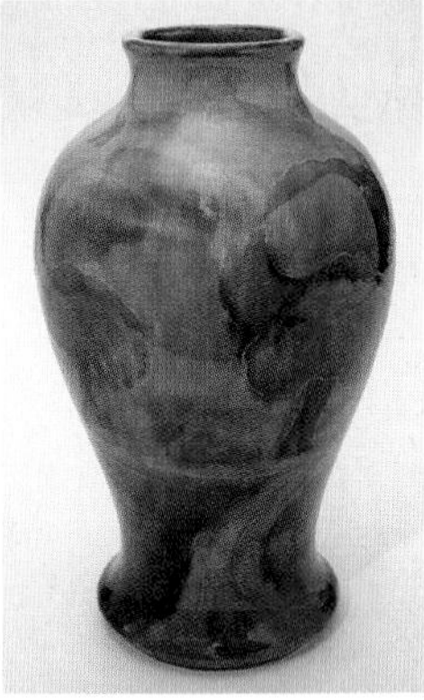

A Moorcroft vase, decorated with Hazeldene pattern, signed, impressed marks, c1914, 9in (23cm) high.
£2,700–3,000
€/ $4,300–4,700 PGO

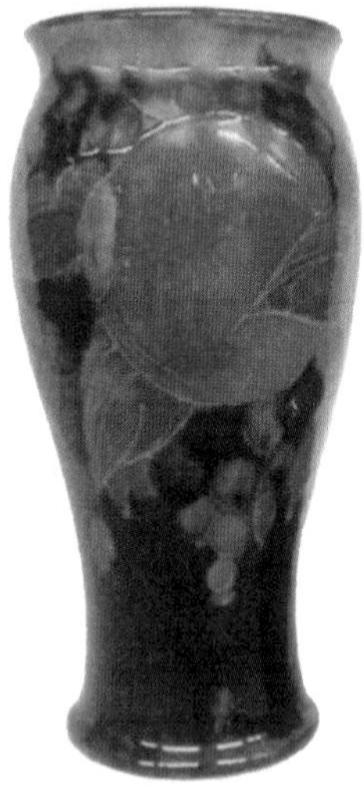

A pair of Moorcroft baluster vases, decorated with Pomegranate pattern, one damaged, painted signature and impressed factory mark, c1916, 8in (20.5cm) high.
£320–375
€/ $500–600 PF

A Moorcroft pottery vase, decorated with Leaves and Fruit pattern, impressed and painted marks and paper label, c1919, 5½in (14cm) high.
£850–1,000
€/ $1,300–1,600 TMA

► A Moorcroft flambé vase, decorated with Eventide pattern, signed, 1925, 10in (25.5cm) high.
£3,000–3,500
€/ $4,700–5,500 GAA

Pomegranate pattern

William Moorcroft's Pomegranate pattern proved one of the pottery's best-selling designs from the moment it was introduced in 1913. The earliest examples can be recognized by the use of a relatively thin cobalt blue that results in large areas of underlying buff pottery being exposed. Later examples from the 1920s and 1930s show a preference for dark cobalt blue glaze.

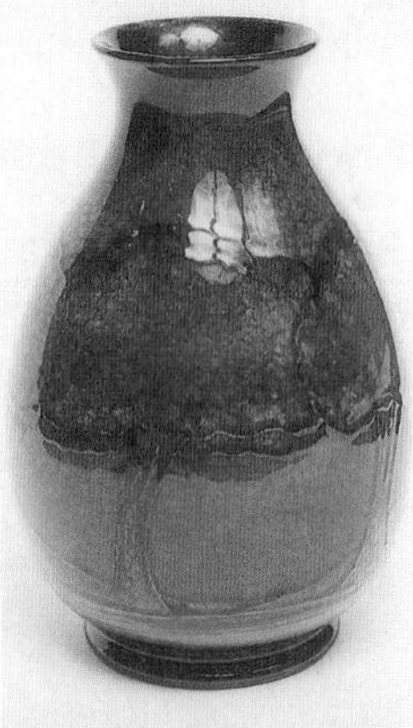

A Moorcroft vase, decorated with Pomegranate pattern, c1925, 4½in (11cm) high.
£350–400
€/ $550–650 PGO
This shape of vase is seldom seen.

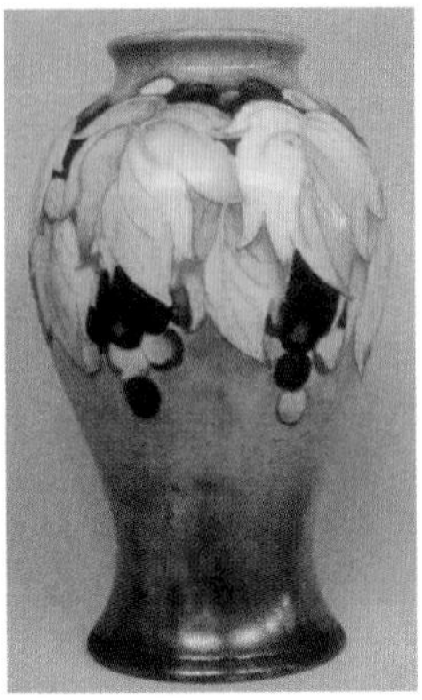

A Moorcroft salt-glazed vase, decorated with Leaf and Grape pattern, impressed mark, signed, c1928, 9½in (24cm) high.
£400–475
€/ $630–750 PF

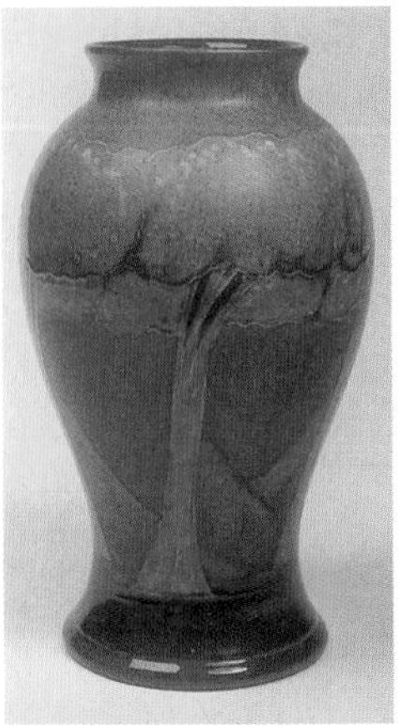

A Moorcroft baluster vase, decorated with Moonlit Blue pattern, signed, 1930, 12½in (32cm) high.
£3,500–4,000
€/ $5,500–6,300 B

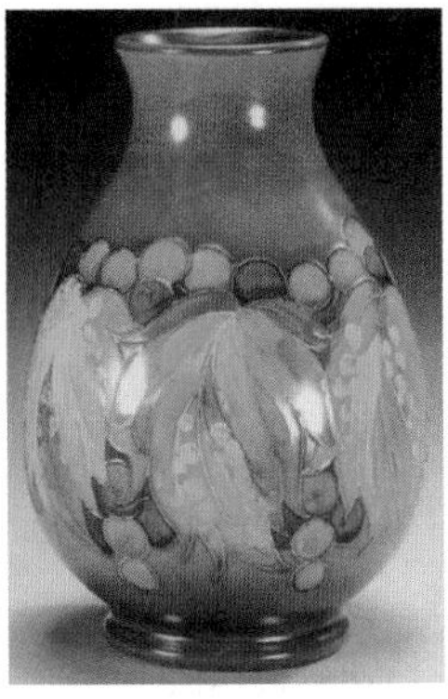

A Moorcroft pottery salt-glazed vase, decorated with Leaf and Berry pattern, impressed marks and facsimile signature, painted signature, 1930s, 9in (23cm) high.
£950–1,100
€/ $1,500–1,700 S(O)

A Moorcroft pottery vase, tube-lined with fish among blooms, impressed marks and painted signature, c1935, 5¾in (14.5cm) high.
£850–1,000
€/ $1,300–1,600 Bea

Art Nouveau Ceramics

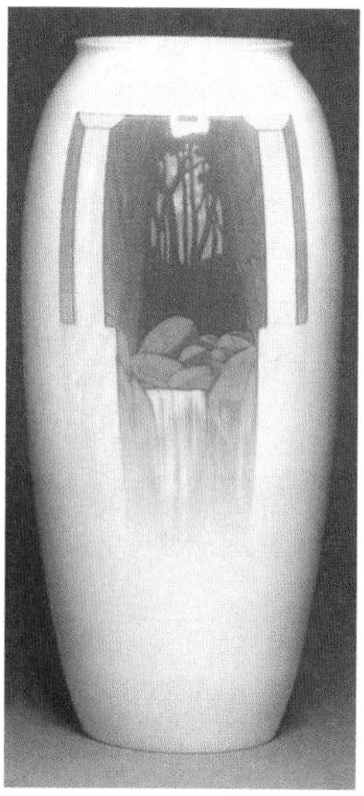

A Berlin porcelain exhibition vase, decorated by Theodor Hermann Schmuz-Baudiss, No. 12073 M.15m, impressed 7218, German, c1904, 18¾in (47.5cm) high.
£3,000–3,500
€/ $4,750–5,500 ⚒ S(NY)

Theodor Hermann Schmuz-Baudiss (1859–1942) served as a director of the underglaze department at the Königliche Porzellanmanufaktur (KPM) in Berlin from 1902–08. He was artistic director from 1908–25, the period of the firm's most innovative production. Schmuz-Baudiss developed his own unique technique of underglaze painting, creating organically shaped ceramic vessels ornamented with naturalistic and fantasy imagery articulated in subtle tones of underglaze. According to the consignor, this vase was exhibited at the St Louis Exposition of 1904.

A Minton Secessionist jardinière, sprig-moulded with stylized foliage, c1910, 10½in (26.5cm) diam.
£200–225
€/ $320–350 ⚒ G(L)

A Boch Frères vase, decorated with copper, silver and metallic glazes, Belgian, c1900, 12in (30.5cm) high.
£350–400
€/ $550–630 ⊞ DSG

The Belgian ceramics firm Boch Frères (established in 1841) was a branch of the German company Villeroy & Boch.

A Meissen *pâte-sur-pâte* vase, by Rudolf Hentschel, heightened with gilt, crossed-swords mark, impressed R151 20, c1898, 4in (10cm) high.
£1,200–1,400
€/ $1,900–2,200 ⚒ S(O)

A Minton earthenware Secessionist stick stand, slip-trailed with stylized flowering stems, printed 'Mintons Ltd no. 62', dated 1920, 22¾in (58cm) high.
£1,700–2,000
€/ $2,700–3,200 ⚒ B
Ex-Minton sale.

A Della Robbia pottery vase, decorated with bluebells and leaves, c1900, 10in (25.5cm) high.
£450–500
€/ $700–800 ⊞ RUSK

The Della Robbia Pottery produced ceramics at Birkenhead from 1894–1906, using the work of the 15th-century Florentine artist Luca Della Robbia as their inspiration.

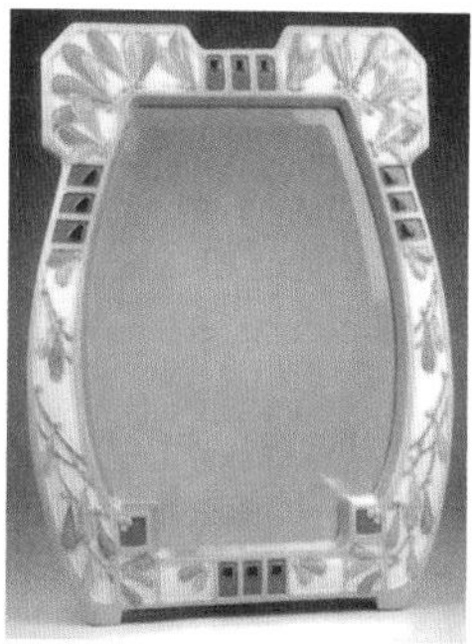

A ceramic wall mirror, by Rudolf Ditmar, the frame with raised floral and geometric decoration, factory stamp and number, Czechoslovakian, Znaim, 1900–10, 25½in (65cm) high.
£1,300–1,500
€/ $2,000–2,400 ⚒ DORO

A Foley Old Chelsea vase, c1890, 6½in (16.5cm) high.
£400–450
€/ $630–700 ⊞ RH

A terracotta plaque, by Alphonse Mucha, Czechoslovakian, c1900, 16in (40.5cm) diam.
£3,200–4,000
€/ $5,100–6,300 ⊞ ASP

A pair of Rookwood earthenware figural vases, with impressed mark, American, 1918, 17in (43cm) high.
£2,700–3,000
€/ $4,300–4,700 ⚒ S(NY)

A Newcomb College Pottery vase, by Joseph Meyer, decorated by Desiree Roman with carved oak trees, marked to underside, American, 1906, 3in (7.5cm) high.
£5,000–5,400
€/ $8,000–8,500 ⊞ CaF

A Royal Dux porcelain bonbon dish, surmounted with a figure, Bohemian, c1915, 7in (18cm) high.
£450–500
€/ $700–800 ⊞ ASP

◄ **A Villeroy & Boch Mettlach Stoneware wall charger,** German, c1890, 15in (38cm) diam.
£850–950
€/ $1,300–1,500 ⊞ ANO

A Pilkington's Royal Lancastrian vase and cover, by Richard Joyce, the cover with a fish knop, the body relief-moulded and decorated with silver and iridescent lustre with carp swimming, painted and impressed marks, date code for 1913, 9in (23cm) high.
£3,000–3,500
€/ $4,750–5,500 ⚒ WW

The value of Pilkington's Royal Lancastrian pottery is dependent upon the degree of control exhibited by the iridescent glaze. Lustrewares could prove notoriously problematic, and a uniform lustre was often the exception rather than the rule. The example shown here displays near perfection, which ensured that it would be keenly contested when offered at auction. The fish knop on the domed cover completed a splendid design that owes much to the influence of Japanese metalwork of the same period.

A Purmurend floor vase, painted with stylized flowers and foliage, painted marks, Dutch, c1900, 24½in (62cm) high.
£4,200–5,000
€/ $6,600–7,900 ⚒ B(NW)

A Rozenburg earthenware pot and cover, decorated with stylized floral motifs, painted and incised marks, Dutch, 1896, 6in (15cm) high.
£1,000–1,100
€/ $1,600–1,700 ⚒ S(Am)

A Wardle jardinière-on-stand, with tube-lined decoration, c1910, 27in (68.5cm) high.
£450–500
€/ $700–800 ⊞ ASP

Items in the Art Nouveau Ceramics section have been arranged alphabetically in factory order.

A Sicardo Ware lustre vase, by Samuel A. Weller, decorated by Jacques Sicard, small chip to rim, painted and impressed marks, American, Ohio, c1905, 7in (18cm) high.
£350–400
€/ $550–630 ⚒ S(O)

► **A porcelain bonbon dish,** by Wahliss, Austrian, c1900, 6in (15cm) diam.
£160–200
€/ $250–320
⊞ ASP

A bisque planter, Austrian, c1910, 9in (23cm) wide.
£180–200
€/ $285–320 ⊞ ASP

Art Nouveau Clocks

An Arnhem Faïence Factory earthenware clock garniture, the clock and two vases decorated with stylized flowers, stamped and painted marks, Dutch, c1920, 14in (35.5cm) high.
£2,000–2,400
€/ $3,200–3,800 S(Am)

► **A bronze mantel clock,** attributed to Jacob van den Bosch, the architectural case with a domed top supported by rows of columns, on a marble base, Dutch, c1915, 15¾in (40cm) high.
£2,000–2,200
€/ $3,200–3,500 S(Am)

A copper and enamel mantel clock, attributed to George Walton, retailer's mark for Goodyers, London, c1900, 13¼in (34cm) wide.
£1,700–2,000
€/ $2,700–3,200 B

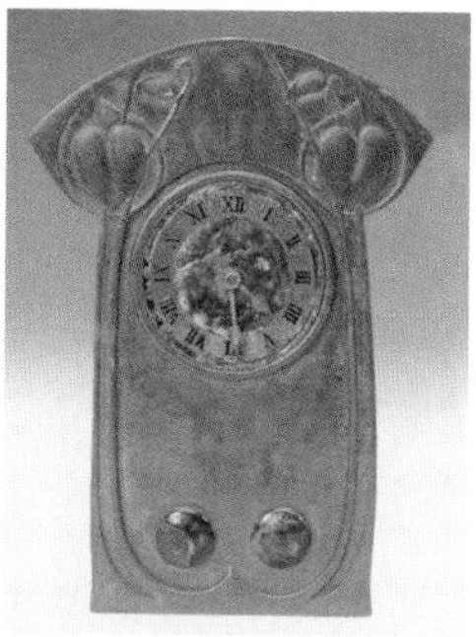

A Liberty & Co Tudric pewter mantel clock, decorated with ivy leaves and tendrils, with Lenzkirch movement, damaged, late 19thC, 8in (20.5cm) high.
£2,000–2,400
€/ $3,200–3,800 TMA

A Liberty & Co Tudric pewter mantel clock, by Archibald Knox, the enamelled-copper dial with Roman numerals, with Lenzkirch movement, c1900, 7¾in (19.5cm) high.
£1,700–2,000
€/ $2,700–3,200 G(L)

► **A silvered-brass and enamelled mantel timepiece,** possibly by George Walton, early 20thC, 8¼in (21cm) high.
£1,800–2,000
€/ $2,800–3,200
S(O)

► **A brass mantel clock,** by J. K. C. Sneltjes, with key and pendulum, surface worn, stamped monogram, Dutch, Haarlem, c1910, 12¼in (31cm) high.
£1,300–1,500
€/ $2,000–2,400 S(Am)

An ebonized hardwood and silver mantel clock, the French drum timepiece movement with a modern lever platform escapement, the front panel hallmarked Birmingham 1909, 12in (30.5cm) high.
£250–300
€/ $400–475 TMA

A silvered-metal table clock, by Wolkenstein & Glückselig, with vertical beaded bands and raised floral decoration, clockwork not functional, impressed factory stamp, Austrian, Vienna, c1915, 7¾in (19.5cm) high.
£700–850
€/ $1,100–1,350 DORO

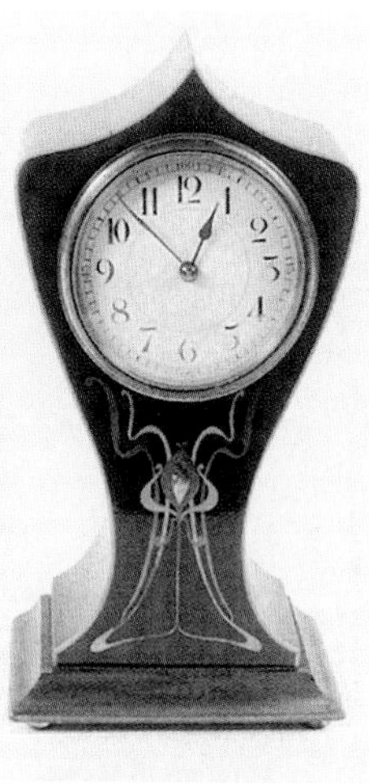

A mahogany mantel clock, late 19thC, 10in (25.5cm) high.
£170–200
€/ $270–320 GAK

◄ **An oak mantel clock,** with electroplated mounts and dial, the eight-day movement striking on a visible bell, above an opaque streaked glass panel, a presentation inscription below, c1911, 14½in (37cm) high.
£475–550
€/ $750–870 DD

Art Nouveau Figures & Busts

A bronze figure, entitled 'L'Otage', by Emmanuel Villanis, signed, French, Paris, 1895, 38½in (98cm) high.
£7,000–8,000
€/ $11,000–13,000 ⊞ MI

A bronze vase, by Charles Korschann, applied with the figure of a young woman, French, c1900, 7in (18cm) high.
£1,000–1,100
€/ $1,600–1,700 ⊞ MI

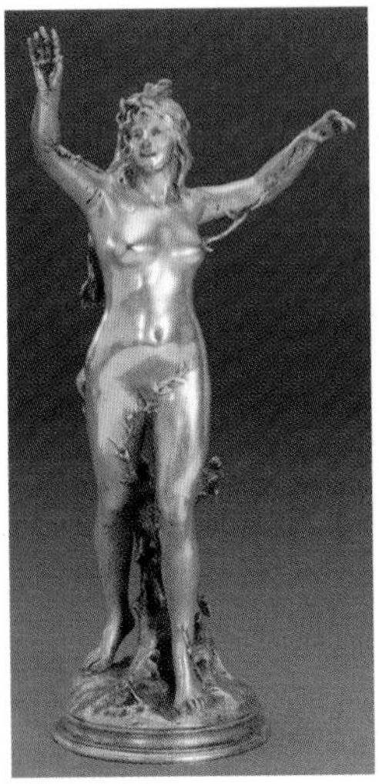

A gilt-bronze figure of The Metamorphosis of Daphne, by Raoul Larche, signed, French, 1900, 12¼in (31cm) high.
£3,000–3,400
€/ $4,700–5,800 ⊞ MI

A Goldscheider terracotta bust of a young woman, inscribed, maker's marks, c1900, 26in (66cm) high.
£1,600–1,800
€/ $2,500–2,800 ⚒ S(O)

A marble and bronze portrait bust, by Schumacher, on a marble base, French, c1900, 7in (18cm) high.
£400–450
€/ $630–700 ⊞ HUM

◄ **A bronze figure,** by R. Varenne, signed, French, Paris, c1900, 9in (23cm) high.
£800–880
€/ $1,300–1,400 ⊞ MI

A Goldscheider terracotta bust, Austrian, Vienna, c1900, 24in (61cm) high.
£1,500–1,800
€/ $2,400–2,800 ⊞ ASP

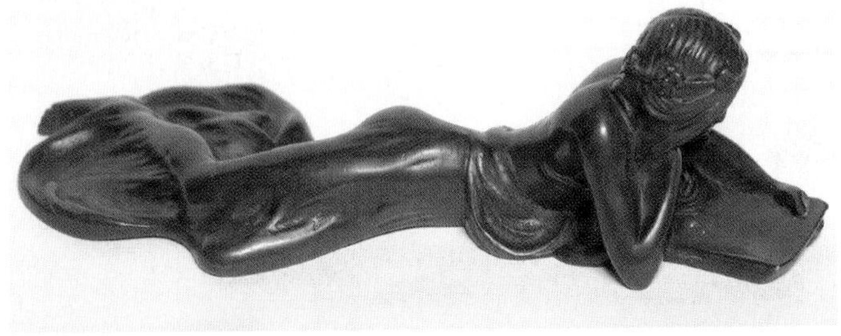

A bronze paperweight, Austrian, c1900, 5in (12.5cm) long.
£350–400
€/ $550–630 ⊞ ANO

A porcelain bust, by Pursol, probably Bohemian, c1910, 19in (48.5cm) high.
£1,400–1,600
€/ $2,200–2,00 ⊞ ASP

◄ **A Royal Dux centrepiece,** decorated in shot enamels, applied pink triangle, impressed marks, minor damage, early 20thC, 16in (40.5cm) high.
£1,100–1,300
€/ $1,700–2,000 S(O)

► **A pair of spelter fairies,** by Auguste Moreau, entitled 'L'Aurore' and 'Le Crépuscule', French, c1910, 9in (23cm) high.
£450–550
€/ $700–870 ASP

► **A Wiener Keramik figure of Girl with Roses,** by Michael Powolny, impressed marks, c1910, 11½in (29cm) high.
£4,500–5,500
€/ $7,000–8,700
DORO

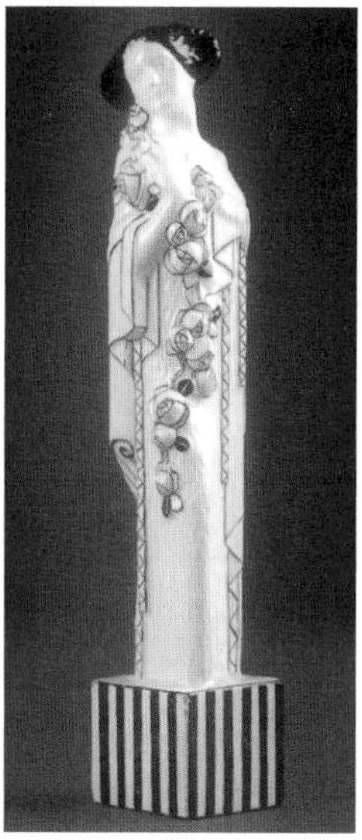

A terracotta bust, signed Barranti Pos, Italian, c1910, 15in (38cm) high.
£450–500
€/ $700–800 ASP

A Goldscheider terracotta bust, Austrian, c1915, 26in (66cm) high.
£2,000–2,200
€/ $3,200–3,500 ASP

Art Nouveau Furniture

An inlaid mahogany cabinet, by Wylie & Lochhead, design No. 6868/4004, c1900, 51¼in (130cm) wide.
£2,500–2,800
€/ $4,000–4,400 S(O)

An inlaid mahogany cabinet, with a mirror-backed open shelf above a central door inlaid with mother-of-pearl and coloured woods, flanked by open shelves, trade label for Robson & Sons, Newcastle-upon-Tyne, c1905, 52¾in (134cm) wide.
£2,200–2,500
€/ $3,500–4,000 TEN

► **A mahogany display cabinet,** c1915, 50in (127cm) wide.
£1,800–2,000
€/ $2,800–3,200 ASP

A Secessionist walnut secretaire cabinet, the fall-front enclosing a fitted interior, over four drawers, Austrian, c1912, 39½in (100.5cm) wide.
£370–450
€/ $580–700 B

A Liberty-style mahogany cabinet, c1900, 36in (91.5cm) wide.
£5,800–6,500
€/ $9,200–10,300 SAW

An oak cabinet, Dutch, c1900, 55¼in (140.5cm) wide.
£2,800–3,200
€/ $4,400–5,000 S(O)

A bentwood rocking chair, by Thonet, Austrian, late 19thC.
£500–550
€/ $800–870 APO

A walnut, ebony-strung and chequerbanded cabinet, attributed to August Ungethum, possibly to designs by Gustav Klimt, the glazed doors with copper glazing bars, two with copper medallion portraits of Apollo and Athene by Georg Klimt, c1900, 60¾in (154.5cm) wide.
£5,500–6,500
€/ $8,700–10,300 B

Ungethum was one of the foremost firms in Vienna in the early years of the 20th century. Many prominent designers including Hoffman and Moser commissioned them to produce their work, and the Wiener Werkstätte were later to become heavily involved with the firm. Other labelled furniture bearing Georg Klimt's panels have been recorded. Georg Klimt was the brother of Gustav and remains best known for producing the work of others, rather than for his own designs.

An inlaid mahogany armchair, c1905.
£520–580
€/ $820–900 APO

► **A stained beech chair,** with replaced canework seat, restored, probably Austrian, Vienna, 1900–10.
£520–620
€/ $820–980 DORO

A rosewood marquetry cabinet, by Louis Majorelle, c1900, 35in (89cm) wide.
£5,600–6,200
€/ $8,800–9,800 APO

An oak, walnut and walnut-veneered display cabinet, by Louis Majorelle, signed, with marquetry decoration, some wear, French, 1905–10, 27¼in (69cm) wide.
£7,500–8,800
€/ $11,800–14,000
DORO

An oak armchair, by Carlo Bugatti, decorated with copper, pewter and nets, parchment seat, Italian, c1900.
£4,800–6,000
€/ $7,600–9,500 DORO

A mother-of-pearl inlaid ebonized wood side chair, designed by Carlo Bugatti, decorated with hammered copper and parchment seat, Italian, c1900.
£5,000–6,000
€/ $8,000–9,500 S(Am)

An Otto Wagner bentwood armchair, by Thonet, after a design by Marcel Kammerer, with a caned seat, Austrian, c1912.
£1,500–1,800
€/ $2,400–2,800 B

An oak, pine and mahogany-veneered chest-of-drawers, by John Moffet & Son, Carlisle, c1900, 15in (38cm) wide.
£1,200–1,500
€/ $1,900–2,400 ASP

A hammered iron and copper fire screen, c1870, 33in (84cm) high.
£160–200
€/ $250–315 EAL

A mahogany double fire screen, with hand-painted decoration, c1900, 36in (91.5cm) wide.
£320–400
€/ $510–630 ASP

Henri van de Velde (1863–1957)

Henri van de Velde initially studied art in Antwerp and Brussels, later turning to architecture and designing several important buildings in Germany. In 1894 he designed his own home near Brussels, including the contents. His early furniture displays medieval influences, but within a short period of time his work began to incorporate the flowing lines that were to eventually emerge as a distinct interpretation of Art Nouveau. His contribution to the 1897 Dresden Exhibition of Arts and Crafts established his reputation as an important designer of international acclaim and led to a significant number of commissions in Germany. His early furniture tended to make use of native woods such as beech and oak, but after 1900 he began to seek out more exotic woods imported from Africa.

His approach to design shows strong similarities to that of Charles Rennie Mackintosh. Like him, his furniture would often be designed for a specific room but when viewed out of the intended setting could appear distinctly odd. Also like Mackintosh, van de Velde designed furniture with a white-painted finish. An all-rounder, he also turned his attention to ceramics, metalwork, jewellery, textiles, wallpaper and book and magazine illustrations.

A fruitwood marquetry hall stand, c1900, 46in (117cm) wide.
£3,500–4,200
€/ $5,500–6,600 S(NY)

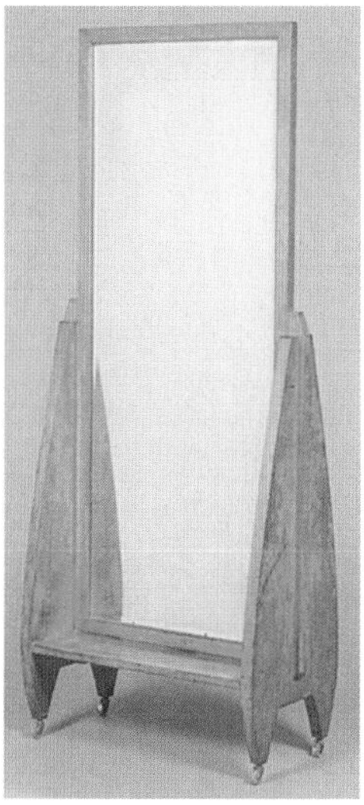

A sycamore dressing mirror, by Henri van de Velde, Belgian, c1905, 31½in (80cm) wide.
£4,300–5,200
€/ $6,800–8,200 S

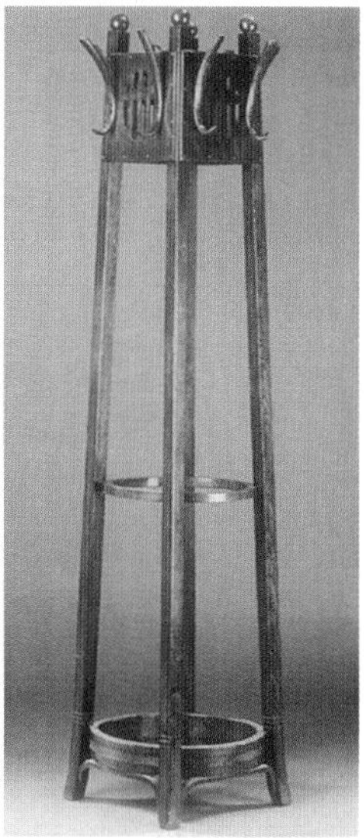

A bentwood hat and coat stand, design attributed to Joseph Hoffmamn, Austrian, early 20thC, 79½in (202cm) high.
£1,000–1,100
€/ $1,600–1,700 S(O)

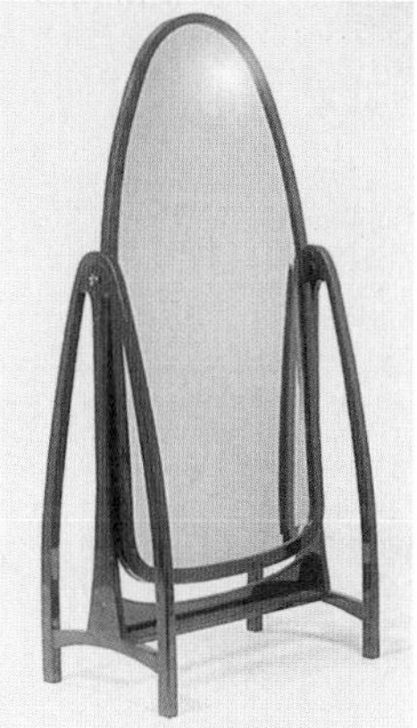

A stained beechwood adjustable hall mirror, probably by Thonet, with bevelled glass, restored, Austrian, Vienna, c1910, 64¼in (163cm) high.
£1,800–2,200
€/ $2,800–3,500 DORO

An oak settle, the back carved with a stylized foliate panel flanked by inset embossed copper panels, with hinged seat, c1910, 50¼in (127.5cm) wide.
£750–875
€/ $1,200–1,400 Bri

An oak sofa, the apron decorated with incised scrollwork, German, c1905, 41in (104cm) wide.
£850–1,000
€/ $1,300–1,600 B

► **A fruitwood stool,** with caned seat, minor damage, American, early 20thC, 20in (51cm) high.
£1,200–1,400
€/ $1,900–2,200 S(Am)

A carved mahogany mirror-back sideboard, by Shapland & Petter, decorated with glass panels overlaid with copper, c1900, 54in (137cm) wide.
£2,700–3,000
€/ $4,300–4,700 ASP

An oak mirror-back sideboard, with label for Gullachsen & Son, Newcastle-on-Tyne, c1900, 67in (170cm) wide.
£250–300
€/ $400–475 B(Ch)

A beechwood salon table, by Thonet, No. 1, with veneered top, repaired, designed pre-1888, 32½in (82.5cm) wide.
£750–875
€/ $1,100–1,400 DORO

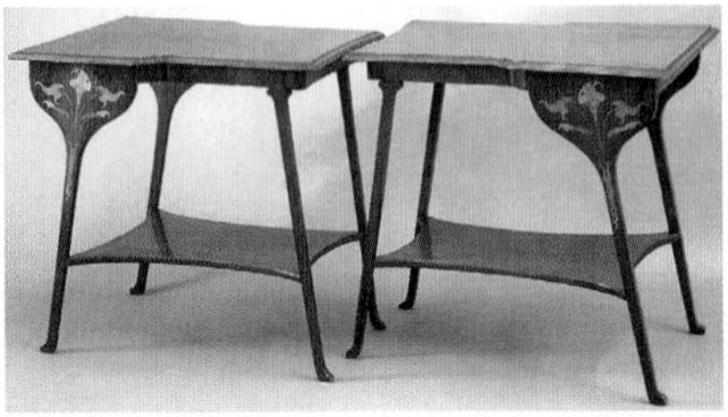

A pair of mahogany side tables, inlaid with lilies, c1900, 30in (76cm) wide.
£800–950
€/ $1,300–1,500 G(L)

An oak, beechwood and marquetry folding occasional table, by Emile Gallé, the top inlaid with a thistle and the Cross of Lorraine, on a pierced scrollwork base, signed, French, early 20thC, 28in (71cm) wide.
£6,000–6,600
€/ $9,500–10,500 S

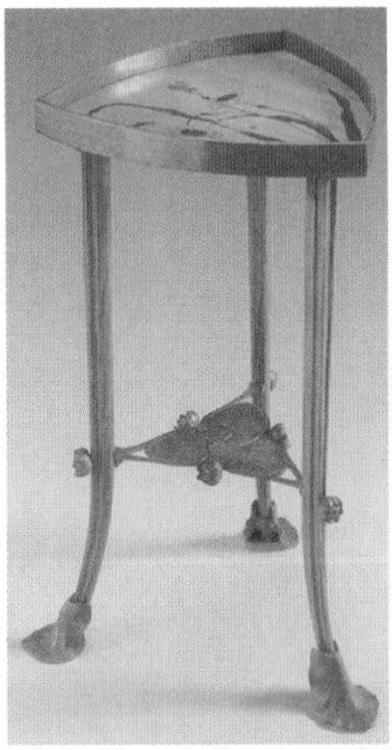

A fruitwood and bronze two-tier lily pad table, by Louis Majorelle, French, c1900, 17½in (44.5cm) wide.
£4,500–5,000
€/ $7,000–8,000 S(NY)

► **A walnut, satinwood and marquetry occasional table,** attributed to Louis Majorelle, the top inlaid with trailing branches and leaves, French, c1910, 25½in (65cm) diam.
£2,500–3,000
€/ $4,000–4,700 B

A pair of Gaudi-style cast-iron tables, with marble tops, c1900, 19¾in (50cm) diam.
£1,700–2,000
€/ $3,700–3,200 S(Am)

Art Nouveau Glass

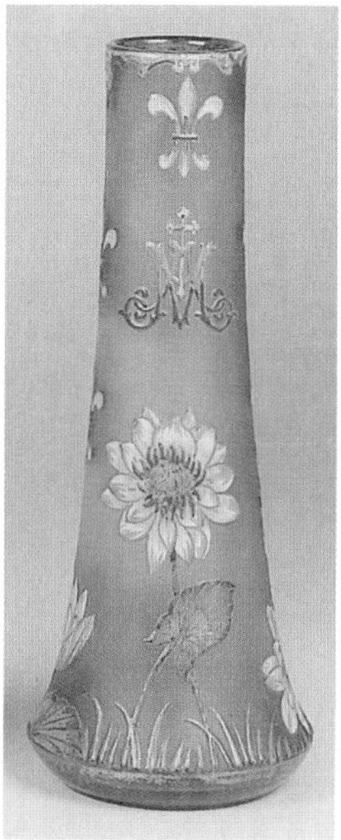

A Burgun, Schverer & Co glass vase, polychrome-decorated with raised flowers, fleurs-de-lys and central monogram 'AM' with a cross, on a matted textured ground, gold signature with thistle, Cross of Lorraine, French, 1897–1903, 15¾in (40cm) high.
£3,000–3,300
€/ $4,700–5,200 DORO

The Lorraine glass-making firm of Burgun, Schverer & Co was established in 1711 and is still operating today under the name Verrerie de Meisenthal. Emile Gallé served a three-year apprenticeship with the company during the late 1860s, and in 1885 they entered into a contract to produce glass for Gallé's own company. Burgun, Schverer & Co are known for their cameo wares with decoration influenced by the local flora, and decorative techniques included acid cutting, foil inclusions, gilding and the use of overlay.

A Cristal Parisiana silver-gilt-mounted glass vase, the flattened body carved on each side with formalized narcissi against a textured bronzed ground, the pierced mounts cast with waterlilies, bulrushes and leaves, etched mark, French, c1900, 8½in (21.5cm) high.
£850–950
€/ $1,300–1,500 S

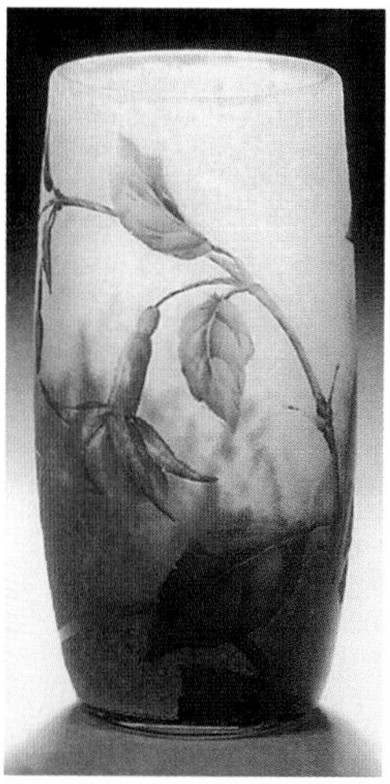

A Daum cameo glass vase, the frosted glass enamelled and etched with fuchsia, signed, Cross of Lorraine, French, c1900, 5in (12.5cm) high.
£1,500–1,800
€/ $2,400–2,800 S(O)

An Emile Gallé opalescent cameo glass dish, carved and etched with wild poppies, incised signature, French, c1900, 16in (40.5cm) wide.
£5,000–5,500
€/ $8,000–8,700 S(O)

A Daum cameo glass vase, decorated with a polychrome wooded landscape, signed, Cross of Lorraine, French, c1900, 5in (12.5cm) high.
£1,200–1,400
€/ $1,900–2,200 HOLL

A Daum cameo glass coupe, decorated in high relief with blackberries, engraved mark, Cross of Lorraine, 1912, 6¼in (16cm) high.
£8,500–10,000
€/ $13,500–15,800 S(P)

A Emile Gallé cameo glass vase, with overlaid decoration of leaves and berries, French, c1900, 7in (18cm) high.
£1,000–1,100
€/ $1,600–1,700 ASA

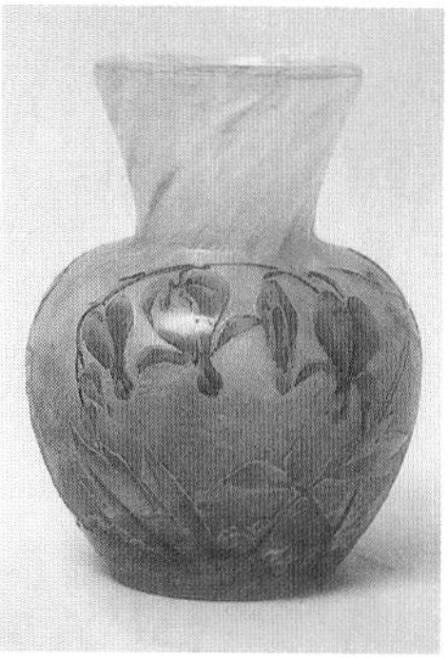

A Daum glass vase, acid-etched and carved with pendant flowers, French, c1900, 3in (7.5cm) high.
£1,100–1,300
€/ $1,700–2,000 OND

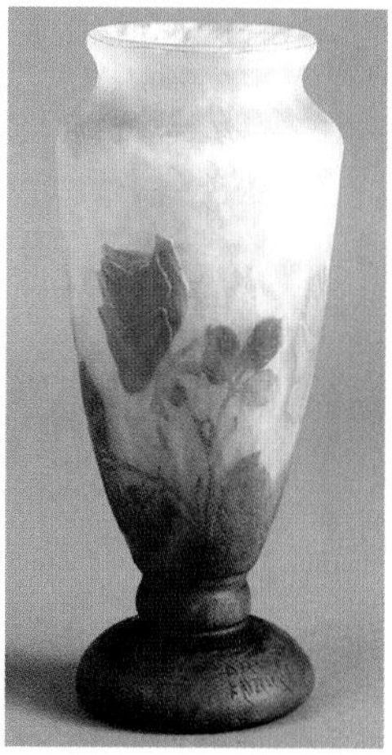

A Daum cameo glass vase, acid-etched and carved with roses and foliage, signed, Cross of Lorraine, French, early 20thC, 7¼in (18.5cm) high.
£750–875
€/ $1,200–1,400 SWO

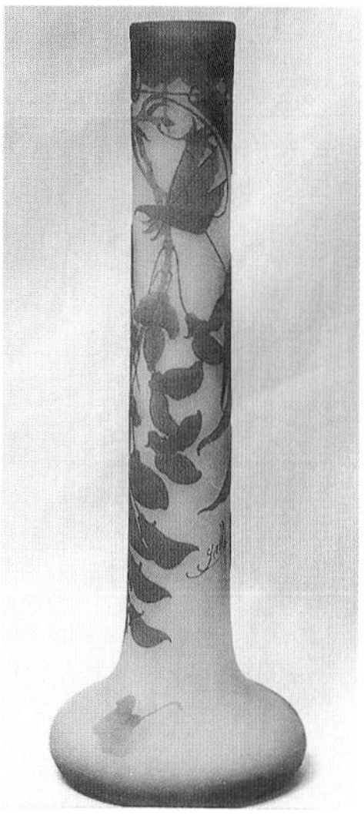

An Emile Gallé cameo glass vase, with acid-etched floral decoration, French, c1900, 14in (35.5cm) high.
£1,100–1,300
€/ $1,700–2,000 OND

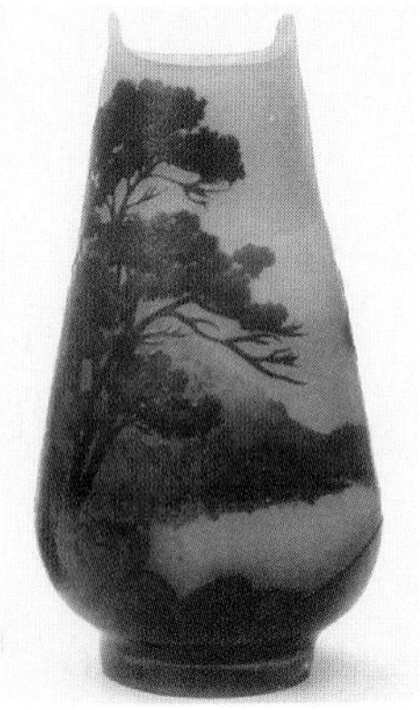

An Emile Gallé cameo glass vase, acid-etched with a wooded mountain scene, engraved signature, French, c1900, 8in (20.5cm) high.
£1,700–2,000
€/ $2,700–3,200 B

An Emile Gallé vase, with enamelled and acid-etched decoration, the flowerheads with applied cabochons, French, c1900, 8in (20.5cm) high.
£1,900–2,100
€/ $3,000–3,300 AFD

Miller's Compares

I. An Emile Gallé cameo glass vase, carved with waterlilies and leaves, cameo mark, French, early 20thC, 7½in (19cm) high.
£1,300–1,500
€/ $2,000–2,400 S

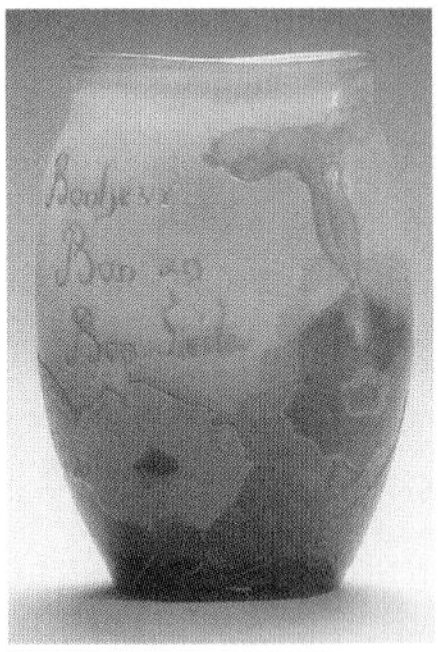

II. An Emile Gallé *marqueterie-sur-verre* and *verre parlant* cameo glas vase, inscribed 'Bonheur Bon an Bon Siècle Gallé', c1900, 5½in (14cm) high.
£5,700–6,300
€/ $9,000–10,000
S(NY)

Item II is 2in (5cm) smaller and less interesting in form than Item I, but has the advantage of the *marqueterie-sur-verre* technique whereby molten glass is carefully embedded into the heated surface to form a flowerhead or leaf design, and as a *vase parlant* is able to speak for itself through its hand-carved inscription. Item I is a standard, industrially-produced vase with overlay and acid carving. Although the decoration is well detailed and polished, it is ultimately less desirable.

A Legras glass vase, enamelled and acid-etched with thistles, signed, French, c1900, 18in (45.5cm) high.
£2,700–3,000
€/ $4,300–4,800 S(Am)

A Legras glass vase, enamelled and acid-cut with full-blown poppies, painted signature, French, early 20thC, 13¾in (35cm) high.
£700–800
€/ $1,100–1,300 S(O)

A Loetz Papillon vase, with all-over iridescent dappling, Austrian, c1890, 6½in (16.5cm) high.
£600–680
€/ $950–1,000 AFD

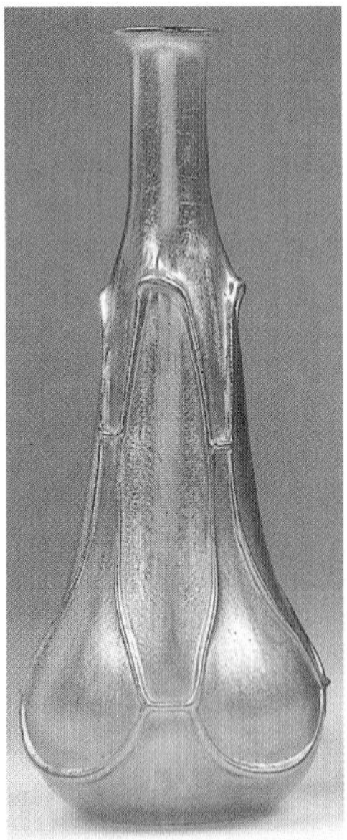

A Loetz iridescent glass vase, decorated with applied raised threads, Austrian, c1900, 9½in (24cm) high.
£1,000–1,200
€/ $1,600–1,900 DORO

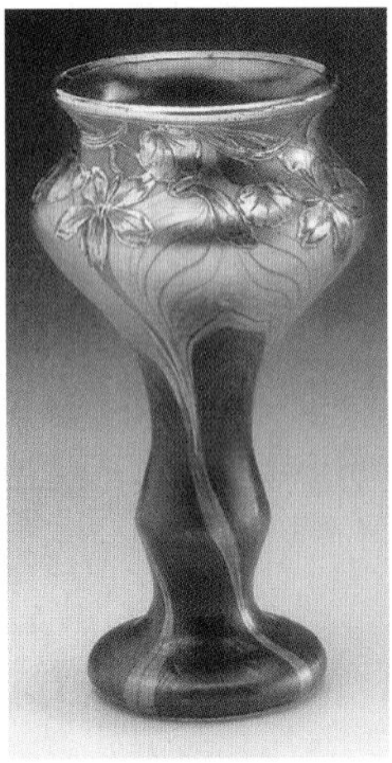

A Loetz iridescent glass vase, decorated with cyclamen, Austrian, c1900, 5¼in (13.5cm) high.
£1,300–1,500
€/ $2,000–2,400 S(P)

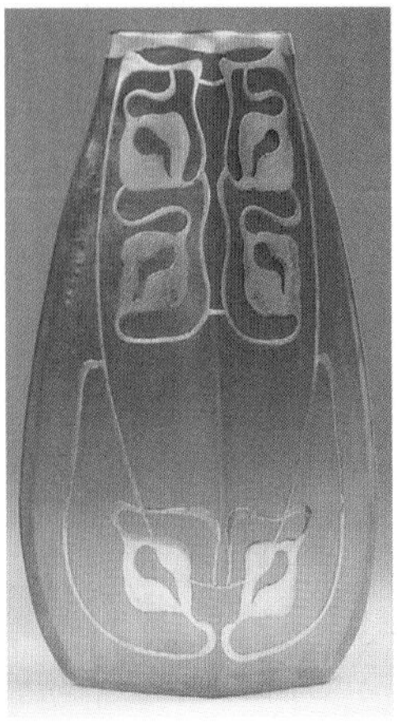

A Loetz iridescent glass vase, with applied silver decoration, ground out inscribed pontil mark, Austrian, c1900, 8¾in (22cm) high.
£3,000–3,500
€/ $4,700–5,500 DORO

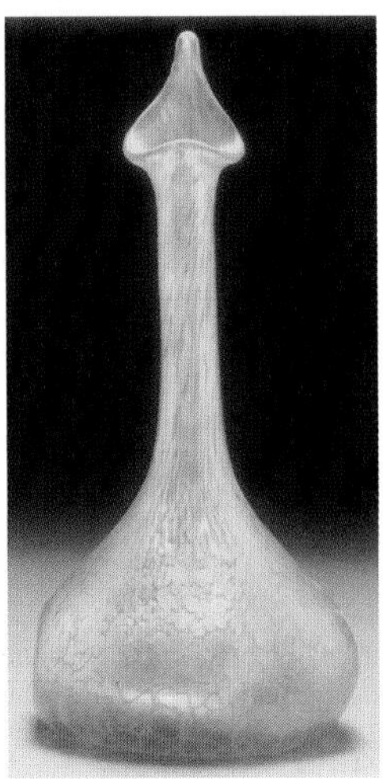

◄ A Loetz goose-neck lustre vase, Austrian, c1900, 9½in (24cm) high.
£1,200–1,400
€/ $1,900–2,200 S

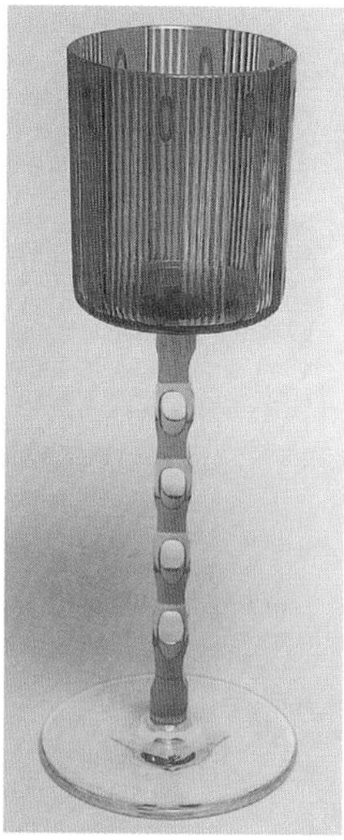

A hock glass, designed by Otto Prutscher, early 20thC, 8½in (21.5cm) high.
£2,800–3,200
€/ $4,400–5,000 ⊞ ALiN
Otto Prutscher (Austrian, 1880–1949) designed many pieces for the Wiener Werkstätte.

A Tiffany Favrile glass vase, American, 1899–1920, 5½in (14cm) high.
£1,500–1,800
€/ $2,400–2,800 ⚒ S(NY)

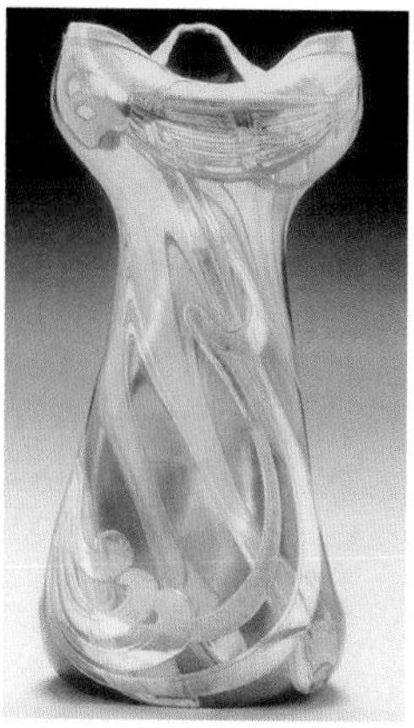

A silver-mounted iridescent glass vase, the pierced overlay incorporating wave, flower and strapwork motifs, probably Austrian, c1905, 7in (18cm) high.
£2,000–2,200
€/ $3,200–3,500 ⚒ S

A glass dish, in a silver-plated mount, c1900, 6in (15cm) diam.
£430–475
€/ $680–750 ⊞ SHa

A glass vase, c1900, 4½in (11.5cm) high.
£250–275
€/ $400–430 ⊞ SHa

A Tiffany Favrile glass dresser box, American, c1910, 5¾in (14.5cm) wide.
£380–450
€/ $600–700 ⚒ DuM

A pair of iridescent glass vases, Bohemian, with silver mounts hallmarked London 1906, 7½in (19cm) high.
£100–125
€/ $160–200 ⚒ PFK

► A bronze and glass vase, French, c1900, 6in (15cm) high.
£450–550
€/ $710–870 ⊞ ASP

A glass vase, c1900, 10in (25.5cm) diam.
£430–475
€/ $680–750 ⊞ SHa

A Tiffany Favrile bowl and plate, American, 1890–1910, plate 7in (18cm) diam.
£750–900
€/ $1,200–1,400 ⊞ ASA

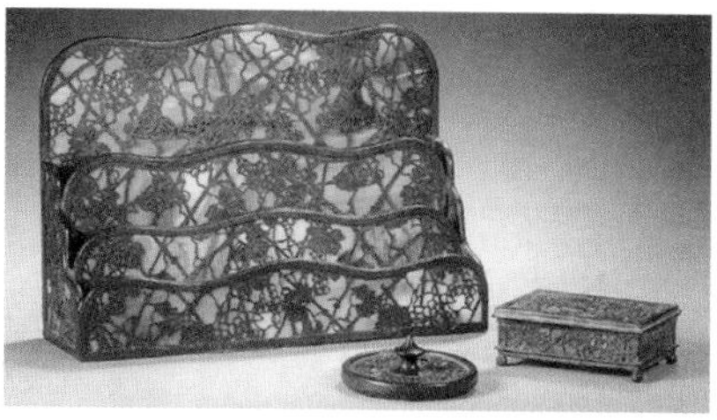

A Tiffany three-piece glass desk set, comprising a stationery rack, stamp box and paperweight, glass missing from paperweight, stamped, American, early 20thC, rack 12½in (32cm) wide.
£1,700–2,000
€/ $2,700–3,200 ⚒ S(O)
Popular during the first two decades of the 20th century as 'Wedding Gift Tiffany', desk sets can be found in 15 various designs including Grape-Vine (above), Pine-Needle, Venetian, American Indian, Louis XVI, Chinese and Adam. The minimum number of pieces deemed to form a set was nine and would include blotter ends, inkstand, pen tray, paper rack, paper knife, rocker blotter, memo pad holder, stamp or utility box and calendar. However, all the pieces were priced and sold individually, and therefore a set can comprise any number of pieces.

Art Nouveau Jewellery

A 9ct gold bracelet, set with turquoise and blister pearls, c1905, 6in (15cm) long.
£600–680
€/ $950–1,000 ⊞ ANO

A 15ct gold brooch, set with a turquoise, c1890, 3in (7.5cm) wide.
£400–450
€/ $630–700 ⊞ ANO

An enamelled brooch, modelled as a lady's head, flowers in her hair, c1890, 1in (2.5cm) wide.
£1,000–1,100
€/ $1,600–1,700 ⊞ NBL

An enamelled triple-leaf brooch, set with pearls, Russian, c1890, 1¼in (3cm) wide.
£1,200–1,400
€/ $1,900–2,200 ⊞ NBL

A 15ct gold brooch, set with a citrine and two diamonds, within a seed pearl border, above a pearl drop, c1900.
£280–325
€/ $440–515 ⚒ BWL

A silver brooch, set with a cabochon, German, 1900–05, 1¼in (3cm) wide.
£270–300
€/ $430–475 ⊞ ANO

A Wiener Werkstätte silver brooch, by Koloman Moser, set with a turquoise within an openwork setting of foliage and rods, the reverse with monogram 'KM', rose mark, Diana's head mark and assay mark, Austrian, designed 1906, 1¾in (4.5cm) high.
£3,800–4,500
€/ $6,000–7,000 ⚒ DORO

A Child & Child pendant necklace, attributed to Edward Burne-Jones, the enamelled wing motif set with a baroque pearl, above two pearl drops, the gold link chain set with six further pearls at intervals, c1900, in a green leather fitted case.
£2,000–2,400
€/ $3,200–3,800 ⚒ G(L)

A 9ct gold Liberty & Co pendant, set with a turquoise, 1900–05, 1¼in (3cm) high.
£450–500
€/ $700–800 ⊞ ANO

A silver and *plique-à-jour* enamel pendant, by Theodor Fahrner, c1900, 1½in (4cm) high.
£600–680
€/ $950–1,000 ⊞ ANO

◄ A silver, marcasite and ivory pendant, by Theodor Fahrner, with enamel and chrysoprase stone, German, c1910, 2in (5cm) long.
£720–800
€/ $1,100–1,300 ⊞ RGA

The German jeweller Theodor Fahrner (1868–1928) produced large quantities of fine jewellery in an abstract Art Nouveau style.

► A silver and carved ivory pendant, German, c1910, 1½in (4cm) high.
£225–250
€/ $350–400 ⊞ RGA

Art Nouveau Lighting

A Daum cameo glass *plafonnier*, etched with hazel leaves and nuts, cameo mark, Cross of Lorraine, French, c1900, 15½in (39.5cm) diam, with twisted hanging cords and metal hooks.
£2,200–2,500
€/ $3,500–4,000 ⚒ S(O)

A leaded glass and bronze table lamp, attributed to Duffner & Kimberly, with finial, impressed 'D', American, c1910, 22½in (57cm) high.
£5,300–6,000
€/ $8,300–9,500 ⚒ S(NY)

A Limoges enamel lamp base, by Camille Fauré, French, c1910, 6¼in (16cm) high.
£1,200–1,300
€/ $1,900–2,000 ⊞ ANO

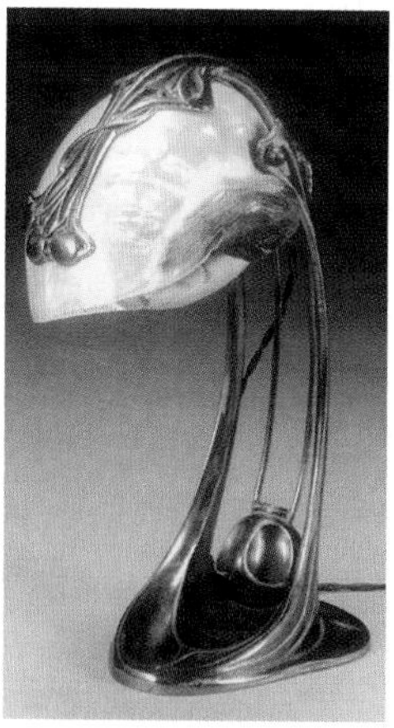

A silvered-metal and shell Nautilus lamp, in the style of Gustav Gurschner, the hinged shade held by twin rods terminating in a counterweight, stamped mark, German, early 20thC, 10¾in (27.5cm) high.
£4,500–5,000
€/ $7,000–8,000 ⚒ S(O)

A Muller Frères cameo glass lamp, acid-etched with anemones, signed, c1900, 22¾in (58cm) high.
£5,000–6,000
€/ $8,000–9,500 ⚒ B

Items in the Art Nouveau Lighting section have been arranged alphabetically by maker, with non-specific pieces appearing at the end.

A Tiffany Favrile glass and bronze Nautilus lamp, impressed mark, American, 1899–1920, 13¼in (33.5cm) high.
£9,000–11,000
€/ $14,200–17,400 S(NY)

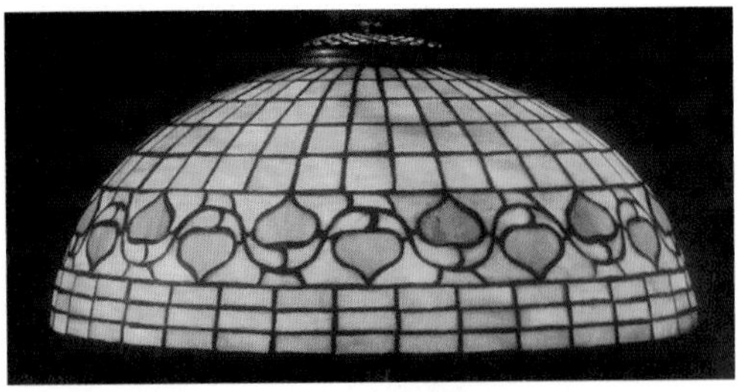

A Tiffany Favrile glass shade, decorated with acorns, impressed mark, American, 1899–1928, 16in (40.5cm) diam.
£5,000–6,000
€/ $8,000–9,500 S(NY)

A Tiffany bronze student lamp, rope coil decoration applied around the oil reservoir and base, with iridescent glass shade, converted for electricity, American, c1910, 28¾in (73cm) high.
£2,800–3,300
€/ $4,400–5,200 B

A patinated-metal and mottled glass two-light table lamp, modelled with two grotesque winged beasts holding pendant lamp shades in their mouths, the body with embossed bronze patinated sides and mounted with leaded glass, c1900, 25in (63.5cm) high.
£3,000–3,300
€/ $4,700–5,200 S(O)

A table lamp, with a leaded glass shade decorated with wistaria, on a reeded patinated-metal stem and arabesque-cast base, c1900, 29½in (75cm) high.
£9,000–10,000
€/ $14,000–16,000 S

A spelter lamp, by E. Villanis, modelled as Fleur de Bohème, French, c1900, 38in (96.5cm) high.
£900–1,000
€/ $1,400–1,600 ASP

Always check that electric lighting conforms to the current safety regulations before using.

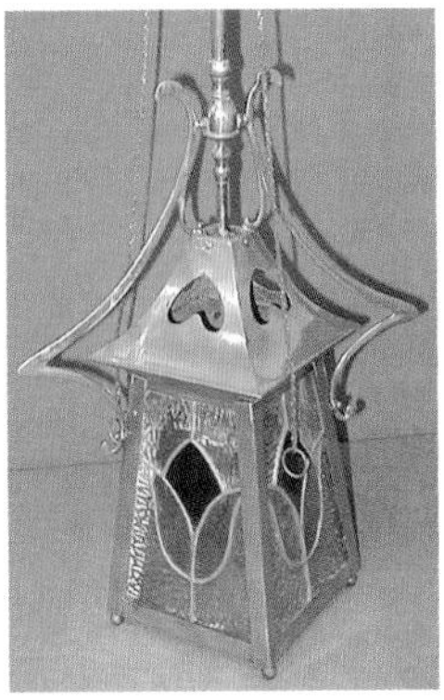

► **A brass 'downer' gas lantern,** with on/off pulls and leaded lights with stylized tulip decoration, early 20thC, 35in (89cm) high.
£300–350
€/ $475–550 TMA

A brass six-arm chandelier, with replacement etched-glass bell shades, Continental, 1910–20, 23in (58.5cm) diam.
£550–600
€/ $870–950 JeH

The Elton John Collection

Elton John unleashed his collection of Decorative Arts onto the world stage at Sotheby's in September 1988. The biggest prices in the four-volume catalogue – now a collector's item in its own right – are to be found in the one devoted to Art Nouveau and Art Deco. Elton John was by no means the only major player in this field: the competition could be tough when up against the likes of Rod Stewart, Joan Collins, Michael Caine and Barbra Streisand. Elton gathered together the best that money could buy and although he purchased from the top dealers he had the distinct advantage of buying on a rising market. More importantly, his decision to sell proved most astute as by the early 1990s the market began to falter in tandem with the Japanese economy and French art glass in particular proved a significant casualty. However, in 1988 the art market was bathed in sunshine. There was plenty of the 'feel good' factor and, as far as the London scene was concerned, no shortage of people with 'loadsamoney'. Elton's collection attracted plenty of bidding from overseas dealers and collectors with several of the top prices paid by American and Japanese buyers.

The sculpture section was led by two bronze and ivory figures by Demêtre Chiparus, with 'The Temple Dancer' enticing a bid of £33,000 (€/ $52,000) and another exotic dancer titled 'Yambo' achieving £48,400 (€/ $76,000). Two Tiffany leaded glass table lamps saw plenty of transatlantic competition with a 'Peacock' lamp selling for £37,400 (€/ $59,000) and a miniature 'Wistaria' lamp secured for £36,300 (€/ $57,000). The most sought-after piece of glass was a Daum internally decorated, applied and carved glass vase which soared to £56,100 (€/ $89,000). The pieces which achieved the highest prices, however, were a McCulloch carpet, designed by John Henry Dearle and woven at the Merton Abbey workshops of Morris & Co, which sold for £71,000 (€/ $112,000) and a salon suite dating from c1925, designed by Raoul Dufy and covered in highly decorative Aubusson tapestries which achieved £90,200 (€/ $143,000). Both pieces were functional as well as decorative, although at these prices one wonders if their new owners were afraid to walk or sit on them!

Eric Knowles

Art Nouveau Metalware

A WMF silver-plated fruit bowl, with glass liner, c1910, 9in (23cm) diam.
£180–200
€/ $285–315 ⊞ TDG

A silver-plated trinket box, with enamel-inset lid and Secessionist design, Continental, early 20thC, 4in (10cm) wide.
£100–120
€/ $160–190 ⚒ G(L)

A silver box, by Horton & Allday, c1904, 4in (10cm) wide.
£450–500
€/ $700–800 ⊞ ANO

A silver leaf-shaped centrepiece, by Georg Jensen, decorated with berries, Danish, Copenhagen c1915, 4in (10cm) wide.
£400–500
€/ $630–800 ⚒ BUK

► A silver cigarette case, by Kate Harris, London c1904, 4in (10cm) wide.
£380–425
€/ $600–675 ⊞ ANO

A copper box, with liner and back stop, c1915, 17in (43cm) wide.
£160–180
€/ $250–280 ⊞ ASP

Items in the Art Nouveau Metalware section have been arranged in alphabetical order.

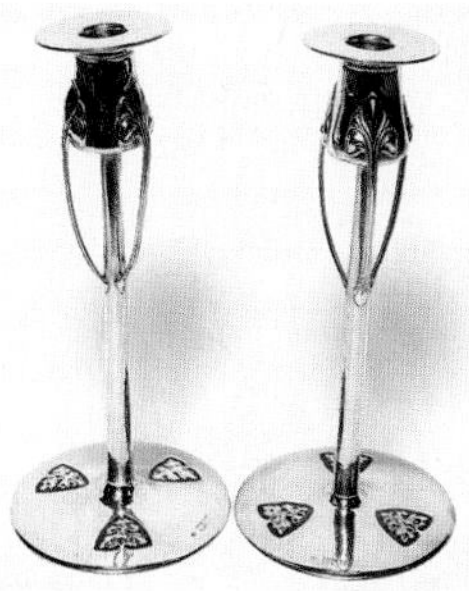

A pair of Mappin & Webb silver and enamel candlesticks, London 1910–11, 9in (23cm) high.
£4,000–4,500
€/ $6,300–7,000 ⊞ NS

A WMF pewter centrepiece, with glass liner, stamped, German, early 20thC, 13½in (34.5cm) wide.
£650–720
€/ $1,000–1,200 ⚒ S(O)

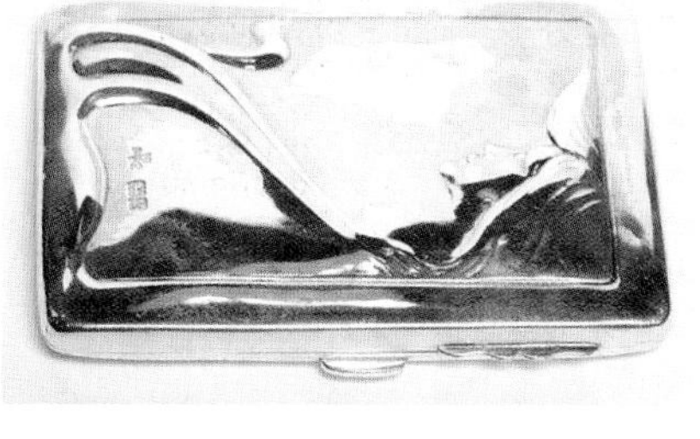

A Liberty & Co pewter biscuit box, decorated with three rows of stylized plant leaves, the cover with twin lug handle, stamped 'English Pewter 0194', c1900, 5½in (14cm) high.
£380–450
€/ $600–700 ⚒ G(L)

A silver and cut-glass trinket box, Birmingham 1903, 4in (10cm) wide.
£120–135
€/ $190–215 ⊞ BrL

A silver centrepiece, with moulded edge, twin foliate scroll and tendril handles and indented bead decoration, presentation inscription, Sheffield 1907, 17¾in (45cm) wide, 58oz.
£750–900
€/ $1,200–1,400 ⚒ TRM

A silver lidded jug, with floral decoration in relief, the knop modelled as a bust, gilt interior, master's mark 'MT', Russian, Moscow c1900, 9in (23cm) high.
£330–400
€/ $520–630 ⚒ DORO

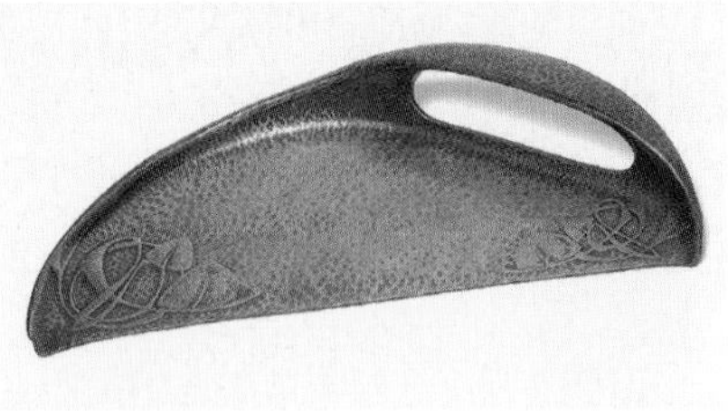

A Liberty & Co pewter crumb tray, by Archibald Knox, c1910, 10in (25.5cm) wide.
£250–280
€/ $400–440 ⊞ AFD

► **A Gorham Manufacturing Co silver three-handled presentation cup,** retailed by Spaulding & Co, Chicago, chased with strapwork enclosing trefoils, etched on one side with a stag, the reverse with presentation inscription, marked and numbered, American, Providence, 1901, 12½in (32cm) high.
£1,400–1,600
€/ $2,200–2,500 ⚒ S(NY)

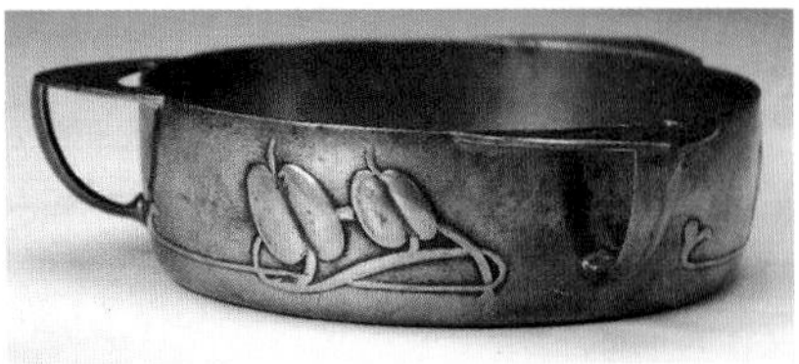

A Liberty & Co Tudric pewter three-handled dish, with stylized foliate decoration, c1900, 6in (15cm) wide.
£280–325
€/ $440–500 ⚒ TMA

► **A WMF pewter dish,** German, c1904, 10in (25.5cm) wide.
£850–950
€/ $1,300–1,500 ⊞ SHa

A silver frame, Sheffield 1902, 13in (33cm) high.
£380–430
€/ $600–680 ⊞ BrL

A silver photograph frame, with repoussé decoration of a woman picking apples, Birmingham 1904, 9½in (24cm) high.
£320–375
€/ $500–600 ⚒ L

A silver double inkstand, by Omar Ramsden and Alwyn Carr, the two lids mounted with wirework and hardstone finials, over hammered sides, a floral cartouche with monogram, the flared base with a penholder inscribed 'Omar Ramsden et Alwyn Carr Me Fecerunt', London 1905, 7¾in (19.5cm) wide, 15.5oz.
£3,200–3,800
€/ $5,000–6,000 ⚒ G(L)

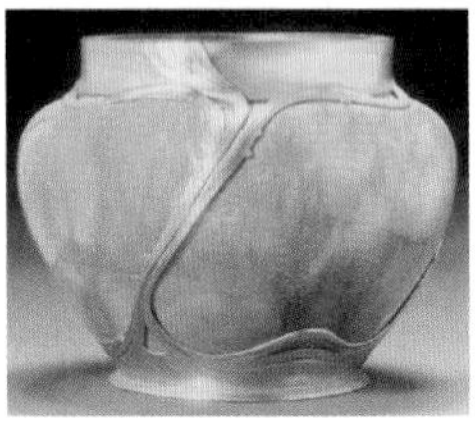

An Orivit gilt-metal-mounted pottery jardinière, the mounts cast and pierced as waves and bubbles, mounts stamped, German, 7¼in (18.5cm) high.
£1,300–1,500
€/ $2,000–2,400 ⚒ S

► **A Liberty & Co Tudric pewter and glass claret jug,** decorated with pomegranate motifs, c1907, 7in (18cm) high.
£270–330
€/ $430–520 ⚒ G(L)

A WMF copper lidded jug, cast in low relief with stylized foliage, cast brass handle, stamped mark and numeral, German, early 20thC, 12in (30.5cm) high.
£275–325
€/ $430–520 ⚒ GH

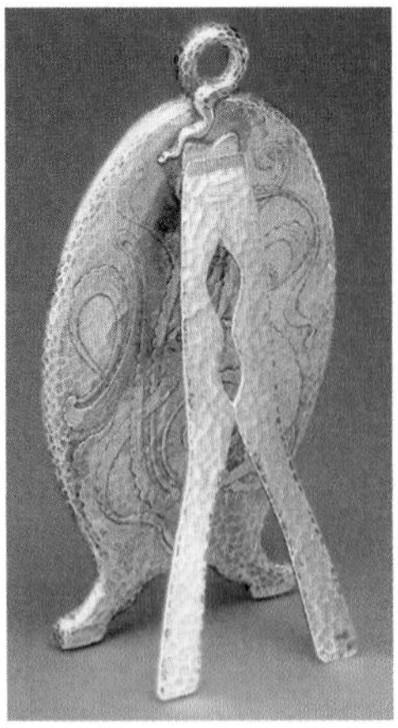

A Tiffany Japanese-style silver easel mirror, the spot-hammered surface etched with tentacle monogram 'NKS', pierced easel and serpent-form loop finial, marked and numbered, American, c1881, 8½in (21.5cm) high.
£1,800–2,200
€/ $2,800–3,500 ⚒ S(NY)

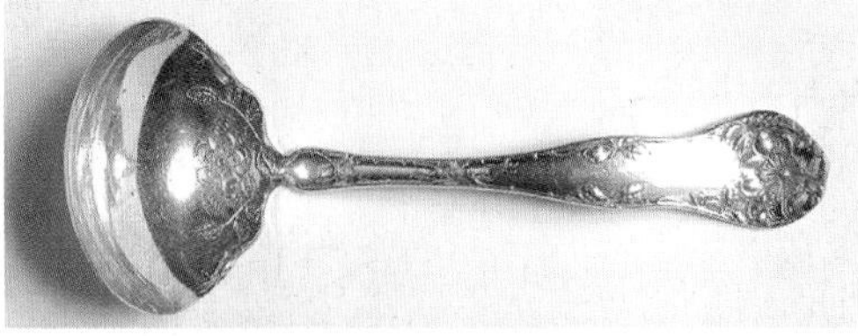

◄ **A silver-plated ladle,** American, 1900–05, 6in (15cm) long.
£110–125
€/ $175–200 ⊞ ANO

A silver christening mug, embossed with stylized leaf devices and applied with a scroll handle, maker's mark 'GW', Sheffield 1903, 3½in (9cm) high.
£120–140
€/ $190–220 BR

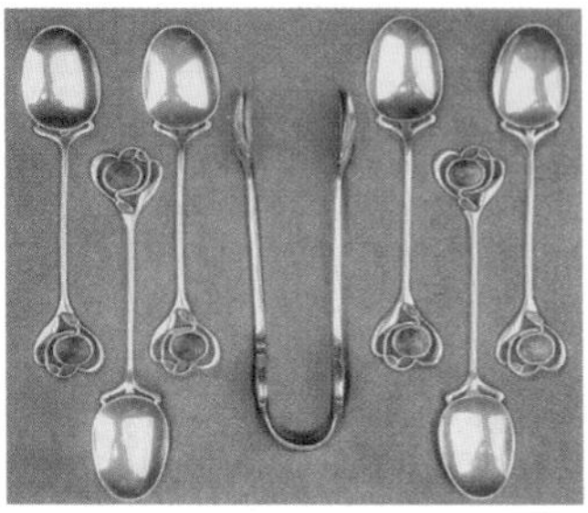

A Liberty & Co cased set of six teaspoons and sugar tongs, each with a pierced scrolling terminal, decorated with an enamel plaque, Birmingham 1907.
£750–875
€/ $1,200–1,400 B(NW)

A Liberty & Co Tudric pewter four-piece tea and coffee service, by Archibald Knox, c1900, 8in (20.5cm) high.
£675–750
€/ $1,000–1,200 WAC

A Connell pewter four-piece tea service, comprising water jug, teapot, sugar basin and milk jug, stamped marks, early 20thC.
£170–200
€/ $270–320 GH

► A Liberty & Co Tudric pewter tankard, 1900, 9in (23cm) high.
£800–900
€/ $1,300–1,400 AFD

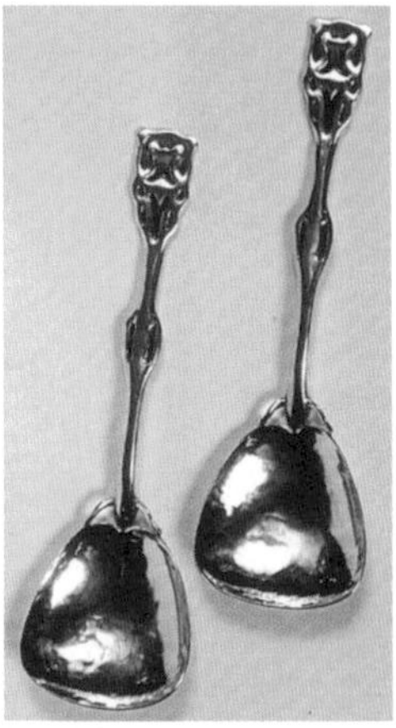

A pair of Liberty Cymric silver and enamelled spoons, 1890–1910, 7in (18cm) long.
£800–900
€/ $1,300–1,400 ASA

◄ A pottery tea canister, with pierced silver overlay, Chester 1904, 4½in (11.5cm) high.
£585–650
€/ $920–1,000 SHa

A bronze vase, by Julien Caussé, cast with overlapping leaves, two of which form the handles, further leaves ending in an opening flower bud, signed, French, c1900, 13in (33cm) high.
£300–350
€/ $475–550 B

◄ A Limoges enamel vase, by Camille Fauré, with landscape decoration, French, c1900, 7in (18cm) high.
£850–950
€/ $1,400–1,500 ANO

◄ A Tiffany silver vase, attributed to Paulding Farnham, etched with scrolling foliate strapwork, engraved monogram 'EH', looped tendril handles, beaded knop and base, marked and numbered, American, c1896, 14¾in (37.5cm) high.
£4,500–5,300
€/ $7,000–8,400 S(NY)

A gilt-bronze vase, by M. Paignant, the two handles surmounted by locusts and cast foliage, signed, Jollet & Cie foundry seal, on a marble plinth, French, c1900, 8in (20.5cm) high.
£2,000–2,200
€/ $3,200–3,500 S

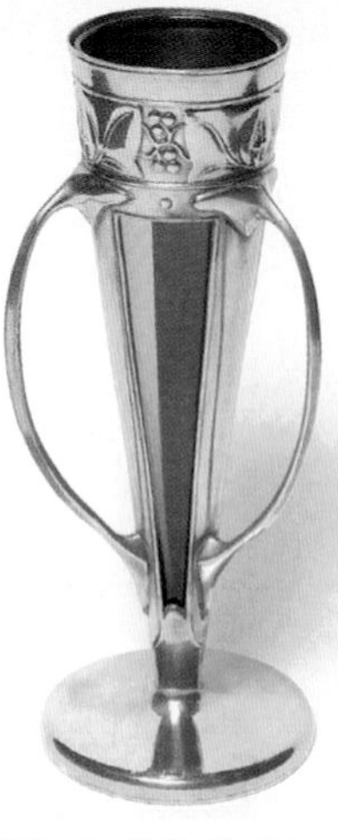

A Liberty & Co Tudric pewter vase, with original glass liner, c1900, 8¾in (22cm) high.
£675–750
€/ $1,000–1,200 SHa

Art Deco Ceramics

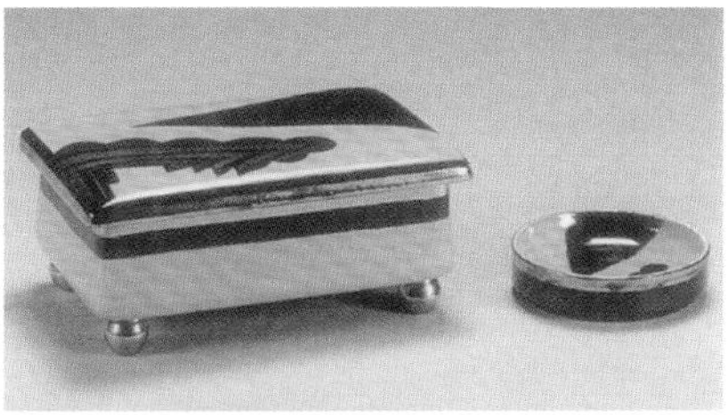

A Carlton Ware Chevrons cigarette box and cover, with matching pin tray, each with silver lustre highlights, the box with pearlescent interior, pattern number 3657, minor wear, 1930s, box 6in (15cm) wide.
£300–360
€/ $475–570 ⚒ S(O)

A Carlton Ware jug, moulded and painted with Spring Flower pattern, 1930s, 10in (25.5cm) high.
£180–200
€/ $285–315 ⊞ PSA

A Carter, Stabler & Adams vase, designed by Truda Adams, painted by Mary Brown with Blue Bird pattern, maker's marks, c1930, 6½in (16.5cm) high.
£130–150
€/ $200–240 ⚒ HoG
Although these wares are invariably referred to as Poole Pottery these days, the company was founded in Poole, Dorset, in 1873 as Carter & Co, and adopted the combined names of its partners, Carter, Stabler & Adams, upon its expansion in 1921. It was not until 1963 that the trade name of Poole Pottery emerged.

A Carter, Stabler & Adams bowl, designed by Truda Carter, c1930, 10in (25.5cm) diam.
£350–400
€/ $550–630 ⊞ HarC

► **A Carter, Stabler & Adams vase,** pattern BM, shape 979, impressed marks, c1930, 8¾in (22cm) high.
£300–350
€/ $475–550 ⚒ GH

LOCATE THE SOURCE

The source of each illustration in Miller's can be found by checking the code letters below each caption with the Key to Illustrations, pages 794–800.

► **A Carter, Stabler & Adams vase,** 1920–30, 7in (18cm) high.
£200–225
€/ $315–350 ⊞ PGO

► **A Claude Coquerel earthenware vase,** signed and monogrammed, c1940, 17in (43cm) high.
£2,000–2,400
€/ $3,200–3,800 ⚒ S(NY)

A Clew's Chameleonware lidded vase, 1930s, 7½in (19cm) high.
£130–150
€/ $200–240 ⚒ WiLP

A Crown Devon jug, decorated with Floral pattern, c1925, 12in (30.5cm) high.
£180–200
€/ $285–315 ⊞ TDG

► **A Crown Devon lustre vase,** c1930, 7½in (19cm) high.
£315–350
€/ $500–550 ⊞ RH

► **A Gouda Kurba vase,** Dutch, c1929, 9½in (24cm) high.
£180–200
€/ $285–315 ⊞ DSG

A Hancock Coronaware bowl, decorated with Springtime pattern, signed 'F. X. Abraham', c1925, 12¼in (31cm) diam.
£240–265
€/ $380–420 ⊞ PIC

A Moravian Pottery & Tile Works tile, Florence Nightingale's lamp, American, c1920, 4in (10cm) square.
£45–50
€/ $70–80 ⊞ KMG

A Myott fan vase, c1930, 9in (23cm) high.
£270–300
€/ $425–475 ⊞ RH

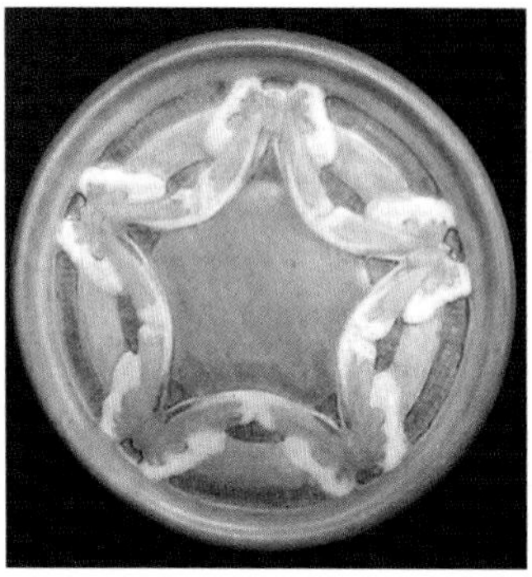

A Newcomb College Pottery plaque, decorated by Sadie Irvine with butterflies, marked, with paper label, American, c1926, 5½in (14cm) diam.
£4,000–4,500
€/ $6,300–7,000 ⊞ CaF

Newcomb College Pottery (American 1895–1941)

The pottery at Newcomb College, New Orleans, has produced some of the rarest and most valuable American art pottery. Operated mainly by women, the distinctive hand-thrown wares were hand-decorated with incised patterns of local flora and fauna highlighted in polychrome slip. Early pieces have a high glaze, while post-1910 wares usually have a semi-matt finish. Larger items are the most collectable, as well as those featuring landscape decoration or pieces decorated by the better artists such as Mary Sheerer, or the founder, Jospeh Meyer.

► A Pilkington's Royal Lancastrian kylix, c1920, 10in (25.5cm) diam.
£135–150
€/ $215–240 ⊞ RUSK

A Newcomb College Pottery vase, decorated by Anna Francis Simpson with egrets against tree trunks, American, c1930, 7¼in (18.5cm) high.
£8,500–9,000
€/ $13,500–15,00 ⊞ CaF

A Pilkington's Royal Lancastrian lustre vase, by William Salter Mycock, 1930s, 7in (18cm) high.
£1,100–1,200
€/ $1,700–1,900 ⊞ ASA

◄ A Shelley Harmony ginger jar, with drip decoration, c1930, 5in (12.5cm) high.
£135–150
€/ $215–240
⊞ BEV

A Roseville Pottery wistaria vase, American, 1933, 8½in (21.5cm) high.
£750–900
€/ $1,200–1,400 ⚒ SPG

A Royal Winton vase, decorated with Flame pattern, c1930, 8in (20.5cm) high.
£145–160
€/ $230–250 ⊞ RH

A Shelley part coffee service, comprising coffee pot and lid, milk jug, sugar bowl, five cups and six saucers, some damage, c1930.
£650–750
€/ $1,000–1,200 ⚒ B(W)

A Shelley Eve shape trio, decorated with Daisy pattern, 1934, cup 3in (7.5cm) high.
£160–180
€/ $250–285 ⊞ BEV

A Wiener Werkstätte earthenware bowl, decorated with stylized birds and flowers, glaze chips, impressed mark and number 336, painted mark 8, Austrian, 1920s, 5in (12.5cm) diam.
£300–360
€/ $474–570 ⚒ S(Am)

A Shelley Queen Anne shape trio, decorated with Blue Iris pattern, c1930, plate 6in (5cm) square.
£80–90
€/ $125–140 ⊞ HarC

A Wedgwood Fairyland lustre bowl, c1930, 8in (205cm) diam.
£350–400
€/ $550–630 ⚒ BWL

► **A J. Wilkinson Tahiti Storm vase,** designed by John Butler, signed, c1930, 17in (43cm) high.
£1,300–1,500
€/ $2,000–2,400 ⊞ BD
John Butler, together with Fred Ridgeway, were Wilkinson's two top designers prior to the arrival of Clarice Cliff in 1920.

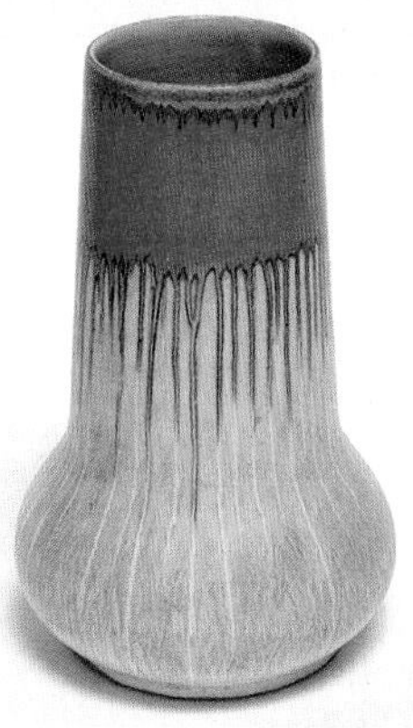

A Shelley drip ware vase, c1930, 7in (18cm) high.
£70–80
€/ $110–125 ⊞ RH

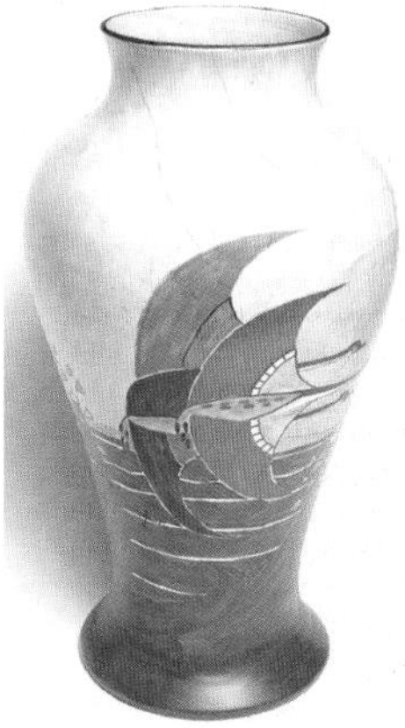

Clarice Cliff

A Clarice Cliff Bizarre bookend, in the shape of a seated Golly, decorated with Sunburst pattern, c1930, 6in (15cm) high.
£1,300–1,500
€/ $2,000–2,400 Bea

A Clarice Cliff Conical bowl, decorated with Garland pattern, c1930, 9in (23cm) diam.
£550–600
€/ $870–950 ⊞ BD

► A Clarice Cliff sugar bowl and tongs, decorated with Autumn pattern, c1930, 3½in (9cm) high.
£500–550
€/ $800–870 ⊞ TDG

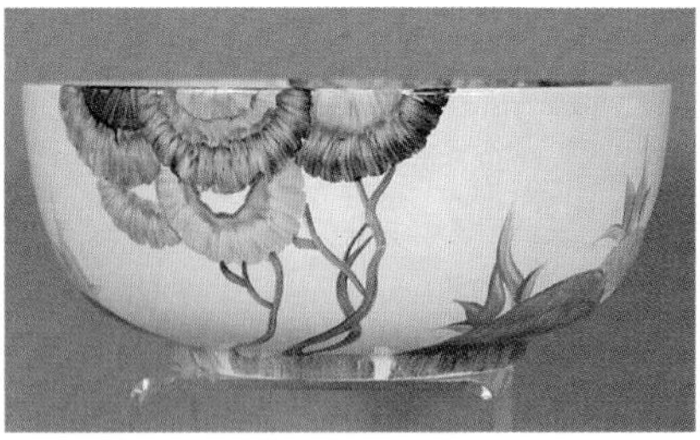

A Clarice Cliff Bizarre bowl, decorated with Aurea pattern, c1930, 7½in (19cm) diam.
£280–320
€/ $440–520 SWO

A Clarice Cliff Fantasque clog, decorated with Windbells pattern, printed marks, restored, 1933–34, 5½in (13.5cm) wide.
£330–400
€/ $520–640 S(O)

A Clarice Cliff pedestal comport, decorated with Rhodanthe pattern, 1930s, 8in (20cm) high.
£550–600
€/ $800–950 ⊞ JOA

A Clarice Cliff Duck egg cup stand, with six egg cups and stand, decorated with Double V pattern, marked, c1929, cup 6¼in (16cm) diam.
£650–750
€/ $1,000–1,200 B

A Clarice Cliff jardinière, decorated with Delecia Iberis pattern, c1930, 11in (28cm) diam.
£200–220
€/ $320–350 GH

► A Clarice Cliff jug, decorated with Sunray pattern, printed marks, restored, c1930, 5½in (14cm) high.
£450–525
€/ $700–830 B

A Clarice Cliff Conical jug, decorated with Summerhouse pattern, c1930, 6½in (16.5cm) high.
£1,800–2,000
€/ $2,800–3,200 ⊞ BD

A Clarice Cliff Bizarre plate, decorated with Devon pattern, c1930, 8½in (21.5cm) diam.
£600–700
€/ $950–1,100 GH

◄ A Clarice Cliff Bizarre plate, produced for Brice Rogers, decorated with Tennis pattern, printed marks, 1930–31, 6¾in (17cm) diam.
£750–875
€/ $1,200–1,400 Bea

A Clarice Cliff plate, decorated with Alton pattern, printed marks, c1934, 9in (23cm) diam.
£280–320
€/ $440–520 PFK

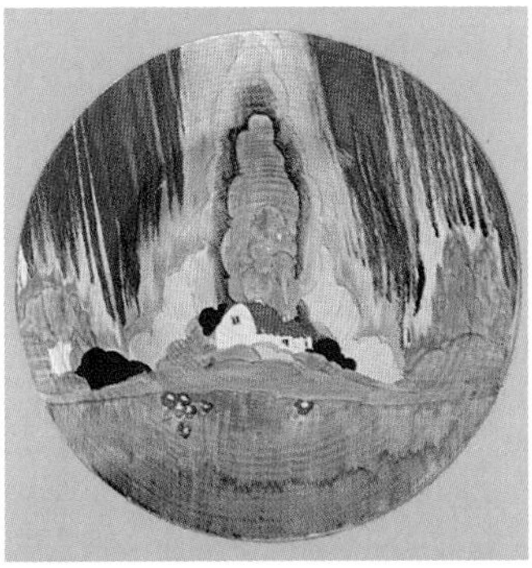

A Clarice Cliff charger, decorated with Forest Glen pattern, printed marks, 1935–37, 18in (45.5cm) diam.
£1,800–2,200
€/ $2,900–3,500 G(B)

A Clarice Cliff Beehive honey pot, decorated with a geometric pattern, signature mark, c1930, 3in (7.5cm) high.
£280–325
€/ $440–515 SWO

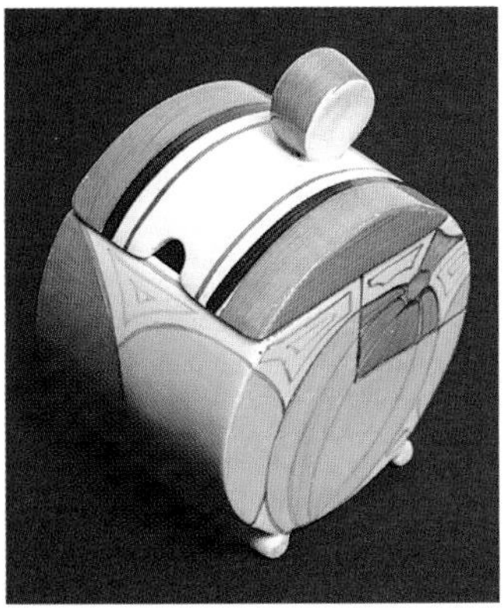

A Clarice Cliff Bonjour jam pot, decorated with Melons pattern, c1930, 4½in (11.5cm) high.
£720–800
€/ $1,100–1,200 BD

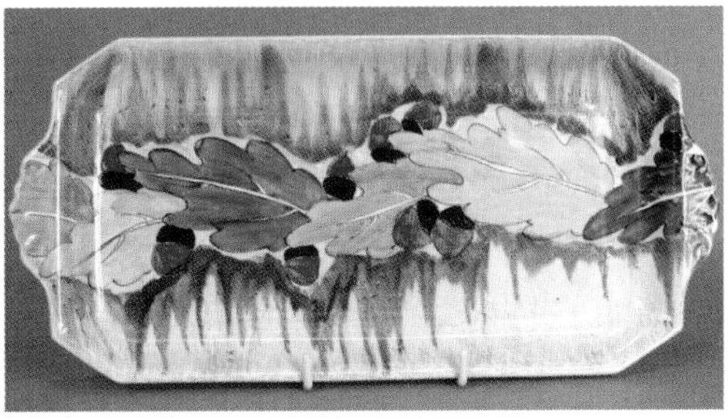

◄ A Clarice Cliff Bizarre sandwich plate, decorated with Acorn pattern, printed marks, 1930s, 11¾in (30cm) wide.
£280–325
€/ $440–500 SWO

A Clarice Cliff Stamford tea set, comprising 10 pieces, painted with a geometric pattern, c1930, teapot 4¾in (12cm) high.
£950–1,100
€/ $1,500–1,700 SWO

A Clarice Cliff sandwich set, comprising seven pieces, decorated with Applique Idyll pattern, c1930, largest 9in (23cm) diam.
£1,700–2,000
€/ $2,700–3,200 GH

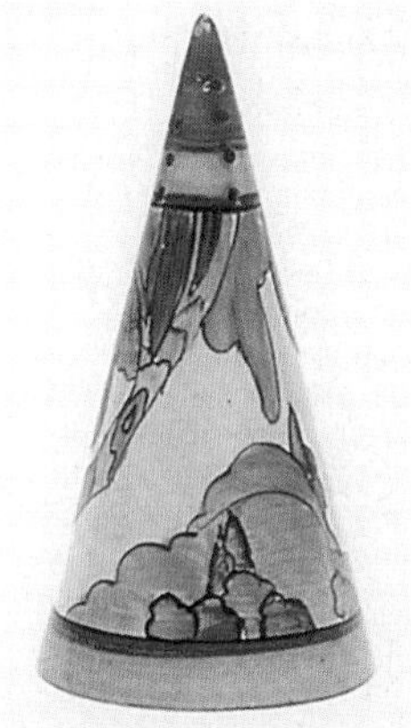

A Clarice Cliff Conical sugar sifter, decorated with a version of Rudyard pattern, printed marks, c1933, 5¼in (13.5cm) high.
£850–1,000
€/ $1,300–1,600 Bea

A Clarice Cliff Bizarre vase, decorated with Blue Firs pattern, c1930, 4in (10cm) high.
£850–1,000
€/ $1,300–1,600 GH

A Clarice Cliff Bizarre vase, decorated with Autumn Crocus pattern, printed and painted marks, c1930, 8¼in (21cm) high.
£675–800
€/ $1,100–1,300 SWO

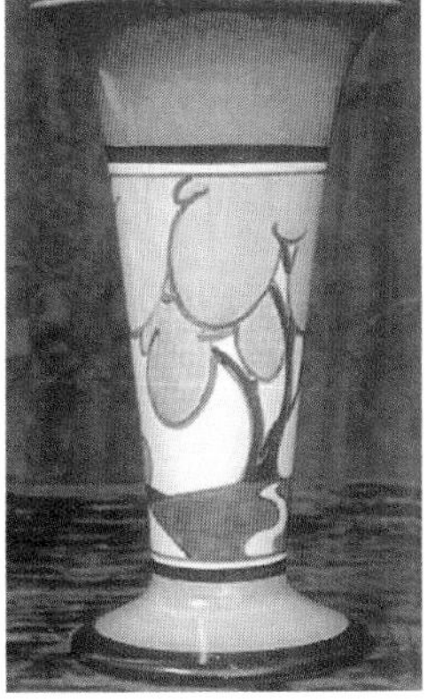

A Clarice Cliff Fantasque vase, decorated with Autumn pattern, marked, c1930, 8in (20.5cm) high.
£600–700
€/ $950–1,100 MAR

A Clarice Cliff Fantasque vase, decorated with Autumn pattern, printed marks, c1930, 7¾in (20cm) high.
£2,200–2,600
€/ $3,500–4,100 TEN

A Clarice Cliff Bizarre vase, decorated with Football pattern, printed marks, 1929–30, 6½in (16.5cm) high.
£2,200–2,500
€/ $3,500–4,000 ⚒ Bea

A Clarice Cliff Isis vase, produced for Lawley's, decorated with Umbrellas and Rain pattern, c1930, 9½in (24cm) high.
£2,200–2,500
€/ $3,500–4,000 ⚒ G(L)

A Clarice Cliff vase, decorated with Latona Red Roses pattern, marked, c1930, 18in (45.5cm) high.
£4,000–4,800
€/ $6,300–7,600 ⚒ B

A Clarice Cliff vase, decorated with Nasturtium pattern, c1930, 10in (25.5cm) high.
£900–1,000
€/ $1,400–1,600 ⊞ BD

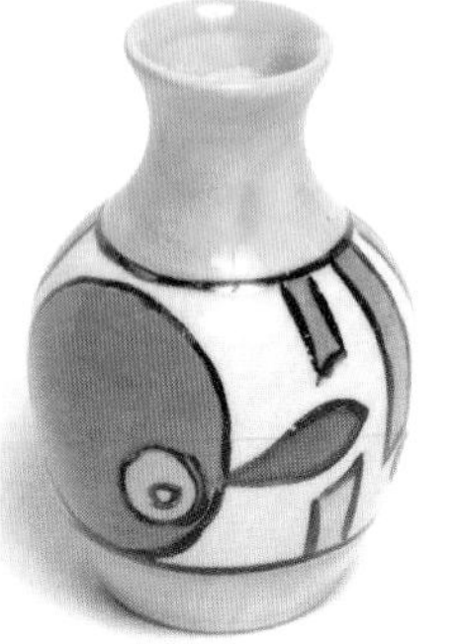

A Clarice Cliff vase, decorated with Orange Battle pattern, c1930, 2in (5cm) high.
£900–1,000
€/ $1,400–1,600 ⊞ BD

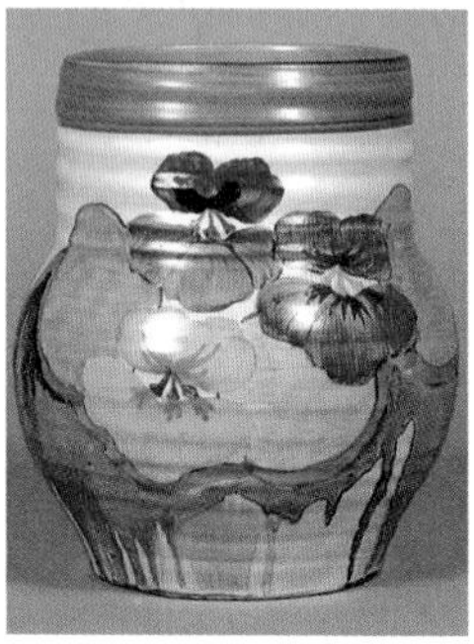

A Clarice Cliff Bizarre vase, decorated with Delecia Pansies pattern, c1930, 5½in (14cm) high.
£320–375
€/ $500–600 ⚒ GH

► A Clarice Cliff vase, decorated with Orange Lily pattern, c1930, 6½in (16.5cm) diam.
£850–950
€/ $1,300–1,500
⊞ TDG

A Clarice Cliff vase, decorated with Windbells pattern, c1930, 8in (20.5cm) high.
£2,700–3,000
€/ $4,300–4,800 ⊞ BD

A Clarice Cliff Yo vase, decorated with Delecia pattern, c1930, 6in (15.cm) high.
£1,200–1,300
€/ $1,900–2,000 ⊞ BD

A Clarice Cliff vase, decorated with Delecia pattern, minor wear, c1930, 7in (18cm) high.
£300–350
€/ $475–550 ⚒ Pott

A Clarice Cliff Bizarre vase, decorated with Whisper pattern, c1930, 7¾in (19.5cm) high.
£900–1,100
€/ $1,400–1,700 ⚒ GH

◄ A Clarice Cliff wall plaque, decorated with Clovelly pattern, depicting cottages, poplars and a full moon, printed marks, c1930, 17½in (44.5cm) diam.
£1,800–2,200
€/ $2,800–3,500
⚒ B

A Clarice Cliff Bizarre vase, printed marks, facsimile signature, c1930, 6in (15cm).
£420–500
€/ $660–790 ⚒ PF

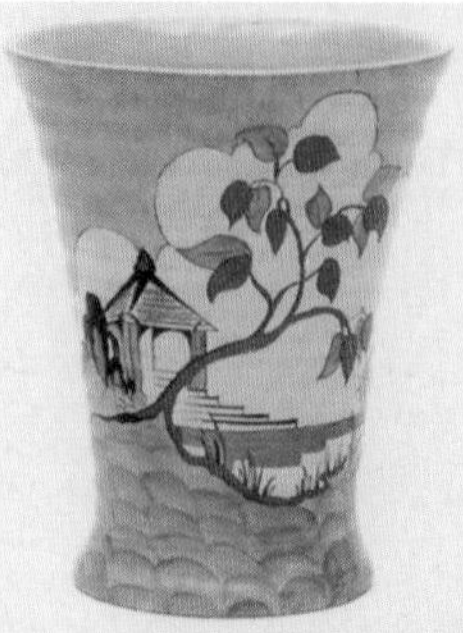

A Clarice Cliff Bizarre vase, decorated with Green Japan pattern, printed marks, 1933–34, 6¾in (17cm) high.
£420–500
€/ $660–790 ⚒ Bea

Susie Cooper

A Susie Cooper Patricia Rose coffee cup and saucer, c1930, 2¼in (5.5cm) high.
£80–90
€/ $125–145 ⊞ **RH**

A Susie Cooper moulded jug, with incised decoration, marks to base, 1930s, 6¾in (17cm) high.
£180–220
€/ $280–350 **SWO**

A Susie Cooper dinner and tea service, comprising 63 pieces, decorated with Fern pattern, c1936.
£220–260
€/ $350–400 **BR**

A Susie Cooper coffee pot, decorated with Assyrian Motif pattern, c1963, 8in (20.5cm) high.
£100–110
€/ $160–175 ⊞ **CHI**

A Susie Cooper jug, decorated with stylized foliage, stamped, c1930, 8¾in (22cm) high.
£100–125
€/ $160–200 **SWO**

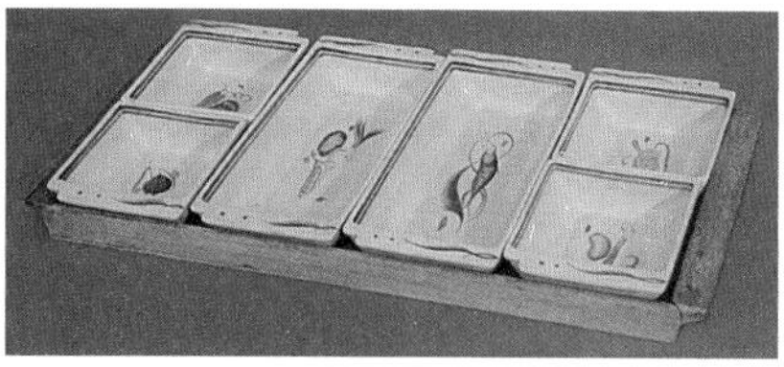

A Susie Cooper six-division entrée dish, decorated with hand-painted vegetables, on an oak tray, c1930, 19¾in (50cm) wide.
£100–120
€/ $160–1900 **WiLP**

► A Susie Cooper mug, with banded decoration, 1930s, 3in (7.5cm) high.
£140–160
€/ $220–250
SWO

A Susie Cooper coffee service, comprising 16 pieces, decorated with Dresden Spray pattern, 1930s.
£140–160
€/ $220–250 **PFK**

◄ A Susie Cooper one pint teapot, decorated with raised enamel polka dots, c1954.
£80–90
€/ $125–145 ⊞ **CHI**

Charlotte Rhead

A Charlotte Rhead Crown Ducal jug, decorated with flowers and stylized leaves, gilded handle, c1930, 14in (35.5cm) high.
£140–160
€/ $220–250 **EH**

A Charlotte Rhead Crown Ducal jug, decorated with a floral design on a mottled ground, printed marks, 1931–43, 8¼in (21cm) high.
£160–200
€/ $250–315 **RIT**

Charlotte Rhead was employed by several Staffordshire pottery factories before joining her father Frederick Rhead at Wood & Sons of Burslem in 1912. In 1926 she moved to Burgess & Leigh who produced Burleigh Ware and by 1937 had moved again to A. G. Richardson, makers of Crown Ducal pottery. Finally, in 1941 she worked once more for Wood's, at H. J. Wood in Burslem.

A pair of Charlotte Rhead Wood & Sons vases, decorated with stylized flowers with gilt detail, printed marks, c1915, 13in (33cm) high.
£850–1,000
€/ $1,300–1,600 **WL**

Art Deco Clocks

Expert's choice

A Night and Day clock, by R. Lalique, c1930, sold by Bonhams, 1989.

I am only too ready to admit that I consider myself incredibly fortunate to have had the opportunity of handling thousands of pieces of Lalique glass and to have overseen some equally amazing sales of Lalique during my many years with Bonhams. Of all the objects I had the pleasure of auctioning, Lalique's Night and Day clock was the item I would truly have loved to have kept, being both stunning and functional. The clock makes clever use of relief and impressed moulding to achieve the tonal qualities of the male and female nude figures whose bodies arch around the central clockface. What made this clock so special was the colour – topaz, not the more usual smoky grey, but a lovely subtle topaz that changed to a vibrant dark amethyst. I've never seen another which is probably just as well for at £80,000 (€/ $126,000) the housekeeping would be under serious pressure.

Eric Knowles

A René Lalique frosted and polished glass mantel clock, *'Quatre Moineaux Du Japon,'* c1928, 8in (20.5cm) square.
£1,400–1,500
€/ $2,200–2,400 ⊞ LBr

An enamelled brass electric wall clock, by Gebr. Arens, Nijmegen, maker's mark, Dutch, c1934, 11¾in (30cm) square.
£1,200–1,400
€/ $1,900–2,200 ⚒ S(Am)

Art Deco Figures & Busts

► A patinated-bronze figure of an armed Amazon, by M. Bouraine, signed, impressed number, French, 1925–30, 32in (81.5cm) wide.
£4,700–5,500
€/ $7,400–8,700 ⚒ DORO

◄ A bronze and ivory figure of a girl, by Dominique Alonzo, signed, French, early 20thC, 9in (23cm) high.
£900–1,100
€/ $1,400–1,700 ⚒ S(O)

► An Art Deco bronze group of a nude girl on a leaping horse, by L. Charles, Verbier, Paris, signed, French, 24½in (62cm) wide.
£1,300–1,500
€/ $2,000–2,400
⚒ TF

A gilt-bronze and carved ivory figure of a girl, by Demêtre Chiparus, entitled 'Chain Dancer', on a marble base, French, original chain missing, c1925, 10½in (26.5cm) high.
£4,500–5,200
€/ $7,000–8,400 ⚒ B

A pair of gilt and silvered-bronze bookends, by Noël Coulon, modelled as Native Americans, signed, French, c1930, 7¼in (18.5cm) high.
£3,000–3,300
€/ $4,700–5,600 ⚒ S(O)

A bronze and ivory figure of a girl, by Gerdago, on an onyx base, German, c1920, 6½in (16.5cm) high.
£4,000–4,500
€/ $6,300–7,000 ⊞ ASA

AUDREY STERNSHINE
AS
ntique Galleries
26 Broad St
Pendleton, Salford
anchester M6 5BY
el: 0161 737 5938
ax: 0161 737 6626
Specialist in Art Nouveau & Art Deco.
T. Preiss

A Goldscheider ceramic figure of a woman, Austrian, c1930, 11in (28cm) high.
£1,000–1,100
€/ $1,600–1,700 ASA

An Art Deco spelter and ivorine group of a woman and two dogs, by Georges Gori, on an onyx base, signed, French, 28in (71cm) wide.
£1,300–1,500
€/ $2,100–2,400 HAM

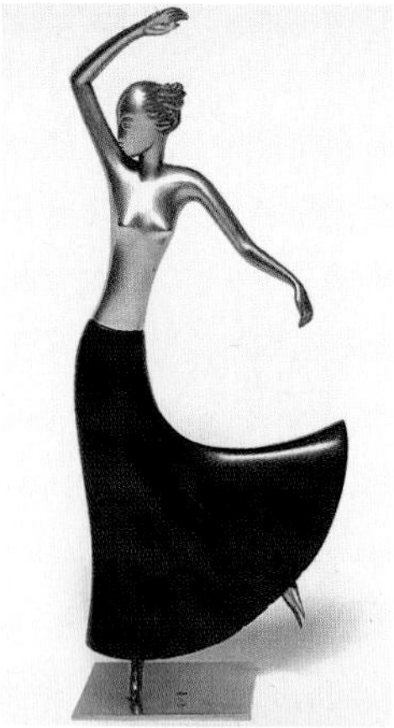

A Hagenauer bronze figure of a woman, signed and stamped to base, Austrian, 1920s, 13½in (34.5cm) high.
£2,700–3,000
€/ $4,300–4,700 TDG

A porcelain group of Pan and Psyche, by Hutschenreuther, German, c1920, 12½in (32cm) high.
£765–850
€/ $1,200–1,300 ANO

A gilt and silver-patinated bronze group, by Alexander Kéléty, entitled 'Hunter with Two Gazelles', on a marble base, French, c1930, 19¾in (50cm) high.
£1,400–1,600
€/ $2,200–2,500 S(P)

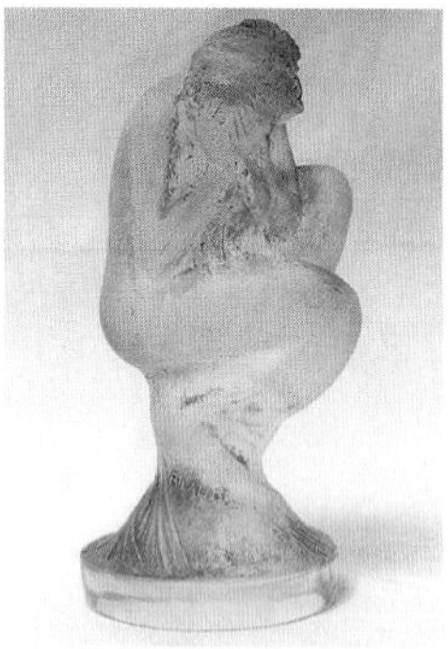

A René Lalique frosted glass figure, entitled 'Sirène', French, c1930, 4in (10cm) high.
£1,300–1,500
€/ $2,100–2,400 OND

► A patinated-bronze figure of Diana, by Pierre Le Faguays, stamped mark, initialled, French, c1930, 25¾in (65.5cm) high.
£3,700–4,200
€/ $5,800–6,600 S

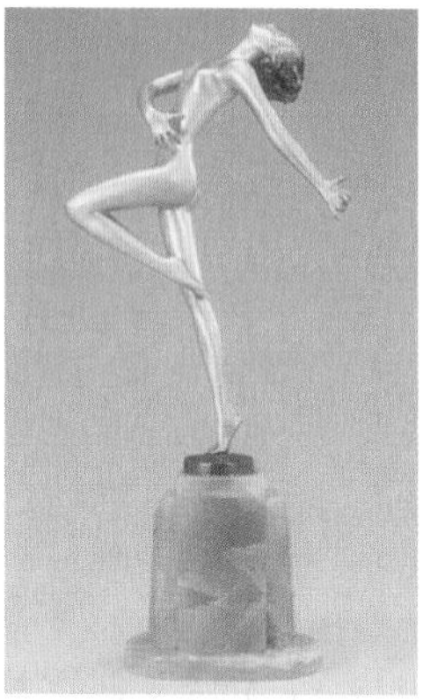

◄ A patinated-bronze figure of a naked woman, by Lorenzl, on an onyx base, signed, 1920s–30s, 11¾in (30cm) high.
£1,100–1,300
€/ $1,700–2,000 BUK

A plaster figure of a woman, by Melani, French, c1930, 24in (61cm) wide.
£240–270
€/ $380–425 ASP

► A silvered- and patinated-bronze figure, by Paul Philippe, entitled 'The Bather', on an onyx base, signed, some damage, 1920s, French, 11in (28cm) high.
£1,300–1,500
€/ $2,100–2,400 G(L)
Paul Philippe was born in Poland but studied in France under Antonin Larroux. He exhibited with success in the Paris salons in the inter-war period.

A bronze and ivory figure, by Ferdinand Preiss, entitled 'Sunshine Girl', German, c1920, 9½in (24cm) high.
£11,000–12,000
€/ $17,000–19,000 ASA

A gilt-bronze group of a woman and a greyhound, by Raymond Léon Rivoire, on a marble base, French, c1925, 15¼in (38.5cm) high.
£5,300–6,000
€/ $8,400–9,500 ⚒ S(NY)

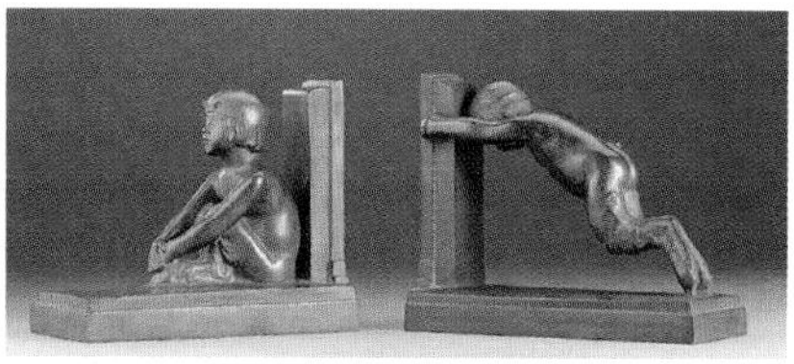

A pair of patinated-bronze bookends, by Paul Silvestre, modelled as two young fauns, signed, French, c1930, 8½in (21.5cm) high.
£1,800–2,000
€/ $2,800–3,200 ⊞ MI

► **A porcelain figure of a female nude,** by Wallendorf, German, c1935, 10in (25.5cm) high.
£180–200
€/ $285–315 ⊞ ASP

A patinated-bronze figure of a female nude, by Felix Weiss, on a marble base, signed, Austrian, 1920s–30s, 24½in (62cm) high.
£1,300–1,500
€/ $2,000–2,400 ⚒ BUK

A carved wood bust of a woman, French, c1915, 15in (38cm) high.
£450–550
€/ $710–870 ⊞ ASP

◄ **A bronze figural table lamp,** in the form of a young woman supporting a coloured glass globe, on a marble base, c1930, 15½in (39.5cm) high.
£420–500
€/ $660–790 ⚒ G(B)

► **A silver-plated figural trophy,** in the form of a dancing lady, c1932, 12¼in (31cm) high.
£450–550
€/ $700–870 ⚒ CHTR

A spelter group of a young girl and a dog, on a marble base, French, c1930, 21in (53.5cm) wide.
£400–450
€/ $630–700 ⊞ ASP

Art Deco Furniture

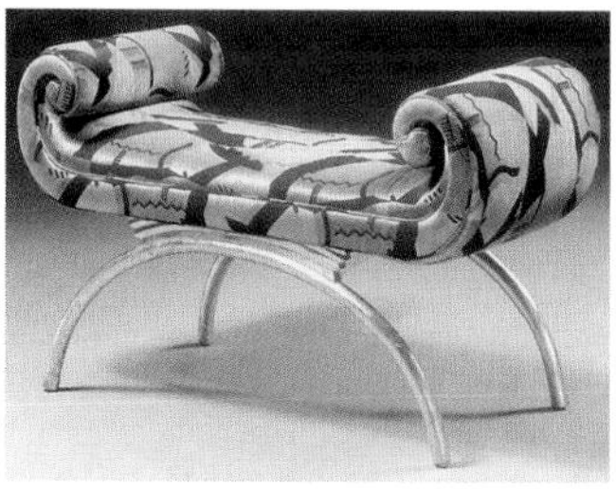

A silvered-wood bench, American, c1930, 42in (106.5cm) wide.
£3,700–4,300
€/ $5,800–6,000 ⚒ S(NY)

► **A pair of sycamore open bookcases,** with block-decorated back-rails above three bays, c1930, 72½in (184cm) wide.
£2,000–2,400
€/ $3,200–3,800 ⚒ B

► **A walnut bookcase,** c1930, 20in (51cm) wide.
£265–300
€/ $415–475 ⊞ GBr

A pair of birchwood bedside cabinets, Swedish, 1920–30, 22¼in (56.5cm) high.
£2,700–3,000
€/ $4,300–4,800 ⊞ CAV

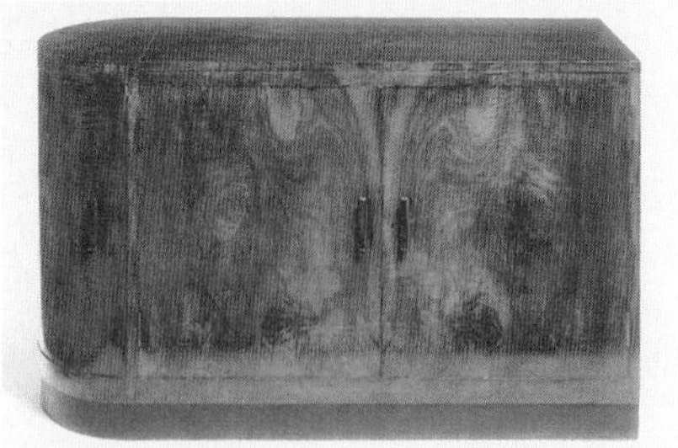

A Bird Iles walnut cocktail cabinet, with a pair of doors enclosing a lead-lined cellaret and curved end door with interior shutters, c1934, 66in (167.5cm) wide.
£230–275
€/ $365–430 B

Jack Bird Iles (1902–85) was one of a group of exclusive designers that included Betty Joel, Syrie Maugham and Sibyl Colefax. They worked in Mayfair and the West End of London between the wars to cater for the taste of many of London's wealthiest inhabitants. Bird Iles was one of the architects of the Dreamland Cinema in Margate, a fine example of a high Art Deco building, and he also provided the interior for the dressing rooms at Elstree Studios. WWII effectively brought an end to Bird Iles' furniture production business due to the shortage of luxury materials and the introduction of purchase tax. However, he continued to work as a decorator into the 1960s.

An oak cabinet, the four doors flanked by silvered and painted fretwork panels, above four drawers, c1930, 42in (107cm) wide.
£320–380
€/ $500–600 B

An oak rocking chair, c1930.
£170–220
€/ $270–350 WiLP

A rosewood secretaire cabinet, the leather-lined fall-front decorated with an ebonized woman's head, with a maple interior, French, c1925, 55in (139.5cm) high.
£4,500–5,000
€/ $7,000–8,000 ⊞ TDG

An André Groult giltwood bergère, with beaded trim, French, c1920.
£10,000–11,000
€/ $15,800–17,000
⊞ NART

André Groult (1884–1967) was an interior decorator and furniture designer whose designs were mainly executed by craftsmen working in his atelier in Paris. His designs invariably demonstrate his preference for curves.

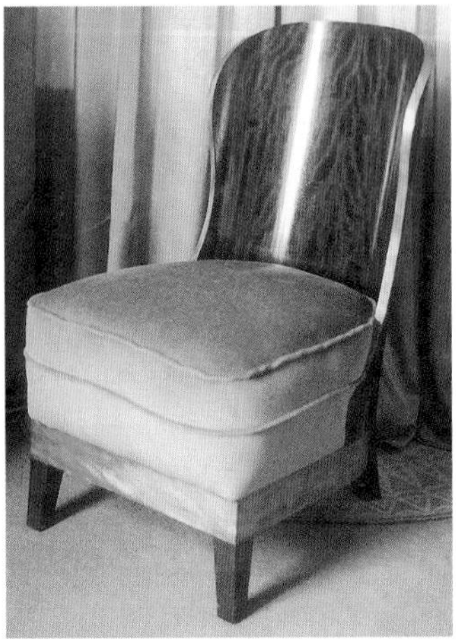

A mahogany and maple salon chair, 1930s.
£400–450
€/ $630–700 ⊞ BDA

A Süe & Mare rosewood and marquetry side cabinet, the top with protruding corners above a frieze drawer, over a pair of doors with shaped panels of stylized floral marquetry enclosing a divided interior, French, c1925, 26½in (67cm) wide.
£2,200–2,500
€/ $3,500–4,000 B

Louis Süe and André Mare, both already established French designers, joined in partnership to set up their *Compagnie des Arts Français* in 1919. It soon became known as Süe et Mare. They produced furniture, both in wood and wrought-iron, that epitomized the opulence of the French high Art Deco style. They also designed co-ordinated interiors, using a large team of prominent designers such as Maurice Marinot.

A burr-walnut armchair, in the style of Pierre Chareau, French, 1920s.
£2,000–2,400
€/ $3,200–3,800 S(Am)

A set of four oak chairs, 1930s.
£520–575
€/ $820–900 ⊞ SAT

A pair of side chairs, by Jacques Adnet, French, 1940s.
£2,200–2,500
€/ $3,500–4,000 S(O)

A wrought-iron reclining chair, upholstered in silk Illusion fabric by Jim Thompson, French, 1940s.
£1,000–1,200
€/ $1,600–1,900 S(Am)

A Hague School oak kneehole desk and chair, by C. Alons, the top lined with linoleum above a central drawer, flanked by two doors opening to shelves and drawers, the reverse with open shelves, with matching chair, Dutch, c1928, 59in (150cm) wide.
£1,500–1,800
€/ $2,400–2,800 S(Am)

◀ **A mahogany dining room suite,** by Jacob van den Bosch, comprising a table, two armchairs and four chairs, Dutch, c1920, table 84in (213.5cm) extended.
£1,200–1,400
€/ $1,900–2,200
S(Am)

A bird's-eye maple and walnut dining room suite, comprising a table, two open armchairs and four chairs, with associated sideboard, c1935, table 72½in (184cm) wide.
£3,500–4,200
€/ $5,500–6,600 B

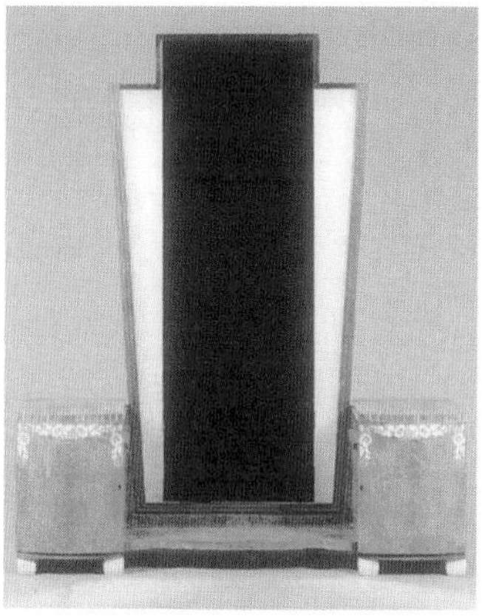

An amboyna-veneered and inlaid dressing table, the tapered mirror flanked by frosted illuminating panels and by pedestal cupboards enclosing shelves, on ivorine feet, c1930, 58¾in (149cm) wide.
£550–650
€/ $870–1,000 S(O)

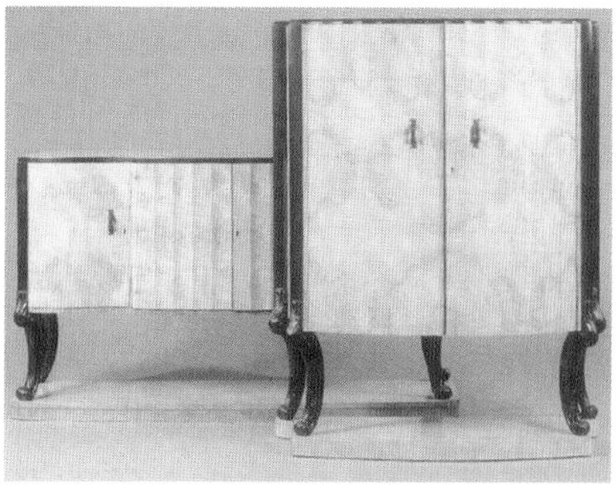

An Epstein burr-walnut dining room suite, comprising a dining table, six chairs, a sideboard and a cocktail cabinet, c1938, table 77½in (197cm) wide.
£9,000–10,000
€/ $14,000–16,000 S(O)

A dressing table, the oval mirror above a central bow-front section with frieze drawer, flanked by pedestal end sections with moulded mirror fronts enclosing shelves and fitted drawers, c1925, 50½in (128cm) wide.
£420–500
€/ $660–790 B

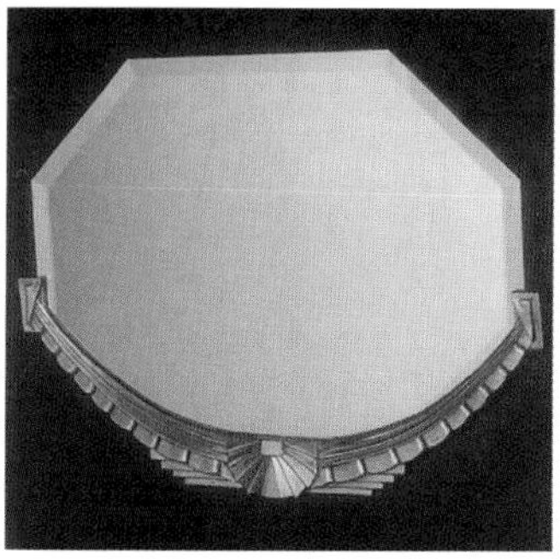

A silvered-bronze wall mirror, above a geometric mount with stylized fan, c1930, 24¾in (63cm) wide.
£600–700
€/ $950–1,100 S(O)

◀ **A William Arthur Chase marquetry inlaid wall mirror,** made for the Rowley Gallery, with a circular glazed panel entitled 'On a bat's wing I do fly', stamped, 1920s, 22¾in (57.5cm) high.
£380–420
€/ $620–740 S(O)

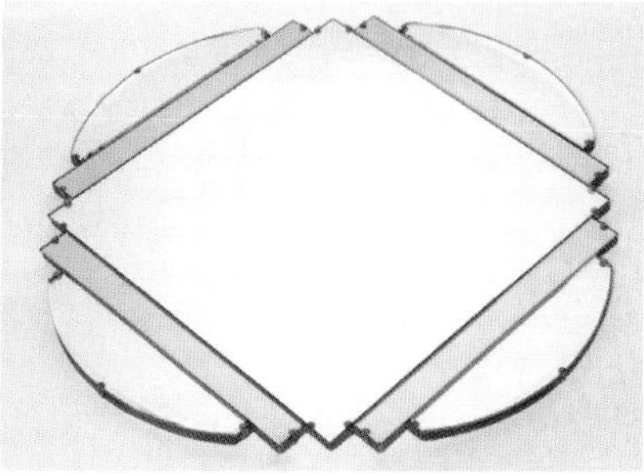

A mirror, with crystal and peach-coloured glass, 1930s, 27in (68.5cm) wide.
£215–235
€/ $340–370 SAT

A four-fold screen, painted by Stuart Scott Somerville in oil on canvas with ornamental birds amid flowering vases, signed and dated 1928, 90in (348cm) wide.
£3,300–4,000
€/ $5,200–6,300 B(EA)

An Edwin Hardy Amies needlework four-fold screen, stitched with Oriental style-flowers, trees and a figure, 1930s, 74in (188cm) wide.
£200–225
€/ $315–350 BIG

A pair of Jean Hanau *verre églomisé* four-panel screens, decorated with stylized figures within hinged black-lacquered frames, marked, French, 1930s, each screen 48¾in (123.5cm) square.
£2,700–3,300
€/ $4,300–5,200 S(O)

An elm fire screen, 1930s, 25in (63.5cm) high.
£150–165
€/ $240–260 ⊞ SAT

► A pine shelf, hand decorated, c1925, 28in (71cm) wide.
£125–140
€/ $200–220 ⊞ SAT

A Heal & Son ebonized and painted sideboard, the design attributed to Ambrose Heal, c1918, 60in (152.5cm) wide.
£2,800–3,200
€/ $4,400–5,000 S(O)

A mahogany and brass sofa, attributed to André Arbus, French, c1940, 57in (145cm) wide.
£12,500–14,000
€/ $20,000–22,000 ⊞ NART

A rosewood and silvered-metal table, attributed to Jules Leleu, French, c1925, 31½in (80cm) diam.
£4,700–5,500
€/ $7,400–8,700 S(NY)

A beech pedestal table, in the style of Emile Jacques Ruhlmann, French, 1920s, 19½in (49.5cm) diam.
£2,200–2,500
€/ $3,400–4,000 S(Am)

A Bird Iles glass and tubular-copper occasional table, the top with an etched band, on bent tubular supports with a glass undertier, c1928, 30in (76cm) diam.
£750–875
€/ $1,200–1,400
B

A painted centre table, by Paul Jouve, the hardstone top above four acanthus scroll supports, French, c1940, 62¼in (158cm) wide.
£1,300–1,500
€/ $2,000–2,400 S(Am)

► An oak-lined walnut wardrobe, c1920, 63in (160cm) wide.
£780–875
€/ $1,200–1,400 ⊞ WiB

► A zebra wood and Macassar ebony wardrobe, attributed to Richter for the Bath Cabinet Makers, c1930, 77in (195.5cm) high.
£3,000–3,300
€/ $4,700–5,200
⊞ TDG

Art Deco Glass

A Charder cameo glass tazza, etched with chestnuts, on an applied foot, cameo mark, French, 1926–33, 13½in (34.5cm) diam.
£1,200–1,400
€/ $1,900–2,200 S(Am)

A Daum acid-cut glass bowl, French, c1930, 8in (20.5cm) diam.
£550–620
€/ $870–980 AFD

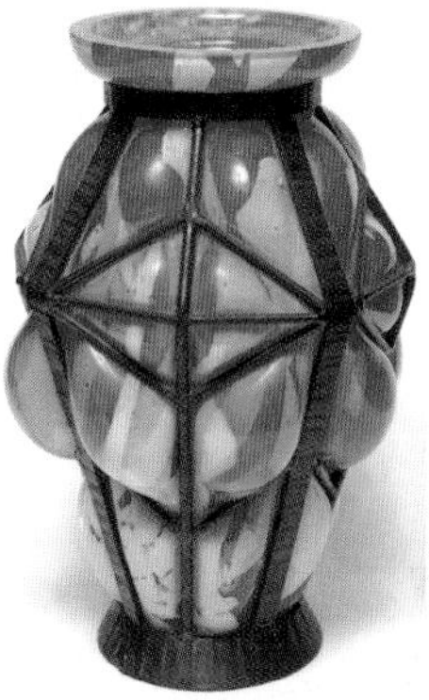

A Daum glass vase, by Louis Majorelle, with wrought-iron mounts, French, c1920, 12in (30.5cm) high.
£800–900
€/ $1,200–1,400 AFD

◄ **A Daum glass vase,** acid-etched with horizontal bands, marked, Cross of Lorraine, French, c1930, 10in (25.5cm) high.
£2,200–2,500
€/ $3,500–4,000 S(O)

► **A Daum glass vase,** acid-etched with foliate decoration, French, c1930, 13in (33cm) high.
£3,400–3,800
€/ $5,400–6,000 GoW

A cameo glass vase, by Degué, French, c1920, 14in (35.5cm) diam.
£1,900–2,100
€/ $3,000–3,300 AFD

A Wiener Werkstätte glass centrepiece, by Josef Hoffmann, small rim chip, acid-etched monogram 'WW', Austrian, designed c1917, 6¾in (17cm) high.
£1,700–2,000
€/ $2,700–3,200 DORO

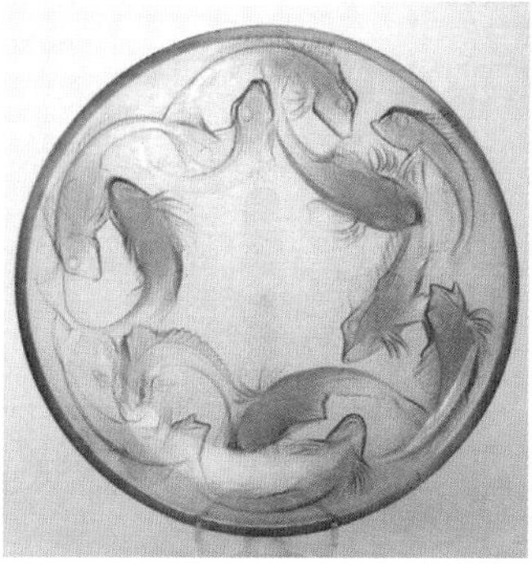

A René Lalique opalescent glass bowl, 'Martigues', No. 377, the underside relief-moulded with swimming fish, nick to rim, moulded mark, wheel cut 'France', designed 1920, 14¼in (36cm) diam.
£1,700–2,000
€/ $2,700–3,200 B

A René Lalique glass bowl, 'Volubilis', No. 383, the underside moulded with three convolvulus flowers, their centres forming three feet, engraved mark and numeral, French, after 1921, 8¼in (21cm) diam.
£800–930
€/ $1,200–1,300 S

◄ **A René Lalique glass vase,** 'Avallon', No. 986, relief-moulded with birds among berried branches, marked, French, pre-1945, 5¾in (14.5cm) high.
£1,300–1,500
€/ $2,000–2,400 SWO

► **A René Lalique glass vase,** 'Gui', French, c1930, 7in (18cm) high.
£1,000–1,100
€/ $1,600–1,800 OND

A Legras enamelled glass vase, French, c1920, 9½in (24cm) high.
£1,000–1,100
€/ $1,600–1,800 ⊞ AFD

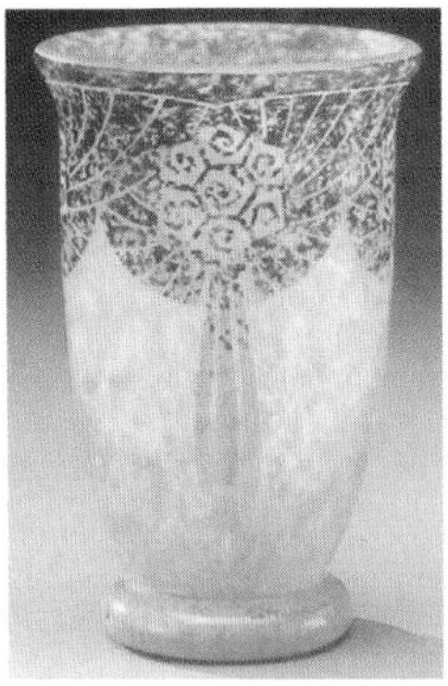

A Le Verre Français cameo glass vase, decorated with stylized rosettes, cameo mark and engraved mark, c1920, 8in (20.5cm) high.
£800–950
€/ $1,200–1,500 ⚒ S(P)

◄ A Le Verre Français cameo glass vase, 'Clochettes', etched with geometrical motifs and stylized flowers, engraved mark, French, c1925, 17¾in (45cm) high.
£2,400–2,700
€/ $4,000–4,300 ⚒ S(Am)

An Orrefors glass vase, by V. Lindstrand, Swedish, c1929, 7½in (19cm) high.
£585–650
€/ $930–1,000 ⊞ SHa

A Loetz glass bowl, by Michael Powolny, Austrian, c1918, 7½in (19cm) diam.
£700–780
€/ $1,100–1,300 ⊞ AFD
Michael Powolny (1871–1954) was principally a ceramics decorator and co-founded Wiener Keramik in 1905 with Bertold Löffler.

A glass vase, by Maurice Marinot, with internal decoration, inscribed, French, c1925, 5¾in (14.5cm) high.
£4,500–5,400
€/ $7,000–8,500 ⚒ S(NY)
Maurice Marinot (1882–1960), a trained technician, chemist and painter, became fascinated with glass when he visited the glassworks of his friends Eugène and Gabriel Viard. At first he designed glassware that the Viard brothers executed, but later he made his own glass. His pieces were all hand-made without the use of mass-production moulded techniques. Many have a clear grey or pale yellow tint. He was not prolific and therefore his work is relatively hard to find.

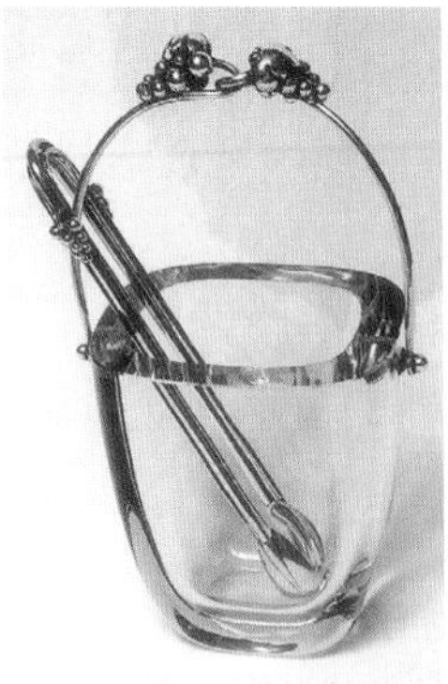

An Orrefors glass ice bucket, with sterling silver mounts, Swedish, c1920, 10in (25.5cm) high.
£1,100–1,300
€/ $1,700–2,000 ⊞ SHa

◄ A mottled glass vase, signed 'Schneider', French, c1930, 10in (25.5cm) high.
£1,500–1,700
€/ $2,400–2,700
⊞ TDG

A Tiffany Favrile glass vase, inscribed, c1915, 3½in (9cm) high.
£3,800–4,500
€/ $6,000–7,000 ⚒ S(NY)

An Almeric Walter *pâte-de-verre* figural inkwell, designed by Henri Bergé, French, c1925, 4¾in (12cm) wide.
£3,800–4,500
€/ $6,000–7,000 ⚒ S(NY)

A glass cocktail shaker, with silver-gilt mounts, the body with vertical cuts above four rows of banding, the integral gilt strainer beneath a domed cover with hammered finish, mounts marked, probably American, 1920s, 7½in (19cm) high.
£450–500
€/ $700–800 ⚒ S(O)

Art Deco Jewellery

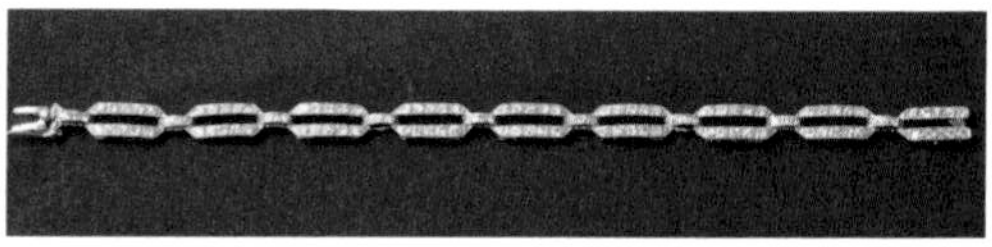

A platinum and diamond link bracelet, French, c1925, 7½in (19cm) long.
£5,200–5,800
€/ $8,200–9,200 WIM

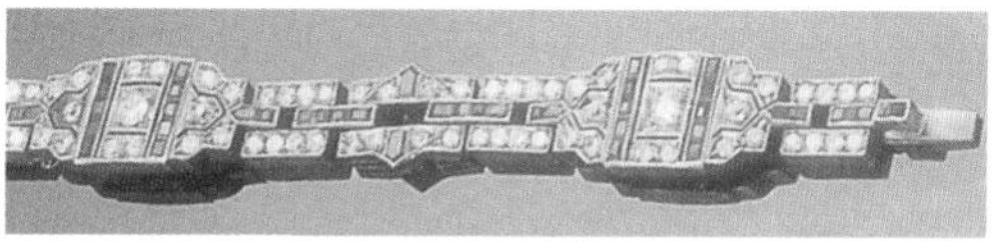

A 14ct rose-gold, diamond, ruby and emerald bracelet, the three geometric saw-pierced panels set with later brilliant-cut diamonds and interspaced with two rows of calibre-cut rubies, set between alternating diamond and ruby panels, with sliding clasp and safety chain, c1940, 6½in (16.5cm) long.
£2,000–2,400
€/ $3,200–3,800 LJ

◄ **A René Lalique frosted glass brooch,** 'Deux Figurines et Masque' in a gilt-metal mount, stamped, French, c1913, 1¾in (4.5cm) diam.
£2,200–2,400
€/ $3,500–3,800 AFD

An emerald and diamond brooch, c1935, in a fitted case by Collingwoods.
£7,500–9,000
€/ $11,900–14,200 WW

◄ **A ruby- and diamond-set dress clip,** with a scroll design, 1940s.
£500–600
€/ $800–950 G(L)

A René Lalique pendant, 'Libellulles', moulded in low relief with two overlapping dragonflies, chipped, intaglio mark, French, designed 1920, 2in (5cm) wide.
£200–225
€/ $315–355 B

► **An Egyptian-revival enamelled silver pendant,** set with moonstones, turquoise, emeralds and mother-of-pearl, c1920, 3½in (9cm) high.
£585–650
€/ $920–1,000 ANO

A sterling silver necklace and earrings, by Fischel and Nessler, American, 1920s, earrings 3in (7.5cm) long.
£400–450
€/ $630–700 RGA

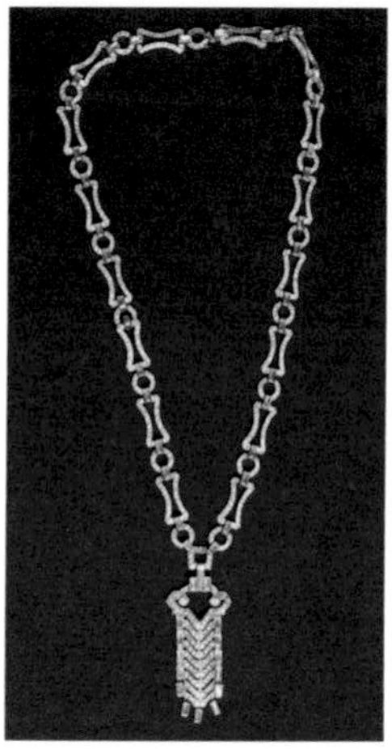

A silver and paste necklace, French, 1920s, 23in (58.5cm) long.
£315–350
€/ $500–550 RGA

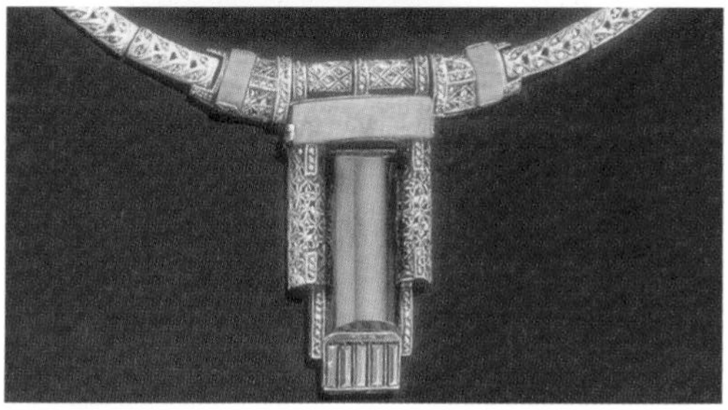

A Fahrner silver, marcasite and amazonite necklace, by Gustav Braendle Forth, stamped marks, German, 1920s.
£2,000–2,200
€/ $3,200–3,500 S(Am)

► **A white metal ring,** set with a light blue stone, the shank with pierced and engraved shoulders, marked 'PT', 1920s.
£200–225
€/ $315–350 PFK

A platinum cockerel pendant, with enamelled head, set with diamonds and a cabochon sapphire, c1930, 1in (2.5cm) wide.
£1,700–1,900
€/ $2,700–3,000 NBL

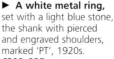

Art Deco Lighting

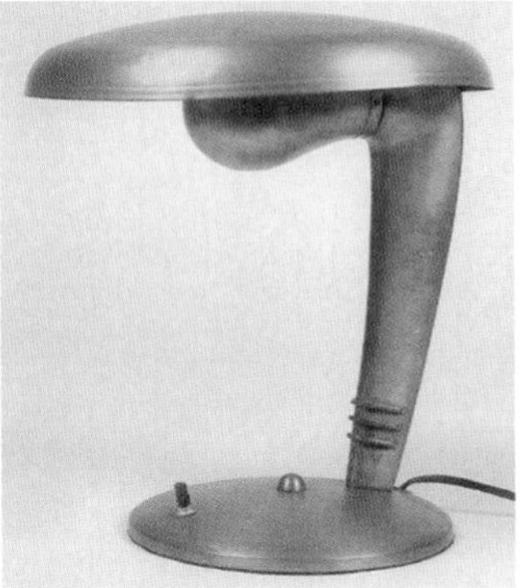

A bronzed-brass table lamp, 'Machine Age', by Norman Bel-Geddes, American, 1930s, 12¼in (31cm) high.
£475–550
€/ $750–870 DORO

A René Lalique frosted and polished glass chandelier, the underside moulded with leafy branches, hanging cords with matching suspension blocks, moulded mark, French, designed 1924, 13½in (34.5cm) diam.
£2,200–2,500
€/ $3,500–4,000 B

A Crown Devon and chrome table lamp, the base modelled with a porcelain figure of a female dancer wearing a flower dress, with original shade, c1930, 15¾in (40cm) high.
£400–475
€/ $630–750 SWO

A Giso glass and metal ceiling lamp, model No. 3051, by Willem Hendrik Gispen, the stepped shade suspended from a nickel-plated metal ceiling cap supporting two satin glass discs, Dutch, c1930, 23¾in (60.5cm) diam, with original invoices.
£2,200–2,600
€/ $3,500–4,100 S(Am)

A patinated-spelter hanging light, by Max le Verrier, signed, French, c1930, shade 13in (33cm) square.
£950–1,100
€/ $1,500–1,700 S(O)

◄ **A Silas Snider & Co patinated-bronze lamp,** 'Family Group', by Concetta Scaravaglione, American, New York, 1945, 32in (81.5cm) high.
£3,000–3,600
€/ $4,700–5,700 S(NY)
Silas Snider & Co produced a line of patinated-bronze limited edition lamps designed by sculptors. They were retailed by Abraham Strauss, among other prestigious department stores.

A Wiener Werkstätte ceramic table lamp, by Vally Wieselthier, with original paper shade, monogrammed 'WW', Austrian, c1928, 16½in (42cm) high.
£2,000–2,400
€/ $3,200–3,800 DORO

LOCATE THE SOURCE
The source of each illustration in Miller's can be found by checking the code letters below each caption with the Key to Illustrations, pages 794–800.

A chrome and Bakelite desk lamp, with swivel shade, c1920, 10in (25.5cm) wide.
£570–635
€/ $900–1,000 NART

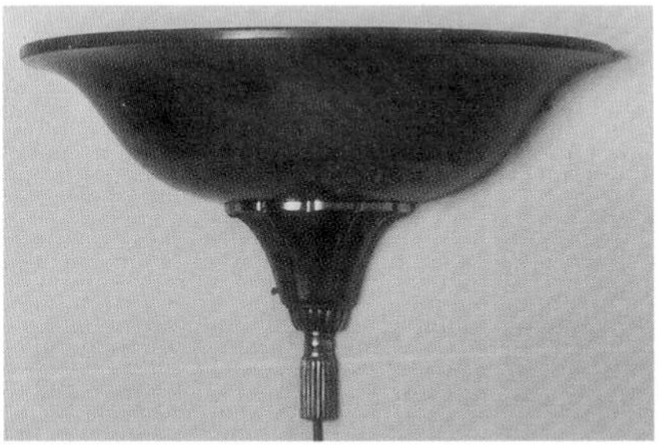

A pair of alabaster wall lights, French, c1925, 16in (40.5cm) wide.
£1,100–1,300
€/ $1,700–2,000 TLG

A pair of onyx lamps, on stepped marble bases, French, c1930, 10½in (26.5cm) high.
£850–1,000
€/ $1,300–1,600 S(P)

Art Deco Metalware

A Hagenauer silvered-bronze bell, Austrian, c1930, 3¾in (9.5cm) high.
£265–300
€/ $420–480 ⊞ ANO

A silver rose bowl, with cast decoration and swing handles, 1940, 6¼in (16cm) diam.
£180–220
€/ $280–350 SWO

A Blanckensee & Son silver bowl, Birmingham 1936, 4¼in (11cm) diam.
£950–1,100
€/ $1,500–1,700 S(O)

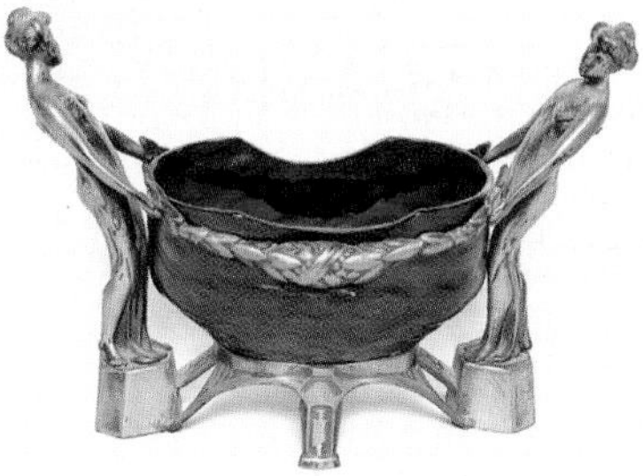

A pewter dish, with glass liner, c1920, 9in (23cm) wide.
£800–900
€/ $1,200–1,400 ⊞ ASP

A Georg Jensen silver centre bowl, designed by Hans Hansen, Danish, 1930s, 7¾in (19.5cm) diam.
£5,500–6,200
€/ $8,700–9,800 ⊞ KK

◄ A pair of patinated-pewter candlesticks, by Just, Danish, c1920, 8in (20.5cm) high.
£850–950
€/ $1,300–1,500 ⊞ SHa

► A pair of silver candlesticks, Birmingham 1924, 8¼in (21cm) high.
£250–300
€/ $400–475 HoG

A Blanckensee & Son silver coffee pot, Birmingham 1923, 8in (20.5cm) high.
£225–250
€/ $350–400 ⊞ WAC

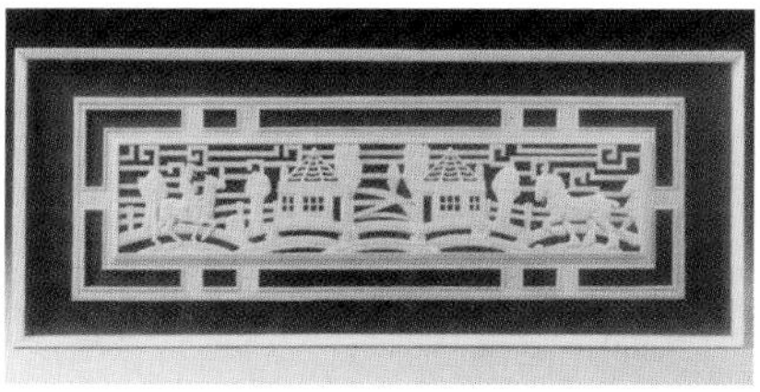

A silvered-metal pierced grille, by Harold Stabler, a distance post inscribed 'HPC VIII', 1932, mounted on a fabric-covered frame, 5½in (14cm) wide.
£850–1,000
€/ $1,400–1,600 S(O)

Harold Stabler (1872–1945) was one of the central figures of the Arts and Crafts movement. He become head of the Keswick School of Industrial Art in 1898, and later joined R. Llewellyn Rathbone in the metalwork department of the Liverpool Art School. After moving to London he was head of the John Cass Technical Institute Art School between 1907 and 1937. Associated for many years with Poole Pottery with his wife Phoebe, he was also a founding member of the Design and Industrial Association in 1915. He was commissioned by the London Passenger Transport Board to design tiles and other fittings for London Underground stations. This piece is a casting of an iron grille installed at Turnpike Lane underground station in 1932.

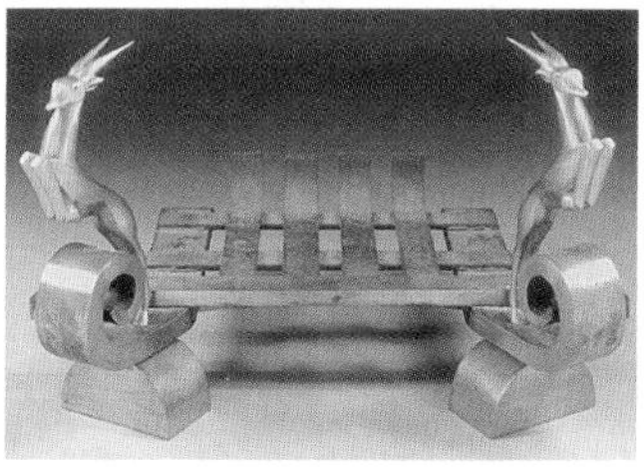

A nickel and steel fire grate, American, 1930s, 27in (68.5cm) wide.
£7,500–9,000
€/ $11,900–14,200 S(NY)

A Georg Jensen silver jug, by Sigvard Bernadotte, Danish, Copenhagen, designed 1938, 6in (15cm) high.
£2,400–2,800
€/ $3,800–4,400 BUK

A Cartier silver cocktail mixing jug and spoon, American, New York c1930, 7in (18cm) high.
£700–800
€/ $1,100–1,300 S(O)

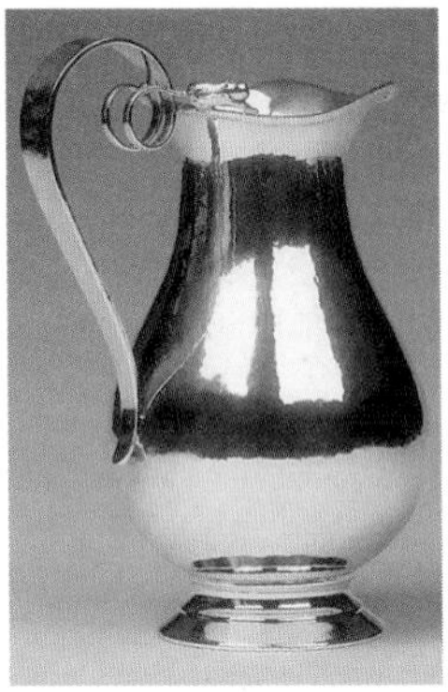

A silver pitcher, by Carl Poul Petersen, with hammered body and blossom-capped C-scroll handle, Canadian, Montreal, mid-20thC, 9in (23cm) high, 19.5oz.
£2,200–2,500
€/ $3,500–3,800 RIT

A set of six Adie Bros silver menu holders, each openwork clip depicting one of a variety of game and other birds, Birmingham 1928, 1¼in (3cm) high, 5.25oz.
£500–600
€/ $800–950 CGC

A four-piece tea and coffee service, with ebonized handles and finials, Sheffield 1938, 1940 and 1942.
£230–275
€/ $360–430 WilP

A Cartier 18ct gold vanity case, c1920, 3½in (9cm) high.
£7,800–8,800
€/ $12,300–14,000 SHa

◄ **A Wiener Werkstätte gilt-metal vase,** by Josef Hoffmann, the bowl hand-hammered in a twisted fluted design, stamped marks, Austrian, c1922, 4¾in (12cm) high.
£1,600–1,800
€/ $2,500–2,800 S

► **A *dinanderie* vase,** with silvered geometric design, signed 'Richmain, France', c1930, 10in (25.5cm) high.
£1,200–1,400
€/ $1,900–2,200 GoW
***Dinanderie* is work in non-precious metals.**

Art Deco Carpets, Rugs & Textiles

An Amsterdam School carpet, by J. Gidding for KVT, Rotterdam, polychrome-decorated with a Tuschinsky-style pattern, Dutch, c1920, 157½ x 115½in (400 x 293.5cm).
£3,200–3,500
€/ $5,000–5,500 S(Am)

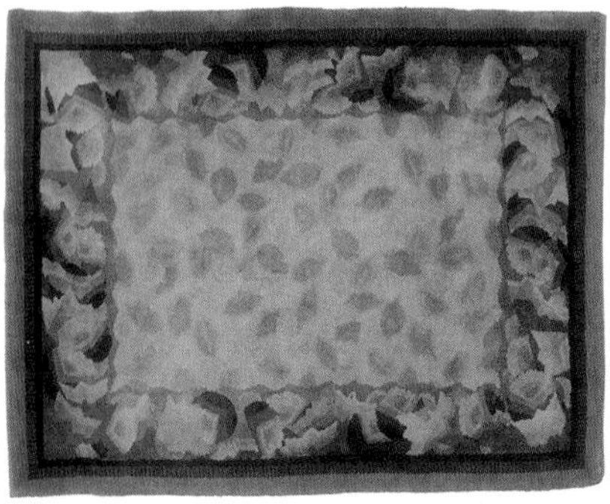

A carpet, by Paul Follot, the central panel decorated with concentric circles and leaves, within an abstract border, woven mark, repair to one corner, French, c1925, 84¼ x 108in (214 x 274.5cm).
£1,200–1,500
€/ $1,900–2,400 S

A rug, by Ben Nicholson, c1930, 44 x 38in (112 x 96.5cm).
£3,000–3,600
€/ $4,700–5,700 S(O)

◄ **A carpet,** by Ashley Havinden, woven monogram, c1930, 97½ x 78½in (247.5 x 199.5cm).
£5,300–5,800
€/ $8,300–9,200 S(NY)

► **A carpet,** by Paule Leleu, woven mark, French, 1940s, 98 x 137in (249 x 348cm).
£5,000–6,000
€/ $8,000–9,500 S(NY)

Twentieth-Century Design

The Modern Movement, an international movement in architecture and design that emerged in Europe in the early 20th century, was, at its core, concerned with breaking down the barriers between technology and society so that high quality pieces could be produced for the masses. In some ways, this was eventually brought about because new materials were developed, such as tubular steel, plywood and polyurethane foam, which gave a new freedom of expression to designers and quicker and less costly methods of production to manufacturers. Nowadays it is common to find white walls and wooden floors complemented by carefully chosen objects from a wide range of disciplines rather than one overriding theme. This change in style has had enormous impact on the market and 20th-century design as a whole is becoming ever more popular and fashionable. The continuous evolution in style and public perception have helped to fuel demand and an acceptance of a 'look' in interior decoration that previously would have been regarded as the taste of a minority.

Always try to buy pieces by known designers. While good quality contemporary pieces by well known designers are rarely inexpensive to buy new, their price on the secondary market can be very reasonable. There follows a period of perhaps 20 to 30 years after design and production when such pieces are uappreciated, after which they tend to be re-evaluated and re-incorporated into popular style. Certain pieces, such as Alvar Aalto's Model No. 60 stool which was designed in 1932, have become iconic and versions of this are now readily available in high street shops. As well as being aware of the designer, you should also buy pieces from the right (usually earliest) edition. For example, the classic Lounge Chair and Ottoman designed by Charles Eames in 1956 was originally made by Herman Miller in the USA and early examples fetch £4,000 (€/ $6,300) or more, whereas the editions produced in Europe by Vitra in the 1980s or later will be worth as little as £1,500 (€/ $2,400), as they can still be bought new for around £2,500 (€/ $4,000). Finally, as with all antiques, condition is all important. Many of the new materials of the 20th century are delicate. For example, some of the early foams used in upholstery have degraded over the last 30 years and are now crumbling beneath their covers. This cannot be restored and so extreme caution should be exercised when looking at such pieces.

Jeremy Morrison and Sarah O'Brien

Ceramics

A Ruskin Pottery high-fired flambé vase, c1920, 7in (18cm) high.
£1,200–1,400
€/ $1,900–2,200 ⊞ DSG

A Bernard Leach earthenware tea set, comprising 15 pieces, impressed 'BL' and St Ives seals, minor chips, c1923, milk jug 3½in (9cm) high.
£2,500–2,800
€/ $4,000–4,400 B

An Oxshott Pottery pitcher, c1925, 9in (23cm) high.
£145–160
€/ $230–250 ⊞ DSG

A Ruskin Pottery high-fired bowl, impressed mark, dated 1925, 12½in (32cm) diam.
£4,500–5,300
€/ $7,000–8,400 B(O)

◄ A Ruskin Pottery lustre glaze jar and cover, c1926, 10in (25.5cm) high.
£600–680
€/ $950–1,100 ⊞ AFD

A Foley tea service, comprising seven pieces, designed by Dame Laura Knight, decorated with Dove pattern, hairline crack, factory marks, signed, c1930, teapot 4in (10cm) high.
£280–325
€/ $440–500 B

Items in the Twentieth-Century Design section have been arranged in date order within each sub-section.

The Albert E. Wade Collection

There are few collectors with as much enthusiasm and energy for their subject as Albert Wade, who identified British art pottery as an interesting collecting area when it was still shunned by many.

From the late 1960s he bought regularly from auctions, markets and in particular Austin's of Peckham, which, during the post-WWII period, was one of the biggest antiques emporia in Europe. It was relatively easy to acquire such pieces because many large Victorian homes in south London were being broken up, and while their furniture was keenly sought, much of the later pottery was overlooked.

Initially, very little was written on the subject of Art Pottery and so collecting it was a far more instinctive occupation than it is today. These days there are many well-researched books on the subject and illustrations of pots from Albert Wade's collection feature heavily in those relating to Moorcroft and Ruskin.

The sale of Wade's collection at Sotheby's Olympia, in two auctions in 2002 included over 2000 items in more than 800 lots and realized over £1,000,000 (€/ $1,580,000). It included the largest collection of Ruskin pottery to have come onto the market in living memory. Among the highlights was a spectacular Chinese-inspired vase dated 1905, which sold for £19,387 (€/ $30,600). This vase was previously in the famous Harriman Judd Collection which Sotheby's sold in a series of sales in New York in 2001. The reason for this extraordinary price was the very fine markings within the glaze, which was notoriously difficult to control in the kiln when the piece was being fired. Other vases of this size, shape and with less exciting glazes were fetching around £3,000 (€/ $4,700) in the UK. **Jeremy Morrison**

A Ruskin Pottery crystalline tazza, c1930, 8¼in (21cm) diam.
£550–600
€/ $870–950 ⊞ DSG

A stoneware footed bowl, by Charles Vyse, with figured tenmoku glaze, incised 'CV', hairline crack, dated 1939, 5¼in (13.5cm) diam.
£400–500
€/ $630–800 ⚒ B
Tenmoku is a high temperature feldspathic glaze deeply stained with iron oxide. The process originated in China during the Tang Dynasty.

A stoneware tile, by Bernard Leach, impressed marks, c1935, 4in (10cm) square, set in an oak frame.
£280–320
€/ $440–500 ⚒ Bea(E)

A pottery bowl, by Waylande Gregory, with sgraffito leaf decoration, the interior gilded, signed, American, mid-20thC, 9in (23cm) diam.
£400–500
€/ $630–800 ⚒ RIT

A Wedgwood bowl, by Keith Murray, signed, c1935, 6½in (16.5cm) diam.
£600–725
€/ $950–1,100 ⚒ B(W)
Murray's black basalt wares are the rarest of all his products.

A Leach Pottery coffee pot, decorated with a mottled glaze, c1950, 9in (23cm) high.
£75–85
€/ $120–130 ⊞ RUSK

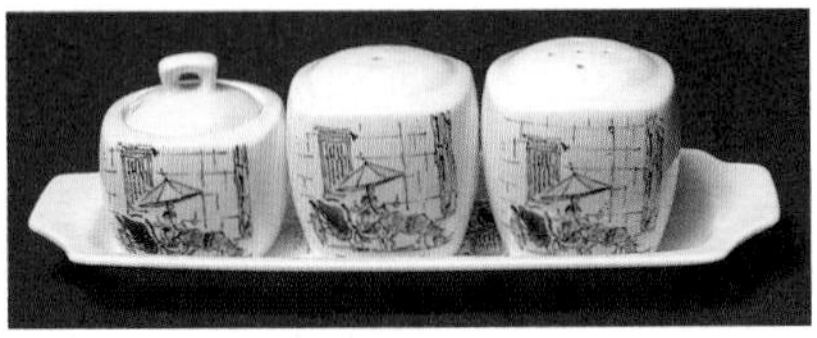

A Midwinter Stylecraft cruet-on-stand, by Hugh Casson, decorated with Riviera pattern, c1954, 9in (23cm) wide.
£85–100
€/ $130–160 ⊞ CHI

▶ **A Madoura pottery jug,** by Pablo Picasso, impressed and inscribed marks, c1955, 12¼in (31cm) high.
£2,000–2,400
€/ $3,200–3,800 ⚒ WW

A Gertrud and Otto Natzler ceramic bowl, with volcanic glaze, signed, American, c1956, 8in (20.5cm) diam.
£3,200–3,500
€/ $5,000–5,500 ⚒ BB(L)

A Rörstrand bottle vase, Swedish, c1960, 6in (15cm) high.
£145–160
€/ $230–250 ⊞ DSG

A Poole Pottery vase, by Robert Jefferson, c1960, 9in (23cm) high.
£630–700
€/ $1,000–1,100 ⊞ HarC
Robert Jefferson was head of design at Poole between 1958 and 1966.

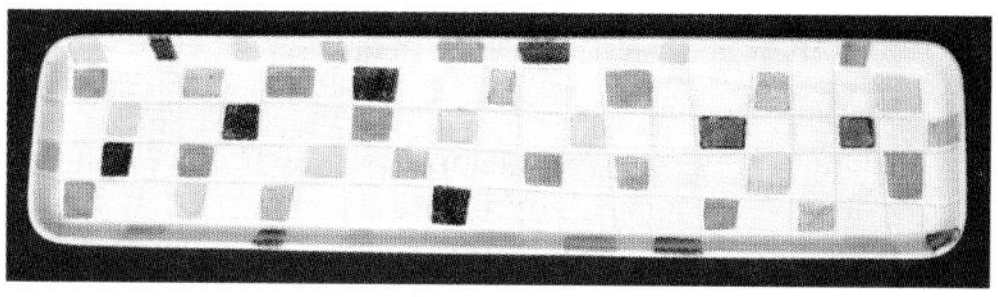

A Midwinter tray, designed by Jessie Tait, decorated with Mosaic pattern, c1960, 22½in (57cm) wide.
£150–165
€/ $240–260 ⊞ CHI

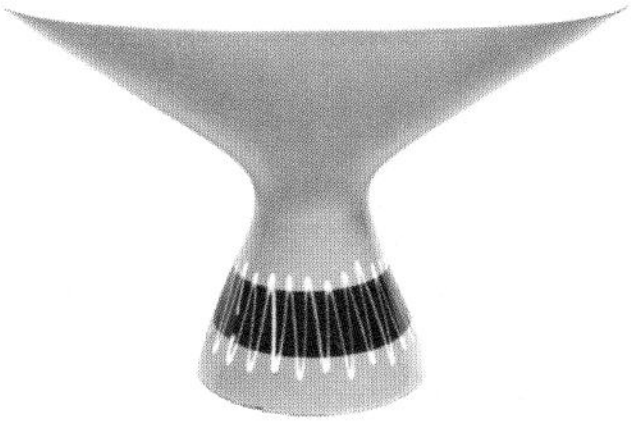

◄ A Hornsea Pottery vase, 1960s, 6in (15cm) high.
£40–45
€/ $64–70
⊞ LUNA

A Poole Pottery Delphis dish, 1960s, 17in (43cm) wide.
£100–120
€/ $160–190 ⊞ CHI

A stoneware charger, by Bryan Newman, impressed marks, c1969, 18in (45.5cm) diam.
£150–175
€/ $240–280 ⚒ GH

A stoneware slab bottle vase, by Bernard Leach, impressed marks, c1970, 7¾in (19.5cm) high, with original receipt and short biography.
£1,100–1,300
€/ $1,800–2,000 ⚒ Bea(E)

A stoneware cup, by Shoji Hamada, with wax resist floral designs, c1962, 3½in (8.5cm) high.
£750–875
€/ $1,200–1,400 ⚒ B

A stoneware vase, by Bernard Rooke, 1960s, 11in (28cm) high.
£60–65
€/ $95–100 ⊞ MARK

A Poole Pottery charger, by Guy Sydenham, c1970, 12in (30.5cm) diam.
£430–480
€/ $680–760 ⊞ HarC

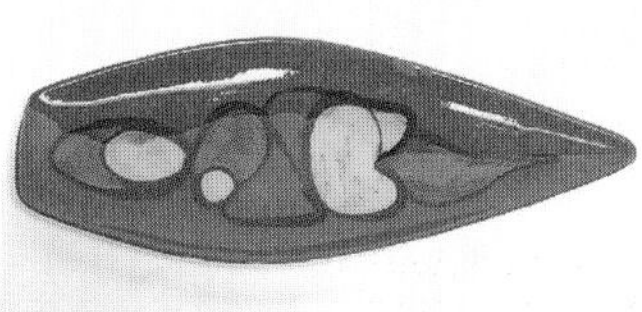

◄ A Poole Pottery dish, 1970s, 18in (45.5cm) wide.
£60–70
€/ $95–110
⊞ LUNA

A Troika mask, painter's mark for Linda Thomas, early 1970s, 10in (25.5cm) high.
£1,000–1,100
€/ $1,600–1,800 ⊞ TRO

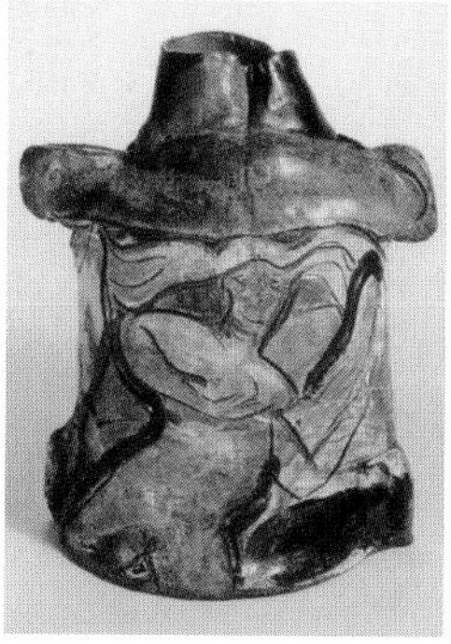

A Rudy Autio stoneware figural vessel, American, c1980, 23½in (59.5cm) high.
£3,000–3,600
€/ $4,800–5,700 ⚒ S(NY)

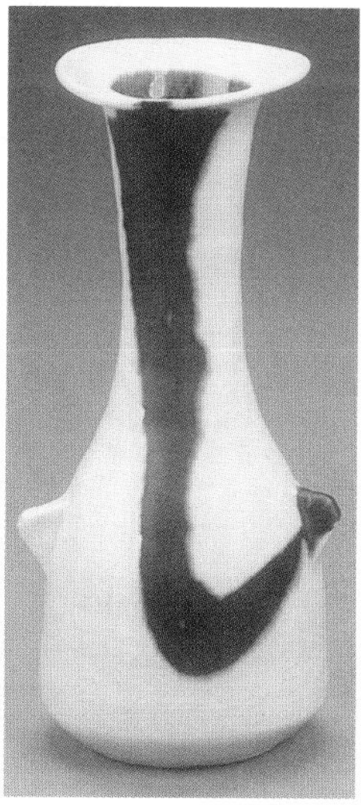

An Elizabeth Woodman glazed earthenware Pillow pitcher impressed 'Woodman', American, c1980, 17¼in (44cm) high.
£4,500–5,500
€/ $7,100–8,700 ⚒ S(NY)

◄ A porcelain vase, by Janet Leach, with two lugs, impressed marks, c1980, 7¾in (19.5cm) high.
£400–500
€/ $640–800 ⚒ B

Furniture

A lacquered-steel and leather LC3 armchair, by Le Corbusier, designed 1928, re-issued by Cassina 1980s, Italian, 39½in (100.5cm) wide.
£750–900
€/ $1,200–1,500 BUK
This design was first made by Thonet Frères, and an original would be highly valuable.

An Isokon bent plywood stool, each foot with two metal reinforcers, three reinforcers missing, designed in 1933, 17¾in (45.5cm) high.
£700–800
€/ $1,100–1,300 S

A velvet-upholstered bentwood Devalle sofa, designed by Carlo Mollino 1939, reissued by Edition Galleria Colombari c1995, Italian, Milan.
£1,300–1,500
€/ $2,000–2,400 DORO

A pair of Barcelona chairs, by Ludwig Mies van der Rohe, German, designed 1929.
£2,200–2,500
€/ $3,500–4,000 S(O)
Designed by Mies van der Rohe for the German Pavilion of the 1929 Barcelona Exhibition, these examples were made c1980. An original would be worth in the region of £40,000 (€/ $63,000).

A pair of Gispen tubular steel armchairs, model No. 414, designed by W. H. Gispen, with curved black Gisolite armrests, upholstered in leatherette, Dutch, designed 1935.
£750–875
€/ $1,200–1,400 S(Am)

A Lloyd Chrome Co Dinette table, designed c1939, American, 36½in (92.5cm) diam.
£380–450
€/ $600–720 BB(L)

◄ **A gilt-iron and mirrored-glass coffee table,** designed by René Prou, French, c1940, 33½in (85cm) diam.
£6,800–7,600
€/ $10,800–12,000 NART

A birch-framed low chair, by Gerald Summers for Makers of Simple Furniture, the seat and back upholstered in vinyl, designed c1933.
£380–450
€/ $600–700 B

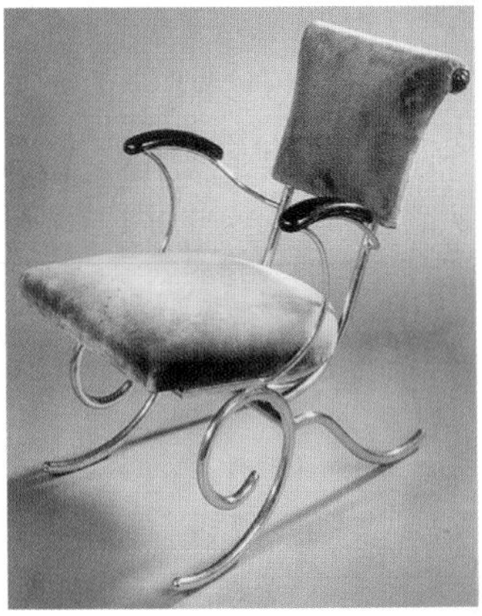

A tubular steel and ebonized wood armchair, designed by S. van Ravesteyn, upholstered in velvet, Dutch, c1936.
£5,800–6,800
€/ $9,200–10,800 S(Am)
Architect and interior designer Sybold van Ravesteyn (1899–1983) began his career as a civil engineer and in the 1920s became acquainted with and influenced by Gerrit Rietveld and other De Stijl members. In the 1930s van Ravesteyn's work took on a more frivolous appearance derived from the baroque and Louis XV styles. Despite being criticized by his more purist colleagues, van Ravesteyn's new work led to many important commissions, such as the renovation of the Tiel Fire Insurance Company, Holland, in 1936 for which he designed this eccentric curvilinear chair. Van Ravesteyn also furnished the interior of the Dutch royal yacht, for which he supplied chairs of the same design.

LOCATE THE SOURCE

The source of each illustration in Miller's can be found by checking the code letters below each caption with the Key to Illustrations, pages 794–800.

◀ **A H. Morris & Co mahogany and laminated birch Allegro chair,** by Sir Basil Spence, with foam-padded leather-covered seat, labelled 'Morris of Glasgow' and impressed number to frame, designed 1947.
£900–1,100
€/ $1,400–1,700 B
This design was not a commercial success as production costs were too high, with each chair taking many hours to create.

A Martyn paroba wood reception desk, by Hugh Casson, Misha Black and John Diamond, the surface covered in goat skin with a raised ebonized surround, above two banks of four drawers and a sliding shelf, with recessed brass drop handles, designed 1952, manufactured 1953, 78in (198cm) wide.
£525–625
€/ $830–1,000 B

A Widdicomb mahogany table, model No. 1764, by T. H. Robsjohn-Gibbings, signed and dated 1952, 48in (122cm) diam.
£2,200–2,500
€/ $3,500–4,000 TREA
T. H. Robsjohn-Gibbings was British-born. He set up a shop in New York's Madison Avenue in 1936 and became one of the most important decorators in the United States in the late 1930s and '40s. He successfully mixed classical elements from Ancient Greece with the Art Deco style in a modern way.

A Swedese Lamino chair, by Yngve Eckström, Swedish, 1950s.
£520–575
€/ $820–900 MARK

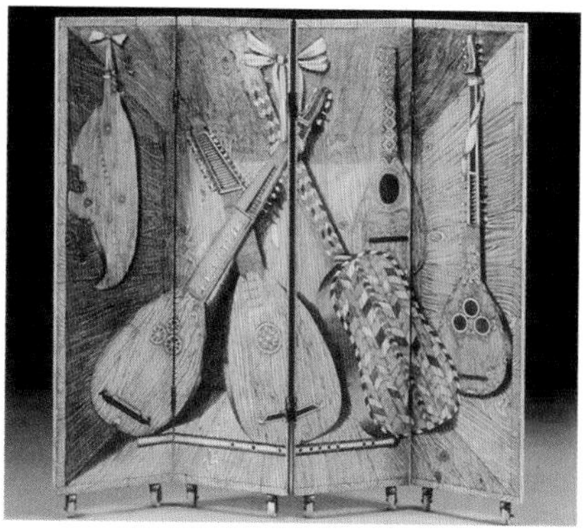

A wood four-panel screen, by Piero Fornasetti, with printed decoration of birds in an aviary on one side and musical instruments in wood-effect on the other, Italian, c1955, each panel 13¾in (35cm) wide.
£8,500–10,000
€/ $13,400–15,800 S(P)

TWENTIETH-CENTURY DESIGN

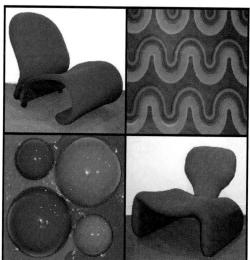

A set of three rosewood and hide stools, Danish, c1960, 20in (51cm) high.
£520–575
€/ $820–900 ⊞ MARK

A G Plan teak swivel chair, 1970s.
£550–600
€/ $870–950 ⊞ TRA

► A dining table, by Paul Evans, American, designed c1970, 94in (239cm) wide.
£2,800–3,200
€/ $4,400–5,000 ⚒ BB(L)

A walnut low table, designed by George Nakashima, American, c1962, 100in (254cm) wide.
£8,500–10,000
€/ $13,400–15,800 ⚒ S(NY)

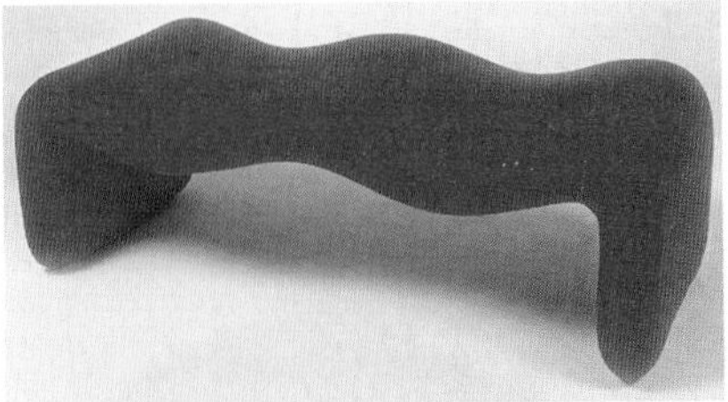

A tubular steel-framed Djinn long bench stool, by Olivier Mourgue for Airborne International, fabric upholstery renewed, French, designed 1965, 49¼in (125cm) wide.
£750–875
€/ $1,200–1,400 ⚒ DORO
The use of pieces such as this in Stanley Kubrick's *2001: A Space Odyssey* made the Djinn series arguably the most famous examples of Pop furniture design, and the first to use urethane foam upholstery over tubular steel frames. The Djinn was named by Mourgue after the Islamic mythological spirit with supernatural powers, who can take human or animal form.

A Knoll rosewood and bronze wire table and four chairs, by Warren Platner, Model No 1725A, the chairs with woollen upholstery, signed, designed 1966, produced 1970s, table 48in (122cm) diam.
£1,700–2,000
€/ $2,700–3,200 ⚒ TREA

An Arkana moulded plastic table and four chairs, after a design by Eero Saarinen, the table with rosewood-veneered top, 1960s, table 47¼in (120cm) diam.
£380–450
€/ $600–720 ⚒ SWO
The American Eero Saarinen's (1910–61) designs used new materials and organic, often futuristic, shapes. He is perhaps best known for his Trans World Airline Terminals at John F. Kennedy Airport in New York and for the design of the Tulip chair which sold in great numbers and was copied extensively in the 1960s.

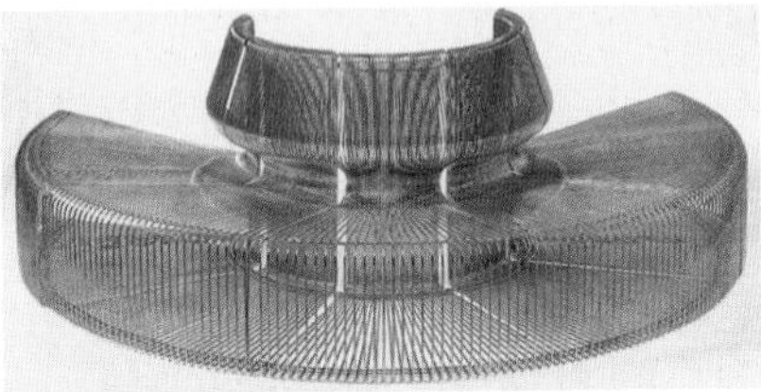

Five Fritz Hansen chromed-steel Wire Furniture Programme seating elements, by Verner Panton, Danish, 1971, each section 29½in (75cm) wide.
£2,800–3,200
€/ $4,400–5,000 ⚒ DORO
These seating elements can be combined in various ways.

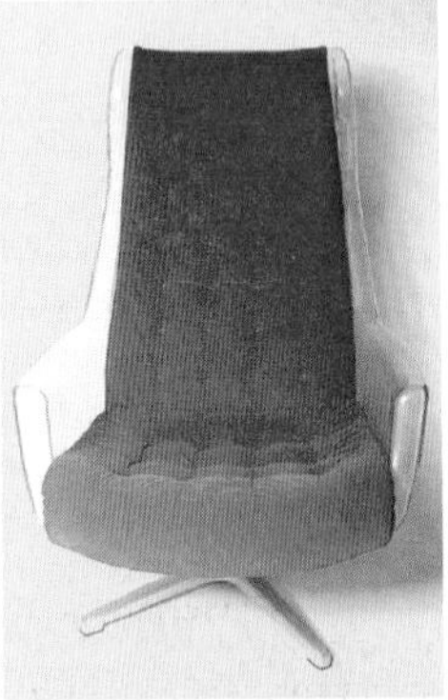

◄ A Perspex chair, with velvet upholstery, 1970s.
£300–330
€/ $475–525
⊞ TWI

A Maxalto rosewood and ebony-inlaid Africa dining suite, by Tobia and Afra Scarpa, comprising a table and eight chairs, stamped 'M', Italian, 1975, table 57in (145cm) diam.
£5,000–5,700
€/ $8,000–9,000 ⚒ S(O)
Tobia Scarpa (b1935) was the son of the architect Carlo Scarpa and after marrying Afra Bianchin they designed furniture for Gavina from 1960. Soon afterwards they opened their own office and went on to design for a number of well known firms including B&B Italia, Knoll, Maxalto and Benetton.

A mahogany rocking chair, by David N. Ebner, American, 1978.
£6,500–7,200
€/ $10,200–11,400 ⚒ S(NY)

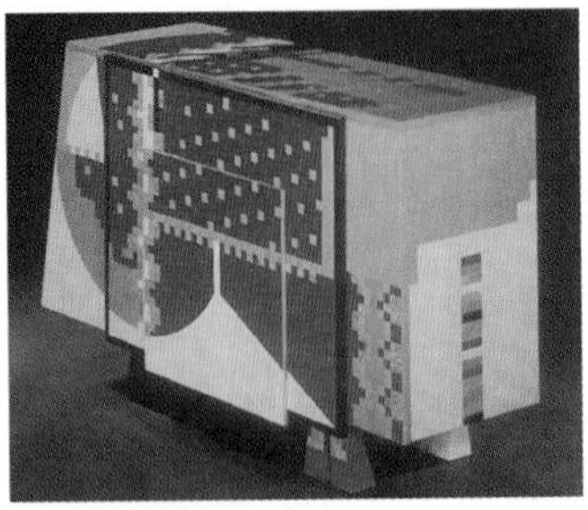

A Nuovo Alchimia/Zabro veneered side cabinet, labelled, Italian, 1985, 52in (132cm) wide.
£2,200–2,500
€/ $3,500–4,000 ⚒ S(O)

Glass

An enamelled glass jug, designed by Dame Laura Knight for the Art in Industry Exhibition at Harrods, factory mark, designed 1934, 7in (18cm) high.
£420–500
€/ $660–790 ⚒ B

In the wake of the Wall Street crash in 1929, British industry was facing a tough challenge. Innovative approaches to design were needed to boost sales and profits. Many critics drew comparisons with the Swedish Exhibition of 1930 which highlighted the successful co-operation between good design and manufacturing. Following a government report, several attempts were made to fuse art with industrial production. In Britain one of the more successful results was the Art in Industry Exhibition at Harrods, named 'Modern Ware for the Table'. Alongside Laura Knight, designs were provided by Vanessa Bell, Graham Sutherland, Frank Brangwyn and others. Laura Knight also designed a range of 'Circus Ware' for Clarice Cliff's Bizarre pottery range for the exhibition.

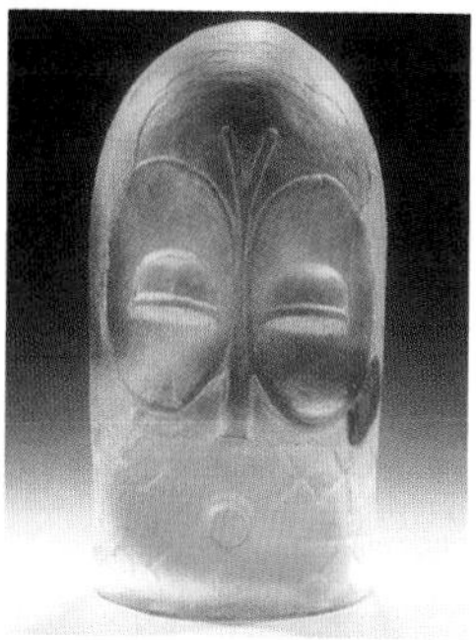

A Seguso Vetri d'Arte Murano glass sculpture, modelled as an ethnic mask, the front unpolished, Italian, Venice, probably 1960s, 15¼in (38.5cm) high.
£1,300–1,500
€/ $2,000–2,400 ⚒ S(Am)

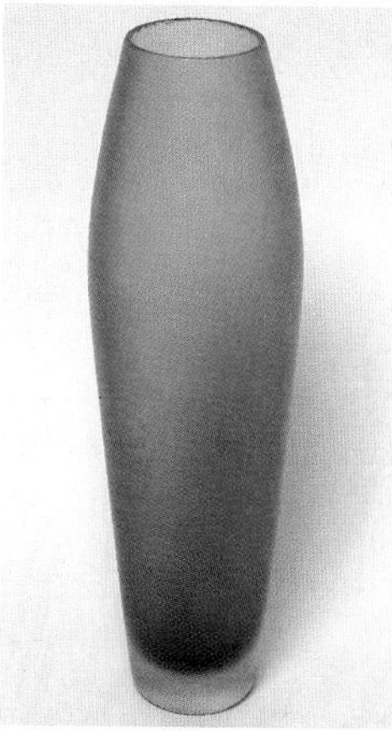

A Venini incised glass vase, signed, Italian, c1950, 16in (40.5cm) high.
£3,800–4,200
€/ $6,000–6,600 ⊞ GoW

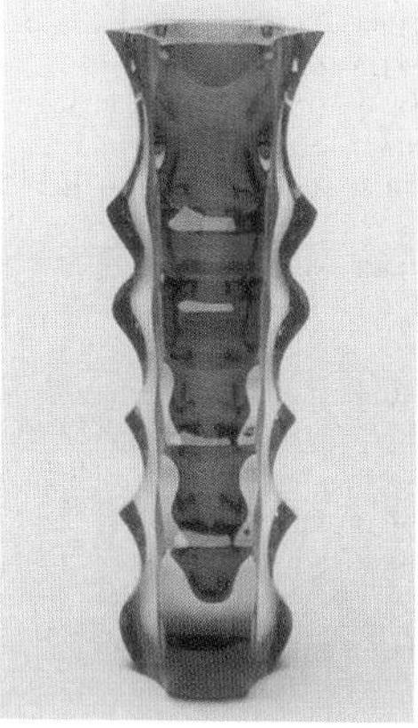

An Exbor Glassworks Sommerso glass vase, attributed to Pavel Hlava, stamped, Czechoslovakian, designed 1960, produced 1970s, 10¾in (27.5cm) high.
£200–225
€/ $320–350 ⚒ B(Kn)

Sommerso is a technique used in Venetian glass-making where one colour is cased (or submerged – hence the name) in clear glass.

A glass sculpture, entitled 'Bronze Solar Riser', by Tom Patti, signed and dated, American, 1979, 4¾in (12cm) high.
£5,700–7,000
€/ $9,000–11,000 ⚒ S(NY)

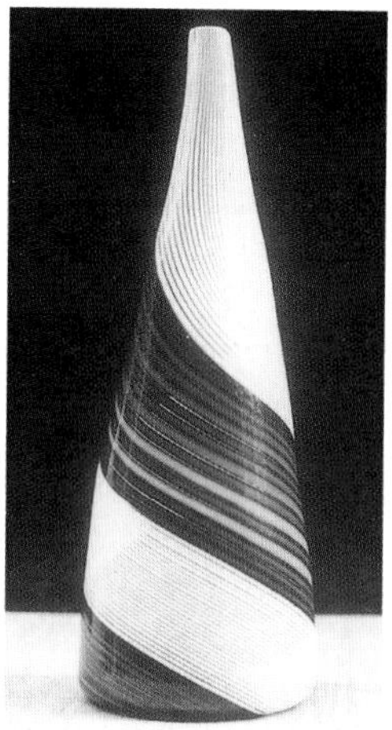

A Murano Filigrana glass bottle, with a dimpled side, Italian, 1950s, 13½in (34.5cm) high.
£1,000–1,100
€/ $1,600–1,700 ⊞ KK

A Salviati Sassi glass vase. by Luciano Gaspari, engraved 'Salviati', with paper label, Italian, designed 1960, produced c1965, 9½in (24cm) high.
£600–700
€/ $950–1,100 ⚒ B(Kn)

An Åfors glass vase, by Bertil Vallien, signed, Swedish, 1970s, 4in (10cm) high.
£45–60
€/ $70–95 ⊞ MARK

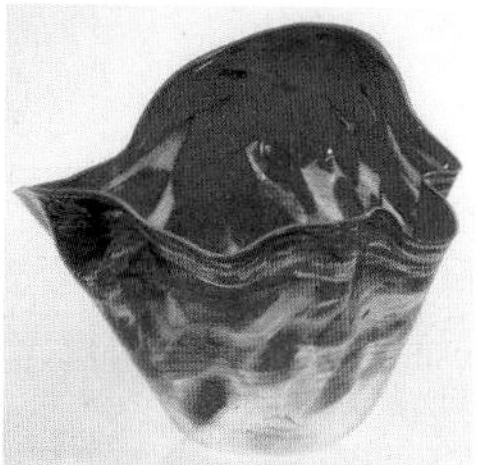

A Kosta green glass vase, by Vicke Lindstrand, Swedish, 1950s, 5in (12.5cm) high.
£55–60
€/ $87–95 ⊞ MARK

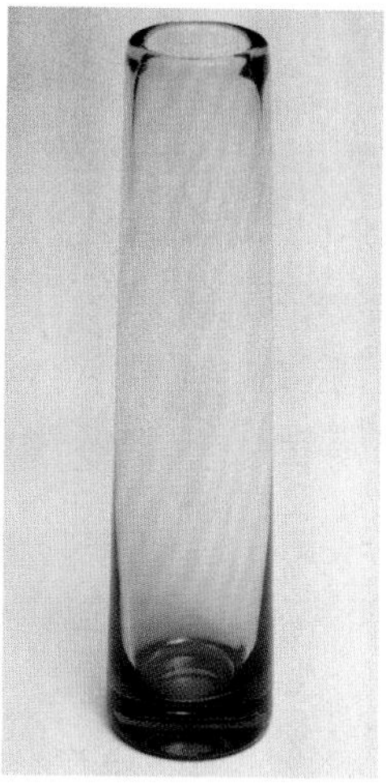

A Holmegaard glass vase, by Per Lutken, Danish, 1950s–60s, 12½in (32cm) high.
£100–120
€/ $160–190 ⊞ ORI

A Misar glass vase, by Ettore Sottsass for Memphis, one handle repaired, Italian, 1982, 12¼in (31cm) high.
£1,500–1,700
€/ $2,400–2,700 ⚒ DORO

This vase was exhibited at the Victoria & Albert Museum, London in 1982.

◀ **A glass bowl,** by Dale Chihuly, signed, American, 1989, 22¾in (58cm) diam.
£3,500–4,000
€/ $5,500–6,300 ⚒ BUK

Jewellery

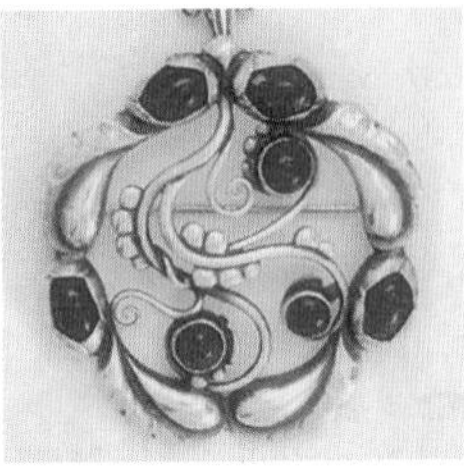

A Jensen & Wendel silver brooch/pendant, by Georg Jensen, set with lapis lazuli, on a silver chain, Danish, Copenhagen, 1945–51, 1¾in (4.5cm) diam.
£500–600
€/ $800–950 BUK

A rhodium pendant, on a chain, 1950s, 3½in (9cm) square.
£35–40
€/ $55–65 SBL

► A Georg Jensen 18ct gold and moonstone brooch, by Nana Ditzel, c1960, 3¼in (8.5cm) wide.
£3,000–3,500
€/ $4,700–5,500
DID

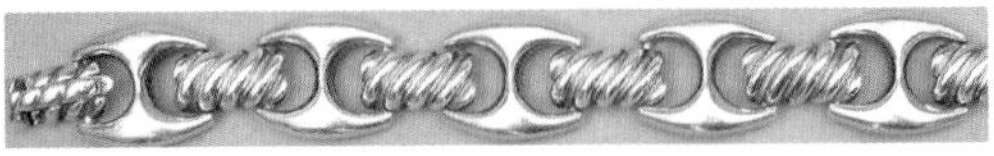

A silver bracelet, Scandinavian, c1970, 2oz.
£160–180
€/ $250–280 G(L)

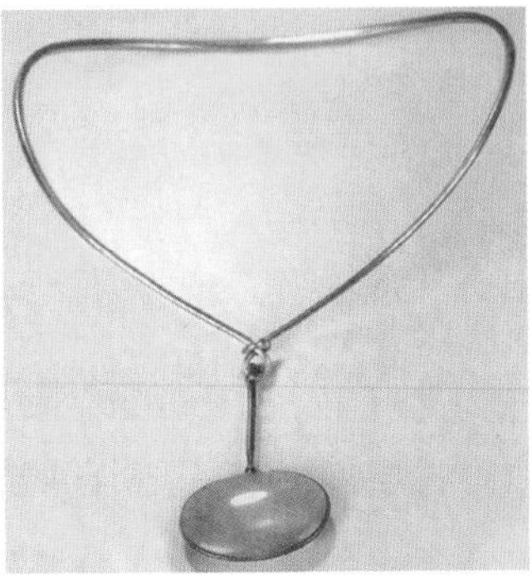

A Georg Jensen silver and quartz necklet and pendant, by Torun Bülow-Hübe, maker's marks, Danish, Copenhagen, London import marks for 1974.
£300–350
€/ $475–550 DN

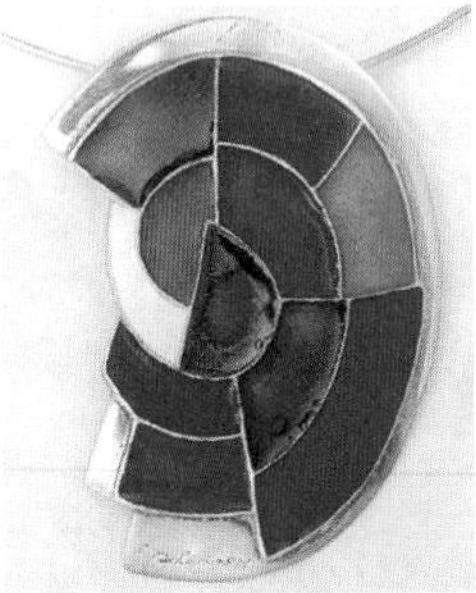

An Artcurial silver and enamel Abstraction pendant, by Sonia Delauney, on a rigid collar, French, designed 1979, pendant 2¾in (7cm) long, in original box with certificate.
£850–1,000
€/ $1,300–1,600 BUK

A silver torque, by Anna Strina Åberg, modelled as stylized flower motifs, with matching ring, Swedish, Nässjo, 1984–87.
£850–1,000
€/ $1,300–1,600 S(O)
Åberg's work is represented at the Swedish National museum and she has created pieces for the Swedish royal family.

Lighting

► A chrome Anglepoise three-step lamp, c1920.
£270–300
€/ $425–475 LUNA

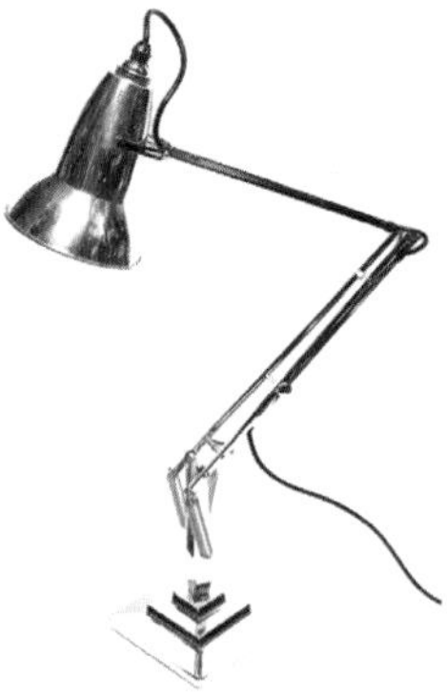

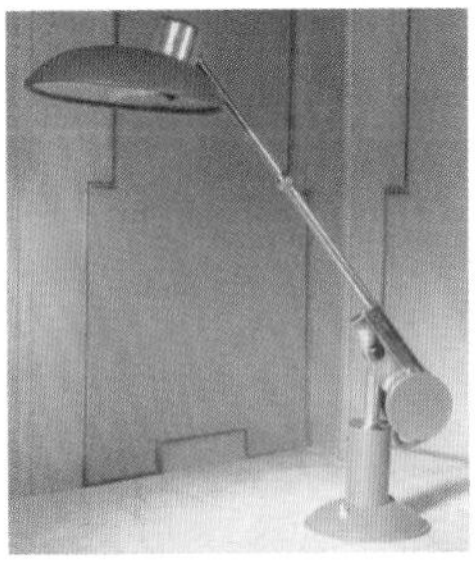

A chrome-plated steel adjustable desk lamp, by F. Solere, with leather shade, French, 1930s, 29½in (75cm) high.
£1,000–1,200
€/ $1,600–1,900 S(Am)

Always check that electric lighting conforms to the current safety regulations before using.

A brass Sputnik light fixture, with decorative bulbs, 1950s, 25in (63.5cm) diam.
£420–500
€/ $660–800 TREA

A gilt-metal and enamel table lamp/radio, by Jospeh Lucas, 1950s, 17¾in (45cm) high.
£60–70
€/ $95–110 L&E

► A painted metal desk light, by Serge Mouille, with adjustable shade, French, c1950, 31½in (80cm) high.
£2,500–2,800
€/ $4,000–4,400 S(O)
Serge Mouille (1922–88) studied as a silversmith and established his own studios in 1945. He designed his first prototype lamp in 1953 for the decorator and architect Jacques Adnet. In 1953 he participated in an exhibition at the Musée des Arts Décoratifs, Paris, before collaborating with Louis Sognot on lighting solutions and going on to be one of the avant-garde designers, including Jean Prouvé, whose modern designs were shown at the Steph Simon gallery, Paris, when it opened in 1956.

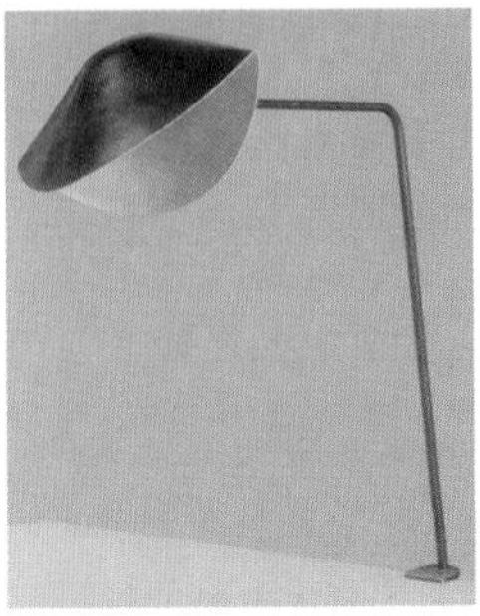

A Poole Pottery Helmet lamp, by Guy Sydenham, c1960, 12in (30.5cm) high.
£1,300–1,500
€/ $2,000–2,400 ⊞ HarC

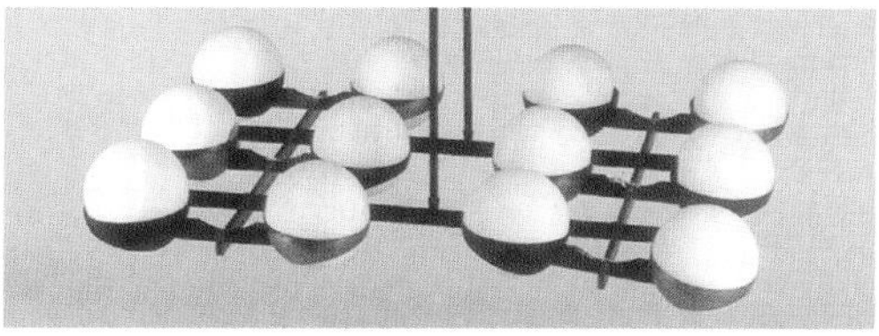

A brass, steel and painted-aluminium hanging light, by Gaetano Scolari, Italian, c1960, 30in (76cm) wide.
£1,100–1,300
€/ $1,700–2,000 ⚒ BB(L)

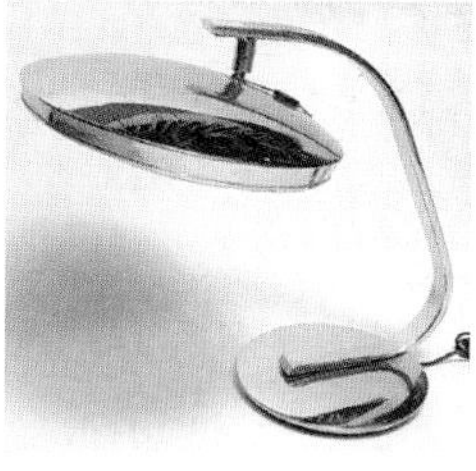

A Fase chrome lamp, Spanish, c1960, 15in (38cm) high.
£250–275
€/ $400–440 ⊞ MARK

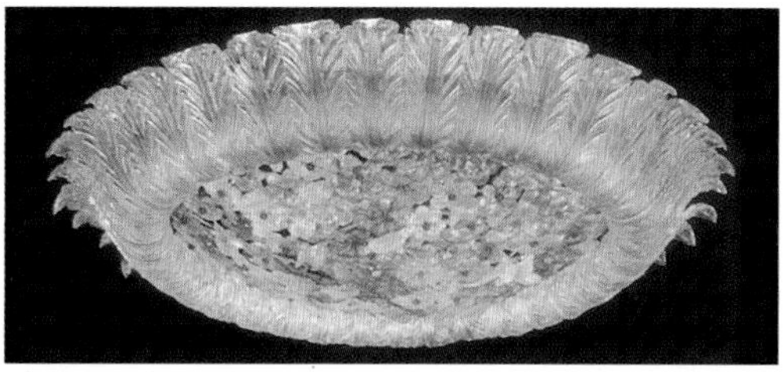

A Murano glass and aventurine *plafonnier*, Italian, Venice, c1960, 39½in (100.5cm) diam.
£3,500–4,200
€/ $5,500–6,600 ⚒ S(P)

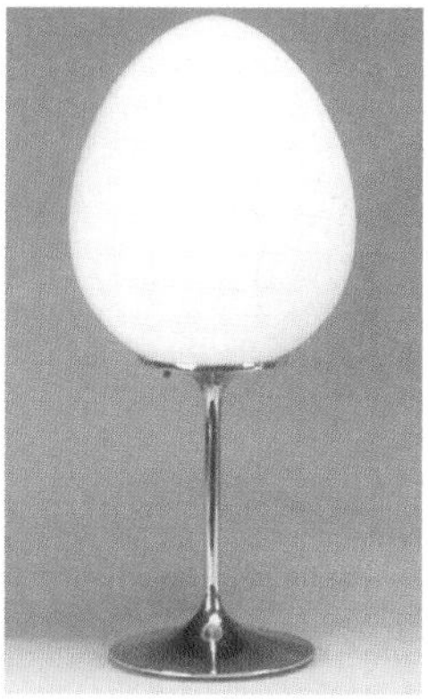

A table lamp, by Bill Curry for Design Line, American, c1968, 21½in (54.5cm) high.
£250–300
€/ $400–475 ⚒ BB(L)

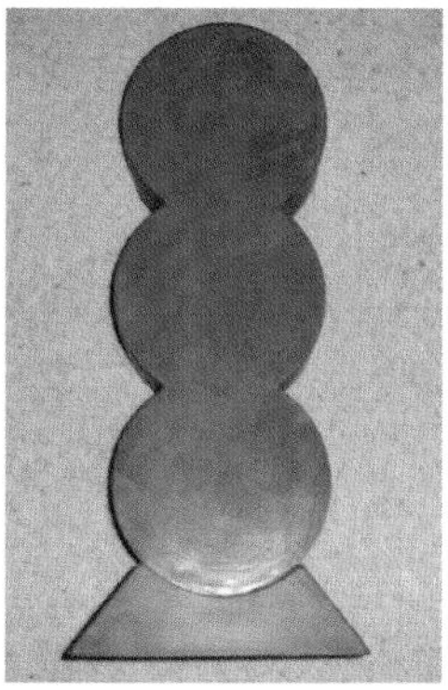

A Troika pottery lamp base, by Lesley Illsley, marked, late 1960s, 15in (38cm) high.
£1,400–1,600
€/ $2,200–2,500 ⊞ TRO

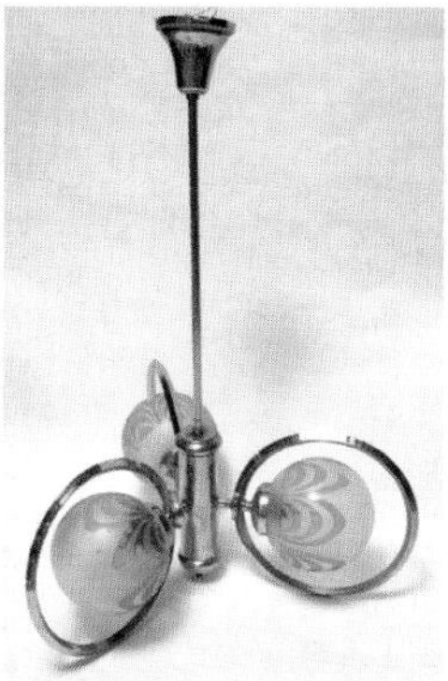

A chrome and glass hanging lamp, c1970, 27in (68.5cm) high.
£35–40
€/ $55–63 ⊞ MARK

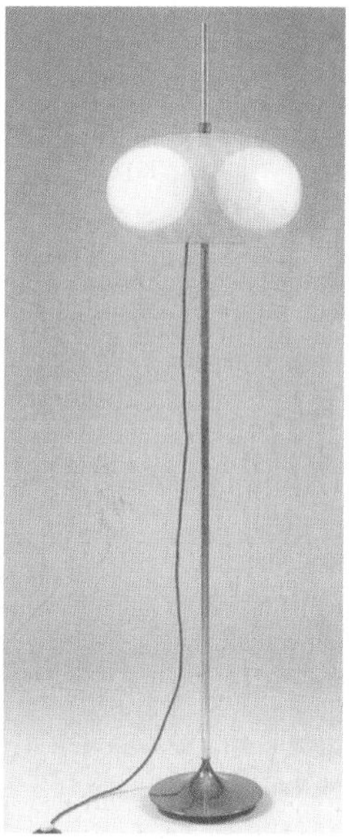

A chromed-metal floor lamp, by Luigi Colani, with plastic shade, German, c1970, 63in (160cm) high.
£320–400
€/ $500–630 ⚒ DORO

◄ A polychromed-metal and laminated wood Tahiti table light, by Ettore Sottsass for Memphis, with label, Italian, designed 1981, 24¾in (63cm) high.
£450–500
€/ $700–800 ⚒ S(O)

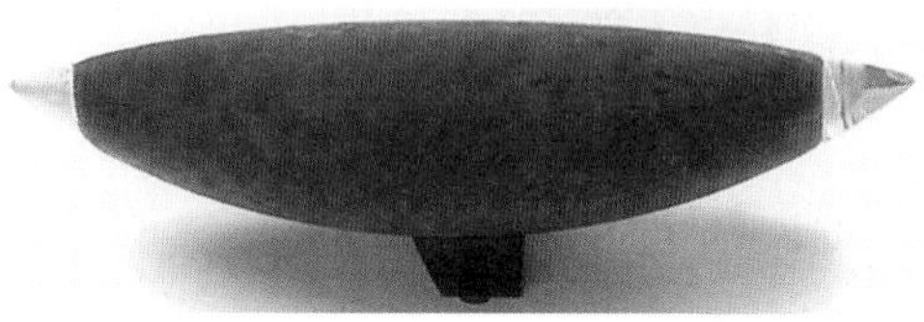

A pair of Vetri VMM glass wall lights, by Barovier & Toso, Italian, c1980, 24in (61cm) wide.
£1,300–1,500
€/ $2,000–2,400 ⚒ DORO

Metalware

A silver napkin ring, by Bernard Cuzner, Birmingham 1952, 1¾in (4.5cm) diam.
£340–375
€/ $540–600 ⊞ SHa

A pair of gilded silver urns, by Pampaloni, Italian, Rome 1960s, 10¼in (26cm) high.
£16,000–18,000
€/ $25,300–28,500 ⊞ KK

A bronze sculpture, by Arman, entitled 'Camera Chopped Up', signed and numbered, French, c1970, 21in (53.5cm) high.
£1,100–1,300
€/ $1,700–2,000 ⊞ MARK

Rugs & Textiles

A tapestry-weave carpet, by Jacques Frank, French, c1950, 119 x 89in (302.5 x 226cm).
£2,700–3,000
€/ $4,300–4,700 S(O)

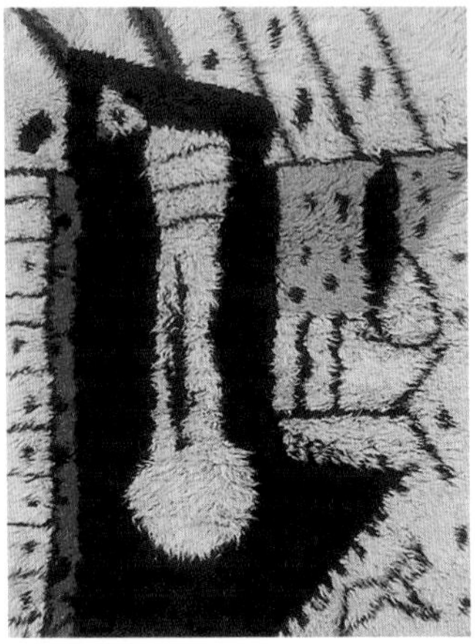

A wool wall rug, after Pablo Picasso, signed 'Picasso', France, 1950s, 80¾ x 59in (205 x 150cm).
£2,000–2,400
€/ $3,200–3,800 DORO

Further reading

Miller's 20th-century Design Buyer's Guide, Miller's Publications, 2003

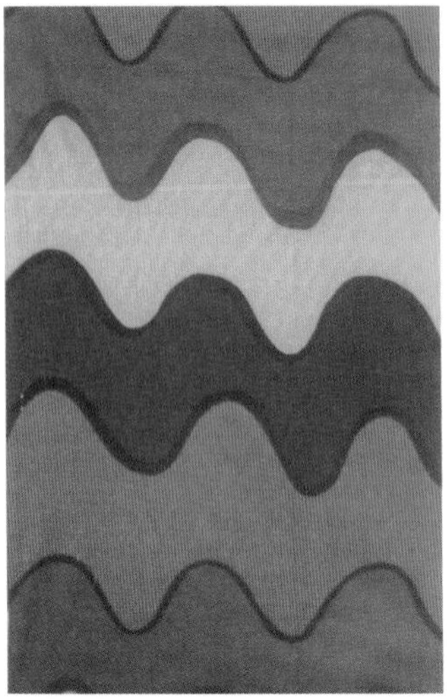

A panel of Marimekko cotton Lokki fabric, by Maija Isola, signed, Finnish, 1961, 60 x 47½in (152.5 x 120.5cm)
£180–200
€/ $285–315 TREA

A panel of linen Allegro fabric, by Lucienne Day for Heal Fabrics, 1952, 53¾ x 50in (135.5 x 127cm).
£850–1,000
€/ $1,300–1,600 B

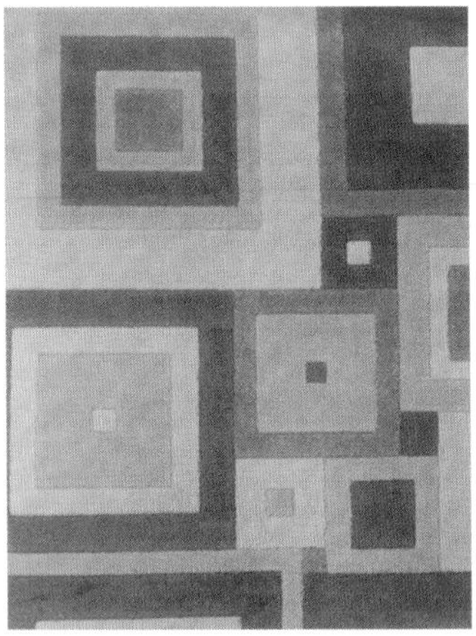

A wool Square Dance carpet, by Ross Litell for Unica Vaev, Danish, Copenhagen, c1960, 124½ x 90¼in (316 x 229cm).
£1,100–1,300
€/ $1,700–2,000 DORO

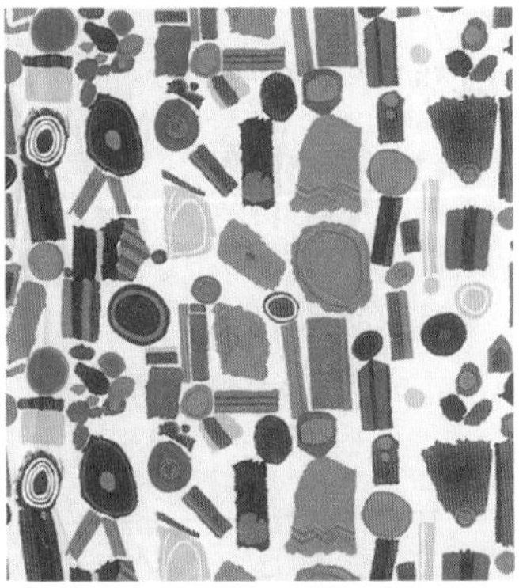

A panel of cotton Top Brass fabric, by Zandra Rhodes for Heal Fabrics, c1967, 78¾x 46¾in (200 x 119cm).
£320–400
€/ $500–630 B

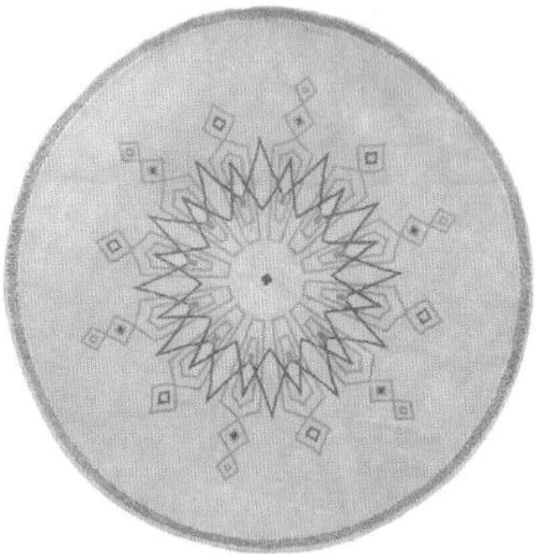

A wool carpet, by Paule Leleu, with woven signature, French, 1950s, 106½in (270.5cm) diam.
£5,700–6,800
€/ $9,000–10,800 S(NY)

A pair of Sanderson & Son Sanderlin fabric Chiesa Della Salute curtains, by John Piper, 1960, 77½in x 46½in (197 x 118cm).
£380–450
€/ $600–700 B

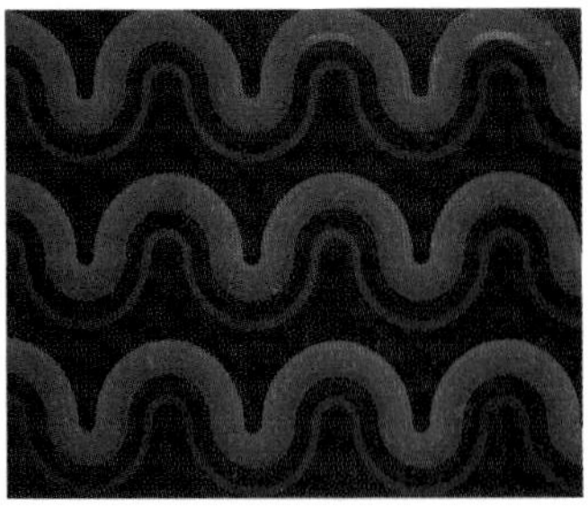

A panel of Wave fabric, by Verner Panton for Mira-X, 1974, 47 x 59in (119.5 x 150cm).
£750–850
€/ $1,200–1,300 MARK

► **A jute Turquoise wall hanging,** by Alexander Calder, signed and dated, American, 1975, 56 x 78in (142 x 198cm).
£2,500–3,000
€/ $4,000–4,700 BB(L)

Lamps & Lighting

Ceiling & Wall Lights

A brass chandelier, drilled for electricity, Flemish, 18thC, 16in (40.5cm) high.
£4,500–5,400
€/ $7,000–8,500 S

A pair of Louis XV ormolu three-light rococo wall sconces, with integral drip pans and candle sconces, drilled for electricity, 26in (66cm) high.
£2,800–3,200
€/ $4,400–5,100 Bri

A pair of patinated metal one-light wall appliques, fitted for electricity, German, 1750–1800, 20½in (52cm) high.
£1,200–1,400
€/ $1,900–2,200 S(Am)

A tin and etched glass hall lantern, one pane damaged, Dutch, 1775–1825, 18¼in (46.5cm) high.
£300–350
€/ $470–550 B(Ch)

A set of four gilt-bronze wall lights, c1870, 8in (20.5cm) high.
£2,500–3,000
€/ $4,000–4,700 S(O)

A pair of giltwood wall appliques, 19thC, 37in (94cm) high.
£1,000–1,100
€/ $1,600–1,700 SWO

A child's sheet tin and waxed paper hanging night light, 19thC, 14in (35.5cm) high.
£430–475
€/ $680–750 SEA

A carved limewood six-light chandelier, Continental, 19thC, 36in (91.5cm) high.
£850–1,000
€/ $1,300–1,600 AH

A cut-glass chandelier, Swedish, 19thC, 36½in (92.5cm) high.
£2,000–2,200
€/ $3,200–3,500 S(O)

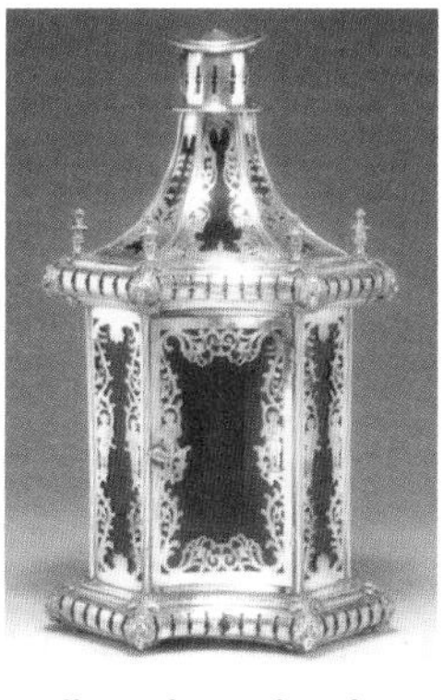

A silvered-metal and glass lantern, Continental, 19thC, 20¼in (51.5cm) high.
£1,700–2,000
€/ $2,700–3,200 S(NY)

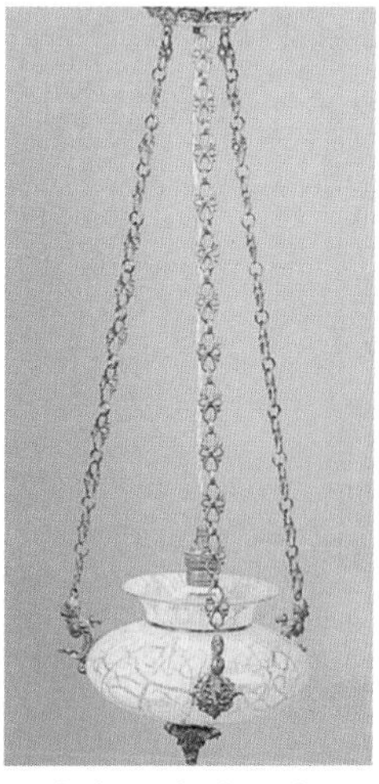

A Biedermeier hanging lantern, fitted for electricity, Austrian, Vienna, 1850–1900, 49½in (125.5cm) long.
£600–720
€/ $950–1,100 DORO

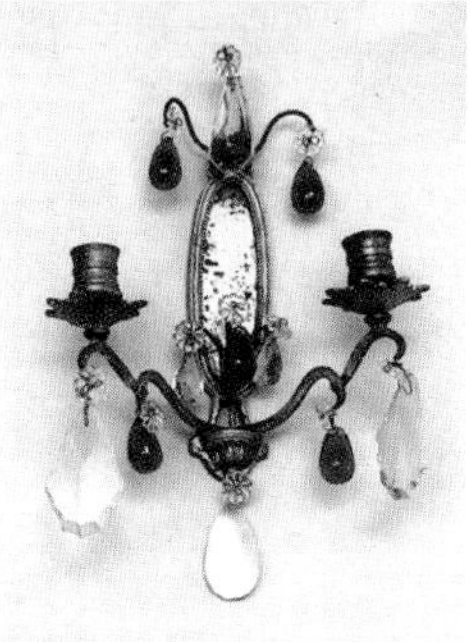

◄ A pair of wall sconces, French, c1880, 13in (33cm) high.
£500–550
€/ $790–870 JPr

◄ A gilded-brass ecclesiastical candle lamp, French, c1890, 35in (89cm) high.
£550–600
€/ $870–950 EAL

A gilded-brass ceiling fitting, with etched glass shades, French, 1890–1900, 36in (91.5cm) high.
£450–500
€/ $700–800 EAL

A brass and stained glass hall lantern, 1875–1925, 10½in (26.5cm) high.
£200–240
€/ $320–380 SWO

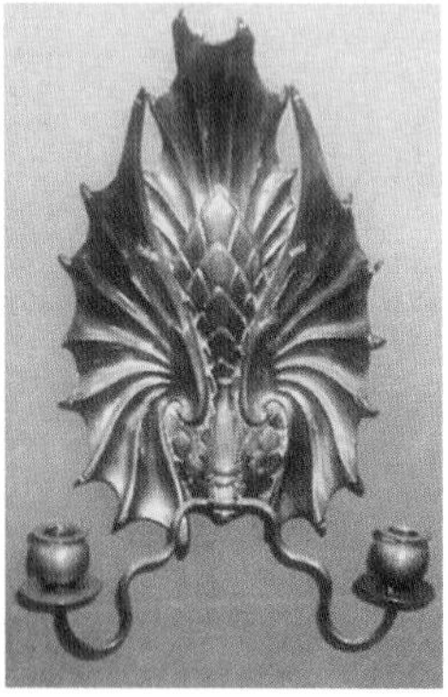

A pair of brass phoenix two-branch candleholders, c1900, 15¾in (40cm) high.
£350–400
€/ $550–630 B(Ch)

A gilt-bronze six-branch ceiling lamp, c1900, 22in (56cm) diam.
£500–550
€/ $790–870 EAL

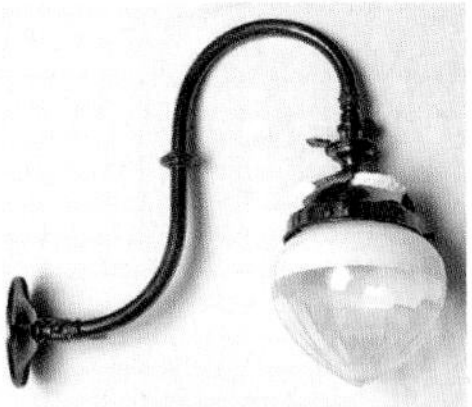

An oxidized brass swan-neck gas bracket, with a period glass shade, converted to electricity, c1900, 12in (30.5cm) high.
£100–110
€/ $160–175 JeH

A gilt-brass hanging lantern, fitted for electricity, 1875–1925, 64¼in (163cm) high.
£2,000–2,200
€/ $3,200–3,500 S

A pair of Louis XVI-style gilt-bronze wall lights, c1900, 21¼in (54cm) high.
£1,200–1,400
€/ $1,900–2,200 S(O)

A gilt-bronze 12-light rococo-style chandelier, late 19thC, 33½in (85cm) high.
£650–750
€/ $1,000–1,200 B

A cut-glass eight-branch chandelier, 1875–1925, 36¼in (92cm) high.
£900–1,000
€/ $1,400–1,600 S(O)

A gilt-bronze and cut-glass chandelier, probably by Agostino Fiorentini, French, c1900, 59in (150cm) high.
£2,000–2,200
€/ $3,200–3,500 S(O)

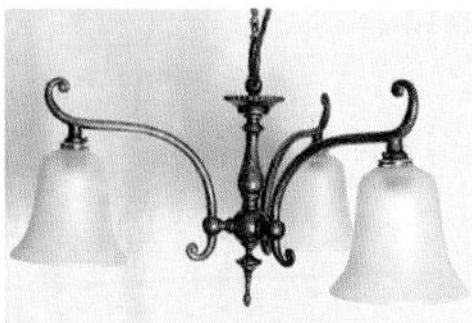

An Edwardian copper oxide three-branch ceiling lamp, with modern shades, 16in (40.5cm) diam.
£175–200
€/ $280–320 JeH

◄ A moulded-glass and brass pendant lamp, by Jefferson, American, c1900, 14in (35.5cm) diam.
£270–300
€/ $430–475 EAL

An antler 12-light chandelier, Scottish, 1875–1925, 33¾in (85.5cm) high.
£3,200–3,800
€/ $5,100–6,000 B(Ed)

A gilt-metal ten-light chandelier, hung overall with faceted teardrop prisms, Continental, c1900, 27in (68.5cm) high.
£380–450
€/ $600–710 NOA

A silver-plated three-branch ceiling lamp, c1900, 16in (40.5cm) diam.
£630–700
€/ $1,000–1,100 EAL

A crystal pendant light, with original brass fitting, c1910, 10in (25.5cm) high.
£115–130
€/ $180–200 JeH

A set of three cast-brass two-arm wall lights, c1910, 12in (30.5cm) wide.
£520–580
€/ $820–920 JeH

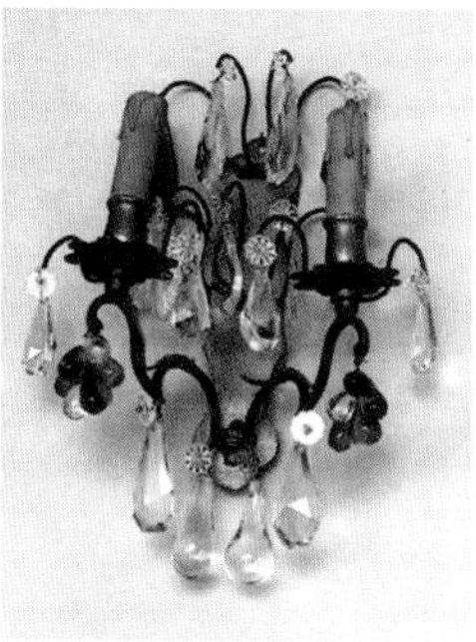

A pair of pewter wall sconces, with beaded drops, rewired, early 20thC, 13in (33cm) high.
£400–450
€/ $630–710 JPr

A brass six-light floral-painted cranberry glass electrolier, with triangular prism drops, Bohemian, early 20thC, 26in (66cm) high.
£200–240
€/ $320–380 G(L)

A moulded glass and gilt-metal eight-light chandelier, with lustre drops and strings of beads, Italian, early 20thC, 33in (84cm) high.
£720–850
€/ $1,100–1,300 S(O)

A gilt-metal and glass drop chandelier, early 20thC, 14½in (37cm) diam.
£230–275
€/ $360–430 SWO

A gilt-bronze and cut-glass electrolier, early 20thC, 33½in (85cm) high.
£420–500
€/ $660–800 B

An Edwardian gilded-brass chandelier, designed for electricity or candles, 29in (73.5cm) high.
£450–500
€/ $700–800 EAL

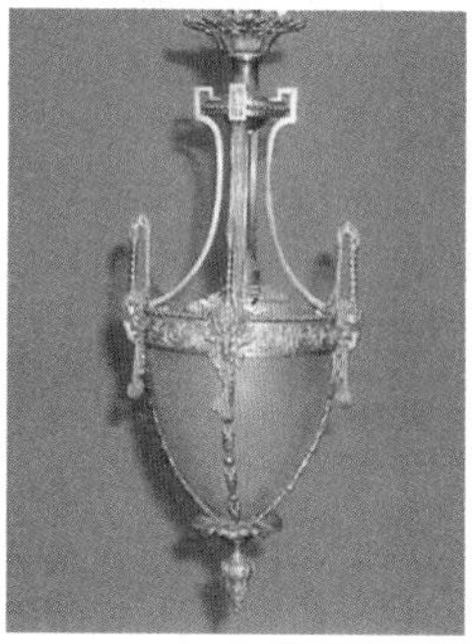

An Edwardian gilt-metal and glass hall lantern, 20in (51cm) high.
£400–480
€/ $630–760 B(Ch)

A white marble ceiling light, carved with cherubs in relief, French, c1920, 19¾in (50cm) diam.
£3,000–3,500
€/ $4,700–5,500 S(O)

An antler chandelier, c1920, 36in (91.5cm) high.
£1,600–1,800
€/ $2,500–2,800 DOA

A set of four gilded-bronze wall lights, French, 1920s, 16in (40.5cm) high.
£585–650
€/ $920–1,000 JPr

Three-branch are more desirable than two-branch or single-branch sconces. Pairs are proportionally worth 50 per cent more than singles and sets of four likewise worth 50 per cent more than two pairs.

A Venetian luster 16-branch chandelier, fitted for electricity, c1930, 35½in (90cm) high.
£2,000–2,400
€/ $3,200–3,800 DORO

Table & Standard Lamps

A gilt-bronze lamp base, by Ferdinand Barbedienne, cast with Classical female figures, signed, c1880, 20in (51cm) high.
£1,000–1,100
€/ $1,600–1,700 ⚒ S(O)

A porcelain lamp, in the form of an owl, with a frosted glass shade, French, late 19thC, 14in (35.5cm) high.
£220–260
€/ $350–410 ⚒ HOLL

A Victorian brass oil lamp, with a reeded brass column, enamelled glass reservoir and glass shade, on a stoneware plinth, 27in (68.5cm) high.
£250–280
€/ $400–440 ⚒ CoH

A late Victorian electroplate candlestick, now fitted as an oil lamp, with a cut crystal reservoir and an opal glass shade, 35½in (90cm) high.
£250–300
€/ $400–475 ⚒ BIG

◄ **A pair of Victorian silver-plated oil lamps,** with moulded glass shades, 14½in (37cm) high.
£200–240
€/ $320–380 ⚒ SWO

A Victorian oil lamp, with enamelled decoration, 13in (33cm) high.
£90–100
€/ $140–160 ⚒ SWO

A pair of silver-plated spelter table lamps, modelled as cavaliers supporting opaque flame shades, late 19thC, 31in (78.5cm) high.
£320–375
€/ $500–590 ⚒ EH

A Victorian oil lamp, 21in (53.5cm) high.
£130–145
€/ $200–230 ⊞ WiB

A gilt and patinated-bronze-mounted porcelain lamp base, with female mask head and wreath-hung handles, the girdle surmounted with a frieze of dancing Classical maidens, the pedestal with anthemion and palmette-cast mounts, late 19thC, 21in (53.5cm) high.
£420–500
€/ $660–800 ⚒ B

◄ **A brass pulpit lamp,** with a cranberry shade, 19thC, 18in (45.5cm) high.
£300–350
€/ $475–550 ⚒ GAK

A pair of porcelain table lamps, with gilt-metal Pan-mask handles, mounts and bases, Continental, possibly Paris, 19thC, 14in (35.5cm) high.
£480–565
€/ $760–890 ⚒ GAK

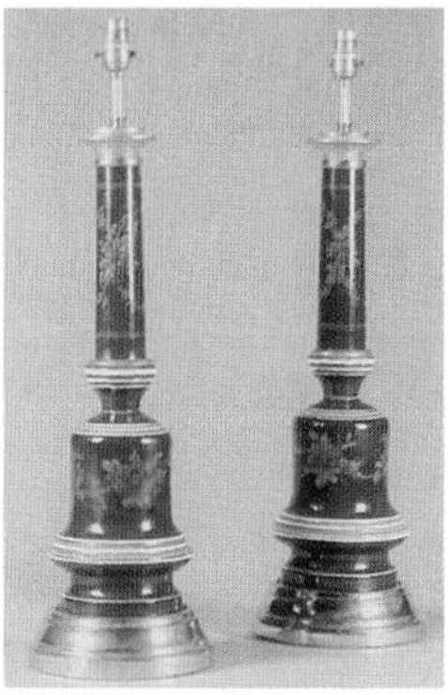

A pair of porcelain lamps, with later mounts, French, 19thC, 26½in (67.5cm) high.
£500–600
€/ $800–950 ⚒ S(O)

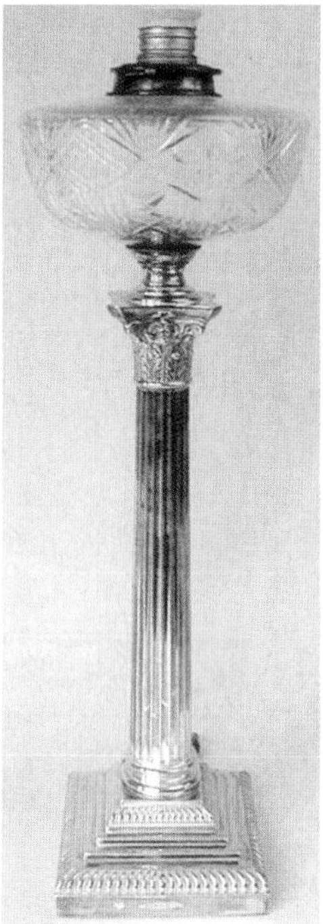

An Edwardian silver-plated Corinthian column oil lamp, with a cut-glass reservoir, converted to electricity, 21in (53.5cm) high.
£280–320
€/ $440–500 ⚒ BR

A metal-mounted hyacinth glass oil lamp, decorated with apple blossom and butterflies, heightened with gilt, Bohemian, 1850–1900, 19¾in (50cm) high.
£250–300
€/ $400–470 ⚒ DORO

A cut-glass Corinthian column table lamp, with an ormolu terminal, 19thC, 22½in (57cm) high.
£1,300–1,500
€/ $2,100–2,400 ⚒ JAd

A carved alabaster figural lampbase and shade, on a tinted base, Italian, 1920s, 29½in (75cm) high.
£650–750
€/ $1,000–1,200 ⚒ B(Ch)

A brass-mounted malachite lamp stand, with an opaque glass flame globe, converted to electricity, 19thC, 30in (76cm) high.
£650–720
€/ $1,000–1,100 ⚒ TMA

A cast silver-plated adjustable table lamp, c1910, 17in (43cm) high.
£135–150
€/ $220–240 ⊞ JeH

A brass table lamp, with a painted glass shade, c1920, 19in (48.5cm) high.
£135–150
€/ $215–240 ⊞ JeH

► An adjustable brass desk lamp, with an opaline shade, c1920, 16in (40.5cm) high.
£170–185
€/ $270–290 ⊞ JeH

A moulded glass and brass Banquet lamp, 19thC, 26in (66cm) high.
£800–950
€/ $1,300–1,500 ⚒ BAu

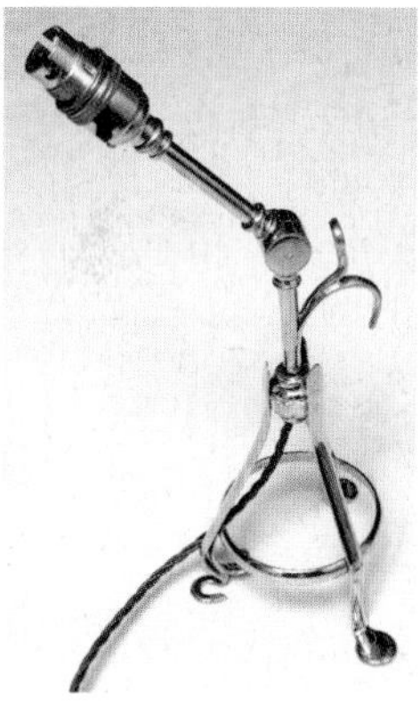

A brass Pullman lamp, with an adjustable arm, 1910–20, 14in (35.5cm) high.
£90–100
€/ $140–160 ⊞ JeH

Rugs & Carpets

An Aubusson carpet, with part metal thread, minor reweaves and damages, French, late 19thC, 233 x 188in (592 x 478cm).
£4,500–5,000
€/ $7,000–8,000 ⚒ S(NY)

A Bessarabian kilim, Moldavian/ Ukrainian, c1930, 117 x 84in (297 x 213.5cm).
£900–1,000
€/ $1,400–1,600 ⚒ S(O)

◄ **A carpet,** after a Cuenca design, Spanish, 1900–25, 212 x 144in (538 x 366cm).
£2,000–2,400
€/ $3,200–3,800 ⚒ S(O)

A needlepoint carpet, 1850–75, 92 x 91in (233.5 x 231cm).
£2,400–2,800
€/ $3,800–4,400 ⚒ S(O)

◄ **An Aubusson carpet,** the field with stylized flowers, centred by a medallion with a scrolling vine border, French, mid-19thC, 133¾ x 118in (339.5 x 299.5cm).
£4,000–4,800
€/ $6,300–7,600 ⚒ B(Ba)

A carpet, European, c1920, 210 x 149½in (533 x 380.5cm).
£2,000–2,200
€/ $3,200–3,500 ⚒ B(Ch)

► **A rug,** minor damages and repairs, Finnish, 19thC, 70½ x 54in (179 x 137cm).
£550–650
€/ $870–1,000 ⚒ BUK

A Donegal carpet, of Portuguese design, Irish, c1920, 203 x 135in (516 x 343cm).
£3,000–3,500
€/ $4,700–5,500 ⚒ S(O)
The unusual design of this carpet, with its corner spandrels depicting European ships, sailors and sea monsters, is taken from a small group of 16th- or 17th-century Safavid or Moghul carpets. Carpets of this group are referred to as 'Portuguese' as their design is thought to depict the story of the death of Bahadur Shah, ruler of Gujurat, who drowned while meeting a Portuguese fleet embarked on a diplomatic mission to the Persian Gulf.

◄ **A Bessarabian carpet,** some wear, Ukrainian, mid-19thC, 111 x 85in (282 x 216cm).
£14,000–16,000
€/ $22,000–25,000 ⚒ WW
Bessarabian carpets are now rare. In design, they are loose copies of French carpets and were made for Russian officers and civil servants unable to afford the originals. As Russia conquered more of the Caucasus, copies of Bessarabians were made in Karabagh and elsewhere.

A Bergama rug, Turkish, 1875–1900, 48 x 38in (122 x 96.5cm).
£1,700–1,900
€/ $2,700–3,000 ⊞ SAM

A Bergama rug, some wear and small repairs, Turkish, mid-19thC, 91 x 70in (231 x 178cm).
£420–500
€/ $800–790 ⚒ WW

A Melas rug, Turkish, mid-19thC, 72 x 48in (183 x 122cm).
£3,200–3,500
€/ $5,000–5,500 ⊞ SAM

A Melas saddlebag, Turkish, c1900, 14 x 20in (35.5 x 51cm).
£675–750
€/ $1,100–1,200 ⊞ SAM

The rugs in this section have been arranged in geographical sequence from west to east, in the following order: Europe, Turkey, Anatolia, Caucasus, Persia, Turkestan, India and China.

► **An Ushak carpet,** Turkish, late 19thC, 139 x 105in (353 x 266.5cm).
£1,800–2,200
€/ $2,800–3,500 ⚒ S(O)

An Ushak carpet, Turkish, late 19thC, 185 x 102in (470 x 259cm).
£1,800–2,000
€/ $2,800–3,200 ⚒ S(O)

An Ushak carpet, Turkish, 1900–25, 151 x 126in (383.5 x 320cm).
£1,800–2,000
€/ $2,800–3,200 ⚒ S(O)

► **An Ushak rug,** slight wear and damage, reduced in size, Turkish, c1900, 106 x 73in (269 x 185.5cm).
£220–250
€/ $350–400 ⚒ WW

A Sivas carpet, central Anatolian, c1900, 133 x 102in (338 x 259cm).
£1,000–1,200
€/ $1,600–1,900 ⚒ S(O)

A Kazak Sewan rug, southwest Caucasian, c1880, 81 x 69in (205.5 x 175.5cm).
£950–1,100
€/ $1,500–1,700 S(O)

A Kazak Chelaberd rug, southwest Caucasian, c1890, 93 x 65in (236 x 165cm).
£1,700–2,000
€/ $2,700–3,200 S(O)

A Gendje long rug, south Caucasian, c1890, 115 x 36in (292 x 91.5cm).
£950–1,100
€/ $1,500–1,700 S(O)

A Shahsavan salt bag, south Caucasian, Karabagh, 1875–1900, 16 x 27in (40.5 x 68.5cm).
£760–850
€/ $1,200–1,300 SAM

◄ **A Chondzoresk rug,** south Caucasian, Karabagh, slight wear, late 19thC, 90 x 44in (228.5 x 112cm).
£3,500–4,000
€/ $5,500–6,300 WW

A rug, south Caucasian, Karabagh, dated 1938, 59 x 94½in (150 x 240cm).
£650–750
€/ $1,000–1,200 B(Ba)

A Kazak Karatchop rug, south Caucasian, c1880, 39 x 64in (99 x 162.5cm).
£3,500–4,000
€/ $5,500–6,300 S(O)

◄ **A Kazak Sewan rug,** south Caucasian, c1890, 56 x 46¾in (142 x 119cm).
£1,100–1,300
€/ $1,700–2,000 S(O)

► **A Kazak Loripambak rug,** south Caucasian, late 19thC, 70 x 91in (178 x 231cm).
£1,100–1,300
€/ $1,700–2,000 S(O)

A Kazak long rug, south Caucasian, dated AH 1320/AD 1902, 136 x 54in (345.5 x 137cm).
£700–800
€/ $1,100–1,300 S(O)

A Kazak prayer rug, south Caucasian, dated AH 1322/AD 1904, 48 x 56in (122 x 142cm).
£2,500–3,000
€/ $4,000–4,700 S(O)

A Moghan-Talish rug, south Caucasian, c1900, 95 x 50in (241.5 x 127cm).
£170–200
€/ $270–320 WW

► **A Bidjov rug,** northeast Caucasian, c1890, 41 x 60in (104 x 152.5cm).
£1,400–1,600
€/ $2,200–2,500 S(O)

A Lesghi rug, northeast Caucasian, c1880, 62 x 38in (157.5 x 96.5cm).
£1,000–1,200
€/ $1,600–1,900 S(O)

A Perepedil rug, east Caucasian, late 19thC, 49 x 64in (124.5 x 162.5cm).
£2,000–2,200
€/ $3,200–3,500 S(O)

A Perepedil rug, east Caucasian, c1900, 75 x 52in (190.5 x 132cm).
£1,000–1,100
€/ $1,600–1,700 S(O)

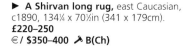

An Akstafa rug, the field with three 'Star of Islam' medallions and three pairs of stylized peacocks, filled with geometric and other symbols, enclosed by a main and two minor borders, southeast Caucasian, c1880, 91 x 55in (231 x 139.5cm).
£1,100–1,200
€/ $1,700–1,900 DNo

A Perepedil rug, east Caucasian, 1900–10, 84 x 53in (213.5 x 134.5cm).
£3,500–4,000
€/ $5,500–6,300 WW

► **A Shirvan long rug,** east Caucasian, c1890, 134¼ x 70½in (341 x 179cm).
£220–250
€/ $350–400 B(Ch)

◄ **A Bidjar *wagireh*,** with leaf, floral and other foliate motifs, northwest Persian, c1880, 83½ x 62in (212 x 157.5cm).
£2,000–2,200
€/ $3,200–3,500 ⚒ RIT

A Heriz carpet, centred by a cruciform medallion with flame palmette pendants, cornered by spandrels and framed by a rosette and palmette border, northwest Persian, c1900, 181¼ x 117¾in (458 x 299cm).
£6,000–7,000
€/ $9,500–11,000 ⚒ B

The rugs in this section have been arranged in geographical sequence from west to east, in the following order: Europe, Turkey, Anatolia, Caucasus, Persia, Turkestan, India and China.

A Tabriz prayer rug, damage and losses, northwest Persian, c1890, 73 x 54in (185.5 x 137cm).
£2,800–3,200
€/ $4,400–5,000 ⚒ S(NY)

A Karadja runner, northwest Persian, c1850, 171 x 43in (434 x 109cm).
£800–900
€/ $1,300–1,400 ⚒ S(O)

A rug, northwest Persian, mid-19thC, 57 x 39in (145 x 99cm).
£320–375
€/ $500–600 ⚒ B(Ba)

► **A Hamadan carpet,** west Persian, c1920, 54 x 83in (137 x 211cm).
£1,000–1,100
€/ $1,600–1,700 ⊞ DNo

A kilim, some damage and repairs, northwest Persian, Senneh/Bidjar, c1903, 80¾ x 53¼in (205 x 135.5cm).
£200–240
€/ $320–380 ⚒ DORO

A Shahsavan kilim, northwest Persian, c1890, 56 x 114in (142 x 289.5cm).
£550–650
€/ $870–1,000 ⚒ S(O)

A Tabriz carpet, outer border missing at either end, northwest Persian, c1900, 30 x 51in (76 x 129.5cm).
£250–280
€/ $400–440 ⊞ DNo

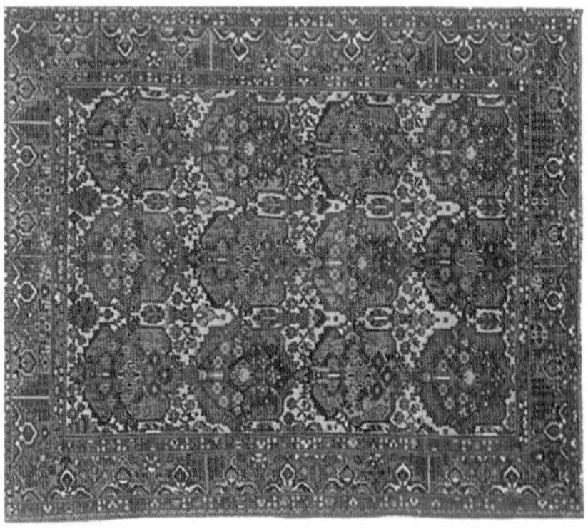

A Bakhtiari carpet, west Persian, early 20thC, 127 x 155in (322.5 x 393.5cm).
£800–900
€/ $1,300–1,400 ⚒ S(O)

A Lori Bakhtiari bedding bag, west Persian, 1875–1900, 39¼ x 55in (99.5 x 139.5cm).
£4,500–5,000
€/ $7,000–8,000 ⊞ SAM

The art of carpet weaving changed fundamentally during the 19th century, when its manufacture was taken over mainly by men. Previously, many carpets, if not all, were woven by women and young girls as dowry pieces and for domestic use. The designs woven were part of their ancient tradition. Once these carpets became sought after by richer nations, the art of carpet making became overtaken by commercial considerations. Most carpets manufactured during the 20th century may last 100 years, but the individuality and the artistic element has for the main part been lost.

A Malayer rug, worn, west Persian, Kurdistan, c1900, 44 x 76in (112 x 193cm).
£325–360
€/ $500–570 ⊞ DNo

A Joshagan carpet, central Persian, c1900, 163 x 125in (414 x 317.5cm).
£2,200–2,500
€/ $3,500–4,000 ⚒ S(O)

A Lori *gabbeh*, west Persian, early 20thC, 47 x 31in (119.5 x 78.5cm).
£1,100–1,300
€/ $1,700–2,000 ⊞ SAM

A Mahal carpet, west Persian, c1890, 133½ x 106in (339 x 269cm).
£2,800–3,200
€/ $4,400–5,000 ⚒ B(Ch)
Although this carpet is in very poor condition, it is very attractive and sympathetic restoration might increase the value.

◄ A Sanjabi Kurds salt bag, west Persian, Kurdistan, c1900, 14 x 26in (35.5 x 66cm).
£675–750
€/ $1,100–1,200 ⊞ SAM

A Kashgai vanity bag, southwest Persian, 1875–1900, 10in (25.5cm) square.
£250–275
€/ $400–440 ⊞ SAM

A Lori runner, west Persian, c1920, 155 x 41in (393.5 x 104cm).
£650–750
€/ $1,000–1,200 ⚒ S(O)

A Sultanabad *kelleh*, west Persian, late 19thC, 123 x 59in (312.5 x 150cm).
£1,700–2,000
€/ $2,700–3,200 ⚒ S(O)

LOCATE THE SOURCE

The source of each illustration in Miller's can be found by checking the code letters below each caption with the Key to Illustrations, pages 794–800.

A Kamo *soffreh*, central Persian, c1900, 35½ x 34in (90 x 86.5cm).
£850–950
€/ $1,300–1,500 ⊞ SAM

◄ **A silk Kashan rug,** central Persian, c1920, 83 x 51in (211 x 129.5cm).
£1,200–1,400
€/ $1,900–2,200 ⚒ S(O)

An Afshar rug, south Persian, 1850–1900, 50 x 70in (127 x 178cm).
£3,500–3,800
€/ $5,500–6,000 ⊞ SAM

A Belouch prayer rug, northeast Persian, c1900, 67 x 36in (170 x 91.5cm).
£1,700–1,900
€/ $2,700–3,000 ⊞ SAM

A Meshad carpet, northeast Persian, c1920, 162 x 129½in (411 x 329cm).
£850–1,000
€/ $1,300–1,600 ⚒ B(Ch)

A Meshad carpet, northeast Persian, Khorasan, c1930, 101 x 126in (256.5 x 320cm).
£150–175
€/ $240–280 ⚒ WW

► **A flatweave,** northeast Persian, 19thC, 57 x 76in (145 x 193cm).
£2,200–2,500
€/ $3,500–4,000 ⊞ SAM

An Afshar carpet, with a rabbit and quail border, southeast Persian, c1890, 74 x 50in (183 x 127cm).
£1,100–1,300
€/ $1,700–2,000 ⊞ DNo

A Kirman carpet, southeast Persian, c1930, 171 x 117¼in (434 x 298cm).
£420–500
€/ $670–800 ⚒ B(Ch)

◄ **A Belouch vanity bag,** southeast Persian, Chakhansur, 1875–1900, 7 x 8in (18 x 20.5cm).
£125–140
€/ $200–220 ⊞ SAM

The Professor Mark Whiting & Dr Jon Thompson Collections

In the first half of the 20th century there were large numbers of Turkmen (Bokhara) weavings to be found in Great Britain, as a result of purchases by military personnel and civil servants posted to the far reaches of the British Empire in the 19th and early 20th centuries. These items included rugs, small bags and other trappings which, as they were largely inexpensive, appealed to many collectors. Dr Jon Thompson and Professor Mark Whiting in the 1960s were among the first people in the UK to take an interest in such pieces and create large collections. Their focused writing in the 1970s helped create a boom for Turkmen products, which collapsed in the early 1980s due to over-optimistic buying. Today there is still a strong interest in Turkmen weaving and the value of rarer pieces remains strong.

Whiting and Thompson both sold their collections in the 1990s. With the collapse of the Soviet Union more Turkmen pieces are appearing on the world market and it is still possible to discover interesting examples. It is an area which still provides rewards for new collectors. **Richard Purdon**

A Yomut saddle cover, northwest Turkestani, 1850–1900, 22in (56cm) square.
£330–400
€/ $515–630 ⚒ S(O)

A Beshir *torba*, west Turkestani, c1880, 18 x 63in (45.5 x 160cm).
£900–1,000
€/ $1,400–1,600 ⚒ S(O)

A wedding trapping, Ersari Turkmen Tribes, west Turkestani, Beshir, mid-19thC, 16 x 51in (40.5 x 129.5cm).
£585–650
€/ $930–1,000 ⊞ SAM

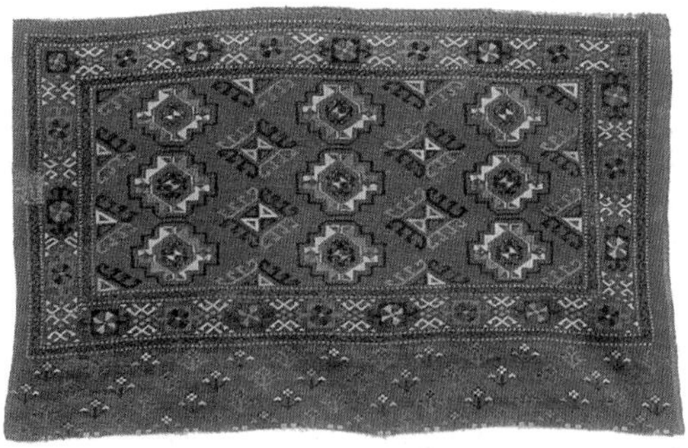

An Ersari *chuval*, southwest Turkestani, 1850–1900, 59 x 34in (150 x 86.5cm).
£575–675
€/ $900–1,100 ⚒ S(O)

A Chodor Turkmen main carpet, north Turkestani, 1880–1900, 89 x 69in (226 x 175.5cm).
£450–525
€/ $700–830 ⚒ WW

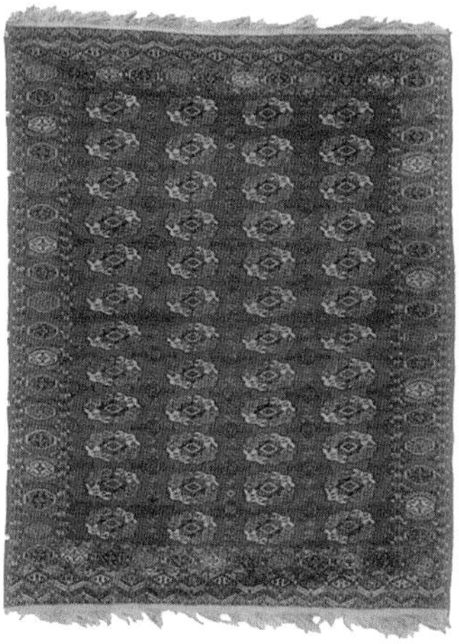

A Tekke carpet, west Turkestani, late 19thC, 115 x 90in (292 x 228.5cm).
£1,400–1,600
€/ $2,200–2,500 ⚒ S(O)

A Tekke Turkmen saddle bag, west Turkestani, early 20thC, 19 x 34in (48.5 x 86.5cm).
£430–475
€/ $675–750 ⊞ SAM

◄ **A Turkmen rug,** west Turkestani, c1920, 38 x 54in (96.5 x 137cm).
£100–120
€/ $160–190 ⚒ WW

European & Eastern rugs & carpets 1977–2002

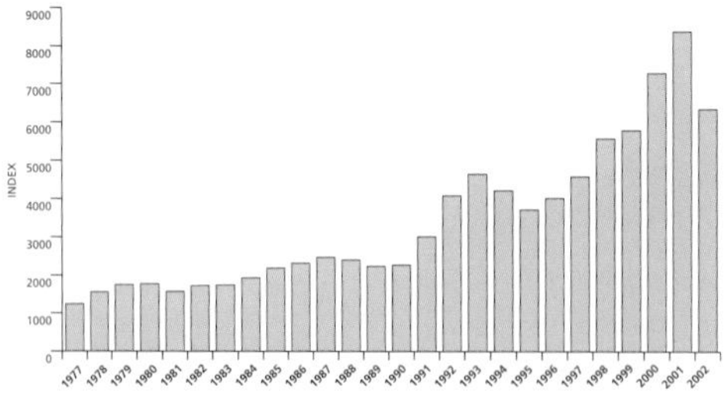

This graph shows the value of European and Eastern rugs and carpets as a whole over the past 25 years. Rugs from particular geographical areas may not follow this graph exactly. ©AMR

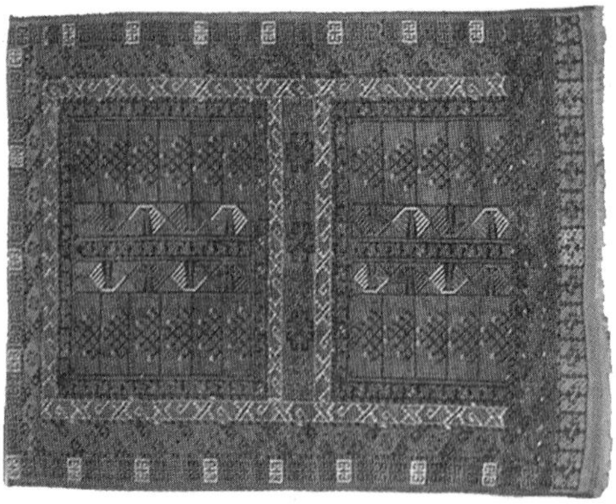

An Afghan *pardah*, slight wear, leather backing sewn on, north Afghani, 1900–20, 82 x 64in (208.5 x 162.5cm).
£150–170
€/ $240–270 WW

A *khordjin* face, Timuri tribes, west Afghani, 1850–1900, 30 x 34in (76 x 86.5cm).
£1,600–1,800
€/ $2,500–2,800 ⊞ SAM
A *khordjin* is a double saddle bag used by nomads and villagers.

► A Khotan silk pile throne rug, the major and minor panels decorated with shrubs and medallions, enclosed by reciprocal T-borders, some wear, east Turkestani, c1870, 66 x 22in (167.5 x 56cm).
£550–600
€/ $870–950 ⊞ DNo

A Khotan carpet, east Turkestani, c1900, 116 x 59in (294.5 x 150cm).
£1,800–2,000
€/ $2,800–3,200 S(O)

A carpet, one hole and one reweave, slight loss to top end, Indian, early 20thC, 136 x 98¾in (345.5 x 251cm).
£2,200–2,500
€/ $3,500–4,000 WW

A rug, north Indian, late 19thC, 104 x 61in (264 x 155cm).
£2,200–2,500
€/ $3,500–4,000 S(O)

◄ An Amritsar rug, north Indian, c1900, 105 x 81in (266.5 x 205.5cm).
£5,300–5,800
€/ $8,400–9,200 S(O)

Pricing antique rugs & carpets

The price of an antique Oriental carpet can never be set in stone, for the factors to be considered have an infinite range of subtleties which are often dependent on the mood of the market. The use of synthetic dyes, which were invented in 1858 and quickly became widely available, is the principal factor that determines value. Rugs made of synthetically dyed materials should be avoided by serious collectors.

Condition is the other major consideration. While most carpets are extremely durable, the presence of visible wear seriously devalues a carpet, especially if it is to be subjected to daily use. In valuable pieces the presence of small holes and damages is not a problem. The rarest examples can still fetch surprising sums at auction despite extensive damage and wear. However, large areas of restoration should only be undertaken with caution by a professional.

A panel from a meditation rug or a seat cover, slight wear, Chinese, Ninghsia, 1850–1900, 30in (76cm) square.
£375–450
€/ $600–700 WW

A silk and metal thread rug, the brocaded metal thread field with an overall floral lattice of flowerheads and vines, within a conforming border, Chinese, Beijing, late 19thC, 108 x 71¾in (274.5 x 182.5cm).
£2,000–2,200
€/ $3,200–3,500 RTo

◄ A silk and metal brocade rug, inscribed 'Made for Palace of Perpetual Harmony', Chinese, possibly Beijing, late 19thC, 98 x 61in (249 x 155cm).
£6,000–7,000
€/ $9,500–11,000 WW

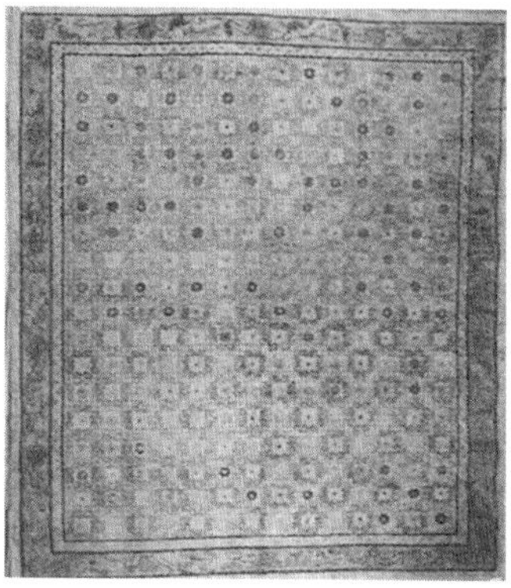

A silk carpet, some pile loss, northeast Chinese, Tianjin, 1875–1925, 118 x 96in (299.5 x 244cm).
£2,000–2,400
€/ $3,200–3,800 WW

► A silk and metal thread carpet, Chinese, c1880, 142½ x 114¼in (362 x 290cm).
£750–875
€/ $1,200–1,400 B(Ch)
The five-toed dragons on this carpet were a restricted emblem for use by the Imperial household until the dissolution of the Empire in 1914.

A carpet, Chinese, c1900, 139¾ x 111½in (355 x 283cm).
£3,000–3,500
€/ $4,700–5,500 S(O)

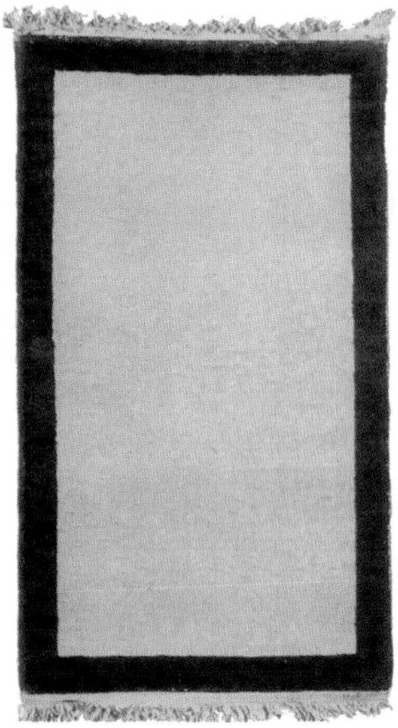

A pair of rugs, Chinese, early 20thC, 40 x 23¾in (101.5 x 60.5cm).
£350–420
€/ $550–670 S(O)

◄ A carpet, Chinese, c1920, 164½ x 123in (418 x 312.5cm).
£950–1,100
€/ $1,500–1,700 S(O)

Textiles

Covers & Quilts

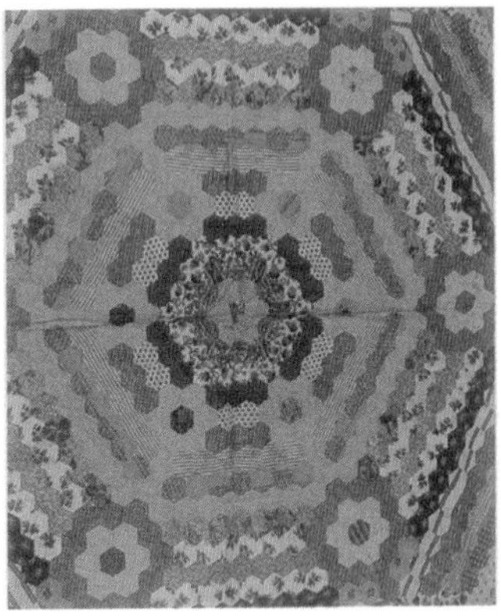

A chintz patchwork coverlet, the patches mainly dress fabric, paper templates intact to reverse, c1845, 84½ x 89in (215 x 226cm).
£420–500
€/ $660–790 S(O)

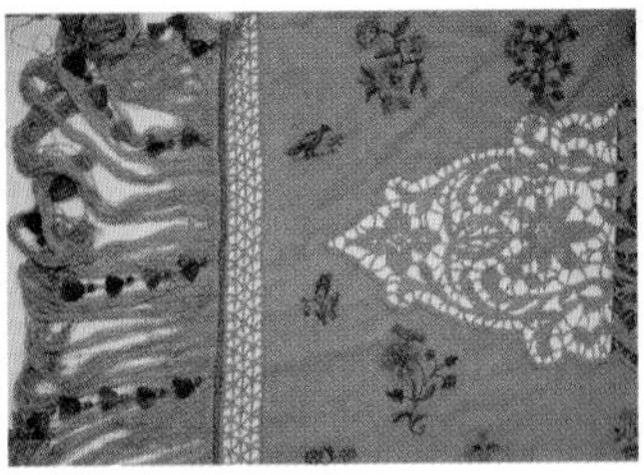

An embroidered linen bed cover, with Bruges lace inserts and woollen tassels, c1860, 118 x 98½in (300 x 250cm).
£550–600
€/ $870–950 JPr

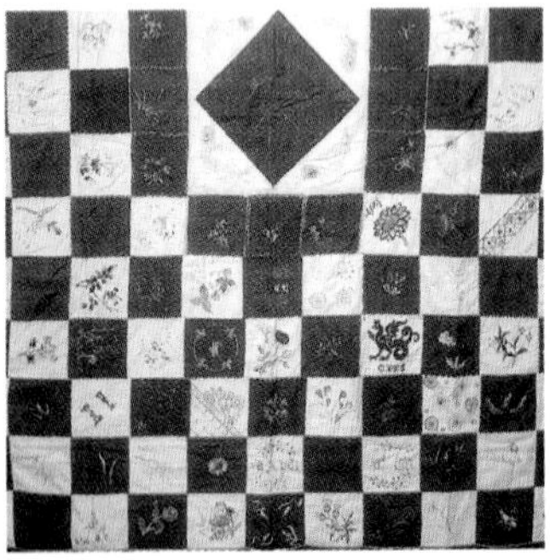

A patchwork coverlet, possibly a 'Friendship Cloth', each square embroidered with a unique design, worked in coloured silks and cottons, with a red scallop-edged border, backed with a cotton twill, late 19thC, 104 x 82¾in (264 x 210cm).
£120–140
€/ $190–220 B(WM)

A Princess Feather appliqué cotton quilt, with floral vine serpentine border, American, c1860, 96in (244cm) square.
£900–1,100
€/ $1,400–1,700 COPA

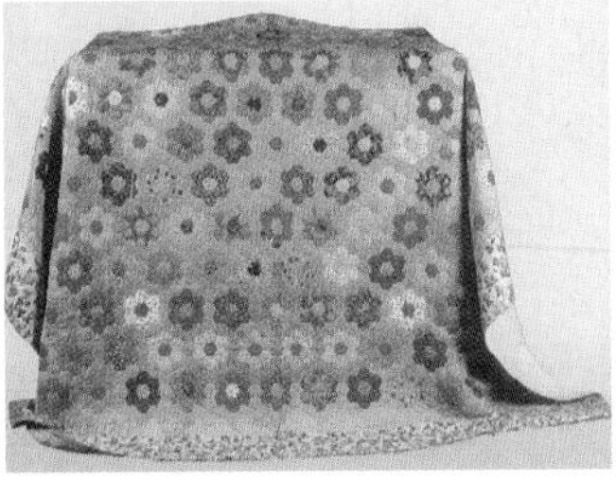

A patchwork quilt, by Isabella Swales, Kepwick, with hexagonal patches in a variety of colours and with a floral-patterned border, 1862, 86 x 96in (218.5 x 244cm).
£220–250
€/ $350–400 Mit

A cotton Bokhara susani, embroidered in silk, Uzbekistan, 19thC, 90½ x 72in (230 x 182cm).
£4,200–5,000
€/ $6,600–7,900 B(Kn)

◄ **A patchwork quilt,** with inset cross-stitch panels, cotton back, late 19thC.
£765–850
€/ $1,200–1,400 JPr

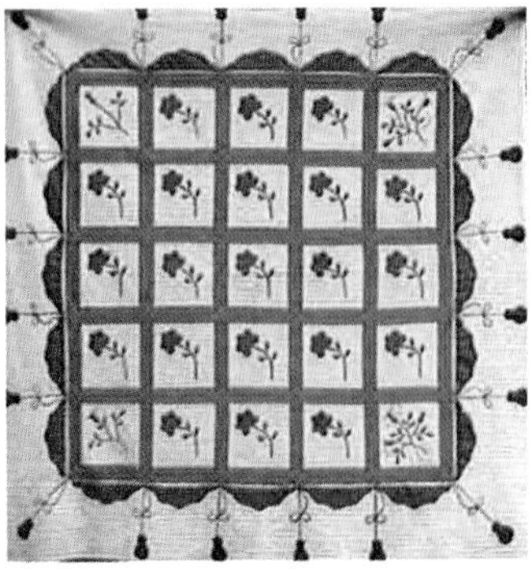

A Rose Appliqué quilt, with swag and tassel borders, American, c1860, 84 x 88in (213.5 x 223.5cm).
£550–600
€/ $870–950 MAQ

A patchwork quilt, with wagon wheel to the centre and a crocheted border, American, dated 1884, 66in (167.6cm) square.
£750–875
€/ $1,200–1,400 COPA

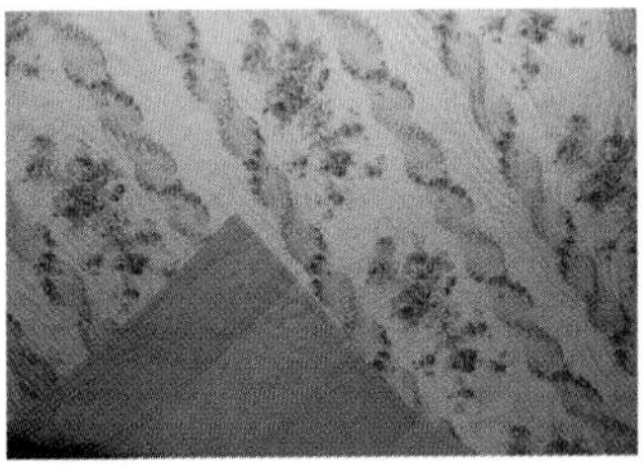

A Victorian double strip quilt, with detailed Durham stitching, 118 x 98½in (300 x 250cm).
£380–420
€/ $600–670 JPr

A patchwork quilt, hand-stitched in the Durham manner, early 20thC, 114¼ x 86in (290 x 260cm).
£350–400
€/ $550–630 JPR

A Durham quilt, hand-stitched, early 20thC, 100 x 110in (254 x 279.5cm).
£315–350
€/ $500–550 ⊞ JPr

A patchwork quilt, with squares in the form of the cross, each square depicting a psalm, American, c1930, 97 x 75in (246.5 x 190.5cm).
£850–1,000
€/ $1,300–1,600 ⚒ COPA

A child's bed sheet, with applied cut-out animals, American, c1920, 54 x 36in (137 x 91.5cm).
£380–420
€/ $600–660 ⚒ COPA

An Aubusson mille fleurs table cover, French, c1920, 58 x 61in (147.5 x 155cm).
£3,500–4,000
€/ $5,500–6,300 ⊞ LGU

A Princess Feather quilt, American, c1930, 86in (218.5cm) square.
£700–800
€/ $1,100–1,300 ⊞ COPA

◄ **A Floral Appliqué quilt,** with rope and diamond quilting, American, c1930, 76in (193cm) square.
£350–400
€/ $550–650 ⊞ MAQ

Embroidery & Needlework

A needlework fragment, in the form of a panel of two joined pieces showing angels on a background of silver thread, 16thC, 7 x 16in (18 x 40.5cm).
£400–450
€/ $630–700 ⊞ JPr

A silkwork picture, depicting the Sacrifice of Isaac, the figures with painted faces, slight damage, 17thC, 9¾ x 10¾in (25 x 27.5cm).
£300–350
€/ $475–550 TEN

A needlework landscape scene, worked in tent stitch with a shepherd and shepherdess, Dutch, mid-17thC, 5¼ x 7in (13.5 x 18cm).
£1,200–1,400
€/ $5,400–6,400 S(O)

A needlework panel, worked in tent stitch and stumpwork with gold and silver wirework and silk, c1660, 12½ x 17in (32 x 43cm).
£750–900
€/ $1,200–1,400 G(L)

A beadwork panel, depicting Adam and Eve in the Garden of Eden, on an ivory satin ground, initialled 'MS', c1660, 11½ x 14½in (29 x 37cm).
£1,700–2,000
€/ $2,700–3,200 S(O)

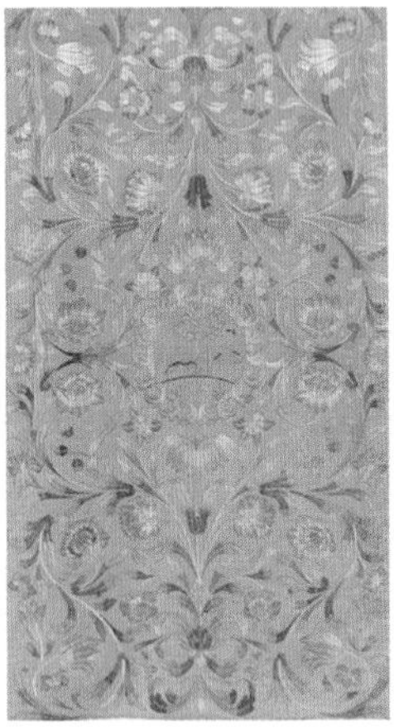

An embroidered panel, worked in silk, Italian or Portuguese, minor damage, c1700, 69¾ x 39¾in (177 x 101cm).
£2,200–2,500
€/ $3,500–4,000 S(Am)

A needlework panel, depicting Elijah and the Ravens, worked in silks, wool and silver thread, early 18thC, 11¼ x 9¾in (28.5 x 25cm).
£2,000–2,200
€/ $3,200–3,500 F&C

Two embroidered needlework panels, one depicting a lady and her parrot and the other a parrot, worked in silk thread on satin, pen and ink details, c1700, framed, 11 x 9½in (28 x 24cm).
£4,500–5,000
€/ $7,000–8,000 ⊞ RYA

► An embroidered chasuble panel, worked in silks on a linen ground with the Annunciation, the faces of painted canvas, probably French, c1720, 56 x 31½in (142 x 80cm).
£850–950
€/ $1,300–1,500 S

► An embroidered panel, worked in tent stitch with wool and silk, c1740, 13in (33cm) square.
£2,000–2,200
€/ $3,200–3,500 S(O)

A needlework panel, depicting Diana, probably from a chair-back, mounted on stretchers, damaged, c1750, 27¼ x 23¼in (69 x 59cm).
£1,500–1,700
€/ $2,400–2,700 ⚒ SWO

A silk embroidery panel, 18thC, 10¾ x 9in (27.5 x 23cm).
£200–240
€/ $320–380 ⚒ SWO

A silk and wool needlework panel, French, 18thC, 7 x13in (18 x 33cm).
£315–350
€/ $475–550 ⊞ LGU

► A silkwork picture, with central oil-painted and embroidered vignette of a girl and lamb, c1790, in a maple frame, 13¾ x 11½in (35 x 29cm).
£420–500
€/ $650–800 ⚒ S(O)

A silkwork picture, by Sarah Brightwell, inscribed on reverse 'attributed to Mrs Potter's school', dated 16 December 1791, 16 x 19in (40.5 x 48.5cm).
£1,300–1,500
€/ $2,100–2,400 ⊞ PSC

◄ A silk needlework picture, French, 18thC, 23 x 18in (58.5 x 45.5cm), in original frame.
£3,000–3,300
€/ $4,700–5,200 ⊞ LGU

An embroidered silk picture, depicting a flautist and his dog, with painted hands, face and background, late 18thC, 7 x 9in (18 x 23cm), framed.
£585–650
€/ $925–1,000 ⊞ WWo
In the late 18th and early 19th century, pictures such as this were probably issued as kits to be filled in with individual colour choices.

A beaded bag, with original kid leather strings, early 19thC, 7in (18cm) high.
£215–240
€/ $135–380 ⊞ JPr

A silkwork and painted picture, worked in chenille, early 19thC, 15½ x 12¼in (39.5 x 31cm).
£475–565
€/ $750–900 ⚒ TEN

A silkwork picture, depicting a shepherdess by a tree, early 19thC, in a *verre églomisé* frame, 11¾ x 9¾in (30 x 25cm).
£320–400
€/ $500–630 ⚒ SWO

A chenille-work silk picture, depicting a wood-gatherer and his dog, early 19thC, 14¼ x 11½in (36 x 29.5cm).
£150–175
€/ $240–280 ⚒ L

An embroidered picture, worked in tent stitch with a basket of flowers, on a black linen ground, early 19thC, 16½ x 21¾in (42 x 55.5cm), in a maple frame.
£420–500
€/ $670–800 ⚒ S(O)

A silkwork and painted picture, depicting Mount Vernon, the sky, faces and hands painted, slight damage, American, probably New England, c1820, 15½ x 20½in (39.5 x 52cm).
£6,000–7,000
€/ $9,500–11,000 ⚒ S(NY)

A silkwork picture, depicting a lady with a donkey and lion, early 19thC, 12¼ x 9½in (31 x 24cm).
£240–275
€/ $380–430 ⚒ SWO

A silkwork mourning picture, with two inscriptions, repaired, American, 1800–25, 19 x 20¼in (48.5 x 51.5cm).
£4,500–5,500
€/ $7,000–8,600 ⚒ S(NY)

◄ An embroidered picture, worked in silk with a woodsman and dogs, painted face, hands and sky, early 19thC, 22¼ x 14¼in (56.5 x 36.5cm).
£240–280
€/ $380–430 ⚒ PFK

A silkwork picture, depicting a lady playing with a child, early 19thC, 6½ x 4½in (16.5 x 11.5cm), in a later frame.
£500–600
€/ $800–950 ⚒ SWO

A Berlin woolwork picture, depicting a lady and two falconers in a palatial setting, 19thC, 32¼ x 26in (82 x 66cm), framed.
£80–100
€/ $125–160 ⚒ PFK

A pair of silkwork banners, worked to each side with a white bird of prey, each with a wooden rail in the form of a bugle, one banner torn, 19thC, each 20in (51cm) square.
£130–150
€/ $200-240 ⚒ PFK

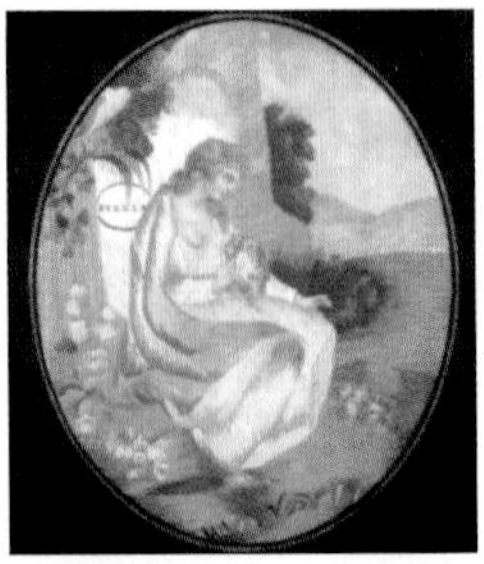

A silkwork and painted picture, entitled 'Stella', the lady holding a wreath of fruit and flowers, c1820, 11in (28cm) high.
£220–250
€/ $350–400 ⚒ HAM

A needlework picture, worked in gros point with a child dressed in tartan and her dog, a ruined castle and cottage behind, 19thC, 17¼ x 15¾in (44 x 40cm).
£375–450
€/ $600–700 TRM

A pair of woolwork pictures, depicting a prince and princess, c1840, 18¼ x 12½in (46.5 x 32cm), in rosewood frames.
£1,100–1,200
€/ $1,700–1,900 S(O)

A wool needlework picture, worked in gros point with a spaniel, the sky unworked, inscribed to reverse, 1842, 11¾ x 15¼in (30 x 38.5cm), in a bird's eye maple frame.
£140–160
€/ $220–250 PFK

A Berlin woolwork picture, depicting a cat and kittens on a cushion, c1850, 10 x 14in (25.5 x 35.5cm), framed.
£180–200
€/ $285–315 JPr

A woolwork picture, depicting a dog on a cushion, c1850, 6in (15cm) square, framed.
£225–250
€/ $350–400 JPr

A pair of embroidered face screens, worked in petit point with flowers, with turned ivory handles, c1850, 20in (51cm) long.
£100–120
€/ $160–190 JPr

A Victorian Berlin woolwork picture, depicting a vase of flowers, with inscription, 22 x 21½in (56 x 54.5cm), in a rosewood frame.
£320–370
€/ $500–580 DMC

A woolwork picture, depicting a bird, c1880, 5in (12cm) wide.
£200–220
€/ $315–350 LGU

An 18thC-style damask panel, depicting a thistle surmounted by a crown, flanked by the Lion of Scotland, the Star and Order of St Andrew, and motto, c1900, 13½ x 11½in (34.5 x 29cm).
£500–575
€/ $800–900 B(Ed)
This design incorporates the defiant symbols found in household linen belonging to supporters of Prince Charles Edward Stuart, manufactured in France after the Battle of Culloden, 1745–46, and widely copied.

An embroidered panel, depicting a parrot, late 19thC, 25¾ x 22in (65.5 x 56cm), framed.
£240–275
€/ $380–440 RTo

A Victorian woolwork picture, depicting two doves on a nest, 16 x 12½in (40.5 x 32cm).
£375–450
€/ $600–700 HYD

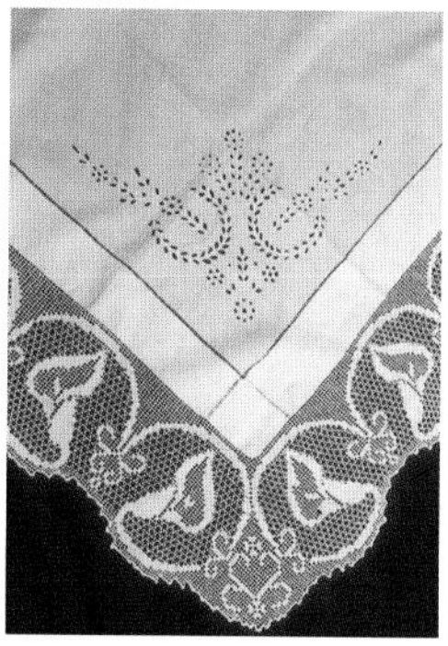

A crochet-edged linen tablecloth, c1900, 54in (137cm) square.
£70–80
€/ $110–125 JuC

Lace

A panel of cut work, probably Italian, late 16thC, 2 x 15in (5 x 38cm).
£55–60
€/ $87–95 ⊞ HL

A panel of needlelace, c1665, 4 x 25in (10 x 63.5cm).
£225–250
€/ $350–400 ⊞ HL

A lace sampler, by Sarah Tyzak, dated 1676, 8 x 9in (23 x 20.5cm).
£1,300–1,500
€/ $2,000–2,400 ⚒ S(O)

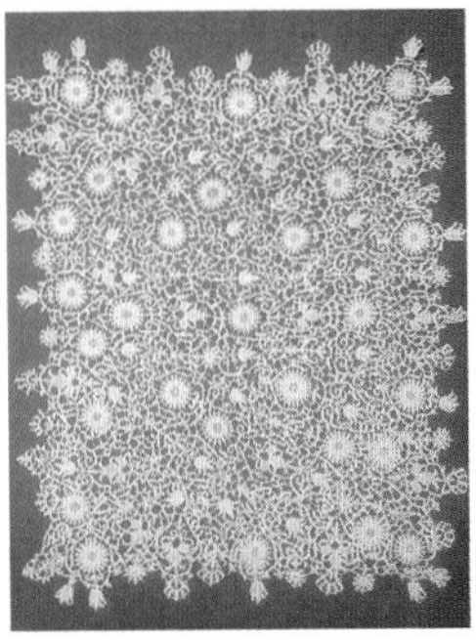

A needlelace cloth, with carnations among tendrils and tulips, late 17thC, 56 x 20in (142 x 52cm).
£850–1,000
€/ $1,300–1,600 ⚒ B(WM)

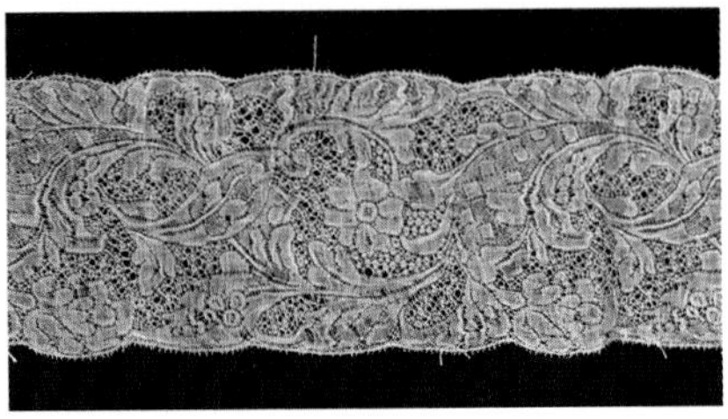

A panel of Valenciennes costume lace, 18thC, 3½ x 44in (9 x 56cm).
£70–75
€/ $110–120 ⊞ HL

► **A panel of Alençon needlelace,** late 18thC, 3½ x 23in (9 x 58.5cm).
£50–55
€/ $80–85 ⊞ HL

A Brussels lace *pointe de gaze* Bertha collar, mid-19thC, 17in (43cm) diam.
£260–285
€/ $400–450 ⊞ HL

A Bedfordshire lace handkerchief, mid–late 19thC, 14in (35.5cm) square.
£70–75
€/ $110–120 ⊞ HL

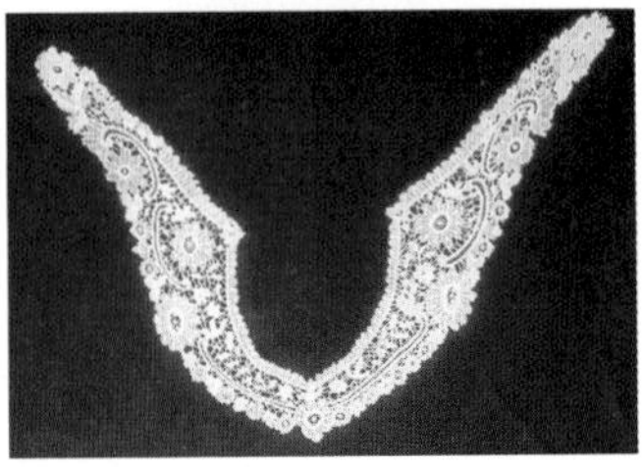

A Brussels needlelace collar, c1890, 10in (25.5cm) long.
£45–50
€/ $70–80 ⊞ JuC

A Honiton lace handkerchief, c1860, 13in (33cm) square.
£140–155
€/ $220–250 ⊞ HL

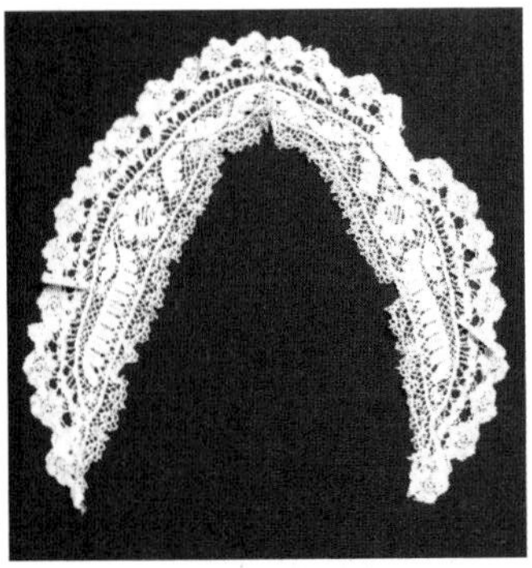

An East Midlands lace collar, late 19thC, 14in (35.5cm) long.
£50–55
€/ $80–87 ⊞ HL

An Edwardian Brussels lace collar, 23in (58.5cm) long.
£60–65
€/ $95–105 ⊞ Ech

Samplers

A band sampler, by Elenor Hines, worked in silks, dated 16th October 1706, 17½in x 8in (44 x 20.5cm, framed.
£650–750
€/ $1,000–1,200 ⚒ B(NW)

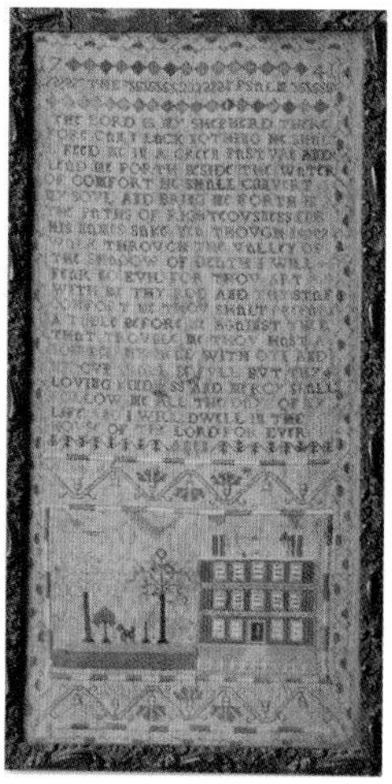

A sampler, 'The Lord is my Shepherd', 1741, 16 x 8in (40.5 x 20.5cm).
£1,350–1,500
€/ $2,100–2,400 ⊞ HIS

A sampler, by Sarah Chamberlain, worked in silks, dated 25 October 1751, 15 x 7½in (38 x 19cm).
£1,000–1,200
€/ $1,600–1,900 ⚒ B(WM)

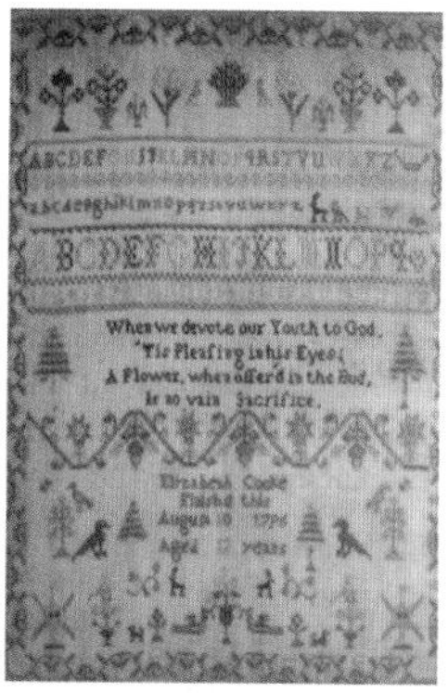

A sampler, by Elizabeth Cooke, aged 12 years, dated 10 August 1796, 16 x 13in (40.5 x 33cm).
£850–1,100
€/ 1,300–1,700 ⚒ FEN

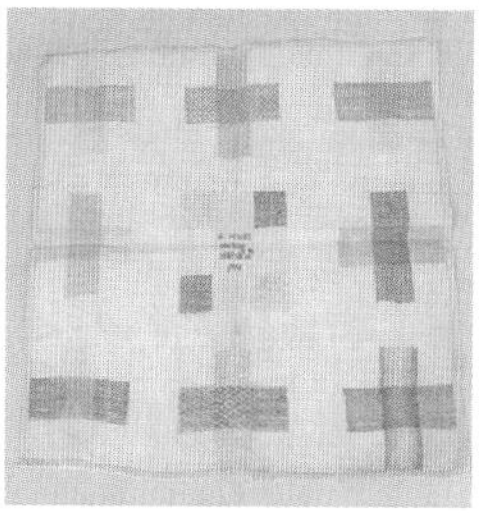

◄ A needlework sampler, by M. Jewitt, Bocking, dated 18 March 1796, 13¾in (35cm) square.
£320–375
€/ $510–590 ⚒ HAM

A sampler, worked in silks and wools, slight damage, c1800, 12½in (32cm) square.
£720–800
€/ $1,100–1,300 ⚒ B(NW)

A sampler, by Mary Vickers, dated 1st November 1800, 12 x 10in (30.5 x 25.5cm).
£360–400
€/ $560–630 ⚒ G(L)

A muslin needlework sampler, depicting the Point to Point on the Delaware, American, c1800, 21 x 18¼in (53.5 x 46.5cm), framed.
£450–500
€/ $700–800 ⚒ S(NY)

Further reading

Miller's Samplers: How to Compare & Value, Miller's Publications, 2002

► A needlework sampler, by Jane Irwin, worked in coloured wools on cream canvas, early 19thC, 17½in (44.5cm) square, framed.
£280–320
€/ $440–500
⚒ RTo

A linen sampler, by Alice Thomson, aged eight, early 19thC, 18½ x 16½in (47 x 42cm), framed.
£720–850
€/ $1,100–1,300 TRM

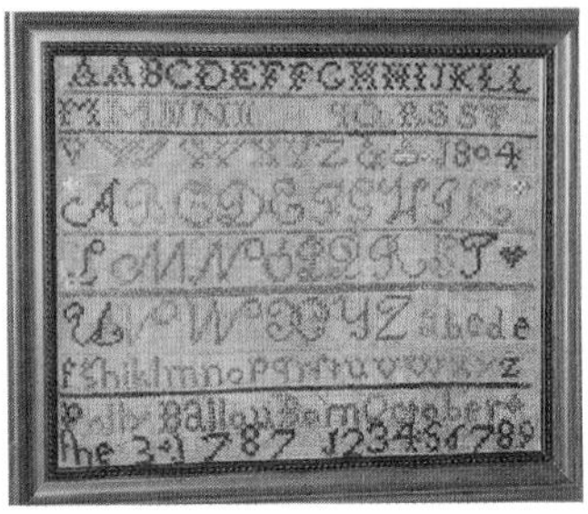

A sampler, by Polly Ballou, American, dated 1804, 12 x 10in (30.5 x 25.5cm), framed.
£315–350
€/ $500–550 HCFA

A needlework sampler, by Martha Pound, 1811, 14¼ x 11½in (36 x 29cm).
£600–700
€/ $950–1,100 L

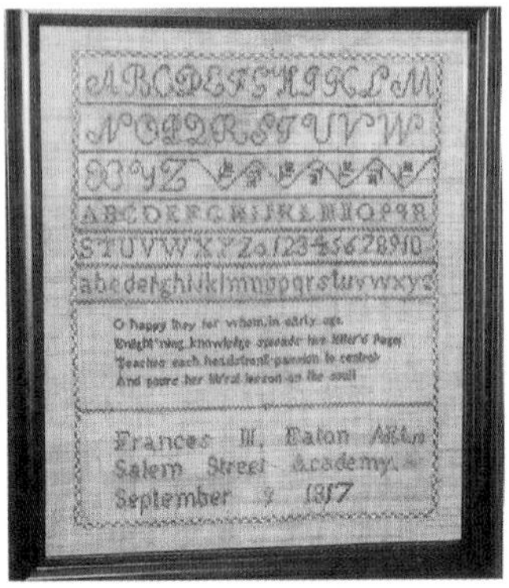

A sampler, by Frances Eaton, aged ten, American, dated 1817, 15 x 13in (38 x 33cm), framed.
£800–880
€/ $1,300–1,400 HCFA

A sampler, worked in silk, with a heart, c1803, 8 x 8½in (20.5 x 21.5cm), framed.
£900–1,000
€/ $1,400–1,600 HIS

A sampler, by Ann Carr, aged 15, worked in silks, dated 1806, 15¼ x 13½in (39 x 34.5cm).
£5,600–6,400
€/ $8,800–10,000 B(NW)

A needlework sampler, by Mary Anne Odem, aged ten, worked in cross-stitch in silks, dated 24 August 1812, 15½ x 11¼in (39.5 x 28.5cm), framed.
£720–850
€/ $1,100–1,300 RTo

A needlework sampler, by Mary Lewis, 1803, 12 x 16½in (30.5 x 42cm).
£300–350
€/ $470–550 RTo

A sampler, by Elisabeth Crane, worked in silks, dated 1807, 17¾ x 13¼in (45 x 33.5cm), framed.
£900–1,100
€/ $1,400–1,700 B(WM)

A needlework sampler, by Jenny Stockton, aged 12, with Adam and Eve beside the Tree of Life, dated 1815, 25 x 17in (63.5 x 43cm).
£700–820
€/ $1,100–1,300 BWL

Auction or dealer?

When buying at auction, prices can be lower than those of a dealer, but a buyer's premium and VAT will be added to the hammer price. Equally, when selling at auction, commission, tax and photography charges will be deducted from the hammer price. Dealers will often restore pieces before putting them back on the market.

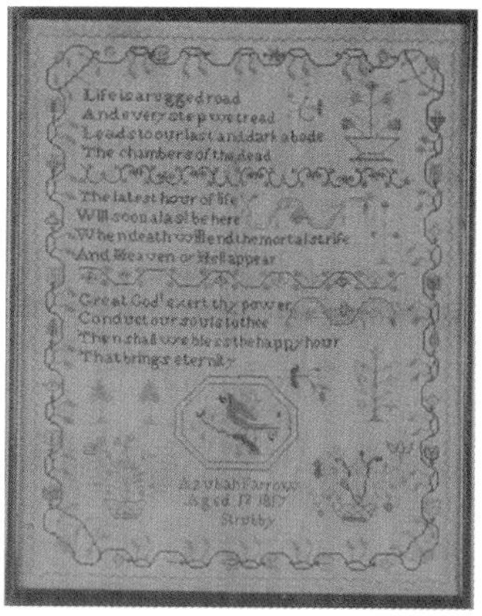

A needlework sampler, by Azubah Farrow, 1817, 14½ x 11½in (36.5 x 29cm), framed.
£600–700
€/ $950–1,100 L

A sampler, by Sarah Lewis Bayly, worked on wool with silks, dated April 1823, 12½ x 13in (31 x 33cm), in an Edwardian oak frame.
£2,200–2,500
€/ $3,500–4,000 S(O)

A sampler, by Eliza Latham, aged eight, faded, c1830, 15 x 12½in (38 x 32cm), in a modern frame.
£800–900
€/ $1,200–1,400 S(O)

Insurance values

Always insure your valuable antiques for the cost of replacing them with similar items, regardless of the original price paid. Both dealers and auctioneers can provide a valuation service for a fee.

A sampler, by Philinda Lamb, aged 13, American, dated 24 July 1820, 14 x 17in (35.5 x 43cm), framed.
£2,000–2,200
€/ $3,200–3,400 COPA

A sampler, by Mary McCorrie, American, dated 1824, 16 x 13in (40.5 x 33cm), in a modern frame.
£500–560
€/ $800–880 HCFA

An embroidered sampler, by HD, worked in silks with a map of Wales, c1830, 16½ x 13in (42 x 33cm).
£4,000–4,500
€/ $6,300–7,000 S(O)

A needlework sampler, by Rebekah Pankhurst, dated 1830, 18¼ x 14¼in (46.5 x 36cm), in a mahogany frame.
£600–720
€/ $950–1,100 L

A needlework sampler, by Martha Lee, dated 1823, 9 x 8in (23 x 20.5cm).
£300–350
€/ $470–550 G(L)

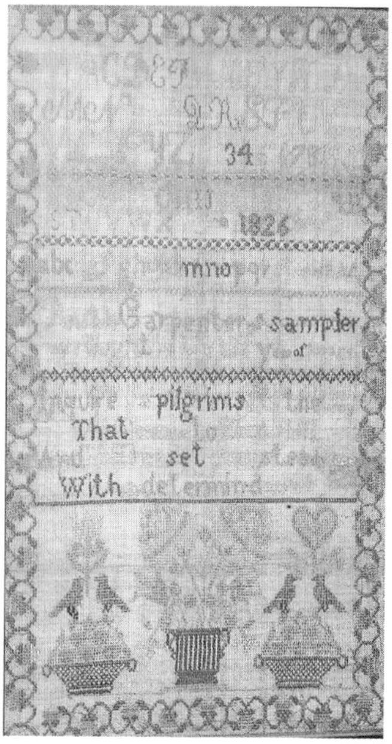

A sampler, by Ruth Carpenter, American, 1826, 20 x 12in (51 x 30.5cm), framed.
£700–770
€/ $1,100–1,200 HCFA

A sampler, by Eliza Thomas, dated 1831, 21¾ x 17¾in (55.5 x 45cm).
£1,100–1,200
€/ $1,700–1,900 PSC

A sampler, by Louisa Oldland, dated 8 March 1833, 17¼ x 13in (44 x 33cm).
£1,100–1,200
€/ $1,700–1,800 S(O)

A sampler, by Elizabeth Kerby, aged 13, dated 1833, 23 x 12in (58.5 x 30.5cm), framed.
£200–225
€/ $320–360 G(L)

A sampler, by Mary Ann White, dated 13 November 1834, 8¼ x 13in (21 x 33cm).
£450–525
€/ $710–830 L

A sampler, by Martha Parnaby, aged 10, dated 16 August 1837, 16½ x 17½in (42 x 44.5cm), in a burrwood frame.
£380–450
€/ $600–710 PFK

A silk sampler, by Susan Wheeler, aged 11, 1835, 13in (33cm) square, framed.
£1,300–1,500
€/ $2,100–2,400 SEA

A sampler, by Louisa Broad, aged 11, dated 11 October 1835, 16 x 12in (41 x 30.5cm), framed.
£350–420
€/ $550–660 Bea(E)

A sampler, by Rachel Walker, Ackworth School, Yorkshire, dated 1842, 6 x 9½in (15 x 24cm), framed.
£720–800
€/ $1,100–1,200 HIS

◄ **A sampler,** inscribed 'MR finished April 10 1838', 16 x 12¾in (40.5 x 32.5cm), in a later frame.
£380–450
€/ $600–710 PF

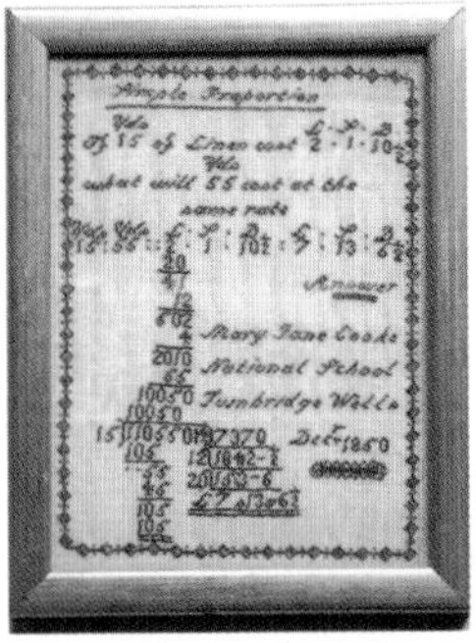

◄ **A school mathematical sampler,** dated 1850, 8 x 6¼in (20.5 x 16cm), framed.
£1,100–1,200
€/ $1,700–1,900 HIS

A sampler, by Mary Fielding, The Shepherd and Shepherdess, dated 1851, 24 x 25in (61 x 63.5cm), framed.
£1,000–1,200
€/ $1,600–1,900 HIS

A sampler, by Sarah Davies, aged 17, Welsh, dated 1864, 16 x 20in (40.5 x 51cm), framed.
£300–350
€/ $470–550 PF

A woolwork sampler, by Elisabeth Preston, dated 1852, 24in (61cm) square, mounted as a fire screen in a painted wood frame.
£280–325
€/ $440–510 AH

Tapestries

A wool and silk tapestry, depicting a hunting scene in a wooded landscape, some damage, Flemish, c1650, 110¼ x 88¼in (280 x 224cm).
£4,000–4,800
€/ $6,300–7,600 ⚒ BUK

A tapestry cushion, 18thC, 10 x 19in (25.5 x 48.5cm).
£350–400
€/ $550–630 ⊞ LGU

An Aubusson tapestry cushion, woven to shape with an urn of blooms, French, late 18thC, 16 x 15½in (40.5 x 39.5cm).
£1,100–1,200
€/ $1,700–1,900 ⚒ S(O)

A tapestry, depicting a 17thC Arcadian scene, Belgian, Ingelmunster, 19thC, 109 x 122in (276 x 310cm).
£1,800–2,200
€/ $2,800–3,500 ⚒ BERN

An armorial tapestry, with the arms of the De Los Rios of Spain, c1650, 128¼ x 115¼in (326 x 292.5cm).
£5,000–6,000
€/ $7,800–9,500 ⚒ S(NY)

A tapestry cushion, woven with flowers, 18thC, 10 x 15in (25.5 x 38cm).
£200–220
€/ $320–350 ⊞ LGU

A wool tapestry, depicting a woodland hunting scene, Flemish, c1800, 60 x 58½in (152.5 x 148.5cm).
£850–1,000
€/ $1,300–1,600 ⚒ B(NW)

An Aubusson verdure tapestry panel, depicting a landscape, French, late 19thC, 75 x 100in (191 x 254cm).
£1,400–1,600
€/ $2,200–2,500 ⚒ S(O)

An Aubusson verdure tapestry, depicting a chateau and a hunting dog, tears, reweaves and restoration, French, early 18thC, 103 x 93in (262 x 236cm).
£2,200–2,500
€/ $3,400–4,000 ⚒ S(P)

A tapestry cushion, 18thC, 9 x 14in (23 x 35.5cm).
£200–220
€/ $320–350 ⊞ LGU

A tapestry cushion, with oak leaf pattern, 18thC, 14 x 10in (35.5 x 25.5cm).
£100–120
€/ $160–190 ⊞ LGU

An Aubusson tapestry cushion, from a larger panel, French, c1880, 11 x 20in (28 x 51cm).
£350–400
€/ $550–630 ⊞ LGU

An Aubusson tapestry cushion, French, c1880, 11 x 17in (28 x 43cm).
£250–280
€/ $400–440 ⊞ LGU

Costume

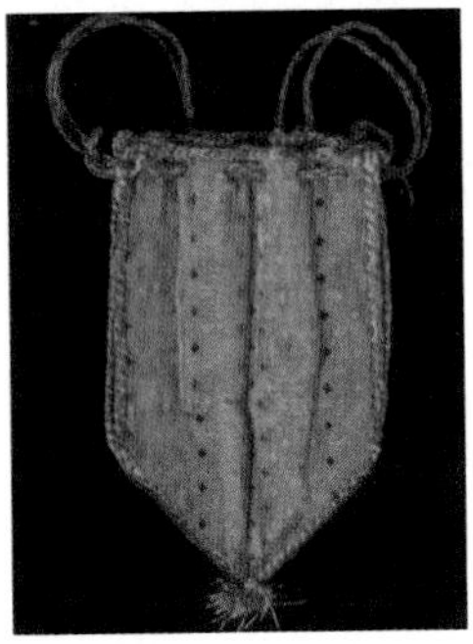

A tapestry draw-string purse, woven with silk crosses, lined with turquoise silk, French, 1650–1700, 4in (10cm) long.
£260–300
€/ $400–475 S(O)

A pair of paste buckles, close set with graduated mixed cut pastes, bright-cut gold bezel, steel back, chape and tongue, c1770.
£100–120
€/ $160–190
WW

A lady's Jacquard woven silk sack-backed open robe, with train and matching petticoat, slight wear, c1780.
£2,500–2,800
€/ $4,000–4,400 B(NW)

A George III gentleman's silk embroidered waistcoat, with blue lining.
£200–240
€/ $320–380 BR

► **A printed cotton bonnet,** c1860.
£50–55
€/ $80–90 CCO

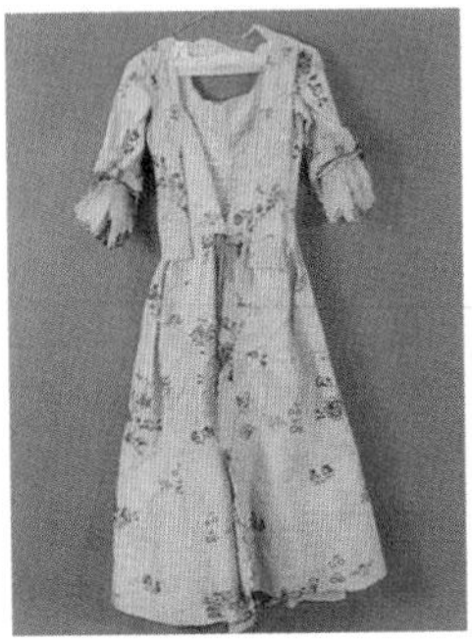

A Spitalfields silk dress, with woven flower decoration, 18thC.
£420–500
€/ $660–790 SWO

A knitted and beaded bonnet, Swiss or German, c1820.
£160–180
€/ $250–285 JuC

A lace afternoon tea dress, 1890s.
£240–265
€/ $380–420 L&L

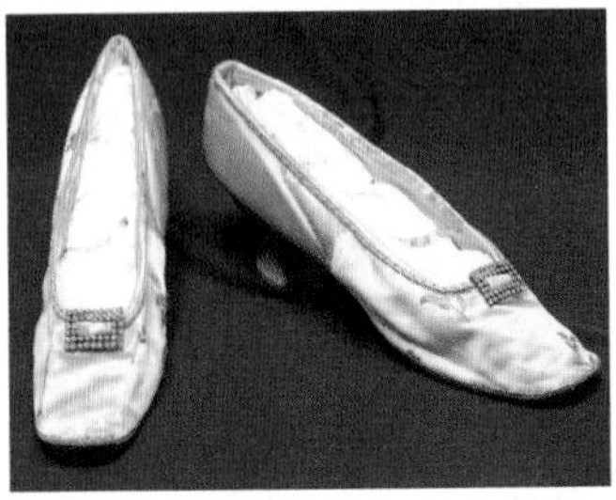

◄ **A pair of silk satin embroidered shoes,** with pink painted heels and diamanté buckles, c1880.
£70–80
€/ $110–125
L&L

◄ **A silk floral panniered dress,** 1870s.
£250–275
€/ $400–440 L&L

A Victorian child's velvet cloak, decorated in brocade-edged silk with plants, the collar trimmed with gold thread, 28in (71cm) long.
£35–45
€/ $55–70 PFK

A Victorian woven silk paisley shawl, 69 x 68in (175.5 x 172.5cm).
£250–275
€/ $400–440 Ech

A Victorian baby's wool and silk carrying cape, with lace edging, 34in (86.5cm) long.
£85–95
€/ $135–150 Ech

A lace dress, with trained skirt, sequin and beaded decoration, labelled 'M. Carey and M. & A. Wall, 8 Bruton Street...London', late 19thC.
£420–500
€/ $660–790 Gam

A Victorian silk cape.
£220–245
€/ $340–380 ⊞ LU

A nurse's embossed and pierced belt buckle, the panels depicting cherubs' faces, Chester 1901, 5½in (14cm) wide.
£55–65
€/ $90–100 ⚒ WilP

An Edwardian Chinese export silk shawl, Canton, 54in (137cm) square.
£150–165
€/ $235–260 ⊞ Ech

An Edwardian pair of lady's leather boots.
£85–100
€/ $135–160 ⊞ Ech

An Edwardian embroidered net blouse.
£40–45
€/ $60–70 ⊞ Ech

An embossed velvet and fur evening coat, 1920s.
£200–225
€/ $320–360 ⚒ SWO

A Continental beaded bag, c1913, 8in (20.5cm) long.
£180–200
€/ $280–320 ⊞ JPr

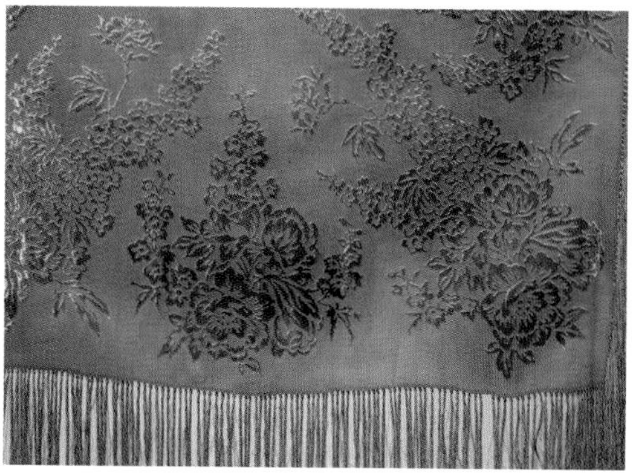

A silk devoré shawl, 1920s, 48in (122cm) square.
£130–150
€/ $200–240 ⊞ Ech

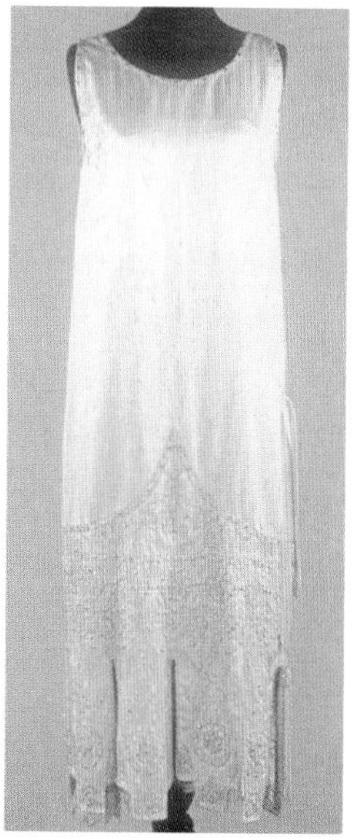

An ivory satin gown, the scalloped hem applied with silver and pearlized studs, crystal beads, tasselled ties, together with underslip, French, 1925.
£450–500
€/ $700–800 ⚒ S(O)
This gown was worn by debutante Susan Rawnsley when she was presented to King George V at court. It is probably by Patou.

A black cotton dress, with all-over bead decoration, 1920s.
£450–500
€/ $700–800 ⊞ Ech

A Chanel-style printed silk chiffon dress, 1920s.
£130–145
€/ $210–230 ⊞ Ech

A flapper dress, with all-over silver beaded decoration and scalloped hem, 1920s.
£630–700
€/ $1,000–1,100 ⊞ Ech

Fans

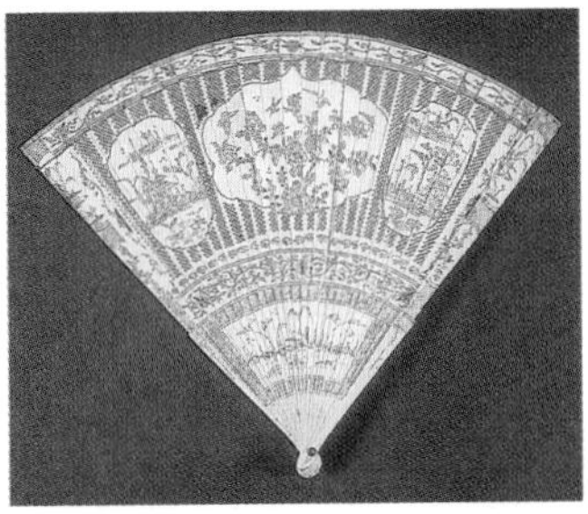

A Chinese export ivory brisé fan, the central cartouche painted in red and gold with birds among blossom branches, above a floral border and Oriental scene, the reverse with mirrored decoration, early 18thC, 10¾in (27cm) long.
£280–320
€/ $440–510 ⚒ B(WM)

A fan, the skin leaf painted with a Biblical scene, the pierced ivory guards and sticks applied with mother-of-pearl and decorated with silver *piqué*, Italian, c1740, 10¾in (27.5cm) long.
£400–480
€/ $630–760 ⚒ S(O)

A fan, the paper leaf painted with a classical scene, the reverse painted with a country dance, with pierced, carved and gilded ivory guards and sticks, c1770, 10¾in (27cm) wide, with associated case.
£1,300–1,500
€/ $2,000–2,400 ⚒ S(O)

A fan, the leaf painted with figures in a landscape, with pierced and gilded mother-of-pearl sticks, 18thC, 18in (45.5cm) wide, framed.
£300–350
€/ $470–550 ⚒ MEA

A lacquered ivory brisé fan, painted with a banquet scene, the reverse with figures in a boat, c1720, 8½in (21.5cm) long.
£1,500–1,800
€/ $2,400–2,800 ⊞ LDC

A fan, the skin leaf painted with Venus and Adonis within a floral border, the reverse painted with a country scene, the mother-of-pearl guards and sticks pierced and carved with figures, French, c1760, 11¾in (30cm) long.
£500–600
€/ $790–950 ⚒ S(O)

► **A fan,** the paper leaf painted with figures on a terrace, c1760, 10in (25.5cm) long.
£55–70
€/ $85–110 ⊞ VB

A fan, painted with figures in a landscape, the tortoiseshell sticks pierced and gilded, French, c1770, 19in (48.5cm) wide, framed.
£420–500
€/ $660–790 ⊞ LDC

A pair of Chinese export ivory brisé fans, pierced with foliate roundels and shields, early 19thC, 10in (25.5cm) long, framed.
£650–750
€/ $1,000–1,200 ⚒ S(O)

A fan, the leaf painted with a classical scene, French, c1730, 11in (28cm) long, with a box labelled 'Duvelleroy' and literature describing the painting.
£1,000–1,200
€/ $1,600–1,800 ⊞ G&G

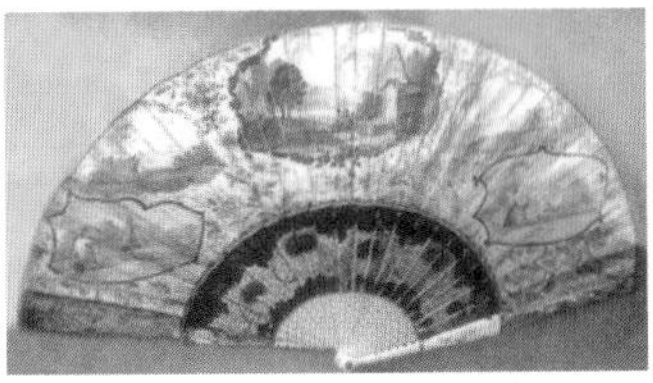

A fan, the paper leaf painted with reserves of figures in landscapes, the pierced ivory sticks painted with scrolls and zigzag shafts, the guards carved with a figure of a woman, with trailing fruit and scrolls, some wear, French, c1760, 21½in (54.5cm) wide.
£220–250
€/ $350–400 ⚒ BR

A fan, the silk leaf painted with a parrot and doves, outlined in gold braid and trimmed with sequins, French, c1775, 19in (48.5cm) wide, framed.
£550–600
€/ $870–950 ⊞ LDC

A fan, the leaf painted with musicians in a landscape, with carved, pierced and gilded horn sticks, c1820, 19in (48.5cm) wide, framed.
£360–400
€/ $570–630 ⊞ LDC

◀ **A fan,** painted with a romantic scene, the reverse with putti holding garlands of flowers, with gilded mother-of-pearl sticks, French, c1840, 11in (28cm) long.
£1,000–1,200
€/ $1,600–1,900 ⚒ S(O)

A fan, the paper leaf painted with figures watching a young shepherd proposing to his lover, signed 'Goslin Maison Dorée', the reverse painted with ribbon-tied floral sprays, with pierced, carved and gilded mother-of-pearl guards and sticks, French, c1840, 11in (28cm) long.
£420–500
€/ $660–790 ⚒ S(O)

A fan, the skin leaf depicting a *fête champêtre*, signed 'Malay Dubois Davernes', the pierced and carved mother-of-pearl sticks gilded in three colours, French, c1849, 10½in (26.5cm) long.
£380–450
€/ $600–700 ⚒ S(O)

A fan, the Chantilly leaf with tortoiseshell guards and sticks, slight damage, mid-19thC, 11in (28cm) long.
£180–200
€/ $280–300 ⊞ HL

A fan, the leaf of Brussels needlepoint appliqué lace, Belgian, c1860, 10in (25.5cm) long.
£220–250
€/ $350–400 ⊞ HL

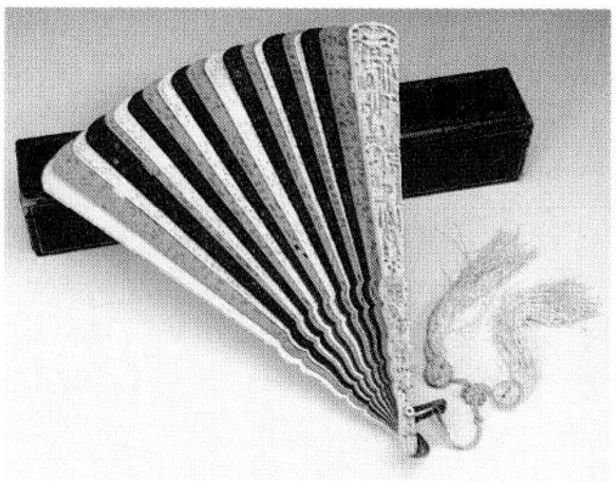

A Chinese export brisé fan, the tortoiseshell, ivory and sandalwood sticks carved with *girures* in domestic and garden settings, the ivory guards with figures, prunus blossom and flowers, 19thC, 13in (33cm) long, with a black and gilt lacquer box.
£550–650
€/ $870–1,000 ⚒ TMA

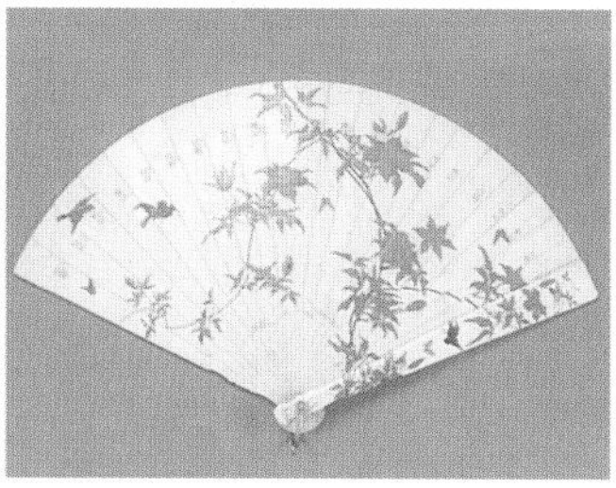

A *shibayama* ivory brisé fan, one side decorated with birds among clematis, the reverse with butterflies and birds in a shrubbery, Japanese, late 19thC, 10¾in (27.5cm) wide.
£2,000–2,200
€/ $3,200–3,500 ⚒ S(O)

A paper and wood fan, advertising Vichy, French, 1880s, 11in (28cm) long.
£90–100
€/ $140–160 ⊞ JUJ

A paper fan, advertising chocolate, French, 1880s, 10in (25.5cm) long.
£90–100
€/ $140–160 ⊞ JUJ

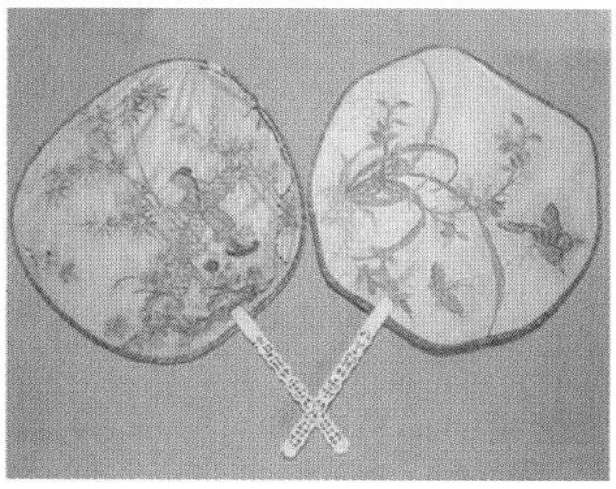

A pair of silkwork fans, with pierced ivory handles, Chinese, early 20thC, 15¾in (40cm) long.
£65–75
€/ $100–120 ⚒ AMB

A lacquered ivory fan, both sides decorated in gold with swallows and plants, with the Imperial *kiku-mon* on both of the outer sticks, silver mount, Japanese, c1900, 9¾in (25cm) long, with lacquered box.
£2,500–3,000
€/ $4,000–4,800 ⚒ S(O)
This fan was an Imperial gift to the Prince of Wales (subsequently Edward VIII), in 1922. He gave it to the lacquer restorer G. Koizumi.

◀ **An Edwardian fan,** the leaf with applied decoration, with gilded wooden sticks and guards, mother-of-pearl detail on the ring, and a silk tassel finger ring, 13in (33cm) long.
£115–125
€/ $180–200
⊞ SAT

FANS

Jewellery

Bangles & Bracelets

An enamel bracelet, with five plaques depicting maidens, each within a turquoise and ruby-set cannetille border, the bracelet strap with a gem-set clasp, damage and losses, Swiss, c1830, 7¾in (19.5cm) long.
£600–700
€/ $950–1,100 B(Kn)

A gold and citrine bracelet, the mixed-cut citrine with a repoussé border with circular-cut citrine accents, with a mesh bracelet, c1850, 6¾in (17cm) long.
£800–900
€/ $1,300–1,400 S(O)

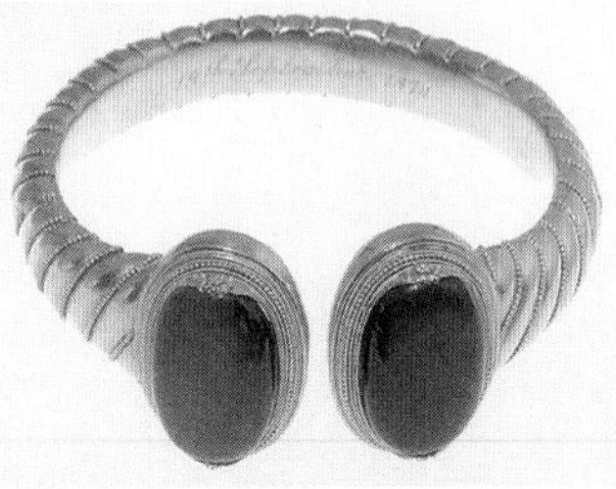

An Estruscan-style gold and lapis lazuli bangle, by Robert Philips & Sons, with applied beaded wirework and two lapis lazuli hinged panels with internal inscription '19th September 1878', with applied maker's marks, 19thC.
£3,500–4,000
€/ $5,500–6,300 Bea

A gold, enamel, diamond and sapphire bracelet, c1880, 6½in (16.5cm) long.
£2,500–3,000
€/ $4,000–4,700 SGr

A two-colour gold jarretière bracelet, with a beaded surround, and buckle clasp, c1890.
£280–320
€/ $440–510 HAM

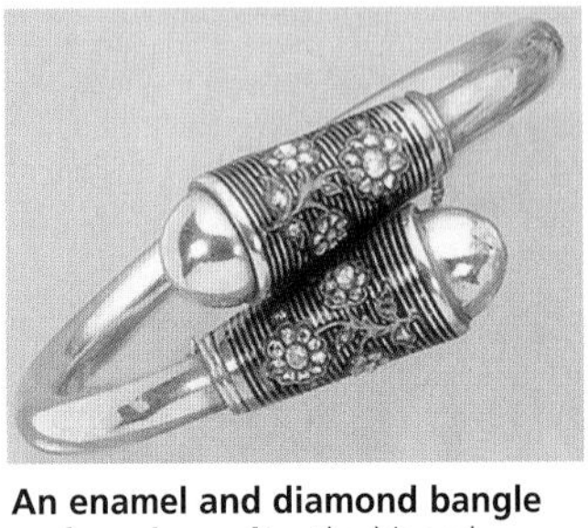

An enamel and diamond bangle and earring suite, the hinged hollow-work bangle with an enamel and rose-cut diamond detail, with a pair of ear studs *en suite*, minor damage, c1890, 2¼in (5.5cm) diam.
£530–630
€/ $840–1,000 B(Kn)

A garnet-set hinged bangle, the front with a flowerhead cluster, 19thC.
£170–200
€/ $270–320 G(L)

A 15ct gold bangle, formed to depict a musical stave, with 'Melba' set in diamonds, c1890, 2½in (6.5cm) diam.
£1,600–1,800
€/ $2,500–2,800 NBL
This bangle was given as a present by the opera singer Dame Nellie Melba.

A late Victorian sapphire and diamond bangle, with case.
£1,000–1,200
€/ $1,600–1,900 GTH

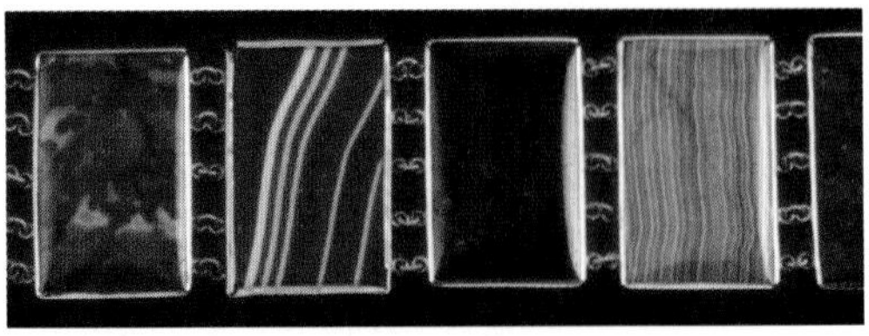

A hardstone bracelet, 19thC, 7½in (19cm) long, with original case by William Robb.
£550–650
€/ $870–1,000 S(O)

◄ **A gold bracelet,** each link with a foliate border and cluster detail to the centre, 19thC, 6¾in (17cm) long.
£400–500
€/ $630–800 B(Kn)

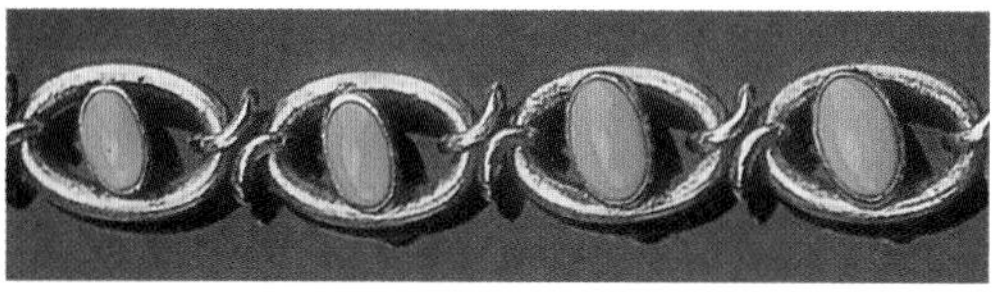

A Victorian bracelet, each link set with a turquoise stone.
£320–375
€/ $510–590 B(O)

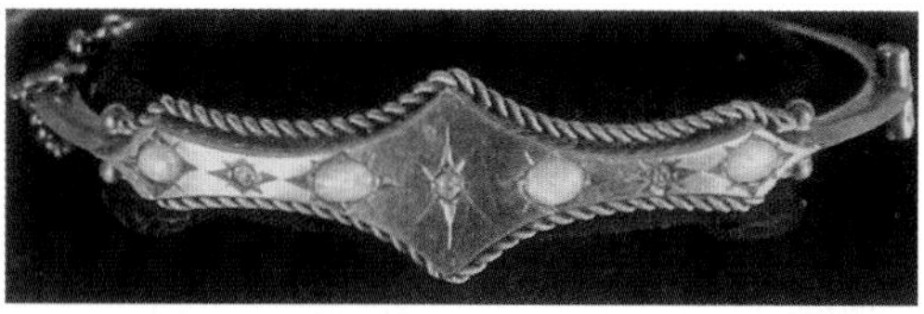

A Victorian 9ct gold opal and diamond-set hinged bangle, with case.
£110–130
€/ $170–210 DMC

A Victorian gold and seed pearl-mounted bangle.
£320–375
€/ $510–590 BIG

An Edwardian gold and amethyst bracelet, 3in (7.5cm) diam, cased.
£350–420
€/ $550–670 B(Kn)

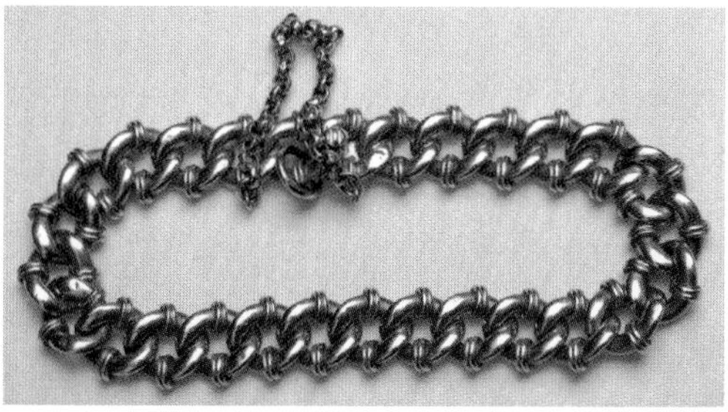

A 15ct gold bracelet, with double curb links, c1910, 3¾in (9.5cm) long.
£550–600
€/ $870–950 WIM

A silver-gilt and enamel bracelet, c1910, 7½in (19cm) long.
£180–200
€/ $280–320 SGr

A gold filigree bracelet, wrought in six sections, each set with a pearl, c1920.
£100–115
€/ $160–180 LCM

A Victorian 15ct gold bracelet, set with multi-coloured gem stones, including sapphire and garnet, 2½in (6.5cm) diam.
£1,800–2,000
€/ $2,800–3,200 WIM

A 15ct gold bracelet, c1900, 3½in (9cm) diam.
£630–700
€/ $1,000–1,100 WIM

An Edwardian gold hinged bangle, set with a row of alternating rubies and pearls within a rope-twist border.
£230–275
€/ $360–430 G(L)

Brooches

A gold brooch, depicting Masonic devices in mother-of-pearl, enamel and gold on a blue glass ground, late 18thC, 1¼in (3cm) wide.
£230–275
€/ $360–430 DN

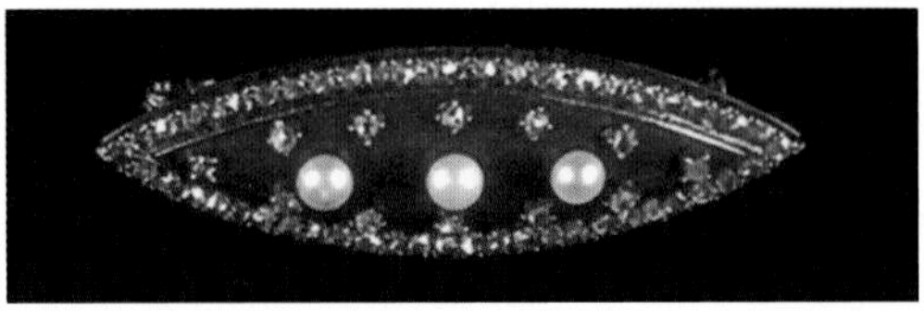

A George III locket brooch, set with pearls and rose-cut diamonds on a *guilloche* enamel ground, within a rose-cut diamond border, with a glazed locket compartment to the reverse, 1½in (4cm) wide.
£650–750
€/ $1,000–1,200 L

► **A Vauxhall glass brooch,** formed as a floral cluster, c1800.
£170–200
€/ $270–315
WW

A 15ct gold-foiled amethyst Maltese cross brooch, with cannetille work, c1830, 2in (5cm) wide.
£800–880
€/ $1,300–1,400 EXC

A Florentine mosaic and gold brooch, set with hardstone flowers including chalcedony, lapiz lazuli and turquoise, the frame with scrolling wirework decoration and a rope-twist border, Italian, mid-19thC, in original case.
£850–1,000
€/ $1,300–1,600 WW

An early Victorian garnet and seed pearl brooch, with a glass compartment containing hair, 1in (2.5cm) wide.
£175–200
€/ $280–320 RIT

► **A carved bog oak brooch,** in the shape of a harp, Irish, c1870, 3in (7.5cm) long.
£90–100
€/ $140–160 STA

A silver and gold kunzite and diamond brooch, c1860.
£1,700–2,000
€/ $2,700–3,200 BUK
Kunzite is a gem variety of the mineral spodumene which fluoresces when illuminated.

A 15ct gold, enamel and pearl brooch, c1890, 1in (2.5cm) wide.
£700–780
€/ $1,100–1,200 SGr

A Victorian gold brooch, set with five amethysts, with wirework decoration and a locket back.
£160–200
€/ $250–315 G(L)

► **A Victorian 18ct gold reverse-painted crystal intaglio brooch,** depicting a fox's head, on a 15ct gold pin, ½in (1cm) diam.
£120–140
€/ $190–220 SWO

A late Victorian diamond brooch, in the form of a Staffordshire knot, the diamonds set in silver and backed in gold.
£850–1,000
€/ $1,300–1,600 WL

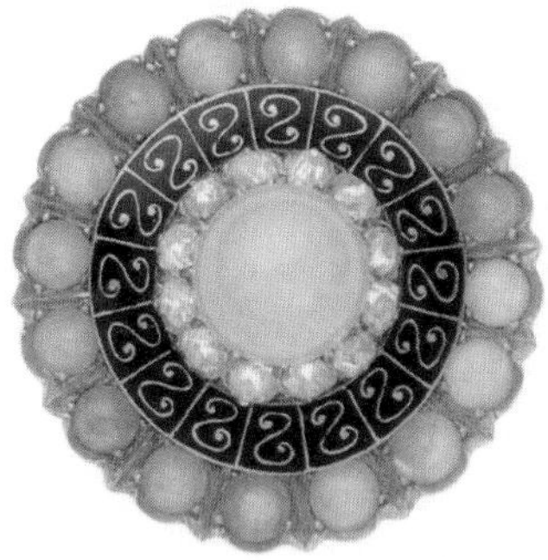

An enamelled gold, sapphire and diamond-mounted brooch, by Carlo Guiliano, the central star sapphire within an enamelled frame surrounding old brilliant-cut diamonds and star sapphires, the pin hinge with applied maker's mark, late 19thC.
£3,500–4,000
€/ $5,500–6,300 Bea

A silver quartz-set Luckenbooth brooch, Scottish, 19thC.
£320–375
€/ $500–590 B(Ed)

A Victorian 15ct gold and turquoise brooch, 1½in (4cm) diam.
£1,000–1,100
€/ $1,600–1,700 WIM

A porcelain and gilt-metal-mounted brooch, painted with the Madonna and child, Continental, late 19thC, 2¼in (5.5cm) long.
£100–120
€/ $160–190 BR

A Victorian gold, enamel and half-pearl brooch, with a locket reverse.
£150–175
€/ $240–275 GTH

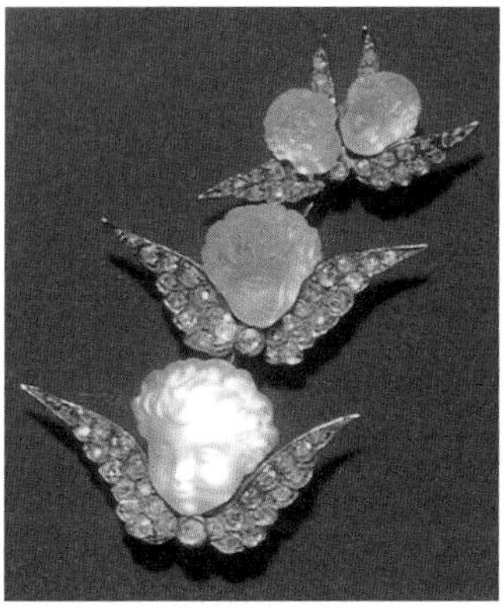

A Victorian diamond and moonstone brooch, designed as four cherub faces with diamond-set wings below.
£4,500–5,200
€/ $7,100–8,200 HYD

◄ **A 15ct gold, enamel and diamond brooch,** c1900, 1in (2.5cm) diam.
£450–500
€/ $700–850 SGr

► **An Edwardian gold-mounted mother-of-pearl brooch,** carved in high relief with figures of a Dutch boy and girl, with a pearl border, 1½in (4cm) diam.
£380–460
€/ $600–720 F&C

A pebble brooch, set with hardstone, 19thC.
£260–320
€/ $400–500 S

A Victorian diamond brooch, in the shape of an anchor with a rope twist, set with 33 graduated old-cut stones, 1¾in (4cm) long.
£2,000–2,400
€/ $3,200–3,800 BWL

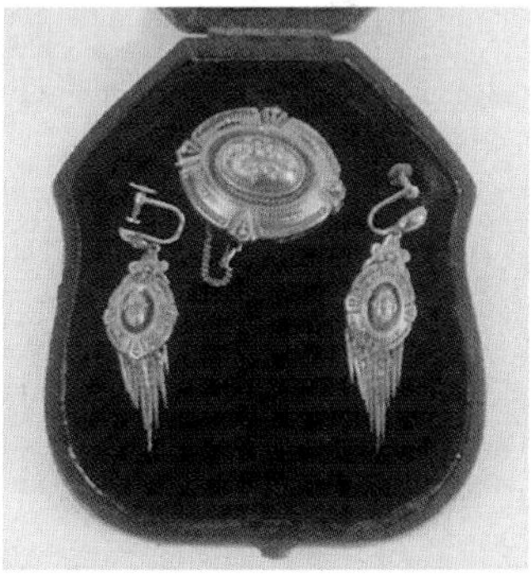

A Victorian gold brooch and earrings set, the brooch with a raised boss centre, the earrings with tassel drops, with case.
£475–565
€/ $750–890 GAK

Cameos

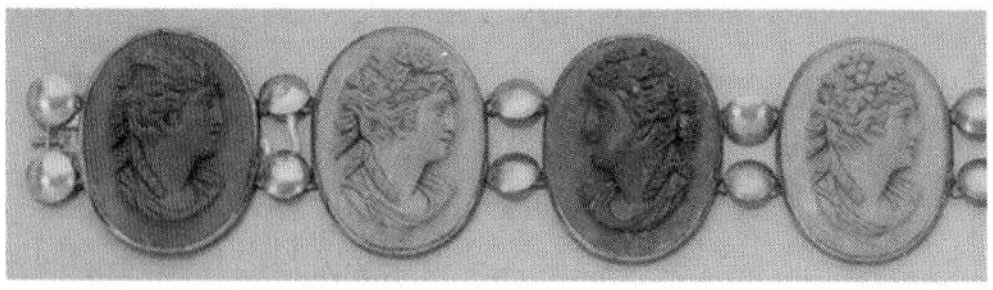

A lava cameo bracelet, the cameos carved to depict classical deities in profile, with a concealed clasp, c1860, 7in (17.5cm) long.
£300–360
€/ $475–575 B(Kn)

A shell cameo pendant brooch, depicting a bacchante, in a gold frame with beaded and rope pattern-twist decoration, Italian, mid-19thC, in original fitted case.
£650–750
€/ $1,000–1,200 WW

A mid-Victorian sardonyx cameo brooch, depicting a neo-classical lady, the frame set with ruby cabochons within a rope-twist border, cased.
£350–420
€/ $550–660 B(L)

A Victorian gold-framed shell cameo brooch/pendant, with a portrait of a gentleman, with a hair-panel back.
£600–700
€/ $950–1,100 GAK

A gold-set cameo pendant, carved with snowdrops, the edge engraved with an inscription, a locket containing hair on the reverse, c1870, ¾in (2cm) long.
£300–325
€/ $475–500 AMC

A gold-framed shell cameo brooch, carved with a classical scene, 19thC.
£250–300
€/ $400–475 Bea

A lava cameo brooch, carved with two putti, within a gold border, c1880, 2in (5cm) long.
£385–460
€/ $600–720 S(O)

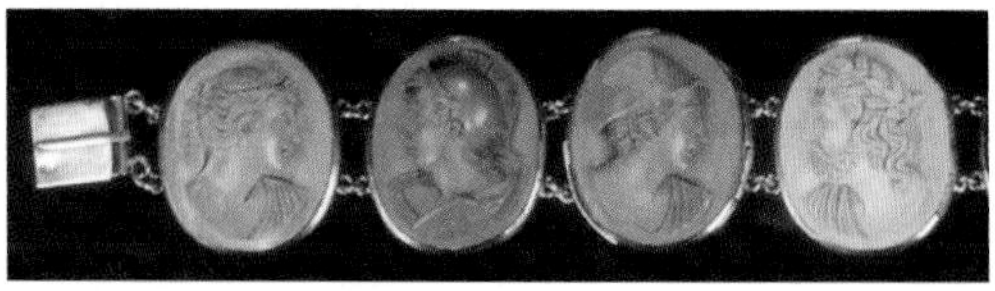

A lava cameo bracelet, the panels carved with classical busts, 19thC.
£280–325
€/ $440–500 DN

A Victorian shell cameo brooch, carved with Apollo, Ayrora and the Sun, in a gold mount.
£1,200–1,400
€/ $1,900–2,200 TEN

◄ **A Victorian cameo brooch,** carved with the bust of a lady with flowers in her hair, in a yellow-metal and turquoise mount.
£450–525
€/ $710–830 CHTR

A 9ct gold shell cameo brooch, carved with a classical female profile, late 19thC.
£230–275
€/ $360–430 G(L)

A pair of late Victorian 15ct gold cameo earrings, 1¾in (4.5cm) long.
£1,200–1,300
€/ $1,900–2,000 WIM

◄ **A cameo brooch,** carved with a Roman bust, set in plain gold mount, c1900, 2¼in (5.5cm) long.
£315–350
€/ $500–550 AMC

Cufflinks

A pair of gold cufflinks, with Essex crystal depictions of game dogs, inscribed 'Eliot Farley', late 19thC.
£1,000–1,200
€/ $1,600–1,900 TEN

A pair of 9ct rose-gold cufflinks, the double-faced plaques engraved with foliate designs, maker's mark SP, hallmarked Birmingham 1906.
£80–100
€/ $130–160 RIT

A pair of reverse intaglio cufflinks, each depicting a dog, mounted on mother-of-pearl, c1900.
£1,600–2,000
€/ $2,500–3,200 S

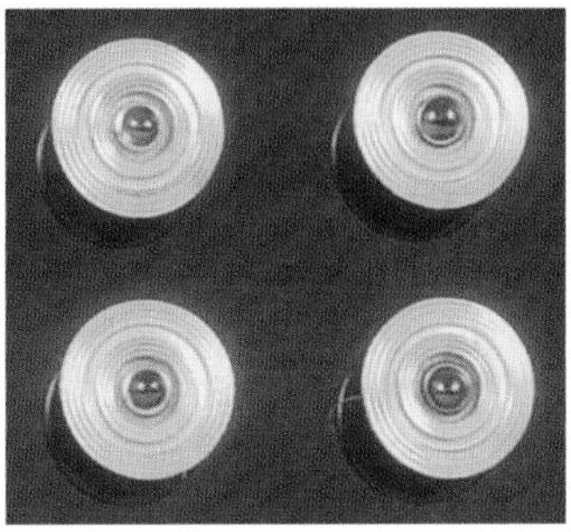

A pair of platinum and sapphire cufflinks, set with cabochon sapphires, within reeded platinum and mother-of-pearl surrounds, c1910.
£220–250
€/ $350–400 HAM

A pair of gold and emerald cufflinks, by Mellerio, French, c1900, ½in (1cm) diam.
£800–900
€/ $1,300–1,400 WIM

A pair of 18ct gold and enamel cufflinks, c1925, ½in (1cm) wide.
£720–800
€/ $1,100–1,300 WIM

Earrings

◄ A pair of diamond and half-pearl pendant earrings, c1890, with fitted case.
£800–950
€/ $1,300–1,500 HAM

A pair of Victorian gold drop earrings.
£100–120
€/ $160–190 L

◄ A pair of platinum and diamond pendant earrings, the whole set with diamonds of 23ct, and with 50 diamonds of 6.5ct, c1945.
£96,000–115,000
€/ $152,000–182,000 S(NY)
From the collection of Eva Peron.

A pair of Victorian 15ct gold earrings, set with armandine garnets, 1½in (4cm) long.
£800–900
€/ $1,300–1,400 WIM

A pair of black opal doublet and diamond pendant earrings, the openwork surmount millegrain-set with single and brilliant-cut diamonds, c1930, 1½in (4cm) long.
£825–1,000
€/ $1,300–1,600 B(Kn)

Necklaces

A paste necklace, composed of a series of stylized floral cluster sections, enclosed in silver, c1775.
£2,800–3,400
€/ $4,400–5,400 ⚒ **WW**

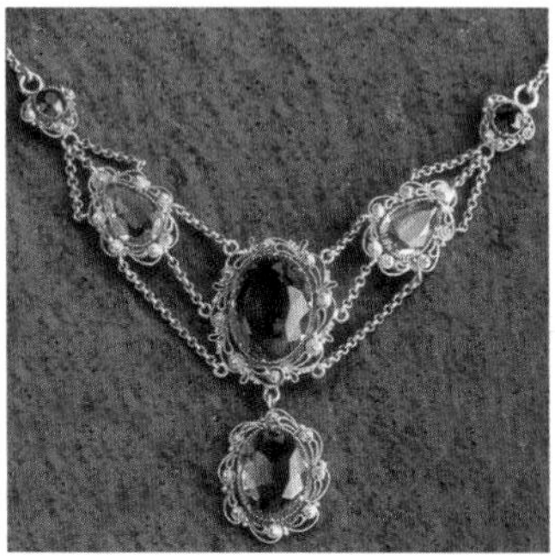

A 9ct gold and amethyst necklace, with cannetille work settings and chain suspensions, on a belcher-link chain, c1830.
£360–450
€/ $575–700 ⚒ **B(O)**

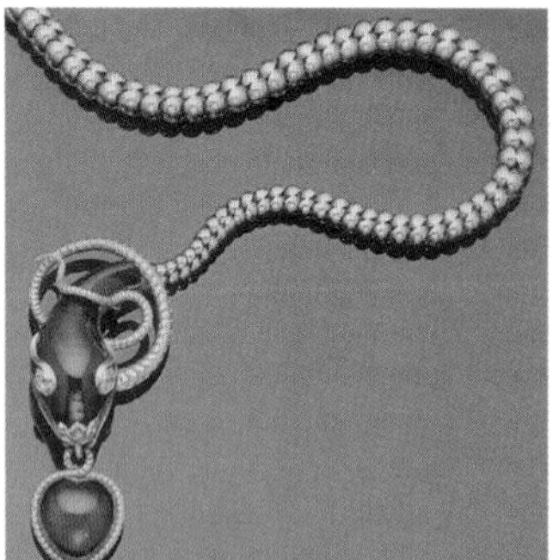

A gold, garnet and diamond serpent necklace, the cabochon garnet serpent's head with rose-diamond eyes and nose, suspending a cabochon garnet heart, a glazed locket to the reverse, on a graduated link chain, with a fitted case, c1845.
£3,500–4,200
€/ $5,500–6,600 ⚒ **WW**

Items in the Jewellery section have been arranged in date order within each sub-section.

A Georgian pinchbeck chain, with a hand clasp, 46in (117cm) long.
£1,300–1,500
€/ $2,000–2,400 ⊞ **WIM**

A gold and amethyst necklace, c1840, 13in (33cm) long.
£3,300–3,600
€/ $5,200–5,700 ⊞ **SGr**

► **A 15ct rose-gold foil-backed amethyst necklace,** c1840, 15in (38cm) long.
£2,000–2,300
€/ $3,200–3,600 ⊞ **EXC**

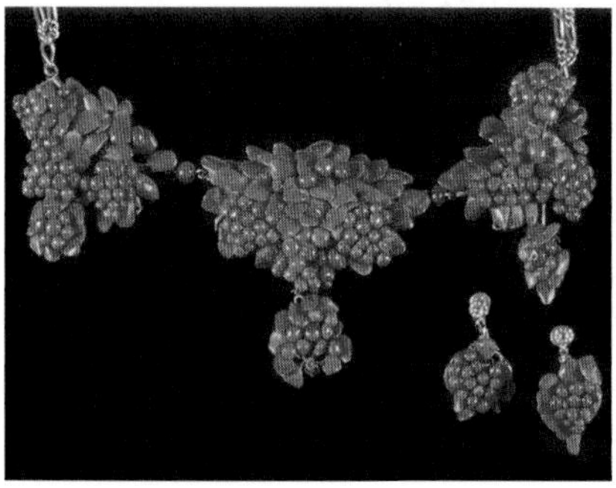

A coral demi-parure, comprising a necklace, bracelet and pendant earrings, each depicting fruiting vines, c1850.
£300–350
€/ $475–550 ⚒ **TEN**

◄ **A diamond fringe necklace,** the reeded tubular link suspending diamond-set flowerheads, mounted in silver and gold, c1880, 14¼in (36cm) long.
£2,000–2,400
€/ $3,200–3,800 ⚒ **HAM**

An early Victorian paste parure, comprising a necklace, two bracelets, a pair of ear pendants and a brooch, with closed back settings, in a fitted case.
£850–1,000
€/ $1,300–1,600 ⚒ **B(Ed)**

A garnet necklace, with floral bud and flower sections in foiled-back gold settings, with a detachable flower drop pendant, c1840, 17¼in (43cm) long.
£1,400–1,600
€/ $2,200–2,500 ⚒ **LJ**

A pendant necklace, the central pierced plaque with a cabochon garnet, Austro-Hungarian, c1880.
£400–480
€/ $630–750 ⚒ **B(Kn)**

A 15ct gold half-pearl necklace, c1890, 8in (20.5cm) long, in a fitted case.
£2,000–2,300
€/ $3,200–3,600 ⊞ WIM

A late Victorian coral necklace, on a box-link chain, the central three cartouches detachable, 15in (38cm) long.
£1,200–1,500
€/ $1,900–2,400 ⚒ B(Kn)

A Victorian garnet necklace, on a trace link chain.
£600–700
€/ $950–1,100 ⚒ TEN

An Edwardian peridot and seed pearl necklace, suspended from lattice work links, on a back chain.
£280–320
€/ $440–500 ⚒ B(O)

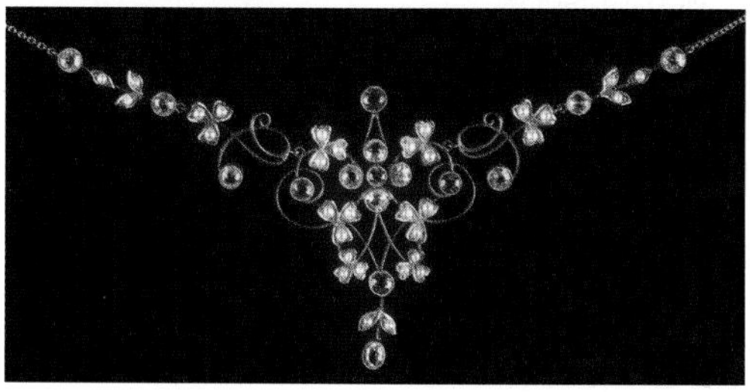

An Edwardian necklace, with aquamarines, pink tourmalines and seed pearls, in a fitted case.
£1,300–1,500
€/ $2,100–2,400 ⚒ L

A late Victorian garnet necklace, on a trace-link chain, 18in (45.5cm) long.
£550–620
€/ $870–980 ⚒ B(Kn)

A Victorian seed pearl necklace, on a curb-link chain, 18in (45.5cm) long.
£650–750
€/ $1,000–1,200 ⚒ B(Kn)

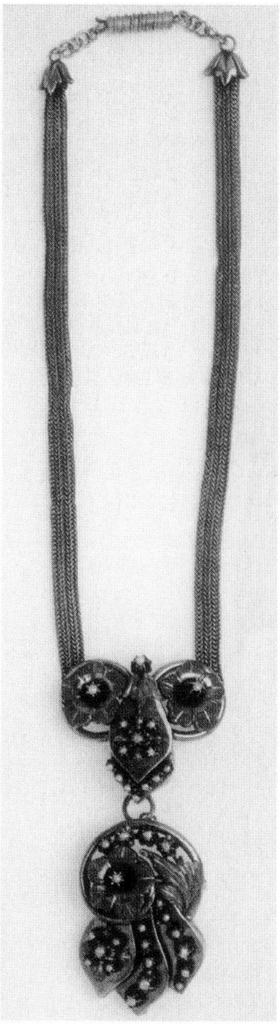

◄ **A 14ct and 10ct two-colour gold necklace and bracelet set,** both pieces inset with small pearls and mother-of-pearl, some losses, c1900.
£200–240
€/ $315–380 ⚒ LCM

A Belle Epoque *sautoir*, the diamond and pearl pendant with a seed pearl tassel, and suspended from a seed pearl necklace, c1910, 17¾in (45cm) long.
£650–720
€/ $1,000–1,100 ⚒ HAM

► **A poured glass demi-parure,** comprising a necklace of graduated flowerheads mounted in gilt metal, and a pair of matching earclips, c1930, with two cardboard Chanel boxes.
£750–880
€/ $1,200–1,400 ⚒ WW

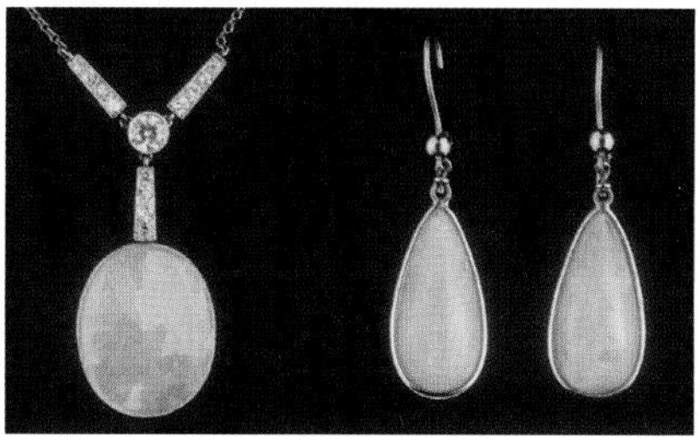

A platinum, diamond and opal necklace, with a pair of earrings *en suite*, c1930.
£2,500–2,800
€/ $4,000–4,400 ⚒ BUK

Pendants

A silver and gold openwork pendant/brooch, of flowerhead foliate design, set with rose-cut diamonds and green paste, Spanish, 18thC, in a fitted case.
£280–320
€/ $440–500 ⚒ G(L)

A turquoise, ruby and diamond-mounted dove pendant, on a simulated seed pearl chain, mid-19thC.
£1,200–1,400
€/ $1,900–2,200 ⚒ Bea

A Victorian diamond and enamel heart pendant, on a gold chain with enamel barrel spacers.
£1,800–2,200
€/ $2,800–3,500 ⚒ B(Ed)

A gold pendant, mounted with a hair plait, with cherub motifs and gold wirework beneath a faceted crystal, 18thC.
£1,000–1,100
€/ $1,600–1,700 ⚒ Bea

An enamelled pendant, by A. Phillips, inset with pearls and rubies, c1860, 3in (7.5cm) long.
£5,800–6,500
€/ $9,200–10,400 ⊞ SGr

◄ A heart-shaped pendant, set with zircons on a diamond ground, c1880, 1in (2.5cm) long.
£2,000–2,200
€/ $3,200–3,500 ⚒ S(O)

An 18ct gold-framed pendant badge, by Isaac Pothecary, with an enamel panel depicting the Tower of London below the crest of the City of London, the reverse with a presentation inscription to the Sheriff of London 1896.
£1,400–1,600
€/ $2,200–2,500 ⚒ CGC

An amethyst, citrine and topaz pendant, with a locket back, 1790–1800, ¾in (2cm) long.
£1,200–1,300
€/ $1,900–2,100 ⊞ WIM

An enamel, gold and pearl pendant, set within a ropework and bead surround, suspending a baroque pearl drop, c1860.
£200–220
€/ $315–350 ⚒ TEN

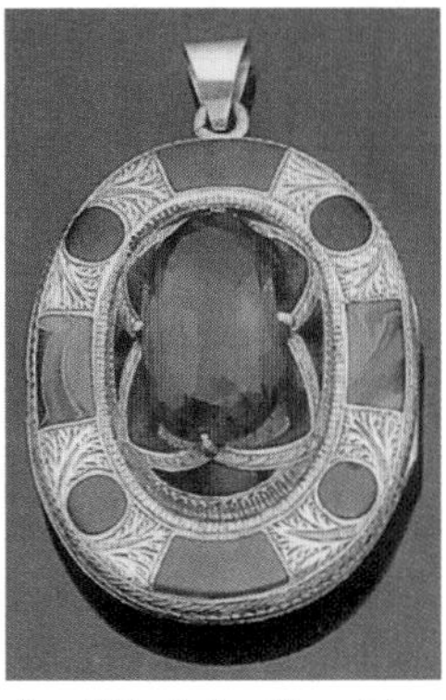

A gold locket, with a citrine in a raised claw setting, on a chased gold surround set with various hardstones, opening to reveal glazed hair compartment, Scottish, 19thC.
£460–550
€/ $720–870 ⚒ WW

► A Victorian gold and coral bead pendant, the reverse with a plaited hair compartment, on a fancy link chain.
£180–220
€/ $280–350 ⚒ G(L)

A rose-cut diamond and enamel cross pendant/brooch, possibly French, c1840, 1¼in (3cm) long.
£1,600–1,800
€/ $2,500–2,800 ⊞ NBL

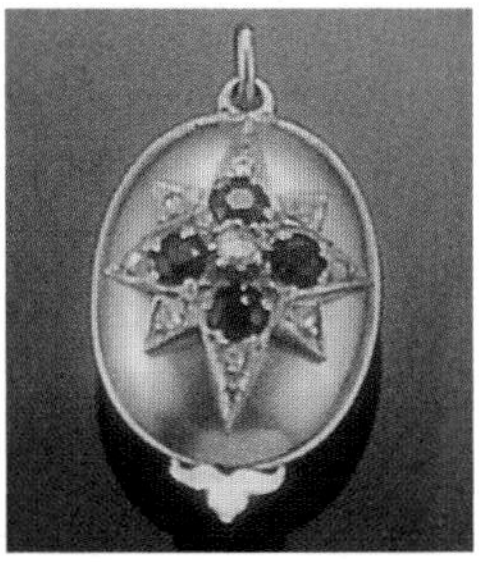

A 15ct gold, diamond and garnet pendant, c1880.
£300–360
€/ $475–570 ⚒ LJ

A Victorian gold and silver rose-diamond-set pendant/brooch, the lattice design over enamel.
£700–820
€/ $1,100–1,300 ⚒ G(L)

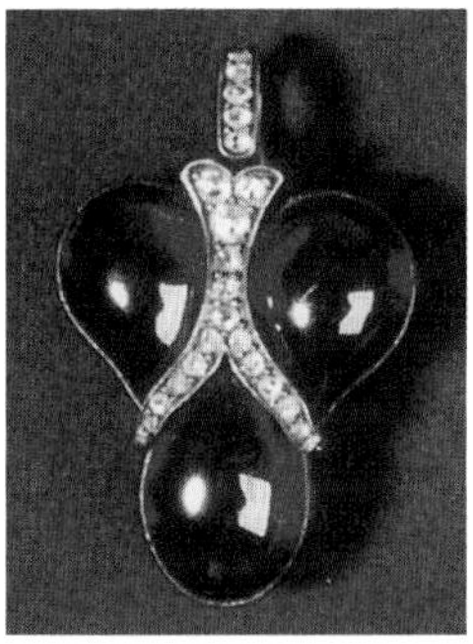

A Victorian pendant, with three cabochon garnets overlaid with a band set with diamonds, the suspension loop set with five diamonds.
£900–1,100
€/ $1,400–1,700 ⚒ HYD

A peridot and half-pearl pendant, c1900.
£420–500
€/ $660–790 ⚒ TEN

An Edwardian 9ct gold pendant, with a central amethyst and seed pearl drop, on an elongated link chain.
£100–120
€/ $160–190 ⚒ G(L)

A gold, enamel, pearl and diamond pendant, in the manner of Giuliano, with a diamond and pearl drop and a cluster suspension loop, 19thC.
£6,500–7,800
€/ $10,300–12,300 ⚒ DN

◀ **A gold pendant,** the amethyst-coloured stone set in a border of seed pearls, surrounded by a border of alternate amethysts and pearls, 1880–1910, 2½in (6.5cm) long.
£350–400
€/ $550–630 ⚒ CGC

An amethyst and seed pearl pendant, of scrolling shield design, Continental, c1900.
£160–200
€/ $250–315 ⚒ B(O)

An Edwardian 15ct gold heart-shaped openwork pendant, set with peridots and seed pearls.
£160–200
€/ $250–315 ⚒ G(L)

A reverse intaglio crystal pendant, depicting a finch among oak leaves, the reverse inset with a miniature portrait of a lady, in a gold bead and wirework frame, 19thC.
£500–600
€/ $800–950 ⚒ G(L)

A Victorian pebble cross pendant, set with bloodstone and variegated agate, mounted in gold, engraved with flowerhead and foliate borders, Scottish.
£780–940
€/ $1,200–1,500 ⚒ B(Ed)

A 9ct gold heart-shaped openwork pendant, set with amethysts and seed pearls, on a fine gold chain, together with a pair of similar earrings, c1900.
£170–200
€/ $270–315 ⚒ G(L)

▶ **A gold and platinum pendant,** set with a carved moonstone, with diamonds and synthetic sapphires and a pearl frame, c1900.
£1,700–2,000
€/ $2,700–3,200 ⚒ BUK

An opal and diamond pendant, c1900, 2in (5cm) long.
£2,200–2,400
€/ $3,500–3,800 ⊞ WIM

▶ **A 15ct gold and platinum black opal pendant,** c1910, 3in (7.5cm) long.
£1,200–1,400
€/ $1,900–2,200 ⊞ WIM

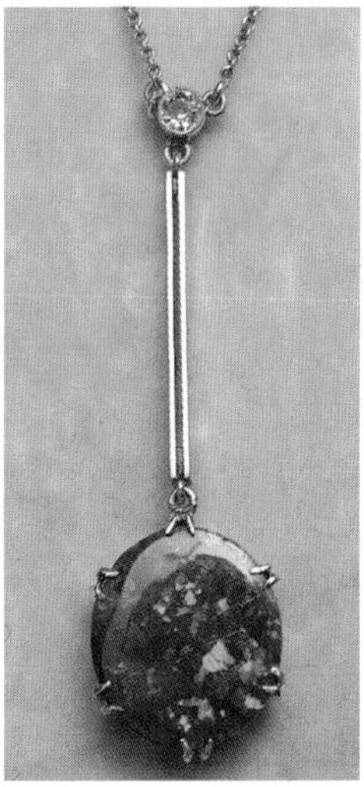

Rings

A Claddagh ring, c1750.
£800–880
€/ $1,300–1,400 ⊞ SAY

An emerald and diamond ring, c1880.
£650–750
€/ $1,000–1,200 ⚒ S(O)

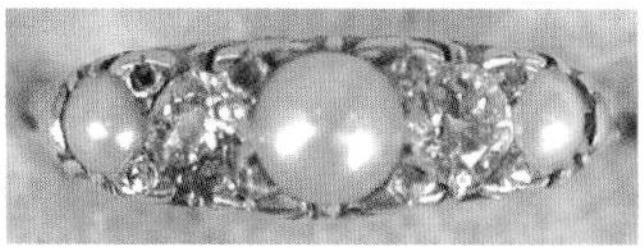

An enamelled gold and garnet mourning ring, with a central skull and crossbones motif beneath a crystal, mid-18thC.
£1,400–1,600
€/ $2,200–2,500 ⚒ Bea

A Victorian 18ct gold snake ring, 1in (2.5cm) diam.
£550–600
€/ $870–950 ⊞ WIM

◄ A Victorian diamond and split-pearl engraved half-hoop ring.
£220–250
€/ $350–400 ⚒ SWO

A gold and platinum ring, set with blue enamel and decorated with the monogram of Maximilian I, with diamond encrustations, and decorated on the laterals with Imperial eagles, Austrian, 1864, with original red velvet case bearing the inscription 'Roth Jeweller of His Majesty the Emperor of Austria Vienna'.
£4,000–4,500
€/ $6,300–7,100 ⚒ LCM

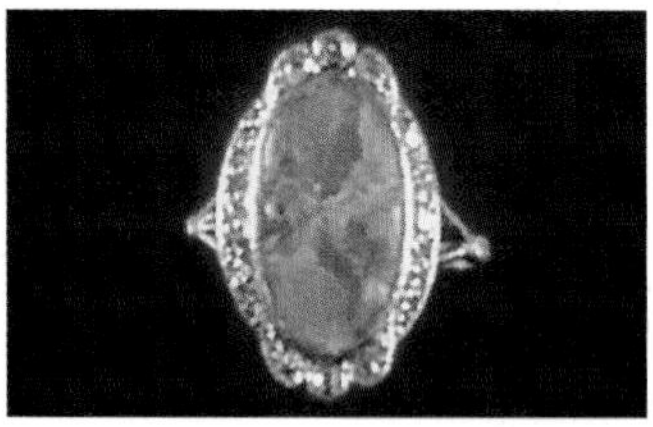

An opal and diamond ring, with pierced shoulders, opal cracked, c1900.
£550–620
€/ $870–980 ⚒ TEN

Stick Pins

An 18ct gold stick pin, by Renée Foy for Boucheron, set with a garnet, c1875, 3½in (9cm) long.
£1,100–1,200
€/ $1,700–1,900 ⊞ WIM

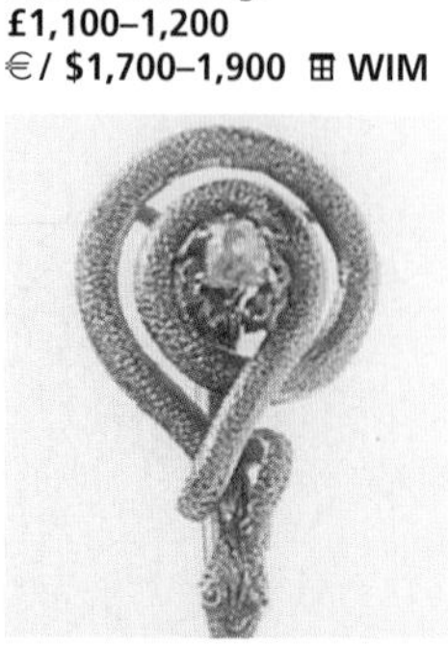

A gold and diamond snake stick pin, 19thC.
£200–220
€/ $315–350 ⚒ Bea

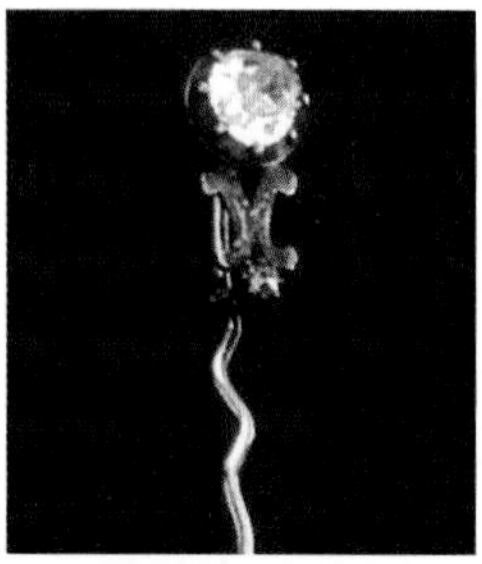

A diamond stick pin, set with a circular-cut diamond and a smaller stone, c1880, 1¾in (4.5cm) long.
£470–550
€/ $740–870 ⚒ S(O)

A Victorian gold, diamond and opal stick pin, the central opal with a serpent surround, set throughout with old-cut diamonds, opal cracked.
£240–260
€/ $380–400 ⚒ B(O)

◄ An enamelled gold double snake stick pin, with diamond eyes, surrounding a banded agate central stone, c1890, 3¼in (8.5cm) long.
£500–550
€/ $790–870 ⊞ ANO

A diamond stick pin, c1890, 2¾in (7cm) long.
£500–600
€/ $790–950 ⚒ S(O)

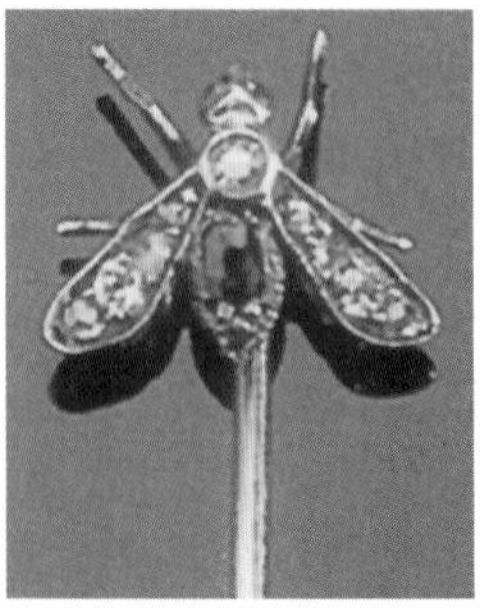

A diamond and sapphire stick pin, the finial modelled as a fly, set with old- and rose-cut diamonds, a sapphire and red stone cabochon eyes, c1890.
£90–110
€/ $140–170 ⚒ B(O)

Enamel

An enamel cosmetic box, the top painted with a couple, the base gilded with a foliate spray, French, 19thC, 2¾in (7cm) diam.
£280–320
€/ $440–500 TMA

An enamel patch box, painted with an exotic bird, butterflies and foliage, c1900, 2in (5cm) wide.
£275–300
€/ $430–480 ⊞ LBr

A silver-gilt and cloisonné enamel snuff box, the top decorated with birds and butterflies, the sides with foliage, Russian, St Petersburg 1908–17, 2¾in (7cm) wide.
£470–550
€/ $740–870 WW

A silver and enamel dressing table set, Birmingham 1947, brush 10½in (26.5cm) long.
£100–120
€/ $160–190 SWO

A pair of gilt-brass and enamel opera glasses, by Prosper Bunouste, Palais Royale, Paris, French, c1860, 4in (10.5cm) wide.
£270–300
€/ $425–475 ⊞ HUM

A silver and cloisonné enamel tea-glass holder, maker's mark 'S.K.', Moscow 1899–1908, Russian, 4¼in (11cm) high.
£700–850
€/ $1,100–1,300 S(O)

◄ **A Limoges-style enamel panel,** depicting a muse and her handmaidens in a sparse landscape, in a cast-bronze frame with floral trophy mantle, French, 19thC, 8in (20.5cm) high.
£340–400
€/ $540–630 HOLL

► **A set of silver-gilt and enamel spoons,** comprising 12 teaspoons and a serving spoon, the backs enamelled with foliage on a gilded stippled ground, Russian, Moscow c1900, largest 5¾in (14.5cm) long.
£1,100–1,300
€/ $1,700–2,000 S(NY)

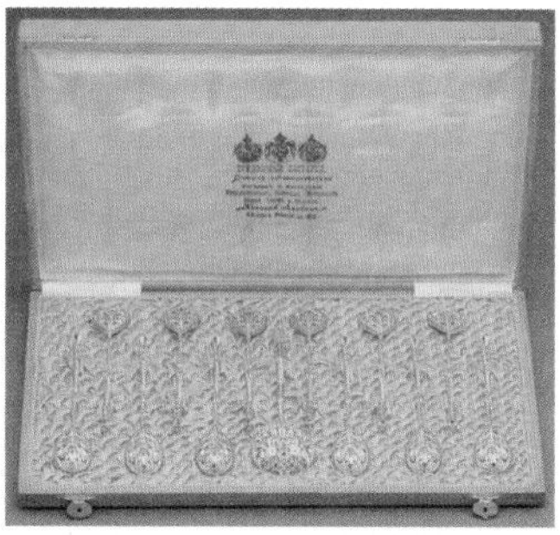

A set of four silver-gilt and enamel salts, with four enamel-backed spoons, Russian, St Petersburg c1900, salts 1¾in (4.5cm) diam, with original case.
£650–780
€/ $1,000–1,200 L

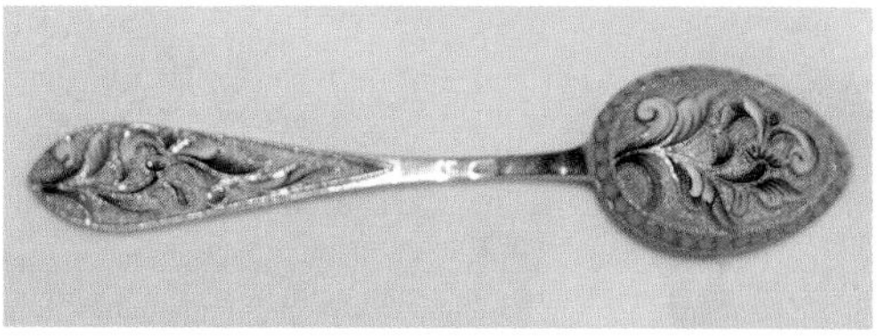

A set of six silver-gilt and cloisonné enamel coffee spoons, by Maria Semenova, Russian, Moscow 1896–1908, 4in (10cm) long.
£1,500–1,700
€/ $2,400–2,700 ⊞ MIR

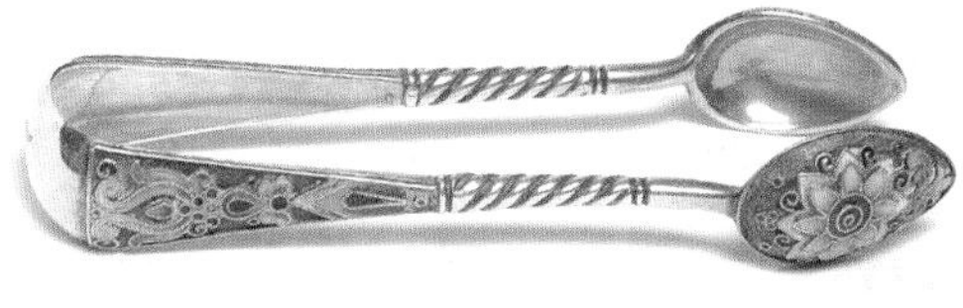

A pair of Imperial cloisonné enamel sugar tongs, 11th Artel, Russian, Moscow, 1908–1917, 4in (10cm) long.
£340–380
€/ $540–600 ⊞ SHa

► **A Limoges enamel tray,** painted with an aristocrat surprising a servant, monogrammed 'F.C.', some damage, 19thC, 4¾in (12cm) square.
£130–160
€/ $200–220 SWO

Fabergé

◄ **A Fabergé silver-gilt and jade bell,** Moscow 1908–17, 2½in (6.5cm) high.
£2,800–3,200
€/ $4,400–5,100 ⚒ DuM

A Fabergé silver and cut-glass bowl, marked 'K. Fabergé', Moscow c1910, 8¾in (22cm) wide.
£3,800–4,500
€/ $6,000–7,100 ⚒ S(NY)

A Fabergé gold, silver and enamel box, workmaster Henrik Wigström, with diamond-chip cluster lip clasp, enamel chipped, marked, import marks for 1911, 2in (5cm) diam.
£550–650
€/ $870–950 ⚒ SWO

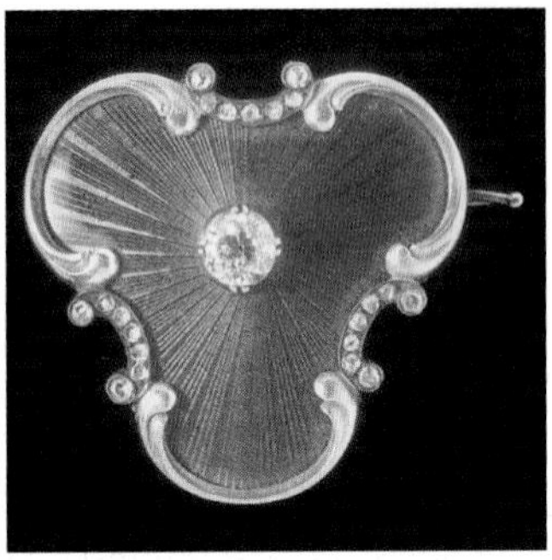

A Fabergé gold, enamel and diamond brooch, marked 'K.F.', Moscow c1900, 1¼in (3cm) wide, in original holly wood box.
£10,000–12,000
€/ $15,800–19,000 ⚒ S(O)

A Fabergé gold cigarette case, workmaster Henrik Wigström, the thumbpiece set with a sapphire, St Petersburg 1908–17, 4in (10cm) high.
£2,300–2,800
€/ $3,600–4,400 ⚒ DORO

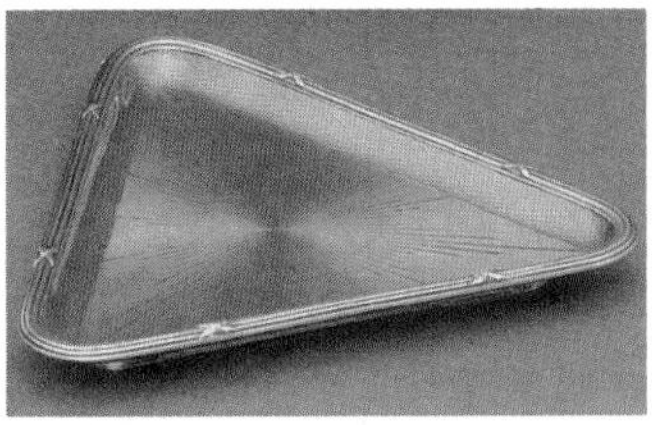

A Fabergé silver and enamel dish, workmaster Karl Gustav Hjalmar Armfelt, the translucent enamel over a *guilloché* ground, St Petersburg, c1890, 4in (10cm) wide.
£5,800–7,000
€/ $9,200–11,000 ⚒ S(NY)

A Fabergé cane handle, workmaster Michael Perchin, the translucent enamel over engine-turned silver, the rim applied with gold, St Petersburg 1896–99, 1½in (4cm) high, in original silk-lined holly wood box.
£5,500–6,500
€/ $8,600–10,200 ⚒ B

A Fabergé miniature egg, gold-mounted rock crystal, the reverse intaglio-enamelled with the flower of St Nicholas, c1905, ½in (1cm) long.
£3,800–4,300
€/ $6,000–6,800 ⊞ SHa

► **A Fabergé silver and wood frame,** workmaster Feodor Afanassiev, St Petersburg c1910, 11½in (29cm) high.
£3,500–4,000
€/ $5,500–6,300 ⚒ S(NY)

Gold

A gold-mounted bottle, the cagework inset with diamonds, emeralds and rubies, French, c1890, 3in (7.5cm) long.
£3,500–3,600
€/ $5,500–5,600 ⊞ LBr

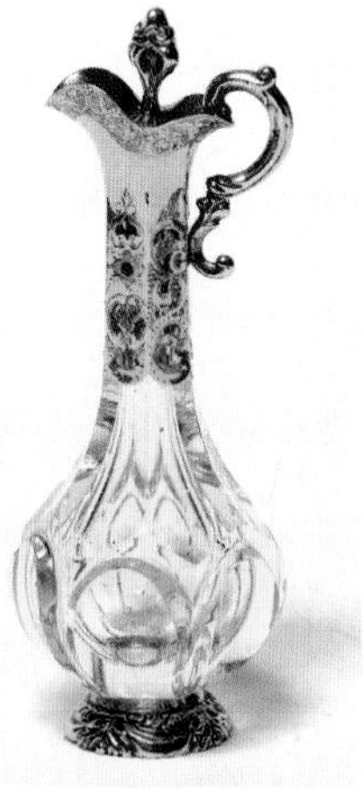

► An 18ct gold-mounted scent bottle, French, c1850, 4in (10cm) high.
£2,000–2,200
€/ $3,200–3,500 ⊞ SHa

An 18ct gold box, by Charles Rowlings and William Summer, London 1844–45, 4in (10cm) wide.
£3,500–4,000
€/ $5,500–6,300 ⊞ NS

A gold box, the lid centred by a medallion, the sides and base with engine-turned panels within chased foliate borders, probably German, early 19thC, 3in (7.5cm) wide.
£520–630
€/ $820–980 ⚒ S(Am)

A gold-mounted jasper snuff box, the sides and border of the lid chased with scrolling foliate decoration, c1745, 2¾in (7cm) long.
£1,300–1,500
€/ $2,000–2,400 ⚒ WW

A gold and enamel snuff box, the lid later inset with a German School portrait miniature of a young lady, maker's mark 'MS' and charge mark of Alaterre, some restoration, late 18thC, 3½in (9cm) long.
£2,800–3,200
€/ $4,400–5,100 ⚒ S(O)

A gold-mounted aventurine snuff box, Italian, c1840, 3in (7.5cm) wide.
£2,000–2,400
€/ $3,200–3,800 ⊞ G&G

A George IV-style 9ct gold engine-turned snuff box, with floral-chased borders and reeded sides, London 1929, 3¼in (8.5cm) wide.
£480–565
€/ $760–890 ⚒ DN

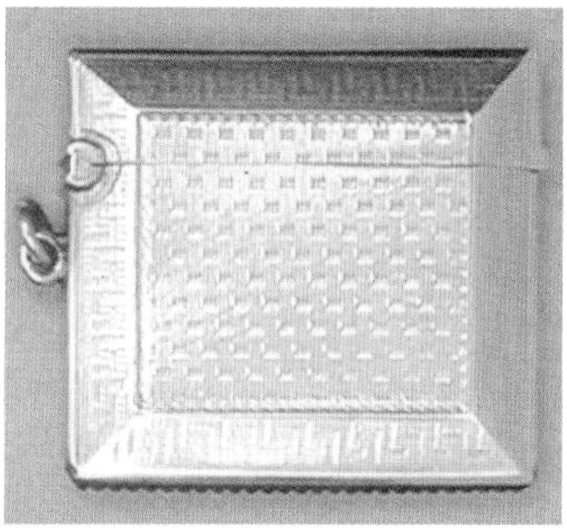

A 9ct gold vesta case, by Joseph Walton & Co, London 1920, 1¾in (4.5cm) wide.
£160–200
€/ $250–315 ⚒ WW

A gold folding telescopic monocular, with a single draw and pendant ring, c1875, 2½in (6.5cm) long, with original morocco case.
£230–275
€/ $360–430 ⚒ WW

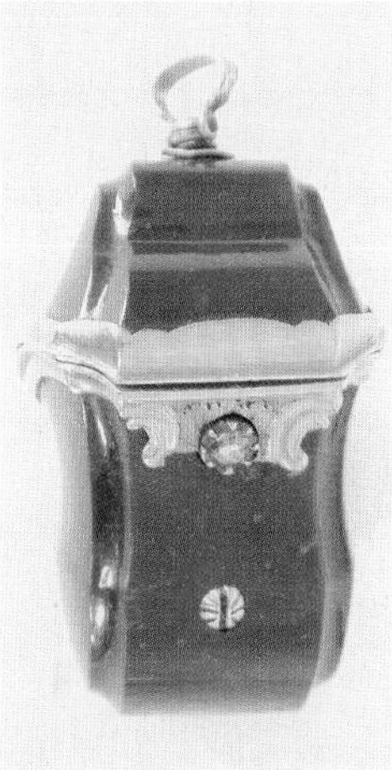

► A gold-mounted bloodstone vinaigrette, the hinged lid with suspension loop and a rose-cut diamond, German, c1760, 1½in (4cm) high.
£600–700
€/ $950–1,100 ⚒ G(L)

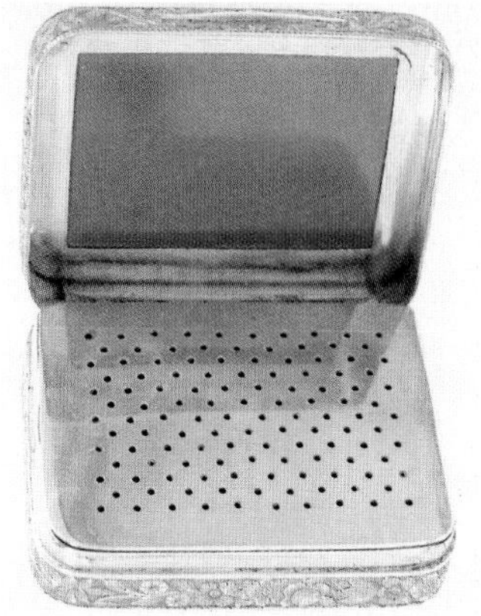

A gold and cornelian vinaigrette, the interior with perforated grille, early 19thC, 1½in (4cm) wide.
£600–700
€/ $950–1,100 ⚒ G(L)

Asian Works of Art

Cloisonné & Enamel

A cloisonné box and cover, the top decorated with the *shou* character and stylized flowerheads, Chinese, Qianlong period, 1736–95, 2¾in (7cm) diam.
£500–550
€/ $800–880 ⊞ G&G

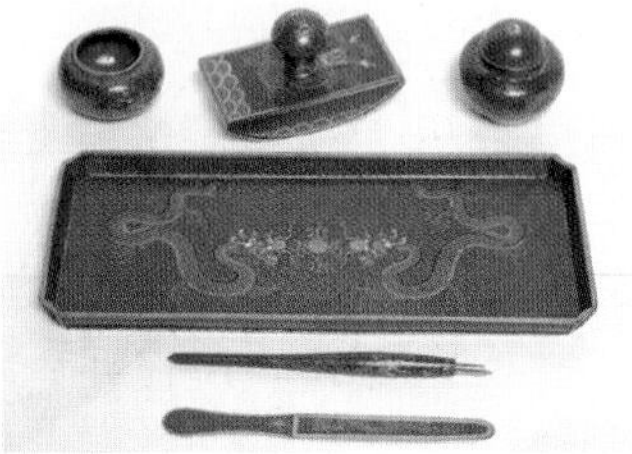

A cloisonné desk set, comprising a tray, ink blotter, inkwell and cover, round pot, pen and letter opener, decorated with dragons chasing the flaming pearl, signed Laotainii Zhi, Chinese, 19thC, tray 11in (28cm) long.
£1,300–1,500
€/ $2,100–2,400 ⊞ AUA

► **A cloisonné plaque,** decorated with cranes perched in flowering branches on a pink ground, Japanese, late 19thC, 19¾in x 12in (50 x 32cm).
£1,400–1,600
€/ $2,200–2,500 ⚒ DN

A pair of cloisonné enamel vases, decorated with peonies, Japanese, late 19thC, 4¾in (12cm) high, with original padded pine box.
£100–110
€/ $160–175 ⚒ PFK

► **A pair of cloisonné vases,** decorated with three panels of spring flowers and birds, Japanese, Meiji period, 1868–1911, 5in (12.5cm) high.
£650–750
€/ $1,000–1,200 ⚒ BUK

A cloisonné jewelled and enamelled box, decorated with flowers and birds, the hinged cover centred with a diamond-set rosette, Indian, 19thC, 2¼in (5.5cm) wide.
£2,200–2,500
€/ $3,500–4,000 ⚒ B(Kn)

A pair of cloisonné jars and covers, decorated with flowers and butterflies on a black ground, Chinese, c1880, 5in (13.5cm) high.
£200–225
€/ $320–350 ⊞ PSA

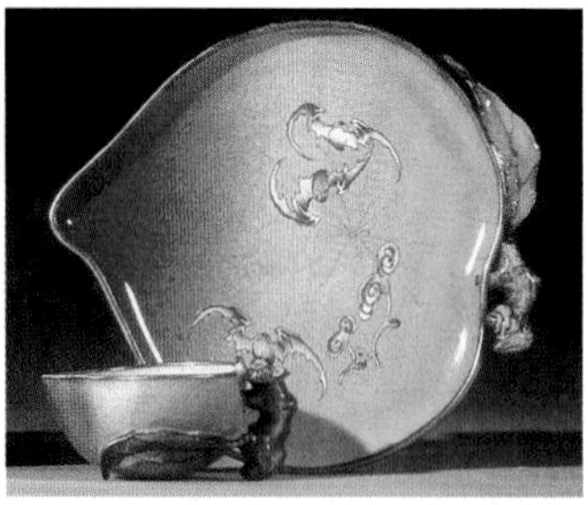

An Imperial Canton enamel cup and saucer, in the shape of a peach, with pointed tip and branch-like handle with blossom and leaves, the interior decorated with two bats, Chinese, Yonzheng/Qianlong period, 18thC, saucer 4¾in (12cm) wide.
£3,800–4,500
€/ $6,000–7,000 ⚒ S(HK)

A cloisonné *koro* and cover, worked in copper wire with a flock of white cranes, Japanese, Meiji period, 1868–1911, 5in (13cm) high.
£800–900
€/ $1,300–1,400 ⚒ S(O)

A cloisonné teapot, Japanese, late 19thC, 3½in (9cm) high.
£120–140
€/ $190–220 ⚒ DuM

A pair of cloisonné vases, decorated with wistaria flowers on a light green ground, Japanese, 19thC, 12½in (32cm) high.
£500–600
€/ $800–960 ⚒ SWO

Glass

A Peking glass box, decorated with coloured stones, Chinese, late 19thC, 6in (15cm) wide.
£170–200
€/ $270–320 BWL

A reverse painting on glass, depicting the Seven Scholars of the Bamboo Grove, inscribed 'Zhu Lin Qi Xian', Chinese, 19thC, 26in (66cm) wide, in original carved wood frame.
£900–1,000
€/ $1,400–1,600 S(O)

A lemon glass vase, Jiaqing mark and period, 1796–1820, Chinese, 7¾in (19.5cm) high.
£4,500–5,500
€/ $7,000–8,400 S(NY)

Jade

A jade brushpot, carved in the form of a tree trunk, with rust-brown inclusions imitating the surface of the bark, 19thC, 5¼in (13.5cm) high.
£1,100–1,200
€/ $1,700–1,900 S(O)

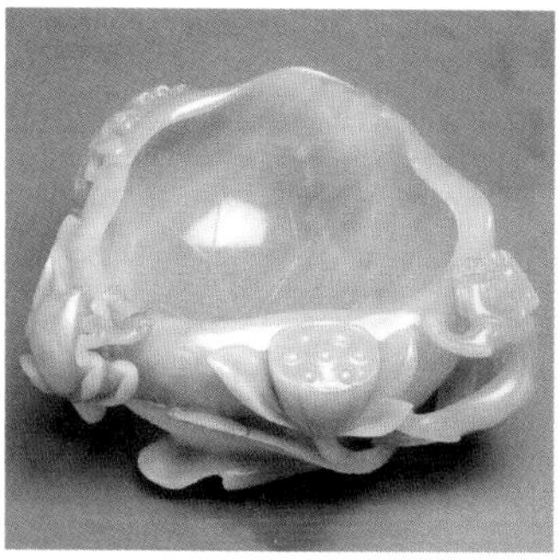

A celadon jade brush washer, carved in the form of a curled lotus leaf, c1700, 6½in (16.5cm) wide.
£2,400–2,800
€/ $3,800–4,400 B

A spinach jade dish, Chinese, 19thC, 9in (23cm) diam.
£900–1,000
€/ $1,400–1,600 GLD

Further reading

Miller's Chinese & Japanese Antiques Buyer's Guide,
Miller's Publications, 1999

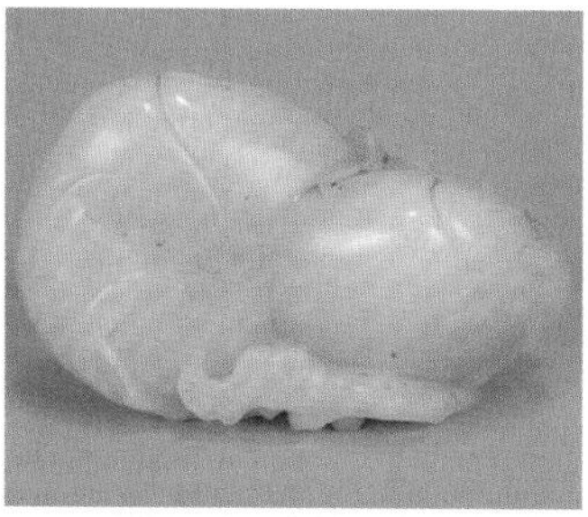

► **A celadon jade group,** carved as two peaches with foliage and five bats, Chinese, Qianlong period, 1736–95, 4¼in (11cm) wide.
£1,700–2,000
€/ $2,700–3,200
L

A celadon jade vesssel, the body with eight lobes flanked by a pair of double ring handles with monster masks, Chinese, 19thC, 12¾in (32.5cm) wide.
£1,400–1,600
€/ $2,200–2,500 S(O)

A pale green jade bottle vase, the sides carved with prunus and rock-work, Chinese, 19thC, 4½in (11.5cm) high, with wooden stand.
£2,200–2,600
€/ $3,500–4,100 DN

A jade bottle vase, carved in relief with palmettes, foliage and geometric design, with ring mask handles, on carved wood fretwork stand, Chinese, late 19thC, 13in (33cm) high.
£280–340
€/ $440–550 SWO

Lacquer

A red lacquer box and cover, carved with lychee and foliage, some damage, Ming Dynasty, 1368–1644, 3in (7.5cm) high.
£1,700–2,000
€/ $2,700–3,200 G(L)

A lacquer box and cover, in the form of three overlapping clam shells, one decorated with autumn plants and two with landscape scenes in gold and *takamakie* and *togidashi* with details in *kirigane*, *aogai* and *e-nashiji*, the interior of *nashiji*, Japanese, 19thC, 5½in (14cm) wide.
£2,400–2,800
€/ $3,800–4,400 S(O)

A lacquer dish, signed Shomosai and Kakihan, Japanese, c1900, 5in (12.5cm) diam.
£315–350
€/ $500–550 G&G

A lacquered rattan betel box, early 20thC, 8in (20.5cm) high.
£145–160
€/ $230–250 QM
This type of box was used to contain a supply of betel leaves for chewing.

A lacquer offerings box, Burmese, early 20thC, 28in (71cm) high.
£340–380
€/ $550–600 QM

A pair of lacquer jars, decorated in gilt, Japanese, 19thC, 13in (33cm) high.
£900–1,000
€/ $1,400–1,600 FRY

► A Chinese export lacquer sewing box, c1860, 14½in (37cm) wide.
£850–950
€/ $1,350–1,500 HAA

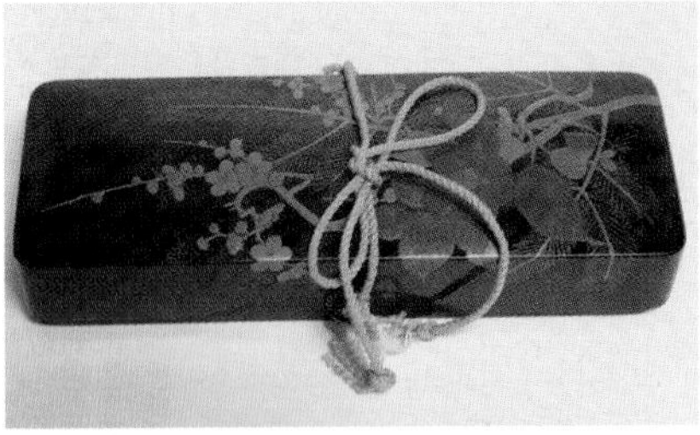

A lacquer box, decorated with cherry blossom, pine and peony in gold and silver, Japanese, 19thC, 9in (23cm) long.
£585–650
€/ $925–1,000 G&G

A lacquer box, with mother-of-pearl inlaid landscape to the cover and flowers to the sides, Chinese, 19thC, 15in (38cm) wide.
£1,300–1,500
€/ $2,000–2,400 BWL

A lacquer box, Chinese, c1890, 7¼in (18.5cm) wide.
£225–250
€/ $350–400 HAA

A lacquer shrine (*Zushi*), the doors with chased gilt-metal mounts, the interior in gilt with the four armed Kannon seated on a pedestal, Japanese, 19thC, 9¾in (25cm) high.
£420–500
€/ $670–800 DN

A Chinese export lacquer tea caddy, on carved dragon feet, c1860, 5in (12.5cm) high.
£1,000–1,200
€/ $1,600–1,900 ⊞ HAA

A pair of *Shibayama* inlaid lacquer vases, with silver-mounted necks, one with a signed red lacquer plaque, one with missing base and damage, Japanese, Meiji period, 1868–1911, 9¼in (23.5cm) high.
£2,800–3,400
€/ $4,400–5,400 ⚒ RTo

A lacquer writing utensil box (*suzuribako*) and cover, decorated with a figure gazing at a rural landscape, the interior with figures pulling barges in a river landscape, some rubbing, Japanese, 19thC, 9in (23cm) wide.
£1,800–2,200
€/ $2,800–3,500 ⚒ DN

Metalware

A bronze basin, with phoenix and fish moulding, old wear, Chinese, Han Dynasty, 206BC–AD220, 17in (43cm) diam.
£3,500–4,000
€/ $5,500–6,300 ⊞ GLD

A bronze buffalo bell, Burmese, 19thC, 4in (10cm) diam.
£160–180
€/ $250–285 ⊞ QM

A cast bronze bell, on a pierced and carved oak stand, Japanese, late 19thC, 44in (112cm) high.
£650–725
€/ $1,000–1,200 ⚒ B(Pr)

A gold and silver-inlaid bronze belt hook (*daigou*), the shaft decorated with gold and silver sheet wire inlay, below a tapering dragon's head hook, Chinese, Warring States Period, 480–221 BC, 5½in (14cm) long.
£580–650
€/ $920–1,000 ⊞ G&G

A cast-iron bowl, the exterior applied in high relief with the Eight Immortals between *chilong* handles, Chinese, Ming Dynasty, 16thC, 8¾in (22cm) diam.
£450–500
€/ $700–800 ⚒ S(O)

For further information on
Metalware see pages 597–603

A bronze tripod censer, with phoenix-shaped handles, on three feet, Chinese, spurious Xuande mark, 19thC, 3½in (9cm) high.
£170–200
€/ $270–320 ⚒ S(O)

A brass incense burner, Indian, early 19thC, 6in (15cm) diam.
£340–375
€/ $550–600 ⊞ SEA

► **A silver-inlaid *huqqa* bottle,** of squat globular form, decorated with panels of flowering shrubs within geometric and foliate-patterned borders, some loss to inlay, Indian, 18th–19thC, 6¼in (16cm) high.
£250–300
€/ $400–475 ⚒ F&C

An iron tripod incense burner and cover, of compressed globular shape, cast in shallow relief with carp rising from tranquil waters, the domed cover cast and pierced with ripples, Japanese, Meiji Period, 1868–1911, 5½in (14cm) diam.
£1,600–1,900
€/ $2,500–3,000 B

A *Shibayama*-panelled silver *koro* and cover, inset with panels of doves, quail, crane, pheasant and other auspicious birds on a gilt ground, with upright dragon handles, finial missing, minor faults, Japanese, Meiji Period, 1868–1911, 6¼in (16cm) high.
£1,300–1,500
€/ $2,000–2,400 RTo

A cast iron mask of Okame, mounted on a pine board, Japanese, 18th–19thC, 8¾in (22cm) high.
£375–425
€/ $600–670 WW
Okame is a character from the No operas. She is the Goddess of laughter, also known as Uzume or Otafuku.

A bronze mask, Japanese, 19thC, 12in (30.5cm) high.
£300–350
€/ $475–550 DuM

A set of ten bronze opium weights, in the form of birds and quadrupeds, Chinese, 18th–19thC, largest 2½in (6.5cm) high.
£350–400
€/ $550–630 AUA

A gilt-bronze paperweight, Chinese, Han Dynasty, 206BC–AD220, 2½in (6.5cm) wide.
£2,000–2,500
€/ $3,200–4,000 GLD

► A pair of bronze vases, cast with dragons, Chinese, 19thC, 9¾in (25cm) high.
£220–250
€/ $350–400 SWO

A parcel-gilt beaker vase (*gu*), the central section and flaring foot with a pair of raised *taotie* on either side and divided by vertical flanges, the neck with four upright plaintain leaves containing stylized *taotie*, the rim and flanges inlaid with silver *leiwen* bands, Chinese, Ming Dynasty, 17thC, 13¾in (35cm) high.
£1,100–1,300
€/ $1,700–2,000 S(Am)

A silver vase, by Shoryusai, engraved in *shibuichi* and gold, with chrysanthemums and a meandering river, Japanese, Taisho period, 1912–26, 7in (18cm) high.
£2,000–2,200
€/ $3,200–3,500 AUA

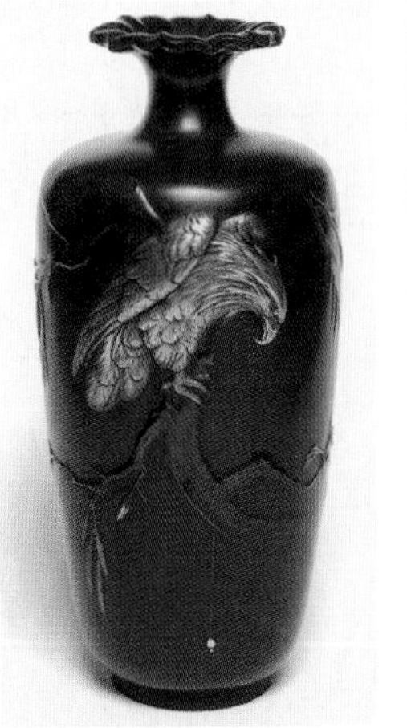

A bronze vase, cast with an eagle worked in *shibuichi, shakudo* and gilt, signed, Japanese, Meiji Period, 1868–1911, 10in (25.5cm) high.
£2,500–2,800
€/ $4,000–4,400 LBO

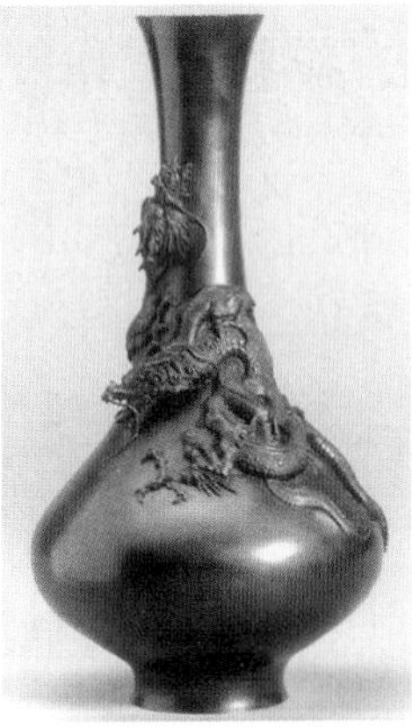

A bronze vase, by Tatsuhiro Akichika, decorated in relief with two dragons struggling for possession of a glass jewel, signed and stamped with a dragonfly, Japanese, Meiji Period, 1868–1911, 13¾in (35cm) high.
£800–900
€/ $1,300–1,400 S(O)

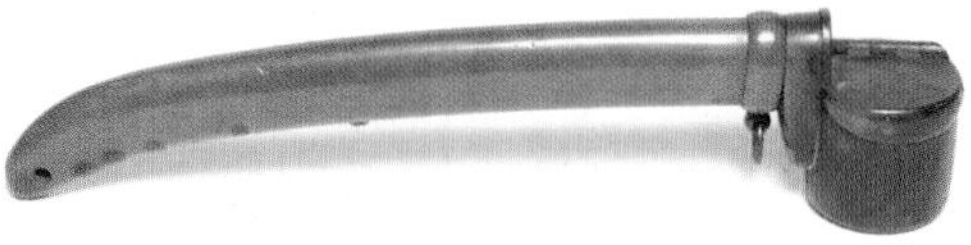

A bronze *yatate*, Japanese, late 19thC, 8in (20.5cm) high.
£120–135
€/ $190–210 FU
A *yatate* is a case to hold a writing brush and ink and is hung from a belt.

Wood

A carved ebony box, Anglo-Indian, c1870, 9in (23cm) wide.
£135–150
€/ $210–240 ⊞ MB

► **A barbed zitan brushpot,** with a plugged base, the wood flecked with vermillion, Chinese, Qing Dynasty, 18thC, 9¼in (23.5cm) high.
£7,000–8,000
€/ $11,000–12,500 ⚒ S(HK)
Zitan is the most desirable of all the Asian woods. It is normally only obtainable in narrow strips as the tree is very small – a strip 9¼in (23.5cm) is very rare for zitan.

A root-wood brushpot, with a hardwood rim and fitted hardwood stand with *ruyi*-head feet, Chinese, 19thC, 5½in (14cm) high.
£700–850
€/ $1,100–1,300 ⚒ S(O)

A bamboo carving of a bunch of grapes, by Qian Kaipang, supported on vine leaves, signed, Chinese, 18thC, 4½in (11.5cm) high.
£2,200–2,500
€/ $3,500–4,000 ⚒ B

A pair of carved wood panels, Chinese, c1850, 15in (38cm) wide.
£120–135
€/ $190–210 ⊞ FU

A pair of carved sycamore corbels, Chinese, c1850, 24in (61cm) high.
£1,600–1,800
€/ $2,500–2,800 ⊞ QM

A wooden needlecase, Chinese, late 19thC, 3in (7.5cm) long.
£100–110
€/ $160–175 ⊞ JCH

A painted wood silk winder, probably for a wedding, Chinese, 19thC, 5½in (14cm) wide.
£40–45
€/ $63–70 ⊞ JCH

A bamboo perfume holder, pierced and carved with a man playing the *qin* within a rocky garden, a boy, a lady and her attendant looking on, with carved horn ends, Chinese, 1775–1825, 8½in (21.5cm) high.
£850–1,000
€/ $1,300–1,600 ⚒ S(O)

A keyaki wood and bronze tobacco/cigarette box (*tabako-bon*), Japanese, c1880, 8in (20.5cm) high.
£1,800–2,000
€/ $2,800–3,200 ⊞ AUA

► **A wooden saddle,** Mongolian, early 20thC, 18in (45.5cm) long.
£225–250
€/ $350–400 ⊞ QM

Arms & Armour

A black-lacquered part armour, laced with silk, with sleeve armour and thigh defence, some age wear, Japanese, 1600–1750.
£1,000–1,200
€/ $1,600–1,900 WAL

A mail shirt, of riveted and plain steel rings, minor holes, Indian, 17th–18thC.
£400–500
€/ $630–800 B(Kn)

► **A lacquer suit of parade armour,** the helmet with gilt-metal covers to the flanges, two fur-covered 'ears', the *mempo* with horsehair moustache, the simulated *hishinui-do* with gilt rivets, all laced and mounted on an upright stand, Japanese, late 19thC.
£5,000–6,000
€/ $8,000–9,500 S(O)

A bronze war helmet, the dome with a boss top above ribbing, and an arched front and back framed by riveting, Chinese, 17thC, 12¼in (31cm) high.
£400–500
€/ $630–800 CGC

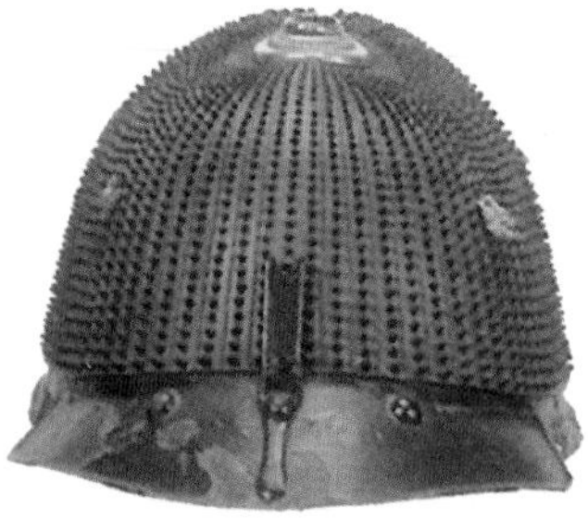

A 62-plate helmet (*Hoshi-Bachi*), with raised rivets, black lacquered peak and holder, and gilt *tehen kanemono*, *shikoro* and a few rivets missing, Japanese, 16thC.
£650–775
€/ $1,000–1,200 WAL

An iron (*mempo*), with wrinkled cheeks, separate ear pieces, half mask and red lacquered interior, one ear piece and detachable nose missing, Japanese, Edo period, 1688–1703, 9½in (24cm) high.
£320–375
€/ $500–600 B(Kn)

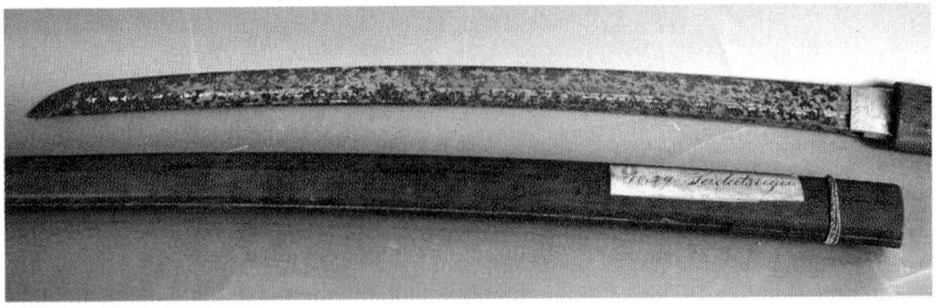

◄ **A *wakizashi* blade,** attributed to Yoshimitsu, with a rusty scabbard, Japanese, Bizen Province, 17thC, 20¼in (51.5cm) long.
£550–620
€/ $870–980 SWO

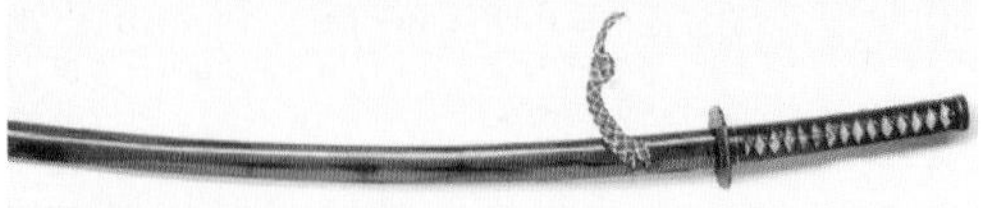

A *shinto katana*, Japanese, c1700, 27¼in (69cm) long.
£2,000–2,200
€/ $3,200–3,500 S(O)

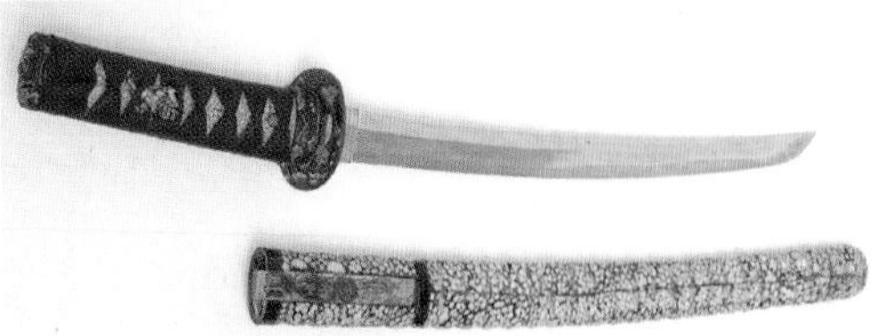

A *wakizashi*, with an 18thC blade, Japanese, 19thC, 24in (61cm) long.
£3,000–3,300
€/ $4,700–5,200 MDL

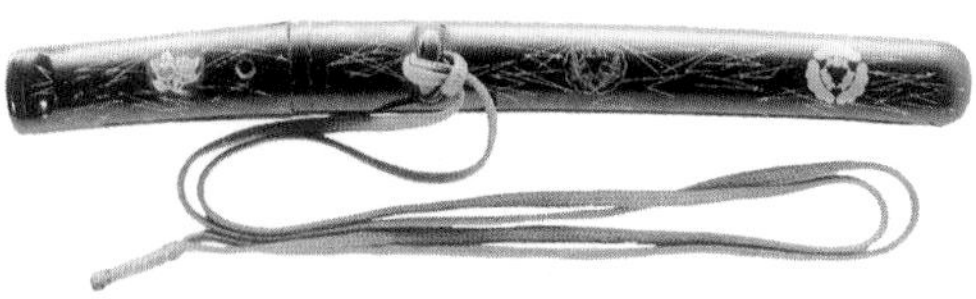

◄ **A *kaiken*,** the guard decorated in gold lacquer with gilt-copper floral *menuki*, Japanese, 19thC, 6¾in (17cm) long.
£850–950
€/ $1,300–1,500 S(O)

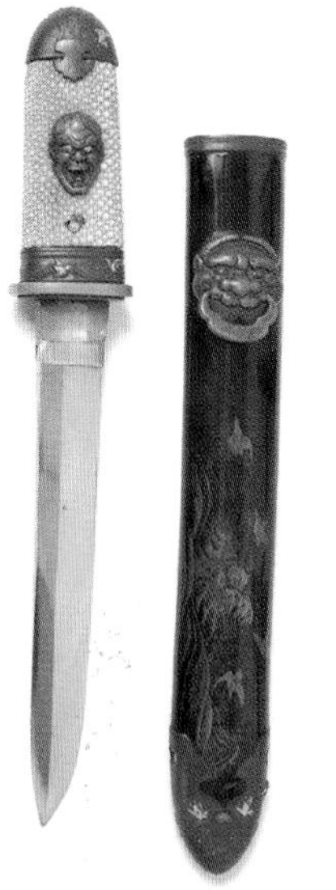

A ***tanto,*** Japanese, 19thC, 15in (38cm) long.
£2,400–2,700
€/ $3,800–4,200 MDL

◄ **An ivory *tanto,*** carved with male and female figures within a landscape, signed in a cartouche, the fitted ivory *kozuka* carved with clouds, Japanese, Meiji Period, 1868–1911, blade 10¼in (26cm) long.
£800–1,000
€/ $1,300–1,600 B(Kn)

A *wakizashi,* Japanese, c1850, 27in (68.5cm) long.
£3,400–3,800
€/ $5,400–6,000 MDL

► **A gold-inlaid *kris,*** Indonesian, 19thC, 18¾in (47.5cm) long.
£150–165
€/ $240–260
SPA

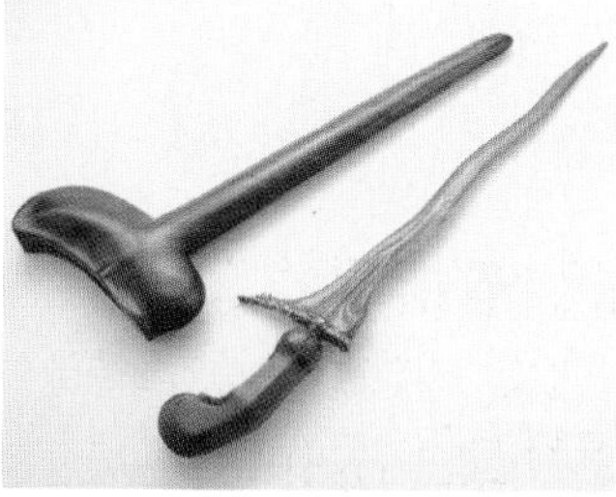

Tsuba

◄ **A Koike Yoshiro School iron *tsuba,*** with pierced and latticed flower design, framed in brass, Japanese, c1600, 3¼in (8.5cm) diam.
£1,200–1,400
€/ $1,900–2,300 LJ

► **An iron *tsuba,*** carved with seashells, Japanese, c1700, 3¼in (8cm) diam.
£520–570
€/ $820–900 LJ

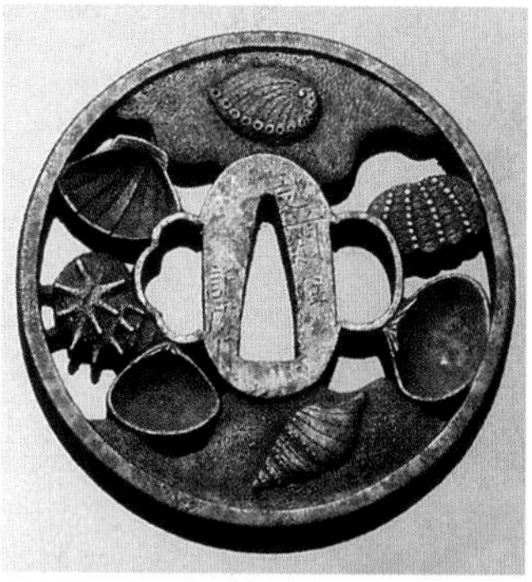

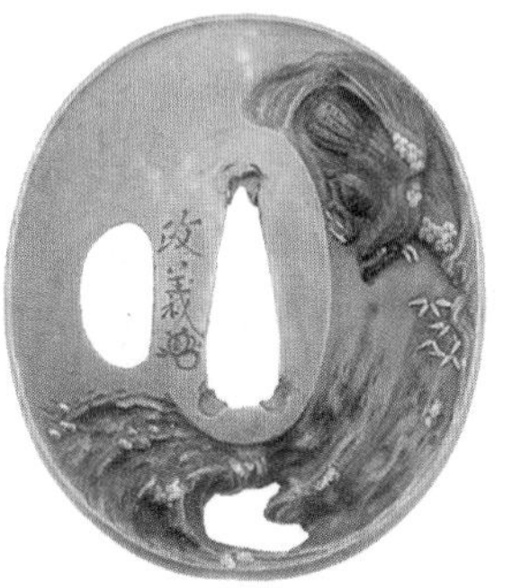

A brass *tsuba,* by Masayoshi, carved and inlaid with an eagle swooping towards a pierced cave with a cowering monkey, Japanese, early 19thC, 2½in (6.5cm) wide.
£1,000–1,100
€/ $1,600–1,750 S(O)

A Choshu School iron *tsuba,* by Tomomichi, carved in relief with monkeys playing around rocks and pine trees, a waterfall on the reverse, signed, Japanese, 19thC, 3in (7.5cm) high.
£900–1,000
€/ $1,400–1,600 S(O)

An iron *tsuba,* by Toshiyoshi, carved and pierced with breaking waves, with spray drops in inlaid silver, signed, Japanese, 19thC, 3in (7.5cm) diam.
£650–720
€/ $1,000–1,100 S(O)

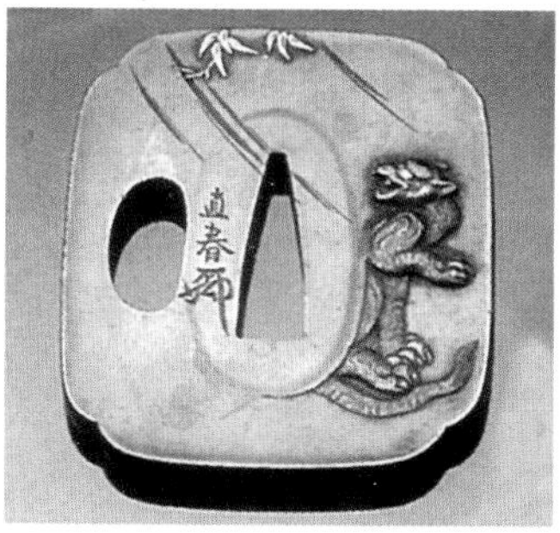

► **An iron Mokko-form *tsuba,*** by Ishiguro Masatsune, inlaid with gold *bonji* character and engraved with *karakusa*, the rim with traces of gold foil, Japanese, 19thC, 3½in (9cm) diam.
£1,200–1,400
€/ $1,900–2,200 S(O)

◄ **A polished iron *tsuba,*** decorated in gold and silver with a tiger under a bamboo tree, signed, Japanese, 19thC, 2¼in (6cm) high.
£450–500
€/ $700–800 LJ

Figures & Models

A grey schist figure of Buddha, halo repaired, surface mottled and encrusted, Gandharan, 2nd–3rdC AD, 18½in (47cm) high.
£2,000–2,200
€/ $3,200–3,500 ⊞ A&O

Gandhara

Gandhara was situated in an area now covered by part of north-west India, Pakistan and Afghanistan. Alexander the Great's expedition to India in 330–325 BC was instrumental in introducing Hellenic influences into the area, but its most creative period was from 1st–3rd centuries AD, when it was visited by pilgrims and travellers from as far afield as China and Greece. Sculpture was in stone, mainly schist, although stucco was increasingly used after the 3rd century AD. Techniques and motifs from classical art are combined with Indian Buddhist iconography to produce a distinctive art form which is noted for its naturalistic modelling.

A grey schist carved model of an elephant, Gandharan, 2ndC AD, 5½in (14cm) wide.
£350–400
€/ $550–630 ⊞ HEL

A terracotta head of a male deity, his turban decorated with crossbands of jewels, Gandharan, 4th–5thC AD, 9¼in (23.5cm) high.
£1,100–1,200
€/ $1,700–1,900 ⚒ S

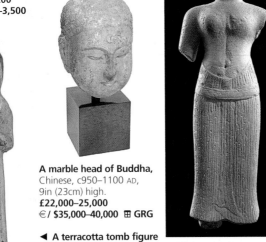

A marble head of Buddha, Chinese, c950–1100 AD, 9in (23cm) high.
£22,000–25,000
€/ $35,000–40,000 ⊞ GRG

◄ A terracotta tomb figure of a courtesan, Chinese, Tang Dynasty, 618–907 AD, 9¼in (23.5cm) high.
£800–875
€/ $1,300–1,400 ⊞ FAC

A Khmer sandstone torso of a female divinity, 11thC, 15¾in (40cm) high.
£2,700–3,000
€/ $4,300–4,700 ⊞ LOP

► A stucco head of a male divinity, traces of lacquer decoration, Burmese, 14th–15thC, 8½in (21.5cm) high.
£1,100–1,200
€/ $1,700–1,900 ⚒ S

A carved sandstone figure of Vishnu, seated and holding a mace and a trident, some losses and pitting, Indian, probably Rajasthan, c12thC, 23in (58.5cm) high.
£2,500–2,800
€/ $4,000–4,400 ⚒ JAA

A bronze incense burner, in the form of a *shishi*, Chinese, Wanli period, 1573–1619, 7in (18cm) high.
£1,400–1,600
€/ $2,200–2,600 ⊞ GLD

A Chieng Saen bronze torso of Buddha, Thai, 16thC, 11½in (29cm) high.
£1,600–1,800
€/ $2,500–2,800 ⊞ LOP

A cast gilt-bronze figure of Sakyamuni, seated on a double lotus throne, the hair with traces of pigment, Tibetan, 16th–17thC, 4½in (11.5cm) high.
£1,300–1,500
€/ $2,100–2,400 ⊞ G&G

A copper alloy head, Laotian, 17thC, 4½in (11.5cm) high.
£850–1,000
€/ $1,400–1,600 ⚒ S

A pair of silver-plated figures of Buddha, Burmese, 17thC, 4¾in (12cm) high.
£315–350
€/ $480–550 ⊞ LOP

A bronze incense burner, modelled as a horse, Chinese, 18thC, 6¼in (16cm) wide.
£420–500
€/ $660–790 ⚒ WW

A bamboo carving of the Hehe Erxian, with the heavenly twins standing on a rocky outcrop, a three-legged toad below, Chinese, Qing Dynasty, 18thC, 11½in (29cm) high.
£3,500–4,000
€/ $5,500–6,300 ⚒ S(NY)

A marine ivory *okimono* of a man seated on a rock with a child, signed, early 19thC, 8in (20.5cm) high.
£400–450
€/ $630–700 ⊞ AMC

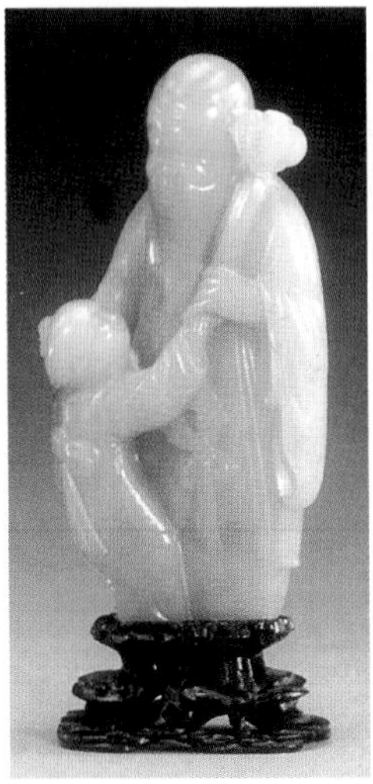

A jade figure of Shou Lao, on a wooden stand, slight damage, Chinese, Qing Dynasty, 18th/19thC, 5in (12.5cm) high.
£380–450
€/ $600–700 ⚒ BUK

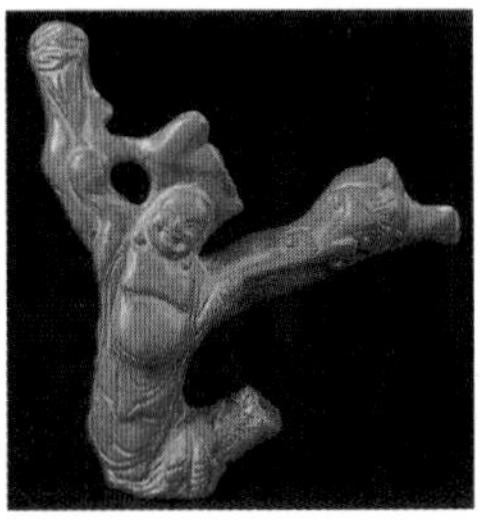

A carved coral figure of Hotei, his outstretched arms clutching symbols, Japanese, early 19thC, 6in (15cm) high.
£140–160
€/ $220–250 ⚒ FEN
Hotei was a Buddhist priest.

A gilt-bronze figure of Buddha, Thai, 18thC, 44in (112cm) high.
£8,500–9,500
€/ $13,300–15,000 ⊞ LOP

A gold-splashed bronze *koro*, modelled as Fukurukuju with his deer, Japanese, mid-19thC, 9½in (24cm) wide.
£2,200–2,300
€/ $3,200–3,600 ⊞ PCA
Fukurukuju is a happy wise man/deity.

A soapstone figure of a deity, in the form of a bearded official wearing a hat and carved flowing robes, Chinese, 18thC, 9in (23cm) high.
£2,200–2,500
€/ $3,500–4,000 ⚒ S

A pair of hardwood models of recumbent Buddhistic lions, minor damage, Indonesian, probably Balinese, 19thC, 39in (99cm) long.
£650–750
€/ $1,000–1,200 ⚒ B

◀ A pair of wooden models of temple guardian dogs, with ivory teeth, Chinese, c1860, 2¼in (5.5cm) wide.
£235–260
€/ $370–400 ⊞ FU

A wooden *deva*, Burmese, 19thC, 36¼in (92cm) high.
£1,100–1,300
€/ $1,700–2,000 ⊞ LOP

A pair of wooden loom pulleys, Burmese, 19thC, 12in (30.5cm) high.
£350–400
€/ $550–630 ⊞ QM

◄ A pair of cloisonné enamel models of cockerels, decorated with gilding, Chinese, 19thC, 9in (23cm) high.
£1,000–1,200
€/ $1,600–1,900
B&L

A bronze scroll weight, in the form of a lion dog, Chinese, 19thC, 3in (7.5cm) high.
£850–950
€/ $1,300–1,500 ⊞ AUA

A bronze figure of Ganesh, seated on a lotus-cast plinth, Indian, 19thC, 23in (58.5cm) high.
£290–320
€/ $460–500 EH

◄ A wooden group of monkeys holding a scroll depicting Shoki, with inlaid mother-of-pearl eyes, signed 'Masayoshi To', Japanese, Meiji period, 1868–1911, 6½in (16.5cm) high.
£2,400–2,700
€/ $3,800–4,300 ⊞ LBO
Shoki is the ancient Chinese queller of demons.

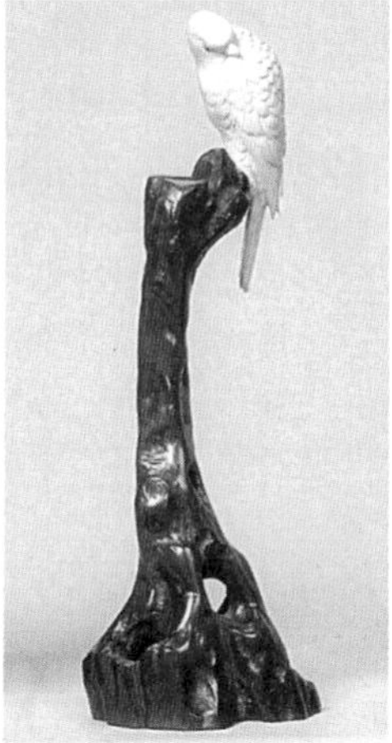

A wood and ivory *okimono*, carved as an exotic tropical bird perched on a branch, Japanese, Meiji period, 1868–1911, 15¾in (40cm) high.
£1,100–1,300
€/ $1,700–2,000 B

An enamelled silver model of a peacock, perched on a branch, Indian, probably Lucknow, c1890, 5½in (14cm) high.
£2,200–2,500
€/ $3,500–4,000 B(Kn)

An ivory *okimono* of a man wrestling with a snake, minor damage to snake, Japanese, Meiji period, 1868–1911, 4in (10cm) high.
£450–500
€/ $700–800 ⊞ AMC

An ivory group of artisans painting a lantern, signed 'Muneyoshi', Japanese, Meiji period, 1868–1911, 4in (10cm) wide.
£2,400–2,700
€/ $3,800–4,300 ⊞ LBO

A bronze seated figure of Jurojin, a staff in his hand, Japanese, 19thC, 5½in (14cm) high.
£100–120
€/ $160–190 WW
Jurojin is a Buddhist sage.

A carved ivory *okimono* of a young girl, holding an apple, three-character marks, Japanese, late 19thC, 5½in (14cm) high.
£140–160
€/ $220–250 SWO

◄ **A bronze *koro*,** in the form of Ebisu and his carp, Japanese, Meiji period, c1880, 10in (25.5cm) wide.
£1,100–1,300
€/ $1,700–2,000
⊞ PCA
Ebisu is the god of fishermen.

A carved ivory and wood figure, of a man chasing a snake from a pumpkin, with enamel and gilt decoration, signed, Japanese, 19thC, 7in (18cm) high.
£2,400–2,800
€/ $3,800–4,400 SWO

A carved ivory *okimono*, of a turbaned man riding a caparisoned camel, a water vessel at his back, on a naturalistic sandy base, Japanese, 19thC, 9in (23cm) high.
£400–500
€/ $630–800 PFK

A cast-bronze group of two Immortals playing Go, Japanese, late 19thC, 7in (18cm) high.
£1,600–1,800
€/ $2,500–2,800 ⊞ PCA

A bronze figure of Buddha, Burmese, Suan States, late 19thC, 17in (43cm) high.
£770–850
€/ $1,200–1,300 ⊞ QM

A carved ivory figure of a male entertainer, holding a baton and a disc, seated on a tree trunk, a box and mask by his feet, red seal mark, Japanese, late 19thC, 5¼in (13.5cm) high.
£900–1,100
€/ $1,400–1,700 AH

A carved ivory *okimono* of a farmer and companion, on a rustic base, red seal mark, Japanese, late 19thC, 4½in (11.5cm) high.
£750–875
€/ $1,200–1,400 AH

An ivory *okimono* of two men and a boy, signed 'Korayoki', Japanese, late 19thC, 6½in (16.5cm) high.
£1,000–1,100
€/ $1,600–1,700 ⊞ AMC

A pair of ivory *okimono*, carved as maidens wearing robes and holding fans and flowers, damaged, Japanese, early 20thC, 10in (25.5cm) high.
£480–550
€/ $750–870 RTo

A carved ivory figure of a farmer and monkey, Japanese, c1900, 16¼in (41.5cm) high.
£1,400–1,600
€/ $2,200–2,500 TEN

A carved and painted wooden figure of a beggar, his body decorated with henna tattoos, Indian, c1900, 20in (51cm) high, on a wooden base.
£280–320
€/ $440–500 PFK

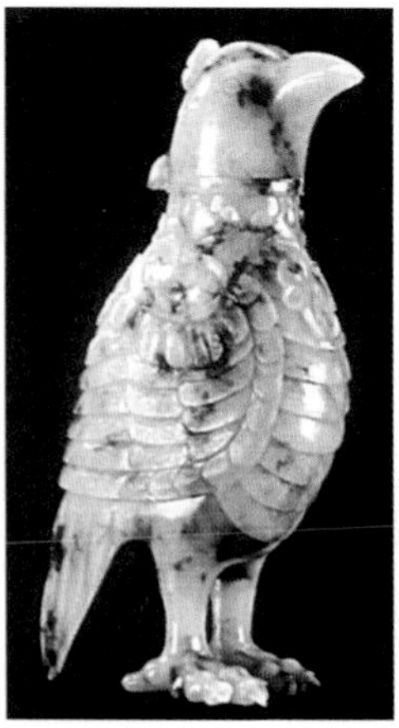

A jadeite vessel, modelled as a bird with detailed plumage, a cloud collar border at the neck, archaistic scrolls at the shoulder, Chinese, c1900, 6¾in (17cm) high.
£900–1,000
€/ $1,400–1,600 S(O)

◄ **A marine ivory *okimono* of a crab fisherman with a boy,** Japanese, c1900, 5in (12.5cm) high.
£350–400
€/ $550–630 ⊞ AMC

ASIAN WORKS OF ART

Furniture

A lacquer bed, Chinese, Shanxi province, 18thC, 94in (239cm) long.
£6,300–7,000
€/ $10,000–11,000 ⊞ QM

An elm bench, with two drawers, late 19thC, 17in (43cm) wide.
£180–200
€/ $285–315 ⊞ OE

A carved elm bureau, Chinese, early 20thC, 33in (84cm) wide.
£400–450
€/ $630–700 ⊞ HiA

► **A lacquer cabinet,** decorated in *hiramakie* and shell inlay with scrolling peony, the interior with a shelf above a fitted drawer, old wear and damage, Japanese, early Edo period, 1620–40, 15½in (39.5cm) wide.
£2,800–3,200
€/ $4,400–5,000 ⚒ B

► **A cabinet,** with brass fittings, Chinese, 18thC, 32in (81.5cm) wide.
£2,800–3,200
€/ $4,400–5,000
⊞ GRG

Chinese domestic furniture

Chinese domestic furniture has been influenced more by tradition than by fashion. Similar styles of furniture have been made over a long period using the same materials and manufacturing techniques. This can make accurate dating of the furniture very difficult.

A Chinese export gilt and lacquer writing cabinet, decorated with figurative scenes, with two doors enclosing a pocket watch holder, two pigeonholes, a mirrored cupboard and six drawers above a portable writing box, the stand decorated with precious objects, decoration worn, mid-19thC, 28¾in (73cm) wide.
£850–1,000
€/ $1,300–1,600 ⚒ BR

A scholar's hardwood cabinet, Chinese, c1880, 33in (84cm) wide.
£875–975
€/ $1,400–1,500 ⊞ Che

◄ **A hardwood and *Shibayama* cabinet-on-stand,** two panels decorated with figures, the others with flowers and birds, Japanese, late 19thC, 21in (53.5cm) high.
£320–375
€/ $500–600 ⚒ DN

A painted cabinet, decorated with a floral pattern, Tibetan, 19thC, 50in (127cm) wide.
£2,000–2,300
€/ $3,200–3,600 ⊞ LOP

A stained cherrywood cabinet, the four shelves with fretted edgings, above two drawers and two cupboard doors, bronze fittings, Chinese, c1900, 37½in (95.5cm) wide.
£400–500
€/ $630–800 ⚒ LCM

An ebony side chair, carved in low relief, on barley-twist legs, Ceylonese, mid-17thC.
£2,400–2,800
€/ $3,800–4,400 TMA

A lacquer money chest, with locking top panel, front feet carved with Greek key pattern, north Chinese, early 19thC, 33in (84cm) wide.
£380–420
€/ $600–670 OE

A George III huali wood architect's desk, the tambour top above a fitted interior and ratcheted writing surface, fitted with one long and two flanking drawers, Anglo-Asian, 36in (91.5cm) wide.
£950–1,200
€/ $1,500–1,900 HOLL

A rosewood plantation chair, Indian, 19thC.
£315–350
€/ $480–560 PAS

A painted chest, with brass fittings, decorated with a textile pattern, Tibetan, 18thC, 33in (84cm) wide.
£1,800–2,000
€/ $2,800–3,200 LOP

A pair of lacquer chests, with canvas covers, decorated with gilt-metal mounts and paulownia, Japanese, Meiji period, 1868–1911, 28in (71cm) wide.
£1,600–2,000
€/ $2,500–3,200 B

A gilt and lacquer eight-fold screen, decorated with pavilions, temples and *dhows*, within a border of opposing dragons chasing the sacred pearl, damaged, Chinese, Qianlong period, 1736–95, 90½in (230cm) wide.
£1,800–2,200
€/ $2,800–3,500 PFK

◄ **An embroidered screen,** with Japanese needlework worked in floss silks and couched metal threads, and European satinwood mounts, 1880s, 57½in (146cm) wide.
£950–1,100
€/ $1,500–1,700 S(O)

► **A hardwood screen,** with mother-of-pearl inlay, Chinese, 19thC, 41in (104cm) wide.
£270–300
€/ $430–475 PaA

A carved hardwood elbow chair, with pierced foliate decoration, Anglo-Indian, c19thC.
£650–750
€/ $1,000–1,200 SWO

A penwork chest-on-stand, decorated with figures and stylized Oriental landscapes on a foliate-carved X-frame, Indian, c1830, 35¾in (91cm) wide.
£7,000–8,000
€/ $11,000–12,700 S(O)

A davenport, carved with foliage, animals and figures, Indian, Bombay, c1880, 22¾in (58cm) wide.
£1,600–1,900
€/ $2,500–3,000 B(Kn)

A William IV padouk settee, with floral-carved back-rail, moquette back and squab, with carved vase form uprights and a floral-carved apron, on gadrooned and turned legs with brass casters, probably Indian, 74½in (189cm) wide.
£1,800–2,200
€/ $2,800–3,500 DMC

An ebony and satin-birch carved sideboard, with three frieze drawers and two cupboard doors enclosing shelves, probably Javanese, c1840, 68½in (174cm) wide.
£3,500–4,200
€/ $5,500–6,600 S(O)

A hardwood stand, with marble-inlaid top, Chinese, c1880, 25in (63.5cm) high.
£570–625
€/ $900–1,000 AUA

A carved wood stand, the top within a raised border, the apron relief-carved with confronting phoenix and Greek key designs, on four bracket feet, Japanese, 1875–1925, 14¼in (36cm) square.
£500–600
€/ $800–950 S(O)

An elm stool, with a rattan top, cloud carving on apron and corners, early 19thC, 21in (53.5cm) square.
£325–360
€/ $515–560 OE

A padouk and brass marquetry card table, the top inlaid with trailing vines and centred by the monogram 'E.H.H.', above a similarly inlaid frieze on detachable cabriole legs and square tapering feet, Anglo-Indian, early 19thC, 36¼in (92cm) wide.
£600–720
€/ $950–1,100 B

A Regency coromandel sofa table, with two drop leaves and two frieze drawers, on splayed legs with brass paw casters, Anglo-Indian, 42in (106.5cm) extended.
£3,000–3,500
€/ $4,700–5,500 MEA

A lacquer work table, decorated in gilt with Chinese families at leisure, on four dragon feet, gilt worn, Chinese, Canton, 19thC, 29in (73.5cm) high.
£1,800–2,200
€/ $2,800–3,500 B

◄ **A walnut occasional table,** with marble top and carved legs, maker's label, Indian, c1870, 15in (38cm) square.
£500–550
€/ $800–870 APO

A jacaranda console table, with brass mounts, Portuguese, Goa, 19thC, 51in (129.5cm) wide.
£6,000–7,000
€/ $9,500–11,000 S(NY)

A cherrywood nest of tables, carved with dragons and scrollwork, on square legs, Chinese, late 19thC, largest 17in (43cm) wide.
£400–475
€/ $630–750 JAd

◄ **A padouk pedestal,** the later rosewood crossbanded top with canted corners and brass border, the pedestal with a baluster-ribbed column and outer scrolling supports, Anglo-Indian, 19thC, 24¾in (63cm) wide.
£1,300–1,500
€/ $2,000–2,400 B

A carved wood washstand, with dragon decoration, Chinese, 19thC, 27½in (70cm) wide.
£1,000–1,100
€/ $1,600–1,700 LOP

Inro

A six-case gold lacquer *inro*, decorated in *hiramakie*, *takamakie* and *kimpun*, *nashiji* interior, signed, with attached wood *ojime* and stag antler *netsuke* pierced and carved with entwined *ruyi* fungus, Japanese, 19thC, 3¾in (9.5cm) high.
£2,300–2,500
€/ $3,600–4,000 ⊞ G&G

► A four-case *inro*, decorated with chrysanthemums in gold *takamakie*, inlaid mother-of-pearl and gold foil, the interior of *nashiji*, signed 'Koma Ankyo' (Yasutada), Japanese, 19thC, 3in (7.5cm) high.
£800–900
€/ $1,200–1,400 ⚒ S(O)

A wood three-case *inro*, by Tadakazu (Chuichi), modelled as a turtle, with head, legs and tail tucked in, the eyes of inlaid horn, signed, Japanese, 19thC, 4in (10cm) high.
£1,800–2,000
€/ $2,800–3,200 ⚒ S(O)

Items in the Asian Works of Art section have been arranged in date order within each sub-section.

An ivory three-case *inro*, each side with a shaped panel carved in low relief with the Seven Gods of Good Fortune, with ivory *ojime* carved with Hotei, signed 'Kosai to', Japanese, 19thC, 3½in (9cm) high.
£1,100–1,300
€/ $1,800–2,000 ⚒ S(O)

Netsuke

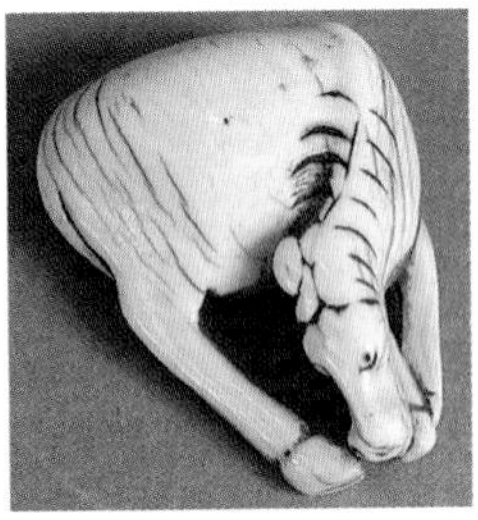

An ivory *netsuke* of a horse, Japanese, 18thC, 4½in (11.5cm) long.
£475–565
€/ $750–900 ⚒ SWO

An ivory *netsuke* of Daikoku with abacus, Japanese, Meiji period, 1868–1911, 1¼in (3cm) high.
£135–150
€/ $215–235 ⊞ AMC

► A carved ivory *netsuke* of a grimacing face, being attacked by a crab and a wasp, signed verso, Japanese, Meiji period, late 19thC, 1¾in (4.5cm) high.
£280–325
€/ $440–515 ⚒ SWO

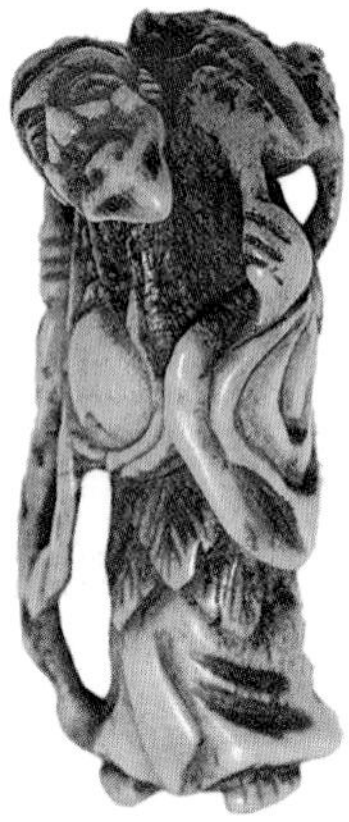

► A horn *netsuke* of Gama Sennin, wearing an oak leaf cloak and carrying a toad on his shoulder, Japanese, early 19thC, 3in (7.5cm) high.
£200–220
€/ $320–350 ⊞ AMC
Gama Sennin is one of the Immortals. He is normally shown with a three-legged toad.

An *okimono*-style ivory *netsuke* of a group of street vendors and entertainers, in a fish basket, Japanese, Meiji period, 1868–1911, 2¼in (5.5cm) high.
£450–525
€/ $700–830 ⚒ G(L)

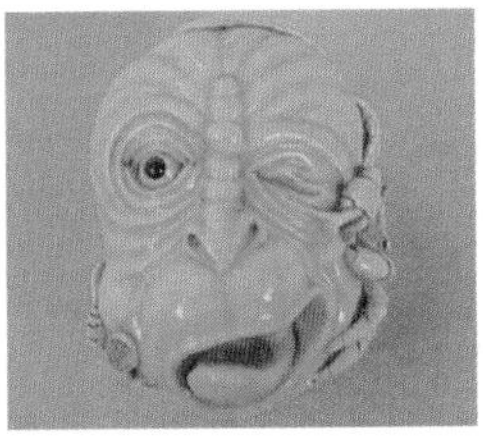

A carved ivory *netsuke* of a street vendor, signed with two characters incised on an inset red *kakihan* beneath his right sandal, Japanese, c1900, 1¾in (4.5cm) high.
£525–625
€/ $830–980 ⚒ TEN

A boxwood *netsuke* of two quail, possibly by Kanetomo of Nanki, Southern Kishu, with jadeite-inset eyes, on a bed of fruit bound by tendril-like leaves, the *himotoshi* formed from one leaf bearing a two-character seal mark, Japanese, Meiji period, 1868–1911, 1¾in (4.5cm) long.
£475–565
€/ $750–900 ⚒ BR

An ivory *netsuke* of a mask of Daikoku, Japanese, early 1900s, 1¼in (3cm) high.
£250–275
€/ $400–430 ⊞ AMC
Daikoku is the god of wealth.

Robes & Costume

An embroidered collar, with cloud motif, Chinese, c1880, 14in (35.5cm) diam.
£175–200
€/ $275–320 ⊞ JCH

A summer court hat, damask silk over a woven bamboo frame, surmounted by a glass hat button indicating a 5th rank civil official, Chinese, Guangxu period, 1875–1908, 35½in (90cm) diam.
£1,100–1,200
€/ $1,700–1,900 ⊞ WRi

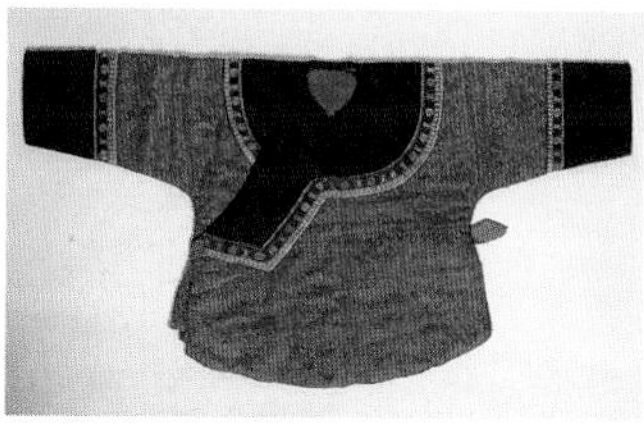

A child's padded jacket, early 20thC, 16in (40.5cm) long.
£110–125
€/ $175–200 ⊞ JCH

A dragon robe, for the Imperial Clan, decorated with clawed dragons, Chinese, c1900.
£1,200–1,400
€/ $1,900–2,200 ⊞ JCH

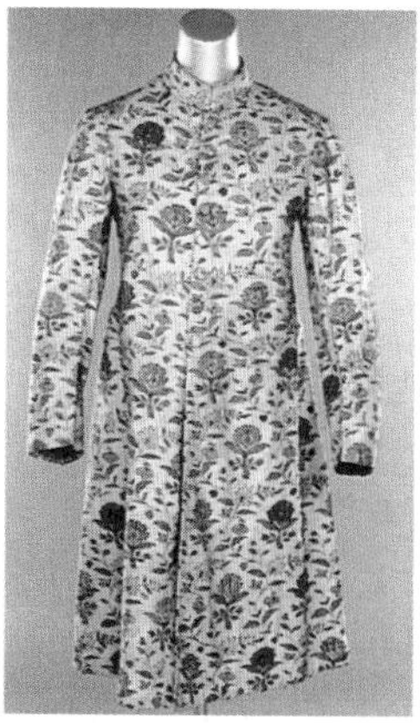

A man's wool coat, woven with flowerheads, darned and repaired, 19thC alterations, fabric Indian, Kashmir, c1800, construction later.
£1,200–1,400
€/ $1,900–2,200 ⚒ S(O)

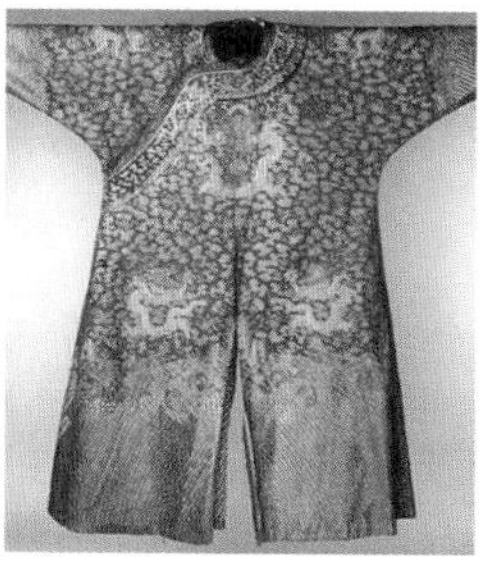

An embroidered outer robe (*chifu*), couched and embroidered in gold and silver threads with coiling dragons and flaming pearls, lining missing, binding frayed, Chinese, mid-19thC.
£1,300–1,500
€/ $2,000–2,400 ⚒ S(O)

A hand-embroidered silk shawl, with silk fringing, Chinese, Canton, late 19thC, 56in (142cm) square.
£225–250
€/ $350–400 ⊞ JPr

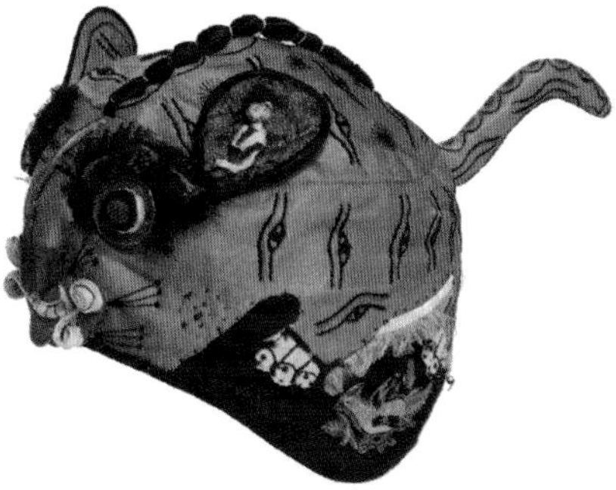

A child's hat, Chinese, late 19thC, 7in (18cm) wide.
£135–150
€/ $215–235 ⊞ JCH

A lady's silk damask front-opening jacket, applied with brocade silk ribbons and embroidered with symbols of good fortune, Chinese, Manchu, Xianfeng period, 1851–61, 26½in (67.5cm) long.
£2,700–3,000
€/ $4,300–4,700 ⊞ WRi

► A woman's vest (*apei*), applied with 9th rank civil badges, the paradise fly catcher in couched gold threads, tasselled hem, Chinese, late 19thC.
£500–600
€/ $800–950
⚒ S(O)

An embroidered damask silk skirt, with ribbon borders, Chinese, Guangxu period, 1875–1908.
£450–500
€/ $700–800 ⊞ WRi

◄ A pair of child's hand-embroidered silk shoes, Chinese, c1890, 5in (12.5cm) long.
£55–60
€/ $85–95 ⊞ JPr

Snuff Bottles

An overlay glass snuff bottle, carved with prunus blossom, bamboo and pine, called The Three Friends of Winter, Chinese, 1780–1850, 2½in (6.5cm) high.
£1,400–1,600
€/ $2,200–2,500 ⊞ RHa

A nephrite snuff bottle, carved in low relief with the formalized design of a bat suspended from a ring above two peaches and lotus, Chinese, 1780–1850, 2¾in (7cm) high.
£1,400–1,600
€/ $2,200–2,500 ⊞ RHa

An agate snuff bottle, carved with fish among weeds, the reverse with a peach and leaf, coral stopper, Chinese, 19thC, 2in (5cm) high.
£260–300
€/ $400–475 ⚒ S(O)

A translucent quartz snuff bottle, moulded with tendrils and leaves, small chip, Chinese, 19thC, 1¾in (4.5cm) high.
£340–375
€/ $550–600 ⚒ G(L)

◄ A silver snuff bottle, inlaid with coral, worked in relief with squirrels eating fruit from a European bowl, with lion-mask handles at the waist, coral-inlaid stopper, Chinese, 19thC, 3in (7.5cm) high.
£350–400
€/ $550–630 ⚒ S(O)

► A puddingstone snuff bottle, carved with bats and cash strings, Chinese, late 19thC, 2¾in (7cm) high.
£400–500
€/ $630–800 ⚒ G(L)

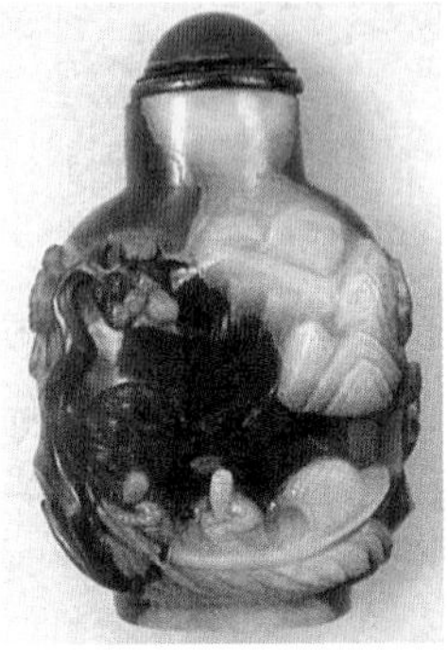

An agate snuff bottle, relief-carved with figures on boats among trees and rocks, the hardstone stopper set with a white metal spatula, Chinese, late 19thC, 3in (7.5cm) high.
£380–450
€/ $600–700 ⚒ BR

Textiles

A brocade altar-table front, decorated with dragons, clouds and waves, floral motifs and longevity symbols, Chinese, 18thC, 38¼in (97cm) long.
£4,500–5,000
€/ $7,000–8,000 ⊞ WRi
This was made for use in a wealthy home, probably for New Year festivities to decorate a table at which the ancestors or household gods were honoured. Among the embroidered motifs are a narcissus flower and a bat with musical chime which are characteristic of New Year decorations.

► A silk brocaded patchwork coverlet, Japanese, late Edo period, c1850, 76in (193cm) long.
£4,000–4,500
€/ $6,300–7,000 ⊞ DAW

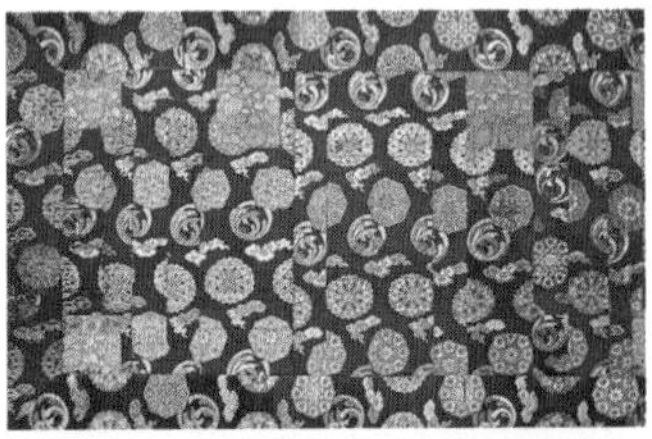

A Chinese export embroidered coverlet, worked with birds, butterflies and bamboo, signed 'Nguyan van Lam, Brodeur a Bac Nimb', late 19thC, 55¼in (140.5cm) long.
£500–600
€/ $800–950 ⚒ S(O)

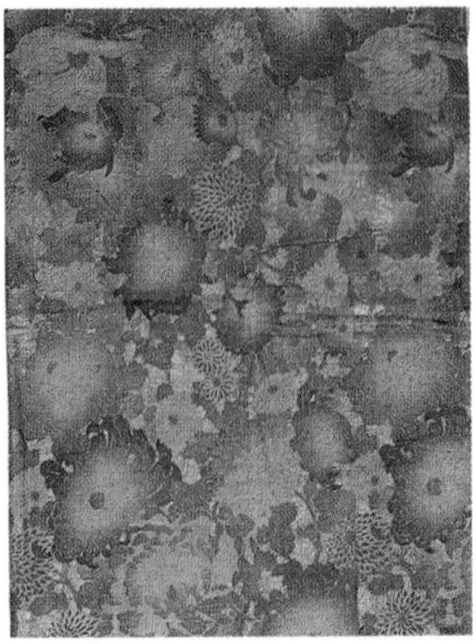

A length of cotton fabric, Japanese, late 19thC, 27in (68.5cm) wide.
£200–220
€/ $320–350 ⊞ JCH

A gentleman's silk fan case, embroidered with silk thread in a geometric design, losses to thread, Chinese, Guangxu period, 19thC, 12¼in (31cm) long.
£400–450
€/ $630–700 ⊞ WRi
The geometric design is based on the complex weaves of ancient silks.

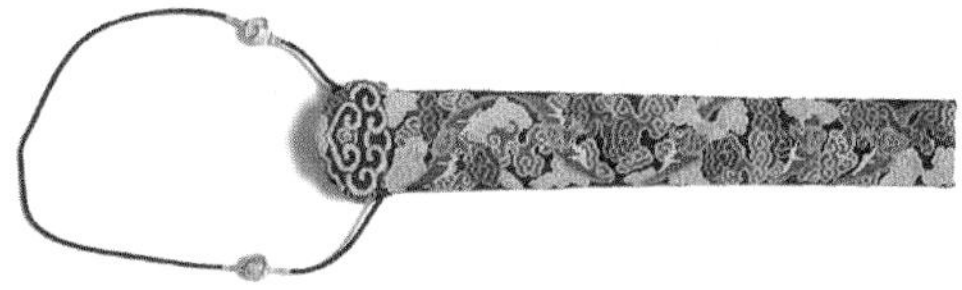

A silk fan case, embroidered with symbols representing The Five Blessings, Chinese, Guangxu period, 1875–1908, 11in (28cm) long.
£180–200
€/ $285–325 ⊞ JCH
The Five Blessings are health, wealth, a long life, the love of virtue and the hope of a natural death.

A silk fragrance pouch, Chinese, late 19thC, 3in (7.5cm) long.
£90–100
€/ $140–160 ⊞ JCH

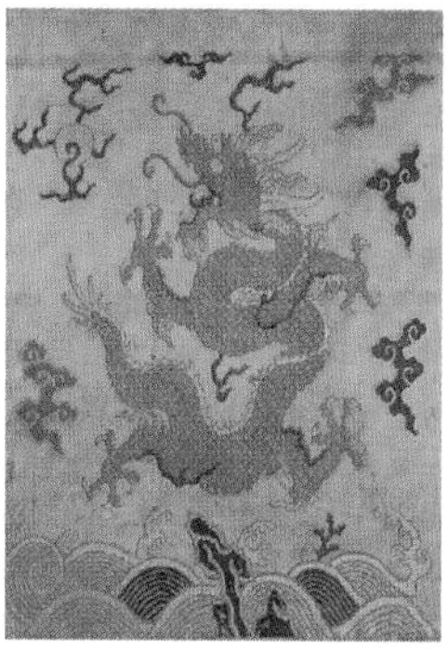

A *thanka*, embroidered with four-clawed dragons, Tibetan, 18thC, 16in (40.5cm) long.
£430–475
€/ $680–750 ⊞ JCH
A *thanka* is a Tibetan representation of divinities. They are used on the walls of temples or shrines as a subject for meditation.

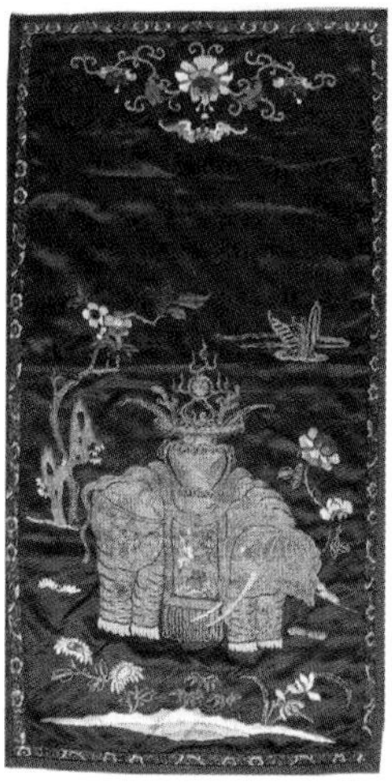

An embroidered panel, depicting an elephant with flowers, Chinese, early 20thC, 33in (84cm) long.
£200–225
€/ $315–350 ⊞ JCH

An embroidered silk panel, with central stylized flowering plants, within rosette borders, Indian, Gujerat, 19thC, 64¼ x 35in (166 x 89cm), mounted.
£800–950
€/ $1,300–1,500 ⚒ B(Kn)

An embroidered panel, decorated with five bats representing The Five Blessings, Chinese, early 20thC, 20in (51cm) wide.
£1,100–1,300
€/ $1,700–2,000 ⊞ JCH

A silk-embroidered rank badge bag, Chinese, late 19thC, 11in (28cm) square.
£100–120
€/ $160–190 ⊞ JPr

A hand-embroidered panel, from an apron skirt, Chinese, c1890, 8 x 12in (20.5 x 30.5cm).
£270–300
€/ $430–475 ⊞ AUA

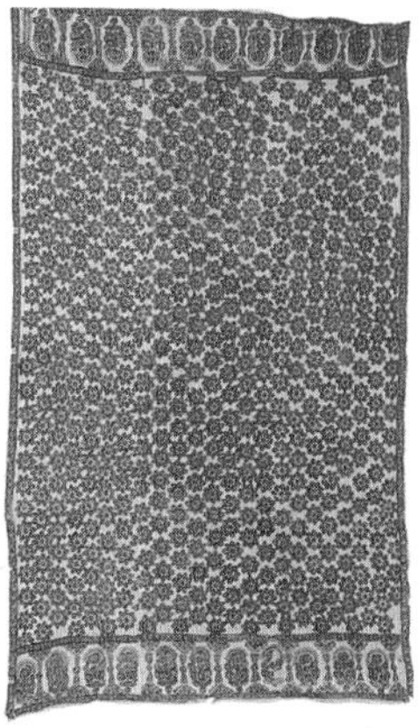

A silk-embroidered panel, Indian, late 19thC, 86¾ x 51¼in (220.5 x 130cm).
£650–720
€/ $1,000–1,100 ⚒ S(O)

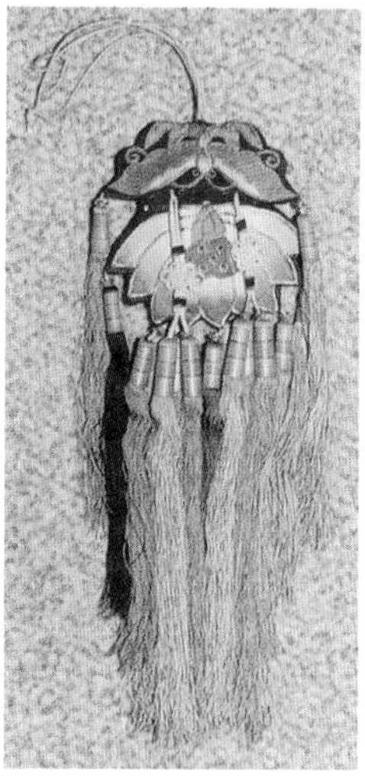

A purse, decorated with a butterfly and multicoloured tasselling, Chinese, 19thC, 9¾in (25cm) long.
£320–350
€/ $500–550 ⊞ WRi

► A 4th rank badge, with appliqué cloud goose surrounded by the eight Buddhist symbols, Chinese, c1890, 12 x 11in (30.5 x 28cm).
£475–525
€/ $750–830
⊞ AUA

◄ A satin wall hanging, couched and embroidered in gold threads and silks with Immortals, grotesque figures and beauties in a garden, Chinese, late 19thC, 115¾ x 88½in (294 x 225cm).
£1,000–1,100
€/ $1,600–1,700 ⚒ S(O)

Islamic Works of Art

Arms & Armour

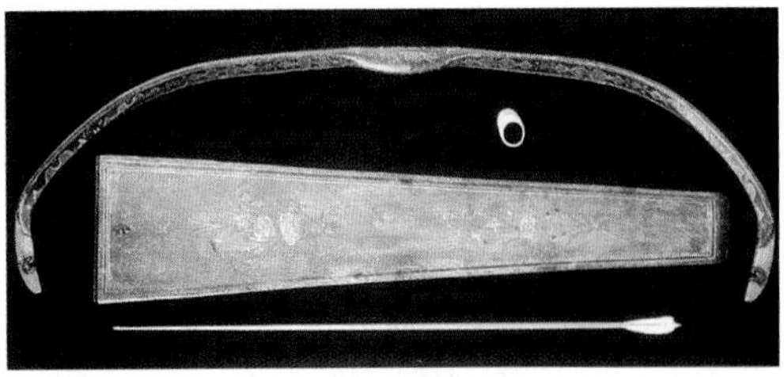

An Ottoman horn bow, wooden arrow-case and ivory thumb-ring, the bow with lacquered gilt decoration, with two associated target arrows, Turkish, 18th/19thC, the bow dated AH1219, bow 27½in (70cm) long.
£4,200–5,000
€/ $6,600–7,900 S

An Ottoman breastplate, the plain rim struck with the mark of the Ottoman Court Arsenal at Hagia Eirene, minor repairs, early 16thC, 13in (33cm) high.
£1,800–2,000
€/ $2,800–3,200 S(O)

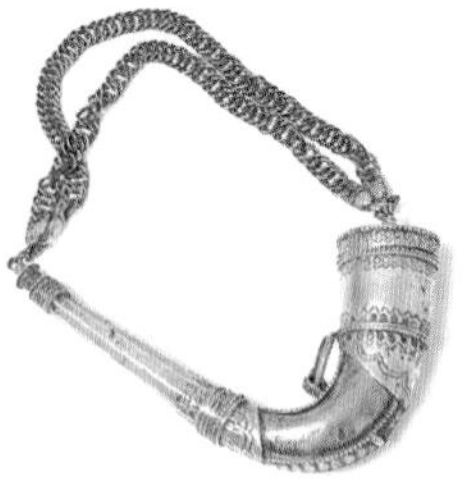

A white metal flask, with pierced and embossed decoration, Persian, c1870, 5in (12.5cm) long.
£200–225
€/ $320–350 MDL

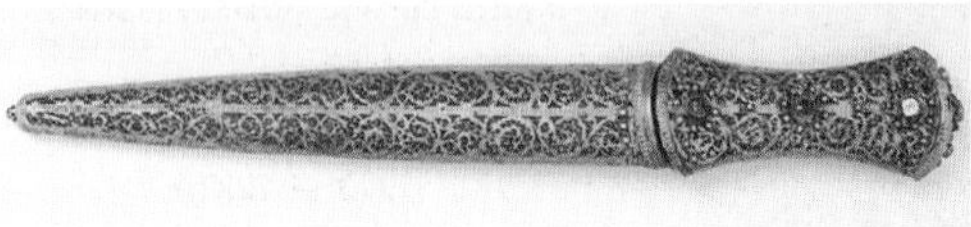

A *jambiya*, with double-edged blade, decorated with gold damascened scrollwork, in original wooden scabbard, Turkish, 19thC, 16in (40.5cm) long.
£2,000–2,200
€/ $3,200–3,500 B(Kn)

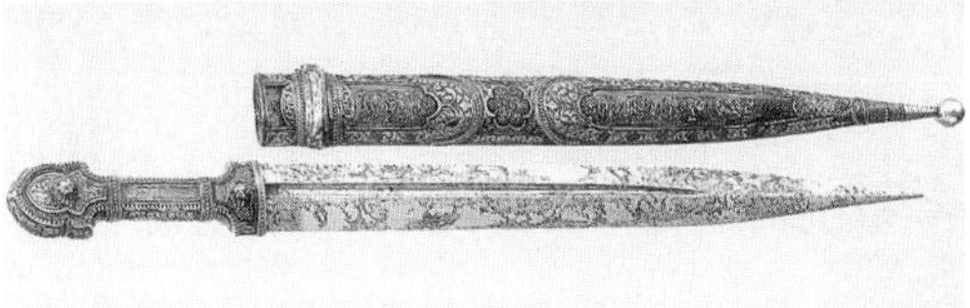

A *kinjal*, with double-edged blade, the nielloed silver grip with gold and ivory decoration, the wooden sheath overlaid in nielloed silver, Dagestan, c1900, 20¼in (51.5cm) long.
£1,700–2,000
€/ $2,600–3,200 Herm

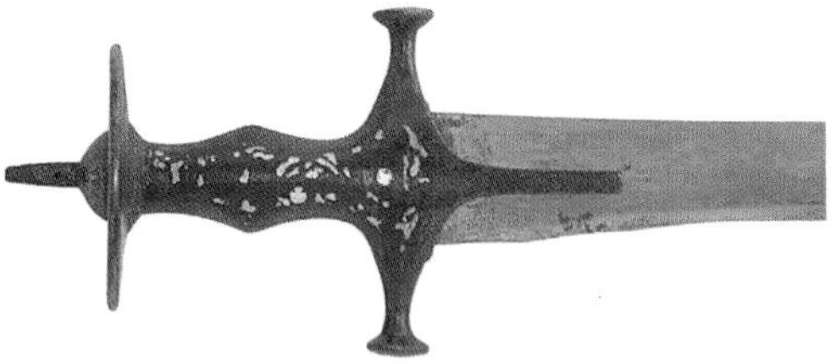

◄ **A Mogul *tulwar*,** the iron hilt with traces of silver overlay and brown patina, early 17thC, blade 30½in (77.5cm) long, with the wooden carcass of the scabbard.
£385–425
€/ $600–700 FAC

Ceramics

An Ilkhanid *lajvardina* pottery bottle, decorated with a phoenix in flight, flowers and scrolls, Persian, 14thC, 8½in (21.5cm) diam.
£2,200–2,500
€/ $3,500–4,000 B(Kn)

A pottery bowl, with incised sgraffito decoration of an abstract bird, Persian, 10th–12thC, 7in (18cm) diam.
£250–275
€/ $400–440 CrF

A Tophane terracotta coffee set, with impressed and gilt decoration and inscriptions, Turkish, dated 1887, ewer 6¼in (16cm) high.
£1,600–2,000
€/ $2,500–3,200 B(Kn)

LOCATE THE SOURCE
The source of each illustration in Miller's can be found by checking the code letters below each caption with the Key to Illustrations, pages 794–800.

◄ **An Iznik pottery dish,** with sloping rim, decorated with a hyacinth flanked by roses and a tulip, Turkish, late 16thC, 12in (30.5cm) diam.
£2,200–2,500
€/ $3,500–4,000 B(Kn)

An Iznik pottery dish, with sloping rim, decorated and gilt with a *saz* leaf, tulips and roses, Turkish, 17thC, 12in (30.5cm) diam.
£1,300–1,500
€/ $2,100–2,400 B(Kn)

A *kalian* or *kendi*, decorated with four panels of Oriental birds in gardens, chips to footrim, Persian, 17thC, 7in (18cm) high.
£1,400–1,600
€/ $2,200–2,500 TEN

A Kubachi pottery dish, the central rosette enclosing floral and foliate motifs, Persian, 17thC, 13¼in (33.5cm) diam.
£7,500–8,500
€/ $12,000–13,500 S

A Kashan lustre-decorated cruciform tile, decorated with palmettes on a ground of scrolls, Persian, 13thC, 8½in (21.5cm) wide.
£250–300
€/ $400–480 S(O)

► **A pair of tiles,** each painted with two exotic birds, roses, foliage and other flowers, Persian, 19thC, 13¼ x 9¾in (34 x 24.5cm).
£200–220
€/ $315–350 CGC

A pottery dish, decorated with Kufic script and characters, Turkish, 18thC, 14¼in (36cm) diam.
£180–200
€/ $280–320 BR

A Timurid carved pottery border tile, with a band of trefoils, central Asian, late 14thC, 9½in (24cm) long.
£800–950
€/ $1,300–1,500 B(Kn)

Furniture

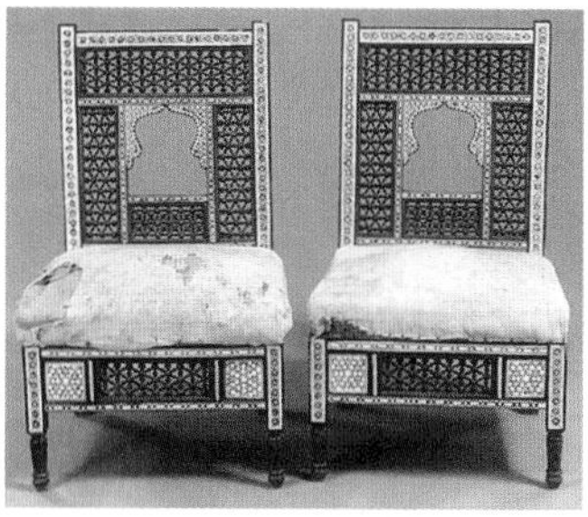

◄ **A pair of mahogany side chairs,** inlaid with mother-of-pearl, each with a bulbous spindle back above a Moorish arch, on turned feet, North African, c1900.
£1,000–1,200
€/ $1,600–1,900 NOA

A walnut and shell-inlaid coffer, Syrian, Damascus, 19thC, 56¾in (144cm) wide.
£800–900
€/ $1,300–1,400 S(O)

An Ottoman serpentine-fronted miniature commode, inlaid with mother-of-pearl, ebony, ivory and bone, Syrian, c1900, 11in (28cm) wide.
£1,000–1,200
€/ $1,600–1,900 CAT

An Ottoman velvet screen, Turkish, 19thC, each panel 59 x 23½in (150 x 60cm).
£3,500–4,200
€/ $5,500–6,600 B(Kn)

A suite of inlaid Damascus-style furniture, early 20thC, davenport 24in (61cm) wide.
£1,800–2,200
€/ $2,800–3,500 S(O)

Glass

A wheel-cut glass bottle, cut with seven circles in relief, Persian, c9thC, 3¾in (9.5cm) high.
£1,000–1,100
€/ $1,600–1,700 B(Kn)

A wheel-cut glass bowl, cut with four rows of indented panels forming a honeycomb design, Persian, c9thC, 4¼in (11cm) diam.
£850–1,000
€/ $1,300–1,600 B(Kn)

A glass flask, with mould-blown decoration of interconnecting circle and dot motifs, Persian, 10th–12thC, 3½in (9cm) high.
£1,600–2,000
€/ $2,200–3,200 S

Manuscripts & Paintings

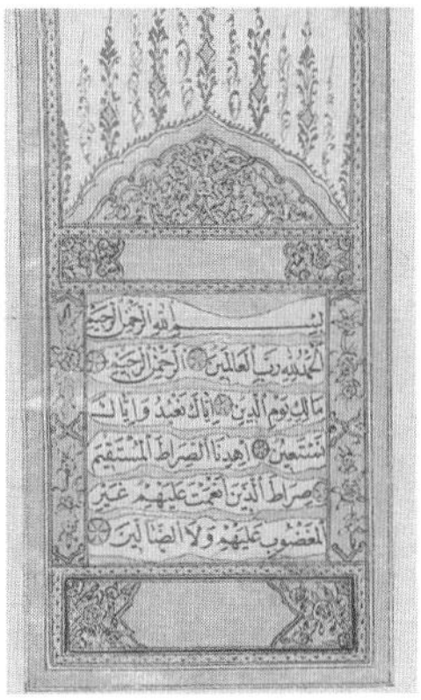

► An Ottoman illuminated Qur'an, 410 leaves, contemporary gold tooled and stamped leather binding, Turkish, 18thC, 6 x 4in (15 x 10cm).
£1,700–2,000
€/ $2,700–3,200
B(Kn)

A miniature painting from a copy of the Sinbadnama, opaque watercolour, ink and gilding on paper, Persian, early 16thC, 2½ x 4¾in (6.5 x 12cm).
£260–300
€/ $400–470 S(O)

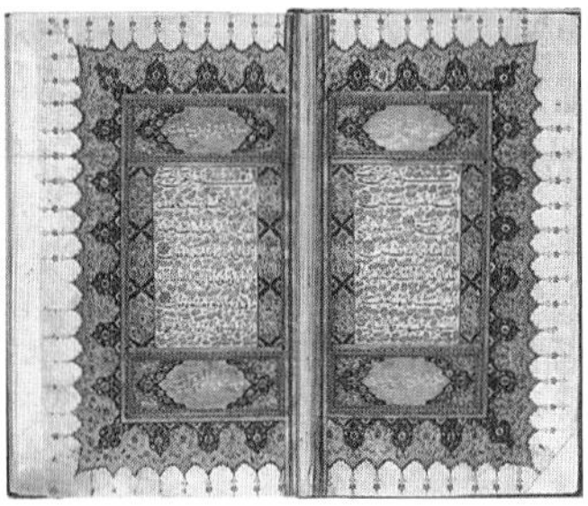

An Arabic illuminated Qur'an, 338 leaves, Turkish, Constantinople, repaired and rebacked, dated 1671, 10¾ x 6¾in (27.5 x 17cm).
£4,200–5,000
€/ $6,600–7,900 S

► An Arabic manuscript on paper, the Psalms of David according to the Coptic Church, 237 leaves, Morocco binding, Egyptian, dated 1784, 5½ x 4in (14 x 10cm).
£3,000–3,500
€/ $4,700–5,500 S

Jewellery

A pair of Qajar enamelled and gold earrings, fringed with seed pearls and glass beads, the hooks set with rubies, Persian, 19thC, 2¼in (6cm) long.
£1,600–2,000
€/ $2,500–3,200 B(Kn)

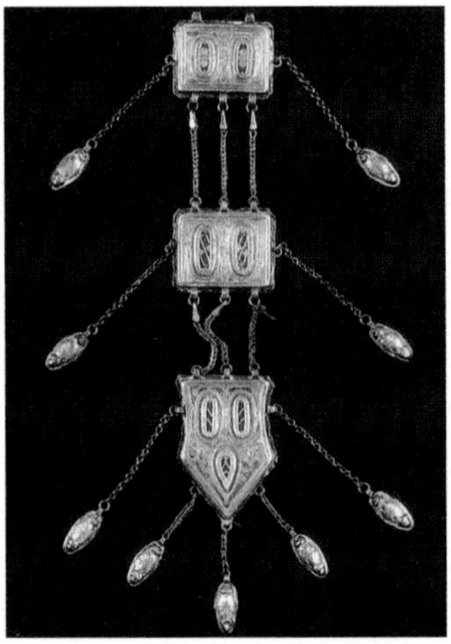

An enamelled gold pendant, set with emeralds, rubies and sapphires, Moroccan, 19thC, 2in (5cm) diam.
£3,200–3,800
€/ $5,100–6,000 S

◄ A Kazak necklace, set with precious stones, Persian, 19thC.
£400–450
€/ $630–710 S

Metalware

A Safavid tinned copper basin, decorated with a band of calligraphy, on a narrow stem foot, Persian, 17thC, 14½in (36.5cm) diam.
£650–750
€/ $1,000–1,200 B(Kn)

A Timurid bronze bowl, with incised calligraphic decoration, Persian, late 15thC, 5¾in (14.5cm) diam.
£1,800–2,200
€/ $2,800–3,500 S

A bronze jug, with bird finial, Persian, damaged, 12thC, 9½in (24cm) high.
£400–480
€/ $630–760 SWO

◄ **A silver box and cover,** chased with a cartouche and repeating floral motifs around the sides, Persian, 19thC, 3in (7.5cm) diam.
£100–120
€/ $160–190 WW

Textiles

A silk brocade panel, Persian, 16th–17thC, 8in (20.5cm) square.
£85–100
€/ $135–160 JCH

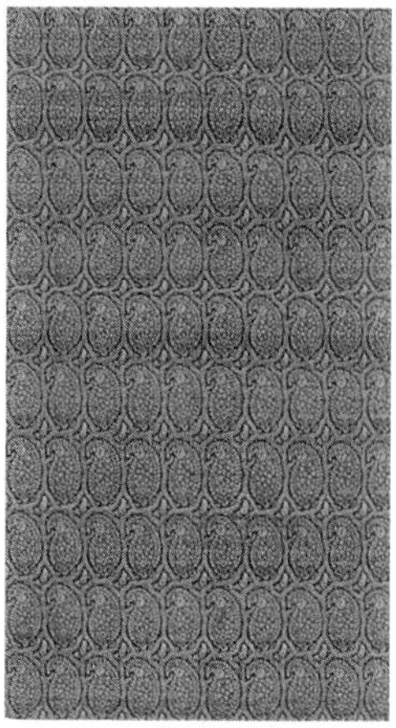

► **A textile fragment of Safavid design,** Persian, 19thC, 45¾ x 27in (116 x 69cm).
£350–400
€/ $550–630 S(O)

An embroidered hanging, worked in cotton on a felted wool ground, slight wear, Persia, Rasht, c1900, 95 x 63in (241.5 x 160cm).
£350–420
€/ $550–660 WW

Miscellaneous

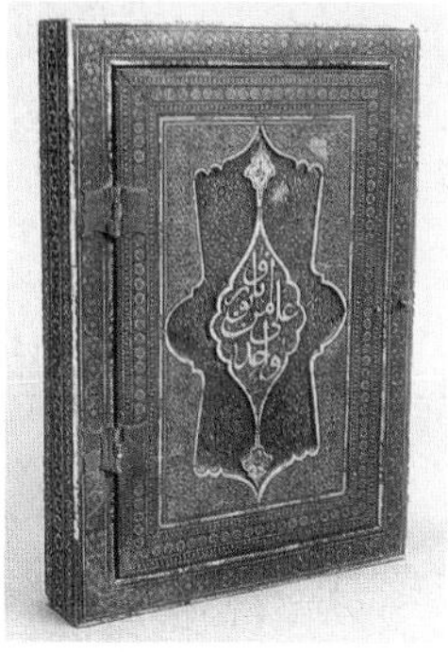

A wooden manuscript box, inlaid with bone and coloured woods, Near Eastern, early 19thC, 8¾ x 6¼in (22.5 x 16cm).
£240–275
€/ $380–430 DN

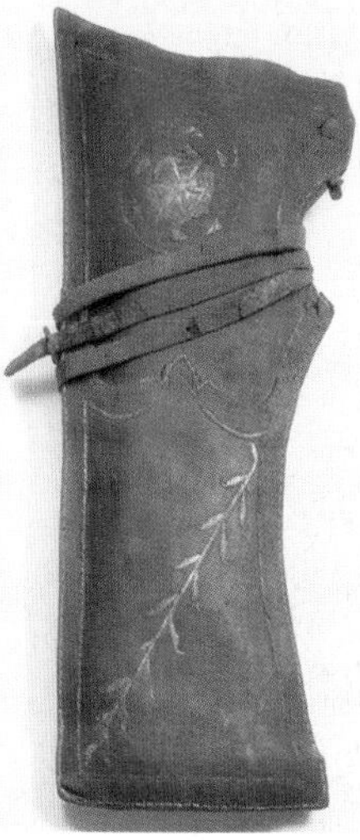

◄ **An Ottoman leather quiver,** embroidered in silver wrapped around a silk core with a roundel containing a large flowerhead, Turkish, c1680, 17in (43cm) long.
£1,700–2,000
€/ $2,700–3,300 B(Kn)

Items in the Miscellaneous section have been arranged in alphabetical order.

► **An Ottoman tombstone,** carved with inscriptions, probably Turkish, c1821, 44in (112cm) high.
£700–850
€/ $1,100–1,300 S(O)

Architectural Antiques

Iron

A Regency painted-iron garden bench, the back with interlaced splats with downswept arms and slatted seat, 50in (127cm) wide.
£750–900
€/ $1,200–1,400 L&E

A cast-iron garden bench, the back pierced with fern leaves, Irish, c1840, 74in (188cm) wide.
£1,000–1,200
€/ $1,600–1,900 ⊞ HON

Items in the Architectural Antiques section have been arranged in alphabetical order.

A cast-iron boot scraper, c1880, 13in (33cm) high.
£110–120
€/ $170–190 ⊞ SMI

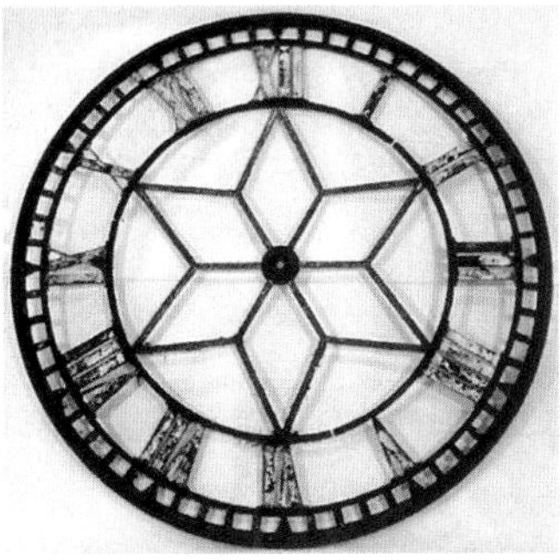

A Victorian cast-iron clock face, c1880, 72in (183cm) diam.
£2,000–2,200
€/ $3,200–3,500 WilP
This clock face came from the Town Hall, Dunstable, Bedfordshire.

A cast-iron royal coat-of-arms, late 19thC, 23in (58.5cm) high.
£900–1,000
€/ $1,400–1,500 ⊞ SWN

A pair of cast-iron door stops, cast as Punch & Judy, Punch dressed as Julius Caesar, c1860, 12in (30.5cm) high.
£500–560
€/ $800–880 ⊞ MFB

A cast-iron door stop, c1870, 8in (20.5cm) high.
£55–60
€/ $85–95 ⊞ GBr

A cast-iron lion-mask down-pipe cover, early 19thC, 10in (25.5cm) high.
£580–650
€/ $920–1,000 ⊞ ChC

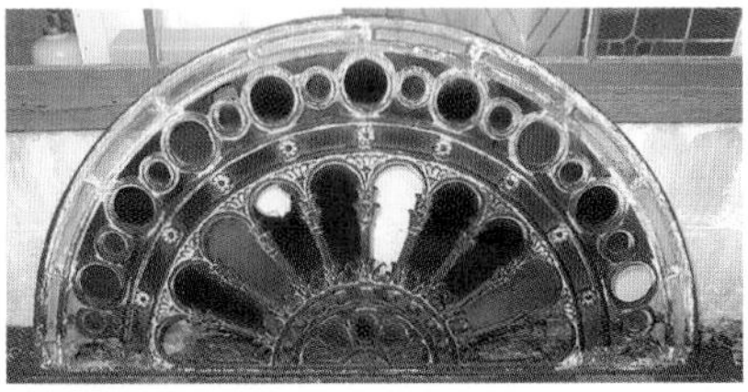

A cast-iron fan light, with coloured glass, minor damage, 19thC, 38in (96.5cm) wide.
£1,100–1,200
€/ $1,700–1,900 ⊞ WRe

► A suite of painted cast-iron garden furniture, comprising five pieces, 19thC, largest 50in (127cm) wide
£3,800–4,500
€/ $6,000–7,100
HOK

A cast-iron fountain, by Handyside Foundry, Derby, on a stepped square base, c1860, 42in (106.5cm) high.
£1,800–2,000
€/ $2,800–3,200 ⚒ S(S)

A Victorian enamelled cast-iron drinking fountain, with brass tap, 37in (94cm) high.
£240–260
€/ $380–420 ⊞ WRe

► A wrought-iron garden gate, with scroll decoration and spiked cresting rail, late 19thC, 53½in (136cm) high.
£700–820
€/ $1,100–1,300
⚒ BR

◄ A cast-iron grid, 1920s, 17in (43.5cm) square.
£85–95
€/ $135–150
⊞ WRe

A cast-iron mask, c1840, 14in (35.5cm) high.
£580–650
€/ $920–1,200 ⊞ RGe

A cast-iron planter, decorated with pierced and trailing foxgloves, zinc liner, 1850–1900, 53in (134.5cm) diam.
£1,000–1,200
€/ $1,600–1,900 ⚒ S(S)

A cast-iron radiator, French, restored, c1900, 61in (155cm) long.
£1,300–1,500
€/ $2,100–2,400 ⊞C&R

◄ A cast- and wrought-iron stove, moulded with a flowering urn and bellflower, Greek key and figural decoration, northern European, c1800, 76in (193cm) high.
£2,000–2,400
€/ $3,200–3,800 ⚒ S(O)

An iron laundry stove, by Thevenot Frères, French, Paris, c1900, 36in (91.5cm) high.
£500–600
€/ $790–950 ⊞ B&R
This stove would have been used for heating flat irons.

◄ A cast-iron and enamel conservatory stove, 19thC, 27¼in (69cm) high.
£140–160
€/ $220–250 ⚒ SWO

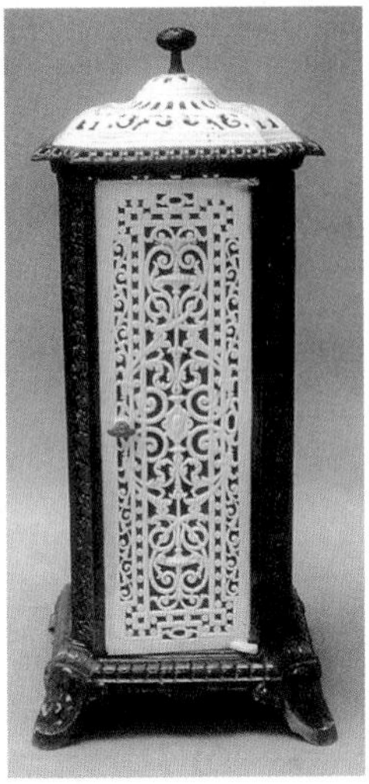

A painted cast-iron and enamel stove, by S. D. F., pierced with strapwork and anthemia, early 20thC, 37¾in (96cm) high.
£300–350
€/ $475–550 DD

◄ A Victorian cast-iron umbrella stand, diamond registration mark, pre-1880, 29in (73.5cm) high,
£350–385
€/ $550–600 RPh

A pair of painted cast-iron urns, the part-ribbed bodies with flared egg-and-dart rims, 19thC, 42in (106.5cm) high.
£1,000–1,200
€/ $1,600–1,900 WW

A pair of Falkirk Foundry cast-iron urns, lobed and reeded, with scroll handles, 1850–1900, 24in (61cm) high.
£900–1,100
€/ $1,400–1,700 S(S)

A pair of cast-iron garden urns, the fluted bodies with scroll handles, labelled 'Corneau Alfred, à Charleville, No 2', French, c1900, 19¼in (49cm) high.
£240–280
€/ $380–440 DMC

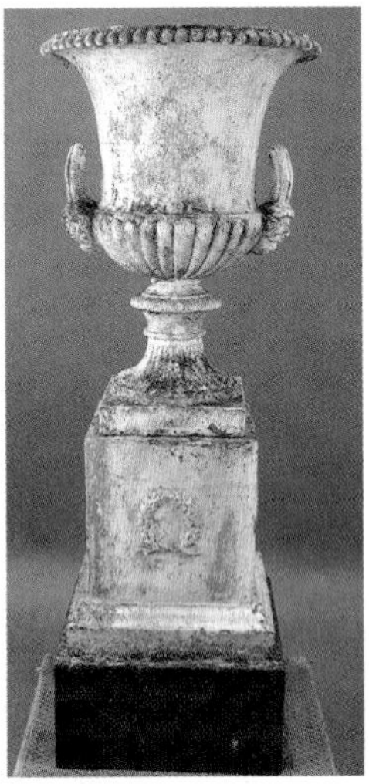

A Victorian cast-iron garden urn, with mask handles on a square plinth, 56¾in (144cm) high.
£1,100–1,300
€/ $1,700–2,000 SWO

An iron garden urn, in the shape of a basket, early 20thC, 35½in (90cm) high.
£650–750
€/ $1,000–1,200 SWO

Sets/pairs

Unless otherwise stated, any description which refers to 'a set' or 'a pair' includes a guide price for the entire set or the pair, even though the illustration may show only a single item.

Bronze

A bronze church bell, by Newcome, 1614, 38in (96.5cm) high.
£2,000–2,500
€/ $3,200–4,000 WEL

A pair of bronze sphinxes, early 20thC, 35in (89cm) high.
£2,000–2,400
€/ $3,200–3,800 JAd

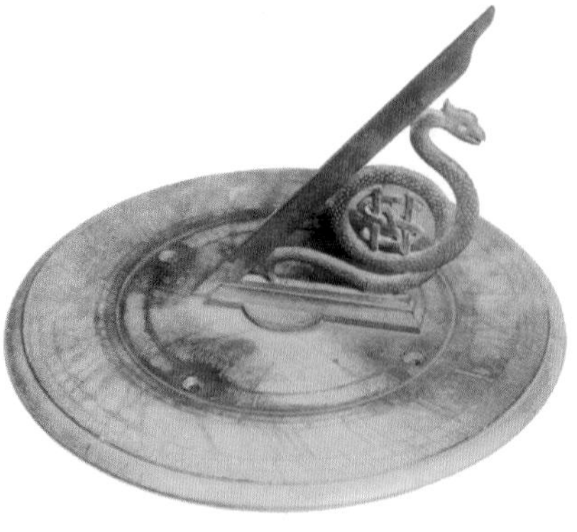

A bronze sundial plate, the dial inscribed with the arms of Cornwall and 'Sol est Lux et Gloria Mundi, Newton Camborne', with pierced gnomon on a coiled serpent, c1900, 14in (35.5cm) diam.
£1,100–1,300
€/ $1,700–2,000 S(S)

Lead

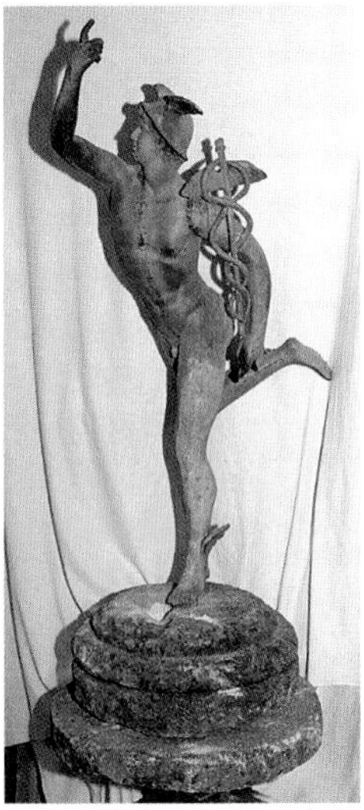

A lead figure of Mercury, by Crowther, c1900, 42in (106.5cm) high.
£1,100–1,200
€/ $1,700–1,900 OLA

A lead figure of a Neapolitan fisher boy, 1900–50, 28in (71cm) high.
£1,700–2,000
€/ $2,700–3,200 S(S)

A length of lead water-pump housing, c1850, 40in (101.5cm) high.
£180–200
€/ $280–320 ⊞ WRe

A lead cistern, the front decorated with strapwork and figures of Neptune, with ownership initials, bronze tap, dated 1764, 44in (112cm) wide.
£8,000–9,500
€/ $12,600–15,000 S(S)

Marble

A pair of Verona marble garden chairs, in the shape of Etruscan thrones flanked by winged lions, the backs centred with a *stemma nobilare*, Italian, 18thC, 33in (84cm) high.
£33,000–40,000
€/ $52,000–63,000 ⊞ W&C
These hand-carved seats are extremely impressive and pieces of such age rarely survive to the 21st century.

A veined marble column, with moulded decoration, late 19thC, 48in (122cm) high.
£550–650
€/ $870–1,000 SWO

A marble figure of a putto, 19thC, 43½in (110.5cm) high.
£2,200–2,500
€/ $3,500–4,000 LVS

A marble figure, 19thC, 47in (119.5cm) high.
£1,100–1,200
€/ $1,700–1,900 ⊞ PAS

A carved marble basket of flowers, French, 19thC, 17in (43cm) wide.
£1,000–1,200
€/ $1,600–1,900 S(S)

A carved marble font, slight damage, probably late 17thC, 23½in (59.5cm) wide.
£650–780
€/ $1,000–1,200 S(S)

Four Victorian marble planters, in the shape of stylized water lilies, 14¼in (36cm) wide.
£2,500–3,000
€/ $4,000–4,700 B(S)

Stone

A carved sandstone birdbath, early 20thC, 29in (74cm) high.
£400–480
€/ $630–760 ⚒ S(S)

A granite mill stone, 19thC, 41in (104cm) diam.
£720–800
€/ $1,100–1,300 ⊞ WRe

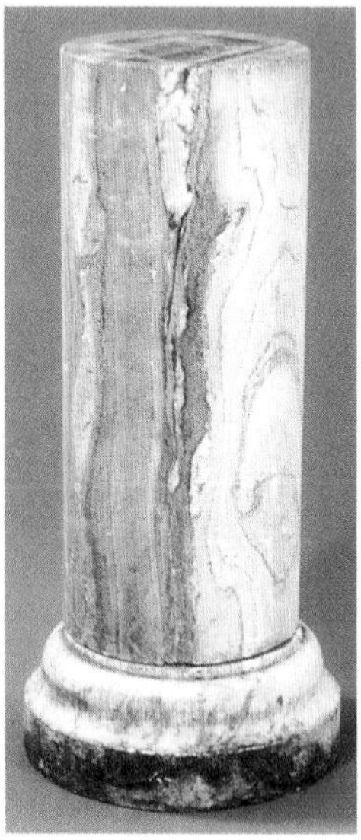

A neo-classical-style variegated stone garden pedestal, on a circular plinth, c1900, 34in (86.5cm) high.
£400–450
€/ $630–710 ⚒ NOA

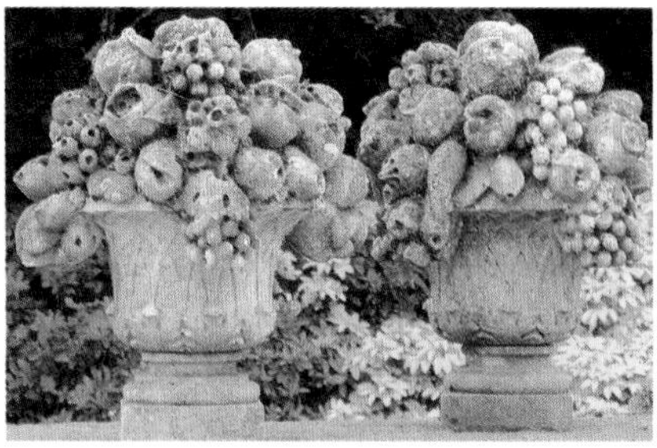

A pair of carved stone baskets of fruit, early 20thC, 22in (56cm) high.
£3,000–3,600
€/ $4,800–5,700 ⚒ S(S)

Two sandstone gate-post finials, with medial bands, 19thC, 12in (30.5cm) high.
£180–220
€/ $280–350 ⚒ PFK

A pair of stone panels, each carved in relief with a bird of paradise with a serpent in its beak, c1900, 34½in (87.5cm) high.
£1,800–2,200
€/ $2,800–3,500 ⚒ S(S)

A carved Bath stone date plaque, 1905, 23in (58.5cm) wide.
£110–120
€/ $175–190 ⊞ WRe

▶ A carved Caen stone planter, French, 19thC, 29in (73cm) wide.
£1,000–1,200
€/ $1,600–1,900 ⚒ S(S)

A pair of carved stone gate-post finials, modelled as pineapples, c1800, 40in (101.5cm) high.
£1,000–1,200
€/ $1,600–1,900 ⚒ S(S)

A Coade stone keystone, carved with the head of a girl, stamped 'Coade, London 1793', 10½in (26.5cm) high.
£1,300–1,500
€/ $2,100–2,400 ⚒ S(S)

Eleanor Coade opened her Lambeth factory for ceramic artificial stone in 1769. Two years later she appointed the sculptor John Bacon as its manager. She was employed by the leading late 18th-century architects. From about 1777 she began creating engraved designs and by 1784 had designed over 700 items. In 1799 the firm became Coade & Sealey, but reverted to the original name in 1821. The London 1774 Building Act reduced exterior woodwork to the absolute minimum to make housing as incombustible as possible, and the Lambeth factory was able to supply a great variety of fireproof decoration for house fronts.

A Bourgogne stone planter, late 19thC, 34in (86.5cm) wide.
£1,500–1,700
€/ £2,400–2,800 ⚒ S(S)

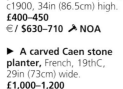

Terracotta

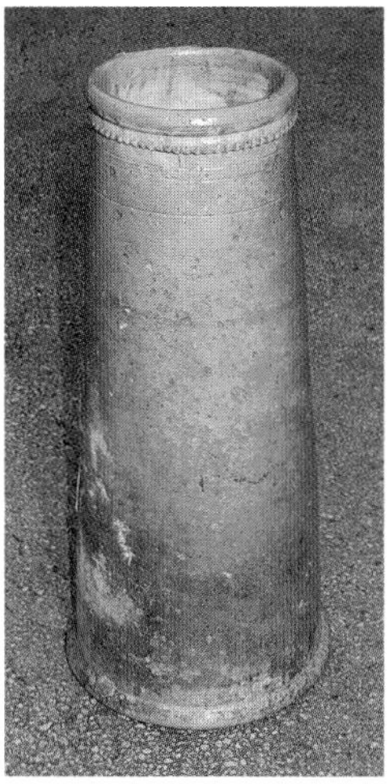

A Victorian terracotta chimney pot, 31in (78.5cm) high.
£90–100
€/ $140–160 ⊞ WRe

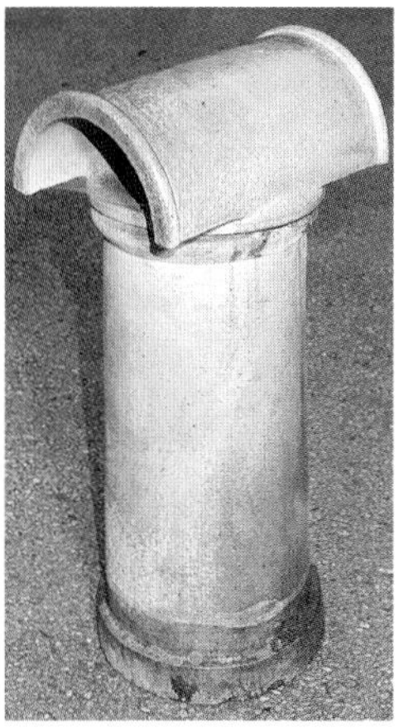

A Victorian terracotta chimney pot, 29in (73.5cm) high.
£45–50
€/ $70–80 ⊞ WRe

A terracotta chimney pot, 1920s, 28in (71cm) high.
£70–80
€/ $110–130 ⊞ WRe

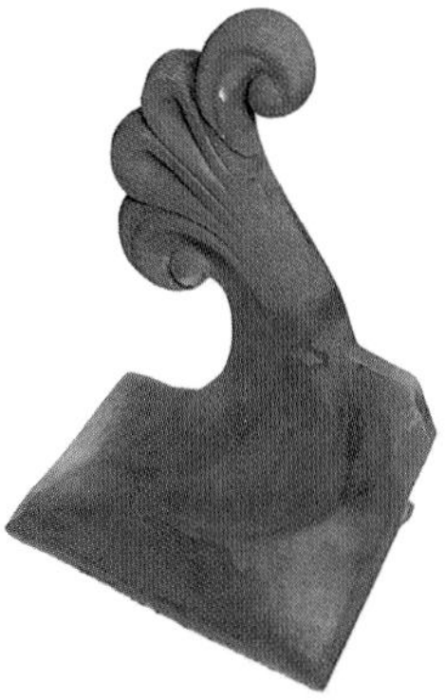

A Victorian terracotta cock's comb finial, 22in (56cm) high.
£60–70
€/ $95–125 ⊞ WRe

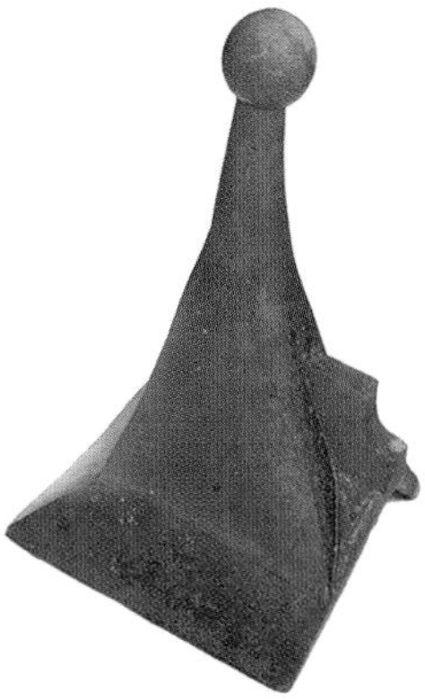

A Victorian terracotta roof finial, 22in (56cm) high.
£55–60
€/ $85–95 ⊞ WRe

A Victorian terracotta garden ornament, in the form of two cherubs, slight damage, 17in (43cm) high.
£200–220
€/ $315–350 ⚒ TMA

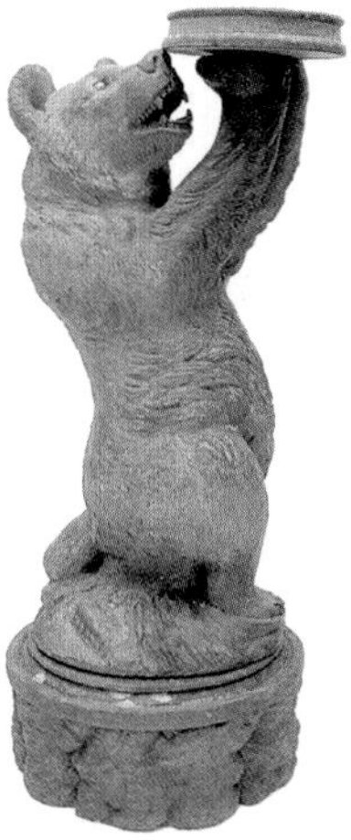

A cast-terracotta jardinière stand, by Withnall, Lancashire, early 20thC, 27½in (70cm) high.
£220–250
€/ $350–400 ⚒ G(L)

A terracotta sundial pedestal, attributed to Compton, with later iron armillary sphere, early 20thC, 63in (160cm) high.
£1,400–1,600
€/ $2,200–2,500 ⚒ S(S)

A Compton terracotta pot, early 20thC, 19in (48.5cm) high.
£550–620
€/ $870–980 ⚒ S(S)

A Di Signa terracotta planter, moulded with cherubs and putti, early 20thC, 37½in (95.5cm) diam.
£500–600
€/ $790–950 ⚒ S(S)

A terracotta roundel, modelled with a dog's head, late 19thC, 20in (51cm) diam.
£650–750
€/ $1,000–1,200 ⚒ S(S)

A matt-glazed terracotta unitile, decorated with a scarab, American, c1918, 16in (40.5cm) wide.
£480–575
€/ $760–900 ⊞ KMG

◄ **A pair of Victorian Doulton terracotta urns,** with egg-and-dart rim, 25in (63.5cm) high.
£500–600
€/ $790–950 ⚒ JAd

Wood

A pair of wooden garden benches, c1900, 48in (122cm) wide.
£2,000–2,300
€/ $3,200–3,600 CAT

► **A carved and painted wooden column,** spiral-carved with grapevines, Italian, c1900, 40in (101.5cm) high.
£170–200
€/ $270–315 NOA

A pair of pine and composition figural corbels, 19thC, 11¾in (30cm) high.
£400–480
€/ $630–760 SWO

A carved wood architectural frame, 1675–1725, some damage, 43¼in (110cm) high.
£1,400–1,600
€/ $2,200–2,500 S(O)

A pair of oak Gothic carved panels, 16thC, 17in (43cm) high.
£1,000–1,100
€/ $1,600–1,700 KEY

A carved oak panel, 16thC, 13in (33cm) square.
£430–480
€/ $680–760 KEY

► **A pair of carved oak panels,** French, 16thC, 21in (53.5cm) wide.
£580–650
€/ $920–1,000 SEA

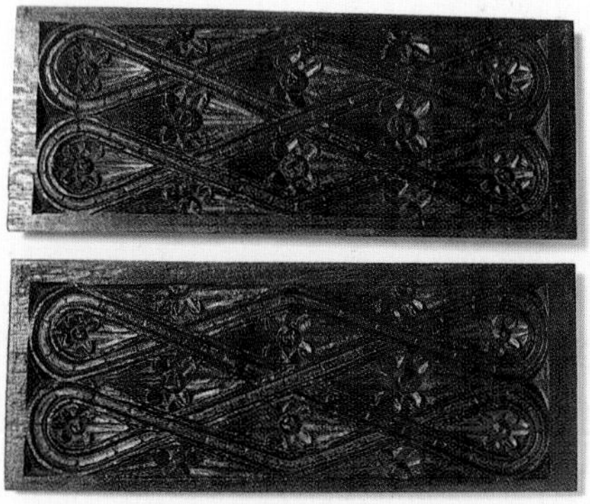

A carved and painted wood pelmet, the fringed drapery suspended from a central tassel-hung bow with two floral and shell wreaths, decorated with fruit and flowers, the fringed tails with tassel terminals, damaged, 19thC, 70½in (179cm) wide.
£2,400–2,800
€/ $3,800–4,400 B

A pair of carved and painted limewood swags, French, c1880, 20in (51cm) wide.
£400–450
€/ $630–700 HUM

A polychrome-painted cluster of wood palm trees, with trailing leaves and fruit and a carved olive tree, northern European, 19thC, 88in (224cm) high.
£1,700–2,000
€/ $2,700–3,200 S(S)
This group was probably part of the background for a large nativity scene.

Bathroom Fittings

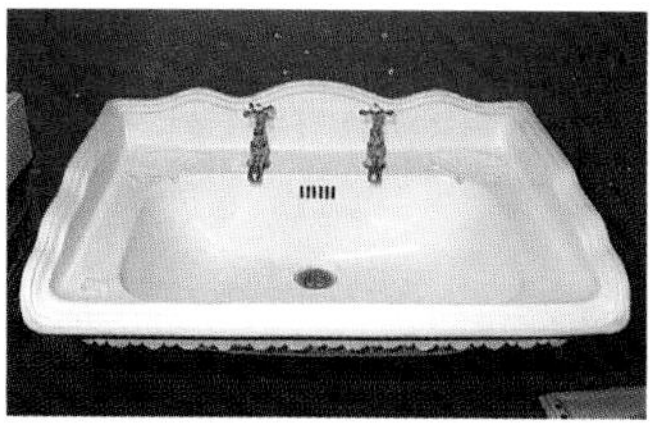

A Victorian basin, with brass taps and decorative cast-iron bracket, 30in (76cm) wide.
£1,700–1,900
€/ $2,700–3,000 ⊞ WRe

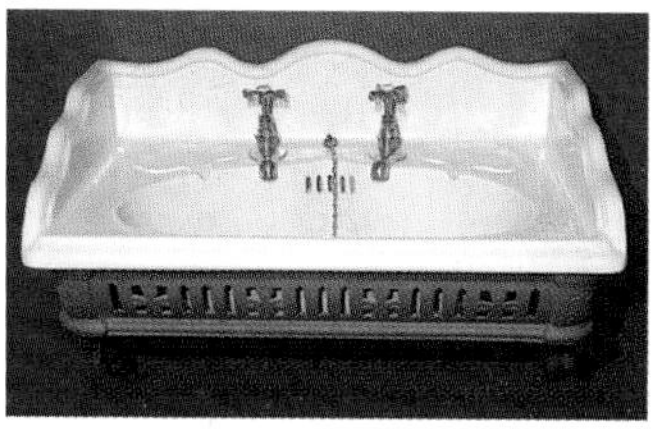

A Victorian basin, with brass taps and cast-iron brackets, 25in (63.5cm) wide.
£1,400–1,600
€/ $2,200–2,500 ⊞ WRe

A pedestal basin, restored, c1900, 34in (86.5cm) wide.
£2,300–2,500
€/ $3,600–4,000 ⊞ C&R

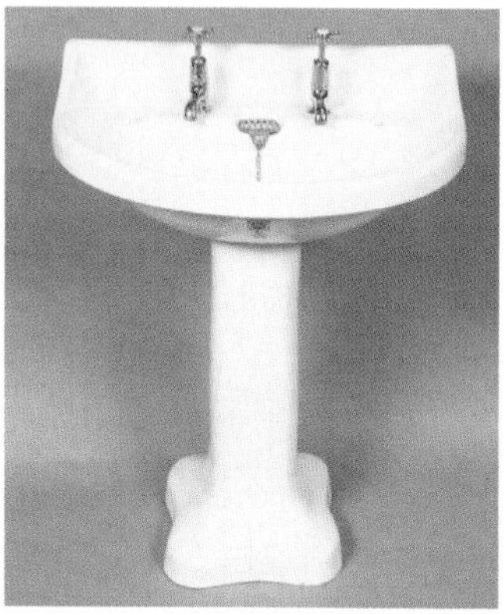

A pedestal basin, c1900, 27in (68.5cm) wide.
£1,300–1,500
€/ $2,100–2,200 ⊞ C&R

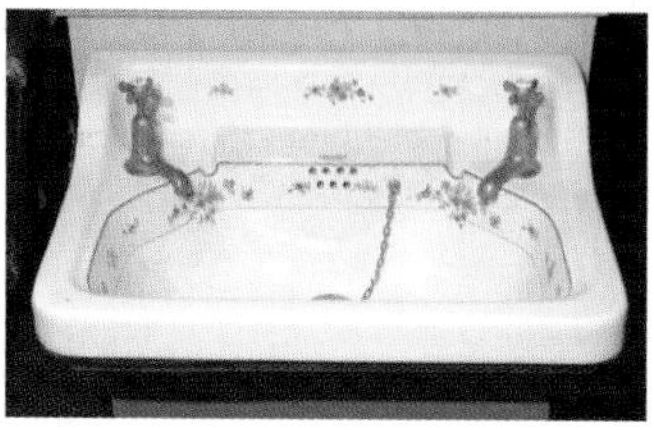

A Shelvas basin, with floral decoration, c1907, 22in (56cm) wide.
£900–1,000
€/ $1,400–1,600 ⊞ WRe

An Edwardian Doulton & Co corner basin, with reconditioned nickel-plated taps and waste, 18in (45.5cm) wide.
£630–700
€/ $1,000–1,100 ⊞ WRe

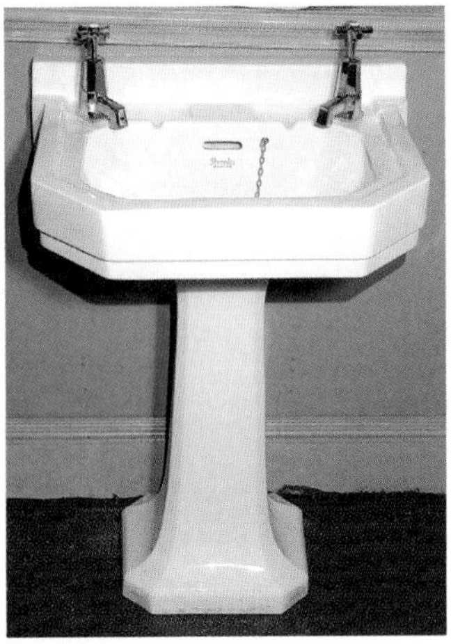

A Shanks & Co pedestal basin, reconditioned, 1930s, 24in (61cm) wide.
£400–450
€/ $630–700 ⊞ WRe

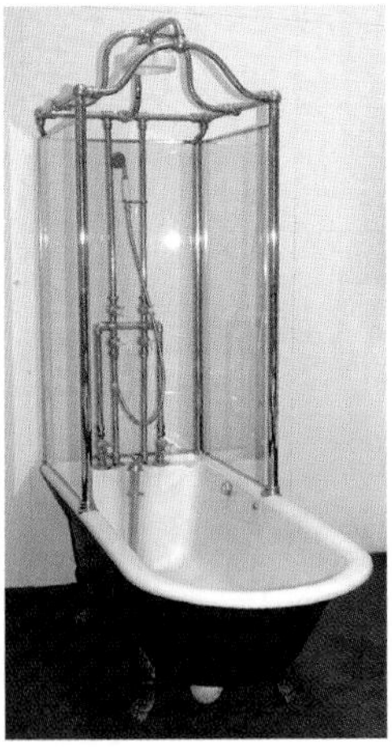

A Shanks & Co canopy bath, c1895, 87in (221cm) high.
£12,000–14,000
€/ $19,000–22,000 ⊞ C&R

A zinc-lined copper bath, with two lift rings on one side, c1900, 69in (175.5cm) long.
£2,800–3,200
€/ $4,400–5,100 ⚒ NOA

An iron bath on wheels, French, c1900, 64in (162.5cm) long.
£1,300–1,500
€/ $2,100–2,400 ⊞ C&R

A Shanks & Co cast-iron bath and shower unit, restored, c1900, 85in (216cm) high.
£11,000–12,000
€/ $17,400–19,000 ⊞ C&R

For further information on Architectural Antiques see the full range of Miller's books at **www.millers.uk.com**

A John Bolding stone bath, c1900, 70in (178cm) long.
£3,500–4,000
€/ $5,500–6,400 ⊞ C&R

A tenement bath, with brass fittings, Scottish, 1920–30, 67in (170cm) long.
£3,500–4,000
€/ $5,500–6,400 ⊞ WRe

A copper geyser, c1900, 41¾in (106cm) high.
£450–500
€/ $720–780 ⊞ C&R

◄ An Oeneas lavatory pan, decorated with English Countryside pattern, c1880, 17in (43.5cm) high.
£1,300–1,400
€/ $2,000–2,200 ⊞ WRe

► A Household Closet lavatory pan, with revolving trap pan, c1895, 17in (43cm) high.
£900–1,000
€/ $1,400–1,600 ⊞ WRe

A Puritas lavatory pan, decorated with a floral pattern, concealed trap, 1891–93, 16in (40.5cm) high.
£900–1,000
€/ $1,400–1,600 ⊞ OLA

A Victorian Adams & Co lavatory pan and cistern, with wooden seat.
£550–600
€/ $870–950 ⊞ OLA

A Doulton Lambeth Patent combination lavatory pan, c1900, 16in (40.5cm) high.
£1,800–2,000
€/ $2,800–3,200 ⊞ C&R

A Victorian Sanitas salt-glazed stoneware lavatory pan, 17in (43cm) high.
£550–600
€/ $870–950 ⊞ WRe

► **An Oeneas lavatory pan, basin and pine washstand,** c1900, stand 41in (104cm) wide.
£6,300–7,000
€/ $10,000–11,000 ⊞ C&R

A pair of brass taps, in the form of swan's necks, c1720, 8in (20.5cm) high.
£585–650
€/ $925–1,000 ⊞ RGe

A mahogany low-level cistern, c1900, 21in (53.5cm) wide.
£450–500
€/ $720–800 ⊞ C&R

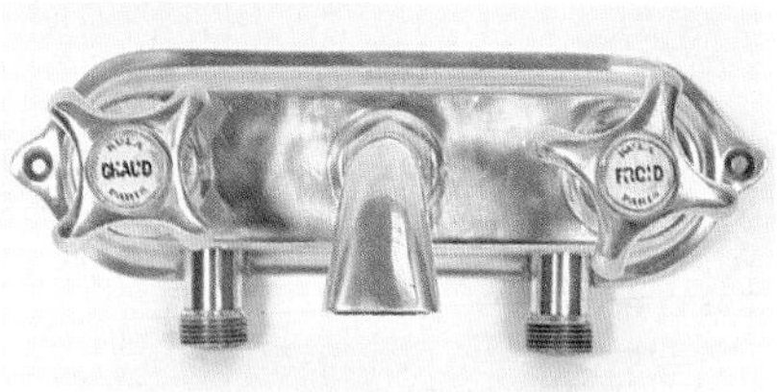

A pair of Kula polished brass bath filler taps, French, c1900, 11in (28cm) wide.
£900–1,000
€/ $1,400–1,600 ⊞ C&R

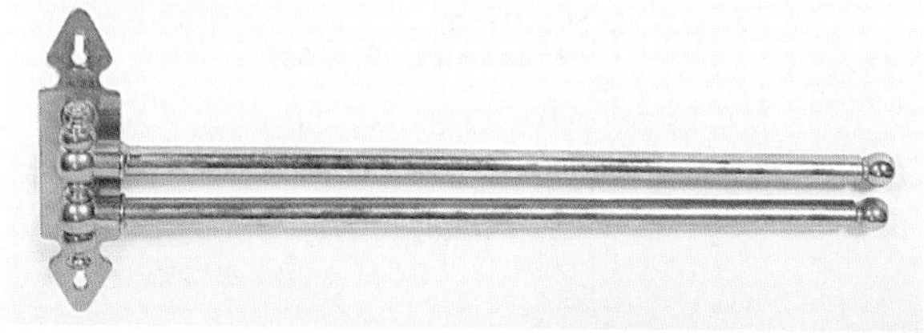

◄ **A nickel-plated double towel rail,** French, c1900, 23¾in (60.5cm) long.
£130–150
€/ $200–220 ⊞ C&R

A Victorian nickel-plated towel rail and radiator, c1900, 44½in (113cm) wide.
£800–1,000
€/ $1,300–1,600 ⊞ C&R

► **A nickel-plated shower mixer and stand pipe,** reconditioned, 1930s, 40in (101.5cm) high.
£800–1,000
€/ $1,300–1,600 ⊞ WRe

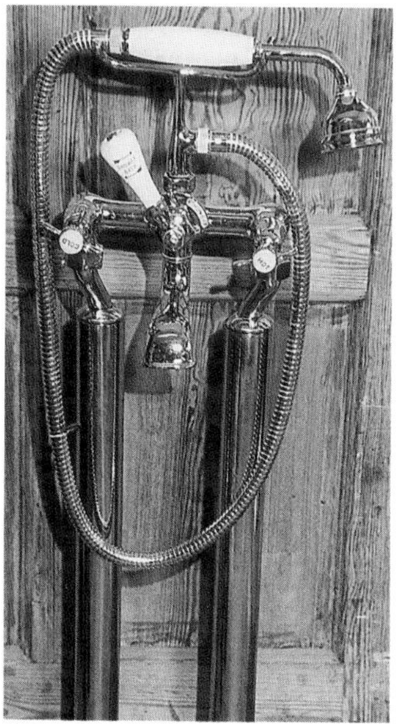

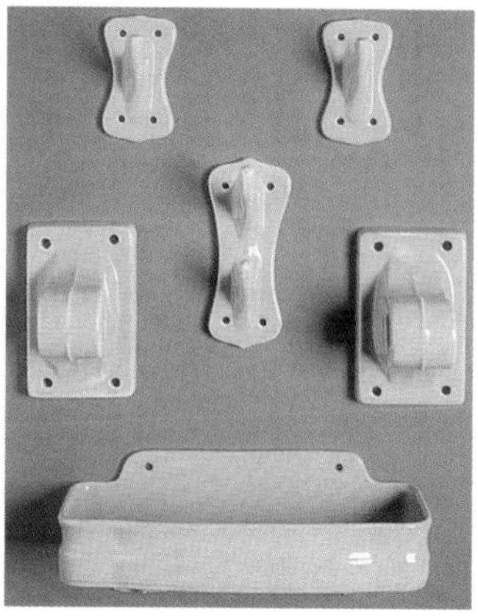

A Minton bathroom set, comprising towel rail brackets, wall shelf, a pair of hooks and a double hook, probably by John Wadsworth, hairline to shelf rim, c1930, shelf 12¼in (31cm) long.
£220–250
€/ $350–400 ⚒ B
Ex-Minton sale.

Bell Pulls

A pair of Regency mahogany and gilt-metal bell pulls, 6in (15cm) high.
£220–250
€/ $350–400 SWO

A brass interior bell push, c1870, 5in (13cm) diam.
£55–60
€/ £85–95 Penn

A brass servants' bell pull, in the form of a lion, early 19thC, 5in (12.5cm) high.
£850–950
€/ $1,300–1,500 ChC

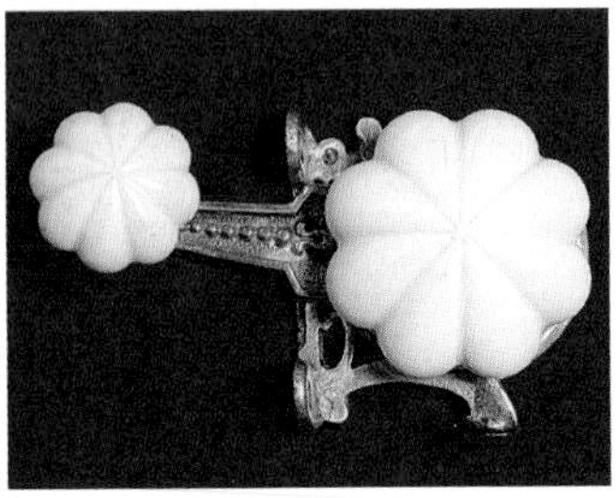

A Victorian brass bell pull, c1860, 9in (23cm) high.
£260–300
€/ $410–475 Penn

◄ A brass and ceramic bell pull, c1890, 5in (12.5cm) high
£60–70
€/ $95–110 Penn

Doors & Door Furniture

◄ A carved pine door, with peep-hole panel, German, early 19thC, 76in (193cm) high.
£350–400
€/ $550–640 HRQ

A pair of oak and pencil-work panelled doors, 19thC, 87¾in (223cm) high.
£2,000–2,200
€/ $3,200–3,500 S(O)

◄ A Kenrick & Sons door knocker and letter plate, registered No 429, c1890, 8in (20.5cm) wide.
£160–180
€/ $250–280 OLA

An Edwardian pine nine-panel front door, 36in (91.5cm) high.
£270–300
€/ $430–480 WRe

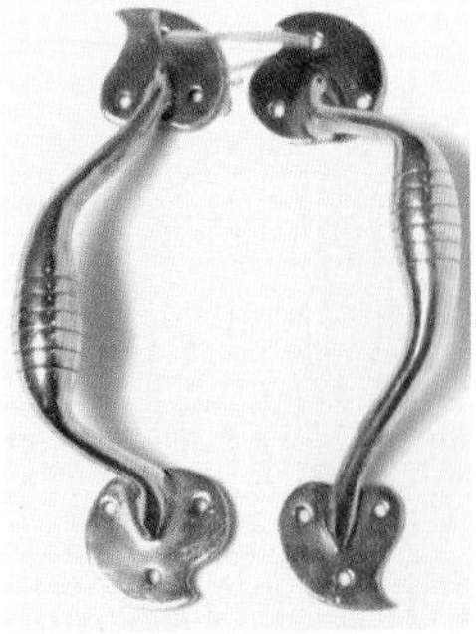

A wrought-iron door knocker, c1770, 7in (18cm) wide.
£180–200
€/ $280–320 SEA

An iron door knocker, c1850, 7½in (19cm) wide.
£110–120
€/ $175–190 Penn

◄ A pair of brass handles, c1890, 9in (23cm) long.
£50–55
€/ $80–85 Penn

Fireplaces

A carved pine fire surround, mid-18thC, 70in (178cm) wide.
£5,000–5,500
€/ $7,900–8,700 ⊞ WRe

A George III inlaid marble fire surround, the frieze centred by a carved tablet, the jambs with fluted banding, 72in (183cm) wide.
£14,000–16,000
€/ $22,000–25,000 ⚒ JAd

A George III pine fire surround, the frieze moulded with key and swag decoration, 58¾in (149cm) wide.
£2,200–2,500
€/ $3,500–4,000 ⚒ CGC

A George III carved pine fire surround, 70½in (179cm) wide.
£650–750
€/ $1,000–1,200 ⚒ SWO

A neo-classical-style black marble and alabaster fire surround, the end blocks decorated with blue john roundels, c1830, 67¾in (172cm) wide.
£10,000–11,000
€/ $15,800–17,400 ⊞ W&C

A marble fire surround, decorated with pomegranates, c1860, 52¾in (134cm) wide.
£9,000–10,000
€/ $14,200–15,800 ⊞ W&C

◄ **A carrara marble fire surround,** c1870, 78in (198cm) wide.
£2,500–2,800
€/ $4,000–4,400
⊞ ASH

A carved pine and gesso fire surround, c1880, 56in (143cm) wide.
£2,200–2,500
€/ $3,500–3,800 ⊞ WRe

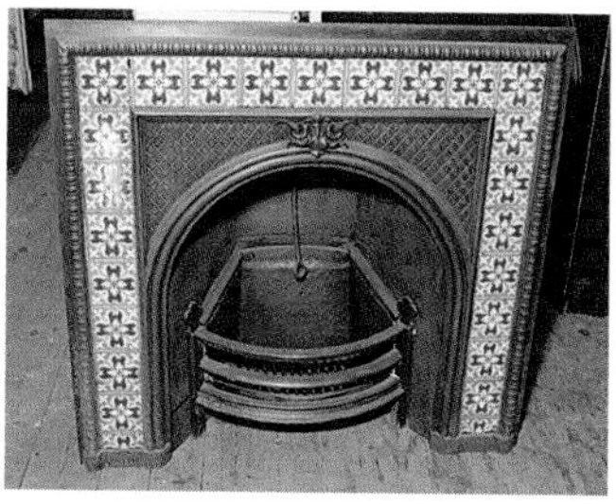

► **A cast-iron and tiled fire surround,** c1880, 40in (101.5cm) wide.
£1,200–1,300
€/ $1,900–2,000
⊞ WRe

A George III-style carved pine and gesso fire surround, 19thC, 56¼in (143cm) wide.
£1,000–1,200
€/ $1,600–1,900 S(O)

A fire surround, early 20thC, 72½in (184cm) wide.
£100–120
€/ $160–190 B(Ba)

A cast-iron hob register grate, early 19thC, 30in (76.5cm) wide.
£500–550
€/ $800–870 WRe

A Victorian cast-iron and tiled fire grate, the jambs decorated with white-glazed Minton tiles, 36in (91.5cm) wide.
£300–350
€/ $475–550 FHF

A Victorian painted wood and composition fire surround, with egg-and-dart decoration, the frieze centred with a mask, 84in (214.5cm) wide.
£2,200–2,500
€/ $3,500–4,000 B(Ch)

A cast-iron fire grate, early 19thC, 36in (91.5cm) wide.
£850–950
€/ $1,300–1,500 WRe

A cast-iron hob register grate, c1820, 32in (81.5cm) wide.
£550–600
€/ $870–950 WRe

A Victorian cast-iron and brass fire grate, late 19thC, 33in (84cm) wide.
£700–850
€/ $1,100–1,300 S(O)

A pine fire surround, Irish, c1880, 51in (129.5cm) wide.
£220–240
€/ $340–380 Byl

A cast-iron hob grate, early 19thC, 28in (71cm) wide.
£315–350
€/ $500–550 WRe

A silvered-brass fire grate, 19thC, 30½in (77.5cm) wide.
£2,400–2,800
€/ $3,800–4,400 WW

LOCATE THE SOURCE

The source of each illustration in Miller's can be found by checking the code letters below each caption with the Key to Illustrations, pages 794–800.

A polished steel fire grate, c1900, 21¾in (55.5cm) wide.
£850–1,000
€/ $1,300–1,600 S(O)

Fireplace Accessories

A pair of wrought-iron andirons, French, c1770, 30in (76.5cm) high.
£630–700
€/ $980–1,100 ⊞ SEA

A pair of Federal polished steel andirons, American, c1800, 23½in (69.5cm) wide.
£1,200–1,400
€/ $1,900–2,200 ⚒ JDJ

A set of mahogany and brass peat bellows, 19thC, 26½in (67.5cm) long.
£170–200
€/ $270–315 ⚒ SWO

A set of walnut, gilt and gesso fire bellows, with 17thC-style armorial decoration and scroll and scallop shell grips, 19thC, 25in (63.5cm) long.
£550–650
€/ $870–1,000 ⚒ G(B)

A walnut and brass coal scuttle, 1880–1900, 13¾in (35cm) high.
£130–150
€/ $200–240 ⚒ SWO

A Victorian *tôle peinte* coal scuttle, the hinged bucket with a *verre églomisé* shield, on a cast-metal base, 48in (122cm) high.
£320–380
€/ $500–600 ⚒ DN

◄ **A copper coal scuttle,** c1910, 18in (45.5cm) high.
£220–245
€/ $350–380 ⊞ WAC

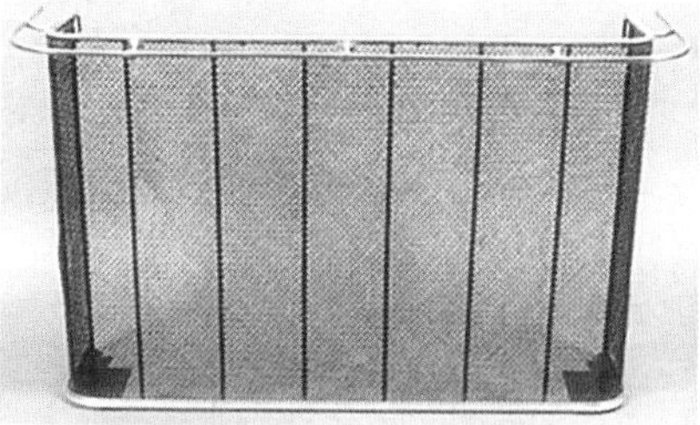

A brass and wire mesh nursery fender, with drying rail, early 19thC, 56¼in (143cm) wide.
£1,000–1,200
€/ $1,600–1,900 ⚒ HOK

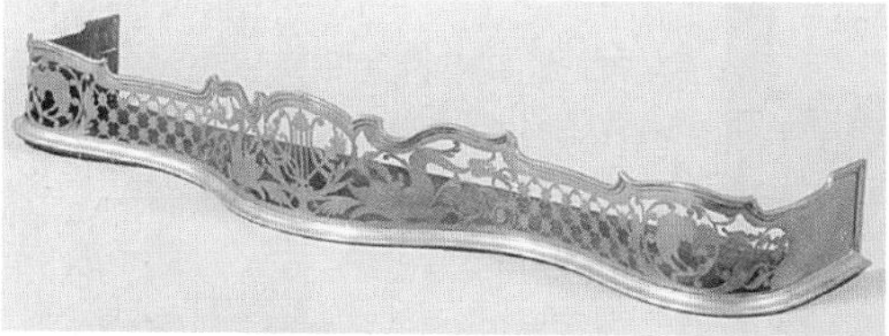

◄ **A George III brass fender,** 56¼in (143cm) wide.
£600–700
€/ $950–1,100 ⚒ S(O)

An armorial cast-iron fireback, 17thC, 19½in (49.5cm) high
£280–320
€/ $440–600 ⚒ F&C

► **A set of steel fire irons,** early 19thC, with associated handles, 29½in (75cm) long.
£770–920
€/ $1,200–1,500 ⚒ S(O)

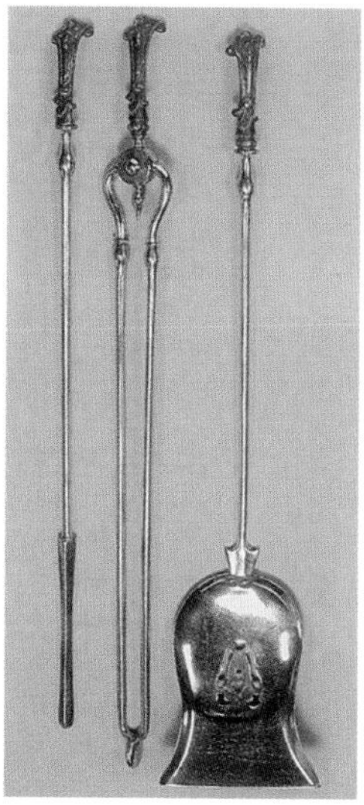

A cast-iron fender, early 19thC, 44in (112cm) wide.
£140–160
€/ $220–250 ⚒ L

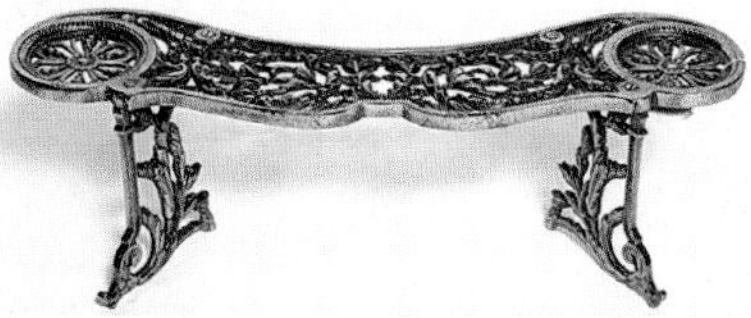

A Victorian cast-iron double trivet, 22in (56cm) wide.
£160–175
€/ $250–275 ⊞ RPh

Sculpture

An ivory group of the Virgin and Child, head of the Virgin replaced, losses, north German, c1230, 3in (7.5cm) high.
£1,500–1,800
€/ $2,400–2,800 S(NY)

An ivory statue of Mary Magdalene, holding an urn, a skull at her feet, on a felt plinth, Flemish, 17thC, statue 3½in (9cm) high.
£530–635
€/ $840–1,000 S(O)

A carved boxwood figure of Christ, 18thC, 18in (45.5cm) high.
£800–1,000
€/ $1,300–1,600 SWO

A limestone corbel head of a queen, modelled with flowing hair beneath a crown, French, 15thC, 6¾in (17cm) high.
£700–950
€/ $1,100–1,500 S

A carved boxwood head of a Doge, wearing a cape, north Italian, c1600, 6in (15cm) high.
£900–1,100
€/ $1,400–1,700 G(L)

A pair of bronze busts of Henry IV of Navarre and the Duc de Sully, Henry IV with curled hair and a beard and wearing a lace ruff and the order of the Saint Esprit, the other wearing a lace ruff and with a sash draped across his armour, on gilt-bronze and marble half columns, 18thC, 10¼in (26cm) high.
£800–1,000
€/ $1,300–1,600 B

An alabaster group of a reclining figure contemplating a skull, Italian, Naples, 17thC, 9in (23cm) wide.
£425–500
€/ $670–790 S(O)

An ivory figure of Ecco Homo, minor defects, Italian, 17thC, 6¾in (17cm) high.
£1,100–1,200
€/ $1,700–1,900 G&G

A terracotta figure of the Virgin and Child, attributed to Walter Pompe, 18thC, 22in (56cm) high.
£1,800–2,200
€/ $2,800–3,500 BERN

A limewood figure of a Roman soldier, with gilt and polychrome decoration, the head with curly hair, wearing a mantle over a cuirass, damaged, arms missing, south German, c1700, 17½in (44.5cm) high.
£900–1,000
€/ $1,400–1,600 S(Am)

An ivory figure of a gardener, resting while smoking his pipe, on an ivory plinth with allegorical masks, Austrian, early 19thC, 12½in (32cm) high.
£4,000–4,500
€/ $6,300–7,000 LBO

A parcel-gilt stained-terracotta figure of a priest with the Christ Child, French, early 19thC, 27½in (70cm) high.
£500–500
€/ $790–950 BERN

A pair of bronze figures of putti, one holding a sickle and a bunch of grapes, the other holding a sheaf of corn, on Siena marble bases, French, 19thC, 8½in (21.5cm) high.
£850–1,000
€/ $1,300–1,600 TEN

An alabaster group of a seated man holding the hand of a maiden, by E. Fiaschi, signed, Italian, 19thC, 33in (84cm) high.
£1,500–1,800
€/ $2,400–2,800 G(B)

A marble bust of a girl, by William Calder Marshall, ARA, signed, nose restored, dated 1849, 21¼in (54cm) high.
£1,200–1,300
€/ $1,900–2,100 S(O)

A patinated-bronze allegorical figure of a woman, 19thC, 11in (28cm) high.
£220–250
€/ $350–400 TMA

A marble bust of a woman, by Pietro Magni, signed, Italian, Milan, c1871, 29½in (75cm) high.
£2,200–2,500
€/ $3,500–4,000 S(NY)

A patinated-bronze group of a girl with a putto and young Bacchus, by Adrien Fourdrin, on a marble base, signed, stamped, dated 1854, 20½in (52cm) high.
£1,300–1,500
€/ $2,100–2,400 BERN

An ivory figure of St George slaying the Dragon, on a later oak base, 19thC, 6¾in (17cm) high.
£400–480
€/ $630–700 S(Am)

A marble figure of a young girl reading a book, signed 'Antonio Bartone', Italian, 19thC, 39in (99cm) high.
£25,000–28,000
€/ $40,000–44,000 CAT
This sculpture is of a good size and by a well-known maker.

A cast bronze figure of Edmund Burke, by J. H. Foley, RA, wearing 18thC costume, base inscribed 'Elkington & Co. Founders & J. H. Foley, RA, London', c1865, 20in (51cm) high.
£2,200–2,500
€/ $3,500–4,000 WL

A bronze figure of The Crouching Venus, after the Antique, on a marble plinth, 19thC, 11½in (29cm) high.
£750–875
€/ $1,200–1,400 Mit

A bronze figure of a gentleman, seated beside a vice, c1880, 15in (38cm) high.
£700–850
€/ $1,100–1,300 BWL

A carved and gilt American eagle, perched on a rocky outcrop, 19thC, 28in (71cm) wide.
£4,000–4,800
€/ $6,300–7,600 S(NY)

A terracotta group of two seated peasants, Italian, 19thC, 10¼in (26cm) high.
£280–320
€/ $440–500 BERN

A bronze figure of a woman, by Charles Veeck, French, 19thC, 11¾in (30cm) high.
£1,900–2,100
€/ $3,000–3,300 G&H

A model of bassett hounds, by Emmanuel Frerniet, entitled 'Ravageot et Ravagerote', c1880, 5½in (14cm) high.
£2,700–3,000
€/ $4,300–4,700 BHa

A Renaissance-style alabaster bust of Laura, by A. Parello, with gilt decoration, signed and titled, Italian, c1880, 20in (51cm) high.
£2,200–2,400
€/ $3,200–3,800 S(O)

A bronze figure of a woman holding a harp, by Georges Coudray, French, late 19thC, 17¼in (44cm) high.
£4,000–4,400
€/ $6,300–7,000 G&H

A carved marble bust of a maiden, by F. Junck, her hair in ringlets and a plait, with a floral bandeau, wearing a wrap-over dress, on an ebonized stepped base, carved signature, Continental, late 19thC, 15½in (39.5cm) high.
£500–600
€/ $790–950 RTo

A bronze figure of a mounted jockey, by J. Willis Good, on a marble base with presentation plaque dated 1884, signed and dated 1895, 12¼in (31cm) high.
£4,500–5,200
€/ $7,100–8,200 B(L)

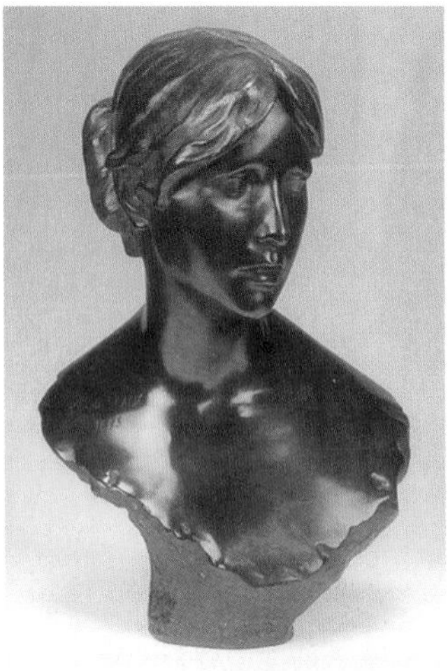

A bronze bust of a female, by Jef Lambeaux, signed and dated 1885, 19¾in (50cm) high.
£900–1,100
€/ $1,400–1,700 BERN

An alabaster bust of a woman, Italian School, socle missing, c1890, 19in (48.5cm) high.
£1,600–1,800
€/ $2,500–2,800 S(O)

A bronze group of two pointers, by Eglantine Lemaître, entitled 'Au Coup de Fusil', signed, foundry stamp, c1890, 17¼in (44cm) wide.
£3,000–3,400
€/ $4,700–5,400 SWO

A bronzed figure of a hound, gnawing a bone, signed 'H. Fouques 1895', 15in (38cm) high.
£500–575
€/ $790–900 L

A naïve carved and painted wood group of a bear and cub, late 19thC, 51¼in (130cm) high.
£1,600–1,800
€/ $2,500–2,800 S(O)

A bronze figure of a seated lady, wearing classical robes, on a low stool with a lyre, signed 'J. Pradier Susse fecit', on a marbleized wooden base, late 19thC, 10¼in (26cm) high.
£400–475
€/ $630–750 B&L

A bronze figure of a warrior, by Eugène Marioton, French, late 19thC, 14¼in (36cm) high.
£2,100–2,300
€/ $3,300–3,600 G&H

A bronze model of a whippet, after Pierre-Jules Mêne, signed, late 19thC, 6in (15cm) high.
£100–120
€/ $160–190 G(L)

A pair of bronze figures of Diana and Hermes, signed, late 19thC, 14¼in (36cm) high.
£1,500–1,800
€/ $2,400–2,800 BERN

A terracotta model of a pug dog, with curled tail and incised coat, collar and glass eyes, repaired, late 19thC, 12½in (32cm) high.
£700–850
€/ $1,100–1,300 B(W)

A pair of bronze figures of Mars and Minerva, on marble bases, Italian, 1875–1925, 12¼in (31cm) high.
£800–900
€/ $1,300–1,400 S(O)

A cold-painted bronze figure of a boy lying on the ground, wearing a fez, Austrian, late 19thC, 5¼in (13.5cm) long.
£500–580
€/ $790–920 RTo

A bronze group of a peasant couple in a sled pulled by horses, by Evgeny Alexandrovich Lanceray, signed, Shtange foundry stamp, Russian, late 19thC, 21in (53.5cm) wide.
£2,200–2,500
€/ $3,500–4,000 S(NY)

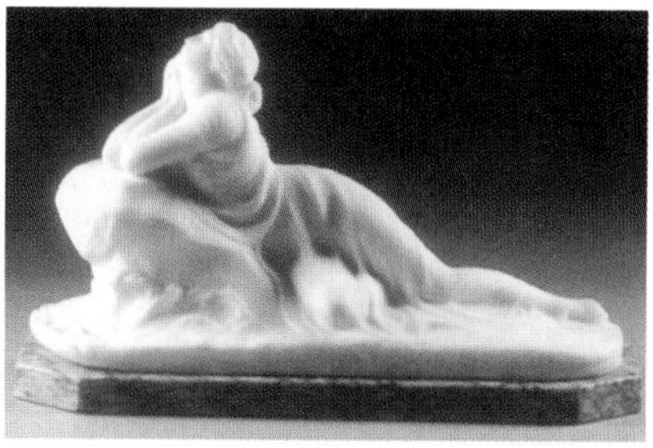

A marble figure of Ida, by Balleux, on a marble base, signed, French, late 19thC, 19¾in (50cm) wide.
£850–1,000
€/ $1,300–1,600 S(O)

A bronze group of two men racing a sail-assisted canoe, by Edouard Drouot, French, c1900, 24in (61cm) wide.
£1,300–1,500
€/ $2,100–2,400 RGa

A cold-painted bronze model of a kingfisher, stamped with Bergman seal, beak possibly bent, Austrian, c1900, 6½in (16.5cm) long.
£240–275
€/ $380–430 ⚒ G(L)

A zinc figure of a woman, stamped 'J. W. Fiske 99 Chambers St, New York', American, c1900, 51in (129.5cm) high.
£3,000–3,400
€/ $4,700–5,400 ⚒ S(NY)

A pair of painted bronze busts of Native Americans, by Franz Bergman, on ebonized plinth bases, impressed seal and numerals, Austrian, c1900, taller 8in (20.5cm) high.
£1,000–1,200
€/ $1,600–1,900 ⚒ S(O)

Paris was considered the home of sculpture in the 19th century and attracted sculptors from all over Europe and the USA. They studied, for the most part, at the Ecole des Beaux Arts and exhibited at the salons, which upheld strong classical traditions. Selected works were displayed at one of the prestigious annual salon exhibitions. As these were attended by important government and institutional purchasers, sculptors were dependent on the commissioning powers of these people for their economic survival. The salons therefore, exercised considerable control over artistic output, which resulted in works displaying a strong classical influence for most of the century.

A bronze bust of a Classical man, by Professor O. Poertzel, on a marble plinth, German, early 20thC, 10¾in (27.5cm) high.
£650–720
€/ $1,000–1,100 ⚒ S(O)

A model of birds sitting in the branch of a tree, by G. Rischmann, signed, German or Austrian, c1900, 11½in (29cm) high.
£850–950
€/ $1,300–1,500 ⊞ BeF

A marble figure of Cupid, by M. Pownall, examining a heart with a magnifying glass, other hearts scattered at his feet, on a naturalistic base, hand restored, signed and dated 1908, 10¾in (27.5cm) high.
£900–1,100
€/ $1,400–1,700 ⚒ B

A bronze figure of Rembrandt van Rijn, by Huib Luns, signed and inscribed, Dutch, early 20thC, 13¾in (35cm) high, with a framed etching of a copy of the drawing.
£800–900
€/ $1,300–1,400 ⚒ S(Am)

◄ A bronze group of Orpheus and Cerberus, by Charles Raoul Verlet, signed and inscribed 'F Barbedienne', underside stamped '/925', French, c1900, 32¼in (82cm) high.
£3,100–3,700
€/ $4,900–5,800 ⚒ B

An ivory and gilt-bronze bust of L'Amour, after the model by Agathon Léonard, inscribed, Paris, numbered 80, c1900, 9¼in (23.5cm) high.
£1,700–2,000
€/ $2,700–3,200 ⚒ Mit
Agathon Léonard (1841–1923) was the pseudonym for Van Weydeveld, a Belgiam artist who moved to France early in his career. He was made a *Chevalier of the Légion d'Honneur* in 1900.

A bronze group of a WWI soldier leading three horses, by Gilbert William Bayes, on a marble base, signed and dated 1915, 10¼in (26cm) wide.
£1,100–1,300
€/ $1,700–2,100 ⚒ S(O)

A bronze figure of a soldier, by Georges Colin, entitled 'Pour la Patrie', the soldier standing on a raft, using his rifle as a rudder, on an ebonized wood base, signed, early 20thC, 33½in (85cm) high.
£1,600–2,000
€/ $2,500–3,200 ⚒ S(Am)

Metalware

Brass

A brass bell, modelled as a pig, c1850, 7in (18cm) wide.
£1,200–1,300
€/ $1,900–2,000 ⊞ RGe

A brass and steel servant's bell, c1900, 8½in (21.5cm) diam.
£90–100
€/ $140–160 ⊞ Penn

A brass ash bucket, Dutch, c1780, 11in (28cm) high.
£525–575
€/ $830–900 ⊞ SEA

A pair of brass candlesticks, c1750, 8in (20.5cm) high.
£620–680
€/ $980–1,000 ⊞ SEA

► **A Victorian gilt-brass casket,** with applied pierced panels, the interior velvet lined, inscribed 'T. A Simpson & Co, 154 Regent St, W', with swing handles, 8¾in (22cm) wide.
£700–820
€/ $1,100–1,300 ⚒ WW

A pair of Regency gilt-metal candlesticks, on triform bases, with later drip pans, 10in (25.5cm) high.
£220–250
€/ $350–400 ⚒ B(Ba)

A Georgian brass coffee pot, with engraved crest, traces of silvering, fruit-wood handle, pseudo-hallmarks to rim, early 18thC, 10in (25.5cm) high.
£2,300–2,800
€/ $3,600–4,400 ⚒ S(O)
This coffee pot has a spout cast in two halves instead of being made in sheet metal.

◄ **A Victorian cast brass doorstop,** modelled as a pineapple, lead weighted, 13¾in (35cm) high.
£200–220
€/ $315–350 ⚒ WW

METALWARE

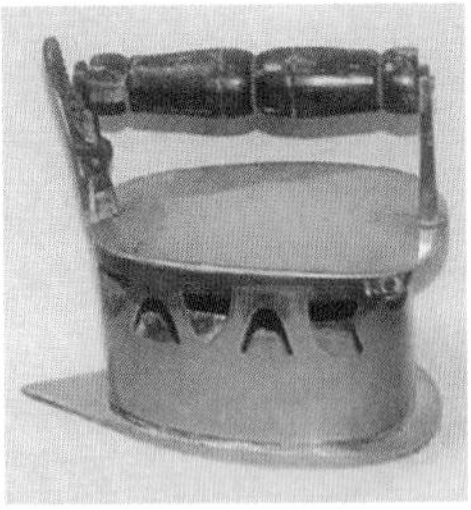

A brass iron, Dutch, 19thC, 8in (20.5cm) wide.
£70–80
€/ $110–130 DuM

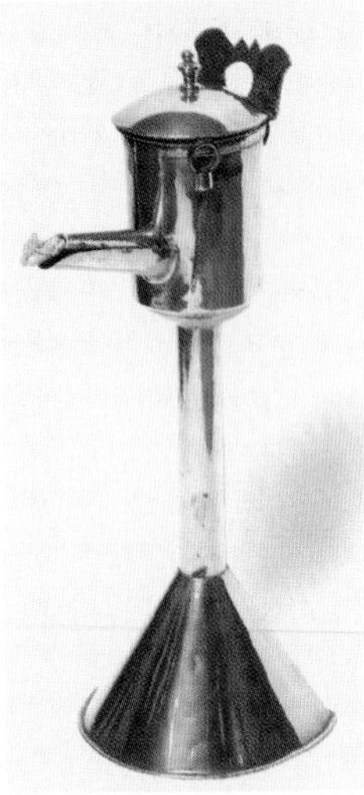

A brass kettle, Dutch, mid-18thC, 12in (30.5cm) high.
£230–255
€/ $360–400 SEA

◄ **A brass lamp,** Dutch, c1795, 13in (33cm) high.
£430–475
€/ $680–750 SEA

► **A brass vinaigrette,** the sides engraved with a hunting scene, the lift-off cover revealing an inner top pierced with the arms of Hanow, Prussian, early 17thC, 1¾in (4.5cm) high.
£1,100–1,200
€/ $1,600–1,900 S(O)

A set of gilt-brass and porcelain letter scales, by S. Mordan & Co, London, c1870, 8in (20.5cm) wide.
£530–630
€/ $840–980 S(O)

Bronze

A bronze rumbler bell, 18thC, 4in (10cm) diam.
£340–375
€/ $550–600 SEA
A rumbler bell is one that contains a small hard object which rattles, and was formerly often used on horses' harnesses.

A leather and gilt-bronze dress box, engraved with royal inscription and decorated with an escutcheon and applied cast bust of Prince Albert on the cover, c1850, 11½in (29cm) diam.
£1,000–1,200
€/ $1,600–1,900 S(O)
This box formerly belonged to H.R.H. Prince Albert.

◄ **A pair of Empire-style bronze and ormolu candlesticks,** the bowls of the campana nozzles cast with leaves above anthemion motifs, on ribbed columns, on three paw feet and bronze tripartite plinth, 19thC, 12¾in (32.5cm) high.
£650–750
€/ $1,000–1,200 CGC

A pair of gilt-bronze two-light candelabra, each foliate-decorated nozzle supported by similarly-decorated arms on a naturalistic base, French, early 19thC, 12½in (32cm) high.
£700–820
€/ $1,100–1,300 B(Nor)

A gilt-bronze Palais Royal four-piece desk stand, the taper inset with jasper and malachite cabochons, on ball feet, 19thC, 8¼in (21cm) wide.
£160–200
€/ $250–320 SWO

◄ **A pair of Renaissance-style patinated-bronze ewers,** with putto's head and serpent handles, cast with classical scenes of Venus and her attendants seated on two dolphins, the reverse with scrolls of birds, dogs and mythical beasts, on cast pedestals and marble circular bases, French, late 19thC, 19in (48.5cm) high.
£750–900
€/ $1,200–1,400 ⚒ B

A gilt-bronze and silvered inkstand, with twin-lidded wells and central glass open well, mid-19thC, 11¾in (30cm) wide.
£330–360
€/ $520–560 ⚒ S(O)

A bronze grisset, c1750, 12in (30.5cm) wide.
£1,800–2,000
€/ $2,800–3,200 ⊞ SEA

A gilt-bronze inkwell, with relief foliage, on griffon supports, the cover cast as two horses, mid-19thC, 9¾in (25cm) high.
£580–700
€/ $900–1,100 ⚒ S(O)

A pair of Regency gilt-bronze mantel lustres, the cast foliate urn nozzles with undulating drip pans and leafy collars hung with later cut-glass prism drops, on scrolling arms centred by a fruiting finial before a model of a greyhound, on a marble plinth, 11¾in (30cm) high.
£1,300–1,500
€/ $2,000–2,400 ⚒ B

A bronze mortar, bearing Charles I's coat-of-arms, c1640, 6in (15cm) high.
£1,800–2,000
€/ $2,800–3,200 ⊞ SEA

For further information on
Kitchenware see pages 220–223

► **A bronze skillet,** Dutch, 16thC, 4in (10cm) high.
£880–980
€/ $1,400–1,500 ⊞ SEA

A gilt-bronze vase and cover, by Pierre Jules Mêne, cast with hunting scenes, associated finial, French, c1849, 15in (38cm) high.
£400–480
€/ $630–750 ⚒ S(O)

A pair of gilt-bronze and patinated models of the Albani vase, each with a fruiting vine rim above a frieze of male masks, on a fluted foot and marble base on lion-paw feet, 19thC, 8¼in (21cm) high.
£2,800–3,200
€/ $4,400–5,000 ⚒ B

A pair of bronze vases, with foliate-decorated rims, one cast with cattle and a ploughing scene, the other with chariot and horse racing scenes, with copper liners, 19thC, 14¼in (36cm) high.
£700–850
€/ $1,100–1,300 ⚒ Bea

METALWARE

Copper

◄ **A copper chocolate pot,** c1850, 11in (28cm) high.
£400–440
€/ $630–700 ⊞ MFB

A copper and wrought-iron-mounted kettle, French, c1900, 24in (61cm) diam.
£435–520
€/ $690–790 ⚒ NOA

A copper two-handled fish kettle, with lid, stamped 'P-S', 19thC, 19in (48.5cm) long.
£70–85
€/ $110–135 ⚒ PFK

◄ **A copper 4-gallon measure,** c1875, 18in (45.5cm) high.
£250–280
€/ $400–440 ⊞ Byl

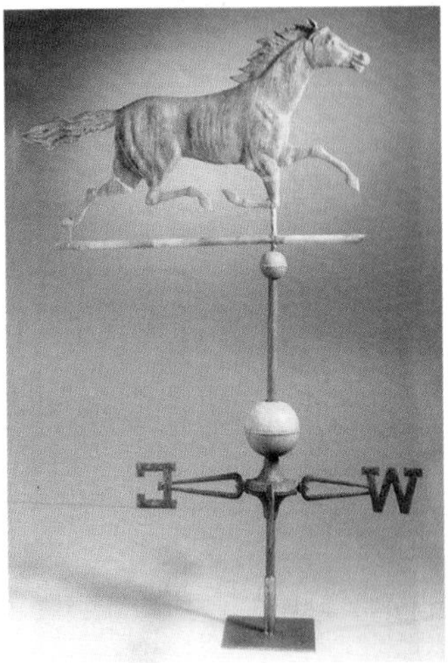

► **A copper weathervane,** the moulded horse on a double-sphere rod with directionals, American, probably New England, c1875, 65in (165cm) high.
£6,500–7,500
€/ $10,300–11,800 ⚒ S(NY)

Iron

A cast-iron bell, in the shape of a pig, with wind-up mechanism, c1860, 7in (18cm) wide.
£1,200–1,400
€/ $1,900–2,200 ⊞ RGe

► **A painted cast-iron offertory box,** c1850, 24in (61cm) high.
£1,600–2,000
€/ $2,500–3,200 ⊞ RYA
This poor house money box was designed to collect money for the needy. Offerings were inserted through the slots in the tower above the dome.

A wrought-iron candle holder and rush nip, c1750, 9in (23cm) high.
£430–480
€/ $680–750 ⊞ SEA

A cast-iron door stop, by Carron, Stirlingshire and Falkirk Foundries, modelled as the Scottish freedom fighter William Wallace, c1890, 13in (33cm) high.
£150–165
€/ $230–260 ⊞ RPh

A set of wrought-iron hanging hooks, Italian, c1770, 22in (56cm) long.
£1,200–1,400
€/ $1,900–2,200 ⊞ SEA

A pair of cast-iron mantel horses, polychrome painted, c1870, 10in (25.5cm) high.
£400–500
€/ $630–800 ⊞ RYA

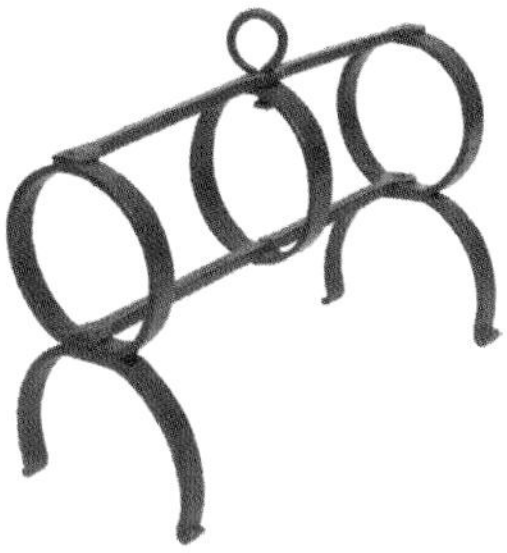

An iron pipe kiln, mid-19thC, 14in (35.5cm) long.
£315–350
€/ $500–550 ⊞ KEY

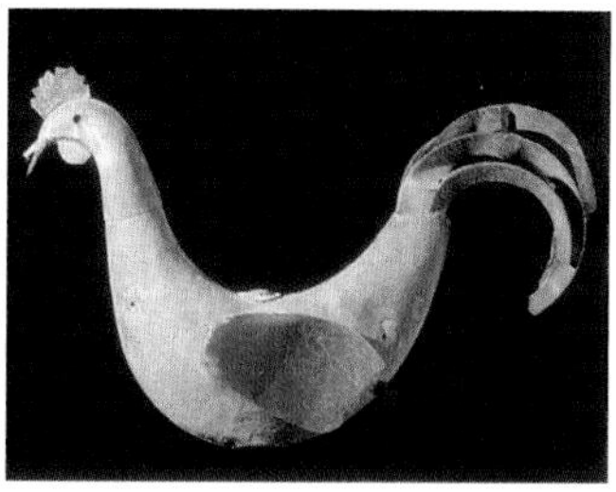

An iron and zinc weathercock, with traces of original paint, probably French, c1890, 35in (89cm) long.
£1,400–1,600
€/ $2,200–2,500 ⊞ RYA

Ormolu

An ormolu box, the centre inset with a painted portrait miniature, signed 'Theo', late 19thC, 4¼in (11cm) wide.
£500–580
€/ $790–920 ⚒ SWO

Two ormolu two-light candelabra, with leaf-and rosette-scrolled arms, tapered half-reeded columns, on anthemion-applied columns, on square bases, larger 13¼in (33.5cm) high.
£1,000–1,200
€/ $1,600–1,900 ⚒ DN

An ormolu, malachite and carnelian-mounted desk set, comprising an ink stand, pen wipe, taper stick and a pounce tazza, each engraved with foliate scrolls and set with cabochons, Russian, mid-19thC, ink stand 4in (10cm) long.
£4,000–4,800
€/ $6,300–7,600 ⚒ BR

Items in the Metalware section have been arranged in alphabetical order within each sub-section.

A late George III ormolu inkstand, in the style of Thomas Weeks, on a marble base, 5¾in (14.5cm) wide.
£700–820
€/ $1,100–1,300 ⚒ WW

► An Empire-style ormolu inkstand, the back gallery with central cartouche, fitted with two ink wells with hinged lids, French, 19thC, 9in (23cm) wide.
£200–240
€/ $315–380
⚒ BR

Pewter

◄ A pewter flask, with cover, stamped 'C. Hertzger', early 18thC, 10in (25.5cm) high.
£200–220
€/ $320–350
⊞ KEY

A pewter lamp, Dutch, 18thC, 11in (28cm) high.
£80–100
€/ $125–160 ⚒ DuM

A pewter *Hannukah* lamp, with lion finials supporting a flagon and a lamp, German, c1800, 7¾in (19.5cm) wide.
£1,500–1,800
€/ $2,400–2,800 ⚒ S(O)

A pewter quart measure, with brass rim, c1860, 6in (15cm) high.
£220–245
€/ $350–380 ⊞ MFB

A pewter pepper pot, c1850, 4¾in (12cm) high.
£45–50
€/ $70–80 ⊞ MFB

A pewter salt, c1870, 3in (7.5cm) diam.
£75–85
€/ $120–135 ⊞ SEA

◄ A glass and pewter scent bottle, c1900, 7in (18cm) high.
£75–85
€/ $120–135 ⊞ WAC

A silver-plated pewter tureen, by C. Saur, Stockholm, Swedish, c1776, 15¼in (39cm) wide.
£1,400–1,700
€/ $2,200–2,700 ⚒ BUK

Toleware

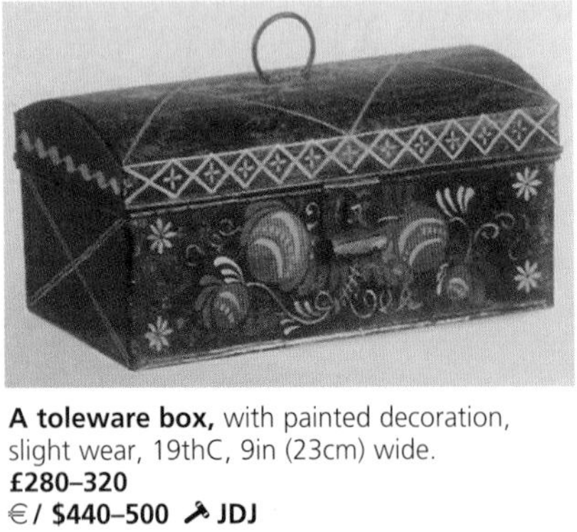

A toleware box, with painted decoration, slight wear, 19thC, 9in (23cm) wide.
£280–320
€/ $440–500 ⚒ JDJ

A toleware tobacco box, the hinged lid painted with a scene of soldiers returning from a defeated army, 19thC, 3in (7.5cm) wide.
£120–140
€/ $190–220 ⚒ TMA

An Edwardian japanned toleware smoker's companion, inscribed in gilt 'H & S 1804', and 'H & S 1904', 10in (25.5cm) high.
£380–450
€/ $600–710 ⚒ PF

A toleware tray, painted with a Georgian domestic scene, twin handles, early 19thC, 28½in (72.5cm) wide.
£550–650
€/ $870–1,000 ⚒ BIG

LOCATE THE SOURCE

The source of each illustration in Miller's can be found by checking the code letters below each caption with the Key to Illustrations, pages 794–800.

A pair of toleware vases, painted with scenes of everyday life and portraits, some damage, early 19thC, 8¾in (22.5cm) high.
£2,000–2,400
€/ $3,200–3,800 ⚒ S(P)

Miscellaneous

A lead tobacco box, with negro head finial, 19thC, 6¾in (17cm) wide.
£250–300
€/ $400–475 ⚒ SWO

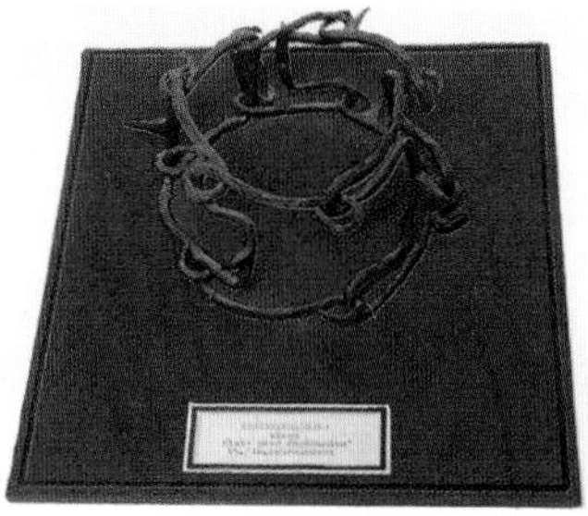

A metal dog collar, 15thC–16thC, 5in (12.5cm) diam.
£500–550
€/ $790–870 ⊞ GGv

◄ A Victorian gilt-metal canary cage, with ebonized finial, 24in (61cm) high.
£130–160
€/ $200–250 ⚒ DA

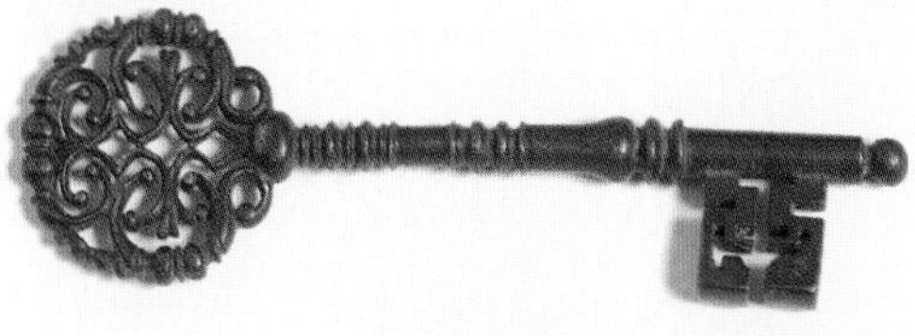

◄ A steel key, late 17thC, 5in (12.5cm) long.
£1,100–1,200
€/ $1,700–1,900 ⊞ KEY

A painted tin letter rack, c1850, 11in (28cm) wide.
£225–250
€/ $350–400 ⊞ SWN

► A Victorian gilt-metal paper clip, modelled as a greyhound's head with inset glass eyes, 19thC, 6in (15cm) long.
£280–340
€/ $440–520 ⚒ SWO

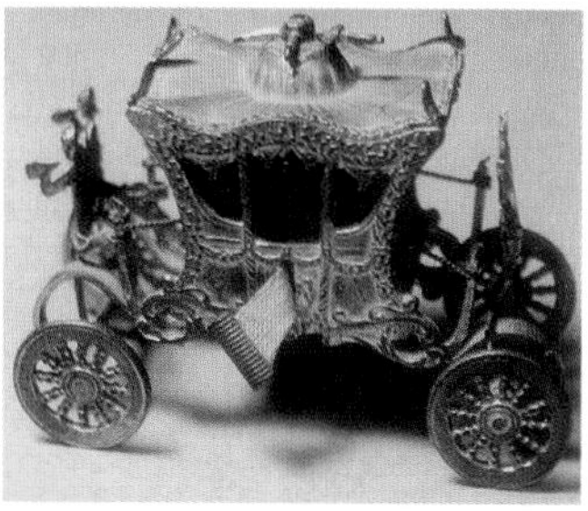

A gilt metal tape measure, in the form of a coronation coach, 19thC, 2in (5cm) high.
£130–150
€/ $200–240 ⚒ AMB

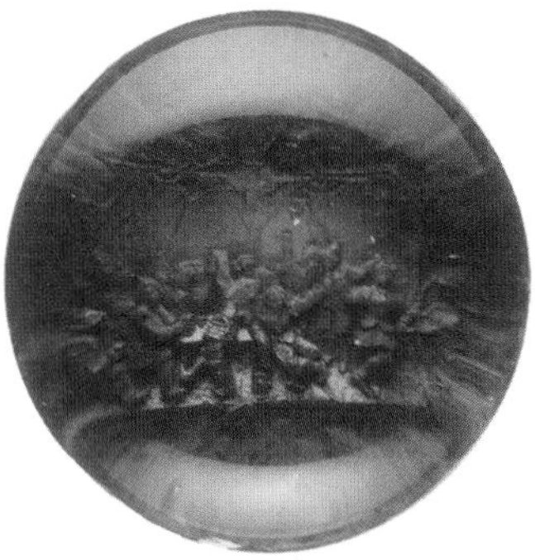

A pinchbeck paperweight, in high relief and gilding with soldiers carousing in a baronial hall, with blue-cloth covered base, mid-19thC, 3¼in (8cm) diam.
£850–1,000
€/ $1,300–1,600 ⚒ S(O)

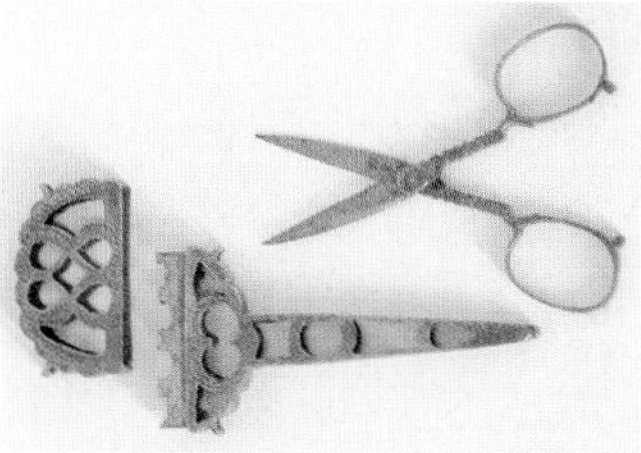

A pair of steel scissors, with engraved decoration, in a pierced engraved case, late 17thC, 3¼in (8.5cm) wide.
£480–550
€/ $760–870 ⚒ G(L)

► A patinated and cold-painted spelter vase, in the style of Louis Hottot, modelled as a reclining camel, French, c1880, 15¾in (40cm) high.
£900–1,100
€/ $1,400–1,800 ⚒ S(Am)
The French sculptor Louis Hottot (1829–1905) specialized in Oriental subjects.

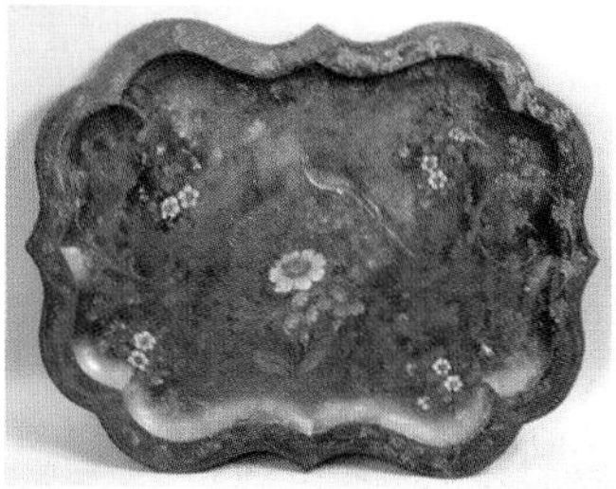

◄ A painted tin tray, worn, 19thC, 30¾in (78cm) wide.
£100–120
€/ $160–190 ⚒ SWO

METALWARE

Leather

A gilt-tooled leather Cumberland wrestling belt, stamped 'Newton Hero 1836', 54½in (138.5cm) long including the brass buckle.
£700–820
€/ $1,100–1,300 PFK

A leather box, Italian, 17thC, 10in (25.5cm) wide.
£850–950
€/ $1,300–1,500 SEA

A brass-studded leather chest, with a domed hinged top, c1740, 48¾in (124cm) wide.
£850–1,000
€/ $1,300–1,600 S(O)

A George IV painted leather fire bucket, with a swing handle, decorated with a crowned 'J.C.' cypher, 11½in (29cm) diam.
£75–90
€/ $120–140 G(L)

A gilt-tooled leather blotter, decorated with a Cardinal's coat-of-arms within floral patterned borders, the spine inscribed 'Pont Roma Pt III', Italian, 18thC, 17 x 12in (43 x 30.5cm).
£360–430
€/ $570–700 G(L)

A leather sewing box, decorated with panels of Dickensian scenes, each signed 'C. Schaub, London, June 4th 1873', 9in (23cm) wide.
£200–240
€/ $315–380 SWO

A brass-studded leather-covered chest, the domed top dated 1668 and initialled 'J.H.', 17thC, 42in (106.5cm) wide.
£1,300–1,500
€/ $2,000–2,400 CGC

A leather dog collar, 1890–1910, 6in (15cm) diam.
£85–95
€/ $135–150 GGv

An Edwardian leather letter holder, with embossed vine leaf decoration, 8in (20.5cm) wide.
£35–40
€/ $55–65 HO

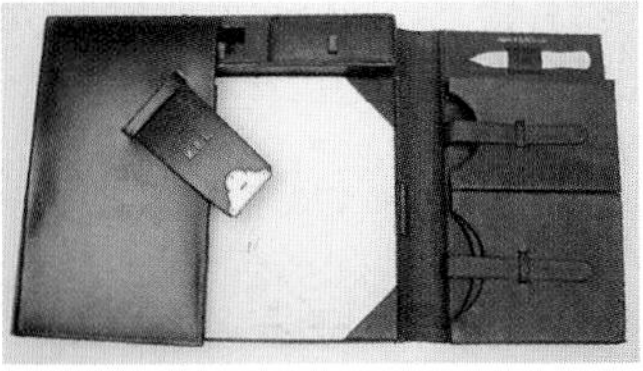

A leather blotter, by Asprey & Co, with a gilt metal lockplate, enclosing inkwells, ivory paper knife and stamp divisions, with key, 19thC, 9½ x 12in (24 x 30.5cm).
£220–250
€/ $350–400 G(L)

An embossed leather casket, with an iron hasp, interior restored, Spanish, 17thC, 19¾in (50cm) wide.
£380–420
€/ $600–650 S(O)

A Spanish-style brass-studded leather-upholstered trunk, with iron carrying handles, on runner feet, Spanish, c1900, 35in (89cm) wide.
£700–830
€/ $1,100–1,300 NOA

A leather and brass dog collar, French, late 19thC, 5¾in (14.5cm) diam.
£200–225
€/ $320–350 GGv

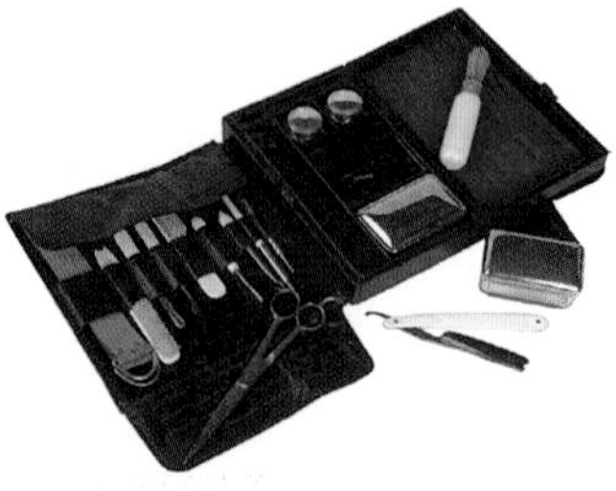

A leather writing and toiletry travel case, the locked flaps enclosing ivory handled tools, some contents replaced, stamped, late 19thC, 8½in (21.5cm) wide.
£135–150
€/ $215–240 ChC

Papier Mâché

A papier mâché box, by the Lukutin Manufactory, the lid painted with a landowner and serfs, early 19thC, 3¾in (9.5cm) diam.
£530–630
€/ $830–1,000 ⚒ S(O)

A papier mâché gaming box, parcel-gilt and inlaid with mother-of-pearl, the interior with four card-deck boxes and a games pieces box *en suite*, late 19thC, 14¼in (36cm) wide.
£500–570
€/ $800–900 ⚒ NOA

A papier mâché tray, by B. Walton & Co, stamped, 19thC, 26in (66cm) diam.
£280–320
€/ $440–500 ⚒ BWL

A Victorian papier mâché and mother-of-pearl inlaid tea caddy, by Lane of Birmingham, with two divisions, painted with floral decoration, 8in (20.5cm) wide.
£170–200
€/ $270–315 ⚒ G(B)

A Victorian papier mâché 'Question Box', the sides painted with figures by a cottage, 6½in (16.5cm) wide.
£180–220
€/ $285–350 ⚒ G(L)

A Regency papier mâché two-handled tray, by Clay, London, the border decorated in gilt with trailing leaves, flowers, moths and butterflies, applied with a pair of C-shaped ormolu handles, some warping and damage, 27½in (70cm) square.
£400–480
€/ $630–710 ⚒ BR

A papier mâché tray, painted in enamels with a floral bouquet, 19thC, 31in (78.5cm) wide.
£520–620
€/ $820–980 ⚒ BWL

A Victorian papier mâché tea caddy, with a hand-painted peacock and floral design, 9¾in (25cm) wide.
£400–480
€/ $630–710 ⚒ WilP

► **A pair of Regency papier mâché bottle stands,** gilt-decorated with shells and scrolling foliage, 5in (12.5cm) diam.
£280–320
€/ $440–500 ⚒ L&E

A papier mâché painted snuff box, by Stobwasser, the lid with a portrait of William IV, the reverse inscribed 'William IV King of Great Britain', damaged, 19thC, 4in (10cm) diam.
£500–600
€/ $800–950 ⚒ SWO

A papier mâché and lacquered tray, decorated with figures in a pagoda garden landscape, heightened with gilt, 19thC, 32in (81.5cm) wide.
£1,200–1,500
€/ $1,900–2,400 ⚒ Bea

A Victorian papier mâché tray, the centre painted with figures fishing in a mountainous landscape, within a gilt-heightened shell and foliate-decorated scalloped border, 21½in (54.5cm) wide.
£950–1,100
€/ $1,500–1,700 ⚒ RIT

Treen

A carved birchwood ale hen, with traces of original paint, Scandinavian, c1780, 8in (20.5cm) wide.
£650–800
€/ $1,000–1,300 ⊞ RYA

A carved oak book lectern, constructed from a single board and carved with fluted scrolls, petals and roundels, with a later heart-shaped metal hook nailed to the right hand edge, 17thC, 13in (33cm) wide.
£2,500–3,000
€/ $4,000–4,700 ⚒ TEN

An oak boot jack, 19thC, 39½in (100cm) high.
£140–160
€/ $220–250 ⚒ S(O)

An elm feeding bowl with handle, turned from one piece of wood, c1850, 9in (23cm) diam.
£170–200
€/ $270–320 ⊞ MFB

A dug-out birchwood ale bowl, Scandinavian, c1790, 18in (45.5cm) wide.
£650–800
€/ $1,000–1,300 ⊞ RYA

A Georgian oak book press, 13in (33cm) wide.
£320–360
€/ $500–570 ⊞ KEY

A turned elm bowl, c1780, 10in (25.5cm) diam.
£100–115
€/ $160–180 ⊞ F&F

A sycamore dairy bowl, c1880, 10in (25.5cm) diam.
£140–160
€/ $220–250 ⊞ SMI

► **A burr-elm box,** the lid carved in relief with portrait busts of Voltaire and Rousseau, interior slightly damaged, French, early 19thC, 3¼in (8.5cm) diam.
£400–450
€/ $630–700 ⚒ G(L)

A beech bird scarer, initialled TF, 19thC, 10in (25.5cm) wide.
£180–200
€/ $280–320 ⊞ SEA

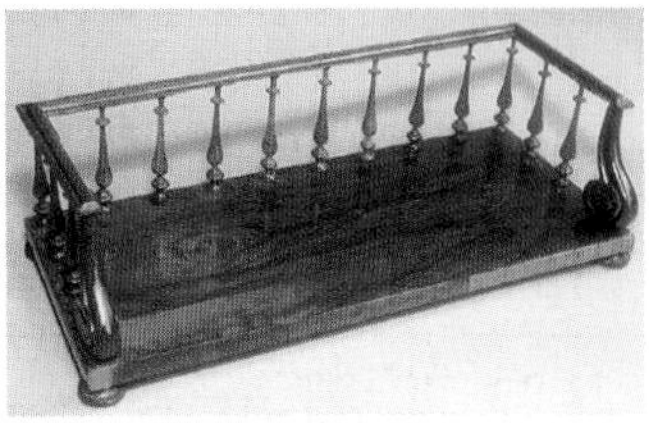

A Regency rosewood bookstand, the gallery with turned supports, on bun feet, 19¼in (49cm) wide.
£200–275
€/ $360–430 ⚒ AMB

A bowl, dug out from a root, Welsh, 18thC, 8in (20.5cm) high.
£500–550
€/ $800–880 ⊞ SEA

A painted and decorated maple bowl, with moulded rim, probably Shaker, American, 19thC, 24in (61cm) diam.
£3,000–3,300
€/ $4,700–5,200 ⚒ S(NY)

A George III oak candle box, 18in (45.5cm) high.
£300–350
€/ $475–550 ⊞ NoC

A *lignum vitae* candlestick, c1660, 12in (30.5cm) high.
£675–750
€/ $1,000–1,200
⊞ SEA

A carved mahogany and wrought-iron pricket candlestick, with bone ball feet, mid-19thC, 9in (23cm) high.
£260–300
€/ $410–475 ⚒ NOA
Pricket sticks were used to light gentlemen's after-dinner cigars.

A turned *lignum vitae* adjustable candelabrum, the campana-shaped holders on a bobbin- and reel-turned support, the screw stem on a circular base, damaged, 19thC, 16½in (42cm) high.
£160–200
€/ $250–315 ⚒ WW

Items in the Treen section have been arranged in alphabetical order.

A pair of Black Forest carved wood candlesticks, in the form of trees with acorns and leaves, each with a bird on the base, German, c1900, 7½in (19cm) high.
£170–200
€/ $270–315 ⚒ DMC

A pair of mahogany open barley-twist candlesticks, on turned bases, c1900, 14in (35.5cm) high.
£250–300
€/ $400–475 ⚒ SWO

A Continental carved and decorated pine centrepiece, holding carved apples, c1880, 6in (15cm) diam.
£230–270
€/ $360–430 ⊞ RYA

A mahogany, oak and inlaid cheese coaster, c1800, 16in (41cm) wide.
£350–400
€/ $550–630 ⚒ S(O)

A George III mahogany cheese cradle, the central ring-turned handle and parallel edges with reeded roundel terminals, 14½in (36.5cm) wide.
£650–780
€/ $1,000–1,200 ⚒ CGC

An elm costrel, c1790, 10in (25.5cm) wide.
£315–350
€/ $500–550 ⊞ SEA

A sycamore lace crimper and board, c1850, 6in (15cm) square.
£45–50
€/ $70–80 ⊞ SEA

► A walnut pedestal grater and cover, carved with leaves, early 19thC, 3in (7.5cm) high.
£80–100
€/ $125–160 ⚒ G(L)

A mahogany 'lazy susan', c1900, 21in (53cm) diam.
£220–250
€/ $350–400 ⚒ SWO

A carved bog oak letter opener, Irish, c1860, 10in (25.5cm) long.
£90–100
€/ $140–160 ⊞ STA

A boxwood nutcracker, 19thC, 5in (12.5cm) long.
£220–250
€/ $350–400 ⊞ SEA

A hand-carved wood photograph frame, dated 1932, 17in (43cm) wide.
£380–420
€/ $600–670 ⊞ WAC

A church warden's thorn pipe, 19thC, 11in (28cm) long.
£335–375
€/ $530–600 ⊞ SEA

An oak piggin, c1850, 18in (45.5cm) diam.
£315–350
€/ $500–550 ⊞ SEA

A birch pounce pot, c1790, 5in (12.5cm) high.
£420–460
€/ $660–720 ⊞ SEA

A laburnum pounce pot, c1800, 5in (12.5cm) high.
£425–475
€/ $670–750 ⊞ SEA

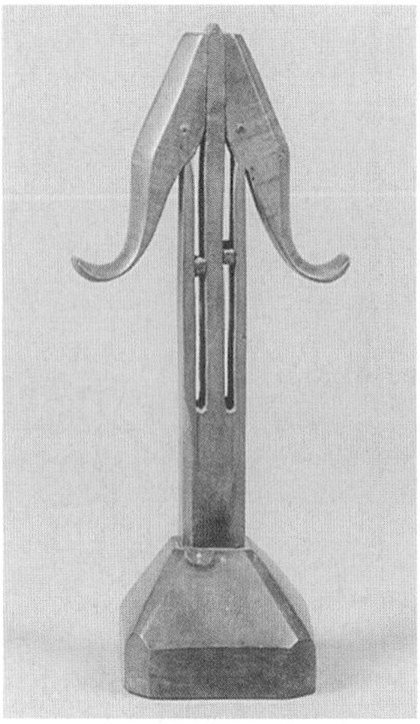

A sycamore rushlight, with twin wood nips, late 19thC, 14¼in (36cm) high.
£240–280
€/ $380–440 ⚒ S(O)

◄ A walnut mould, in the form of a rabbit, late 19thC, 19in (48.5cm) high.
£900–1,000
€/ $1,400–1,600
⊞ ChC
This mould was used to make a papier mâché model of a rabbit. The papier mâché was built up around the mould and then cut off to make the model.

A pitch pine salt, Scottish, c1820, 4in (10cm) high.
£350–400
€/ $550–630 ⊞ SEA

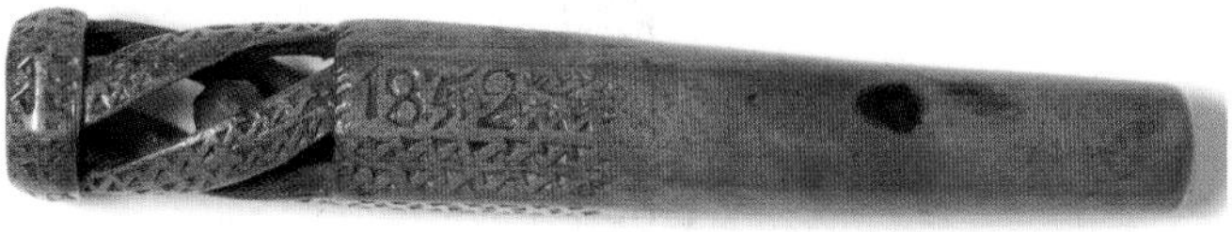

A child's carved maple rattle, dated 1852, 6in (15cm) long.
£700–775
€/ $1,100–1,200 ⊞ SEA

A sycamore snuff box, in the form of a frog, c1800, 5¼in (13.5cm) long.
£530–630
€/ $850–1,000 ⚒ S(O)

◄ A carved love spoon, Welsh, early 19thC, 12in (30.5cm) long.
£1,000–1,200
€/ $1,600–1,900 ⊞ SEA

A carved burr-birchwood peg tankard, Norwegian, c1780, 12in (30.5cm) high.
£900–1,000
€/ $1,400–1,700 ⊞ RYA

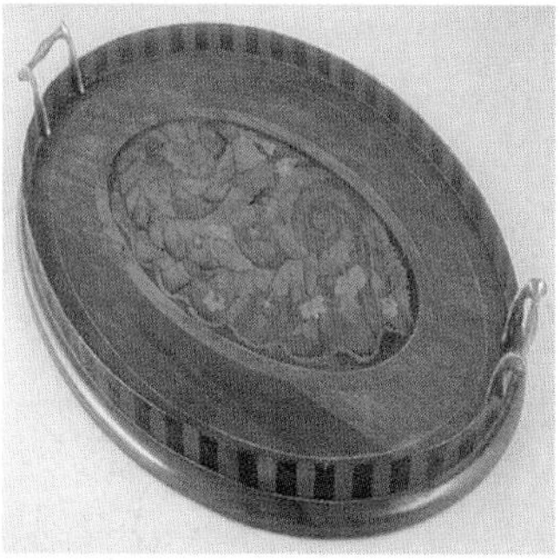

An Edwardian mahogany drinks tray, with two open brass handles, inlaid with a marquetry shell with foliage and stringing, 22¾in (58cm) wide.
£160–200
€/ $250–315 ⚒ WW

► A carved olivewood flared-footed vase, Italian, early 19thC, 19in (48.5cm) high.
£900–1,100
€/ $1,400–1,700
⚒ NOA

◄ A turned mahogany wig or bonnet stand, c1820, 14in (35.5cm) high.
£80–90
€/ $125–140
⊞ F&F

A mahogany snuff shoe, with brass inlay and hinged cover, dated 1870, 4in (10cm) long.
£420–500
€/ $660–790 ⚒ BWL

A sycamore tazza, c1780, 7in (18cm) diam.
£450–500
€/ $700–800 ⊞ SEA

An Edwardian mahogany tray, with shaped gallery and brass handles, inlaid with marquetry, 25¾in (65.5cm) wide.
£160–200
€/ $250–315 ⚒ SWO

Further reading

Miller's Antiques Under £1000, Miller's Publications, 2003

A fruitwood snuff box, in the form of a butterfly, the cover with mother-of-pearl and ebonized inlay, c1900, 4in (10cm) wide.
£1,300–1,500
€/ $2,000–2,400 ⚒ S(O)

A pearwood tea caddy, with iron hinge and escutcheon, traces of foil lining and blush decoration, c1800, 6½in (16.5cm) high.
£4,200–5,000
€/ $6,600–7,900 ⚒ GH

A carved birch vessel, with a copper rim, Baltic or Norwegian, early 19thC, 13½in (34cm) diam.
£380–420
€/ $600–660 ⚒ S(O)
This vessel may have been a boat baler.

An oak and beech wool winder and counter, c1660, 24in (61cm) high.
£450–500
€/ $700–800 ⊞ SEA

Tunbridge Ware

A Victorian Tunbridge ware rosewood book rack, decorated with two views of a castle, 13in (33cm) long.
£170–200
€/ $270–315 ⚒ G(L)

A Tunbridge ware box, by H. Hollamby, decorated with a view of the Pantiles, Tunbridge Wells, c1880, 9½in (24cm) wide.
£2,000–2,300
€/ $3,200–3,600 ⊞ PGO

A Victorian Tunbridge ware-banded walnut jewellery box, 11¾in (30cm) wide.
£240–280
€/ $380–440 ⚒ WilP

To order Miller's books in the USA please ring AOL/Time Warner on 1-800-759-0190

A Regency Tunbridge ware white-wood work box, decorated with a coloured engraving of Upton Cottage near Broadstairs, on a simulated rose-wood ground with dog's tooth cross-banding, some repair, 4¼in (11cm) wide.
£150–175
€/ $240–275 ⚒ BR

A Tunbridge ware box, the hinged lid decorated with a central panel of figures before a tower, some wear, early 19thC, 6¼in (16cm) high.
£200–220
€/ $315–350 ⚒ SWO

A Tunbridge ware burr-walnut glove box, the cover with a tesserae panel flanked by lozenges, 19thC, 8¾in (22cm) long.
£170–200
€/ $270–320 ⚒ BR

A Tunbridge ware coromandel cotton reel box, the lid with a tesserae bouquet within geometric crossbanding, the sides with running rose banding, enclosing a removable stand with five brass reel pins, 19thC, 6½in (16.5cm) long.
£420–500
€/ $670–800 ⚒ BR

A lady's Tunbridge ware writing box, decorated with a view of Tonbridge Castle, c1875, 11in (28cm) wide.
£1,300–1,500
€/ $2,100–2,400 ⊞ HAA

► **A Tunbridge ware rosewood magnifying glass,** 19thC, 6in (15cm) long.
£350–420
€/ $550–660 ⚒ TMA

A Tunbridge ware box, with floral mosaic decoration, c1810, 4in (10cm) wide.
£100–110
€/ $160–175 ⊞ AMH

A Tunbridge ware rosewood box, with mosaic inlay, 19thC, 3½in (9cm) wide.
£70–80
€/ $110–125 ⊞ MB

A Tunbridge ware maple stationery box, by Henry Hollamby, the top with a tesserae rose spray within tesserae crossbanding, the sides with a rose and scroll border, maker's paper label to underside, with key, 19thC, 6¼in (16cm) wide.
£700–820
€/ $1,100–1,300 ⚒ BR

A Tunbridge ware desk stand, with three lidded compartments and a cut-glass bottle, applied label of Edmund Nye, Tunbridge Wells, 19thC, 11¾in (30cm) wide.
£230–275
€/ $360–430 ⚒ SWO

A Tunbridge ware picture, restored, 1810–80, 9¼ x 7¼in (23.5 x 18.5cm).
£1,300–1,500
€/ $2,100–2,400 ⊞ PGO

► A Tunbridge ware rosewood and stickware-inlaid pin dish, c1840, 4in (10cm) diam.
£65–70
€/ $100–110 ⊞ MB

A Tunbridge ware whitewood sewing clamp, the body painted with stylized leaves and printed with a view of Brighton Pavilion, early 19thC, 7½in (19cm) high.
£320–380
€/ $500–600 BR

A Tunbridge ware picture, attributed to Henry Hollamby, depicting a view of The Pantiles, in a tesserae frame, 19thC, 7 x 9in (18 x 23cm).
£600–700
€/ $950–1,100 BR

A Tunbridge ware pin cushion, with one drawer, mid-19thC, 8in (20.5cm) wide.
£530–585
€/ $830–930 ⊞ PGO

A Tunbridge ware sovereign holder, in the shape of a ball, c1860, 1¾in (4.5cm) diam.
£300–350
€/ $475–550 VB

◄ A Tunbridge ware tea caddy, c1880, 8½in (21.5cm) wide.
£440–485
€/ $700–770 ⊞ PrB

A Tunbridge ware rosewood wine table, possibly by Wise, the top with marble, half square and Van Dyke borders, damage, 1840–50, 20in (51cm) square.
£2,000–2,400
€/ $3,200–3,800 BR

► A Tunbridge ware rosewood combination thermometer stand and compass, the ivory scale signed 'H. Hollamby, Tunbridge Wells', between two tesserae-banded sides, late 19thC, 5in (12.5cm) high.
£475–565
€/ $750–900 BR

A Victorian Tunbridge ware desk thermometer, by H. Hollamby, Tunbridge Wells, supported by two columns on a base, 5in (12.5cm) high.
£200–220
€/ $315–350 WW

Boxes

The popularity of antique boxes has risen steadily over the past 25 years, and prices therefore have been affected rather dramatically. Without doubt the largest increases have occurred in tea caddies, especially tortoiseshell, ivory and turned fruit-shaped examples. English and Continental finely painted caddies have also proved to be favourites. However, stationery boxes, games compendiums, sewing/work boxes, snuff boxes and stamp boxes have also seen significant rises in value. These have the additional benefit that they can still be used for their original intended purpose.

While we do not doubt that antique boxes will remain popular, prospective buyers should be aware of the possible pitfalls of purchasing such items. One should look out for outright fakes, badly or over-restored boxes as well as altered or adorned pieces.

The fake caddy in particular has become prolific and can be found at auctions, fairs and unfortunately, even vetted shows. Currently there are a number of Dutch-style tortoiseshell caddies in circulation which are actually made of plastic tortoiseshell veneered onto a plywood carcass. They have no lock or escutcheon and the interior is lined with modern baize. We have seen such examples on dealers' stands dated as c1850 as well as offered at auction. Other commonly faked caddies include inlaid oval and octagonal examples in the George III style and various fruitwood pieces, particularly the melon-shaped. A slightly more clever deception is the making of a tortoiseshell-embossed caddy using panels of an embossed tortoiseshell visiting card case which have been veneered onto the front of the carcass of the caddy. Genuine examples of this type always have embossed panels on all four sides.

Poor restoration is certainly not acceptable. Antique boxes that have been stripped and repolished have the least chance of a return on one's investment. All too often the trade papers read 'this box would have fetched considerably more if it had not been badly or over restored.'

The market for antique boxes is still strong. Americans and Europeans alike appreciate the value of good quality antique boxes and are always keen buyers. We feel that in the short term price increases will probably be smaller than in the past ten years. However, while one should never advocate the buying of antiques purely for investment, the fact is that if one buys well, bearing in mind the salient points mentioned here then a return to some extent should be expected.

Alan and Kathy Stacey

A chinoiserie lacquer lace box, c1700, 21in (53.5cm) wide.
£950–1,100
€/ $1,500–1,800 ⊞ TWh

A mahogany tea caddy, fitted with three lidded containers, c1770, 9in (23cm) wide.
£700–750
€/ $1,100–1,200 ⊞ AKS

A mahogany tea caddy, the top with barber's pole inlay, the interior with three sections, lock missing, some faults, c1780, 10¼in (26cm) wide.
£400–475
€/ $630–750 ⚒ BR

The Robert Harman Collection

The Robert Harman Collection of tea caddies was sold at Sotheby's London in November 1999. Comprising some 40 lots, this collection offered a wide and varied selection, including some rare examples.

Arguably the tour de force was a George III marquetry caddy, the front panel of which was modelled with an architectural view of a house façade. This sold for £28,750 (€/ $45,000), although the highest price achieved was approximately £34,500 (€/ $55,000) for a Regency ivory, tortoiseshell and polychrome japanned caddy. A wonderful pair of George III painted caddies, in the manner of Henry Clay, and in good original condition, sold for £21,850 (€/ $35,000).

Many of the more standard offerings sold above market value, aided no doubt by the added attraction of being offered in a collection. There was a handful of unsold lots, including an attractive ivory and gold-mounted decagonal caddy, c1790. This possibly failed because of the high reserve and severe cracking to some of its ivory panels.

The long-term investment on many of these caddies will be positive, with the added benefit of owning such beautiful objects.

Alan Stacey

A George III mahogany knife box, outlined with holly stringing, the divided interior inlaid with ebony and boxwood, 9in (23cm) wide.
£1,100–1,300
€/ $1,700–2,000 ⊞ JC

A mahogany tea caddy, the top with bail handle attached to a silver-plated back plate engraved with a battle scene and inscribed 'Gibraltar Sept. 13th 1782', the escutcheon similarly engraved, the interior previously fitted with three sections, 18thC, 10in (25.5cm) wide.
£250–300
€/ $400–480 ⚒ M

The plate and escutcheon engravings commemorate the last attack of the Great Siege of Gibraltar by the Combined Fleet of France and Spain on 13 September 1782.

An inlaid mahogany and fruitwood-edged tea caddy, c1800, 7in (18cm) wide.
£270–300
€/ $430–470 ⊞ MB

An ivory box, the top inset with a silhouette, c1790, 4in (10cm) wide.
£1,600–1,800
€/ $2,500–3,000 ⊞ SHa

A tortoiseshell miniature travel writing set, decorated with silver piqué, c1800, 1½in (4cm) high.
£1,100–1,200
€/ $1,700–1,900 ⊞ HAA

► A stained straw-work box, decorated with figures in relief, c1800, 2¼in (5.5cm) diam.
£230–270
€/ $360–430 ⚒ G(L)

A harewood tea caddy, with floral marquetry, c1790, 4½in (11.5cm) high.
£1,400–1,600
€/ $2,200–2,600 ⊞ HAA

A sycamore and marquetry-inlaid jewellery box, German, c1800, 6¾in (17cm) wide.
£80–100
€/ $125–150 ⚒ BR

A George III mahogany crossbanded tea caddy, inlaid with stars, the interior now with three lidded containers, 10in (25.5cm) wide.
£275–325
€/ $435–520 L

A Regency rosewood tea caddy, with four canisters, a bowl and later spoons, 17in (43cm) wide.
£2,200–2,500
€/ $3,500–4,200 ⊞ Penn

A Mauchline and penwork tea caddy, the top with a scene of Loch Lomond, the interior with two canisters, Scottish, early 19thC, 9¾in (25cm) wide.
£700–820
€/ $1,100–1,300 B(Ed)

A Regency mahogany tea caddy, inlaid with satinwood and rosewood, the interior with a bowl and two lidded compartments, 13in (33cm) wide.
£600–700
€/ $950–1,100 B(L)

A painted and incised compass-drawn box, American, Pennsylvania, early 19thC, 7in (18cm) wide.
£5,000–5,500
€/ $8,000–8,700 S(NY)

◄ **A Regency penwork and fruitwood desk box,** the interior lined with marbelized Florentine papers, 12½in (32cm) wide.
£620–700
€/ $980–1,100 NOA

A Regency ebony-banded rosewood tea caddy, with two lidded canisters and a glass bowl, 14in (35.5cm) wide.
£320–375
€/ $500–600 AH

► **A Regency penwork tea caddy,** decorated with chinoiserie scenes within vine borders, 8¼in (21cm) wide.
£800–900
€/ $1,300–1,400
S(O)

◄ **A rosewood tea caddy,** on brass ball feet, c1820, 8in (20.5cm) wide.
£220–250
€/ $350–400
⊞ MB

► **A tortoiseshell tea caddy,** with mother-of-pearl appliqué decoration, c1820, 6½in (16.5cm) high.
£3,800–4,200
€/ $6,000–6,600
⊞ HAA

BOXES

An oyster-veneered yew wood box, the lift-out four-division tray possibly associated, c1820, 13in (33cm) wide.
£1,300–1,500
€ / $2,000–2,400 S(O)

◀ **A tortoiseshell box,** the lid inset with an ivory-mounted bronze portrait of Peter the Great, c1820, 2½in (6.5cm) diam.
£180–200
€ / $285–340 MB

A George IV mahogany and brass-bound box, the lid engraved with a crest, the lock stamped 'Bramah Piccadilly', 12in (30.5cm) wide.
£800–900
€ / $1,300–1,400 S(O)

A Regency tortoiseshell tea caddy, with ivory banding and pewter stringing, c1825, 5in (13cm) wide.
£3,600–4,000
€ / $5,700–6,300 AKS

A rosewood inlaid work box, with a named cartouche to the inside of the lid 'Maria Borgen', c1825, 12in (30.5cm) wide.
£340–380
€ / $540–600 STA

▶ **A Mauchline snuff box,** the lid painted with a scene entitled 'The Blessing', the sides and base painted with a tartan pattern, Scottish, early 19thC, 3½in (9cm) wide.
£320–400
€ / $500–600 B(Ed)

A sycamore and penwork tea caddy, Belgian, c1830, 4½in (11.5cm) wide.
£1,800–2,000
€/ $2,800–3,400 ⊞ AKS

A burr-walnut writing box, with brass fretwork, c1850, 10in (25.5cm) wide.
£270–300
€/ $425–475 ⊞ MB

A gilt-brass-mounted burrwood jewel casket, by Halstaff & Hannaford, London, with velvet-lined fitted interior, the fall-front reveals a spring-action jewel drawer and a secret morocco-upholstered slide, 1850–75, 12¾in (32.5cm) wide.
£1,300–1,500
€/ $2,100–2,400 ⚒ NOA

A marquetry-inlaid kingwood and holly wood jewel casket, lined with satin, 1850–75, 12in (30.5cm) wide.
£900–1,000
€/ $1,400–1,700 ⚒ NOA

► **An olivewood stationery box,** 19thC, 9in (23cm) wide.
£380–450
€/ $600–700 ⚒ WilP

A William IV rosewood and brass-inlaid tea caddy, with fitted interior, 14¾in (37.5cm) wide.
£400–475
€/ $630–750 ⚒ SWO

A Victorian figured-walnut writing slope, the lid with inscribed silver plaque enclosing boxwood compartments behind a removable rosewood-veneered dipped pen tray and two ink bottles, the original hide-covered writing surface above a bird's-eye maple-lined compartment and a side drawer, 18¾in (47.5cm) wide.
£1,200–1,300
€/ $1,800–2,000 ⊞ JC

► **A tea caddy,** with ivory-faced interior and translucent top, Dutch, c1850, 4½in (11.5cm) wide.
£1,600–1,800
€/ $2,500–2,800 ⊞ AKS

A William IV mahogany tea caddy, with fitted interior, 16in (40.5cm) wide.
£250–300
€/ $400–475 ⚒ TMA

A silver-mounted ivory *aide memoire*, c1850, 5in (12.5cm) wide.
£80–90
€/ $125–140 ⊞ MB

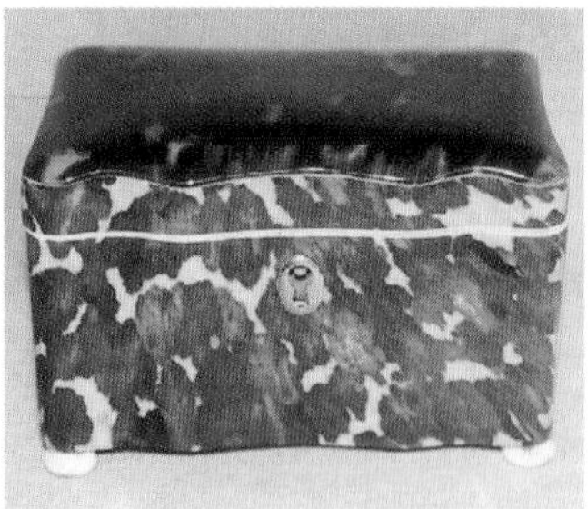

Tortoiseshell boxes

Check for the following faults when buying tortoiseshell tea caddies and boxes:

- the presence of plastic filler used for repair (often coloured, so check carefully) at the extremities, eg pagoda corners, plinths, etc.
- poorly-cut-in patches of tortoiseshell on damaged areas.
- damage around the hinge area, both on the tortoiseshell and on the inner ivory edgings.
- missing or incorrect feet, escutcheons, cartouches, finials and interior knobs.
- orange-peel effect on the shell caused by French polishing, lacquering or incorrect burnishing.
- excessive carcass movement with particular regard to 'smiling' (when the lid does not fit close to the base).
- the caddy is either brand new or reveneered onto an old wooden carcass.

A buyer may still decide to purchase a box with some of these faults evident but damage or restoration should be reflected in the price.

An ivory trinket box, the lid carved with lions, 19thC, 4¾in (12cm) wide.
£180–220
€/ $285–350 ⚒ WilP

A mother-of-pearl jewellery box, with ivory edging and silver feet, c1860, 5in (12.5cm) wide.
£330–370
€/ $520–620 ⊞ AKS

A shell-decorated box, c1860, 7in (18cm) wide.
£175–200
€/ $280–340 ⊞ F&F

A horn snuff box, French, 19thC, 5in (12.5cm) wide.
£315–350
€/ $500–550 ⊞ SEA

An arbutus wood box, inlaid with a view of Muckross Abbey, Killarney, Irish, c1866, 9in (23cm) square.
£350–400
€/ $550–630 ⊞ STA

A brass-banded olivewood box, c1870, 10in (25.5cm) wide.
£215–235
€/ $340–370 ⊞ MB

An ebonized letter box, inlaid with mother-of-pearl and tulipwood, with rosewood fitted interior, French, c1870, 16in (40.5cm) wide.
£900–1,000
€/ $1,400–1,700 ⊞ MB

A burr-holly wood writing slope, inlaid with mother-of-pearl, nickel silver, malachite, agate and marble, Austrian, c1870, 13in (33cm) wide.
£320–350
€/ $500–550 ⊞ MB

A Victorian brass-banded oak scent casket, bottles damaged, French, c1870, 8in (20.5cm) wide.
£270–300
€/ $425–450 ⊞ MB

An Imperial lacquer box, by Vichnaikov, Russian, c1880, 6¼in (16cm) wide.
£585–650
€/ $920–1,000 ⊞ SHa

A micro-mosaic and ormolu jewel case, the lid and sides inset with scenes of Rome, with buttoned silk interior, Italian, 19thC, 5in (12.5cm) wide.
£3,800–4,500
€/ $6,000–7,200 ⚒ TRM

Age & patina

Wooden tea caddies and boxes often suffer from the over-zealous use of paint stripper and wire wool. In a few short minutes hundreds of years of age are wiped away, together with a high percentage of the value of the piece. Any box that has been subject to this treatment must be avoided. Only buy boxes with good original patination. This will enhance the object's beauty, integrity and value.

A lacquer dressing table box, the lid hand-painted with a courting couple, small cracks, late 19thC, 4in (10cm) diam.
£160–200
€/ $250–300 ⚒ SWO

A tortoiseshell and silver casket, by G.F., with embossed mounts of lion's masks, putti and flowers, 1901, 7½in (19cm) wide.
£1,700–2,000
€/ $2,700–3,200 ⚒ L

A Victorian mother-of-pearl tea caddy, with two interior lidded compartments, 5½in (14cm) wide.
£400–480
€/ $630–750 ⚒ BWL

A Victorian figured-walnut and rosewood writing/work box, with fitted lift-out tray, the front opens to form a slope with two velvet-lined flaps enclosing compartments, 12in (30.5cm) wide.
£240–275
€/ $380–440 ⚒ PF

A pietra dura and ebony jewellery box, inset with a hardstone panel depicting a flower, Italian, late 19thC, 10in (25.5cm) wide.
£380–450
€/ $600–720 ⚒ BR

A Victorian rosewood and mother-of-pearl inlaid tea caddy, with fitted interior, 14½in (37cm) wide.
£320–400
€/ $500–630 ⚒ DMC

A Victorian tortoiseshell manicure set, with six unmarked silver fittings, damaged, 6½in (16.5cm) wide.
£200–240
€/ $320–380 ⚒ IM

A late Victorian stained and carved wood letter box, the fall-front with pierced aperture and inscribed 'Letters', minor damage, 11¾in (30cm) wide.
£200–220
€/ $320–350 ⚒ TRM

An oak stationery box, the fall-front opening to reveal a writing surface and fitted interior, c1900, 16in (40.5cm) wide.
£400–480
€/ $630–750 ⚒ NOA

◄ An Edwardian mahogany writing cabinet, the fitted interior with drop-down fascia, with brass handles, labelled 'Dimlock & Son, Norwich', 12¼in (31cm) wide.
£370–450
€/ $580–700 ⚒ AH

Music

Cylinder Musical Boxes

A cylinder musical box, playing eight airs, with two layers of circular engraved bells, in a burr-walnut case, mid-19thC, 22¾in (58cm) wide.
£1,500–1,800
€/ $2,400–2,800 ⚒ L&E

A cylinder musical box, by Paillard, playing eight airs, with matching table and extra cylinders, Swiss, c1880, 43in (109cm) wide.
£7,000–8,000
€/ $11,000–12,700 ⊞ GWe

► **A cylinder musical box,** by Ami Riveric, playing eight airs, with original tune sheet and finish to case, movement restored, c1880, 14in (35.5cm) wide.
£1,300–1,500
€/ $2,000–2,400 ⊞ PGO

◄ **A tremolo cylinder musical box,** by Nicole Frères, the 15in (38cm) cylinder playing 12 airs, indicator with fast/slow lever, in a burr-walnut and burr-maple-veneered case, with tune sheet, Swiss, c1880, 30in (76cm) wide.
£3,000–3,600
€/ $4,700–5,700 ⚒ S(O)

A cylinder musical box, by Nicole Frères, playing eight airs, restored, Swiss, c1865, 21in (53.5cm) wide.
£3,400–3,800
€/ $5,400–6,000 ⊞ KHW

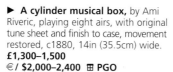

A cylinder musical box, by M. M. & Co, the double main spring barrel playing 12 airs, in a repolished buffet case, movement overhauled, Swiss, c1895, 30in (76cm) wide.
£4,700–5,200
€/ $7,400–8,200 ⊞ PGO

A cylinder musical box, by L'Epée, with individually played bells, reconditioned, French, c1895, 22in (56cm) wide.
£3,000–3,900
€/ $4,700–6,200 ⊞ KHW

A late Victorian cylinder musical box, by National, playing six airs, in a *faux* coromandel case, 14¼in (36cm) wide.
£240–280
€/ $380–440 ⚒ SWO

Disc Musical Boxes

A Symphonion disc musical box, with eight discs, contained in a walnut case, late 19thC, discs 7½in (19cm) diam.
£350–400
€/ $550–630 SWO

A Symphonion disc musical box, contained in a rosewood case, with associated discs, German, 19thC, 10in (25.5cm) wide.
£260–315
€/ $400–480 SWO

A Polyphon 19⅝in coin-operated disc musical box, with 13 discs, with twin-comb mechanism, contained in a walnut case with glazed door and pierced foliate frets flanked by turned pilasters, the base with a frieze drawer and side winding handle, German, c1900.
£4,000–4,800
€/ $6,300–7,600 S(O)

► **A Polyphon disc musical box,** with original disc, movement serviced, German, c1900, disc 8¼in (21cm) diam.
£1,300–1,500
€/ $2,000–2,400 PGO

A Symphonion 11⅞in disc musical box, contained in a walnut-veneered case, German, c1895, 19in (48.5cm) wide.
£2,000–2,400
€/ $3,200–3,800 GWe

A Polyphon disc musical box, with nine discs, contained in a floral transfer-decorated case with offset lithograph to interior of lid, German, late 19thC, 8in (20.5cm) wide.
£420–500
€/ $660–790 AMB

A Symphonion disc musical box, with ten 12in (30.5cm) discs, contained in a wooden case with rococo decoration, German, c1900, 18in (45.5cm) wide.
£5,000–5,500
€/ $7,900–8,600 KHW

An Ariston organette, by Paul Ehrlich, Leipzig, with 13in (33cm) card discs and 24 notes, German, c1895, 16in (40.5cm) wide.
£1,800–2,000
€/ $2,800–3,200 KHW

A Polyphon disc musical box, 'The Dandy Fifth', with ten 19⅝in (49.5cm) discs, contained in a walnut-veneered case, restored, German, Leipzig, c1898, 50in (127cm) high.
£8,700–9,500
€/ $13,700–15,000 KHW

A Symphonion 11⅞in disc musical box, contained in a carved wood case, the interior of the lid with a silk picture, German, c1900, 18in (45.5cm) wide.
£4,500–5,000
€/ $7,000–8,000 GWe

► **A Monopol disc musical box,** with ten 7¼in (18.5cm) discs, contained in an ebonized fruitwood cabinet, unrestored, German, c1905, 12in (30.5cm) square.
£1,600–1,800
€/ $2,500–2,800 KHW

A Britannia disc musical box, by B. H. Abrahams, with ten discs, contained in a smoker's cabinet with original finish, movement overhauled, Swiss, St Croix, c1900, 21in (53.5cm) high.
£2,000–2,200
€/ $3,200–3,500 PGO

A Polyphon disc musical box, with 12 bells and 14½in (37cm) disc, restored, German, c1900, 19in (48.5cm) wide.
£5,000–5,500
€/ $7,900–8,700 KHW

Mechanical Music

◄ **An ivory musical box,** c1890, 6½in (16.5cm) wide.
£770–850
€/ $1,200–1,300 ⊞ HAA

◄ **A hurdy-gurdy,** inlaid with ebony and ivory inked design, the finial surmounted by a male head, labelled, body stamped with maker's details, French, 1873.
£1,000–1,200
€/ $1,600–1,900 ⚒ B

A musical animated scene, with a ship, windmill and soldiers, beneath a glass dome, French, 19thC, 21in (53.5cm) high.
£1,800–2,000
€/ $2,800–3,200 ⊞ AUTO

A singing bird in a cage automaton, with clockwork mechanism, French, c1880, 20in (51cm) high.
£4,000–4,500
€/ $6,300–7,100 ⊞ AUTO

► **A Serinette miniature barrel organ,** by Thibouville-Lamy, Mirecourt, with ten notes, French, c1850, 10in (25.5cm) wide.
£1,800–2,000
€/ $2,800–3,200 ⊞ KHW
This would have been used to teach singing birds popular tunes.

► **A hand-cranked parlour barrel organ,** by Preston, London, the 18in (45.5cm) barrel playing ten airs, the mahogany case with hinged lid revealing hand-written tune sheets for five barrels, the base with hinged side panel enclosing two further pinned barrels, stop panel signed, early 19thC, 57½in (146cm) high.
£1,700–2,000
€/ $2,700–3,200 ⚒ S(O)

Gramophones

An HMV gramophone, in a mahogany case, c1926, 37in (94cm) high.
£270–300
€/ $425–475 ⊞ GM

A Victor Monarch gramophone, with exhibition soundbox, brass and black-painted witch's hat horn with Nipper transfer, the oak case with fluted corner pillars and maker's label, 1910, 13in (33cm) square.
£380–440
€/ $600–700 ⚒ B(WM)

◄ **A concert gramophone,** by E. M. Ginn, with papier mâché horn, the oak cabinet with later electric turntable, c1925, 21¼in (54cm) wide.
£950–1,100
€/ $1,500–1,700 ⚒ S(O)

Musical Instruments

◄ **A cello,** by Ludovicus Guersan, Paris, labelled, restorations, French, 1766, length of back 28in (71cm).
£8,500–10,000
€/ $13,500–15,800 ⚒ B

An English School cello, minor restorations, c1820, length of back 29¼in (74.5cm).
£3,500–4,200
€/ $5,500–6,600 ⚒ B

◄ **A cello,** labelled 'Nicolaus Amatus...', probably Dutch, early 19thC, length of back 29¼in (74.5cm).
£6,000–7,000
€/ $9,500–11,000 ⚒ GH

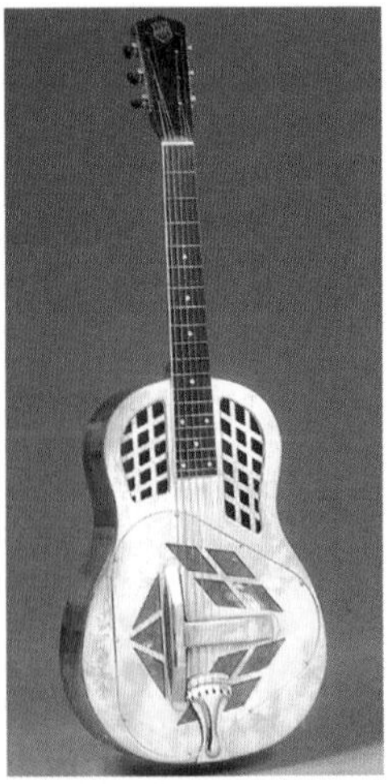

A Simatone steel-bodied guitar, by Simon Beuscher, stamped, 1953.
£850–1,000
€/ $1,300–1,600 ⚒ B

◄ **A carved giltwood, brass and maple harp,** by Francis Serouet, London, signed, 1800–25, 68in (172.5cm) high.
£3,500–4,000
€/ $5,500–6,300 ⚒ NOA

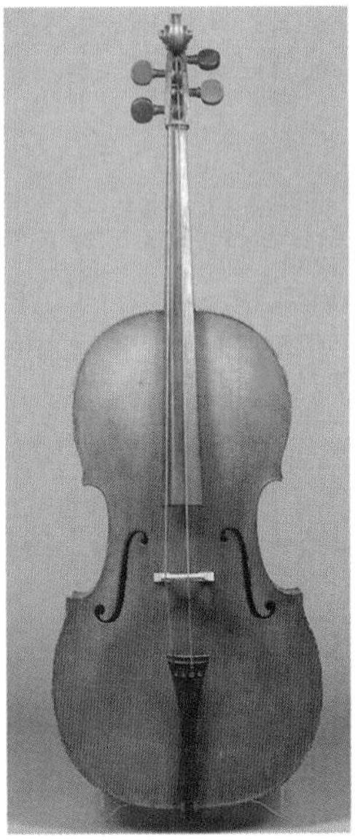

A cello, by Sebastian Dallinger, Vienna, stamped, Austrian, 1786, length of back 29¾in (75.5cm).
£6,500–7,500
€/ $10,300–11,800 ⚒ B

A cello, attributed to Lockey Hill, London, minor blemishes, manuscript label, fingerboard numbered 'P705', c1820, length of back 29in (73.5cm).
£9,500–11,000
€/ $15,000–17,400 ⚒ B

► **A salon harp,** by Sebastian Eraros & Pierre, London, with Gothic-style decoration above a column mounted with five carved angels playing musical instruments, on winged beast feet, late 19thC, 69in (175.5cm) high.
£2,400–2,800
€/ $3,800–4,400 ⚒ HYD

A cello, by Simon Kriner, Mittenwald, labelled, fingerboard stamped 'W. E. Hill & Sons, Reg No. 79606', c1812, length of back 29¾in (75.5cm).
£3,000–3,600
€/ $4,700–5,700 ⚒ B

A walnut and parcel-gilt triple-strung concert harp, brass plate inscribed in Welsh and English 'Eisteddfod, Llandovery May 1872, 1st Prize', Welsh, 19thC, 78in (198cm) high.
£1,000–1,200
€/ $1,600–1,900 ⚒ PF

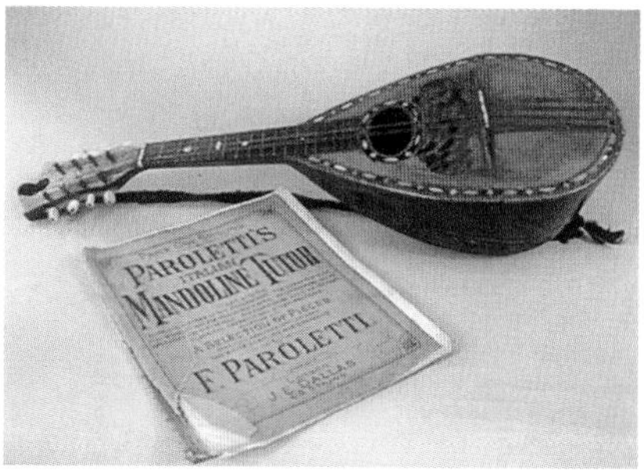

A mandolin, by F. D. E. Mureda, Italian, Naples, dated 1898, with case and sheet music.
£140–160
€/ $220–250 SWO

► **An ophicleide,** by J. Pask, London, minor damage, engraved maker's shield, 1800–50, 39½in (100.5cm) long, with two modern photographs reproducing early newspaper cuttings.
£900–1,100
€/ $1,400–1,600 F&C

The ophicleide (keyed serpent) was invented by the Frenchman Halary in 1817. One of the most celebrated ophicleide parts is that in Mendelssohn's 'A Midsummer Night's Dream'. In Victorian times it was a popular instrument in brass bands and orchestras, the pre-cursor of the tuba.

Items in the Musical Instruments section have been arranged in alphabetical order.

A carved walnut piano, by Wetzels, with ivory inlay, 31 panels depicting various scenes from classical literature, two depicting Classical nudes, on winged lion pedestals, some losses, paper label inscribed 'No. 800/31', French, c1810, 48in (122cm) wide.
£2,000–2,400
€/ $3,200–3,800 JAA

A mahogany and inlaid square piano, by Wasterman & Co, early 19thC, 71¾in (182.5cm) wide.
£380–450
€/ $600–710 SWO

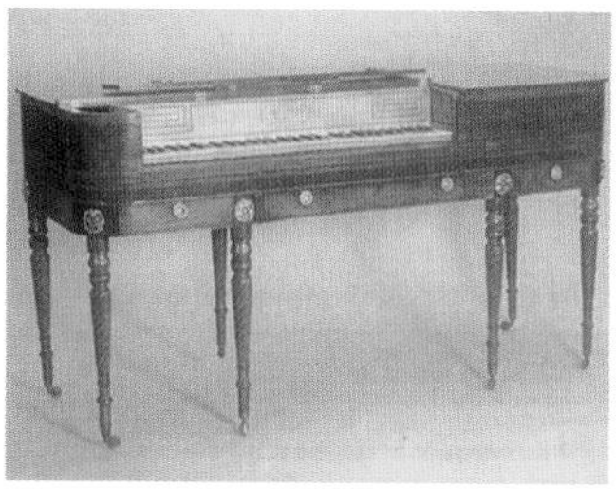

A Regency mahogany piano, with satinwood banding and chequer stringing, inscribed 'New Patent, Willm Phillips...London', the three frieze drawers with later handles, 67in (170cm) wide.
£550–620
€/ $870–980 WW

A Regency mahogany and rosewood-banded piano, by John Broadwood & Sons, with ebony inlay, the front interior in satinwood, on lion-paw feet, inscribed, 42in (106.5cm) wide.
£12,000–14,000
€/ $19,000–22,000 MEA

A flame-mahogany grand piano, by Boisselot et Fils, Marseille, with boxwood inlay stringing, restored, French, c1835, 60in (152.5cm) long.
£20,000–23,000
€/ $31,500–36,000 PPC

A walnut and gilt-bronze upright piano, by Erard, London, with marquetry decoration, signed and dated 1856, 59½in (151cm) wide.
£4,200–5,000
€/ $6,600–7,900 S(O)

A rosewood and mahogany square piano, by Clementi & Co, with crossbanding, brass inlay and gilt-metal mounts, 19thC, 68½in (174cm) wide.
£550–620
€/ $870–980 AH

A burr-walnut grand piano, by J. Kuhse, Dresden, German, 1875–1900, 59½in (151cm) wide.
£1,300–1,500
€/ $2,000–2,400 NOA

An ebonized grand piano, by Pleyel, Paris, with chinoiserie decoration, restored, 1886, 75in (190.5cm) long.
£25,000–28,000
€/ $39,500–44,000 PPC

An ebonized grand piano, by Irmler, c1895, 66in (167.5cm) wide.
£700–800
€/ $1,100–1,300 PEx

A mahogany grand piano, by Bösendorfer, Austrian, Vienna, 1901, 67in (170cm) long.
£2,800–3,300
€/ $4,400–5,200 S(Am)

A tulipwood piano, by W. Knabe, American, 1876, 85in (216cm) wide.
£5,500–6,000
€/ $8,700–9,500 LCM

A rosewood grand piano, by Steinway, c1890, 88in (223.5cm) long.
£8,000–10,000
€/ $12,600–15,800 PEx

An Adam revival-style satinwood and inlaid grand piano, by C. Bechstein, c1900, 59in (150cm) wide.
£8,500–10,000
€/ $13,400–15,800 S(O)

A mahogany baby grand piano, by Steck, c1930, 54in (137cm) wide.
£1,000–1,200
€/ $1,600–1,900 PEx

► **A black-lacquered grand piano,** by Werlein, New Orleans, American, c1975, 68in (172.5cm) long, with matching stool.
£2,000–2,200
€/ $3,200–3,500 NOA

A rosewood concert grand piano, by Steinway, 1886, 108in (274.5cm) wide.
£12,000–14,000
€/ $19,000–22,000 PEx

A rosewood grand piano, by John Brinsmead, c1892, 72in (183cm) wide.
£400–500
€/ $630–790 PEx

A carved mahogany grand piano, by Bechstein, c1900, 72in (183cm) wide.
£7,000–9,000
€/ $11,000–14,000 PEx

PIANO-EXPORT
WHOLESALERS AND EXPORTERS OF QUALITY SECONDHAND PIANOS
C.BECHSTEIN
Specialists in Grand Pianos with many in stock by
★ STEINWAY ★
★ BECHSTEIN ★
★ BLUTHNER ★
★ BOSENDORFER ★
★ ERARD ★ PLEYEL ★
★ BROADWOOD ★
Many with highly decorated inlaid and carved cases in all types of exquisite veneers
ALL STEINWAY GRANDS WANTED
For more details telephone or write to:
PIANO-EXPORT, Bridge Road, Kingswood, Bristol BS15 4FW, England Tel: 0117 956 8300 · International: +44 117 956 8300

A violin, attributed to Antonio Stradivari, Cremona, labelled, Italian, 1679, length of back 14in (35.5cm).
£230,000–270,000
€/ $360,000–425,000 B

A violin, neck straightened, base bar repaired, 1775–1825, length of back 14in (35.5cm).
£350–420
€/ $550–660 RTo

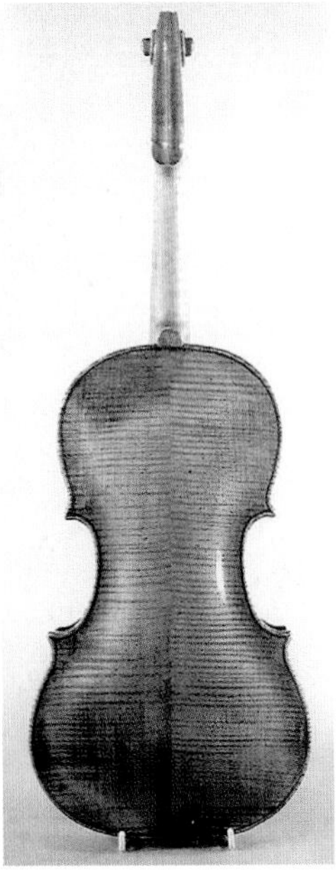

A violin, labelled 'Sympertus Niggell Lauten und Geigen Macher in Fussen 1777', length of back 14in (35.5cm), with case.
£1,500–1,800
€/ $2,400–2,800 GH

A violin, c1800, length of back 14in (35.5cm).
£3,500–4,200
€/ $5,500–6,600 B

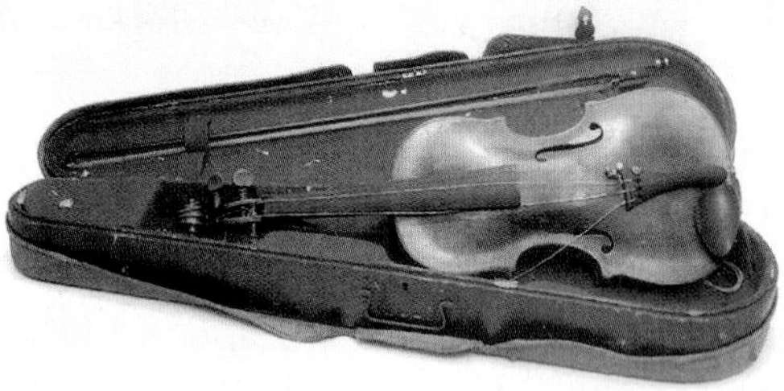

A mahogany violin and bow, some damage, the interior with a hand-written label 'Saul Malcor?, 1807', 23in (58.5cm) long, in matched case with canvas cover.
£320–380
€/ $500–600 FHF

A School of Guadagnini viola, enlarged, labelled, Italian, c1800, length of back 16¼in (41.5cm), with case.
£15,000–18,000
€/ $24,000–28,000 B

A violin, by Matthew Hardie, Edinburgh, fingerboard numbered 'G180', c1810, length of back 14in (35.5cm).
£3,000–3,500
€/ $4,700–5,500 B

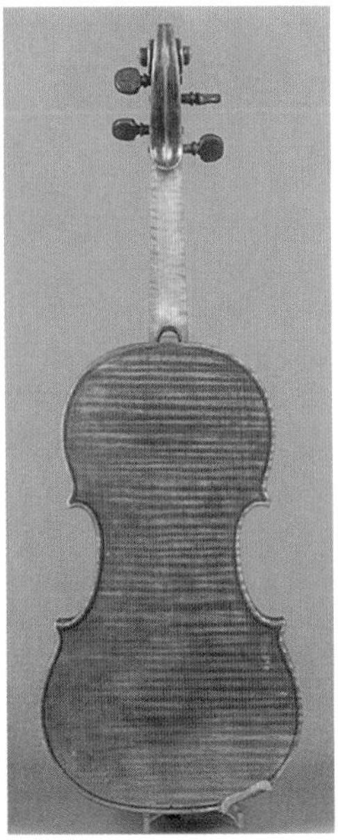

► **A Turin School violin,** labelled 'Joannes Franciscus Pressenda...Taurini...1836?', length of back 14in (35.5cm), with case.
£15,000–18,000
€/ $23,700–28,500 B

A violin, of the school of J. B. Vuillaume, Paris, labelled, French, c1840, length of back 14in (35.5cm).
£8,000–9,500
€/ $12,600–15,000 B

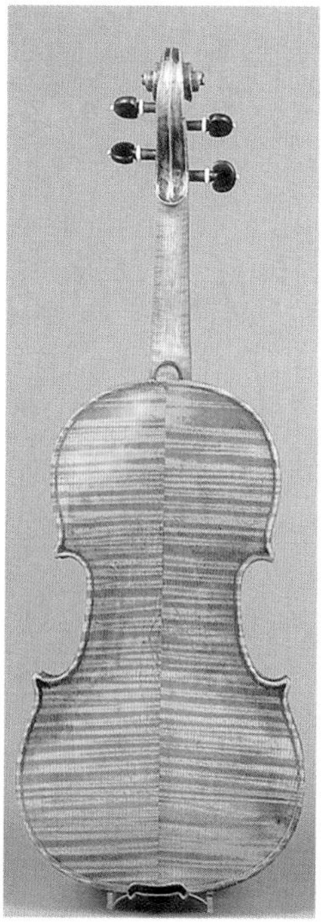

A violin, by C. A. Maucotel, Paris, labelled, French, 1855, length of back 14in (35.5cm).
£7,000–8,500
€/ $11,000–13,500 ⚒ B

A violin, slight damage, strings missing, marked 'A la Ville de Cremonne/D.Nicolas ainé' and 'par hipplite Boedier, musicien...le 30 mars 1878', 24in (61cm) long, with case and two bows.
£580–680
€/ $920–1,100 ⚒ FHF

A violin, by Alfonso della Corte, Napoli, labelled, fingerboard numbered '1067', Italian, 1883, length of back 14in (35.5cm), with case.
£7,500–9,000
€/ $11,800–14,200 ⚒ B

◄ **A violin,** by A. Poller, Vienna, labelled, Austrian, 1912, length of back 14in (35.5cm).
£4,500–5,200
€/ $7,100–8,200 ⚒ B

A violin, by Richard Weichold, Dresden, labelled, German, 1899, length of back 14in (35.5cm).
£3,800–4,500
€/ $6,000–7,100 ⚒ B

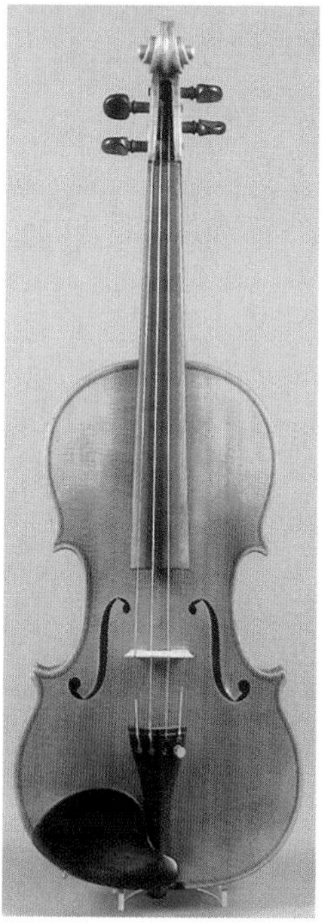

A violin, attributed to Carolus Joseph Dvorak, Prague, labelled, Czechoslovakian, 1928, length of back 14in (35.5cm), with case.
£3,000–3,500
€/ $4,700–5,500 ⚒ B

► **A violin,** by Paul Kaul, Paris, labelled, French, 1945, length of back 14½in (37cm), with case.
£4,200–5,000
€/ $6,600–7,900 ⚒ B

Icons

An icon of the Virgin of Vladimir, with a silver oklad, Russian, 15thC, 12¼ x 10½in (31 x 26.5cm).
£7,700–8,500
€/ $12,200–13,500 ⊞ TeG

An icon of Metropolitan Alexei of Moscow, Russian, 16thC, 12¼ x 9¾in (31 x 25cm).
£3,500–3,800
€/ $5,500–6,000 ⊞ TeG

► A roundel icon of the Mother of God, 'Platyera', Greek, 17thC, 8¾in (22cm) diam.
£1,300–1,500
€/ $2,000–2,400 ⊞ TeG

An icon of the Enthroned Saviour, Greek, 17thC, 17¼ x 11in (44 x 28cm).
£12,000–14,000
€/ $19,000–22,000 ⚒ S(O)

An icon of St Parasceva, Byzantine, 15thC, 8¾ x 7in (22.5 x 18cm).
£5,500–6,000
€/ $8,700–9,500 ⊞ RKa

An icon of the Vladimir Mother of God, the halos embellished with *faux* gemstones, Russian, c1650, 11¾ x 9¼in (30 x 23.5cm).
£950–1,100
€/ $1,500–1,700 ⚒ JAA

An icon of the Mother of God of Tenderness, Eleousa, Cretan, late 15thC, 10in (25.5cm) square.
£16,000–18,000
€/ $25,000–28,000 ⊞ RKa

An icon of Christ Washing the Feet of His Disciples, on a gold ground, within an 18thC Venetian frame, Ionian Islands, 17thC, 15¼ x 14in (38.5 x 35.5cm).
£6,500–7,800
€/ $10,300–12,300 ⚒ S(O)

An icon of St Markari, Russian, c1700, 14¼ x 12¾in (36 x 32.5cm).
£1,600–1,800
€/ $2,500–2,800 ⊞ TeG

◄ An icon of the Akhtuirskaya Mother of God, the borders overlaid with a repoussé silver oklad, with an ornate silver halo, Cyrillic maker's marks for Yaroslav Frolov, Moscow, the icon with a fragment of the signature of Ivanov, Russian, c1780, 14 x 12in (35.5 x 30.5cm).
£1,000–1,200
€/ $1,600–1,900 ⚒ JAA

A brass icon of St John the Evangelist, Russian, 18thC, 4 x 2¼in (10 x 5.5cm).
£350–380
€/ $550–600 ⊞ RKa

An icon of the Resurrection and Descent into Hell, Anastasis, Russian, late 18thC, 14 x 11¾in (35.5 x 30cm).
£2,200–2,500
€/ $3,500–4,000 ⊞ RKa

An icon of the Kazan Mother of God, set within a gilt-metal mount composed of elements from an earlier panel, the veil decorated with seed pearls, turquoises and pastes, later oklad, Russian, 18thC, 12½ x 10¾in (32 x 27.5cm).
£1,100–1,300
€/ $1,700–2,100 S(O)

An icon of the Saviour, Russian, late 18thC, 11¾ x 9½in (30 x 24cm).
£1,300–1,500
€/ $2,000–2,400 ⊞ TeG

An icon of St Demetrius, Russian, c1800, 15¾ x 14¼in (40 x 36cm).
£3,200–3,500
€/ $5,000–5,500 ⊞ TeG

An icon of St Nicholas the Wonderworker, Russian, 18thC, 34¾ x 26½in (88.5 x 67.5cm).
£4,500–5,000
€/ $7,000–7,900 ⊞ TeG

An icon of the Virgin in St Anna's Sanctuary, Bulgarian, c1800, 18½ x 16¾in (47 x 42.5cm).
£1,300–1,400
€/ $2,000–2,200 ⊞ RKa

◄ **An icon of the Shui-Smolensk Odigitria Mother of God,** overlaid with an oklad sewn with mother-of-pearl beads, Russian, c1800, 13 x 11in (33 x 28cm).
£1,700–2,000
€/ $2,700–3,200 JAA

An icon of the Three-handed Mother of God, overlaid with an oklad sewn with coloured beads and pastes, Russian, c1801, 13 x 11½in (33 x 29cm).
£2,000–2,400
€/ $3,200–3,800 JAA

◄ **A painted icon of the Holy Venerable Paul of Thebes,** Russian, c1875, 8¾ x 6½in (22 x 16.5cm).
£375–450
€/ $600–700 JAA

A painted icon of St Theodosiy, Bishop, Russian, c1890, 10½ x 9in (26.5 x 23cm).
£375–450
€/ $600–700 JAA

An icon of the Mother of God, set in a silver oklad, each figure with crowns set with coloured stones, the borders of the oklad decorated with strapwork and Cyrillic inscriptions, workmaster's mark and initials 'D.I.', Russian, mid-19thC, 10¼ x 8½in (26 x 21.5cm).
£2,200–2,600
€/ $3,500–4,100 LAY

An icon of Saints Afanasi and Kyril, Russian, 19thC, 12¼ x 9¾in (31 x 25cm).
£1,300–1,500
€/ $2,000–2,400 TeG

► An icon of the Archangel Gabriel, Russian, 19thC, 12 x 10in (30.5 x 25.5cm).
£1,300–1,500
€/ $2,000–2,400 TeG

An icon of Christ Pantocrator, Russian, late 19thC, 8½ x 6½in (21.5 x 16.5cm).
£220–280
€/ $350–440 WW

An icon of St Nicholas, with scenes from his life, Russian, 19thC, 14 x 12¼in (35.5 x 31cm).
£2,500–2,800
€/ $4,000–4,400 RKa

◄ An icon of the Madonna and Child, the silver frame and enamel-mounted oklad with gilt highlights, moulded clothing and an enamelled halo, hallmarked 'A.C1896', Russian, 12¼ x 10¾in (31 x 27.5cm).
£875–1,000
€/ $1,400–1,600 JDJ

An icon of the Sign Mother of God, Russian, c1900, 12½ x 10¾in (32 x 27.5cm).
£600–720
€/ $950–1,100 JAA

An icon of the Kazan Mother of God, set with a silver and *cloisonné* enamel oklad, maker's mark 'S.G.', Russian, Moscow, late 19thC, 10½ x 9in (26.5 x 23cm).
£1,200–1,400
€/ $1,900–2,200 S(O)

An icon of the Archangel Michael Voyevoda, Russian, 19thC, 12¼ x 10½in (31 x 26.5cm).
£3,200–3,500
€/ $5,100–5,500 TeG

An icon of the Virgin of Vladimir, Russian, 19thC, 12¼ x 11in (31 x 28cm).
£800–900
€/ $1,300–1,400 ⊞ TeG

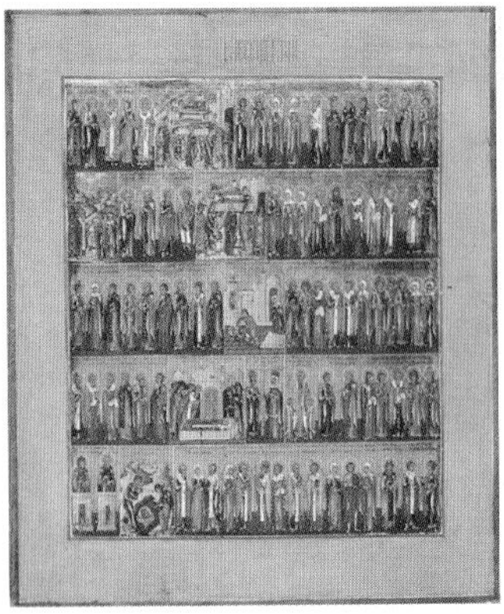

An icon of the Calendar for the Month of June, Russian, 19thC, 12¼ x 10¼in (31 x 26cm).
£1,600–1,800
€/ $2,500–2,800 ⊞ TeG

An icon of the Mother of God of the Sign, Russian, 19thC, 12¼ x 10¼in (31 x 26cm).
£1,300–1,500
€/ $2,000–2,400 ⊞ RKa

An icon of the Four Metropolitans of Moscow, Russian, 19thC, 7 x 5¾in (18 x 14.5cm).
£850–950
€/ $1,300–1,500 ⊞ TeG

An icon of Hodigitria, with a silver oklad, Russian, 19thC, 7¼ x 6in (18.5 x 15cm).
£550–600
€/ $870–950 ⊞ TeG

An icon of the Saints of Vologda, Russian, 19thC, 14 x 12in (35.5 x 30.5cm).
£900–1,100
€/ $1,400–1,700 ⚒ S(NY)

An icon of Christ Pantocrator, Russian, 19thC, 15 x 12¼in (38 x 31cm).
£450–550
€/ $700–870 ⚒ JDJ

An icon of the Council of the Archangel Michael, Russian, 19thC, 15¾ x 12½in (40 x 32cm).
£220–260
€/ $350–400 ⚒ JDJ

An icon, depicting an elderly male saint, with silver-coloured metal oklad, stamped, Russian, 1875–1925, 4¼ x 3½in (11 x 9cm).
£120–140
€/ $190–220 ⚒ GTH

An embossed and pierced silver icon, marked, Russian, 1875–1925, 8¾ x 7in (22 x 18cm).
£100–120
€/ $160–190 ⚒ SWO

◄ **An icon of St Seraphim of Sarov,** overlaid with an engraved silver-gilt oklad with applied *cloisonné* halo and corners, hallmarked, Cyrillic maker's mark 'S.G.', probably Sergiy Gupkin, Russian, Moscow, c1903, 23 x 18in (58.5 x 45.5cm), in a carved custom-fitted *kiot*.
£1,800–2,200
€/ $2,800–3,500 ⚒ JAA

► **An icon of the Fiery Ascension of the Prophet Elijah,** inscribed, Russian, dated 1922, 14 x 12in (35.5 x 30.5cm).
£400–480
€/ $630–760 ⚒ JAA

Portrait Miniatures

A pair of portrait miniatures of a lady and gentleman, Spanish School, oil on copper, c1600, 3in (7.5cm) high, in modern giltwood frames.
£700–820
€/ $1,100–1,300 ⚒ S(O)

A portrait miniature of Sir Gerald Aylmer, 6th Bt of Donadea, inscribed on reverse, c1726, 1¾in (4.5cm) high, in a papier mâché frame.
£1,700–2,000
€/ $2,700–3,200 ⚒ TEN

A portrait miniature of a lady, by Charles Dixon, hair panel on reverse, c1750, 2in (5cm) high, in a gold locket frame.
£3,000–3,400
€/ $4,700–5,400 ⊞ BHa

A portrait miniature of a lady, in Renaissance costume, on ivory, named on reverse 'Mary Stuart', late 16thC, 3¼in (8.5cm) high.
£330–400
€/ $520–630 ⚒ TMA

A portrait miniature of a gentleman, by Nathaniel Hone, watercolour on ivory, monogrammed and dated 1763, 1½in (4cm) high, mounted in a gold-mounted carton pierre snuff box.
£1,400–1,600
€/ $2,200–2,500 ⚒ G(L)

A portrait miniature of a lady, by Richard Cosway, c1780, 2in (5cm) high, in a gold bracelet clasp frame.
£2,200–2,500
€/ $3,500–4,000 ⊞ BHa

◄ **A portrait miniature of a lady,** signed with initial V, c1780, 1½in (3.5cm) high, in a gold frame.
£450–520
€/ $710–820 ⚒ B

A portrait miniature of a gentleman, by Susan Penelope Rosse, on vellum, late 17thC, 1½in (4cm) high.
£3,250–3,750
€/ $5,000–6,000 ⊞ SHa

◄ **A portrait miniature of a lady,** by C. F. Zincke, on enamel, monogram on reverse, c1730, 2in (5cm) high, in a gold frame.
£3,000–3,300
€/ $4,700–5,200 ⊞ BHa

► **A portrait miniature of a lady,** by Gervase Spencer, gold bracelet clasp mount, signed and dated 1748, 1½in (4cm) high.
£500–600
€/ $790–950 ⚒ B

A portrait miniature of a gentleman, wearing armour, 17thC, 3in (8cm) high, in a damaged leather case.
£2,000–2,400
€/ $3,200–3,800 ⚒ Bea(E)

A portrait miniature of a gentleman, on ivory, c1790, 4½in (11.5cm) high, in a gold bracelet clasp frame.
£1,300–1,500
€/ $2,100–2,400 ⚒ WL

A portrait miniature of an officer, probably of the 12th Light Dragoons, by William Denton, the reverse glazed to reveal a gold monogram 'ML' on plaited hair, signed and dated 1794, 2½in (6.5cm) high.
£1,500–1,800
€/ $2,400–2,800 ⚒ B

► A Georgian portrait miniature of a lady, 1¾in (4.5cm) high, in a white metal foliate and scroll frame set with old-cut diamonds.
£1,800–2,000
€/ $2,800–3,200 ⚒ DMC

A portrait miniature of a lady, by Hurter, on ivory, Swiss, c1790, 3in (7.5cm) high, in a gold frame.
£850–950
€/ $1,300–1,500 ⊞ SHa

► A portrait miniature of a lady, watercolour on ivory, c1800, 4in (10cm) high.
£180–200
€/ $275–300 ⊞ PSC

A portrait miniature of a lady, by J. T. Mitchell, signed and dated 1798, 2¾in (7cm) high, in a gold frame.
£450–500
€/ $700–800 ⚒ B

◄ A portrait miniature of a boy, by Henry Eldridge, c1790, 2¾in (7cm) high, the frame with plaited two-coloured hair surround.
£3,500–4,000
€/ $5,400–6,300 ⊞ BHa

A portrait miniature of a gentleman, by Henry Bone, RA, signed with monogram and dated 1793, 2¼in (5.5cm) high, in a gilt-metal frame.
£600–700
€/ $950–1,100 ⚒ B

A portrait miniature of a lady, English School, watercolour on ivory, 18thC, 2in (5cm) high, in a gold locket frame.
£380–450
€/ $600–710 ⚒ G(L)

A portrait miniature of Admiral Foot, by C. Hayter, the reverse with interwoven hair panel, c1800, 3½in (9cm) wide, in a gold locket frame.
£3,500–4,000
€/ $5,500–6,300 ⊞ BHa

A portrait miniature of a gentleman, on ivory, c1800, 3½in (9cm) high.
£2,000–2,200
€/ $3,200–3,500 SHa

A portrait miniature of a staff officer, English School, the enamelled back set with a lock of hair, early 19thC, 2¾in (7cm) high, in a gilt-metal frame.
£450–475
€/ $710–750 Bea(E)

A portrait miniature of a gentleman, attributed to Richard Bull, the reverse with a blue glass border and gold-mounted aperture with seed pearl monogram 'CH' surrounded by hair adorned with pearls, Irish, c1800, 3in (7.5cm) high, in a gold frame.
£650–750
€/ $1,000–1,200 B

A portrait miniature of a lady, said to be Jane Barlow, English School, early 19thC, 1½in (4cm) high, in a gold frame with hair-plait back.
£320–380
€/ $510–600 Bea(E)

A portrait miniature of a gentleman, on ivory, English School, early 19thC, 2¾in (7cm) high, in a papier mâché frame.
£1,000–1,200
€/ $1,600–1,900 AH

A portrait miniature of J. G. Muirhead, on ivory, Continental School, the convex glass panel back enclosing an enamelled inscribed plaque, early 19thC, 2¾in (7cm) high, in a gilt-metal frame.
£300–350
€/ $475–550 BR

► **A portrait miniature of the Marquess of Thomand,** by Henry Bone, enamel on copper, inscribed and dated 1808, 5½in (14cm) high, in a gilded frame.
£3,300–4,000
€/ $5,200–6,300 BWL

A portrait miniature of a gentleman, on ivory, English School, early 19thC, 3¼in (8cm) high.
£280–340
€/ $440–540 B(S)

A portrait miniature of John Noble, engraved with his name and dates, early 19thC, 1¾in (4.5cm) high, in a later 9ct gold frame, with leather case.
£200–220
€/ $320–350 BR

A portrait miniature of a gentleman, said to be William Steenbergen, attributed to Lawrence Sully, c1800, 2¾in (7cm) high.
£800–950
€/ $1,300–1,500 S(NY)

A portrait miniature of Anne Barnes, watercolour on ivory, 1810, 4in (10cm) high.
£200–220
€/ $320–350 ⊞ PSC

A portrait miniature of a lady, on ivory, French, 1820, 3¼in (8.5cm) high, in a gold frame.
£3,400–3,800
€/ $5,400–6,000 ⊞ SHa

► A portrait miniature of a girl, on ivory, English School, c1835, 4¼in (11cm) high.
£480–550
€/ $760–870 ⚒ L

A portrait miniature of Archibald Cochrane, aged 19, by J. V. Dupont, enamel, painted in Geneva, 1837, 2in (5cm) high.
£1,700–1,900
€/ $2,700–3,000 ⊞ BHa

A portrait miniature of a gentleman, attributed to J. J. Gillespie, c1815, 5in (12.5cm) high.
£250–275
€/ $400–440 ⊞ PSC

A portrait miniature of a Russian officer, by René Louis Letronne, French, signed and dated 1825, 7½in (19cm) high, in a veneered wood frame.
£1,800–2,000
€/ $2,800–3,200 ⚒ S(O)

A portrait miniature of a lady, attributed to Johann Heusinger, German, signed and dated 1820, 3½in (9cm) high, in a gilded carved wood frame.
£500–600
€/ $790–950 ⚒ B

A portrait miniature of an officer, by Louis Gross, signed, c1830, Austrian, Vienna, 3in (7.5cm) high.
£3,200–3,500
€/ $5,000–5,500 ⊞ BHa

A portrait miniature of Mrs William Donald, by T. Carlyle, signed, inscribed and dated 1833, 4in (10cm) high.
£400–480
€/ $630–760 ⚒ TEN

◄ A portrait miniature of a gentleman, watercolour on ivory, 19thC, 2in (5cm) high.
£120–140
€/ $190–220 ⚒ G(L)

A portrait miniature of a lady, watercolour on ivory, c1840, 5¼in (13.5cm) high, in original carved wood frame.
£250–275
€/ $400–440 ⊞ PSC

A Victorian portrait miniature of Richard Doughty, inscribed 'born 26th May 1850, aged one year and four months', lock of hair to reverse, 2¾in (7cm) high, in a yellow metal frame.
£330–400
€/ $520–630 ⚒ BR

A portrait miniature of a lady, 19thC, 3¼in (8.5cm) high.
£200–220
€/ $320–350 ⚒ WW

A portrait miniature of a lady, French School, c1840, 2½in (6.5cm) high, in a gilt locket frame.
£1,700–1,900
€/ $2,700–3,000 ⊞ BHa

A portrait miniature of a lady, by John Thomas Gullick, on ivory, inscribed on reverse, c1865, 5¼in (13cm) high, in a gilt frame.
£380–450
€/ $600–710 ⚒ SWO

A portrait miniature of a lady, on ivory, 19thC, 4¼in (11cm) high.
£480–550
€/ $760–870 ⚒ DMC

◄ A portrait miniature of a French lady, on ivory, 19thC, 3½in (9cm) high, in original gilt acanthus leaf-scroll frame.
£380–450
€/ $600–710 ⚒ BWL

► A portrait miniature of a gentleman in uniform, on ivory, early 20thC, 2¾in (7cm) high, in a silver and white enamel frame, hallmarked London 1910.
£200–220
€/ $320–350 ⚒ DMC

A portrait miniature of an officer, in 18thC uniform, English School, pinchbeck bracelet clasp mount with plaited hair bracelet, mid-19thC, 1½in (4cm) high.
£400–480
€/ $630–760 ⚒ B

A portrait miniature of a gentleman, wearing a Masonic chain, watercolour on ivory, c1880, 5¼in (13cm) high.
£175–200
€/ $280–315 ⊞ PSC

A portrait miniature of a gentleman and a lady, on ivory, 19thC, 2½in (6.5cm) diam.
£500–600
€/ $790–950 ⚒ DuM

Silhouettes

A silhouette of a gentleman, by Richard Jorden, painted on glass, c1780, 4in (10cm) high, in a hammered brass frame.
£240–275
€/ $380–430 G(L)

A silhouette of an officer, wearing a Tarleton helmet, English School, painted on flat glass backed with silk, c1800, 6in (15cm) high, in a hammered brass frame.
£500–600
€/ $790–950 B

A silhouette of a gentleman, by Michael Rowed, painted on card, c1820, 3in (7.5cm) high.
£160–175
€/ $250–275 PSC

A silhouette of a lady and gentleman taking tea, painted on card, c1784, 11 x 15in (28 x 38cm).
£6,000–7,000
€/ $9,500–11,000 G(L)

A silhouette of Lady Marland's child, by J. Watkins, painted on paper, signed, early 19thC, 4¼in (11cm) high, in an ormolu and papier mâché frame.
£520–620
€/ $820–980 G(L)

A silhouette of HRH The Duke of Sussex, by W. Mason, painted on card, c1826, 3¼in (8.5cm) high, in a papier mâché frame.
£520–620
€/ $820–980 G(L)

◄ **A silhouette of a young boy,** painted on card, 19thC, 2½in (6.5cm) high, in a maple frame.
£130–150
€/ $200–240 AH

A silhouette of a lady, by Miss Mary Lightfoot, painted on card, c1785, 3¾in (9.5cm) high, in a papier mâché frame.
£380–450
€/ $600–710 B

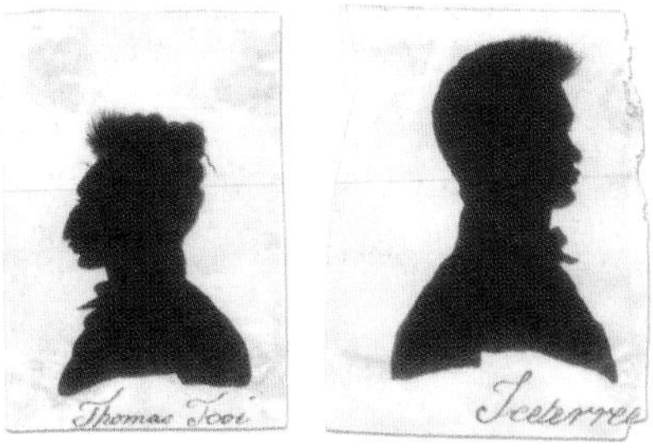

Two black ink silhouettes, inscribed 'Thomas Tooi' and 'Teeterree', c1818, larger 2¾in (7cm) high.
£2,800–3,200
€/ $4,400–5,100 F&C

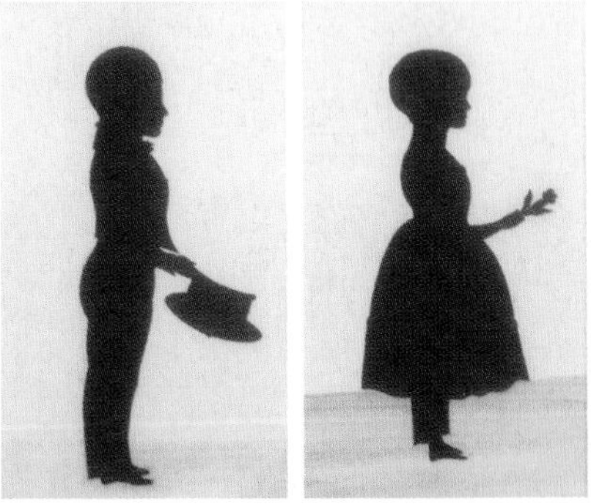

A set of four silhouettes of the children of the 1st Earl of Cottenham, by J. Gapp, cut-outs on card, inscribed and dated 1830, 6½in (16.5cm) high, in maple frames.
£1,400–1,600
€/ $2,200–2,500 B

◄ **A Victorian silhouette of Mrs Raymond,** 10 x 8in (25.5 x 20.5cm).
£380–450
€/ $600–710
WW

Artists' Materials

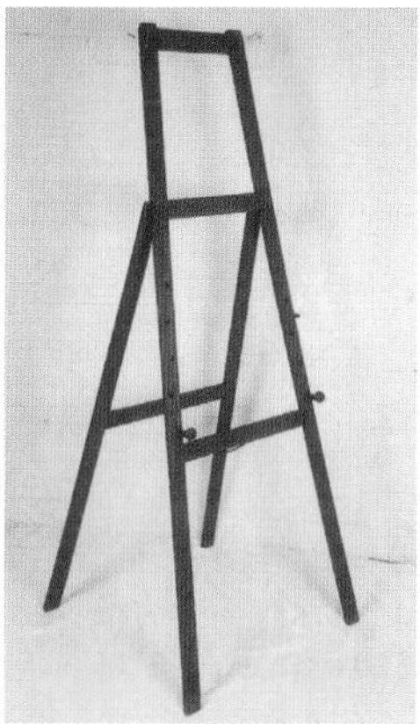

A wooden easel, c1900, 70in (178cm) high.
£55–60
€/ $85–95 ⊞ AL

► **An oak adjustable studio easel,** by Robertson & Co, with triple-screw mechanism and handle, on trestle supports, labelled, late 19thC, 25½in (65cm) wide.
£1,500–1,800
€/ $2,400–2,800 ⚒ B(WM)

A satinwood marquetry easel, the broken pediment centred by a medallion, above a frieze inlaid with garlands, c1900, 75½in (192cm) high.
£3,000–3,500
€/ $4,700–5,400 ⚒ S(Am)

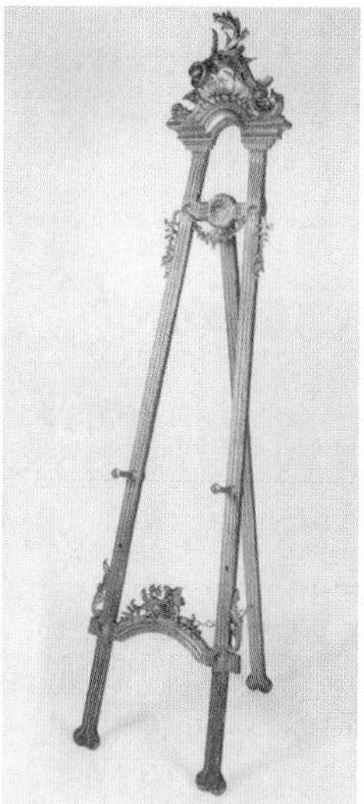

A Victorian giltwood easel, decorated with floral swags, surmounted by a pierced rococo shell and leaf pediment, 92in (233.5cm) high.
£1,800–2,200
€/ $2,800–3,200 ⚒ HYD

◄ **A Victorian mahogany paint box,** the compartmented interior and one long drawer partially fitted with original contents, 10in (25.5cm) wide.
£30–40
€/ $47–63 ⚒ G(L)

A Regency mahogany paint box, trade label for Rowney & Forster, with fitted interior, 8¾in (22cm) wide.
£230–275
€/ $360–430 ⚒ WW

◄ **An artist's mahogany table,** each side with a baize-lined slide, c1790, 20in (51cm) wide.
£950–1,100
€/ $1,500–1,700 ⚒ S(O)

An artist's satinwood table, banded with purpleheart and strung with boxwood and ebony, with a removable ledge and a pair of candleslides to the side, the frieze drawer enclosing a fitted compartment, on turned tapering legs, brass cappings and casters, c1800, 22½in (57cm) wide.
£22,000–25,000
€/ $34,700–40,000 ⚒ S

Items in the Artists' Materials section have been arranged in alphabetical order.

► **An artist's mahogany travelling box,** with velvet-lined folding easel slope over a box with one long drawer, early 19thC, 11in (28cm) wide.
£200–240
€/ $315–380 ⚒ TMA

Antiquities

A terracotta bowl, with an upturned rim, the interior red burnished, Egyptian, Pre-Dynastic, c4000–3000 BC, 9½in (24cm) diam.
£700–820
€/ $1,100–1,300 B(Kn)

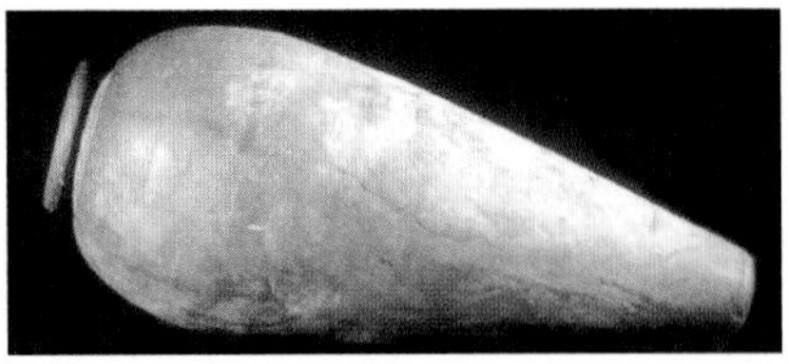

A ceramic storage jar, the shoulder decorated with a stylized wave pattern, cracked, Egyptian, c3000 BC, 23½in (59.5cm) high.
£1,200–1,400
€/ $1,900–2,200 S(Am)

An Abydos ware flagon, Jordan/Israel area, c3000BC, 12in (30.5cm) high.
£230–270
€/ $360–430 AnAr
Abydos wares were found in the royal tombs of the 1st and 2nd Dynasties at Abydos, Middle Egypt. They were an import from the Jordan/Israel area.

The items in this section have been arranged chronologically in sequence of civilizations, namely Egyptian, Near Eastern, Greek, Roman, Byzantine, western European, British, Anglo-Saxon and Medieval.

A painted wooden head of a man, wearing a wig of short tiered curls, Egyptian, 6th Dynasty, 2360–2195 BC, 5¼in (13.5cm) high.
£600–700
€/ $950–1,100 S

◄ **A wooden headrest,** carved in three sections, Egyptian, probably 18th Dynasty, 1540–1292 BC , 2½in (6.5cm) high.
£3,000–3,500
€/ $4,750–5,500
S(NY)

Egyptian gods

The pantheon of the gods of ancient Egypt is enormous. Legend had it that the gods lived and ruled in Egypt long before the arrival of man. The Greek historian Herodotus (c450 BC), wrote that most animals were sacred to the Egyptians, and the practice of representing many of the gods as humans with animal or birds' heads was abhorrent to the Classical world.

Many of the human-headed gods can be recognized by the hieroglyphic symbol on their heads. For instance, Isis has a small throne and Serkhet, the scorpion goddess, has a small scorpion on her head. There were also several sacred family trinities: the major one being Osiris, god of the dead, his wife Isis and their son Horus. Other family trinities were particularly venerated in different parts of the country.

Representations of the various gods occur in all materials and sizes, those most often seen being the small faïence images, pierced for suspension, that served as protective amulets. Common among bronze statuettes are standing figures of Osiris, and seated figures of Isis nursing her son Horus. Many gods are still obscure and not easily identified.

A bronze figure of Anubis, including the top part of the attached column from the standard, Egyptian, Late Dynastic Period, 6th–4thC BC, 1¾in (4.5cm) high.
£115–125
€/ $180–200 ANG
This figure represents Anubis (Wepwawet), the 'Opener of the Ways', the jackal god of embalming, and Protector of Osiris. It is standing with characteristically sloping back legs which is how the creature is portrayed on standards carried before the Pharaoh in processions.

A bronze figure of Osiris, Egyptian, 26th Dynasty, c664–525 BC, 9½in (24cm) high.
£2,400–2,800
€/ $3,800–4,400 B(Kn)

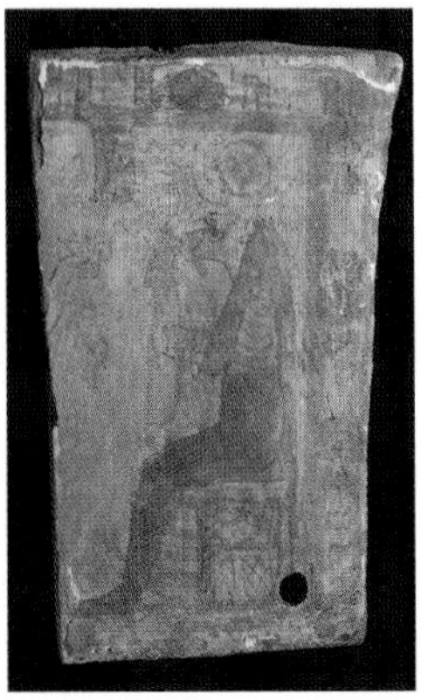

◄ **A gesso-painted wooden sarcophagus fragment,** showing an ape-headed mummiform deity seated, small piercing in the bottom right-hand corner, on a black velvet mount, Egyptian, post-300 BC, 9½in (24cm) high.
£340–375
€/ $550–600 ANG
The representation is of the god Hapi, one of the Four Sons of Horus. He guarded the lungs of the deceased.

Gesso

Gesso is a plaster made of whiting and glue. It was used on a large scale from the 18th Dynasty for applying to wood as a ground for painting and gilding. Later it was used for mummy masks and coffins made of cartonnage. Cartonnage consists of layers of linen and gesso.

A carved limestone eye idol, of stylized form, Mesopotamian, Tell Brak, c3000 BC, 2in (5cm) high.
£550–600
€/ $870–950 ⊞ HEL

A stone jar, the shoulder carved with a rope-twist band of decoration interspersed with four pierced miniature lugs, one lug chipped, Mesopotamian, 3000–2000 BC, 4¾in (12cm) high.
£750–875
€/ $1,200–1,400 ⚒ B(Kn)

A pottery cuneiform trade or taxation pierced docket, inscribed 'City of Uruk', repeated twice, Mesopotamian, 2500–2200 BC, 1½in (3.5cm) high.
£400–450
€/ $630–700 ⊞ HEL

A stone vessel, in the form of a crouching frog with a deep cavity on the back, Greater Syria, first half of 2nd millennium BC, 4¼in (11cm) wide.
£3,800–4,200
€/ $6,000–6,600 ⚒ S(NY)

◄ A clay cuneiform tablet, with ten lines of Babylonian on the obverse and reverse, some damage and repair, Old Babylonian, 1900–1700 BC, 1¾in (4.5cm) high.
£260–285
€/ $400–450 ⊞ A&O
These tablets were a type of balance sheet for products from a large economic organization.

► A bronze dagger, the flanged hilt with a finger grip, a narrow guard and an elongated blade, with a 4in (10cm) section of the original wooden hilt, Ancient Iran, c1250–950 BC, 16½in (42cm) long.
£400–450
€/ $630–700
⊞ A&O

A pottery model of a wagon, with incised decoration, Syrian, 2nd–1st millennium BC, 10½in (26.5cm) high.
£1,100–1,200
€/ $1,700–1,900 ⚒ S(O)

A bronze bowl, Persian, Luristan, c1200–1000 BC, 6in (15cm) diam.
£230–270
€/ $360–430 ⊞ AnAr

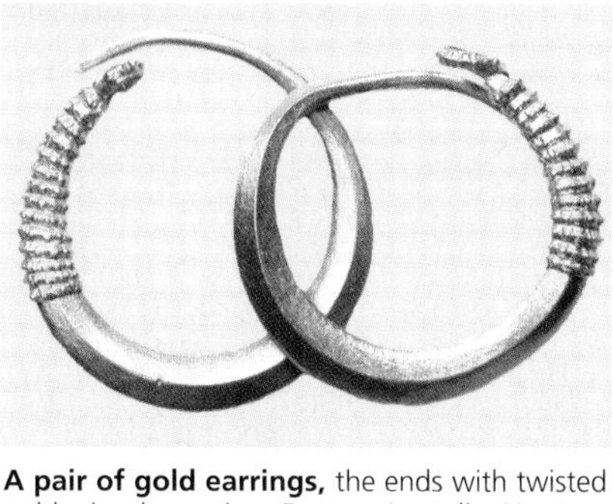

A pair of gold earrings, the ends with twisted gold wire decoration, Eastern Anatolia, Urartu, c800 BC, ½in (1cm) diam.
£250–275
€/ $400–440 ⊞ A&O

A burnished pottery jug, Phoenician, 8th–7thC BC, 5in (13cm) high.
£200–220
€/ $315–350 ⊞ HEL

A gypsum carved head of a god or king, Achaemenid, 5thC BC, 3in (8cm) high.
£200–220
€/ $315–350 ⊞ HEL

The Desmond Morris Collection

Desmond Morris, zoologist, anthropologist, television personality and broadcaster, was 'hooked' on the art of Bronze Age Cyprus the moment he walked into Room Two of the Cyprus Museum in Nicosia. He bought his first Cypriot piece in 1967 and, over the next nine years, formed a magnificent collection of over 1,100 pieces. The culmination of his dedication was his publication of the collection, *The Art of Ancient Cyprus* (1985), a magnificently illustrated and researched study that has become a seminal reference work.

Having achieved his objective, Dr Morris decided to sell the collection. He hoped that it could be kept together, perhaps bought by a museum or institution as there was no doubt that the collection was the finest of its kind outside Cyprus. Many of the pieces had provenance and origins from other major collections, some formed over 100 years ago. Not able to keep such a large collection intact, Dr Morris put the most important pieces into auction in November 2001. Many of the major pieces, notably the so-called 'Scenic Compositions', were hotly pursued in the saleroom, going high above estimate, with the Getty Museum in Malibu, California, a major purchaser.

Peter Clayton

A pottery footed cup, the sides painted with two undulating lines and concentric circles inside, Minoan or Mycenaean, c15th–14thC BC, 4¾in (12cm) diam.
£550–600
€/ $870–950 S

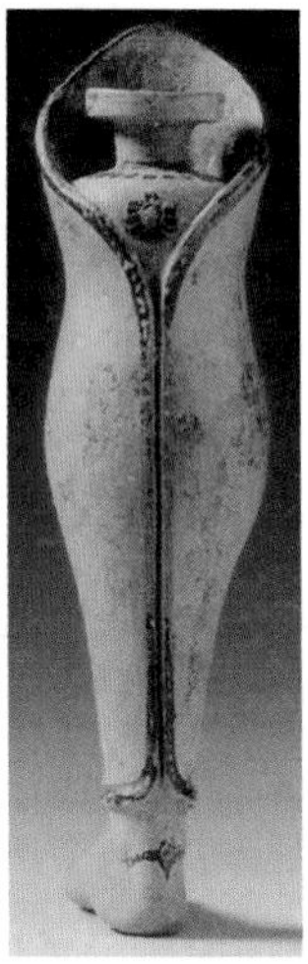

◄ **A pottery aryballos,** in the form of a vessel contained inside a greave open at the back, an incised contour line on the inner calf, alternating red and black tongues on the disk rim, tongues on the shoulder, a palmette below, restored, Greek, Rhodes, first half of the 6thC BC, 5½in (14cm) high.
£5,300–5,800
€/ $8,500–9,200
S(NY)

A terracotta flagon, with painted geometric decoration, Cyprus, early Iron Age, c1200 BC, 10in (25.5cm) high.
£320–400
€/ $500–630 AnAr

A pottery cup, painted with a geometric design, Cypriot, early Iron Age, 1050–650 BC, 4¾in (12cm) diam.
£270–300
€/ $430–475 HEL

► **A core-formed glass alabastron,** the applied handles with spurs, neck and rim missing, some iridescence, Greek, c6th–5thC BC, 4½in (11.5cm) high.
£650–750
€/ $1,000–1,200 B(Kn)

A terracotta figure, of a lady offerant wearing a polos headdress, Greek, 5thC BC, 12in (30.5cm) high.
£1,000–1,200
€/ $1,600–1,900
AnAr

A pottery nestoris, painted with palmette and lotus motifs, the flat handles with rotelles, Apulian, Messapian, 5th–4thC BC, 11½in (29cm) high.
£700–800
€/ $1,100–1,300 S

A Red Figure kantharos, depicting the head of a Lady of Fashion, Magna Graecia, 4thC BC, 8½in (21.5cm) high.
£1,000–1,200
€/ $1,600–1,900 AnAr

◄ **A gold wreath,** composed of 11 sheet-gold myrtle leaves, connecting wire missing, Greek, c4th–3rdC BC, 8¼in (21cm) diam.
£3,200–3,500
€/ $5,000–5,500
S(NY)

A terracotta fragment, depicting a male with a kantharos, Greek, 4th/3rdC BC, 4½in (11.5cm) high.
£130–160
€/ $200–250 AnAr

A carved marble foot, wearing a sandal, Roman, 1stC AD, 6in (15cm) long.
£1,500–1,700
€/ $2,400–2,700 ⊞ HEL

A marble fragment from a sarcophagus, carved with the muse Polyhymnia facing to the right and holding a scroll, a theatre mask at her feet, Roman, c200 AD, 30in (76cm) high.
£5,000–5,500
€/ $7,900–8,700 ⚒ S
Polyhymnia, muse of Sacred Poetry and of Mime, is often shown veiled, with a pensive look on her face. She is the seventh of the nine muses of Ancient Greece.

A marble profile portrait of a youth, restored, Roman, c1stC AD, 5¼in (13.5cm) high.
£900–1,100
€/ $1,400–1,700 ⚒ S(Am)

A marble relief fragment from a sarcophagus, carved with the head of Dionysos, his right arm raised above his head, Roman, c3rdC AD, 6¾in (17cm) high.
£1,500–1,700
€/ $2,400–2,700 ⚒ S

A bronze vessel attachment, in the form of the god Pan, Roman, Carnuntum, 2ndC AD, 2¾in (7cm) high.
£270–300
€/ $430–475 ⊞ ANG
This is a complete figure with a semi-circular attachment for fitting to the outside rim of a situla (table vessel).

◄ **A bronze chest fitting,** cast and chased in the form of a lion's head, with a loop handle, remains of three iron fixing nails or studs, repair to two stud holes, Roman Syria or Near East, c2ndC AD, 5¼in (13.5cm) diam.
£350–400
€/ $550–650 ⊞ ANG

A bronze fitting, in the form of a bacchante, probably from a tripod leg, set on an integral ridged base, with L-shaped attachment bar to her back, both arms missing from the elbows, mounted, Roman, c2ndC AD, 4½in (11.5cm) high.
£850–950
€/ $1,350–1,500 ⊞ A&O

A bronze grotesque figure of a male, standing on one leg, on a wooden display stand, Roman, 2ndC AD, 3¼in (8.5cm) high.
£175–200
€/ $275–320 ⊞ ANG

A bronze lamp, the handle plate in the form of Medusa's head, the calyx pierced for attachment of the missing lid, Roman, 1st–2ndC AD, 7in (18cm) long.
£2,700–3,000
€/ $4,300–4,800 ⚒ S(NY)

A bronze lamp, in the form of a wild sow, with the nozzle between her tusks, the coiled tail forming the handle, Roman or Byzantine, c4thC AD, 6in (15cm) long.
£1,300–1,500
€/ $2,000–2,400 ⚒ S(NY)

Roman lamps

Roman pottery lamps are among the most collectable of Roman antiquities. Examples from the 1st and 2nd century AD often have a scene represented on the discus (the top) depicting aspects of daily life: gladiators fighting, chariot racing, actors, harbours, buildings, and quite highly prized (and priced) erotic encounters. Many gods are represented, both classical and 'oriental', the latter including the Egyptian Anubis and Isis, and Cybele, Mother Goddess of Asia Minor. The base of the lamp often carries an impressed maker's mark so the factory can often be identified.

The red-fired pottery lamps of Christian Roman North Africa often have Biblical scenes, such as the Sacrifice of Isaac, the Children in the Fiery Furnace or, extremely rare, Christ surrounded by the heads of the twelve disciples. Other Christian symbols include the Chi-Rho monogram (the first two letters of Christ's name in Greek), a Christogram cross, a fish, or a chalice with doves. Some very rare lamps have a seven-branched candlestick, the Jewish menorah.

Many 1st-century AD lamps made in Italy are found in North Africa, where they were imported before local lamp factories were established there. These operated mainly between AD 350 and 425, when the Vandalic invasions destroyed most of them.

Collecting Roman lamps can be very rewarding because of their variety. It is possible to concentrate on a single theme, such as animals, ships, gods etc, or perhaps study the maker's marks to give the collection a more personal touch.

A terracotta oil lamp, the discus decorated with an actor wearing a comic theatre mask, the base with maker's name L. M. Adiec, Roman, early 2ndC AD, 5in (12.5cm) long.
£215–240
€/ $340–380 ⊞ A&O

Lucius Munetus Adiectus was a central Italian manufacturer who exported much of his products to Roman North Africa.

A redware oil lamp, decorated with the Chi-Rho symbol of Christianity, the edge of the discus with decorative geometric symbols, Roman North Africa, c350–420 AD, 5¾in (14.5cm) long.
£215–240
€/ $340–380 ⊞ A&O

A glass double balsamarium, with applied glass handles, one handle damaged, Roman, c3rd–4thC AD, 4½in (11.5cm) high.
£320–375
€/ $500–600 ⚒ B(Kn)

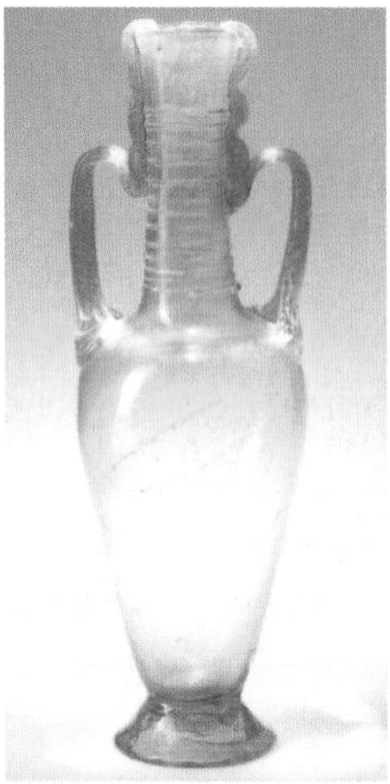

A glass amphora, with trail decoration around the neck, the handles applied with trailed glass extending to the rim, Roman, c4thC AD, 9in (23cm) high.
£900–1,100
€/ $1,400–1,700 ⚒ B(Kn)

LOCATE THE SOURCE

The source of each illustration in Miller's can be found by checking the code letters below each caption with the Key to Illustrations, pages 794–800.

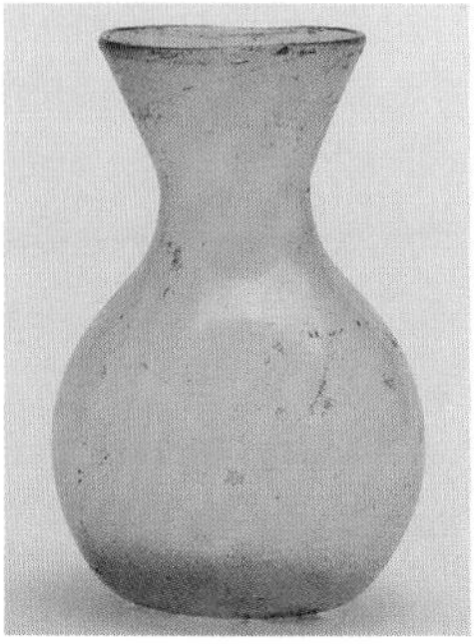

A glass jar, with an everted mouth, Roman, 4thC AD, 5in (12.5cm) high.
£160–200
€/ $250–315 ⊞ AnAr

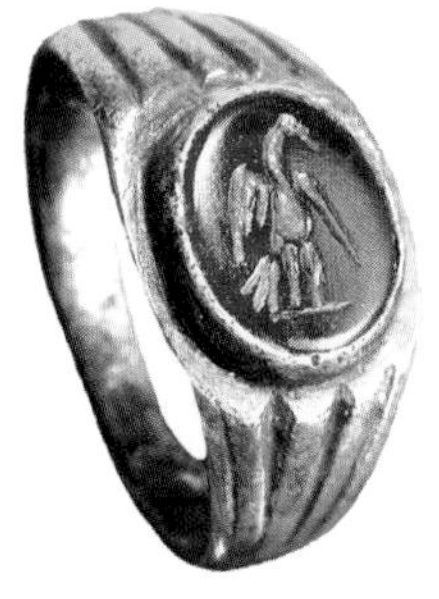

A silver ring, the carnelian intaglio carved with a stylized eagle, Roman, c2nd–3rdC AD.
£200–225
€/ $315–350 ⊞ A&O

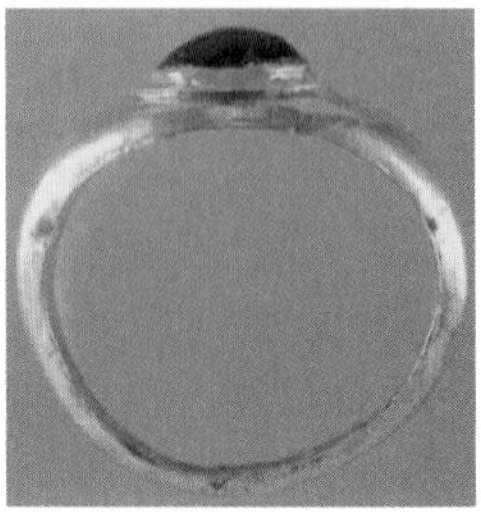

A gold finger ring, mounted with a garnet cabochon, Roman, c2nd–4thC AD.
£3,000–3,500
€/ $4,700–5,500 ⚒ WW

A limestone reliquary shrine, the entablatures carved in relief with guilloche and other motifs, Byzantine, c6thC AD, 6¼in (16cm) high.
£4,500–5,000
€/ $7,000–7,900 S(NY)

◄ **A bronze fibula,** the pin with a poppy-head terminal, the bow with a coiled loop at either end and twisted central section, Italic, c9th–8thC BC, 10in (25.5cm) long.
£275–325
€/ $430–515 B(Kn)

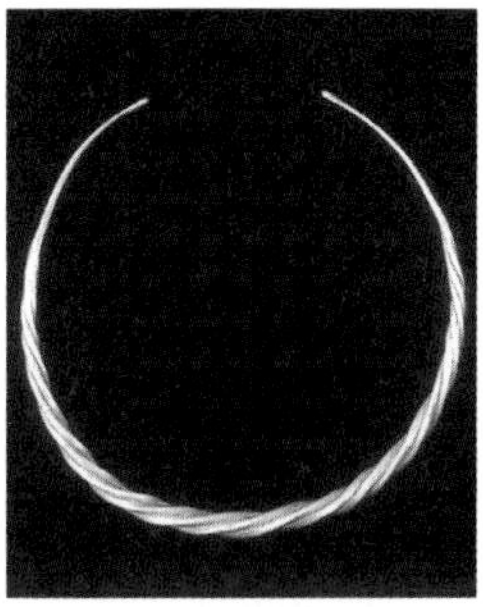

A twisted silver torq, Celtic, c4th–3rdC BC, 7in (18cm) diam.
£800–1,000
€/ $1,300–1,600 B(Kn)

A bronze figure of a discus thrower, on a wooden stand, right leg missing, Italic, 4thC BC, 3in (7.5cm) high.
£175–200
€/ $275–320 ANG

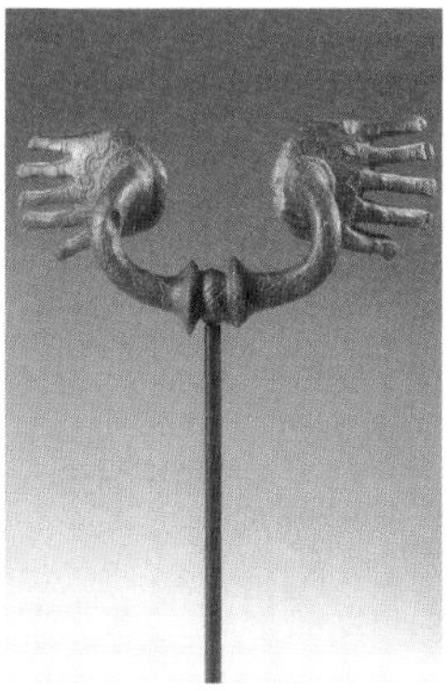

A bronze cauldron handle, the attachments formed as a pair of hands incised with knuckle and fingernail details, the wrist area decorated with a meander and dot pattern, mounted, Celtic, c4th–1stC BC, 8½in (21.5cm) wide.
£550–650
€/ $870–1,000 B(Kn)

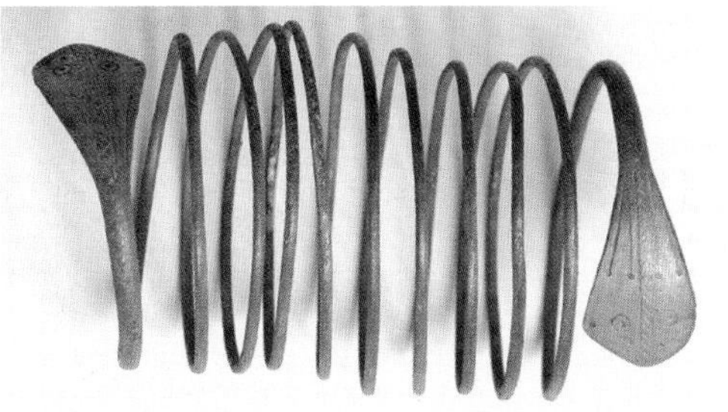

A Celtic silver coiled arm bracelet, with serpent terminals, Thracian, c1stC BC, 4¾in (12cm) long.
£250–275
€/ $400–440 ANG

► **A bronze spearhead,** the hollow socle pierced on either side, the hipped leaf-shaped blade with medial rib, mounted, Bronze Age, c1200–800 BC, 10½in (26.5cm) long.
£800–950
€/ $1,300–1,500 B(Kn)

A bronze openwork buckle, in the form of a sphinx, pin and backplate missing, British, Norfolk, late 2nd–early 3rdC AD, 1¾in (4.5cm) wide.
£130–145
€/ $200–230 ANG
This is a rare piece and, until now, unknown in Britain.

A Migdale-type copper-alloy flat axe, Humberside, early Bronze Age, c1800 BC, 4½in (11.5cm) wide.
£260–285
€/ $410–450 A&O

A bronze cosmetic grinding set, the boat-shaped mortar with knobbed terminals, with suspension loops, the pestle with a swan-neck loop, Norfolk, c1stC BC, mortar 3in (7.5cm) wide.
£350–385
€/ $550–600 A&O

A rabbit brooch, complete with pin, Romano-British, c1st–2ndC AD, ¾in (2cm) wide.
£100–120
€/ $160–190 A&O

A bronze vesica seal, with central decorative fleur-de-lys, and inscription 'S'LETICIE FIL WILL GISSO', c14thC, 1¾in (4.5cm) high.
£80–90
€/ $125–145 A&O
This seal would have been for personal use.

Pre-Columbian Art

A standing terracotta figure, Ecuador, Manabi, 500 BC–AD 500, 9¾in (25cm) high.
£220–250
€/ $350–400 BERN

A pottery human effigy vessel, with traces of geometric devices, old repairs, Mexican, Jalisco, c150 BC–AD 250, 8in (20.5cm) high.
£225–250
€/ $350–400 SK

A terracotta vase, Mayan, Late Classic period, AD 600–900, 6¾in (17cm) high.
£450–550
€/ $700–870 BERN

► A pottery figure, with perforations for attachments, minor damage, Columbia, Quimbaya, AD 500–1500, 9in (23cm) high.
£320–380
€/ $500–600 SK

A Mezcala stone figure, Mexican, Late Pre-Classic 300–100 BC, 4in (10cm) high.
£300–325
€/ $475–515 A&O

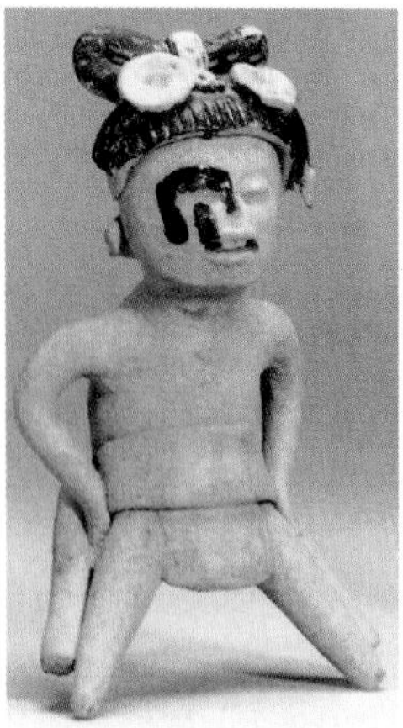

A pottery war figure, with a built-in whistle at the back, pigment details on the head, some losses, Mexican, Vera Cruz, AD 150– 250, 9½in (24cm) high.
£280–320
€/ $440–500 SK

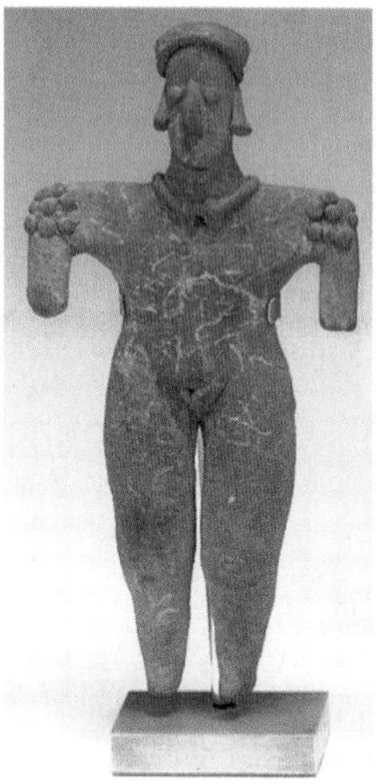

A female terracotta flat figure, on a stand, Mexican, Colima, Protoclassic Period, 100 BC–AD 250, 7¾in (19.5cm) high.
£150–175
€/ $240–280 BERN

► A terracotta head, from a large hollow figure, the face with a pierced mouth showing teeth and wearing earrings, some hair and flange missing, chips and repairs, Mexican, Veracruz, AD 250–450, 13½in (34.5cm) high.
£800–950
€/ $1,300–1,500 S(P)

A painted pottery figure, the body with geometric painting, Mexican, Jalisco, c100 BC–AD 250, 10½in (26.5cm).
£350–400
€/ $550–650 SK

◄ A double-chambered figural vessel, the front chamber modelled as a king wearing a crown, his mouth forming the spout, Peruvian, Chimu, AD 1000–1200, 7in (18cm) long.
£350–400
€/ $550–650
A&O

A pair of earthenware cuchimilco figures, Peruvian, Chancay, AD 1100–1400, 18½in (46.5cm) high.
£1,300–1,500
€/ $2,100–2,400 BERN
Cuchimilco means 'with upraised arms'.

Tribal Art

An Inuit child's pair of fur moccasins, c1880, 5in (12.5cm) long.
£160–180
€/ $250–285 JPr

◄ An Inuit model of a kayak, with a wooden figure wearing a skin anorak, the skin cover with ivory fittings, inscribed 'White Fish Islands 1862', 21in (53.5cm) long.
£450–525
€/ $710–830
B(Kn)

A pair of Dakota beaded hide spirit moccasins, Native American, c1900, 10¼in (26cm) long.
£475–550
€/ $750–870 DuM
The design symbolizes an opening to the spirit world.

► An Inuit carved green stone swimming whale, signed and dated '81' to the underside, 20in (51cm) long.
£350–425
€/ $550–670 RIT

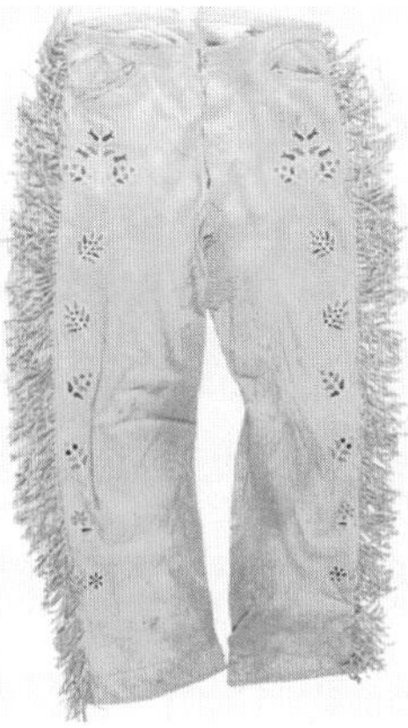

A pair of Eastern Sioux beaded deerskin trousers, with a silver buckle, three metal buttons, and nickel-brass catch, the outer seams with seven beaded floral panels and fringing, Native American, late 19thC, legs 38in (96.5cm) long.
£475–550
€/ $750–870 JDJ

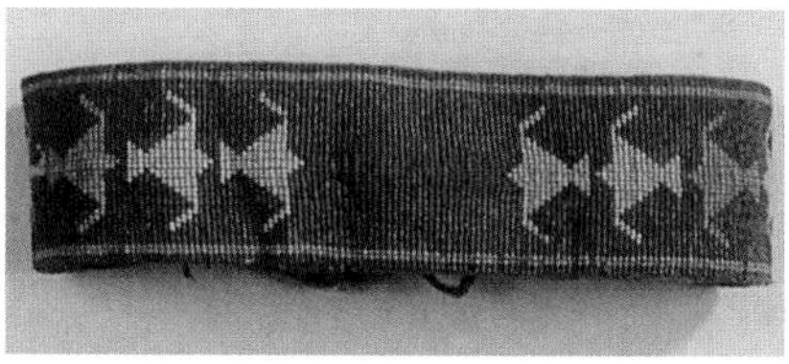

A Great Lakes choker, the beaded strip attached to birch bark, with a blue silk liner, tanned hide ties, minor damage, Native American, mid-19thC, 5in (12.5cm) diam.
£1,000–1,100
€/ $1,600–1,700 SK

A pair of Southern Plains high top moccasins, with beaded feet and two double bands of beading on the upper portion of the leggings, some holes, Native American, 19thC, 20in (51cm) long.
£600–725
€/ $950–1,100 JDJ

A pair of beaded cuffs, decorated with a stylized flower motif, with fringed beaded loops, Native American, probably Plains, 19thC, 8in (20.5cm) long.
£130–150
€/ $200–240 DN

A pair of moccasins, Native American, Iroquois, c1880.
£160–180
€/ $250–280 JPr

◄ A Navajo weaving, minor damage, some wool loss, Native American, late 19thC, 40 x 15½in (101.5 x 39.5cm).
£2,200–2,700
€/ $3,500–4,300 SK

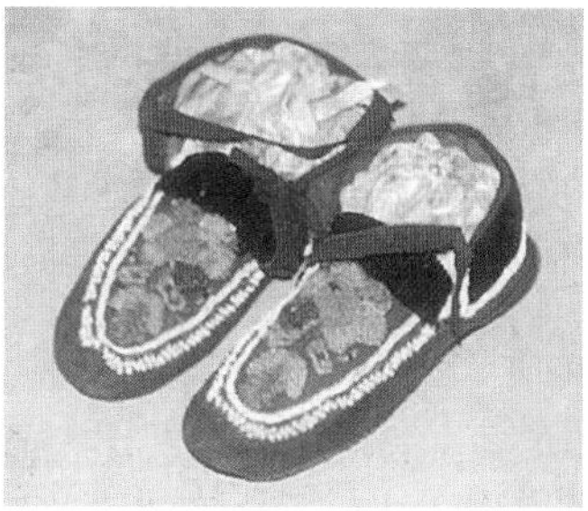

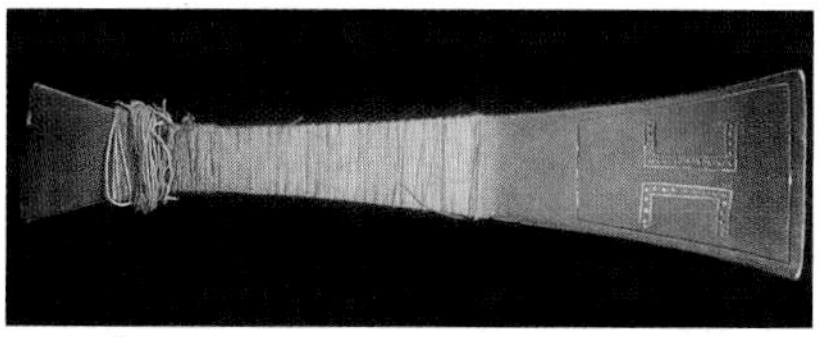

A ceremonial club, with incised motifs to either side, the central section wrapped in string binding, inscribed '44-1957', South American, Surinam, 16¼in (41.5cm) long.
£2,000–2,400
€/ $3,200–3,800 S

◄ A pair of beaded hide moccasins, Native American, c1910, 10½in (26.5cm) long.
£230–275
€/ $360–440 DuM

A wooden mask, minor damage, Liberian, Bassa, 9¾in (25cm) high.
£2,000–2,400
€/ $3,200–3,800 S(P)

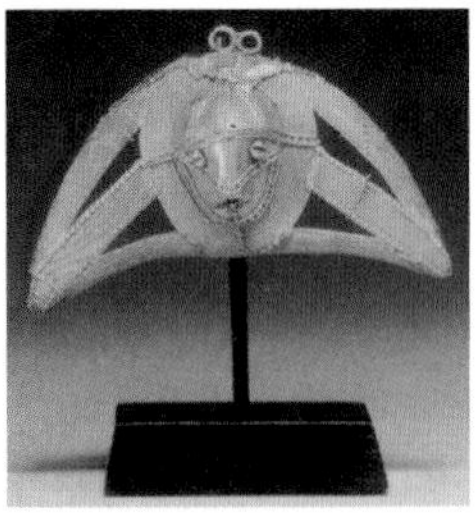

An Ebrie or Baule gold pendant, African, Ivory Coast, 3¾in (9.5cm) wide.
£1,200–1,400
€/ $1,900–2,200 S(NY)
The eastern coast of the Ivory Coast comprises an area of lagoons. The Ebrie, while influenced stylistically by the neighbouring Akan and Baule groups, have a distinctive style of elaborate gold jewellery. Made using the lost-wax process, it is characterized by fine linear geometric-relief decoration. The nature of the lost-wax process means that each piece is unique.

A male Chiwara wooden antelope headdress, with metal strips on the brow, African, Bambara, Mali, 42in (106.5cm) high.
£200–220
€/ $320–350 RIT
This stylized antelope headdress would have surmounted a basketwork cap worn at agricultural festivals. Two dancers, one wearing a male Chiwara headdress, the other a female, would be disguised in fibre costumes and would perform ritual dances to promote the fertility of the soil.

A Senufo wooden loom heddle, with spool, African, Ivory Coast, 7¾in (19.5cm) high.
£330–400
€/ $520–630 BERN
These pulleys are designed to hold the thread in the loom and are elaborately carved with either figurative or zoomorphic decoration. They are created purely for aesthetic satisfaction and have no magical purpose.

A female wooden Akuaba doll, African, Ghana, Ashanti, 9¼in (23.5cm) high.
£300–360
€/ $480–580 BERN
The Akuaba doll is a symbol of fertility to Ghanaian women. A doll is carried either to induce conception or, in the case of a pregnant woman, to ensure the well-being of the unborn child.

► **A Fon wooden cyclopic female figure,** African, Ivory Coast, 25in (63.5cm) high.
£600–700
€/ $950–1,100 S(O)

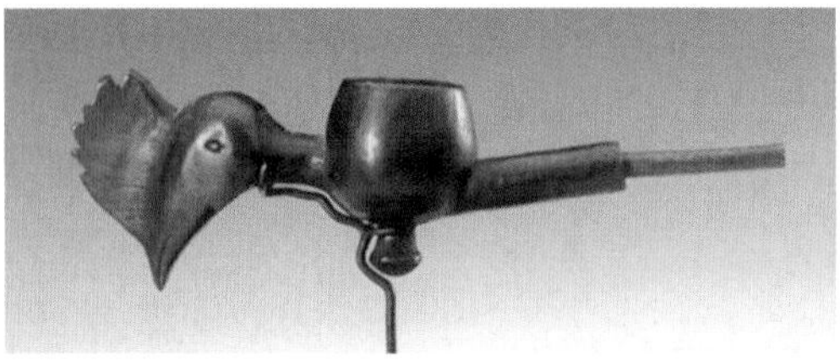

A Baule or Guro wooden pipe bowl, carved as a chicken, African, Ivory Coast, 5½in (14cm) long.
£700–800
€/ $1,100–1,300 HUR

◄ **A Bwa wooden mask,** with polychrome decoration, African, Burkina Faso, c1885, 48in (122cm) high.
£170–200
€/ $270–320 ARTi
This mask was worn by the Bwa in farming rituals. The protuberance over the stylized human face evokes an abstract head of a bird.

► **A wooden mask,** carved as a water spirit, crowned by four men and a boat, with red pigmentation and scarification marks, African, Cirhobo, Nigeria, 1930s, 19in (48.5cm) high.
£1,000–1,100
€/ $1,600–1,700 GRG

A Yoruba carved wood stool, Africa, Nigeria, 14in (35.5cm) high.
£600–700
€/ $950–1,100 S(O)

A pair of female Yoruba Ibeji twins, the heads of carved wood, decorated with beads and cowrie shells, African, Nigeria, 1940s, 10in (25.5cm) high.
£900–1,000
€/ $1,400–1,600 ⊞ Cas
The Yoruba, in Nigeria, have the highest rate of twin births in the world. Twins are considered a blessing to a family. If a twin died, a figure was commissioned and the mother would feed, clothe and care for it, to look after its soul and prevent it from taking the surviving twin. In the event of both twins dying, a pair of twins would be carved.

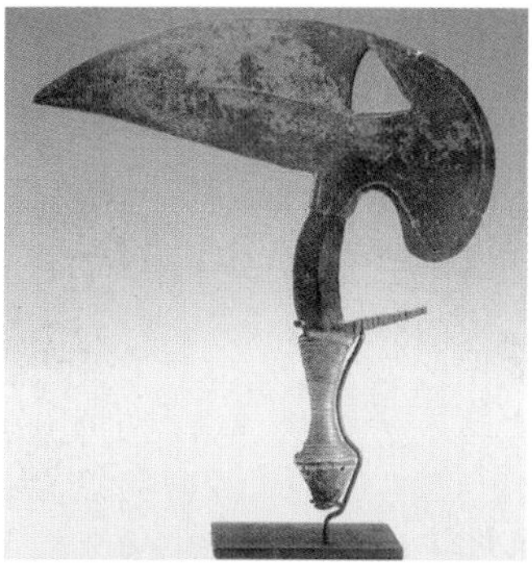

A Kota or Fang iron and brass bird's-head knife, African, Gabon, 13in (33cm) high.
£1,400–1,600
€/ $2,200–2,500 ⊞ HUR
Taking the form of the revered hornbill, the knife was used for ceremonial purposes. It was also a prestige item which could be traded as currency as part of a bride price.

A Fang soft wood Ngil mask, African, Gabon, c1940, 16in (40.5cm) high.
£625–700
€/ $1,000–1,100 ⊞ Cas
Ngil is the judiciary association within the Fang people who policed ceremonies.

► An Azande wooden figure of a female, the head incised with a hatched grid pattern, the shoulders and torso with geometric panels of decoration, African, Democratic Republic of Congo, 37½in (95.5cm) high.
£1,000–1,200
€/ $1,600–1,900 ⚒ B(Kn)
Collected by John Hilberth, a Swedish missionary in Angola and the Congo during the 1940s.

A chief's carved wood staff, African, Ovimbundu, Angola, 21¼in (54cm) high.
£2,500–3,000
€/ $4,000–4,700 ⚒ S(P)

A Ngbandi or Yakoma knife and scabbard, the knife forged from iron and copper, the scabbard made from hide and fibre, decorated with glass beads, Central African Republic, knife 14¼in (36cm) long.
£1,400–1,600
€/ $2,200–2,500 ⊞ HUR
The Ngbandi and related peoples who live along the Zaire River are among the most skillful swordsmiths of Central Africa, with a repertoire of blades ranging from long swords to curved sabres and short spatulate knives with intricate designs. Blades such as this were intended for use as weapons and also for display in ceremonies in veneration of deceased leaders.

A Kuba wooden ceremonial table, on nine chip-carved tapering legs, with a dark red patina, African, Democratic Republic of Congo, 19thC, 20in (51cm) diam.
£320–375
€/ $500–600 ⚒ F&C

A Lozi wooden double bowl, carved as a duck, African, Zambia, 1950s, 17in (43cm) long.
£150–170
€/ $240–270 ⊞ Trib

Items in the Tribal Art section have been arranged geographically from west to east.

◄ A Karamojong feather, pigment-coloured clay and human hair head-dress, African, Karamoja, Uganda, 1950–60, 10in (25.5cm) high.
£340–380
€/ $550–600 ⊞ Trib

◄ A Nyamwezi wooden figure of a female, African, Tanzania, early 20thC, 23½in (59.5cm) high.
£3,800–4,200
€/ $6,000–6,600 ⊞ Trib

A terracotta bowl, modelled as an abstract turtle, with traces of pigment, New Guinea, Lower Sepik River, 10in (25.5cm) diam.
£600–700
€/ $950–1,100 ⚒ S(NY)

A wooden ceremonial bowl, crack to underside, Papua New Guinea, Massim region, 31in (78.5cm) diam.
£3,200–3,800
€/ $5,000–6,000 ⚒ S(P)

A wooden *gope* board, with encrusted natural earth pigments, New Guinea, Papuan Gulf, 1915, 46½in (118cm) high.
£4,300–4,600
€/ $6,800–7,300 ⚒ S

A cane spear thrower, with a stylized carved wood figure mounted with rattan to the centre, New Guinea, north coast, 19thC, 33½in (85cm) long.
£330–360
€/ $520–570 ⊞ FAC

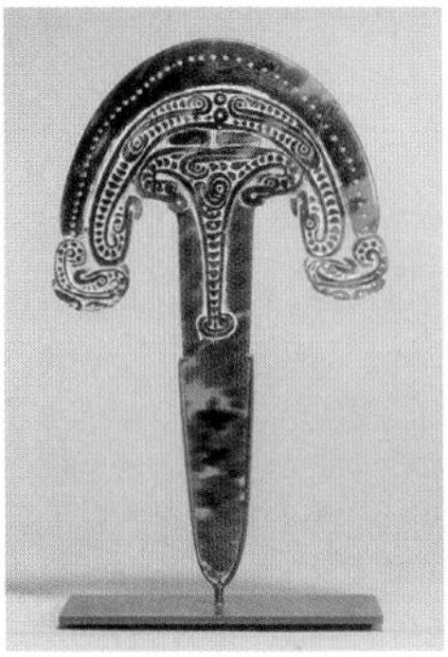

A turtleshell ceremonial spatula, with traces of white pigment, New Guinea, Milne Bay Province, 8¼in (21cm) high.
£3,000–3,500
€/ $4,700–5,500 ⚒ S(NY)
The spatulate form of this finely carved turtleshell object belies its real use. Made only on the Louisiade Archipelago and possibly only on Tagula and Wanim, these 'spatulas' were items of great value used for both display and trade. They were part of a group of very specific objects used in exchange throughout the Massim area on the south eastern part of New Guinea in a highly organized network of trade relations called *kula*.

► A carved wood figure of a female, with traces of red ochre pigments, minor losses, crack, New Caledonian, 23in (58.5cm) high.
£5,500–6,500
€/ $8,700–10,300 ⚒ S(P)

A carved wood Garuda, decorated with coloured pigments, Indonesian, Bali, 1975–95, 41in (104cm) high.
£225–250
€/ $350–400 ⊞ ARTi
Garuda is a mythical man-bird figure.

A Tau-Tau wooden torso, the face stained with white pigment, the neck socket passing through a separately carved hollow torso, Indonesian, 29in (73.5cm) high.
£700–820
€/ $1,100–1,300 ⚒ B(Kn)

◄ A Dyak *mandau*, the carved antler grip with hair tufts, with a woven rattan grip over a horn base terminal, the carved wood scabbard with original pig-hide back compartment, the shoulder straps decorated with shells, Borneo, 19thC, 20in (51cm) long.
£500–550
€/ $800–870 ⊞ FAC

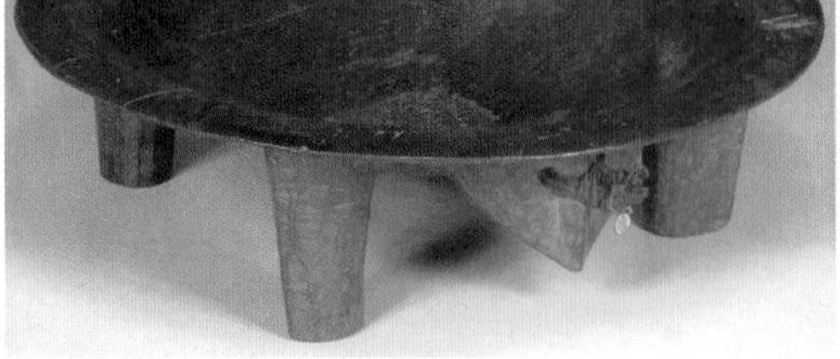

A wooden ceremonial kava bowl, on four tapering adzed legs, with a pendant flange pierced through for suspension, Fijian, 23in (58.5cm) diam.
£5,500–6,500
€/ $8,700–10,300 ⚒ S(P)
Kava is a milky, intoxicating drink made from the crushed root of the pepper tree. The communal drinking of kava was an integral part of religious, economic and political life throughout the Pacific. It still retains great significance in Fiji, but it is now drunk as a social custom as well as a ceremony.

A wooden figure of a male, the eyes inset with obsidian, inscribed '15-1957', Easter Island, 17½in (44.5cm) high.
£2,700–3,000
€/ $4,300–4,700 S

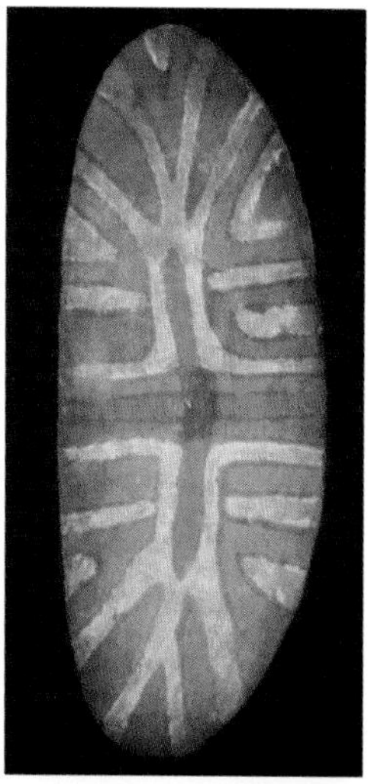

An Aboriginal wooden spear thrower, 'woomera', with carved decoration, Western Australian, 19thC, 24½in (62cm) long.
£200–240
€/ $320–380 F&C

◄ An Aboriginal wooden shield, decorated with natural pigments, inscribed '1973 C.Q.', Australian, northeast Queensland, 34in (86.5cm) high.
£7,800–8,500
€/ $12,300–13,500 S

A Maori carved wood treasure box, the fitted lid pierced at the ends for suspension and decorated with two splayed Tiki figures, the heads carved in relief, the eyes inset with *haliotis* shell, New Zealand, 24¼in (61.5cm) wide.
£2,800–3,200
€/ $4,400–5,000 S(NY)
These boxes are called *wakahuia* and are used to store small valuables and feathers. They were usually suspended from the rafters and viewed from below, which is why the underside is so elaborately decorated.

A Maori Kauri gum portrait head, the face with moko ornament, black-painted hair, minor damage, New Zealand, 19thC, 4in (10cm) high.
£160–200
€/ $250–320 F&C
Moko is the ceremonial tattooing of the face of Maoris. It was believed that after death elaborate facial tattoos would be a passport to the afterlife.

Books & Book Illustrations

Henry C. Andrews, *The Botanists' Repository of New and Rare Plants*, 1797, 4°, vol 1, 64 of 72 hand-coloured engravings, contemporary blue morocco with stamped gilt decoration.
£650–750
€/ $1,000–1,200 ⚒ DW

George Ashdown Audsley, *Gems of Japanese Art and Handicraft*, 1913, 2°, 66 chromolithographed plates, bound in modern green morocco, probably by the Ashley Bindery, japanese paper endpapers and slip-case.
£700–820
€/ $1,100–1,300 ⚒ BBA

William Beattie, *The Ports, Harbours, Watering-Places, and Coast Scenery of Great Britain*, published by George Virtue, 1842, 4°, 2 vols, engraved additional titles, portrait and 122 plates after W. H. Bartlett, maroon polished roan gilt.
£230–275
€/ $360–430 ⚒ L

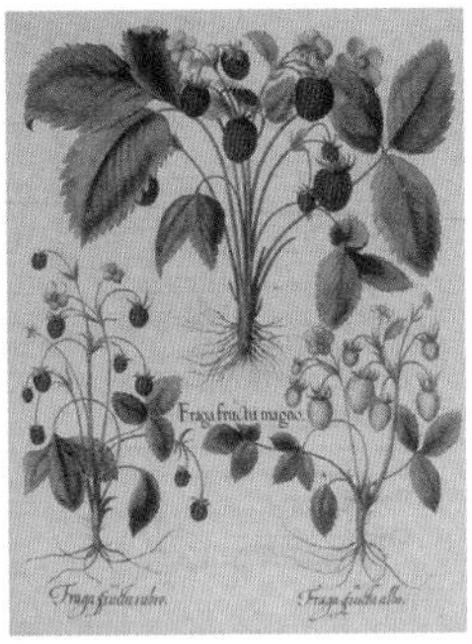

Basilius Besler, *Fraga Fructu Magno*, and two other strawberry plants on one plate, published by Eichstatt and Nuremberg, 1613, 19 x 15¾in (48.5 x 40cm), copper engraving with hand-colouring.
£800–950
€/ $1,300–1,500 ⚒ BBA

► **The Holy Bible,** 1864, 13 x 10in (33 x 25.5cm), original gilt-tooled leather, with brass clasps.
£110–120
€/ $175–190
⊞ PaA

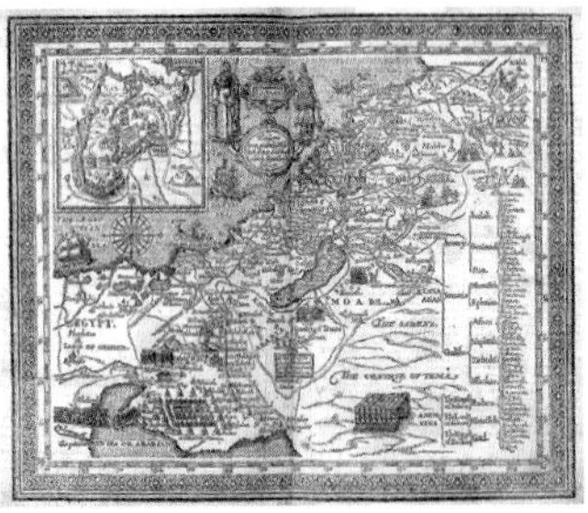

The Holy Bible, printed by Robert Barker, London, 1612, 8°, New Testament title page in cordiform cartouche within a woodcut border, bound with the 1614 *Booke of Psalmes*, inserted engraved map of Canaan, general title page missing, antique calf.
£1,500–1,800
€/ $2,400–2,800 ⚒ S(NY)

Items in the Books & Book Illustrations section have been arranged in alphabetical order by author.

◄ **The Holy Bible,** late 19thC, 13 x 11in (33 x 28cm), with colour illustrations and maps, leather with brass clasps.
£90–100
€/ $140–160
⊞ PaA

The Holy Bible, printed by Christopher Barker, London, 1584, 4°, bound with Sternhold & Hopkins *Book of Psalmes*, printed by John Daye, London 1584, with woodcut borders and map, upper cover detached, lower cover missing, contemporary calf.
£1,200–1,400
€/ $1,900–2,200 ⚒ F&C

Rev William Bradford, *Sketches of the Country, Character, and Costume, in Portugal and Spain, made during the Campaign, and on the Route of the British Army, in 1808 and 1809*, 1813?, 2°, 2 vols in 1, 53 hand-coloured plates, worn and covers near detached, contemporary boards.
£850–1,000
€/ $1,300–1,600 ⚒ DW

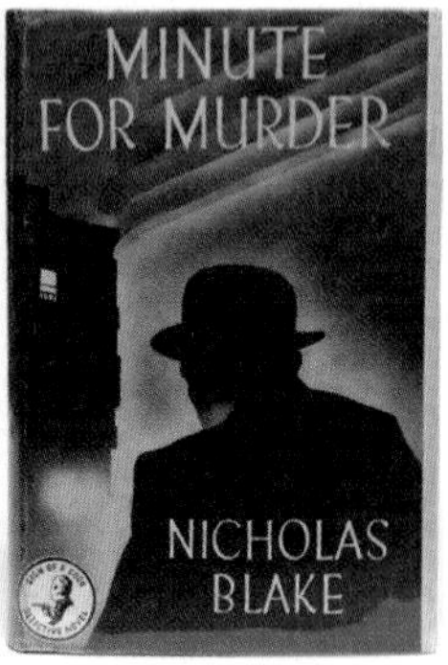

Nicholas Blake, *Minute for Murder*, published by Collins Crime Club, 1947, 7½ x 5in (19 x 12.5cm).
£160–175
€/ $250–280 ⊞ BIB

Nicholas Blake was the pseudonym of British poet Cecil Day Lewis (1904–72). The future Poet Laureate secretly turned to crime writing in order to pay for repairs on his house, and used an assumed name in order to preserve his poetic identity. Nicholas Strangeways, his sleuth, is said to resemble his friend and fellow poet W. H. Auden.

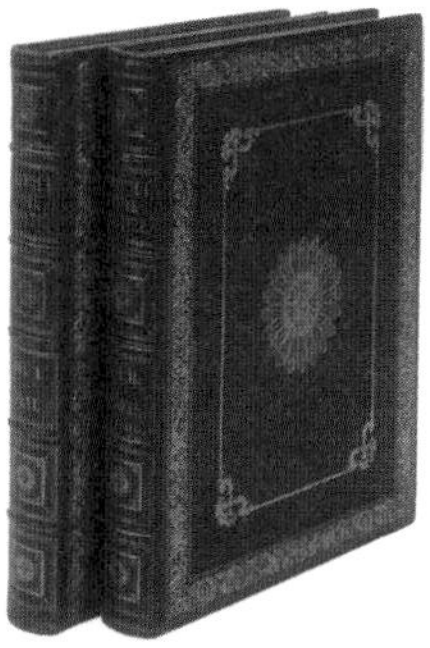

John Browne, *The History of the Metropolitan Church of St. Peter, York*, 1847, 4°, 2 vols, 150 engraved plates, including 10 hand-coloured plates, contemporary morocco with gilt decoration.
£240–280
€/ $380–440 DW

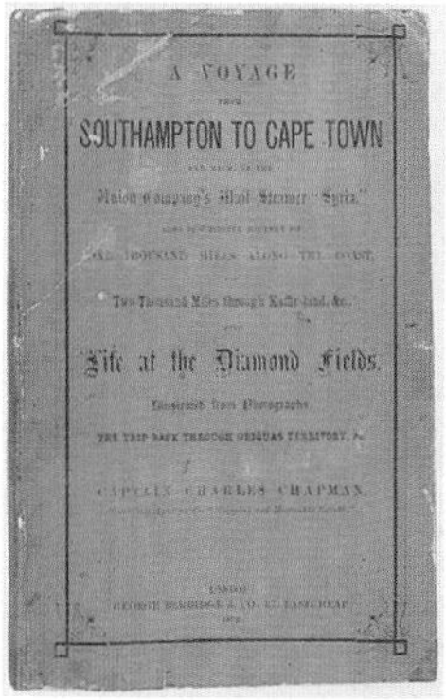

Arabella B. Buckley, *The Fairy-Land of Science*, published by Edward Stanford, 1899, 7½ x 5in (19 x 12.5cm).
£100–110
€/ $160–175 ⊞ TDG

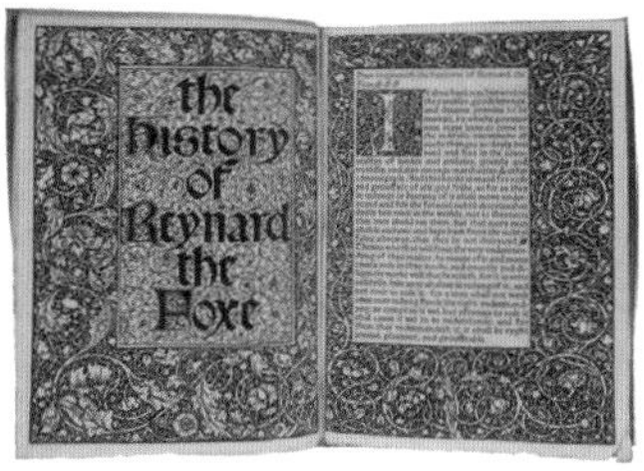

William Caxton (Translator), *The History of Reynard the Foxe*, published by Kelmscott Press, 1892, 4°, one of 300 copies, original limp vellum with ties, uncut.
£1,300–1,600
€/ $2,000–2,500 BBA

◄ **Captain Charles Chapman,** *A Voyage from Southampton to Cape Town and Back, in the Union Company's Mail Steamer* Syria, published by George Berridge & Co, 1872, 8°, recased with original printed wrappers laid on.
£700–840
€/ $1,100–1,300 BBA

► ***The Poetical Works of Thomas Campbell,*** The Lansdowne Poets series, published by Frederick Warne & Co, 1870s, 7 x 5in (18 x 12.5cm).
£120–130
€/ $190–200
⊞ TDG

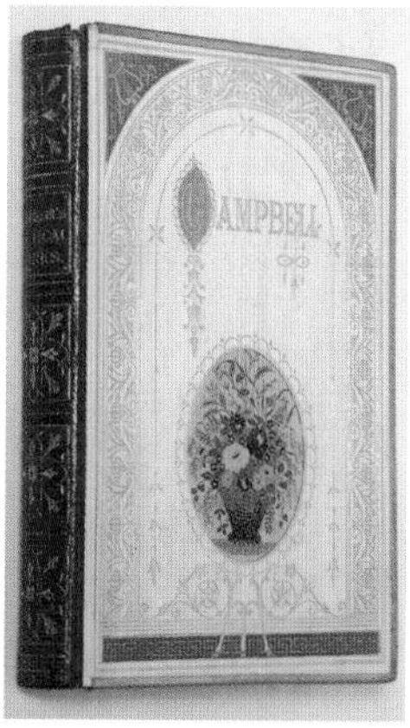

A. Chapuis and E. Gélis, *Le Monde des Automates*, French, 1928, 11 x 9in (28 x 23cm), 2 vols, No. 148 of 1,000.
£1,300–1,500
€/ $2,000–2,400 ⊞ AUTO

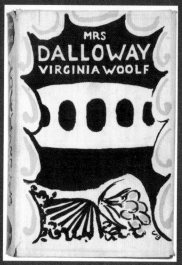

Agatha Christie, *The Body in the Library*, published by Collins Crime Club, first edition, 1942, 7½ x 5¼in (19 x 13.5cm).
£1,200–1,400
€/ $1,900–2,200 ⊞ BIB

Arthur Conan Doyle, *The Case-Book of Sherlock Holmes*, published by John Murray, first edition, 1927, 8 x 5in (20.5 x 12.5cm).
£5,200–5,800
€/ $8,200–9,200 ⊞ NW

For further information on antique books see the full range of Miller's books at
www.millers.uk.com

Rev Charles Lutwidge Dodgson (Lewis Carroll), *Alice's Adventures in Wonderland*, first edition, illustrated by Harry Rountree, published by Nelson, 1908, 4°, 92 colour illustrations, pictorial cloth with gilt decoration to spine and colour illustration to upper cover.
£1,100–1,200
€/ $1,700–1,900 ⊞ JON

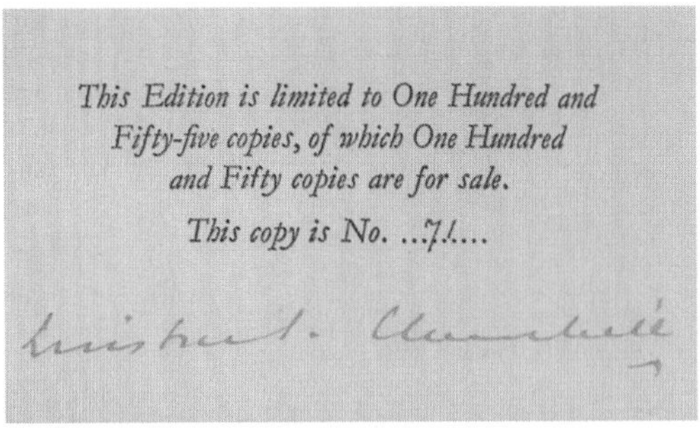
This Edition is limited to One Hundred and Fifty-five copies, of which One Hundred and Fifty copies are for sale.

This copy is No. ..71....

Sir Winston S. Churchill, *Marlborough His Life and Times, 1933–38*, published by Leighton-Straker, first edition, 8°, 4 vols, signed, 71 of 155 copies, contemporary gilt morocco.
£3,800–4,500
€/ $6,000–7,000 ⚒ L

Arthur Conan Doyle, *The Hound of The Baskervilles*, published by George Newnes, first edition, 1902, 8 x 5in (20.5 x 12.5cm).
£1,300–1,500
€/ $2,000–2,400 ⊞ NW
Only about three copies of this book are known to exist in its original dust-jacket, and only one has ever appeared at auction, selling at Sotheby's for over £80,000 (€/ $126,000) in 1998.

▶ **Dalziel Brothers (engravers),** *The Spirit of Praise*, 1867, 10in (25.5cm) high.
£120–135
€/ $190–215 ⊞ TDG

Daphne du Maurier, *Jamaica Inn*, published by Victor Gollancz, 1936, 8 x 6in (20.5 x 15cm), signed.
£900–1,000
€/ $1,400–1,600 ⊞ ADD

William Curtis, *Flora Londinensis*, 1777, 2°, vols 1 and 3, 288 hand-coloured engraved plates, half green-stained calf.
£3,200–3,800
€/ $5,100–6,000 ⚒ L

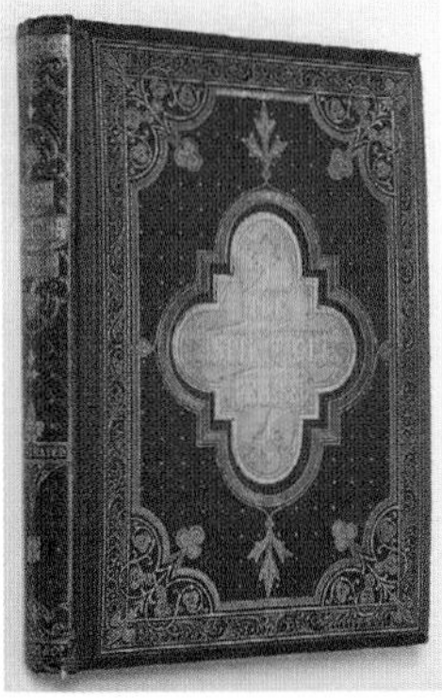

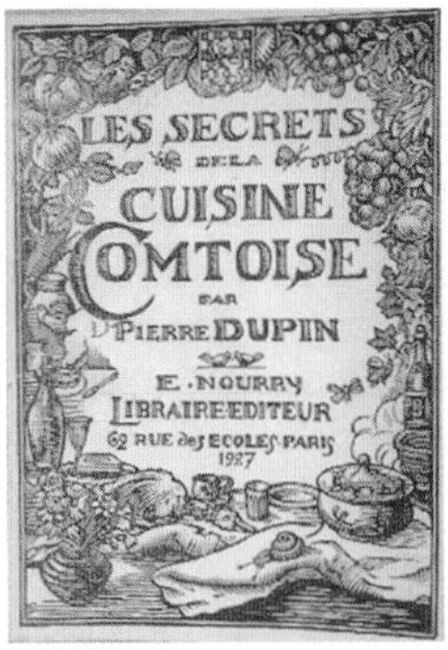

Pierre Dupin, *Les Secrets de la Cuisine Comtoise*, published by E. Nourry, Paris, 1927, five wood-engraved plates, original printed wrappers.
£100–120
€/ $160–190 ⚒ WW

Church Services, published by Oxford University Press, 1855, 6in (15cm) high, mother-of-pearl and paua shell boards.
£225–250
€/ $350–400 ⊞ TDG

Dalziel Brothers (engravers), *Golden Thoughts from Golden Fountains*, published by F. Warne & Co, 1870, 10in (25.5cm) high.
£165–180
€/ $260–285 ⊞ TDG

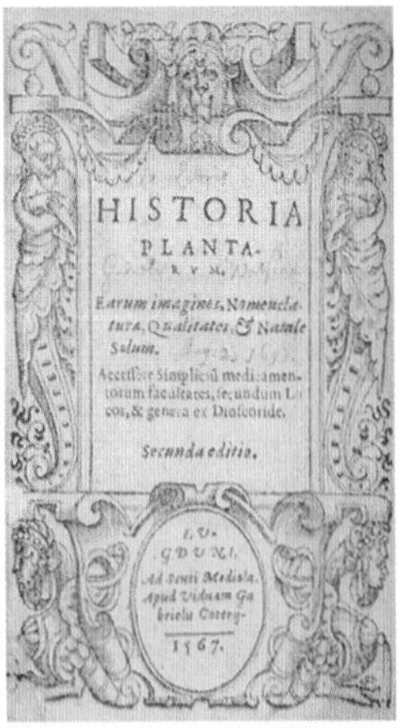

Antoine Dupinet, *Historia Plantarum, Earum Imagines, Nomenclatura, Qualitates, & Natale Solum*, published by Vidua Gabrielis Coterii, Lyon second edition, 1567, 16°, woodcut title border, several hundred woodcut illustrations, contemporary limp vellum.
£600–700
€/ $950–1,100 ⚒ BBA

James Dwight, *Practical Lawn Tennis*, published by Harper, New York, 1893, 8°, 25 black and white plates, original gilt cloth.
£300–360
€/ $475–570 ⚒ DW

T. S. Eliot, *Old Possum's Book of Practical Cats*, published by Faber & Faber, first edition, 1939, small 4°, original cloth, dust-jacket.
£230–275
€/ $360–430 ⚒ BBA

William Faulkner, *The Sound and the Fury*, introduction by Richard Hughes, published by Chatto & Windus, first edition, 1931, 8°, original cloth and dust-jacket with opinions of Faulkner's previous novel *Soldiers' Pay* printed on the reverse.
£420–500
€/ $660–790 ⚒ DW

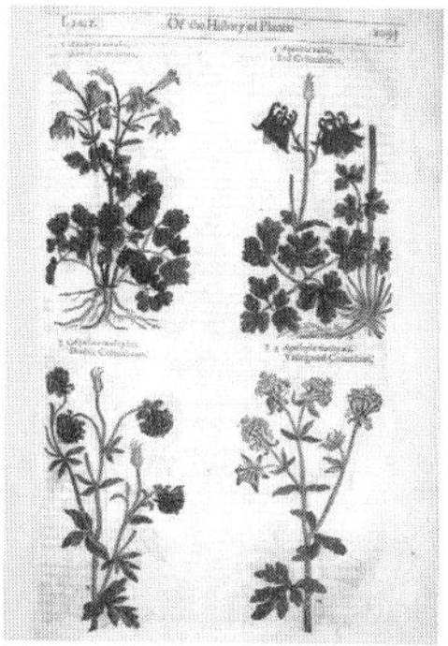

John Gerarde, *The Herball or Generall Historie of Plantes*, 1633, 2°, woodcut illustrations and hand-colouring, 18thC tree calf.
£2,200–2,600
€/ $3,500–4,100 ⚒ WW

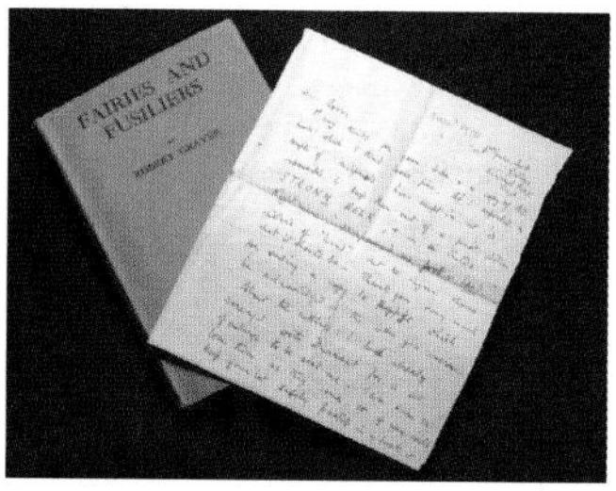

Robert Graves, *Fairies and Fusiliers*, published by William Heinemann, first edition, 1917, 7 x 5in (18 x 12.5cm), with a letter to Robbie Ross.
£900–1,000
€/ $1,400–1,600 ⊞ ADD
Robbie Ross was a writer, critic and art dealer who acted as Oscar Wildes literary executor.

► Ernest Hemingway, *A Farewell to Arms*, published by Jonathan Cape, first edition, 1929, 8 x 5½in (20.5 x 14cm).
£400–450
€/ $630–700
⊞ BIB

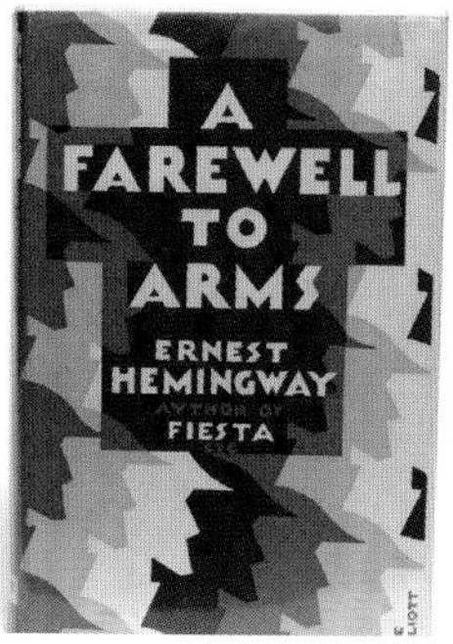

G. A. Henty, *The Young Colonists*, published by Routledge, first edition, 1885, 8°, pictorial gilt cloth.
£650–775
€/ $1,000–1,200 ⚒ DW

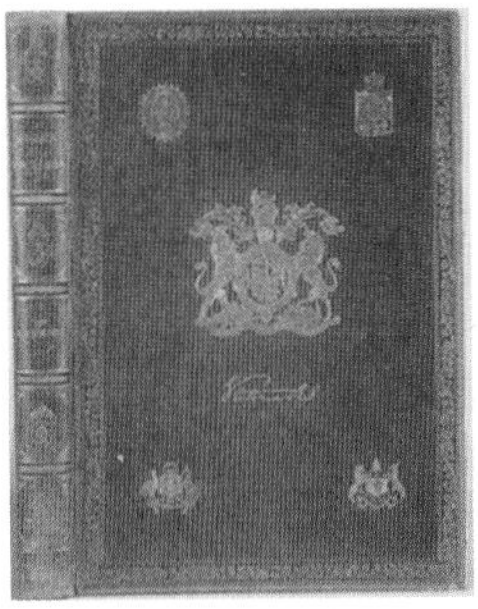

Richard Rivington Holmes, *Queen Victoria*, published by Boussod, Valadon & Co, London & New York, 1897, hand-coloured frontispiece and 40 plates, No. 255 of 350, contemporary morocco with royal coat-of-arms by Zaehnsdorf.
£140–160
€/ $220–250 DN

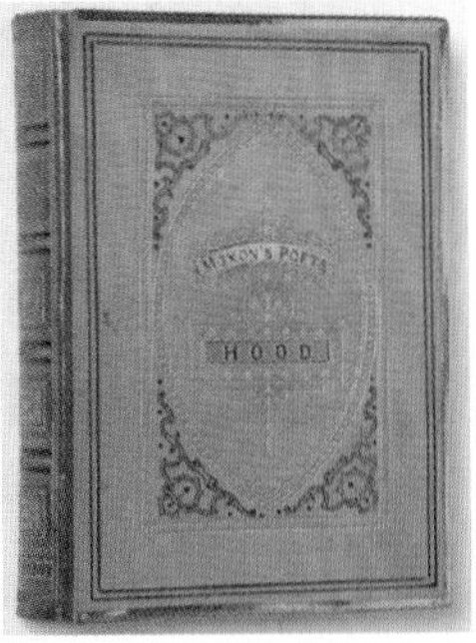

The Poetical Works of Thomas Hood, edited by William Rossetti, illustrated by Gustav Doré, published by E. Moxon, Son & Co, first edition, 1856, 7½in (19cm) high.
£160–175
€/ $250–280 TDG

Rev John Hutchins, *The History and Antiquities of the County of Dorset*, first edition, 1774, 2°, 2 vols, engraved map, plates and plans, calf-backed boards.
£700–800
€/ $1,100–1,300 L

George M. Kelson, *The Salmon Fly: How to Dress It and How to Use It*, 1895, illustrated, gilt cloth.
£320–375
€/ $500–590 CHTR

Jessie M. King, *Mummy's Bedtime Storybook by "Marion"*, 1929, 4°, 12 full-page colour illustrations, decorated endpapers, pictorial boards, glassine dust-jacket.
£1,000–1,200
€/ $1,500–1,900 DW

Marie Laurencin (illustrator), *The Garden Party and Other Stories*, by Katherine Mansfield, published by the Verona Press, 1939, 4°, No. 656 of 1,200, coloured plates, original decorative cloth, slip-case.
£900–1,100
€/ $1,400–1,700 L

Hugh Lofting, *Doctor Dolittle and the Secret Lake*, published by Jonathan Cape, London, first edition, 1949, 8°, colour frontispiece, black and white illustrations after Lofting, original cloth, dust-jacket.
£40–50
€/ $65–80 RTo

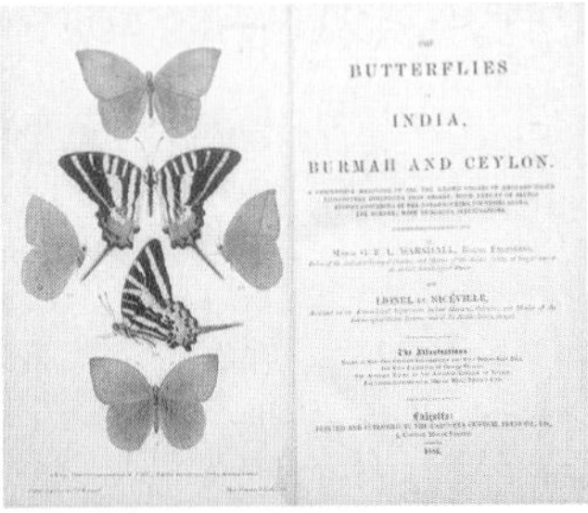

G. Marshall and L. Niceville, *The Butterflies of India, Burmah and Ceylon*, published by Calcutta Central Press, 1882–90, 3 vols, polished calf.
£400–475
€/ $630–750 HYD

Gerrit S. Miller, Jr, *Fauna of the N. E. United States*, Albany, 1900, 62 pages, with coloured illustrations in pen and ink with watercolour and gouache, over pencil, defects, lower cover missing.
£550–650
€/ $870–1,000 BBA

A. A. Milne, *Now We Are Six*, with illustrations by E. H. Shepard, published by Methuen, first edition, 1927, 8 x 5in (20.5 x 12.5cm), limp leather.
£225–250
€/ $325–400 ADD

◄ **Nancy Mitford,** *Wigs on the Green*, published by Thornton Butterworth, London, first edition, 1935, 8°, original cloth, two pages torn, dust-jacket designed by Bip Pares.
£120–140
€/ $190–220
RTo

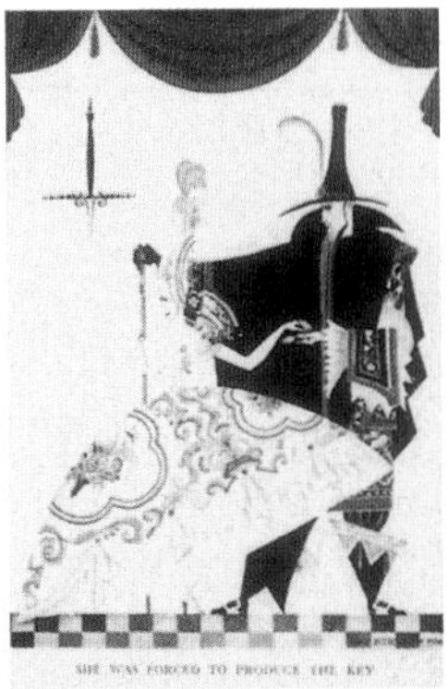

◄ **Kay Nielsen (illustrator),** *Red Magic: A Collection of the World's Best Fairy Tales from all Countries*, edited by Romer Wilson, published by Cape, 1930, 8°, eight colour plates and numerous black and white illustrations, original cloth.
£650–775
€/ $1,000–1,200 DW

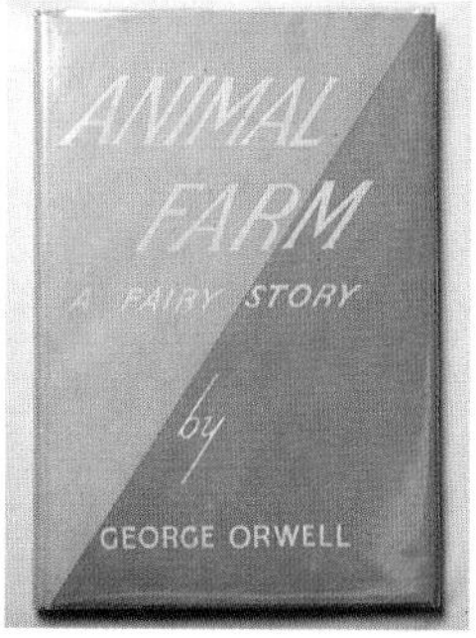

George Orwell, *Animal Farm*, published by Secker & Warburg, second edition, printed within a month of the first, 1945, 8 x 5in (20.5 x 12.5cm).
£175–200
€/ $275–320 ⊞ ADD

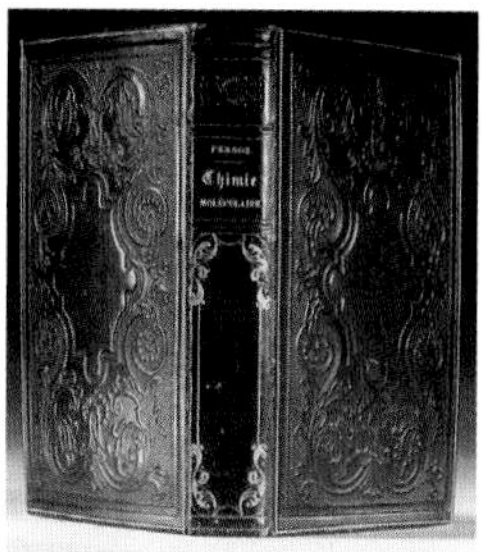

Jean-François Persoz, *Introduction à l'étude de la chimie moléculaire*, published by Mathias, Lagny Frères, Beaujouan & Jourdan, Paris, Derivaux, Strasbourg, 1839, 8¼ x 5in (21 x 12.5cm), nine folding letterpress tables, one engraved plate, gilt calf.
£230–275
€/ $360–430 ⚒ S(NY)

Beatrix Potter, *Peter Rabbit's Painting Book*, published by F. Warne & Co, first edition, 1911, 8°, illustrated in colour with a picture of Peter Rabbit, paper-covered boards.
£2,200–2,500
€/ $3,500–4,000 ⊞ JON
Because of the nature of a children's painting book, very few have survived and most known copies have been coloured or painted. At the time of publication Beatrix Potter suggested to Warne that in addition to the book itself they might sell separate sheets of the outline drawings for children to paint. This would allow them to hang their finished work and also take into account 'some particular children, as well as the parents, (who) do not like to spoil the book.' Perhaps this copy belonged to one of these 'particular' children.

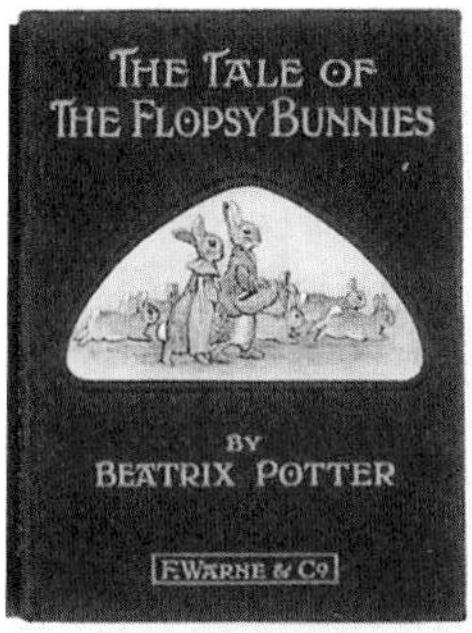

Beatrix Potter, *The Tale of the Flopsy Bunnies*, published by F. Warne & Co, first edition, 1909, 16°, early issue with Notice Board in picture on p14, colour illustrations, inscription to reverse of frontispiece, original pictorial boards, original printed glassine dust-jacket.
£800–950
€/ $1,300–1,500 ⚒ BBA

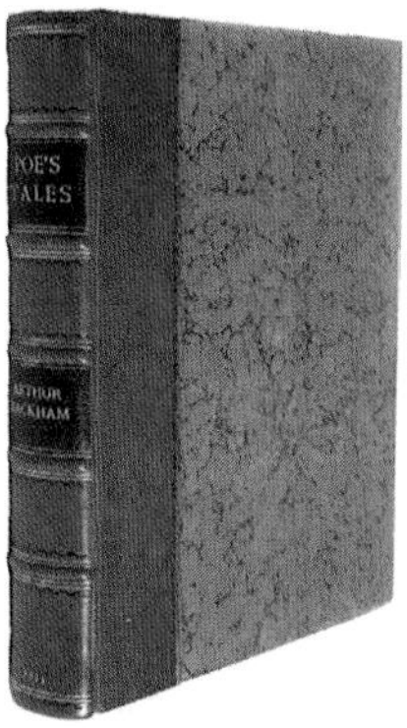

Arthur Rackham (Illustrator), *Poe's Tales*, first edition, 1935, 10 x 8in (25.5 x 20.5cm), original endpapers, gilt morocco.
£350–400
€/ $550–630 ⊞ ADD

Andrew Smith, *Illustrations of the Zoology of South Africa*, 1849, 4°, 5 vols bound in three, 279 lithographed plates, mostly hand-coloured, later buckram.
£4,000–4,700
€/ $6,300–7,400 ⚒ DW

Margaret Tempest (Illustrator), original artwork for *Little Grey Rabbit*, watercolour, 1936, 4in (10cm) square.
£4,700–5,200
€/ $7,500–8,200 ⊞ BRG

◄ **J. R. R. Tolkien,** *The Hobbit* or *There and Back Again*, published by Allen & Unwin, first edition, 1937, 8°, signed by the author on the half-title page, original green cloth with blue designs on the boards, dust-jacket designed by the author, in a custom-made quarter-leather clamshell box.
£90,000–100,000
€/ $142,000–158,000 ⊞ JON
On a summer afternoon in the late 1920s, J. R. R. Tolkien was marking School Certificate papers. His mind began to wander, and then across the top paper in his pile he wrote, 'In a hole in the ground lived a Hobbit.' In that moment a great literary classic was born. Only 1,500 copies of the first edition were printed and they sold out within a couple of months. Tolkien was a reclusive character and avoided contact with the public. Consequently signed copies of his work are very rare. The rarely-found dust-jacket is also without damage or restoration. The combination here of an exceptionally well-preserved copy, signed by the author, makes it an extremely desirable item.

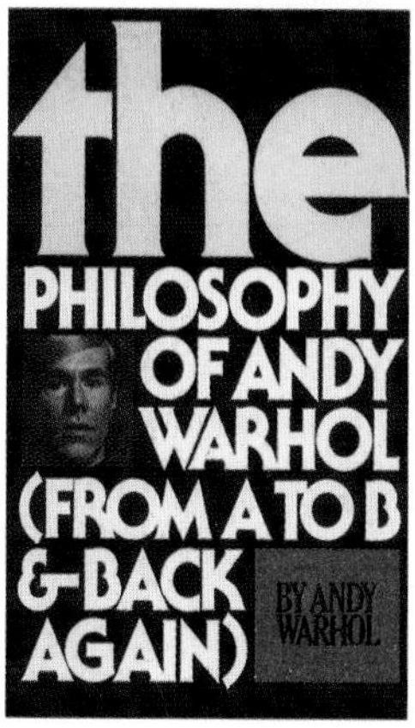

◄ **Andy Warhol,** *The Philosophy of Andy Warhol (From A to B and Back Again)*, published by Harcourt Brace Jovanovich, New York, first edition, 1975, 8½ x 5¾in (21.5 x 14.5cm), inscribed and signed, dust-jacket.
£765–850
€/ $1,200–1,500
⊞ ASC

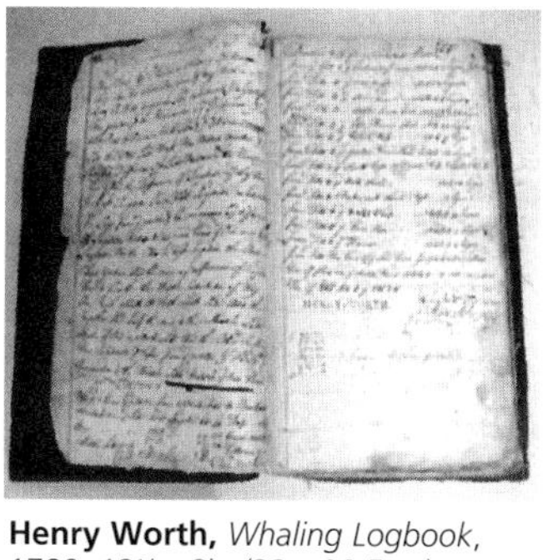

Henry Worth, *Whaling Logbook*, 1789, 12½ x 8in (32 x 20.5cm), probably original, leather binder.
£5,000–6,000
€/ $7,900–9,500 ⚒ JDJ

Paul Wytsman, *Genera Avium*, Brussels, 1905–14, 4°, original printed wrappers.
£150–180
€/ $240–285 ⚒ DW

Maps & Atlases

World

G. Valk, a copperplate map of the world, original colour, Dutch, Amsterdam, c1658, 23 x 20in (58.5 x 51cm).
£6,500–7,200
€/ $10,300–11,400 ⊞ JOP

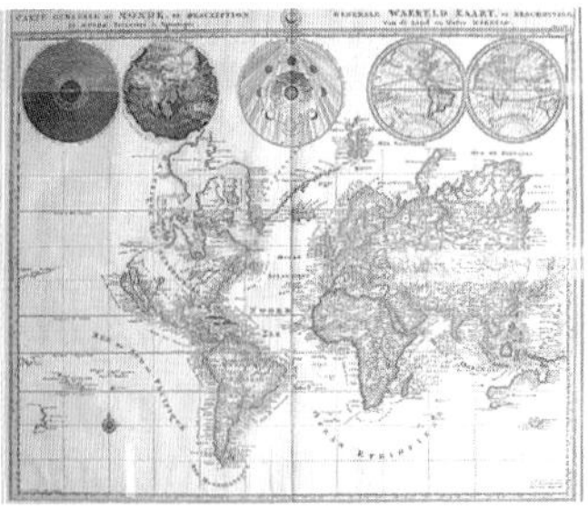

Mercator's Projection of the World, by Covens and Mortier, 1700, 15 x 19in (38 x 48.5cm).
£2,700–3,000
€/ $4,300–4,700 ⊞ APS

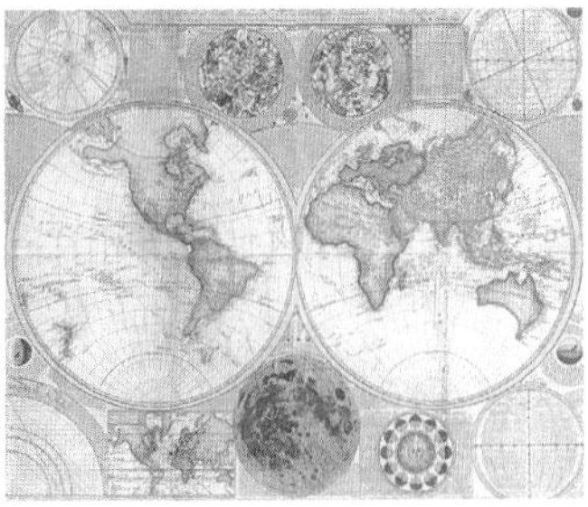

Samuel Dunn, *Scienta terrarum et coelorum,* from *The General Atlas*, published by Robert Sayer, 1772, hand-coloured engraved, printed on four sheets, joined, 41½ x 51in (105.4 x 129.5cm).
£3,800–4,500
€/ $6,000–7,100 ⚒ S(NY)

LOCATE THE SOURCE
The source of each illustration in Miller's can be found by checking the code letters below each caption with the Key to Illustrations, pages 794–800.

J. Henry, a woodblock map of the world, French, Paris, 1835, 19 x 13in (48.5 x 33cm).
£540–600
€/ $850–950 ⊞ JOP

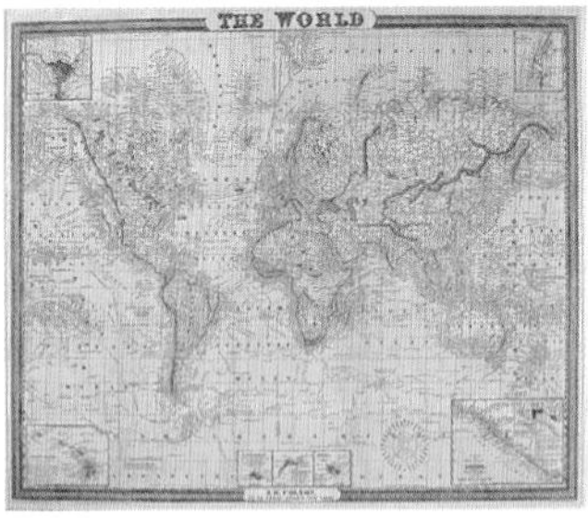

◄ **J. H. Colton,** a map of the world, coloured lithograph, American, 1842, 25 x 20in (63.5 x 51cm).
£450–500
€/ $700–800 ⊞ JOP

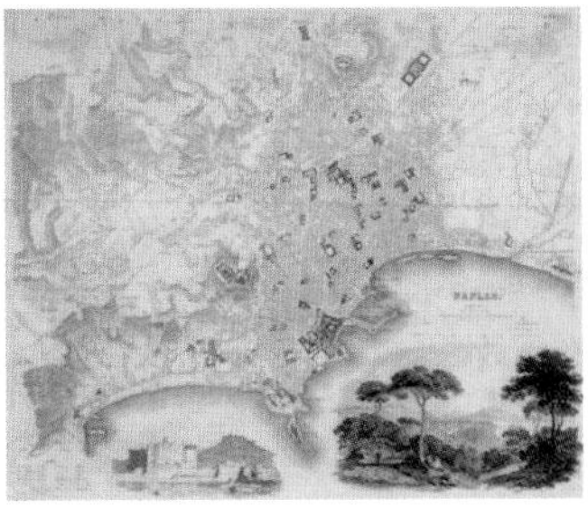

Maps of the Society for the Diffusion of Useful Knowledge, two vols, 215 engraved plates, two missing, half calf, bindings loose, 1844, 2°.
£1,500–1,800
€/ $2,400–2,800 ⚒ CHTR

Africa

Willem Blaeu, *Africa nova descriptio*, hand-coloured double-page engraved map, Dutch text to verso, c1650, 16 x 21¾in (41 x 55.5cm).
£1,700–2,000
€/ $2,700–3,200 ⚒ B

► **F. de Wit,** a copperplate map of Africa, coloured, Dutch, Amsterdam, c1680, 23 x 20in (58.5 x 51cm).
£900–1,000
€/ $1,400–1,600 ⊞ JOP

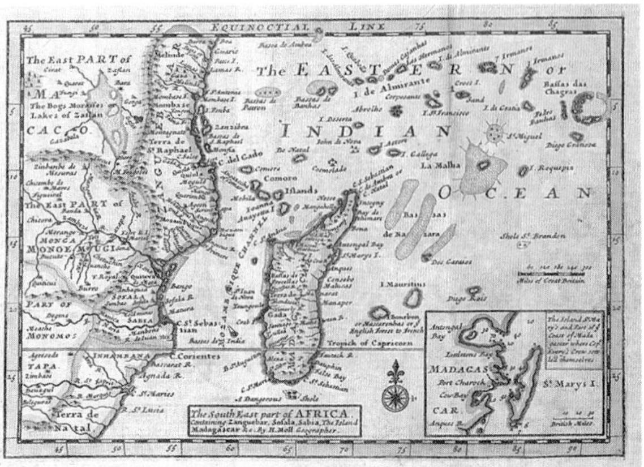

► **Herman Moll,** a map of Madagascar and part of the east coast of Africa, 1719, 8 x 11in (20.5 x 28cm).
£80–100
€/ $125–160 ⊞ MAG

Americas

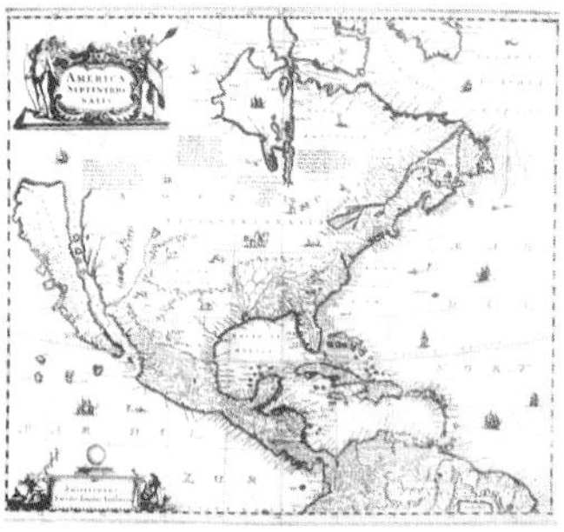

◀ **Johannes Jansson,** *America Septentrionalis*, c1640, 18½ x 21½in (47 x 55cm).
£1,400–1,700
€/ $2,200–2,700 ⚒ DW
California is shown as an island.

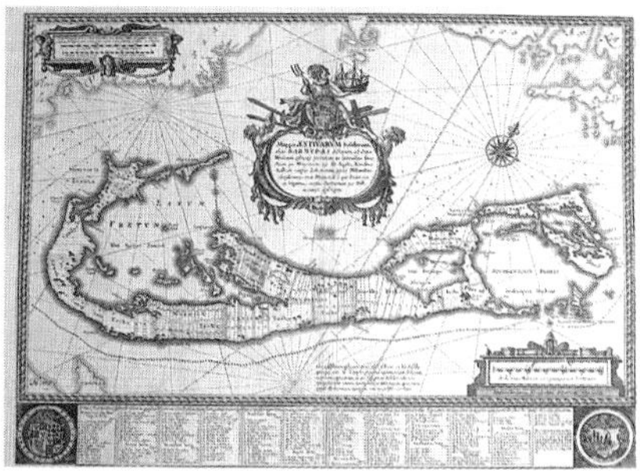

Willem Blaeu, a copperplate map of Bermuda, hand-coloured, 1662, 20 x 23in (51 x 58.5cm).
£2,100–2,300
€/ $3,300–3,600 ⊞ APS

G. & L. Valk, a copperplate map of the Americas, original colour, Dutch, c1700, 24 x 20in (61 x 51cm).
£1,600–1,800
€/ $2,500–2,800 ⊞ JOP

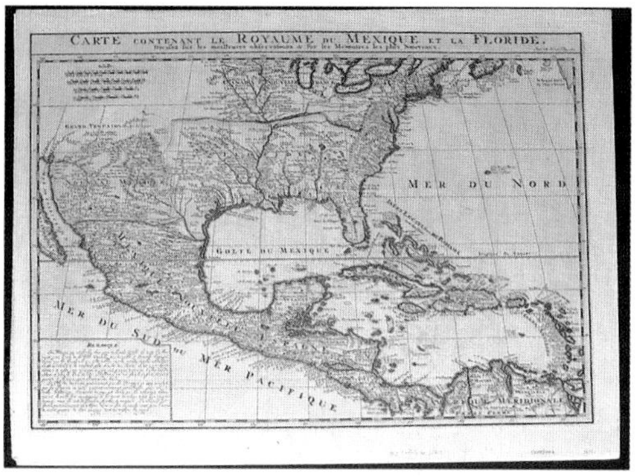

H. A. Chatelain, a map of the Gulf of Mexico, 1719, 18 x 22in (45.5 x 56cm).
£2,200–2,500
€/ $3,500–4,000 ⊞ APS

Asia

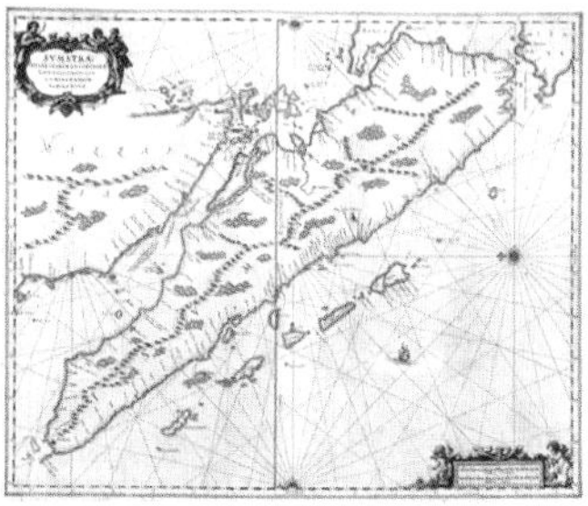

Jan Jansson, *Sumatrae*, engraved map with original outline hand colouring, re-margined, slight damage, c1650, 16¾ x 20¾in (42.5 x 52.5cm).
£370–430
€/ $570–680 ⚒ BBA

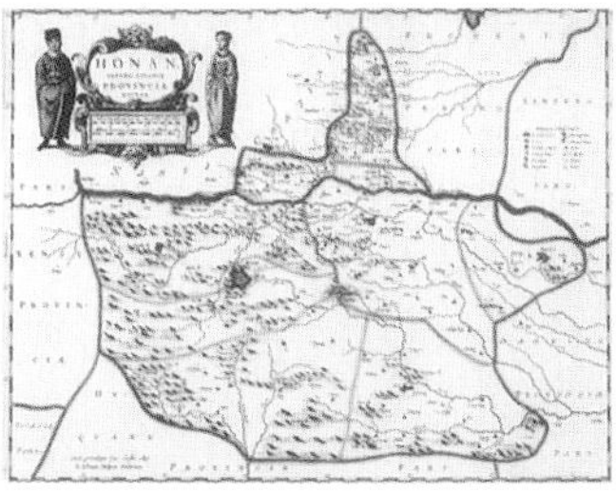

Joan Blaeu, *Honan*, and nine other hand-coloured double-page engraved maps of provinces of China from the same atlas, c1655, 16 x 19¼in (40.5 x 49cm).
£900–1,100
€/ $1,400–1,700 ⚒ B

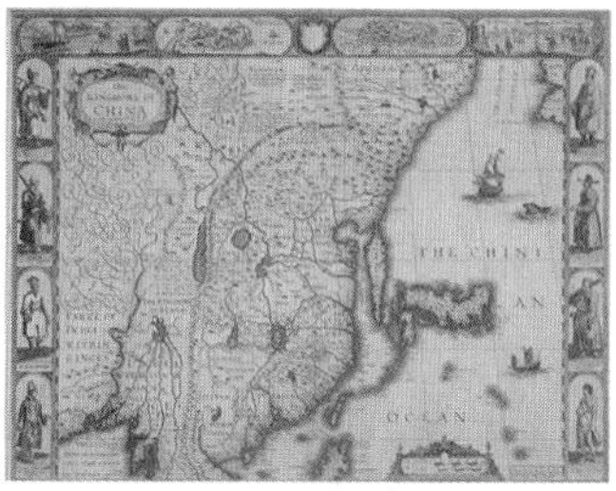

John Speed, *The Kingdome of China*, hand-coloured engraved map, repaired splits, c1676, 15¾ x 20¼in (40 x 51.5cm).
£1,300–1,500
€/ $2,000–2,400 ⚒ BBA

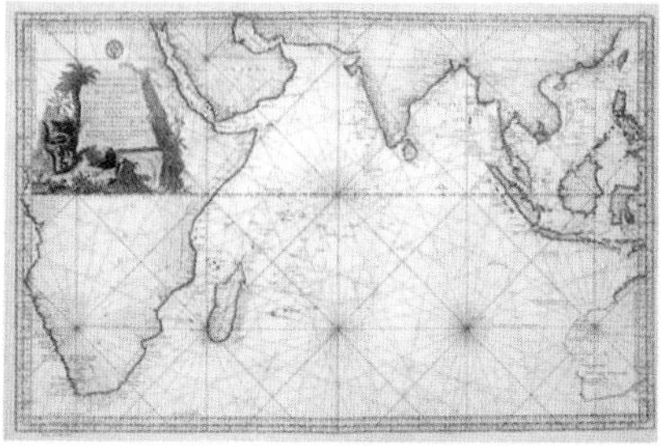

J. N. Bellin, *Carte Réduite de L'Ocean Oriental ou Mer des Indes*, hand-coloured chart of the Indian Ocean, including Sri Lanka, Madagascar and Borneo, French, 1757, 22¾ x 35¼in (58 x 89.5cm).
£500–570
€/ $790–900 ⚒ BBA

A woodblock map, depicting Mount Fuji and its environs, Japanese, late 19thC, 13¼ x 38¼in (33.5 x 97cm).
£65–75
€/ $100–120 ⚒ SWO

Europe & the Middle East

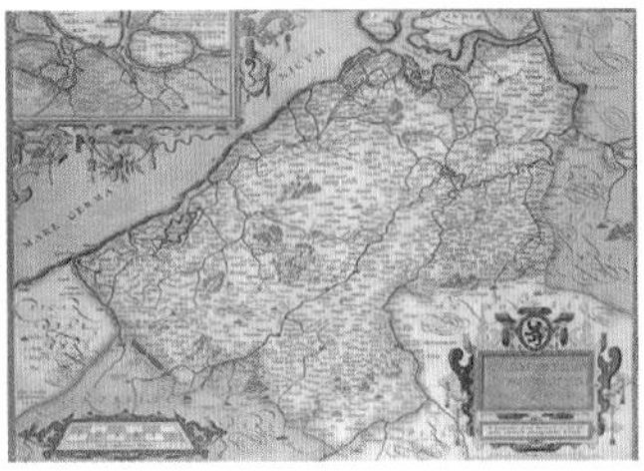

Abraham Ortelius, *Flandriae Comitatus Descriptio*, hand-coloured copper engraving, printed in Antwerp by Christopher Plantin, Flemish, 1592, 18 x 22½in (45.5 x 57cm).
£2,200–2,500
€/ $3,500–4,000 S
Abraham Ortelius and his sisters became map illuminators and colourists following the death of their father. He was first established as an antiques dealer and from 1558 onwards he was recorded as purchasing multiple copies of maps in order to colour them whilst building up a substantial personal collection.

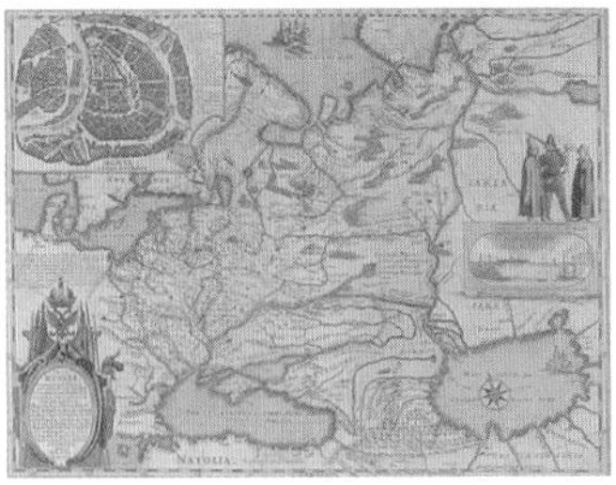

Joan and Willem Blaeu, *Tabula Russiae*, from the North Sea to the Caspian Sea, engraved map with original hand-colouring, Dutch, Amsterdam, c1650, 17 x 21½in (43 x 54.5cm).
£775–900
€/ $1,200–1,400 BBA
The Blaeu family publishing house was founded by Willem Janszoon Blaeu (1571–1638). Originally specializing in sea charts, he published his first world atlas, the *Atlantis Appendix* in 1630. Blaeu maps are renowned for the high level of care and attention given to every stage of the production, using only the best paper with the finest engraved plates and highest standard of printing.

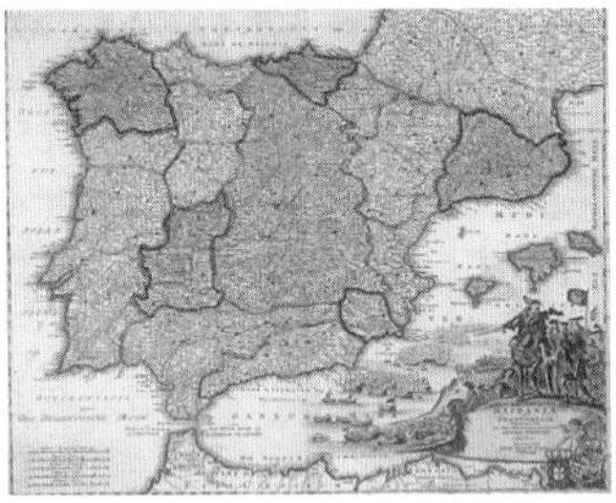

◄ **Johann Baptist Homann,** *Regnorum Hispaniae et Portugalliae*, engraved map of the Spanish peninsula, in original hand-colouring, slight damage, c1740, 19¼ x 22½in (49 x 57cm).
£420–500
€/ $660–790 BBA

Frederick de Wit, *Insula Malta*, engraved map of Malta and Gozo with original outline hand-colouring, c1680, 17½ x 21½in (44.5 x 55cm).
£500–600
€/ $800–950 BBA

John Tallis, *Switzerland*, 1850, 10 x 13in (25.5 x 33cm).
£60–65
€/ $95–120 MAG

Great Britain & Ireland

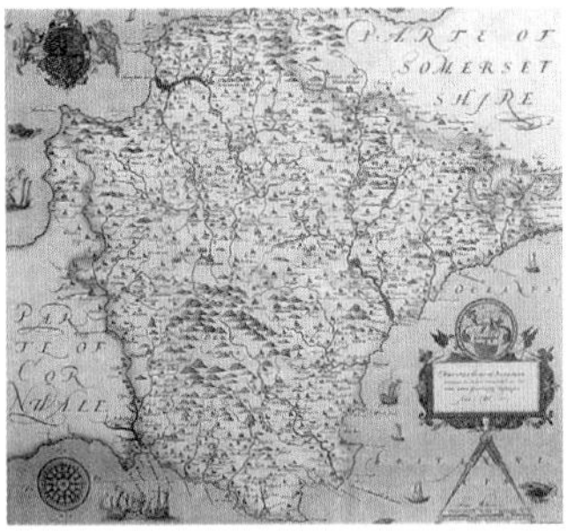

Christopher Saxton, a map of Devon, later hand colouring, 1575, 16¼ x 18¼in (41.5 x 46.5cm).
£80–100
€/ $125–160 FHF

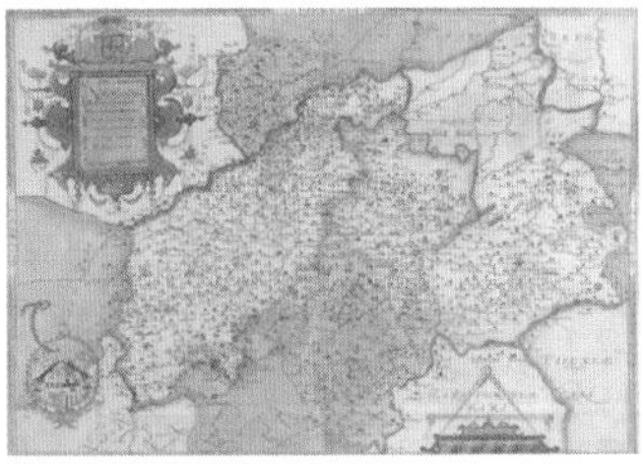

Christopher Saxton, a map of Northamptonshire, Bedfordshire, Cambridgeshire, Huntingdonshire and Rutland, engraved and hand-coloured, paper repair, c1576, 15¾ x 20½in (40 x 52cm).
£2,200–2,500
€/ $3,500–4,000 DW

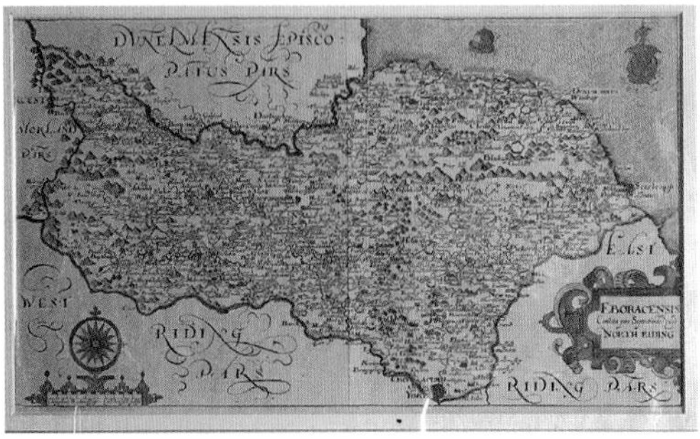

◄ **Christopher Saxton,** *North Riding of Yorkshire*, engraved by Hole, 1610, 8 x 14in (20.5 x 35.5cm).
£330–370
€/ $520–600
APS

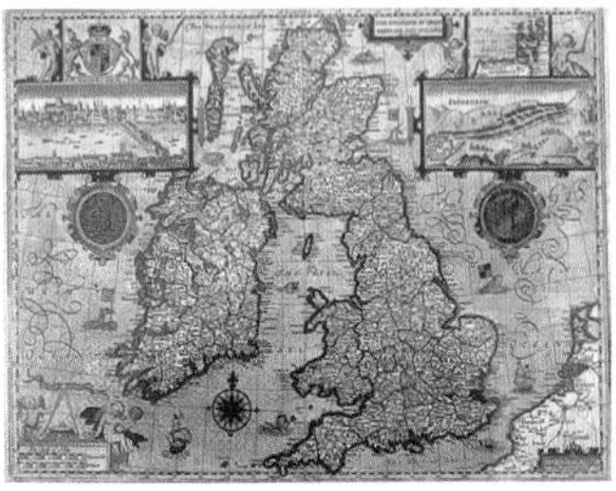

John Speed, *The Kingdome of Great Britaine and Ireland*, published by Basset & Chiswell, hand-coloured, double page map, inset with views of London and Edinburgh, English text to verso, c1611, 15 x 20in (38 x 51cm).
£1,700–2,000
€/ $2,700–3,200 B(B)

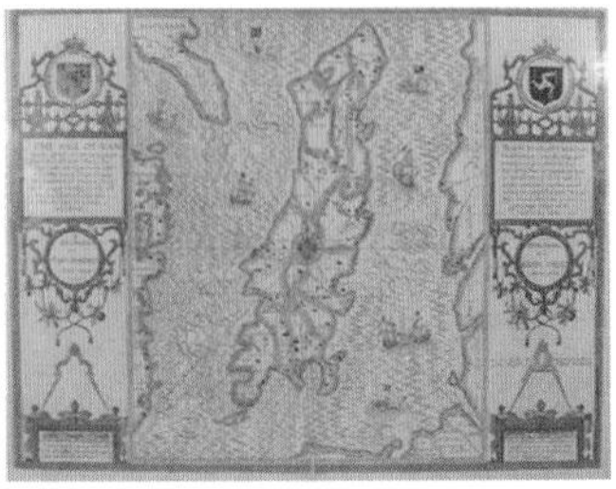

John Speed, *The Isle of Man*, hand-coloured in outline, 1610, 15¼ x 20in (39 x 51cm).
£200–240
€/ $320–380 WilP

John Speed, *England, Wales, Scotland and Ireland Described and Abridged with ye Historie Relation of Things Worthy Mention from a Farr Larger Volume...*, engraved title, 63 maps, 1627, oblong 8°, reversed calf.
£2,000–2,200
€/ $3,200–3,500 ⚒ B(B)

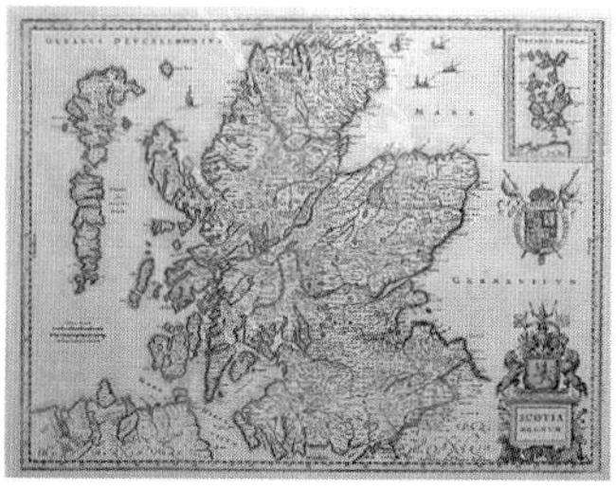

Joannes Jansson, *Scotland*, 1646, 16 x 22in (40.5 x 56cm).
£1,400–1,600
€/ $2,200–2,500 ⊞ APS

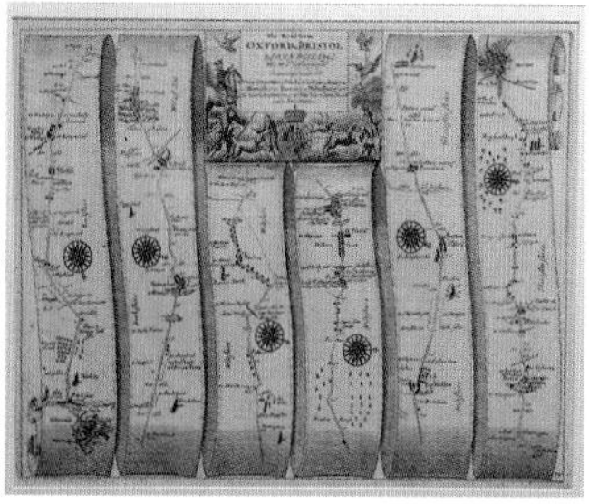

John Ogilby, a strip road map of Oxford to Bristol, 1675, 13 x 18in (33 x 45.5cm).
£350–400
€/ $550–630 ⊞ MAG

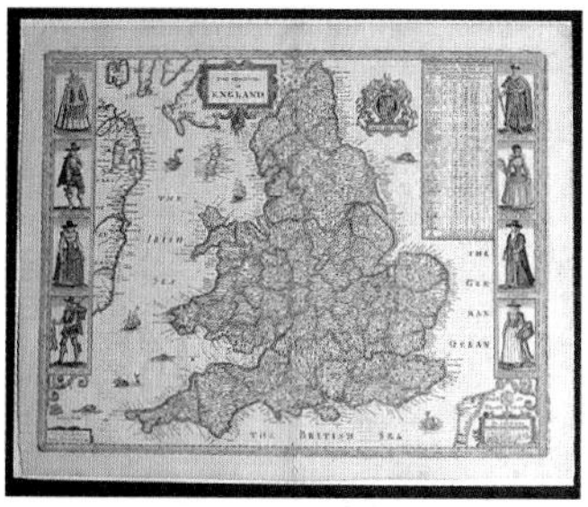

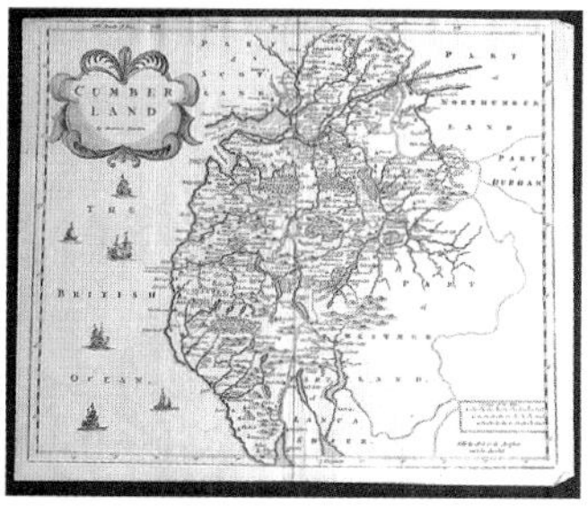

Robert Morden, *Cumberland*, 1695, 15 x 17in (38 x 43cm).
£250–280
€/ $400–440 ⊞ APS

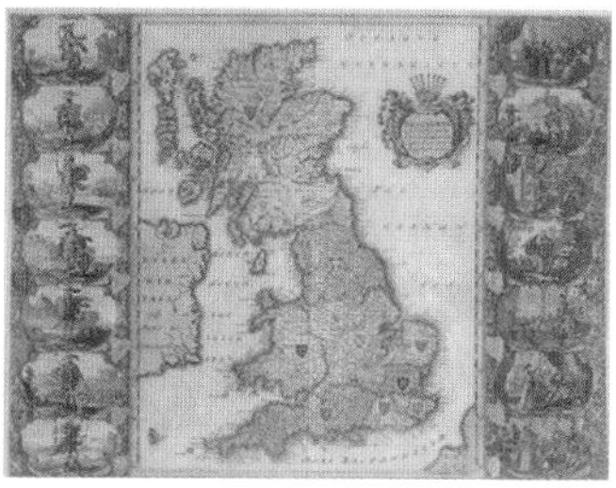

Joan Blaeu, *Great Britain*, hand-coloured engraved map, heightened with gold, Spanish text to verso, c1640, 16½ x 21in (42 x 53cm).
£1,400–1,600
€/ $2,200–2,500 ⚒ DW

► **Joan Blaeu,** *Annandale*, hand-coloured, 1663, 16½ x 20in (42 x 51cm).
£70–80
€/ $110–130 ⚒ TRM

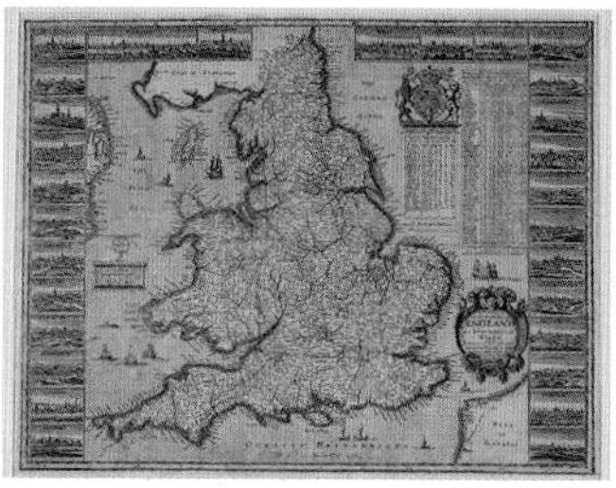

P. Stent, a copperplate map of England and Wales, coloured, 1662–67, 20 x 16in (51 x 40.5cm).
£1,600–1,800
€/ $2,500–2,800 ⊞ JOP

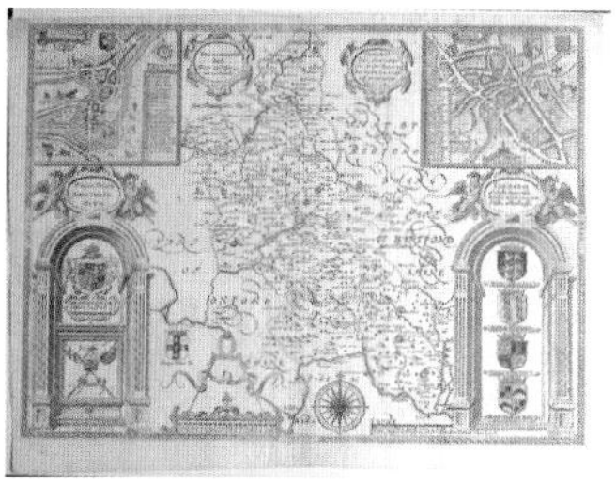

John Speed, *Buckinghamshire*, 1676, 16 x 21in (40.5 x 53.5cm).
£1,200–1,300
€/ $1,900–2,000 ⊞ APS

◄ **John Speed,** *The Kingdome of England*, 1676, 17 x 22in (43 x 56cm).
£1,800–2,000
€/ $2,800–3,200 ⊞ APS

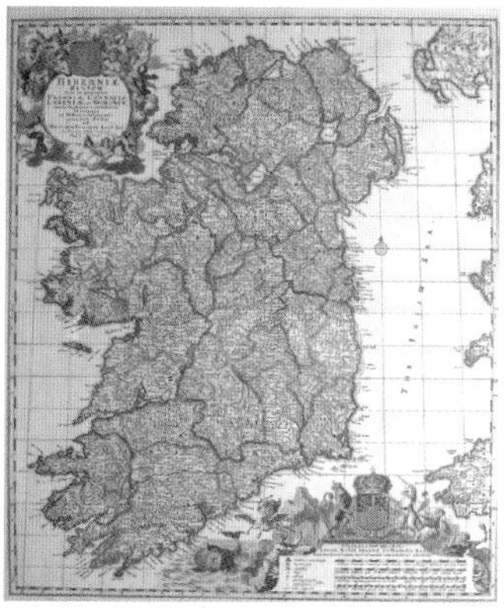

Claes Janszoon Visscher, *Ireland*, 1695, 24 x 19in (61 x 48.5cm).
£2,700–3,000
€/ $4,300–4,800 ⊞ APS

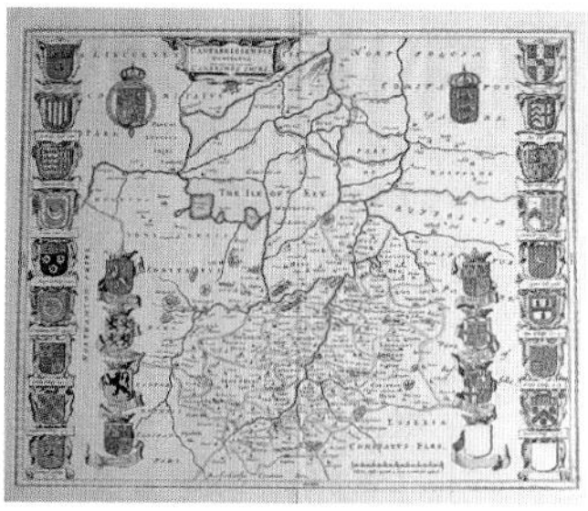

Joan Blaeu, *Cambridgeshire*, 1645, 20 x 33in (51 x 84cm).
£900–1,000
€/ $1,400–1,600 ⊞ APS

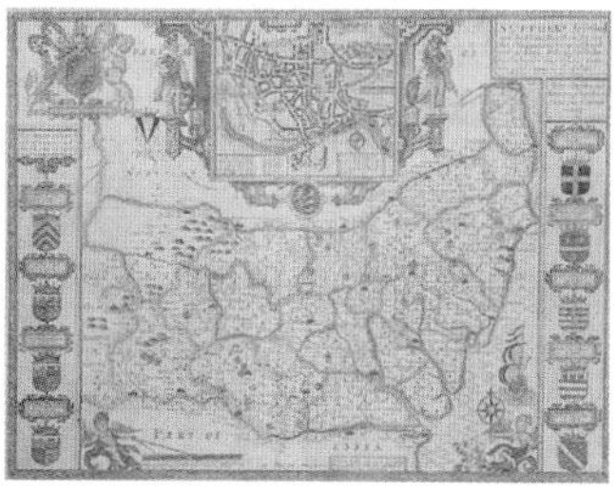

John Speed, *Suffolk*, hand-coloured copper engraving, c1676, 20 x 15½in (39.5 x 51.5cm).
£450–525
€/ $700–830 ⚒ B(EA)

Robert Morden, *Oxfordshire*, c1695, 14 x 16in (35.5 x 40.5cm).
£220–250
€/ $350–400 ⊞ SAT

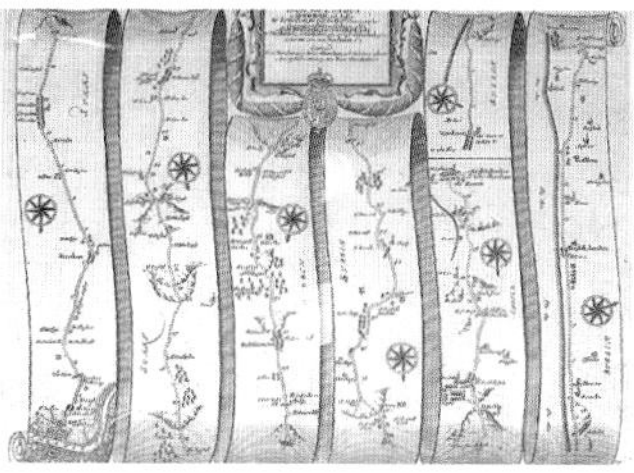

John Ogilby, a strip road map of London to Newhaven, 1695, 14 x 17in (35.5 x 43cm).
£400–450
€/ $630–700 ⊞ APS

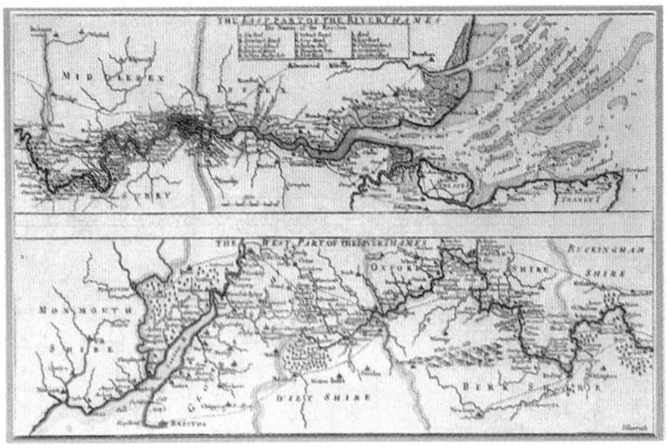

◀ **Thomas Cox,** *The East and West Parts of the Thames from Magna Britannica*, 1724, 15 x 9in (38 x 23cm).
£450–500
€/ $720–800 ⊞ SAT

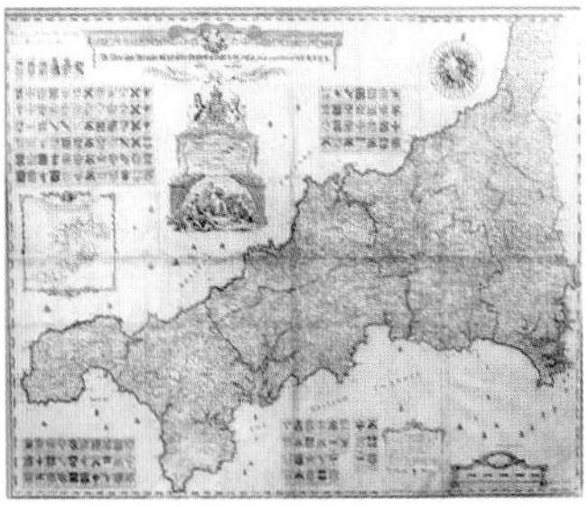

Thomas Martyn, *A New and Accurate Map of the County of Cornwall*, inset with the Isles of Scilly, 1816, 57 x 71in (145 x 180cm), framed.
£1,200–1,400
€/ $1,900–2,200 ⚒ B(Pr)

▶ **W. R. Gardner,** *Plan of the County of Westmorland*, in four sections from survey taken in 1823, contemporary colouring, London, 1828, 28 x 32in (71 x 81.5cm).
£300–360
€/ $475–570 ⚒ PFK

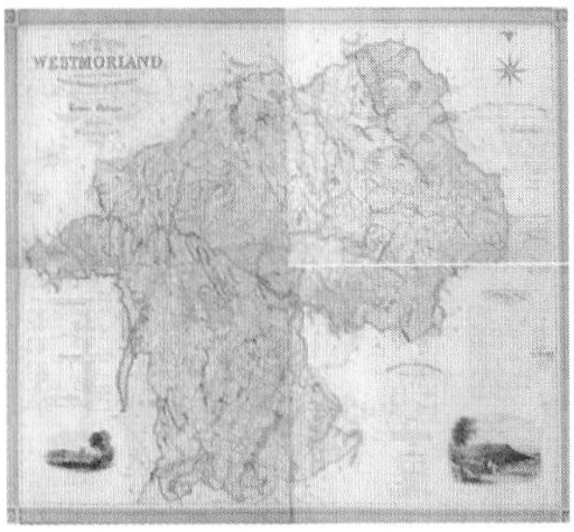

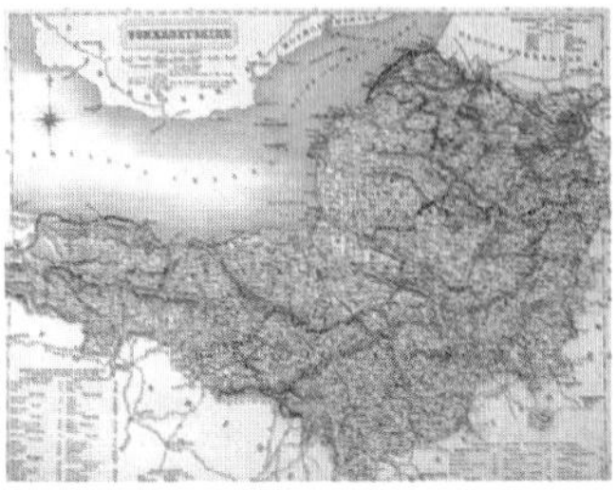

J. & C. Walker, *British Atlas, Comprising Separate Maps of Every County in England*, engraved title and 47 maps, hand-coloured in outline, dated March 1, 1837, large 4°, upper cover detached.
£400–480
€/ $630–760 ⚒ L

C. & J. Greenwood, *Map of the County of Essex*, original colour, steelplate, 1831, 17 x 24in (43 x 61cm).
£250–280
€/ $400–440 ⊞ JOP

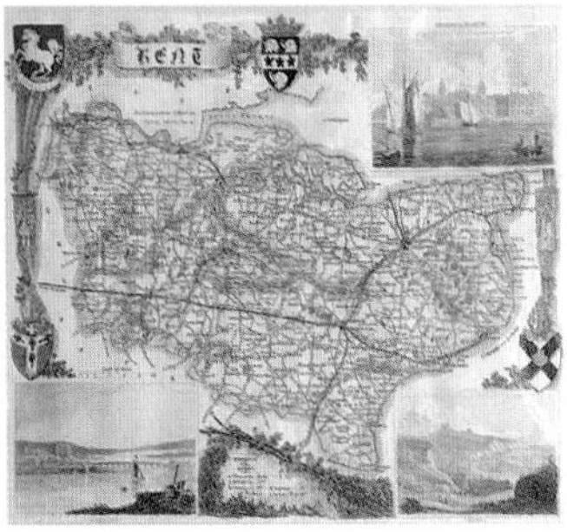

◀ **Thomas Moule,** *Kent*, 1845, 8 x 10in (20.5 x 25.5cm).
£200–220
€/ $320–350 ⊞ APS

MAPS & ATLASES

Town & City Plans

S. Munster, town plan of Amsterdam, coloured woodblock, Swiss, 1544–50, 16 x 11in (40.5 x 28cm).
£470–520
€/ $750–820 ⊞ JOP

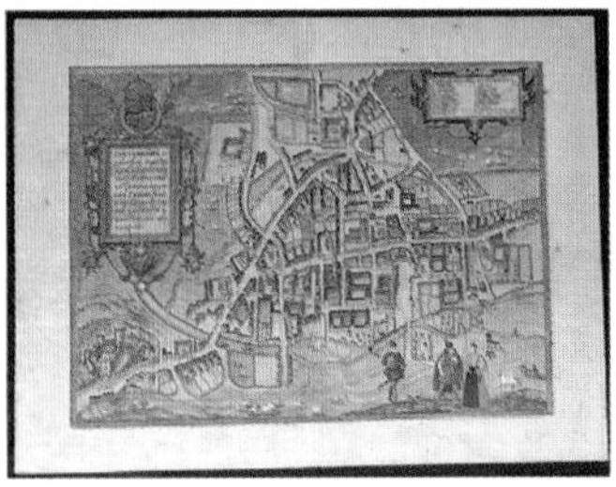

Georg Braun and Franz Hogenberg, a town plan of Cambridge, 1575, 16 x 21in (40.5 x 53.5cm).
£1,300–1,500
€/ $2,100–2,400 ⊞ APS

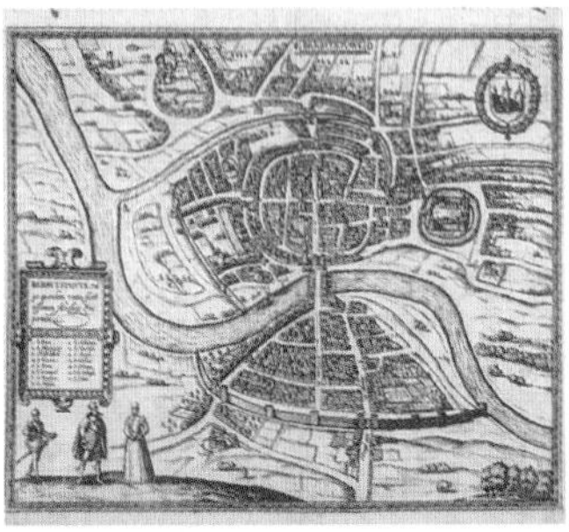

Georg Braun and Franz Hogenberg, a town plan of Brightstowe, c1581, 13¾ x 17¼in (35 x 44cm).
£350–420
€/ $550–660 ⚒ DW

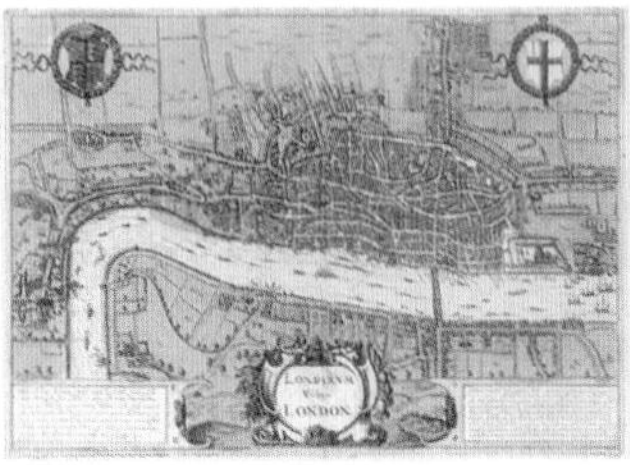

John Speed, *Midle-Sex described with the most famous Cities of London and Westminster*, hand-coloured engraved map, printed by George Humble 1610, but 1627 or later, 15 x 20in (38 x 50.5cm).
£400–450
€/ $630–700 ⚒ B

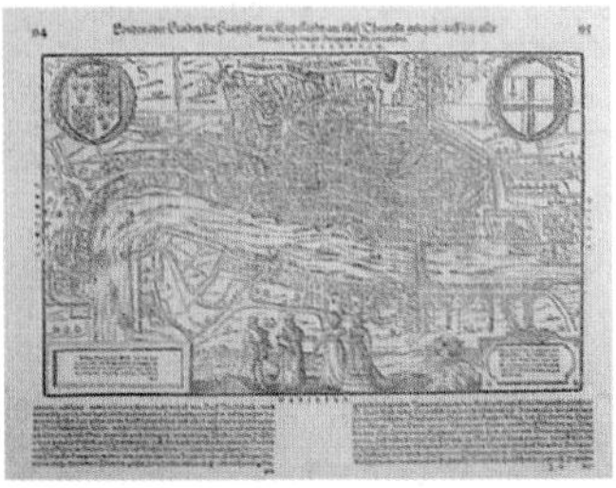

Sebastian Munster, *Londen oder Lunden*, a woodcut map of London, German text to verso, repaired tear, c1628, 12½ x 16½in (32 x 42cm).
£900–1,000
€/ $1,400–1,600 ⚒ BBA

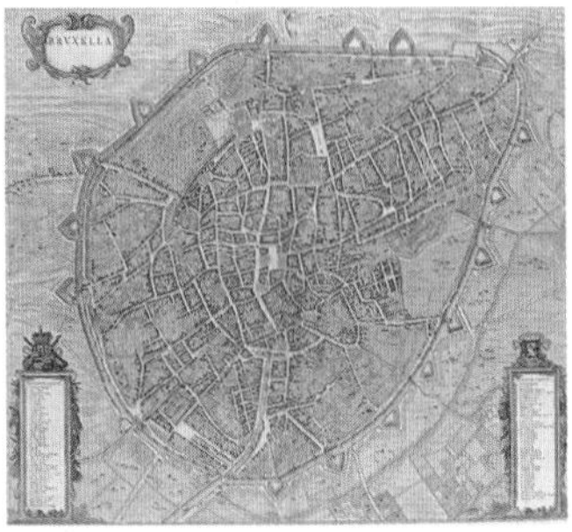

Joan Blaeu, *Bruxella*, hand-coloured copper engraving of Brussels, Amsterdam, 1649, 20 x 24in (51 x 61cm).
£2,200–2,500
€/ $3,500–4,000 ⚒ S

Dolls

Selected Makers

An Alt, Beck & Gottschalck bisque-headed doll, with fixed glass eyes, closed mouth and stuffed cloth body, bisque arms, later wig, German, c1890, 29½in (75cm) high.
£800–1,000
€/ $1,300–1,600 YC

► **A Bru Jeune Empress Eugénie bisque-headed doll,** with glass eyes, closed mouth and plaited wig, gusset-jointed kid leather body, silk shirt and muslin jacket, marked 'E' on head and left shoulder, French, c1875, 15½in (39.5cm) high.
£2,100–2,500
€/ $3,300–4,000 THE

An Ernest Descamps bisque-headed *bébé* doll, with fixed paperweight eyes and open mouth, a double-jointed composition body, incised 'E.9.D', re-made clothing, c1900, 19in (48.5cm) high.
£1,200–1,400
€/ $1,900–2,200 YC

An Alt, Beck & Gottschalck bisque-headed doll, with weighted eyes and open mouth, five-piece composition body, impressed '1361 50', German, 1912, 22in (56cm) high.
£330–400
€/ $520–630 VEC

A Cuno & Otto Dressel bisque-headed Poppy doll, with glass eyes and closed mouth, composition arms and stuffed cotton body, German, c1912, 9¾in (25cm) high.
£160–200
€/ $250–320 YC

A Bähr & Pröschild bisque-headed character doll, with open mouth, two teeth and glass eyes, original Sonneburg composition jointed body, new wig, body partially repainted, marked '204', German, c1910, 16½in (42cm) high.
£345–415
€/ $540–660 THE

A Bru Jeune bisque-headed doll, with original mohair wig and composition Girard body, two original outfits, French, c1890, 21in (53.5cm) high, in original labelled box.
£10,000–11,000
€/ $15,800–17,400 Beb

► **An EFFanBEE character doll,** by Dewees Cochran, 'Anne-Shirley', with sleeping eyes, closed mouth and blonde wig, composition body, marked, hairline cracks to thigh, American, 1930s, 21in (53.5cm) high.
£525–625
€/ $830–1,000 SK(B)

A Belton Bru-style doll, with composition body, German, c1880, 10in (25.5cm) high.
£1,000–1,100
€/ $1,500–1,700 BaN

A DEP bisque-headed doll, with weighted glass eyes, fully-jointed composition body, produced for the French market, German, c1910, 18in (45.5cm) high, in original box.
£350–420
€/ $550–670 B(Ch)

A Fleischmann & Bloedel Eden *bébé* doll, with original wig, French, 1890s, 24in (61cm) high.
£1,800–2,000
€/ $2,800–3,200 ⊞ BaN

A François Gaultier bisque-headed *bébé* doll, with weighted eyes, closed mouth and blonde wig, eight-ball articulated wood and composition body, impressed 'F 6 G', French, c1880, 16in (40.5cm) high, with assorted original clothing.
£3,200–3,800
€/ $5,000–6,000 ⚒ SK(B)

An Ernst Heubach bisque-headed doll, model No. 320, with sleeping eyes, open mouth and jointed baby body, German, c1920, 25¼in (64cm) high.
£180–220
€/ $280–350 ⊞ YC

A bisque-headed doll, attributed to François Gaultier, with glass eyes, closed mouth, blonde wig and leather body, wearing a silk gown, marked '3', French, c1875, 16in (40.5cm) high.
£1,400–1,700
€/ $2,200–2,700 ⊞ THE

A Heinrich Handwerck bisque-headed doll, with sleeping glass eyes, open mouth and double-jointed composition body, incised 'GG', wearing a later wig and clothes, German, c1910, 21in (53cm) high.
£450–500
€/ $700–800 ⊞ YC

An Ernst Heubach bisque-headed doll, mould 350, with sleeping eyes and composition body, German, c1925, 10in (25.5cm) high.
£250–275
€/ $400–440 ⊞ BaN

Gebrüder Heubach (German 1820–c1945) & Ernst Heubach (German 1887–1930)

These two companies which both operated from the German state of Thuringia are often confused for each other but are unconnected.

Gebrüder Heubach were based near Wallendorf, and initially produced figurines and bisque dolls' heads, but by 1905 the firm was registered as making entire dolls. Above all they are renowned for the variety of their bisque-headed character dolls. Among the firm's other products were small bisque figurines, known as 'piano babies', and mantelpiece figures.

Ernst Heubach of Koppelsdorf made a range of more affordable bisque dolls including characters, babies and jointed girl dolls. Body types varied and included jointed, bent-limb and baby. Ernst's daughter Beatrix married the son of the famous doll manufacturer Armand Marseille, also of Koppelsdorf, and in 1919 the two factories merged to become the Koppelsdorf Porcelain Factory.

A Julius Hering bisque-headed doll, with sleeping eyes, open mouth and composition hands and feet, stamped 'Victoria, J.H.', flag symbol, German, 1875–1925, 24½in (62cm) high.
£140–170
€/ $220–260 ⚒ DMC

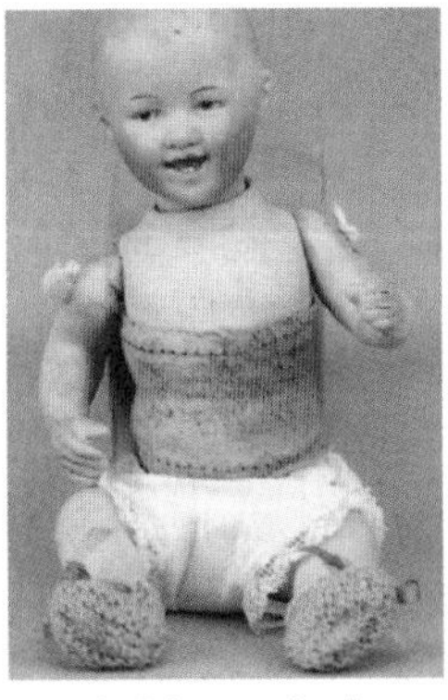

A Gebrüder Heubach bisque-headed doll, with intaglio eyes, open/closed mouth, two teeth, and five-piece curved limb composition body, sprung squeaker not working, chipped, arms restrung and one repaired, German, c1912, 6¼in (16cm) high.
£280–320
€/ $440–510 ⚒ VEC

An Ernst Heubach bisque-headed doll, with bisque lower arms and kid and cloth body, marked 'Hch 6/0 H' with horseshoe, German, late 19thC, 17in (43cm) high.
£160–200
€/ $250–315 ⚒ JDJ

A Gebrüder Heubach bisque-headed character doll, with sleeping eyes, closed mouth and double-jointed toddler body, original wig, wearing a modern sailor outfit, German, c1912, 14¼in (36cm) high.
£1,100–1,200
€/ $1,700–1,900 ⊞ YC

A Gebrüder Heubach bisque-headed doll, with sleeping eyes, blonde hair and composition body, German, early 20thC, 13in (33cm) high, with original black and white photograph of a boy with the doll.
£160–200
€/ $250–315 TMA

A Jumeau bisque-headed *bébé* doll, with brown paperweight eyes, closed mouth and composition body, incised mark 'Déposé Jumeau', French, 1880s, 27in (68.5cm) high, with the doll's own doll.
£3,800–4,500
€/ $6,000–7,200 SK(B)

A Jumeau bisque-headed doll, with paperweight eyes, closed mouth and brown wig-over-cork pate, wood and composition fully-jointed body, repainted limbs, marked, French, c1886, 22in (56cm) high.
£2,400–2,900
€/ $3,800–4,600 THE

A Gebrüder Heubach bisque-headed doll, with intaglio eyes, blonde sculpted hair and wood and composition ball-jointed body, wearing a corduroy suit, a shirt and leather shoes, marked '5896 Germany', c1915, 11in (28cm) high.
£260–300
€/ $410–475 THE

A Jumeau bisque-headed *bébé* doll, French, c1885, 21in (53.5cm) high.
£3,000–3,500
€/ $4,700–5,500 Beb

A Tête Jumeau bisque-headed doll, head and body stamped, c1890, 20in (51cm) high.
£1,300–1,500
€/ $2,100–2,400 BaN

A Gebrüder Heubach Piano Baby doll, with moulded and painted hair, closed mouth, broken finger, stamped with trademark and marked 'Dep', German, c1915, 4in (10cm) high.
£85–100
€/ $130–160 THE

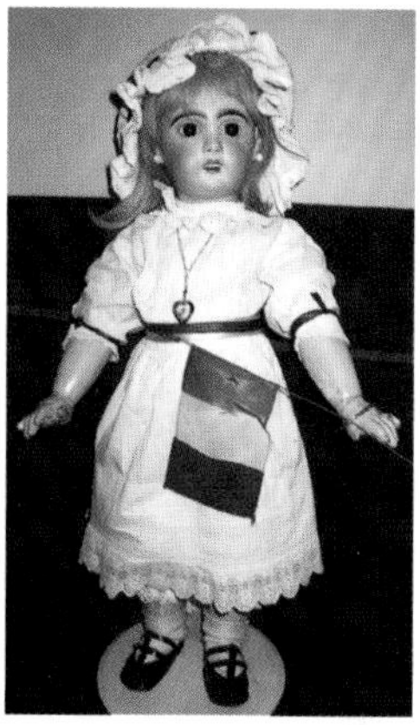

A Jumeau bisque-headed *bébé* doll, with paperweight eyes and composition body, French, 1885–90, 25in (63.5cm) high.
£2,700–3,000
€/ $4,200–4,800 Beb

A Jumeau bisque-headed doll, with fixed glass eyes, open mouth and fully-jointed composition body, hairline cracks, French, c1910, 20in (51cm) high.
£600–700
€/ $950–1,100 B(Ch)

A Jumeau *bébé* doll, with paperweight eyes, French, c1880, 32in (81.5cm) high.
£7,200–8,000
€/ $11,400–12,600 Beb

A Jumeau bisque-headed doll, with glass paper-weight eyes, closed mouth and double-jointed composition body, marked 'Déposé Tête Jumeau - B.T.E. S.D. G.D.', French, c1885, 15in (38cm) high.
£3,000–3,500
€/ $4,800–5,500 YC

A Kämmer & Reinhardt bisque-headed character doll, 'Gretchen', with painted features, original wig and double-jointed composition body, later dress, German, c1908, 19¾in (50cm) high.
£3,600–4,500
€/ $5,700–7,000 YC

A pair of Marion Kaulitz Munich Art dolls, with painted composition heads and closed mouths, on fully-jointed composition bodies, German, c1911, 13in (33cm) high.
£1,000–1,200
€/ $1,600–1,900 B(Ch)

A J. D. Kestner bisque-headed doll, with weighted eyes, wood and composition ball-jointed body, chips, impressed '192 9', German, c1910, 20in (51cm) high.
£450–525
€/ $710–830 VEC

A J. D. Kestner bisque-headed Oriental character baby doll, with brown glass sleeping eyes, black wig and composition body, wearing Chinese silk costume, some damage, impressed 'Made in Germany 243 JDK', German, 1920s, head circumference 10in (25.5cm).
£520–620
€/ $830–980 SK(B)

A Kämmer & Reinhardt bisque-headed character doll, No. 115/A, with sleeping eyes and closed mouth, double-jointed composition toddler body, German, c1910, 13½in (34.5cm) high.
£1,800–2,000
€/ $2,800–3,200 YC

A J. D. Kestner Excelsior bisque-headed doll, with weighted glass eyes, open mouth, upper teeth and fully-jointed wood and composition body, incised, stamped 'Excelsior D.R.P, no 70685', German, c1910, 21in (53.5cm) high.
£420–500
€/ $660–800 B(Ch)

A J. D. Kestner bisque-headed character doll, 'Hilda', with sleeping eyes, open mouth and composition body, original clothes, incised mark, German, c1910, 11½in (29cm) high.
£1,600–2,000
€/ $2,500–3,200 YC

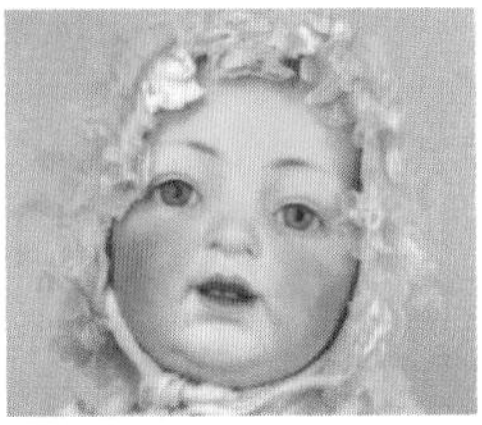

A J. D. Kestner bisque-headed baby doll, with sleeping eyes, open mouth and painted hair, marked 'JDK, Made in-14- Germany', wearing baby clothes, early 20thC, 18in (45.5cm) high.
£275–330
€/ $430–520 JDJ

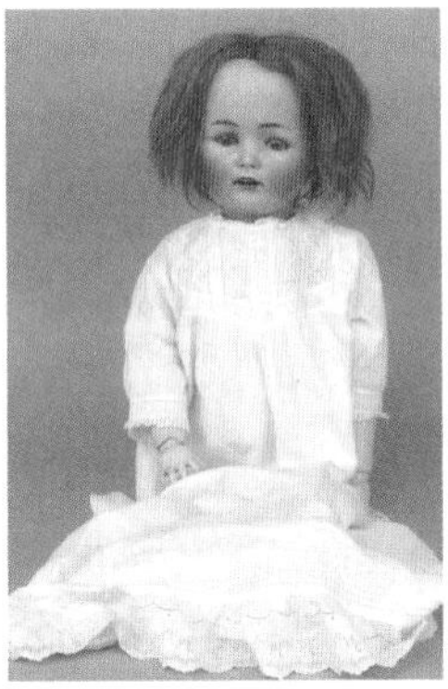

A J. D. Kestner bisque-headed doll, with weighted glass eyes, open mouth and wig, a wood and composition ball-jointed body, impressed 'J.D.K. 260 63 71', minor chip, German, c1916, 25½in (65cm) high.
£550–625
€/ $870–990 VEC

◄ **A Buddy Lee composition doll,** with a painted face, five-piece body, wearing denim dungarees labelled 'Lee-Union Made', American, c1922, 12in (30.5cm) high.
£185–225
€/ $290–360 THE

A J. D. Kestner bisque-headed character doll, No. 239, with sleeping eyes, open mouth, double-jointed composition body, original clothing, new wig, German, c1910, 19in (48.5cm) high.
£500–600
€/ $790–950 YC

Condition

The condition is absolutely vital when assessing the value of an antique. Damaged pieces on the whole appreciate much less than perfect examples. However a rare desirable piece may command a high price even when damaged.

A Käthe Kruse cloth doll, with painted eyes, wearing original school uniform, German, c1930, 20in (51cm) high.
£1,200–1,400
€/ $1,900–2,200 B(Ch)

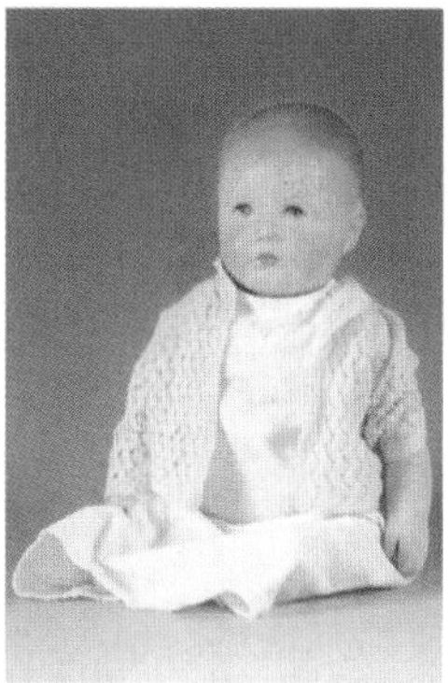

A Käthe Kruse Du Mein sand baby doll, with magnesite head, painted eyes and closed mouth, foam-filled body covered with stockinet, stamped on right foot, German, c1940, 21in (53.5cm) high.
£1,300–1,500
€/ $2,100–2,400 B(Ch)

A Käthe Kruse cloth doll, with painted face, moulded ears, jointed at hips, marked '120437', German, c1940, 18in (45.5cm) high.
£600–700
€/ $950–1,100 B(Ch)

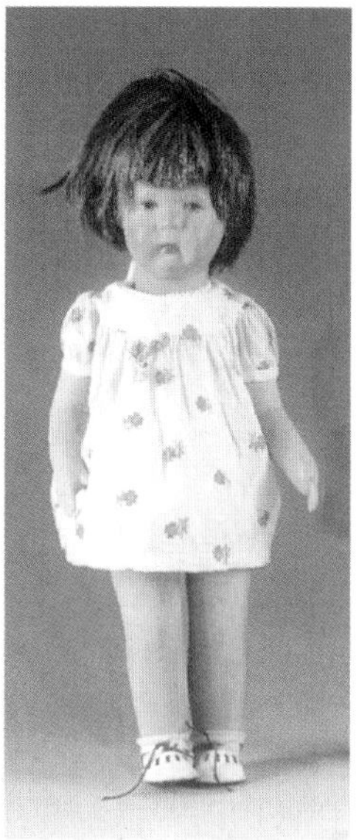

A Käthe Kruse doll, 'Little German child', with hard plastic head, painted eyes and short wig, cloth body, German, c1950, 18in (45.5cm) high.
£450–525
€/ $710–830 B(Ch)

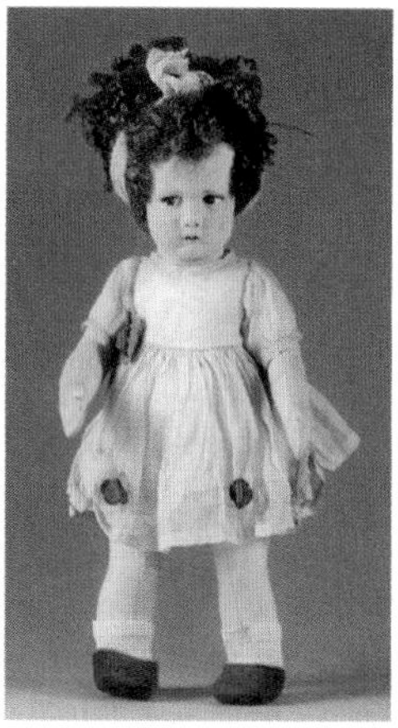

A Lenci cloth doll, with painted features, curly mohair wig, swivel neck and jointed shoulders and hips, Italian, c1930, 17in (43cm) high.
£300–350
€/ $475–550 B(Ch)

A Lenci felt character doll, with painted eyes, closed mouth and a blonde mohair wig, jointed neck and limbs, wearing a sailor's outfit, Italian, 1930s, 22½in (57cm) high.
£1,400–1,700
€/ $2,200–2,700 SK(B)

An Armand Marseille bisque-headed doll, mould 390, with cloth body and composition arms, original wig, 1890s, 26in (66cm) high.
£430–470
€/ $680–750 BaN

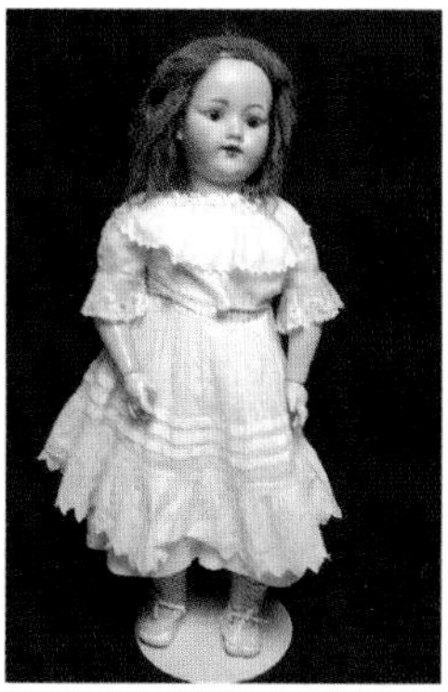

An Armand Marseille bisque-headed doll, mould 390, German, c1900, 34in (86.5cm) high.
£580–650
€/ $920–1,000 BaN

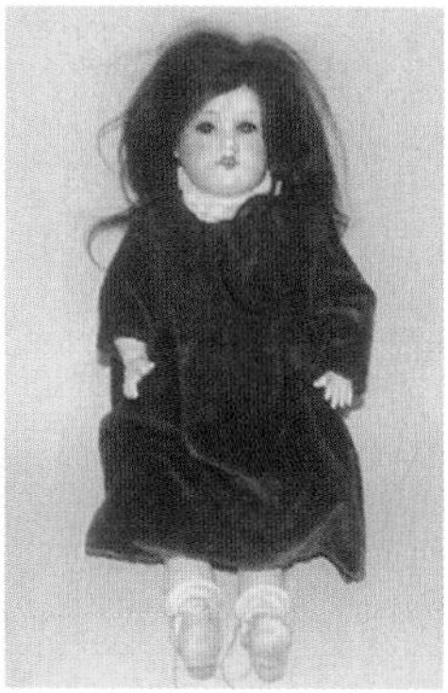

An Armand Marseille bisque-headed doll, mould 370, the kid body with jointed limbs, impressed mark, early 20thC, 15¾in (40cm) high.
£220–250
€/ $350–400 PFK

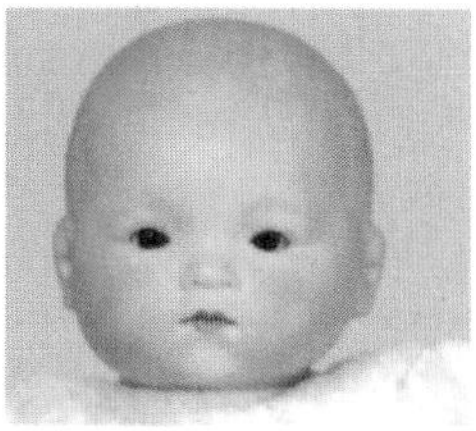

► **An Armand Marseille Dream Baby doll,** with sleeping eyes, composition hands and cloth body, hands repainted, German, early 20thC, 16in (40.5cm) high.
£100–120
€/ $160–190 JDJ

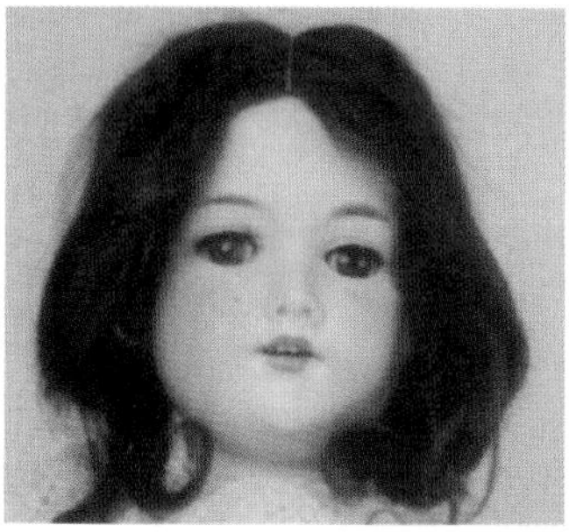

An Armand Marseille bisque-headed doll, mould 390, with sleeping eyes, marked, c1900, 22in (56cm) high.
£90–110
€/ $140–170 JDJ

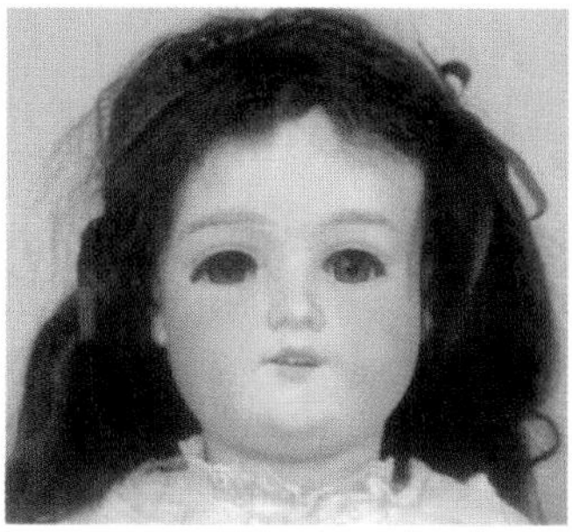

An Armand Marseille bisque-headed doll, mould 390, with glass eyes, new wig, one leg broken, marked, c1900, 27in (68.5cm) high.
£145–160
€/ $230–250 JDJ

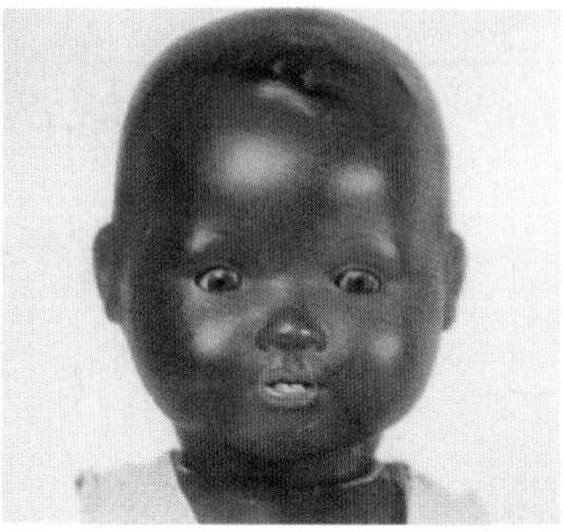

An Armand Marseille bisque baby doll, mould 351, with painted hair, some damage, marked, early 20thC, 20in (51cm) high.
£425–475
€/ $670–750 JDJ

DOLLS

An Armand Marseille doll, mould 390, fully jointed, wearing a fairy costume, marked, German, early 20thC, 16in (40.5cm) high, with original Kalitu Production ticket.
£220–260
€/ $350–400 BWL

◄ An Armand Marseille bisque-headed Googly doll, mould 323, with sleeping eyes, closed mouth, composition toddler body, new clothes, German, c1912, 10¼in (26cm) high.
£900–1,100
€/ $1,400–1,700 ⊞ YC

A Kewpie bisque doll, signed by Rose O'Neill, American, c1915, 6in (15cm) high.
£300–350
€/ $475–550 ⊞ THE

A Kewpie bisque doll, 'The Traveller', incised Rose O'Neill, American, c1915, 6in (15cm) high.
£345–400
€/ $545–630 ⊞ THE

A poured wax doll, possibly by Pierotti, c1870, 30in (76cm) high.
£2,700–3,000
€/ $4,300–4,800 ⊞ Beb

A Bye-Lo doll, with sleeping eyes, cloth body and celluloid hands, marked 'Grace Putnam', early 20thC, 14in (35.5cm) high.
£125–150
€/ $200–240 JDJ

► A Franz Schmidt bisque-headed doll, with sleeping glass eyes and jointed composition toddler body, original wig, c1912, 21in (53.5cm) high.
£400–500
€/ $630–800 ⊞ YC

An S. F. B. J. bisque-headed doll, with weighted brown eyes and a wood and composition body, impressed '301 7', French, c1910, 20in (51cm) high.
£130–150
€/ $210–240 VEC

An S. F. B. J. bisque-headed doll, with weighted blue glass eyes, open mouth and moulded teeth, fully-jointed composition body, hairline crack to head, French, c1910, 31in (78.5cm) high.
£380–450
€/ $600–710 B(Ch)

A Simon & Halbig bisque-shoulder-headed doll, with fixed glass eyes, wig with plaited bun, on a twill-over-wood jointed body, wearing original striped dress, one thumb broken, German, c1870, 10½in (26.5cm) high, in original box with trousseau.
£2,000–2,400
€/ $3,200–3,800 B(Ch)

Further reading

Miller's Antiques & Collectables: The Facts At Your Fingertips, Miller's Publications, 2000

A Simon & Halbig bisque doll, wearing an antique outfit, German, c1890, 14in (35.5cm) high.
£500–600
€/ $870–950 ⊞ Beb

A Simon & Halbig bisque doll, with weighted eyes, wood and composition ball-jointed body, impressed 'S & H 1079 DEP 11', cracked, German, c1892, 22¾in (58cm) high.
£150–175
€/ $240–275 VEC

A Simon & Halbig bisque-headed doll, with sleeping glass eyes, wig and amber-tinted composition ball-jointed body, wearing silk costume, marked 'Simon&Halbig-Germany-1329-5', repainted arms and legs, German, c1900, 18in (45.5cm) high.
£760–900
€/ $1,200–1,400 ⊞ THE

A Simon & Halbig bisque-headed doll, mould 1009, with glass sleeping eyes, double-jointed wood and composition body, wearing original outfit, produced for the French market, German, c1895, 20½in (52cm) high.
£600–700
€/ $950–1,100 ⊞ YC

A Simon & Halbig bisque-headed doll, with sleeping eyes, on jointed body, wearing original costume, impressed 'S and H 1078 Simon and Halbig 6', German, c1910, 14½in (37cm) high.
£360–430
€/ $580–680 BWL

► **A Simon & Halbig bisque-headed doll,** mould 1249, 'Santa', with sleeping glass eyes, on a double-jointed composition body, wearing original baby clothes, German, c1905, 15in (38cm) high.
£550–600
€/ $870–950
⊞ YC

A Simon & Halbig bisque-headed doll, German, c1910, 27in (68.5cm) high.
£750–850
€/ $1,200–1,300 ⊞ BaN

A Simon & Halbig/Kämmer & Reinhardt bisque-shoulder-headed doll, with weighted glass eyes, original wig on a cloth body, bisque lower arms, wearing regional costume, German, c1910, 16in (40.5cm) high, in original card box, lid missing.
£320–375
€/ $510–590 B(Ch)

◄ **A Jules Steiner bisque-headed doll,** with glass paperweight eyes, on a double-jointed composition body, wearing original costume, marked 'Steiner Paris', French, c1890, 21¼in (54cm) high.
£3,500–4,000
€/ $5,500–6,200 ⊞ YC

Auction or dealer?

When buying at auction, prices can be lower than those of a dealer, but a buyer's premium and VAT will be added to the hammer price. Equally, when selling at auction, commission, tax and photography charges will be deducted from the hammer price. Dealers will often restore pieces before putting them back on the market.

► **A Walther & Sohn bisque-headed doll,** with googly sleeping eyes, composition bent-limb body, marked '208.121', German, c1920, 7in (18cm) high.
£280–320
€/ $440–510
AH

DOLLS

Unknown Makers

A wooden doll, with painted features and peg-jointed body, one arm and leg possible replacements, American, early 19thC, 5¼in (13.5cm) high.
£240–300
€/ $380–475 ⚒ SK(B)
This doll was found in New England and a note with her states 'this doll was the plaything of Eliza Thornton, sister of Lydia Thornton Cram'.

A poured wax doll, with fixed eyes, cloth body with wax lower arms and legs, head repaired, c1870, 28in (71cm) high.
£1,500–1,700
€/ $2,400–2,800 ⊞ BaN

A late Victorian bisque-headed doll, with jointed composition body, 23¾in (60.5cm) high.
£140–160
€/ $220–250 ⚒ SWO

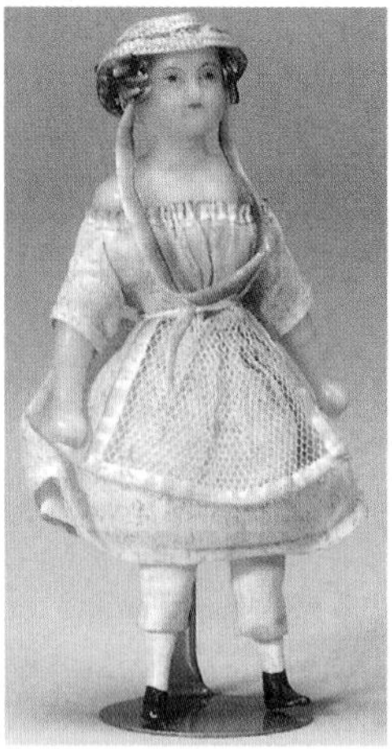

A wax doll, with painted eyes, closed mouth, with composition lower legs, original dress and apron, c1860, 6in (15cm) high.
£350–380
€/ $550–600 ⚒ SK(B)

A bisque shoulder-headed fashion doll, made for Simmone, with glass eyes and closed mouth, stuffed kid body, original wig and dress, c1880, 16½in (42cm) high.
£1,600–1,800
€/ $2,500–2,800 ⊞ YC

► **A doll,** with fixed glass eyes, open mouth with applied teeth and moulded hair, on a jointed composition body, French, c1910, 20in (51cm) high.
£1,400–1,600
€/ $2,200–2,500 ⚒ AH

A poured wax shoulder-headed doll, with fixed eyes, cloth body and wax-over-composition lower arms and legs, cracks, damage, c1860, 23in (58.5cm) high.
£160–200
€/ $250–320 ⚒ VEC

A bisque-headed doll, with paperweight eyes and closed mouth, pierced ears with original earrings, jointed composition body, marked 'M10', French, c1890, 22¾in (58cm) high.
£2,200–2,500
€/ $3,500–4,000 ⚒ Bri

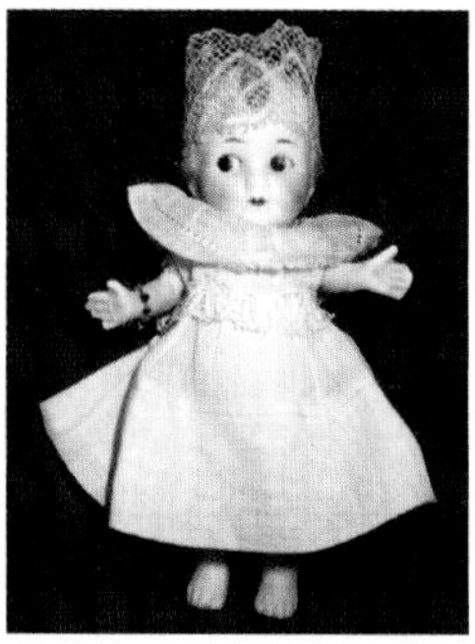

A bisque Googly doll, c1910, 6in (15cm) high.
£550–650
€/ $870–1,000 ⊞ Beb

► **A doll,** with painted features, cloth body with composition arms, French, c1930, 12½in (32cm) high.
£65–75
€/ $100–120 ⊞ YC

A china-headed doll, 'Grape Lady', with blue painted eyes, and a cluster of iridescent cobalt blue grapes beneath white ruffled gold snood, cloth body with china limbs, wearing original beige silk and wool dress, German, 1860s, 17in (43cm) high.
£1,300–1,500
€/ $2,000–2,400 ⚒ SK(B)

A wax doll, with closed mouth, curly wig, 19thC, 22in (56cm) high.
£260–320
€/ $410–500 ⚒ SWO

A wax-over-composition doll, with fixed glass eyes and cloth body, 19thC, 16in (40.5cm) high.
£145–160
€/ $230–250 ⊞ BaN

DOLLS

Dolls' Houses

A painted wooden dolls' house, with a painted tiled roof, the front opening to reveal six rooms, hallway and staircase, mid-19thC, 38in (97cm) wide.
£1,000–1,200
€/ $1,600–2,000 B(Ch)

A painted wooden dolls' house, the front opening in two sections to reveal four rooms, c1860, 30in (76cm) wide.
£480–570
€/ $760–900 B(Ch)

A wooden dolls' house, with four furnished rooms, c1870, 29in (73.5cm) wide.
£3,200–3,500
€/ $5,000–5,500 Beb

A wooden dolls' house, damaged, late 19thC, 29in (73.5cm) wide.
£400–500
€/ $600–800 S(O)

A Moritz Göttschalk painted wooden dolls' house, with single opening front revealing two rooms, with original wallpaper and floor coverings, German, c1900, 11in (28cm) wide.
£600–700
€/ $950–1,100 B(Ch)

A painted wooden dolls' house, with lift-off front and side opening, dated 1914, 23¾in (60.5cm) wide.
£350–420
€/ $550–650 S(O)

A wooden dolls' house, rendered in white stucco, the front opening in two sections to reveal four rooms, hallway, staircase and landing, all with original floor coverings and fireplaces, 1920s, 36in (91.5cm) wide.
£130–160
€/ $210–250 B(Ch)

A Tri-ang mock-Tudor wooden dolls' house, 'Albert Cottage', No. 77, the exterior painted with flowers to the walls, the front opening in two sections to reveal four rooms, hall, staircase and built-in garage with double doors, 1930s, 33½in (85cm) wide.
£200–240
€/ $320–380 WAL

An 'Amersham' dolls' house, with cream-painted exterior and *faux* slate roof, the front opening to reveal two rooms with fitted fireplace, late 1930s, base 16½in (42cm) square.
£80–100
€/ $125–160 WAL

◄ **A Tri-ang wooden dolls' house,** 'Fashionable Tudor House', No. 93, the exterior painted cream with flowers to the walls and half-timbered gables, the front opening in four sections to reveal five rooms, hall and staircase, built-in garage with opening double doors, with original wall and floor coverings and electric lighting, with furniture and many accessories, c1950, 47in (119.5cm) wide.
£800–950
€/ $1,300–1,500 B(Ch)

Teddy Bears

A Chad Valley curly mohair teddy bear, with glass eyes and rexine pads, labelled, 1940s, 14in (35.5cm) high.
£270–300
€/ $430–480 ⊞ BBe

A Clemens teddy bear, German, 1940s, 18in (45.5cm) high.
£400–450
€/ $630–700 ⊞ Beb

This teddy bear comes from a collection formed by the Volpps, an American couple who wrote many story books with teddy bears as the main characters.

◄ A Dean's Tru-to-Life mohair teddy bear, designed by Sylvia Wilgoss, with rubber nose, feet and pads, labelled, early 1950s, 22in (56cm) high.
£2,200–2,500
€/ $3,500–4,000 ⊞ BBe

A Chad Valley Magna mohair teddy bear, with glass eyes and cotton pads, labelled, 1950s, 12in (30.5cm) high.
£350–400
€/ $550–630 ⊞ BBe

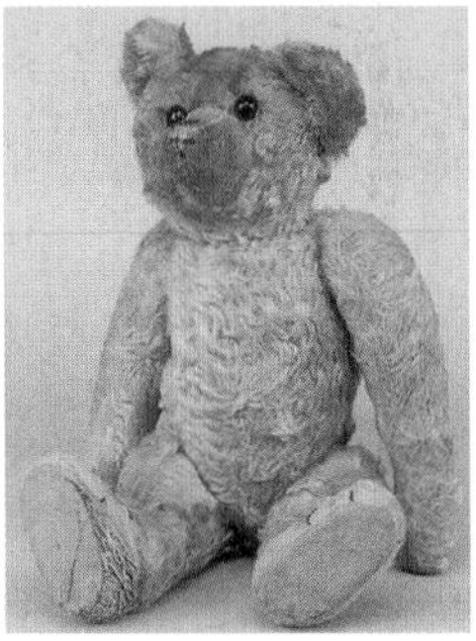

A Farnell mohair teddy bear, replaced glass eyes, head sewn on, repaired, worn, 1920s, 15in (38cm) high.
£800–950
€/ $1,300–1,500 ⚒ VEC

A Merrythought teddy bear, with glass eyes and original cotton pads, wishbone button in one ear, labelled, 1930s, 18in (45.5cm) high.
£315–350
€/ $500–550 ⊞ BBe

Further reading

Miller's Teddy Bears: A Complete Collector's Guide, Miller's Publications, 2001

A Dean's Rag Book mohair mouse-eared teddy bear, pads require restoration, 1930s, 16in (40.5cm) high.
£550–600
€/ $870–950 ⊞ BBe

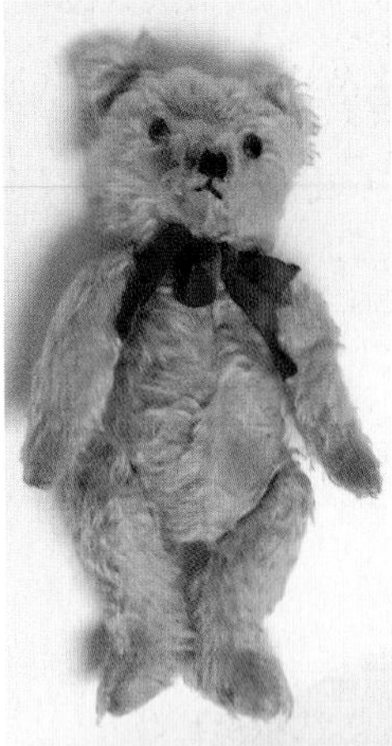

A Joy Toys mohair teddy bear, with glass eyes, Australian, 1940s, 14in (35.5cm) high.
£260–300
€/ $400–480 ⊞ BBe

A Merrythought mohair teddy bear, with glass eyes and cotton paw feet, labelled, 1930s–40s, 15in (38cm) high.
£350–400
€/ $550–630 ⊞ BBe

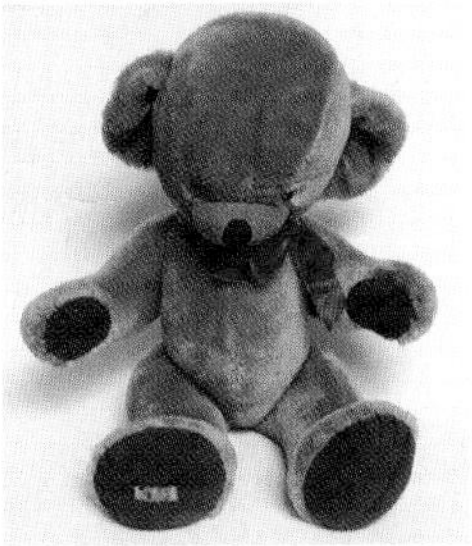

A Merrythought Cheeky mohair teddy bear, with plastic eyes, 1960, 24in (61cm) high.
£675–750
€/ $1,100–1,200 ⊞ BBe

Merrythought's Cheeky design was first registered in 1957. Sought-after by collectors today, it was a very popular bear in the late '50s and early '60s and was produced in a number of sizes and versions. Identifying features include bells inside the ears and the Merrythought label sewn to the foot. Over the years felt pads often became worn and were replaced so labels can be missing.

A Steiff plush teddy bear, with black boot-button eyes, centrally-stitched snout, hump back and button in ear, German, c1908, 22½in (57cm) high.
£2,200–2,500
€/ $3,500–4,000 ⚒ TEN

A Steiff mohair teddy bear, with boot-button eyes, fully jointed, some wear, German, c1908, 15½in (39.5cm) high.
£1,200–1,400
€/ $1,900–2,200 ⚒ VEC

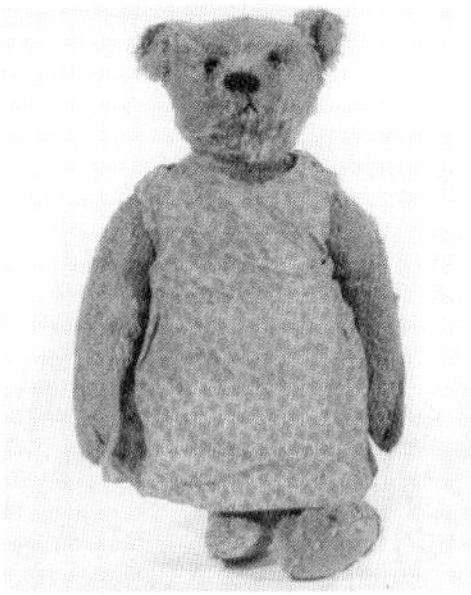

A Steiff plush teddy bear, with button eyes, jointed limbs and button to ear, straw-filled, German, c1910, 12in (30.5cm) high.
£1,400–1,600
€/ $2,200–2,500 ⚒ AH

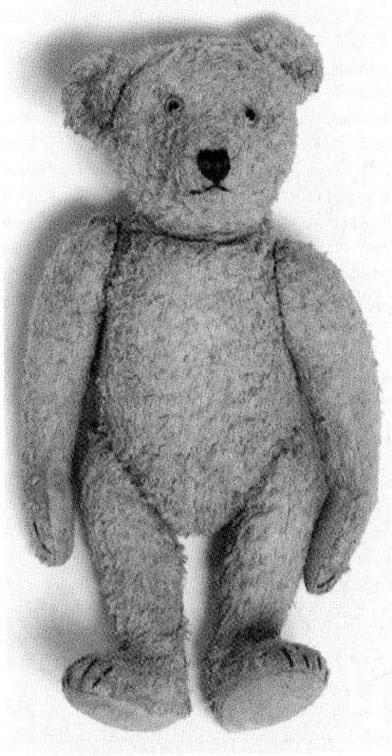

► A Steiff plush teddy bear, with glass eyes and cotton pads, German, 1940s, 16in (40.5cm) high.
£1,300–1,500
€/ $2,000–2,400 ⊞ BBe

A Tara Toys plush teddy bear, with jointed limbs, Irish, c1950, 18in (45.5cm) high.
£100–120
€/ $160–190 ⚒ G(L)

A mohair teddy bear, with glass eyes and felt pads, 1920s, 15in (38cm) high.
£350–400
€/ $550–630 ⊞ BBe

Soft Toys

A Wendy Boston mohair dog nightdress case, with plastic eyes, leather collar and original label, 1950s, 16in (40.5cm) long.
£60–65
€/ $95–100 ⊞ BBe

► **A Chad Valley cloth golly,** with cardboard label 'By Appointment to HM Queen Elizabeth the Queen Mother', small hole to back of head, one felt nostril missing, late 1950s–early 1960s, 24in (61cm) high.
£140–160
€/ $220–250 ⚒ VEC

► **A Chad Valley velvet Bonzo dog,** with painted features, swivel head and jointed limbs, card-lined feet, original collar with button attached, c1920, 10¼in (26cm) high.
£280–325
€/ $440–510 ⚒ DA

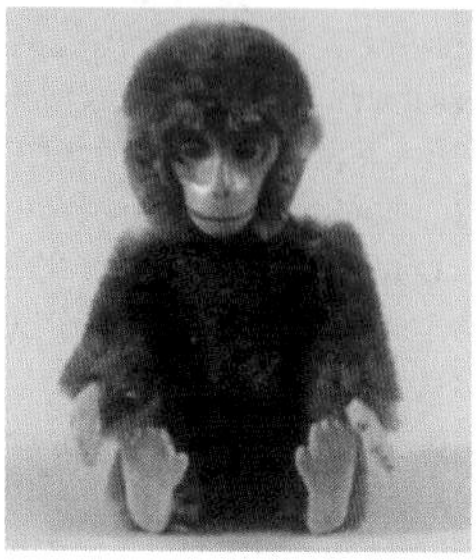

A Schuco mohair Yes/No monkey, German, 1920s, 4¾in (12cm) high.
£145–170
€/ $230–270 ⚒ JDJ

A Schuco Goofy, German, 1950s, 14in (35.5cm) high.
£160–180
€/ $250–280 ⚒ TQA

A Steiff mohair giraffe, with original buttons, ear tag, squeaker boot and button eyes, German, 1950s, 11in (28cm) high.
£60–65
€/ $95–100 ⊞ BBe

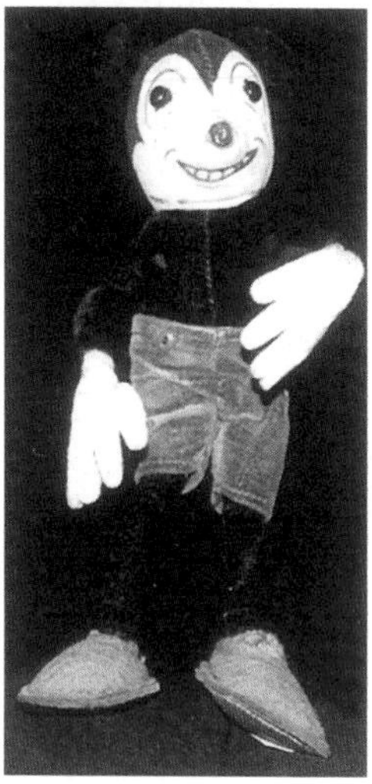

A velvet Mickey Mouse, slightly worn, some repair, c1930, 9in (23cm) high.
£140–160
€/ $220–250 ⚒ DA

A plush miniature monkey, with tin face, jointed head and limbs, early 20thC, 2¼in (5.5cm) high.
£75–90
€/ $120–140 ⚒ SWO

A felt Mickey and Minnie Mouse, after 1945, 13½in (34.5cm) high.
£35–40
€/ $55–65 ⚒ G(L)

Further reading

Miller's Soft Toys: A Collector's Guide, Miller's Publications, 2000

◄ **A cloth lion,** with glass eyes, 1950s, 12in (30.5cm) high.
£27–30
€/ $40–45 ⊞ YC

► **A Soo puppet,** from *Sooty & Sweep*, 1950s, 9in (23cm) high.
£10–15
€/ $16–24 ⊞ CCO

A fur monkey, with glass eyes, c1960, 14in (35.5cm) high.
£22–25
€/ $35–40 ⊞ YC

Toys

Over the many years that I have been involved in the antiques business I have found that collectors of toys generally fall into four main categories. I always advise the 'Pure Investor' to select an area to collect, research it inside out, find the rarest pieces and purchase the best examples one can afford. This will usually ensure that the items will command the best possible prices when they come to be sold at a later date. The 'Serious Collector' is looking for excellent condition and knows his subject. He also enjoys the fun of the hunt, the pure delight of arriving home from the auction or fair with the piece that has eluded him for so many months, and which is then lovingly placed in the cabinet. The 'Hobbyist' collects for the sheer joy of it and all one requires is an example of the type. Nothing has to be perfect and indeed, the fact that in years gone by a youngster has had fun with it just adds to its attraction and therefore a mint, boxed example is not necessary. The 'Limited Edition Collector' collects mainly modern models, perhaps the many series representing vehicles used in television programmes and films. These collectors should bear in mind that in the long term these items are unlikely to be a good investment, since once the craze for collecting a particular range of models has passed, the value often falls quickly.

Modern limited editions should not be confused, however, with early television- and film-related vehicles, which have become increasingly popular over the last 25 years. For example, in the 1960s Corgi and Dinky produced a range which included the *Man From U.N.C.L.E.* Oldsmobile, the James Bond Aston Martin DB5, and various *Captain Scarlet* vehicles, among others. These are very sought after today and can command extremely high prices, particularly in comparison to many other die-cast vehicles of the same period. They have proved to be an excellent investment: as an example, a mint, boxed Corgi James Bond Toyota 2000 GT which cost £18 (€/ $28) in c1980 would now cost about £375 (€/ $590). This, I feel, is mainly due to the role that film and television plays in our lives today.

Reruns on the television of the old classics such as James Bond films, *Doctor Who*, *Thunderbirds* and the like awaken feelings of nostalgia in adults who can now afford to collect toys which remind them of perhaps more carefree days. The field is immense and encompasses die-cast, tinplate and even plastic examples. The hobby is driven by a worldwide audience which is no doubt helping to push up prices.

Glenn Butler

Aeroplanes

A Dinky Toys Imperial Airways airliner, 1930s, 4in (10cm) long.
£120–135
€/ $190–215 ⊞ CBB

A Dinky Toys Short Shetland Flying Boat, 1940s, 7in (18cm) long.
£250–280
€/ $400–440 ⊞ CBB

A Fanfare Models aircraft hanger, with pilot, ground crew, mechanics and RAF personnel, and a copy of a Britain's Autogyro, c1930, 23in (58.5cm) wide.
£160–200
€/ $250–320 ⚒ VEC

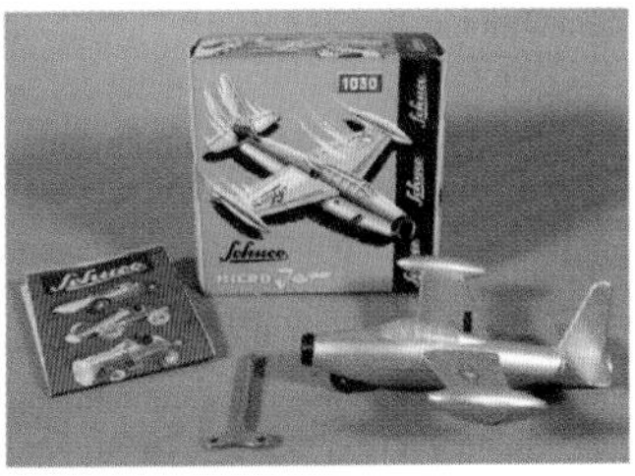

► A Schuco 1030 Micro Jet, German, 1950s, with box, 5½in (14cm) square.
£40–50
€/ $63–80 ⚒ TQA

A Schuco 1031 Micro Jet, German, 1950s, with box, 5in (12.5cm) square.
£40–45
€/ $63–70 ⚒ TQA

◄ A tinplate bi-plane, c1930, 18in (45.5cm) wide.
£200–220
€/ $315–350
⚒ VEC

Boats

◄ **A Bing clockwork battleship,** one secondary turret missing, German, c1920, 20in (51cm) wide.
£1,000–1,200
€/ $1,600–1,900 B(Ch)

A Bing tinplate clockwork U boat, with detachable flag, 1930s, 13½in (34.5cm) wide.
£475–550
€/ $750–870 WAL

A Schuco 3003 clockwork police boat, German, 1950s, 5in (12.5cm) wide.
£100–125
€/ $160–200 TQA

Tinplate

The term tinplate covers a vast range of items, including boats, trains, cars, buses, automata and space ships. If your budget is relatively small – under £150 (€/ $240) – then the 1960s to 1970s is the best period to focus on. Battery-powered examples made in Japan, China, and some eastern European countries are plentiful. If you are looking to spend more, you should collect earlier items as far back as the Victorian era, where in many cases a great deal has to be spent to secure these childhood playthings.

The rules for investment buying are: buy the best examples you can find; make sure the action works; check that battery-powered examples do not show signs of battery leakage, and look for pieces in original packaging.

◄ **A Schuco clockwork 3006 Pitt boat,** German, 1950s, 11in (28cm) wide.
£100–125
€/ $160–200 TQA

► **A motor boat,** the spirit-fired brass boiler with oscillating engine, Japanese, 1930s, 10in (25.5cm) wide.
£140–160
€/ $220–250 HoG

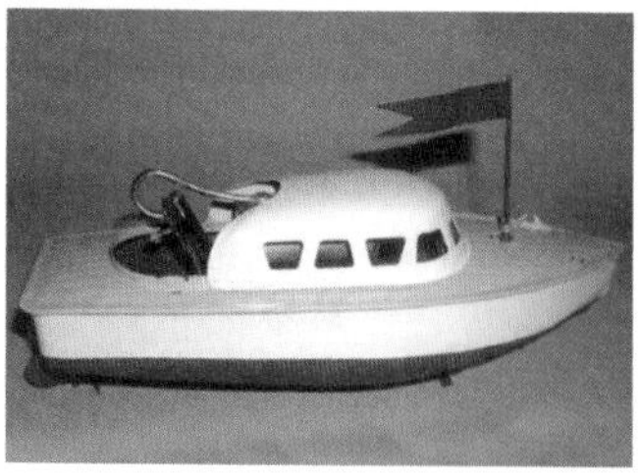

Mechanical Toys

A Brimtoy Pocketoy 9/501 clockwork steamroller, 1950s, 4in (10cm) wide, boxed.
£60–65
€/ $95–105 GTM

► **A Fontaine Fox clockwork painted tin trolley car,** 'Toonerville Trolley', with driver, American, 1920s, 5in (12.5cm) high.
£420–500
€/ $660–800 BAu

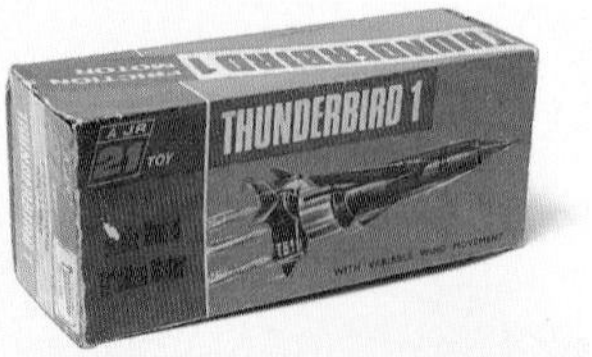

A JR 21 Toys Thunderbird 1, with friction motor, c1966, 8in (20.5cm) wide, boxed.
£90–100
€/ $140–160 GTM

► **A Lambert musical automaton of a Spanish dancer,** clothes replaced, French, c1895, 21in (53.5cm) high.
£2,700–3,000
€/ $4,300–4,700 KHW

A Rock Valley Toys battery-operated bubble-blowing monkey, Japanese, 1950s, 11in (28cm) high.
£125–140
€/ $200–230 CBB

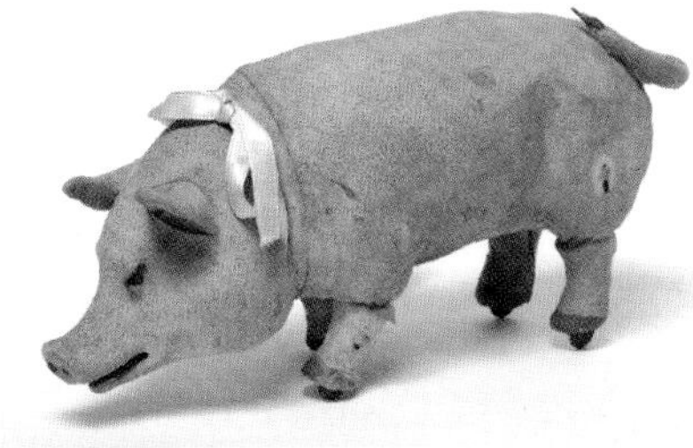

An automaton walking pig, possibly by Roullet et Decamps, covered with skin, French, c1900, 11in (28cm) long.
£765–850
€/ $1,200–1,300 ⊞ BaN

◄ **A pair of Schuco felt-covered tinplate clockwork pigs,** one plays a fiddle, the other a drum, German, 1920–30, 4½in (11.5 cm) high.
£300–360
€/ $475–575 ⚒ F&C

► **A flock-covered papier mâché bulldog,** with bark and nodding head, French, c1900, 21in (53.5cm) long.
£1,000–1,100
€/ $1,600–1,700 ⊞ AUTO

A clockwork toy of two dancing dolls, with bisque heads, c1930, 8in (20.5cm) high.
£585–650
€/ $925–1,000 ⊞ AUTO

A tinplate clockwork swan, Japanese, 1950s, 7in (18cm) long, boxed.
£115–130
€/ $180–200 ⊞ CBB

◄ **A tinplate battery-operated X-7 Flying Saucer,** Japanese, 1960s, 8in (20.5cm) diam.
£175–200
€/ $275–315 ⊞ GTM

Money Boxes

A cast-iron Bulldog Bank money box, with glass eyes, losses, American, dated 1880, 7¾in (19.5cm) high.
£200–225
€/ $315–350 ⚒ HAM

A cast-iron money box, in the form of a golly, c1910, 6½in (16.5cm) high.
£360–400
€/ $570–630 ⊞ MFB

◄ **A cast-iron mechanical money box,** the dog performs a trick, American, c1930, 9in (23cm) wide.
£360–400
€/ $570–630
⊞ HAL

Noah's Arks

A painted pine Noah's Ark, with a collection of painted pine and composition figures and animals, losses and damage, Swiss, mid-19thC, 18½in (47cm) wide.
£600–720
€/ $950–1,100 BR

► A painted Noah's Ark, with seven figures and 39 animals, German, mid-19thC, 6¼in (16cm) wide.
£1,600–1,800
€/ $2,500–2,800 SK(B)

◄ A painted wooden Noah's Ark, with five figures and approximately 65 animals, slight damage, German, late 19thC, 28in (71cm) wide, together with a quantity of wooden farmyard fencing, trees and animals.
£1,400–1,600
€/ $2,200–2,500 VEC

Rocking Horses

A Victorian rocking horse, on traditional rocker base, restored, 80in (203cm) long.
£1,400–1,600
€/ $2,200–2,500 JM

A carved- and painted-wood rocking horse, c1900, 51¼in (130cm) long.
£350–400
€/ $550–630 SWO

A carved- and painted-wood rocking horse, with horsehair mane and tail, original leather bridle and saddle, on a safety stand, marked for Henry's, Winchester, c1880, 44in (122cm) high.
£700–800
€/ $1,100–1,300 B(Ch)

An F. Ayres ponyskin rocking horse, with horsehair mane and tail, original leather bridle, saddle and metal stirrups, on a safety rocker, minor losses, c1900, 53in (134.5cm) high.
£600–700
€/ $950–1,100 B(Ch)

◄ A rocking horse, with hair mane and leather saddle, on a pine stand, restored, early 20thC, 48in (122cm) wide.
£800–950
€/ $1,300–1,500 EH

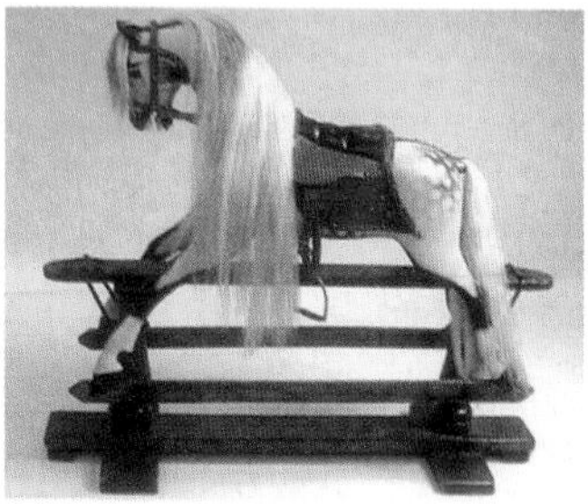

An F. Ayres painted rocking horse, on a trestle base, restored by Stevenson Bros, c1890, 39½in (100.5cm) high.
£1,100–1,300
€/ $1,700–2,000 BR

A rocking horse, with padded body and wooden base, possibly eastern European, early 20thC, 34¼in (87cm) wide.
£220–250
€/ $350–400 SWO

An F. Ayres carved and painted rocking horse, with horsehair mane and tail, remains of leather bridle and saddle, with leg rest for side saddle, on safety rockers, embossed Ayres signature, c1920, 47in (119.5cm) high.
£1,100–1,300
€/ $1,700–2,000 B(Ch)

Soldiers

◄ **A Britains set of Germanic 16th Lancers,** comprising nine figures including officer and trumpeter, with moveable arms and twistable pennons, in associated box, losses, 1893.
£2,000–2,400
€/ $3,200–3,800 B(Ch)

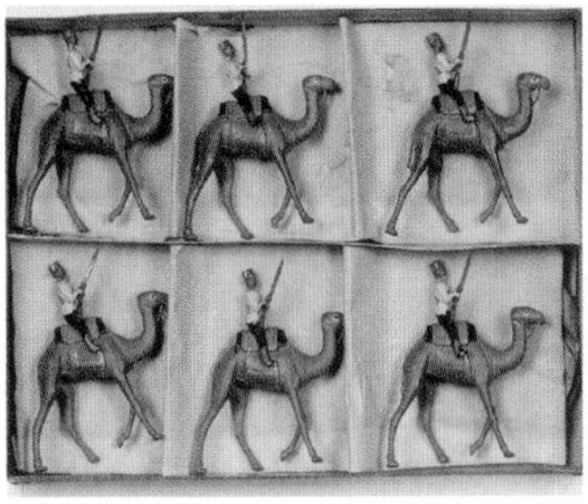

A Britains set of Egyptian Camel Corps, set No. 48, with wire tails and removable riders, in original box, 1899.
£550–650
€/ $870–1,000 B(Ch)

A Britains set of 21st Lancers, set No. 94, comprising four mounted Lancers and a mounted officer, minor damage, 1901, boxed.
£400–475
€/ $630–750 VEC

A Britains Middlesex Regiment, set No. 76, comprising eight figures, 1903.
£180–220
€/ $285–350 B(Ch)

► **A Britains set of US Infantry,** comprising 10 marching infantrymen, 1906.
£250–300
€/ $400–475 VEC

Three Britains American mounted soldiers, from set No. 149, 1907–16.
£550–650
€/ $870–1,000 VEC

A Britains Mountain Artillery group, set No. 28, comprising six gunners, a mounted officer, four mules and dismantled R. A. gun, 1910.
£160–200
€/ $250–315 VEC

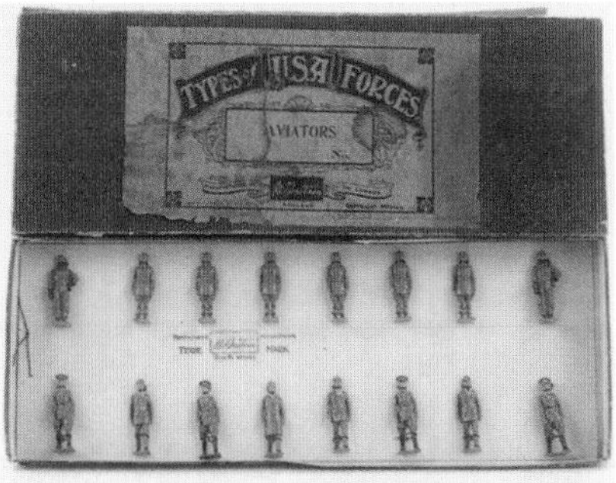

◄ **A Britains USA Aviation Display set,** set No. 336, comprising 16 figures of aviators and marching privates, boxed, 1929.
£600–725
€/ $950–1,100 VEC

A Britains Royal Horse Artillery group, set No. 318, with artillerymen mounted on standing horses, mounted officer and fumed metal limber and gun, standing artillery men missing, 1930.
£850–1,000
€/ $1,300–1,600 B(Ch)
This is a rare set, because boys wanted the horse cantering or trotting – standing still was in effect dull.

A Britains set of Royal Navy Bluejackets and Whitejackets, set No. 254, comprising nine figures including Petty Officer, some retouching to paint, 1935.
£100–125
€/ $160–200 B(Ch)

► **A Britains set of Royal Welch Fusiliers,** set No. 2124, with officer and goat mascot, in original box, 1958.
£140–160
€/ $220–250 B(Ch)

Trains

A Bassett-Lowke gauge 0 live steam 4–6–0 Enterprise locomotive and tender, 6285, c1935, together with other items including original Bassett-Lowke bill of sale, spare wick and spring, filler, two cans of rocket oil and two cans of cylinder oil.
£500–575
€/ $800–900 AH

An American Flyer gauge 0 electric train, roof repainted, c1935, 21in (53.5cm) long.
£175–200
€/ $275–315 WOS

Gauges

Trains of various gauges are one of the most popular collecting fields within the toy and model world. Z and N gauge are the very small pieces normally purchased to run rather than collect, ideal for when space is at a premium. 0 and 00 are the two gauges mainly collected by people looking to invest and also run.

Frank Hornby's products, the 0 and Dublo series, are much sought after. Bassett-Lowke, Bing, Märklin, and other well-known manufacturers also have a very strong following. If you have a budget of about £350 (€/ $500) you will be able to buy many examples of these gauges.

The rarer ones can cost as much as £1,000 (€/ $1,600) or more. The rules for investment buying are: buy the best example you can find; watch for professionally restored examples as these can sometimes be passed off as mint originals; check the wheels are not later replacements; look for dents/creases that have been removed; check the condition of the clockwork or electric motor, and take a key to test the clockwork mechanism. A reputable vendor will not mind you doing this.

A Bassett-Lowke gauge 0 electric 0–6–0 tank locomotive, RN 68211, in BR livery, 1950s, boxed.
£320–375
€/ $500–600 B(Ch)

◄ **A Bing gauge 0 live steam 0–4–0 locomotive and tender,** finished in black with red lining, early 20thC.
£320–400
€/ $510–630 LAY

A Bing plastic signal box, restored, 1930s, 10in (25.5cm) high.
£40–45
€/ $65–70 WOS

A Karl Bub tinplate gauge 0 clockwork 4–4–0 locomotive, RN 1632, with six-wheel tender and two bogie carriages with opening doors and side-hinged roof, minor damage, German, early 20thC.
£550–650
€/ $870–1,000 WAL

► **A Carette gauge 1 eight-wheeled carriage,** with opening doors, German, c1910.
£270–300
€/ $425–475 WOS

A Fleischmann gauge H0 D.B. 4–6–2 mainline heavy duty locomotive and tender, German, 1950s.
£90–100
€/ $140–160 WOS

A Hornby gauge 0 Pullman coach, c1930, boxed.
£135–150
€/ $215–240 GTM

TOYS

A Hornby gauge 0 No. 2 corridor brake end coach, with opening windows, compensating bogies with reduced Mansell wheels, mid-1930s.
£230–275
€/ $365–440 WAL

► **A Hornby gauge 0 E2E engine shed,** with two three-rail roads, details to one side only, mid-1930s.
£370–425
€/ $585–670
WAL

A Hornby gauge 0 clockwork 0–4–0 No. 1 Tank locomotive, c1937.
£38–42
€/ $60–65 VJ

A Hornby Dublo gauge 00 LMR 8F electric freight locomotive and tender, 1958–61, with original box.
£115–125
€/ $180–200 GTM

A Hornby two-rail BR diesel locomotive, 1950s.
£65–75
€/ $100–120 WOS

Colour variations

Two frequently asked questions are: why are cars produced in different colourways? why is one more valuable than the other?

One answer is that at the end of a working week, quite often at the end of a month, the supply of paint on a particular production line might have run out. Rather than stop production, a similar paint would be requisitioned from another line and painters would continue until the shift ended. Maybe only a few hundred toys would have been made in the new unrecorded colour. Another scenario is that a company would commission a limited number in their own livery for promotional purposes. Values for these limited pieces can be greatly in excess of those for normal production pieces.

A Hornby gauge 0 tinplate station, electric lights not original, bulbs missing, 1950s, 32in (81.5cm) wide.
£75–85
€/ $120–135 WOS

A Hornby Dublo LMS passenger train set, comprising 4–6–2 Duchess of Atholl locomotive and tender, track, controller, spanner and oil, repaired, with original box, 1950s.
£280–325
€/ $440–520 VEC

A Hornby gauge 0 clockwork 4–4–2 No. 2 Special Tank locomotive, No. 6, 1930s.
£280–325
€/ $440–500 VEC

A Lionel electric 2–6–2 streamlined locomotive and tender, with three-rail pickup, American, 1930s, 18in (45.5cm) long.
£150–165
€/ $240–260 WOS

A Leeds Model Co gauge 0 Brighton Belle Pullman coach, Hazel, minor wear, 1930s.
£100–120
€/ $160–190 WAL

A Lionel gauge 0 electric locomotive, No. 1668.E, and four tinplate rolling stock, with track, marked, American, mid-20thC.
£80–100
€/ $125–160 SWO

► A Märklin gauge H0 Swiss railway Bo–Bo twin pantograph mainline locomotive, German, 1950s, boxed.
£200–225
€/ $315–350
WOS

A Märklin four-wheeled crane truck, No. 1668, German, 1930s.
£170–200
€/ $270–300 VEC

A Milbro gauge 0 bogie passenger coach, RN 8173, third class, corridor, 1930s.
£110–130
€/ $170–200 WAL

► A Rivarossi gauge H0 plastic station 5511, Italian, c1965, 21in (54cm) long, boxed.
£60–65
€/ $95–100 WOS

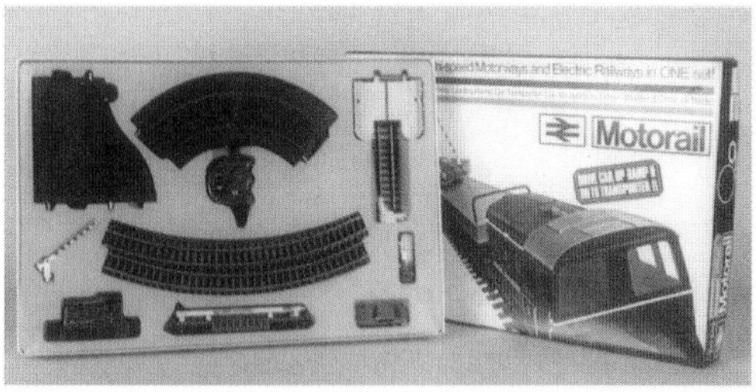

A Tri-ang Hornby Minic RMD motorail set, comprising Dock Authority diesel shunter, rail transporter, Aston Martin, track and hand controller, c1967, boxed.
£250–300
€/ $400–475 VEC

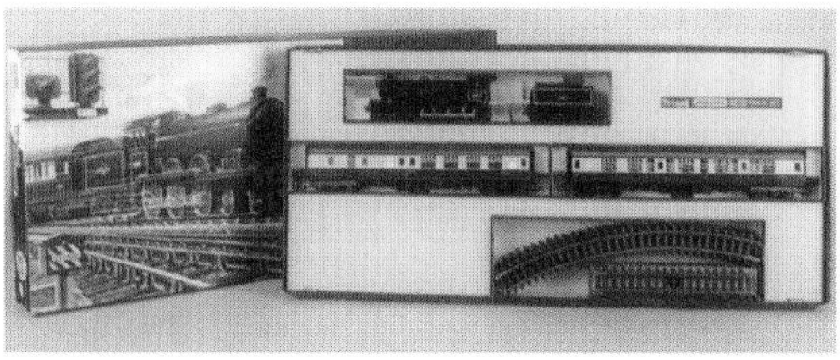

A Tri-ang RS29 Local Passenger train set, comprising 4–6–0 B12 locomotive and tender, two Mark I coaches and track, c1964, boxed.
£80–100
€/ $125–160 VEC

A pair of Wrenn gauge 00 Pullman coaches, The Brighton Belle, 1970s.
£160–175
€/ $250–275 WOS

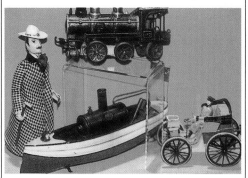

Vehicles

A Britains Napier Bluebird record car, c1937, 4in (10cm) long, boxed.
£180–220
€/ $285–350 IM

A Chad Valley diecast clockwork Wee Kin cable layer toy, 1949–53, 4½in (11.5cm) long.
£80–90
€/ $125–140 GTM

A Corgi Toys Green Hornet car, 1960s, 5in (12.5cm) long, boxed.
£315–350
€/ $500–550 HAL

◄ **A Crescent Toys D-type Jaguar,** No. 1292, 1957–60, 4in (10cm) long, boxed.
£115–130
€/ $180–200 CBB

► **A Dinky Toys tinplate petrol filling station,** No. 48, 1930s, in original box.
£350–420
€/ $550–670 WAL

► **A Dinky Toys MG Magic Midget,** No. 11, 1930s.
£230–275
€/ $360–430
B(Ch)

Dinky Toys

Frank Hornby launched his brand new Modelled Miniatures range of lead diecast toys in 1931. He could not have known that some 70 years later millions of pounds would still be spent every year on them by collectors worldwide. In 1934 they became known as Dinky Toys apparently after a visit to his grand-mother one Sunday afternoon; Hornby showed her one of his new range to be used along side his 0 gauge railway. 'What a dinky toy that is,' she is supposed to have said, and the name stuck. Over 1000 different toys and vehicles were produced until the factory closed in 1979.

Pre-WWII Dinky Toys have thin axles with smooth wheel hubs, unlike the post-war Dinkys. Watch for metal fatigue on these early examples. This is not an issue with the very early vehicles which were made of lead. Look at any prospective purchase carefully: many Dinkys have been restored; some so well you might be fooled into thinking that they are unrestored examples. Check for traces of the original paint in hard-to-get-at areas, see if the wheels have been taken off, and if parts have been replaced.

► **A Jo Hill Co land speed record car,** c1929, 5½in (14cm) long.
£175–200
€/ $275–315
CBB

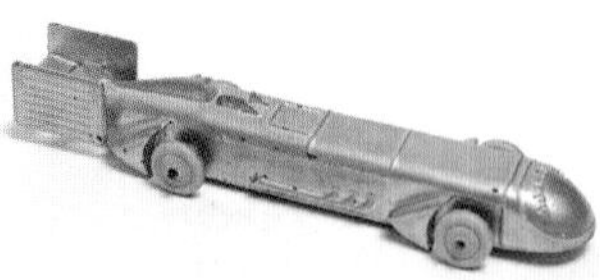

A Kingsbury fire engine, American, 1930s, 32in (81.5cm) long.
£220–250
€/ $350–400 VEC

TOYS

The Bob Ewers Collection

During the last 18 years many toy collections have gone through the system, but only a few come to mind as being special. One of those was owned by a man named Bob Ewers.

Bob's collection was different because for over 40 years he nurtured a passion for collecting Matchbox Series Vehicles made by Moko Lesney. There were 75 vehicles in the series, and every few years the range would change as the series was updated. The boxes were also changed as time progressed. Bob would collect each series as it came out, but would then find as many wheel, colour and export variations as he could. In those days these were regarded simply as toys, and no major value could be put to his growing collection. Only in later years, when the hobby grew to become a major player in the collecting world, did the reward come home. Sadly Bob died just before his collection was sold in 2001, and therefore did not get to see the two auctions needed to sell his hobby, which totalled over £54,000 (€/ $85,300). **Glenn Butler**

A Mettoys BOAC van, c1953, 6in (15cm) long.
£100–110
€/ $160–170 ⊞ GTM

► A Moko Lesney Matchbox American Ford station wagon, No. 31, boxed.
£300–350
€/ $475–550 ⚒ VEC

A Schuco battery-operated dump truck, No. 6077, German, 1950s, 10in (25.5cm) long.
£380–450
€/ $600–700 ⚒ TQA

◄ A Schuco tinplate clockwork Examico 4001 car, German, 1940s, 6in (15cm) long.
£135–150
€/ $220–240
⊞ HAL

◄ A Tri-ang Minic police car, c1948, 5in (12.5cm) long.
£63–70
€/ $100–110
⊞ HAL

A Tri-ang double decker bus, c1950, 7in (18cm) long, boxed.
£230–255
€/ $360–400 ⊞ CBB
The harlequin box is scarce.

◄ A Victory Industries battery-operated Triumph TR2, early 1960s, 9in (23cm) long, boxed.
£225–250
€/ $350–400
⊞ UCO

TOYS

Miscellaneous

Items in the Toys Miscellaneous section have been arranged in alphabetical order.

► **A Tri-ang Brooklands pedal car,** c1950, 46in (117cm) long.
£765–850
€/ $1,200–1,300 ⊞ JUN

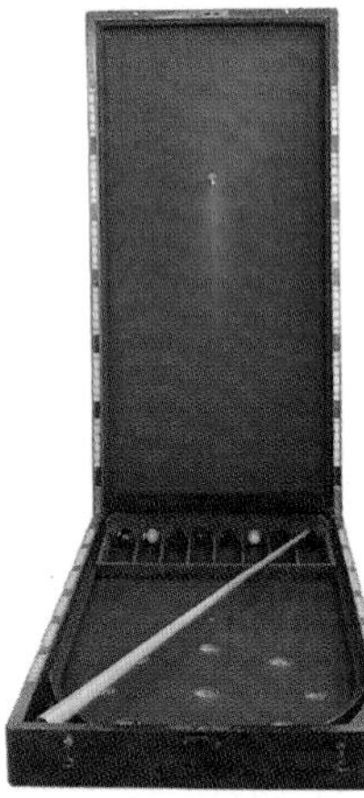

A mahogany folding bagatelle board, with numbered arched bridge and nine balls, 19thC, 94in (239cm) wide.
£170–200
€/ $270–315 ⚒ BWL

An Edinburgh ivory chess set, c1860, king 3in (7.5cm) high.
£650–750
€/ $1,000–1,200 ⚒ CO

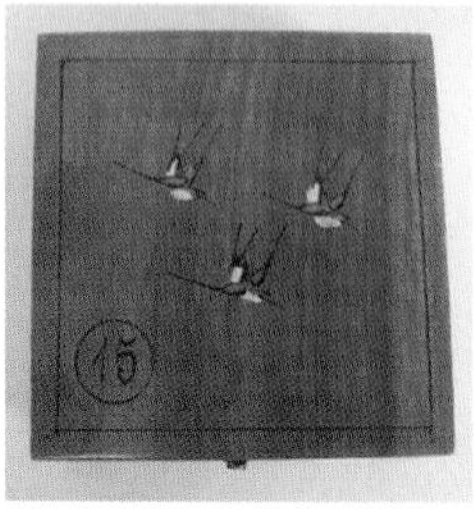

An olivewood games box, with roulette wheel, early 20thC, 4¼in (11cm) square.
£120–140
€/ $190–220 ⚒ TMA

◄ **A Meier tinplate 'penny toy' open landau,** with horse and driver, 1920s, 4in (10cm) long.
£280–315
€/ $440–500 ⊞ RGa

A carved pine and gesso toy horse on wheels, with leather details, c1880, 11in (28cm) long.
£450–500
€/ $700–800 ⊞ RYA

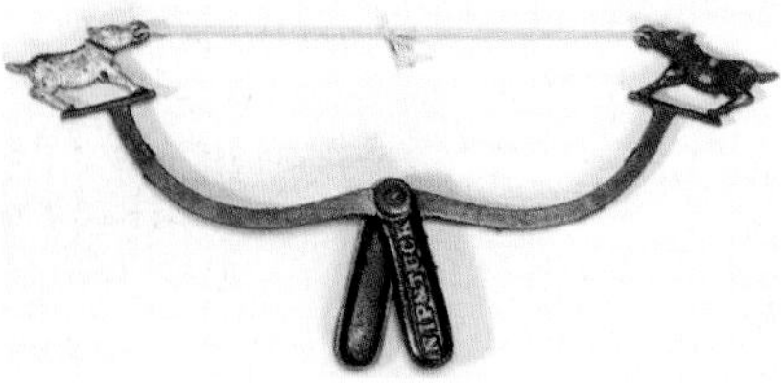

A cast-iron 'Nip & Tuck' toy, the painted dogs pulling on a string, c1875, 9in (23cm) wide.
£700–800
€/ $1,100–1,300 ⚒ SK(B)

A walnut-veneered Deluxe arcade pinball table, c1930, 36in (91.5cm) wide.
£900–1,000
€/ $1,400–1,600 ⊞ ChC

A Pelham Puppets Duchess string puppet, with standard control and metal knee joints, pre-1955, 11¾in (30cm) high, boxed.
£200–225
€/ $315–350 ⚒ B(Ch)

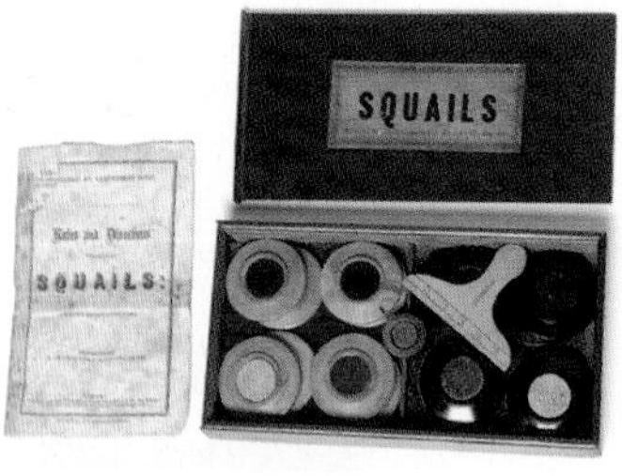

◄ **A J. Jaques Squails game,** c1870, in a mahogany case 9 x 5in (23 x 12.5cm).
£135–150
€/ $220–240 ⊞ HUM

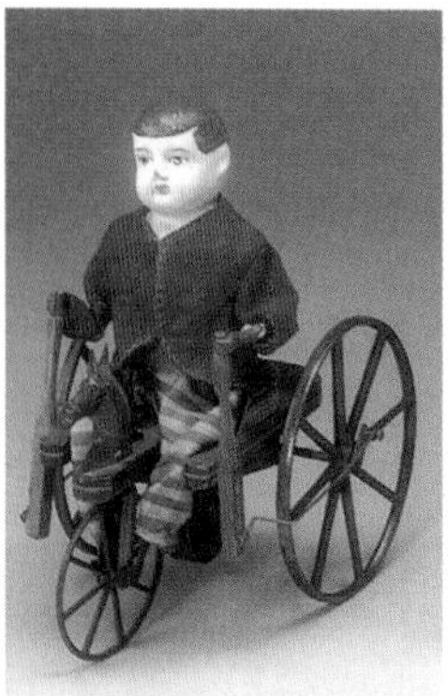

◄ **An Ives Boy on a Velocipede,** with twin propulsion rods, spring motor and steering mechanism, American, 1870s, 8in (20.5cm) long.
£8,000–9,000
€/ $12,500–14,000 ⚒ SK(B)

► **A papier mâché and wood ventriloquist's dummy,** with book, photograph, case and flag, c1920, 42in (106.5cm) high.
£1,300–1,500
€/ $2,100–2,400 ⊞ AUTO

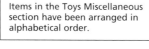

Ephemera

Annuals & Comics

◀ ***Hobbies,*** issue No. 1840, published by George Newnes, with Mickey Mouse cover and cut-out Mickey and Minnie Mouse portraits insert, 1931.
£50–60
€/ $80–95
CBP

Mickey Mouse Weekly, issue Nos. 48–99, complete year including Coronation with cover art by Walt Disney, Easter, Fireworks and Christmas issues, 1937.
£300–360
€/ $470–560 CBP

The Beano, issue No. 46, 1939.
£150–180
€/ $240–280 CBP

The Dandy Monster Comic, 1950.
£380–450
€/ $600–700 CBP

◀ ***Young Marvelman Annual,*** issue No. 1, 1954.
£50–60
€/ $80–95 CBP

▶ ***Marvelman Annual,*** issue No. 2, 1955.
£80–95
€/ $125–150 CBP

Action Comics, issue No. 265, June 1960, 10 x 7in (25.5 x 18cm).
£18–20
€/ $25–30 NOS

Detective Comics, issue No. 325, published by DC Comics, 1964, 10 x 7in (25.5 x 18cm).
£12–14
€/ $16–20 CoC

Viz, issue No. 1, with free ice cream, 1979.
£250–300
€/ $400–470 CBP

The Amazing Spider-Man, issue No. 300, 25th Anniversary Issue, May 1988.
£35–40
€/ $55–65 CBP

Autographs

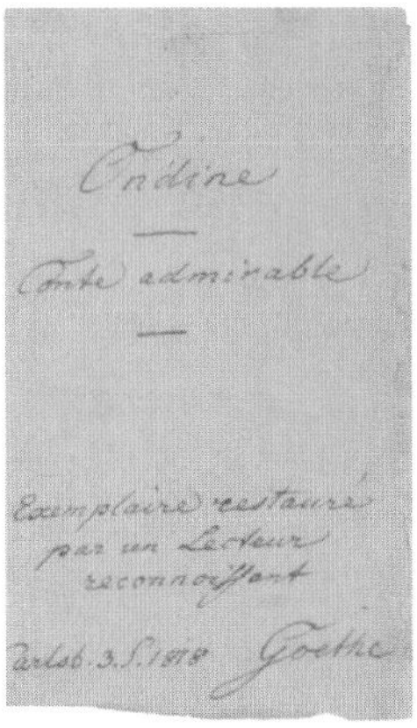

J. W. von Goethe, autograph note, 1818, 1 page, 8°.
£2,400–2,800
€/ $3,800–4,400 ⚒ S
This note was probably written on a flyleaf of Goethe's copy of the French translation of *Undine*, Friedrich de la Motte Fouqué's fairytale of 1811.

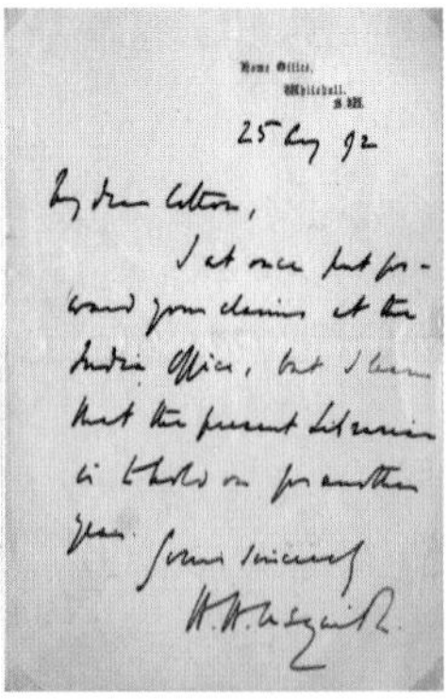

Herbert Henry Asquith, a signed letter, 1892.
£45–50
€/ $70–80 ⊞ AEL

Robert E. Lee, signed *carte de visite*, signed on the front 'R. E. Lee' and inscribed on the back 'Miss Cummings from her friend Mary C. Lee, Lexington Jan'y 18th 1869'.
£1,300–1,500
€/ $2,100–2,400 ⚒ SK(B)

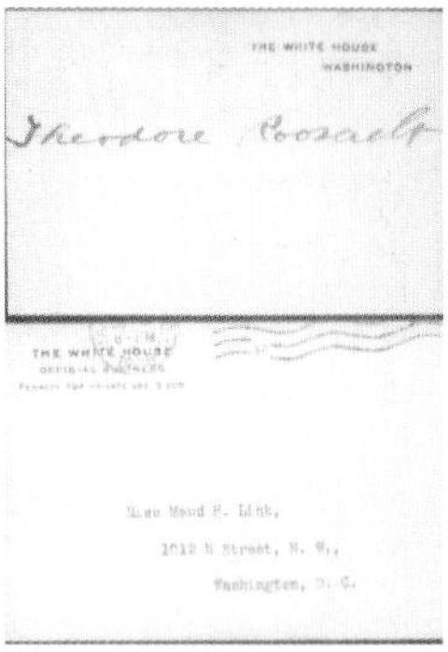

Theodore Rooseveldt, signed official White House card, with envelope, dated 1908.
£100–120
€/ $160–190 ⚒ DW

► **King George V,** a signed photograph, 1923, 8 x 6in (20.5 x 15cm).
£630–700
€/ $1,000–1,100 ⊞ AEL

Queen Alexandra, a pre-printed letter of thanks for condolences sent following the death of Edward VII, in a silver frame, on a V-shaped foliate-engraved frame, hallmarked for London 1910, 6in (15cm) wide.
£280–320
€/ $440–500 ⚒ GAK

Edward, Prince of Wales, a signed photograph, 1915, 9 x 5in (23 x 12.5cm).
£850–950
€/ $1,300–1,500 ⊞ AEL

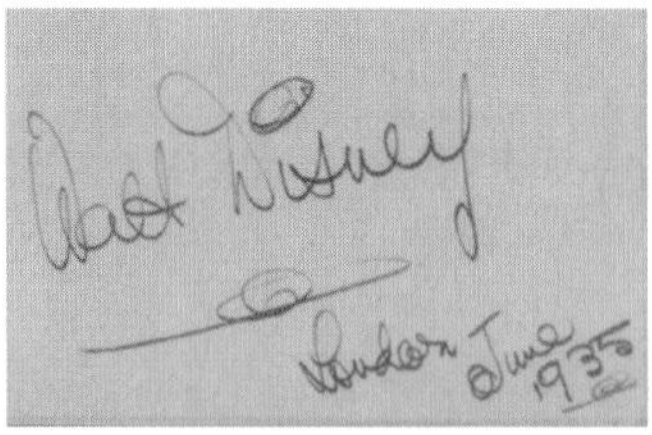

◄ **Walt Disney,** an autograph on an album page, 1935, 4 x 6in (10 x 15cm).
£1,500–1,800
€/ $2,400–2,800 ⚒ S(O)

► **Adriana Caselotti,** a signed composite image showing Caselotti as Snow White, with an image of Snow White and the Seven Dwarfs from Disney's animated cartoon, c1937, 8 x 10in (20.5 x 25.5cm).
£70–80
€/ $110–130 ⚒ VS

Winston Churchill, a signed photograph, 1947, 7 x 4½in (18 x 11.5cm), framed and glazed.
£2,400–2,800
€/ $3,800–4,400 ⚒ VS

Yuri Gagarin, a signed photograph, wearing his Russian spacesuit, c1961, 4½ x 3½in (11.5 x 9cm).
£280–320
€/ $440–510 ⚒ VS

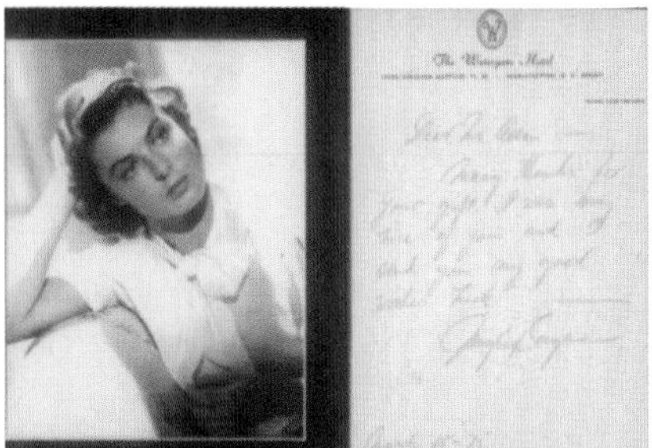

Ingrid Bergman, a signed, hand-written letter of thanks, dated 15 March 1975, 11 x 16in (28 x 40.5cm).
£200–240
€/ $315–380 ⚒ CO

Cigarette Cards

Allen & Ginter, Celebrated American First Nation Chiefs, set of 50, 1888.
£1,300–1,500
€/ $2,000–2,400 ⊞ MUR

R. C. Brown & Co, one of a set of five Capadura cigar cartoon cards, issued 1876–79.
£170–200
€/ $270–315 ⚒ B

Godfrey Phillips, Indian Series, set of 25, c1908.
£170–200
€/ $270–315
⚒ VS

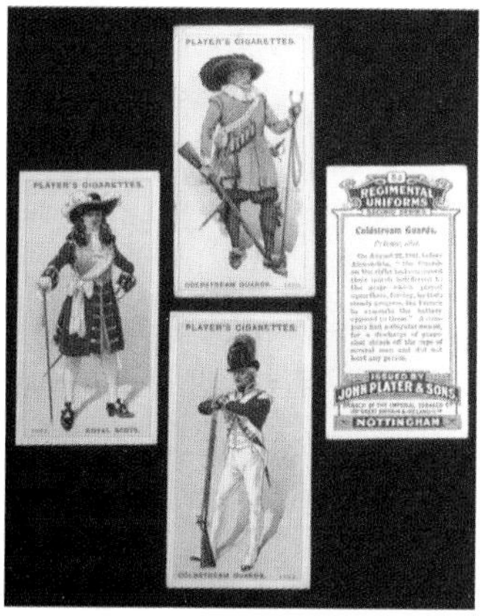

W. D. & H. O. Wills, Beauties, set of 52, 1875–1925.
£70–80
€/ $110–130
⚒ VS

Ogden's, Trainers, and Owners' Colours, set of 25, first series, 1925.
£45–50
€/ $70–80 ⊞ MUR

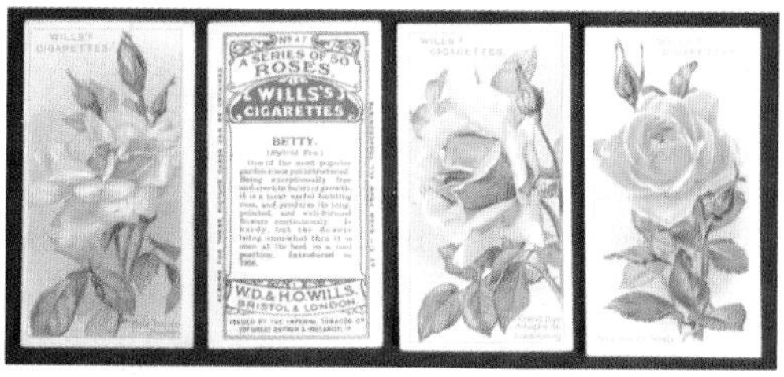

W. D. & H. O. Wills, Roses, set of 50, 1912.
£55–60
€/ $85–95 ⊞ MUR

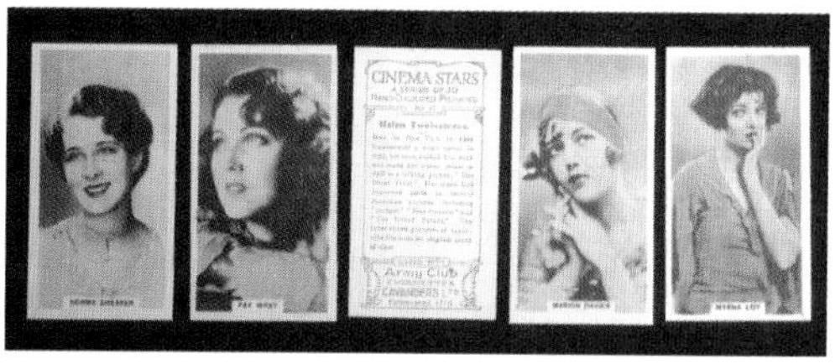

Cavanders, Cinema Stars, set of 30, 1934.
£30–35
€/ $50–55 ⊞ MUR

Hignett Bros, Greetings of the World, set of 25, 1907.
£55–63
€/ $85–100 ⊞ MUR

J. A. Pattreiouex, Builders of the British Empire, set of 50, c1929.
£60–70
€/ $95–110 ⚒ VS

◄ **John Player & Sons,** Regimental Uniforms, set of 50, 1914.
£80–90
€/ $125–145 ⊞ MUR

Postcards

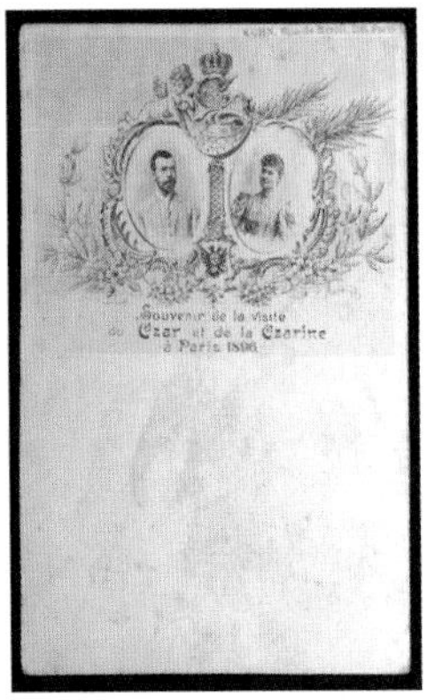

A souvenir postcard, of the visit of the Czar and Czarina to Paris, unused, French, 1896, 6 x 4in (15 x 10cm).
£22–25
€/ $35–40 ⊞ S&D

Four postcards, 'Les Petites Ouvrières', by Théophile-Alexandre Steinlen, unused, c1900, 5½ x 3½in (14 x 9cm).
£140–170
€/ $220–270
VSP

A postcard, No. VIII, 'Enfants de la Mer', by Raphael Kirchner, c1902.
£34–38
€/ $55–60 VS

A pair of patriotic royalty postcards, depicting Kaiser Wilhelm II and his wife, postally used, German, c1903, 6 x 4in (15 x 10cm).
£18–20
€/ $28–32 ⊞ S&D

Items in the Postcards section have been arranged in date order.

An L & NW Railways Co transportation photographic postcard, c1905, 6 x 4in (15 x 10cm).
£15–18
€/ $25–28 ⊞ S&D

A postcard, depicting the flight of Paulhan in his Farman plane, from the 'Aviation' series for the *Daily Mail*, published by E. L. D., in French and English, early 20thC.
£70–85
€/ $110–135 VS

A Hamburg-America Line postcard, depicting the *Cleveland*, c1908, 6 x 4in (15 x 10cm).
£15–18
€/ $25–28 ⊞ S&D

A Fry's Cocoa advertising postcard, with postal mark, c1908, 4 x 6in (10 x 15cm).
£12–14
€/ $18–22 ⊞ S&D

A Royal Mail Steam Packet Co postcard, depicting the dining room of the *Aragon*, c1908, 4 x 6in (10 x 15cm).
£13–15
€/ $20–23 ⊞ S&D

A postcard, depicting the launch of the *Shamrock IV*, 1914, 4 x 6in (10 x 15cm).
£20–25
€/ $30–40 ⊞ S&D

A B & I Line postcard, depicting the SS *Lady Longford*, c1930, 4 x 6in (10 x 15cm).
£11–12
€/ $16–19 ⊞ S&D

A postcard, depicting Wittersham Road Station, Kent, dated 1937.
£40–50
€/ $65–80 VS

Posters

A Napoleonic poster, printed by J. Biettell for J. Hatchard, calling for Englishmen to mobilize against the Corsican tyrant, c1800, 22 x 18in (56 x 45.5cm), framed and glazed.
£200–225
€/ $315–360 HAM

A Red Star Line poster, 'Anvers New York', by Henri Cassiers, Belgian, 1898, 32¾ x 18½in (83 x 47cm).
£600–700
€/ $950–1,100 VSP

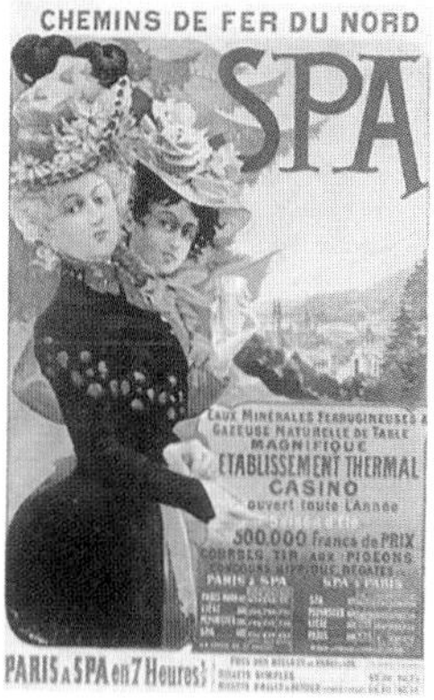

A Chemins de Fer du Nord poster, by George Blott, French, Paris, 1899, 42½ x 29½in (108 x 75cm).
£430–500
€/ $660–800 VSP

A Crawford American Cycles poster, printed by Hazell, Watson & Viney, on linen-backed paper support, damage and repairs, c1900, 58¾ x 40in (149 x 101.5cm).
£420–500
€/ $660–790 BBA

A Teppichhaus poster, by Burkhard Mangold, printed by J. E. Wolfensberger, Zürich, 1911, 49¼ x 37½in (125 x 95.5cm).
£330–400
€/ $540–630 VSP

A poster, by J. Gabriel, advertising 'Cernay Cottage Hotel, Vallée de Chevreuse', on linen, French, c1930, 61¾ x 44¾in (157 x 113.5cm).
£230–280
€/ $360–440 VSP

► **A poster,** No. 132, 'Forward! Forward to Victory Enlist Now', by Lucy Kemp Welch, published by the PRC, printed by David Allen, mounted on linen, 1915, 59½ x 39in (151 x 99cm).
£850–1,000
€/ $1,300–1,600 ONS

An LMS Railway lithographic poster, after R. T. Roussel, advertising Southend-On-Sea, printed by McCorquadale, early 20thC, 47¾ x 37¾in (121.5 x 96cm).
£500–600
€/ $790–950 RTo

A Southern Electric poster, No. 4346, by Chas Pears, advertising 'Summer Services for Winter Visitors to Portsmouth, Southsea & Isle of Wight', printed by Waterlow, 1937, 50 x 40¼in (127 x 102cm).
£1,300–1,500
€/ $2,100–2,400 ONS

A Chemin de Fer du Nord poster, 'Nord Express', by A. M. Cassandre, printed by Hachard & Co, mounted on japanese paper, repaired tear, slight fading, 1927, 41¼ x 29¼in (105 x 74.5cm).
£4,200–5,000
€/ $6,600–7,900 ONS

► **A Wood-Milne Adjustable Soles advertising poster,** creases, 1930s, 19½ x 14¼in (49.5 x 36cm).
£75–90
€/ $120–140 BBR

A foyer poster, advertising *Tondelaya* (White Cargo), with Hedy Lamarr and Walter Pidgeon, 1942, 23 x 15in (58.5 x 38cm).
£115–125
€/ $180–200 ⊞ MARK

An Aga Radio lithographic poster, by Gunnar Brandt, printed by J. Olsen, Stockholm, creases, Swedish, 1947, 39½ x 27¼in (100.5 x 69cm).
£125–150
€/ $200–240 ⚒ BUK

A poster, advertising Dartmouth Winter Carnival, 1947, 34 x 22in (86.5 x 56cm).
£180–220
€/ $280–350 ⚒ SK(B)

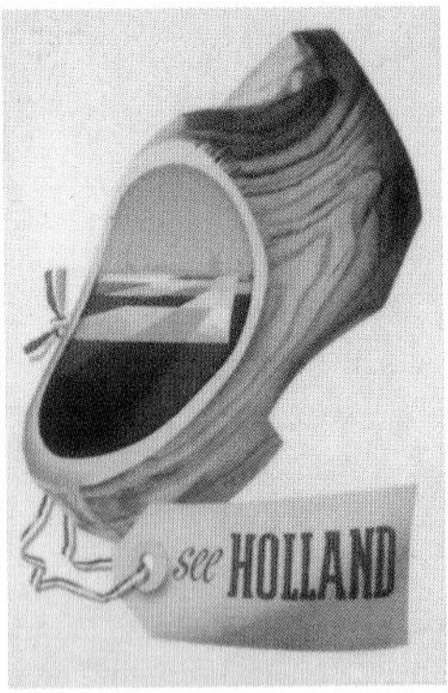

A poster, by Cornelius van Velsen, 'See Holland', on linen, Dutch, 1948, 38 x 24½in (96.5 x 62cm).
£150–175
€/ $240–280 ⚒ VSP

A poster, by Pablo Picasso, advertising an exhibition at the Maison De La Pensée Française, French, 1949, 28¾ x 20½in (73 x 52cm).
£165–185
€/ $260–290 ⚒ VSP

► **An MGM lithographic poster,** depicting Greta Garbo, printed by J. Olsen, Stockholm, creases and tears, 1953, 39½ x 27¼in (100.5 x 69cm).
£250–300
€/ $400–475
⚒ BUK

An American President Lines lithographic poster, by J. Clift, advertising Bangkok, American, 1958, 34 x 23¾in (86.5 x 60.5cm).
£80–95
€/ $130–150 ⚒ VSP

A United Artists film poster, advertising *The Magnificent Seven* with Yul Brynner, Eli Wallach and Steve McQueen, American, 1960, 16 x 11½in (40.5 x 29cm).
£220–250
€/ $350–400 ⚒ CO

A Samuel Goldwyn film poster, advertising *Stronger Than Fear*, with Dana Andrews and Farley Granger, on linen-backed paper support, minor damage, 1950s, 30 x 39¾in (76 x 101cm).
£50–60
€/ $80–95 ⚒ BBA

Further reading

Miller's Movie Collectibles, Miller's Publications, 2002

A foyer poster, advertising *Vénus Imperiale*, with Gina Lollobrigida, French, 1963, 15 x 23in (38 x 58.5cm).
£115–125
€/ $180–200 ⊞ MARK

A UFA film poster, advertising *Voulez Vous Danser avec Moi?*, with Brigitte Bardot, 1965, 31½ x 23in (80 x 58.5cm).
£210–250
€/ $330–390 ⚒ VSP

◄ **A poster,** by John Burningham, advertising coach travel, 1961, 29¾ x 20in (75.5 x 51cm).
£100–120
€/ $160–190 ⚒ VSP

Rock & Pop

Over the last 25 years there has been a streamlining of rock and pop artists whose memorabilia people wish to acquire. The field of collecting at the high end has largely narrowed down to The Beatles, The Rolling Stones, Elvis Presley, The Who, Led Zeppelin, Pink Floyd, Buddy Holly and Bob Dylan. The gulf between these artists and others further down the scale is considerable and seemingly ever widening – although to an extent this disparity does not seem to have any basis in reason. For example, why should a good set of Beatles' signatures sell for thousands, yet a set of the Beach Boys' autographs – a band that created music of equal, or arguably superior, quality – might only realize £100 (€/ $160)? Similarly, the memorabilia of many other extremely influential artists such as Chuck Berry and Gene Vincent continues to be of low value.

The Beatles have been at the top of the league since the market in memorabilia was established c1980 and have continued to dramatically increase their points lead over their nearest rivals. This is mainly due to their immense popularity in the 1960s which is reflected today by the number of people collecting ephemera associated with them. There is a wide range to collect, as they produced more merchandise than other artists, and putting money into Beatles collectables is seen as a sound investment. However, a significant, ever-widening gap is opening up between the price of rare, unique and personal items such as concert posters, good autographed items and clothing and that of more common pieces such as tour programmes or mass-produced novelty items.

In second place in the league table are The Rolling Stones. In the last couple of years prices of concert posters, handbills and novelty items in particular, have gained great momentum, perhaps a side effect of the rise in value of Beatles memorabilia. Interest in The Who and Pink Floyd has been very strong recently, and Led Zeppelin has also started to accelerate, having largely been overlooked for the past several years. Interestingly, collecting Elvis Presley continues to be mainly an American phenomenon.

The other striking and important trend in collecting has been that of an increasing concern among collectors over condition. It is items in excellent to mint condition that now command a price well in excess of book value while items in less than perfect condition tend to sell below estimate. This is no doubt due to the investment factor associated with Rock and Pop and this trend has also been reflected in the market for vinyl records. **Paul Wane**

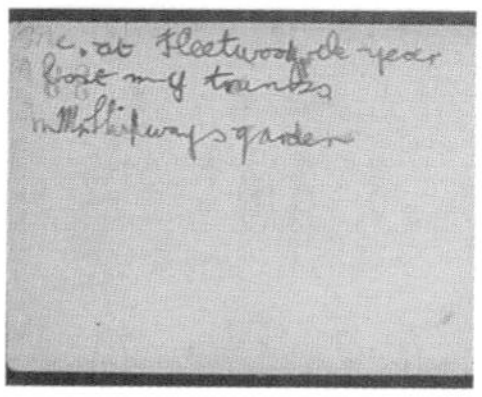

John Lennon, a photograph, the reverse inscribed 'Me at Fleetwood the year I lost my trunks. In Mr Shipway's garden', late 1940s, 2¼ x 3¼in (5.5 x 8.5cm).
£2,500–3,000
€/ $4,000–4,700 S(O)

A Fender Telecaster electric guitar, butterscotch blonde single cutaway ash body and maple neck, serial number 28637, owned by Tim Rose on which he devised the arrangement of 'Hey Joe', 1958.
£5,500–6,300
€/ $8,700–10,000 CO
Also included is a letter from Tim Rose which reads 'I entered a bluegrass music contest in Warrenton, Virginia... I heard a song about a guy shooting his girlfriend and taking off for Mexico... I started a group with a few friends when I began doing an arrangement of that song. By now I called it 'Hey Joe'... I finally recorded it in 1966 for CBS Records. Chas Chandler heard my record at Harlow's Discotheque in New York City and took it back to London for Jimi'.

A Buddy Holly & The Crickets UK Tour autographed programme, signed on the back cover, 1958.
£650–750
€/ $1,000–1,200 S(O)

◄ **A Beatles demonstration single record,** 'Love Me Do' and 'P.S. I Love You', by Parlophone, with misspelled credit 'Lennon – McArtney', 1962, with paper sleeve.
£1,700–2,000
€/ $2,700–3,200 B(Ch)
Only 250 demonstration singles were produced with the misspelling of 'McArtney' and distributed to the band, their management, the press and radio disc jockeys. This unique demo was the first official pressing featuring John, Paul, George and Ringo on the same single.

A red label Beatles single record, 'Please Please Me' and 'Ask Me Why' by Parlophone, 1963, signed on the A side by the Beatles.
£2,200–2,500
€/ $3,500–4,000 S(O)

A knitted silk tie, owned by Ringo Starr, the prize in a competition run by *The Viewer,* with a letter from the magazine and a print of the Beatles wearing similar ties, dated 15 January 1964, 24 x 32½in (61 x 82.5cm).
£700–800
€/ $1,100–1,300 S(O)

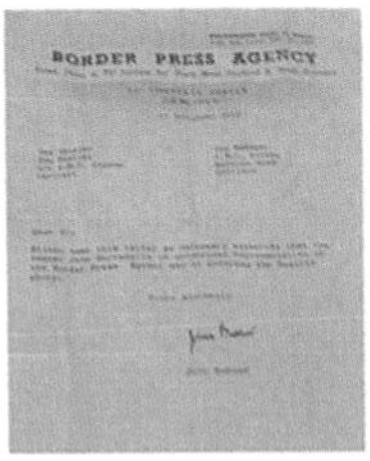

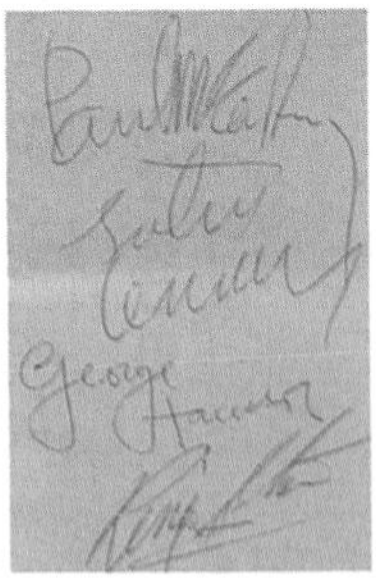

A letter from the Border Press Agency, signed on the reverse by all four members of the Beatles in blue ballpoint, giving press authority to the manager of the ABC cinema for the Beatles' visit to Carlisle on 21 November 1963.
£3,800–4,500
€/ $6,000–7,200 TRM

A Beatles one-sided 7in demo record, 'Wait', by Emidisc, with hand-written label, 1965.
£420–500
€/ $660–800 CO

◄ A silkscreen print, 'The Rolling Stones, Red Cage', signed by the photographer Gered Mankowitz, c1966, 16 x 20in (40.5 x 51cm).
£300–350
€/ $480–550 CO

A Nashville Teens and The Truth concert poster, the Town Hall, Liskeard, c1966, 30 x 20in (76 x 21cm).
£90–100
€/ $140–160 ⊞ CTO

Elvis Presley, a signed Christmas card, dedicated 'To Mary from Elvis Presley' dated 1966, 8½ x 5½in (16 x 14cm).
£400–475
€/ $640–750 CO

► A Radio England souvenir programme, for a concert featuring the Small Faces, Koobas and Dave Berry, 1966, 12 x 9in (30.5 x 23cm) with a ticket to the concert.
£45–50
€/ $70–80 ⊞ CTO

A programme for The Beatles North American tour, sold at US tour venues, 1966.
£140–160
€/ $220–250 CO

A Martin Sharp silkscreen poster of Bob Dylan, 'Blowing in the Mind', 1967, 30 x 20in (76 x 51cm).
£300–325
€/ $475–515 ⊞ ASC

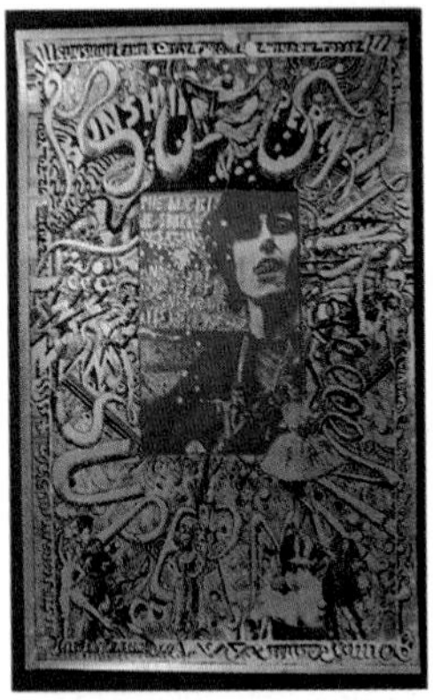

◄ A Martin Sharp silk-screen poster of Donovan, 'Sunshine Superman', 1967, 30 x 20in (76 x 51cm).
£135–150
€/ $215–240 ⊞ ASC

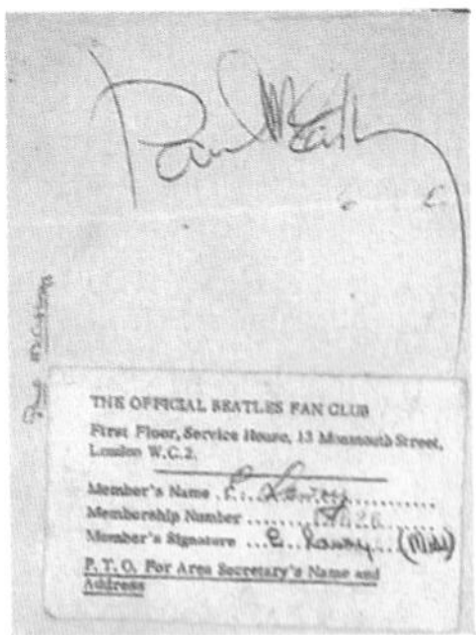

Paul McCartney, a signed album page, together with an Official Beatles Fan Club membership ticket, 1960s.
£160–200
€/ $250–320 VS

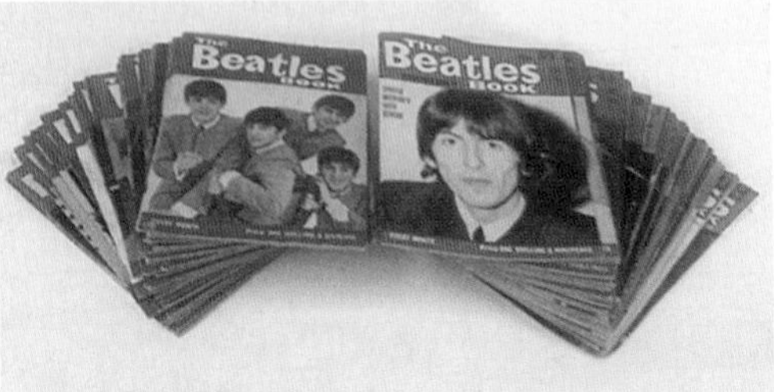

The Beatles Book, complete set of the monthly magazines, comprising 77 issues, 1960s.
£420–500
€/ $650–800 CO

◄ A Big Brother & The Holding Company Jack the Ripper poster, American, 1967, 22 x 16in (56 x 41.5cm).
£180–200
€/ $280–320 VSP

Expert's choice

The sale of the manuscript lyrics to *A Day in the Life*, the final song on The Beatles' *Sgt. Pepper's Lonely Hearts Club Band* LP, at Sotheby's, London, on 27 August 1992 was important in several respects. Firstly, in achieving a hammer price of £40,000 (€/ $63,000) plus commission, it put the hand-written lyrics of Lennon and McCartney in the same price bracket as some of the other eminent composers of the last three centuries and at the same time affirmed the importance, in relation to other composers, of the famous song-writing team from Liverpool. Secondly, in respect of the market for Beatles and pop memorabilia in general, it established manuscript lyrics of Beatles songs as the holy grail of rock 'n' roll collectables. Thirdly, the sale was significant in that it helped to establish Beatles lyrics as an important medium for investors. Fans could invest in their lyrics, enjoy owning them and at the same time watch their money grow!

Paul Wane

Jimi Hendrix, a photograph by Bruce Fleming, taken at Monterey Rock Festival, signed on the reverse by the photographer, No. 3 of an edition of 50, June 1967, 19¾ x 23¾in (50 x 60.5cm).
£280–320
€/ $440–500 B(Ch)

A Beatles Magical Mystery Tour paper sign, September 1967, 59 x 19in (150 x 48.5cm).
£4,500–5,200
€/ $7,000–8,200 CO
The vendor and her family were holidaying in Devon and Cornwall. Driving along a cliff top road en route for the beach, they came upon some filming and stopped to watch the proceedings. The vendor and her sister were very excited to find the Beatles there and took some photographs of them and also obtained their autographs. Their father however, sought a greater souvenir for his daughters and carefully peeled the Magical sign from the side of the bus!

Brian Jones, a photograph, c1967, 24 x 16in (61 x 40.5cm).
£500–600
€/ $800–950 S(O)

A Sgt Pepper cloth badge, made to John Lennon's specifications, c1967, 3in (7.5cm) diam.
£170–200
€/ $270–315 CO

A Jimi Hendrix Experience LP record, 'Are You Experienced', by Reprise, signed on the front 'Douglas – Stay Groovy Jimi Hendrix x, Love! Mitch Mitchell and Noel', 1968.
£1,400–1,600
€/ $2,200–2,500 CO

A Great Society with Grace Slick LP record, 'Conspicuous only in its Absence', by CBS, 1968.
£45–50
€/ $70–80 BNO

► A Bill Graham poster, advertising Eric and The Animals in concert, designed by Lee Conklin, signed by Eric Burdon, American, c1968, 20 x 14in (51 x 35.5cm).
£80–100
€/ $130–160 CO

A Family Dog poster, advertising The Velvet Underground, Iron Butterfly and Chrome Cyrcus at the Avalon Ballroom, San Francisco, designed by Schnepf, American, June 1968, 20 x 13in (51 x 33cm).
£100–120
€/ $160–190 CO

A Jimi Hendrix Experience concert poster, Hallendstadion, Zurich, 30–31 May 1968, 28¼ x 19¼in (72 x 49cm).
£3,800–4,500
€/ $6,000–7,200 B(Ch)

An Island Artists promotional poster, for Spooky Tooth, late 1960s, 30 x 20in (76 x 51cm).
£320–375
€/ $500–600 CO

A Yellow Submarine film poster, by King Features, Polish, 1968, 23 x 15in (58.5 x 38cm).
£130–150
€/ $200–240 B(Ch)

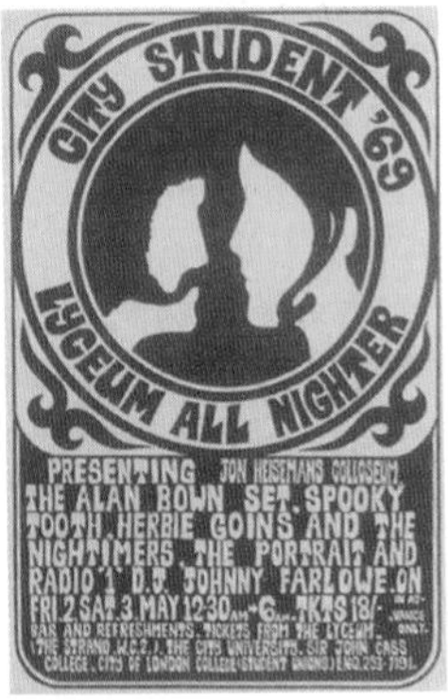

A City Student Lyceum All Nighter promotional poster, 2–3 May 1969, 30 x 20in (76 x 51cm).
£320–375
€/ $500–600 CO

A Bill Graham Fillmore West concert poster, advertising Chuck Berry and Jethro Tull, designed by David Singer, signed by Ian Anderson of Jethro Tull, c1969, 14 x 20in (35.5 x 51cm).
£65–75
€/ $100–120 CO

◄ **A Blind Faith LP record cover,** 'Faith', by Polydor Records, an alternative UK issue for the American market, 1969.
£180–200
€/ $280–320
BNO

A wooden hookah pipe, owned by John Lennon, hand painted, late 1960s, 10in (25.5cm) long.
£1,700–2,000
€/ $2,700–3,200 CO

An Isle of Wight festival programme, featuring Jimi Hendrix, The Doors, The Who and Free, 1970, 11½ x 8in (29 x 20.5cm).
£170–200
€/ $270–315 CO

◄ **A fringed suede waistcoat,** owned by Elvis Presley, c1971.
£600–700
€/ $950–1,100 S(O)

► **A David Bowie and The Spiders from Mars single record,** 'John, I'm Only Dancing', by RCA, signed 'Love David Bowie, Mick Ronson, Trevor Boulder and Woody', 1972, 11½in (29cm) square, framed.
£400–475
€/ $630–750 CO

Bob Marley, photographed by Dennis Morris, a matt fibre print, 1973, 20 x 15in (51 x 38cm).
£320–375
€/ $500–600 CO

A reproduction Rolling Stones concert poster, for the cancelled concert at Cardiff and Pembroke castles 1973, No. 4500 of an edition of 5000, with facsimile autographs of Mick Jagger, Charlie Watts and Keith Richards, 17 x 23in (43 x 58.5cm).
£80–100
€/ $130–160 CO

Freddie Mercury, a photograph by Mick Rock, signed by the photographer, 1974, 48in (122cm) square.
£330–400
€/ $520–640 ⚒ CO

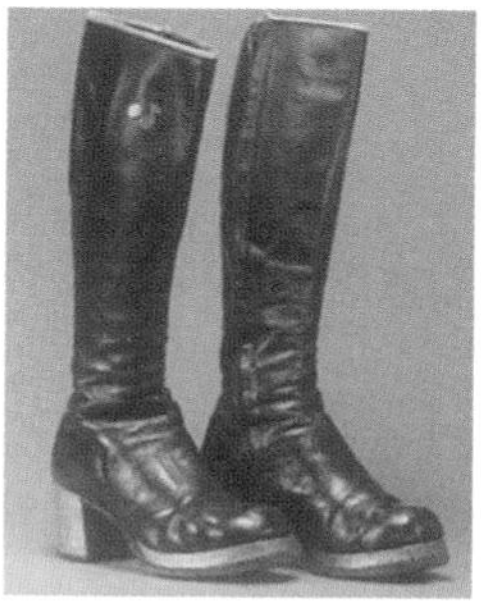

A pair of platform boots, owned by Elton John, late 1970s.
£530–630
€/ $840–1,000 ⚒ S(O)

► **A Sex Pistols single record,** 'God Save The Queen' and 'Did You No Wrong', signed, 1977.
£1,100–1,200
€/ $1,700–1,900 ⚒ S(O)

A pistol pin charm, removed from a leather jacket owned by Sid Vicious, with original safety pin attached to a piece of paper signed and dedicated 'CBGB for Helen SID', with a bloody finger print, c1978, with a Helen Wheels and the Skeleton Crew concert flyer and a Helen Wheels business card.
£800–950
€/ $1,300–1,500 ⚒ CO
Sid Vicious and Helen Wheels were friends and became 'blood brother and sister', hence the print on the paper.

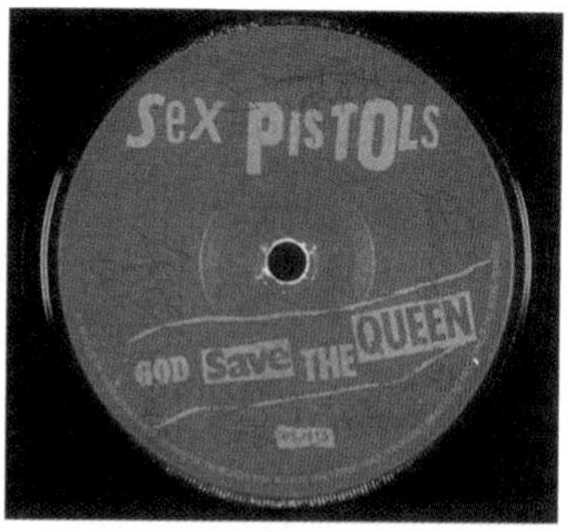

A sales award for the Abba album 'Arrival', named to Anna Frid Lyngstad, 1980, 15¼ x 17in (39 x 43cm).
£1,100–1,200
€/ $1,700–1,900 ⚒ S(O)
This was awarded for sales of over 100,000 copies in the Netherlands.

◄ **The Clash,** a photograph by Bob Gruen of the US Tour, signed by the photographer, 1979, 16 x 20in (40.5 x 51cm).
£330–400
€/ $520–640 ⚒ CO

Scientific Instruments

Calculating Instruments

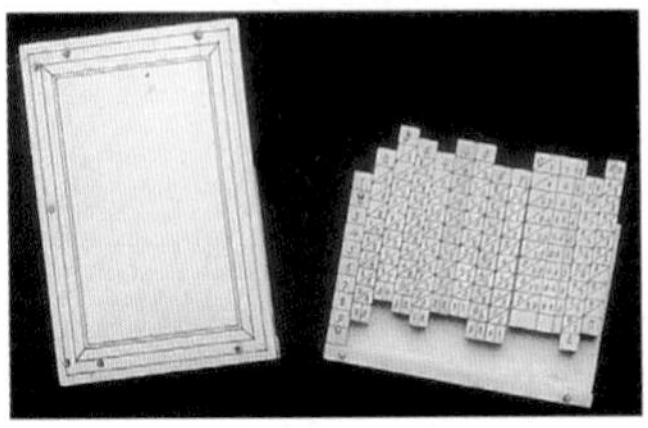

A set of ivory Napiers bones, with a fixed rod, ten individual ivory rods and a three-section tablet, each punched with numerals, in an ivory case with slide cover, case damaged, late 17thC, 2in (5cm) wide.
£5,000–5,500
€/ $7,900–8,700 ⚒ S(O)
Napiers bones are used to make calculations based on the logarithm system.

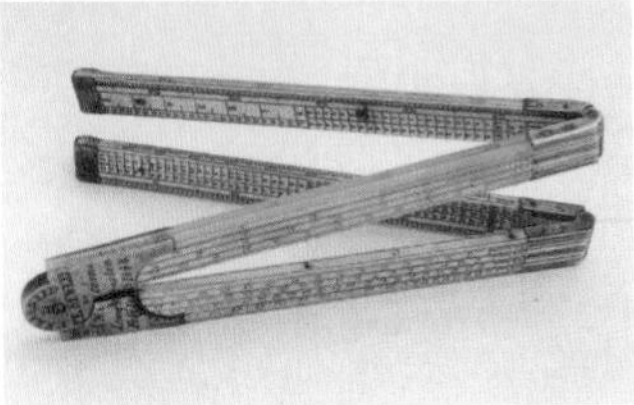

An ivory four-fold rule, with ironmonger's scales and presentation inscription, dated 1848, 24in (61cm) long.
£250–300
€/ $400–475 ⊞ TOM

A boxwood slide rule, early 18thC, 12in (30.5cm) long.
£250–300
€/ $400–475 ⊞ TOM

Miller's Compares

I. **A brass arithmometer,** by Thomas de Colmar, with 12 digit display windows, seven smaller digit displays and six sliding indices, French, late 19thC, 18¼in (46.5cm) wide, in an oak case with engraved silvered plaque to lid.
£2,000–2,200
€/ $3,200–3,500 ⚒ S(O)

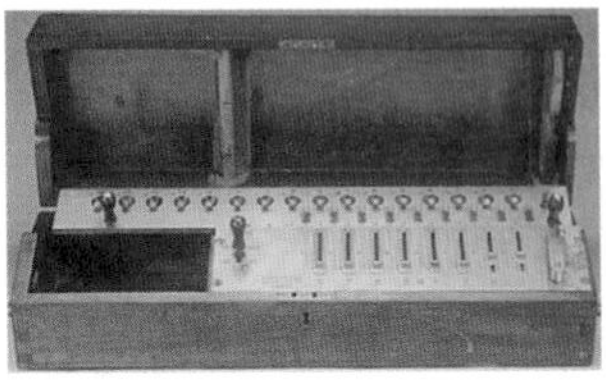

II. **A brass arithmometer,** by C. & E. Layton, with 16 digit display windows, nine smaller windows, c1900, 23¾in (60.5cm) wide, in a mahogany case with brass carrying handles.
£1,300–1,500
€/ $2,000–2,400 ⚒ S(O)

Thomas de Colmar was the inventor of this type of calculator, and therefore one made by him is more sought after. The turned ivory operating handles and original lacquer of Item I are also desirable features. Item II has ebony operating handles rather than ivory, and it is missing an opaque glass panel on the left-hand side, both factors which contribute to its lower price.

Compasses & Dials

► An ivory diptych dial, attributed to the Ducher family workshop, Nuremberg, with pin gnomon dials for Italian hours, string horizontal dial, the compass bowl decorated with four wind motifs, the scaphe dial with zodiacal symbols, two crowned snake punch marks attributed to Hans II, Hans III or Thomas Ducher, German, 1595–1645, 3in (7.5cm) wide.
£6,500–7,200
€/ $10,200–11,400 ⚒ S(O)

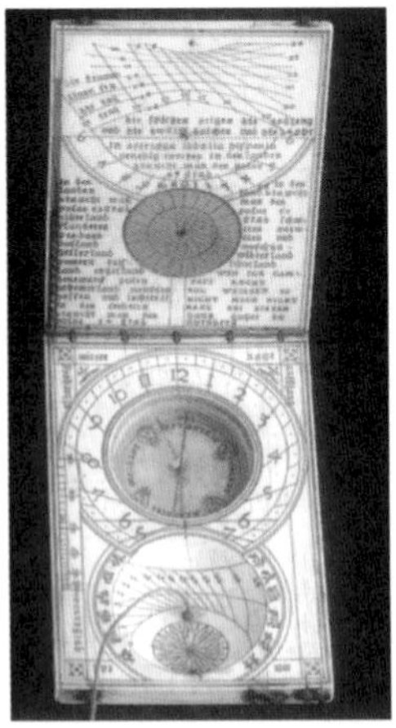

◄ An ivory diptych dial, by Lienhart Miller, German, c1680, 2½in (6.5cm) wide.
£2,000–2,400
€/ $3,200–3,800 ⊞ DJH

► An ivory diptych dial, French, Dieppe, late 17thC, 2½in (6.5cm) square.
£1,600–1,800
€/ $2,500–2,800 ⊞ DJH

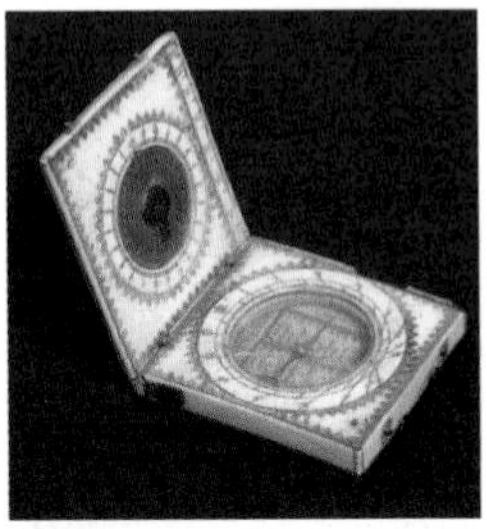

A bronze horizontal plate sundial, by John Troughton, the hour scale divided IIII=XII=VIII and reading to two minutes, with a projecting gnomon, signed, dated 1755, 6in (15cm) diam.
£570–675
€/ $900–1,000 ⚒ S(O)

A brass astrolabe, with five plates, one drawn for the southern latitudes, Indo-Persian, mid/late 17thC, 3½in (9cm) diam.
£10,000–11,000
€/ $15,800–17,400 ⚒ S(O)
Plates for southern latitudes are unusual in astrolabes otherwise designed for northern use, but are not without utility in low latitudes of the northern hemisphere. They are therefore sometimes found in instruments produced in Lahore with which school of astrolabe-making the present instrument may be linked by its style and arrangement.

A universal equinoctial dial, with later brass sight, glass broken, probably Augsburg, late 18thC, 2¼in (5.5cm) diam, with original leather-covered card case.
£600–700
€/ $950–1,100 S(O)

Expert's choice

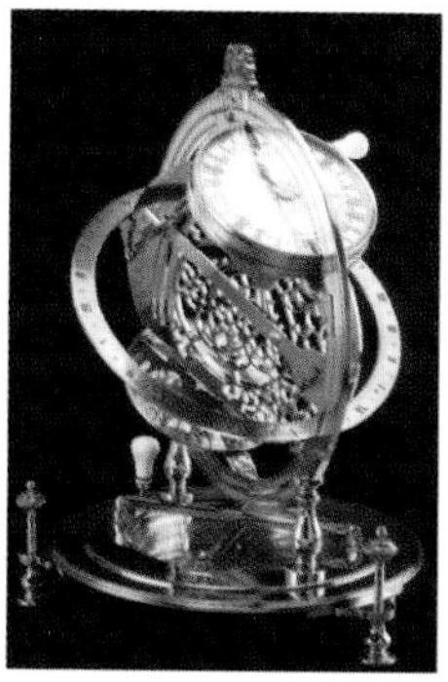

A silvered-brass mechanical equinoctial standing ring-dial, c1720, sold as part of the Time Museum Collection, New York, in December 1999.

The mechanical ring-dial by Richard Glynne, c1720, included as part of the Time Museum auction in New York in December 1999, broke barriers in two respects. Scientific instruments have had a very specialist and small following throughout the 20th century, and it took the Time Museum Collection auction to promote the esoteric field of instruments to a far wider public.

Measuring almost 24in (61cm) in height, the instrument, which tells the time accurately using sunlight and precision mechanical adjustment, has great sculptural quality combined with fine technical design and a high-quality finish. It appealed to collectors who had never bought a scientific instrument before; this stimulated the bidding to more than triple the low estimate, and achieved a hammer price of £600,000 (€/ $950,000). Not only was this a world record price for an instrument of this type, but it took the whole field of scientific instruments to a new level of appreciation. **Jon Baddeley**

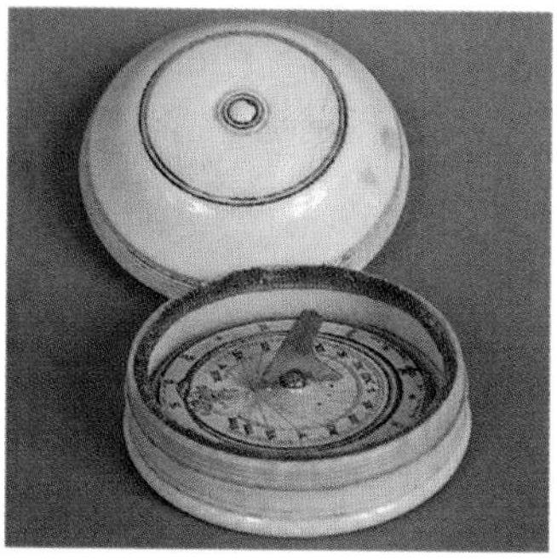

A magnetic sundial, by S. Porter, c1824, 2in (5cm) diam, in an ivory case with paper label to lid.
£360–425
€/ $575–675 SWO

► **A surveying compass,** by James Gregory, Birmingham, with silver dial and folding sights, c1870, in a mahogany case, 5in (12.5cm) wide.
£500–550
€/ $790–870 WAC

Globes & Armillary Spheres

A 12in terrestrial globe, by N. Hill, 'New Globe of the Earth', on a mahogany stand with three cabriole legs, labelled 'Sold by Bennett Instrument Maker to Ye Duke of Gloucester... Henry Prince Frederick in Crown Court, St Ann's, Soho', dated 1759, 24in (61cm) high.
£4,500–5,200
€/ $7,000–8,200 ⚒ Gam

A pocket terrestrial globe, by George Adams, London, in a sharkskin case, c1760, 3in (7.5cm) diam.
£6,000–6,500
€/ $9,500–10,200 ⊞ HUM

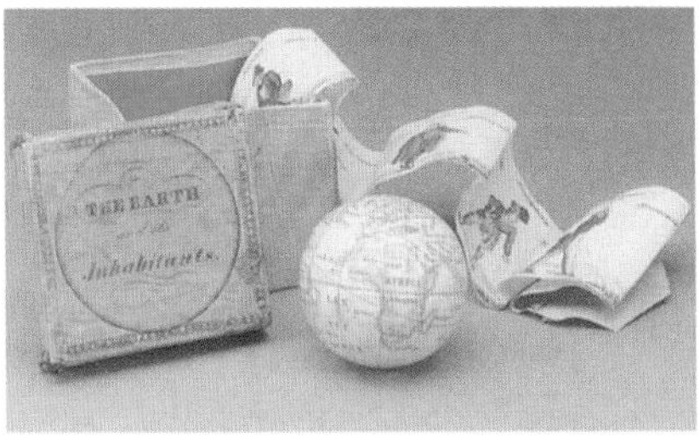

A 1½in terrestrial globe, with coloured prints of inhabitants, the hand-coloured paper gores laid onto the wooden sphere, German, 1800–25, in original card box inscribed 'The Earth and its Inhabitants', 2¼in (5.5cm) wide.
£1,300–1,500
€/ $2,000–2,400 ⚒ S(O)

◄ A 3in pocket terrestrial globe, by Holbrook & Co, the hand-coloured paper gores applied to a hinged wooden sphere opening to reveal a world map with cartouche, American, c1840.
£1,300–1,500
€/ $2,000–2,400 ⚒ S(O)

A 4in table terrestrial globe, by Lebègue, Brussels, the paper gores on a papier mâché sphere, on a gilt-brass stand with tripod base, Belgian, c1850, in original wooden case 8in (20.5cm) high.
£1,100–1,200
€/ $1,700–1,900 ⚒ S(O)

◄ A 1½in miniature globe, by Johann Georg Klinger, lithographed by C. Danzinger, with original outline hand-colouring, slight surface wear and scratches, on a modern Perspex stand, German, Nuremberg, mid-19thC.
£225–275
€/ $350–430 ⚒ BBA

Two globes, by C. Adams, Berlin, with compass, on ebonized stands, German, the terrestrial dated 1865, the celestial dated 1867, 27in (68.5cm) high.
£9,000–10,000
€/ $14,200–15,800 ⊞ DJH

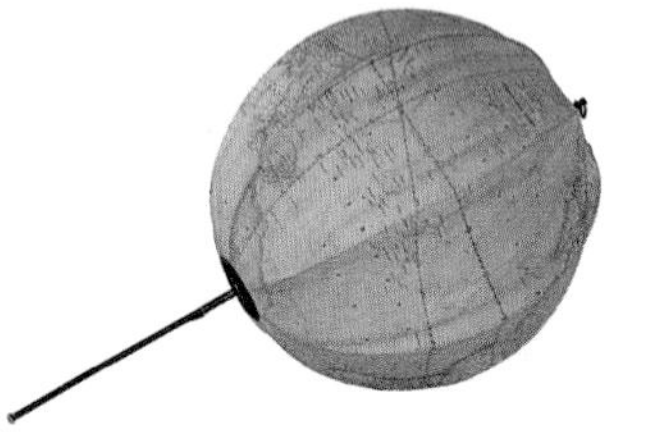

A collapsible New Portable silk terrestrial globe, by George Philip & Son, after the original Betts patents, c1880, 15in (38cm) diam.
£340–375
€/ $550–600 ⊞ ChC
This globe is opened and closed by an umbrella mechanism to allow for ease of transport and originally would have had a box. Although sturdy when opened, the nature of its operation no doubt led to the silk often becoming damaged, thus rendering them relatively rare.

A 16in terrestrial globe, by Smith's, with hand-coloured gores, engraved brass meridian ring, on a printed and coloured zodiac horizon, on three reeded legs joined by a signed compass, needle and glass missing, 19thC, 45in (114.5cm) high.
£3,800–4,500
€/ $6,000–7,000 ⚒ B

◄ A 3in pocket terrestrial globe, the paper segments showing voyages by Columbus, Cook and Vancouver, with a steel axis pin, damaged, label inscribed 'A new terrestrial globe from the best authorities by J. Smith and sold by C. Smith, 172 Strand', 19thC, in a fishskin-covered case, the interior with a celestial chart.
£2,000–2,200
€/ $3,200–3,500 ⚒ SWO

Medical & Dental

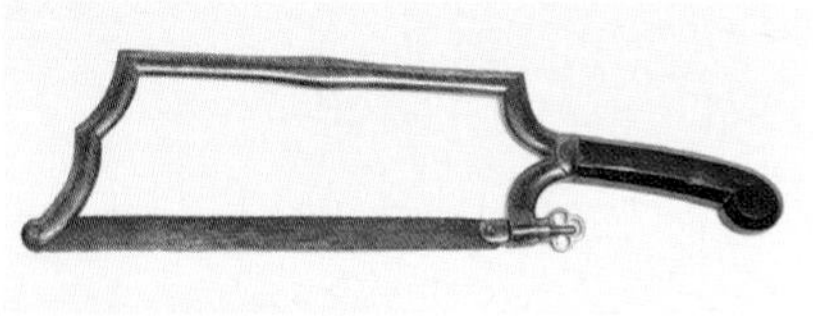

A metal amputation saw, with a wooden handle, c1820, 18in (45.5cm) long.
£400–450
€/ $630–700 ⊞ CuS

◄ **A silver-plated auroscope,** c1900, in a box 4in (10cm) square.
£150–165
€/ $240–260 ⊞ CuS

A metal anaesthetic inhaler, c1900, 8in (20.5cm) high.
£270–300
€/ $425–475 ⊞ CuS

A brass spring fleam, c1820, 2¾in (7cm) long, in original case.
£220–245
€/ $350–380 ⊞ CuS
This instrument was used for blood letting.

A figured-walnut dentist's cabinet, with original brass fittings, c1880, 33in (84cm) wide.
£3,200–3,500
€/ $5,000–5,500 ⊞ MTay

A dental tool sterilizer, in a panelled mahogany case with nickeled-brass fittings, with a compartment with alcohol burner and steam boiler fitted to a zinc-lined copper cavity with three removable wooden slat racks, 19thC, 11¾in (30cm) wide.
£450–500
€/ $700–790 ⚒ JAA

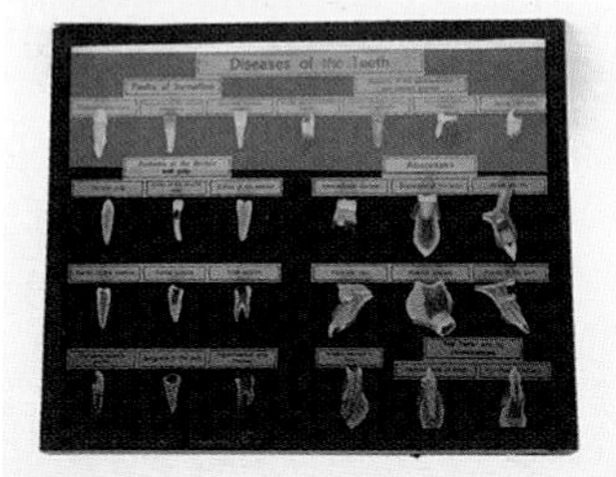

A display case of wax teeth, c1900, 12 x 10½in (30.5 x 26.5cm).
£250–275
€/ $400–430 ⊞ CuS

► **A japanned metal enema pump,** French, c1850, 10in (25.5cm) high.
£265–300
€/ $420–470 ⊞ CuS

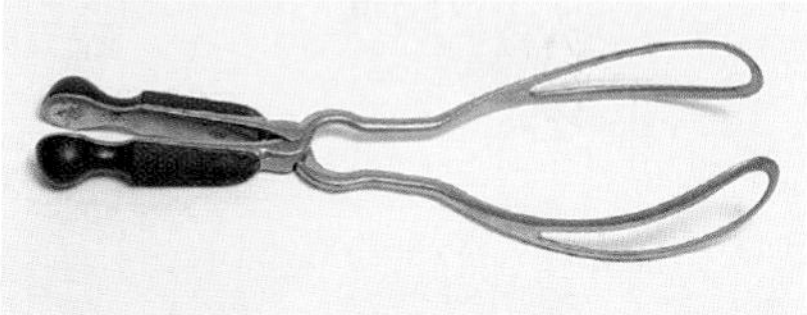

A pair of metal forceps, c1880, 14½in (37cm) long.
£165–185
€/ $260–300 ⊞ CuS

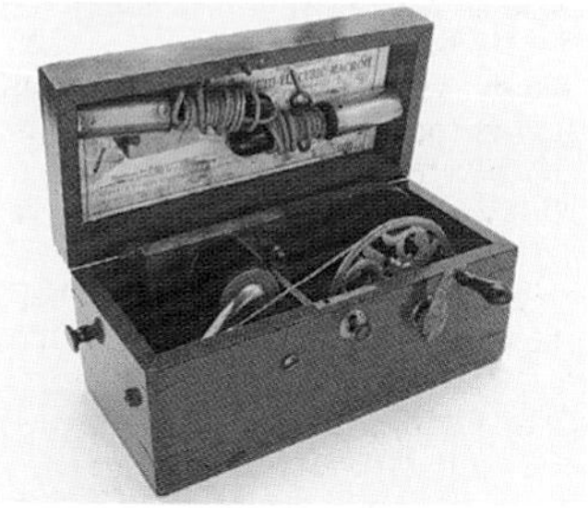

A magneto-electric machine, by S. Maw, Son & Thompson, c1900, 10in (25.5cm) wide.
£160–175
€/ $250–275 ⊞ SPA

A mahogany medicine chest, the hinged lid with a marquetry conch shell, opening to reveal six glass bottles with stoppers, above a base drawer, early 19thC, 6½in (16.5cm) wide.
£380–450
€/ $600–700 ⚒ WW

◄ **A Victorian homeopathic sample case,** comprising 60 named glass phials in an embossed leather hinged case, within a slip case, 6¼in (16cm) high.
£320–375
€/ $500–600 ⚒ WW

A mahogany and brass-mounted medicine chest, the hinged top enclosing a fitted interior, above two drawers, early 19thC, 10in (25.5cm) wide.
£220–250
€/ $350–400 G(L)

Medicine chests

Medicine chests were popular with the upper classes throughout the 19th century as a means to treat everyday ailments rather than having to resort to the expense of calling in the local doctor. They always accompanied the family and were therefore designed for travel. Often in brass-bound mahogany cases, the glass bottles and accessories were securely contained in fitted drawers. It is important to ensure that all the bottles fit snugly and are therefore original to the case. In the back of the case there is often a secret sliding panel that originally held poison bottles, and a drawer in the base for a pestle and mortar and a set of scales.

A mahogany medicine chest, c1860, 8½in (21.5cm) wide.
£600–675
€/ $950–1,000 ⊞ CuS

A mahogany medicine chest, with accessories including bottles and scales, late 19thC, 9½in (24cm) wide.
£400–475
€/ $630–750 SWO

A mahogany medicine chest, with sunken brass handles, the hinged front enclosing bottle compartment and drawers, the back with a slide, 19thC, 12in (30.5cm) wide.
£750–900
€/ $1,200–1,400 WW

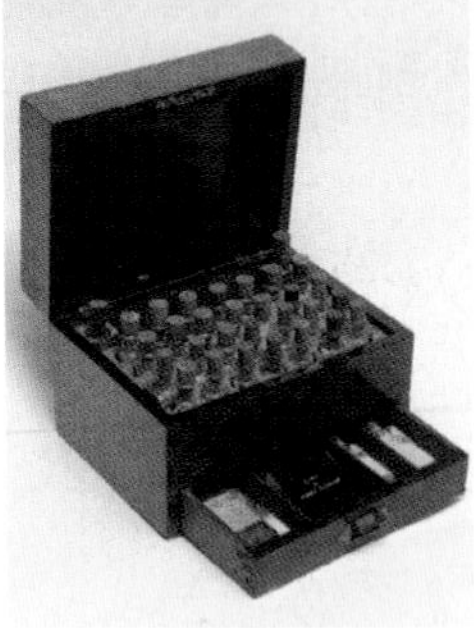

A walnut-veneered homeopathic medicine chest, c1880, 8½in (21.5cm) wide.
£240–265
€/ $380–420 ⊞ CuS

◄ A demonstration eye, c1890, in a box 7½in (19cm) wide.
£315–350
€/ $500–550 ⊞ CuS
This would be used by students to identify diseases in the eye.

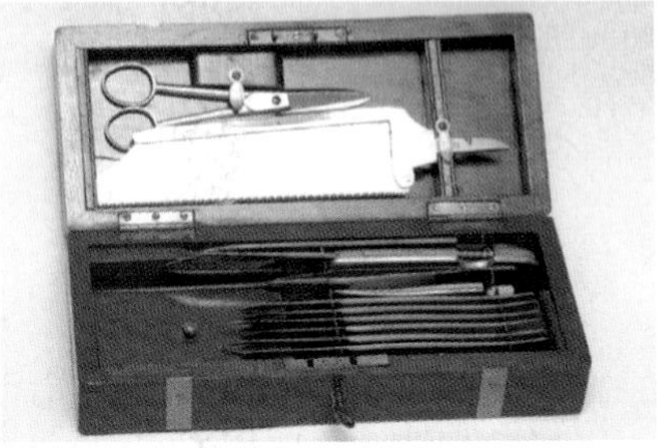

A field operating kit, in a brass-bound mahogany box, c1890, 10in (25.5cm) wide.
£330–365
€/ $520–580 ⊞ CuS

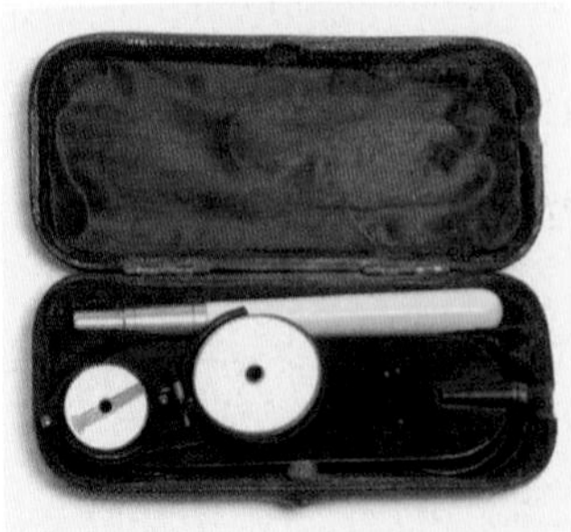

An ophthalmoscope, c1880, in original fitted case, 4½in (11.5cm) wide.
£150–165
€/ $240–260 ⊞ CuS

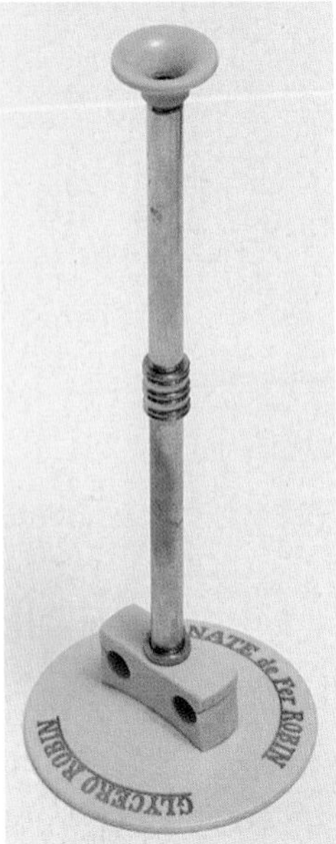

► A metal and ivory stethoscope, c1890, 7in (18cm) long.
£240–265
€/ $380–420 ⊞ CuS

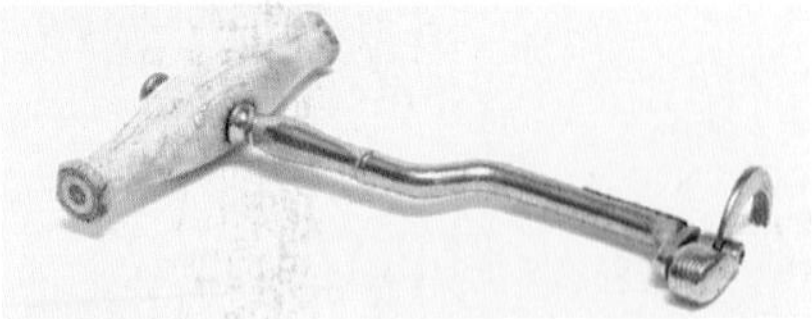

A tooth key, with ivory handle, c1850, 6in (15cm) long.
£200–225
€/ $320–350 ⊞ CuS

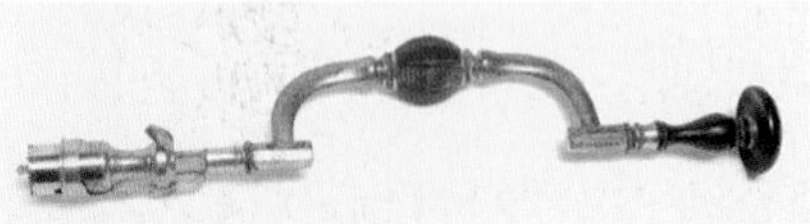

A metal trepanning brace, c1860, 12in (30.5cm) long.
£450–500
€/ $700–790 ⊞ CuS

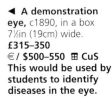

Microscopes

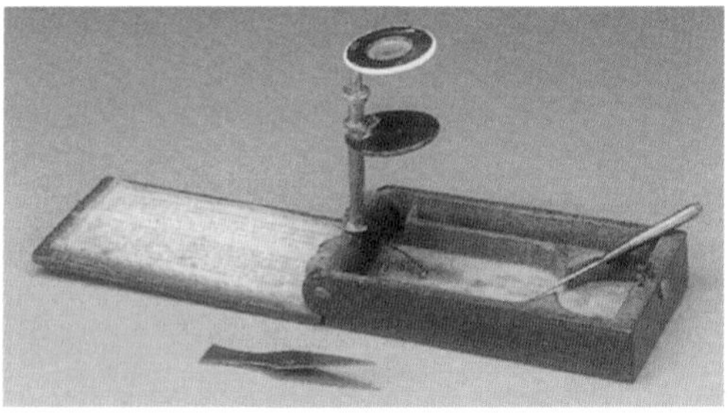

A brass Withering-style botanical microscope, the lens mounted with ivory and a blackened ivory stage, with tweezers and a spike, in a wooden case with instruction label to interior of lid, c1795, case 4¾in (12cm) wide.
£500–600
€/ $800–950 S(O)

A Victorian brass monocular compound microscope, by R. & J. Beck, London, with rack-and-pinion focusing, a polarizing lens on a brass stand, and two brass objectives, maker's stamp, 10in (25.5cm) high, in a mahogany case with brass carrying handle.
£170–200
€/ $270–320 PFK

A mid-Victorian brass binocular compound microscope, by Negretti & Zambra, the lacquered and gilded-brass frame with knurled adjusters, in original box with an assortment of sleeved and named objectives, case 16½in (42cm) high.
£950–1,100
€/ $1,500–1,700 BIG

A compound Nuremberg microscope, the box-form base with an adjustable mirror, surmounted by a compound optical tube covered with paper, on a wooden base beneath a glass dome, German, 1800–25, 15in (38cm) high.
£600–700
€/ $950–1,100 S(O)

► **A brass compound binocular microscope,** with rack-and-pinion focusing and double nosepiece, over a fixed stage with substage condenser and plano concave mirror on a Y-shaped base, in a case with a single drawer containing accessories including a bull's-eye condenser, five eye-pieces and two objectives, late 19thC, box 16¼in (41.5cm) high.
£320–375
€/ $500–600 B(Kn)

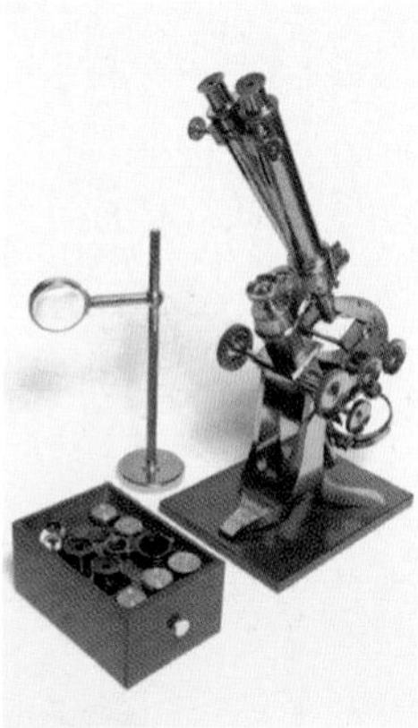

A binocular microscope, No. 1, by Ross, in a mahogany case, with accessories, c1860, 20in (51cm) high.
£5,500–6,000
€/ $8,700–9,500 ETO

Surveying & Drawing Instruments

A George III mahogany travelling draughtsman's box, with compartmented lateral drawer, the reverse with a folio stand, 27½in (70cm) wide.
£720–850
€/ $1,100–1,300 S(O)

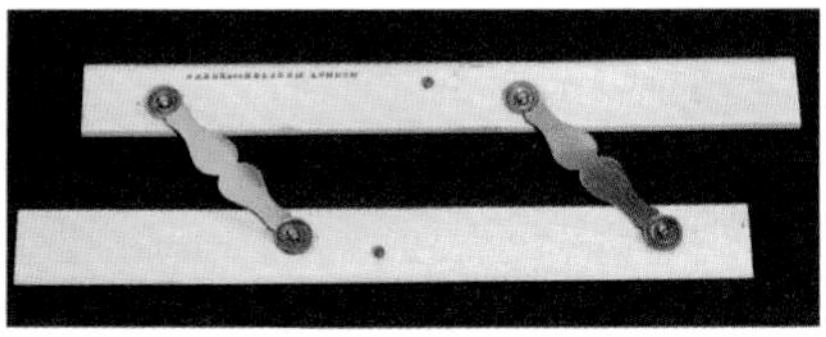

An ivory parallel rule, by Baker, Holborn, London, c1870, 7in (18cm) long.
£70–80
€/ $110–125 ETO

► **A drawing instrument set,** c1740, with a silver-mounted fishskin pocket case, signed 'S. Saunders', 6½in (16.5cm) high.
£3,500–4,200
€/ $5,500–6,600 G(L)

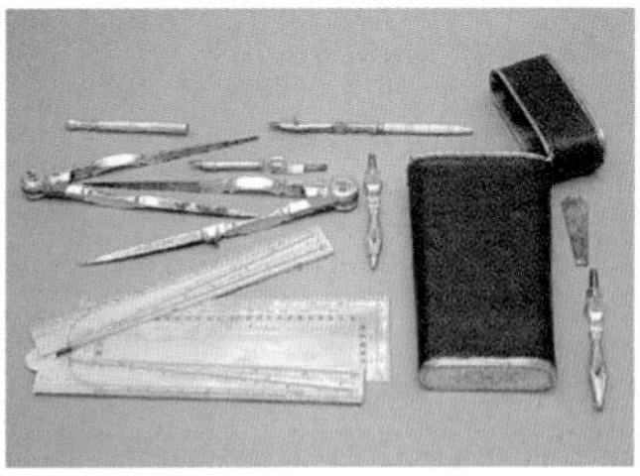

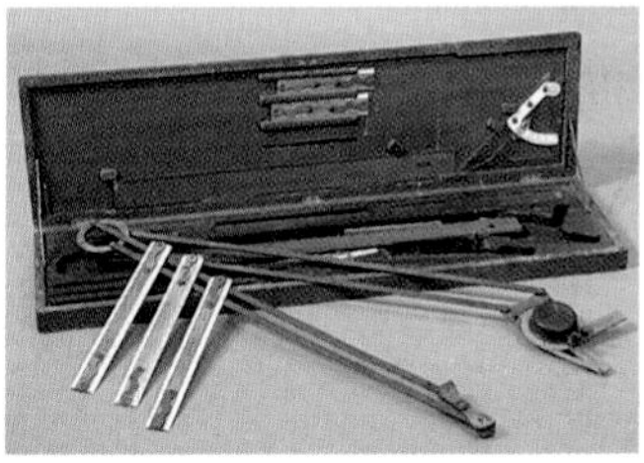

A pantograph, by Universal Drafting Machine Co, American, Cleveland, Ohio, early 20thC, 35½in (90cm) long, in a fitted mahogany box with accessories.
£130–150
€/ $200–240 SWO

A brass theodolite, by Cary, London, c1820, 17½in (44.5cm) high.
£1,100–1,200
€/ $1,700–1,900 PHo

Telescopes

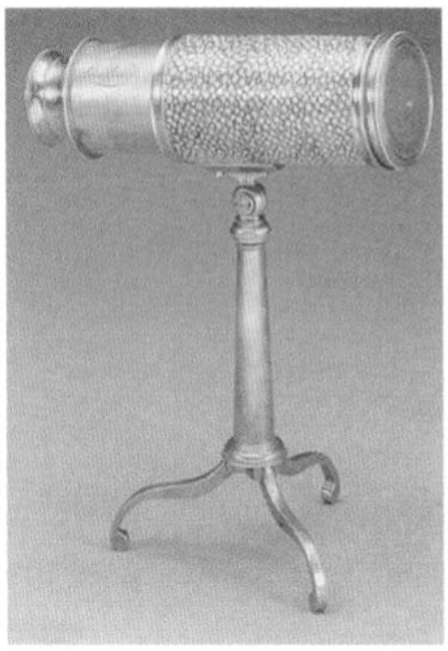

A 1½in table refracting telescope, by Dollond, the signed brass tube with shagreen cover, on a tapering pillar and three scrolled folding legs, mid-18thC, 7½in (19cm) high.
£2,000–2,200
€/ $3,200–3,500 S(O)

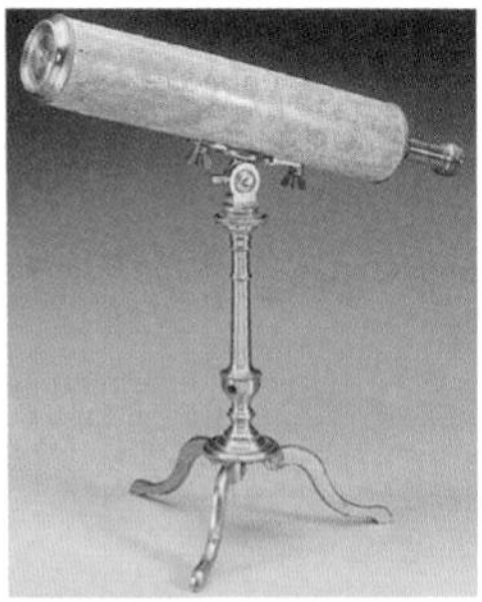

A 3in reflecting telescope, the rayskin-covered brass body with screw adjustment, on a brass pillar with folding tripod feet, French, mid-18thC, 17in (43cm) long, in an associated wooden case with Passemant trade label to interior of lid.
£2,800–3,200
€/ $4,400–5,000 S(O)

An ivory and *lignum vitae* pocket refracting telescope, with card inner tubes, probably Continental, mid-18thC, 7¼in (18.5cm) long.
£570–675
€/ $900–1,000 S(O)

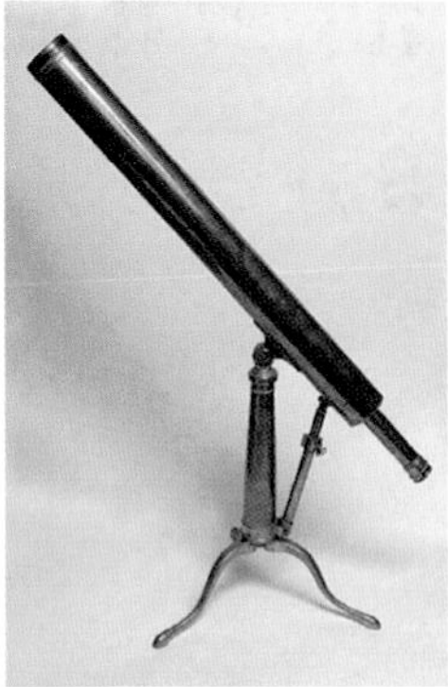

A brass refracting telescope, by Jessie Ramsden, London, c1780, barrel 31in (78.5cm) long, in original box.
£2,200–2,500
€/ $3,500–4,000 HUM

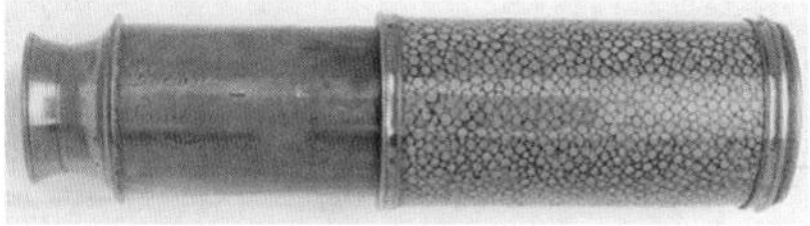

A 1½in pocket refracting telescope, by Dollond, the body covered with shagreen, signed, early 19thC, 4¾in (12cm) long.
£330–400
€/ $520–630 S(O)

A brass eight-draw telescope, by V. Somalvico & Co, London, with leather-covered body and lens cap, 19thC, 28¼in (72cm) extended.
£130–150
€/ $200–240 DMC

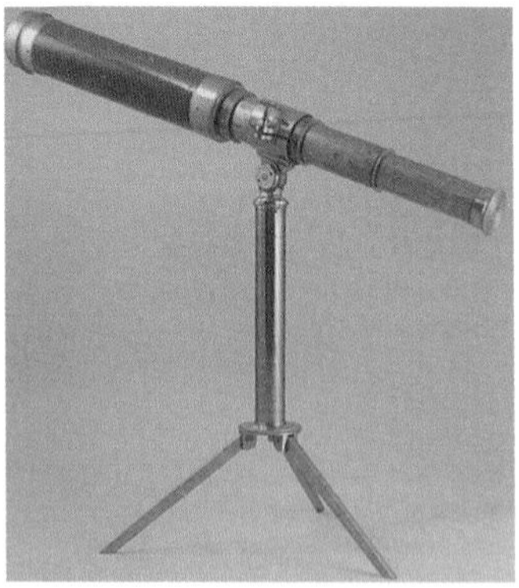

A brass four-draw telescope, with mahogany hand grip, on a folding tripod stand, inscribed 'Cary, London', mid-19thC, 14in (35.5cm) high.
£280–320
€/ $440–500 WW

A Victorian telescope, by J. H. Steward, London, with leather-covered body, silvered applied maker's plaque and engraved pull-out drawer, on an associated mahogany and brass stand, 46½in (118cm) extended.
£700–800
€/ $1,100–1,300 S(O)

Weights & Measures

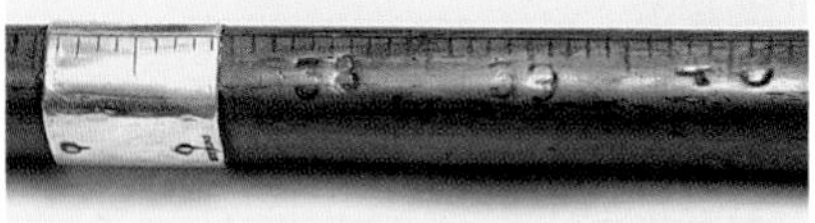

A wooden measuring stick, with silver band and inches marked, c1850, 54in (137cm) long.
£160–175
€/ $250–275 GBr

A folding pocket guinea balance, made and retailed by H. Bell & Co, Prescot, Lancashire, with original paper labels, without weights, early 19thC, 6in (15cm) long.
£55–65
€/ $85–100 TMA

► **A set of parcel scales,** with graduated brass weights, on a platform base, 19thC.
£200–240
€/ $320–380 BWL

A set of brass scales, by Avery, Birmingham, with faceted baluster stem and four weights, late 19thC, 29in (73.5cm) high.
£425–500
€/ $670–800 S(O)

A set of brass Nuremberg cup weights, German, c1780, 2in (5cm) diam.
£430–475
€/ $680–750 RGe

Marine

Barometers

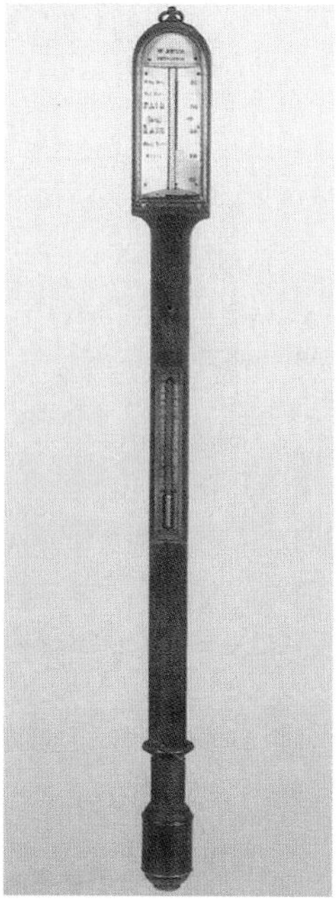

A Regency mahogany marine barometer, with vernier and mercury thermometer, brass cistern cover, inscribed 'W. Atkin, Newcastle', 38in (96.5cm) high.
£1,800–2,200
€/ $2,800–3,500 ⚒ Mit

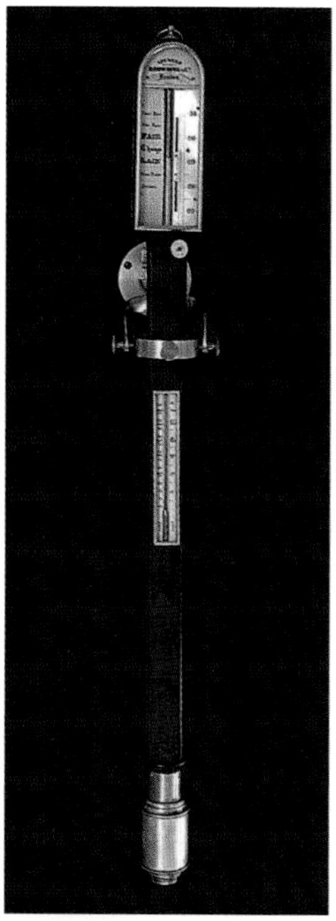

A mahogany marine barometer, inscribed 'Spencer Browning & Co', on contemporary gimbals, c1840, 36in (91.5cm) high.
£3,400–3,800
€/ $5,400–6,000 ⊞ AW

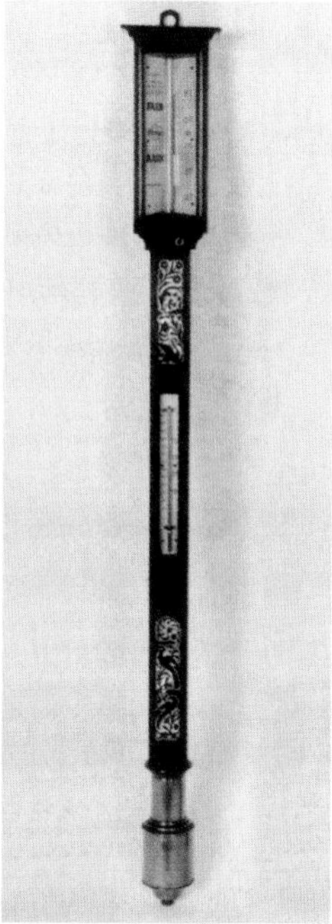

An early Victorian rosewood marine barometer, by I. Mackrow, London, decorated with mother-of-pearl, brass cistern, 36in (91.5cm) high.
£1,400–1,600
€/ $2,200–2,500 ⚒ HYD

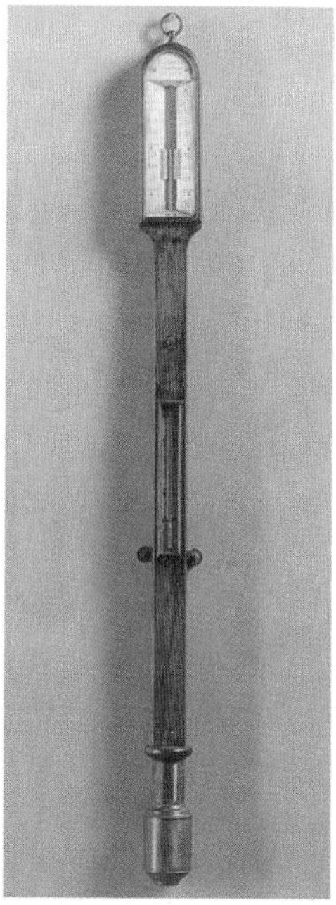

A rosewood marine barometer, signed 'J. Jeacock, London', with two-day ivory plates and verniers, thermometer and brass cistern, c1850, 37¾in (96cm) high.
£2,400–2,700
€/ $3,800–4,300 ⚒ S(O)

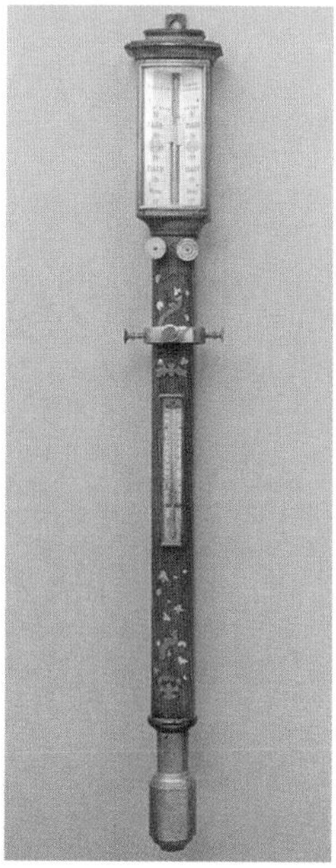

A brass and mother-of-pearl-inlaid rosewood marine barometer, by McGregor & Co, Glasgow & Greenock, brass cistern cover, Scottish, mid-19thC, 38½in (98cm) high.
£3,500–4,200
€/ $5,500–6,600 ⚒ B

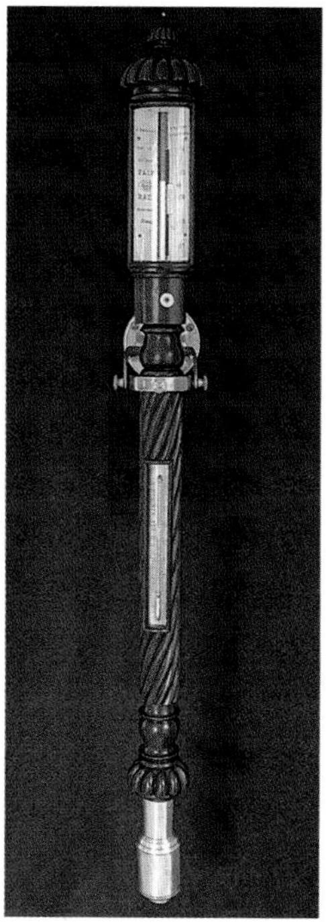

A carved walnut marine barometer, by John Graham, Liverpool, with ivory plates, c1860, 38in (96.5cm) high.
£4,500–5,000
€/ $7,000–8,000 ⊞ AW

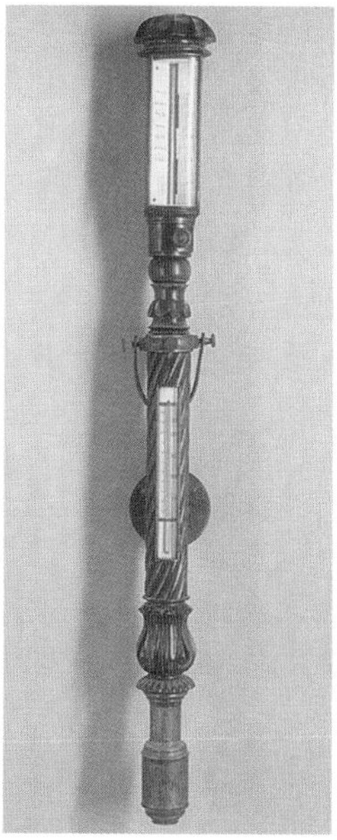

A mahogany marine barometer, by B. Palasca, Liverpool, with ivory plates and single vernier, thermometer and brass cistern cover, with brass gimbal wall mount, c1860, 37in (94cm) high.
£5,000–5,500
€/ $8,000–8,700 ⚒ S(O)

A brass marine barometer, by Kelvin, White & Hutton, with thermometer, iron cistern cover and gimbal wall fitting, Scottish, c1910, 36¼in (92cm) high.
£1,100–1,200
€/ $1,700–1,900 ⚒ S(O)

Chronometers & Timekeepers

A two-day freesprung marine chronometer, by John Poole, London, helical hairspring and bimetallic balance with Poole's auxiliary compensation, Earnshaw-type detent escapement with maintaining power, in a brass-inlaid mahogany case, mid-19thC, 7in (18cm) wide.
£1,200–1,400
€/ $1,900–2,200 B

John Poole was born in 1818. He worked from various London addresses, but 57 Fenchurch Street was used between 1858–85. He established himself as a chronometer maker in 1840 and became one of the great names. He invented his own compensation, which was first applied c1850, and his ideas and movements were used by many others. He committed suicide in 1867.

A two-day marine chronometer, by D. McGregor & Co, Glasgow & Greenock, in an ebony and brass-strung case, with outer deck box, Scottish, c1870, 7in (18cm) wide.
£5,000–5,500
€/ $8,000–8,700 JeF

A brass and mahogany nautical mantel timepiece, French, c1890, 14in (35.5cm) high.
£1,300–1,500
€/ $2,100–2,400 MSh

A two-day marine chronometer, the silvered dial with subsidiaries and signed 'J. P. Dupont & Zoon, Rotterdam', movement with spotted plates, detent escapement with compensation balance and helical spring, in a mahogany box, with possibly later travelling case, c1870, 6¾in (17cm) high.
£1,400–1,700
€/ $2,200–2,700 S(Am)

An officer's of the watch clock, by Seth Thomas, striking the hours on a saucer bell, American, 1880–90, 10in (25.5cm) high.
£340–380
€/ $550–600 OLD

► **A chromed-metal chronometer deck watch,** by Hamilton Watch Co for the US Navy, 21 jewels, compensation balance, adjusted to temperatures and six positions, in a mahogany box, 1941, 2¾in (7cm) diam.
£900–1,100
€/ $1,400–1,700 S(Am)

Model Ships

◄ **An unrigged dockyard model of a two-deck 94-gun ship of the line,** with carved bust figurehead and catheads, on a mahogany stand, minor damage, mid-19thC, 16¼in (41.5cm) long.
£600–720
€/ $950–1,100 DN

A fruitwood half-block model of a yacht, c1920, 20in (51cm) long.
£135–150
€/ $220–240 BoC

A Victorian carved wood model of a boat, in a mahogany case, the back painted with a Mediterranean coastal scene, 26in (66cm) wide.
£320–375
€/ $500–600 WW

◄ **A pond yacht,** with full rigging and sails, painted wood hull and metal counterweight, later additions, c1910, 68in (172.5cm) long.
£220–250
€/ $350–400 AH

Nautical Handicrafts

An ivory-inlaid wood love token box, made by the captain of the SS *Gloster*, American, 1871, 11in (28cm) wide.
£4,000–4,800
€/ $6,300–7,600 S(NY)
American folk art is highly collectable. Had this piece been British the price would have been much less.

An alabaster-framed reverse painting on glass, depicting an East Indiaman in Bombay harbour, early 19thC, 5½in (14cm) diam.
£250–280
€/ $400–440 HUM

A miniature reverse painting on glass of a frigate, the reverse inscribed 'The frigate Arenensius(?) on her maiden voyage at Plymouth S**** 24 Oct 1854, 224 tonnes R. Westfall Skipper White Star Line', c1854, 4¼in (11cm) wide, framed.
£600–720
€/ $950–1,100 S(O)
Captain Westfall was skipper on board the frigate on her maiden voyage from Plymouth to Darwin.

A sailor's woolwork picture of a three-masted man-o-war, a paddle steamer and other vessels, with a coal store, Royal Naval buildings and a hill, possibly of Chatham, Kent, 19thC, 20 x 24in (51 x 61cm).
£6,500–7,500
€/ $10,300–12,000 CHTR
This sold for a high price because the dyes used in such pieces were not very fast and it is therefore very unusual to get such strong colours and a very complicated design.

Woolwork pictures

Little is known about the sailor's skills with a needle and thread beyond the practical purpose of mending sails and patching clothes. However, a number of pictures made of wool, known as 'woollies', are assumed to have been made by sailors while on board ship. Their design is often quite naïve and they therefore appeal to collectors of both samplers and folk art.

Prices have risen considerably over the past few years on the strength of the American market, with fine examples fetching up to £10,000 (€/ $16,000). Collectors are looking for well-designed images of marine interest in good condition. The dye used in the wool is not fast and the pictures are liable to both fading and moth damage. Original maple frames also add to the desirability of such woolwork pictures.

► **A sailor's woolwork picture,** 'Leisure Hours in India', c1870, 23 x 29in (58.5 x 73.5cm), framed.
£1,600–1,800
€/ $2,500–2,800 SWN

A coquilla nut snuff box, carved with maritime scenes, late 19thC, 4in (10cm) wide.
£250–300
€/ $400–475 TMA

Navigational Instruments

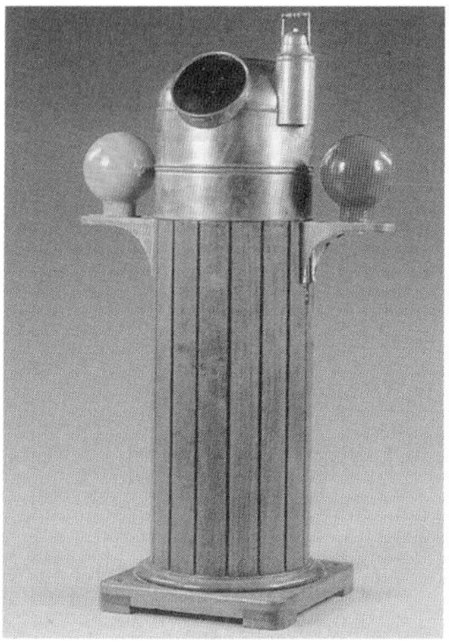

◄ **A teak binnacle compass,** the brass cover housing the gimple-mounted floating compass card, flanked by two iron compensation spheres, with binnacle lamp, c1920, 56¾in (144cm) high.
£530–630
€/ $840–1,000 S(O)

A Victorian brass navigational plotting protractor, by Blackburne, 13in (33cm) long.
£75–85
€/ $120–135 WiB

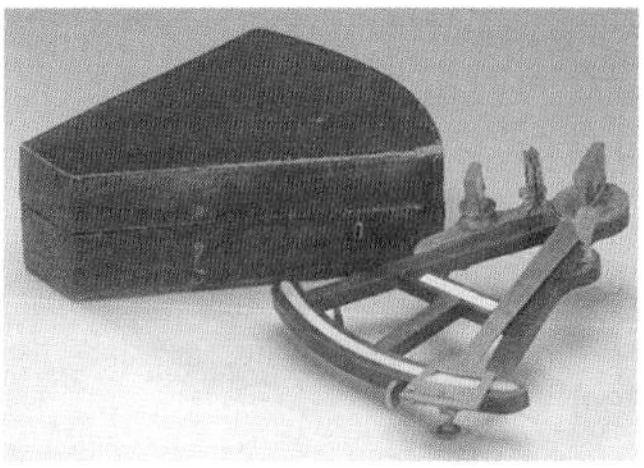

An ebony octant, by Spencer, Browning & Co, with ivory name plaque, scale and vernier, brass index arm, one set of interchangeable filters, in a wooden case, early 19thC, 11¾in (30cm) radius.
£450–550
€/ $700–870 S(O)

Sea Chests

◄ **An iron-bound oak sea captain's chest,** fitted with decanters and glasses, on a later stand, 18thC, 15in (38cm) high.
£550–650
€/ $870–1,000 E

A ship's surgeon's oak chest, with brass plaque inscribed 'Elmina R.Y.S', on a later stand, 19thC, 21¼in (54cm) wide.
£170–200
€/ $270–320 WilP

◄ **An elm sea chest,** the top inscribed 'The Admiral', 19thC, 38¼in (97cm) wide.
£2,500–3,000
€/ $4,000–4,700 S(O)

Ship's Fittings

► **A ship's bell,** engraved 'SS *Commissioner*, 1905, Graton' and 'Hall, Russell & Co Ltd, Aberdeen, engineers and shipbuilders', c1905, 10¾in (27.5cm) diam.
£280–325
€/ $440–500 SWO

► **A brass-bound mahogany ship's wheel,** c1860, 60in (152.5cm) diam.
£850–950
€/ $1,300–1,500
HON

◄ **A carved wood and gesso figurehead,** 19thC, 30½in (77.5cm) high.
£10,000–11,000
€/ $15,800–17,400 S(O)
Figureheads endured the brunt of the sea being mounted at the prow of the ship. Examples in good condition such as this one are therefore very rare and this is reflected in its high price.

◄ **A brass-bound mahogany ship's wheel,** 19thC, 48½in (123cm) diam.
£650–750
€/ $1,000–1,200
SWO

MARINE

Miscellaneous

A pair of brass binoculars, by Alexandre LaFleur, Paris, with leather grips, fitted with sliding shades to the objects lens, in a velvet-lined mahogany presentation case.
£550–625
€/ $870–1,000 B

A White Star Line brochure, 16 pages, c1911, 6 x 8in (15 x 20.5cm).
£1,300–1,500
€/ $2,000–2,400 HAld

► **A lacquered brass three-draw telescope,** by Gome, Paris, with morocco cover and extending shade, French, 19thC, 32in (81.5cm) extended.
£65–75
€/ $100–120 PFK

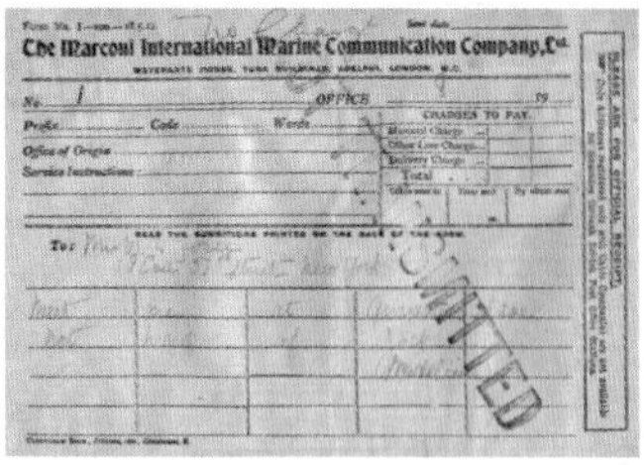
The Marconi International Marine Communication Company, Ltd.

A Marconigram, sent from the *Titanic*'s rescue ship *Carpathia*, by Madeline Astor, dated 15 April 1912, 7 x 8in (18 x 20.5cm).
£11,000–13,000
€/ $17,000–20,000 HAld

Admiral Lord Nelson

A diamond anchor brooch, with scrolled initials 'H' and 'N' for Horatio Nelson, mounted in silver and gold, c1801, 2½in (6.5cm) long.
£150,000–180,000
€/ $237,000–285,000 S
Ex-Alexander Davison Collection. This brooch is believed to have been a personal gift from Nelson to Emma, Lady Hamilton. It was placed in Alexander Davison's custody after Nelson's death.

A pictorial silk embroidery, depicting Admiral Lord Nelson and Lady Hamilton, with a verse below, early 19thC, 10¾ x 13¾in (27.5 x 35cm), framed.
£750–875
€/ $1,200–1,400 AH

► **A Staffordshire Nelson jug,** modelled standing beside a canon, on a titled base, 1850–75, 11¾in (30cm) high.
£400–500
€/ $630–800 S(O)

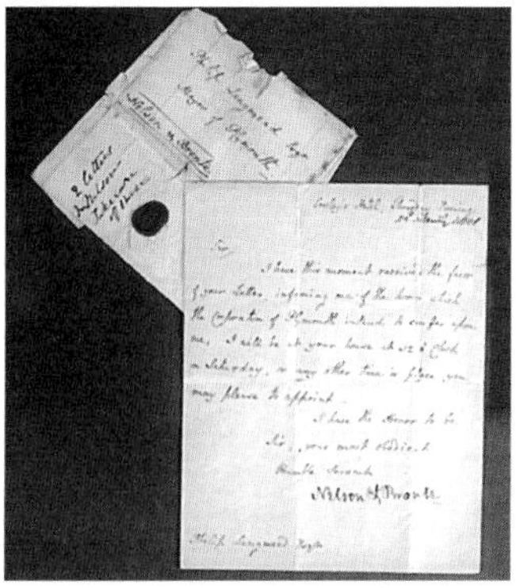

Horatio Nelson, single page letter with integral blank leaf, signed 'Nelson & Bronte' to Philip Longmead, Mayor of Plymouth, in his secretary's hand with Nelson's signature, discussing the honour which the 'corporation of Plymouth intend to confer upon me', 4°, with envelope bearing red seal, dated 22 January 1801, with George Tetley's *Old Times and New* (London, 1904).
£1,500–1,700
€/ $2,500–2,700 DN

The Alexander Davison Collection

This collection of Nelson memorabilia sold by Sotheby's in 2002 was doubly exciting. Not only did it include letters, jewellery, ceramics, coinage and personal effects directly relating to Admiral Lord Nelson, but the collection was also initially unknown to historians and collectors alike.

The Sotheby's jewellery expert was called in by the direct descendants of Alexander Davison to advise them of the value of some jewellery. He subsequently discovered a hoard of material that had been owned by Davison, who was Nelson's intimate friend, treasurer, prize agent and closest advisor. The two men met in 1782 in Quebec when Nelson, at 23, was a rising post-captain. Davison was eight years older and had amassed a fortune as a ship owner and government contractor through the recent American war. He remained a constant figure in Nelson's life. At Nelsons's funeral 23 years later Davison, as one of the four principal members of his household, broke his white stave of office to be placed on the coffin as it was lowered into the vault of St Paul's Cathedral.

The fabulous prices achieved at auction for sometimes quite humble pieces reflect the immense importance paid by collectors for historic pieces with impeccable provenance, and in this case, belonging to someone who is still considered one of Britain's greatest heroes.

Jon Baddeley

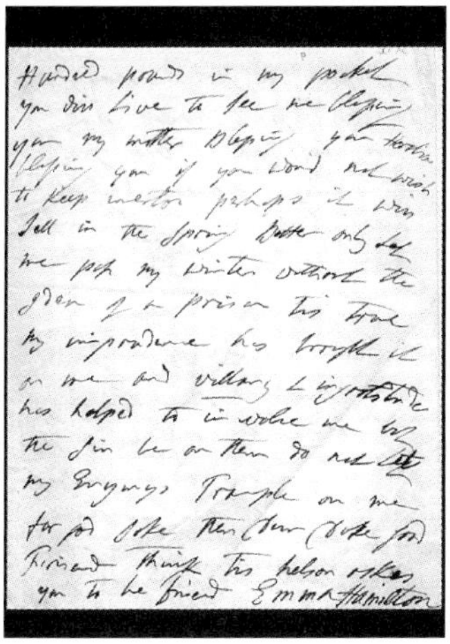

◄ **Emma Hamilton,** a signed letter to the Duke of Queensbury begging him 'for my sake for Nelsons sake for the good I have done my country...Tis Nelson asks you' – to buy Merton '...that I may live free from fear that every debt may be paid I think & hope fifteen thousand pounds will do for every thing... purchase it take it only giving me the portraits of Sir William...I wish not for more than will pay my debts', four pages, 4°, with a transcript of a letter by Emma and copy of *Baily's Biography and Iconography*, 4 September 1808.
£2,000–2,400
€/ $3,200–3,800 B
This letter, begging Queensbury to buy 'Paradise Merton' – the house which Emma and Nelson shared and from which Nelson departed for Trafalgar – can be seen as marking the end of a dream. The letter's recipient, the Duke of Queensbury, was an immensely rich and very ancient roué, familiarly known as 'Old Q'. He was possessed of such a wide circle of female acquaintance – all desperate to inherit his vast fortune – that he was likened to the Grand Turk with his seraglio. At the time of writing, Emma was living in one of the Duke's properties, Heron Court in Richmond. Unfortunately her plea was unsuccessful. The Duke declined to buy, Merton having been valued at £12,000 (€/ $19,000) rather than the £15,000 (€/ $24,000) asked for.

A silver Alexander Davison medal for the Battle of the Nile, the obverse decorated with a figure of Peace standing with an anchor, holding an olive branch and a shield with a profile portrait of Nelson, with the legend 'Europe's Hope and Britain's Glory', the reverse with a view of the engagement in Aboukir Bay, signed 'C. H. Küchler' and 'Victory of the Nile August 1. 1798' in exergue, 1¾in (4.5cm) diam.
£600–700
€/ $950–1,100 ⚒ S(O)

The practice of awarding official naval campaign medals began in 1794, when captains and flag officers present at the Battle of the Glorious First of June were awarded gold medals. They were highly prized by their recipients, but with these early medals no provision was made for junior officers or men. Therefore in 1798 Alexander Davison decided to issue a 'Tribute of Regard' to mark Nelson's victory at Aboukir Bay and to reward, for the first time, every participant in the Battle of the Nile. Gold medals were presented primarily to Nelson and to captains of his fleet, while silver examples were offered to officers, copper-gilt to petty officers and bronzed-copper to seamen, marines and others. Davison's motives were not entirely philanthropic, as he was hoping with this undertaking to consolidate his position as Nelson's prize agent and was thereby currying favour with the British fleet, Royalty and, to some extent, the public at large.

A souvenir of the Battle of the Nile, painted alabaster and reverse-painted convex glass, depicting the stern of HMS *Vanguard*, Nelson's flag and the fleets in action, inscribed 'Adml Nelson's Victory', 18thC, 6in (15cm) diam.
£550–625
€/ $870–1,000 ⚒ LAY

A copper medal, by T. Wyon Sr, commemorating the Battle of Trafalgar, minor damage, 1805, 1¾in (4.5cm) diam.
£220–250
€/ $350–400 ⚒ DNW

A gold-mounted pine snuff box, belonging to Alexander Davison, the cover set with a gold plaque engraved 'This is made from the *Victory* main mast close to which the Immortal Nelson fell on the 21st October 1805, Alexr, Davison', c1805, 2¾in (7cm) wide.
£50,000–60,000
€/ $79,000–95,000 ⚒ S

Ex-Alexander Davison Collection. Davison may have commissioned a number of similar boxes as mementos for distribution. The masts on the *Victory* were largely shot away during the action at Trafalgar, and it was to the main mast, on the middle deck, that the barrel holding Nelson's body was secured for the long passage home. After her return to England bearing Nelson's body in a barrel of spirits, HMS *Victory* was paid off to be refitted at Chatham. She served in the Baltic until 1812 when she returned to Portsmouth for an extensive refit. She later acted as the Port Admiral's flagship and was twice visited by Queen Victoria. Although she was popular to sightseers while moored in Gosport, as the 19th century wore on and memories of Trafalgar faded, she fell into disrepair, often being stripped of materials, and suffering the final indignity of being rammed and badly damaged by HMS *Neptune* in 1903. In 1922 she was eventually moved to Portsmouth, where she remains today. In the early 20th century, a 'Save the *Victory*' campaign was launched funding the major restoration of 1922–27. In 1941 she was damaged by enemy action yet again. HMS *Victory* is still in commission.

A silver-gilt vinaigrette, engraved with a portrait of Nelson, Birmingham 1805, 1¾in (4.5cm) wide.
£1,300–1,500
€/ $2,000–2,500 ⚒ G(L)

A hand-painted silk panel, portraying two escutcheons bearing the impaled arms of Lord and Lady Nelson, one of six made for the velvet pall which covered Nelson's coffin during its journey up the River Thames, and from the Admiralty to St Paul's Cathedral, London, for burial on 9 January 1806, 17 x 23in (43 x 58.5cm), framed.
£35,000–40,000
€/ $55,000–63,000 ⚒ DN

Formerly the property of the Rev Alexander John Scott (1768–1840), and thence by direct descent. Scott was Chaplain to HMS *Victory* and acted as the Admiral's interpreter, Nelson being – by his own admission – a 'poor linguist'. He was also the individual who held and supported Nelson as he lay dying in the *Victory*'s cockpit. He afterwards wrote to Emma Hamilton '...what an affectionate, fascinating little fellow he was... I become stupid with grief for what I have lost...'.

Lord Nelson's green silk purse, with 13⅓ guineas in gold and a manuscript *Money, Coins in Lord Nelson's Pocket, Purse &c when Killed,* 1805, 11¾in (30cm) long.
£250,000–300,000
€/ $400,000–475,000 ⚒ S

Ex-Alexander Davison Collection. This purse was from the Admiral's personal effects carried aboard HMS *Victory* at the Battle of Trafalgar, and at the time of his death passed to Alexander Davison.

Cameras

A Butcher's Cameo folding plate camera, c1920.
£25–30
€/ $40–48 ⊞ VCL

A Canon F-1 camera, c1970.
£180–200
€/ $285–320 ⊞ VCL

A Coronet Midget black Bakelite camera, c1935.
£70–80
€/ $110–125 ⊞ APC

A FED Type 2 camera, early Leica copy, Russian, 1935–39.
£135–150
€/ $215–240 ⊞ HEG

A Dallmeyer mahogany and brass-plate studio camera, on an adjustable stand, 1875–80.
£1,000–1,200
€/ $1,600–1,900 ⚒ B(WM)

◄ A FED camera, early Leica copy, Russian, 1930s–40s.
£90–100
€/ $140–190
⊞ HEG

A Houghton Butcher oxidized brass Butcher's No. 6 tropical watch pocket carbide camera, with 4in anastigmatic f4.5 lens, c1920.
£130–145
€/ $210–230 ⊞ WAC

A Houghton Butcher Ensignette miniature camera, c1930.
£35–40
€/ $55–63 ⊞ VCL

A Kiev 3A Contax copy 35mm film camera, with Rangefinder and light meter, c1950.
£70–80
€/ $110–125 ⊞ HEG

A Kodak 1st Model No. 4 cartridge camera, c1900.
£90–100
€/ $140–160 ⊞ VCL

◄ A Kodak Panoramic Model A camera, c1900.
£200–220
€/ $320–350 ⊞ VCL

► A Kodak No. 2 Stereo Brownie camera, c1910.
£320–350
€/ $510–550 ⊞ APC

A Kodak Vanity Series 111 VPK camera, c1930.
£270–300
€/ $430–480 ⊞ APC

A Lumière & Cie subminiature roll-film camera, French, 1936–46.
£50–60
€/ $80–95 ⊞ HEG

A Steky 16mm subminiature cassette camera, minor variations, 1950–55.
£70–80
€/ $110–125 ⊞ HEG

A Kodak Vanity Ensemble camera, c1930, with box.
£1,300–1,500
€/ $2,100–2,400 ⊞ APC

A Leica II Hektor nickel camera, c1935.
£500–600
€/ $790–950 ⊞ VCL

A Thornton Pickard Triple Imperial half-plate camera, c1910.
£270–300
€/ $430–480 ⊞ APC

A Vollenda horizontal folding roll-film camera, with various lenses, 1931–32.
£70–80
€/ $110–125 ⊞ HEG

◄ A Zeiss Ikon camera, c1940.
£50–55
€/ $80–88 ⊞ JOA

A Kodak Beau Brownie box camera, c1930.
£70–80
€/ $110–125 ⊞ APC

A Nikon S camera, with a Nikkor-S f1.4/5cm lens and instructions, 1952, with original inner and outer boxes.
£550–650
€/ $870–1,000 ⚒ B(Kn)

A Voigtlander Bessamatic 35mm SLR camera, with light meter, c1963.
£90–100
€/ $40–160 ⊞ VCL

A United Optical Co Merlin camera, with black crackle finish, 1936.
£60–70
€/ $95–110 ⊞ APC

Further reading

Miller's Collecting Science & Technology, Miller's Publications, 2001

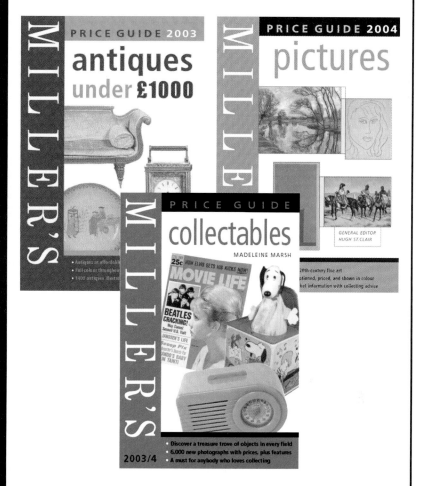

Optical Devices & Viewers

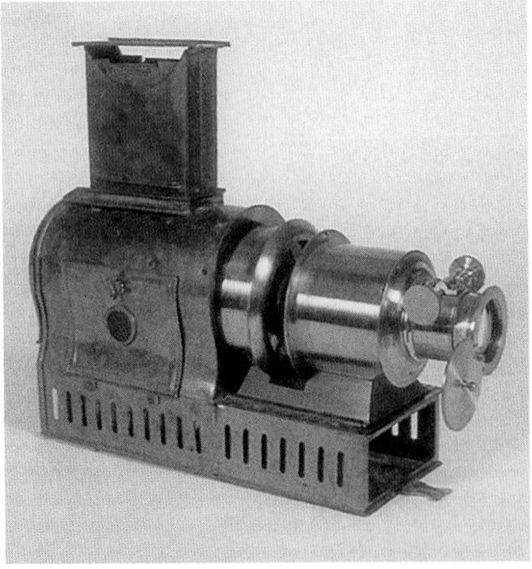

A steel and brass magic lantern and slides, with 3¼in (8.5cm) slides, oil illuminant, condenser, lens, chimney, slide carrier and carrying box with five wood-mounted circular slides, and other boxes of slides and sundries, c1880.
£200–220
€/ $320–350 B(WM)

A walnut-veneered stereo graphoscope, with brass and glass fittings, the single lens on brass slides and hinged double stereo lenses, fretwork card stand and adjustable support, c1875, 16in (41cm) long.
£250–300
€/ $400–475 BBA

A Rowsell's Patent walnut-veneered stereo graphoscope, with brass and bone fitments, filigree rest and manufacturer's name disc, with some stereocards, late 19thC, 23in (58.5cm) wide.
£280–325
€/ $440–515 DW

A walnut stereo graphoscope, with decorative stringing, 5½in (14cm) lens and binocular focusing stereo lenses, built-in ebonized folding shade and mirror for glass or daguerrean views, string and pulley focusing for the easel with control knobs on each side, stamped 'Brevette SGBG', French, late 19thC, base 18½in (47cm) long.
£380–450
€/ $600–710 B(WM)

A burr-walnut stereoscopic viewer and cards, 19thC, 21¼in (54cm) high.
£350–420
€/ $550–660 SWO

A mahogany Stereo Classeur stereoscope, Le Taxiphote, the case with a moulded-edge top, fitted with two sliding drawers containing slides, late 19thC, slides 2¼ x 5¼in (5.5 x 13cm).
£480–570
€/ $760–900 TRM

A Richard Verascope stereo viewer, with glass slides, c1910, 4¾in (12cm) wide.
£90–100
€/ $140–160 APC

A rosewood Zograscope, the turned and inlaid stand flanked by brass candle sconces, 19thC, 25¼in (64cm) high.
£300–350
€/ $475–550 SWO

► **A George III mahogany Zograscope,** the mirror inlaid with diced stringing to the border and fold-over viewing glass, on an adjustable column and circular base.
£170–200
€/ $270–315
HOLL

A George III mahogany Zograscope, 27in (68.5cm) high.
£430–475
€/ $680–750 APO

Photographs

Berenice Abbott, 'Hanover Square, Manhattan', annotated by a Federal Art Project assistant in pencil and with stamped letters on reverse, American, 1936, 7½ x 9½in (19 x 24cm).
£3,800–4,500
€/ $6,000–7,000 ⚒ S(NY)

Berenice Abbott was hired in 1935 by the Federal Art Project and the Museum of the City of New York to photograph New York as it constantly evolved and changed.

Berenice Abbott, 'West Street Row II: 217–221 West Street, Manhattan', annotated by a Federal Art Project assistant in pencil and with stamped letters on the reverse, American, 1936, 7½ x 9½in (19 x 24cm).
£3,200–3,800
€/ $5,000–6,000 ⚒ S(NY)

This section of West Street Row, between North Moore and Franklin Streets, was razed in the 1960s. The Borough of Manhattan Community College, completed in 1980, now stands on this spot.

Ansel Adams, 'Mudhills, Arizona', plate 2 from *Portfolio V*, mounted, signed by the photographer and numbered 'V-2-97/110', No. 97 of 110, matted, American, 1947, printed later, 14¾ x 19¼in (37.5 x 49cm), framed.
£2,000–2,200
€/ $3,200–3,500 ⚒ S(NY)

Emmy Andriesse, 'Germaine Richier', silver print, mounted on card along the upper edge, photographer's stamp 'Amstel 248 Amsterdam', Dutch, 1948, 10½ x 9¼in (26.5 x 23.5cm).
£1,000–1,100
€/ $1,600–1,700 ⚒ S(Am)

D. F. Barry, 'Chief Gall', American, 1891, 11 x 5¾in (28 x 14.5cm).
£550–625
€/ $870–1,000 ⚒ DuM

Samuel Bourne, 'Poplar Avenue, Srinagar, Kashmir', albumen print from wet collodion negative, c1865, 11½ x 9½in (29 x 24cm).
£150–200
€/ $240–320 ⊞ RMe

► **Brassaï,** 'Conchita with Sailors, Place d'Italie, Paris', signed, titled and numbered, French, dated 1932, printed later, 8¼ x 12in (21 x 30.5cm), framed.
£2,500–3,000
€/ $4,000–4,700 ⚒ S(NY)

Items in the Photographs section have been arranged in alphabetical order.

Bill Brandt, from a fashion series on beach wear, gelatin silver print, 1948, 10 x 12in (25.5 x 30.5cm).
£500–600
€/ $790–950 ⊞ RMe

► **James Bray (Attributed),** a silver gelatin *carte de visite* photograph of Dan Kelly, Burman copy of an original, Australian, 1877–78, 3½ x 2¼in (9 x 5.5cm).
£475–550
€/ $750–870 ⚒ LJ

European & American photography 1976–2002

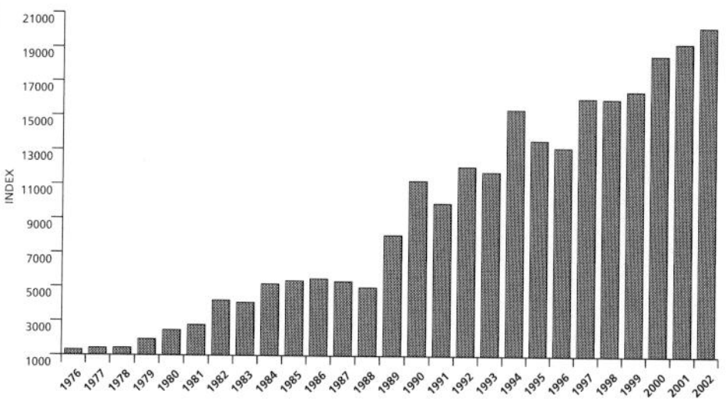

This graph shows the increasing value of European and American photography as a whole over the past 25 years. Individual collecting areas may not follow this graph exactly. ©AMR

Antoine Claudet, 'Portraits of a Lady and Gentleman', a pair of stereoscopic daguerreotypes, hand-coloured, gilt highlights, maker's engraved label, 1850s, in a fitted leather case with gilt stamp.
£1,100–1,200
€/ $1,700–1,900 ⚒ BBA

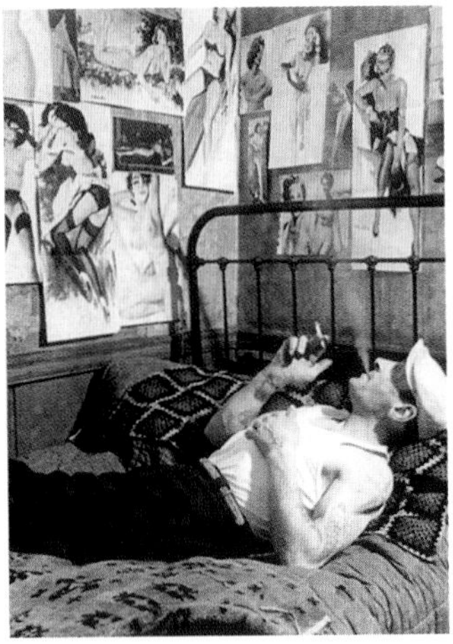

Robert Doisneau, 'Créatures de Rêve', silver print, mounted on card along the upper edge, signed in ink, French, 1952, printed later, 12¼ x 10½in (31 x 26.5cm).
£1,200–1,400
€/ $1,900–2,200 ⚒ S(Am)

Arthur Fellig (Weegee), 'Children's Performance', silver gelatin print, 1940s, 12½ x 10in (32 x 25.5cm).
£900–1,100
€/ $1,400–1,700 ⚒ NOA

Marjorie Content, 'Still Life with Calla and Spotted Leaf', signed and dated by the photographer, American, c1928, 3½ x 2¾in (9 x 7cm).
£2,200–2,500
€/ $3,500–4,000 ⚒ S(NY)

Frantisek Drtikol, 'Portrait of L. Janácek', albumen print, mounted on card along the upper edge, Polish, c1925, 9 x 6½in (23 x 16.5cm).
£300–360
€/ $475–575 ⚒ S(Am)

William Henry Fox Talbot, 'The Fruit Sellers', Lacock Abbey', salt print from calotype negative, c1842, in a frame 6¾ x 8¼in (17 x 21cm).
£5,000–5,500
€/ $7,900–8,700 ⚒ S(Am)

► **Eugene Omar Goldbeck,** 'Albert Einstein & Wife with Hopi Indians, Arizona, 1922', silver gelatin print, American, printed 1970s, 7 x 9in (18 x 23cm).
£280–320
€/ $440–500 ⚒ NOA

Baron Adolf De Meyer, 'Claude Monet', signed by the photographer on the reverse, matted, 1921, 8½ x 6in (21.5 x 15cm).
£3,000–3,300
€/ $4,700–5,200 ⚒ S(NY)

Andreas Feininger, 'New York, Downtown Manhattan from Brooklyn Bridge', silver print, titled and inscribed 'New York 1940', by the photographer, American, 1940, 13¾ x 11¼in (35 x 28.5cm).
£2,200–2,500
€/ $3,500–4,000 ⚒ S(Am)

Francis Frith (Possibly), 'Kashmiri Policemen', albumen print, 1860–65, 7½ x 6in (19 x 15cm).
£450–500
€/ $700–800 ⊞ RMe

Hachenberger, Bullfighters, Mexico, from a set of 30 gelatin silver prints depicting life in the country, c1930, 5 x 7in (12.5 x 18cm).
£780–850 the set
€/ $1,200–1,300 ⊞ RMe

J. Jackson, 'Burma', a set of 16 albumen prints mounted on 12 card leaves, several signed, 1865–70, 5½ x 8¾in (14 x 22cm), in original cloth folder.
£280–325
€/ $440–515 ⚒ DW

W. E. Kilburn, a man in full military uniform with plumed hat on a table, 9th plate daguerreotype, c1850, 2½ x 1½in (6.5 x 4cm).
£200–250
€/ $300–400 ⊞ RMe

Gustave Le Gray, 'Etude de nuages, clair-obscur', albumen print of a Normandy cloudscape from a collodion glass negative, signed, mounted on cut-down card, c1856, 11½ x 16¼in (29 x 41.5cm).
£8,500–10,000
€/ $13,500–15,800 ⚒ DW

David Octavius Hill and Robert Adamson, 'St Andrews, The College Church of St Salvator', calotype, 1845, 8½ x 6½in (21.5 x 16.5cm)
£500–600
€/ $790–950 ⊞ HEG

Willy Kessels, 'Orchids', silver print, mounted on card along the upper edge, Belgian, c1936, 7 x 9½in (18 x 24cm).
£575–675
€/ $900–1,000 ⚒ S(Am)

Aart Klein, 'Rachmaninoff', silver print, mounted on card along the upper edge, 1936, 6½ x 9½in (16.5 x 24cm).
£1,000–1,100
€/ $1,600–1,700 ⚒ S(Am)

Hill & Adamson, Newhaven fisherman, carbon print from the original negative by Jessie Bertram, original c1845, print 1914, 7 x 5in (18 x 12.5cm).
£550–600
€/ $870–950 ⊞ RMe

W. E. Kilburn, 'Portrait of a Gentleman', a daguerreotype, c1850, 4¼ x 3¼in (11 x 8.5cm).
£550–600
€/ $870–950 ⊞ HEG

Joseph Lawton, Buddha, Ceylon, from an album of views and archaeological sites in Ceylon, albumen prints, c1870, 10 x 8in (25.5 x 23cm).
£2,000–2,500 album
€/ $3,200–4,000 ⊞ RMe

◄ Angus McBean, 'Hepburn Desert', silver print, mounted on card, signed and dated 1951, printed 1986, 17½ x 12¾in (44.5 x 32.5cm).
£1,500–1,700
€/ $2,400–2,700 ⚒ S(Am)
This photograph is inscribed 'Audrey Hepburn's first published picture. Picked out from the chorus of the revue *Sauce* at the Cambridge Theatre 1951. One of my very few commercial jobs – The beauty which dares to come close'.

◄ **Herbert Ponting,** Captain Oates and ponies in the stable on the ship *Terra Nova*, gelatin silver contact print, 1911, 4 x 6in (10 x 15cm).
£450–500
€/ $700–800
⊞ RMe

Man Ray, 'Paddle Wheel of a Water Mill', silver print, mounted on card, undated, c1936, 3½ x 5½in (9 x 14cm).
£3,000–3,300
€/ $4,700–5,200 ⚒ S(P)

André Rogi (Rosa Klein), 'Portrait of Dora Maar', contemporary silver print, semi-matt, signed and dated 1941, 11½ x 9in (29 x 23cm).
£3,700–4,200
€/ $5,900–6,600 ⚒ S(P)

Southworth and Mawe's, 'Portrait of Robert Charles Winthrop', a daguerreotype, c1849, 6¼ x 4¾in (17 x 12cm)
£3,200–4,000
€/ $5,000–6,300 ⊞ HEG
Robert Charles Winthrop was the Speaker of the US House of Representatives, 1838–40.

Paul Strand, 'Portrait of a Farmer, Luzzara, Italy', mounted, 1953, 4½ x 6in (11.5 x 15cm).
£2,700–3,200
€/ $4,300–5,000 ⚒ S(NY)

Carleton E. Watkins, 'The best general view of the Yosemite Valley from the Mariposa Trail 6', albumen print, captioned and numbered on the original card mount, 1865–66, 15½ x 20½in (39.5 x 52cm).
£650–750
€/ $1,000–1,200 ⚒ B(WM)

Johan van der Keuken, 'Ile Saint Louis, Paris', silver print, mounted on card along the upper edge, photographer's stamp, Dutch, 1956, printed later, 11½ x 15½in (29 x 39.5cm).
£1,100–1,300
€/ $1,700–2,000 ⚒ S(Am)

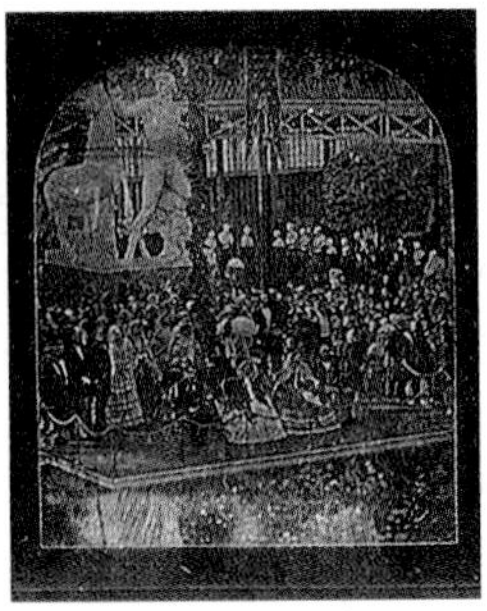

T. R. Williams (attributed), a stereo daguerreotype of Queen Victoria, Prince Albert, Emperor Napoleon III and Empress Eugenie on the podium during their visit to the Crystal Palace, 20 April 1855, on a black mount with gold lining, 3 x 4in (7.5 x 10cm).
£2,500–3,000
€/ $4,000–4,700 ⚒ B(WM)

Anon, 'Women from Sarawak', from an album of native people and views in Malaysia, Sarawak and Indonesia, albumen print, c1870, 12 x 15in (30.5 x 38cm).
£8,000–9,000 album
€/ $12,500–14,000 ⊞ RMe

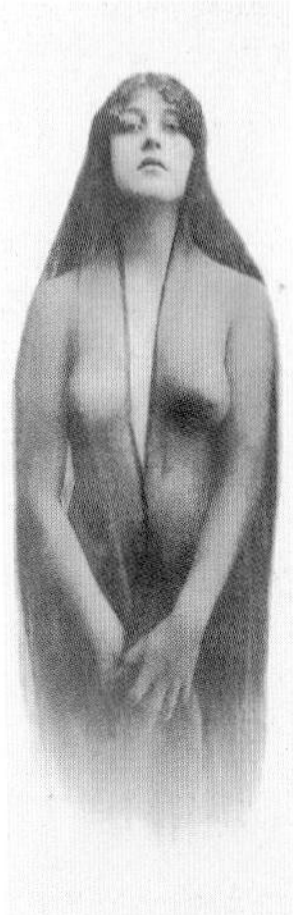

◄ **Mrs Wyatt Earp,** an anonymous photograph of her wearing a veil, c1860, 10 x 4in (25.5 x 10cm).
£3,000–3,500
€/ $4,700–5,500
⊞ ASP

◄ **Anon,** a mandarin's wife in court costume, 1870–80, 12 x 10in (30.5 x 25.5cm).
£650–800
€/ $1,000–1,300 ⊞ RMe

Arms & Armour

Armour

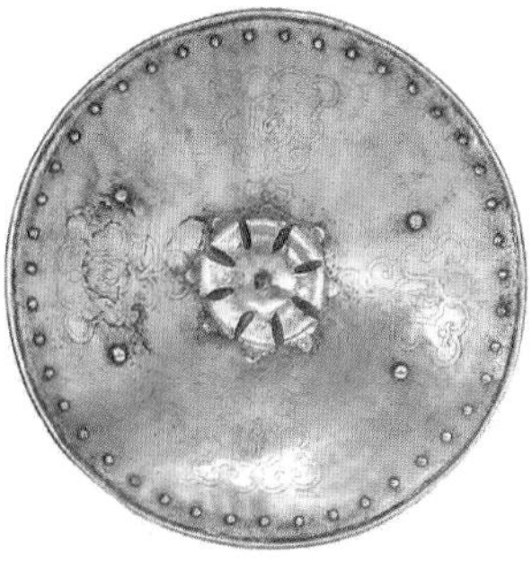

An iron shield, the perimeter with a row of some leather remaining, some rust and spot staining, Italian, c1550, 22in (56cm) diam.
£6,750–7,500
€/ $10,500–11,800 ⊞ FAC

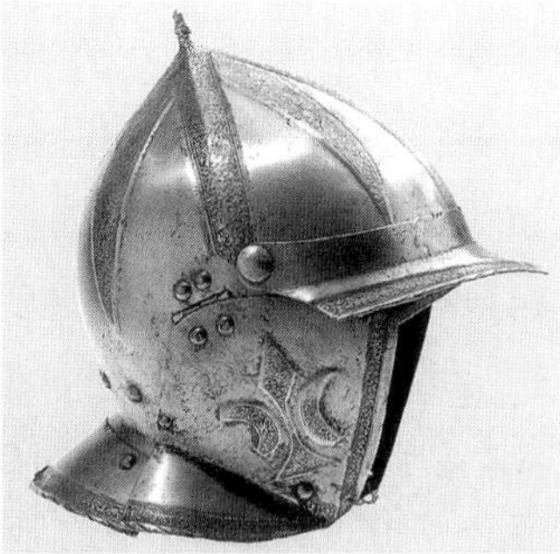

An iron helmet, with brass rivets, the hinged cheek flaps with fleur-de-lys decoration, German, Berlin, 1560–70, 10½in (26.5cm) high.
£3,000–3,500
€/ $4,800–5,400 ⚒ Herm

A morion, with a high comb, with all-over chased decoration, German, c1580, 11in (28cm) high.
£2,700–3,200
€/ $4,300–5,000 ⚒ Herm

► A close-helmet, Italian, possibly Milanese, late 16thC, 11½in (29cm) high.
£4,000–4,800
€/ $6,300–7,600
⚒ B(Kn)

A chainmail shirt, German, 16thC, 26¾in (68cm) long.
£1,600–2,000
€/ $2,500–3,200 ⚒ Herm

A composite full armour, partly Flemish, 16thC.
£7,600–9,200
€/ $12,000–14,500 ⚒ S(O)

◄ A cuirassier's helmet, with a lattice visor, German, 1610–20.
£7,700–8,500
€/ $12,200–13,400 ⊞ FAC

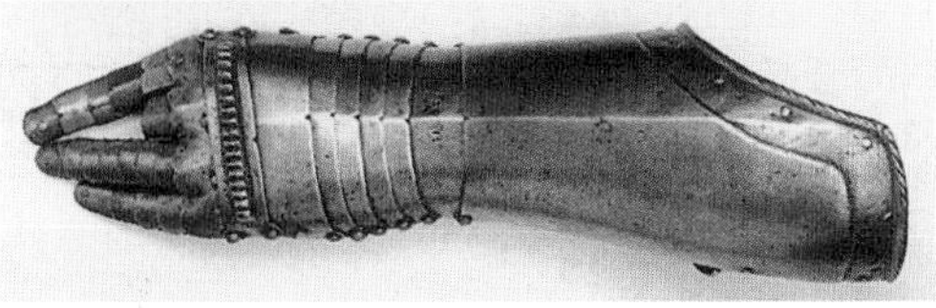

A bright steel bridle-gauntlet, most finger scales either missing or replaced, 1575–1625, 16½in (42cm) long.
£850–1,000
€/ $1,300–1,600 ⚒ B(Kn)

► A lobster-tail helmet, European, 17thC, 11in (28cm) high.
£1,000–1,100
€/ $1,600–1,700 ⊞ MDL

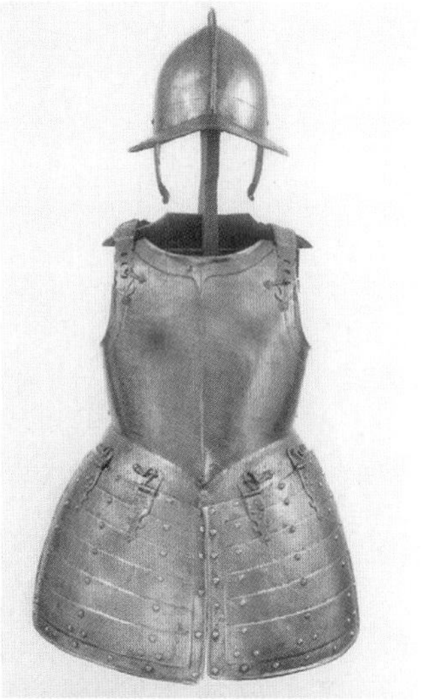

A pikeman's helmet, with moulded brim, nasal bar, plume holder missing, some damage, 17thC, 6in (15cm) high.
£220–250
€/ $350–400 F&C

◀ **A composite steel pikeman's armour,** rust-patinated and polished overall, c1650.
£3,800–4,500
€/ $6,000–7,100 B(Kn)

A black-and-white comb morion, one washer missing, German, 1600–25, 11½in (29cm) high.
£2,600–3,200
€/ $4,100–5,000 S(O)

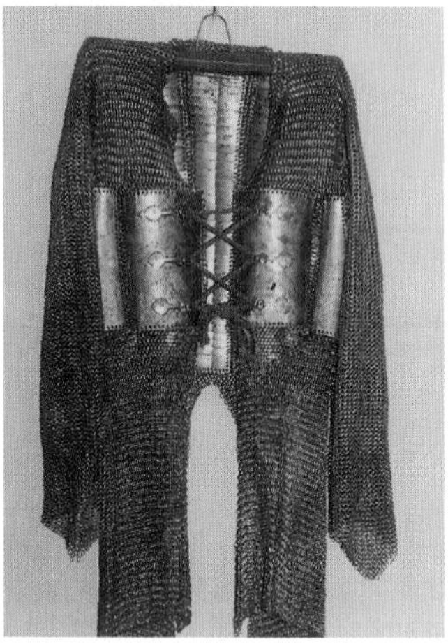

A chainmail shirt, Indian, c1700.
£1,000–1,200
€/ $1,600–1,900 ARB

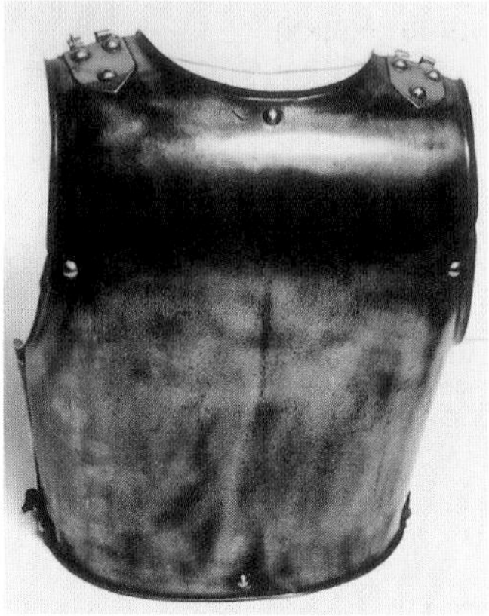

A steel and brass backplate, French, numbered and dated 1828, 16in (40.5cm) high.
£350–400
€/ $550–630 ARB

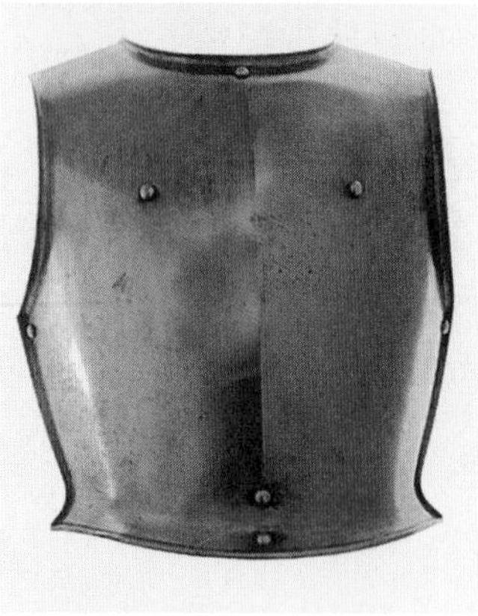

A breastplate, French, made in August, 1876.
£250–300
€/ $400–475 JDJ

Cannons

A bronze cannon barrel, decorated in relief with mouldings, with scroll lifting handles modelled as dolphins, on a later wheeled wooden stepped carriage, late 17thC, barrel 17½in (44.5cm) long.
£850–1,000
€/ $1,300–1,600 B(Kn)

LOCATE THE SOURCE
The source of each illustration in Miller's can be found by checking the code letters below each caption with the Key to Illustrations, pages 794–800.

A bronze signal cannon, on a stepped teak carriage with brass mounts, 1750–1800, barrel 21in (53.5cm) long.
£2,200–2,500
€/ $3,500–4,000 S(O)

▶ **A bronze miniature cannon,** in Flemish or German mid-16thC style, cast in relief, on a mahogany stepped carriage with quoin and four trucks, late 19th/early 20thC, barrel 16¼in (41.5cm) long.
£760–900
€/ $1,200–1,400 S(O)

A half-pounder bronze signal mortar, on a stepped wooden carriage with brass mounts, late 18thC, barrel 9in (23cm) long.
£2,200–2,600
€/ $3,500–4,100 S(O)

Edged Weapons

A left-hand dagger, with silver pellet inlay and a spirally-fluted wire-wrapped grip, c1590, 11in (28cm) long.
£5,800–6,500
€/ $9,200–10,200 ⊞ FAC

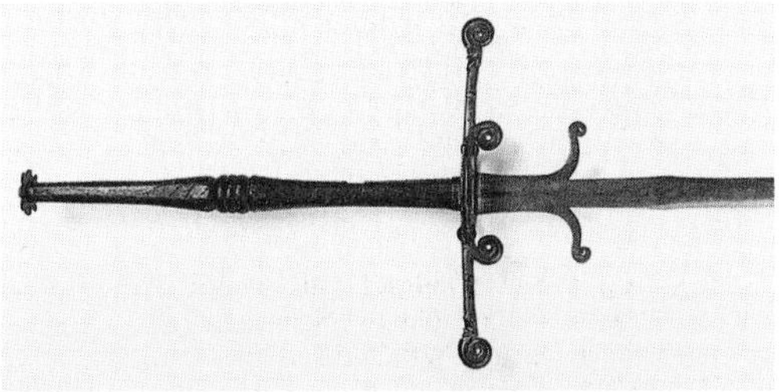

A two-hand processional sword, the iron hilt with incised decoration comprising side-rings each with stylized monsters' heads and a button terminal, the quillons each with a scroll beneath and a scrolled monster-head terminal, later star-shaped pommel and wooden grip, some worming and minor damage, cover missing, German, 1575–1625, blade 58in (147.5cm) long.
£2,200–2,500
€/ $3,500–4,000 B(Kn)

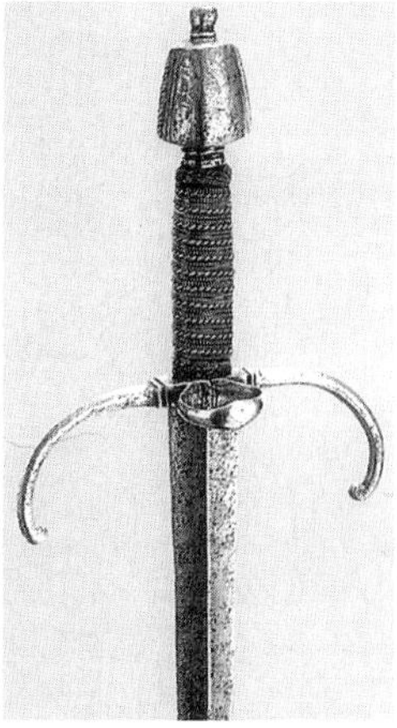

A left-hand dagger, with downswept quillon and iron blade, the hilt with a conical pommel, German, c1600, 19¾in (50cm) long.
£1,700–2,000
€/ $2,700–3,200 Herm

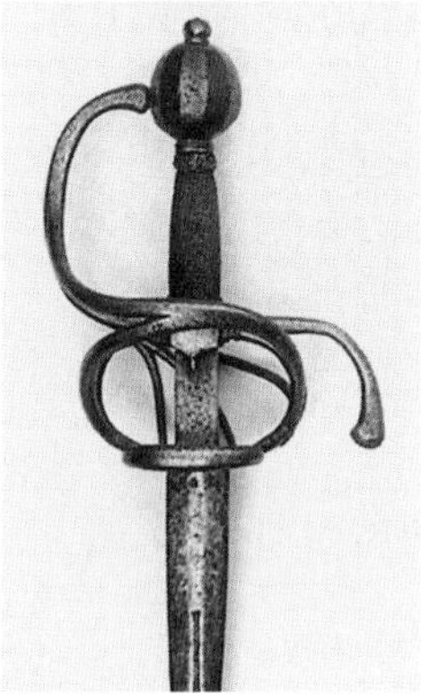

A swept-hilt rapier, stamped 'Tomas De Ayala' within the fuller, the grip later bound with twisted steel wire, early 17thC, blade 39¾in (101cm) long.
£1,700–2,000
€/ $2,700–3,200 B(Kn)

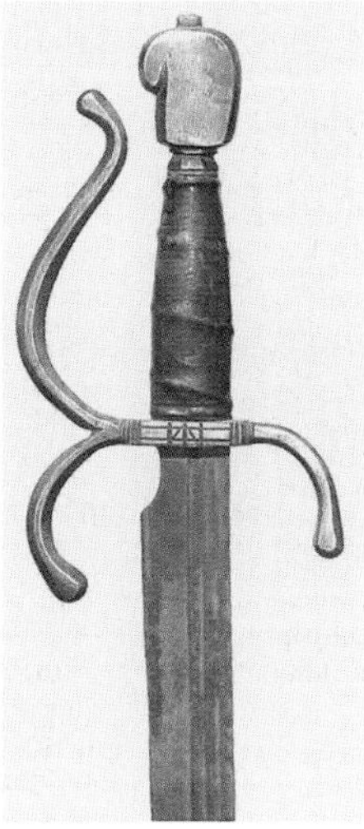

A falchion, with a curved blade, Italian, c1620, 31in (78.5cm) long.
£3,000–3,300
€/ $4,700–5,200 ⊞ FAC

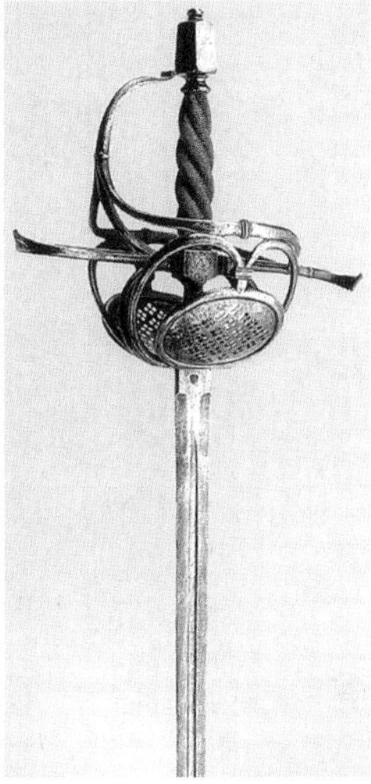

A stick rapier, by Johannes Hoppe, German, Solingen, c1630, 47¼in (120cm) long.
£2,800–3,200
€/ $4,500–5,000 Herm

A rapier, with a diamond section blade, the hilt with alternating pierced and solid panels, the quillons with curled ends, engraved pommel, the wood grip with Turks' heads, grip wire missing, c1630, blade 36¼in (92cm) long.
£1,400–1,600
€/ $2,200–2,500 B(L)

A rapier, the double-edged blade stamped with illegible letters, chiselled throughout with a foliage design, later grip, rust-patinated overall, c1640, blade 37in (94cm) long.
£1,700–2,000
€/ $2,700–3,200 B(Kn)

A dish-hilted rapier, signed 'Sahagom' in the central fuller, the hilt chased with leaves against a stippled ground, replacement grip, counter guard section missing, patinated overall, c1640, blade 38½in (98cm) long.
£1,400–1,700
€/ $2,200–2,700 B(L)

A transitional rapier, chiselled with stylized faces and foliage, the grip with copper wire binding, c1650, blade 31in (78.5cm) long.
£1,600–1,800
€/ $2,500–2,800 ⊞ ASB

A basket-hilted backsword, one bar from hilt missing, grip wire loose, worn overall, mid-17thC, blade 34¾in (88.5cm) long.
£1,000–1,200
€/ $1,600–1,900 B(L)

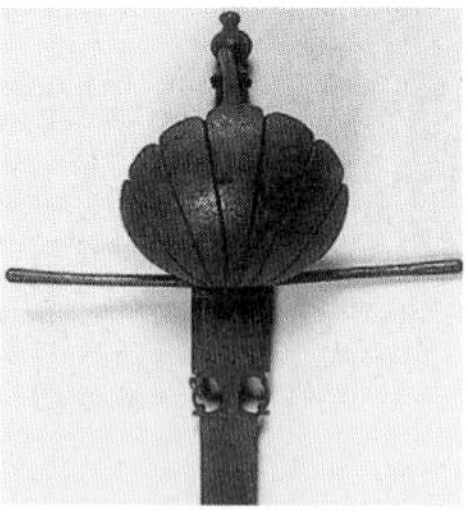

A left-hand dagger, the wood grip retaining one Turk's head, grip wire missing, rust patinated, possibly Italian, 17thC, blade 14½in (37cm) long.
£600–700
€/ $950–1,100 ⚒ B(L)

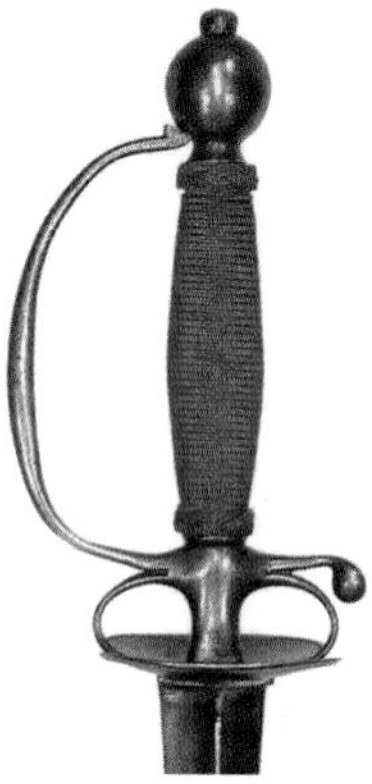

An iron-hilted smallsword, with plain knuckle bow and pommel, and brass wire-wrapped grip, c1740, blade 31¾in (80.5cm) long.
£750–825
€/ $1,200–1,300 ⊞ FAC

A smallsword, the iron hilt with a faceted stylized urn-shaped pommel, slight wear and oxidation, European, 1780–1800, blade 31¾in (80.5cm) long.
£600–650
€/ $950–1,000 ⊞ FAC

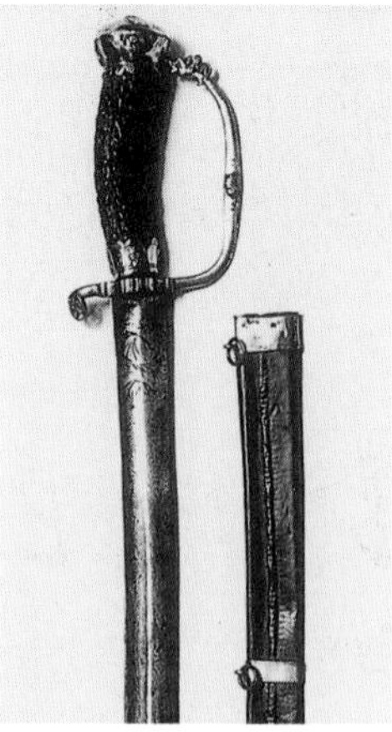

A silver-hilted hanger sword, with a stag horn grip, and running wolf blade, c1680, 26in (66cm) long.
£2,500–3,000
€/ $4,000–4,700 ⊞ ARB

A silver-gilt smallsword, with a hollow triangular blade, the hilt cast and chased with faceted beads, French, c1750, 31½in (80cm) long.
£2,200–2,500
€/ $3,500–4,000 ⊞ FAC

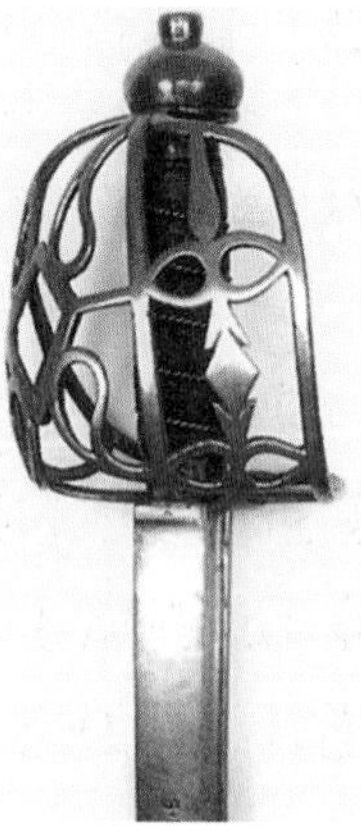

A hanger, the gilt-brass hilt with a sculpted shell guard and stipple chased foliage, with gold within the chiselling, with an ebony pistol grip and flattened diamond-section blade, European, c1680, blade 27¼in (69cm) long.
£900–1,000
€/ $1,400–1,600 ⊞ FAC

An infantry officer's sabre for Bern Canton, the brass hilt with a lion-head pommel, double shell guard and three bar guards, the curved blade partly etched with foliage, trophies of arms and a motto, Swiss, c1750, blade 28¼in (72cm) long.
£1,400–1,500
€/ $2,200–2,400 ⊞ FAC

A brass-hilted hanger, with a curved fullered blade, the two-piece grip cast with scrolls, strapwork and foliage terminating in a stylized lion-head pommel, some wear, pitting and repair, 1650–1700, blade 26½in (67.5cm) long.
£480–575
€/ $760–910 ⚒ B(Kn)

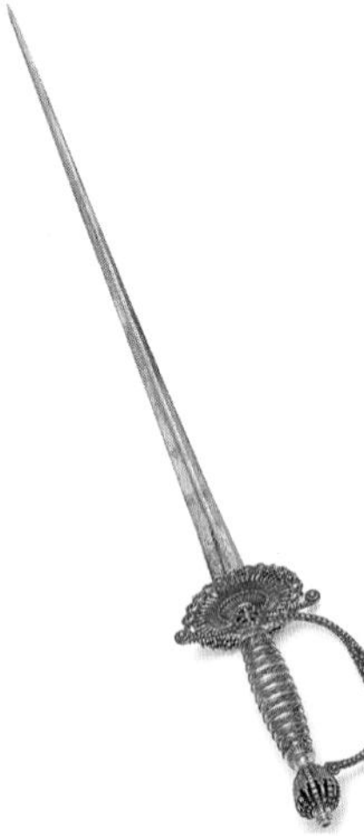

A silver-hilted smallsword, with an etched trefoil blade and detailed hilt, c1770, 88in (223.5cm) long.
£1,000–1,200
€/ $1,600–1,900 ⊞ MDL

◄ **A dragoon sabre,** stamped 'S. Harvey', the steel half-basket guard with diamond pattern, flattened bun pommel and brass wire-bound fishskin-covered grip, grip restored, blade reseated, mid-18thC, curved blade 30in (76cm) long.
£2,200–2,500
€/ $3,500–4,000 ⚒ WAL

A basket-hilted military backsword, wooden grip split, binding missing, some rust patination overall, Scottish, mid-18thC, blade 38½in (98cm) long.
£900–1,100
€/ $1,400–1,700 ⚒ B(Kn)

A hunting knife, with diamond-section damascus blade, the hilt with steeled blue mounts chiselled with gilt scrolling foliage, with a ribbed ivory grip, in a velvet-covered wood scabbard with decorated steel mounts, slight wear to mounts and velvet worn, probably Russian, late 18thC, blade 10¼in (26cm) long.
£700–800
€/ $1,100–1,300 ⚒ B(L)

ARMS & ARMOUR

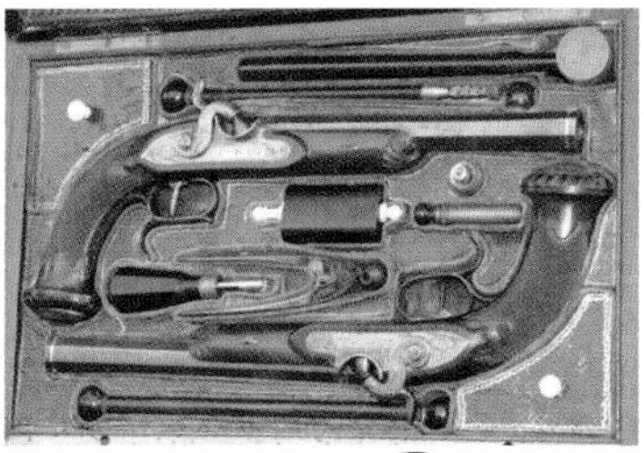

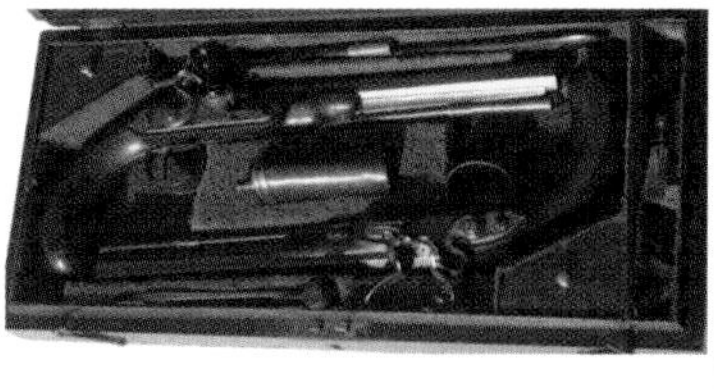

Garth Vincent

Antique Arms, Armour & Medals

LAPADA MEMBER

THE GUN TRADE ASSOCIATION

I have customers worldwide and I am interested in purchasing single items or complete collections, advice freely given

Dealer in antique and reproduction arms and armour for the collector, investor and interior decorator

Commission buying at auction

Access & Visa accepted

Brochure available

The Old Manor House
Allington, Nr Grantham
Lincolnshire NG32 2DH
Telephone: 01400 281358
Fax: 01400 282658
Mobile: 07785 352151

Email: garthvincent@aol.com
Website: http://www.guns.uk.com

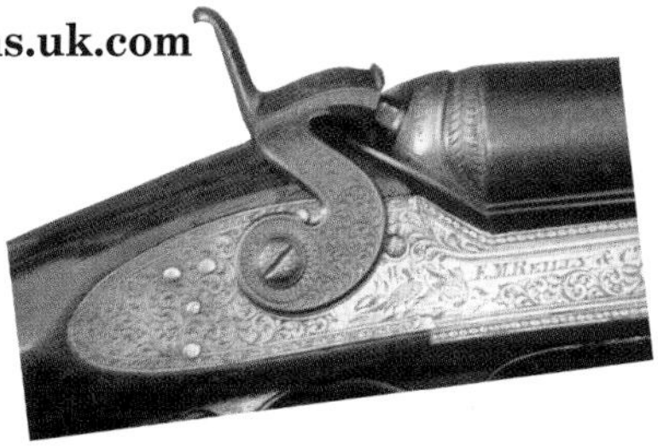

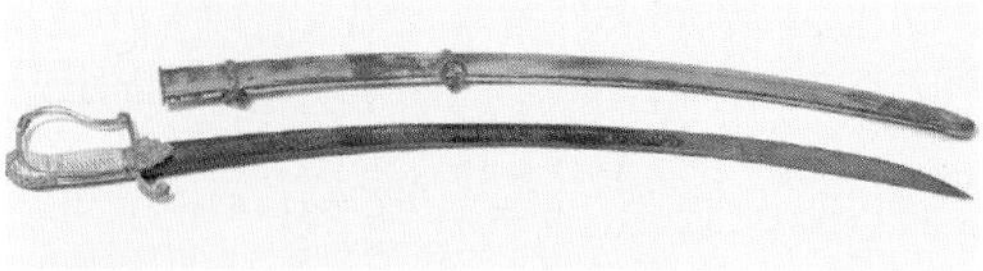

An officer's horseman's sword, with carved ivory grip, gilt stirrup hilt with lion-head pommel, the blade engraved with blue and gilt decoration, the gilt scabbard engraved with a leaf design, American, c1800, 36in (91.5cm) long.
£2,200–2,500
€/ $3,500–4,000 ⊞ MDL

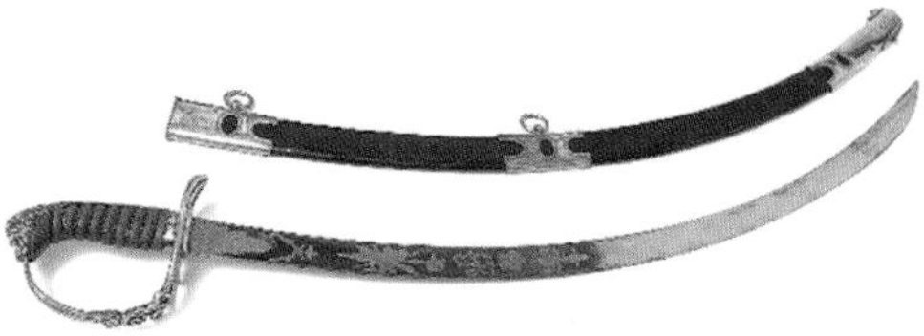

A cavalry sabre, with lion-head pommel and brass hilt, the damascas-etched blade with a leather scabbard, c1800, 41in (104cm) long.
£1,500–1,700
€/ $2,400–2,700 ⊞ MDL

An 1803 pattern officer's light infantry blue and gilt sword, early 19thC, 34in (86.5cm) long.
£1,100–1,200
€/ $1,700–1,900 ⊞ MDL

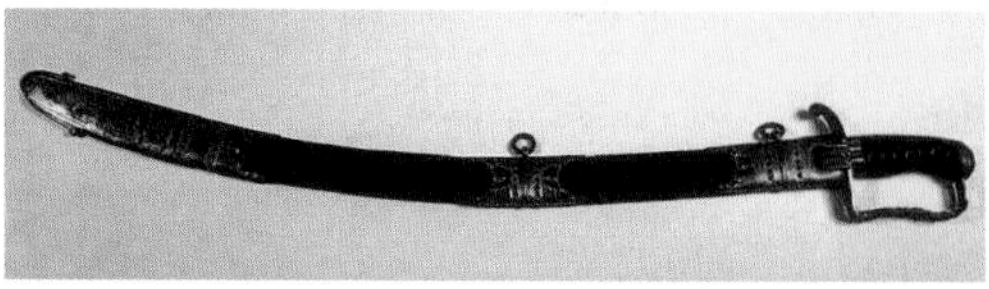

A gilt-mounted cavalry sabre, by Brunn, the blade engraved and gilded, the gilt-brass stirrup hilt engraved, with pierced knucklebow, the leather scabbard with engraved and pierced brass mounts, c1800, 37in (94cm) long.
£2,000–2,300
€/ $3,200–3,600 ⊞ WSA

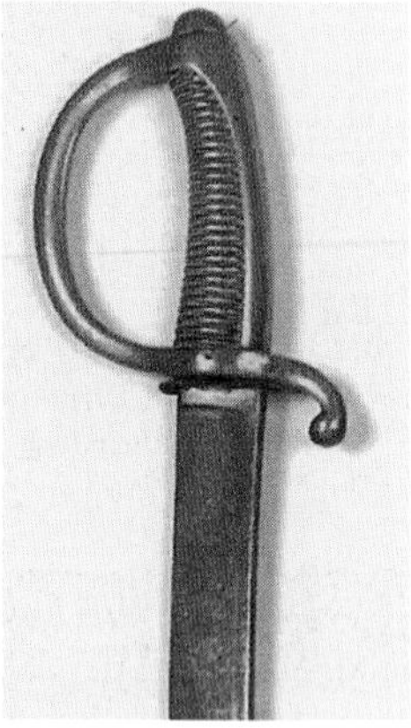

A Model AN XI infantryman's shortsword briquet, with regulation one-piece brass stirrup hilt, associated brass-mounted leather scabbard, some wear, French, 1802–03, blade 23¼in (59cm) long.
£100–120
€/ $160–190 ⚒ WAL

A grenadier guard's hanger, the blade with regimental markings at the forte, the brass hilt with a D-form guard and ribbed grip, some staining, c1838, blade 20¾in (52.5cm) long.
£560–625
€/ $900–1,000 ⊞ FAC

A cavalry trooper's sword, the hilt with remains of original blackened finish, the grip wrap and covering complete, c1843, blade 35½in (90cm) long.
£280–325
€/ $440–520 ⊞ FAC

A King Ludwig Ist civil servant's sword, by Stroblberger, Munich, with finely-gilded blade, German, mid-19thC, blade 34¾in (88.5cm) long.
£700–800
€/ $1,100–1,300 ⚒ Herm

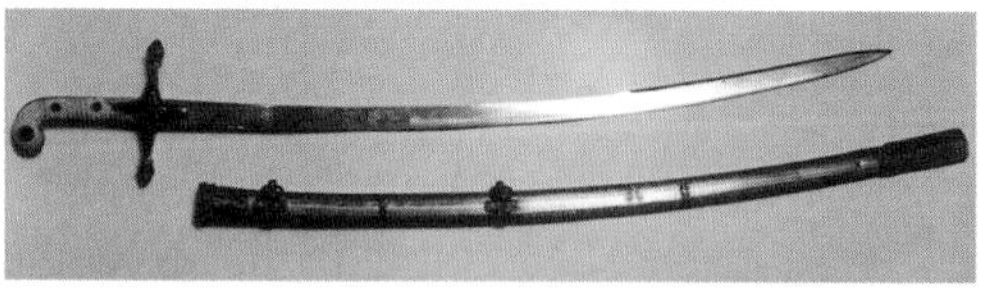

A 15th Hussars officer's sword, with gilt-brass cross quillon, ivory handle and gilt-brass scabbard, c1860, 36in (91.5cm) long.
£1,350–1,500
€/ $2,000–2,400 ⊞ ARB

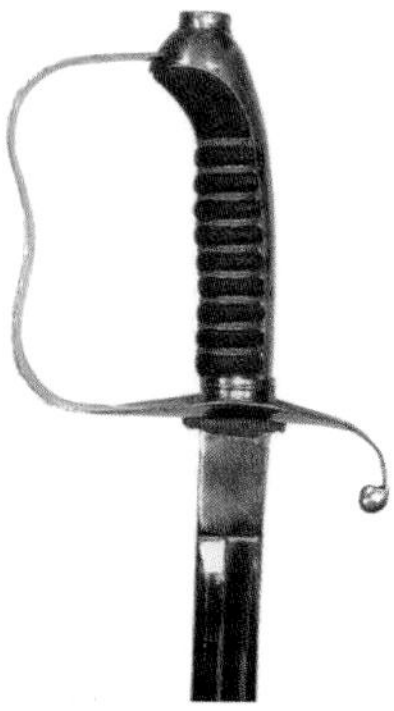

► An infantry officer's sabre, Wagner No. 150, by Weyersberg & Co, Solingen, with curved broad fullered blade, wire-wrapped sharkskin-covered grip, plated hilt, blade and scabbard, minor discolouration, Austrian, c1861, blade 32¼in (82cm) long.
£475–525
€/ $750–830 ⊞ FAC

◄ An assembled Confederate presentation sword, by Millar, Dayville, New York, the double fuller sword with dog-head pommel, iron scabbard with brass mountings and presentation inscription, slight rust, American, c1862, blade 35in (89cm) long.
£700–800
€/ $1,100–1,300 ⚒ JDJ

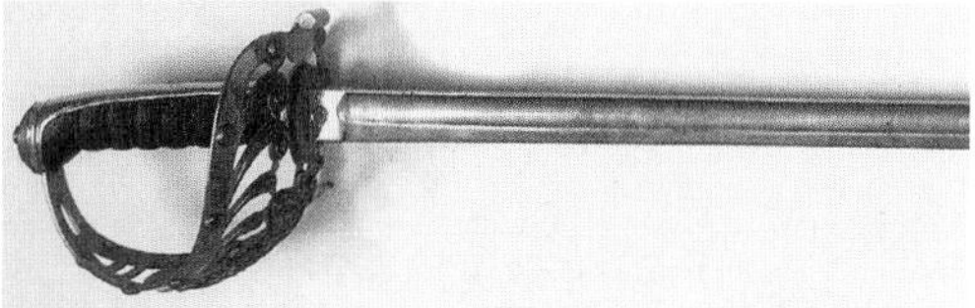

An 1834 pattern 1st life guard's NCO's dress and undress sword, No. 13748, the pierced guard applied with a brass-crowned regimental device, scrolls and border studs, plated gripstrap, stepped brass pommel and wire-bound fishskin grip, c1865, the Wilkinson blade 39in (99cm) long.
£900–1,100
€/ $1,400–1,700 ⚒ WAL

A dirk, the straight blade decorated with a coat-of-arms, flowers and Latin inscription, the finely-carved ebony and gilt handle engraved with a reciprocal coat-of-arms, Scottish, c1874, 18½in (47cm) long.
£1,200–1,400
€/ $1,900–2,200 ⚒ Herm

A staff and field officer's sword, by Schuyler, Hartley & Graham, New York, with diamond-section double-edged blade, the guard cast with an applied sterling silver spread-winged eagle and shield beneath an American flag, the tortoiseshell-bound grip with a triple-wire wrap, the silver-plated iron scabbard with engraved brass furniture, minor losses to grip wire, hilt loose, American, 1865–75, blade 31½in (80cm) long.
£1,300–1,500
€/ $2,000–2,400 ⚒ JDJ

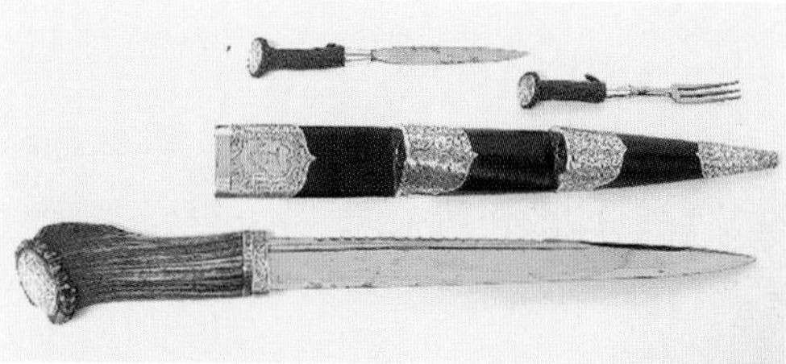

A silver-mounted dirk, with the owner's crest, the stag-horn grip with floral-engraved mounts, the scabbard with companion knife and fork, all mounted *en suite* with silver mounts, Scottish, c1880, blade 10½in (26.5cm) long.
£1,100–1,200
€/ $1,700–1,800 ⊞ MDL

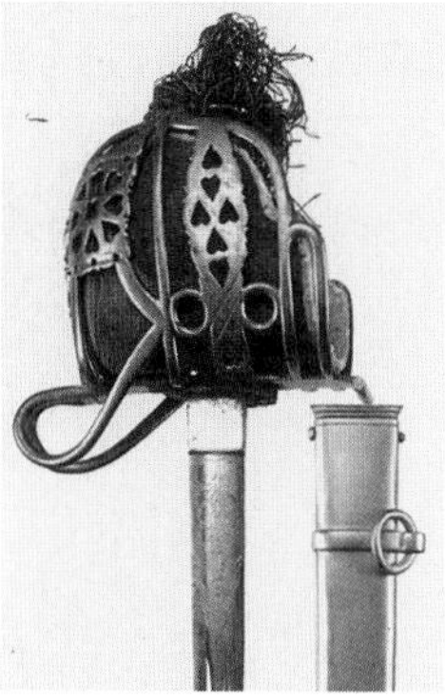

A Victorian Highland officer's basket-hilted broadsword, with etched blade, original liner and silk tassel, in associated nickel-plated scabbard, blade 31½in (80cm) long.
£700–800
€/ $1,100–1,300 ⚒ S(O)

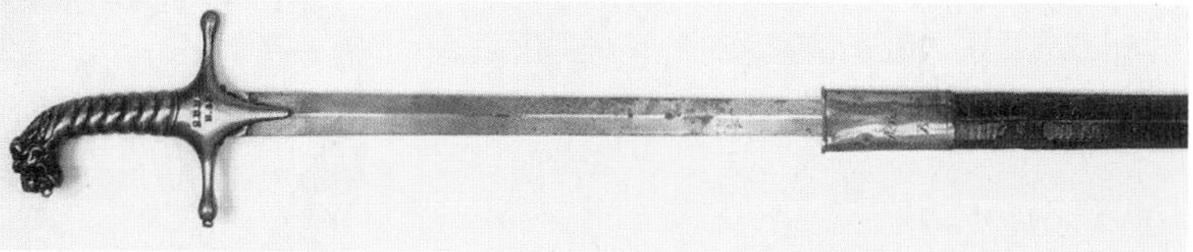

A Victorian bandsman's sword, of the Royal Bucks Militia Band, the one-piece brass hilt stamped 'RBM B18' on both sides, the spiral grip with lion-head pommel, the leather scabbard with engraved locket, minor rust stains, knucklechain and chape missing, leather worn and shortened, blade 24¾in (63cm) long.
£130–150
€/ $210–240 ⚒ WAL

A Venezuelan officer's Prussian model 1889 pattern sword, the gilt-brass hilt with the arms of Venezuela flanked by foliage, over a motto ribbon and cornucopia above, the grip with a 'R de V' monogram, German, dated 1900, blade 31¼in (79.5cm) long.
£500–550
€/ $800–870 ⊞ FAC

An infantry officer's Prussian model 1889 pattern presentation sword, the damascus blade etched with scrollwork, the outer face with presentation inscription, the hilt inscribed '1893–1911', in original blackened steel scabbard, German, c1911, blade 31½in (80cm) long.
£770–850
€/ $1,200–1,400 ⚒ S(O)

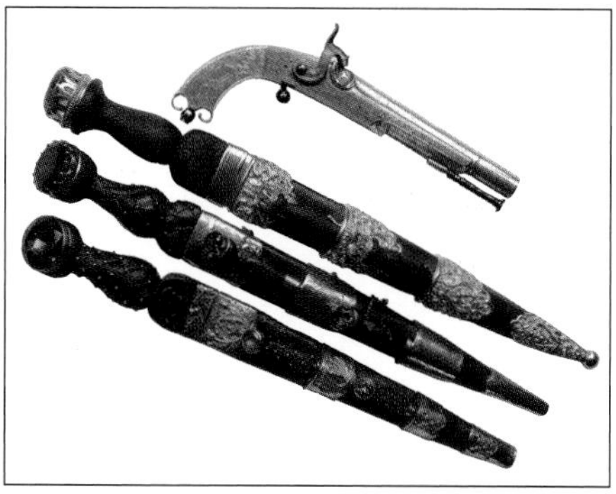

Firearms

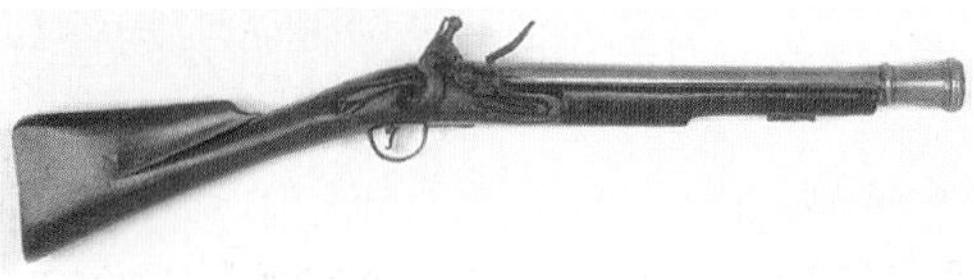

A flintlock blunderbuss, with London proof marks, rounded Brown Bess-style military lock with swan-neck cock, walnut full stock, brass mounts, ramrod missing, minor damage, c1770, 34in (86.5cm) long.
£1,200–1,400
€/ $1,900–2,200 WAL

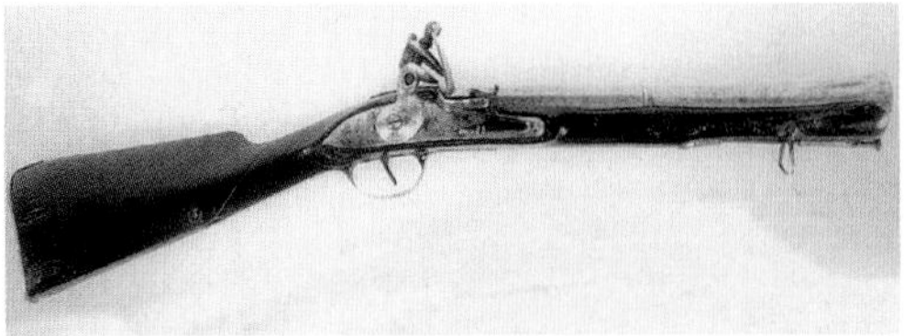

A George III flintlock blunderbuss, with brass-edge mahogany stock and steel tower lock, 28in (71cm) long.
£800–950
€/ $1,300–1,500 LVS

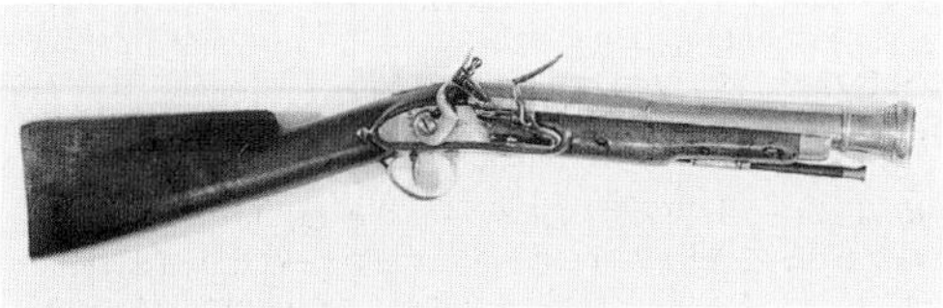

A brass-barrelled flintlock blunderbuss, with walnut stock, inscribed 'Rigby, Dublin', nickel-plated steel action, brass rounded trigger guard fore end and butt plate, Irish, 19thC, 30in (76cm) long.
£1,500–1,800
€/ $2,400–2,800 AH

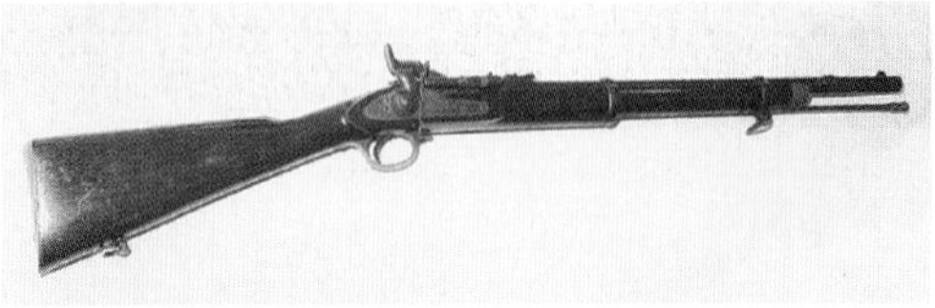

A .577 Snider 2 band Mk III artillery carbine, by BSA, full military marks, 1866, 40in (101.5cm) long.
£1,600–1,800
€/ $2,500–2,800 SPA

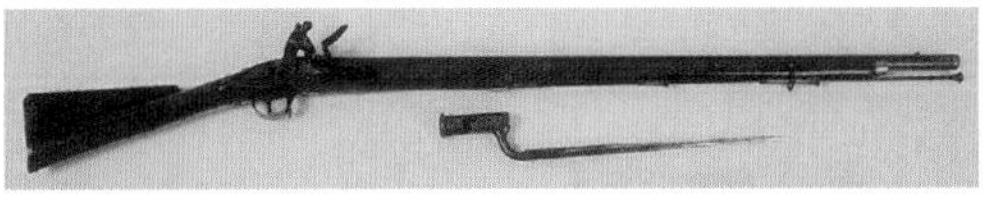

A .75 calibre Indian pattern Brown Bess flintlock musket with bayonet, 1809 reinforced lock, bayonet marked Osborn & Grundy, introduced 1797, barrel 39in (99cm) long.
£1,100–1,300
€/ $1,700–2,000 BWL

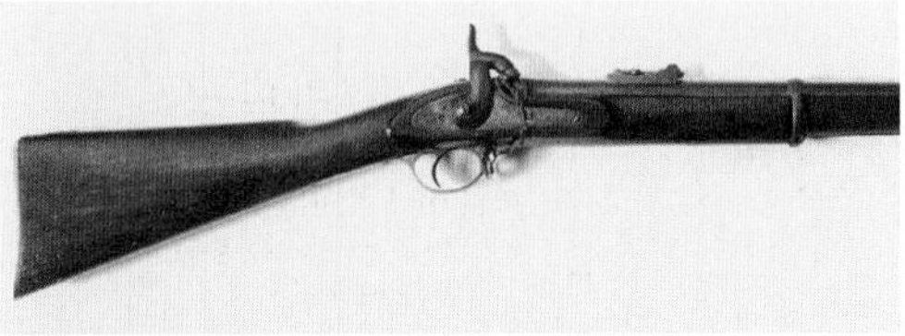

A .577 calibre 1853 pattern fourth model percussion rifled musket, the sighted barrel with three bands, calibrated folding adjustable back-sight, dated lock stamped 'Tower', steel ramrod, dated 1868, barrel 39¼in (99cm) long.
£660–800
€/ $1,000–1,300 B(Kn)

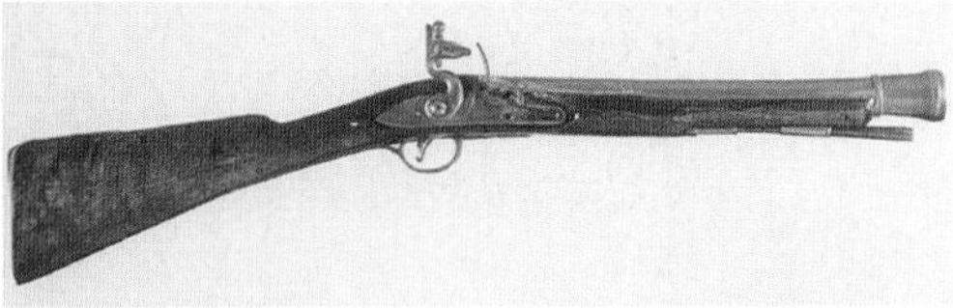

A flintlock blunderbuss, by Steele, with figured-walnut full stock, three-stage brass barrel, signed lock engraved with foliage, full brass mounts, original brass-tipped wooden ramrod, lock spring replaced, c1780, 29½in (75cm) long.
£1,300–1,500
€/ $2,000–2,400 S(O)

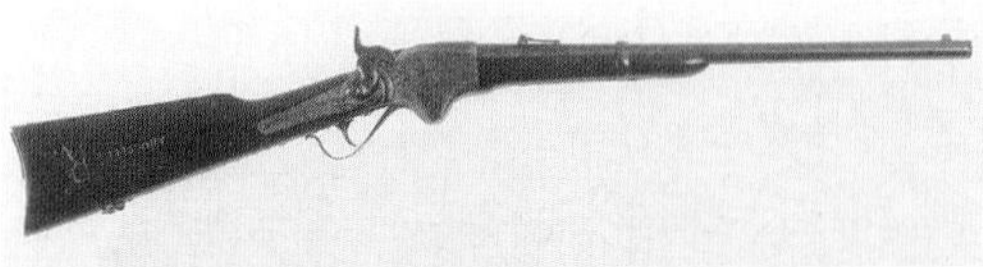

A Spencer Civil War repeating carbine, square base front sight and ladder rear sight, top of receiver marked, inspector's marks, stamped 'J. Russell' to buttstock, 19thC, barrel 21in (53.5cm) long.
£1,400–1,600
€/ $2,200–2,600 JDJ

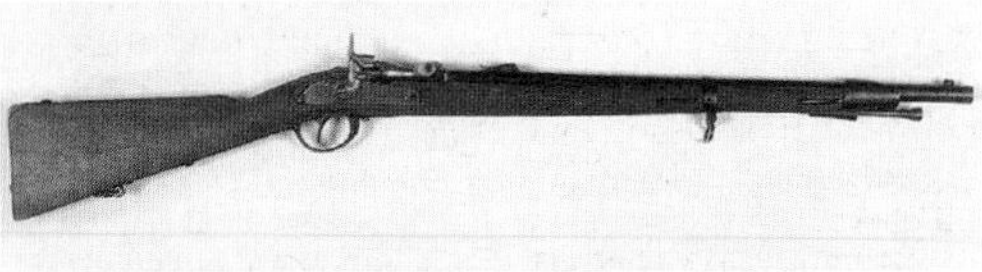

A Wanzl hinged breech SS military carbine, the full stock with steel mounts, sling swivels, breech tang stamped 'W. Mashek', plain lock stamped '863', Austrian, 1863, barrel 23¾in (60.5cm) long.
£300–360
€/ $475–570 WAL

► **A Derringer-style six-shot pin fire pepperbox pistol,** with wooden grips, folding trigger and side gate, Continental, 19thC, 5in (12.5cm) long.
£270–300
€/ $430–470
MDL

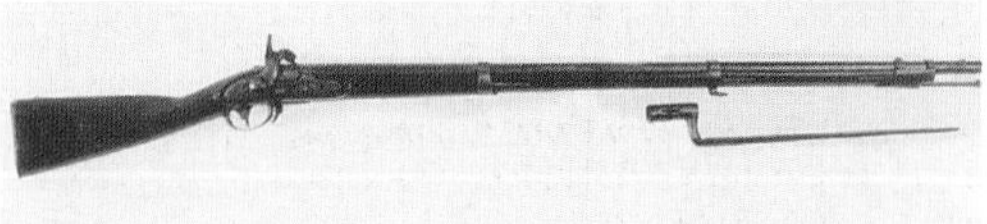

A .69 calibre Pomeroy model 1821 converted musket with bayonet, Belgian-style conversion with cone in barrel, issue marks '3-F' painted on stock, lockplate and barrel tang dated 1822, barrel 42in (106.5cm) long.
£360–430
€/ $575–675 JDJ

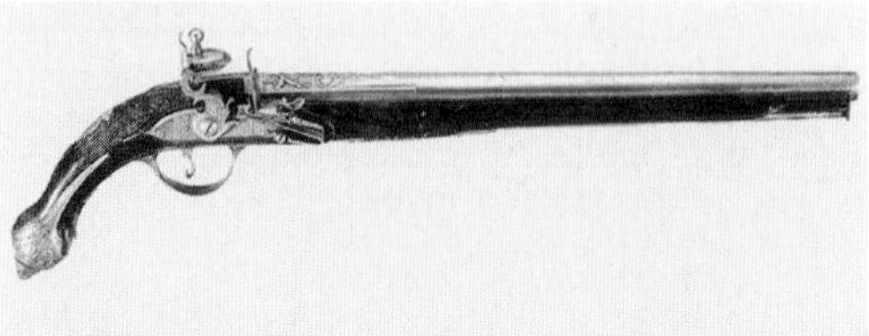

A flintlock pistol, with floral-carved wooden stock and engraved iron mounts, iron ramrod, engraved lock with signature 'P. Alberti', marked 'L.LA-Zarino', probably for export to eastern Europe, fore end and butt restored, Italian, 1720–30, 19¼in (49cm) long.
£1,000–1,200
€/ $1,600–1,900 Herm

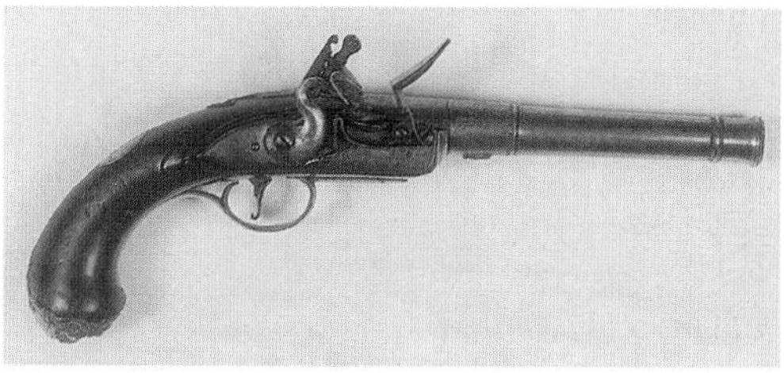

A flintlock cannon-barrelled pistol, by W. Turvey, London, the three-stage turn-off barrel with ringed muzzle, signed breech, replacement cock, c1740, barrel 5¼in (13.5cm) long.
£900–1,100
€/ $1,400–1,700 ⚒ B(L)

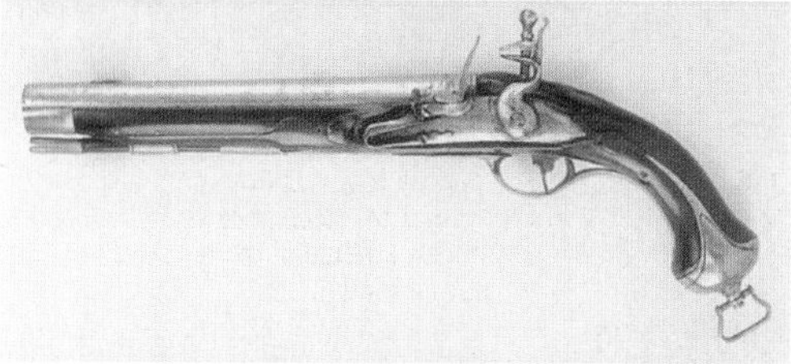

A .700 calibre Saxon regulation flintlock cavalry pistol, with moulded walnut full stock and regulation brass mounts, the sighted barrel struck with 'SS' mark on the tang, left-hand lock, ramrod pipes and ramrod replacement repairs, 1760–70, 17¼in (44cm) long.
£850–950
€/ $1,300–1,500 ⚒ S(O)

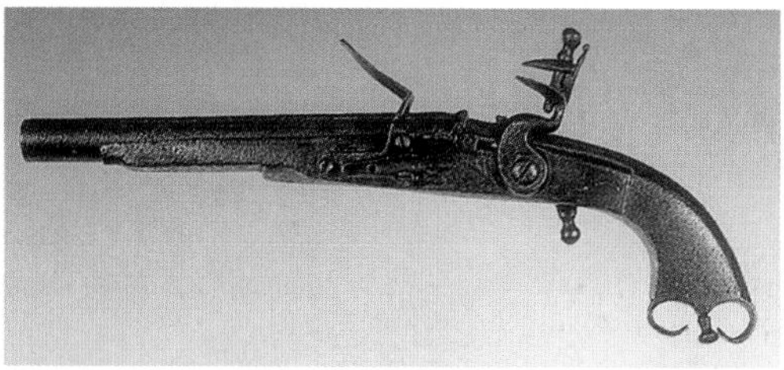

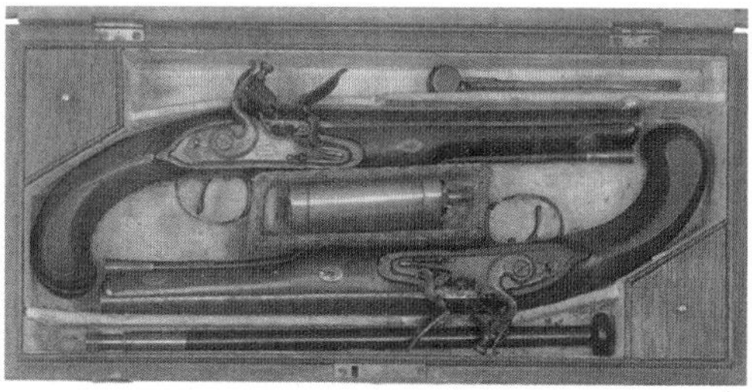

A pair of 24 bore flintlock duelling pistols, by Bennett, London, the walnut full stocks with chequered butts and ribbed finials, steel mounts including engraved French-style trigger guards with pineapple finials and single set triggers, maker's proof marks, c1795, 15in (38cm) long, cased.
£1,800–2,200
€/ $2,800–3,500 ⚒ WAL

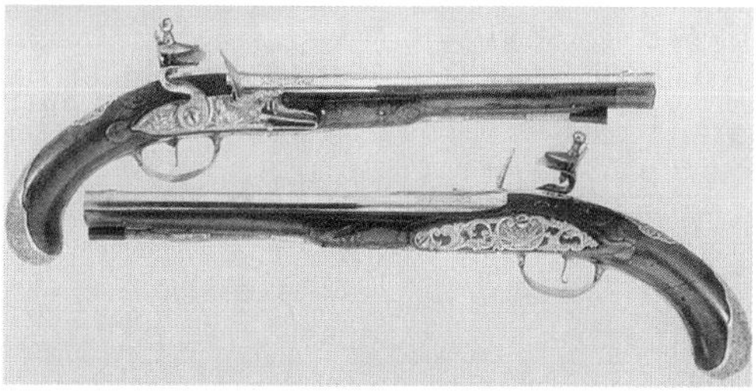

A pair of flintlock pistols, the walnut stock with floral carving, pierced brass mounts in relief, struck mark 'ZK' underneath, 'MW' to the side, minor restoration, German, Suhl, mid-18thC, 18¼in (46.5cm) long.
£1,700–2,000
€/ $2,700–3,200 ⚒ Herm

A pair of silver-mounted and engraved Queen Anne-style flintlock carriage pistols, by Delany, with London proofs and foreigner's mark, the figured-walnut butts with silver wire inlay and carved with rocailles, silver furniture, signed, c1740, 12½in (32cm) long.
£3,400–3,800
€/ $5,400–6,000 ⊞ WSA

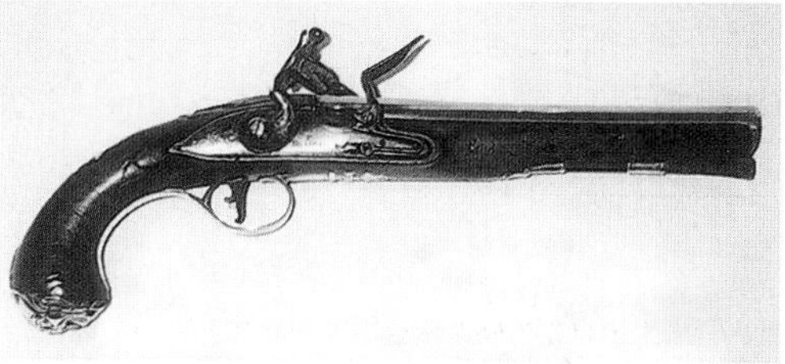

A pair of silver-mounted brass barrel holster pistols, by Bradley, Liverpool, with Birmingham proofs, the walnut full stocks with cast and engraved silver mounts, c1765, barrels 8¼in (21cm) long.
£5,000–5,500
€/ $7,900–8,700 ⊞ WSA

◄ **A steel flintlock belt pistol,** the lock with traces of foliate engraving, the stock with ram's-horn butt, ball trigger, part of belt hook missing, action faulty, Scottish, c1780, barrel 7¾in (19.5cm) long.
£550–625
€/ $870–990 ⚒ B(Ed)

A percussion travelling pistol, the walnut full stock relief-carved with scrolls, the two-stage barrel with beaded mouldings, inlaid with silver scrolling tendrils, rebuilt from miquelet-lock, later ramrod, Spanish, late 18thC, 7in (18cm) long.
£700–850
€/ $1,100–1,300 S(O)

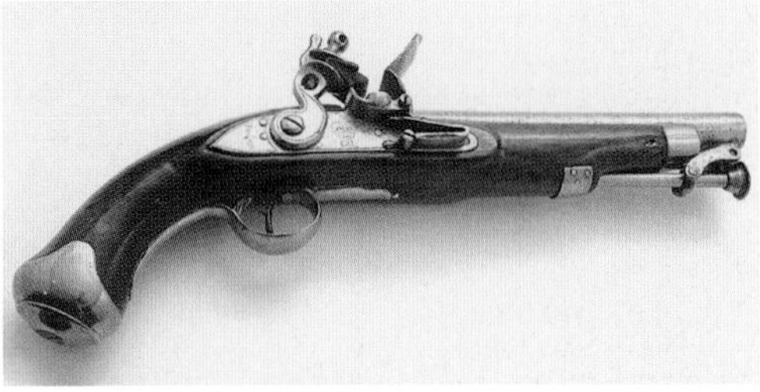

A Newland patent flintlock pistol, with brass plate to reinforce throat, swivel ramrod, c1800, 15in (38cm) long.
£800–900
€/ $1,200–1,400 ⊞ SPA

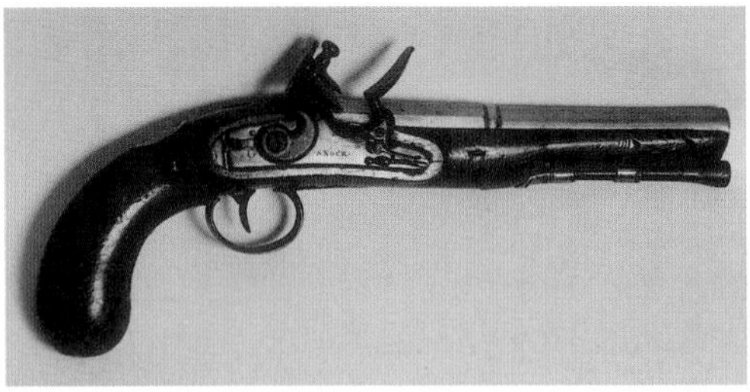

A flintlock pistol, by S. Nock, with walnut full stock and brass barrel, c1800, 13½in (34.5cm) long.
£1,300–1,500
€/ $2,100–2,400 ⊞ ARB

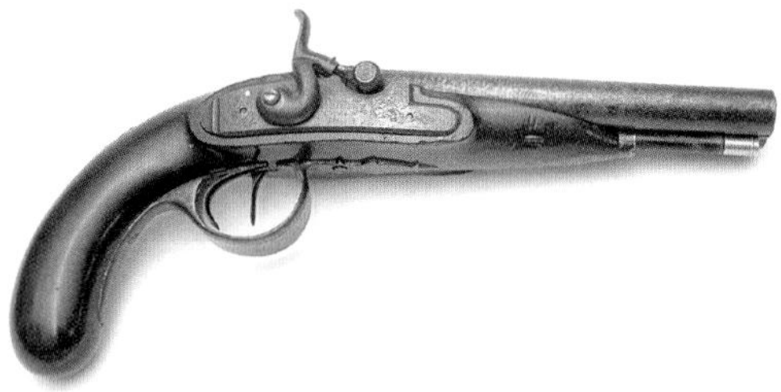

A double-barrel pistol, by Leech, with steel mounts, percussion lock and mahogany stock, early 19thC.
£420–500
€/ $660–790 G(L)

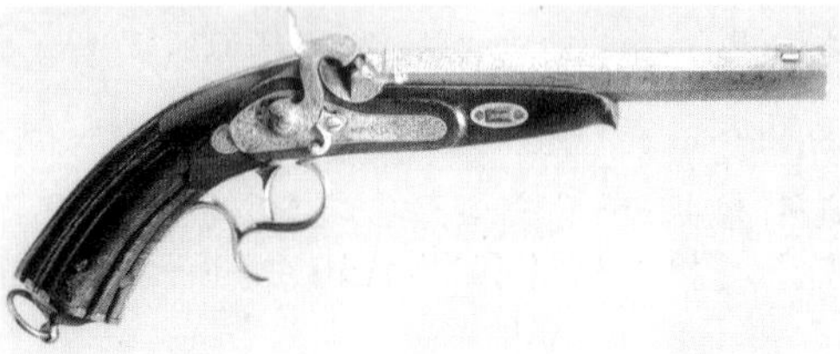

A pair of percussion pistols, by C. Freyer, Dresden, with walnut full stock and iron mounts, German, 1820–30, 15in (38cm) long.
£1,300–1,500
€/ $2,000–2,400 Herm

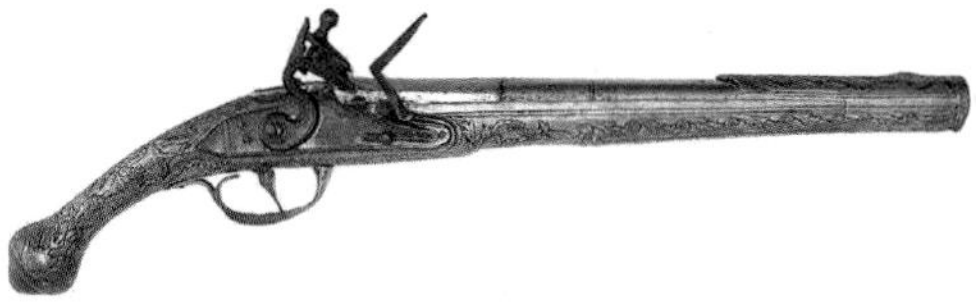

A flintlock pistol, relief-decorated in niello with military trophies, foliage and rococo moulding, Montenegrin, 18th–19thC, 15in (38cm) long.
£3,200–3,500
€/ $5,000–5,500 ⊞ FAC

A 16 bore officer's flintlock holster pistol, by Prosser, London, the walnut full stock with chequered butt, steel mounts including engraved trigger guard with pineapple finial, swivel ramrod, c1800, 15in (38cm) long.
£850–1,000
€/ $1,300–1,600 WAL

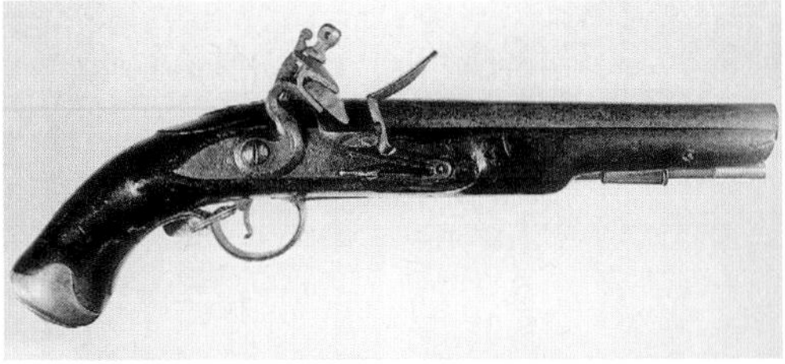

A 16 bore flintlock Light Dragoon holster pistol, with walnut full stock, the barrel with tower proofs, regulation brass furniture, lock marked crown, GR cypher and 'T. Richards', with later ramrod, full stock cracked, c1800, 9in (23cm) long.
£360–440
€/ $560–700 WD

A pocket percussion pistol, with walnut stock engraved 'Jackson, London' and stamped 'W. P.', early 19thC, 5¾in (14.5cm) long.
£250–300
€/ $400–475 SWO

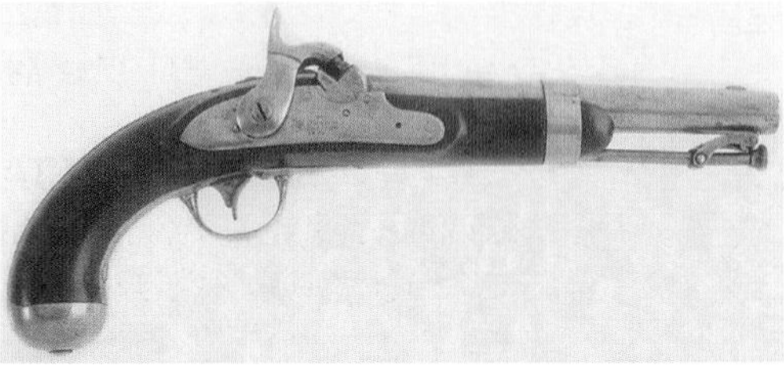

A .54 calibre converted Johnson 1836 model martial pistol, hammer screw replaced, the lock dated 1836, barrel 8½in (21.5cm) long.
£900–1,000
€/ $1,400–1,600 JDJ

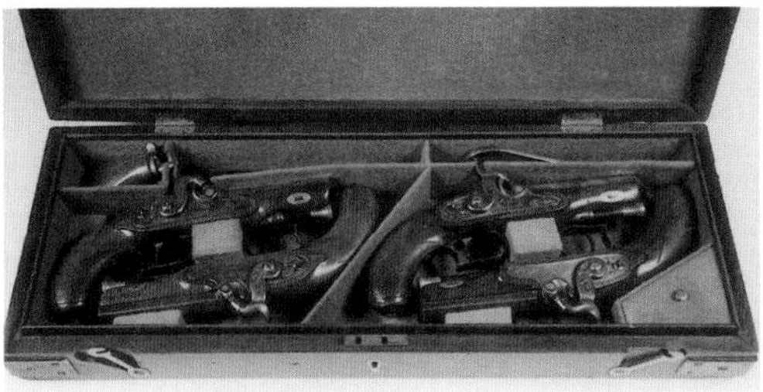

A set of four bank pistols, with walnut full stocks, the twist barrels signed 'London', the engraved sidelocks signed 'Rimmer', engraved steel furniture, brass-tipped ramrods, c1840, barrels 4in (10cm) long, in a relined case with accessories.
£4,300–4,800
€/ $6,800–7,600 ⊞ WSA

A knife pistol, the octagonal barrel with percussion nipple, slab horn sides, two knife blades and folding trigger, Continental, c1850, 7in (18cm) long, with leather holster.
£560–625
€/ $870–985 ⊞ MDL

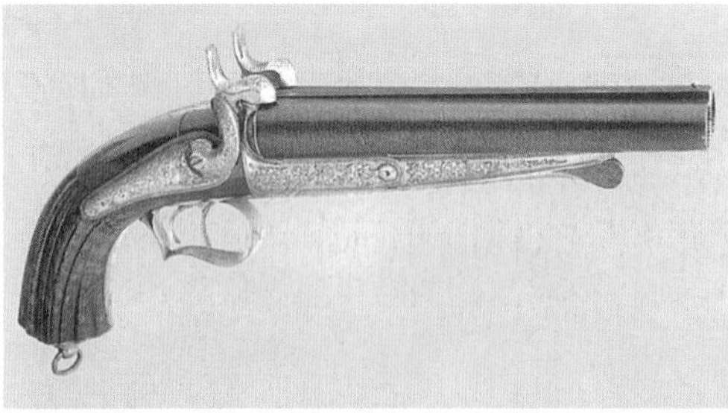

A pair of double-barrelled pistols, by F. P. Gastinne-Renette, with walnut grip, engraved iron butt cap and lock plates, underlever breakdown action, signed, French, Paris, c1860, 14in (35.5cm) long.
£2,400–2,800
€/ $3,800–4,400 ⚒ Herm
F. P. Gastinne-Renette was court gunmaker to the King of Spain and Napoleon II of France.

A palm pistol, by Chicago Firearms Co, American, c1870, 5in (12.5cm) long.
£800–900
€/ $1,200–1,400 ⊞ MDL

► **A Colt Navy revolver,** c1855, in a box 15in (38cm) wide.
£6,300–7,000
€/ $10,000–11,000 ⊞ WSA

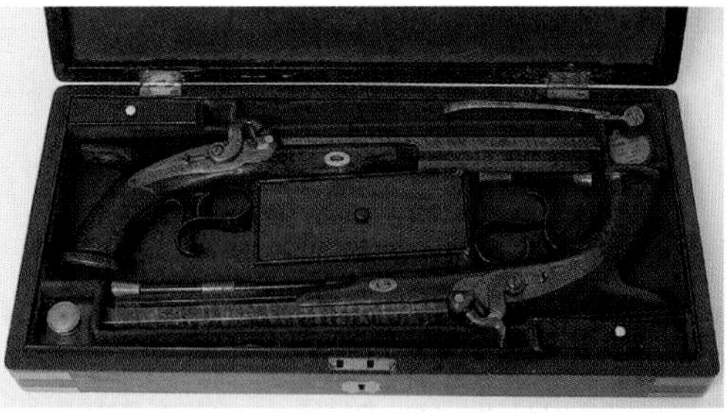

A pair of saw-handle percussion pistols, by Cole, the octagonal-twist barrels engraved 'Belfast', stocks with saw grip and horn fore end, brass-tipped ebony ramrods with embossed three-way flask, bullet mould, oil bottle and cap tin, c1850, in a brass-bound case 19in (48.5cm) wide.
£3,900–4,300
€/ $6,200–6,800 ⊞ MDL

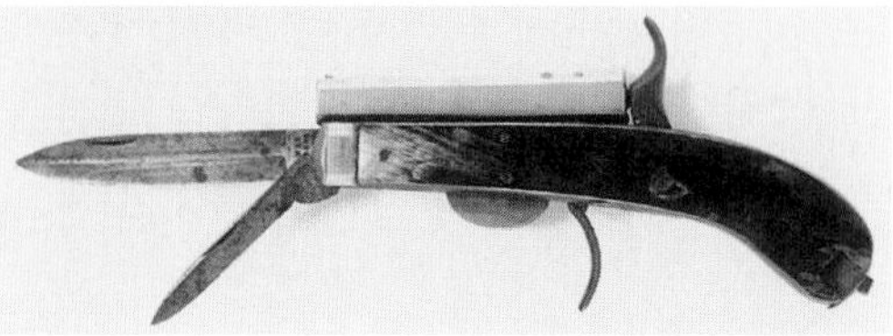

A Roger's patent percussion knife pistol, with Birmingham proof marks and German silver barrel, the butt with hinged German silver trap, folding trigger and two folding knife blades, one signed 'James Rogers', bullet mould and another accessory missing, mid-19thC, 6¾in (17cm) long.
£450–500
€/ $700–790 ⚒ S(O)

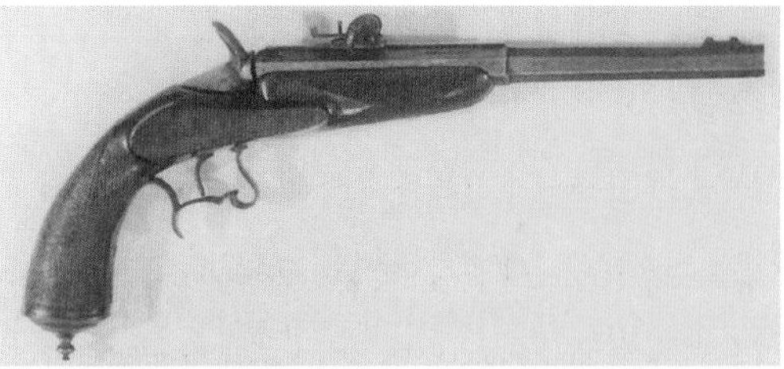

A percussion salon pistol, with chequered walnut stock and grip with baluster-turned end cap, octagonal barrel, quadrant rear sight on a graduated dovetailed rail, shaped grip trigger guard, Belgian, 19thC, 17¾in (45cm) long.
£200–240
€/ $315–380 ⚒ AH

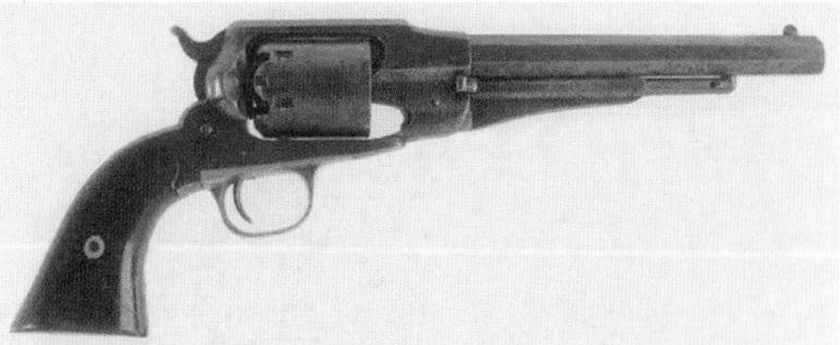

A .44 calibre Remington model 1858 New Model army revolver, with pinched front sight, walnut grips with outline of cartouche visible and various inspector marks, brass trigger guard, American, 19thC, barrel 8in (20.5cm) long.
£1,000–1,200
€/ $1,600–1,900 ⚒ JDJ

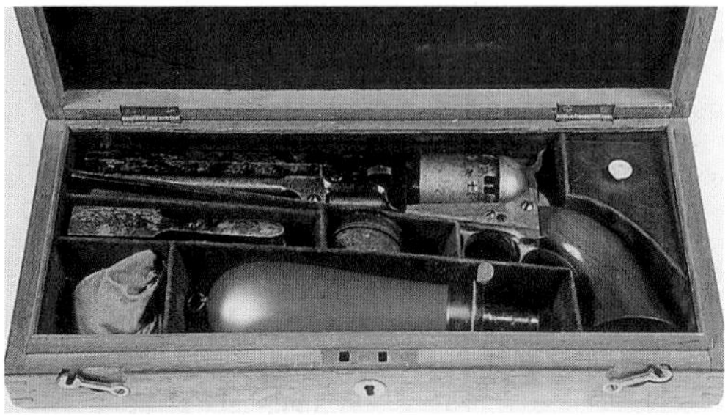

A percussion revolver, No. 2628, by V. Dreyse, the walnut grip with fishscale carving, signed, German, Sömmerda, c1865, 11¾in (30cm) long.
£2,800–3,200
€/ $4,400–5,000 ⚒ Herm

A Colt Bisley model single-action revolver, No. 233312, case-hardened frame with rampant Colt motif and patent dates, chequered and hard rubber grips, c1875, barrel 7½in (19cm) long.
£650–750
€/ $1,000–1,200 ⚒ WD

► A .44 calibre percussion full stock rifle, by J. A. Lechler, lock marked 'Josh Golcher', rear sight installed backwards, some damage, American, mid-19thC, barrel 36½in (92.5cm) long.
£450–550
€/ $700–840 ⚒ JDJ

A six-shot pepperbox percussion revolver, with leaf-chased brass action, inscribed 'Boston, Wakefield', chased steel hammer and rounded trigger guard, chequered walnut grip, hinged chased steel grip cap box, 19thC, 9½in (24cm) long.
£420–500
€/ $660–790 ⚒ AH

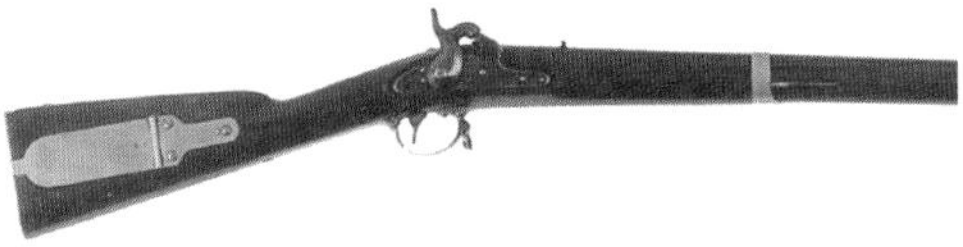

A Whitney model 1842 Mississippi rifle, the walnut stock with 'SM', 'W.A.T' and 'JH' cartouches, minor repairs, American, lock and barrel dated 1850, barrel 33in (84cm) long.
£3,200–3,800
€/ $5,000–6,000 ⚒ JDJ

Polearms & Axes

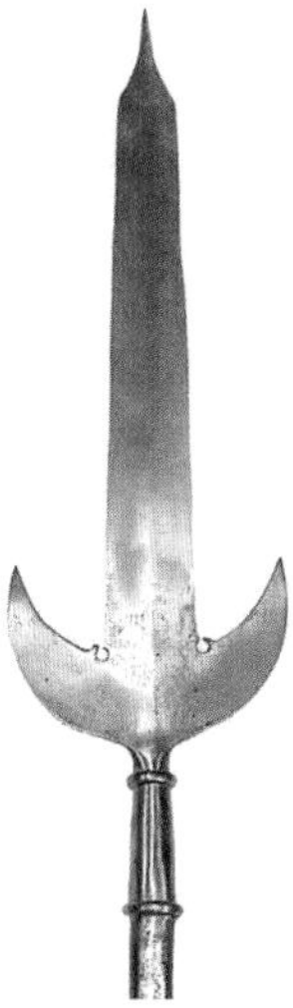

A partisan, the crescent base with forged 'eyes', the diamond-section tapering blade with thickened elongated point, integral double-banded socket and integral cheek straps, tapering haft inlet for a base shoe now missing, French, c1630, 104in (264cm) long.
£2,100–2,300
€/ $3,300–3,600 ⊞ FAC

A military pioneer's axe, the crescent head with spear point beak, on a wooden haft with brass ferrule and boss, 19thC, 35½in (90cm) long.
£200–240
€/ $315–380 ⚒ WAL

A military camp axe, stamped 'H Macneal Gordon Highlanders', on original wooden haft, 19thC, head 7in (18cm) long.
£280–325
€/ $440–515 ⚒ WAL

Militaria

Collectors of Militaria have a seemingly endless variety of fields on which to focus their interests, such as uniforms, regimental headdress, drums, regimental histories, Army, Air Force and Navy lists and, for the serious addict, even vehicles. Campaign medals are, in most cases, named around the rim or on the back with the number, rank, name and unit of the person to whom they were awarded. It is therefore possible to research the recipient's story and the campaigns in which they took part, making collecting even more interesting. Smaller items, such as military buttons and cap badges can be acquired for a modest amount and will demonstrate how a particular regiment or corps has changed since its inception. Sweetheart brooches or pins, usually a smaller version of the regimental badge, and produced by jewellers to sell to servicemen to present to their loved ones, can be found in precious metals and stones or in base metal and paste. They are a fascinating collecting area on their own and also pleasing to the eye.

Over the years collecting Militaria has proved to be a good investment as there is an enthusiastic international market and of course a limited supply of items which have survived to the present day. Some examples are: a group of eight medals awarded to a Colonel in the King's Own Yorkshire Light Infantry which sold for £85 (€/ $135) in 1973 and for £4,600 (€/ $7,300) 30 years later; a complete Trooper's uniform of the 16th Lancers, c1899 which sold for £200 (€/ $320) in 1976 and recently realized £1,100 (€/ $1,700) at auction, and a Victorian officer's helmet of the 5th Royal Irish Lancers which was worth £600 (€/ $950) in the early 1980s and revalued at over £5,000 (€/ $8,000) in 2003. It is clear that the market for Militaria is very strong at the moment, and in particular for gallantry medals, drums and cap badges.

One can never overestimate the joy for the enthusiast of adding to his collection and the golden rule is of course to always buy something because you like it, but the satisfaction of finding that there is also a financial reward at some future date can also not be denied!

John Wright

Badges

A Crimean War die-struck brass badge, Russian, c1853, 4½in (11.5cm) diam.
£150–175
€/ $240–280 WAL

A Royal Aberdeen Highlanders Militia other ranks' white metal glengarry badge, 1874–81.
£140–160
€/ $220–250 DNW

◄ A Victorian South Indian Railway Volunteer Rifle Corps other ranks' white metal Maltese Cross hat badge.
£70–80
€/ $110–130 WAL

A Gordon Highlanders, 4th Donside Highland Volunteer Battalion officer's die-cast silver-plated glengarry/bonnet badge, c1893–1908.
£140–160
€/ $220–250 DNW

A Victorian Pretoria Volunteers Corps bronze manufacturer's sample Shako badge and helmet plate, on original card, 6 x 7in (15 x 18cm).
£550–600
€/ $870–950 Q&C

A Victorian 1st and 2nd Battalion The Buffs officer's silver-plated pouch belt badge, slight wear.
£100–120
€/ $160–190 WAL

A Victorian Engineer Volunteers other ranks' white metal glengarry badge, possibly Colonial.
£100–120
€/ $160–190 WAL

A 1st Gurkha Rifles gilt-metal puggaree badge, c1900, some staining.
£350–400
€/ $550–630 WAL

◄ **A Duke of Cornwall's Light Infantry silver cap badge,** hallmarked F&S, Birmingham 1910.
£170–200
€/ $270–320 WAL

A Victorian 1st Devon Militia other ranks' brass glengarry badge.
£70–80
€/ $110–130 WAL

Costume

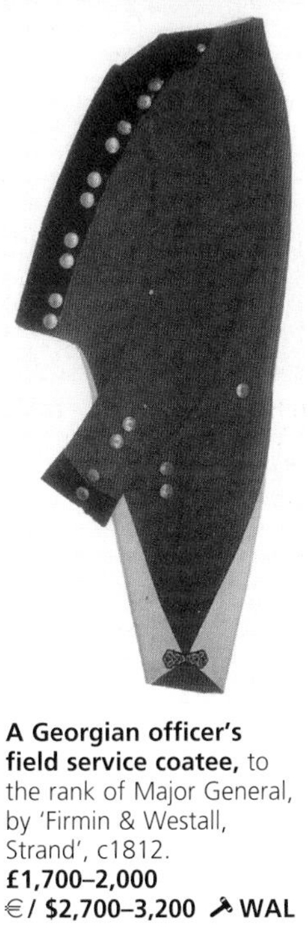

A Georgian officer's field service coatee, to the rank of Major General, by 'Firmin & Westall, Strand', c1812.
£1,700–2,000
€/ $2,700–3,200 WAL

► **A Victorian Bombay Volunteer Rifles Lieutenant's uniform,** comprising torrin cap, tunic, shoulder belt and waist belt, a sword knot, a pair of box spurs and a pair of shoulder cords with buttons, whistle and chains missing.
£750–900
€/ $1,200–1,400 WAL

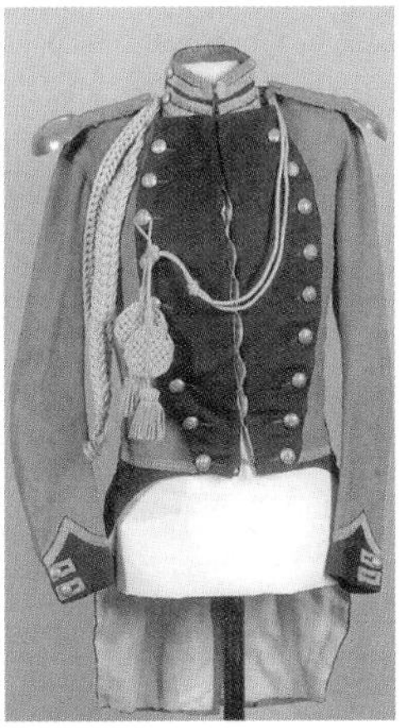

◄ **A militia Cavalry coatee,** American, two buttons missing, c1855.
£500–600
€/ $800–950 JAd

► **A Victorian Royal Field Artillery Staff Sergeant's uniform,** comprising pill box hat, frock, sidecap and overalls.
£550–625
€/ $870–1,000 WAL

A Lifeguard Hussars Regiment's Sergeant's coat and cap, German, 1915.
£2,000–2,200
€/ $3,200–3,500 Herm

A 20th Artillery Captain's service dress uniform, comprising peaked cap, tunic, shoulder belt and metal pouch, breeches, knee boots, waistbelt and sword, Italian, WWII.
£400–475
€/ $630–750 WAL

Helmets & Headdresses

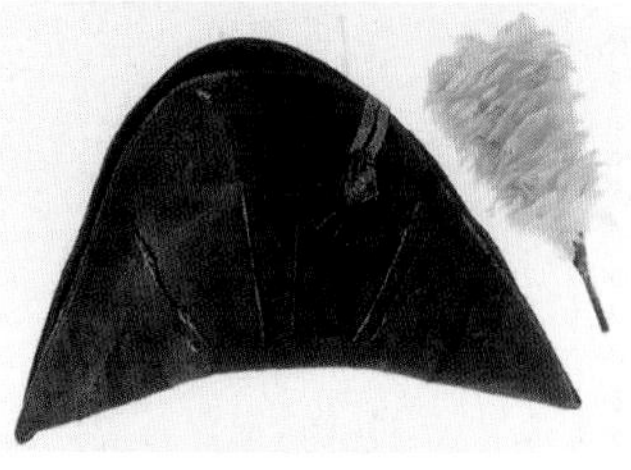

A militia officer's beaver felt bicorn dress hat, American, 1815–25.
£2,400–2,800
€/ $3,800–4,400 JDJ

A Kingdom of the Two Sicilies 1st Batallion National Guard of Sicily helmet, Italian, 1848–60.
£1,700–2,000
€/ $2,700–3,200 Herm

A 1st Volunteer Batallion Border Regiment other ranks' helmet, leather missing from chin chain, c1880.
£450–500
€/ $700–790 MDL

A Royal Hohenzollern-Hechinger Infantry officer's shako, German, 1820–45.
£3,500–4,000
€/ $5,500–6,300 Herm

A Dragoon officer's brass and leather helmet, Swedish, c1850.
£500–570
€/ $790–900 MDL

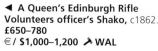

◄ **A Queen's Edinburgh Rifle Volunteers officer's Shako,** c1862.
£650–780
€/ $1,000–1,200 WAL

A 1st/Duke of Manchester's Mounted Volunteers helmet, horsehair plume associated, back peak bent, c1865.
£1,300–1,500
€/ $2,000–2,400 WAL

► **A Sherwood Foresters officer's cloth-covered helmet,** Hawkes & Co maker's stamp to the skull, c1880.
£675–750
€/ $1,100–1,200 MDL

A Gendarmerie officer's shako, Imperial German State, 1831–37.
£2,200–2,500
€/ $3,500–4,000 Herm

A Worcestershire Yeomanry Cavalry leather and white metal helmet, with horsehair plume and chin chain, c1860.
£1,700–1,900
€/ $2,700–3,000 MDL

An Infantry officer's model 1868 Raupenhelm, with full gilt-metal mounts, plume missing, some damage, Bavarian, c1870.
£600–675
€/ $950–1,000 S(O)

◄ **A Durham Light Infantry cloth-covered helmet,** stamped Hawkes & Co, c1890.
£650–725
€/ $1,000–1,100 ⊞ MDL

A Victorian 4th (Queen's Own) Hussars officer's cloth torrin cap.
£300–350
€/ $475–550 ⚒ WAL

A Victorian 4th (Queen's Own) Hussars officer's pillbox hat.
£220–250
€/ $350–400 ⚒ WAL

A Victorian 5th Royal Hussar's shako.
£800–900
€/ $1,300–1,400 ⊞ Q&C

◄ **A late Victorian 19th Hussars officer's busby,** with hat box and plume holder.
£675–750
€/ $1,100–1,200
⊞ Q&C

► **A Border Regiment officer's 1878 pattern cloth-covered helmet,** sweat band and silk liner missing, with associated 1884–1901 pattern helmet plate.
£500–575
€/ $800–900
⚒ DNW

A 1st King's Dragoon Guards officer's 1871 pattern helmet, lining missing, 1901–10.
£2,000–2,200
€/ $3,200–3,500 ⚒ S(O)

A Royal Naval bicorn hat and epaulettes, in a tin box, WWI.
£350–400
€/ $550–630 ⊞ MDL

A Prussian Infantry other ranks' leather and brass *Pickelhaube*, Berlin maker's stamp inside crown, brass peak trim missing, some wear, Imperial German, early 20thC.
£280–320
€/ $440–500 ⚒ WAL

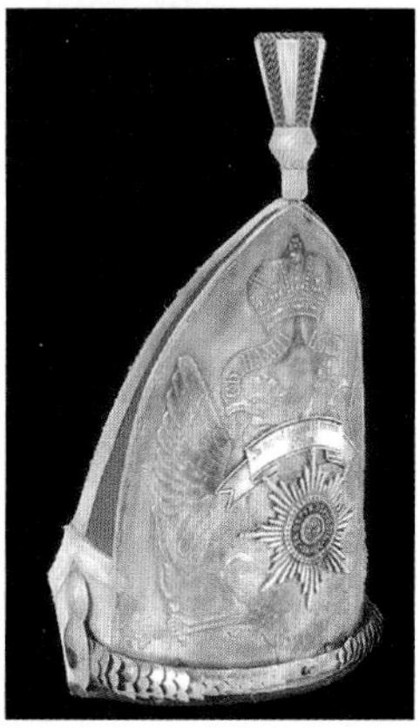

A Grenadier's cloth and brass mitre cap, hessian liner with storekeeper's stamp dated 1910, Imperial Russian.
£2,000–2,200
€/ $3,200–3,500 ⚒ WAL

Helmet Plates & Shoulder Belt Plates

A 63rd (West Suffolk) Regiment officer's gilt-copper shoulder belt plate, gilt loss, 1830–55.
£470–530
€/ $740–840 DNW

A 26th Regiment other ranks' brass helmet plate, one loop missing, Russian, 1854–55.
£100–120
€/ $160–190 WAL

A gilt-copper helmet plate, for a bell-top shako, c1840.
£420–465
€/ $670–720 MDL

A Victorian 1st Middlesex Engineer Volunteers other ranks white metal helmet plate, cleaned, repairs to back.
£170–200
€/ $270–320 WAL

A gilt-copper and silver helmet plate, for a bell-top shako, c1840.
£265–300
€/ $420–475 MDL

A Pretoria Volunteer Rifle Corps officer's silver-plated helmet plate, with a double pole to the wagon, late 19thC.
£220–260
€/ $350–400 WAL
The double pole to the wagon is a rare variation. The shafts of the wagon pointing downwards indicates volunteers.

Historical Medals

◄ **A silver medal,** for the Attempted Invasion of Scotland, by G. Hautsch, the obverse with a bust of Anne, the reverse with the English fleet in pursuit of the French, the coast of Scotland in the distance, the edge inscribed 'Sic Pueri Nasum Rhinocerotis Habent' (Thus Boys have the Nose of a Rhinoceros), 1708, 1½in (4cm) diam.
£340–375
€/ $550–600 TML
The epigram on the edge comes from Martial – the attempted invasion was so ridiculous that even small boys turn their noses up at it.

► **A silver medal,** for the British Army Entering Madrid, by T. and P. Wyon, the obverse with a bare-headed bust of Wellington, the reverse with a tablet of victories surmounted by shields of Britain, Portugal and Spain, enclosed by military trophies, 1812, 1¾in (4.5cm) diam.
£300–350
€/ $475–550 DNW

A silver medal, for the Battle of Culloden, 16 April 1746, by Richard Yeo, the obverse with a bust of Cumberland, the reverse with the Duke, as Hercules, trampling on Discord and raising Britannia, edge engraved, 1746, 2in (5cm) diam.
£250–285
€/ $400–450 TML

LOCATE THE SOURCE
The source of each illustration in Miller's can be found by checking the code letters below each caption with the Key to Illustrations, pages 794–800.

Orders & Medals

A General Service Medal, awarded to Private Robert Willis, 3rd Dragoon Guards, with Toulouse, Vittoria, Albuhera and Talavera bars, 1793–1814.
£1,700–2,000
€/ $2,700–3,200 Bri

Aged 13, Robert Willis signed up for Volunteer Service at Salisbury two days after Christmas, 1798. He rose through the ranks to Sergeant Major, holding that rank for his last ten years and 332 days. His discharge papers list his reason for leaving 'being worn out in the service' in June 1821.

A Victorian Military Service medal, awarded to Richard Charlesworth, 84th Foot, two bars, Nivelle and Nive.
£850–1,000
€/ $1,300–1,600 BAL

Miller's Compares

I. A Waterloo medal, awarded to Sergeant Richard Spencer, 2nd Battalion 95th Regiment Foot, 1815.
£2,000–2,400
€/ $3,200–3,800 WAL

II. A Hanoverian Waterloo medal, awarded to Michael Wedekind, Landwehr Battalion Alfield, 1815.
£380–450
€/ $600–710 WAL

Pictured above are two medals awarded to soldiers fighting in the Battle of Waterloo: Item I to a British soldier and Item II to a soldier of the Prussian Army who fought alongside the British. The Prussian Army was virtually an army of mercenaries, being paid for by the English Parliament, and records are almost non existent. Hanoverian Waterloo Medals were authorized by the Prince Regent on behalf of his father King George III in his capacity as Elector of Hanover. All British-issued medals were named around the rim with the recipient's name and unit, but not all German ones were. It is therefore much easier to verify a medal to a British soldier from the Regimental Medal Rolls held at the Public Records Office at Kew than it is to a member of the German Legion whose records have in most cases been lost. Value is also increased by what the Regiment did in the battle, such as in the case of Item I where the recipient's unit was in the thick of it with losses of 246 out of an original 585 men. Moreover, medals awarded to officers such as Item I command a higher price because there were fewer of them and their part in the action is well documented.

A Crimean campaign group of six, awarded to Lieutenant-Colonel Lord George Bingham, Coldstream Guards, Aide-de-Camp to the Earl of Lucan: Silver Coronation medal 1902; Coronation medal 1911; Crimea medal 1854–56, three bars; Legion of Honour Second Empire medal; Order of the Medjidie; Turkish Crimea medal, Sardinian issue.
£2,800–3,200
€/ $4,400–5,000 DNW

◀ **A silver Military Service medal,** by J. Ries, Imperial German, 1870 and 1914–18, in original case.
£850–1,000
€/ $1,300–1,600 Herm

A pair of medals, awarded to Corporal William Shaw, York & Lancaster Regiment, late 55th Foot: First China War medal, 1842, original suspension; Volunteer Force Long Service Victoria medal.
£650–750
€/ $1,000–1,200 BAL

A pair of medals, awarded to Cornet D. Gibson, Royal Scots Greys: Crimea medal 1854–56, two bars, Balaklava, Sebastopol; Turkish Crimea medal, Sardinian issue, fitted with replacement suspension.
£950–1,100
€/ $1,500–1,700 Gle

An Indian Mutiny medal, awarded to T. Ledsham, 2nd Dragoon Guards, edge knocks, one bar Lucknow 1857–58.
£320–375
€/ $500–600 WAL

A group of three medals, awarded to Lieutenant-Colonel the Honorable Ranulf Allsopp, Royal Artillery & Honourable Artillery Company: Egypt & Sudan medal, 1882, one bar; Khedive's Star, 1882; Turkey, silver and enamel Order of Medjidjie 4th class breast badge, in a damaged case marked 'Metcalf of London'.
£950–1,100
€/ $1,500–1,700 BAL

A pair of medals, awarded to F. E. Quinton: East and West Africa medal 1892, one bar, Benin 1897; Naval LS and GC medal, Edward VII issue.
£220–250
€/ $350–400 WAL

The Order of St Stanislav, a gold and enamel decoration with the Stanislav coat-of-arms, Imperial Russian, c1890.
£1,100–1,300
€/ $1,700–2,000 SHa

◄ **A group of five medals,** awarded to Private Phillip Williams, Royal Marine Light Infantry: Sierra-Leone 1898–99; 1914 Star; British War and Victory medals; George V Good Service medal.
£600–700
€/ $950–1,100 BR

A group of three medals, awarded to Captain H. M. Birch, British South Africa Police: British South Africa Company medal 1897; British War and Victory medals, with miniatures mounted for wear.
£420–500
€/ $670–790 L

A group of eight medals, awarded to Captain and Group Adjutant T. J. Higgins, City of London Rifle Volunteers, late Coldstream Guards: Queens South Africa medal 1899–1902, six bars; King's South Africa medal 1901–02, two bars; 1914–15 Star; British War and Victory Medals, M.I.D. oak leaf; Army Long Service and Good Conduct, EVIIR; Army Meritorious Service Medal, G.VI.R., first issue; Serbian Cross of Karageorge, second class, with swords, dated 1914–16.
£1,000–1,200
€/ $1,600–1,900 DNW

A Queen's South Africa medal, awarded to Supr A. C. Chatfield, R E, with four bars, South Africa 1902, Transvaal, OFS, Cape Colony.
£80–100
€/ $125–160 CHTR

◄ **A pair of medals,** awarded to Lieutenant B. M. Byrne, Conn. Rang.: Africa General Service medal 1902–56, two bars; S. Nigeria, 1902–03.
£950–1,100
€/ $1,500–1,700 BAL

A Great War Military Cross and double M.S.M. group of eleven, awarded to Regimental Sergeant-Major William Lawrance, 1st Battalion, The Rifle Brigade: Military Cross, G.V.R.; Queen's South Africa medal 1899–1902, six bars; King's South Africa medal 1901–02, two bars; 1914 Star; British War and Victory medals; Defence medal; Jubilee medal 1935; Army L.S. & G.C., G.V.R., first issue; Meritorious Service medal, G.V.R., first issue; Meritorious Service medal, G.VI.R., third issue.
£3,000–3,500
€/ $4,700–5,500 DNW

A group of six medals, awarded to Sergeant-Major G. Jakeman, 25th Sge.Bry, R.G.A.: 1914–15 Star; British War and Victory medals; Distinguished Conduct medal G.V.; Army Long Service and Good Conduct medal; Special Constabulary Long Service Medal.
£950–1,100
€/ $1,500–1,700 G(L)

A group of ten medals, mounted as worn to a Warrent Officer, 1st Class, Royal Electrical and Mechanical Engineers: 1939–45 Star; Pacific Star; Defence Medal; War Medal; General Service Medal, one bar Malaya; British Korea; United Nations Korea; Campaign Service Medal, one bar Northern Ireland; 1977 Silver Jubilee; Regular Army Long Service and Good Conduct medal.
£540–600
€/ $850–950 ⊞ Q&C

► **A group of eight medals,** awarded to Staff Sergeant M. Antoniszewski, Polish Army Staff: Poland Cross of Valour, two bars; Monte Cassino Cross; Army Active Service Medal; Great Britain Military Medal, G.VI.R.; 1939–45 Star; Africa Star; Italy Star; Defence Medal.
£1,700–2,000
€/ $2,700–3,200 ⚒ DNW

◄ **A group of nine medals,** awarded to Wing Commander T. S. Tull, Royal Air Force: Distinguished Service Order South East Asia; Commander of the British Empire; Order of the British Empire; 1939–45 Star; Burma Star; Defence Medal; 1939–45 War Medal; General Service Medal, with bar; Air Efficiency Award.
£3,250–3,600
€/ $5,100–5,700 ⊞ RMC

Pouches

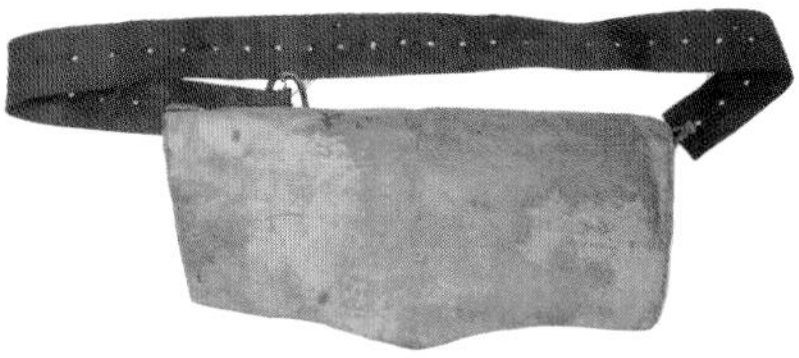

A doeskin bullet pouch, German, c1720, 14in (35.5cm) wide.
£585–650
€/ $920–1,000 ⊞ FAC

► **A British Indian Army Regiment leather pouch and belt,** c1900, 17in (43cm) long.
£80–90
€/ $125–140 ⊞ MDL

► **A Victorian Royal Artillery officer's full dress shoulder belt and embroidered pouch,** with ornamental gilt buckle, tip and slide, and pouch mounts, with a velvet-lined foul weather cover.
£550–625
€/ $870–1,000 ⚒ WAL

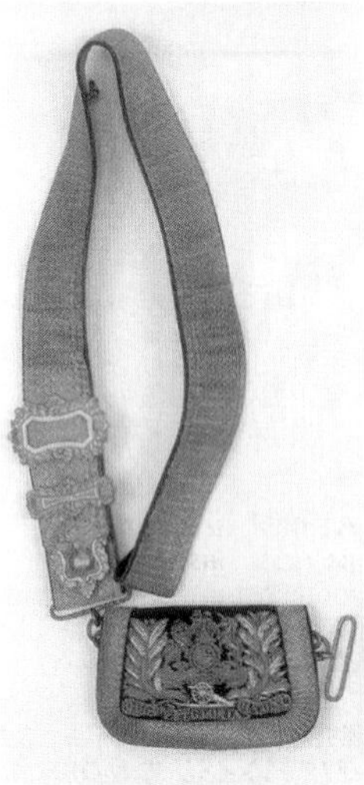

Powder Flasks & Horns

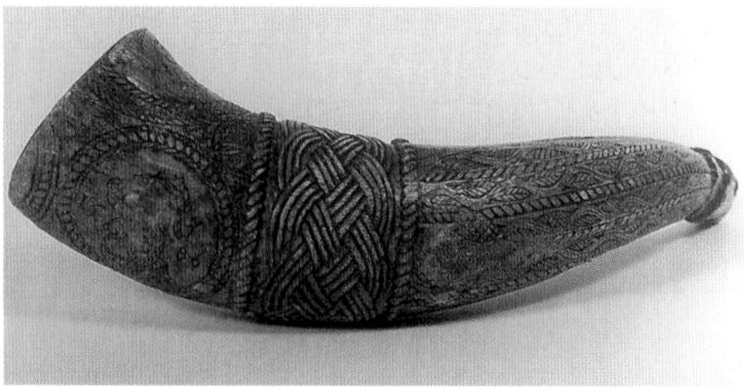

A powder horn, Spanish, dated 1586, 9in (23cm) long.
£1,300–1,500
€/ $2,000–2,400 ⊞ SEA

► **A musketeer's flask,** the curved wood body with iron mounts including a pierced plate, an iron belt hook to the rear, sprung cut-off and sprung cap to the tapered nozzle, four forged suspension rings, Nuremberg Town mark to top, German, c1630, 11in (28cm) long.
£850–950
€/ $1,300–1,500 ⊞ FAC

Items in the Militaria section have been arranged in date order within each sub-section.

A musketeer's powder flask, the leather-covered wooden body with steel edging and scrolling corner mounts, the reverse with belt hook, the sides with suspension rings, the nozzle with spring cut-off, worn, German, 17thC, 8¼in (21cm) high.
£450–525
€/ $700–830 ⚒ B(L)

An enamelled bronze priming flask, the centre and edge decorated with a raised geometric motif, the tapered baluster spout with sprung pivoting cap, hinged suspension rings and three rings below for tassels, Russian, 17thC, 2in (5cm) diam.
£850–950
€/ $1,300–1,500 ⊞ FAC

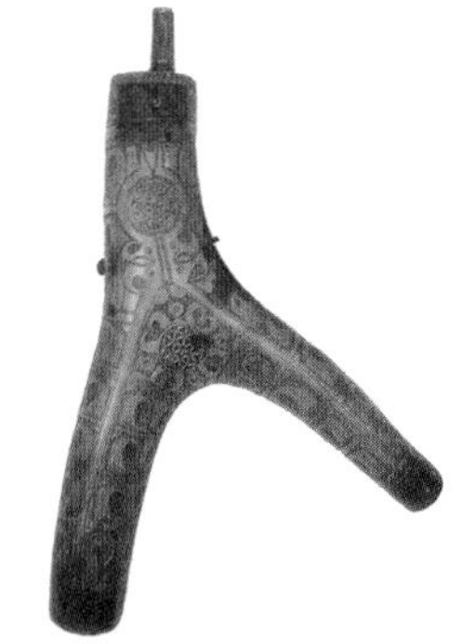

A powder horn, made from a stag's antler section, engraved with hook and geometric decoration, fixed spout, one iron hanging ring, ring rusted, Transylvanian, 17thC, 12½in (32cm) long.
£420–500
€/ $670–800 ⚒ WAL

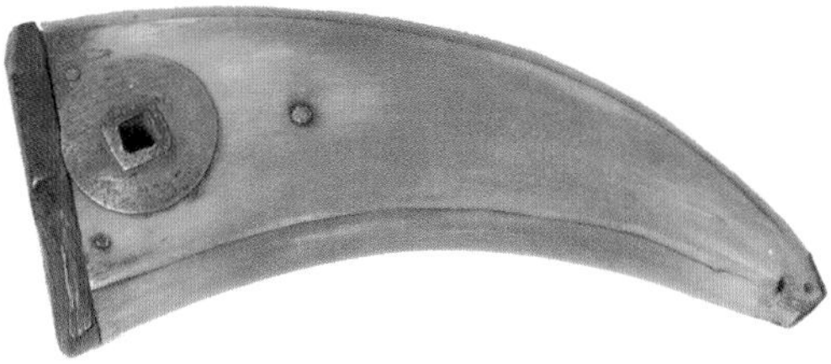

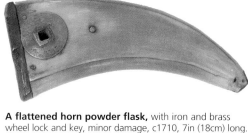

A flattened horn powder flask, with iron and brass wheel lock and key, minor damage, c1710, 7in (18cm) long.
£150–165
€/ $240–260 ⊞ MDL

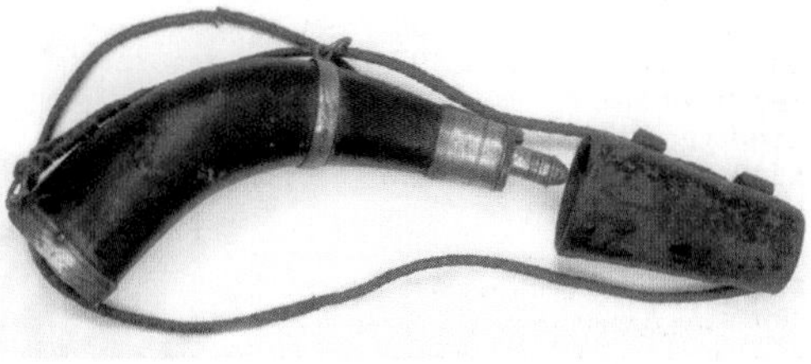

A brass-mounted cowhorn powder flask, probably for Rifle Volunteers, the common brass tip with sprung lever and adjustable nozzle, brass hanging band with suspension loop, concave brass base with suspension loop, original leather charger cover and woven leather-covered suspension cords, late 18thC, 11in (28cm) long.
£350–420
€/ $550–670 ⚒ WAL

► A wood and leather powder flask, Indian, c1800, 5in (12.5cm) wide.
£70–80
€/ $110–125 ⊞ ARB

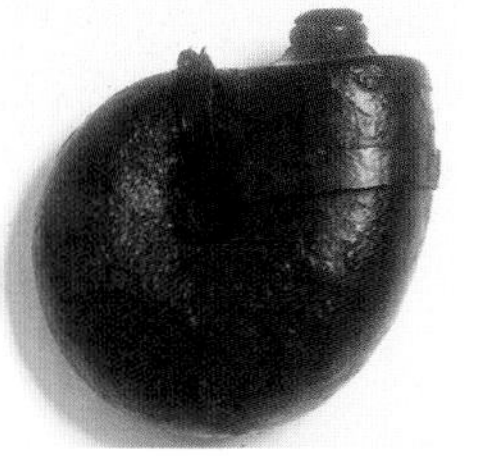

A polished coconut powder flask, with silver mounts, the side straps with three hanging rings, charger top, c1850, 6in (15cm) long.
£350–400
€/ $550–630 ⊞ MDL

A brass and horn rifle powder flask, c1850, 12in (30.5cm) long.
£130–145
€/ $200–230 ⊞ MDL

◄ A gunner's powder flask, with horn inspection window to each side, paint chipped, Italian, 19thC, 6¾in (17cm) long.
£300–350
€/ $475–550 ⚒ B(Kn)

Sabretaches

An East Lothian Yeomanry leather sabretache, with gilt crown above reversed VR cypher enclosed in a thistle wreath with silvered scrolls, mid-19thC, 10in (25.5cm) wide.
£570–635
€/ $900–1,000 ⊞ MDL

► A Victorian Royal Artillery officer's full dress embroidered sabretache, with a gilt-lace border, in a velvet-lined foul weather cover, some wear.
£475–550
€/ $750–870 ⚒ WAL

◄ An 8th (The King's Royal Irish) Hussars officer's full dress leather sabretache, the cloth-covered face with gold shamrock-pattern train lace enclosing the regimental distinctions, light cavalry crown, motto, 'VR', royal crest over the Harp & Maid battle honour scrolls from Laswarree and Hindoostan to Central India and Afghanistan, with foul weather cover, some damage, c1880.
£950–1,100
€/ $1,500–1,700 ⚒ DNW

Miscellaneous

A Victorian ambrotype of a Royal Horse Artillery mounted officer, wearing full dress with tall busby, his overalls with leather reinforcements.
£150–175
€/ $240–275 B

An ambrotype is an early type of photograph where the glass negative is backed with black varnish so that it appears as a positive image.

A 65th (2nd York North Riding) Regiment gilt-coloured belt buckle, pre-1881.
£200–240
€/ $320–380 WAL

A carved and painted wood bust of a French cavalry officer, possibly an advertising figure, the reverse with pierced suspension lugs, and a metal ring, 19thC, 37¾in (96cm) high.
£2,200–2,500
€/ $3,500–4,000 FEN

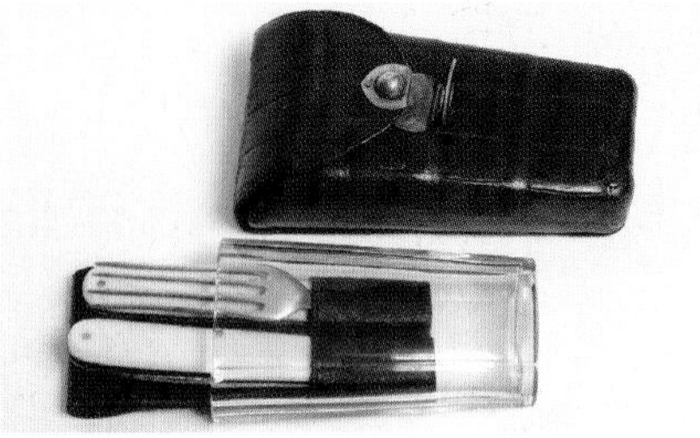

A campaign cutlery set, in a glass, within a crocodile skin case, c1890, 4in (10cm) high.
£90–100
€/ $140–160 MB

A Victorian Lord Lieutenant's full dress epaulettes, 4in (10cm) long, in a tin.
£450–500
€/ $700–800 MDL

A snare drum, the leather sliders decorated with five-pointed stars, late 19thC, with two sets of sticks and a chamois beater.
£150–180
€/ $240–280 JDJ

A 2nd Battalion The Irish Guards half shallow drum, post-WWI, 14in (35.5cm) wide.
£225–250
€/ $350–400 Q&C

A Civil War 34-star flag, American, 1860–62, 53 x 65in (134.5 x 165cm).
£1,500–1,800
€/ $2,400–2,800 JDJ

A recruitment poster, depicting a Tommy with rifle, WWI, 29 x 19in (73.5 x 48.5cm).
£280–325
€/ $440–515 WAL

◄ **An Edwardian carved teak table top,** for a Royal Horse Artillery regiment, Indian, 27in (68.5cm) diam.
£350–400
€/ $550–630 Q&C

The Potter Collection

The Potter Collection of antique drums, sold by Bosley's of Marlow on 9th June 1999, was amassed over a period of 150 years by George Potter & Co of London and Aldershot. The firm was started in the 1850s by two brothers who were ex-service musicians in the British Army. They supplied musical instruments, including regimental drums, to every regiment and corps in the British Armed Forces, as well as the British Indian Army and most of the Commonwealth forces. Many of the drums included in the sale were of great historical importance, the highlight being a bass drum that was played at the Battle of Waterloo by the Coldstream Guards, which realized £5,000 (€/ $8,000). Also on offer were miniature drums made by apprentices and used as samples by salesmen to show to prospective buyers, and plaques made from the outer wooden casing of drums which had been straightened out and framed to display the heraldry included in the decoration. The Potter Collection drums have now been scattered to the four corners of the globe so a sale such as this can never be repeated. At the time the prices achieved were very reasonable and it is likely that many pieces will have doubled in value by now. **John Wright**

Sport

Archery

◄ **A tile,** depicting an archer with bows and arrows, Dutch, 17thC, 5in (12.5cm) square.
£65–80
€/ $100–125 TMA

► **A walnut sporting crossbow,** with ivory inlay, German, c1750, 27in (68.5cm) long.
£3,600–4,000
€/ $5,700–6,000 ARB

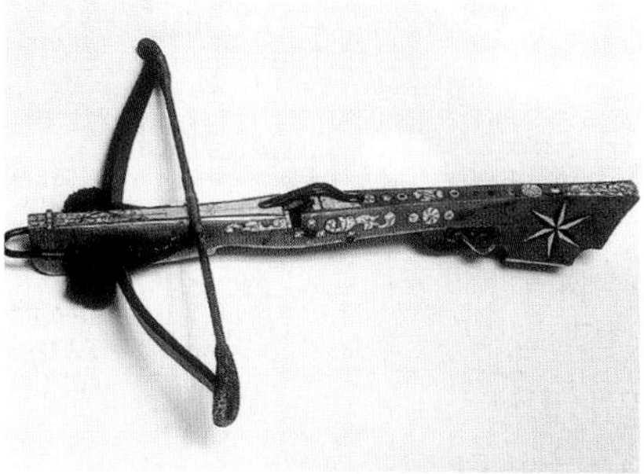

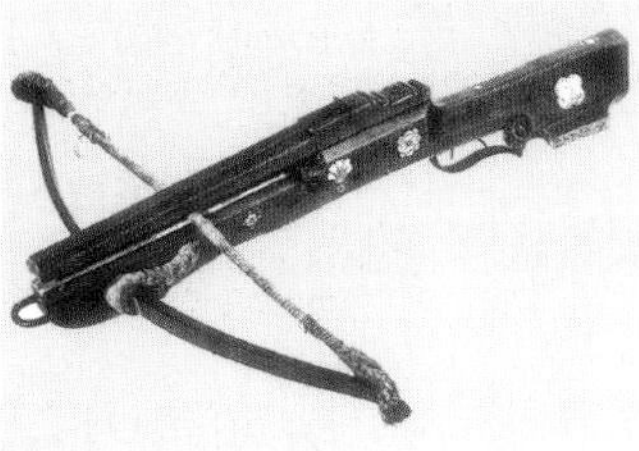

A carved fruitwood crossbow, with horn inlay of shells and blossom, the butt end with a coat-of-arms and marked 'Laukol', iron mounts, German, 18thC, 24¼in (61.5cm) long.
£800–950
€/ $1,300–1,500 Herm

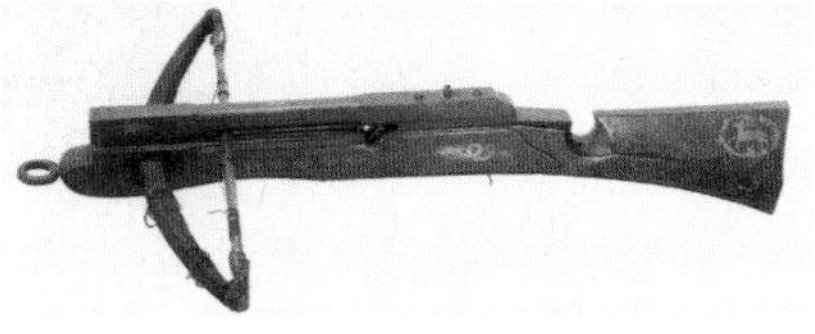

A 17thC-style steel and wood sporting crossbow, the engraved stock inlaid with pewter wire scrollwork, the butt with an engraved pewter stag and foliage, losses, German, 19thC, 35¾in (91cm) long.
£420–500
€/ $630–800 B(Kn)

For further information on sporting antiques see the full range of Miller's books at **www.millers.uk.com**

An 18ct gold World Championship medal, won at Raglan Castle in 1891.
£200–240
€/ $315–380 BWL

Billiards

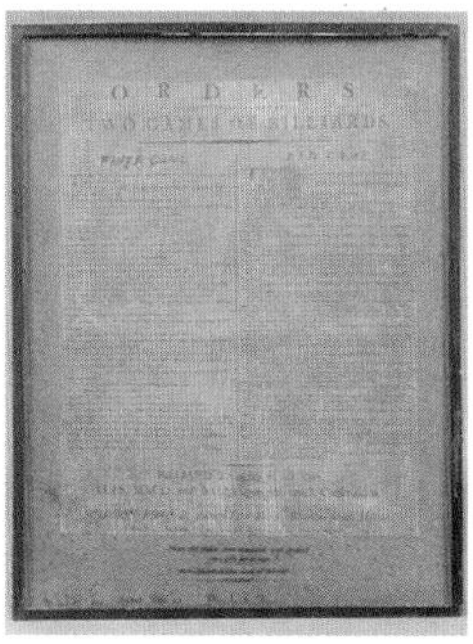

A copy of the printed rules for billiards, published by Solomon Erwood, London, on a card mount, repairs, framed, c1720, with a letter from the makers, Thurston & Co, dating this set of rules 'to be prior to 1730'.
£800–900
€/ $1,300–1,400 S(O)

► **A set of nine ivory billiard balls,** early 19thC.
£650–780
€/ $1,000–1,200
S(O)

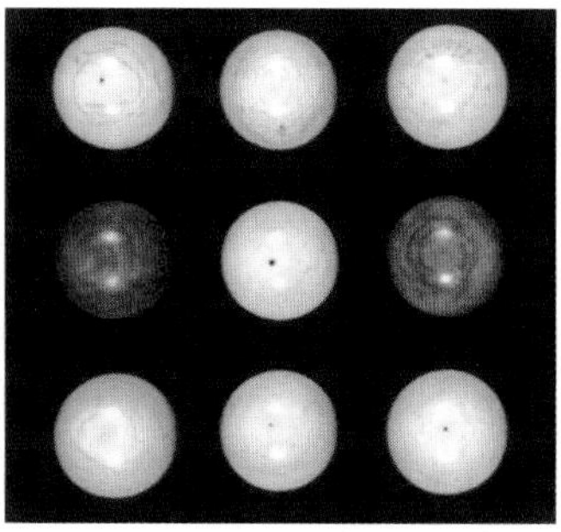

► **A Victorian mahogany revolving cue stand,** the top centred by a finial on a turned and ringed column, with cues and rests.
£800–950
€/ $1,300–1,500 B(S)

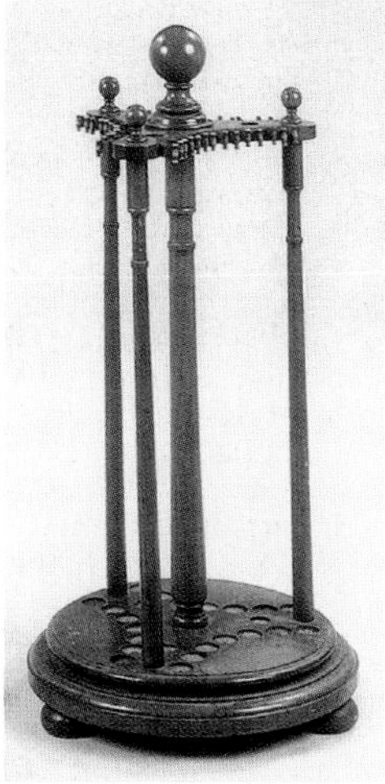

► **An oak revolving cue stand,** c1890, 45in (114.5cm) high.
£1,400–1,600
€/ $2,200–2,500 MSh

Items in the Sport section have been arranged in date order within each sub-section.

► **A painted walnut firescreen,** entitled 'When my cue comes call me', depicting a gentleman beside a billiards table, early 20thC, 31¼in (80cm) high.
£950–1,100
€/ $1,500–1,700 S(O)

A walnut, burr-walnut and ebonized billiards table, Swedish, 1850s, 144 x 72in (366 x 183cm).
£27,000–30,000
€/ $43,000–47,000 ⊞ WBB

A Cox & Yeoman burr-yew billiards table, 1860s, 144 x 72in (366 x 183cm).
£22,000–25,000
€/ $34,750–38,500 ⊞ WBB

A Gillows mahogany billiards table, 1880s, 144 x 72in (366 x 183cm).
£22,000–25,000
€/ $34,750–38,500 ⊞ WBB

A Burroughs & Watts mahogany billiards table, 1880s, 120 x 60in (305 x 152.5cm).
£4,500–5,000
€/ $7,000–8,000 ⊞ WBB

► **An Ashcroft walnut and burr-walnut billiards table,** 1880s, 144 x 72in (366 x 183cm).
£13,000–15,000
€/ $20,500–24,000 ⊞ WBB

A Riley oak billiards table, 1920s, 144 x 72in (366 x 183cm).
£4,000–4,500
€/ $6,300–7,000 ⊞ WBB

► **A beech and brass billiard cue tipper,** c1900, 6½in (16.5cm) long.
£60–65
€/ $95–100 ⊞ MSh

Bowling

A wooden ball, French, c1900, 7in (18cm) diam.
£30–35
€/ $50–55 ⊞ TRA

A set of four *lignum vitae* bowls, 1920s, 5in (12.5cm) diam.
£65–70
€/ $95–110 ⊞ MINN

A silver-mounted *lignum vitae* bowl, c1923, 5in (12.5cm) diam.
£45–50
€/ $70–75 ⊞ MINN

Boxing

A colour engraving, after the original painting by Gem Ward, depicting the fight between Tom Sayers and J. C. Heenan, 19thC, 43 x 31in (109 x 78cm), framed.
£650–750
€/ $1,000–1,200 B(NW)
This fight took place on 17 April 1860, for the championship of England and America.

► A Wood pearlware figure of a pugilist, representing Gentleman Humphreys, restored, c1785, 8in (20.5cm) high.
£3,000–3,500
€/ $4,700–5,500 S(O)

A pair of Staffordshire pearlware figures of Tom Cribb and Tom Molineux, 1812–15, taller 8½in (21.5cm) high.
£5,000–6,000
€/ $8,000–9,000 S(NY)
Known as the 'Black Diamond' from his occupation as a coal porter, Tom Cribb was the foremost pugilist of his day in England, becoming champion in 1809. His most celebrated matches were fought against Tom Molineux, a freed slave from Virginia.

Jack Johnson, a signed photograph, 'From Champion Jack Johnson to Carl Brooke', c1914, 6 x 4in (15 x 10.5cm).
£1,000–1,200
€/ $1,600–1,900 HYD

A pair of child's leather boxing gloves, 1950s, 7in (18cm) long.
£45–50
€/ $70–75 TRA

Cricket

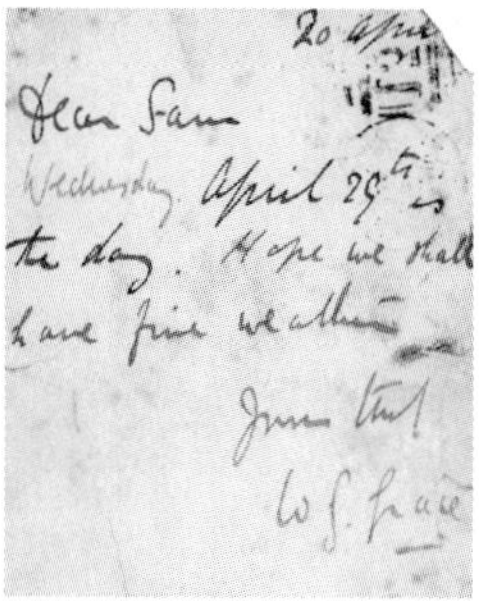
20 April
Dear Sam
Wednesday April 29th is the day. Hope we shall have fine weather
Yours truly
W. G. Grace

W. G. Grace, a handwritten postcard, dated 29 April 1896.
£180–220
€/ $285–350 B(Ch)

A photograph of the Australian cricket team, signed by 15 members, 1930, 14½ x 17in (37 x 43cm).
£350–420
€/ $550–630 S(O)

A photograph of the Australian cricket team, signed by every member, 1934, 19¾in (50cm) square.
£850–1,000
€/ $1,300–1,600 B(NW)

A Victorian cricket bat, by G. G. Hearne, London, 35in (89cm) long.
£135–150
€/ $215–240 MINN

A Victorian cricket bat, by Wisden, 35in (89cm) long.
£135–150
€/ $215–240 MINN

► A child's cricket bat, by Sandham & Strudwick, signed by the 1934 England and Australian cricket teams of the Oval Test, the reverse signed by the 1933–34 Chelsea football squad.
£650–780
€/ $1,000–1,200 S(O)

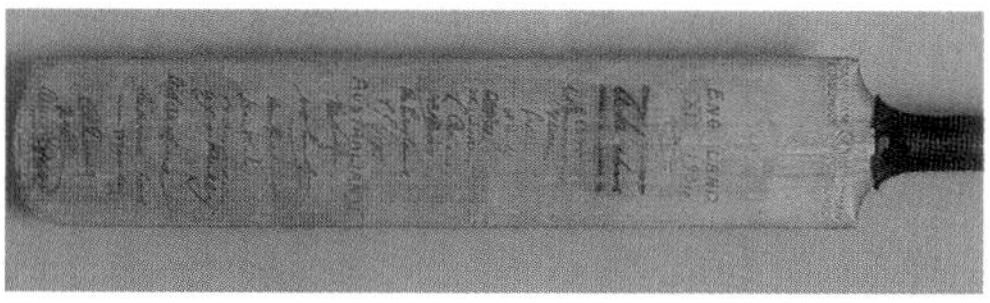

◄ **A cricket cap worn by Australia's Ian Chappell,** sold with an invitation and menu to the Anglo-American Sporting Club Dinner, London, signed by Don Bradman, Godfrey Evans, Denis Compton, Alec Bedser and Keith Miller, 1968.
£2,300–2,700
€/ $3,600–4,200 ⚒ S(O)
This cap was purchased at the after-dinner auction. Sir Donald Bradman was guest of honour on this occasion and it was his last official appearance in England.

W. D. & H. O. Wills, Cricketers 1908, set of 50, 1908.
£90–110
€/ $140–175 ⚒ VS

A Fletcher & Co creamware commemorative mug, one side printed with a view of a cricket match at Lord's, the reverse with a view of the Oatland Stakes at Ascot, c1795, 7in (17.5cm) high.
£5,400–6,500
€/ $8,500–10,300 ⚒ WW

A pottery dish, with a sepia portrait of Jack Hobbs, c1926, 3½in (9cm) diam.
£55–65
€/ $85–100 ⚒ SAS
Jack Hobbs played in 61 test matches between 1907–30, and as captain in 1926 he achieved the highest score at Lords of 316 runs. He was knighted in 1953.

◄ **A late Victorian wooden novelty ink stand,** with cricket ball inkwell and stumps pen rest, 5in (12.5cm) diam.
£180–220
€/ $280–350 ⚒ TMA

► **A photographic collage,** of the Canterbury Jubilee cricket match 1891, 17 x 32in (43 x 81.5cm).
£400–450
€/ $630–700 ⊞ MSh

Equestrian

A pair of leather riding boots, with steel studs, 18thC.
£420–500
€/ $670–790 ⚒ S(O)

◄ **A pair of leather riding boots,** with trees, 1890s.
£100–110
€/ $160–175 ⊞ RGa

► **A pair of leather field boots,** with trees, c1910.
£130–145
€/ $200–220 ⊞ SPT

An ivory box, decorated with a horse race, c1890, 9in (23cm) long.
£1,800–2,000
€/ $2,800–3,200 ⊞ RGa

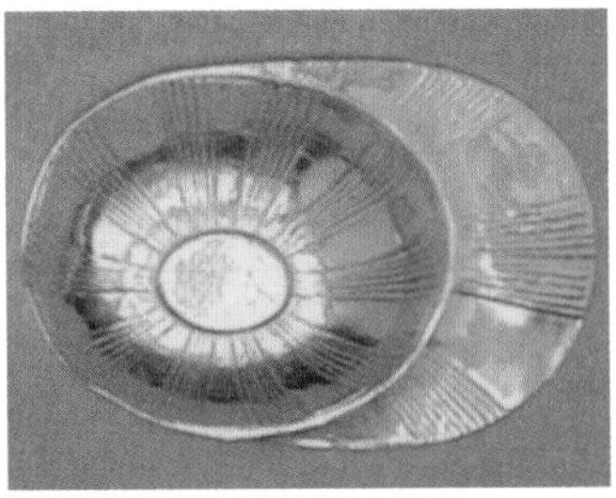

◄ **A George III silver caddy spoon,** in the shape of a jockey's cap, initialled 'I.RK.', lion passant and duty marks, c1805, 2in (5cm) wide.
£260–315
€/ $400–480 ⚒ WW

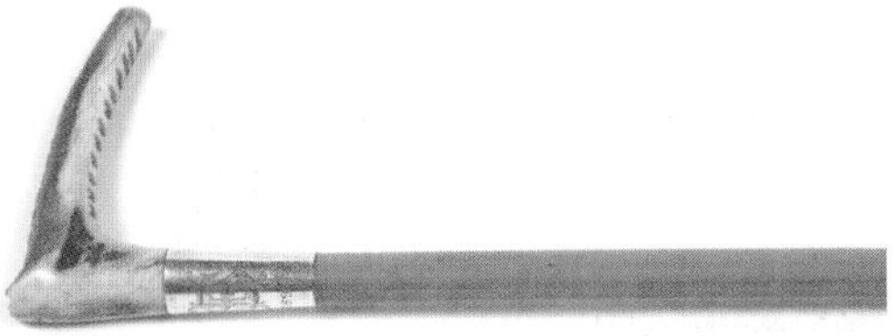

► **A silver-mounted horn and wood riding crop,** monogrammed, c1900, 26in (66cm) long.
£72–80
€/ $110–125 ⊞ RGa

◄ **A silver-mounted riding crop,** c1919, 21in (53.5cm) long.
£55–60
€/ $90–100 ⊞ GBr

A silver presentation cup, by Emes & Barnard, inscribed 'Northallerton Races 1835, the Duke of Leeds, the Honble Coll Arden, Stewards', the cover with an equine finial, 1825, 15¼in (39.5cm) high, 82oz.
£3,300–4,000
€/ $5,200–6,300 TEN

A silver trophy, inscribed 'The Pendle Forest Hunt...', London 1934, 10¾in (27.5cm) high, 24oz.
£100–120
€/ $160–190 SWO

A silver-plated cruet set, by Elkington & Co, in the form of a horseshoe with riding boots, hat and riding crop-shaped spoons, c1890, 4in (10cm) high.
£1,900–2,100
€/ $3,000–3,300 ⊞ RGa

An inkwell, the top in the shape of a jockey's cap, the pen rest in the shape of a saddle, late 19thC, 6in (15cm) high.
£850–930
€/ $1,300–1,500 ⊞ RGA

A Neale & Co creamware dish, the centre decorated with a racehorse and the name 'High Flyer' on a ribbon, impressed mark, c1780, 11½in (29cm) wide.
£230–275
€/ $360–430 SAS

A cut-glass hunting decanter, by T. J. London, with a silver top and leather case, 1893, 9in (23cm) high.
£130–150
€/ $200–240 FEN

► **A horseshoe letter clip,** centred with a stirrup, on an oak base, late 19thC, 11in (28cm) wide.
£430–475
€/ $680–750 ⊞ RGa

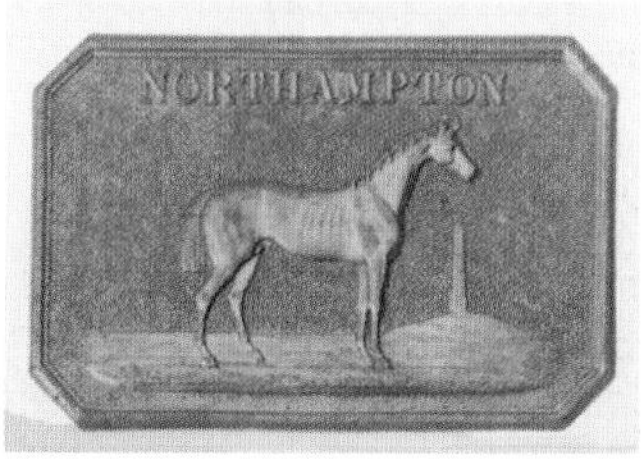

A pair of white metal Northampton Race Course member's passes, issued to Earl Spencer, c1830, 22½in (57cm) wide.
£1,200–1,400
€/ $1,900–2,200 ⊞ TML

A Copeland & Garrett soup plate, transfer-printed with Racehorses pattern from the Field Sports series, 1846–47, 10in (25.5cm) diam.
£170–200
€/ $270–300 ⊞ DSA

A silver tea-glass holder, repoussé-decorated with two horses' heads, Russian, Moscow, 1908–12, 4½in (11.5cm) high.
£240–280
€/ $380–440 S(O)

A Davies & McDonald tile, American, c1930, 8in (20.5cm) square.
£400–450
€/ $550–650 ⊞ KMG

Fishing

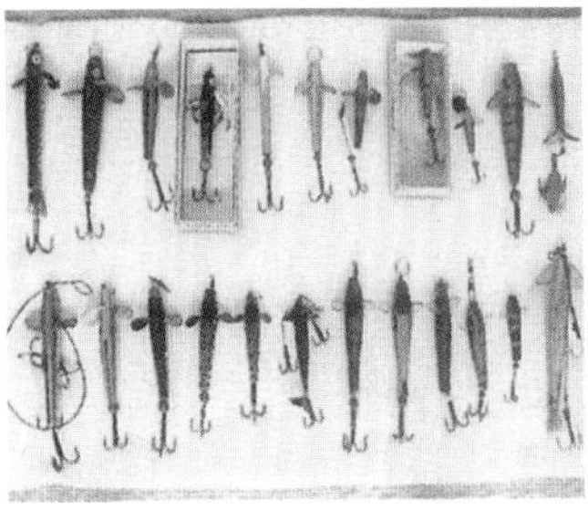

A collection of baits, including Wadhams 'Spangaloid' Clipper and Devon Minnows, with ten different Hardy baits, five Allcock 'Feathoro' Minnows and others, 1910–50, in a glazed wooden case.
£220–250
€/ $350–400 ⚒ MUL

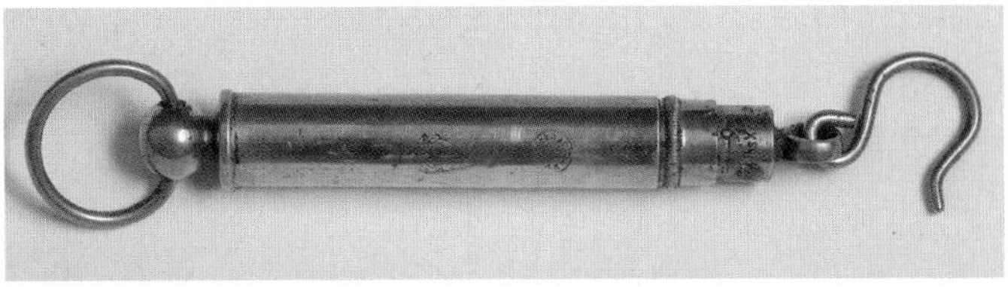

A Hardy 10lb trout balance, 1930s, 4in (10cm) long.
£23–25
€/ $35–40 ⊞ OTB

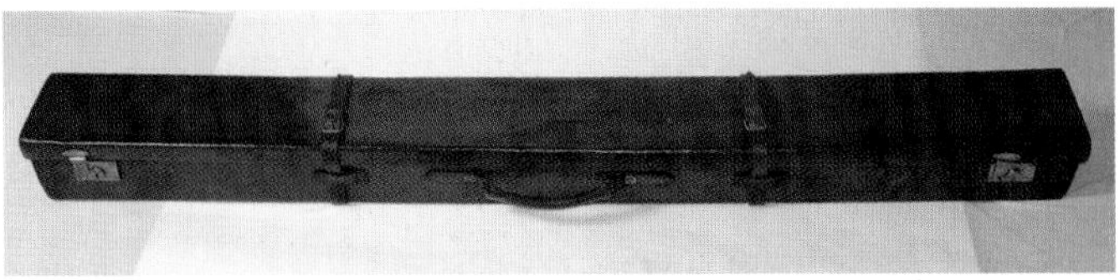

A leather fishing rod case, with brass fittings, 1880s, 69¼in (176cm) long.
£625–685
€/ $980–1,000 ⊞ MSh

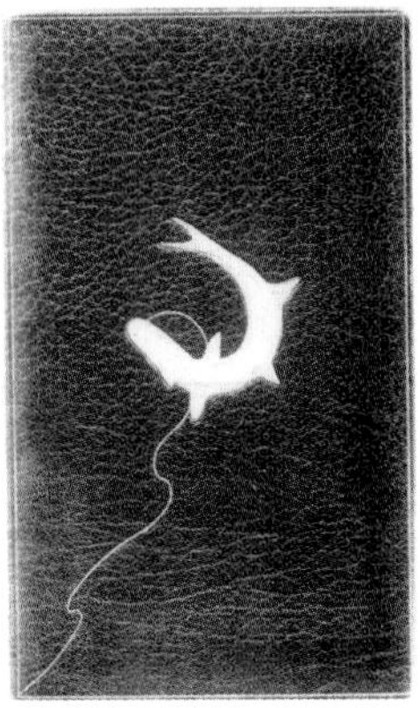

► **Eldridge Reeves Johnson,** *Tarpomania – The Madness of Fishing*, New York, 1908, 8°, photographic plates, inscribed and signed by the author, full green morocco with white- and gilt-inlaid tarpon, some damage.
£325–375
€/ $500–600 ⚒ F&C

Items in the Sport section have been arranged in alphabetical order within each sub-section.

► **A French reed creel,** c1900, 26¾in (68cm) wide.
£80–90
€/ $125–140
⊞ MINN

A stuffed and mounted grayling, in a bowfronted case, inscribed 'Grayling, taken by Mr T. Blatchley from the River Costa September 12th 1889, weight 2lbs 6ozs', case 24in (61cm) wide.
£700–850
€/ $1,100–1,300 ⚒ AH

A stuffed and mounted dace, by J. Cooper & Sons, in a bowfronted case, inscribed in gilt 'Dace, 11 inches, 10½ozs, caught at Thetford, Sept 28th 1897, by W. Ransom, Lychnobrite Angling Society', case 16in (40.5cm) wide.
£1,800–2,200
€/ $2,800–3,200 ⚒ SWO

A stuffed and mounted rudd, by J. Cooper & Sons, in a gilt-lined bowfronted case, inscribed 'Rudd 1lb 5½oz specimen 1906', with a framed copy of the 1906 minutes from the Swindon Golden Carp AA.
£725–875
€/ $1,100–1,400 B(W)

A stuffed and mounted perch, by J. Cooper & Sons, in a bowfronted case, 1909, 18in (45.5cm) wide.
£450–500
€/ $700–800 OTB

A stuffed and mounted rainbow trout, by J. Cooper & Sons, in a gilt-lined bowfronted case, c1920, 29¼in (74.5cm) wide.
£850–1,000
€/ $1,300–1,600 MUL

A stuffed and mounted pike, by A. J. Ponchard, in a bowfronted case, 1932, 45in (114.5cm) wide.
£850–950
€/ $1,300–1,500 MSh

► A stuffed and mounted brown trout, inscribed in gilt 'Killed by E. M. Knott, River Sense 30th May 1933, weight 2lb 11oz', case 23in (58.5cm) wide.
£450–530
€/ $710–830 L&E

Insurance values

Always insure your valuable antiques for the cost of replacing them with similar items, regardless of the original price paid. Both dealers and auctioneers can provide a valuation service for a fee.

A stuffed and mounted bream, by J. Cooper & Sons, in a bowfronted case, inscribed in black and gilt 'Bream 5lbs caught by R. W. Draper Jnr, 4th Aug 1947', case 24¾in (63cm) wide.
£550–650
€/ $870–1,000 SWO

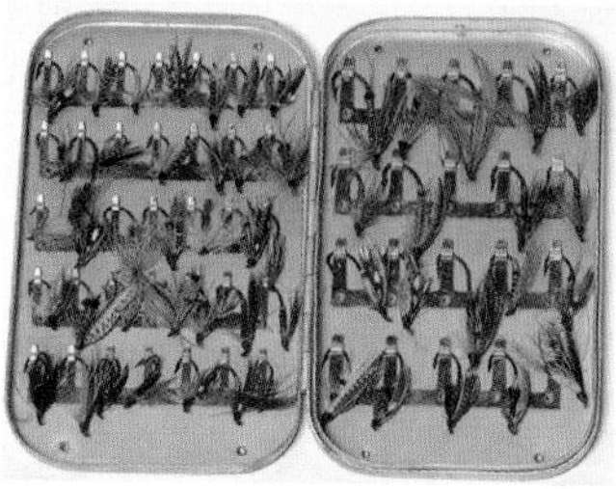

A collection of salmon flies, in a Wheatley aluminium case, 1920s, 6in (15cm) wide.
£70–80
€/ $110–125 MINN

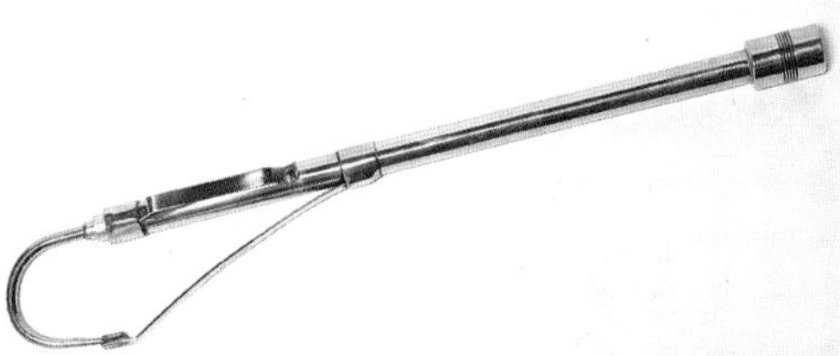

An Allcock & Co priest gaff, 1930s, 14in (35.5cm) long.
£70–80
€/ $110–125 MINN

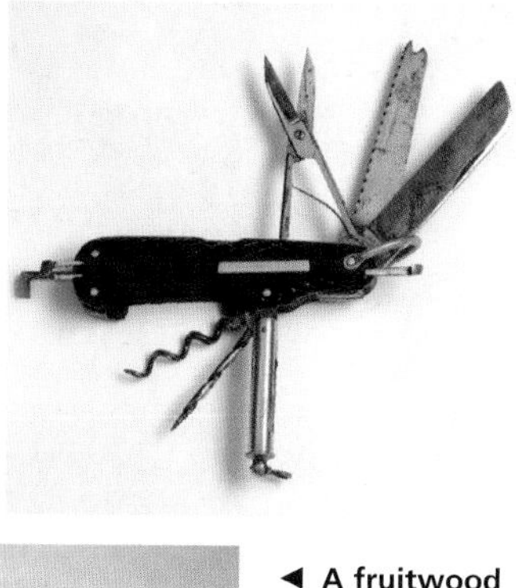

► A horn-cased angler's knife, early 20thC, 4¼in (11cm) long.
£400–450
€/ $630–700
OTB

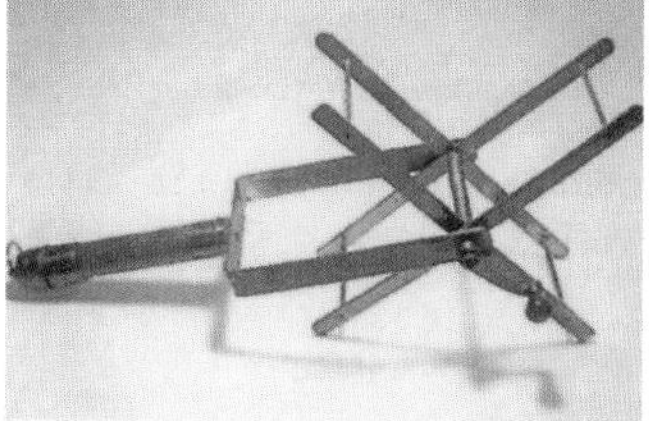

◄ A fruitwood and brass line drier, stamped 'Army & Navy Stores, London', c1905, 16in (40.5cm) long.
£130–150
€/ $200–240
MUL

A chromium-plated car mascot, inscribed 'Fly fishers' club', c1920, 5in (12.5cm) long.
£200–225
€/ $315–350 L

An enamelled menu holder, by Goldsmiths & Silversmiths Co, Chester 1905, the centre panel depicting a black bass leaping, 1½in (3.5cm) diam.
£300–350
€/ $375–550 B(W)

A folding trout net, by Millwards, with a wooden handle, measure and brass fittings, 1920s, 40in (101.5cm) long.
£105–115
€/ $160–180 MINN

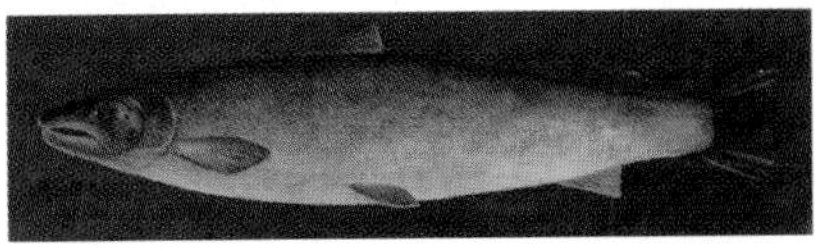

A painting of a trophy fish, caught on the River Wye, inscribed 'May 6th 1913', on wood, 50½in (128.5cm) wide.
£900–1,000
€/ $1,400–1,500 MINN

A Jones 4in brass fly reel, with leather case, c1880.
£110–120
€/ $170–190 MINN

A Malloch 2¾in Sun and Planet brass and ebonite fly reel, with nickel-silver rims, fixed check, triple pillared cage, rosewood handle, brass handleplate stamped 'Patent', c1880.
£220–250
€/ $350–400 MUL

A Hardy Hercules 4in Special Pattern Fly Reel, with raised constant check housing to front plate, waisted brass foot pierced twice, quadruple pillared cage and ivorine handle, c1890.
£220–250
€/ $350–400 MUL

A Prickman Hercules-style 2¼in reel, with constant check, triple pillared cage, horn handle and raised brass winding plate, c1895.
£160–200
€/ $250–315 MUL

A brass crank wind reel, probably by Reuben Heaton of Birmingham, with fixed check and transluscent amberite handle knob, 1890–1910.
£120–130
€/ $190–200 OTB

A J. Bernard & Son 3½in gunmetal salmon reel, c1900.
£110–120
€/ $175–190 MINN

An Eaton & Deller Hercules-style 2¾in brass salmon fly reel, maker's mark, c1900.
£55–60
€/ $85–95 OTB

A Hardy Perfect 4¼in salmon fly reel, brass rim, 1905 check, Turk's head locking nut, ivory handle and brass foot, in Hardy card box.
£400–475
€/ $630–750 B(W)

A Hardy Perfect 4in salmon fly reel, c1906.
£675–750
€/ $1,100–1,200 MSh

A Farlow 4¼in Patent lever salmon fly reel, the back plate with half coin-shaped drag control, 1907–15, with original stamped block leather case.
£90–100
€/ $145–160 OTB

An Allcock 3½in Schooling reel, Model No. 1, perforated and brass-flanged ebonite drum, wooden core and single handle with counter balance, engraved, c1915.
£450–500
€/ $700–800 OTB

An Allcock Aerial 3½in centrepin reel, the six spoke drum with ventilated front and ebonite rear flange, drum removal fork and spoke tension, optional brass check button, ivorine handles and brass foot, c1915.
£400–475
€/ $630–750 MUL

◄ **A Hardy Silex 3½in multiplying reel,** first model with smooth brass foot and rim-mounted casting trigger, 1925–26 only.
£800–900
€/ $1,300–1,400 OTB

A Hardy Eureka 4in centrepin trotting reel, with perforated drum, telephone-shaped latch and engraved black-leaded back plate, c1930.
£155–170
€/ $240–260 OTB

An Eaton & Deller Hardy Uniqua-style 3in trout fly reel, with horseshoe-shaped latch and interior stamped 'D', for Walter Dingley, c1930.
£55–60
€/ $85–95 OTB
Walter Dingley was an ex-Hardy engineer who began his own business and made several reels in the Hardy style.

A Hardy Hardex No. 1 Mk II fixed spool reel, with chromed flier, half bail arm and brass lever spool clutch, 1930s.
£65–75
€/ $100–110 MUL

A Hardy Duck's Foot Altex Mk I fixed spool reel, with 'turned up' body shape, spool clutch, ebonite spool and non-folding handle, stamped 'Patent Applied For', 'Mark 1', c1932.
£325–400
€/ $500–630 MUL

► **A Hardy Altex No. 1 Mk II fixed spool reel,** with original leatherette case, c1940, case 6in (15cm) wide.
£80–90
€/ $125–140
OTB

► **A Hardy Jock Scott multiplying bait casting reel,** with line drier, oil bottle and leather-pouched reel spanner, 1938–52, in fitted teak case 6in (15cm) wide.
£720–800
€/ $1,100–1,200 OTB

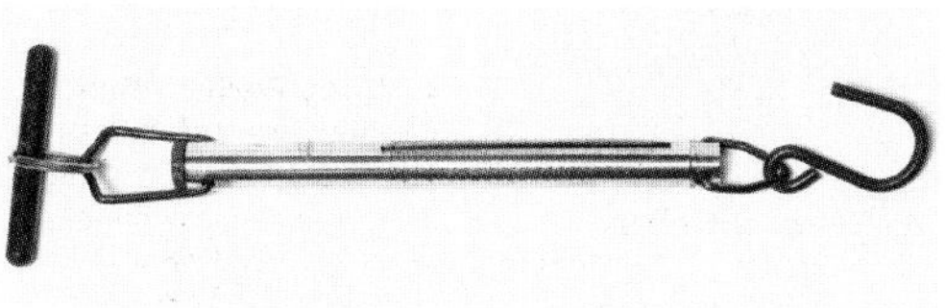

A set of brass salmon scales, 1930s, 13in (33cm) long.
£23–25
€/ $35–40 MINN

A selection of Hardy and Farlow line greaser and rod ferrule grease tins, 1930s–40s, largest 3in (7.5cm) diam.
£10–12
€/ $15–18 OTB

Football

Five James Hurst Cherry Balsam football cards, 'Play Up Oldham', featuring football players, c1900, 3in (7.5cm) high.
£170–200
€/ $270–320 ⚒ BBR

A leather football, signed by the Ipswich Town squad, 1936–37 season.
£800–900
€/ $1,300–1,400 ⚒ S(O)

A 9ct gold and enamel medal, inscribed 'Liverpool Charity Match, 1913'.
£320–375
€/ $500–600 ⚒ S(O)

An England v Scotland International cap, worn by Dicky Bond, 1906, with a print of Bond wearing an England shirt and cap.
£1,700–2,000
€/ $2,700–3,200 ⚒ S(O)
Richard Bond of Preston North End, and later Bradford City, won a total of eight England caps between 1905–10. This cap was awarded to the outside-right for his appearance in the England v Scotland match at Hampden Park, 7 April 1906. Scotland won 2-1.

A Football Association representative cap, from the tour of Canada, inscribed 'F.A. England, Canada, 1931'.
£630–750
€/ $1,000–1,200 ⚒ S(O)

A leather football, signed by the members of the British Isles Amateur Football team, Australia Tour 1937, and the Australian cricket team, including Don Bradman.
£280–320
€/ $440–510 ⚒ SWO

◀ **A Scotland v England International woollen jersey,** worn by Jimmy Quinn, 1909.
£950–1,100
€/ $1,500–1,700 ⚒ S(O)
Jimmy Quinn of Celtic won a total of 11 Scottish International caps between 1905–12.

▶ **A menu card,** for a dinner relating to the Ireland v England Amateur International match, held at the Imperial Hotel, Dublin, on 15 December 1906, signed by 13 members of the England party.
£900–1,100
€/ $1,400–1,700 ⚒ S(O)

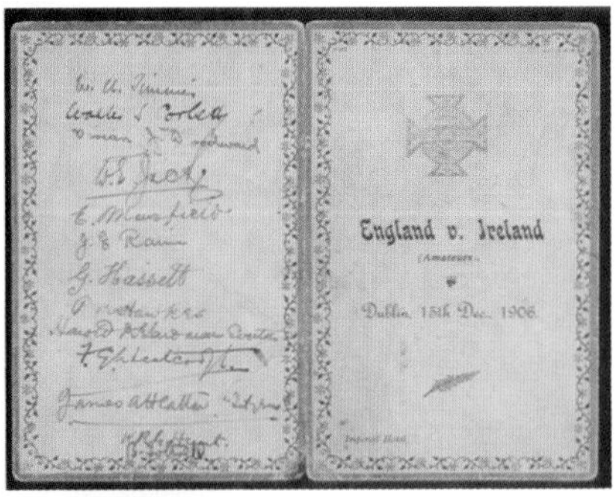

A photograph of the Arsenal squad, 1888, 24 x 20in (61 x 51cm), framed.
£220–250
€/ $350–400 ⚒ CO

◀ **An Arsenal team photograph,** signed by the team, c1934, 7½ x 9½in (19 x 24cm).
£450–525
€/ $710–830 ⚒ S(O)

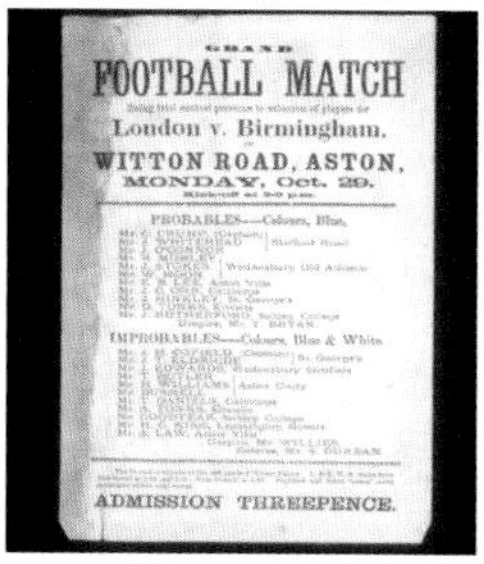

A trial match programme, between Probables and Improbables to represent Birmingham v London at Witton Road, Aston, 29th October 1877.
£2,300–2,800
€/ $3,600–4,400 S(O)

A Newcastle United v Bradford City FA Cup Final souvenir programme, contains portraits of the teams, 12 views of London and statistical information, 1911.
£3,900–4,600
€/ $6,200–7,300 S(O)

A pewter commemorative tankard, for the London F.A. v Frankfurt Inter-Cities Cup match, Wembley, 26 October 1955, with an enamelled badge bearing the crest of the London F.A., with a ruby glass base.
£480–575
€/ $760–910 S(O)
This tankard was presented to one of the Frankfurt players in the above match. This historic game was the first to be played in the competition that was the forerunner of all European football tournaments. This match was also the first game to be played under floodlights at Wembley Stadium.

A silver pocket watch, inscribed 'Presented by the Labrador Watch Company, to Mr J. Graham, Captain of the Millwall Athletic Football Club Champion Team 1st Division Southern League 1894/5', hallmarked.
£300–350
€/ $475–550 B(Ch)

A gilt-metal pocket watch, by Polito, the case decorated with a football scene, signed, Swiss, c1910.
£370–450
€/ $580–700 S(O)

Golf

A gutty ball, hand-hammered, c1860.
£530–630
€/ $840–1,000 S(O)

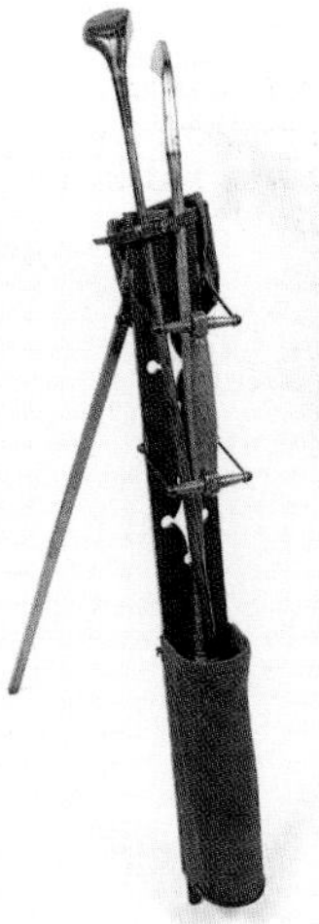

◄ A Bussey automatic caddy golf bag, c1890, 36in (91.5cm) long.
£1,400–1,600
€/ $2,200–2,600 MSh

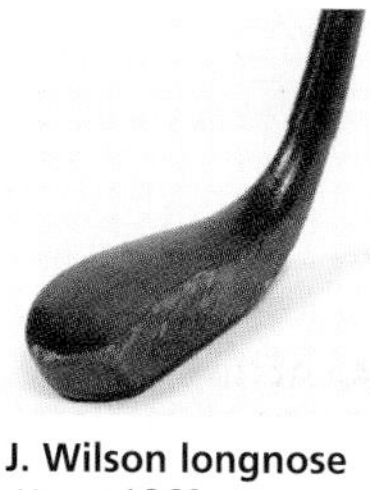

A J. Wilson longnose putter, c1860.
£2,300–2,500
€/ $3,600–3,800 MSh

A silver bowl, inscribed 'Beckenham Golf Club, Captain's Prize 1943, won by Frank Bartlett', maker's mark 'H.H. & S', Birmingham, 6in (15cm) high, 11.5oz.
£85–100
€/ $135–160 BR

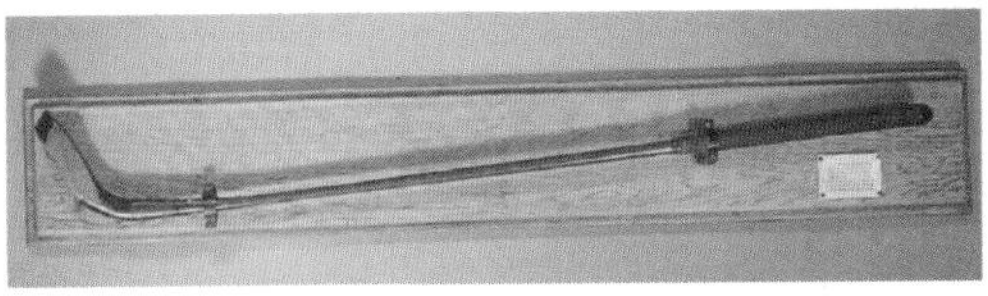

A Robert Forgan & Son fruitwood-headed longnose putter, greenheart shaft, stamped, leather grip replaced, minor damage, c1885, mounted on an oak display board with inscription plaque.
£1,400–1,700
€/ $2,200–2,700 S(O)

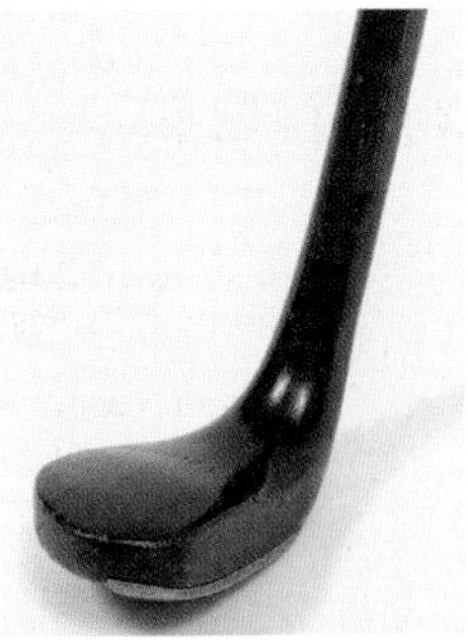

A Sunday golf club, with lead weight and alloy sole insert, c1900.
£230–260
€/ $360–400 MSh

A Bradwell aluminium head driver, with gutta percha face, c1900.
£160–180
€/ $250–280 MSh

A Slazenger driver, c1910, American, 40in (101.5cm) long.
£65–70
€/ $100–110 MINN

An Antishank club, c1910, 38in (96.5cm) long.
£65–70
€/ $100–110 MINN

A silver-plated figure of a golfer, by Zwick, c1920, 7in (18cm) high.
£1,200–1,300
€/ $1,900–2,000 MSh

A Royal Doulton Kingsware dish, after C. Crombie, c1920, 4½in (11.5cm) diam.
£250–280
€/ $400–440 MSh

Charles Crombie, *The Rules of Golf Illustrated*, red lettering on green cloth boards, c1905, 11¾ x 18¼in (30 x 46cm).
£340–400
€/ $540–630 SWO

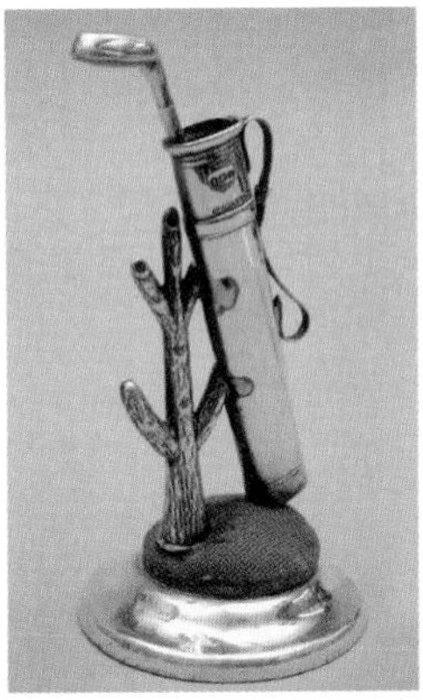

► **A silver novelty hatpin stand/ring holder,** modelled as a golf club and caddy, Birmingham 1910, 4½in (11.5cm) high.
£325–375
€/ $500–600 G(L)

A Doulton Lambeth stoneware tyg and cover, decorated with embossed golfing scenes, with metal rim and cover, c1900, 8in (20.5cm) high.
£3,000–3,600
€/ $4,700–5,700 S(O)

Lacrosse

A pair of Victorian leather lacrosse or hockey boots.
£75–85
€/ $120–135 SA

A photograph, of the North of England men's lacrosse team, 1928–29, 8 x 11in (20.5 x 28cm).
£60–65
€/ $95–100 SA

◄ **A wood and leather lacrosse stick,** 1920s, 49in (124.5cm) long.
£35–40
€/ $55–65 SPT

Olympic Games

◀ **A silvered-bronze and enamel Olympic Games umpire's badge,** London, 1908.
£1,500–1,800
€/ $2,400–2,800 ⚒ S(O)

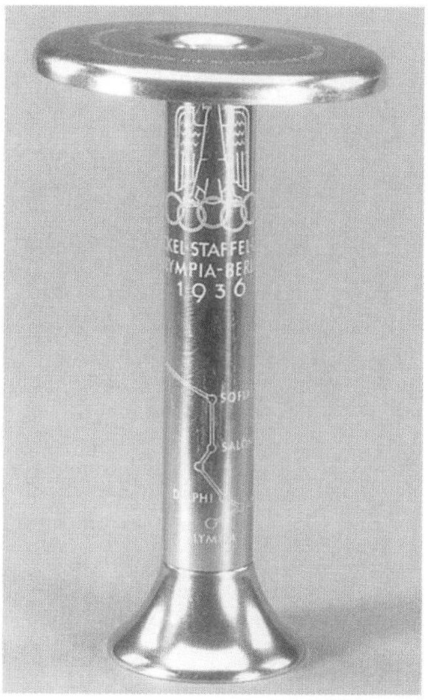

▶ **A white metal Olympic Games bearer's torch,** from the XIth Olympiad in Berlin, the handle engraved with an eagle, Olympic rings and inscribed with the route from Olympia to Berlin, 1936, 10½in (27cm) high.
£2,000–2,400
€/ $3,200–3,800 ⚒ S(O)
The tradition of the Olympic torch relay was inaugurated at the Berlin Games of 1936. The 3,422 bearers each ran 1km.

An Olympic Games bid book, leather-covered with metal and enamel emblem, with fold-out artists' impressions of proposed stadiums, and signed and sealed letters by the Governor of the State of Victoria and the Lord Mayor of Melbourne, 1956.
£420–500
€/ $670–800 ⚒ B(NW)
This book was presented to the International Olympic Committee as the successful attempt to win the 1956 games for Melbourne.

Shooting

A silver ring casket, embossed with pheasants and gun dogs, late 19thC, 3¾in (9.5cm) wide.
£140–160
€/ $220–250 ⚒ G(L)

A leather and brass cartridge magazine, c1900, 16in (40.5cm) wide.
£340–375
€/ $540–600 ⊞ MINN

A leather cartridge bag, 1920s, 9in (23cm) wide.
£55–60
€/ $85–95 ⊞ MINN

An enamel cigarette case, the hinged case decorated with a shooting scene, Continental, late 19thC, 3½in (9cm) wide.
£370–450
€/ $585–700 ⚒ AH

A Britannia metal gun oil container, by J. Dicksons & Sons, Sheffield, c1840, 3in (7.5cm) diam.
£50–60
€/ $80–90 ⊞ ARB

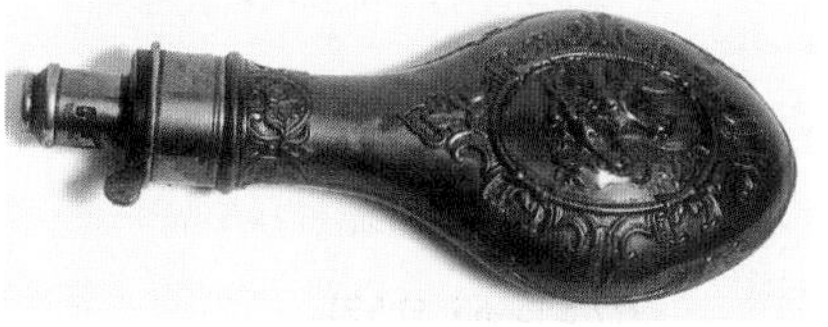

◀ **A copper and brass sporting powder flask,** by Hawksley, Sheffield, with a variable nozzle, c1850, 8in (20.5cm) long.
£135–150
€/ $220–240 ⊞ ARB

A Staffordshire figure of a hunter and his dog, c1820, 6in (15cm) high.
£765–850
€/ $1,200–1,300 ⊞ JHo

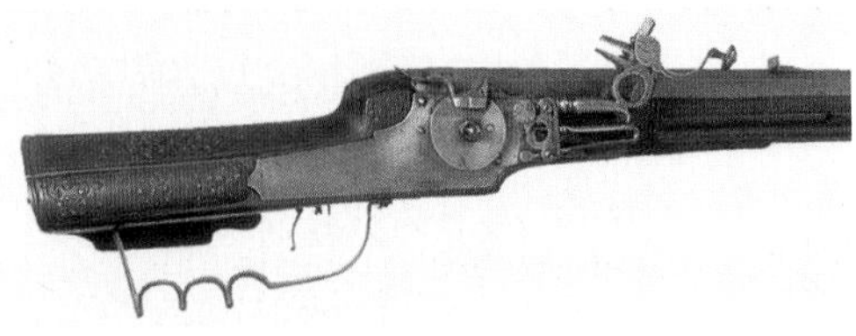

A wheel-lock sporting rifle, by Martin Gummi, with swamped octagonal sighted barrel, figured hardwood full stock, iron trigger guard, with original steel-tipped ramrod, German, c1650, barrel 31½in (80cm) long.
£2,600–3,200
€/ $4,100–5,000 ⚒ S(O)

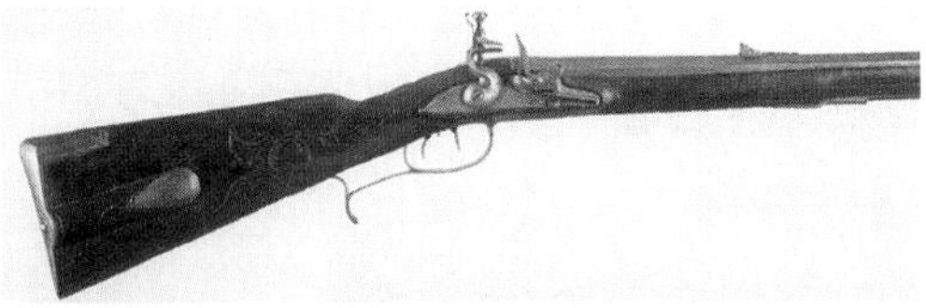

A rifled flintlock sporting carbine, with sighted barrel signed 'Iohann Friedrich Limmer in Bamberg' and dated 1716, the butt carved with rococo ornaments, brass mounts, original brass-tipped ramrod, Bavarian, c1750, barrel 29¾in (74.5cm) long.
£1,500–1,800
€/ $2,400–2,800 ⚒ S(O)

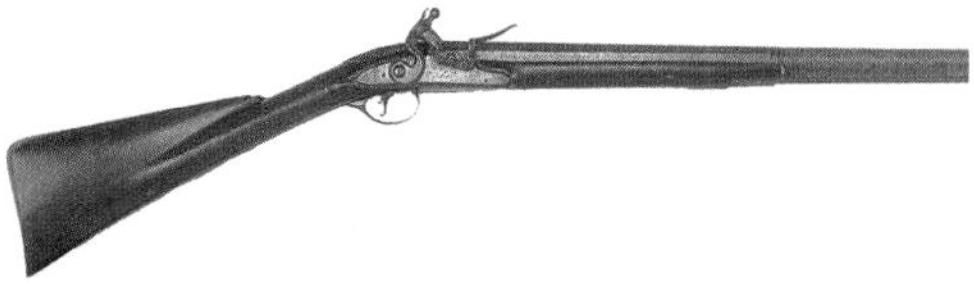

An SB 12 bore flintlock sporting gun, by W. Bailes, London, the barrel with London proof marks, plain walnut half stock, the wrist inlaid with silver wire foliage, steel mounts and ramrod, converted from full stock, c1800, 49¾in (126.5cm) long.
£670–800
€/ $1,100–1,300 ⚒ WAL

A 20 bore flintlock sporting gun, with chequered walnut stock, engraved brass butt-plate and trigger guard, lock stamped 'W.S.', ramrod missing, early 19thC, 54¼in (138cm) long.
£150–180
€/ $240–280 ⚒ F&C

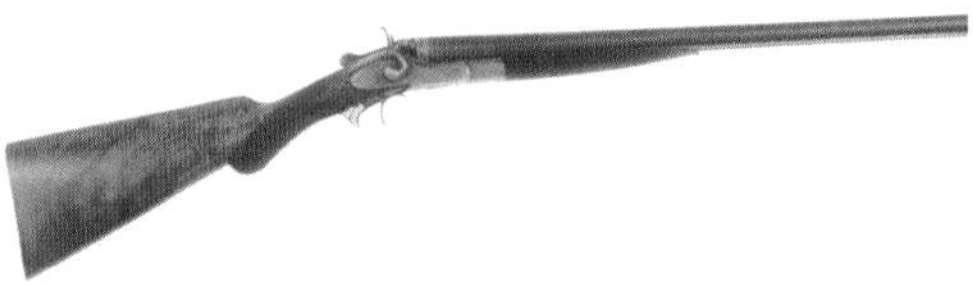

A Winchester match-grade double barrel shotgun, rib marked 'Winchester Repeating Arms Co (Match Gun) New Haven Conn. USA', the receiver engraved with a game scene, double triggers and extractors, 1879–84, barrel 29¾in (75.5cm) long.
£3,000–3,600
€/ $4,700–5,600 ⚒ JDJ

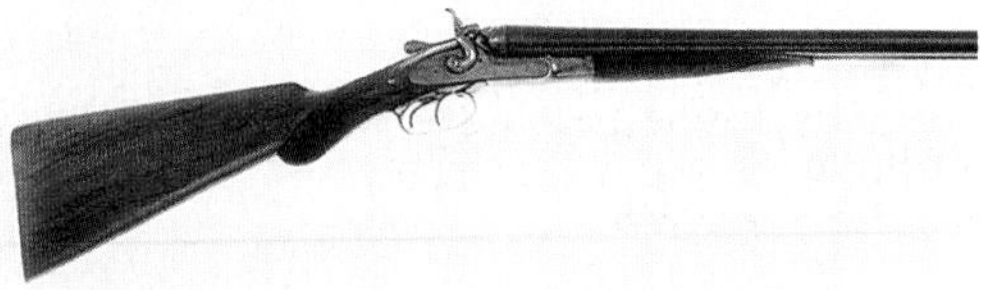

A Winchester Class B double barrel shotgun, rib marked 'Winchester Repeating Arms Co (Class B) New Haven Conn. USA', the receiver engraved with arabesque pattern, double triggers and extractors, 1879–84, barrel 30in (76cm) long.
£2,600–3,000
€/ $4,100–4,800 ⚒ JDJ

The two Winchester shotguns (above and left) are double barrel hammer-type and breech loading, made to order in England by the Winchester Repeating Arms Co. In 1879 Winchester purchased these shotguns from several various makers to test the double-barrel breech loading shotgun market in the US. They did so well that Winchester followed with several more orders, finally designing their own pattern and placing their own name on them. Most of these were made to order by Edmond Redman of Birmingham, with several other makers also being used. These were marked 'Winchester Repeating Arms Co' on the rib and were divided into five classes, the 'Match' gun and 'A', 'B', 'C', 'D', the Match gun being the highest quality. Of approximately 10,000 of these shotguns imported by Winchester, less than 2,000 were made to their specifications and marked with their name. It is estimated that only about three per cent have survived. These shotguns come with extensive documentation and reference material and are exceedingly rare.

A pair of 50 bore percussion target pistols, by Johann Contriner, with signed sighted barrels, figured half stocks and steel mounts, ramrod missing, Austrian, Vienna, c1830, barrels 11¼in (28.5cm) long.
£1,000–1,200
€/ $1,600–1,900 ⚒ B(Kn)

A Royal Doulton Lambeth stoneware trophy jug, Wimbledon Rifle Contest, inscribed and dated 1860–89, 5¼in (13.5cm) high.
£120–140
€/ $190–220 ⚒ SAS

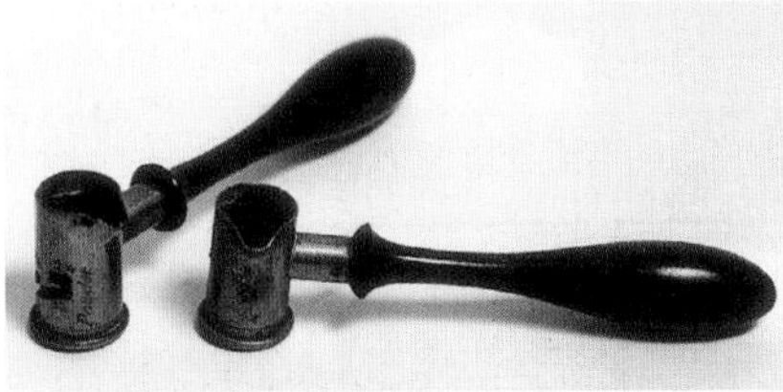

A pair of brass and rosewood calibrated powder and shot measures, c1840, 5in (12.5cm) long.
£80–90
€/ $125–140 ⊞ ARB

► **An Edwardian bamboo and brass shooting stick,** 28in (71cm) high.
£115–125
€/ $180–195 ⊞ MINN

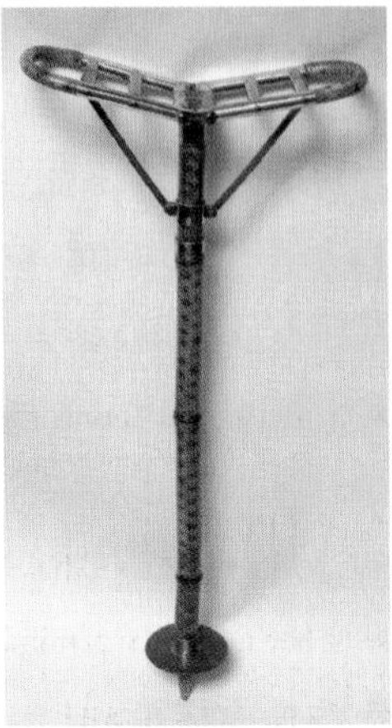

Tennis

A sealed tin of Slazenger patent tennis balls, patent No. 103442, 27 July 1916, 8in (20.5cm) high.
£330–400
€/ $520–630 S(O)

The Annals of Tennis, by Julian Marshall, c1878, 10 x 7½in (25.5 x 19cm).
£2,100–2,300
€/ $3,300–3,600 MSh

A History of Tennis, two volumes by E. B. Noel and J. O. M. Clark, c1924, 11¼ x 8in (28.5 x 20.5cm).
£1,300–1,400
€/ $2,000–2,200 MSh

A silver tennis brooch, pin missing, P.O.D.R. mark for 1880, maker's initials 'J.T.', 1¾in (4.5cm) wide.
£300–350
€/ $475–550 S(O)

W. D. & H. O. Wills, Lawn Tennis, set of 25, 1931.
£150–170
€/ $220–260 VS

► **A spelter figure of a tennis player,** on a marble base, c1920, 10in (25.5cm) high.
£500–550
€/ $800–870
MSh

An oak and brass dinner gong, c1890, 13½in (33cm) high.
£850–950
€/ $1,300–1,500 MSh

► **A mahogany tennis racket press,** for four rackets, with brass fittings, 1890s, 13in (33cm) wide.
£180–200
€/ $280–320 MSh

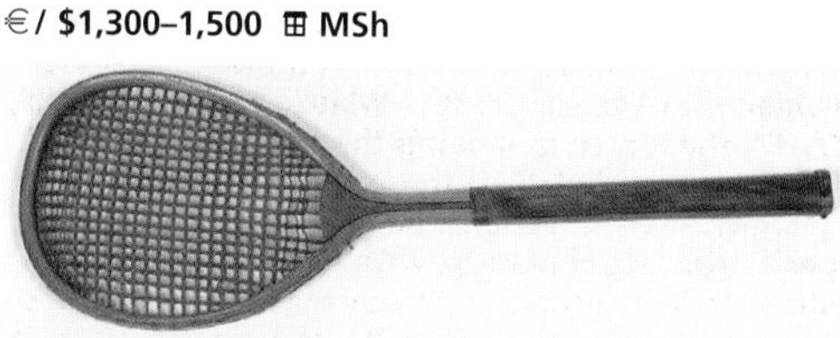

A Mark Bailey tennis racket, with double stringing, 1870s.
£2,300–2,500
€/ $3,600–4,000 MSh

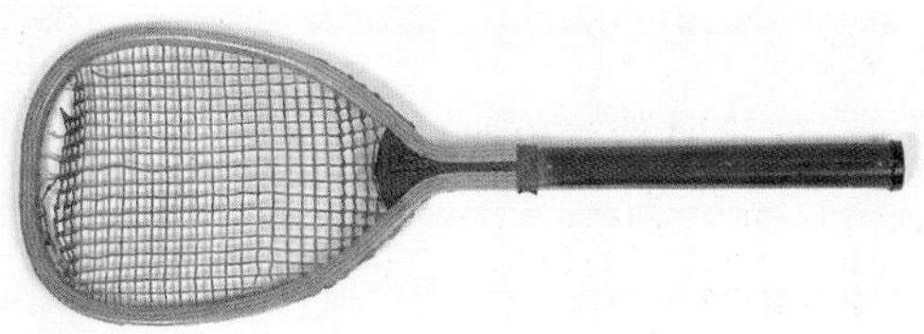

A Sparke flat top tennis racket, 1880s.
£400–450
€/ $630–700 MSh

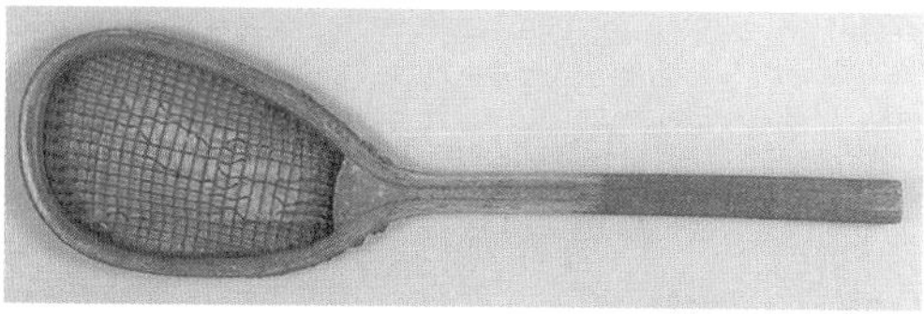

A Brouaye Real Tennis racket, with tilted head, coarse gut strings and lop-sided green morocco wedge, stamped, late 19thC.
£700–840
€/ $1,100–1,300 S(O)

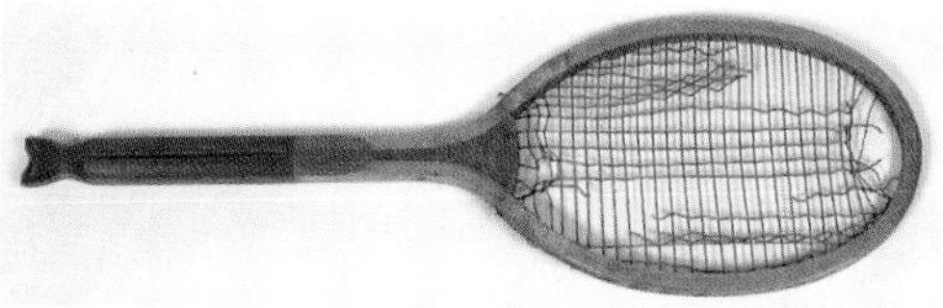

A Slazenger Special Design tennis racket, c1910.
£120–130
€/ $190–200 MSh

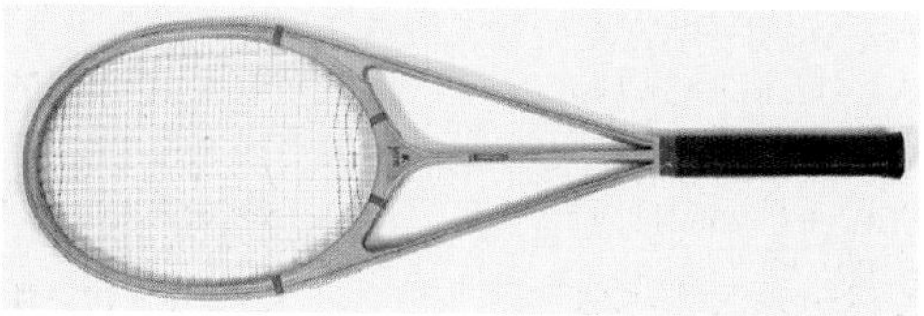

► **A hazelwood Steamline junior tennis racket,** 1930s.
£580–650
€/ $920–1,000 MSh

Glossary

Below are explanations of some of the terms that you will come across in this book.

agate ware: 18thC pottery, veined or marbled to resemble the mineral agate.

Agatin: Marbled glass intended to resemble agate, created by the use of metallic oxides.

albarello: Pottery vessel used for storing pharmaceutical ingredients.

anchor escapement: Said to have been invented c1670 by Robert Hooke or William Clement. A type of escape mechanism shaped like an anchor, which engages at precise intervals with the toothed escape wheel. The anchor permits the use of a pendulum (either long or short), and gives greater accuracy than was possible with the verge escapement.

***aogai*:** Japanese lacquer technique.

arabesque: Scrolling foliate decoration.

associated: Term used in antiques, in which one part of an item is of the same design but not originally made for it. *See marriage*.

automaton: Any moving toy or decorative object, usually powered by a clockwork mechanism.

bezel: Ring, usually brass, surrounding the dial of a clock, and securing the glass dial cover.

Biedermeier: Style of furniture made principally in the 1820s and 1830s in Austria, Germany and parts of Scandinavia and characterized by simple, heavy Classical forms. It is named after a fictional character who symbolized the German bourgeoisie of the early 19thC.

biggin: Form of coffee percolator invented c1799 by George Biggin.

***bijin*:** Japanese term for a beautiful woman.

bisque: French term for biscuit ware, or unglazed porcelain.

***blanc-de-chine*:** Translucent white Chinese porcelain, unpainted and with a thick glaze, made at kilns in Dehua in the Fujian province from the Song Dynasty and copied in Europe.

blind fret carving: Fretwork either glued to, or carved upon, a solid surface and therefore unable to be seen through.

***Bodhisattva*:** Attendant of Buddha.

***boteh*:** Stylized design of a floral bush found on rugs, similar to a Paisley design.

bracket clock: Originally a 17thC clock which had to be set high up on a bracket because of the length of the weights; now sometimes applied to any mantel or table clock.

Britannia Standard: Higher standard of silver required between 1697 and 1720. Denoted by Britannia and a lion's head in profile on the hallmark.

***bureau de dame*:** Writing desk of delicate appearance and designed for use by ladies. Usually raised above slender cabriole legs and with one or two external drawers.

***bureau plat*:** French writing table with a flat top and drawers in the frieze.

cabaret set: Tea set on a tray for three or more people.

calamander: Hardwood, imported from Sri Lanka (of the same family as ebony), used in the Regency period for making small articles of furniture, as a veneer and for crossbanding.

cameo glass: Two or more layers of coloured glass in which the top layer/s are then cut or etched away to create a multi-coloured design in relief. An ancient technique popular with Art Nouveau glassmakers in the early 20thC.

cartouche: Ornate tablet or shield surrounded by scrollwork and foliage, often bearing an inscription, monogram or coat-of-arms.

cavetto: Quarter-round concave moulding.

celadon: Chinese stonewares with an opaque grey-green glaze, first made in the Song Dynasty and still made today, principally in Korea.

cellaret: Lidded container on legs designed to hold wine. The interior is often divided into sections for individual bottles.

***champlevé*:** Enamelling on copper or bronze, similar to cloisonné, in which a glass paste is applied to the hollowed-out design, fired and ground smooth.

chapter ring: Circular ring on a clock dial on which the hours and minutes are engraved, attached or painted.

character doll: One with a naturalistic face, especially laughing, crying, pouting, etc.

***chilong*:** Chinese mythical dragon-type lizard.

Chinese Imari: Chinese imitations of Japanese blue, red and gold painted Imari wares, made from the early 18thC.

chinoiserie: The fashion, prevailing in the late 18thC, for Chinese-style ornamentation on porcelain, wall-papers, fabrics, furniture and garden architecture.

***chuval*:** Turkic word meaning bag.

cistern tube: Mercury tube fitted into stick barometers, the lower end of which is sealed into a boxwood cistern.

***cizhou*:** Chinese porcelain wares characterized by bold shapes and decoration on a slip-covered body. They were named after the most important centre of production, Cixian (Cizhou), but were also produced in many different places in northern China.

clock garniture: Matching group of clock and vases or candelabra made for the mantel shelf. Often highly ornate.

cloisonné: Enamelling on metal with divisions in the design separated by lines of fine metal wire. A speciality of the Limoges region of France in the Middle Ages, and of Chinese craftsmen to the present day.

coin silver: Silver of the standard used for coinage, ie .925 or sterling.

coromandel: Imported wood from the Coromandel coast of India, of similar blackish appearance to calamander and used from c1780 for banding, and for small pieces of furniture.

countwheel: Wheel with segments cut out of the edge or with pins fitted to one face, which controls the striking of a clock. Also known as a locking plate.

***cwpwrdd deuddarn*:** Welsh variety of the press cupboard with two tiers.

Cymric: Trade-name used by Liberty & Co for a mass-produced range of silverware inspired by Celtic art, introduced in 1899 and often incorporating enamelled pictorial plaques.

deadbeat escapement: Type of anchor escapement, possibly invented by George Graham and used in precision pendulum clocks.

Delft: Dutch tin-glazed earthenwares named after the town of Delft, the principal production centre, from the 16thC onwards. Similar pottery made in England from the late 16thC is also termed 'delft' or 'delftware'.

***deutsche Blumen*:** Naturalistically painted flowers, either single or tied into bunches, used as a popular decorative motif on 18thC pottery and porcelain.

***deva*:** Asian female deity.

diaper: Surface decoration composed of repeated diamonds or squares, often carved in low relief.

dog of *Fo*: Buddhist guardian lion.

doucai: Decoration on Chinese porcelain using five colours.

***écuelle*:** 17th and 18thC vessel, usually of silver, but sometimes ceramic, for serving soup. Has a shallow, circular bowl, two handles and a domed cover. It often comes complete with a stand.

***ensi*:** Rug used as a tent door by Turkoman tribes.

EPNS: Electroplated nickel silver.

escapement: Means or device which regulates the release of the power of a timepiece to its pendulum or balance.

***façon de Venise*:** Literally 'in the Venetian Style', used to describe high quality, Venetian-influenced glassware made in Europe during the 16th–17thC.

faïence: Tin-glazed earthenwares named after the town of Faenza in Italy, but actually used to describe products made anywhere but Italy, where they are called maiolica.

***famille jaune/noire/rose/verte*:** Chinese porcelain in which yellow, black, pink or green respectively are the predominant ground colours.

***fauteuil*:** French open-armed drawing room chair.

fielded panel: Panel with bevelled or chamfered edges.

filigree: Lacy openwork of silver or gold thread, produced in large quantities since the end of the 19thC.

firing glass: Low drinking glass with a short, thick stem and a thick foot, used on ceremonial occasions when, after toasting, the glass would be hammered on the table to make a sound like gunfire.

flashed: Method of colouring glass that involves applying a thin layer of coloured glass to a vessel, either by painting it or dipping it into a pot of colourant. Flashed glass can also be carved to produce a less expensive version of overlay glass.

flatware (1): Collective name for flat pottery and porcelain, such as plates, dishes and saucers.

flatware (2): Cutlery.

fluted: Border that resembles a scalloped edge, used as a decoration on furniture, glass, silver and porcelain items.

frit: Powdered glass added to fine white clay to make a type of soft-paste porcelain.

fusee: 18thC clockwork invention; a cone-shaped drum, linked to the spring barrel by a length of gut or chain. The shape compensates for the declining strength of the mainspring thus ensuring constant timekeeping.

***gabbeh*:** Word meaning 'unclipped' used to describe thick long piled rugs produced by the tribes of Fars.

gadroon: Border or ornament comprising radiating lobes of either curbed or straight form. Used from the late Elizabethan period.

girandole: Carved and gilt candle sconce incorporating a mirror.

***goncalo alves*:** Brazilian timber sometimes mistaken for rosewood.

***gope*:** Board presented to New Guinea warriors to commemorate an act of bravery.

***grisaille*:** Monochrome decoration, usually grey, used on ceramics and furniture during the 18th and 19thC.

***guéridon*:** Small circular table designed to carry some form of lighting.

***guilloche*:** Pattern of twisting bands, spirals, double spirals or linked chains.

***gül*:** From the Persian word for flower – usually used to describe a geometric flowerhead on a rug.

halberd: Spear fitted with a double axe.

hard paste: True porcelain made of china stone (petuntse) and kaolin; the formula was long known to, and kept secret by, Chinese potters but only discovered in the 1720s at Meissen, Germany, from where it spread to the rest of Europe and the Americas. Recognized by its hard, glossy feel.

***herati*:** Overall repeating design of a flowerhead within a lozenge issuing small leaves. Used in descriptions of rugs.

***himatoshi*:** Japanese term for the two cord holes in a *netsuke*.

***hiramakie*:** Japanese term for sponged gold applied level with the surface.

***hirame*:** Japanese lacquer decorated with gold and silver leaf.

Historismus: Late 19thC revival of medieval decorative themes.

***hongmu*:** Type of wood used in the manufacture of Chinese furniture.

***ho-o*:** Mythical Chinese bird, similar to a phoenix, symbolizing wisdom and energy.

***huanghuali*:** Type of Oriental wood, much admired for its colour.

***huqqa* (hookah):** Oriental pipe for smoking marijuana, tobacco etc, consisting of a container of water or liquid from which smoke is drawn by means of one or more flexible stems. Also known as a hubble-bubble pipe.

Hyalith: Black opaque glass, developed in Czechoslovakia by Count Bucquoy c1807. Became popular c1840, especially with gold decoration. Also made by Friedrich Egermann.

Ibeji: Nigerian cult whereby if a twin died, a wooden figure of it would be commissioned and the mother would feed, clothe and care for it, to look after it and prevent it from taking the surviving twin. If both twins died a pair would be carved.

Imari: Export Japanese porcelain of predominantly red, blue and gold decoration which, although made in Arita, is called Imari after the port from which it was shipped.

***indianische Blumen*:** Indian flowers; painted on porcelain in the Oriental style, especially on mid-18thC Meissen.

***inro*:** Japanese multi-compartmental medicine or seal container, carried suspended from the sash of a kimono.

ironstone: Stoneware, patented 1813 by Charles James Mason, containing ground glassy slag, a by-product of iron smelting, for extra strength.

jadeite: Type of jade, normally the best and most desirable.

Kakiemon: Family of 17thC Japanese porcelain decorators who produced wares decorated with flowers and figures on a white ground in distinctive colours: azure, yellow, turquoise and soft red. Widely imitated in Europe.

kalian cup: Part of a hookah or hubble-bubble pipe.

***katana*:** Long Japanese sword.

***kelleh*:** Long narrow carpets which are wider than runners.

***kendi*:** Chinese or Japanese globular drinking vessel which is filled through the neck, the liquid being drunk through the spout.

***kiku mon*:** Japanese stylized chrysanthemum.

***kilin*:** Chinese mythical beast with a lion's tail, cloven hooves and the scales of a dragon.

***kirigane*:** Decoration of rectilinear cut gold foil particles on Japanese items.

***kirin*:** Japanese mythical beast.

knop: Knob, protuberance or swelling in the stem of a wine glass, of various forms which can be used as an aid to dating and provenance.

***koro*:** Japanese incense burner.

***kovsh*:** Russian vessel used for measuring drink, often highly decorated for ornamental purposes.

***kozuka*:** Small Japanese utility knife.

***kraak porselein*:** Dutch term for porcelain raided from Portuguese ships, used to describe the earliest Chinese export porcelain.

krater: Ancient Greek vessel for mixing water and wine in which the mouth is always the widest part.

***kufic*:** Arabic angular script – used in rugs to refer to stylized geometric calligraphy.

kylix: Ancient Greek shallow two-handled drinking vessel.

latticinio: Fine threads of white or clear glass forming a filigree mesh effect enclosed in clear glass.

***leiwen*:** Chinese pattern known as 'thunder pattern', used as a decorative motif, usually on bronzes.

***lingzhi*:** Type of fungus or mushroom, used as a motif on Chinese works of art.

Lithyalin: Polished opaque glass resembling hardstones, patented by Friedrich Egermann in 1829 at his factory in Haida, northern Bohemia.

loaded: In silverware, a hollow part of a vessel, usually a candlestick, filled with pitch or sand for weight and stability.

***lohan*:** Saintly or worthy Chinese man.

Long Eliza: Elongated female figure found on Kangxi blue and white export porcelain. The name derives from the Dutch 'lange lijsen'.

lunette: Semi-circular decorative motif popular for carved friezes in the Jacobean and Victorian periods.

made up: Piece of furniture that has been put together from parts of other pieces of furniture. *See marriage*.

maiolica: Tin-glazed earthenware produced in Italy from the 15thC to the present day.

majolica: Heavily-potted, moulded ware covered in transparent glazes in distinctive, often sombre colours, developed by the Minton factory in the mid-19thC.

***mandau*:** Bornean short sword.

marriage: Joining together of two unrelated parts to form one piece of furniture. *See associated and made up*.

***martelé*:** Term for silverware with a fine, hammered surface, first produced in France and later revived by the American silversmiths Gorham Manufacturing Co during the Art Nouveau period.

***meiping*:** Chinese for cherry blossom, used to describe a tall vase with high shoulders, small neck and narrow mouth, used to display flowering branches.

***menuki*:** Hilt ornaments for Japanese sword mountings.

merese: Flat disc of glass which links the bowl and stem, and sometimes the stem and foot, of a drinking glass.

***mihrab*:** Prayer niche with a pointed arch; the motif which distinguishes a prayer rug from other types.

millefiori: Multi-coloured, or mosaic, glass, made since antiquity by fusing a number of coloured glass rods into a cane, and cutting off thin sections; much used to ornament paperweights.

***nashiji*:** Multitude of gold flakes in Japanese lacquer.

nestoris: Ancient Greek pot noted for its high-reaching and sharply-angled handles.

***netsuke*:** Japanese carved toggles made to secure *sagemono* (hanging things) to the *obi* (waist belt) from a cord; usually of ivory, lacquer, silver or wood, from the 16thC.

niello: Black metal alloy or enamel used for filling in engraved designs on silverware.

***ojime*:** Japanese word meaning bead.

***okimono*:** Small, finely carved Japanese ornament.

oklad: Silver or gold icon cover, applied as a tribute or in gratitude for a prayer answered. Also known as a riza or basma.

***oni*:** Chinese devil.

ormolu: Strictly, gilded bronze but used loosely for any yellow metal. Originally used for furniture handles and mounts but, from the 18thC, for inkstands, candlesticks etc.

overlay: In cased glass, the top layer, usually engraved to reveal a different coloured layer beneath.

palmette: In rugs, a cross-section through a stylized flowerhead or fruit.

pardah: Rug which is suspended in a tent doorway.

***pâte-de-verre*:** Translucent glass created by melting and applying powdered glass in layers or by casting it in a mould.

***pâte-sur-pâte*:** 19thC Sèvres porcelain technique, much copied, of applying coloured clay decoration to the body before firing.

penwork: Type of decoration applied to japanned furniture, principally in England in the late 18th/early 19thC. Patterns in white japan were applied to a piece which had already been japanned black, and then the details and shading were added using black Indian ink with a fine quill pen.

pier glass: Mirror designed to be fixed to the pier, or wall, between two tall window openings, often partnered by a matching pier table. Made from the mid-17thC.

***pietra dura*:** Italian term for hardstone, applied to a mosaic pattern of semi-precious stones and marble.

***plique-à-jour*:** Enamelling technique in which a structure of metal strips is laid on a metal background to form enclosed areas which are then filled with transparent enamels. When the backing is removed, a transparent 'stained glass' effect is achieved.

plum pudding: Type of figuring in some veneers, produced by dark oval spots in the wood. Found particularly in mahogany.

pole screen: Small adjustable screen mounted on a pole and designed to stand in front of an open fire to shield a lady's face from the heat.

***poudreuse*:** French dressing table.

powder flask: Device for measuring out a precise quantity of priming powder, suspended from a musketeer's belt or bandolier and often ornately decorated. Sporting flasks are often made of antler and carved with hunting scenes.

powder horn: Cow horn hollowed out, blocked at the wide end with a wooden plug and fitted with a measuring device at the narrow end, used by musketeers for dispensing a precise quantity of priming powder.

prie-dieu: Chair with a low seat and a tall back designed for prayer. Usually dating from the 19thC.

printie: Circular or oval scoop out of glass, sometimes called a lens.

prunt: Blob of glass applied to the stem of a drinking vessel both as decoration and to stop the glass from slipping in the hand.

Puritan spoon: Transitional style of silver spoon, linking early English to modern types. Similar to a slip top but with a broader stem, its name derives from its plain form.

pushti: Rug measuring approximately 3ft x 2ft.

***qilin*:** Alternative spelling of *kilin* – a Chinese mythical beast.

***qin*:** Type of Japanese harp.

quarter-veneered: Four consecutively cut, and therefore identical, pieces of veneer laid at opposite ends to each other to give a mirrored effect.

register plate: Scale of a barometer against which the mercury level is read.

regulator: Clock of great accuracy, thus sometimes used for controlling or checking other timepieces.
rocaille: Shell and rock motifs found in rococo work.
rotelles: Circular decorative 'studs' at the junction of handles on ancient pots.
rummer: 19thC English low drinking goblet.
***ruyi*:** Chinese presentation sceptre.
***sancai*:** Three-colour decoration on Chinese porcelain.
***sang-de-boeuf*:** (lit. ox-blood) Bright red glaze used extensively on Chinese ceramics during the Qing Dynasty.
S.F.B.J.: Société de Fabrication de Bébés et Jouets; association of doll makers founded 1899 by the merger of Jumeau, Bru and others.
sgraffito: Form of ceramic decoration incised through a coloured slip, revealing the ground beneath.
***shakudo*:** Japanese term for an alloy of copper and gold.
***Shibayama*:** Lacquer applied with semi-precious stones and ivory.
***shibuichi*:** Japanese term for an alloy of copper and silver.
***shikoro*:** Neck guard of a Japanese helmet.
***shinto*:** Japanese sword blades made after c1600.
***shishi*:** Japanese mythical beast, a lion-dog.
shoulder-head: Term for a doll's head and shoulders below the neck.
shoulderplate: Area of a doll's shoulder-head below the neck.
***shou* symbol:** Formal, artistic version of the Chinese character shou, meaning long-life.
siphon tube: U-shaped tube fitted into wheel barometers where the level of mercury in the short arm is used to record air pressure.
***soffreh*:** Persian bread cloth.
soft paste: Artificial porcelain made with the addition of ground glass, bone-ash or soap-stone. Used by most European porcelain manufacturers during the 18thC. Recognized by its soft, soapy feel.
spadroon: Cut-and-thrust sword.
spandrel: Element of design, closing off a corner.
spelter: Zinc treated to look like bronze and much used as an inexpensive substitute in Art Nouveau appliqué ornament and Art Deco figures.
spontoon: Type of halberd often carried by junior infantry officers and senior non-commissioned officers.
strapwork: Repeated carved decoration suggesting plaited straps.
stuff-over: Descriptive of upholstered furniture where the covering extends over the frame of the seat.
stumpwork: Embroidery which incorporates distinctive areas of raised decoration, formed by padding certain areas of the design.
***sugán*:** Twisted lengths of straw: referring to a type of Irish country chair which has a seat of this type.
***susani*:** Central Asian hand-embroidered bridal bed-cover.
sympiesometer: Instrument that uses a gas and coloured oil to record air pressure.
***takamakie*:** Technique used in Japanese lacquerware in which the design is built up and modelled in a mixture of lacquer and charcoal or clay dust, and then often gilded.
***tanto*:** Japanese dagger.
***Taotie*:** Chinese mythical animal which devours wrong-doers.
tassets: Overlapping plates in armour for the groin and thighs.
tazza: Wide but shallow bowl on a stem with a foot; ceramic and metal tazzas were made in antiquity and the form was revived by Venetian glassmakers in the 15thC. Also made in silver from the 16thC.
teapoy: Piece of furniture in the form of a tea caddy on legs, with a hinged lid opening to reveal caddies, mixing bowl and other tea drinking accessories.
tear: Tear-drop shaped air bubble in the stem of an early 18thC wine glass, from which the air-twist evolved.
term: Pillar or pedestal terminating in a carving of a human head or torso, usually armless.
tester: Wooden canopy over a bedstead supported on either two or four posts. It may extend fully over the bed, known as a full tester, or only over the bedhead half, known as a half tester.
tête-à-tête: Tea set for two people.
***togidashi*:** Japanese lacquer technique in which further layers of lacquer are added to *hiramakie*.
thuyawood: Reddish-brown wood with distinctive small 'bird's-eye' markings, imported from Africa and used as a veneer.
timepiece: Clock that does not strike or chime.
tin glaze: Glassy opaque white glaze of tin oxide; re-introduced to Europe in the 14thC by Moorish potters; the characteristic glaze of delftware, faïence and maiolica.
toleware: Items made from tinplated sheet iron which is varnished and then decorated with brightly coloured paints.
***torba*:** Turkmen textile bag.
touch: Maker's mark stamped on much, but not all, early English pewter. Their use was strictly controlled by the Pewterer's Company of London: early examples consist of initials, later ones are more elaborate and pictorial, sometimes including the maker's address.
trumeau: Section of wall between two openings; a pier mirror.
***tsuba*:** Guard of a Japanese sword, usually consisting of an ornamented plate.
Tudric: Range of Celtic-inspired Art Nouveau pewter of high quality, designed for mass-production by Archibald Knox and others, and retailed through Liberty & Co.
tulipwood: Yellow-brown wood with reddish stripe, imported from Central and South America and used as a veneer and for inlay and crossbanding.
tyg: Mug with three or more handles.
verge escapement: Oldest form of escapement, found on clocks as early as 1300 and still in use in 1900. Consisting of a bar (the verge) with two flag-shaped pallets that rock in and out of the teeth of the crown or escape wheel to regulate the movement.
vernier scale: Short scale added to the traditional 3in (7.5cm) scale on stick barometers to give more precise readings than had previously been possible.
***verre églomisé*:** Painting on glass. Often the reverse side of the glass is covered in gold or silver leaf through which a pattern is engraved and then painted black.
vesta case: Ornate flat case of silver or other metal for carrying vestas, an early form of match. Used from the mid-19thC.
***vetro a fili*:** Type of glass decorated with threads.
***vetro a retorti*:** Type of glass decorated with twisted threads bedded into the main body.
vitrine: French display cabinet which is often of bombé or serpentine outline and ornately decorated with marquetry and ormolu.
Vitruvian scroll: Repeated border ornament of scrolls that resemble waves.
***wagireh*:** Knotted sampler used by rug weavers showing part of the field design and a section of the border and guard stripe.
***wakizashi*:** Japanese sword shorter than a *katana*.
WMF: Short for Württembergische Metallwarenfabrik, a German foundry that was one of the principal producers of Art Nouveau metalware.
***wucai*:** Type of five-colour Chinese porcelain decoration.
***yen yen*:** Chinese term for a long-necked vase with a trumpet mouth.

Directory of Specialists

If you wish to be included in next year's directory, or if you have a change of address or telephone number, please contact Miller's Advertising Department by April 2004. We advise readers to make contact by telephone before visiting a dealer, therefore avoiding a wasted journey.

20TH CENTURY
Kent
20th Century Marks, 12 Market Square, Westerham TN16 1AW Tel: 01959 562221 Mobile: 07831 778992 lambarda@btconnect.com www.20thcenturymarks.co.uk
20thC furniture and design.

Nottinghamshire
Luna, 23 George Street, Nottingham NG1 3BH Tel: 0115 924 3267 info@luna-online.co.uk www.luna-online.co.uk
20thC objects for the home. Open Mon–Sat 10–5.30pm. Stock includes lighting, furniture, ceramics, glass, telephones, etc.

AMERICANA
USA
American West Indies Trading Co Antiques & Art, 27315 Barbuda Lane, Summerland Key, Florida 33042 Tel: 305 872 3948 awindies@att.net www.goantiques.com/members/awindiestrading
Ethnographic, Folk, Tribal, Spanish Colonial, Santos & Retablos, American Indian, Indonesian Keris, southeast Asian antiquities, orientalia, Art Deco, Floridiana.

ANTIQUE DEALERS ASSOCIATION
Oxfordshire
T.V.A.D.A., The Old College, Queen Street, Dorchester-on-Thames OX10 7HL Tel: 01865 341639 antiques@tvada.co.uk www.tvada.co.uk

Republic of Ireland
Irish Antique Dealers Association, Main Street, Adare, Co Limerick Tel: 00 353 61 396 409

ANTIQUITIES
Dorset
Ancient & Gothic, PO Box 5390, Bournemouth BH7 6XR Tel: 01202 431721
Antiquities from before 300,000 BC to about 1500 AD

USA
Hurst Gallery, 53 Mt Auburn Street, Cambridge MA 02138 Tel: 617 491 6888 manager@hurstgallery.com www.hurstgallery.com
Art of the Pacific, Africa, Asia, The Americas and the ancient world.

ARCHITECTURAL ANTIQUES
Cheshire
Nostalgia, Hollands Mill, 61 Shaw Heath, Stockport SK3 8BH Tel: 0161 477 7706 www.nostalgia-uk.com

Gloucestershire
Minchinhampton Architectural Salvage Company, Cirencester Road, Chalford, Stroud GL6 8PE Tel: 01285 760886 masco@catbrain.com www.catbrain.com
Architectural antiques, garden statuary, bespoke chimney pieces and traditional flooring. MASCo specializes in large architectural features and garden ornaments. The company also carries extensive stocks of hard and soft wood flooring as well as reclaimed building materials. Call or email for further details. Subscribers to the SALVO code. We also offer a Garden Design service.

Kent
Catchpole & Rye, Saracens Dairy, Jobbs Lane, Pluckley, Ashford TN27 0SA Tel: 01233 840840 info@crye.co.uk www.crye.co.uk

Surrey
Drummonds Architectural Antiques Ltd, The Kirkpatrick Buildings, 25 London Road (A3), Hindhead GU26 6AB Tel: 01428 609444 www.drummonds-arch.co.uk
Open 7 days.

ARMS & MILITARIA
Cheshire
Armourer – The Militaria Magazine, Published by Beaumont Publishing Ltd, 1st Floor Adelphi Mill, Bollington SK10 5JB Tel: 01625 575700 editor@armourer.co.uk www.armourer.co.uk
A bi-monthly magazine for military antique collectors and military history enthusiasts offering hundreds of contacts for buying and selling, articles on all aspects of militaria collecting plus the dates of UK militaria fairs and auctions. Available on subscription.

Gloucestershire
Q & C Militaria, 22 Suffolk Road, Cheltenham GL50 2AQ Tel: 01242 519815 Mobile: 07778 613977 qcmilitaria@btconnect.com www.qcmilitaria.com

Kent
Sporting Antiques, 10 Union Square, The Pantiles, Tunbridge Wells TN4 8HE Tel: 01892 522661
Specialist dealers in antique arms, armour, pistols – sporting and military inclusive of all accessories and tools. Books and prints. We buy and sell.

Lincolnshire
Garth Vincent, The Old Manor House, Allington, Nr Grantham NG32 2DH Tel: 01400 281358 garthvincent@aol.com www.guns.uk.com

Surrey
Alan Cook, Walton on Thames Tel: 01932 228328 Mobile: 07785 252120 antiquearms@btinternet.com www.antiquearms.co.uk
Callers by appointment.

West Street Antiques, 63 West Street, Dorking RH4 1BS Tel: 01306 883487 weststant@aol.com www.antiquearmsandarmour.com

East Sussex
Wallis & Wallis, West Street Auction Galleries, Lewes BN7 2NJ Tel: 01273 480208 auctions@wallisandwallis.co.uk www.wallisandwallis.co.uk
Auctioneers of militaria, arms and armour and medals.

Warwickshire
London Antique Arms Fairs Ltd, 15 Burbury Court, Emscote Road, Warwick CV34 5LD Tel: 01432 355416 & 01926 883665 Mobile: 07801 943983 www.antiquearmsfairsltd.co.uk

USA
Fagan Arms, Inc, Box 425, Fraser MI48026 Tel: 586 465 4637 info@faganarms.com www.faganarms.com

BAROGRAPHS
Somerset
Richard Twort Tel: 01934 641900 Mobile: 07711 939789

BAROMETERS
Berkshire
Alan Walker, Halfway Manor, Halfway, Nr Newbury RG20 8NR Tel: 01488 657670 Mobile: 07770 728397 www.alanwalker-barometers.com

Somerset
Knole Barometers, Bingham House, West Street, Somerton TA11 7PS Tel: 01458 241015 Mobile: 07785 364567 dccops@btconnect.com

Warwickshire
Summersons, 172 Emscote Road, Warwick CV34 5QN Tel: 01926 400630 clocks@summersons.com www.summersons.com
We offer a complete restoration service for antique clocks and barometers. We also undertake the following: Dial restoration, cabinetwork and French polishing, wheel cutting, one-off parts made, clock hands cut, fretwork, silvering/gilding, polishing/lacquering, restoration parts and materials, insurance valuations, free estimates and advice. WANTED: Clocks and barometers purchased in any condition.

West Yorkshire
Weather House Antiques, Kym S. Walker, Foster Clough, Hebden Bridge HX7 5QZ Tel: 01422 882808/886961 Mobile: 07889 750711 kymwalker@btinternet.com

Wiltshire
P. A. Oxley Antique Clocks & Barometers, The Old Rectory, Cherhill, Calne SN11 8UX Tel: 01249 816227 info@paoxley.com www.british-antiqueclocks.com

USA
Medford Clock & Barometer, 3 Union Street, Medford, New Jersey 08055 Medlock@aol.com

BEDS
Wales
Seventh Heaven, Chirk Mill, Chirk, Wrexham, County Borough LL14 5BU Tel: 01691 777622/773563 requests@seventh-heaven.co.uk www.seventh-heaven.co.uk

Worcestershire
S. W. Antiques, Newlands (road), Pershore WR10 1BP Tel: 01386 555580 sw-antiques@talk21.com www.sw-antiques.co.uk

BOOKS
London
Biblion, Grays Antique Market, 1–7 Davies Mews W1K 5AB Tel: 020 7629 1374 info@biblion.com www.biblion.com www.biblionmayfair.com
Antiquarian books, maps and prints.

Middlesex
John Ives, 5 Normanhurst Drive, Twickenham TW1 1NA Tel: 020 8892 6265 jives@btconnect.com
Reference books on antiques and collecting.

Surrey
David Aldous-Cook, PO Box 413, Sutton SM3 8SZ Tel: 020 8642 4842 aldous-cook@statacom.net
Reference books on antiques and collectables.

Wiltshire
Dominic Winter Book Auctions, The Old School, Maxwell Street, Swindon SN1 5DR Tel: 01793 611340 info@dominicwinter.co.uk www.dominicwinter.co.uk

BOXES & TREEN
Berkshire
Mostly Boxes, 93 High Street, Eton, Windsor SL4 6AF Tel: 01753 858470
Open Mon–Sat 10am–6.30pm.

London
Hampton Antiques, The Crown Arcade, 119 Portobello Road W11 2DY Tel: 01604 863979 Mobile: 07779 654879 info@hamptonantiques.co.uk www.hamptonantiques.co.uk

Gerald Mathias, Antiquarius, 135–142 Kings Road, Chelsea SW3 4PW Tel: 020 7351 0484 fineantiqueboxes@geraldmathias.com www.geraldmathias.com

Somerset
Alan & Kathy Stacey Appointment only Tel: 01963 441333 Mobile: 07810 058078 info@antiqueboxes.uk.com www.antiqueboxes.uk.com
Tea caddies and fine boxes. Specialist dealers in tortoiseshell, ivory, mop, shagreen, exotic timber pieces. Professional conservation services, consultancy, valuations. Members of LAPADA and BAFRA. Each piece comes with 100% guarantee of quality and authenticity.

BRITISH ANTIQUE FURNITURE RESTORERS' ASSOCIATION
BAFRA Head Office, The Old Rectory, Warmwell, Dorchester DT2 8HQ Tel: 01305 854822 headoffice@bafra.org.uk www.bafra.org.uk

Bedfordshire
Duncan Michael Everitt, DME Restorations Ltd, 11 Church Street, Ampthill MK45 2PL Tel: 01525 405819 duncan@dmerestorations.com www.dmerestorations.com
A full restoration service of antique furniture.

Berkshire
Ben Norris & Co., Knowl Hill Farm, Knowl Hill, Kingsclere, Newbury RG20 4NY Tel: 01635 297950
Gilding, carving and architectural woodwork. Antique furniture restorer.

Cambridgeshire
Ludovic Potts, Unit 1 & 1A, Haddenham Business Park, Station Road, Ely CB6 3XD Tel: 01353 741537 mail@restorers.co.uk www.restorers.co.uk
Traditional repairs, boulle, walnut, oak, veneering, upholstery, cane, rush and gilding.

Derbyshire
Anthony Allen, The Old Wharf Workshop, Redmoor Lane, New Mills, High Peak SK22 3JL Tel: 01663 745274
Conservation and restoration of furniture, clocks and artifacts.

Devon
Tony Vernon, 15 Follett Road, Topsham, Exeter EX3 0JP
Tel: 01392 874635
tonyvernon@antiquewood.co.uk
www.antiquewood.co.uk
All aspects of conservation and restoration including gilding, carving, upholstery, veneering and polishing. Accredited member of BAFRA.

Dorset
Michael Barrington, The Old Rectory, Warmwell, Dorchester DT2 8HQ Tel: 01305 852104
headoffice@bafra.org.uk
The conservation and restoration of antique and fine furniture and clocks. Clock dials and movements, barometers, upholstery, mechanical music, automata and toys, antique metalwork ferrous and non-ferrous.

Essex
Clive Beardall, 104B High Street, Maldon CM9 5ET Tel: 01621 857890 www.clivebeardall.co.uk
Open Mon–Fri 8am–5.30pm, Sat 9am–3pm.

Brian Harris, 24 Town Street, Thaxted CM6 2LA
Tel: 01371 832832

Gloucestershire
Alan Hessel, The Old Town Workshop, St George's Close, Moreton-in-Marsh GL56 0LP
Tel: 01608 650026
Our skilled craftsmen have restored fine furniture since 1976. We accept commissions from galleries and private collections. Our specialism is from the late 17thC to early 19thC furniture.

Hampshire
David C. E. Lewry, Wychelms, 66 Gorran Avenue, Rowner, Gosport PO13 0NF Tel: 01329 286901
Furniture. Consultancy only.

Tankerdale Limited, Johnson's Barns, Waterworks Road, Sheet, Petersfield GU32 2BY Tel: 01730 233792 mail@tankerdale.co.uk
www.tankerdale.co.uk
We offer a comprehensive restoration and conservation service for furniture and historic woodwork, including carving, gilding, marquetry, polishing, lacquer and decorated surfaces. Accredited by BAFRA and UKIC, advisors to the National Trust.

Hertfordshire
John B. Carr, Charles Perry Restorations Ltd, Praewood Farm, Hemel Hempstead Road, St Albans AL3 6AA Tel: 01727 853487
cperry@praewood.freeserve.co.uk
Specialists in restoration and conservation of all types of antique furniture.

Kent
Timothy Akers, The Forge, 39 Chancery Lane, Beckenham BR3 6NR Tel: 020 8650 9179
www.akersofantiques.com
Longcase and bracket clocks, cabinet-making, French polishing.

Benedict Clegg, Rear of 20 Camden Road, Tunbridge Wells TN1 2PT Tel: 01892 548095
All aspects of 17th–19thC furniture.

Bruce Luckhurst, Little Surrenden Workshops, Ashford Road, Bethersden, Ashford TN26 3BG
Tel: 01233 820589
restoration@woodwise.newnet.co.uk
www.bruceluckhurst.co.uk
1 Year Course available, also weekend and 5 day courses.

Lancashire
Eric Smith Antique Restorations, The Old Church, Park Road, Darwen BB3 2LD Tel: 01254 776222
eric.smith@restorations.ndo.co.uk
www.ericsmithrestorations.co.uk
Accredited member of the British Antique Furniture Restorers Association. Consultant to Galway Claire Castle Galway Ireland. Workshop is included on the Conservation register maintained by the United Kingdom Institute for Conservation in London.

Lincolnshire
Michael Czajkowski BSc, E. Czajkowski & Son, 96 Tor O Moor Road, Woodhall Spa LN10 6SB Tel: 01526 352895
michael.czajkowski@ntlworld.com
Conservation and restoration of antique furniture, clocks (dials, movements and cases) and barometers. Skills include: marquetry Buhle and inlaywork; carving and gilding; lacquerwork, re-upholstery and upholstery conservation; clockwork and associated metalwork. Regular collection service to the East Midlands and London. Member of BAFRA and Accredited Member United Kingdom Institute of Conservation.

London
Oliver Clarke Heritage Restorations, 96 Webber Street SE1 0QN Tel: 020 7928 3624
18th & 19thC furniture specialist.

Rodrigo Titian, Titian Studio, 32 Warple Way, Acton W3 0DJ
Tel: 020 8222 6600
enquiries@titianstudios.co.uk
www.titianstudios.co.uk
Carving, gilding, lacquer, painted furniture and French polishing. Caning and rushing.

Norfolk
Michael Dolling, Church Farm Barns, Glandford, Holt NR25 7JR
Tel: 01263 741115 *Also at: 44 White Hart Street, East Harling NR16 2NE. Tel: 01953 718658. Restoration of antique and fine furniture including marquetry, carving, gilding, upholstery and caning.*

Roderick Nigel Larwood, The Oaks, Station Road, Larling, Norwich NR16 2QS Tel: 01953 717937
rodlar@tinyworld.co.uk
Restorers of fine antiques and traditional finishers.

Scotland
William Trist, 135 St Leonard's Street, Edinburgh EH8 9RB
Tel: 0131 667 7775
BAFRA. Registered with the Museum and Galleries commission and Historic Scotland. Restoration and Conservation of antique furniture. Cabinet making, desk leathers, architectural mouldings, French polishing, cane and rush seating, traditional upholstery, chairmaking, materials and fittings. Shop with 18th and 19thC furniture.

Shropshire
Richard Higgins Conservation, The Old School, Longnor, Nr Shrewsbury SY5 7PP
Tel: 01743 718162
All fine furniture, clocks, movements, dials and cases, casting, plating, boulle, ivory, tortoiseshell, gilding, lacquerwork, carving, period upholstery.

Somerset
Stuart Bradbury, M. & S. Bradbury, The Barn, Hanham Lane, Paulton, Bristol BS39 7PF Tel: 01761 418910
enquiries@mandsbradbury.co.uk
Antique furniture conservation and restoration.

Alan & Kathy Stacey Appointment only Tel: 01963 441333
Mobile: 07810 058078
info@antiqueboxes.uk.com
www.antiqueboxes.uk.com
Tea caddies and fine boxes. Specialist dealers in tortoiseshell, ivory, mop, shagreen, exotic timber pieces. Professional conservation services, consultancy, valuations. Members of LAPADA and BAFRA. Each piece comes with 100% guarantee of quality and authenticity.

North Somerset
Robert P. Tandy, Lake House Barn, Lake Farm, Colehouse lane, Kenn, Clevedon BS21 6TQ
Tel: 01275 875014
robertptandy@hotmail.com
Traditional antique furniture restoration and repairs.

Staffordshire
Stefan Herberholz, Middleton Hall, Middleton B78 2AE
Tel: 01827 282858

Surrey
Hedgecoe & Freeland Antique Furniture Restoration & Upholstery, 21 Burrow Hill Green, Chobham, Woking GU24 8QP
Tel: 01276 858206/07771 953870
hedgecoefreeland@aol.com

Timothy Naylor, 24 Bridge Road, Chertsey KT16 8JN
Tel: 01932 567129
timothy.naylor@talk21.com

West Sussex
Simon Paterson, Whitelands, West Dean, Chichester PO18 0RL
Tel: 01243 811900
sp@hotglue.fsnet.co.uk
Boullework, marquetry, clock case and general restoration and repair.

Albert Plumb, Albert Plumb Furniture Co., Briarfield, Itchenor Green, Chichester PO20 7DA
Tel: 01243 513700
Cabinet making and upholstery.

West Midlands
Phillip Slater, 93 Hewell Road, Barnt Green, Birmingham B45 8NL
Tel: 0121 445 4942
Inlaywork and marquetry.

Wiltshire
William Cook, High Trees House, Savernake Forest, Nr Marlborough SN8 4NE Tel: 01672 512561
wcook_uk@yahoo.com

Worcestershire
Jeffrey Hall, Malvern Studios, 56 Cowleigh Road, Malvern WR14 1QD Tel: 01684 574913

CAMERAS
Lincolnshire
Antique Photographic Co Ltd Tel: 01949 842192 alpaco47@aol.com

CERAMICS
Surrey
Julian Eade Tel: 01491 575059
Mobile: 07973 542971
Doulton Lambeth stoneware and Burslem wares. Royal Worcester, Minton and Derby.

CLOCKS
Cheshire
Coppelia Antiques, Holford Lodge, Plumley Moor Road, Plumley WA16 9RS Tel: 01565 722197
www.coppeliaantiques.co.uk
Open 7 days by appointment.

G. K. Hadfield, Beck Bank, Great Salkeld, Penrith CA11 9LN
Tel: 01768 870111
gkhadfield@dial.pipex.com
www.gkhadfield-tilly.co.uk

Devon
Carnegie Paintings & Clocks, 15 Fore Street, Yealmpton, Plymouth Pl8 2JN Tel: 01752 881170
www.paintingsandclocks.com

Musgrave Bickford Antiques, 15 East Street, Crediton EX17 3AT
Tel: 01363 775042

Essex
Bellhouse Antiques, Chelmsford
Tel: 01268 710415
Bellhouse.Antiques@virgin.net

It's About Time, 863 London Road, Westcliff-on-Sea SS0 9SZ
Tel: 01702 472574
sales@antiqueclock.co.uk
www.antiqueclock.co.uk

Gloucestershire
Jeffrey Formby, The Gallery, Orchard Cottage, East Street, Moreton-in-Marsh GL56 0LQ
Tel: 01608 650558
www.formby-clocks.co.uk
Visitors by appointment.

The Grandfather Clock Shop, Styles of Stow, The Little House, Sheep Street, Stow-on-the-Wold GL54 1JS Tel: 01451 830455
info@stylesofstow.co.uk
www.stylesofstow.co.uk
Open all day Mon–Sat or by appointment.

Greater Manchester
Northern Clocks, Boothsbank Farm, Worsley, Manchester M28 1LL Tel: 0161 790 8414
Mobile: 07970 820258
info@northernclocks.co.uk
www.northernclocks.co.uk
Open Thurs, Fri and Sat 10am–5pm or by appointment.

Hampshire
Bryan Clisby Antique Clocks at Andwells Antiques, High Street, Hartley Wintney RG27 8NY
Tel: 01252 716436 or 842305
www.bryanclisby-antiqueclocks.co.uk

The Clock-Work-Shop (Winchester), 6A Parchment Street, Winchester SO23 8AT Tel: 01962 842331 Mobile: 07973 736155
www.clock-work-shop.co.uk

Kent
Campbell & Archard Ltd, Lychgate House, Church Street, Seal TN15 0AR Tel: 01732 761153
campbellarchard@btclick.com
www.campbellandarchard.co.uk
Open by appointment.

Gaby Gunst, 140 High Street, Tenterden TN30 6HT
Tel: 01580 765818
Closed Sun.

The Old Clock Shop, 63 High Street, West Malling ME19 6NA
Tel: 01732 843246
theoldclockshop@tesco.net
www.theoldclockshop.co.uk
Open Mon–Sat 9am–5pm.

Derek Roberts, 25 Shipbourne Road, Tonbridge TN10 3DN Tel: 01732 358986 drclocks@clara.net
www.qualityantiqueclocks.com

London
The Clock Clinic Ltd, 85 Lower Richmond Road, Putney SW15 1EU Tel: 020 8788 1407
clockclinic@btconnect.com
www.clockclinic.co.uk
Open Tues–Fri 9am–6pm, Sat 9am–1pm. Closed Mon.

Gavin Douglas Fine Antiques Ltd, 75 Portobello Road W11 2QB
Tel: 01825 723441/0207 221 1121
Mobile: 07860 680521
gavin@antique-clocks.co.uk
www.antique-clocks.co.uk

Pendulum, King House, 51 Maddox Street W1R 9LA
Tel: 020 7629 6606
www.pendulumofmayfair.co.uk

Roderick Antique Clocks, 23 Vicarage Gate W8 4AA
Tel: 020 7937 8517
rick@roderickantiqueclocks.com
www.roderickantiqueclocks.com

W. F. Turk, 355 Kingston Road, Wimbledon Chase SW20 8JX
Tel: 020 8543 3231
www.wfturk.com

Oxfordshire
Craig Barfoot Antique Clocks, Tudor House, East Hagbourne OX11 9LR Tel: 01235 818968
Mobile: 07710 858158
craig.barfoot@tiscali.co.uk

Scotland
John Mann Antique Clocks, The Clock Showroom, Canonbie, Near Carlisle, Galloway DG14 0SY
Tel: 013873 71337/71827
Mobile: 07850 606 147
jmannclock@aol.com
www.johnmannantiqueclocks.co.uk

Somerset
Kembery Antique Clocks Ltd, Bartlett Street Antiques Centre, 5 Bartlett Street, Bath BA1 2QZ Tel: 0117 956 5281 Mobile: 07850 623237 kembery@kdclocks.co.uk
www.kdclocks.co.uk

Staffordshire
The Essence of Time, Antique Clocks, Unit 2, Curborough Antiques & Craft Centre, Watery Lane, (off Eastern Bypass), Lichfield WS13 8ES Tel: 01543 418239
Mobile: 07944 245064
Open Wed, Thurs, Fri, Sat and Sun 10.30am–5pm. Closed Mon–Tues.

Surrey
Antique Clocks by Patrick Thomas, 62a West Street, Dorking RH4 1BS
Tel: 01306 743661
clockman@fsmail.net
www.antiqueclockshop.co.uk

The Clock House, 75 Pound Street, Carshalton SM5 3PG Tel: 020 8773 4844 Mobile: 07850 363 317
markcocklin@theclockhouse.co.uk
www.theclockhouse.co.uk
Open Tues–Fri 9.30am–4.30pm, Sat 9am–6pm or by appointment.

The Clock Shop, 64 Church Street, Weybridge KT13 8DL Tel: 01932 840407/855503
Open Mon–Sat 10am–6pm. Closed Wed.

Horological Workshops, 204 Worplesdon Road, Guildford GU2 9UY Tel: 01483 576496
enquiries@horologicalworkshops.com
www.HorologicalWorkshops.com

East Sussex
Sam Orr Antique Clocks, 34–36 High Street, Hurstpierpoint, Nr Brighton BN6 9RG Tel: 01273 832081 Mobile: 07860 230888
clocks@samorr.co.uk
www.samorr.co.uk

Warwickshire
Summersons, 172 Emscote Road, Warwick CV34 5QN Tel: 01926 400630 clocks@summersons.com
www.summersons.com
We offer a complete restoration service for antique clocks and barometers. We also undertake the following: Dial restoration, cabinetwork & French polishing, wheel cutting, one-off parts made, clock hands cut, fretwork, silvering/gilding, polishing/lacquering, restoration parts and materials, insurance valuations, free estimates and advice. WANTED: Clocks and barometers purchased in any condition.

West Midlands
Woodward Antique Clocks, 14 High Street, Tettenhall, Wolverhampton WV6 8QT
Tel: 01902 745608

Wiltshire
P. A. Oxley Antique Clocks & Barometers, The Old Rectory, Cherhill, Calne SN11 8UX Tel: 01249 816227 info@paoxley.com
www.british-antiqueclocks.com
Open Mon–Sat 9.30am–5pm. Closed Wed or by appointment.

Allan Smith Clocks, Amity Cottage, 162 Beechcroft Road, Upper Stratton, Swindon SN2 7QE Tel: 01793 822977
Mobile: 07778 834342
allansmithclocks@lineone.net
www.allansmithantiqueclocks.co.uk

Yorkshire
Brian Loomes, Calf Haugh Farm, Pateley Bridge HG3 5HW
Tel: 01423 711163
www.brianloomes.com
Established 37 years.

Time & Motion, 1 Beckside, Beverley HU17 0PB
Tel: 01482 881574

Republic of Ireland
Jonathan Beech, Westport, Co Mayo Tel: 00 353 98 28688
www.antiqueclocks-ireland.com
Member of the Irish Antique Dealers' Association.

USA
Medford Clock & Barometer, 3 Union Street, Medford, New Jersey 08055 Medlock@aol.com

R. O. Schmitt Fine Art, Box 1941, Salem, New Hampshire 03079
Tel: 603 893 5915
bob@roschmittfinearts.com
www.antiqueclockauction.com
Specialist antique clock auctions.

Setniks In Time Again, 815 Sutter Street, Suite 2, Folsom, California 95630 Tel: 916 985 2390 Toll Free 888 333 1715 setniks@pacbell.net
setniksintimeagain.com

COMICS

London
Comic Book Postal Auctions Ltd, 40–42 Osnaburgh Street NW1 3ND Tel: 020 7424 0007
comicbook@compuserve.com
www.compalcomics.com

DECORATIVE ARTS

Dorset
Market Street Gallery Ltd T/A Delf Stream Gallery, Bournemouth Tel: 07974 926137 oastman@aol.com
www.delfstreamgallery.com

Gloucestershire
Ruskin Decorative Arts, 5 Talbot Court, Stow-on-the-Wold, Cheltenham GL54 1DP
Tel: 01451 832254
william.anne@ruskindecarts.co.uk
Specializing in the Decorative Arts 1860–1930. Arts and Crafts, Art Nouveau and Art Deco items. Cotswold School Movement including Guild of Handicraft, Gordon Russell and Gimson and The Barnsleys, Heals.

Greater Manchester
A. S. Antique Galleries, 26 Broad Street, Pendleton, Salford M6 5BY Tel: 0161 737 5938
Mobile: 07836 368230
as@sternshine.demon.co.uk
Open Thurs, Fri and Sat or by appointment.

Kent
The Design Gallery 1850–1950, 5 The Green, Westerham TN16 1AS Tel: 01959 561234
Mobile: 07974 322858
sales@thedesigngallery.uk.com
www.thedesigngallery.uk.com

London
Artemis Decorative Arts Ltd, 36 Kensington Church Street W8 4BX Tel: 020 7376 0377
Artemis.w8@btinternet.com
www.artemisdecorativearts.com

Crafts Nouveau, 112 Alexander Park Road, Muswell Hill N10 2AE Tel: 020 8444 3300
Mobile: 07958 448 380
craftsnouveau@btconnect.com
www.craftsnouveau.co.uk

Rumours, 4 The Mall, Upper Street, Camden Passage, Islington N1 0PD Tel: 020 7704 6549/078 36 277274 Mobile: 07831 103748
Rumdec@aol.com
Moorcroft.

Shapiro & Co., Stand 380, Gray's Antique Market, 58 Davies Street W1K 5LP Tel: 020 7491 2710
Fabergé.

Northamptonshire
Aspidistra Antiques, 51 High Street, Finedon, Wellingborough NN9 5JN Tel: 01933 680196
Mobile: 07768 071948
info@aspidistra-antiques.com
www.aspidistra-antiques.com

Scotland
decorative arts @ doune, Stand 26, Scottish Antique and Arts Centre, By Doune, Stirling FK16 6HD Tel: 01786 461 439 or 0141 946 3571 Mobile: 07778 475 974
decorativearts.doune@btinternet.com
www.decorativearts-doune.com

Yorkshire
Muir Hewitt, Art Deco Originals, Halifax Antiques Centre, Queens Road Mills, Queen's Road/Gibbet Street, Halifax HX1 4LR Tel: 01422 347377 muir.hewitt@virgin.net
www.muirhewitt.com
Clarice Cliff.

Republic of Ireland
Mitofsky Antiques, 8 Rathfarnham Road, Terenure, Dublin 6
Tel: 00 353 1 492 0033
info@mitofskyartdeco.com
www.mitofskyartdeco.com

EPHEMERA

Nottinghamshire
T. Vennett-Smith, 11 Nottingham Road, Gotham NG11 0HE
Tel: 0115 983 0541
info@vennett-smith.com
www.vennett-smith.com
Ephemera auctions.

EXHIBITION & FAIR ORGANISERS

Devon
Trident Exhibitions, West Devon Business Park, Tavistock PL19 9DP
Tel: 01822 614671
info@trident-exhibitions.co.uk
www.tridentexhibitions.co.uk
www.interfine.co.uk
www.surreyantiquesfair.co.uk
www.buxtonantiquesfair.co.uk

Nottinghamshire
DMG Fairs, PO Box 100, Newark NG24 1DJ Tel: 01636 702326
www.dmgantiquefairs.com

Warwickshire
London Antique Arms Fairs Ltd, 15 Burbury Court, Emscote Road, Warwick CV34 5LD Tel: 01432 355416 & 01926 883665
Mobile: 07801 943983
www.antiquearmsfairsltd.co.uk

West Midlands
Antiques for Everyone Fair, NEC House, National Exhibition Centre, Birmingham B40 1NT
Tel: 0121 780 4141
antiques@necgroup.co.uk
www.antiquesforeveryone.co.uk

EXPORTERS

Devon
Pugh's Antiques, Pugh's Farm, Monkton, Nr Honiton EX14 9QH
Tel: 01404 42860
sales@pughsantiques.com
www.pughsantiques.com
Open Mon–Sat.

Gloucestershire
Piano-Export, Bridge Road, Kingswood, Bristol BS15 4FW
Tel: 0117 956 8300
Open Mon–Fri.

Nottinghamshire
Antiques Across the World, James Alexander Building, London Road/Manvers Street, Nottingham NG2 3AE Tel: 0115 979 9199 tonyrimes@btopenworld.com

Staffordshire
Acorn G.D.S. Ltd, 183 Queens Road, Penkhull, Stoke-on-Trent ST4 7LF Tel: 01538 399670 acorn@acorn-freight.co.uk www.acorn-freight.co.uk

East Sussex
International Furniture Exporters Ltd, Old Cement Works, South Heighton, Newhaven BN9 0HS Tel: 01273 611251 ife55@aol.com www.int-furniture-exporters.co.uk

The Old Mint House, High Street, Pevensey BN24 5LF Tel: 01323 762337 antiques@minthouse.co.uk www.minthouse.co.uk *Open Mon–Fri 9am–5.30pm, Sat 10.30am–4.30pm or by appointment.*

Wiltshire
North Wilts. Exporters, Farm Hill House, Brinkworth SN15 5AJ Tel: 01666 510876 Mobile: 07836 260730 mike@northwilts.demon.co.uk www.northwiltsantiqueexporters.com *Open Mon–Sat 8am–6pm or by appointment.*

FISHING

Hampshire
Evans & Partridge, Agriculture House, High Street, Stockbridge SO20 6HF Tel: 01264 810702 *Sporting auctions.*

Kent
Old Tackle Box, PO Box 55, Cranbrook TN17 3ZU Tel: 01580 713979 Mobile: 07729 278 293 tackle.box@virgin.net

London
Angling Auctions, PO Box 2095 W12 8RU Tel: 020 8749 4175/07785 281349 neil@anglingauctions.demon.co.uk

FURNITURE

Berkshire
Hill Farm Antiques, Hill Farm, Shop Lane, Leckhampstead, Nr Newbury RG20 8QG Tel: 01488 638541/638361 Mobile: 07836 503561 beesley@hillfarmantiques.demon.co.uk *Specialists in antique dining tables.*

The Old Malthouse, Hungerford RG17 0EG Tel: 01488 682209 hunwick@oldmalthouse30.freeserve.co.uk

Cumbria
Anthemion, Cartmel, Grange Over Sands LA11 6QD Tel: 015395 36295 Mobile: 07768 443757

Derbyshire
Spurrier-Smith Antiques, 28, 30, 39 Church Street, Ashbourne DE6 1AJ Tel: 01335 343669/342198/344377

Devon
Musgrave Bickford Antiques, 15 East Street, Crediton EX17 3AT Tel: 01363 775042

Pugh's Antiques, Pugh's Farm, Monkton, Nr Honiton EX14 9QH Tel: 01404 42860 sales@pughsantiques.com www.pughsantiques.com *Open Mon–Sat.*

Jane Strickland & Daughters, 71 High Street, Honiton EX14 1PW Tel: 01404 44221 JSandDaughtersUk@aol.com www.janestricklanddaughters.co.uk

Essex
F. G. Bruschweiler (Antiques) Ltd, 41–67 Lower Lambricks, Rayleigh SS6 8DA Tel: 01268 773 761/773 932 info@fgbantiques.com www.fgbantiques.com *Member of LAPADA.*

Gloucestershire
Christopher Clarke (Antiques) Ltd, The Fosseway, Stow-on-the-Wold GL54 1JS Tel: 01451 830476 cclarkeantiques@aol.com www.campaignfurniture.com *Specialists in Campaign furniture and travel items, including furniture, leather goods, luggage, boxes, candlesticks, personal items and artwork, etc. Annual exhibition.*

Hertfordshire
Collins Antiques, Corner House, Wheathampstead AL4 8AP Tel: 01582 833111

Kent
Flower House Antiques, 90 High Street, Tenterden TN30 6JB Tel: 01580 763764

Pamela Goodwin, 11 The Pantiles, Royal Tunbridge Wells TN2 5TD Tel: 01892 618200 mail@goodwinantiques.co.uk www.goodwinantiques.co.uk *Antique furniture, clocks, oil lamps, mirrors and decorative items.*

Jeroen Markies Antiques & Furniture Exchange Uk.Com, 25 High Street, Edenbridge TN8 5AB Tel: 01732 867687 jeroen@furnitureexchange.uk.com www.furnitureexchange.uk.com

Sutton Valence Antiques, North Street, Sutton Valence, Nr Maidstone ME17 3AP Tel: 01622 843333/01622 675332 svantiques@aol.com www.svantiques.co.uk

Swan Antiques, Stone Street, Cranbrook TN17 3HF0 Tel: 01580 712720

Lincolnshire
Seaview Antiques, Stanhope Road, Horncastle LN9 5DG Tel: 01507 524524 tracey@seaviewantiques.co.uk www.seaviewantiques.co.uk

London
Oola Boola Antiques London, 139–147 Kirkdale SE26 4QJ Tel: 020 8291 9999 Mobile: 07956 261252 oola.boola@telco4u.net

Middlesex
Phelps Antiques, 133–135 St Margaret's Road, Twickenham TW1 1RG Tel: 020 8892 1778/7129 antiques@phelps.co.uk www.phelps.co.uk *Mon–Fri 9am–5.30pm, Sat 9.30am–5.30pm, Sun 12am–4pm.*

Oxfordshire
Blender Antiques, Cotefield Farm, Oxford Road, Bodicote, Nr Banbury OX15 4AQ Tel: 01295 254754 blenderantiques@btopenworld.com www.blenderantiques.co.uk

The Chair Set, 18 Market Place, Woodstock OX20 1TA Tel: 01428 707301 Mobile: 07711 625 477 allanjames@thechairset.com www.thechairset.com *Specialists in sets of chairs, furniture and accessories for the dining room.*

Rupert Hitchcox Antiques, Warpsgrove, Nr Chalgrove, Oxford OX44 7RW Tel: 01865 890241 www.ruperthitchcoxantiques.co.uk

Georg S. Wissinger Antiques, Georgian House Antiques, 2, 21 & 44 West Street, Chipping Norton OX7 5EU Tel: 01608 641369

Surrey
Dorking Desk Shop, J. G. Elias Antiques Limited, 41 West Street, Dorking RH4 1BU Tel: 01306 883327/880535 info@dorkingdeskshop.co.uk www.desk.uk.com *Antique desks.*

J. Hartley Antiques Ltd, 186 High Street, Ripley GU23 6BB Tel: 01483 224318

East Sussex
The Old Mint House, High Street, Pevensey BN24 5LF Tel: 01323 762337 antiques@minthouse.co.uk www.minthouse.co.uk *Open Mon–Fri 9am–5.30pm, Sat 10.30am–4.30pm or by appointment.*

Pastorale Antiques, 15 Malling Street, Lewes BN7 2RA Tel: 01273 473259 or 01435 863044 pastorale@btinternet.com *Large showrooms. Genuine Georgian and Victorian furniture as seen in Miller's Antiques Price Guide. Also French provincial and old pine. A further 3,000 sq ft now available for serious traders. Phone for details.*

West Sussex
British Antique Replicas, 22 School Close, Queen Elizabeth Avenue, Burgess Hill RH15 9RX Tel: 01444 245577 www.1760.com *Antique replica furniture.*

Stable Antiques, Adrian Hoyle, 98a High Street, Lindfield RH16 2HP Tel: 01444 483662 Mobile: 07768 900331 ahoyle@msn.com *Regency furniture.*

Warwickshire
Apollo Antiques Ltd, The Saltisford, Birmingham Road, Warwick CV34 4TD Tel: 01926 494746/494666 mynott@apolloantiques.com www.apolloantiques.com

Coleshill Antiques & Interiors, 12–14 High Street, Coleshill B46 1AZ Tel: 01675 467416 enquiries@coleshillantiques.com www.coleshillantiques.com *Dealers in fine antiques and exclusive interiors.*

West Midlands
Martin Taylor Antiques, 323 Tettenhall Road, Wolverhampton WV6 0JZ Tel: 01902 751166/07836 636524 enquiries@mtaylor-antiques.co.uk www.mtaylor-antiques.co.uk

Wiltshire
Cross Hayes Antiques, Units 6–8 Westbrook Farm, Draycot Cerne, Chippenham SN15 5LH Tel: 01249 720033 david@crosshayes.co.uk www.crosshayes.co.uk *Shipping furniture.*

USA
Antique Associates at West Townsend, PO Box 129W, 473 Main Street, West Townsend MA 01474 Tel: (978) 597 8084 drh@aaawt.com

Dragonflies Antiques & Decorating Center, Frank & Cathy Sykes, New England Events Mgt, PO Box 678, 24 Center Street, Wolfeboro, New Hampshire 03894 Tel: 603 569 0000 Dragonflies@metrocast.net *Also Folk Art, mahogany speed boat models, maps and antiquarian books.*

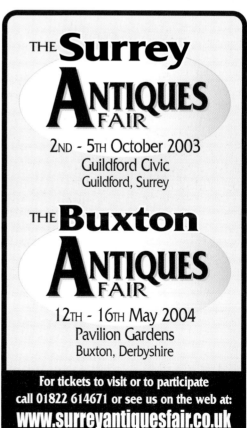

Warehouse Provence, 1120 Massachusetts Ave, (Rte 111) Boxborough, Maine MA 01719 Tel: 978 266 0200 warehouseprovence@aics.net www.warehouseprovence.com

GLASS
Somerset
Somervale Antiques, 6 Radstock Road, Midsomer Norton, Bath BA3 2AJ Tel: 01761 412686 Mobile: 07885 088022 ronthomas@somervaleantiquesglass.co.uk www.somervaleantiquesglass.co.uk

Staffordshire
Gordon Litherland, 25 Stapenhill Road, Burton on Trent DE15 9AE Tel: 01283 567213 Mobile: 07952 118987 pubjugs@aol.com *Bottles, breweriana and pub jugs, advertising ephemera and commemoratives.*

ICONS
London
The Temple Gallery, 6 Clarendon Cross, Holland Park W11 4AP Tel: 020 7727 3809 info@templegallery.com www.templegallery.com

IRISH ANTIQUE DEALERS ASSOCIATION
Northern Ireland
Marion Langham Limited, Claranagh, Tempo, County Fermanagh BT94 3FJ Tel: 028 6654 1247 marion@ladymarion.co.uk www.ladymarion.co.uk *Belleek and paperweights specialist.*

Republic of Ireland
Jonathan Beech, Westport, Co Mayo Tel: 00 353 98 28688 www.antiqueclocks-ireland.com

IVORY & TORTOISESHELL
Somerset
Alan & Kathy Stacey Appointment only Tel: 01963 441333 Mobile: 07810 058078 info@antiqueboxes.uk.com www.antiqueboxes.uk.com *Tea caddies and fine boxes. Specialist dealers in tortoiseshell, ivory, mop, shagreen, exotic timber pieces. Professional conservation services, consultancy, valuations. Members of LAPADA and BAFRA. Each piece comes with 100% guarantee of quality and authenticity.*

JEWELLERY
London
Sarah Groombridge, Stand 335, Grays Market, 58 Davies Street W1K 5LP Tel: 020 7629 0225 Mobile: 07770 920277 sarah.groombridge@totalise.co.uk

Wimpole Antiques, Stand 349, Grays Antique Market, 58 Davies Street W1K 5LP Tel: 020 7499 2889 WimpoleAntiques@compuserve.com

Canada
Fiona Kenny Antiques, PO Box 11, 18 Front Street North, Thorold, Ontario Tel: 905 682 0090 merday@cogeco.ca www.trocadero.com/merday *18th–20thC jewellery and antiques, sterling and silver plate, china and pottery, 20thC modern, collectibles and advertising.*

KITCHENWARE
Gloucestershire
Bread & Roses, Durham House Antique Centre, Sheep Street, Stow on the Wold GL54 1AA Tel: 01451 870404/01926 817342

Lincolnshire
Skip & Janie Smithson Antiques Tel: 01754 810265 Mobile: 07831 399180 *Dairy bygones, enamel wares, laundry items and advertising.*

East Sussex
Ann Lingard, Ropewalk Antiques, Rye TN31 7NA Tel: 01797 223486 ann-lingard@ropewalkantiques.freeserve.co.uk

LIGHTING
Devon
The Exeter Antique Lighting Co, Cellar 15, The Quay, Exeter EX2 4AP Tel: 01392 490848 Mobile: 07702 969438 www.antiquelightingcompany.com *Antique lighting and stained glass specialists.*

Somerset
Joanna Proops Antique Textiles & Lighting, 34 Belvedere, Lansdown Hill, Bath BA1 5HR Tel: 01225 310795 antiquetextiles@aol.co.uk www.antiquetextiles.co.uk

USA
Lamps: By The Book, Inc, 514 14th West Palm Beach, Florida 33401 Tel: 561 659 1723 booklamps@msn.com www.lampsbythebook.com *Gift lamps. Also buy leather-bound books.*

MARKETS & CENTRES
Derbyshire
Chappells Antiques Centre – Bakewell, King Street, Bakewell DE45 1DZ Tel: 01629 812496 ask@chappellsantiquescentre.com www.chappellsantiquescentre.com *30 established dealers inc BADA and LAPADA members. Quality period furniture, ceramics, silver, plate, metals, treen, clocks, barometers, books, pictures, maps, prints, textiles, kitchenalia, lighting and furnishing accessories from the 17th–20thC, scientific, pharmaceutical and sporting antiques. Open Mon–Sat 10–5pm, Sun 12–5pm. Closed Christmas Day, Boxing Day and New Year's Day. Please ring for brochure, giving location and parking information.*

Matlock Antiques, Collectables & Riverside Café, 7 Dale Road, Matlock DE4 3LT Tel: 01629 760808 bmatlockantiques@aol.com www.matlock-antiques-collectables.cwc.net *Proprietor W. Shirley. Over 70 dealers. Open 7 days 10am–5pm including Bank Holidays. Parking available.*

Devon
Colyton Antiques Centre, Dolphin Street, Colyton EX24 6LU Tel: 01297 552339 colytonantiques@modelgarage.co.uk www.modelgarage.co.uk

Essex
Debden Antiques, Elder Street, Debden, Saffron Walden CB11 3JY Tel: 01799 543007 info@debden-antiques.co.uk www.debden-antiques.co.uk *Mon–Sat 10am–5.30pm, Sun and Bank Holidays 11am–4pm. 30 quality dealers in a stunning 17thC Essex barn. Large selection of 16th–20thC oak, mahogany and pine furniture, watercolours and oil paintings, rugs, ceramics, silver and jewellery. Plus garden furniture and ornaments in our lovely courtyard.*

Gloucestershire
The Antiques Emporium, The Old Chapel, Long Street, Tetbury GL8 8AA Tel: 01666 505281 *Open Mon–Sat 10am–5pm, Sun 1–5pm. 38 dealers. Jewellery, clocks, antiquities, books, furniture, treen, flatware, glass, china, porcelain and decorative accessories.*

Gloucester Antiques Centre, The Historic Docks, 1 Severn Road, Gloucester GL1 2LE Tel: 01452 529716 www.antiques.center.com *The Gloucester Antiques Centre makes a fine day out, with antiques and collectibles of every description. There is something for everyone, even those that are not antiques collectors will find items to decorate any home. Collectors of modern items are catered for. Open Mon–Sat 10am–5pm Sun 1pm–5pm.*

Jubilee Hall Antiques Centre, Oak Street, Lechlade on Thames GL7 3AY Tel: 01367 253777 mail@jubileehall.co.uk www.jubileehall.co.uk

Kent
Malthouse Arcade, High Street, Hythe CT21 5BW Tel: 01303 260103

Lancashire
The Antique Centre, 56 Garstang Road, Preston PR1 1NA Tel: 01772 882078 info@paulallisonantiques.co.uk www.paulallisonantiques.co.uk *Open 7 days a week.*

GB Antiques Centre, Lancaster Leisure Park, (the former Hornsea Pottery), Wyresdale Road, Lancaster LA1 3LA Tel: 01524 844734 *Over 140 dealers in 40,000 sq ft of space. Showing porcelain, pottery, Art Deco, glass, books and linen. Also a large selection of mahogany, oak and pine furniture. Open 7 days a week 10am–5pm.*

Kingsmill Antique Centre, Queen Street, Harle Syke, Burnley BB10 2HX Tel: 01282 431953 *Open 7 days 10am–5pm, 8pm Thurs. 8,500 sq ft. Trade welcome.*

Leicestershire
Oxford Street Antique Centre, 16–26 Oxford Street, Leicester LE1 5XU Tel: 0116 255 3006

Lincolnshire
Hemswell Antique Centres, Caenby Corner Estate, Hemswell Cliff, Gainsborough DN21 5TJ Tel: 01427 668389 info@hemswell-antiques.com www.hemswell-antiques.com *Open 7 days 10am–5pm.*

London
Antiquarius Antiques Centre, 131/141 King's Road, Chelsea SW3 5ST Tel: 020 7351 5353 antique@dial.pipex.com *Open Mon–Sat 10am–6pm.*

Atlantic Antiques Centres, Chenil House, 181–183 Kings Road SW3 5EB Tel: 020 7351 5353 antique@dial.pipex.com

Bond Street Antiques Centre, 124 New Bond Street W1Y 9AE Tel: 020 7351 5353 antique@dial.pipex.com *Open Mon–Sat 10am–5.30pm.*

The Mall Antiques Arcade, Camden Passage, Islington N1 Tel: 020 7351 5353 antique@dial.pipex.cpm *Open Tues, Thurs and Fri 10am–5pm, Wed 7.30am–5pm anf Sat 9am–6pm.*

Nottinghamshire
Antiques Trade Space, Brunel Drive, Newark NG24 2DE Tel: 01636 651444 info@antiquestradespace.com www.antiquestradespace.com

Newark Antiques Warehouse Ltd, Old Kelham Road, Newark NG24 1BX Tel: 01636 674869 Mobile: 07974 429185 enquiries@newarkantiques.co.uk www.newarkantiques.co.uk

Oxfordshire
Chipping Norton Antiques Centre, Ivy House, Middle Row, Market Place, Chipping Norton Tel: 01608 644212

The Swan at Tetsworth, High Street, Tetsworth, Nr Thame OX9 7AB Tel: 01844 281777 antiques@theswan.co.uk www.theswan.co.uk *Over 80 dealers displaying 40 showrooms of quality Georgian antiques right through to Art Deco in Grade II Elizabethan Coaching Inn. Open every day 10am –6pm. 5 mins junctions 6/8 M40 motorway. Award winning restaurant. Tel 01844 281777 for brochure or visit website www.theswan.co.uk*

Shropshire
Old Mill Antiques Centre, Mill Street, Low Down, Bridgnorth W15 5AG Tel: 01746 768778 www.oldmill-antiques.co.uk

East Sussex
Church Hill Antiques Centre, 6 Station Street, Lewes BN7 2DA Tel: 01273 474 842 churchhilllewes@aol.com www.church-hill-antiques.co.uk

Hastings Antique Centre, 59–61 Norman Road, St Leonards-on-Sea TN38 0EG Tel: 01424 428561

Wales
Afonwen Craft & Antique Centre, Afonwen, Nr Caerwys, Nr Mold, Flintshire CH7 5UB Tel: 01352 720965 *Open all year Tues–Sun 9.30am–5.30pm, closed Mon, open Bank Holidays. The largest centre in North Wales and the borders. 14,000 sq ft, 40 dealers. Fabulous selection of antiques, china, silver, crystal, quality collectables, fine furniture, oak, walnut, mahogany, pine from around the world. Excellent restaurant, free entrance, free large car park.*

Offa's Dyke Antique Centre, 4 High Street, Knighton, Powys LD7 1AT Tel: 01547 528635/520145 *Open Mon–Sat 10am–1pm, 2pm–5pm. 12 dealers in 18th–20thC ceramics including Delft and slipware, glass, books on antiques, general antiques and collectables.*

Warwickshire
Barn Antiques Centre, Station Road, Long Marston, Nr Stratford-upon-Avon CV37 8RB Tel: 01789 721399 www.barnantique.co.uk *Huge old barn crammed full of affordable antiques. Over 13,000 sq ft and 50 established dealers. Open daily 10am–5pm, Sun 12pm–6pm. Large free car park. Licensed bistro.*

Yorkshire
Cavendish Antique & Collectors Centre, 44 Stonegate, York YO1 8AS Tel: 01904 621666 www.cavendishantiques.co.uk *Open 7 days 9am–6pm. Browse at leisure. Over 70 dealers on three floors. Jewellery, silver, porcelain, glass engravings and prints, furniture, oils and watercolours, watches, collectables.*

The Chapel Antiques Centre, 99 Broadfield Road, Heeley, Sheffield S8 0XQ Tel: 0114 258 8288 enquiries@antiquesinsheffield.com www.antiquesinsheffield.com *Open 7 days, over 25 dealers displaying a wide range of antiques and collectables including specialists in clocks, Art Deco, French furniture, books, pine, fabrics, porcelain, and much more. Services: upholstery, furniture restoration, re-caning, pottery restoration, French polishing and delivery.*

The Court House, 2–6 Town End Road, Ecclesfield, Sheffield S35 9YY Tel: 0114 257 0641 Mobile: 07973 409505

MEDALS
Roxburghshire
Romsey Medal Centre, The Grapes Hotel, 16 Douglas Square, Newcastleton TD9 0QD Tel: 013873 75245 post@romseymedals.co.uk www.romseymedals.co.uk

MINIATURES
Gloucestershire
Judy & Brian Harden Antiques, PO Box 14, Bourton-on-the-Water, Cheltenham GL54 2YR Tel: 01451 810684 Mobile: 07831 692252 harden@portraitminiatures.co.uk www.portraitminiatures.co.uk *Portrait miniatures.*

MONEY BOXES
Yorkshire
John & Simon Haley, 89 Northgate, Halifax HX1 1XF Tel: 01422 822148/360434 toysandbanks@aol.com

MUSICAL INSTRUMENTS
Gloucestershire
Keith Harding's World of Mechanical Music, The Oak House, High Street, Northleach GL54 3ET Tel: 01451 860181 keith@mechanicalmusic.co.uk www.mechanicalmusic.co.uk *Mechanical music and automata, antique and modern. Also antique musical boxes and clocks.*

Piano-Export, Bridge Road, Kingswood, Bristol BS15 4FW Tel: 0117 956 8300 *Open Mon–Fri.*

Kent
Stephen T. P. Kember, Pamela Goodwin, 11 The Pantiles, Royal Tunbridge Wells TN2 5TD Tel: 01959 574067 Mobile: 07850 358067 steve.kember@btinternet.com www.antique-musicboxes.co.uk *Antique cylinder and disc musical boxes.*

Nottinghamshire
Turner Violins, 1–5 Lily Grove, Beeston NG9 1QL Tel: 0115 943 0333 info@turnerviolins.co.uk

OAK & COUNTRY
Cambridgeshire
Mark Seabrook Antiques, PO Box 396, Huntingdon PE28 0ZA Tel: 01480 861935 Mobile: 07770 721931 enquiries@markseabrook.com www.markseabrook.com

Kent
Douglas Bryan Antiques, The Old Bakery, St David's Bridge, Cranbrook TN17 3HN Tel: 01580 713103 Mobile: 07774 737303 *By appointment only.*

London
Robert Young Antiques, 68 Battersea Bridge Road SW11 3AG Tel: 020 7228 7847 *Country furniture and Folk Art.*

Northamptonshire
Paul Hopwell, 30 High Street, West Haddon NN6 7AP Tel: 01788 510636 Mobile: 07836 505950 paulhopwell@antiqueoak.co.uk www.antiqueoak.co.uk

Oxfordshire
Key Antiques of Chipping Norton, 11 Horsefair, Chipping Norton OX7 5AL Tel: 01608 644992 info@keyantiques.com www.keyantiques.com

Surrey
The Refectory, 38 West Street, Dorking RH4 1BU Tel: 01306 742111 www.therefectory.co.uk *Oak & Country – Refectory table specialist.*

Anthony Welling, Broadway Barn, High Street, Ripley GU23 6AQ Tel: 01483 225384 ant@awelling.freeserve.co.uk

ORIENTAL
London
R & G McPherson Antiques, 40 Kensington Church Street W8 4BX Tel: 020 7937 0812 Mobile: 07768 432 630 rmcpherson@orientalceramics.com www.orientalceramics.com *Specialists in shipwreck ceramics.*

Somerset
Lopburi Art & Antiques, 5 Saville Row, Bath BA1 2QP Tel: 01225 322947 mail@lopburi.co.uk www.lopburi.co.uk

USA
Mimi's Antiques, 8763 Carriage Hills Drive, Columbia MD 21046 Tel: 410 381 6862/443 250 0930 mimisantiques@comcast.net www.mimisantiques.com www.trocadero.com/mimisantiques *18th and 19thC Chinese export porcelain, American and English furniture, Continental porcelain, paintings, Sterling, Oriental rugs.*

PACKERS & SHIPPERS
Dorset
Alan Transport Franklin, 26 Blackmoor Road, Ebblake Industrial Estate, Verwood, BH31 6BB Tel: 01202 826539

Gloucestershire
The Shipping Company, Bourton Industrial Park, Bourton-on-the-Water, Cheltenham GL54 2HQ Tel: 01451 822451 enquiries@theshippingcompanyltd.com www.theshippingcompanyltd.com

Middlesex
Sterling Art Services, Unit 5, Cypress Court, Harris Way, Sunbury on Thames TW16 7EL Tel: 01932 771442 salis@sterlingartservices.co.uk www.sterlingartservices.co.uk

PAPERWEIGHTS
Cheshire
Sweetbriar Gallery Paperweights Ltd, Sweetbriar House, Robin Hood Lane, Helsby WA6 9NH Tel: 01928 723851 Mobile: 07860 907532 sales@sweetbriar.co.uk www.sweetbriar.co.uk

Northern Ireland
Marion Langham Limited, Claranagh, Tempo, County Fermanagh BT94 3FJ Tel: 028 895 41247 marion@ladymarion.co.uk www.ladymarion.co.uk

USA
The Dunlop Collection, PO Box 6269, Statesville NC 28687 Tel: (704) 871 2626 or Toll Free Tel: (800) 227 1996

PHOTOGRAPHS
London
Jubilee Photographica, 10 Pierrepoint Row, Camden Passage N1 8EE Mobile: 07860 793707 *Specialist shop and gallery dealing in rare and collectable photographs from the 19th and 20thC. We sell and hold a large and constantly changing stock of cartes de visite, stereocards, daguerreotypes and ambrotypes, albums of travel, topographical and ethnic photographs, art photographs and a range of books on the art and history of photography. We also have magic lanterns and lantern slides, and stereoscopic viewers. The shop is open Wed–Sat 10am–4pm.*

PINE
Cornwall
Julie Strachey, Trevaskis Barn, Gwinear Road, Nr Hayle TR27 5JQ Tel: 01209 613750 *Antique farm and country furniture in pine, oak, etc. Ironwork and interesting pieces for the garden (no repro). By appointment. Junction 9 M40 2 miles. Established 27 years.*

Cumbria
Ben Eggleston Antiques, The Dovecote, Long Marton, Appleby CA16 6BJ Tel: 01768 361849 ben@benegglestonantiques.co.uk www.benegglestonantiques.co.uk *Trade only.*

Essex
English Rose Antiques, 7 Church Street, Coggeshall CO6 1TU Tel: 01376 562683 Mobile: 07770 880790 & 0049 (0)1719 949541 englishroseantiques@hotmail.com www.englishroseantiques.co.uk www.Delta-Line-Trading.com *Large selection of English and Continental pine furniture. Open Mon–Sun 10am–5.30pm. Closed Wed.*

Gloucestershire
Cottage Farm Antiques, Stratford Road, Aston Subedge, Chipping Campden GL55 6PZ Tel: 01386 438263 info@cottagefarmantiques.co.uk www.cottagefarmantiques.co.uk

Hampshire
Pine Cellars, 39 Jewry Street, Winchester SO23 8RY Tel: 01962 777546/867014

Kent
Up Country, The Old Corn Stores, 68 St John's Road, Tunbridge Wells TN4 9PE Tel: 01892 523341 www.upcountryantiques.co.uk

Lancashire
David Roper Antiques, Hill View Farm, Gill Lane, Longton, Preston PR4 4ST Tel: 01772 615366 Mobile: 07803 134851 davidroper@supanet.com *Mostly English 18th–20thC pine and country furniture. Trade suppliers. No reproductions.*

Nottinghamshire
A. B. Period Pine, The Barn, 38 Main Street, Farnsfield, Newark NG22 8EA Tel: 01623 882288 alan@abperiodpine.fsnet.co.uk www.abperiodpine.co.uk

Harlequin Antiques, 79–81 Mansfield Road, Daybrook, Nottingham NG5 6BH Tel: 0115 967 4590 sales@antiquepine.net www.antiquepine.net

Somerset
Gilbert & Dale Antiques, The Old Chapel, Church Street, Ilchester, Nr Yeovil BA22 8ZA Tel: 01935 840464 *Painted pine and country.*

Westville House Antiques, Westville House, Littleton, Nr Somerton TA11 6NP Tel: 01458 273376 Mobile: 07941 510823 antique@westville.co.uk www.westville.co.uk

East Sussex
Ann Lingard, Ropewalk Antiques, Rye TN31 7NA Tel: 01797 223486 ann-lingard@ropewalkantiques.freeserve.co.uk

Graham Price, Apple Store, Chaucer Industrial Estate, Dittons Road, Polegate BN26 6JF Tel: 01323 487167 www.grahampriceantiques.co.uk

Warwickshire
Pine & Things, Portobello Farm, Campden Road, Nr Shipston-on-Stour CV36 4PY Tel: 01608 663849 www.pinethings.co.uk

Wiltshire
North Wilts Exporters, Farm Hill House, Brinkworth SN15 5AJ Tel: 01666 510876 Mobile: 07836 260730 mike@northwilts.demon.co.uk www.northwiltsantiqueexporters.com *Open Mon–Sat 8am–6pm or by appointment.*

Republic of Ireland
Bygones of Ireland Ltd, Lodge Road, Westport, Co Mayo Tel: 00 353 98 26132/25701 bygones@anu.ie www.bygones-of-ireland.com

Delvin Farm Antiques, Gormonston, Co Meath Tel: 00 353 1 841 2285 info@delvinfarmpine.com john@delvinfarmpine.com www.delvinfarmpine.com

Ireland's Own Antiques, Alpine House, Carlow Road, Abbeyleix, Co Laois Tel: 00 353 502 31348 *Ireland's own antiques have a fine stock of original country furniture, which for years has been collected from country cottages and mansions all over Ireland by Peter and Daniel Meaney. Years of experience in the art of packing and shipping, and have many customers. This is a well worth while call for overseas buyers.*

PORCELAIN
Essex
Barling Porcelain Tel: 01621 890058 stuart@barling.uk.com www.barling.uk.com

Bellhouse Antiques, Chelmsford Tel: 01268 710415 Bellhouse.Antiques@virgin.net

Gloucestershire
Judy & Brian Harden Antiques, PO Box 14, Bourton-on-the-Water, Cheltenham GL54 2YR Tel: 01451 810684 harden@meissenfigures.co.uk www.meissenfigures.co.uk *Meissen figures.*

Hampshire
The Goss & Crested China Club & Museum, incorporating Milestone Publications, 62 Murray Road, Horndean PO8 9JL Tel: (023) 9259 7440 info@gosschinaclub.demon.co.uk www.gosscrestedchina.co.uk *Goss and Crested china.*

London
Diana Huntley Antiques, 8 Camden Passage, Islington N1 8ED Tel: 020 7226 4605 diana@dianahuntleyantiques.co.uk www.dianahuntleyantiques.co.uk

Marion Langham Limited Tel: 020 7730 1002 marion@ladymarion.co.uk www.ladymarion.co.uk *Belleek.*

Shropshire
Harvey Antiques, Corve Villa, 30A Corve Street, Ludlow SY8 1GB Tel: 01584 876375 christopher-harvey@tesco.net *By appointment only.*

East Sussex
Tony Horsley, PO Box 3127, Brighton BN1 5SS Tel: 01273 550770 *Candle extinguishers, Royal Worcester and other fine porcelain.*

Warwickshire
Coleshill Antiques & Interiors, 12–14 High Street, Coleshill B46 1AZ Tel: 01675 467416 enquiries@coleshillantiques.com www.coleshillantiques.com

Wiltshire
Andrew Dando, 34 Market Street, Bradford on Avon BA15 1LL Tel: 01225 865444 www.andrewdando.co.uk
English, Oriental and Continental porcelain.

Yorkshire
The Crested China Co, Highfield, Windmill Hill, Driffield YO25 5YP Tel: 01377 257042 dt@thecrestedchinacompany.com www.thecrestedchinacompany.com
Goss and Crested china.

POTTERY

Berkshire
Special Auction Services, Kennetholme, Midgham, Reading RG7 5UX Tel: 0118 971 2949 www.invaluable.com/sas/
Specialist auctions of commemoratives, pot lids and Prattware, Fairings, Goss and Crested, Baxter and Le Blond prints.

Buckinghamshire
Gillian Neale Antiques, PO Box 247, Aylesbury HP20 1JZ Tel: 01296 423754/07860 638700 gillianneale@aol.com www.gilliannealeantiques.co.uk
Blue and white transfer-printed pottery 1780–1860.

Dorset
Greystoke Antiques, 4 Swan Yard, (off Cheap Street), Sherborne DT9 3AX Tel: 01935 812833
Established 28 years. Adjacent to town centre car park. 10am–4.30pm daily. Closed Wed. Also blue transfer-printed pottery 1800–50. Always some 200–300 pieces in stock.

Hampshire
Millers Antiques Ltd, Netherbrook House, 86 Christchurch Road, Ringwood BH24 1DR Tel: 01425 472062 mail@millers-antiques.co.uk www.millers-antiques.co.uk
Majolica and Quimper, decorative items, English and Continental furniture.

Kent
Serendipity, 125 High Street, Deal CT14 6BB Tel: 01304 369165/01304 366536 dipityantiques@aol.com
Staffordshire pottery.

London
Jonathan Horne, 66 Kensington Church Street W8 4BY Tel: 020 7221 5658 JH@jonathanhorne.co.uk www.jonathanhorne.co.uk
Early English pottery.

Oxfordshire
Key Antiques of Chipping Norton, 11 Horsefair, Chipping Norton OX7 5AL Tel: 01608 644992 info@keyantiques.com www.keyantiques.com

Surrey
Judi Bland Antiques Tel: 01276 857576 or 01536 724145
18th and 19thC English Toby jugs and Bargeware.

Tyne & Wear
Ian Sharp Antiques, 23 Front Street, Tynemouth NE30 4DX Tel: 0191 296 0656 iansharp@sharpantiques.demon.co.uk www.sharpantiques.demon.co.uk
Tyneside and Wearside ceramics.

Wiltshire
Andrew Dando, 34 Market Street, Bradford on Avon BA15 1LL Tel: 01225 865444 www.andrewdando.co.uk
English, Oriental and Continental pottery.

PUBLICATIONS

Cheshire
Armourer – The Militaria Magazine, Published by Beaumont Publishing Ltd, 1st Floor Adelphi Mill, Bollington SK10 5JB Tel: 01625 575700 editor@armourer.co.uk www.armourer.co.uk
A bi-monthly magazine for military antique collectors and military history enthusiasts offering hundreds of contacts for buying and selling, articles on all aspects of militaria collecting plus the dates of UK militaria fairs and auctions. Available on subscription.

West Midlands
Antiques Magazine, H. P. Publishing, 2 Hampton Court Road, Harborne, Birmingham B17 9AE Tel: 0121 681 8000 Subs 01562 701001 copy@antiquesmagazine.com www.antiquesmagazine.com

RESTORATION

Northamptonshire
Leather Conservation Centre, University College Campus, Boughton Green Road, Moulton Park, Northampton NN2 7AN Tel: 01604 719766 lcc@northampton.ac.uk
Conservation and restoration of leather screens, wall hangings, car, carriage and furniture upholstery, saddlery, luggage, firemens' helmets and much, much more. The Centre is included on the Register maintained by the United Kingdom Institute for Conservation.

ROCK & POP

Cheshire
Collector's Corner, PO Box 8, Congleton CW12 4GD Tel: 01260 270429 dave.popcorner@ukonline.co.uk

Lancashire
Tracks, PO Box 117, Chorley PR6 0UU Tel: 01257 269726 sales@tracks.co.uk
Beatles and rare pop memorabilia.

London
Cooper Owen, 10 Denmark Street WC2H 8LS Tel: 020 7240 4132 www.CooperOwen.com

RUGS & CARPETS

Gloucestershire
Samarkand Galleries, 7–8 Brewery Yard, Sheep Street, Stow-on-the-Wold GL54 1AA Tel: 01451 832322 mac@samarkand.co.uk www.samarkand.co.uk
Antique rugs from Near East and Central Asia. Antique Nomadic weavings. Decorative carpets. Tribal artefacts. Unique contemporary Rugs. Contact: Brian MacDonald FRGS.

Scotland
Samarkand Galleries, 16 Howe Street, Edinburgh EH3 6TD Tel: 0131 225 2010 howe@samarkand.co.uk www.samarkand.co.uk
Antique rugs from Near East and Central Asia. Antique Nomadic weavings. Decorative carpets. Tribal artefacts. Unique contemporary Rugs. Contact: Brian MacDonald FRGS.

SCIENTIFIC INSTRUMENTS

Cheshire
Charles Tomlinson, Chester Tel: 01244 318395 charles.tomlinson@lineone.net www.lineone.net/-charles.tomlinson

Kent
Sporting Antiques, 10 Union Square, The Pantiles, Tunbridge Wells TN4 8HE Tel: 01892 522661
Theodolites, sextants, levels, marine and military compasses, microscopes, telescopes and drawing instruments. We buy and sell.

Scotland
Early Technology, Monkton House, Old Craighall, Musselburgh, Midlothian EH21 8SF Tel: 0131 665 5753 Mobile: 07831 106768 michael.bennett-levy@virgin.net www.earlytech.com www.tvhistory.tv
Open any time by appointment.

Surrey
Eric Tombs, 62a West Street, Dorking RH4 1BS Tel: 01306 743661 ertombs@aol.com www.dorkingantiques.com

SERVICES

Essex
The National Clock Register Tel: 08707 422485 www.nationalclockregister.co.uk
Clock anti-theft register.

Hampshire
Securikey Ltd, PO Box 18, Aldershot GU12 4SL Tel: 01252 311888 enquiries@securikey.co.uk www.securikey.co.uk
Underfloor safes.

Surrey
The Internet Fine Art Bureau, The Elms, Alma Way, Farnham GU9 0QN Tel: 01252 640 666 enquiries@interfine.com www.interfine.com
Specialist designers of websites for the antiques and fine art trade.

SILVER

Dorset
Greystoke Antiques, 4 Swan Yard, (off Cheap Street), Sherborne DT9 3AX Tel: 01935 812833
Adjacent to town centre car park. 10am–4.30pm daily. Closed Wed. Georgian, Victorian and later silver.

London
Daniel Bexfield, 26 Burlington Arcade W1J 0PU Tel: 020 7491 1720 antiques@bexfield.co.uk www.bexfield.co.uk

Lyn Bloom & Jeffrey Neal, Vault 27, The London Silver Vaults, Chancery Lane WC2A 1QS Tel: 020 7242 6189 Mobile: 07768 533055 bloomvault@aol.com www.bloomvault.com
We stock fine quality silver items ranging from £70 to £20,000 which includes anything from silver napkin rings and flatware to large centrepieces. Our speciality is a range of over 200 antique miniature silver toys.

Shropshire
Harvey Antiques, Corve Villa, 30A Corve Street, Ludlow SY8 1GB Tel: 01584 876375 christopher-harvey@tesco.net
By appointment only.

SPORTS & GAMES

Kent
Sporting Antiques, 10 Union Square, The Pantiles, Tunbridge Wells TN4 8HE Tel: 01892 522661
Fishing rods, reels, trophies, books and prints. Golf and general antique sporting goods.

Nottinghamshire
T. Vennett-Smith, 11 Nottingham Road, Gotham NG11 0HE Tel: 0115 983 0541 info@vennett-smith.com www.vennett-smith.com
Sporting auctions.

TEDDY BEARS

Gloucestershire
Bourton Bears, Bourton-on-the-Water Tel: 01451 821466 mel@strathspey-bed-fsnet.co.uk www.bourtonbears.com

Oxfordshire
Teddy Bears of Witney, 99 High Street, Witney OX28 6HY Tel: 01993 702616/706616

TEXTILES

London
Erna Hiscock & John Shepherd, Chelsea Galleries, 69 Portobello Road W11 Tel: 01233 661407 Mobile: 0771 562 7273 erna@ernahiscockantiques.com www.ernahiscockantiques.com
Antique samplers. Sat 7am–3pm.

Somerset
Joanna Proops Antique Textiles & Lighting, 34 Belvedere, Lansdown Hill, Bath BA1 5HR Tel: 01225 310795 antiquetextiles@aol.co.uk www.antiquetextiles.co.uk

USA
Antique European Linens, PO Box 789, Gulf Breeze, Florida 32562-0789 Tel: 850 432 4777 Cell 850 450 463 name@antiqueeuropeanlinens.com www.antiqueeuropeanlinens.com
Hungarian goose down pillows and European duvets.

TOYS

Berkshire
Special Auction Services, Kennetholme, Midgham, Reading RG7 5UX Tel: 0118 971 2949 www.invaluable.com/sas/
Specialist auctions of toys for the collector including Dinky, Corgi, Matchbox, lead soldiers and figures, tinplate and model railways, etc.

Kent
The Collector's Toy & Model Shop, 52 Canterbury Road, Margate CT9 5BG Tel: 01843 232301 Mobile: 07973 232778 www.collectorstoyandmodelshop.com

East Sussex
Wallis & Wallis, West Street Auction Galleries, Lewes BN7 2NJ Tel: 01273 480208 grb@wallisandwallis.co.uk www.wallisandwallis.co.uk
Auctioneers of diecast toys, model railways, tinplate toys and models.

Yorkshire
John & Simon Haley, 89 Northgate, Halifax HX1 1XF Tel: 01422 822148/360434 toysandbanks@aol.com

USA
Joyce M. Leiby, PO Box 6048, Lancaster PA 17607 Tel: (717) 898 9113 joyclei@aol.com
Early German Christmas Santas and decorations, also Easter toys.

TRIBAL ART

USA
Hurst Gallery, 53 Mt. Auburn Street, Cambridge MA 02138 Tel: 617 491 6888 manager@hurstgallery.com www.hurstgallery.com
Art of the Pacific, Africa, Asia, The Americas and the ancient world.

TUNBRIDGE WARE

Kent
Bracketts, The Auction Hall, The Pantiles, Tunbridge Wells TN2 5QL Tel: 01892 544500 sales@bfaa.co.uk www.bfaa.co.uk
Tunbridge ware auctioneers.

WATCHES

Kent
Tempus, Tunbridge Wells Antique Centre, Union Square, The Pantiles, Tunbridge Wells Tel: 01932 828936 tempus.watches@tinyonline.co.uk www.tempus-watches.co.uk

London
Pieces of Time, (1–7 Davies Mews), 26 South Molton Lane W1Y 2LP Tel: 020 7629 2422 info@antique-watch.com www.antique-watch.com

Directory of Auctioneers

Auctioneers who hold frequent sales should contact us by April 2004 for inclusion in the next edition.

UNITED KINGDOM

Bedfordshire

W&H Peacock, 26 Newnham Street, Bedford MK40 3JR Tel: 01234 266366

Berkshire

Cameo Auctions, Kennet Holme Farm, Bath Road, Midgham, Reading RG7 5UX Tel: 01189 713772 cameo-auctioneers@lineone.net

Dreweatt Neate, Donnington Priory, Donnington, Newbury RG14 2JE Tel: 01635 553553 fineart@dreweatt-neate.co.uk www.auctions.dreweatt-neate.co.uk

Law Fine Art, Firs Cottage, Church Lane, Brimpton RG7 4TJ Tel: 0118 971 0353 info@lawfineart.co.uk www.lawfineart.co.uk

Padworth Auctions, 30 The Broadway, Thatcham RG19 3HX Tel: 01734 713772

Shiplake Fine Art, 31 Great Knollys Street, Reading RG1 7HU Tel: 01734 594748

Special Auction Services, Kennetholme, Midgham, Reading RG7 5UX Tel: 0118 971 2949 www.invaluable.com/sas/

Buckinghamshire

Amersham Auction Rooms, Station Road, Amersham HP7 0AH Tel: 01494 729292 info@amershamauctionrooms.co.uk www.amershamauctionrooms.co.uk

Bosley's, 42 West Street, Marlow SL7 2NB Tel: 01628 488188

Bourne End Auction Rooms, Station Approach, Bourne End SL8 5QH Tel: 01628 531500

Dickins Auctioneers Ltd, The Claydon Saleroom, Calvert Road, Middle Claydon, MK18 2EZ Tel: 01296 714434 info@dickens-auctioneers.com www.dickens-auctioneers.com

Cambridgeshire

Cheffins, Clifton House, Clifton Road, Cambridge CB1 7EA Tel: 01223 213343 www.cheffins.co.uk

Rowley Fine Art, The Old Bishop's Palace, Little Downham, Ely CB6 2TD Tel: 01353 699177 mail@rowleyfineart.com www.rowleyfineart.com

Willingham Auctions, 25 High Street, Willingham CB4 5ES Tel: 01954 261252 www.willinghamauctions.com *Contact Colin. Quality auctions held every three weeks. Furniture, clocks, silver, china, glass and collectables. Six different sale rooms. Cafe and extensive parking on site.*

Channel Islands

Bonhams and Langlois, Westaway Chambers, 39 Don Street, St Helier, Jersey JE2 4TR Tel: 01534 722441

Cheshire

Bonhams, New House, 150 Christleton Road, Chester CH3 5TD Tel: 01244 313936 www.bonhams.com

Halls Fine Art Auctions, Booth Mansion, 30 Watergate Street, Chester CH1 2LA Tel: 01244 312300/312112

Frank R. Marshall & Co, Marshall House, Church Hill, Knutsford WA16 6DH Tel: 01565 653284

Maxwells of Wilmslow inc Dockree's, 133A Woodford Road, Woodford SK7 1QD Tel: 0161 439 5182

Wright Manley, Beeston Castle Salerooms, Tarporley CW6 9NZ Tel: 01829 262150 www.wrightmanley.co.uk

Cleveland

Vectis Auctions Ltd, Fleck Way, Thornaby, Stockton-on-Tees TS17 9JZ Tel: 01642 750616 admin@vectis.co.uk www.vectis.co.uk *Vectis Auctions Limited, one of the world's leading toy auctioneers, holding over 50 auctions yearly, with a superior internet site giving a full and up-to-date picture of the company.*

Cornwall

Bonhams, Cornubia Hall, Eastcliffe Road, Par PL24 2AQ Tel: 01726 814047

Lambrays, Polmorla Walk Galleries, The Platt, Wadebridge PL27 7AE Tel: 01208 813593

W. H. Lane & Son, Jubilee House, Queen Street, Penzance TR18 2DF Tel: 01736 361447

David Lay ASVA, Auction House, Alverton, Penzance TR18 4RE Tel: 01736 361414

Martyn Rowe, The Truro Auction Centre, Triplets Business Park, Poldice Valley, Nr Chacewater, Truro TR16 5PZ Tel: 01209 822266 www.invaluable.com/martynrowe

Cumbria

Bonhams, 48 Cecil Street, Carlisle CA1 1NT Tel: 01228 542422

Kendal Auction Rooms, Sandylands Road, Kendal LA9 6ES Tel: 01539 720603 or 07713 787509 www.kendalauction.co.uk *Regular sales of antique & quality reproduction furniture held at this Lake District based auction room. Situated 10 minutes from Junction 36 or 37 of M6 motorway.*

Mitchells Auction Company, The Furniture Hall, 47 Station Road, Cockermouth CA13 9PZ Tel: 01900 827800

Penrith Farmers' & Kidd's plc, Skirsgill Salerooms, Penrith CA11 0DN Tel: 01768 89078 penrith.farmers@virgin.net

Thomson, Roddick & Medcalf Ltd, Coleridge House, Shaddongate, Carlisle CA2 5TU Tel: 01228 528939

Devon

Bearnes, St Edmund's Court, Okehampton Street, Exeter EX4 1DU Tel: 01392 422800 nsaintey@bearnes.co.uk www.bearnes.co.uk

Bonhams, Dowell Street, Honiton EX14 1LX Tel: 01404 41872

Bonhams, 38/39 Southernhay East, Exeter EX1 1PE Tel: 01392 455 955

Michael J. Bowman, 6 Haccombe House, Netherton, Newton Abbot TQ12 4SJ Tel: 01626 872890

Eldreds Auctioneers & Valuers, 13–15 Ridge Park Road, Plympton, Plymouth PL7 2BS Tel: 01752 340066

Robin A. Fenner & Co, The Stannary Gallery, Drake Road, Tavistock PL19 0AX Tel: 01822 617799 sales@rafenner.com www.rafenner.com

S. J. Hales, 87 Fore Street, Bovey Tracey TQ13 9AB Tel: 01626 836684

Honiton Galleries, 205 High Street, Honiton EX14 1LQ Tel: 01404 42404 sales@honitongalleries.com www.honitongalleries.com

The Plymouth Auction Rooms, Edwin House, St John's Rd, Cattedown, Plymouth PL4 0NZ Tel: 01752 254740

Rendells, Stonepark, Ashburton TQ13 7RH Tel: 01364 653017 stonepark@rendells.co.uk www.rendells.co.uk

G. S. Shobrook & Co, 20 Western Approach, Plymouth PL1 1TG Tel: 01752 663341

John Smale & Co, 11 High Street, Barnstaple EX31 1BG Tel: 01271 42000/42916

Martin Spencer-Thomas, Bicton Street, Exmouth EX8 2SN Tel: 01395 267403

Dorset

Bonhams, Long Street Salerooms, Sherborne DT9 3BS Tel: 01935 815271

Chapman, Moore & Mugford, 9 High Street, Shaftesbury SP7 8JB Tel: 01747 852400

Charterhouse, The Long Street Salerooms, Sherborne DT9 3BS Tel: 01935 812277 enquiry@charterhouse-auctions.co.uk www.charterhouse-auctions.co.uk

Cottees of Wareham, The Market, East Street, Wareham BH20 4NR Tel: 01929 552826 www.auctionsatcottees.co.uk

Hy Duke & Son, Dorchester Fine Art Salerooms, Dorchester DT1 1QS Tel: 01305 265080

Onslow's Auctions Ltd, The Coach House, Manor Road, Stourpaine DT8 8TQ Tel: 01258 488838

Riddetts of Bournemouth, 177 Holdenhurst Road, Bournemouth BH8 8DQ Tel: 01202 555686 auctions@riddetts.co.uk www.riddetts.co.uk

Semley Auctioneers, Station Road, Semley, Shaftesbury SP7 9AN Tel: 01747 855122/855222

Essex

Ambrose, Ambrose House, Old Station Road, Loughton IG10 4PE Tel: 020 8502 3951

Leigh Auction Rooms, John Stacey & Sons, 88–90 Pall Mall, Leigh-on-Sea SS9 1RG Tel: 01702 477051

Saffron Walden Auctions, 1 Market Street, Saffron Walden CB10 1JB Tel: 01799 513281 www.saffronwaldenauctions.com *Contact Colin. Sales held every six weeks on Sunday's at 11 o'clock.*

Sworders, 14 Cambridge Road, Stansted Mountfitchet CM24 8BZ Tel: 01279 817778 www.sworder.co.uk

Gloucestershire

Bristol Auction Rooms, St John's Place, Apsley Road, Clifton, Bristol BS8 2ST Tel: 0117 973 7201 www.bristolauctionrooms.com

Bruton, Knowles & Co, 111 Eastgate Street, Gloucester GL1 1PZ Tel: 01452 521267

The Cotswold Auction Company Ltd, incorporating Short Graham & Co and Hobbs and Chambers Fine Arts, The Coach House, Swan Yard, 9–13 West Market Place, Cirencester GL7 2NH Tel: 01285 642420 info@cotswoldauction.co.uk www.cotswoldauction.co.uk

Mallams, 26 Grosvenor Street, Cheltenham GL52 2SG Tel: 01242 235712

Moore, Allen & Innocent, The Salerooms, Norcote, Cirencester GL7 5RH Tel: 01285 646050 fineart@mooreallen.co.uk www.mooreallen.co.uk

Specialised Postcard Auctions, 25 Gloucester Street, Cirencester GL7 2DJ Tel: 01285 659057

Tayler & Fletcher, London House, High Street, Bourton-on-the-Water, Cheltenham GL54 2AP Tel: 01451 821666 bourton@taylerfletcher.com www.taylerfletcher.com

Wotton Auction Rooms, Tabernacle Road, Wotton-under-Edge GL12 7EB Tel: 01453 844733 info@wottonauctionrooms.co.uk www.wottonauctionrooms.co.uk

Greater Manchester

Bonhams, The Stables, 213 Ashley Road, Hale WA15 9TB Tel: 0161 927 3822

Capes Dunn & Co, The Auction Galleries, 38 Charles Street, Off Princess Street M1 7DB Tel: 0161 273 6060

Hampshire

Bonhams, 54 Southampton Road, Ringwood BH24 1JD Tel: 01425 473333

Evans & Partridge, Agriculture House, High Street, Stockbridge SO20 6HF Tel: 01264 810702

Jacobs & Hunt, 26 Lavant Street, Petersfield GU32 3EF Tel: 01730 233933 www.jacobsandhunt.co.uk

George Kidner, The Old School, The Square, Pennington, Lymington SO41 8GN Tel: 01590 670070 info@georgekidner.co.uk www.georgekidner.co.uk

May & Son, The Old Stables, 9A Winchester Road, Andover SP10 2EG Tel: 01264 323417 office@mayandson.com www.mayandson.com

D. M. Nesbit & Co, Fine Art and Auction Department, Southsea Salerooms, 7 Clarendon Road, Southsea PO5 2ED Tel: 023 9286 4321 auctions@nesbits.co.uk www.nesbits.co.uk

Odiham Auction Sales, Unit 4, Priors Farm, West Green Road, Mattingley RG27 8JU Tel: 01189 326824 auction@dircon.co.uk

Herefordshire

Brightwells Fine Art, The Fine Art Saleroom, Ryelands Road, Leominster HR6 8NZ Tel: 01568 611122 fineart@brightwells.com www.brightwells.com

Morris Bricknell, Stroud House, 30 Gloucester Road, Ross-on-Wye HR9 5LE Tel: 01989 768320 morrisbricknell@lineone.net www.morrisbricknell.com

Nigel Ward & Co, The Border Property Centre, Pontrilas HR2 0EH Tel: 01981 240140 www.nigel-ward.co.uk

Williams & Watkins, Ross Auction Rooms, Ross-on-Wye HR9 7QF Tel: 01989 762225

Hertfordshire

Sworders, The Hertford Saleroom, 42 St Andrew Street, Hertford SG14 1JA Tel: 01992 583508 www.sworder.co.uk

Tring Market Auctions, The Market Premises, Brook Street, Tring HP23 5EF Tel: 01442 826446 sales@tringmarketauctions.co.uk www.tringmarketauctions.co.uk

Kent

Bonhams, 49 London Road, Sevenoaks TN13 1AR Tel: 01732 740310

Bracketts, The Auction Hall, The Pantiles, Tunbridge Wells TN2 5QL Tel: 01892 544500 sales@bfaa.co.uk www.bfaa.co.uk

Calcutt Maclean Standen, The Estate Office, Stone Street, Cranbrook TN17 3HD Tel: 01580 713828

The Canterbury Auction Galleries, 40 Station Road West, Canterbury CT2 8AN Tel: 01227 763337 auctions@thecanterburyauctiongalleries.com www.thecanterburyauctiongalleries.com

Mervyn Carey, Twysden Cottage, Scullsgate, Benenden, Cranbrook TN17 4LD Tel: 01580 240283

Gorringes, 15 The Pantiles, Tunbridge Wells TN2 5TD Tel: 01892 619670 www.gorringes.co.uk

Ibbett Mosely, 125 High Street, Sevenoaks TN13 1UT Tel: 01732 456731 auctions@ibbettmosely.co.uk www.ibbettmosely.co.uk

Lambert & Foster, 102 High Street, Tenterden TN30 6HT Tel: 01580 762083 saleroom@lambertandfoster.co.uk www.lambertandfoster.co.uk

Wealden Auction Galleries, Desmond Judd, 23 Hendly Drive, Cranbrook TN17 3DY Tel: 01580 714522

Lancashire

Smythe's, 174 Victoria Road West, Cleveleys FY5 3NE Tel: 01253 852184

Tony & Sons, 4–8 Lynwood Road, Blackburn BB2 6HP Tel: 01254 691748

Leicestershire

William H. Brown, Warner Auction Rooms, 16–18 Halford Street, Leicester LE1 6AS Tel: 0116 255 9900

Gildings, 64 Roman Way, Market Harborough LE16 7PQ Tel: 01858 410414 sales@gildings.co.uk www.gildings.co.uk

Heathcote Ball & Co, Castle Auction Rooms, 78 St Nicholas Circle, Leicester LE1 5NW Tel: 0116 253 6789 heathcote-ball@clara.co.uk www.heathcote-ball.clara.co.uk

Lincolnshire

DDM Auction Rooms, Old Courts Road, Brigg DN20 8JD Tel: 01652 650172

Thomas Mawer & Son, Dunston House, Portland Street, Lincoln LN5 7NN Tel: 01522 524984 mawer.thos@lineone.net

Marilyn Swain Auctions, The Old Barracks, Sandon Road, Grantham NG31 9AS Tel: 01476 568861

Walter's, No. 1 Mint Lane, Lincoln LN1 1UD Tel: 01522 525454

London

Academy Auctioneers & Valuers, Northcote House, Northcote Avenue, Ealing W5 3UR Tel: 020 8579 7466 www.thesaurus.co.uk/academy/

Angling Auctions, PO Box 2095 W12 8RU Tel: 020 8749 4175 neil@anglingauctions.demon.co.uk

Bloomsbury Book Auctions, 3 & 4 Hardwick Street, Off Rosebery Avenue EC1R 4RY Tel: 020 7833 2636/7 & 020 7923 6940 info@bloomsbury-book-auct.com www.bloomsbury-book-auct.com

Bonhams, 65–69 Lots Road, Chelsea SW10 0RN Tel: 020 7393 3900 www.bonhams.com

Bonhams, 101 New Bond Street W1S 1SR Tel: 020 7629 6602 www.bonhams.com

Bonhams, 10 Salem Road, Bayswater W2 4DL Tel: 020 7313 2700 www.bonhams.com

Bonhams, Montpelier Street, Knightsbridge SW7 1HH Tel: 020 7393 3900 www.bonhams.com

Bonhams, 101 New Bond Street W1S 1SR Tel: 020 7629 6602 www.bonhams.com

Christie, Manson & Woods Ltd, 8 King Street, St James's SW1Y 6QT Tel: 020 7839 9060

Christie's South Kensington Ltd, 85 Old Brompton Road SW7 3LD Tel: 020 7581 7611 christies.com

Comic Book Postal Auctions Ltd, 40–42 Osnaburgh Street NW1 3ND Tel: 020 7424 0007 comicbook@compuserve.com www.compalcomics.com

Cooper Owen, 10 Denmark Street WC2H 8LS Tel: 020 7240 4132 www.CooperOwen.com

Criterion Salerooms, 53 Essex Road, Islington N1 2BN Tel: 020 7359 5707

Dix-Noonan-Webb, 1 Old Bond Street W1S 4PB Tel: 020 7499 5022

Glendining's (A division of Bonhams specialising in coins & medals), 101 New Bond Street W1S 1SR Tel: 020 7493 2445

Harmers of London, 111 Power Road, Chiswick W4 5PY Tel: 020 8747 6100 auctions@harmers.demon.co.uk www.harmers.com

Lloyds International Auction Galleries, Lloyds House, 9 Lydden Road, Earlsfield SW18 4LT Tel: 020 8788 7777 www.lloyds-auction.co.uk

Lots Road Auctions, 71–73 Lots Road, Chelsea SW10 0RN Tel: 020 7351 7771 marketing@lotsroad.com www.lotsroad.com

Morton & Eden Ltd, in association with Sotheby's, 45 Maddox Street W1S 2PE Tel: 020 7493 5344 info@mortonandeden.com

Proud Oriental Auctions, Proud Galleries, 5 Buckingham Street WC2N 6BP Tel: 020 7839 4942

Rosebery's Fine Art Ltd, 74/76 Knights Hill SE27 0JD Tel: 020 8761 2522 auctions@roseberys.co.uk

Sotheby's, 34–35 New Bond Street W1A 2AA Tel: 020 7293 5000 www.sothebys.com

Sotheby's Olympia, Hammersmith Road W14 8UX Tel: 020 7293 5000 www.sothebys.com

Spink & Son Ltd, 69 Southampton Road, Bloomsbury WC1B 4ET Tel: 020 7563 4000

Merseyside

Cato Crane & Co, Liverpool Auction Rooms, 6 Stanhope Street, Liverpool L8 5RF Tel: 0151 709 5559 johncrane@cato-crane.co.uk www.cato-crane.co.uk

Outhwaite & Litherland, Kingsway Galleries, Fontenoy Street, Liverpool L3 2BE Tel: 0151 236 6561

Middlesex

West Middlesex Auction Rooms, 113–114 High Street, Brentford TW8 8AT Tel: 0208 568 9080

Norfolk

Garry M. Emms & Co Ltd, Great Yarmouth Salerooms, Beevor Road (off South Beach Parade), Great Yarmouth NR30 3PS Tel: 01493 332668 g_emms@gt-yarmouth-auctions.com www.gt-yarmouth-auctions.com

Thomas Wm Gaze & Son, Diss Auction Rooms, Roydon Road, Diss IP22 4LN Tel: 01379 650306 sales@dissauctionrooms.co.uk www.twgaze.com

Horners Professional Valuers & Auctioneers, incorporating Howlett & Edrich and Jonathan Howlett, North Walsham Salerooms, Midland Road, North Walsham NR28 9JR Tel: 01692 500603

Keys, Off Palmers Lane, Aylsham NR11 6JA Tel: 01263 733195 www.aylshamsalerooms.co.uk

Knight's, Cuckoo Cottage, Town Green, Alby, Norwich NR11 7HE Tel: 01263 768488

Northamptonshire

Merry's Auctioneers, Northampton Auction & Sales Centre, Liliput Road, Brackmills, Northampton NN4 7BY Tel: 01604 769990

Northern Ireland

Anderson's Auction Rooms Ltd, Unit 7, Prince Regent Business Park, Prince Regent Road, Castereagh, Belfast BT5 6QR Tel: 028 9040 1888

Northumberland

Jack Dudgeon, The New Saleroom, 76 Ravensdowne, Berwick-upon-Tweed TD15 1DQ Tel: 01289 332700 jack@jackdudgeon.co.uk www.jackdudgeon.co.uk

Nottinghamshire

Bonhams, 57 Mansfield Road, Nottingham NG1 3PL Tel: 0115 947 4414

Arthur Johnson & Sons Ltd, The Nottingham Auction Centre, Meadow Lane, Nottingham NG2 3GY Tel: 0115 986 9128 arthurjohnson@btconnect.com

Mellors & Kirk, The Auction House, Gregory Street, Lenton Lane, Nottingham NG7 2NL Tel: 0115 979 0000

Neales, 192 Mansfield Road, Nottingham NG1 3HU Tel: 0115 962 4141 fineart@neales.co.uk www.neales-auctions.com

C. B. Sheppard & Son, The Auction Galleries, Chatsworth Street, Sutton-in-Ashfield NG17 4GG Tel: 01773 872419

T. Vennett-Smith, 11 Nottingham Road, Gotham NG11 0HE Tel: 0115 983 0541 info@vennett-smith.com www.vennett-smith.com

Oxfordshire

Bonhams, 39 Park End Street, Oxford OX1 1JD Tel: 01865 723524

Holloway's, 49 Parsons Street, Banbury OX16 5PF Tel: 01295 817777 enquiries@hollowaysauctioneers.co.uk www.hollowaysauctioneers.co.uk

Mallams, Bocardo House, 24 St Michael's Street, Oxford OX1 2EB Tel: 01865 241358 oxford@mallams.co.uk

Simmons & Sons, 32 Bell Street, Henley-on-Thames RG9 2BH Tel: 01491 612810 www.simmonsandsons.com

Soames County Auctioneers, Pinnocks Farm Estates, Northmoor OX8 1AY Tel: 01865 300626

Scotland

Bonhams, 65 George Street, Edinburgh EH2 2JL Tel: 0131 225 2266

Bonhams, 176 St Vincent Street, Glasgow G2 5SG Tel: 0141 223 8866

Christie's Scotland Ltd, 164–166 Bath Street, Glasgow G2 4TG Tel: 0141 332 8134

William Hardie Ltd, 15a Blythswood Square, Glasgow G2 4EW Tel: 0141 221 6780

Loves Auction Rooms, 52 Canal Street, Perth PH2 8LF Tel: 01738 633337

Lyon & Turnbull, 33 Broughton Place, Edinburgh EH1 3RR Tel: 0131 557 8844 john.mackie@lyonandturnbull.com

Macgregor Auctions, 56 Largo Road, St Andrews, Fife KY16 8RP Tel: 01334 472431

Shapes Fine Art Auctioneers & Valuers, Bankhead Avenue, Sighthill, Edinburgh EH11 4BY Tel: 0131 453 3222 auctionsadmin@shapesauctioneers.co.uk www.shapesauctioneers.co.uk

L. S. Smellie & Sons Ltd, Within the Furniture Market, Lower Auchingramont Road, Hamilton ML10 6BE Tel: 01698 282007 or 01357 520211

Sotheby's, 112 George Street, Edinburgh EH2 4LH Tel: 0131 226 7201 www.sothebys.com

Thomson, Roddick & Medcalf Ltd, 60 Whitesands, Dumfries DG1 2RS Tel: 01387 279879

Thomson, Roddick & Medcalf Ltd, 20 Murray Street, Annan DG12 6EG Tel: 01461 202575

Thomson, Roddick & Medcalf Ltd, 43/4 Hardengreen Business Park, Eskbank, Edinburgh EH22 3NX Tel: 0131 454 9090

Shropshire

Halls Fine Art Auctions, Welsh Bridge, Shrewsbury SY3 8LA Tel: 01743 231212

McCartneys, Ox Pasture, Overture Road, Ludlow SY8 4AA Tel: 01584 872251

Mullock & Madeley, The Old Shippon, Wall-under-Heywood, Church Stretton SY6 7DS Tel: 01694 771771 auctions@mullockmadeley.co.uk www.mullockmadeley.co.uk

Nock Deighton, Livestock & Auction Centre, Tasley, Bridgnorth WV16 4QR Tel: 01746 762666

Welsh Bridge Salerooms, Welsh Bridge, Shrewsbury SY3 8LH Tel: 01743 231212

Somerset

Aldridges, Newark House, 26–45 Cheltenham Street, Bath BA2 3EX Tel: 01225 462830

Bonhams, 1 Old King Street, Bath BA1 2JT Tel: 01225 788 988

Clevedon Salerooms, The Auction Centre, Kenn Road, Kenn, Clevedon, Bristol BS21 6TT Tel: 01934 830111 clevedon.salerooms@blueyonder.co.uk www.clevedon-salerooms.com

Gardiner Houlgate, The Bath Auction Rooms, 9 Leafield Way, Corsham, Nr Bath SN13 9SW Tel: 01225 812912 gardiner-houlgate.co.uk www.invaluable.com/gardiner-houlgate

Greenslade Taylor Hunt Fine Art, Magdelene House, Church Square, Taunton TA1 1SB Tel: 01823 332525

Lawrence Fine Art Auctioneers, South Street, Crewkerne TA18 8AB Tel: 01460 73041

Tamlyn & Son, 56 High Street, Bridgwater TA6 3BN Tel: 01278 458241

Staffordshire

Louis Taylor Auctioneers & Valuers, Britannia House, 10 Town Road, Hanley, Stoke-on-Trent ST1 2QG Tel: 01782 214111

Potteries Specialist Auctions, 271 Waterloo Road, Cobridge, Stoke-on-Trent ST6 3HR Tel: 01782 286622

Wintertons Ltd, Lichfield Auction Centre, Fradley Park, Lichfield WS13 8NF Tel: 01543 263256 enquiries@wintertons.co.uk www.wintertons.co.uk

Suffolk

Abbotts Auction Rooms, Campsea Ashe, Woodbridge IP13 0PS Tel: 01728 746323

Boardman Fine Art Auctioneers, Station Road Corner, Haverhill CB9 0EY Tel: 01440 730414

Bonhams, 32 Boss Hall Road, Ipswich IP1 5DJ Tel: 01473 740494

Diamond Mills & Co, 117 Hamilton Road, Felixstowe IP11 7BL Tel: 01394 282281

Dyson & Son, The Auction Room, Church Street, Clare CO10 8PD Tel: 01787 277993 info@dyson-auctioneers.co.uk www.dyson-auctioneers.co.uk

Lacy Scott and Knight, Fine Art Department, The Auction Centre, 10 Risbygate Street, Bury St Edmunds IP33 3AA Tel: 01284 763531

Neal Sons & Fletcher, 26 Church Street, Woodbridge IP12 1DP Tel: 01394 382263

Olivers, Olivers Rooms, Burkitts Lane, Sudbury CO10 1HB Tel: 01787 880305 oliversauctions@btconnect.com

Vost's, Newmarket CB8 9AU Tel: 01638 561313

Surrey

Bonhams, Millmead, Guildford GU2 4BE Tel: 01483 504030

Clarke Gammon, The Guildford Auction Rooms, Bedford Road, Guildford GU1 4SJ Tel: 01483 880915

Ewbank Auctioneers, Burnt Common Auction Room, London Road, Send, Woking GU23 7LN Tel: 01483 223101 antiques@ewbankauctions.co.uk www.ewbankauctions.co.uk

Lawrences Auctioneers Limited, Norfolk House, 80 High Street, Bletchingley RH1 4PA Tel: 01883 743323 sarah@lawrencesbletchigley.co.uk www.lawrencesbletchingley.co.uk

John Nicholson, The Auction Rooms, Longfield, Midhurst Road, Fernhurst GU27 3HA Tel: 01428 653727

Richmond & Surrey Auctions Ltd, Richmond Station, Kew Road, Old Railway Parcels Depot, Richmond TW9 2NA Tel: 020 8948 6677 rsatrading.richmond@virgin.net

P. F. Windibank, The Dorking Halls, Reigate Road, Dorking RH4 1SG Tel: 01306 884556/876280 sjw@windibank.co.uk www.windibank.co.uk

East Sussex

Burstow & Hewett, Abbey Auction Galleries and Granary Salerooms, Lower Lake, Battle TN33 0AT Tel: 01424 772374 www.burstowandhewett.co.uk

Gorringes Auction Galleries, Terminus Road, Bexhill-on-Sea TN39 3LR Tel: 01424 212994 bexhill@gorringes.co.uk www.gorringes.co.uk

Gorringes inc Julian Dawson, 15 North Street, Lewes BN7 2PD Tel: 01273 472503 auctions@gorringes.co.uk www.gorringes.co.uk

Edgar Horns, 46–50 South Street, Eastbourne BN21 4XB Tel: 01323 410419 sales@edgarhorns.com www.edgarhorns.com

Raymond P. Inman, 98a Coleridge Street, Hove BN3 5AA Tel: 01273 774777 www.invaluable.com/raymondinman

Rye Auction Galleries, Rock Channel, Rye TN31 7HL Tel: 01797 222124 sales@ryeauction.fsnet.co.uk

Scarborough Perry Fine Art, Hove Auction Rooms, Hove Street, Hove BN3 2GL Tel: 01273 735266

Wallis & Wallis, West Street Auction Galleries, Lewes BN7 2NJ Tel: 01273 480208 auctions@wallisandwallis.co.uk grb@wallisandwallis.co.uk www.wallisandwallis.co.uk

West Sussex

Henry Adams, Fine Art Auctioneers, Baffins Hall, Baffins Lane, Chichester PO19 1UA Tel: 01243 532223 enquiries@henryadamsfineart.co.uk www.henryadamsfineart.co.uk

John Bellman Auctioneers, New Pound Business Park, Wisborough Green, Billingshurst RH14 0AZ Tel: 01403 700858 jbellman@compuserve.com

Peter Cheney, Western Road Auction Rooms, Western Road, Littlehampton BN17 5NP Tel: 01903 722264 & 713418

Denham's, The Auction Galleries, Dorking Road, Nr Horsham RH12 3RZ Tel: 01403 255699 info@denhams-auctions.com www.denhams-auctions.com

R. H. Ellis & Sons, 44–46 High Street, Worthing BN11 1LL Tel: 01903 238999

Sotheby's Sussex, Summers Place, Billingshurst RH14 9AD Tel: 01403 833500 www.sothebys.com

Stride & Son, Southdown House, St John's Street, Chichester PO19 1XQ Tel: 01243 780207

Rupert Toovey & Co Ltd, Spring Gardens, Washington RH20 3BS Tel: 01903 891955 auctions@rupert-toovey.com www.rupert-toovey.com

Worthing Auction Galleries Ltd, Fleet House, Teville Gate, Worthing BN11 1UA Tel: 01903 205565 info@worthing-auctions.co.uk www.worthing-auctions.co.uk

Tyne & Wear

Anderson & Garland (Auctioneers), Marlborough House, Marlborough Crescent, Newcastle-upon-Tyne NE1 4EE Tel: 0191 232 6278

Boldon Auction Galleries, 24a Front Street, East Boldon NE36 0SJ Tel: 0191 537 2630

Bonhams, 30–32 Grey Street, Newcastle Upon Tyne NE1 6AE Tel: 0191 233 9930

Sneddons, Sunderland Auction Rooms, 30 Villiers Street, Sunderland SR1 1EJ Tel: 0191 514 5931

Wales

Anthemion Auctions, 2 Llandough Trading Park, Penarth Road, Cardiff CF11 8RR Tel: 029 2071 2608

Bonhams, 7–8 Park Place, Cardiff CF10 3DP Tel: 029 2072 7980 cardiff@bonhams.com www.bonhams.com

Peter Francis, Curiosity Sale Room, 19 King Street, Carmarthen SA31 1BH Tel: 01267 233456 Peterfrancis@valuers.fsnet.co.uk www.peterfrancis.co.uk

Morgan Evans & Co Ltd, 30 Church Street, Llangefni, Anglesey, Gwynedd LL77 7DU Tel: 01248 723303/ 421582 llangefni@morganevans.demon.co.uk www.morganevans.com

Rogers Jones & Co, The Saleroom, 33 Abergele Road, Colwyn Bay LL29 7RU Tel: 01492 532176 www.rogersjones.co.uk

J. Straker Chadwick & Sons, Market Street Chambers, Abergavenny, Monmouthshire NP7 5SD Tel: 01873 852624

Wingetts Auction Gallery, 29 Holt Street, Wrexham, Clwyd LL13 8DH Tel: 01978 353553 auctions@wingetts.co.uk www.wingetts.co.uk

Warwickshire

Bigwood Auctioneers Ltd, The Old School, Tiddington, Stratford-upon-Avon CV37 7AW Tel: 01789 269415

Locke & England, 18 Guy Street, Leamington Spa CV32 4RT Tel: 01926 889100 www.auctionsonline.com/locke

West Midlands

Bonhams, The Old House, Station Road, Knowle, Solihull B93 0HT Tel: 01564 776151

Fellows & Sons, Augusta House, 19 Augusta Street, Hockley, Birmingham B18 6JA Tel: 0121 212 2131 info@fellows.co.uk www.fellows.co.uk

Weller & Dufty Ltd, 141 Bromsgrove Street, Birmingham B5 6RQ Tel: 0121 692 1414 wellerdufty@freewire.co.uk www.wellerandduffy.co.uk

Wiltshire

Henry Aldridge & Son, Unit 1, Bath Road Business Centre, Devizes SN10 1XA Tel: 01380 729199 andrew.aldridge@virgin.net www.henry-aldridge.co.uk

Finan & Co, The Square, Mere BA12 6DJ Tel: 01747 861411 post@finanandco.co.uk www.finanandco.co.uk

Kidson Trigg, Estate Office, Friars Farm, Sevenhampton, Highworth, Swindon SN6 7PZ Tel: 01793 861000

Dominic Winter Book Auctions, The Old School, Maxwell Street, Swindon SN1 5DR Tel: 01793 611340 info@dominicwinter.co.uk www.dominicwinter.co.uk

Woolley & Wallis, Salisbury Salerooms, 51–61 Castle Street, Salisbury SP1 3SU Tel: 01722 424524 mail@salisbury.w-w.co.uk www.w-w.co.uk

Worcestershire

Andrew Grant, St Mark's House, St Mark's Close, Worcester WR5 3DJ Tel: 01905 357547

Philip Laney, The Malvern Auction Centre, Portland Road, off Victoria Road, Malvern WR14 2TA Tel: 01684 893933 PhilipLaney@compuserve.com

Philip Serrell, The Malvern Saleroom, Barnards Green Road, Malvern WR14 3LW Tel: 01684 892314

Yorkshire

BBR, Elsecar Heritage Centre, Wath Road, Elsecar, Barnsley S74 8HJ Tel: 01226 745156 sales@bbrauctions.co.uk www.onlinebbr.com

Bonhams, 17a East Parade, Leeds LS1 2BH Tel: 0113 2448011

Boulton & Cooper, St Michael's House, Market Place, Malton YO17 7LR Tel: 01653 696151

H. C. Chapman & Son, The Auction Mart, North Street, Scarborough YO11 1DL Tel: 01723 372424

Cundalls, 15 Market Place, Malton YO17 7LP Tel: 01653 697820

Dee, Atkinson & Harrison, The Exchange Saleroom, Driffield YO25 6LD Tel: 01377 253151 exchange@dee-atkinson-harrison.co.uk www.dahauctions.com

David Duggleby, The Vine St Salerooms, Scarborough YO11 1XN Tel: 01723 507111 auctions@davidduggleby.freeserve.co.uk www.davidduggleby.com

David Duggleby, The Paddock Salerooms, Whitby YO23 3DB Tel: 01947 820033 auctions@davidduggleby.freeserve.co.uk www.davidduggleby.com

ELR Auctions Ltd, The Nichols Building, Shalesmoor, Sheffield S3 8UJ Tel: 0114 281 6161

Andrew Hartley, Victoria Hall Salerooms, Little Lane, Ilkley LS29 8EA Tel: 01943 816363 info@andrewhartleyfinearts.co.uk www.andrewhartleyfinearts.co.uk

Lithgow Sons & Partners, The Auction Houses, Station Road, Stokesley, Middlesbrough TS9 7AB Tel: 01642 710158 info@lithgowsauctions.com www.lithgowsauctions.com

Malcolm's No. 1 Auctioneers & Valuers Tel: 01977 684971 info@malcolmsno1auctions.co.uk www.malcolmsno1auctions.co.uk

Christopher Matthews, 23 Mount Street, Harrogate HG2 8DQ Tel: 01423 871756

Morphets of Harrogate, 6 Albert Street, Harrogate HG1 1JL Tel: 01423 530030

Sheffield Railwayana Auctions, 43 Little Norton Lane, Sheffield S8 8GA Tel: 0114 274 5085 ian@sheffrail.freeserve.co.uk www.sheffieldrailwayana.co.uk

Tennants, The Auction Centre, Harmby Road, Leyburn DL8 5SG Tel: 01969 623780 enquiry@tennants-ltd.co.uk www.tennants.co.uk

Tennants, 34 Montpellier Parade, Harrogate HG1 2TG Tel: 01423 531661 enquiry@tennants-ltd.co.uk www.tennants.co.uk

Wilkinson & Beighton Auctioneers, Woodhouse Green, Thurcroft, Rotherham SY3 8LA Tel: 01709 700005

Wombell's Antiques & General Auction, The Auction Gallery, Northminster Business Park, Northfield Lane, Upper Poppleton, York YO26 6QU Tel: 01904 790777 www.invaluable.com/wombell

AUSTRIA

Dorotheum, Palais Dorotheum, A–1010 Wien, Dorotheergasse 17 Tel: 0043 1 515 60 354

AUSTRALIA

Leonard Joel Auctioneers, 333 Malvern Road, South Yarra, Victoria 3141 Tel: 03 9826 4333 decarts@ljoel.com.au or jewellery@ljoel.com.au www.ljoel.com.au

Shapiro Auctioneers, 162 Queen Street, Woollahra, Sydney NSW 2025 Tel: 00 612 9326 1588

BELGIUM

Bernaerts, Verlatstraat 18–22, 2000 Antwerpen/Anvers Tel: +32 (0)3 248 19 21 edmond.bernaerts@ping.be www.auction-bernaerts.com

CANADA

Bailey's Auctions, 467 Elmira Road, North Guelph, Ontario N1H 6J4 Tel: 001 519 823 1107 auctioneer@baileyauctions.com www.baileyauctions.com

Robert Deveau Galleries Fine Art Auctioneers, 297–299 Queen Street, Toronto, Ontario M5A 1S7 Tel: 00 416 364 6271

Ritchies Inc, Auctioneers & Appraisers of Antiques & Fine Art, 288 King Street East, Toronto, Ontario M5A 1K4 Tel: (416) 364 1864 auction@ritchies.com www.ritchies.com

A Touch of Class Auctions, 92 College Crescent, Barrie, Ontario L4M 5C8 Tel: 001 705 726 2120 krista.richards@rogers.com www.atouchofclassauctions.com

Waddington's Auctions, 111 Bathurst Street, Toronto MSV 2RI Tel: 001 416 504 9100 vb@waddingtonsauctions.com www.waddingtonsauctions.com

When the Hammer Goes Down, 440 Douglas Avenue, Toronto, Ontario M5M 1H4 Tel: 001 416 787 1700 TOLL FREE 1 (866) BIDCALR (243 2257) BIDCALR@rogers.com www.bidcalr.com

CHINA

Christie's Hong Kong, 2203–5 Alexandra House, 16–20 Chater Road, Hong Kong Tel: 00 852 2521 5396

Sotheby's, Li Po Chun Chambers, 18th Floor, 189 Des Vouex Road, Hong Kong Tel: 852 524 8121 www.sothebys.com

DENMARK

Bruun Rasmussen-Havnen, Pakhusvej 12, DK–2100, Copenhagen Tel: +45 70 27 60 80 havnen@bruun-rasmussen.dk www.bruun-rasmussen.dk

FINLAND

Bukowskis, Horhammer, Iso Roobertink, 12 Stora Robertsg, 00120 Helsinki, Helsingfors Tel: 00 358 9 668 9110 www.bukowskis.fi

Hagelstam, Bulevardi 9 A, II kerros, 00120 Helsinki Tel: 358 (0)9 680 2300 www.hagelstam.fi

FRANCE

Sotheby's France SA, 76 Rue du Faubourg, Saint Honore, 75008 Paris Tel: 00 33 147 42 22 32 www.sothebys.com

GERMANY

Auction Team Koln, Postfach 50 11 19, 50971 Koln Tel: 00 49 0221 38 70 49 auction@breker.com

Hermann Historica OHG, Postfach 201009, 80010 Munchen Tel: 00 49 89 5237296

Sotheby's Berlin, Palais anmFestungsgraben, Unter den Linden, Neue Wache D–10117 Tel: 49 (30) 2010521www.sothebys.com

Sotheby's Munich, Odeonsplatz 16, D–80539 Munchen Tel: 49 (89) 291 31 51 www.sothebys.com

ISRAEL

Sotheby's Israel, Gordon 38, Tel Aviv 63414 Tel: 972(3)522 3822 www.sothebys.com

ITALY

Christie's Rome, Palazzo Massimo, Lancellotti, Piazza Navona 114, Rome 00186 Tel: 00 396 687 2787

Sotheby's, Palazzo Broggi, Via Broggi, 19, 20129 Milano Tel: 02 295001 www.sothebys.com

Sotheby's Rome, Piazza d'Espana 90, 00187, Rome Tel: 39(6) 69941791/6781798 www.sothebys.com

MEXICO

Galeria Louis C. Morton, GLC A7073L IYS, Monte Athos 179, Col. Lomas de Chapultepec CP11000 Tel: 52 5520 5005 glmorton@prodigy.net.mx www.lmorton.com

MONACO

Christie's (Monaco), S.A.M., Park Palace, Monte Carlo 98000 Tel: 00 337 9325 1933

Sotheby's Monaco, Le Sporting d'Hiver, Place du Casino, 98001 Cedex Tel: 00 377 93 30 8880 www.sothebys.com

NETHERLANDS

Christie's Amsterdam, Cornelis Schuystraat 57, Amsterdam 107150 Tel: (3120) 57 55 255

Sotheby's Amsterdam, De Boelelaan 30, 1083 HJ, Amsterdam Tel: 00 31 20 550 22 00 www.sothebys.com

Van Sabben Poster Auctions, PO Box 2065, 1620 EB Hoorn Tel: 31 229 268203 uboersma@sabbenposterauctions.nl www.vsabbenposterauctions.nl

REPUBLIC OF IRELAND

James Adam & Sons, 26 St Stephen's Green, Dublin 2 Tel: 00 3531 676 0261 www.jamesadam.ie

Christie's Dublin, 52 Waterloo Road, Dublin 4 Tel: 00 353 1 6680 585

Hamilton Osborne King, 4 Main Street, Blackrock, Co. Dublin Tel: 353 1 288 5011 blackrock@hok.ie www.hok.ie

Mealy's, Chatsworth Street, Castle Comer, Co Kilkenny Tel: 00 353 56 41229 info@mealys.com www.mealys.com

Whyte's Auctioneers, 38 Molesworth Street, Dublin 2 Tel: 00 353 1 676 2888 info@whytes.ie www.whytes.ie

SINGAPORE

Christie's, Unit 3 Park Lane, Goodwood Park Hotel, 22 Scotts Road Tel: (65) 235 3828

Sotheby's (Singapore) Pte Ltd, 1 Cuscaden Road, 01–01 The Regent Tel: (65) 732 8239 www.sothebys.com

SWEDEN

Bukowskis, Arsenalsgatan 4, Stockholm-SE111 47 Tel: 00 46 (0)8 614 08 00 info@bukowskis.se www.bukowskis.se

SWITZERLAND

Christie's (International) S.A., 8 Place de la Taconnerie, 1204 Geneva Tel: 00 4122 319 1766

Phillips, Kreuzstrasse 54, 8008 Zurich Tel: 00 41 1 254 2400

Phillips Geneva, 9 rue Ami-Levrier, Geneva CH–1201 Tel: 00 41 22 738 0707

Sotheby's, 13 Quai du Mont Blanc, Geneva CH–1201 Tel: 00 41 22 908 4800 www.sothebys.com

Sotheby's Zurich, Gessneralee 1, Zurich CH–8021 Tel: 00 41 1 226 2200 www.sothebys.com

USA

Bloomington Auction Gallery, 300 East Grove St, Bloomington, Illinois 61701 Tel: 001 309 828 5533 joyluke@aol.com www.joyluke.com

Frank H. Boos Gallery, 420 Enterprise Court, Bloomfield Hills, Michigan 48302 Tel: 001 248 332 1500

Braswell Galleries, 125 West Ave, Norwalk CT06854 Tel: 001 203 899 7420

Butterfields, 220 San Bruno Avenue, San Francisco CA 94103 Tel: 00 1 415 861 7500

Butterfields, 7601 Sunset Boulevard, Los Angeles CA 90046 Tel: 00 1 323 850 7500

Butterfields, 441 W. Huron Street, Chicago IL 60610 Tel: 00 1 312 377 7500

Christie, Manson & Woods International Inc, 502 Park Avenue, (including Christie's East), New York 10022 Tel: 001 212 636 2000

Christie's East, 219 East 67th Street, New York NY10021 Tel: 001 212 606 0400

Copake Auction, Inc., PO Box H, Copake NY 12516 Tel: 518 329 1142 info@copakeauction.com www.copakeauction.com

William Doyle Galleries, 175 East 87th Street, New York 10128 Tel: 212 427 2730

Du Mouchelles, 409 East Jefferson, Detroit, Michigan 48226 Tel: 001 313 963 6255

Eldred's, Robert C Eldred Co Inc, 1475 Route 6A, East Dennis, Massachusetts 0796 02641 Tel: 00 1 508 385 3116

Freeman Fine Art Of Philadelphia Inc., 1808 Chestnut Street, Philadelphia PA 19103 Tel: 001 215 563 9275

The Great Atlantic Auction Company, 2 Harris & Main Street, Putnam CT 06260 Tel: 001 860 963 2234 www.thegreatatlanticauction.com

Gene Harris Antique Auction Center, 203 S. 18th Avenue, PO Box 476, Marshalltown, Iowa 50158 Tel: 641 752 0600 geneharris@geneharrisauctions.com geneharrisauctions.com

Hunt Auctions, 75 E. Uwchlan Avenue, Suite 130, Exton, Pennsylvania 19341 Tel: 001 610 524 0822 info@huntauctions.com www.huntauctions.com

Randy Inman Auctions Inc, PO Box 726, Waterville, Maine 04903–0726 Tel: 001 207 872 6900 inman@inmanauctions.com www.inmanauctions.com

Jackson's Auctioneers & Appraisers, 2229 Lincoln Street, Cedar Falls IA 50613 Tel: 00 1 319 277 2256

MastroNet, Inc, 1515 W.22nd Street, Suite 125, Oak Brook, Illinois 60523 Tel: 001 630 472 1200 lauraharden@mastronet.com www.mastronet.com

Paul McInnis Inc Auction Gallery, 21 Rockrimmon Road, Northampton, New Hampshire 03862–2336 Tel: 001 603 964 1301

New Orleans Auction Galleries, Inc, 801 Magazine Street, AT 510 Julia, New Orleans, Louisiana 70130 Tel: 00 1 504 566 1849

Northeast Auctions, 93 Pleasant St, Portsmouth NH 03810–4504 Tel: 001 603 433 8400 neacat@ttlc.net

Phillips New York, 406 East 79th Street, New York NY10021 Tel: 00 1 212 570 4830

R. O. Schmitt Fine Art, Box 1941, Salem, New Hampshire 03079 Tel: 603 893 5915 bob@roschmittfinearts.com www.antiqueclockauction.com

Skinner Inc, 357 Main Street, Bolton MA 01740 Tel: 00 1 978 779 6241

Skinner Inc, The Heritage On The Garden, 63 Park Plaza, Boston MA 02116 Tel: 001 617 350 5400

Sotheby's, 1334 York Avenue, New York 10021 Tel: 00 1 212 606 7000 www.sothebys.com

Sotheby's, 9665 Wilshire Boulevard, Beverly Hills, California 90212 Tel: (310) 274 0340 www.sothebys.com

Sotheby's, 215 West Ohio Street, Chicago, Illinois 60610 Tel: 00 1 312 670 0010 www.sothebys.com

Sprague Auctions, Inc., Route 5, Dummerston VT 05301 Tel: 802 254 8969 bob@spragueauctions.com www.spragueauctions.com

Swann Galleries Inc, 104 East 25th Street, New York 10010 Tel: 00 1 212 2544710

Theriault's, PO Box 151, Annapolis MD21401 Tel: 001 800 638 0422 info@theriaults.com www.theriaults.com

Treadway Gallery Inc and John Toomey Gallery, 2029 Madison Road, Cincinnati, Ohio 45208 Tel: 001 513 321 6742 www.treadwaygallery.com

TreasureQuest Auction Galleries Inc, 2581 Jupiter Park Drive, Suite E 9, Jupiter, Florida 33458 Tel: 561 741 0777 www.tqag.com

Weschler's, 909 E. Street NW, Washington. DC2004 Tel: 202 628 1281/ 800 331 14630 judy@weschlers.com www.weschlers.com

Wolfs Gallery, 1239 W. 6th Street, Cleveland OH 44113 Tel: 216 575 9653

SIMMONS & SONS

CHARTERED SURVEYORS · INDEPENDENT SINCE 1802

32 Bell Street, Henley-on-Thames, Oxfordshire
Telephone: 01491 571111
Fax: 01491 579833
www.simmonsandsons.com

AUCTIONEERS & VALUERS OF
ANTIQUES, FINE ART & CHATTELS

CAMEO

Fine Art Auctioneers and Valuers

Good quality entries welcomed for our sales – comprehensive advertising and detailed catalogue descriptions enable the best possible prices!

We specialise in:

- Monthly Antique Furniture and Quality Collectables Auctions
- Valuations for insurance and probate
- House clearances and deceased effects
- Friendly, experienced and confidential advice
- We work for many estate agents, solicitors, courts and charities in the area and have over 20 years of experience in the business.

CAMEO, Kennet Holme Farm, Bath Road, Midgham, Reading, Berks RG7 5UX
(On the main A4, next to The Berkshire Arms, only 5 miles from Newbury and 8 miles from M4 Jct 12.)

Tel 01189 713772 Fax 01189 710330
Email cameo-auctioneers@lineone.net

Easy parking and refreshments available on site

1964

LAWRENCES

AUCTIONEERS LIMITED

Regular Sales of Fine Art & Chattels
Single Items or Complete House Contents
Free Auction Estimates
Valuation for Probate & Insurance
Collection & Delivery Available
26 years experience in Auctions

Norfolk House, 80 High Street
Bletchingley, Surrey RH1 4PA

Telephone: 01883 743323

www.lawrencesbletchingley.co.uk

Ibbett Mosely

AUCTIONEERS & VALUERS

A Regular Programme of Sales

of Antique, Victorian and Edwardian Furniture, Works of Art, Silver, Glass, Watches, China, Musical Instruments, Jewellery, etc. etc.

Held in our Saleroom at Otford, Nr. Sevenoaks, Kent

Also valuations carried out for Probate, Insurance and Family Division

Complete house clearances undertaken with personal supervision

Storage facilities available for short periods pending sale

125 High Street, Sevenoaks, Kent TN13 1UT

Telephone: 01732 456731 Fax: 01732 740910

Email: auctions@ibbettmosely.co.uk Website: www.ibbettmosely.co.uk

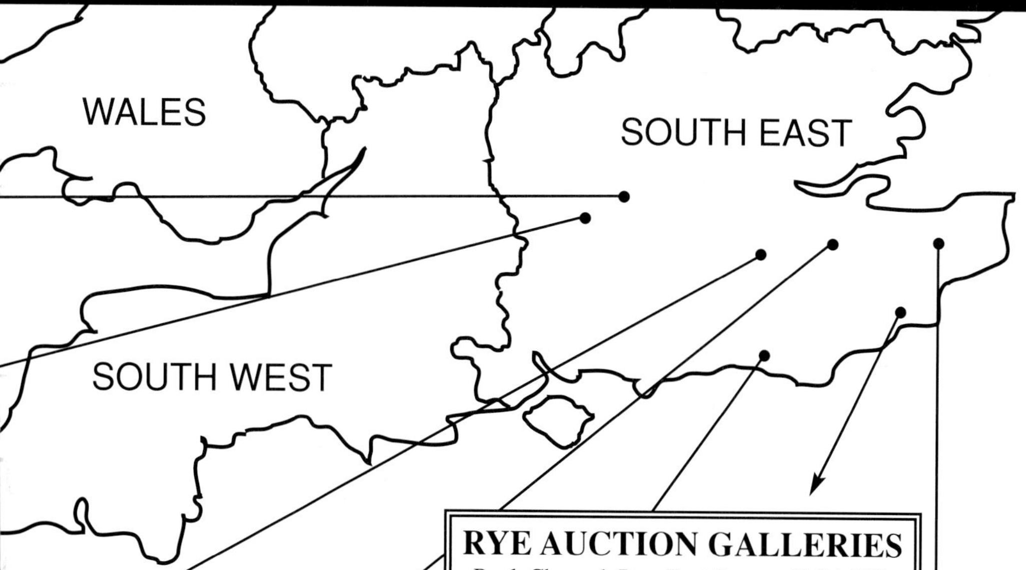

RYE AUCTION GALLERIES

Rock Channel, Rye, East Sussex, TN31 7HL
Tel: 01797 222124 Fax: 01797 222126
Email: sales@ryeauction.fsnet.co.uk

SALES HELD 1ST AND 3RD FRIDAYS OF EACH MONTH

Valuations for Probate, Insurance, Family division and auction
House clearances undertaken

WORTHING AUCTION GALLERIES
FINE ARTS & CHATTELS

Two day monthly sales of antique, 20th Century and reproduction furniture, ceramics, glass, silver, silver plate, jewellery, clocks, books, pictures and collectables.

AT: Fleet House, Teville Gate
Worthing, West Sussex BN11 1UA
Tel: 01903 205565
E-Mail: info@worthing-auctions.co.uk
Website: www.worthing-auctions.co.uk

Auctioneers & Valuers of Fine Art, Antiques & Collectors' Items

The CANTERBURY AUCTION Galleries

KENT'S leading Independent Auctioneers and Valuers offer a fully professional yet personal service throughout the South East for the sale of Fine Art, Antiques and Collectors' Items. Detailed Valuations for Insurance, Probate, Family Division and Sale by Auction.

Member of the society SOFAA *of Fine Art Auctioneers*

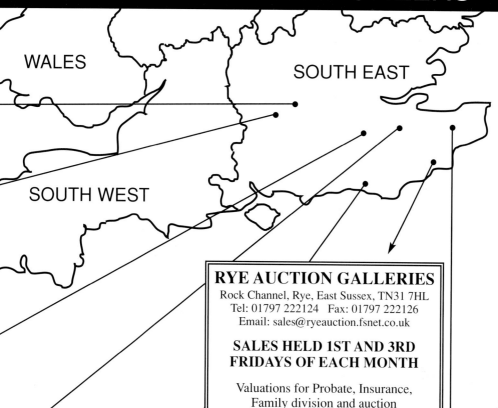

40 STATION ROAD WEST, CANTERBURY, KENT CT2 8AN
TELEPHONE: 01227 763337 FAX: 01227 456770
www.thecanterburyauctiongalleries.com

WALES
SOUTH WEST
SOUTH EAST

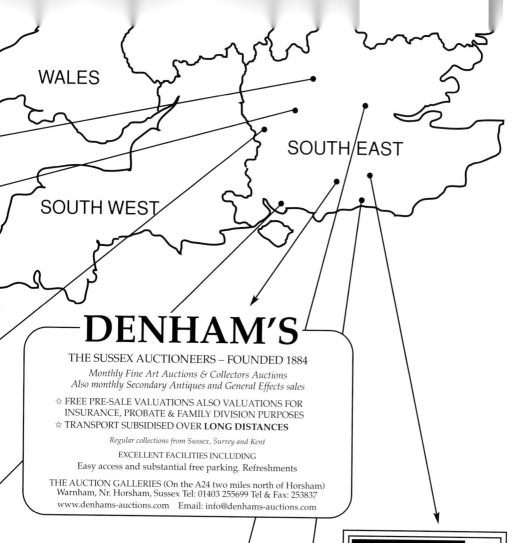

LLOYDS INTERNATIONAL
AUCTION GALLERIES

ESTABLISHED 1944

REGULAR AUCTIONS of ANTIQUES & COLLECTABLES

To include Georgian, Victorian & Edwardian Furniture, China, Silver, Clocks, Glassware, Books, Paintings and Prints
For Sale Dates, Previews and a Free Catalogue Download
Visit our Website at **www.lloyds-auction.co.uk**

LLOYDS HOUSE 9 LYDDEN ROAD LONDON SW18 4LT
Tel: 020 8788 7777 Fax: 020 8874 5390

Valuations for Auction & Probate Undertaken

Odiham Auction Sales

(Stephen R. Thomas)

ANTIQUE AUCTIONS HELD FORTNIGHTLY.
QUALITY ITEMS ACCEPTED.
HOUSE CLEARANCES ETC.
VALUATIONS FOR PROBATE.

SALES HELD AT: NORTH WARNBOROUGH VILLAGE HALL, NR. ODIHAM, HANTS (JUNCTION 5, M3)
FOR DETAILS CALL:

TEL: 01189 326824
FAX: 01189 326797
E-mail: auction@dircon.co.uk

Office & Store:
Unit 4, Priors Farm, West Green Road, Mattingley RG27 8JU

P.F. WINDIBANK
FINE ART AUCTIONEERS AND VALUERS

The Dorking Halls,
Reigate Road, Dorking,
Surrey RH4 1SG

Tel: 01306 884556/876280
Fax: 01306 884669
Email: sjw@windibank.co.uk
Website: www.windibank.co.uk

Established 1945

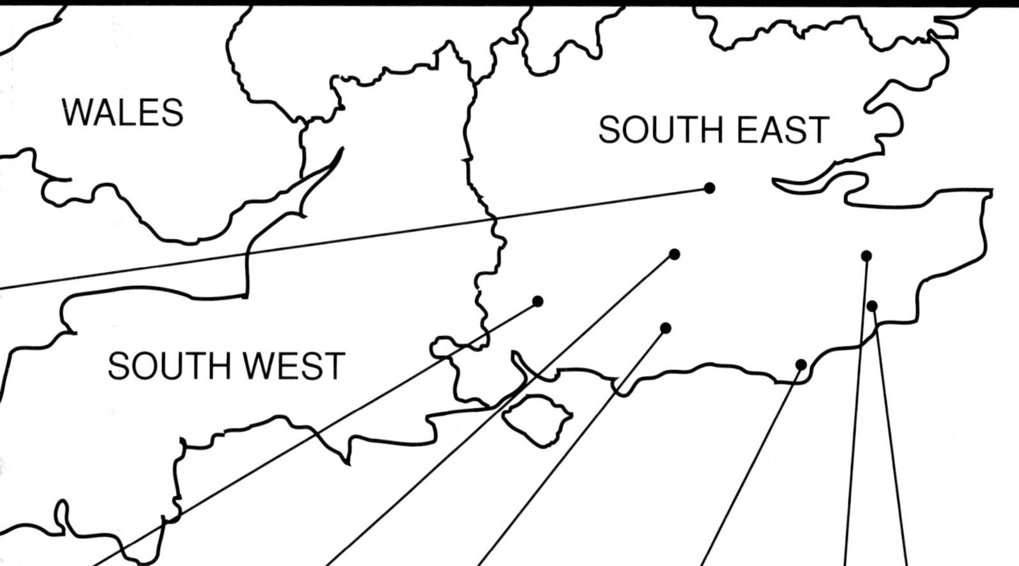

RUPERT TOOVEY

AUCTIONEERS & VALUERS

Professional Members of the Royal Institution of Chartered Surveyors

SPRING GARDENS
WASHINGTON
WEST SUSSEX RH20 3BS
01903 891955
www.rupert-toovey.com

BURSTOW *Auctioneers* **& HEWETT** *Valuers*

ESTABLISHED 1790
ROBERT ELLIN FSVA IRRV
MARK ELLIN FNAVA

ABBEY
AUCTION GALLERIES

Lower Lake, Battle, E. Sussex
Tel: 01424 772374
Fax: 01424 772302

Illustrated website:
www.burstowandhewett.co.uk

Monthly Sales of Antique and Fine Furniture, Silver, Jewellery, Paintings, etc.
Valuations for all purposes
House clearance undertaken

The Fine Art Auction Group

EDGAR HORNS

• AUCTIONEERS •

The Leading Fine Art Auctioneers in Eastbourne

Regular Fine Art & Antique Auctions
Free Auction Estimates
House Clearance Service
Insurance and Probate Valuations

Professional advice on all aspects of buying and selling at auction

01323 410419

Enquiries: sales@edgarhorns.com

46-50 South Street, Eastbourne, East Sussex BN21 4XB
www.edgarhorns.com
Edgar Horns is part of The Fine Art Auction Group

The Fine Art Auction Group

BRACKETTS

• AUCTIONEERS •

The Leading Fine Art Auctioneers in Tunbridge Wells

Regular Fine Art & Antique Auctions
Free Auction Estimates
House Clearance Service
Insurance and Probate Valuations

Professional advice on all aspects of buying and selling at auction

01892 544500

Enquiries: sales@bfaa.co.uk

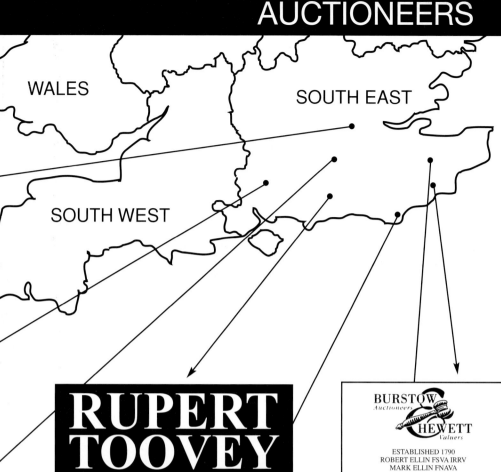

The Auction Hall, The Pantiles, Tunbridge Wells, Kent TN2 5QL
www.bfaa.co.uk
Bracketts is part of The Fine Art Auction Group

- Leading Provincial Auction House Established 1857
- Over 2000 Lots every Week – Fridays & many Saturdays

- Fine Furniture & Collectables
- Architectural Salvage
- Modern Design
- Pop Memorabilia
- 19th & 20th Century Paintings
- Rural & Domestic Bygones
- Decorative Arts
- Shipping Goods etc. etc.
- Online catalogues & calendars ▶ www.twgaze.com

Thos.Wm. GAZE & SON

Chartered Surveyors Est.1857

- **DISS AUCTION ROOMS**
  ROYDON ROAD DISS NORFOLK IP22 4LN
- tel 01379 650306
- sales@dissauctionrooms.co.uk

DYSON & SON

AUCTIONEERS & VALUERS

REGULAR THREE WEEKLY SATURDAY AUCTIONS OF ANTIQUE, OTHER FURNITURE AND EFFECTS.

VIEWING FRIDAY 9 A.M. TO 9 P.M.
SATURDAY FROM 9 A.M. SALE STARTS 11 A.M.
APPROXIMATELY 700 LOTS.
PLEASE PHONE FOR COMPLIMENTARY YEARLY AUCTION DATE CALENDAR OR VENDORS TERMS.

VISA, MASTERCARD AND DEBIT CARDS ACCEPTED.

The Auction Room, Church Street, Clare, Suffolk. CO10 8PD
Tel: 01787 277993 Fax: 01787 277996
Web site: www.dyson-auctioneers.co.uk
E-mail: info@dyson-auctioneers.co.uk

OLIVERS

AUCTIONEERS & VALUERS

REGULAR SALES OF ANTIQUES & WORKS OF ART

FORTNIGHTLY SALES OF VICTORIAN & LATER FURNITURE & HOUSEHOLD EFFECTS

VALUATIONS FOR INSURANCE PROBATE AND FAMILY DIVISION

SPECIALISTS IN HOUSE CLEARANCES FOR DECEASED ESTATES

Members of the society SOFAA of Fine Art Auctioneers

The Saleroom, Burkitts Lane, Sudbury, Suffolk CO10 1HB
Telephone 01787 880305 Fax 01787 883107
Email: oliversauctions@btconnect.com

SWORDERS

FINE ART AUCTIONEERS & VALUERS SINCE 1782

Monthly Fine Art Sales
Fully Illustrated Catalogues
General Sales Every Thursday at 11am
Valuations for all Purposes

www.sworder.co.uk

Member of the Society of Fine Art Auctioneers

14 Cambridge Rd, Stansted Mountfitchet, Essex CM24 8BZ
Tel: 01279 817778 Fax: 01279 817779
42 St. Andrew St., Hertford SE14 1JA. Tel/Fax: 01992 583508

PETER CHENEY

Auctioneers & Valuers

MONTHLY AUCTION SALES
ANTIQUES, FURNITURE, PICTURES, SILVER, PORCELAIN AND COLLECTORS ITEMS
NO BUYERS PREMIUM
VALUATIONS FOR INSURANCE & PROBATE

Western Road Auction Rooms, Western Road, Littlehampton, West Sussex BN17 5NP
Tel: 01903 722264 & 713418
Fax: 01903 713418

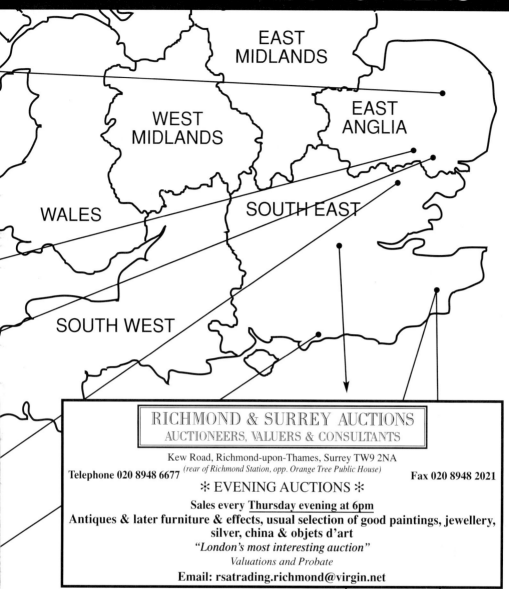

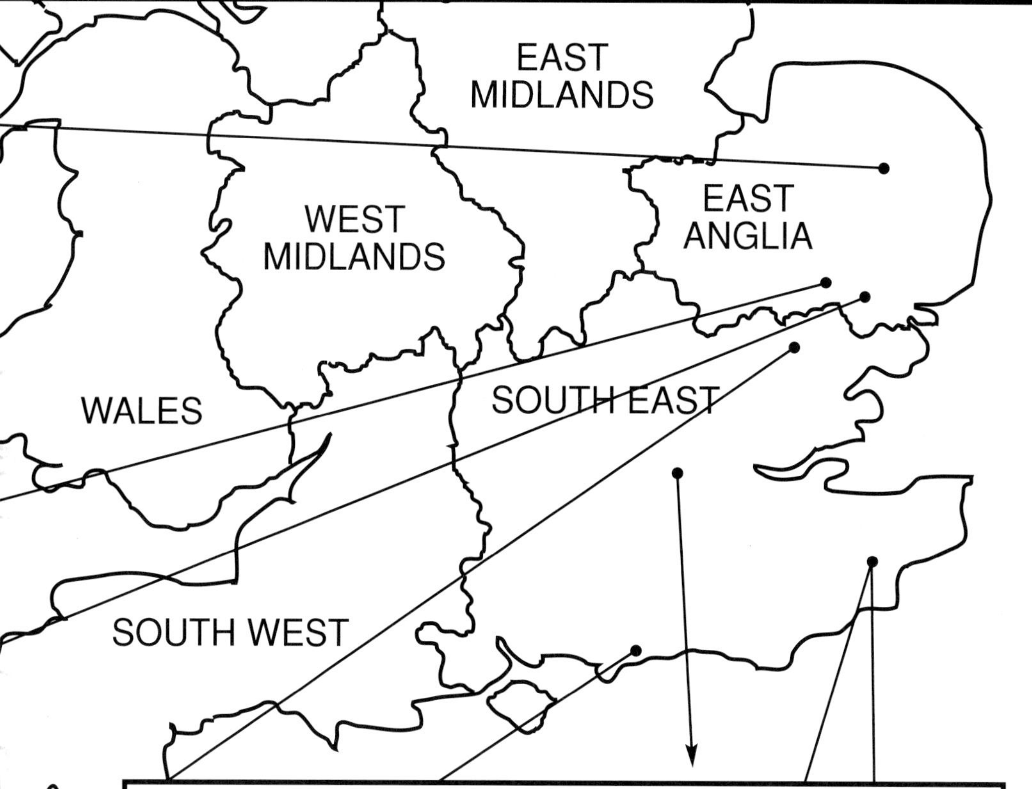
EAST
MIDLANDS
WEST
MIDLANDS
EAST
ANGLIA
WALES
SOUTH EAST
SOUTH WEST

WALES
SOUTH EAST
SOUTH WEST

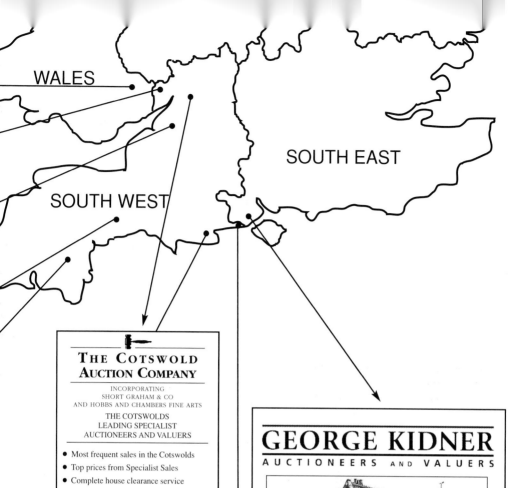

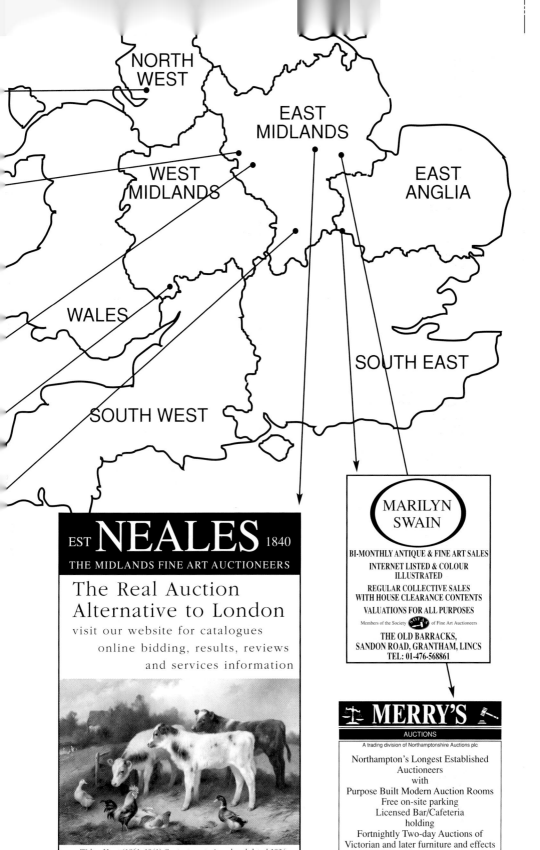

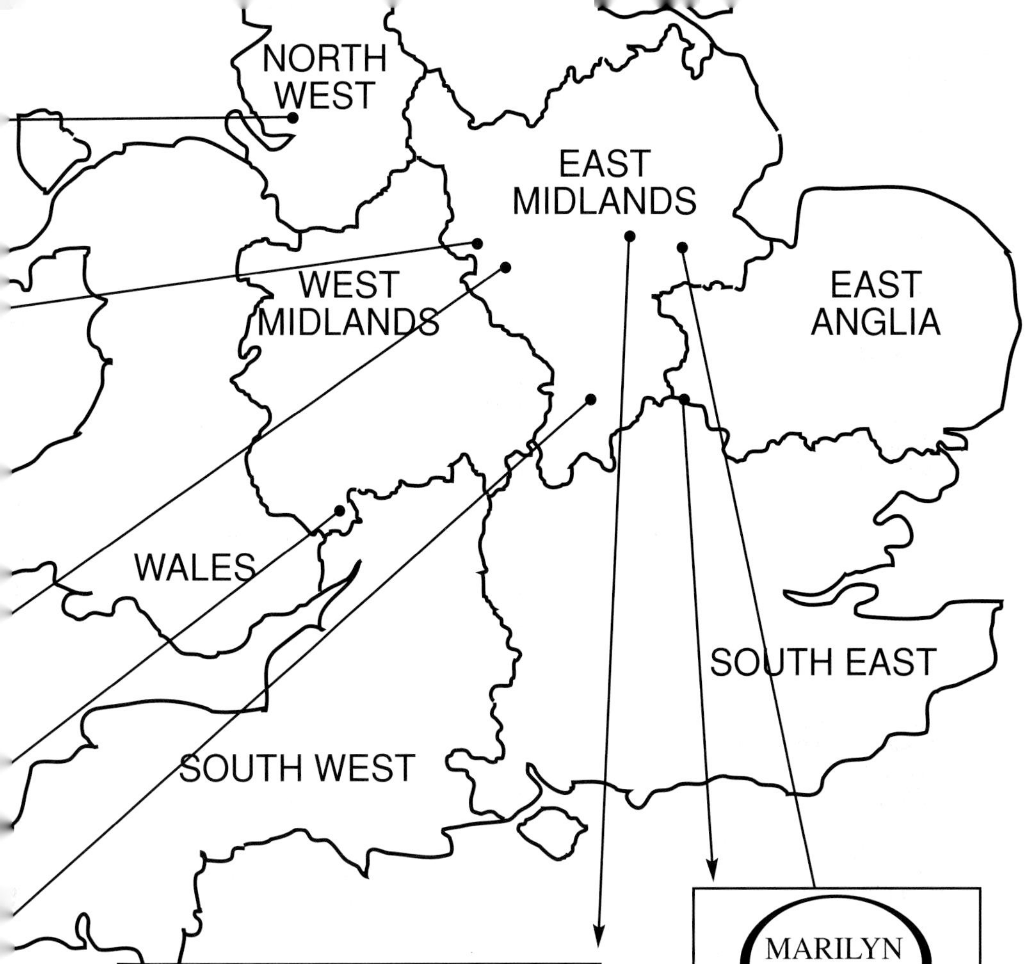
NORTH WEST
EAST MIDLANDS
WEST MIDLANDS
EAST ANGLIA
WALES
SOUTH EAST
SOUTH WEST

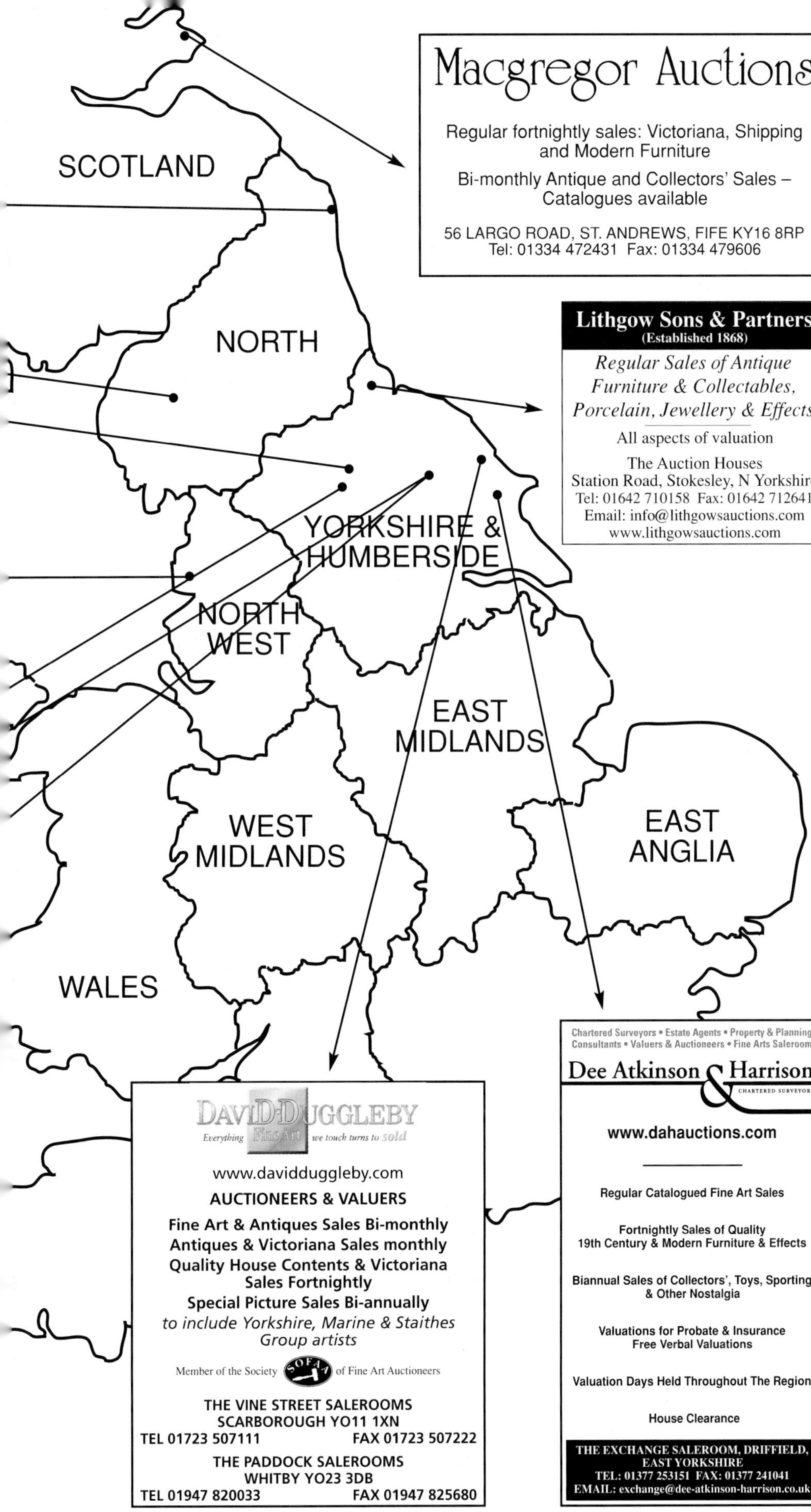
SCOTLAND
NORTH
YORKSHIRE & HUMBERSIDE
NORTH WEST
EAST MIDLANDS
WEST MIDLANDS
EAST ANGLIA
WALES

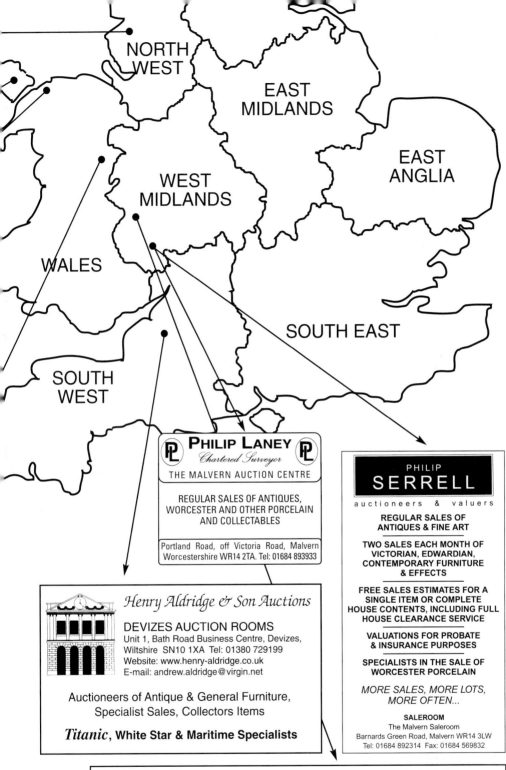

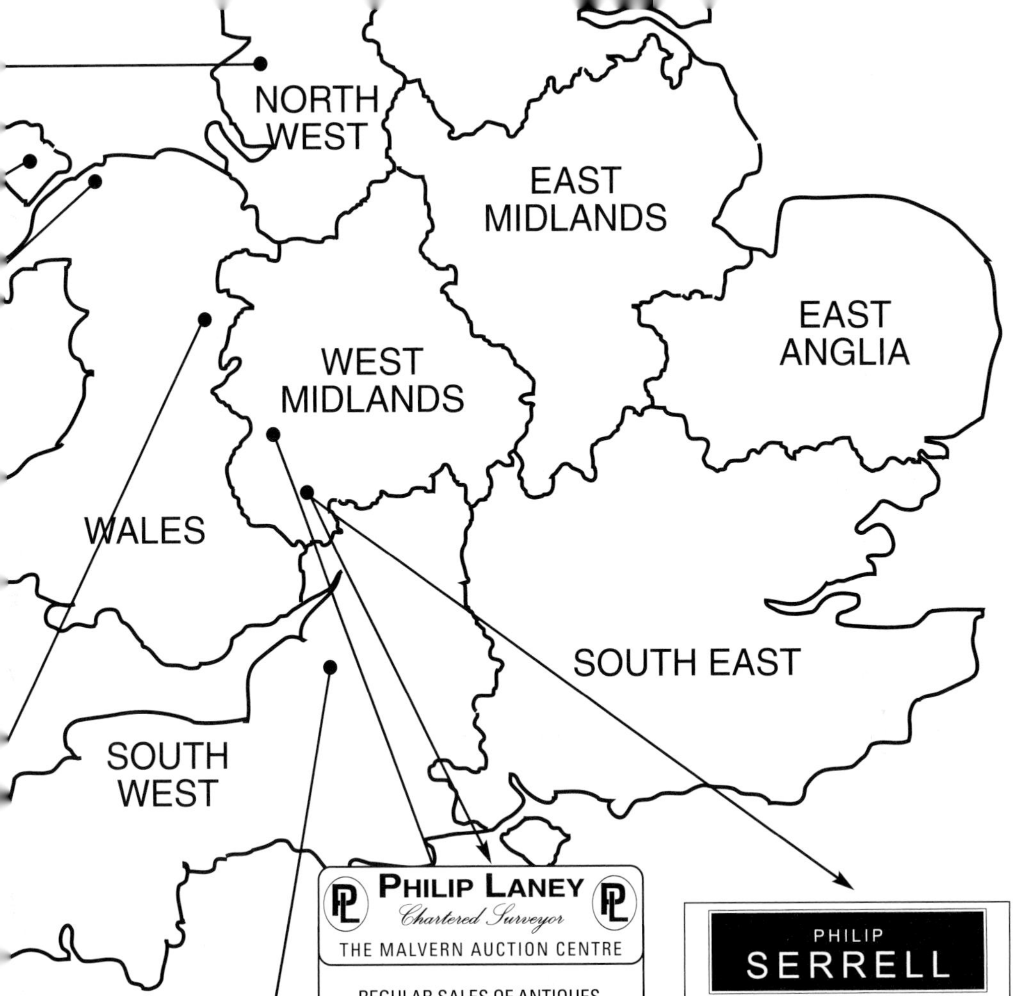
NORTH WEST
EAST MIDLANDS
EAST ANGLIA
WEST MIDLANDS
WALES
SOUTH EAST
SOUTH WEST

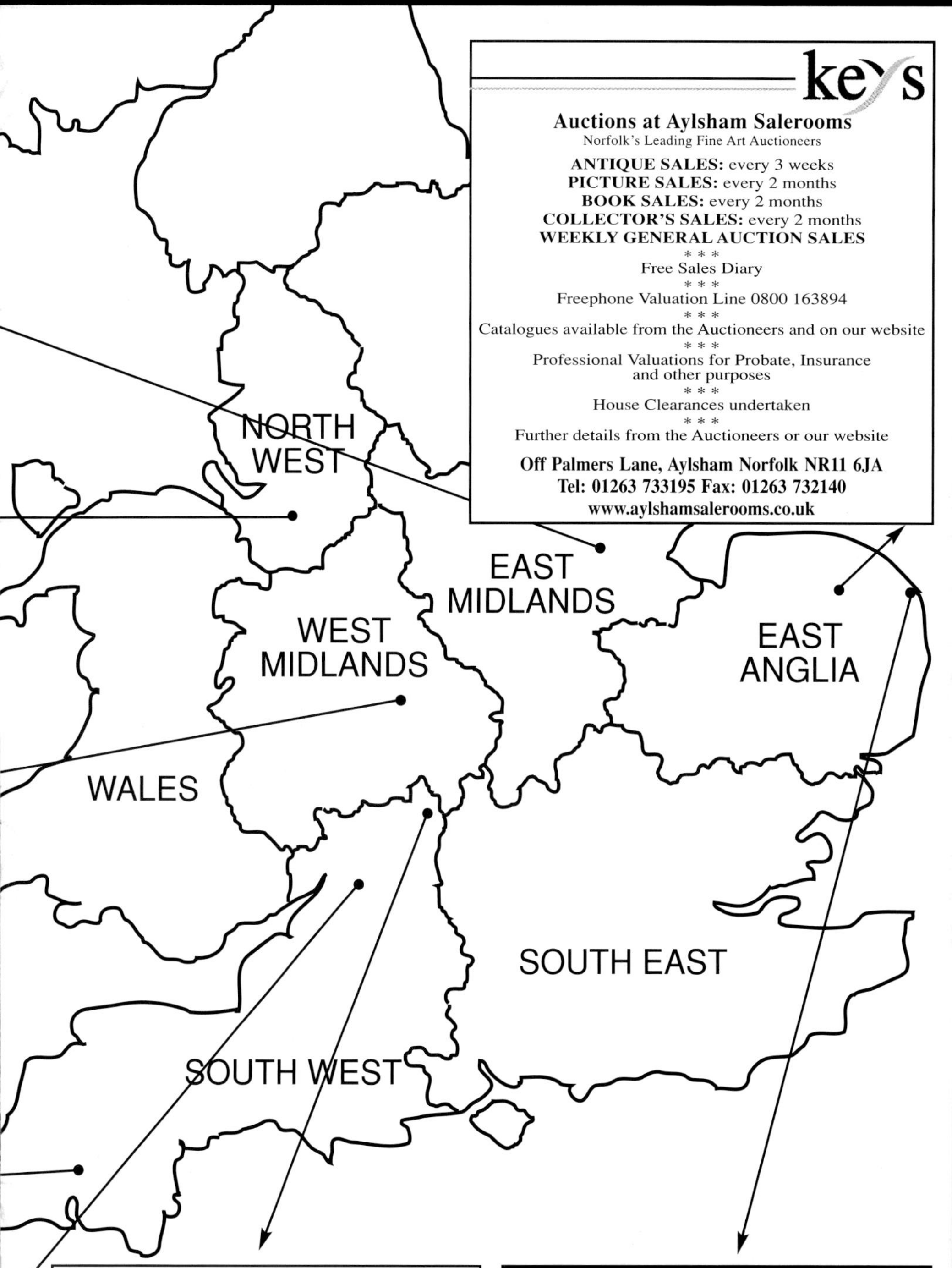

keys

Auctions at Aylsham Salerooms

Norfolk's Leading Fine Art Auctioneers

ANTIQUE SALES: every 3 weeks
PICTURE SALES: every 2 months
BOOK SALES: every 2 months
COLLECTOR'S SALES: every 2 months
WEEKLY GENERAL AUCTION SALES

* * *

Free Sales Diary

* * *

Freephone Valuation Line 0800 163894

* * *

Catalogues available from the Auctioneers and on our website

* * *

Professional Valuations for Probate, Insurance and other purposes

* * *

House Clearances undertaken

* * *

Further details from the Auctioneers or our website

Off Palmers Lane, Aylsham Norfolk NR11 6JA
Tel: 01263 733195 Fax: 01263 732140
www.aylshamsalerooms.co.uk

HOLLOWAY'S

Auctioneers and Valuers of Fine Art and Furniture

Regular Fine Art Specialist and General Sales
Valuations for all purposes
Catalogues on website or by post

SOFAA

49 Parsons Street, Banbury, Oxfordshire OX16 5PF
Tel: 01295 817777 Fax: 01295 817701
E-mail: enquiries@hollowaysauctioneers.co.uk
Website: www.hollowaysauctioneers.co.uk

Garry M. Emms & Co. Ltd

AUCTIONEERS, VALUERS & AGENTS

GREAT YARMOUTH SALEROOMS

Auctions of Antique, Reproduction, Furniture and Effects held most Wednesdays at Great Yarmouth Salerooms, Beevor Road (off South Beach Parade), Great Yarmouth, Norfolk NR30 3PS.

Bi-monthly Picture Sales
Plus Special Sales and On-Site Auctions etc.
Appointed Auctioneer for both Lowestoft and Great Yarmouth County Courts and Norfolk Constabulary.
We offer Free Valuations and of course a full and comprehensive House Clearance Service.
Valuations also for Probate and Family Division.
Shipping arranged, Small Removals and Carriage undertaken.
For further help and advice please contact:

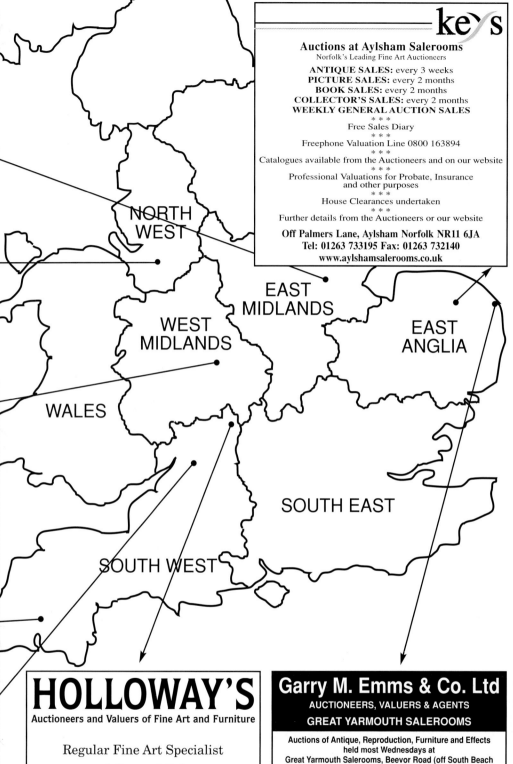

Saleroom: 01493 332668 Fax: 01493 728290
Email: g_emms@gt-yarmouth-auctions.com
www.gt-yarmouth-auctions.com

Key to Illustrations

Each illustration and descriptive caption is accompanied by a letter code. By referring to the following list of auctioneers (denoted by ⚒) and dealers (⊞) the source of any item may be immediately determined. Inclusion in this edition in no way constitutes or implies a contract or binding offer on the part of any of our contributors to supply or sell the goods illustrated, or similar articles, at the prices stated. Advertisers in this year's directory are denoted by †.

If you require a valuation for an item, it is advisable to check whether the dealer or specialist will carry out this service and if there is a charge. Please mention Miller's when making an enquiry. Having found a specialist who will carry out your valuation it is best to send a photograph and description of the item to the specialist together with a stamped addressed envelope for the reply. A valuation by telephone is not possible.

Most dealers are only too happy to help you with your enquiry; however, they are very busy people and consideration of the above points would be welcomed.

A&O ⊞ Ancient & Oriental Ltd Tel: 01664 812044 alex@antiquities.co.uk www.antiquities.co.uk

AB ⊞ The Antique Barometer Company, 5 The Lower Mall, 359 Upper Street, Camden Passage, London N1 0PD Tel: 020 7226 4992 sales@antiquebarometer.com www.antiquebarometer.com

ACO ⊞ Angela & Clive Oliver, 68 Watergate Street, Chester CH1 2LA Tel: 01244 312306/335157

ADD ⊞ Addyman Books, 39 Lion Street, Hay-on-Wye, Herefordshire HR3 5AD Tel: 01497 821136 www.hay-on-wyebooks.com

AEL ⊞ Argyll Etkin Ltd, 1–9 Hills Place, Oxford Circus, London W1F 7SA Tel: 020 7437 7800 philatelists@argyll-etkin.com www.argyll-etkin.com

AFD ⊞ Afford Decorative Arts Tel: 01827 330042 Mobile: 07831 114909 afforddecarts@fsmail.net

AG ⚒ Anderson & Garland (Auctioneers), Marlborough House, Marlborough Crescent, Newcastle-upon-Tyne, Tyne & Wear NE1 4EE Tel: 0191 232 6278

AGR ⊞ Anthony Green Antiques, Unit 39, The Bond Street Antique Centre, 124 New Bond Street, London W1S 1DX Tel: 020 7409 2854 vintagewatches@hotmail.com www.anthonygreen.com

AH ⚒† Andrew Hartley, Victoria Hall Salerooms, Little Lane, Ilkley, Yorkshire LS29 8EA Tel: 01943 816363 info@andrewhartleyfinearts.co.uk www.andrewhartleyfinearts.co.uk

AKS ⊞† Alan & Kathy Stacey Tel: 01963 441333 Mobile: 07810 058078 By appointment only info@antiqueboxes.uk.com www.antiqueboxes.uk.com

AL ⊞† Ann Lingard, Ropewalk Antiques, Rye, East Sussex TN31 7NA Tel: 01797 223486 ann-lingard@ropewalkantiques.freeserve.co.uk

ALiN ⊞ Andrew Lineham Fine Glass, The Mall, Camden Passage, London N1 8ED Tel: 020 7704 0195 andrew@andrewlineham.co.uk www.andrewlineham.co.uk

ALS ⊞† Allan Smith Clocks, Amity Cottage, 162 Beechcroft Road, Upper Stratton, Swindon, Wiltshire SN2 7QE Tel: 01793 822977 Mobile: 07778 834342 allansmithclocks@lineone.net www.allansmithantiqueclocks.co.uk

AMB ⚒ Ambrose, Ambrose House, Old Station Road, Loughton, Essex IG10 4PE Tel: 020 8502 3951

AMC ⊞ Amelie Caswell Tel: 0117 9077960

AMH ⊞ Amherst Antiques, Monomark House, 27 Old Gloucester Street, London WC1N 3XX Tel: 01892 725552 Mobile: 07850 350212 amherstantiques@monomark.co.uk

AMR Art Market Research, 71 Oxford Gardens, London W10 5UJ Tel: 020 8968 9999 artmarketsearch@easynet.co.uk www.artmarketresearch.com

AMS ⊞ Andy & Margaret Shannan, 28 Plymouth Road, Buckfastleigh, Devon TQ11 0DB Tel: 01364 644624 Mobile: 07971 590395

AnAr ⊞ Ancient Art, 85 The Vale, Southgate, London N14 6AT Tel: 020 8882 1509 ancient.art@btinternet.com www.ancientart.co.uk

ANG ⊞† Ancient & Gothic, PO Box 5390, Bournemouth, Dorset BH7 6XR Tel: 01202 431721

ANO ⊞ Art Nouveau Originals Tel: 01733 244717 Mobile: 07774 718 096 cathy@artnouveauoriginals.com www.artnouveauoriginals.com

APC ⊞ Antique Photographic Company Ltd Tel: 01949 842192 alpaco47@aol.com

APO ⊞† Apollo Antiques Ltd, The Saltisford, Birmingham Road, Warwick CV34 4TD Tel: 01926 494746/494666 mynott@apolloantiques.com www.apolloantiques.com

APS ⊞ The Antique Print Shop, 11 Middle Row, East Grinstead, West Sussex RH19 3AX Tel: 01342 410501 printsandmaps@www.theantiqueprintshop.com www.theantiqueprintshop.com

ARB ⊞ Arbour Antiques Ltd, Poet's Arbour, Sheep Street, Stratford-on-Avon, Warwickshire CV37 6EF Tel: 01789 293453

ARTi ⊞ Artifactory, 641 Indiana Avenue NW, Washington DC 20004, USA Tel: 202 393 2727 artifactorydc@msn.com www.artifactorydc.com

ASA ⊞† A. S. Antique Galleries, 26 Broad Street, Pendleton, Salford, Greater Manchester M6 5BY Tel: 0161 737 5938 Mobile: 07836 368230 as@sternshine.demon.co.uk

ASB ⊞ Andrew Spencer Bottomley, The Coach House, Thongs Bridge, Holmfirth, Yorkshire HD7 2TT Tel: 01484 685234 andrewbottomley@compuserve.com

ASC ⊞ Andrew Sclanders, 32 St Paul's View, 15 Amwell Street, London EC1R 1UP Tel: 020 7278 5034 sclanders@beatbooks.com www.beatbooks.com

ASH ⊞ Adrian Ager Ltd, Great Hall, North Street, Ashburton, Devon TQ13 7QD Tel: 01364 653189 afager@tinyworld.co.uk www.adrianager.co.uk

ASP ⊞ Aspidistra Antiques, 51 High Street, Finedon, Wellingborough, Northamptonshire NN9 5JN Tel: 01933 680196 info@aspidistra-antiques.com www.aspidistra.antiques.com

AUA ⊞ Austin's Antiques, PO Box 4723, Ringwood, Hampshire BH24 2DN austinsantiques@ukonline.co.uk www.austins-antiques.co.uk

AUTO ⊞ Automatomania, M13 Grays Mews, 58 Davies Street, London W1K 5LP Tel: 020 7495 5259 Mobile: 07790 719097 magic@automatomania.com www.automatomania.com

AW ⊞† Alan Walker, Halfway Manor, Halfway, Nr Newbury, Berkshire RG20 8NR Tel: 01488 657670 Mobile: 07770 728397 www.alanwalker-barometers.com

B ⚒† Bonhams, 101 New Bond Street, London W1S 1SR Tel: 020 7629 6602 www.bonhams.com

B(Ba) ⚒ Bonhams, 10 Salem Road, Bayswater, London W2 4DL Tel: 020 7313 2700

B(Ch) ⚒ Bonhams, 65–69 Lots Road, Chelsea, London SW10 0RN Tel: 020 7393 3900

B(EA) ⚒ Bonhams, 32 Boss Hall Road, Ipswich, Suffolk IP1 5DJ Tel: 01473 740494

B(Ed) ⚒ Bonhams, 65 George Street, Edinburgh EH2 2JL, Scotland Tel: 0131 225 2266

B(Kn) ⚒ Bonhams, Montpelier Street, Knightsbridge, London SW7 1HH Tel: 020 7393 3900

B(L) ⚒ Bonhams, 17a East Parade, Leeds, Yorkshire LS1 2BH Tel: 0113 2448011

B(Nor) ⚒ Bonhams, The Market Place, Reepham, Norwich, Norfolk NR10 4JJ Tel: 01603 871443

B(NW) ⚒ Bonhams, New House, 150 Christleton Road, Chester CH3 5TD Tel: 01244 313936

B(O) ⚒ Bonhams, 39 Park End Street, Oxford OX1 1JD Tel: 01865 723524

B(Pr) ⚒ Bonhams, Cornubia Hall, Eastcliffe Road, Par, Cornwall PL24 2AQ Tel: 01726 814047

B(S) ⚒ Bonhams, 49 London Road, Sevenoaks, Kent TN13 1AR Tel: 01732 740310

B(SW) ⚒ Bonhams, 7–8 Park Place, Cardiff CF10 3DP, South Wales Tel: 029 2072 7980

B(W) ⚒ Bonhams, Dowell Street, Honiton, Devon EX14 1LX Tel: 01404 41872

B(WM) ⚒ Bonhams, The Old House, Station Road, Knowle, Solihull, West Midlands B93 0HT Tel: 01564 776151

B&L ⚒ Bonhams and Langlois, Westaway Chambers, 39 Don Street, St Helier, Jersey JE2 4TR, Channel Islands Tel: 01534 722441

B&R ⊞† Bread & Roses, Durham House Antique Centre, Sheep Street, Stow-on-the-Wold, Gloucestershire GL54 1AA Tel: 01451 870404/01926 817342

BAL ⊞ A. H. Baldwin & Sons Ltd, Numismatists, 11 Adelphi Terrace, London WC2N 6BJ Tel: 020 7930 6879

BaN ⊞ Barbara Ann Newman Tel: 07850 016729

BAu ⚒† Bloomington Auction Gallery, 300 East Grove St, Bloomington, Illinois 61701, USA Tel: 309 828 5533 joyluke@aol.com www.joyluke.com

BB(L) ⚒ Butterfields, 7601 Sunset Boulevard, Los Angeles CA 90046, USA Tel: 323 850 7500

BBA ⚒ Bloomsbury Book Auctions, 3 & 4 Hardwick Street, Off Rosebery Avenue, London EC1R 4RY Tel: 020 7833 2636/7 & 0207923 6940

info@bloomsbury-book-auct.com www.bloomsbury-book-auct.com

BBe † Bourton Bears, Bourton-on-the-Water, Gloucestershire Tel: 01451 821466 mel@strathspey-bed-fsnet.co.uk www.bourtonbears.com

BBo Bazaar Boxes Tel: 01992 504 454 Mobile: 07970 909 206 bazaarboxes@hotmail.com commerce.icollector.com/BazaarBoxes/

BBR BBR, Elsecar Heritage Centre, Wath Road, Elsecar, Barnsley, Yorkshire S74 8HJ Tel: 01226 745156 sales@bbrauctions.co.uk www.onlinebbr.com

BD Banana Dance Ltd, 16 The Mall, Camden Passage, 359 Upper St, Islington, London N1 0PD Tel: 020 8699 7728 Mobile: 07976 296987 jonathan@bananadance.com www.bananadance.com

BDA Briar's C20th Decorative Arts, Skipton Antiques & Collectors Centre, The Old Foundry, Cavendish Street, Skipton, Yorkshire BD23 2AB Tel: 01756 798641

Bea/ Bea(E) Bearnes, St Edmund's Court, Okehampton Street, Exeter, Devon EX4 1DU Tel: 01392 422800 nsaintey@bearnes.co.uk www.bearnes.co.uk

Beb Bebes et Jouets, c/o Post Office, Edinburgh EH7 6HW, Scotland Tel: 0131 332 5650 Mobile: 0771 4374995 bebesetjouets@u.genie.co.uk you.genie.co.uk/bebesetjouets

BeF Bevan Fine Art, PO Box 60, Uckfield, East Sussex TN22 1ZD Tel: 01825 766649 Mobile: 07711 262022 bevanfineart@quista.net

BELL † Bellhouse Antiques, Chelmsford, Essex Tel: 01268 710415 Bellhouse.Antiques@virgin.net

BERA Berry Antiques, 3 High Street, Moreton-in-Marsh, Gloucestershire GL56 0AH Tel: 01608 652929 chris@berryantiques.com berryantiques.com berryantiques.co.uk

BERN Bernaerts, Verlatstraat 18–22, 2000 Antwerpen/Anvers, Belgium Tel: +32 (0)3 248 19 21 edmond.bernaerts@ping.be www.auction-bernaerts.com

BEV Beverley, 30 Church Street, Marylebone, London NW8 8EP Tel: 020 7262 1576

BEX † Daniel Bexfield, 26 Burlington Arcade, London W1J 0PU Tel: 020 7491 1720 antiques@bexfield.co.uk www.bexfield.co.uk

BHa † Judy & Brian Harden Antiques, PO Box 14, Bourton-on-the-Water, Cheltenham, Gloucestershire GL54 2YR Tel: 01451 810684 Mobile: 07831 692252 harden@portraitminiatures.co.uk www.portraitminiatures.co.uk

BIB † Biblion, Grays Antique Market, 1–7 Davies Mews, London W1K 5AB Tel: 020 7629 1374 info@biblion.com www.biblion.com www.biblionmayfair.com

BIG Bigwood Auctioneers Ltd, The Old School, Tiddington, Stratford-upon-Avon, Warwickshire CV37 7AW Tel: 01789 269415

BLm Lyn Bloom & Jeffrey Neal, Vault 27, The London Silver Vaults, Chancery Lane, London WC2A 1QS Tel: 020 7242 6189 Mobile: 07768 533055 bloomvault@aol.com www.bloomvault.com

BMi Bobbie Middleton, 58 Long Street, Tetbury, Gloucestershire GL8 8AQ Tel: 01666 502761 Mobile: 07774 192660 bobbiemiddleton@lineone.net

BNO Beanos, Middle Street, Croydon, London CR0 1RE Tel: 020 8680 1202 enquiries@beanos.co.uk www.beanos.co.uk

Bns Brittons Jewellers, 4 King Street, Clitheroe, Lancashire BB7 2EP Tel: 01200 425555 info@brittons-watches.co.uk www.brittons-watches.co.uk www.antique-jewelry.co.uk

BoC Bounty Antiques Centre, 76 Fore Street, Topsham, Devon EX3 0HQ Tel: 01392 875007 Mobile: 07939 526504

BR † Bracketts, The Auction Hall, The Pantiles, Tunbridge Wells, Kent TN2 5QL Tel: 01892 544500 sales@bfaa.co.uk www.bfaa.co.uk

Bri Bristol Auction Rooms, St John's Place, Apsley Road, Clifton, Bristol, Gloucestershire BS8 2ST Tel: 0117 973 7201 www.bristolauctionrooms.com

BrL The Brighton Lanes Antique Centre, 12 Meeting House Lane, Brighton, East Sussex BN1 1HB Tel: 01273 823121 Mobile: 07785 564337 peter@brightonlanes-antiquecentre.co.uk www.brightonlanes-antiquecentre.co.uk

BROW David Brower, 113 Kensington Church Street, London W8 7LN Tel: 0207 221 4155 David@davidbrower-antiques.com www.davidbrower-antiques.com

BrW Brian Watson Antique Glass, Foxwarren Cottage, High Street, Marsham, Norwich, Norfolk NR10 5QA Tel: 01263 732519 By appointment only brian.h.watson@talk21.com

BUK Bukowskis, Arsenalsgatan 4, Stockholm SE111 47, Sweden Tel: 00 46 (0)8 614 08 00 info@bukowskis.se www.bukowskis.se

BUK(F) Bukowskis, Horhammer, Iso Roobertink, 12 Stora Robertsg, 00120 Helsinki Helsingfors, Finland Tel: 00 358 9 668 9110 www.bukowskis.fi

BWL † Brightwells Fine Art, The Fine Art Saleroom, Ryelands Road, Leominster, Herefordshire HR6 8NZ Tel: 01568 611122 fineart@brightwells.com www.brightwells.com

Byl † Bygones of Ireland Ltd, Lodge Road, Westport, Co Mayo, Republic of Ireland Tel: 00 353 98 26132/25701 bygones@anu.ie www.bygones-of-ireland.com

C&A † Campbell & Archard Ltd, Lychgate House, Church Street, Seal, Kent TN15 0AR Tel: 01732 761153 campbellarchard@btclick.com www.campbellandarchard.co.uk

C&R † Catchpole & Rye, Saracens Dairy, Jobbs Lane, Pluckley, Ashford, Kent TN27 0SA Tel: 01233 840840 info@crye.co.uk www.crye.co.uk

CaF Caren Fine, USA Tel: 301 854 6262 jdcicca@bellatlantic.net

CAL Cedar Antiques Ltd, High Street, Hartley Wintney, Hampshire RG27 8NY Tel: 01252 843222 or 01189 326628

Cas John & Barbara Gair, Castle Antiques, Essex www.castle-antiques.com

CAT Lennox Cato, 1 The Square, Church Street, Edenbridge, Kent TN8 5BD Tel: 01732 865988 Mobile: 07836 233473 cato@lennoxcato.com www.lennoxcato.com

CAV Rupert Cavendish Antiques, 610 King's Road, London SW6 2DX Tel: 020 7731 7041 www.rupertcavendish.co.uk

CB Christine Bridge, 78 Castelnau, London SW13 9EX Tel: 07000 445277

CBB Colin Baddiel, Gray's Mews, 1–7 Davies Mews, London W1Y 1AR Tel: 020 7408 1239/020 8452 7243

CBP † Comic Book Postal Auctions Ltd, 40–42 Osnaburgh Street, London NW1 3ND Tel: 020 7424 0007 comicbook@compuserve.com www.compalcomics.com

CCO Collectable Costume, Showroom South, Gloucester Antiques Centre, 1 Severn Road, Gloucester GL1 2LE Tel: 07980 623926

CGA Castlegate Antiques Centre, 55 Castlegate, Newark, Nottinghamshire NG24 1BE Tel: 01636 700076 Mobile: 07860 843739

CGC Cheffins, Clifton House, Clifton Road, Cambridge CB1 7EA Tel: 01223 213343 www.cheffins.co.uk

CHAC † Church Hill Antiques Centre, 6 Station Street, Lewes, East Sussex BN7 2DA Tel: 01273 474 842 churchhilllewes@aol.com www.church-hill-antiques.co.uk

ChC Christopher Clarke (Antiques) Ltd, The Fosseway, Stow-on-the-Wold, Gloucestershire GL54 1JS Tel: 01451 830476 cclarkeantiques@aol.com www.campaignfurniture.com

Che Chevertons of Edenbridge Ltd, 67–73 High Street, Edenbridge, Kent TN8 5AL Tel: 01732 863196

CHI Chinasearch, 9 Princes Drive, Kenilworth, Warwickshire CV8 2FD Tel: 01926 512402 helen@chinasearch.uk.com jackie@chinasearch.uk.com www.chinasearch.uk.com

CHT Catherine Hunt Antique Oriental Ceramics, PO Box 743, Cheltenham, Gloucestershire GL52 5ZB Tel: 01242 227794 cathyhunt@btinternet.com

CHTR Charterhouse, The Long Street Salerooms, Sherborne, Dorset DT9 3BS Tel: 01935 812277 enquiry@charterhouse-auctions.co.uk www.charterhouse-auctions.co.uk

CO Cooper Owen, 10 Denmark Street, London WC2H 8LS Tel: 020 7240 4132 www.CooperOwen.com

CoA Country Antiques (Wales), Castle Mill, Kidwelly, Carmarthenshire SA17 4UU, Wales Tel: 01554 890534

CoC Comic Connections, 4a Parsons Street, Banbury, Oxfordshire OX16 5LW Tel: 01295 268989 comicman@freenetname.co.uk

CoCo Country Collector, 11–12 Birdgate, Pickering, Yorkshire YO18 7AL Tel: 01751 477481

COF Cottage Farm Antiques, Stratford Road, Aston Subedge, Chipping Campden, Gloucestershire GL55 6PZ Tel: 01386 438263 info@cottagefarmantiques.co.uk www.cottagefarmantiques.co.uk

CoH Cooper Hirst Auctions, The Granary Saleroom, Victoria Road, Chelmsford, Essex CM2 6LH Tel: 01245 260535

CoHA Corner House Antiques and Ffoxe Antiques, The Old Ironmongers Centre, 5 Burford Street, Lechlade, Gloucestershire GL7 3AP Tel: 01367 860078 jdhis007@btopenworld.com www.corner-house-antiques.co.uk

COPA † Copake Auction, Inc, PO Box H, Copake NY 12516, USA Tel: 518 329 1142 info@copakeauction.com www.copakeauction.com

CoS Corrine Soffe Tel: 01295 730317 soffe@btinternet.co.uk

CrF Crowdfree Antiques, PO Box 395, Bury St Edmunds, Suffolk IP31 2PG Tel: 0870 444 0791 info@crowdfree.com www.crowdfree.com

CS Christopher Sykes, The Old Parsonage, Woburn, Milton Keynes, Buckinghamshire MK17 9QM Tel: 01525 290259

CTO † Collector's Corner, PO Box 8, Congleton, Cheshire CW12 4GD Tel: 01260 270429 dave.popcorner@ukonline.co.uk

CuS Curious Science, 319 Lillie Road, Fulham, London SW6 7LL Tel: 020 7610 1175 Mobile: 07956 834094 curiousscience@medical-antiques.com

DA Dee, Atkinson & Harrison, The Exchange Saleroom, Driffield, East Yorkshire YO25 6LD Tel: 01377 253151 exchange@dee-atkinson-harrison.co.uk www.dahauctions.com

DAC No longer trading

DAD decorative arts@doune, Stand 26, Scottish Antique and Arts Centre, By Doune, Stirling FK16 6HD, Scotland Tel: 01786 461 439/0141 946 3571 Mobile: 07778 475 974 decorativearts.doune@btinternet.com www.decorativearts-doune.com

DAN Andrew Dando, 34 Market Street, Bradford on Avon, Wiltshire BA15 1LL Tel: 01225 865444 www.andrewdando.co.uk

DAU Dickins Auctioneers Ltd, The Claydon Saleroom, Calvert Road, Middle Claydon, Buckinghamshire MK18 2EZ Tel: 01296 714434 info@dickens-auctioneers.com www.dickens-auctioneers.com

DAV Hugh Davies, The Packing Shop, 6–12 Ponton Road, London SW8 5BA Tel: 020 7498 3255

DAW Douglas Dawson, Dawson Gallery, 222 West Huron, Chicago, Illinois 60610, USA

DD David Duggleby, The Vine St Salerooms, Scarborough, Yorkshire YO11 1XN Tel: 01723 507111 auctions@davidduggleby.freeserve.co.uk www.davidduggleby.com

DeA Delphi Antiques, Powerscourt Townhouse Centre, South William Street, Dublin 2, Republic of Ireland Tel: 00 353 1 679 0331

DeG Denzil Grant, Suffolk Fine Arts, Drinkstone House, Drinkstone, Bury St. Edmunds, Suffolk IP30 9TG Tel: 01449 736576

Del Delomosne & Son Ltd, Court Close, North Wraxall, Chippenham, Wiltshire SN14 7AD Tel: 01225 891505

DFA Delvin Farm Antiques, Gormonston, Co Meath, Republic of Ireland Tel: 00 353 1 841 2285 john@delvinfarmpine.com www.delvinfarmpine.com

DHA Durham House Antiques Centre, Sheep Street, Stow-on-the-Wold, Gloucestershire GL54 1AA Tel: 01451 870404

DHu Diana Huntley Antiques, 8 Camden Passage, Islington, London N1 8ED Tel: 020 7226 4605 diana@dianahuntleyantiques.co.uk www.dianahuntleyantiques.co.uk

DIA Mark Diamond Tel: 020 8508 4479

DID Didier Antiques, 58–60 Kensington Church Street, London W8 4DB Tel: 020 7938 2537/07836 232634

DJH David J. Hansord & Son, 6 & 7 Castle Hill, Lincoln LN1 3AA Tel: 01522 530044 Mobile: 07831 183511

DLP The Dunlop Collection, PO Box 6269, Statesville NC 28687, USA Tel: (704) 871 2626 or Toll Free Telephone (800) 227 1996

DMa David March, Abbots Leigh, Bristol, Gloucestershire BS8 Tel: 0117 937 2422

DMC Diamond Mills & Co, 117 Hamilton Road, Felixstowe, Suffolk IP11 7BL Tel: 01394 282281

DMe Ireland's Own Antiques, Alpine House, Carlow Road, Abbeyleix, Co Laois, Republic of Ireland Tel: 00 353 502 31348

DN Dreweatt Neate, Donnington Priory, Donnington, Newbury, Berkshire RG14 2JE Tel: 01635 553553 fineart@dreweatt-neate.co.uk www.auctions.dreweatt-neate.co.uk

DNo Desmond & Amanda North, The Orchard, 186 Hale Street, East Peckham, Kent TN12 5JB Tel: 01622 871353

DNW Dix-Noonan-Webb, 1 Old Bond Street, London W1S 4PB Tel: 020 7499 5022

DOA Dorchester Antiques, 3 High Street, Dorchester-on-Thames, Oxfordshire OX10 7HH Tel: 01865 341 373

DORO Dorotheum, Palais Dorotheum, A–1010 Wien, Dorotheergasse. 17, 1010 Austria Tel: 0043 1 515 60 354

DSA David Scriven Antiques, PO Box 1962, Leigh-on-Sea, Essex SS9 2YZ Mobile: 07887 716677 david@david-scriven-antiques.fsnet.co.uk

DSG Market Street Gallery Ltd T/A Delf Stream Gallery, Bournemouth, Dorset Tel: 07974 926137 oastman@aol.com www.delfstreamgallery.com

DUK Dukeries Antiques Centre, Thoresby Park, Budby, Newark, Nottinghamshire NG22 9EX Tel: 01623 822252

DuM/ Dum/DUM Du Mouchelles, 409 East Jefferson, Detroit, Michigan 48226, USA Tel: 313 963 6255

DW Dominic Winter Book Auctions, The Old School, Maxwell Street, Swindon, Wiltshire SN1 5DR Tel: 01793 611340 info@dominicwinter.co.uk www.dominicwinter.co.uk

DY Dycheling Antiques, 34 High Street, Ditchling, Hassocks, West Sussex BN6 8TA Tel: 01273 842929 Mobile: 07785 456341 www.antiquechairmatching.com

E Ewbank Auctioneers, Burnt Common Auction Room, London Road, Send, Woking, Surrey GU23 7LN Tel: 01483 223101 antiques@ewbankauctions.co.uk www.ewbankauctions.co.uk

EAL The Exeter Antique Lighting Co, Cellar 15, The Quay, Exeter, Devon EX2 4AP Tel: 01392 490848 Mobile: 07702 969438 www.antiquelightingcompany.com

Ech Echoes, 650a Halifax Road, Eastwood, Todmorden, Yorkshire OL14 6DW Tel: 01706 817505

EH Edgar Horns, 46–50 South Street, Eastbourne, East Sussex BN21 4XB Tel: 01323 410419 sales@edgarhorns.com www.edgarhorns.com

ETO Eric Tombs, 62a West Street, Dorking, Surrey RH4 1BS Tel: 01306 743661 ertombs@aol.com www.dorkingantiques.com

EXC Excalibur Antiques, Taunton Antique Centre, 27–29 Silver Street, Taunton, Somerset TA13DH Tel: 01823 289327/07774 627409 pauldwright@btinternet.com www.excaliburantiques.com

F Freshfords, High Street, Freshford, Bath, Somerset BA3 6EF Tel: 01225 722111 Mobile: 07714 362863 antiques@freshfords.com www.freshfords.com

F&C Finan & Co, The Square, Mere, Wiltshire BA12 6DJ Tel: 01747 861411 post@finanandco.co.uk www.finanandco.co.uk

F&F Fenwick & Fenwick, 88–90 High Street, Broadway, Worcestershire WR12 7AJ Tel: 01386 853227/841724

FAC Fagan Arms, Inc, 22952 E Fifteen Mile Road, Clinton Township, MI 48035, USA Tel: 586 465 4637 info@faganarms.com www.faganarms.com

FEN See **RbF**

FHF Fellows & Sons, Augusta House, 19 Augusta Street, Hockley, Birmingham, West Midlands B18 6JA Tel: 0121 212 2131 info@fellows.co.uk www.fellows.co.uk

FRY Curiosities and Collectables, Gloucester Antiques Centre, The Historic Docks, 1 Severn Road, Gloucester GL1 2LE Tel: 01452 529716

FU Fu Ts'ang Lung, Rotherham, Yorkshire Tel: 01709 829805 futsanglung@hotmail.com

G(B) Gorringes Auction Galleries, Terminus Road, Bexhill-on-Sea, East Sussex TN39 3LR Tel: 01424 212994 bexhill@gorringes.co.uk www.gorringes.co.uk

G(L) Gorringes inc Julian Dawson, 15 North Street, Lewes, East Sussex BN7 2PD Tel: 01273 472503 auctions@gorringes.co.uk www.gorringes.co.uk

G&CC The Goss & Crested China Club & Museum, inc Milestone Publications, 62 Murray Road, Horndean, Hampshire PO8 9JL Tel: (023) 9259 7440 info@gosschinaclub.demon.co.uk www.gosscrestedchina.co.uk

G&G Guest & Gray, 1–7 Davies Mews, London W1K 5AB Tel: 020 7408 1252 info@chinese-porcelain-art.com www.chinese-porcelain-art.com

G&H Garret & Hazlehurst Tel: 07976 247942 garhaz.com@btopenworld.com

GAA Gabrian Antiques Tel: 01923 859675 gabrian.antiques@virgin.net

GAK Keys, Off Palmers Lane, Aylsham, Norfolk NR11 6JA Tel: 01263 733195 www.aylshamsalerooms.co.uk

Gam Clarke Gammon, The Guildford Auction Rooms, Bedford Road, Guildford, Surrey GU1 4SJ Tel: 01483 880915

GBr Geoffrey Breeze Antiques, 6 George Street, Bath, Somerset BA1 2EH Tel: 01225 466499

GD Gilbert & Dale Antiques, The Old Chapel, Church Street, Ilchester, Nr Yeovil, Somerset BA22 8ZA Tel: 01935 840464

GDO Gavin Douglas Fine Antiques Ltd, 75 Portobello Road, London W11 2QB Tel: 01825 723441/0207 221 1121 Mobile: 07860 680521 gavin@antique-clocks.co.uk www.antique-clocks.co.uk

GGv G. G. van Schagen Antiquair Tel: 0031 229 275692 Mobile: 06 51 393975 g.schagen@wxs.nl

GH Gardiner Houlgate, The Bath Auction Rooms, 9 Leafield Way, Corsham, Nr Bath, Somerset SN13 9SW Tel: 01225 812912 gardiner-houlgate.co.uk www.invaluable.com/gardiner-houlgate

GKe Gerald Kenyon, 6 Great Strand Street, Dublin 1, Republic of Ireland Tel: 00 3531 873 0625/873 0488

GLD Glade Antiques, PO Box 873, High Wycombe, Buckinghamshire HP14 3ZQ Tel: 01494 882818 Mobile: 07771 552 328 sonia@gladeantiques.com www.gladeantiques.com

Gle Glendining's (A division of Bonhams specializing in coins & medals), 101 New Bond Street, London W1S 1SR Tel: 020 7493 2445

GM Philip Knighton, Bush House, 17B South Street, Wellington, Somerset TA21 8NR Tel: 01823 661618 philip.knighton@btopenworld.com

GN Gillian Neale Antiques, PO Box 247, Aylesbury, Buckinghamshire HP20 1JZ Tel: 01296 423754/07860 638700 gillianneale@aol.com www.gilliannealeantiques.co.uk

GoW Gordon Watson Ltd, 50 Fulham Road, London SW3 Tel: 020 7589 3108

GRe Greystoke Antiques, 4 Swan Yard, (off Cheap Street), Sherborne, Dorset DT9 3AX Tel: 01935 812833

GRG Gordon Reece Galleries, Finkle Street, Knaresborough, Yorkshire HG5 8AA Tel: 01423 866219 www.gordonreecegalleries.com

GRI Grimes House Antiques, High Street, Moreton-in-Marsh, Gloucestershire GL56 0AT Tel: 01608 651029 grimes_house@cix.co.uk www.grimeshouse.co.uk www.cranberryglass.co.uk

GS Ged Selby Antique Glass Tel: 01756 799673 By appointment only

GTH Greenslade Taylor Hunt Fine Art, Magdelene House, Church Square, Taunton, Somerset TA1 1SB Tel: 01823 332525

GTM Gloucester Toy Mart, Ground Floor, Antique Centre, Severn Road, Old Docks, Gloucester GL1 2LE Tel: 07973 768452

GWe Graham Webb, 59 Ship Street, Brighton, East Sussex BN1 1AE Tel: 01273 321803

H&G Hope & Glory, 131A Kensington Church Street, London W8 7LP Tel: 020 7727 8424

HA Hallidays, The Old College, Dorchester-on-Thames, Oxfordshire OX10 7HL Tel: 01865 340028/68 Mobile: 07860 625917 antiques@hallidays.com www.hallidays.com

HAA Hampton Antiques, The Crown Arcade, 119 Portobello Road, London W11 2DY Tel: 01604 863979 info@hamptonantiques.co.uk www.hamptonantiques.co.uk

HAL John & Simon Haley, 89 Northgate, Halifax, Yorkshire HX1 1XF Tel: 01422 822148/360434 toysandbanks@aol.com

HAld Henry Aldridge & Son, Unit 1, Bath Road Business Centre, Devizes, Wiltshire SN10 1XA Tel: 01380 729199 andrew.aldridge@virgin.net www.henry-aldridge.co.uk

HAM Hamptons International, Baverstock House, 93 High Street, Godalming, Surrey GU7 1AL Tel: 01483 423567 fineartauctions@hamptons-int.com www.hamptons.co.uk

HarC Hardy's Collectables Tel: 07970 613077

HARP Harpers Jewellers Ltd, 2/6 Minster Gates, York YO1 7HL Tel: 01904 632634 harpersyork@btopenworld.com www.vintage-watches.co.uk

HCA Hilltop Cottage Antiques, 101 Portobello Road, London W11 Tel: 01451 844362 Mobile: 0777 365 8082 noswadp@aol.com

HCFA Henry T. Callan, 162 Quaker Meeting House Road, East Sandwich MA 02537–1312, USA Tel: 508 888 5372

HEG Stuart Heggie, 14 The Borough, Northgate, Canterbury, Kent CT1 2DR Tel: 01227 470422 heggie.cameras@virgin.net

HEL Helios Gallery, 292 Westbourne Grove, London W11 2PS Tel: 077 11 955 997 heliosgallery@btinternet.com www.heliosgallery.cpm

Herm Hermann Historica OHG, Postfach 201009, 80010 Munchen, Germany Tel: 00 49 89 5237296

HiA Rupert Hitchcox Antiques, The Garth, Warpsgrove, Nr Chalgrove, Oxford OX44 7RW Tel: 01865 890241 www.ruperthitchcoxantiques.co.uk

HIS Erna Hiscock & John Shepherd, Chelsea Galleries, 69 Portobello Road, London W11 Tel: 01233 661407 Mobile: 0771 562 7273 erna@ernahiscockantiques.com www.ernahiscockantiques.com

HL Honiton Lace Shop, 44 High Street, Honiton, Devon EX14 1PJ Tel: 01404 42416 shop@honitonlace.com www.honitonlace.com

HO Houghton Antiques, Houghton, Cambridgeshire Tel: 01480 461887 Mobile: 07803 716842

HoG Honiton Galleries, 205 High Street, Honiton, Devon EX14 1LQ Tel: 01404 42404 sales@honitongalleries.com www.honitongalleries.com

HOK Hamilton Osborne King, 4 Main Street, Blackrock, Co Dublin, Republic of Ireland Tel: 353 1 288 5011 blackrock@hok.ie www.hok.ie

HOLL Holloway's, 49 Parsons Street, Banbury, Oxfordshire OX16 5PF Tel: 01295 817777 enquiries@hollowaysauctioneers.co.uk www.hollowaysauctioneers.co.uk

HON Honan's Antiques, Crowe Street, Gort, County Galway, Republic of Ireland Tel: 00 353 91 631407 www.honansantiques.com

HOW John Howard at Heritage, 6 Market Place, Woodstock, Oxfordshire OX20 1TA Tel: 0870 4440678 Mobile: 07831 850544 john@johnhoward.co.uk www.antiquepottery.co.uk

HRQ Harlequin Antiques, 79–81 Mansfield Road, Daybrook, Nottingham NG5 6BH Tel: 0115 967 4590 sales@antiquepine.net www.antiquepine.net

HUM Humbleyard Fine Art, Unit 32 Admiral Vernon Arcade, Portobello Road, London W11 2DY Tel: 01362 637793 Mobile: 07836 349416

HUN The Country Seat, Huntercombe Manor Barn, Henley-on-Thames, Oxfordshire RG9 5RY Tel: 01491 641349

HUR Shana Dumont, Hurst Gallery, 53 Mt Auburn Street, Cambridge, MA 02138, USA Tel: 617 491 6888 manager@hurstgallery.com www.hurstgallery.com

HYD Hy Duke & Son, Dorchester Fine Art Salerooms, Dorchester, Dorset DT1 1QS Tel: 01305 265080

IM Ibbett Mosely, 125 High Street, Sevenoaks, Kent TN13 1UT Tel: 01732 456731 auctions@ibbettmosely.co.uk www.ibbettmosely.co.uk

IS Ian Sharp Antiques, 23 Front Street, Tynemouth, Tyne & Wear NE30 4DX Tel: 0191 296 0656 iansharp@sharpantiques.demon.co.uk www.sharpantiques.demon.co.uk

JAA Jackson's Auctioneers & Appraisers, 2229 Lincoln Street, Cedar Falls IA 50613, USA Tel: 319 277 2256

JAd James Adam & Sons, 26 St Stephen's Green, Dublin 2, Republic of Ireland Tel: 00 3531 676 0261 www.jamesadam.ie

JAK Clive & Lynne Jackson Tel: 01242 254375 Mobile: 0410 239351

JAY Jaycee Bee Antiques, Hampshire

JBL Judi Bland Antiques Tel: 01276 857576 or 01536 724145

JC J. Collins & Son, The Studio, 28 High Street, Bideford, Devon EX39 2AN Tel: 01237 473103

JCH Jocelyn Chatterton, 126 Grays, 58 Davies St, London W1Y 2LP Tel: 020 7629 1971 Mobile: 07798 804 853 jocelyn@cixi.demon.co.uk www.cixi.demon.co.uk

JDJ James D. Julia, Inc, PO Box 830, Rte. 201, Skowhegan Road, Fairfield ME 04937, USA Tel: 207 453 7125 jjulia@juliaauctions.com www.juliaauctions.com

JE Julian Eade Tel: 01491 575059 Mobile: 07973 542971

JeF Jeffrey Formby, The Gallery, Orchard Cottage, East Street, Moreton-in-Marsh, Gloucestershire GL56 0LQ Tel: 01608 650558 www.formby-clocks.co.uk

JeH Jennie Horrocks Tel: 07836 264896 gallery@aw18.fsnet.co.uk info@artnouveaulighting.co.uk artnouveaulighting.co.uk

JF Julia Foster, 84 York Street, London W1H 1DP Tel: 07973 146610 By appointment only

JHa Jeanette Hayhurst Fine Glass, 32a Kensington Church Street, London W8 4HA Tel: 020 7938 1539

JHo Jonathan Horne, 66 Kensington Church Street, London, W8 4BY Tel: 020 7221 5658 JH@jonathanhorne.co.uk www.jonathanhorne.co.uk

JIL Jillings Antique Clocks, Croft House, 17 Church Street, Newent, Gloucestershire GL18 1PU Tel: 01531 822100 Mobile: 07973 830110 clocks@jillings.com www.Jillings.com

JM Maxwells of Wilmslow inc Dockree's, 133A Woodford Road, Woodford, Cheshire SK7 1QD Tel: 0161 439 5182

JNic John Nicholson, The Auction Rooms, Longfield, Midhurst Road, Fernhurst, Surrey GU27 3HA Tel: 01428 653727

JOA Joan Gale Antiques Dealer, Tombland Antiques Centre, 14 Tombland, Norwich, Norfolk NR3 1HF Tel: 01603 619129 joan.gale@ukgateway.net

JOL Kaizen International Ltd, 88 The High Street, Rochester, Kent ME1 1JT Tel: 01634 814132

JON Jonkers, 24 Hart Street, Henley-on-Thames, Oxfordshire RG9 2AU Tel: 01491 576427 bromlea.jonkers@bjbooks.co.uk www.bjbooks.co.uk

JOP Jonathan Potter Ltd Antique Maps, 125 New Bond Street, London W1S 1DY Tel: 020 7491 3520 jpmaps@attglobal.net www.jpmaps.co.uk

JPr/JPR Joanna Proops Antique Textiles & Lighting, 34 Belvedere, Lansdown Hill, Bath, Somerset BA1 5HR Tel: 01225 310795 antiquetextiles@aol.co.uk www.antiquetextiles.co.uk

JRe John Read, 29 Lark Rise, Martlesham Heath, Ipswich, Suffolk IP5 7SA Tel: 01473 624897

JSt Jane Strickland & Daughters, 71 High Street, Honiton, Devon EX14 1PW Tel: 01404 44221 JSandDaughtersUk@aol.com www.janestricklanddaughters.co.uk

JuC Julia Craig, Bartlett Street Antiques Centre, 5–10 Bartlett Street, Bath, Somerset BA1 2QZ Tel: 01225 448202/310457 Mobile: 07771 786846

JUJ Just Jewellery

JUN Junktion, The Old Railway Station, New Bolingbroke, Boston, Lincolnshire PE22 7LB Tel: 01205 480068

JUP Jupiter Antiques, PO Box 609, Rottingdean, East Sussex BN2 7FW Tel: 01273 302865

K&D Kembery Antique Clocks Ltd, Bartlett Street Antiques Centre, 5 Bartlett Street, Bath, Somerset BA1 2QZ Tel: 0117 956 5281 Mobile: 07850 623237 kembery@kdclocks.co.uk www.kdclocks.co.uk

KES Keystones, PO Box 387, Stafford ST16 3FG Tel: 01785 256648

KEY Key Antiques of Chipping Norton, 11 Horsefair, Chipping Norton, Oxfordshire OX7 5AL Tel: 01608 644992 info@keyantiques.com www.keyantiques.com

KHW Keith Harding's World of Mechanical Music, The Oak House, High Street, Northleach, Gloucestershire GL54 3ET Tel: 01451 860181 keith@musicbox10.demon.co.uk www.mechanicalmusic.co.uk

KK Karl Kemp & Associates, Ltd Antiques, 36 East 10th Street, New York NY 10003, USA Tel: (212) 254 1877 info@karlkemp.com www.karlkemp.com

KMG Karen Michelle Guido, Karen Michelle Antique Tiles, PO Box 62, Blairsville PA 15717, USA Tel: (724) 459 6669 Karen@antiquetiles.com www.antiquetiles.com

L Lawrence Fine Art Auctioneers, South Street, Crewkerne, Somerset TA18 8AB Tel: 01460 73041

L&E Locke & England, 18 Guy Street, Leamington Spa, Warwickshire CV32 4RT Tel: 01926 889100 www.auctions-online.com/locke

L&L ⊞ Linen & Lace, Shirley Tomlinson, Halifax Antiques Centre, Queens Road/Gibbet Street, Halifax, Yorkshire HX1 4LR Tel: 01422 366657 Mobile: 07711 763454

LAY ⚒ David Lay ASVA, Auction House, Alverton, Penzance, Cornwall TR18 4RE Tel: 01736 361414

LBO ⊞ Laura Bordignon Antiques, PO Box 6247, Finchingfield, Essex CM7 4ER Tel: 01371 811 791 Mobile: 07778 787929 laurabordignon@hotmail.com

LBr ⊞ Lynda Brine, Assembly Antiques, 6 Saville Row, Bath, Somerset BA1 2QP Tel: 01225 448488 lyndabrine@yahoo.co.uk www.scentbottlesandsmalls.co.uk

LCM ⚒ Galeria Louis C. Morton, GLC A7073L IYS, Monte Athos 179, Col. Lomas de Chapultepec CP11000, Mexico Tel: 52 5520 5005 glmorton@prodigy.net.mx www.lmorton.com

LDC ⊞ L. & D. Collins Tel: 020 7584 0712

LFA ⚒† Law Fine Art, Firs Cottage, Church Lane, Brimpton, Berkshire RG7 4TJ Tel: 0118 971 0353 info@lawfineart.co.uk www.lawfineart.co.uk

LGU ⊞ Linda Gumb, Stand 123, Grays Antique Market, 58 Davies Street, London W1K 5LP Tel: 020 7629 2544 linda@lindagumb.com

LJ ⚒ Leonard Joel Auctioneers, 333 Malvern Road, South Yarra, Victoria 3141, Australia Tel: 03 9826 4333 decarts@ljoel.com.au or jewellery@ljoel.com.au www.ljoel.com.au

LOP ⊞† Lopburi Art & Antiques, 5/8 Saville Row, Bath, Somerset BA1 2QP Tel: 01225 322947 mail@lopburi.co.uk www.lopburi.co.uk

LU ⊞ Lucia Collectables, Stalls 57–58 Admiral Vernon Antique Arcade, Portobello Road, London (open Saturdays) Tel: 01793 790607 sallie_ead@lycos.com

LUNA ⊞ Luna, 23 George Street, Nottingham NG1 3BH Tel: 0115 924 3267 info@luna-online.co.uk www.luna-online.co.uk

LVS ⚒ Loves Auction Rooms, 52 Canal Street, Perth PH2 8LF, Scotland Tel: 01738 633337

M ⚒ Morphets of Harrogate, 6 Albert Street, Harrogate, Yorkshire HG1 1JL Tel: 01423 530030

MAA ⊞ Mario's Antiques Tel: 020 7226 2426 Mobile: 07956 580772 marwan@barazi.screaming.net www.marios_antiques.com

MAG ⊞ Magna Gallery, Antiques on High, 85 High Street, Oxford OX1 5BG Tel: 01285 750753 info@magna-gallery.com

MAQ ⊞ Marie Miller Antique Quilts, 1489 Route 30, PO Box 983, Dorset VT 05251, USA Tel: 802 867 5969 www.antiquequilts.com www.antiquehookedrugs.com www.antiquequimper.com

MAR ⚒ Frank R. Marshall & Co, Marshall House, Church Hill, Knutsford, Cheshire WA16 6DH Tel: 01565 653284

MARK ⊞† 20th Century Marks, 12 Market Square, Westerham, Kent TN16 1AW Tel: 01959 562221 Mobile: 07831 778992 lambarda@btconnect.com www.20thcenturymarks.co.uk

MB ⊞† Mostly Boxes, 93 High Street, Eton, Windsor, Berkshire SL4 6AF Tel: 01753 858470

MCA ⚒† Mervyn Carey, Twysden Cottage, Scullsgate, Benenden, Cranbrook, Kent TN17 4LD Tel: 01580 240283

McP ⊞† R. & G. McPherson Antiques, 40 Kensington Church Street, London W8 4BX Tel: 020 7937 0812 Mobile: 07768 432 630 rmcpherson@orientalceramics.com www.orientalceramics.com

MDL ⊞ Michael D. Long Ltd, 96–98 Derby Road, Nottingham NG1 5FB Tel: 0115 941 3307 sales@michaeldlong.com www.michaeldlong.com

MEA ⚒ Mealy's, Chatsworth Street, Castle Comer, Co Kilkenny, Republic of Ireland Tel: 00 353 56 41229 info@mealys.com www.mealys.com

MER ⊞ Mere Antiques, 13 Fore Street, Topsham, Exeter, Devon EX3 0HF Tel: 01392 874224

MFB ⊞ Manor Farm Barn Antiques Tel: 01296 658941 Mobile: 07720 286607 mfbn@btinternet.com btwebworld.com/mfbantiques

MHA ⊞ Merchant House Antiques, 19 High Street, Honiton, Devon EX14 1PR Tel: 01404 42694/44406 antiquesmerchant@ndirect.co.uk

MI ⊞† Mitofsky Antiques, 8 Rathfarnham Road, Terenure, Dublin 6, Republic of Ireland Tel: 00 353 1 492 0033 info@mitofskyartdeco.com www.mitofskyartdeco.com

MINN ⊞ Geoffrey T. Minnis, Hastings Antique Centre, 59–61 Norman Road, St Leonards-on-Sea, East Sussex TN38 0EG Tel: 01424 428561

MIR ⊞ Mir Russki Tel: 01506 843973 Mobile: 07979 227779 info@russiansilver.co.uk www.russiansilver.co.uk

Mit ⚒ Mitchells Auction Company, The Furniture Hall, 47 Station Road, Cockermouth, Cumbria CA13 9PZ Tel: 01900 827800

ML ⊞ Memory Lane, Bartlett Street Antiques Centre, 5/10 Bartlett Street, Bath, Somerset BA1 2QZ Tel: 01225 466689

MLa ⊞† Marion Langham Limited Tel: 020 7730 1002 marion@ladymarion.co.uk www.ladymarion.co.uk

MLL ⊞† Millers Antiques Ltd, Netherbrook House, 86 Christchurch Road, Ringwood, Hampshire BH24 1DR Tel: 01425 472062 mail@millers-antiques.co.uk www.millers-antiques.co.uk

MPC ⊞ M. C. Tel: 01244 301800 Sales@Moorcroftchester.co.uk www.Moorcroftchester.co.uk

MSB ⊞ Marilynn and Sheila Brass, PO Box 380503, Cambridge MA 02238–0503, USA Tel: 617 491 6064 mpbkitty@aol.com

MSh ⊞ Manfred Schotten, 109 High Street, Burford, Oxfordshire OX18 4RG Tel: 01993 822302 www.antiques@schotten.com

MTay ⊞† Martin Taylor Antiques, 323 Tettenhall Road, Wolverhampton, West Midlands WV6 0JZ Tel: 01902 751166/07836 636524 enquiries@mtaylor-antiques.co.uk www.mtaylor-antiques.co.uk

MUL ⚒ Mullock & Madeley, The Old Shippon, Wall-under-Heywood, Church Stretton, Shropshire SY6 7DS Tel: 01694 771771/07803 276394 auctions@mullockmadeley.co.uk www.mullockmadeley.co.uk

MUR ⊞ Murray Cards (International) Ltd, 51 Watford Way, Hendon Central, London NW4 3JH Tel: 020 8202 5688 murraycards@ukbusiness.com www.murraycard.com/

NART ⊞ Newel Art Galleries, Inc, 425 East 53rd Street, New York 10022, USA Tel: 212 758 1970 info@newel.com www.Newel.com

NAW ⊞† Newark Antiques Warehouse Ltd, Old Kelham Road, Newark, Nottinghamshire NG24 1BX Tel: 01636 674869 Mobile: 07974 429185 enquiries@newarkantiques.co.uk www.newarkantiques.co.uk

NBL ⊞ N. Bloom & Son (1912) Ltd, 12 Piccadilly Arcade, London SW1Y 6NH Tel: 020 7629 5060 nbloom@nbloom.com www.nbloom.com

NMA ⊞ Noel Mercer Antiques, Aurora House, Hall Street, Long Melford, Sudbury, Suffolk CO10 9RJ Tel: 01787 311882/01206 323558

NOA ⚒ New Orleans Auction Galleries, Inc, 801 Magazine Street, AT 510 Julia, New Orleans, Louisiana 70130, USA Tel: 504 566 1849

NoC ⊞ No.1 Castlegate Antiques, 1–3 Castlegate, Newark, Nottinghamshire NG24 1AZ Tel: 01636 701877 Mobile: 07850 463173

NOS ⊞ Nostalgia and Comics, 14–16 Smallbrook Queensway, City Centre, Birmingham, West Midlands B5 4EN Tel: 0121 643 0143

NS ⊞ Nicholas Shaw Antiques, Virginia Cottage, Lombard Street, Petworth, West Sussex GU28 0AG Tel: 01798 345146/01798 345147 Mobile: 07885 643000/07817 572746 silver@nicholas-shaw.com www.nicholas-shaw.com

NW ⊞ Nigel Williams Rare Books, 22 & 25 Cecil Court, London WC2N 4HE Tel: 020 7836 7757

OE ⊞ Orient Expressions, Assembly Antiques Centre, 5–8 Saville Row, Bath, Somerset BA1 2QP Tel: 01225 313399 Mobile: 07747 691128

OLA ⊞ Olliff's Architectural Antiques, 19–21 Lower Redland Road, Redland, Bristol, Gloucestershire BS6 6TB Tel: 0117 923 9232 marcus@olliffs.com www.olliffs.com

OLD ⊞ Oldnautibits, PO Box 67, Langport, Somerset TA10 9WJ Tel: 01458 241816 geoff.pringle@oldnautibits.com www.oldnautibits.com

OND ⊞ Ondines Tel: 01865 882465

ONS ⚒ Onslow's Auctions Ltd, The Coach House, Manor Road, Stourpaine, Dorset DT8 8TQ Tel: 01258 488838

ORI ⊞ Origin 101, Gateway Arcade, Islington High Street, London N1 Tel: 07769 686146/07747 758852 David @origin101.co.uk www.naturalmodern.com www.origin101.co.uk

OTB ⊞† Old Tackle Box, PO Box 55, Cranbrook, Kent TN17 3ZU Tel: 01580 713979 Mobile: 07729 278 293 tackle.box@virgin.net

P&T ⊞ Pine & Things, Portobello Farm, Campden Road, Nr Shipston-on-Stour, Warwickshire CV36 4PY Tel: 01608 663849 www.pinethings.co.uk

PaA ⊞ Pastorale Antiques, 15 Malling Street, Lewes, East Sussex BN7 2RA Tel: 01273 473259 or 01435 863044 pastorale@btinternet.com

PAO ⊞† P. A. Oxley Antique Clocks & Barometers, The Old Rectory, Cherhill, Calne, Wiltshire SN11 8UX Tel: 01249 816227 info@paoxley.com www.british-antiqueclocks.com

PAS ⊞ Tina Pasco, Waterlock House, Wingham, Nr Canterbury, Kent CT3 1BH Tel: 01227 722151 tinapasco@tinapasco.com www.tinapasco.com

PAY ⊞ Payne & Son, 131 High Street, Oxford OX1 4DH Tel: 01865 243787 silver@payneandson.co.uk www.payneandson.co.uk

PCA ⊞ Patricia Cater Tel: 01451 830944 Patriciacaterorg@aol.com www.PatriciaCater-OrientalArt.com

Penn ⊞ Penny Fair Antiques Tel: 07860 825456

PEx ⊞† Piano-Export, Bridge Road, Kingswood, Bristol, Gloucestershire BS15 4FW Tel: 0117 956 8300

PF ⚒† Peter Francis, Curiosity Sale Room, 19 King Street, Carmarthen SA31 1BH, South Wales Tel: 01267 233456 Peterfrancis@valuers.fsnet.co.uk www.peterfrancis.co.uk

PFK ⚒† Penrith Farmers' & Kidd's plc, Skirsgill Salerooms, Penrith, Cumbria CA11 0DN Tel: 01768 890781 penrith.farmers@virgin.net

PGO ⊞† Pamela Goodwin, 11 The Pantiles, Royal Tunbridge Wells, Kent TN2 5TD Tel: 01892 618200 mail@goodwinantiques.co.uk www.goodwinantiques.co.uk

PHA ⊞† Paul Hopwell, 30 High Street, West Haddon, Northamptonshire NN6 7AP Tel: 01788 510636 Mobile: 07836 505950 paulhopwell@antiqueoak.co.uk www.antiqueoak.co.uk

PHo ⊞ Paul Howard Mobile: 07881 862 375 scientificantiques@hotmail.com

PIC ⊞ David & Susan Pickles Tel: 01282 707673

PICA ⊞ Piccadilly Antiques, 280 High Street, Batheaston, Bath BA1 7RA Tel: 01225 851494 Mobile: 07785 966132 piccadillyantiques@ukonline.co.uk

Pott ⚒ Potteries Specialist Auctions, 271 Waterloo Road, Cobridge, Stoke on Trent, Staffordshire ST6 3HR Tel: 01782 286622

PPC ⊞ Period Piano Company, Park Farm Oast, Hareplain Road, Biddenden, Nr Ashford, Kent TN27 8LJ Tel: 01580 291393 www.periodpiano.com

PrB ⊞ Pretty Bizarre, 170 High Street, Deal, Kent CT14 6BQ Tel: 07973 794537

PSA ⊞ Pantiles Spa Antiques, 4, 5, 6 Union House, The Pantiles, Tunbridge Wells, Kent TN4 8HE Tel: 01892 541377 Mobile: 07711 283655 psa.wells@btinternet.com www.antiques-tun-wells-kent.co.uk

PSC ⊞ Peter & Sonia Cashman, Bartlett Street Antique Centre, 5–10 Bartlett Street, Bath, Somerset BA1 2QZ Tel: 01225 469497 Mobile: 0780 8609860

PT ⊞† Pieces of Time, (1–7 Davies Mews), 26 South Molton Lane, London W1Y 2LP Tel: 020 7629 2422 info@antique-watch.com www.antique-watch.com

PTh ⊞ Antique Clocks by Patrick Thomas, 62a West Street, Dorking, Surrey RH4 1BS Tel: 01306 743661 clockman@fsmail.net www.antiqueclockshop.co.uk

PVD ⊞ Puritan Values at the Dome, St Edmunds Business Park, St Edmunds Road, Southwold, Suffolk IP18 6BZ Tel: 01502 722211 Mobile: 07966 371676 sales@puritanvalues.com www.puritanvalues.com

Q&C ⊞† Q & C Militaria, 22 Suffolk Road, Cheltenham, Gloucestershire GL50 2AQ Tel: 01242 519815 Mobile: 07778 613977 qcmilitaria@btconnect.com www.qcmilitaria.com

QM ⊞ The Quiet Man, Core One, The Gas Works, 2 Michael Road, London SW6 2AN Tel: 020 7736 3384 cullis24@hotmail.com

RAN ⊞ Ranby Hall-Antiques, Barnby Moor, Retford, Nottinghamshire DN22 8JQ Tel: 01777 860696 Mobile: 07860 463477 paul.wyatt@virgin.net www.ranbyhall.antiques-gb.com

RAP ⊞ Rapparee Antiques at Louisa Frances Fine Antiques, High Street, Brasted, Westerham, Kent TN16 1JB Tel: 01959 561222 or 020 8777 4016

RAV ⊞ Ravenwood Antiques Tel: 01886 884 456 alan@arthur81.freeserve.co.uk

RAY ⊞ Derek & Tina Rayment Antiques, Orchard House, Barton Road, Barton, Nr Farndon, Cheshire SY14 7HT Tel: 01829 270429 Mobile: 07860 666629 and 07702 922410 raymentantiques@aol.com www.antique-barometers.com

RbF ⚒† Robin A. Fenner & Co, The Stannary Gallery, Drake Road, Tavistock, Devon PL19 0AX Tel: 01822 617799 sales@rafenner.com www.rafenner.com

RdeR ⊞ Rogers de Rin, 76 Royal Hospital Road, London SW3 4HN Tel: 020 7352 9007

RdV ⊞ Roger de Ville Antiques Tel: 01629 812496 Mobile: 07798 793857 www.rogerdeville.co.uk

REF ⊞† The Refectory, 38 West Street, Dorking, Surrey RH4 1BU Tel: 01306 742111 www.therefectory.co.uk

REI ⊞ Reindeer Antiques Ltd, 43 Watling Street, Potterspury, Northamptonshire NN12 7QD Tel: 01908 542200 nicholasfuller@btconnect.com www.reindeerantiques.co.uk

RGA ⊞ Richard Gibbon, Shop 4, 34/34a Islington Green, London N1 8DU Tel: 020 7354 2852 Mobile: 07958 674447 neljeweluk@aol.com

RGa ⊞ Richard Gardner Antiques, Swanhouse Market Square, Petworth, West Sussex GU28 0AN Tel: 01798 343411

RGe ⊞ Rupert Gentle Antiques, The Manor House, Milton Lilbourne, Nr Pewsey, Wiltshire SN9 5LQ Tel: 01672 563344

RH ⊞ Rick Hubbard Art Deco, 3 Tee Court, Bell Street, Romsey, Hampshire SO51 8GY Tel: 01794 513133 Mobile: 07767 267607 rick@rickhubbard-artdeco.co.uk www.rickhubbard-artdeco.co.uk

RHa ⊞ Robert Hall, 15c Clifford Street, London W1X 1RF Tel: 020 7734 4008

RIT ⚒ Ritchies Inc, Auctioneers & Appraisers of Antiques & Fine Art, 288 King Street East, Toronto, Ontario M5A 1K4, Canada Tel: (416) 364 1864 auction@ritchies.com www.ritchies.com

RKa ⊞ Richardson & Kailas Tel: 020 7371 0491 By appointment only

RMC ⊞† Romsey Medal Centre, The Grapes Hotel,16 Douglas Square, Newcastleton, Roxburghshire TD9 0QD Tel: 013873 75245 post@romseymedals.co.uk www.romseymedals.co.uk

RMe ⊞ Jubilee Photographica, 10 Pierrepoint Row, Camden Passage, London N1 8EE Tel: 07860 793707

ROSc ⚒† R. O. Schmitt Fine Art, Box 1941, Salem, New Hampshire 03079, USA Tel: 603 893 5915 bob@roschmittfinearts.com www.antiqueclockauction.com

RPh ⊞† Phelps Antiques, 133–135 St Margaret's Road, Twickenham, Middlesex TW1 1RG Tel: 020 8892 1778/7129 antiques@phelps.co.uk www.phelps.co.uk

RTo ⚒† Rupert Toovey & Co Ltd, Spring Gardens, Washington, West Sussex RH20 3BS Tel: 01903 891955 auctions@rupert-toovey.com www.rupert-toovey.com

RTW ⊞† Richard Twort Tel: 01934 641900 Mobile: 07711 939789

RUSK ⊞ Ruskin Decorative Arts, 5 Talbot Court, Stow-on-the-Wold, Cheltenham, Gloucestershire GL54 1DP Tel: 01451 832254 william.anne@ruskindecarts.co.uk

RYA ⊞† Robert Young Antiques, 68 Battersea Bridge Road, London SW11 3AG Tel: 020 7228 7847

S ⚒ Sotheby's, 34–35 New Bond Street, London W1A 2AA Tel: 020 7293 5000 www.sothebys.com

S(Am) ⚒ Sotheby's Amsterdam, De Boelelaan 30, 1083 HJ, Amsterdam, Netherlands Tel: 00 31 20 550 22 00 www.sothebys.com

S(G) ⚒ Sotheby's, 13 Quai du Mont Blanc, Geneva, Switzerland CH–1201 Tel: 00 41 22 908 4800 www.sothebys.com

S(HK) ⚒ Sotheby's, Li Po Chun Chambers, 18th Floor, 189 Des Vouex Road, Hong Kong, China Tel: 852 524 8121 www.sothebys.com

S(NY) ⚒ Sotheby's, 1334 York Avenue, New York NY 10021, USA Tel: 212 606 7000 www.sothebys.com

S(O) ⚒ Sotheby's Olympia, Hammersmith Road, London W14 8UX Tel: 020 7293 5000 www.sothebys.com

S(P) ⚒ Sotheby's France SA, 76 Rue du Faubourg, Saint Honore, 75008 Paris, France Tel: 00 33 147 42 22 32 www.sothebys.com

S(S) ⚒ Sotheby's Sussex, Summers Place, Billingshurst, West Sussex RH14 9AD Tel: 01403 833500 www.sothebys.com

S&D ⊞ S. & D. Postcards, Bartlett Street Antique Centre, 5–10 Bartlett Street, Bath, Somerset BA1 2QZ winstampok@netscapeonline.co.uk

SA ⊞ Sporting Antiques, St Ives, Cambridgeshire Tel: 01480 463891 john.lambden@virgin.net

SAM ⊞ Samarkand Galleries, 7–8 Brewery Yard, Sheep Street, Stow-on-the-Wold, Gloucestershire GL54 1AA Tel: 01451 832322 mac@samarkand.co.uk www.samarkand.co.uk

SAM ⊞ Samarkand Galleries, 16 Howe Street, Edinburgh EH3 6TD, Scotland Tel: 0131 225 2010 howe@samarkand.co.uk www.samarkand.co.uk

SAS ⚒† Special Auction Services, Kennetholme, Midgham, Reading, Berkshire RG7 5UX Tel: 0118 971 2949 www.invaluable.com/sas/

SAT ⊞ The Swan at Tetsworth, High Street, Tetsworth, Nr Thame, Oxfordshire OX9 7AB Tel: 01844 281777 antiques@theswan.co.uk www.theswan.co.uk

SAW ⊞ Salisbury Antiques Warehouse Ltd, 94 Wilton Road, Salisbury, Wiltshire SP2 7JJ Tel: 01722 410634 Mobile: 07703 211151 kevin@salisbury-antiques.co.uk

SAY ⊞ Charlotte Sayers, 360 Grays Antique Market, 58 Davies St, London W1K 5LP Tel: 020 7499 5478

SBL ⊞ Twentieth Century Style Tel: 01822 614831

SCO ⊞ Peter Scott Tel: 0117 986 8468 Mobile: 07850 639770

SDA ⊞ Stephanie Davison Antiques, Bakewell Antiques Centre, King Street, Bakewell, Derbyshire DE45 1DZ Tel: 01629 812496 Mobile: 07771 564 993 bacc@chappells-antiques.co.uk www.chappells-antiques.co.uk

SEA ⊞† Mark Seabrook Antiques, PO Box 396, Huntingdon, Cambridgeshire PE28 0ZA Tel: 01480 861935 Mobile: 07770 721931 enquiries@markseabrook.com www.markseabrook.com

SeH ⊞† Seventh Heaven, Chirk Mill, Chirk, Wrexham, County Borough LL14 5BU, Wales Tel: 01691 777622/773563 requests@seventh-heaven.co.uk www.seventh-heaven.co.uk

SER ⊞ Serendipity, 125 High Street, Deal, Kent CT14 6BB Tel: 01304 369165/01304 366536 dipityantiques@aol.com

SET ⊞† Setnik's In Time Again, 815 Sutter Street, Suite 2, Folsom, California 95630, USA Tel: 916 985 2390 Toll Free 888 333 1715 setniks@pacbell.net setniksintimeagain.com

SGr ⊞ Sarah Groombridge, Stand 335, Grays Market, 58 Davies Street, London W1K 5LP Tel: 020 7629 0225 Mobile: 07770 920277 sarah.groombridge@totalise.co.uk

SHa ⊞† Shapiro & Co, Stand 380, Gray's Antique Market, 58 Davies Street, London W1K 5LP Tel: 020 7491 2710

SIE ⊞ Sieff, 49 Long Street, Tetbury, Gloucestershire GL8 8AA Tel: 01666 504477 sieff@sieff.co.uk www.sieff.co.uk

SJH ⚒ S. J. Hales, 87 Fore Street, Bovey Tracey, Devon TQ13 9AB Tel: 01626 836684

SK Skinner Inc, The Heritage On The Garden, 63 Park Plaza, Boston MA 02116, USA Tel: 001 617 350 5400

SK(B) Skinner Inc, 357 Main Street, Bolton MA 01740, USA Tel: 978 779 6241

SMI Skip & Janie Smithson Antiques Tel: 01754 810265 Mobile: 07831 399180

Som Somervale Antiques, 6 Radstock Road, Midsomer Norton, Bath, Somerset BA3 2AJ Tel: 01761 412686 Mobile: 07885 088022 ronthomas@somervaleantiquesglass.co.uk www.somervaleantiquesglass.co.uk

SPA Sporting Antiques, 10 Union Square, The Pantiles, Tunbridge Wells, Kent TN4 8HE Tel: 01892 522661

SPF Scarborough Perry Fine Art, Hove Auction Rooms, Hove Street, Hove, East Sussex BN3 2GL Tel: 01273 735266

SPG Sprague Auctions, Inc, Route 5, Dummerston, VT 05301, USA Tel: 802 254 8969 bob@spragueauctions.com www.spragueauctions.com

SPT Sporting Times Gone By, Warehouse (Clubhouse) Tel: 01903 885656 Mobile: 07976 942059 www.sportingtimes.co.uk

SSW Spencer Swaffer, 30 High Street, Arundel, West Sussex BN18 9AB Tel: 01903 882132

STA Michelina & George Stacpoole, Main St, Adare, Co Limerick, Republic of Ireland Tel: 00 353 61 396 409 stacpool@iol.ie

SuA Suffolk House Antiques, High Street, Yoxford, Suffolk IP17 3EP Tel: 01728 668122 Mobile: 07860 521583

SWA S. W. Antiques, Newlands (road), Pershore, Worcestershire WR10 1BP Tel: 01386 555580 sw-antiques@talk21.com www.sw-antiques.co.uk

SWB Sweetbriar Gallery Paperweights Ltd, Sweetbriar House, Robin Hood Lane, Helsby, Cheshire WA6 9NH Tel: 01928 723851 Mobile: 07860 907532 sales@sweetbriar.co.uk www.sweetbriar.co.uk

SWN Swan Antiques, Stone Street, Cranbrook, Kent TN17 3HF Tel: 01580 712720

SWO Sworders, 14 Cambridge Road, Stansted Mountfitchet, Essex CM24 8BZ Tel: 01279 817778 www.sworder.co.uk

TDG The Design Gallery 1850–1950, 5 The Green, Westerham, Kent TN16 1AS Tel: 01959 561234 Mobile: 07974 322858 sales@thedesigngallery.uk.com www.thedesigngallery.uk.com

TDS The Decorator Source, 39a Long Street, Tetbury, Gloucestershire GL8 8AA Tel: 01666 505358

TeG The Temple Gallery, 6 Clarendon Cross, Holland Park, London W11 4AP Tel: 020 7727 3809 info@templegallery.com www.templegallery.com

TEM Tempus, Tunbridge Wells Antique Centre, Union Square, The Pantiles, Tunbridge Wells, Kent Tel: 01932 828936 tempus.watches@tinyonline.co.uk www.tempus-watches.co.uk

TEN Tennants, The Auction Centre, Harmby Road, Leyburn, Yorkshire DL8 5SG Tel: 01969 623780 enquiry@tennants-ltd.co.uk www.tennants.co.uk

TEN Tennants, 34 Montpellier Parade, Harrogate, Yorkshire HG1 2TG Tel: 01423 531661 enquiry@tennants-ltd.co.uk www.tennants.co.uk

TF Tayler & Fletcher, London House, High Street, Bourton-on-the-Water, Cheltenham, Gloucestershire GL54 2AP Tel: 01451 821666 bourton@taylerfletcher.com www.taylerfletcher.com

TH Tony Horsley, PO Box 3127, Brighton, East Sussex BN1 5SS Tel: 01273 550770

THE Theriault's, PO Box 151, Annapolis MD21404, USA Tel: 410 224 3655 info@theriaults.com www.theriaults.com

TLG The Lamp Gallery, Talbot Walk Antiques Centre, The Talbot Hotel, High Street, Ripley, Surrey GU23 6BB Tel: 01483 211724

TMA Tring Market Auctions, The Market Premises, Brook Street, Tring, Hertfordshire HP23 5EF Tel: 01442 826446 sales@tringmarketauctions.co.uk www.tringmarketauctions.co.uk

TML Timothy Millett Ltd, Historic Medals and Works of Art, PO Box 20851, London SE22 0YN Tel: 020 8693 1111 Mobile: 07778 637 898 tim@timothymillett.demon.co.uk

TOM Charles Tomlinson, Chester Tel: 01244 318395 charles.tomlinson@lineone.net www.lineone.net/-charles.tomlinson

TPC Pine Cellars, 39 Jewry Street, Winchester, Hampshire SO23 8RY Tel: 01962 777546/867014

TQA Treasure Quest Auction Galleries, Inc, 2581 Jupiter Park Drive, Suite E9, Jupiter, Florida 33458, USA Tel: 561 741 0777 www.tqag.com

TRA Tramps, Tuxford Hall, Lincoln Road, Tuxford, Newark, Nottinghamshire NG22 0HR Tel: 01777 872 543 info@trampsuk.com

TREA Treadway Gallery, Inc, 2029 Madison Road, Cincinnati, Ohio 45208, USA Tel: 513 321 6742 www.treadwaygallery.com

TRI Trident Antiques, 2 Foundry House, Hall Street, Long Melford, Suffolk CO10 9JR Tel: 01787 883388 Mobile: 07860 221402 tridentoak@aol.com

Trib Tribal Gathering, No. 1 Westbourne Grove Mews, Notting Hill, London W11 2RU Tel: 020 7221 6650 bryan@tribalgathering.com www.tribalgatheringlondon.com

TRL Thomson, Roddick & Medcalf Ltd, Coleridge House, Shaddongate, Carlisle, Cumbria CA2 5TU Tel: 01228 528939

TRM Thomson, Roddick & Medcalf Ltd, 60 Whitesands, Dumfries, Scotland DG1 2RS Tel: 01387 279879

TRM Thomson, Roddick & Medcalf Ltd, 20 Murray Street, Annan, Scotland DG12 6EG Tel: 01461 202575

TRM Thomson, Roddick & Medcalf Ltd, 43/4 Hardengreen Business Park, Eskbank, Edinburgh EH22 3NX, Scotland Tel: 0131 454 9090

TRO The Troika Man Tel: 01535 273088 thetroikaman@aol.com www.troikapottery.org

TSC The Silver Collection Ltd Tel: 01442 890954 Mobile: 07802 447813

TUN Tunbridge Wells Antiques, 12 Union Square, The Pantiles, Tunbridge Wells, Kent TN4 8HE Tel: 01892 533708

TWh Tim Wharton, 24 High Street, Redbourn, Nr St Albans, Hertfordshire AL3 7LL Tel: 01582 794371 Mobile: 07850 622880

TWI Twinkled, High St Antiques Centre, 39 High Street, Hastings, East Sussex TN34 Tel: 01424 460068 info@twinkled.net www.twinkled.net

UCO Unique Collections, 52 Greenwich Church Street, London SE10 9BL Tel: 020 8305 0867 glen@uniquecollections.co.uk www.uniquecollections.co.uk

US Ulla Stafford Tel: 0118 934 3208 Mobile: 07944 815104

VB Variety Box, 16 Chapel Place, Tunbridge Wells, Kent TN1 1YQ Tel: 01892 531868

VCL Vintage Cameras Ltd, 256 Kirkdale, Sydenham, London SE26 4NL Tel: 020 8778 5416 info@vintagecameras.co.uk www.vintagecameras.co.uk

VEC Vectis Auctions Ltd, Fleck Way, Thornaby, Stockton-on-Tees, Cleveland TS17 9JZ Tel: 01642 750616 admin@vectis.co.uk www.vectis.co.uk

VJ Ventnor Junction, 48 High Street, Ventnor, Isle of Wight PO38 1LT Tel: 01983 853996 shop@ventjunc.freeserve.co.uk

VS T. Vennett-Smith, 11 Nottingham Road, Gotham, Nottinghamshire NG11 0HE Tel: 0115 983 0541 info@vennett-smith.com www.vennett-smith.com

VSP Van Sabben Poster Auctions, PO Box 2065, 1620 EB Hoorn, Netherlands Tel: 31 229 268203 uboersma@sabbenposterauctions.nl www.vsabbenposterauctions.nl

W&C Westland & Co, St Michael's Church, Leonard Street (off Great Eastern Street), London EC2A 4ER Tel: 020 77398094 westland@westland.co.uk www.westland.co.uk

WAC Worcester Antiques Centre, Reindeer Court, Mealcheapen Street, Worcester WR1 4DF Tel: 01905 610680 WorcsAntiques@aol.com

WAL Wallis & Wallis, West Street Auction Galleries, Lewes, East Sussex BN7 2NJ Tel: 01273 480208 auctions@wallisandwallis.co.uk grb@wallisandwallis.co.uk www.wallisandwallis.co.uk

WAW Warwick Antiques Warehouse, Unit 7, Cape Road Industrial Estate, Cattell Road, Warwick CV34 4JN Tel: 01926 498849 aboylin1@tiscali.co.uk

WBB William Bentley Billiards, Standen Manor Farm, Hungerford, Berkshire RG17 0RB Tel: 01488 861711 www.billiards.co.uk

WD Weller & Dufty Ltd, 141 Bromsgrove Street, Birmingham, West Midlands B5 6RQ Tel: 0121 692 1414 wellerdufty@freewire.co.uk www.welleranddufty.co.uk

WeA Wenderton Antiques Tel: 01227 720295 By appointment only

WEL Wells Reclamation & Co, Coxley, Nr Wells, Somerset BA5 1RQ Tel: 01749 677087

WELD J. W. Weldon, 55 Clarendon Street, Dublin 2, Republic of Ireland Tel: 00 353 1 677 1638

WELL Anthony Welling, Broadway Barn, High Street, Ripley, Surrey GU23 6AQ Tel: 01483 225384 ant@awelling.freeserve.co.uk

WiB Wish Barn Antiques, Wish Street, Rye, East Sussex TN31 7DA Tel: 01797 226797

WilP/ WiLP W. & H. Peacock, 26 Newnham Street, Bedford MK40 3JR Tel: 01234 266366

WIM Wimpole Antiques, Stand 349, Grays Antique Market, 58 Davies Street, London W1K 5LP Tel: 020 7499 2889 WimpoleAntiques@compuserve.com

WL Wintertons Ltd, Lichfield Auction Centre, Fradley Park, Lichfield, Staffordshire WS13 8NF Tel: 01543 263256 enquiries@wintertons.co.uk www.wintertons.co.uk

WMa William Macadam, Edinburgh, Scotland Tel: 0131 466 0343

WOS Wheels of Steel, Grays Antique Market, Stand A12–13, Unit B10 Basement, 1–7 Davies Mews, London W1Y 2LP Tel: 020 7629 2813

WRe Walcot Reclamations, 108 Walcot Street, Bath, Somerset BA1 5BG Tel: 01225 444404

WRi Linda Wrigglesworth, 34 Brook Street, London W1K 5DN Tel: 020 7408 0177 linda@wrigglesworth.demon.co.uk www.artnet.com/chinesetextileswrigglesworth.html

WSA West Street Antiques, 63 West Street, Dorking, Surrey RH4 1BS Tel: 01306 883487 weststant@aol.com www.antiquearmsandarmour.com

WW Woolley & Wallis, Salisbury Salerooms, 51–61 Castle Street, Salisbury, Wiltshire SP1 3SU Tel: 01722 424524 mail@salisbury.w-w.co.uk www.w-w.co.uk

WWo Woman's Work Tel: 020 8940 2589 Mobile: 07971 691748

WWW WW Warner, The Forge, The Green, Brasted, Kent TN16 1JL Tel: 01959 563698

YC Yesterday Child, Angel Arcade, 118 Islington High Street, London N1 8EG Tel: 020 7354 1601

Index to Advertisers

A. B. Period Pine....204
Acorn G.D.S. Ltd....2
Henry Aldridge....791
David Aldous-Cook....12
Amersham Auction Rooms....779
American West Indies Trading Co....651
Ancient & Gothic....643
Angling Auctions....750
Anthemion....145
Antique European Linens....525
Antiques Across the World....15
Antiques for Everyone Fair....6
Antiques Magazine....*back end paper*
Antiques Trade Space....13
Apollo Antiques Ltd....57
Artemis Decorative Arts Ltd....477
A S Antique Galleries....465, 487
Atlantic Antiques Centres....473
BAFRA....18
Craig Barfoot Antique Clocks....397
Barling Fine Porcelain....291
Clive Beardall Antiques....73
Jonathan Beech....418
Bellhouse Antiques....305, 393
Daniel Bexfield Antiques....355
Biblion....655
Judi Bland Antiques....255
Blender Antiques....13
Bonhams....*back jacket*
Boulton & Cooper Ltd....788
Bourton Bears....672
Bracketts....611, 781
Bread & Roses....221
Brightwells....791
British Antique Replicas....5, *front end paper*
F. G. Bruschweiler (Antiques) Ltd....7
Douglas Bryan....187
Burstow & Hewett....781
Cameo Auctions....776
Campbell & Archard Ltd....429
Canterbury Auction Galleries....777
Mervyn Carey....783
Carnegie Paintings & Clocks....388
Catchpole & Rye Ltd....585
Cato Crane & Co....786
The Chair Set....59
Peter Cheney....782
Church Hill Antiques Centre....10
Bryan Clisby....416
The Clock Clinic Ltd....389
The Clock House....407
The Clock Shop (Weybridge)....380
The Clock - Work - Shop....381
Collectors Corner....695
The Collectors Toy & Model Shop....685
Collins Antiques....55
Comic Book Postal Auctions Ltd....687
Alan S. Cook....727
Coppelia Antiques....400
The Court House....18
Crafts Nouveau....461
The Cotswold Auction Company....785
Cottees of Wareham....784
The Crested China Company....273
Cross Hayes Antiques....12
Crundalls....788
Dee Atkinson & Harrison....789
decorative arts@doune....455
Delvin Farm Antiques....201
Denham's....779
DMG Fairs....*back end paper*
The Dorking Desk Shop....85
Gavin Douglas Fine Antiques Ltd....387
Dreweatt Neate....778
Drummonds....579
Jack Dudgeon....788
David Duggleby....789
Dyson & Son....782
Julian S. Eade....457
Early Technology....700, 701
Ben Eggleston Antiques Ltd....205
Garry M. Emms & Co Ltd....793
Ewbank....779
English Rose Antiques....195
The Essence of Time....423

Evans & Partridge 753
The Exeter Antique Lighting Co 511
Fagan Arms 721
Fellows & Sons 792
R. A. Fenner & Co 792
Flower House Antiques..............................61
Jeffrey Formby Antiques 379
Peter Francis 790
Alan Franklin Transport..............................14
Thos W. M. Gaze & Son 782
Gilbert & Dale..215
Gilding's 786
Pamela Goodwin 103
The Goss & Crested China Club 272
Gaby Gunst 382
G. K. Hadfield..405
John and Simon Haley 677, 683
Hampton Antiques 614
Judy & Brian Harden Antiques 307, 633
Keith Harding's..621
Harlequin Antiques..................................199
Andrew Hartley 788
J. Hartley Antiques Ltd...............................39
Hemswell Antique Centres 12
Hill Farm Antiques 121
Erna Hiscock & John Shepherd 531
Rupert Hitchcox Antiques ....
....49, 67, 115, 175
Holloway's...793
Honiton Galleries....................................784
Paul Hopwell Antiques 160, 161
Edgar Horns 781
Jonathan Horne.......................................235
Horological Workshops............................426
Tony Horsley Antiques 287
Ibbett Mosely 776
Raymond P. Inman 779
International Furniture Exporters................13
The Internet Fine Art Bureau.........................
....*front end paper*
It's About Time.......................................385
John Ives 2
Arthur Johnson & Sons 792
Jubilee Hall Antiques 14
Stephen T. P. Kember 619
Kembery Antique Clocks 401
Key Antiques of Chipping Norton.....179, 253
Keys 793
George Kidner 785
Knole Barometers 441
Lambert & Foster 783
Philip Laney 791
Marion Langham Ltd 275, 348
Law Fine Art 778
Lawrences Auctioneers Ltd 776
Ann Lingard 193, 217
Gordon Litherland 341
Lithgow Sons & Partners..........................789
Lloyds International 24, 780
The London Antique Arms Fairs 733
Brian Loomes...413
Lopburi Art & Antiques............................563
MacGregor Auctions 789
John Mann Fine Antique Clocks 411
Market Street Gallery Ltd.........................481
Gerald Mathias 613
Maxwells of Wilmslow.............................790
R & G McPherson Antiques 317
Merry's 787
Millers Antiques Ltd.................................257
Miller's Publications.................597, 631, 715
Mitofsky Antiques 451
Moore, Allen & Innocent 792
Morgan Evans & Co 790
Morris Bricknell..784
Mostly Boxes 617
National Clock Register............................392
Gillian Neale 261
Neales 787
D. M. Nesbit & Co 778
Newark Antiques Warehouse Ltd 105
Northern Clocks 417
North Wilts. Exporters..............................207
Nostalgia 589
Odiham Auction Sales 780
The Old Clock Shop.................................384
The Old Malthouse 47
Old Mill Antique Centre 8
The Old Mint House Antiques.......................9
The Old Tackle Box 751

Olivers 782
Oola Boola 133
Samuel Orr Antique Clocks.......................409
P. A. Oxley..403
Pendulum 406
Penrith Farmers' & Kidd's 788
Phelps Antiques...51
Piano-Export...................................623, 625
Pieces of Time 433
The Pine Cellars..............................203, 213
Graham Price Antiques Ltd 197
Joanna Proops 527
Pugh's Antiques 10
Q & C Militaria 737
The Refectory 169
Rendells..784
Richmond & Surrey Auctions 783
Riddetts 785
Derek Roberts..419
Roderick Antique Clocks...........................391
Rogers Jones Co 790
Romsey Medals 741
Rumours..459
Rye Auction Galleries...............................777
Mark Seabrook Antiques 183
Seaview Antiques 135
Securikey 2
Philip Serrell..791
Setniks in Time Again 765
Seventh Heaven...29
Shapiro & Co 552
Ian Sharp Antiques 265
The Shipping Company 2
Simmons & Sons......................................776
Allan Smith 399
Skip & Janie Smithson Antiques................223
Smythes..788
Somervale Antiques.................................333
Special Auction Services 247, 684
Spurrier-Smith Antiques.............................95
Stable Antiques 119
Alan & Kathy Stacey 615
Sterling Art Services...................................15
Styles of Stow..415
Sutton Valence Antiques 10
S. W. Antiques 27
Marilyn Swain Auctions 787
Swan Antiques 165
Sweetbriar Gallery 347
Sworders 782
20th Century Marks 503
Martin Taylor Antiques 11
Louis Taylor 786
Teddy Bears of Witney.............................673
Tempus 435
Tennants 788
Time & Motion 383
Charles Tomlinson 699
Rupert Toovey 781
Tracks...697
Trident Exihibitions ....
.....................................767, *back end paper*
Tring Market Auctions 778
W. F. Turk 421
Turner Violins 627
TVADA 18
Richard Twort..444
Up Country 197
T. Vennett-Smith 689, 755
Garth Vincent..725
Alan Walker 437
Wallis & Wallis................................681, 731
Nigel Ward & Co 784
Warehouse Provence.............*front end paper*
Weather House Antiques..........................439
Anthony Welling 171
West Street Antiques...............................729
Westville House Antiques 211
Williams & Watkins..................................786
Wimpole Antiques...................................541
P. F. Windibank 780
Wingetts..790
Dominic Winter Book Auctions.................653
Wintertons 786
Georg S. Wissinger Antiques 117
Woodward Antique Clocks.......................425
Worthing Auction Galleries.......................777
Wotton Auction Rooms 784
Wright Manley 792
Robert Young Antiques 163

Index

Bold numbers refer to information and pointer boxes

A

Abbott, Berenice 717
Åberg, Anna Strina 506
Aboriginal art 651
Abraham, F.X. 480
Abraham, Jacob 437
Abrahams, B.H. 620
Absolon, William 337
Adam, Robert **336**
Adam-style pedestals 82
Adams, Ansel 717
Adams, C. 702
Adams, E.H. 383
Adams, G. 437
Adams, George 702
Adams, William 261
Adams & Co 587
Addison, Faulkener & Co 264
Adie Bros 498
Admiral Fitzroy barometers 439–40
Adnet, Jacques 491
aeroplanes, toy 675
Aesthetic Movement 445–7
ceramics 445
furniture 446–7
metalware 447
Afanassiev, Feodor 552
Afghan rugs 522
Åfors 505
African tribal art 648–9
Afshar rugs and carpets 520
agate snuff bottles 572
agateware 245
Agatin 339
Airborne International 504
Akichika, Tatsuhiro 558
Akstafa rugs 517
alabaster: lamp bases 513
sculpture 592–4
Alcock, Samuel 282
ale bowls 606
ale glasses 334, 336, 337
Alençon lace 530
Alibert 385
Allcock & Co 751–3
Allen & Ginter 689
Alner Coe & Co 444
Alons, C. 491
Alonzo, Dominique 486
Alpine chests 167
Alt, Beck & Gottschalck 663
Amadio, J. 439
Amatus, Nicolaus 622
ambrotypes 744
American: architectural antiques 583
armchairs 58, 60
arms and armour 726, 727, 732–3
barographs 444
barometers 438
bedroom suites 113
beds 26
benches 489
bookcases 33, 34
boxes 614
cabinets 43, 46, 49
ceramics 448, 480, 500, 501
chairs 64, 162, 164, 165, 193, 446, 504
chests of drawers 72, 74, 75, 77, 79, 170, 171, 194, 195
clocks 427–8
cupboards 198
desks 84
dolls 663, 666, 668, 670
dressing tables 124
fire screens 97
fireplace accessories 591
glass 347, 471, 494, 505
jewellery 495
lap desks 192
lighting 473, 474, 496, 507, 510
marine 708, 709
metalware 497, 600
militaria 735, 736, 744
mirrors 94
musical instruments 624
needlework 528
photographs **717**, 717, 718
posters 692
pottery 247, 250, 254
quilts 524–5
samplers 531, 533
scientific instruments 705
sculpture 596
secretaire chests 78
settees 184
shooting 758
sideboards 103
silver 353, 355, 358–61, 364, 366, 369, 447, 476, 478, 497
silver plate 375
sofas 99
sport 749, 756
stools 468
tables 115, 118, 120, 125, 126, 129, 138, 140, 190, 447, 450, 502, 504
textiles 508
toys 677, 682–4
treen 606
wardrobes 146
watches 432
whatnots 219
American Encaustic Tiling Co 448
American Flyer 680
Amies, Edwin Hardy 492
Amritsar rugs 522
Amsterdam School 498
Anatolian carpets 515
andirons 591
Andrews, Henry C. 652
Andrews, William 367
Andriesse, Emmy 717
aneroid barometers 443
Angell, John 358, 370
Angell, Joseph 358, 365, 370
Angell, Messrs 366
anglaise style carriage clocks **392**, 392
Anglepoise 506
Anglo-Indian: furniture 568, 569
wood 559
animals: bears 224, 595
boars 309
bulls 225
camels 227, 309
cats 226, 268
chicken 224–6
Chinese ceramics 309–10
cows 225, 226, 228, 353
deer 228, 353
dogs 224–8, 263, 267, 268, 304, 309, 310, 594, 595
elephants 228, 304, 562
fish 353
goats 224, 228
hedgehogs 228, 353
horses 225, 226, 309, 595, 596
leopards 267
lions 225, 226
monkeys 228, 268
mules 267
pigs 225
porcelain 267–8
pottery 224–8, 263
sheep 225, 228, 309
silver 353
water buffalo 224
zebras 228
annuals 687
antiquities 640–5
apothecary chests 194, 206
apothecary jars 245
apple corers 220
apprentice furniture 195
Arbu 434
Arbus, André 492
archery 745
architects' tables 114, 568
architectural antiques 578–91
bathroom fittings 585–7
bell pulls 588
bronze 580
doors and door furniture 588
fireplace accessories 591
fireplaces 589–90
iron 578–80
lead 581
marble 581
stone 582
terracotta 583
wood 584
Arens, Gebr. 486
Arita 327, 328, 330, 331
Arkana 504
Arman 507
armchairs 55–63
Art Deco 490
Art Nouveau 466–7
Arts and Crafts 449
bergères 63
open 55–60
twentieth-century 502
upholstered 61–2
see also chairs
Armfelt, Karl Gustav Hjalmar 552
armillary spheres 702
armoires 175–7, 199
arms and armour 721–33
antiquities 641, 645
armour 721–2
Asian 560–1
cannons 722
edged weapons 723–7
firearms 728–33
Islamic 574
polearms and axes 733
Arnhem Faïence Factory 463
Arnold, London 382
Art Deco 479–98
carpets, rugs and textiles 498
ceramics 479–86
Charlotte Rhead **485**, 485
Clarice Cliff 482–4
clocks 486
figures and busts 486–9
furniture 489–92
glass 493–4
jewellery 495
lighting 496
metalware 497–8
Susie Cooper 485
watches 436
Art Nouveau 461–78
ceramics 461–2
clocks 463
figures and busts 464–5
furniture 466–8
glass 469–71
jewellery 472
lighting 473–4
metalware 475–8
Artcurial 506
artists' materials 639
Arts and Crafts 448–60
ceramics 448
clocks 449
Doulton 457–8
furniture 449–50
jewellery 452
lighting 452–3
Martin Brothers 459
metalware 454–6
Moorcroft 459–60
Ashbee, Charles Robert 454
Ashcroft 746
Ashworth 448
Asian 554–73
arms and armour 560–1
cloisonné and enamel 554, 565
figures and models 562–6
furniture 567–9
glass 555
inro 570
jade 555
lacquer 556–7
metalware 557–8
netsuke 570
robes and costume 571
snuff bottles 572
textiles 572–3
tsuba 561
wood 559
asparagus dishes 232
Asprey, Charles and George 357
Asprey & Co 604
Astbury 253
astrolabes 698
Atkin, W. 707
Atkins Clock Co 427
atlases 658–62
Aubusson 514, 525, 535
Audsley, George Ashdown 652
Ault 448
Australian: photographs 717
teddy bears 672
Austrian: armchairs 467
arms and armour 728
bronzes 464
busts 464, 465
cabinets 41, 466
ceramics 288, 462, 481
chairs 466
clocks 386, 426, 430, 463
coat stands 467
figures 488, 489
glass 470, 493, 494
jewellery 472, 550
lighting 496, 509
metalware 497, 498
mirrors 467
musical instruments 622, 624, 627
portrait miniatures 636
sculpture 592, 595, 596
shooting 758
silver 365, 370, 373
watches 431
Austro-Hungarian jewellery 546
Autio, Rudy 501
autographs 688, 693, 694, 711, 747
automata 621
Avard, Joseph 404
Avenell, Philip 398
Avenell, William 398
Avery 706
axes 733
Ayres, F. 678

B

Baccarat 339, 347
bachelor's chests of drawers 73
bacon dishes 375
badges 734–5, 757
bagatelle boards 686
bags 537
Bähr & Pröschild 663
Bailes, W. 758
Bailey, Annie 280
Bailey, James 226
Baker, Charles 129
Baker, Holborn 705
Baker, John 370
Baker, R. 440
Bakhtiari carpets 518
baking tins 220
Ball, Tomkins & Black 360
Balleux 595
Ballou, Polly 532
balls, sport 745, 746, 754, 755, 759
Baltic: bonheurs du jour 32
mirrors 96
tables 118
bamboo 219, 564
bangles 540–1
banners 528
Barbe, Jules 343
Barbedienne, Ferdinand 512
barber's bowls 230, 327
Barbour Silver Co 447
Barlow, Hannah 458
Barnard, E.J. & W. 354, 368
Barnard, Edward 360, 362, 364
Barnard, Walter and John 368
Barnard Bros 361, 362
barographs 444
barometers 437–43, 707
Baron, William 448
Barovier & Toso 507
Barr, Flight & Barr 273
Barr, William 429
barrel organs 621
Barry, D.F. 717
Bartley & Eggert 412
Bartone, Antonio 593
basins 311, 585–6
baskets: porcelain 268–9
pottery 229, 259
silver 354
silver plate 374
Bassett-Lowke 680
Bateman, Ann 354, 371
Bateman, Hester 359, 363
Bateman, Peter 354, 371, 373
Bateman, William 371, 373
Bath Cabinet Makers 492
bathroom fittings 585–7
bats, cricket 747
Baume & Mercier 434
Baxter, Thomas 296
Bayes, Gilbert William 457, 486, 596
Bayly, Sarah Lewis 533
B.B. & Crescent 356
beadwork 526, 528
beakers: glass 339
porcelain 303, 304
Royal Doulton 457
silver 354
Beal, Samuel 414

INDEX

The Beatles 693–6
Beattie, William 652
Bechstein, C. 624
Beck, R. & J. 705
Becker, Gustav 390, 427
Beckmann, R. 439
bed covers 524–5, 572
bed steps 110
bedroom suites 113, 446, 449
beds 26–30
  Asian 567
  campaign 152
  four-poster 152
  miniature 90
  oak and country 156–7
  pine 191
bedside cabinets 41–2, 201, 202, 218, 446, 489
bedside tables 114
beer sets 258
Beilby 335
Bel-Geddes, Norman 496
Belgian: barometers 438
  boxes 616
  glass 339
  globes 702
  mirrors 467
  photographs 719
  posters 691
  tables 120
Bell, H. & Co 706
Bell, Jn. 404
Bell, John 287–8
bell pulls 588
Belle Epoque beds 30
Belleek: animals 267
  baskets 268
  bowls 269–70
  boxes 271
  centrepieces 273
  figures 285
  jugs 294
  plates 289
  teapots 275
  trays 299
  vases 267, 300
Bellin, J.N. 659
bellows 591
bells: Asian 557
  brass 597
  bronze 497, 580
  Fabergé 552
  iron 600
  ship's 710
  silver 370
Belman, W. 404
Belouch rugs 520
Belter, John Henry 58
Belton 663
belts 604
benches 31, 100
  Art Deco 489
  Asian 567
  garden 578, 584
  oak and country 156
Benet Fink & Son 375
Bennett, Sir John 383
Bennett, London 729
Benson, J.W. 434
Benson, W.A.S. 452–3, 455, **456**, 456
bentwood chairs 466
Bérain, J. 256
Bergama rugs 515
bergères 63, 99, 490
Bergman, Franz 596
Berlin porcelain 274, 279, 283, 285, 289, 461
Berlin woolwork 528, 529
Bernadotte, Sigvard 497
Bernard, J. & Son 752
Berthoud 394
Bertrand 596
Beshir rugs 521
Besler, Basilius 652
Bessarabian rugs 514
Beuscher, Simon 622
Bevington, John 274
Bezant, A.M. 383
Bible boxes 158
Bibles 652
Bickelman, Phillip Jacob 431
Bidjov rugs 517
Biedermeier: armchairs 60
  benches 31
  cabinets 48, 49
  chairs 66
  clocks 417, 426
  cupboards 198
  lighting 509
  linen presses 81
  secretaire chests 78
  tables 120, 142
  wardrobes 147, 216
Biggs, E.T. 382
bijouterie tables 123
Bilbie, E. 401
billiards 745–6
Bing 676, 680
binoculars 710
bird cages 603
Bird Iles, Jack **490**, 490, 492
bird scarers 606
birdbaths 582
birds: ceramic 224–8, 267, 268, 304, 310, 457
  sculpture 596
  silver 353
Birge, Peck & Co 427
Birge & Fuller 427
Birks, Alboin 290
Birley 420
Birmingham Guild of Handicrafts 454
Birtwell, W. 416
biscuit boxes 271, 374, 475
biscuit figures 286, 288
biscuit tins 223
bisque dolls 663–70
Black, James 245
Black, John 412
Black, Misha 503
Black, Starr & Frost 366
black basalt 257
Black Forest: clocks 424, 427
  treen 607
Blackburne 709
Blaeu, Joan 659, 660, 662
Blaeu, Willem 658–60
Blake, Nicholas 652
blanc-de-chine 316, 326
Blanckensee & Son 497
blanket chests 71, 192, 194
Blaylock 404
Bloor Derby 295, 300
Blott, George 691
blotters 604
blouses 537
Blundell, Thomas 412
blunderbusses 728
boats, toy 676
Boch Frères 461
Bohemian: busts 464
  ceramics 281, 288, 294, 302
  glass 332, 337–9, 341–6, **345**, 349, 351, 352, 471
  lighting 511, 513
Boisselot et Fils 623
Bolding, John 586
bonbon dishes 363, 462
bonbonnières 303
Bone, Henry 634, 635
bonheurs du jour 31–2
bonnet stands 609
bonnets 536
book lecterns 606
book presses 606
bookcases **33**, 33–7
  Art Deco 489
  Arts and Crafts 449
  bamboo 219
  book racks 606, 610
  bureau 35
  campaign 152
  low 36
  miniature 90
  oak and country 156
  pine 191
  revolving 36
  secretaire 37
bookends 482
books and book illustrations 652–7, 759
boot jacks 606
boot scrapers 578
Booth, Enoch 229
boots 537, 697, 748, 756
Bosch, Jacob van den 463, 491
Bose, Charlotte 279
Bösendorfer 624
Boston, Wendy 674
Boston & Sandwich Glass Co 347
bottle openers 376
bottle stands 110, 605
bottles 340, 572, 576
  see also scent bottles
Boucheron 550
Bouillat, Edmé-François 270
Bouillat, Geneviève-Louise 270
boulle: clocks 388–90
  tables 117
Boullemier, Antonin 290
Boullemier, Lucien 299
Boulton, Matthew 374, 376
bouquetières 256
Bouraine, M. 486
Bourne, Samuel 717
Bow: baskets 268
  coffee cups 279
  figures 285
  jugs 294
  mugs 295
  sauce boats 297
  saucer dishes 289
bowling 746
bowls: Aesthetic Movement 447
  antiquities 640
  Art Deco 479–81
  Arts and Crafts 454
  Chinese ceramics 310–11
  Clarice Cliff 482
  Fabergé 552
  glass 342, 471, 493, 494, 505, 576
  Japanese ceramics 327
  Martin Brothers 459
  Moorcroft 459
  porcelain 269–71
  pottery 229–30, 259, 263
  silver 355, 447, 454, 497, 755
  silver plate 475
  treen 606
  tribal art 649–50
  twentieth-century 499, 500
box stools 184
boxes 612–18
  age and patina **618**
  Art Nouveau 475
  artist's 639
  Arts and Crafts 454
  Bible 158
  blanket 192
  boxes-on-stands 38
  bronze 598
  campaign 152–3
  candle 192, 607
  Chinese ceramics 312
  cloisonné 554
  cutlery 220
  document 192
  enamel 551
  Fabergé 552
  glass 342, 471, 555
  gold 553
  iron 600
  Islamic 577
  ivory 748
  lacquer 556, 557
  leather 604
  love token 709
  maid's 221
  oak and country 158
  ormolu 601
  papier mâché 605
  pine 192
  porcelain 271, 304
  pottery 258
  sewing 38, 556, 604
  silver 356, 475, 757
  toleware 602
  tool 192
  tortoiseshell 615, **616**, 618
  treen 606, 607
  Tunbridge ware 610
  wood 559
  writing 153, 158, 610, 613, 616, 618
  see also snuff boxes
boxing 747
bracelets 472, 495, 506, 540–1, 645
bracket clocks 379, **380**, 381, 383, 384, 389
brackets, wall 145
Bradford, Rev William 652
Bradley, Liverpool 729
Bradwell 756
Brandt, Gunnar 692
brandy decanters 377
brandy saucepans 376
brass 597–8
  Aesthetic Movement 447
  Arts and Crafts 450, 454–6
  Asian 557
  beds 27, 30
  bell pulls 588
  chandeliers 509
  clocks 392–3, 395, 424, 449, 463
  fenders 591
  kitchenware 221–3
  lighting 452–3, 474
Brassaï 717
Braun, Georg 662
Bray, James 717
bread and cheese cupboards 176
bread baskets 354
breakfast cups 279
breakfast dishes 363
Breguet 431, 432
Breitling 434
Bretby 244
Breton: beds 157
  chairs 165
  cupboards 177
Bridge, John 364
Brightwell, Sarah 527
Brimtoy 676
Brinsmead, John 624
Bristol: glass 340
  pearlware 258
  porcelain 295, 303
Bristol delft 229, 240, 241, 243, 245
Britains 679, 684
Broad, Louisa 534
Broadwood, John & Sons 623
bronze 598–9
  antiquities 640, 641, 643–5
  architectural antiques 580
  Art Deco 497
  Art Nouveau 478
  Asian 557, 558
  clocks 424
  figures 464, 486–9, 565–6
  Islamic 577
  lighting 474
  sculpture 592–6
  twentieth-century 507
brooches 542–3, 711
  antiquities 645
  Art Deco 495
  Art Nouveau 472
  Fabergé 552
  sporting 759
  twentieth-century 506
Brown, James 405
Brown, Mary 479
Brown, Nath. 405
Brown, R.C. & Co 689
Brown, Thomas 402
Brown-Westhead and Moore 227
Browne, John 653
Bru Jeune 663
Brühl, Count Heinrich von 307
Brunelot 392
Brunn 726
Brunwin, Henry 408
brushpots 312, 555, 559
Brussels lace 530, 539
BSA 728
Bub, Karl 680
buckets 38, 597, 604
buckles 331, 452, 536, 537, 645, 744
Buckley, Arabella B. 653
Budgen, Thomas 398
buffets 38, 158
buffets à deux corps 158, 204
Bugatti, Carlo 467
buildings, pottery 230, 331
Bulgarian icons 629
Bull, Richard 635
Bullock, George 135
Bülow-Hübe, Torun 506
Bunning, John Anton 354
Bunouste, Prosper 551
bureau bookcases 35
bureau cabinets 43, 159
bureau de dame 40
bureaux 39–40
  Asian 567
  campaign 153
  oak and country 159
  pine 203
Burgomaster chairs 58
Burgun, Schverer & Co 469
Burlington & Co 381
Burmantofts 445, 448
Burmese: figures 562, 564–6
  lacquer 556
  metalware 557
Burne, Thomas George **248**
Burne-Jones, Edward 472
Burningham, John 692
Burns, Robert 247
Burroughs & Watts 746
Burton 437
Burton, James 380
busts: Art Deco 489
  Art Nouveau 464–5
  bronze 594, 596
  porcelain 272, 305
  pottery 231
  wood 592, 744
Butcher's 713
butcher's blocks 218
Butler, Frank 457
Butler, John 481
butler's cupboards 198
butler's trays 144
butter churns 220
butter dishes 224, 233
butter prints 220
butter wheels 220
Bye-Lo 668
Byzantine: antiquities 645
  icons 628

C

cabaret services 252, 276, 445
cabaret trays 299
cabinet cups 280, 281
cabinet plates 289, 290, 307
cabinets 41–53
Aesthetic Movement 446
Art Nouveau 466
Asian 567
bedside 41–2, 201, 202, 218, 446, 489
bureau 43, 159
cabinets-on-chests 43, 177
cabinets-on-stands 53, 174
campaign 153
cocktail 490
corner 44–5, 446
dentist's 703
display 45–7, 149, 449, 466
drinks 38
miniature 90
music 48, 219
oak and country 176, 177
pedestal **48**, 48
secretaire 49, 449, 466, 490
side 50–2, 90, 177, 182, 207–8, 490, 504
table 53
twentieth-century 504
caddy spoons 356, 748
Cadogan teapots **322**, 322
cake baskets 354, 374
cake stands 107, 374
calculating instruments 698
Calder, Alexander 508
Calder Marshall, William 593
Callaghan & Co 444
Caltagirone 256
cameo glass 349, 469–70, 473, 493, 494
cameos 544
cameras 713–14
Camerer, Kuss & Co 384
Camozzi, C. 441
campaign furniture 152–5
Canadian: pottery 226, 245
silver 498
canapés 100, 101
candelabra 374, 453, 598, 601
candle boxes 192, 607
candle holders 310, 600
candle snuffers 286, 305
candle stands 110
candlesticks: Arts and Crafts 454
brass 597
bronze 598
pewter 497
porcelain 273, 305
pottery 231
silver 356, 475, 497
silver plate 374
treen 607
cane handles 552
caneware 229
cannons 722
Canon 713
canterburies 54
capes 536–7
caqueteuses 162
car mascots 752
carafes 341, 352
card cases 357
card tables 115–17, 155, 569
card trays 299
cards: cigarette 689, 748, 759
postcards 690, 747
care of furniture **76**
Carette 680
Carlton House desks 84, 86
Carlton Ware 479
Carlyle, T. 636
Carpenter, Ruth 533
carpets *see* rugs and carpets
Carr, Alwyn 476
Carr, Ann 532
Carr, John 266
carriage clocks 360, 392–3, **393**
carriage lamps 366
Carroll, Lewis 654
Carron 600
cartel clocks **394**, 394, **426**
Carter, John 370
Carter, Stabler & Adams 479
Carter, Truda 479
Cartier 434, 497, 498
carver chairs 56, 164
Cary 705, 706
Cash & Skilbeck 394
caskets 342, 597
Cassandre, A.M. 691
Cassiers, Henri 691
Cassina 502
cassolets 257
Casson, Hugh 500, 503
cassones 71
cast iron *see* iron
Castelli 245
casters, silver **357**, 357
Caucasian rugs 516–17
Caughley: bowls 270, 271
coffee and tea services 277
coffee pots 275
cream boats 297
custard cups 282
dishes 283
eye baths 303
jugs 294
spoon trays 299
tea bowls 279
Cauldon 282
Caussé, Julien 478
Cavanders 689
Caxton, William 653
Caygill, Christopher 408
ceiling lights 509–11
celadon: dishes 317
figures 316
garden seats 320
vases 325
cellarets 150–1
cellos 622
Celtic antiquities 645
censers 557
centre tables 118–19, 186, 447, 492
centrepieces: Art Nouveau 465, 475
glass 343–4, 493
porcelain 267, 273–4
silver 358, 475
silver plate 374
treen 607
ceramics: Aesthetic Movement 445
antiquities 640–2, 644
Art Deco 479–86
Art Nouveau 461–2
Arts and Crafts 448
Chinese 308–26
Doulton 457–8
Islamic 574–5
Martin Brothers 459
Moorcroft 459–60, **460**
Pre-Columbian 646
twentieth-century 499–501
see also porcelain; pottery
Ceylonese furniture 568
Chad Valley 672, 674, 684
chairs 63–70
Aesthetic Movement 446
Art Deco 490–1
Art Nouveau 466–7
Asian 568
bamboo 219
campaign 153
chair tables 162
children's 63, 166
corner 64
dining 64–7, 165
hall 68
Islamic 575
library 68
nursing 69
oak and country 162–6
piano 112
pine 193
rocking 58, 60, 164, 166, 446, 466, 490, 504
salon 69, 490
side 70, 446, 467, 491, 568, 575
twentieth-century 502–4
valuing sets **65**
see also armchairs
chaise longues 71
chamber pots 263
Chamberlain, Sarah 531
Chamberlain Worcester: animals 268
cups 281
custard cups 282
dishes 284
inkwells 293
plates 291
tapersticks 273
tea services 278
trays 299
wine coolers 292
chambersticks 273, 305, 356, 454
Champagne decanters **345**, 345
Champion Bristol 279
chandeliers 452–3, 474, 496, 509–11
Channel Islands silver 355
Chapman, Captain Charles 653
Chapuis, A. 653
Chapuis, Jean-Joseph 114
character jugs 254–5
Charder 493
Chareau, Pierre 490
chargers: Art Nouveau 462
Arts and Crafts 454
Clarice Cliff 483
Japanese ceramics 329
pottery 239–41
porcelain 290
twentieth-century 500
Chase, William Arthur 491
Chatelain, H.A. 659
Chawner, Henry 361, 362, 372
cheese coasters 259
cheese cradles 607
cheese domes 231
Chelsea: clocks 279
dishes 283
figures 285
plates 289
tea bowls 279
vases 300
chenets 454
cheroot cases 359
chess sets 686
Chesterfield sofas 101
chests 71
Asian 568
campaign 153
leather 604
medicine 703–4, **704**
miniature 90
oak and country 166–8
pine 194
sea 710
chests of drawers 72–80, **75**
Art Nouveau 467
campaign 154
chests-on-chests 77, 172
chests-on-stands 78–9, 172–3
miniature 90
oak and country 170–2
pine 194–6
secretaire 78, 154
Wellington 80, 90
cheval mirrors 91
Chicago Firearms Co 732
chiffoniers 50, 51, 154, 207, 208
Chihuly, Dale 505
Child & Child 472
children's furniture: chairs 63, 166, 193
tables 138, 186
chiming clocks **381**
chimney pots 583
Chinese: arms and armour 560
cloisonné 554
costume 571
figures 562–6
furniture **567**, 567–9
glass 555
jade 555
lacquer 556–7
metalware 557, 558
rugs and carpets 523
snuff bottles 572
textiles 572–3
wood 559
Chinese ceramics 308–26
animals 309–10
bowls 310–11
boxes 312
brushpots 312
cups 313–14
dishes 314–15, 317–18
ewers and *kendi* 315
figures 316
flatware 317–19
garden seats 320
jars 320–1
jugs 321
marks 308
mugs and tankards 322
tea, chocolate and coffee pots 322–3
tureens 323
vases 324–6
Chinese Chippendale 55, 145
Chinese export: chocolate pots 323
fans 538, 539
figures 316
flatware 318, 319
mugs 322
shawls 537
tea bowls 314
tea canisters 326
tureens 323
vases 324
chinoiserie: cabinets 41, 44, 219
desks 219
salon suites 113
Chiparus, Demêtre 486
Chippendale style **26**
armchairs 60, 61
beds 26
bureaux 39
cabinets 45
chairs 64
chests of drawers 171
dressing tables 124
fire screens 97
linen presses 80
sofas 99, 101
tables **134**, 134, 137
wine coolers 150
chocolate cups 280
chocolate moulds 222
chocolate pots 322–3, 358, 600
Chodor Turkmen carpets 521
Chondzoresk rugs 516
Choshu School 561
christening bowls 355
christening mugs 354, 367, 478
Christian, John 408
Christian's Liverpool 276, 301
Christie, Agatha 654
chronometers 708
Churchill, Winston 654
cider kegs 220
cigar cabinets 53
cigar cases 359
cigar cutters 374
cigarette boxes 479
cigarette cards 689, 748, 759
cigarette cases 359, 475, 552, 757
cisterns 581, 587
claret jugs 476
Clark, Alexander 355
Clarke, C. 376
Clarke, Chris 408
Claudet, Antoine 718
Clay, London 605
Clayton, David 366
Clemens 672
Clementi & Co 623
Clérissy 256
Clews 259, 260, 479
Clichy 343, 347–8
Cliff, Clarice 482–4
Clift, J. 692
cloaks 536
clocks 378–430, 578
American 427–8
Art Deco 486
Art Nouveau 463
Arts and Crafts 449
British bracket, mantel and table clocks 378–84, **380**, 449
carriage 360, 392–3, **393**
cartel **394**, 394, **426**
Continental bracket, mantel and table clocks 279, 385–90
electric 394
garnitures 395, 449, 463
lantern 395
longcase 396–22, **397**, **402**, **414**
marine 708
novelty 424
porcelain 279
regulators 429–30, **430**
silver 360
skeleton 424
spring-driven **379**
striking/chiming/musical **381**
table 463
wall 425–8, **426**, 486
clockwork toys 676–7
clogs, ceramic 482
cloisonné, Asian 554, 565
clothes presses 80–1, 173
Clows, John 396
Coade stone 582
coal boxes 41, 455
coal scuttles 455, 591
Coalbrookdale 107
Coalport: baskets 268
chambersticks 273
cups 279, 280
dessert services 282
ice pails 292
jardinières 293
plates 289
spoon trays 299
tea services 276
coasters 376
coat stands 107, 467
coats 537, 571
coats-of-arms 578
Cobb, John 132
cocktail cabinets 490
cocktail jugs 497
cocktail shakers 494
cocktail watches 436
coffee biggins 374
coffee cups and cans 279–80, 314, 327, 485
coffee grinders 220
coffee pots: brass 597
Chinese ceramics 322–3
porcelain 275–6

pottery 253, 259
silver 358–9, 497
Susie Cooper 485
twentieth-century 500
coffee services: Art Deco 480, 498
Islamic 574
Japanese ceramics 330
pewter 478
porcelain 277–8
Royal Doulton 457
silver 360–1, 455
silver plate 375
Susie Cooper 485
coffee tables 502
coffers 71, 166–8, 194, 450, 575
Colani, Luigi 507
Cole 732
Cole, George H. 297
Cole, Thomas 392
Colin, Georges 596
collars: Asian 571
dog 375, 603, 604
lace 530
collector's cabinets 45, 53
Collingwoods 495
Collins, James 356
Collinson & Lock 86
Colmar, Thomas de 698
colour, valuing furniture **119**
Colt 732–3
Colton, J.H. 658
columns 82, 581, 584
comics 687
commemorative ceramics 242, 246, 259, 266, 290, 457, 748
commodes 52, 72–6, 171, 196, 575
commodes, night 41, 42, 110, 162, 166
compactum 147
Compagnie des Indes 322, 323
compasses 698–9, 709
comports 259, 274, 482
Compton 583
comtoise clocks 420
Comyns, Richard 486
Comyns, William 356, 357, 360, 367, 370
condiment pots 258, 361
Connell 456, 478
console tables 120, 569
consoles desserte 38
Content, Marjorie 718
Continental: armchairs 58, 60
beds 27, 157, 191
cabinets 50
ceramics 274, 288
chairs 67, 68, 193
chests of drawers 72, 76, 195, 196
coffers 167
commodes 171
desks 203
frames 88
glass 349–51
jardinières 89
jewellery 543
lighting 474, 509, 510, 513
porcelain 296
regulators 430
scientific instruments 706
sculpture 594
settles 210
shoe benches 218
side cabinets 208
silver 353, 355, 365, 369, 370
silver plate 475
treen 607
Contriner, Johann 758
conversation seats 100
Cooke, Elizabeth 531
Cookworthy, William 274, **295**, 295
Cooper, J. & Sons 750–1
Cooper, Susie 485
Copeland: busts 272
coffee sets 361
cups and saucers 259
figures 285
meat dishes 261
plates 289
Copeland & Garrett 251, 262, 276, 749
copper 600
Art Nouveau 475, 476
Arts and Crafts 450, 454–6
Islamic 577
kitchenware 222
lighting 453
Coquerel, Claude 479
corbels 584, 592
cordial glasses 333
Cordingley 412
Corgi Toys 684
corkscrews 376
corner chairs 64
corner cupboards 44–5, 175–7, 198–202, 446
Coronet 713
Corti, John 440
costume 536–7
Asian 571
militaria 735
tribal 647
Cosway, Richard 633
Cotswold School 450
Coudray, Georges 594
Coulon, Noël 486
counter boxes 356
coupes 469
cow creamers 232, 353
Cox, London 438
Cox, Robert 378
Cox, Thomas 662
Cox & Yeoman 746
Crace & Co 122
cradles 27, 156
Craig, John 358
cranberry glass 345, 352, 511
Crane, Elisabeth 532
cream boats 297–8
cream jugs 245, 295, 364, 447
cream pails 220
creamware: animals 224
butter dishes 233
coffee pots 253, 259
dishes 749
figures 234
flatware 241
jugs 264
moulds 222
mugs 248, 748
sauce boats 258
strainers 233
tureens 256
credenzas 45–6, 51, 52, 446
Crescent Toys 684
Cretan icons 628
cricket 747–8
cricket tables 186, 188–90, 211, 212
Cristal Parisiana 469
crocus pots 228
Crombie, Charles 756
crossbows 745
Crown Devon 479, 496
Crowther 581
cruet bottles 340
cruet stands 455
cruets: silver 362
silver plate 749
twentieth-century 500
crumb trays 476
cuckoo clocks **426**, 427
cufflinks 545
cupboard cases, for campaign chests 154
cupboards: corner 44–5, 175–7, 198–202, 446
food 174, 177, 218
hall 450
hanging 446
oak and country 174–8
pine 198–202
spice 178
see also cabinets; clothes presses; linen presses; wardrobes
cups: Chinese ceramics 313–14
cloisonné 554
Japanese ceramics 327
porcelain 279–81, 305
pottery 258, 259, 501
silver 362, 476, 749
Susie Cooper 485
curio cabinets 46
Currer, R. 420
Curry, Bill 507
Curry & Paxton 440
curtains 508
Curtis, William 654
cushions 535
custard cups 282
Cutbush, Robert 397
Cuthbert, John 367
cutlery: campaign 744
glass 352
silver 362
silver plate 375
cutlery boxes 220
Cuzner, Bernard 507
cylinder bureau bookcases 35
cylinder bureaux 40
cylinder musical boxes 619
Cypriot antiquities 642
Czech: ceramics 462
glass 505
musical instruments 627

D

daggers 723–4
daily care, furniture **123**
Dallinger, Sebastian 622
Dallmeyer 713
Dalziel Brothers 654
Dancer, J.B. 439
Daniell, Jabez 357
Daniell, Thomas 357, 362
Danish: armchairs 58
carpets 508
glass 338, 505
jewellery 506
pewter 497
pottery 254
seating 504
silver 365, 475, 497
stools 504
Darker, William 355
Darvel chairs 165
Daum 469, 473, 493
Davenport 256, 257, 259
davenports 82–3, **83**, 568
Davies, Sarah 534
Davies & McDonald 749
Davis, Joseph 440
Davison, Alexander **711**
Daws, Robert 56
Dawson, Stewart 369
Dawson's 262, 264
Day, Lewis F. 449
Day, Lucienne 508
daybeds 83, 156
De Morgan, William 448
De Porceleyne Claeuw 224
de Wit, Frederick 658, 660
Dean's 672
Dearling 426
decanter boxes 377
decanters 340–1, 350, 749
Champagne decanters **345**, 345
decorative arts 445–98
Aesthetic Movement 445–7
Art Deco 479–98
Art Nouveau 461–78
Arts and Crafts 448–60
decorative features, furniture **46**
Degué 493
Delamain, Henry 252
Delany 729
Delaunay, Sonia 506
delft **240**
flatware 242
inkstands 243
pots 250
tankards 248
see also Bristol delft; Dublin delft; Dutch Delft; English delft; London delft
della Corte, Alfonso 627
Della Robbia 461
Delvaux, Paul 291
Denby 223, 448
Dent, M.F. 433
dental instruments 703–4
Denton, William 634
DEP 663
Derby **280**
coffee cups 280
dishes 284
figures 285–6
ice pails 292
jugs 294
plates 289
scent bottles 298
services 282
teapots 275
tureens 300
vases 300
Derby Crown Porcelain Co 276, 280
Derbyshire cupboards 199
Descamps, Ernest 663
Design Line 507
desk lamps 496, 506, 513
desk sets and stands 373, 471, 554, 598, 601, 610
desks 84–6
Asian 568
bamboo 219
Carlton House 84, 86
kneehole 84–6, 178, 491
lady's 85, 86
oak and country 178
partner's 84, 86, 203
pedestal 84, 85, 178, 203
pine 203
twentieth-century 503
dessert plates 290
dessert services 251, 282–3
details, decorative **46**
Devon: settles 210
slipware 246
Dewsberry, David 458
Deykin, Thomas 398
dials 698–9
Diamond, John 503
diamonds: jewellery 495, 540–50, 711
watches 432, 433, 436
Dicksons, J. & Sons 757
Dilger & Barclay 418
dinanderie 498
dining chairs 64–7, 165
dining suites 491, 504
dining tables 121–3, 155, 190, 212, 450, 504
Dinky Toys 675, **684**, 684
dinner services 251, 262, 282–3, 485, 500
Dion family 244
Directoire style: mirrors 96
tables 114
disc musical boxes 620
dish rings and crosses 363, 375
dish wedges 373
dishes: Art Nouveau 462
Chinese ceramics 314–15, 317–18
Fabergé 552
glass 352, 471
jade 555
Japanese ceramics 328
lacquer 556
pewter 476, 497
porcelain 283–4
pottery 232–3, 239, 259–61
silver 363, 455
sporting 748, 749, 756
twentieth-century 500
dispatch boxes 152
display cabinets 45–7, 149, 449, 466
display tables 123
Ditmar, Rudolf 461
Ditzel, Nana 506
Dixey, G. & C. 441
Dixon, Charles 633
Dixon, James & Sons 356, 365
Dixon & Co 263, 264, 266
Doccia 289
document boxes 192
Dodge, Arther 431
dog collars 375, 603, 604
dog-kennel armchairs 162
Doisneau, Robert 718
Dollond 437, 439, 706
dolls 663–70
dolls' houses 671
Donegal carpets 514
door stops 578, 597, 600
doors and door furniture 588
dough bins 178
Doulton 457–8, 756, 583, 585, 587
dowry chests 166, 168, 172, 194
Doyle, Arthur Conan 654
drabware 252
drainers 233
dram glasses 337
drawing instruments 705
Dresden porcelain 271, 298, 302
Dressel, Cuno & Otto 663
Dresser, Christopher 445, 455, 456
dresser bases 207–8
dressers 179–82, 204–6
dresses 536, 537
dressing chests and tables 73, 208
dressing table mirrors 91–2
dressing table sets 364, 551
dressing tables 124–5, 189, 491
Drew & Sons 366
Dreyse, V. 733
De Drie Klokken 245
Dring & Fage 442
drinking glasses 332–8
drinking sets 350
drinks cabinets 38
Drocourt 392
drop-leaf tables 125, 186, 211–14
Drouot, Edouard 595
Drtikol, Frantisek 718
drug jars 245
drum tables 126
drums, militaria 744
du Maurier, Daphne 654
Du Paquier 294, 303
Dubberly 416
Dublin delft 252
Duchêne Compagnie 432
Ducher family 698
Duchess of Sutherland's Cripples Guild of Handicrafts **455**, 455, 456
duet stands 109
duet stools 112
Duffner & Kimberly 473
dumb waiters **87**, 87
Duncan, Alex 405
Dunhill 390
Dunn, Samuel 658

Dupin, Pierre 654
Dupinet, Antoine 654
Dupont, J.P. & Zoon 708
Dupont, J.V. 636
Durham, Joseph 285
Durham quilts 524–5
Durlach 232, 252, 256
Dutch: armchairs 502
barometers 708
boxes 616
bureaux 40
cabinets 41, 42, 50, 466
carpets 498
ceramics 254, 462, 479
chairs 64, 65, 70
chests 168
chests of drawers 73–6, 171
clocks 425, 463, 486
commodes 73
cupboards 174, 200
desks 491
dining suites 491
glass 340
lighting 496, 509
maps 658–60
metalware 597–9, 601
musical instruments 622
needlework 526
photographs 717, 719
posters 692
sculpture 596
sport 745
tables 118, 127, 135, 140, 142
watches 431
Dutch Delft: animals 224, 226
flatware 239–42
tiles 254
tobacco jars 245
vases 256
Dutton, David 427
Duval 420
Duvivier, Fidelle 270
Dvorak, Carolus Joseph 627
Dwight, James 655

E

Earnshaw, Thomas 432
earrings 495, 544, 545, 576, 641
earthenware: beer sets 258
bowls 230
flower pots 244
jardinières 244
vases 257
easels 639
East Midlands lace 530
eastern European: chests of drawers 196
cupboards 200, 202
dressers 205, 206
Eaton, Frances 532
Eaton, William 373
Eaton & Deller 752, 753
Eberlein, J.F. 306
Ebner, David N. 504
Ecalle, A. 393
Eckström, Yngve 503
écuelles 271
Edgecumbe, John 407
Edington, James Charles 345
Edition Galleria Colombari 502
Edwards, Charles 456
Edwards, D. & C. 377
Edwards & Roberts 142, 143
EFFanBEE 663
egg cups 305, 482
egg stands 260
eggs, Fabergé 552
eggshell porcelain **330**, 330
Egyptian: antiquities **640**, 640
manuscripts 576
Ehrlich, Paul 620
elbow chairs 55, 56, 60, 164
Eldridge, Henry 634
electric clocks 394
electroliers 511
electroplate 374
Eley, Thomas 377
Eley, W. 369
Eley, William 356
Eliot, T.S. 655
Elkin & Newbon 262
Elkington, Frederick 377
Elkington & Co 361, 368, 374, 593, 749
embroidery 526–9, 573, 577, 711
Emes, John 370
Emes, Rebecca 362, 364
Emes & Barnard 749
Empire: beds 26, 28
candlesticks 598
chairs 70
chests of drawers 75
clocks 390
dressing tables 124
dumb waiters 87
glass 350
pedestals 82
sofas 99
enamel 551
Art Nouveau 478
Asian 554
cigarette cases 757
jewellery 472, 540
lamp bases 473
end tables 190
English delft: bowls 229
flatware 239–41
tiles 254
entrée dishes 363, 485
L'Epaute 431
L'Epée 619
épergnes 343–4, 358
ephemera 687–92
annuals and comics 687
autographs 688, 693, 694
cigarette cards 689, 748, 759
postcards 690, 747
posters 691–2, 694–6, 744
L'Epine Horologers du Roy 431
Epstein 491
equestrian 748–9
Erard 109, 622, 623
Erickson, Oscar 444
Ernst, Petter 400
Ersari rugs 521
escritoires 85
Eska Watch Co 434
etagères 87
étuis 353
Eureka Clock Co 394
Eureka Pottery 247
Evans, Paul 504
ewers: bronze 599
Chinese ceramics 315
glass 345
porcelain 294–5
pottery 247, 259
Royal Doulton 457
silver 364
Ewers, Bob **685**
Exbor Glassworks 505
eye baths 303

F

Fabergé 552
façon de Venise glass 332, 343, 352
Factory X 295
Fahrner, Theodor 472, 495
faïence: barber's bowls 230
butter dishes 233
dishes 232
figures 234
flatware 239, 240
plaques 249
snuff boxes 258
stands 252
tankards 248
tea canisters 252
tureens 256
vases 256, 257
fakes, furniture **138**
Falkirk Foundry 580
famille rose: bowls 311
boxes 312
brushpots 312
candle holders 310
coffee pots 323
dishes 315
figures 316
flatware 318, 319
jars 321
mugs 322
tea bowls 313
tea canisters 326
teapot stands 314
tureens 323
vases 325, 326
famille verte: animals 310
basins 311
brushpots 312
flatware 318
garden seats 320
tea bowls 313
teapots 322
vases 324
fan cases 573
fan lights 578
Fanfare Models 675
fans 538–9
Farlow 752, 753
farmhouse tables 189, 190
Farnell 672
Farnham, Paulding 478
Farraday & Son 453
Farrar Pottery 245, 246
Farrow, Azubah 533
Fase 507
Faulkner, William 655
Fauré, Camille 473, 478
fauteuils 55, 58, 60, 62
Fayrer, Thomas 405
Fearn, W. 369
FED 713
Federal: chests of drawers 74
fireplace accessories 591
mirrors 94
sideboards 103
sofas 99
tables 120, 126, 138
Feininger, Andreas 718
Fell, Thomas 262
Fellig, Arthur 718
fenders 591
Fiaschi, E. 593
Fielding, Mary 534
figureheads, ship's 710
figures: antiquities 640, 642, 643, 645
Art Deco 486–9
Art Nouveau 464–5
Asian 562–6
Chinese ceramics 316
Japanese ceramics 328
lead 581
marble 581
matching pairs **288**
porcelain 285–8, 305–6, 489
pottery 234–8, 747, 757
Pre-Columbian 646
silver 365
silver plate 756
spelter 759
tribal art 649–51
see also animals; sculpture
film posters 692
finials 457, 582, 583
Finnish: barographs 444
rugs 514
textiles 508
Fiorentini, Agostino 510
fire buckets 604
fire screens 97–8, 467, 745
firearms 728–33, 758
fireplace accessories 591
fireplaces 450, 589–90
firing glasses 337
Fischel and Nessler 495
fish kettles 600
fish slices 220
fishbowls 326
fishing 750–3
Fishley 246
Fiske, J.W. 596
flags 744
flasks: glass 344, 576
Japanese ceramics 331
pewter 601
powder 742–3
silver 365
flatware: Chinese ceramics 317–19
Japanese ceramics 328–9
porcelain 289–92
pottery 239–42, 260–1, 266
see also cutlery
Fleischmann 680
Fleischmann & Bloedel 664
Fleming, William 376
Flemish: arms and armour 721
chests 168
cupboards 174
lighting 509
maps 660
sculpture 592
tables 190
Fletcher, Robert 402
Fletcher & Co 748
Flight & Barr 296
Flight, Barr & Barr 276, 281, 293, 302
Flint, W. 410
flour barrels 220
flower bricks 243
flower pots 244
Fly, C. 431
fob watches 433
Fogelberg, Andrew 364
Foley 448, 461, 499
Foley, J.H. 593
folio stands 108
Follot, Paul 498
Fontaine Fox 676
fonts 581
food cupboards 174, 177, 218
Foot 406
football 754–5
footman 455
footstools 111, 112
Forbes, William 360
Forester, Thomas & Sons 231
Forgan, Robert & Son 756
Fornasetti, Piero 503
Forth, Gustav Braendle 495
Fountain, William 360
fountains 579
Fouques, H. 594
four-poster beds 27, 28, 152
Fourdrin, Adrien 593
Fox, Charles and George 353
Fox Talbot, William Henry 718
Foy, Renée 550
frames 88
architectural antiques 584
Fabergé 552
silver 365, 476
treen 608
Franchini 348
Frank, Jacques 508
Frankenthal 286
French: architectural antiques 579, 581, 582, 584, 586, 587
armchairs 55, 61–3, 490
armoires 175–7
arms and armour 722, 724, 726, 732, 733
barographs 444
barometers 441, 442, 443
beds 27, 30, 157
benches 157
bergères 490
bonheurs du jour 31, 32
bookcases 157
boxes 617
bronze 478
buffets 158
buffets à deux corps 204
bureaux 40
cabinets 42, 44, 47, 49–51, 53, 176, 466, 490
cameras 714
carpets 498, 508, 514
chairs 69, 164, 166, 491
chests 166
chests of drawers 75
clocks 279, 385–90, 392–5, 398, 420, 424, **426**, 426, 430
costume 536
cupboards 177, 198, 201
daybeds 83
desks 85
dolls 663–5, 668–70
dough tables 178
dressers 180, 182
dressing tables 124
enamel 478, 551
fans 538–9
figures 464, 465, 486–9
fireplace accessories 591
folio stands 108
glass 342, 343, 347–8, 469–71, 493–4
gold 553
jardinières 89
jewellery 495, 506, 545, 548
kitchenware 220, 223
leather 604
lighting 473, 474, 496, 506, 509–12
maps 658, 659
marine 708, 710
mechanical music 621
metalware 498, 598–600, 601, 603
mirrors 92, 95, 96
musical boxes 619
musical instruments 622–7
needlework 526, 527
optical devices 716
pedestals 82
photographs 717, 718
plant stands 109
porcelain 271, 280, 284, 288, 290, 294
portrait miniatures 636, 637
postcards 690
posters 691, 692
pottery 228, 232, 240, 244
quilts 525
scientific instruments 698, 703, 706
sculpture 507, 593–6
settees 100, 101, 184
sideboards 158
silver 354, 363, 373
sofas 492
sport 746, 750
stools 504
tables 114, 117, 120, 123, 128, 129, 139, 142, 188–90, 214, 468, 492, 502
tapestries 535
toys 676–7
treen 606
washstands 148
watches 431, 432

INDEX

whatnots 149
French Empire *see* Empire
Frerniet, Emmanuel 594
Freyer, C. 730
friggers 352
Frith, Francis 718
Fritsche, William **345**
Frodsham, Charles 432
Frolov, Yaroslav 628
fruit baskets 354
fruit bowls 269, 270, 342, 475
Fukugawa 329
funnels, wine 376
furniture 26–155
Aesthetic Movement 446–7
Art Deco 489–92
Art Nouveau 466–8
Arts and Crafts 449–50
Asian 567–9
bamboo and wicker 219
colour and patination **119**
daily care **123**
fakes **138**
Islamic 575
marriages **138**
oak and country 156–90
pine 191–218
twentieth-century 502–4
waxing **127**
Furnival Pottery 230
Fürstenberg 276, 280, 298, 299

G

G Plan 504
Gabriel, J. 691
Gainsborough chairs 55, 60
Gallé, Emile 468–70
Gamble, Henry 410
game pie dishes 233
games tables 126, 212
Gandhara **562**, 562
Gapp, J. 638
Garden, John 429
garden furniture 578
garden seats, ceramic 243, 261, 320
Gardner, W.R. 662
garnitures, clock 395, 449, 463
Garrard, Sebastian 361
Garrison Pottery 266
gas lighting 510
Gaskin, George 452
Gaspari, Luciano 505
Gastinne-Renette, F.P. 732
Gatehouse, John 159
gateleg tables 186–8
gates 579
Gaudi, Antoni 468
Gaudy Welsh 271
Gaultier, François 664
Gendje rugs 516
Gerarde, John 655
Gerdago 486
German: animals 224
arms and armour 721–3, 726, 727, 729, 730, 733
barometers 439
beds 156, 191
boxes 613
cabinets 43, 45, 49
chairs 502
chests 194
chests of drawers 75
clocks 390, 395, 404, 422, 424, **426**, 427
coat stands 107
copper 476
costume 536
cupboards 177, 198
desks 203
dolls 663–70
dolls' houses 671
doors 588
figures 486, 488
flatware 239
glass 339, 346
gold 553
jewellery 472, 495
lighting 473, 507, 509
metalware 601
militaria 736, 737, 742
musical boxes 620
musical instruments 624, 627
pewter 475, 476
porcelain 267, 268, 274, 276, 279, 280, 283, 285–7, 290, 292, 296, 303, 489
portrait miniatures 636
postcards 690
pottery 232, 233, 244, 245, 248, 256, 462, 476
scientific instruments 698, 699, 702, 705, 706
sculpture 592, 596
shooting 758
sideboards 106
silver 370
sofas 468
soft toys 674
sport 745
tables 142, 212, 215
teddy bears 672, 673
toys 675–8, 680, 683, 685
wardrobes 216, 217
gesso **640**
geysers 586
Gibb 431
Gibson, J. 376
Gidding, J. 498
Gilbert, William L. 428
Giles, James 314, **336**, **349**, 349
Giles Workshop 335
Gillespie, J.J. 636
Gillett & Healey 425
Gillow & Co: billiard tables 746
bureaux 40
cabinets 446
chairs 68
mirrors 92
piano stools 112
settees 99
sideboards 104
tables 118, 139, 142
wardrobes 146
washstands 148
Gilmour, Margaret 454
gilt furniture **94**
ginger jars 480
Ginn, E.M. 621
Giso 496
Gispen, Willem Hendrik 496, 502
Giuliano, Carlo 543, 549
Glasgow School 450, 453
glass 332–52
ale, spirit and wine glasses 332–8
antiquities 642, 644
Art Deco 493–4
Art Nouveau 469–71
Asian 555
beakers and tumblers 339
bottles, carafes and decanters 340–1
bowls 342, 471, 493, 494, 505, 576
boxes 342, 471, 555
centrepieces 343–4, 493
decanters 350, 749
dishes 352, 471
figures 488
flasks 344
inkwells 494
Islamic 576
jugs and ewers 345, 505
lustres 346
mugs and tankards 346
neo-classical **336**
panels and pictures 346, 555
paperweights 347–8
scent bottles 349
sculpture 505
sets and services 350
sweetmeat and jelly dishes 350
twentieth-century 505
vases and urns 350–1, 469–71, 493–4, 505, 555
globes 702
glove boxes 610
Glynne, Richard 699
goblets: glass 332, 337, 338
silver 362
Godwin, E.W. 447
Goff, Bertha Lilian 452
goffering irons 221
gold 553
antiquities 641, 642, 644
Fabergé 552
jewellery 472, 495, 506, 540–50
watches 431–6
Goldbeck, Eugene Omar 718
Goldscheider 464, 465, 488
Goldsmiths & Silversmiths Co 360, 363, 752
golf 755–6
Gome 710
gongs, dinner 759
Good, J. Willis 594
Gorham Manufacturing Co 353, 358, 361, 447, 476
Gori, Georges 488
Goss, W.H. 272, 286, 290
Gothic: armchairs 62
beds 30
cabinets 177
chairs 66, 165
clocks 388, 427
sideboards 105
Gothic revival: bookcases 34
clocks 421
desks 84
hall stands 88
linen presses 173
tables 127, 129, 211
Göttschalk, Moritz 671
Gough 440
Graham, John 707
grain bins 218
Grainger's Worcester 271, 295, 302
gramophones 621
graphoscopes 716
graters 607
grates 497, 590
Graves, Robert 655
Greatbatch, William 253
Greek: antiquities 642
icons 628
Greek revival, clocks 428
Green, T.G. 223
Greenaway, Kate 369
Greenwood, C. & J. 662
Gregory, James 699
Gregory, Waylande 500
Grendey, Giles 134
griddles 221
Griffith, Richard 416
grilles 497
Grimes, William 396
Gross, Louis 636
Groult, André 490
Guadagni 626
guéridon tables 129
Guersan, Ludovicus 622
Guild of Handicraft 452, 454
guitars 622, 693
Gullachsen & Son 468
Gullick, John Thomas 637
Gummi, Martin 758
Gunn, Martha 255
guns 728–33, 758
Gupkin, Sergiy 632
gurgler jugs 228
Gurschner, Gustav 473

H

Hachenberger 719
Hackwood, William 231, 262
Hadfield, T. 412
Hadley Ware 302
Hagenauer 488, 497
Hague School 491
half-hunter watches 433, 435
half-tester beds 27, 28, 90
Halford, Thomas 371
Hall, Martin & Co 359
hall benches 31
hall chairs 68
hall cupboards 177, 450
hall stands 88, 450, 467
Halsey, Jabez 359
Halstaff & Hannaford 616
Hamada, Shoji 501
Hamadan carpets 518
Hamann, Adolph 270
Hambly, William 379
hambone holders 221
Hames, Thomas 356
Hamilton Watch Co 708
Hanau, Jean 492
Hancock 480
Hancock, H.S. 284
handkerchiefs 530
handles 588
Handley & Moore 380
Handyside Foundry 579
hanging cupboards 198
Hansen, Fritz 504
Hansen, Hans 497
Harden, Charles 432
Harden, George 406
Hardie, Matthew 626
Hardy 750, 752, 753
Harman, Robert **612**
harps 622
Harrach Glasshouse 337, 345
Harris, Charles Stuart 355, 361, 369
Harris, Kate 475
Harrison, John & Co 371
Harrocks, Joshua 400
Hart, S. 382
Hart, W. 250
Harvey, Abergavenny 412
Haseler, W.H. 371
Haseler & Haseler 357
hat pins 452
hat stands 107
Hatcher cargo 310, 315
hats 571
Haviland, Frank 283
Havinden, Ashley 498
Hawksley 757
Hawksworth, Eyre & Co 373
Hay, J. 355
Hay, John 438
Hayter, C. 634
Haywood-Wakefield 219
Heal, Ambrose 492
Heal & Son 124, 446, 492
Heal Fabrics 508
Healer, G. 413
Hearne, G.G. 747
Heath, J.T. 366
Heath Pottery 259
Heathman, J.H. 209
Heaton, Reuben 752
Heckert, Fritz 341
Hegge, William van der 431
Heinrich Handwerck 664
helmet plates 738
helmets 560, 721–2, 736–7
Hemingway, Ernest 655
Henan 310
Hennell, R. & S. 377
Henri, F. 458
Henrikstorp 339
Henry, J. 658
Hentschel, Rudolf 461
Henty, G.A. 655
Hepplewhite style: chairs 64, 164
mirrors 92
secretaire bookcases 37
tables 136
Herculaneum 262
Hering, Julius 664
Heriz carpets 518
Herter Brothers 70, 446
Heubach, Gebrüder **664**, 664–5
Heusinger, Johann 636
Hewlett, Andrew 398
Hicks & Meigh 233, 251
high chairs 63
Hignett Bros 689
Hilditch 276
Hill, David Octavius 719
Hill, Jo 684
Hill, N. 702
Hill & Millard 154
Hille, S. & Co 41
Hines, Elenor 531
Hinnenburg Goblet 338
hip flasks 365
Hipp, Matthäus 394
Hispano-Moresque pottery 229, 239
Hitchcock, L. 60
Hlava, Pavel 505
HMV 621
hob grates 590
Höchst 286, 300
hock glasses 471
Hoffmann, Josef 467, 493, 498
Holbrook & Co 702
Hollamby, Henry 610, 611
Holland & Sons 120, 127
Holmegaard 505
Holmes, Richard Rivington 656
Homann, Johann Baptist 660
Hone, Nathaniel 633
honey pots 483
Honiton lace 530
Hood 656
Hope, Thomas 111, 134
Hoppe, Johannes 723
horn: beakers 354
boxes 617
netsuke 570
powder flasks 742–3
vinaigrettes 372
Hornby 680–2
Horner, Charles 452
Hornsea Pottery 501
horses: equestrian 748–9
rocking 678
Horton & Allday 373, 475
Hösel, Eric 304
hot water jugs 364, 373
hot water urns 375, 447
Hottot, Louis 603
Houghton Butcher 713
Household Closet 586
housekeeper's cupboards 176, 199
Howard & Son 211, 446
Howard-style armchairs 62
Howden, James 402
Howse, Richard 442
Hukin & Heath 455, 456
Humberstone, Simon 257
Hungarian chairs 193
Hunt, John Samuel 364
hurdy-gurdies 621
Hürten, Charles Ferdinand 289
Hurter 634
Hutchins, Rev John 656
Hutschenreuther 488

Hutton, William & Son 366
Hyde, T. 428
Hynam, Robert 400

I

ice buckets 292, 494
ice cups 303
ice houses **151**
icons 628–32
Illsley, Lesley 507
Imari: bowls 327
chargers 329
chocolate pots 323
dishes 315, 328
figures 328
fishbowls 326
jars 329
jugs 321
koros 329
plates 318
tankards 322
tea bowls 327
teapots 322
vases 324, 325, 330, 331
Imperial Porcelain Manufactory 270
incense burners 557, 558, 562, 564
incense pots 329
Indian: arms and armour 560, 722
cloisonné 554
costume 571
figures 562, 565
furniture 568, 569
metalware 557
rugs and carpets 522
textiles 573
Indonesian: arms and armour 561
figures 564
Ingraham, E. & Co 428
inkstands and inkwells: bronze 599
glass 352, 494
ormolu 601
porcelain 293
pottery 235, 243
silver 366, 476
sporting 748, 749
Innes, Robert 369
inro 570
International Silver Co 364
International Watch Co 434
Inuit art 647
Ipsen, P. 254
Irish: armchairs 55
arms and armour 728
bookcases 191
boxes 192
bureaux 203
carpets 514
ceramics 267–70, 275, 289, 294
chairs 165, 193
chests 168
chests of drawers 172
chiffoniers 207, 208
clocks 412
cupboards 199–202
dressers 204, 205
glass 345, 350
jewellery 542
kitchenware 221
linen presses 81
plate racks 218
silver 355, 358, 362, 363, 367, 368, 376
tables 115, 120, 127, 128, 132, 211, 212, 214
treen 608
wardrobes 216
watches 432
Irmler 624
iron 600–1
architectural antiques 578–80
Asian 557, 558
daybeds 83
door furniture 588
fire surrounds 589
fireplace accessories 591
grates 590
kitchenware 221, 223
money boxes 677
stick stands 107
wine coolers 377
irons 221, 598
Ironstone 233, **246**, 251
see also Mason's Ironstone
Irvine, Sadie 480
Irwin, Jane 531
Islamic 574–7
arms and armour 574
ceramics 574–5
furniture 575
glass 576
jewellery 576
manuscripts and paintings 576
metalware 577
textiles 577
Isokon 502
Isola, Maija 508
Italian: armchairs 58, 60, 467, 502
arms and armour 721, 723, 724, 728
beds 30
boxes 618
buffets 158
bureaux 40
busts 465
cabinets 42, 43, 51, 53, 504
ceramics 287, 289
chairs 467
chests 71
chests of drawers 170
commodes 73
dining suites 504
dolls 667
flatware 239
frames 88
glass 505
gold 553
jewellery 542
lace 530
leather 604
lighting 507, 511, 513
metalware 600
militaria 736, 743
mirrors 93
musical instruments 623, 626, 627
needlework 526
screens 97, 503
sculpture 592–4
settees 101
silver 359, 507
sofas 502
tables 123, 133
toys 683
treen 609
window seats 150
ivory: boxes 613, 616, 748
fans 538–9
figures 486, 488, 564–6
netsuke 570
sculpture 592, 593, 596
Iznik pottery 574–5

J

jackets 571
Jackfield-style animals 226, 227
Jackson, J. 719
Jackson & Graham 446
Jacobean revival: bookcases 157
clocks 422
Jacobs, Samuel 371
jade 555, 564
Jagetet Pinon 301
jam pots 459, 483
Jansson, Jan 659
Jansson, Joannes 659, 661
Japanese: arms and armour 560–1
cloisonné 554
figures 564–6
furniture 567–9
inro 570
lacquer 556
maps 659
metalware 557, 558
netsuke 570
textiles 572
toys 676, 677
tsuba 561
wood 559
Japanese ceramics 327–31
bowls 327
cups 327
dishes 328
figures 328
flatware 328–9
jars 329
koros 329
tea and coffee services 330
vases 330–1
japanned: bonheurs du jour 31
cabinets 41, 44
linen presses 81
tables 134
Japonaise glass 351
Japy Frères 387, 389, 430
jardinières 89, 109
Art Nouveau 461, 462, 476
Arts and Crafts 448
bamboo 219
Chinese ceramics 326
Clarice Cliff 482
Doulton 457
Japanese ceramics 331
Martin Brothers 459
porcelain 293
pottery 244
silver 353
terracotta 583
jars: Arts and Crafts 448
Chinese ceramics 320–1
cloisonné 554
Japanese ceramics 329
lacquer 556
pottery 245
twentieth-century 499
jasper ware 249, 253, 257
Javanese furniture 569
Jeacock, J. 707
Jefferson 510
Jefferson, Robert 501
jelly dishes 350
jelly moulds 222
Jenkins, Merthyr 429
Jennens & Bettridge 31
Jensen, Georg 475, 497, 506
Jensen & Wendel 506
jewellery 540–50
antiquities 641, 642, 644, 645
Art Deco 495
Art Nouveau 472
Arts and Crafts 452
bangles and bracelets 472, 495, 506, 540–1, 645
brooches 472, 495, 506, 542–3, 552, 645, 711, 759
cameos 544
cufflinks 545
earrings 495, 544, 545, 576, 641
Islamic 576
necklaces 452, 472, 495, 506, 546–7, 576
pendants 452, 472, 495, 506, 548–9, 576
rings 495, 550, 644
stick pins 550
twentieth-century 506
jewellery boxes 610, 613, 616–18
Jewitt, M. 531
Johnson, Eldridge Reeves 750
Johnson, George 278
Johnson, Liverpool 425
joint stools 184–5
Jolliffe 450
Jones 752
Jones, A.E. 455, 456
Jones, George 229–31, 243, 252, 296
Jorden, Richard 638
Joshagan carpets 519
Jouve, Paul 492
Joy Toys 672
Joyce, Richard 462
JR 21 Toys 676
jugs: Aesthetic Movement 445
antiquities 641
Art Deco 479
Art Nouveau 475, 476
Charlotte Rhead 485
Chinese ceramics 321
Clarice Cliff 482
cream 245, 295, 364, 447
glass 345, 505
gurgler 228
Martin Brothers 459
milk 230
Moorcroft 459
porcelain 294–5, 306
pottery 230, 245–7, 261–5, 758
puzzle 246
silver 364, 373, 447, 475, 497
Susie Cooper 485
Toby and character **254**, 254–5
twentieth-century 500
Jumeau 665
Junck, F. 594
Junyao 310, 317, 320
Just 497
Justice, Thomas & Co 46

K

Kakiemon 327, 328
Kalabergo, G. 441
Kämmer & Reinhardt 665–6, 669
Kammerer, Marcel 467
Kamo rugs 520
Kändler, J.J. 304–7
Kanetomo of Nanki 570
Kangxi 326
Kanjiro, Kawai 500
Karadja rugs 518
Kashan rugs 520
Kashgai bags 519
Kaul, Paul 627
Kaulitz, Marion 666
Kazak rugs 516–17
Kéléty, Alexander 488
Kellett, Samuel 411
Kelson, George M. 656
Kelvin, White & Hutton 707
kendi 315
Kenrick & Sons 588
Kent, W.W. 429
Kenway, James 408
Ker, James 358
Kerby, Elizabeth 534
Kessels, Willy 719
Kestner, J.D. 666
Keswick School of Industrial Art 450, 454
kettle stands 108
kettles: brass 447, 455, 598
copper 600
silver 366
silver plate 375
Keuken, Johan van der 720
Kewpie dolls 668
keys 603
keystones 582
Khmer figures 562
Khotan rugs 522
Kiev 713
Kilburn, W.E. 719
kilims 514, 518
King, Jessie M. 656
King, Stephen 406
King Street Derby **280**
Kingsbury 684
Kinkozan Studio 330
Kirchner, Raphael 690
Kirman carpets 520
Kirschner, Gottlieb Friedrich 276
Kit-Kat wine glasses 333
kitchenware 220–3
Klein, Aart 719
Klimt, Gustav 466
Klinger, Johann Georg 702
Klingert, Gustav 373
Kloster Veilsdorf 267
Knabe, W. 624
kneehole desks 84–6, 178, 491
knife boxes 612
Knight, George 372
Knight, Dame Laura 499, 505
knives, angler's 751
knockers 588
Knoll 504
Knöll, Frank 373
Knox, Archibald 452, 463, 476, 478
Kny, Frederick **345**
Kodak 713–14
Koike Yoshiro School 561
koros 329, 554, 558, 566
Korschann, Charles 464
Koshov, M. 354
Kosta 339, 505
kovsh 373
kraak porselein **317**, 317
Kramer, Louis 445
Kriner, Simon 622
Kruse, Käthe 666–7
Kubachi 575
Kuhse, J. 624
Kula 587
Kurdistan rugs 519
Kutani vases 331
kylixes 480

L

labels, wine 377
lace 530
lace crimpers 607
lacquer: Asian 556–7, 567, 568
boxes 617
cabinets 44, 45
tables 219
trays 144
lacrosse 756
ladders 209
ladles 221, 369, 476
LaFleur, Alexandre 710
Lalique, René 486, 488, 493, 495, 496
Lamb, Philinda 533
Lamb of Manchester 52, 67, 119, 447
Lambeaux, Jef 594
Lambert 676
lambing chairs **164**, 164
Lamerie, Paul de 373
lamp stands 110
lamps and lighting 509–13
antiquities **644**, 644
Art Deco 496
Art Nouveau 473–4
Arts and Crafts 452–3
brass 598
ceiling and wall lights 509–11
pewter 601
silver 366
table and standard lamps 512–13
twentieth-century 506–7

Lancashire dressers 181
Lancashire chests 73, 74
Lanceray, Evgeny Alexandrovich 595
Lane of Birmingham 605
lantern clocks 395
lanterns 453, 473, 509–11
Laotian figures 564
lap desks 192
Larche, Raoul 464
larder cupboards 199, 200
Larsson, Ola 414
Latham, Eliza 533
latticinio glass 332
Laurence, Richard 379
Laurencin, Marie 656
lavatory pans 586–7
Lawrence, Bristol 417
Lawton, Joseph 719
Layton, C. & E. 698
lazy Susans 252, 608
Le Corbusier 502
Le Coultre 434
Le Faguays, Pierre 488
Le Gray, Gustave 719
Le Hongre, Etienne 285
Le Nove 287
Le Roy & Fils 432
le Verrier, Max 496
Leach, Bernard 499–501
Leach, Janet 501
Leach Pottery 500
lead, architectural antiques 581
leather 604
Lebègue 702
Lechler, J.A. 733
Lee, Buddy 666
Lee, Martha 533
Leech 730
Leeds Model Co 682
Leeds pottery 248, 256, 258
Legras 470, 494
Leica 714
Leleu, Jules 492
Leleu, Paule 498, 508
Lemaître, Eglantine 594
Lenci 667
Léonard, Agathon 596
Lesghi rugs 517
Letronne, René Louis 636
letter boxes 617, 618
letter clips 749
letter openers 608
letter racks 603
letter scales 598
letters 711
Lewis, Gravesend 411
Lewis, Mary 532
Lias, Henry 356, 447
Liberty & Co: clocks 449, 463
furniture 449, 450
jewellery 472
pewter 475–8
silver 478
library furniture: chairs 68
steps 110
tables 127, 215
Licas, Jospeh 506
lighters 373
Lightfoot, Mary 638
lighting *see* lamps and lighting
Limbach 287
Limehouse 268, 284
Limoges 283, 478, 551
Lincolnshire chiffoniers 208
Lindstrand, Vicke 494, 505
Lindström, C.A. 394
linen presses 80–1
miniature 90
oak and country 173
pine 199, 209
Linke, François 142
Lionel 682–3
liqueur stands 377
Litell, Ross 508
Lithyalin glass 339
lits en bateau 26
Liverpool delft 232, 243, 254
Liverpool porcelain 276
livery cupboards 174, 176
Lizars, J. 444
Lloyd Chrome Co 502
Lobmeyr 339, 341, 343, 345
Lock, Joseph 372
Locke & Co 302
lockets 544, 548
Lockey Hill 622
Lockwood, Benjamin 402
Lockwood, Richard 370
Loetz 470, 494
Lofting, Hugh 656
London delft: dishes 232
drainers 233
flatware 240
flower bricks 243
jars 245
stands 252
vases 256
longcase clocks 396–22, **397**, **402**, **414**
Longines 433, 434
Longton Hall 301
Lorenzl 488
Lori rugs 519
love seats 100
love spoons 609
loving cups 258
Low, J. 413
low bookcases 36
Low Countries, boxes 158
low dressers 181–2
Low Lights Pottery 266
lowboys 89, 182
Lowestoft 276, 280, 294, 298
Lozano, Thomas 402
Lucas, Daniel 295
Lück, C. 286
Ludwigsburg 276
luggage stands 110, 155
Lukutin Manufactory 605
Lumière & Cie 714
Lumpkin, Thomas 396
Lund & Blockley 384
Luns, Huib 596
lustres 346, 599
lustreware 263–6
animals 263
bowls 229, 263, 481
chamberpots 263
flatware 239
jugs 263–5
mugs 265
plaques 266
vases 266, 448, 479
Lutken, Per 505
Luvate, A. 442
'Lynn' wine glasses 336

M

McBean, Angus 719
McCabe, James 378, 381, 426
McCorrie, Mary 533
McGregor & Co 707, 708
Machin & Potts 247
McIntire, Samuel Field 115
Mack, Williams & Gibton 132
Mackay, J. 364
Mackrow, I. 707
Madoura 500
magic lanterns 716
Magni, Pietro 593
Mahal carpets 519
maid's boxes 221
maiolica: apothecary jars 245
bowls 229
dishes 239
vases 256
majolica: baskets 229
bowls 230
candlesticks 231
cheese domes 231
dishes 232
figures 238
flatware 242
game pie dishes 233
garden seats 243
gurgler jugs 228
jardinières 244
jars 245
jugs 247, 445
mugs 249
services 251, 252
stick stands 227, 258
teapots 253
tobacco boxes 228
Majorelle, Louis 466, 468, 493
Makers of Simple Furniture 502
Makkum 249
Malayer rugs 519
Malizard 443
Malloch 752
Maltese clocks 426
Manchester clocks 400
mandolins 623
Mangan Bros 200
mangles 221
Mangold, Burkhard 691
Mann & Co 242
mantel clocks 279, 380–90, 449, 463, 486
manuscripts, Islamic 576
Maori art 651
Maple & Co 76, 81, 85, 86, 421
Mappin & Webb 360, 363, 367, 422, 475
maps and atlases 658–62
marble: antiquities 643
architectural antiques 581
busts 464
fire surrounds 589
sculpture 593, 595, 596
Marc, Henry 389
Marcus & Co 355
Mare, André **490**
Marieberg 233, 257, 258, 282
Marimekko 508
marine 707–12
Admiral Lord Nelson 711–12
barometers 707
chronometers and timekeepers 708
model ships 708
nautical handicrafts 709
navigational instruments 709
sea chests 710
ship's fittings 710
Marinot, Maurice **494**, 494
Marioton, Eugène 595
Märklin 683
marks, Chinese ceramics 308
Marks, Henry Stacy 258
marquetry **129**
boxes 616
boxes-on-stands 38
bureaux 40
cabinets 41, 46, 50, 51, 466
chairs 64, 70
chests of drawers 75
chests-on-stands 79
clocks 396
desks 86
mirrors 491
tables 114, 118, 128, 130, 132, 135, 138, 142
Marrenzeller 430
marriage chests 168, 194
marriage cupboards 199
marriages: furniture **138**
longcase clocks **397**
Marseille, Armand 667–8
Marshall, G. 656
Marshall, Greenside 416
Marshall, Mark V. 458
Marshall, William 356
Marti 388, 395
Martin, Benjamin 400
Martin, Richard 396
Martin & Hall 377
Martin Brothers 459
Martinelli, L. & Son 442
Martyn 503
Martyn, Thomas 662
Masatsune, Ishiguro 561
Masayoshi 561
masks 558, 579, 648, 649
Mason 260
Mason, W. 638
Mason, William 401
Masonic jugs 264
Mason's Ironstone: drainers 233
jugs 246, 247
mugs 249
services 251
tureens 256
Massey 432
Massy, Jacob 397
Matthew, William 356, 362
Matthews, Henry 354
Mauchline ware 614, 615
Maucotel, C.A. 627
Maule, William 430
Maw, S. Son & Thompson 703
Maxalto 504
Mayer & Newbold 301
measures 602, 706
meat dishes 260–1, 319
mechanical music 621
mechanical toys 676–7
medals 712, 738–42, 745, 754
medical instruments 703–4
medicine chests 703–4, **704**
Meier 686
meiping 324
Meir, John 262
Meissen 304–7, 323, 461
Melani 488
Melas rugs 515
Mellor, Thomas 276
Memphis 505, 507
Mêne, Pierre Jules 599
menu holders 367, 498, 752
Meraux, Joseph **390**
Mercer, William 407
Meridien Britannia Co 375
Merrythought 672–3
Meshad carpets 520
Mesnil 386
Mesopotamian antiquities 641
metalware 597–603
Aesthetic Movement 447
Art Deco 497–8
Art Nouveau 475–8
Arts and Crafts 454–6
Asian 557–8
brass 597–8
bronze 598–9
copper 600
iron 600–1
Islamic 577
ormolu 601
pewter 601–2
toleware 602
twentieth-century 507
metamorphic furniture: library chairs 68
library steps 110
settles 184
tables 136, 184
Mettoys 685
Mexican art 646
Meyer, Baron Adolf de 718
Meyer, D. 425
Meyer, Joseph 462
Meyr's Neffe 339
micro-mosaic 96, 618
microscopes 705
Middleton, J.H. 366
Midwinter 500, 501
Mies van der Rohe, Ludwig 502
Milbro 683
milchglas 345
Miles, Septimus 380
militaria 734–44
badges 734–5
costume 735
helmet plates and shoulder belt plates 738
helmets and headdresses 736–7
historical medals 738
orders and medals 739–42
pouches 742
powder flasks and horns 742–3
sabretaches 743
milk boilers 221
milk cans 221
milk jugs 230
milk skimmers 222
milking stools 185
mill stones 582
Millar, Andrew 382
Millar, Dayville 726
Miller, A. 427
Miller, Gerrit S. Jr 656
Miller, Lienhart 698
Mills, Nathaniel 357, 359, 370, 372
Mills, Thomas 118
Millwards 752
Milne, A.A. 656
Ming Dynasty marks 308
miniature furniture 90
miniatures, portrait 633–7
Minton: bathroom fittings 587
beer sets 258
bowls 230, 259
busts 272
cabaret sets 276
candlesticks 231
centrepieces 274
dinner services 262
dishes 232, 260
figures 287–8
game pie dishes 233
garden seats 243
jardinières 461
jars 245
jugs and ewers 247
plates 290
services 251, 283
stick stands 461
teapots 253
tiles 590
trays 299
vases 267, 301, 445
Minton & Hollins 233
Mira-X 508
mirrors 91–6, **92**
Art Deco 491
Art Nouveau 461, 467, 476
Arts and Crafts 450
campaign 155
cheval 91
dressing table 91–2, 365
silver 367
wall 93–6, 491
Mitchell, B. 406
Mitchell, Henry 291
Mitchell, J.T. 634
Mitford, Nancy 656
Mitin, Alexander N. 366
moccasins 647
models: Asian 562–6
pottery 263

ships 708
Moffet, John & Son 467
Moghan-Talish rugs 517
Moko Lesney 685
Moll, Herman 658
Mollino, Carlo 502
Molteno & Baroni 442
money boxes 230, 677
Mongolian wood 559
Monkhouse, Jas. 410
monk's benches 183
monoculars 553
Monopol 620
monteiths 270
Monti, Raphael 272, 285
Moody, William 359
Moorcroft 459–60, **460**
Moore, Edward 369
Moore Bros 267
Moravian Pottery & Tile Works 480
Morden, Robert 661
Moreau, Auguste 465
Moreau, Math. 388
Morgan, Jeremiah 362
Moroccan jewellery 576
Morris, Desmond **642**
Morris, H. & Co 503
Morris, Henry 291
Morris & Co 98
mortars 599
Mosbach 233, 256
Moseley 413
Moser, Koloman 472
mother-of-pearl 617, 618
Mouille, Serge **506**, 506
moulds: kitchenware 222
treen 608
Moule, Thomas 662
Mourgue, Olivier 504
Moustier 240, 256
Movado 434
Mucha, Alphonse 462
mugs: Chinese ceramics 322
glass 346
porcelain 295–6
pottery 248–9, 262, 265, 748
silver 367, 478
Susie Cooper 485
mule chests 71, 166–8, 194
Muller, P. 367
Muller Frères 473
Munster, Sebastian 662
Murano Filigrana 505
Murano Glass Co 338, 507
Mureda, F.D.E. 623
Murphy, H.G. 456
Murray, Keith 500
Murrle Bennet 452
music 619–27
cylinder musical boxes 619
disc musical boxes 620
gramophones 621
mechanical 621
musical instruments 622–6
rock and pop 693–7
music cabinets 48, 219
music canterburies 54
music stands 109
music stools 112
musical clocks **381**
muskets 728
mustard pots 237, 353, 361
Mycock, William Salter 480
Myott 480

N

Nailsea 340
Nakashima, George 504
Nanking cargo 311
Nantgarw 290, 300
Napiers bones 698
napkin rings 368, 507
Nash, Gawn 372
Native American art 647
Natzler, Gertrud and Otto 500
nautical handicrafts 709
navigational instruments 709
Neale & Co 229, 246, 256, 749
necklaces 452, 472, 495, 506, 546–7, 576
needle cases 303, 559
needlepoint carpets 514
needlework 492, 526–9
Negretti & Zambra 439, 443, 444, 705
Nekola, Karol 249
Nelson, Admiral Lord 711–12
neo-classical: armchairs 56
glass **336**
neo-Renaissance silver 358
nests of tables 128, 569
netsuke 570
Neuberg-Gieshübl 290
New Guinea tribal art 650
New Hall 276, 278, 280, 294
Newcastle Pottery 264
Newcomb College Pottery 462, **480**, 480
Newcome 580
Newell Harding & Co 373
Newlyn 454
Newman, Bryan 501
Nicholas, John 425
Nicholls of Canterbury 410
Nicholson, Ben 498
Nicole Frères 619
Niderviller 288
Nielsen, Kay 656
night lights 509
Nikon 714
Noah's arks 678
Nock, S. 730
North African furniture 575
North Shields Pottery 264
Northumberland Pottery 265
Norton, Eardley 410
Norwegian: chests 194
treen 609
Nöstetangen 336
Nottingham pottery 248, 258
novelty clocks 424
NTE Opticien 438
Nuovo Alchimia 504
nursery ware 242, 249
nursing chairs 69
nut crackers 222
Nye, Edmund 610
Nylander, Jonas 354
Nymphenburg 280, 292, 293

O

oak and country furniture 156–90
beds, cradles and daybeds 156–7
benches 157
bookcases 157
boxes 158
buffets 158
bureau cabinets 159
bureaux 159
chairs 162–6
chests and coffers 166–8
chests of drawers 170–3
clothes and linen presses 173
cupboards 174–8
desks 178
dough bins 178
dressers 179–82
lowboys 182
settles and seats 183–4
stools 184–5
tables 186–90
Oakley, George 50
oatmeal crushers 222
occasional tables 128–9, 155, 186, 447, 450, 468, 492, 569
Odem, Mary Anne 532
Oeneas 586, 587
Ogden, Thomas 410
Ogden's 689
Ogilby, John 661
oil jugs 331
oil lamps 512, 513, **644**, 644
okimono 565, 566, 570
Old Hickory-style chairs 165
Oldland, Louisa 534
Oliphant, A. 411
Olive, Thos. 407
olivewood **129**
Olympics 757
Omega 435
O'Neill, Rose 668
opaline glass 341
open armchairs 55–60
opera glasses 551
optical devices and viewers 716
Orange Order 249
Orivit 476
Orm, George & Son 433
ormolu 601
clocks 385–8, **386**, 395
Orrefors 494
Ortelius, Abraham 660
Orwell, George 657
Ottoman: arms and armour 574
furniture 575
manuscripts 576
quivers 577
tombstones 577
ottomans 97
ovens 222
overmantel mirrors 96
Owen, George 271
Owen, Watkin 408
Oxford T/L test, Chinese ceramics 309
Oxshott Pottery 499
oyster dishes 232

P

Paignant, M. 478
paint boxes 639
paintings: glass 346, 555, 709
Islamic 576
portrait miniatures 633–7
see also pictures
pairs, pedestal cabinets **48**
Palais Royal 598
Palasca, B. 707
Pampaloni 507
panels: enamel 551
glass 346
needlework 526–7, 529, 573
stone 582
wood 559, 584
Pankhurst, Rebekah 533
Pantin 348
Panton, Verner 504, 508
pap feeders 262
paper clips 603
paperweights: bronze 464, 558
glass 347–8
pinchbeck 603
papier mâché **141**, 605
bonheurs du jour 31
boxes 605
tea caddies 605
trays 605
Papworth, E. 285
parasol handles 353
Parello, A. 594
Parian: animals 267
busts 272
figures 285, 287–8
Paris porcelain 278, 280, 290, 301
Parker, William **336**
Parkington Collection **333**
Parkinson & Frodsham 381
Parnaby, Martha 534
parquetry **129**
bonheurs du jour 32
bureaux 40
cabinets 43
commodes 73
tables 128, 129
Parr, Thomas 236
Parry Collection 72
Parsons 384
partner's desks 84, 86, 203
partners' writing tables 142
Pascoe, H. 438
Pask, J. 623
pastille burners 303
pastry cutters 222
patch boxes 551
patch pots 352
patchwork quilts 524–5, 572
pâte-sur-pâte: cabaret sets 276
centrepieces 274
plaques 296
plates 290
tiles 254
vases 461
Patek Philippe 432, 435
patination: valuing furniture **119**
wooden boxes 618
Patou 537
Patti, Tom 505
Pattreiouex, J.A. 689
Peacock, Jno 413
Pearce, Stafford 417
pearl jewellery 547, 549, 550
pearlware: animals 225
baskets 229, 259
boxes 258
busts 231
condiment sets 258
figures 234–6, 747
flatware 242
jugs 246, 262
mugs 248
punch pots 253
tankards 248
tea bowls 259
Toby jugs 255
tureens 256
vases 257
Pears, Chas 691
Pearson, John 454
peat buckets 38
pedestal cabinets **48**, 48
pedestal desks 84, 85, 178, 203
pedestals 82, 569, 582, 583
Pedrone, Louis 438
Pegg, 'Quaker' 289
Pelham Puppets 686
pelmets 584
Pembroke tables 130, 139, 140, 155
pendants 452, 472, 495, 506, 548–9, 576
Pennington's Liverpool 297
penwork 568, 614, 616
pepper casters **357**, 357, 602
Perchin, Michael 552
Perepedil rugs 517
Perigal, Francis 379
Perry, Frederick 366
Persian: antiquities 641
ceramics 574, 575
glass 576
jewellery 576
metalware 577
paintings 576
rugs and carpets 518–20
textiles 577
Persoz, Jean-François 657
pestles and mortars 222
Petersen, Carl Poul 498
Petit, Jacob 279
Peugeot Frères 220
Pewsey 430
pewter 601–2
Art Deco 497
Art Nouveau 475–8
clocks 463
kitchenware 222
tankards 755
Pezé Pilleau 366
Pfeiffer, Anton Heinrich 338
Pfränger 267
Philip, George & Son 702
Philippe, Paul 488
Philips, Robert & Sons 540
Phillips, A. 548
Phillips, Godfrey 689
photograph frames *see* frames
photographs 717–20
autographs 688
sport 747, 748, 754, 756
photography 713–14
Phyfe, Duncan 111
piano chairs 112
piano stools 112
pianos 623–4
Pibus, W. 418
Picasso, Pablo 500, 508, 692
pickle dishes 259, 284
pickle stands 274
pictures: silhouettes 638
silkwork 526–8
tile 254
Tunbridge ware 611
woolwork 528–9, **709**, 709
see also paintings
pier cabinets 51
pier mirrors 94
pier tables 120
Pierce 435
Pierotti 668
pietra dura 53
Pilkington's Royal Lancastrian 462, 480
Pillement, Jean 291
pin cushions 353, 611
pinball tables 686
Pinder & Bourne 445
pine 191–218
beds 191
bookcases 191
boxes 192
chairs 193
chests and coffers 194
chests of drawers 194–6
cupboards 198–202
desks and bureaux 203
doors 588
dresser bases and side cabinets 207–8
dressers 204–6
dressing chests and tables 208
fire surrounds 589–90
ladders and steps 209
linen presses 199, 209
settles and settees 210
tables 211–15
wardrobes 216–17
washstands 217
Piper, John 508
pipes, Prattware 258
Pirrie 420
pistols 728–32
pitchers 247, 364, 498–500
plafonniers 473, 507
plant stands 109
planters: Aesthetic Movement 445
Art Nouveau 462
cast-iron 579
marble 581

INDEX

stone 582
terracotta 583
see also jardinières
plaques: Art Deco 480
Art Nouveau 462
Clarice Cliff 484
cloisonné 554
porcelain 296
pottery 249, 266
plastic furniture 504
plate racks 218
plates: Arts and Crafts 448
Chinese ceramics 317–19
Clarice Cliff 482–3
porcelain 289–92, 307
pottery 239–42, 260, 261, 266
Royal Doulton 458
silver 373
platinum: jewellery 495, 545, 547, 550
watches 436
Platner, Warren 504
platters 373
Plaue 274
Player, John & Sons 689
Pleyel 624
plique-à-jour enamel 472
Plummer, William 354, 361
pocket watches 431–3, 755
Poertzel, O. 596
pole screens 97–8
polearms 733
Polish photographs 718
Polito 755
Pollard, William 293
Polyphon 620
polytechnic barometers **440**
Pompe, Walter 592
Ponchard, A.J. 751
pond yachts 708
Pons of Paris 386
Ponting, Herbert 720
Poole, John 708
Poole of London 384
Poole Pottery 501, 507
porcelain 267–307
animals 267–8
baskets 268–9
beakers 304
bowls 269–71
boxes 271, 304
busts 272, 305, 464
candlesticks and chambersticks 273, 305
centrepieces 273–4
clocks 279
coffee and teapots 275–6, 307
cups 279–81, 305
custard cups 282
dishes 283–4
eggshell porcelain **330**, 330
figures 285–8, 305–6, 489
flatware 289–92
ice pails and wine coolers 292
inkstands and inkwells 293
jardinières 293
jugs and ewers 294–5, 306
lamp bases 512, 513
Meissen 304–7
mugs and tankards 295–6
plaques 296
pot-pourri jars and vases 297
reticulation **271**
sauce and cream boats 297–8
scent bottles 285, 288, 298
services 277–8, 282–3
tea canisters 299
trays 299
tureens 300
vases 300–2, 307
wall brackets 302
see also Chinese ceramics; Japanese ceramics
porringers 270, 456
Porter, S. 699
Porthouse, John I 401
Portobello 263
portrait miniatures 633–7
Portuguese: needlework 526
tables 118
Pos, Barranti 465
posset pots 250
postcards 690, 747
posters 691–2, 694–6, 744
'postman's alarm' clocks **426**
posy vases 351
pot board dressers 179
pot cupboards 199
pot lids 250
pot-pourri jars and vases 297
pot racks 218
potato presses 223
Pothecary, Isaac 548
Potschappel 274
Potter, Beatrix 657
pottery 224–66
animals 224–8, 263
baskets 229, 259
bowls 229–30, 259, 263
boxes 258
buildings 230, 331
busts 231
candlesticks 231
cheese coasters 259
cheese domes 231
comports 259
covered dishes 233
cow creamers 232
cups 259
dishes 232, 239, 259–61
drainers and strainers 233
ewers 259
figures 234–8
flatware 239–42, 260–1, 266
flower bricks 243
garden seats 243, 261
inkstands and inkwells 243
jardinières 244
jars 245
jugs and ewers 245–7, 261–5
lustreware 263–6
models 263
mugs and tankards 248–9, 262, 265
plaques 249, 266
pot lids 250
pots 250
services 251–2, 262
stands 252
tankards 262
tea canisters 252
tea, coffee and punch pots 253, 259, 262
tiles 254
Toby and character jugs 254–5
transfer-printed 259–62
tureens 256, 262
vases and urns 256–7, 266
see also Chinese ceramics; Japanese ceramics
Potts, James 413
pouches, militaria 742
pounce pots 608
Pound, Martha 532
powder flasks and horns 742–3, 757
Pownall, M. 596
Powolny, Michael 465, 494
Pratt-style: plaques 249
punch pots 253
Prattware **253**, 744
animals 225
cow creamers 232
figures 234
money boxes 230
pipes 258
tea canisters 252
Toby and character jugs 254, 255
prayer rugs 517, 518, 520
Pre-Columbian art 646
Predary, J. 441
Preiss, Ferdinand 488
press cupboards 174–6
Preston, Elisabeth 534
Preston, London 621
Prickman 752
prie-dieus 70
Priest, William 402
programmes 694, 755
Prou, René 502
Prutscher, Otto 471
Pugin, A.W.N. 100
pulpit lamps 512
punch bowls 230, 355
punch ladles 369
punch pots 253
puppets 674, 686
Puritas 586
Purmurend 462
purses 373, 536, 573, 712
Pursol 464
Pursell Cornhill 222
puzzle jugs 246

Q

Qian Kaipang 559
Qing Dynasty marks 308
quaiches 232, 355
quartetto tables 128
quilts 524–5
quivers 577

R

rackets, tennis 759
Rackham, Arthur 657
radiators 579
radios 506
Raingo Frères 386, 387
Ramsden 437
Ramsden, Jessie 706
Ramsden, Omar 476
Randall, William 414
ratafia flutes 335
rattles 368, 608
Rauschmann in Ofen 430
Ravesteyn, Sybold van **502**, 502
Ravilious, Eric 500
Ravrio 386
Ray, Man 720
Raymond, Charles 401
Read, David 420
reading tables 131
records, rock and pop 693–7
red ware 253
Reed, Clement 362
reels, fishing 752–3
refectory tables 186–8, 190
Reformed Gothic 33
Regency period **134**
register grates 590
regulators 429–30, **430**
Reily, Charles 359, 360
Reily, Samuel 368
Remington 732
Renaissance revival: armchairs 58
beds 27
bookcases 34
tables 125
repairs, furniture **42**
Restauration armchairs 56, 63
restoration, furniture **42**
reticulation, porcelain **271**
reverse glass paintings 346, 555, 709
revolvers 732–3
revolving bookcases 36
Rhead, Charlotte **485**, 485
Rhodes, Zandra 508
Ricardo, Halsey 448
Richard, Jules 444
Richardson of Hull 142
Richardson's of Stourbridge 350
Richter 492
Ricketts 270
Ridgway 260, 261, 283
Riemer 283
rifles 758
Riley 746
Riley, J. & R. 272
ring holders 756
rings 495, 550, 644
rinsers 352
Rischmann, G. 596
Riva, G. & Co 442
Rivarossi 683
Riveric, Ami 619
Rivoire, Raymond Léon 489
Robb, William 540
Roberts, William 416
Roberts, Florence 458
Robertson & Co 639
robes 536, 571
Robsjohn-Gibbings, T.H. **503**, 503
rock and pop 693–7
Rock Valley Toys 676
rocking chairs 58, 60, 164, 166, 446, 466, 490, 504
rocking horses 678
Rockingham **294**, 294, 298, 301
Rococo revival: armchairs 55
bureau bookcases 35
clocks 279
dressing tables 124
tables 118
Rodgers, Richard & Thomason 248
roemers 338
Rogers 261
Rogi, André 720
Rolex 435–6
Roman: antiquities 643–4
lamps **644**
Romanian: chests of drawers 196
kitchenware 223
pot racks 218
settles 210
side cabinets 208
Rooke, Bernard 501
Rookwood 448, 462
Roper, Martin 414
Rörstrand 232, 256, 501
rose bowls 342, 355, 497
Rosendorf, Yelizaveta V. 290
Roseville Pottery 480
rosewood **86**
Ross 705
Ross & Co 153–5
Rosse, Susan Penelope 633
Roughsedge, Richard 417
Roullet et Decamps 677
Rous Lench Collection **248**
Roussel, R.T. 691
Rowed, Michael 638
Rowlings, Charles 553
Rowney & Forster 639
Rowsell's 716
Royal Crown Derby 274, 276, 282, 293, 301
Royal Doulton 221, 457–8, 756, 758
Royal Dux 288, 462, 465
Royal Winton 480
Royal Worcester: animals 268
bowls 270
coffee sets 278
cups 281
dishes 284
figures 288
jardinières 293
jugs 295
plaques 296
plates 292
pot-pourri jars 297
reticulation **271**, 271
services 283
vases 302
wall brackets 302
see also Worcester
Rozenburg 462
rugs and carpets 514–23, **519**
Art Deco 498
pricing **523**
twentieth-century 508
Ruhlmann, Emile Jacques 492
rumbler bells 598
rummers 337
rushlights 608
Ruskin Pottery 450, 499–500
Russian: arms and armour 724
boxes 617
cameras 713
ceramics 270, 286, 290
commodes 76
enamel 551
glass 342
icons 628–32
jewellery 472
militaria 734, 737, 740, 743
sculpture 595
silver 354, 359, 366, 370, 373, 475, 749

S

Saarinen, Eero 504
sabretaches 743
saddle covers 521
saddlebags 515, 521
Saddleton, James Parlett 379
Sadler, Robert 396
Sadler & Green 241
Safavid metalware 577
safety, children's furniture 63
Sagar, E. 402
Saget, Jean-Nicholas 354
St Anthony's Pottery 266
Saint Cloud 268
St Louis 348
salon chairs 69, 490
salon suites 113
salt bags 516, 519
salt-glazed stoneware: animals 224
finials 457
flatware 241
loving cups 258
mugs 248
pots 250
teapots 253
tureens 256
wall pockets 258
salt spoons 369
salts: enamel 551
glass 352
pewter 602
porcelain 306
silver 361
treen 608
salvers 368
Salviati 338, 505
samovars 375, 456
samplers 530, 531–4
Sampson Mordan & Co **349**, 349, 367, 369, 598
Samson 293, 299
Sanderson & Son 508
Sandham & Strudwick 747
Sandland, Edwin 247
sandwich plates 483
Sanitas 587
Sanjabi Kurds salt bags 519
sardine boxes 233
Sarreguemines 228, 232
Satsuma: belt buckles 331

bowls 327
figures 328
incense pots 329
jardinières 331
jars 329
models 331
tea services 330
vases 330–1
Satzger, Johann Martin 370
sauce boats 258, 297–8, 369
saucer dishes 289, 291
saucers: Chinese ceramics 318, 319
see also cups
Saur, C. 602
Savona 252
Savonarola armchairs 58
Saxton, Christopher 660
scales 223, 706
Scandinavian: chairs 65
mirrors 95
secretaire chests 78
treen 606
Scarpa, Tobia and Afra **504**, 504
scent bottles: glass 349
gold 553
pewter 602
porcelain 285, 288, 298
silver 369
Schachtenbach 337
Schenk, Frederick 296
Schlaggenwald 281
Schmidt, Franz 668
Schmuz-Baudiss, Theodor Hermann 461
Schneider 494
Schuco 674–7, 685
Schumacher 464
Schuyler, Hartley & Graham 727
Schwarzlot glass 339
scientific instruments 698–706
calculating instruments 698
compasses and dials 698–9
globes and armillary spheres 702
medical and dental 703–4
microscopes 705
surveying and drawing instruments 705
telescopes 706
weights and measures 706
scissors 603
Scolari, Gaetano 507
sconces 456, 509, 511
Scott, Anthony 264–6
Scott, Robert 382
Scottish: animals 225
architectural antiques 586
arms and armour 724, 727
barometers 437, 438, 442, 707, 708
boxes 615
clocks 411–13, 418, 420
glass 340
jewellery 543, 548
kitchenware 221, 222
lighting 510
metalware 454
silver 355, 356, 358, 377
treen 608
screens 97–8
Art Deco 492
Asian 568
embroidered 529
fire 97–8, 467, 745
Islamic 575
twentieth-century 503
sculpture 592–6
antiquities 643
bronze 507
glass 505
see also figures
sea chests 710
seats, oak and country 183–4
Sebright, Richard 283
secretaire bookcases 37
secretaire cabinets 49, 449, 466, 490
secretaire chests 78, 154
secrétaires à abattant 49
Seguso Vetri d'Arte 505
Semenova, Maria 551
Serouet, Francis 622
services: glass 350
porcelain 277–8, 282–3
pottery 251–2, 262
serving dishes 374
serving implements 369
serving tables 131
Seth Thomas Clock Co 428
settees 99–101, **100**
Asian 569
oak and country 184
pine 210
settles: Art Nouveau 468
oak and country 183–4
pine 210
Sèvres: bowls 270
boxes 271
busts 272
cups 281
dishes 284
ice cups 303
jugs 294
trays 299
vases 301
sewing boxes 38, 556, 604
sewing chairs 70
sewing tables 126, 141
S.F.B.J. 668
Shahsavan: kilims 518
salt bags 516
Shaker lap desks 192
Shanks & Co 586
Shapland & Petter 449, 450, 468
Sharp, Robert 356
shaving mugs 373
shaving stands 109
shawls 536, 537, 571
Sheffield plate 374
Sheilds, Hugh 165
Sheldon, C.E. 221
shell work 617
Shelley 480–1
Shelvas 585
shelves 102, 492
Shepherd, Thomas 359
Sheraton style: armchairs 63
bureau bookcases 35
cabinets 47, 52
chairs 64
desks 85, 86
dressing tables 125
sideboards 103, 104, 106
tables 115, 116, 130
trays 144
window seats 150
Sherratt, Obadiah 225, 236
Sherwood, Thomas 380
shields 721
ships: model 708
toy 676
see also marine
ships' fittings 710
Shirvan rugs 517
shoe benches 218
shoes 536, 571
Shoolbred, James & Co 109
shooting 757–8
shop counters 218
Short & Mason 444
Shoryusai 558
shrines 556
Sicardo Ware 462
side cabinets 50–2
Art Deco 490
miniature 90
oak and country 177, 182
pine 207–8
twentieth-century 504
side chairs 70, 467, 491, 568, 575
side tables 132–3
Art Nouveau 468
Arts and Crafts 450
oak and country 186–90
pine 211–13, 215
sideboards 102–6, **105**
Aesthetic Movement 446–7
Art Deco 492
Art Nouveau 468
Arts and Crafts 450
Asian 569
oak 158
silhouettes 638
silk: carpets 523
Islamic 577
silkwork pictures 526–8
silver 353–73
Aesthetic Movement 447
animals 353
antiquities 644, 645
Art Deco 497–8
Art Nouveau 475–8
Arts and Crafts 454–6
Asian 558
baskets 354
beakers 354
bowls 355, 447, 454, 497, 755
boxes 356, 475, 757
caddy spoons 356
candlesticks and chambersticks 356, 475, 497
card cases 357
casters **357**, 357
centrepieces 358, 475
chocolate, coffee and teapots 358–9
cigar and cigarette cases 359, 475
clocks and watches 360
coffee and tea services 360–1
condiment pots 361
covered dishes 363
cruets 362
cups and goblets 362, 476, 749
cutlery 362
dish rings and crosses 363
dishes 363, 455
dressing table sets 364
Fabergé 552
figures 365
flasks 365
frames 365, 476
inkstands and inkwells 366, 476
Islamic 577
jewellery 452, 472, 495, 506, 542, 543, 548
jugs and ewers 364, 373, 447, 475, 497
kettles 366
lamps 366
medals 738–9
menu holders 367, 498
mirrors 367
mugs and tankards 367, 478
napkin rings 368, 507
rattles 368
salvers and trays 368
sauce boats 369
scent bottles 369
serving implements 369
snuff bottles 572
snuff boxes 370
snuffer trays 370
spoons 456, 478, 748
table bells 370
tea caddies 371
tea-glass holders 749
toast racks 371
trophies 749
twentieth-century 507
vases 478
vesta cases 371
vinaigrettes 372, 712
watches 431, 433, 434
wax jacks 372
wine antiques 376–7
silver plate 374–5
Art Nouveau 475, 476
Arts and Crafts 450, 456
cruet sets 749
figures 756
kitchenware 221
table lamps 513
trophies 489
silver tables 134, 187
Silvestre, Paul 489
Simm, James 418
Simmance, Eliza 458
Simon & Halbig 668–9
Simpkins, Thomas Barton 364
Simpson, Anna Francis 480
Sinsson, Jacques-Nicolas 281
Sivas carpets 515
skeleton clocks 424
skillets 599
skirts 571
Slazenger 756, 759
Sleath, Gabriel 358
slide rules 698
slop bowls 259
Smith, Andrew 657
Smith, Daniel 356
Smith, Edwin & Theophilus 107
Smith, George 109
Smith & Gamble 432
Smith's 702
smoker's companions 602
Smythe, James 400
Snelling, James 378
Sneltjes, J.K.C. 463
Snider, Silas & Co 496
Snow, William I 397
snuff bottles 572
snuff boxes: enamel 551
gold 553
horn 617
Mauchline 615
nautical handicrafts 709, 712
papier mâché 605
porcelain 268
pottery 258
silver 370
treen 609
snuffer trays 370
sofa tables 134–5, 569
sofas 99–101
Art Deco 492
Art Nouveau 468
twentieth-century 502
soft toys 674
soldiers, toy 679
Solere, F. 506
solitaires 278
Solomon, Samuel 442
Somalvico, Lione & Co 441
Somalvico, V. & Co 706
Somerville, Stuart Scott 492
Sothers, Orchard & Co 365
Sottsass, Ettore 505, 507
soup ladles 369
soup plates 241, 290, 307, 318, 749
soup tureens 323
Southwick Pottery 264–6
Southworth and Mawe 720
sovereign holders 611
Sozan 330
Spanish: armchairs 55
arms and armour 730
carpets 514
ceramics 267
leather 604
lighting 507
militaria 742
portrait miniatures 633
pottery 229
tables 127, 189
Speed, John 659–62
spelter: clocks **388**, 388
figures 465, 489, 759
lighting 474, 496
table lamps 512
vases 603
Spence, Sir Basil 503
Spencer Browning & Co 707, 709
spice cupboards 178
spice towers 223
spill vases 226–8, 235–8, 257, 267
Spitalfields silk 536
spittoons 303
Spode: centrepieces 274
comports 259
dishes 260, 284
drainers 233
egg stands 260
meat dishes 260
pastille burners 303
pot-pourri jars 297
scent bottles 298
slop bowls 259
tureens 300
vases 301
spongeware 241, 242, 255
spoon-back armchairs 61
spoon trays 299, 315
spoon warmers 375
spoons: caddy 356, 748
enamel 551
love 609
porcelain 303
silver 362, 369, 456, 478
sport 745–59
archery 745
billiards 745–6
bowling 746
boxing 747
cricket 747–8
equestrian 748–9
fishing 750–3
football 754–5
golf 755–6
lacrosse 756
Olympics 757
shooting 757–8
tennis 759
spring-driven clocks **379**
Sputnik 506
staartkloks 425, **426**
Stabler, Harold **497**, 497
Staffordshire: animals 224–8, 263
baskets 229
bowls 230
buildings 230
busts 231
butter dishes 233
figures 234–8, 747, 757
inkwells 293
jugs 245, 294–5, 711
lustreware 263, 264
meat dishes 261
pipes 258
services 251, 252, 278, 283
teapots 253
Toby and character jugs 254, 255
tureens 256
vases 257, 301
watch stands 230
stained glass windows 346
standard lamps 512–13
stands 107–10
Asian 569
cake 107

INDEX

coat 467
folio 108
hall 88, 450, 467
hat and stick 107
kettle and urn 108
luggage 155
music 109
plant 109
pottery 252
shaving 109
umbrella 580
Starr, Theo B. 430
stationery boxes 610, 616, 618
Steck 624
Stedman 380
Steele 728
Steiff 673, 674
Steiner, Jules 669
Steinlen, Théophile-Alexandre 690
Steinway 624
Steky 714
Stening, C. 384
Stent, P. 661
Stephenson, George 416
steps 110, 209
stereoscopes 716
Stevenson, Andrew 259, 260
Steward, J.H. 706
stick-back chairs 165
stick barometers 437–40, **438**
stick pins 550
stick stands 107, 227, 258, 461
Stickley, Gustav 450
Stinton, John 292, 296
Stobwasser 605
Stockton, Jenny 532
stoelkloks **426**
Stoltz, Sam 453
stone: antiquities 641, 643, 645
architectural antiques 582
sculpture 592
stone china 251
stoneware **243**
bowls 500
cheese domes 231
Chinese ceramics 324
inkwells 243
jugs 245, 246, 758
Martin Brothers 459
tiles 500
tygs 756
vases 458, 500
see also salt-glazed stoneware
stools 111–12
Art Nouveau 468
Asian 569
music 112
oak and country 184–5
tribal 648
twentieth-century 502, 504
Stopes, Aylmer 398
storage jars 223
Storer, George 359, 360
Storr, Paul 354, 371
Stourbridge 342, 343, 349, 350
stoves 579–80
Stowe, J.W. Smith 438
Stradivari, Antonio 626
strainers 233
Strand, Paul 720
straw-work 613
strawberry dishes 232
Strigels, George Philip 379
striking clocks **381**
Stroblberger 726
Stromier, Josh. 420
sucriers 229, 271
Süe & Mare **490**, 490
sugán chairs 165
sugar baskets 354
sugar bowls: Clarice Cliff 482
porcelain 269
pottery 230
silver 447
sugar boxes 342
sugar sifters 483
sugar tongs 551
sugar urns 373
Suggate, George 410
suites: bedroom 113, 446, 449
dining 491, 504
salon 113
Sully, Lawrence 635
Sultanabad rugs 519
Summer, William 553
Summerhayes, R. 414
Summers, Gerald 502
Sunderland lustreware 263–6
sundials 580, 583, 698–9
surveying instruments 705
Sutherland tables 136, 450
Swales, Isabella 524
Swansea **291**
centrepieces 274
cow creamers 232
cups 281
plates 242
soup plates 291
tea services 278
tureens 300
Swatow 310
Swedish: armchairs 60
beds 26
cabinets 48, 53, 489
ceramics 282, 286, 501
chairs 66, 70, 164, 503
chaise longues 71
chests of drawers 195
clocks 394, 400, 414, 417, 418
glass 332, 339, 494, 505
jewellery 506
lighting 509
metalware 602
militaria 736
pottery 232, 233, 256, 257
side cabinets 207
silver 354, 358, 362
sofas 99
sport 746
tables 211
sweetmeat dishes 232, 350
Swift 408
Swiss: arms and armour 724
clocks 394
costume 536
glass 352
jewellery 540
musical boxes 619, 620
toys 678
watches 431–6, 755
swords 560–1, 723–7
Sydenham, Guy 501, 507
Symphonion 620
Syrian: antiquities 641
furniture 575

T

table bells 370
table cabinets 53
table clocks 378–82, **380**, 384, 463
table lamps 473–4, 489, 496, 507, 512–13
tablecloths 529
tables 114–42
architects' 114, 568
Art Deco 492
Art Nouveau 468
artist's 639
Asian 569
bamboo 219
bedside 114
billiards 746
campaign 155
card 115–17, 155, 569
centre 118–19, 186, 447, 492
chair tables 162
coffee 502
console and pier 120, 569
cricket 186, 188–90, 211, 212
dining 121–3, 155, 190, 212, 450, 504
display 123
dough 178
dressing 124–5, 189
drop-leaf 125, 186, 211–14
drum 126
farmhouse 189, 190
folding 190
games 126, 212
gateleg 186–8
library 127, 215
metamorphic 184
nests of tables 128, 569
oak and country 186–90
occasional 128–9, 155, 186, 447, 450, 468, 492, 569
Pembroke 130, 139, 140, 155
pine 211–15
reading 131
refectory 186–8, 190
serving 131
sewing 126, 141
side 132–3, 186–90, 211–13, 215, 450, 468
silver 134, 187
sofa 134–5, 569
Sutherland 136, 450
tavern 188
tea 136–7, 155
tilt-top 188, 189
tray 144
trestle 189
tripod 137–8, 188
twentieth-century 502–4
two-tier 139
wine 188, 214, 611
work 139–41, 569
writing 136, 141–2, 155, 447
Tabriz rugs and carpets 518
Tadakazu (Chuichi) 570
Tait, Jessie 501
Taizan 331
Tallis, John 660
tambour-top bureaux 39
tankards: Chinese ceramics 322
glass 346
pewter 478, 755
porcelain 295–6
pottery 248, 262
silver 367
treen 609
Tanner, W. 381
tantaluses 377
tape measures 603
tapersticks 273
tapestries 535
taps 585–7
Tara Toys 673
Tatham, Charles 150
tavern clocks 425, **426**
tavern tables 188
Taylor, John & Son 178
Taylor, Joseph 372
tazzas: glass 343, 493
pottery 500
silver plate 374
treen 609
tea bowls: Chinese ceramics 310, 313–14
Japanese ceramics 327
Meissen 305
porcelain 280, 281
transfer-printed 259
tea caddies and canisters 612–16, 618
Chinese ceramics 326
lacquer 557
Mauchline ware 614
papier mâché 605
penwork 614, 616
porcelain 299
pottery 252, 478
silver 356, 371
silver plate 375
tortoiseshell 614, 615
treen 609
Tunbridge ware 611
tea caddy bowls 342
tea-glass holders 373, 551, 749
tea services: Art Deco 498
Clarice Cliff 483
Japanese ceramics 330
pewter 478
porcelain 277–8
pottery 252
silver 360–1, 456
silver plate 375
Susie Cooper 485
twentieth-century 499
tea tables 136–7, 155
teapot stands 314
teapots: Cadogan **322**, 322
Chinese ceramics 322–3
cloisonné 554
Japanese ceramics 331
porcelain 275–6, 307
pottery 253, 262
silver 358–9
silver plate 375
Susie Cooper 485
teapoys 143
teddy bears 672–3
Tek Sing cargo 314
Tekke carpets 521
telescopes 706, 710
Tempest, Margaret 657
tennis 759
terracotta: architectural antiques 583
busts 464, 465
figures 562
plaques 462
sculpture 592–5
Terry & Williams 376
tester beds 26, 27
textiles 524–37
Asian 572–3
costume 536–7
covers and quilts 524–5
embroidery and needlework 526–9
Islamic 577
lace 530
samplers 531–4
tapestries 535
twentieth-century 508
Thai figures 562, 564
Theresienthal 338
thermometers, Tunbridge ware 611
thermos flasks 456
Thevenot Frères 579
Thibouville-Lamy 621
Thieme, Carl 274
Thomas, Eliza 533
Thomas, Linda 501
Thomas, Seth 708
Thompson, Jim 491
Thompson, Dr Jon **521**
Thomson, Alice 532
Thonet 466–8
Thorndike, Samuel 408
Thornton Pickard 714
Thorpe, T. 398
Thuilly 431
Thuringian tankards 248
Tibetan: figures 562
furniture 567, 568
rugs 522
textiles 573
Tiffany & Co: glass 471, 494
lighting 474
silver 363, 369, 476, 478
watches 436
tiles 254, 745
Art Deco 480
Arts and Crafts 448
Islamic 575
twentieth-century 500
tilt-top tables 188, 189
Timurid metalware 577
tinplate: toys **676**, 676
trays 603
tins, biscuit 223
Tinworth, George 458
Titanic 710
Tittensor, Charles and John 234
toast racks 262, 371
tobacco boxes 228, 602, 603
tobacco jars 245, 448
Toby jugs **254**, 254–5
Todd, Charles Stewart 448
toddy lifters 352
Toft, Charles 247
toilet sets 458
tôle peinte 591
toleware 220, 602
Tolkien, J.R.R. 657
tombstones 577
Tomomichi 561
tongs, sugar 551
Tonks of Birmingham 155
tool boxes 192
torchères 143
torques 506
Torricelli 443
tortoiseshell: boxes 615, **616**, 618
clocks 393
Toshiyoshi 561
Tournai 297
towel rails 144, 218, 587
Townsend, Charles 355
toys 675–86
aeroplanes 675
boats 676
mechanical 676–7
money boxes 677
Noah's arks 678
rocking horses 678
soft toys 674
soldiers 679
trains 680–3
vehicles 684–5
trains, toy 680–3
transfer-printed pottery 259–62
Transylvanian militaria 743
travel cases 604
trays 144
ceramic 501
copper 456
enamel 551
papier mâché 605
porcelain 299
silver 368
silver plate 375
snuffer 370
tin 603
toleware 602
treen 609
treen 606–9
Tregent, James 407
trembleuse saucers 280
Trent Tile Co 254
trestle tables 189
Tri-Ang 671, 683, 685, 686
tribal art 647–51
trinket boxes 475
trios 481
tripod tables 137–8, 188
trivets 456, 591
Troika 501, 507
trophies 489, 749, 758

Trotter, Alex 437
Troughton, John 698
trunks: campaign 155
leather 604
pine 194
tsuba 561
tub chairs 56, 62, 70
tubular steel furniture 502, 504
Tudor & Leader 354
tulip vases 256
tumblers 339
Tunbridge ware 112, 610–11
tureens: Chinese ceramics 323
pewter 602
porcelain 300
pottery 256, 262
silver plate 456
Turkestani rugs and carpets 521–2
Turkish: ceramics 574–5
manuscripts 576
rugs and carpets 515
Turkmen rugs 521
Turnbull, John 402
Turvey, W. 729
twentieth-century design 499–508
ceramics 499–501
furniture 502–4
glass 505
jewellery 506
lighting 506–7
metalware 507
rugs and textiles 508
two-tier tables 139
tygs 458, 756
Tyneside lustreware 264
Tyzak, Sarah 530

U

Uago 441
Ukrainian carpets 514
umbrella stands 580
Ungethum, August 466
Unica Vaev 508
United Optical Co 714
Universal Drafting Machine Co 705
upholstered armchairs 61–2
uranium glass 343
urn stands 108
urns: cast-iron 580
glass 350
pottery 257
silver 507
terracotta 583
Ushak carpets 515
Uzbekistani quilts 524

V

Vacheron & Constantin 436
Val St Lambert 339
Vale, H. & Co 363
Valenciennes lace 530
Valk, G. 658, 659
Vallien, Bertil 505
valuing furniture: colour and patination **119**
sets of chairs **65**
Van Briggle 448
van Velsen, Cornelius 692
vanity cases 498
Varenne, R. 464
vases: Aesthetic Movement 445
Art Deco 479–81, 498
Art Nouveau 461, 462, 478
Arts and Crafts 448
bronze 558, 599
Charlotte Rhead 485
Chinese ceramics 324–6
Clarice Cliff 483–4
cloisonné 554
Doulton 458
glass 350–1, 469–71, 493–4, 505, 555
jade 555
Japanese ceramics 330–1
lacquer 557
Moorcroft 460
porcelain 300–2, 307
pottery 256–7, 266
Royal Doulton 458
silver 478
spelter 603
toleware 602
treen 609
twentieth-century 499–501
Vauchez 431
Vauxhall 281, 284
Veeck, Charles 594
vehicles, toy 684–5
Velde, Henri van de **467**, 467
veneers: marquetry **129**
parquetry **129**
Venetian stands 110
Venini 505
Verbier 486
verge watches 431
Verlet, Charles Raoul 596
verre églomisé 492
Le Verre Français 494
vesta cases 371, 553
Viardot, Gabriel 27, 52, 53
Vickers, Mary 531
Victor gramophones 621
Victory Industries 685
Vienna porcelain: coffee services 278
cups 281
dessert services 283
figures 288
jugs 295
sauce boats 298
tea services 278
trays 299
tureens 300
Vienna-style clocks 427
Villanis, Emmanuel 464, 474
Villeroy & Boch 462
vinaigrettes: brass 598
glass 352
gold 553
silver 372, 712
Viner & Co 381
violins 626–7
Visscher, Claes Janszoon 661
vitrine tables 123
vitrines 46
Vodrey, Frederick 448
Voigtlander 714
Vollenda 714
Vuillaume, J.B. 626
Vung Tau cargo 311, 313, 321
Vyse, Charles 500

W

Wade, William 94
wager cups 365
Wagner, Otto 467
Wagstaff & Brunt 261
Wahliss 462
wainscot armchairs **162**, 162
waistcoats 536
Waite, Thomas 426
wake tables 125
Wakely, James 447
Wales & McCulloch 383
Walker, J. & C. 662
Walker, Rachel 534
Walker Ltd 393
wall brackets 145
Martin Brothers 459
porcelain 302
wall clocks 425–8, **426**, 486
wall lights 507, 509–11
wall mirrors 93–6, 491
wall pockets 258, 303, 500
wall racks 218
Wallendorf 489
Walsh, John Walsh **343**, 343
Walter, Almeric 494
Waltham Clock Co 428, 432
Walther & Sohn 669
Walton, B. & Co 605
Walton, George 449, 463
Walton, Joseph & Co 553
Wardle 244, 462
wardrobes 146–7
Art Deco 492
bamboo 219
pine 216–17
Warhol, Andy 657
wash sets 258
washstands 148, 587
Asian 569
bamboo 219
campaign 155
pine 217
Wasterman & Co 623
watch stands 230
watches 431–6
pocket 431–3, 755
silver 360
wristwatches 434–6
water jugs 345, 364
Watkins, Carleton E. 720
Watkins, J. 638
Watney collection **298**
Watson, John 378
Watts, Chas. 382
wax dolls 668, 670
wax holders 373
wax jacks 372
waxing furniture **127**
weapons *see* arms and armour
weathervanes 600, 601
Webb, Stephen 86
Webb, Thomas & Sons 343, **345**, 351
Webster, James 401
Webster, Percy 421
Wedgwood: animals 228
baskets 229
bowls 481, 500
busts 231, 272
candlesticks 231
cups and saucers 258
dinner services 500
flatware 241
jardinières 219
jugs 246
lazy Susans 252
plates 291
punch bowls 230
vases 257, 500
wall pockets 500
Wedgwood & Bentley 257
Weeks, Thomas 601
Weichold, Richard 627
weights 558, 706
Weiss, Felix 489
Welch, E.N. 428
Welch, Lucy Kemp 691
Welcher, E. 302
Welder, Samuel 357
Weller, Samuel A. 462
Wellington chests 80, 90
Welsh: barometers 442
bookcases 34
ceramics 278
chairs 166
clocks 408, 412, 413, 416
coffers 168
cupboards 175, 177
dressers 179–80, 204, 205
kitchenware 220
musical instruments 622
settles 183, 210
tables 211, 214
treen 606, 609
Wemyss: baskets 230
ewers 247
flatware 242
flower pots 244
jardinières 244
mugs 249
pots 250
quaiches 232
wash sets 258
Werlein 624
West, F.L. 443
West & Son 371
West Country: chests 166
kitchenware 220
Westerwald 245
Wetzels 623
Weyersberg & Co 726
whatnots 149, 219
Wheatley, Samuel 376
wheel barometers 440–3
Wheeler 443
Wheeler, Susan 534
Whieldon, Thomas 224, **241**, 241
whistles 225, 365
Whitby, W.P. 406
White, Mary Ann 534
White Star Line 710
Whitehurst & Son 381, 411
Whitfield, George 255
Whiting, Professor Mark **521**
Whitney 733
Whittingham, E. 400
wicker 219
Widdicomb 503
Wiener Keramik 465
Wiener Werkstätte: ceramics 481
glass 493
jewellery 472
lighting 496
metalware 498
Wieselthier, Vally 496
wig stands 609
Wigström, Henrik 552
Wileman & Co 445
Wilgoss, Sylvia 672
Wilkinson, J. 481
Willets Manufacturing Co 302
Williams, T.R. 720
Williams & Gibton 127
Willmore, Joseph 368, 369
Wills, W.D. & H.O. 689, 748, 759
Wilson 222, 243
Wilson, Askrigg 401
Wilson, George 418
Wilson, J. 440, 755
Winchester Repeating Arms Co 758
window seats 150
Windsor chairs 164, 166, 193
wine antiques 376–7
wine bottles 340
wine coolers 150–1, **151**
cast iron 377
porcelain 292
silver 377
wine cups 313
wine flasks 331
wine glasses 332–8
wine kettles 326
wine pots 326
wine tables 188, 214, 611
Winfield, R.W. & Co 58
wing armchairs 61, 62
Winstanley 404
Winter, James & Sons 38
Winterhalder & Hofmeier 390, 395, 422
Wisden 747
Witek, Josef 370
Withnall 583
WMF 475, 476
Wolkenstein & Glückselig 463
wood: architectural antiques 584
Asian 559
busts 489
figures 563–4, 566
kitchenware 220
olivewood **129**
sculpture 592, 595
treen 606–9
Wood, Enoch 249, 255
Wood, Ralph 224–5, 234, 254
Wood & Caldwell 231
Wood & Son 485
Wood family **234**, 234, 747
wood-turner's chairs 165
Woodman, Elizabeth 501
woolwork pictures 528–9, **709**, 709
Worcester: baskets 269
cream boats 298
cups 281
dishes 284, 291
inkwells 293
jardinières 293
jugs 295
mugs 296
porringers 270
sauce boats 298
spittoons 303
tea canisters 299
teapots 276
vases 302
wall pockets 303
see also Royal Worcester
work boxes 615, 618
work tables 139–41, 569
Worth, Henry 657
Wrenn 683
Wright & Mansfield 85
Wrigley, James 404
wristwatches 434–6
writing boxes 153, 158, 610, 613, 616, 618
writing cabinets 53
writing desks 84
writing slopes 616, 617
writing tables 136, 141–2, 155, 447
wrought iron *see* iron
wucai 313, 314, 320–1
Wylie & Lochhead 466
Wyon, E.W. 272
Wyon, T. Sr 712
Wytsman, Paul 657

X

X-framed chairs 58

Y

Yarmouth rummers 337
Yeats, Jack B. 210
Yingqing ware 315
Yixing ware 323
Yoell 422
Yomut saddle covers 521
Yorkshire: chairs 162
cow creamers 232
Young, William Weston 248
Ysart, Salvador 348
Yue ware 315

Z

Zabro 504
Zanetti, Giulio II 359
Zeiss 714
Zenith 436
Zethelius, Pehr 358, 362
Zimmermann, A. & J. 357, 367
Zincke, C.F. 633
Zittau 239
Zograscopes 716
Zwick 756